Blankets

Blankets

an illustrated novel by
CRAIG THOMPSON

TOP SHELF PRODUCTIONS
Marietta, Georgia

This graphic novel is based on personal experiences,
though the names have been changed, and certain characters,
places, and incidents have been modified in the service of the story.

Thompson, Craig.
Blankets / Craig Thompson
ISBN 1-891830-43-0
1. Graphic Novels 2. Cartoons 3. Fiction

First Printing, July 2003. **PRINTED IN CANADA**

Contents:

*For my
family,
with love*

I

Cubby Hole

When we were young, my little brother
Phil and I shared the same bed.

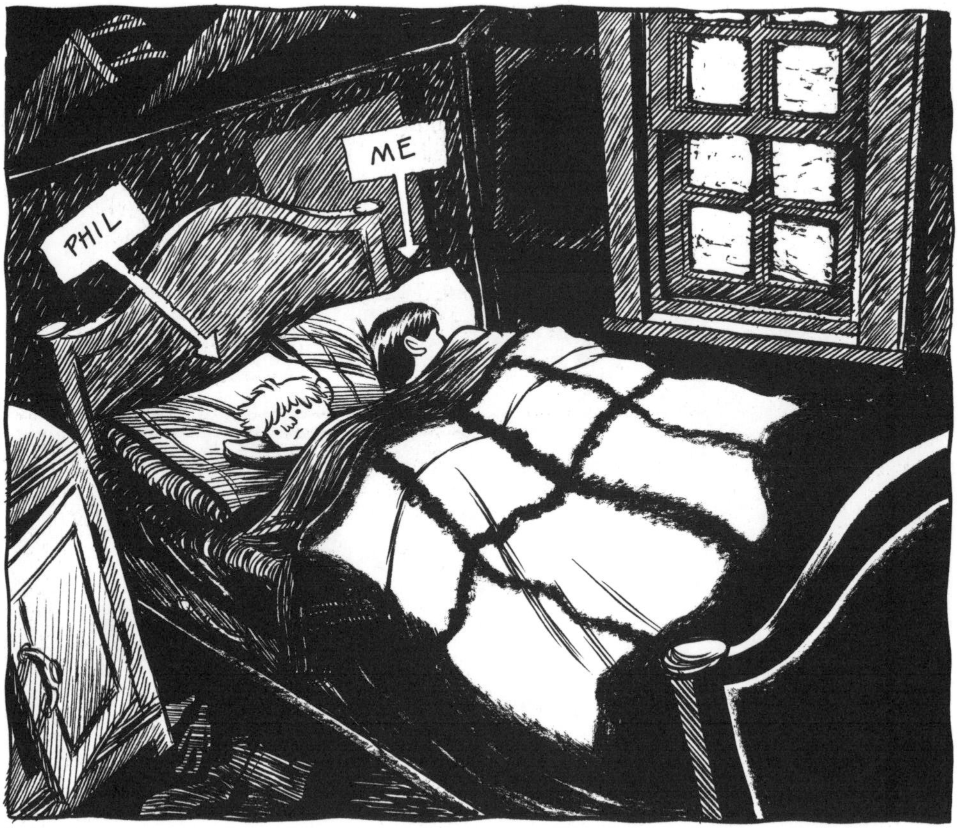
ME
PHIL

"SHARED" is the sugar-coated way of saying we were TRAPPED in the same bed, as we were children and had no say in the matter.

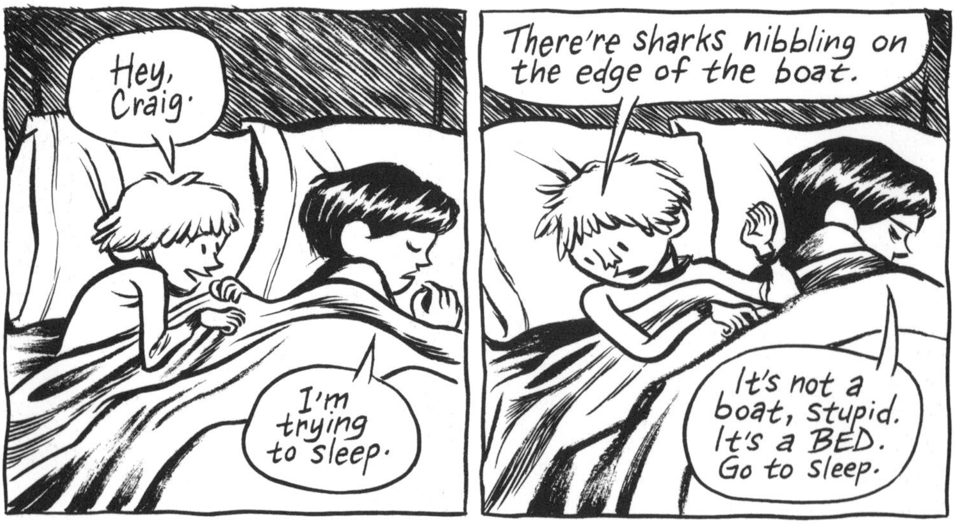
Hey, Craig.
I'm trying to sleep.
There're sharks nibbling on the edge of the boat.
It's not a boat, stupid. It's a BED. Go to sleep.

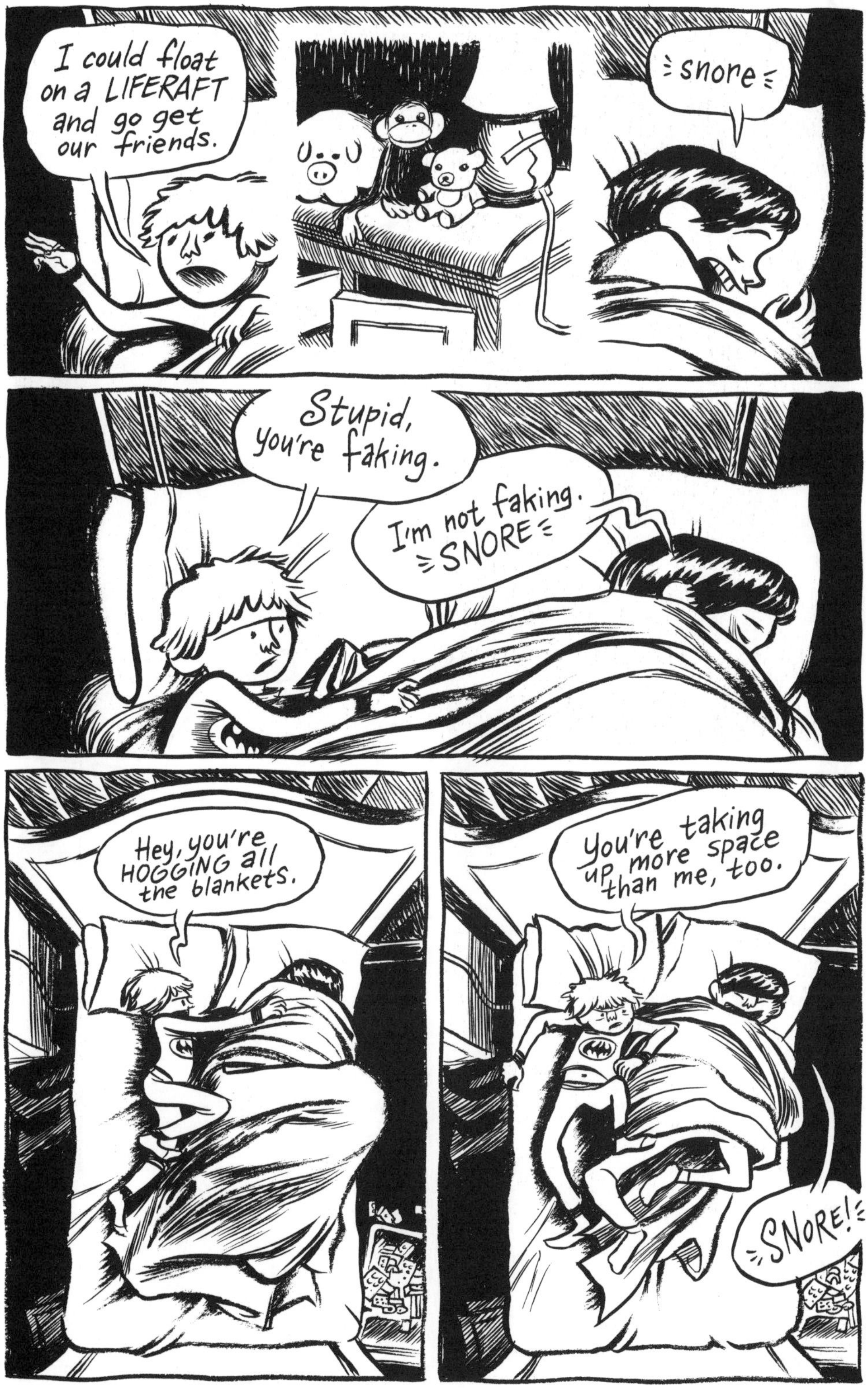
I could float on a LIFERAFT and go get our friends.
snore
Stupid, you're faking.
I'm not faking. SNORE
Hey, you're HOGGING all the blankets.
You're taking up more space than me, too.
SNORE!

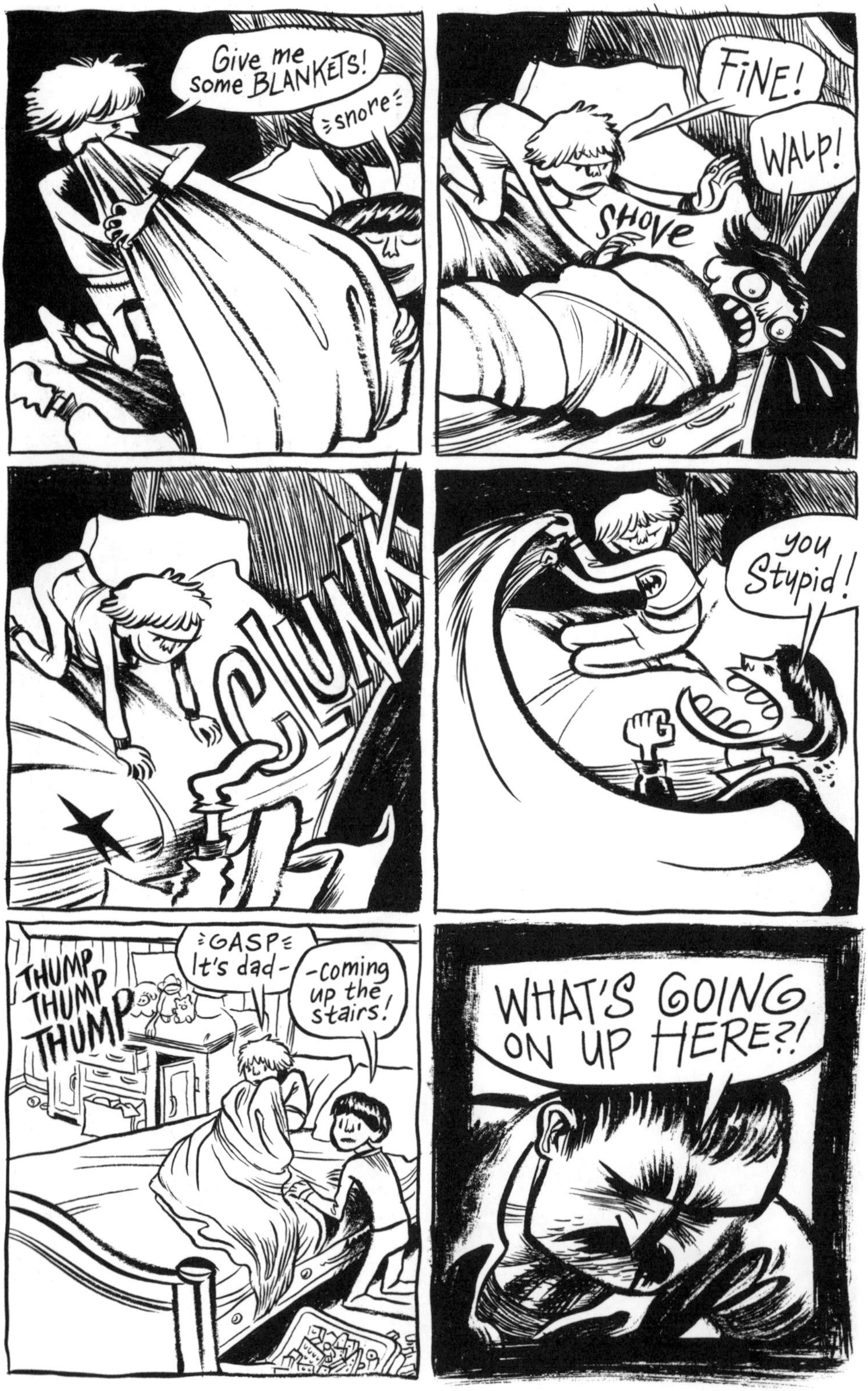
Give me some BLANKETS!
snore
FINE!
WALP!
SHOVE
CLUNK
you Stupid!
THUMP THUMP THUMP
GASP It's dad-
-coming up the stairs!
WHAT'S GOING ON UP HERE?!

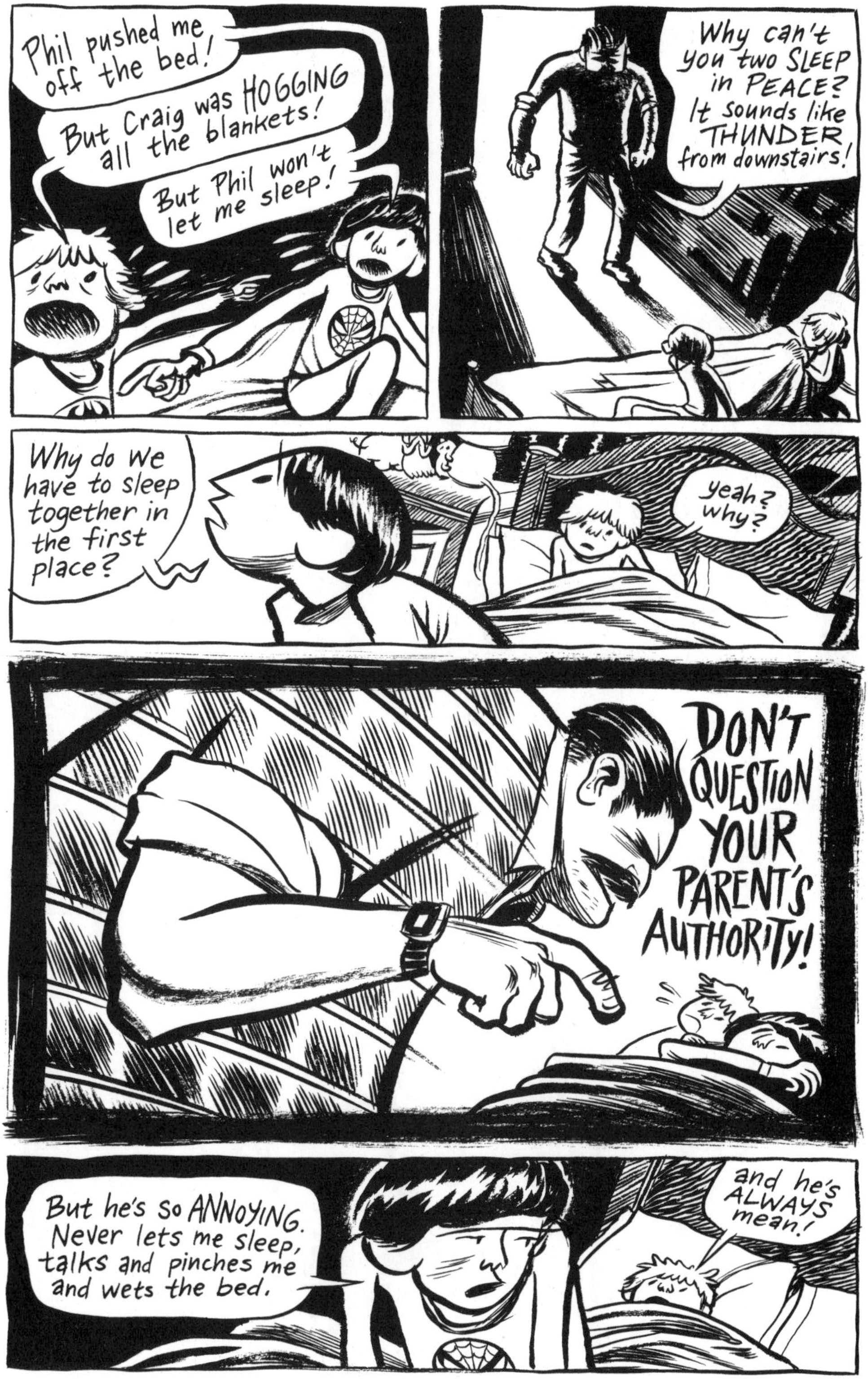
Phil pushed me off the bed!
But Craig was HOGGING all the blankets!
But Phil won't let me sleep!
Why can't you two SLEEP in PEACE? It sounds like THUNDER from downstairs!
Why do we have to sleep together in the first place?
yeah? why?
DON'T QUESTION YOUR PARENT'S AUTHORITY!
But he's so ANNOYING. Never lets me sleep, talks and pinches me and wets the bed.
and he's ALWAYS mean!

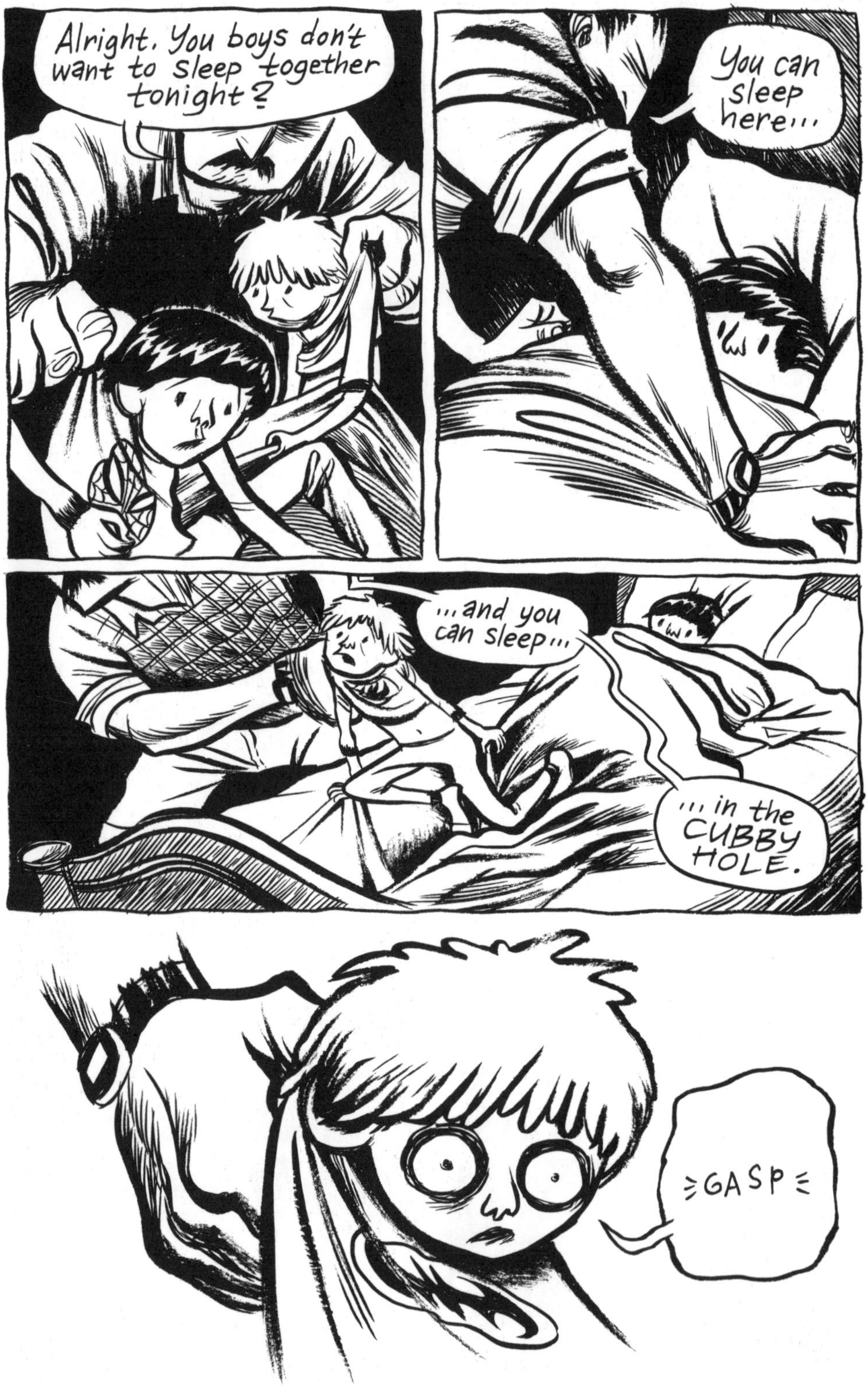
Alright. You boys don't want to sleep together tonight?
You can sleep here...
...and you can sleep...
...in the CUBBY HOLE.
GASP

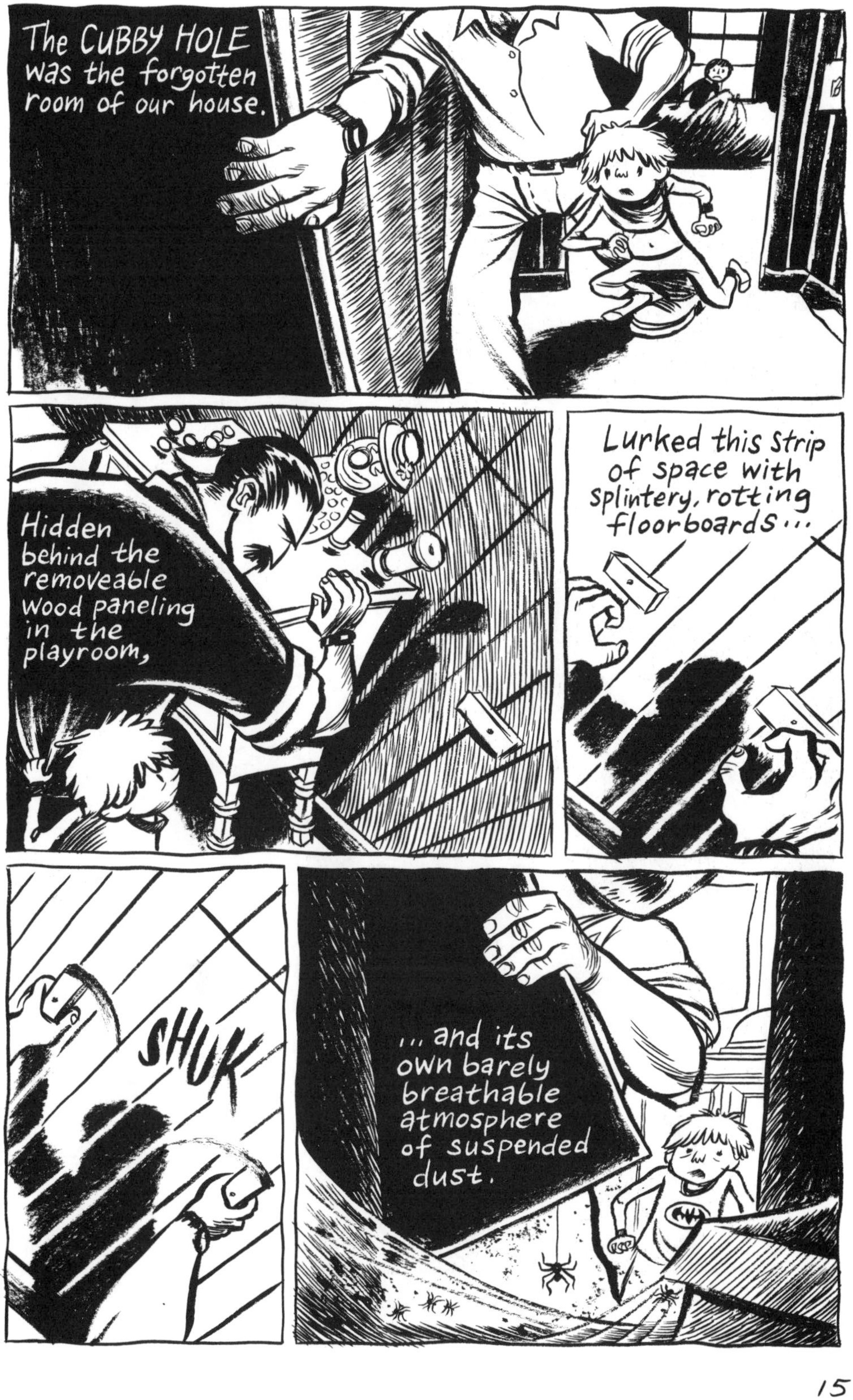
The CUBBY HOLE was the forgotten room of our house.
Hidden behind the removeable wood paneling in the playroom,
Lurked this strip of space with splintery, rotting floorboards...
SHUK
...and its own barely breathable atmosphere of suspended dust.

Uninsulated, unlit, and uninhabited – except by spiders and vermin (we heard skittering within the walls at night) and a few dust-filled cardboard boxes,

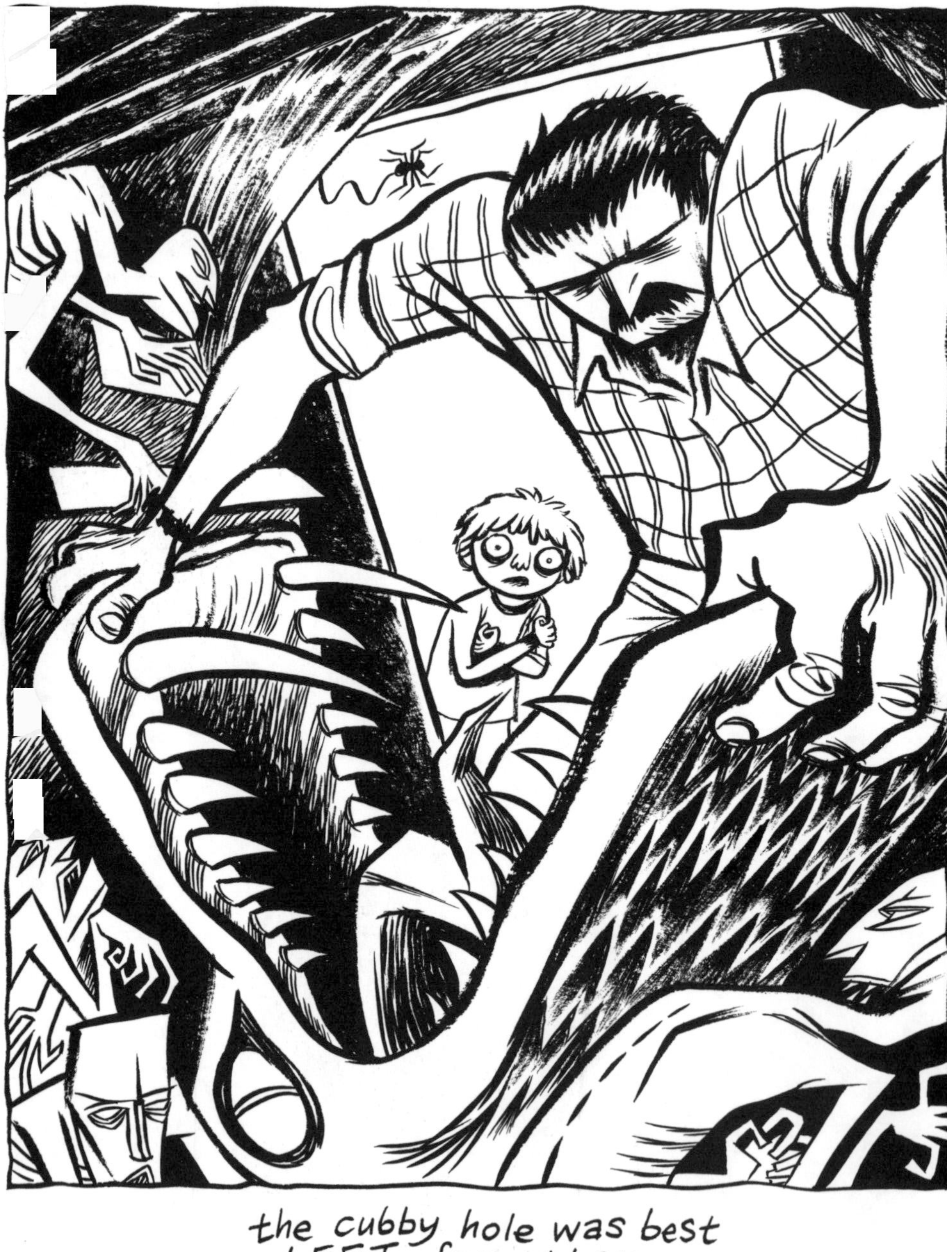

the cubby hole was best LEFT forgotten.

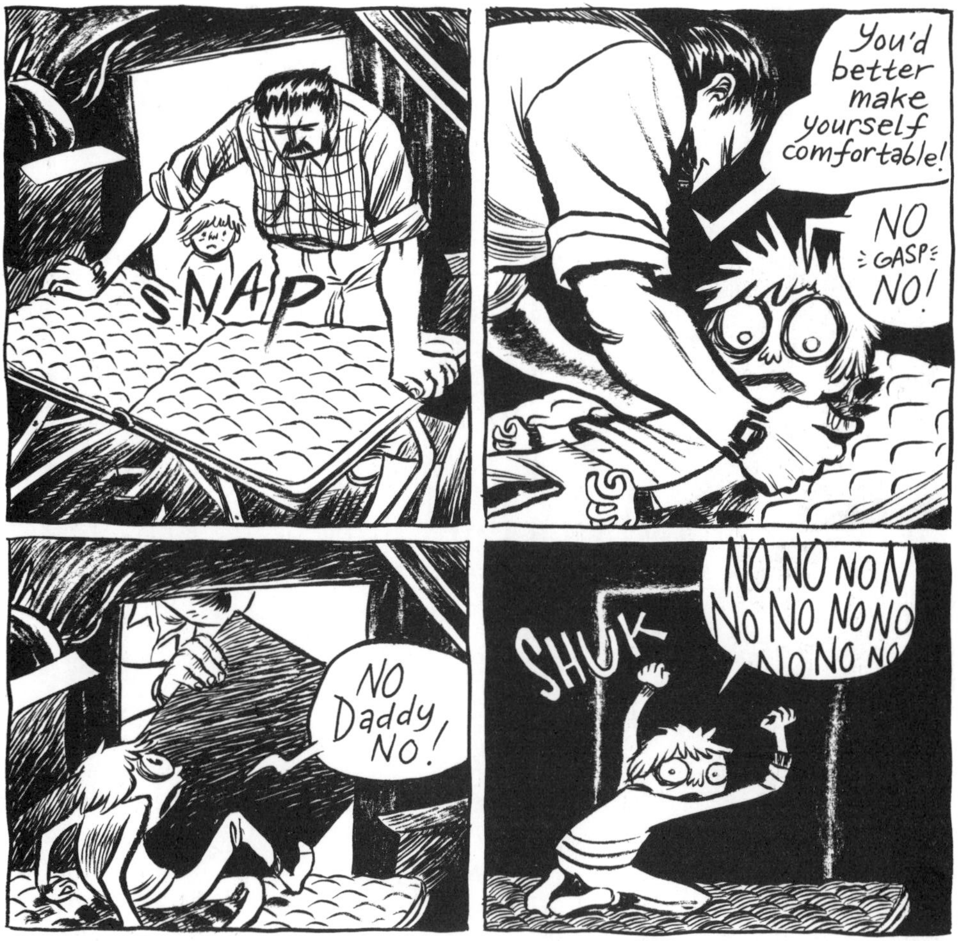
SNAP
You'd better make yourself comfortable!
NO GASP NO!
NO Daddy NO!
SHUK
NO NO NON
No No No No

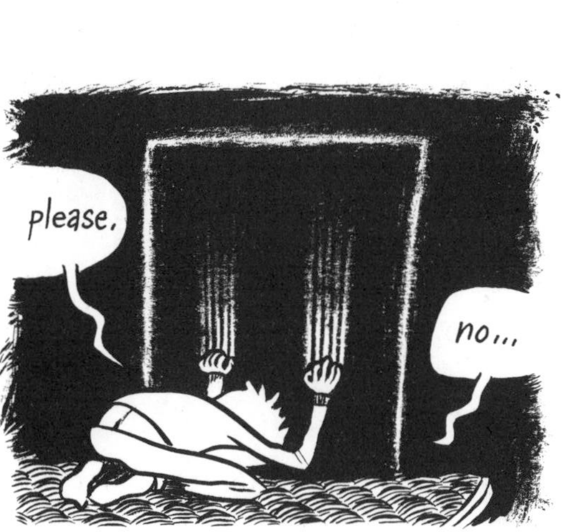
please.
no...

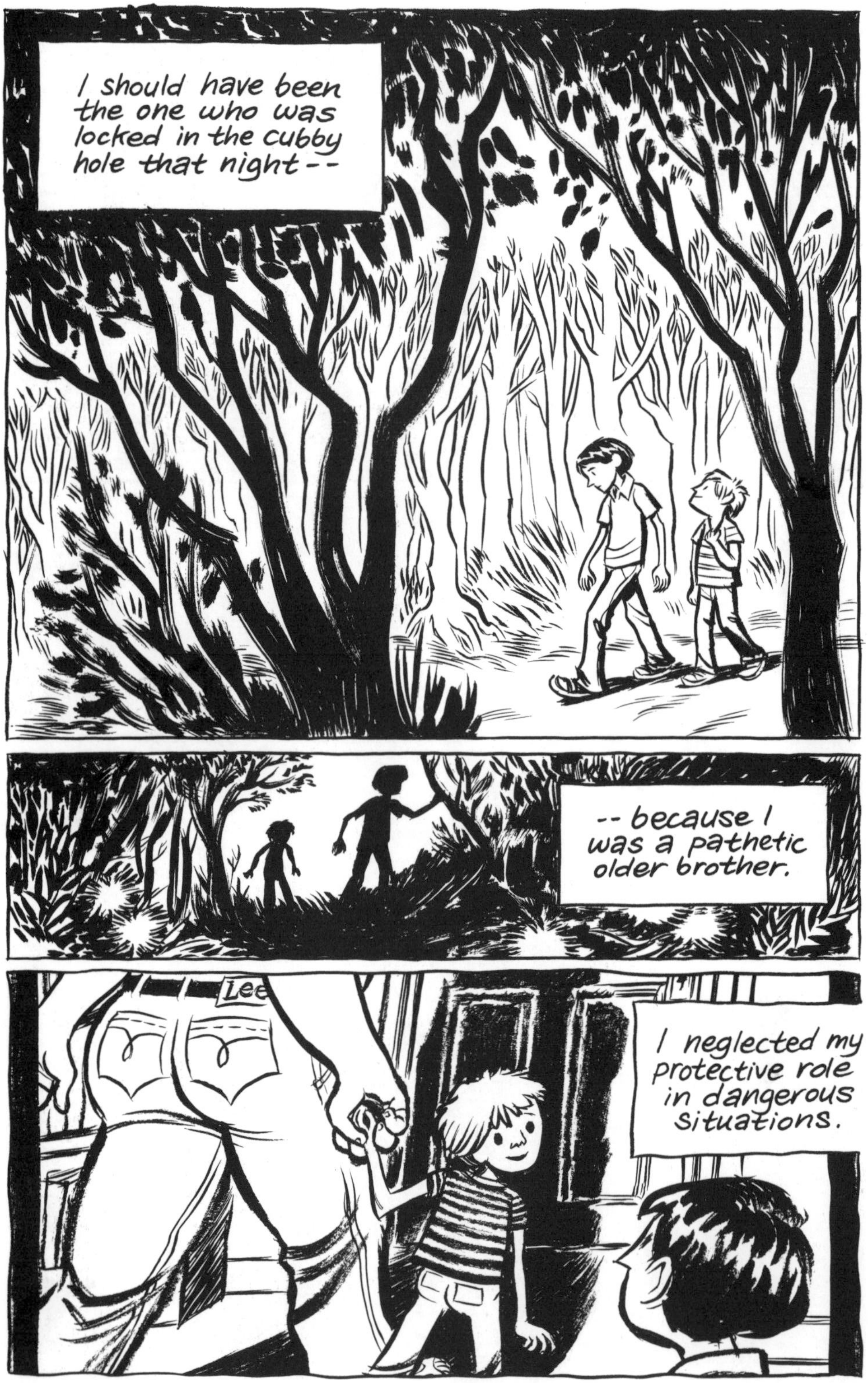
I should have been the one who was locked in the cubby hole that night--
-- because I was a pathetic older brother.
Lee
I neglected my protective role in dangerous situations.

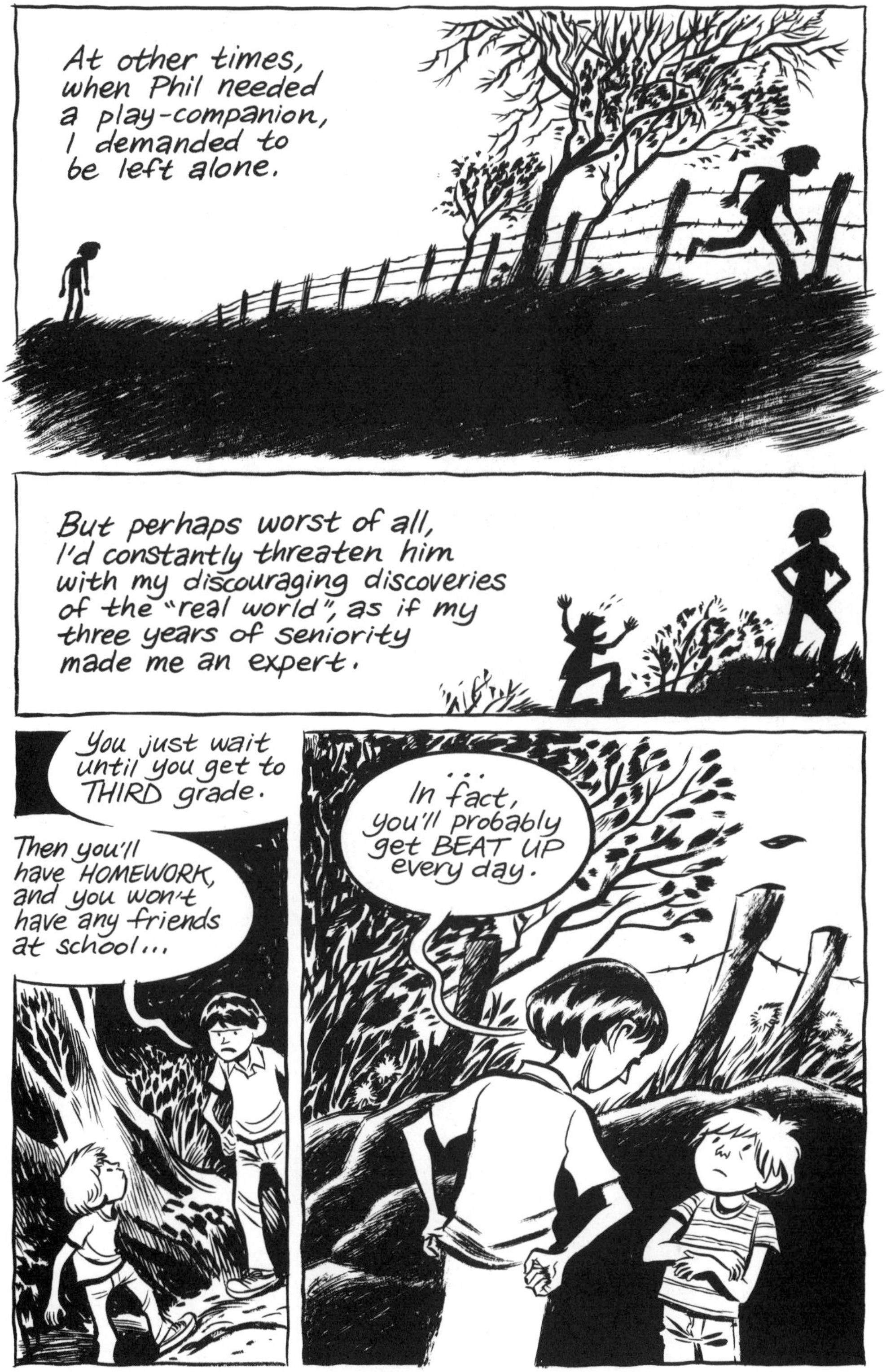
At other times, when Phil needed a play-companion, I demanded to be left alone.
But perhaps worst of all, I'd constantly threaten him with my discouraging discoveries of the "real world", as if my three years of seniority made me an expert.
You just wait until you get to THIRD grade.
Then you'll have HOMEWORK, and you won't have any friends at school...
...
In fact, you'll probably get BEAT UP every day.

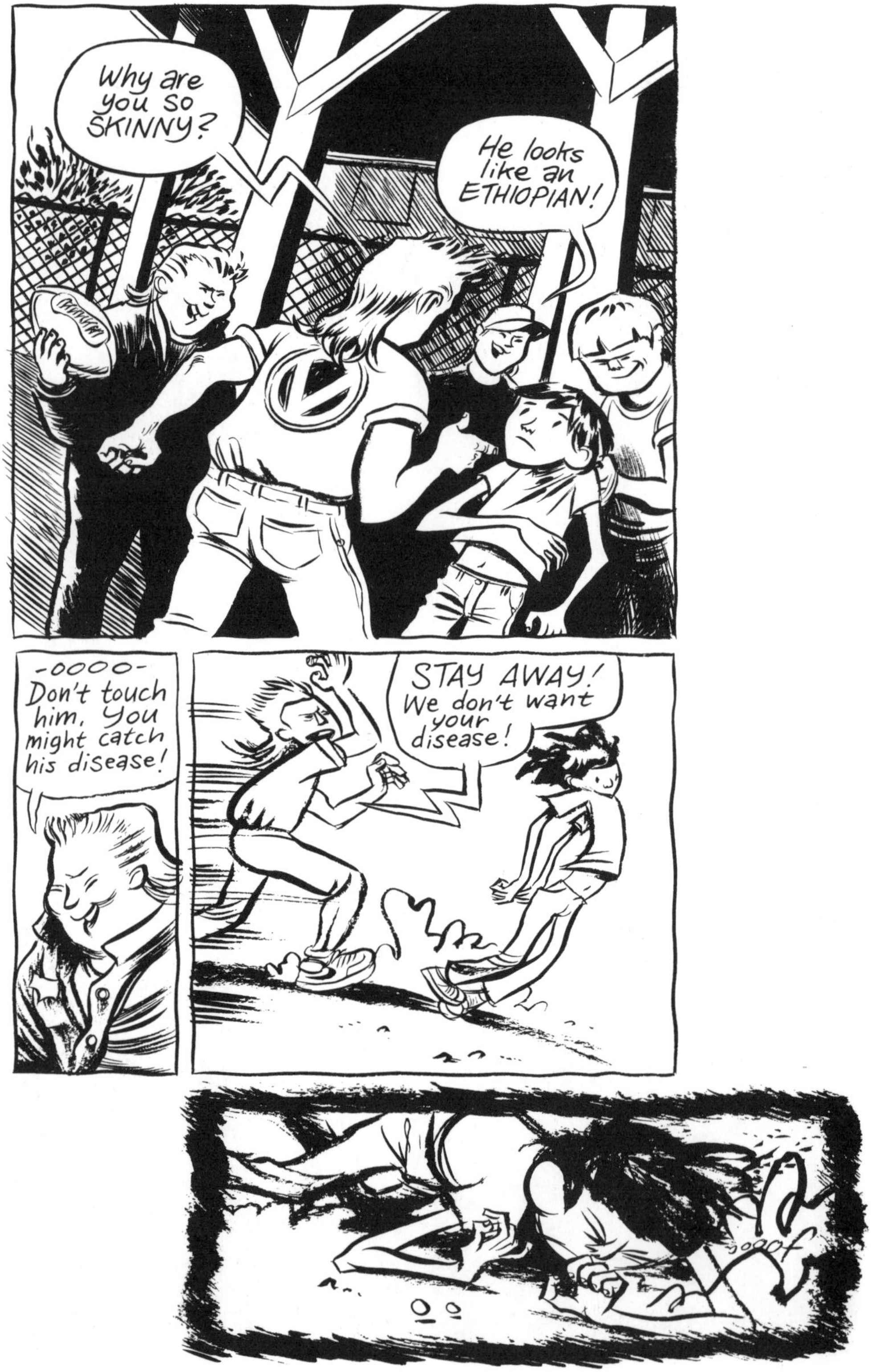
Why are you so SKINNY?
He looks like an ETHIOPIAN!
-OOOO- Don't touch him, You might catch his disease!
STAY AWAY! We don't want your disease!

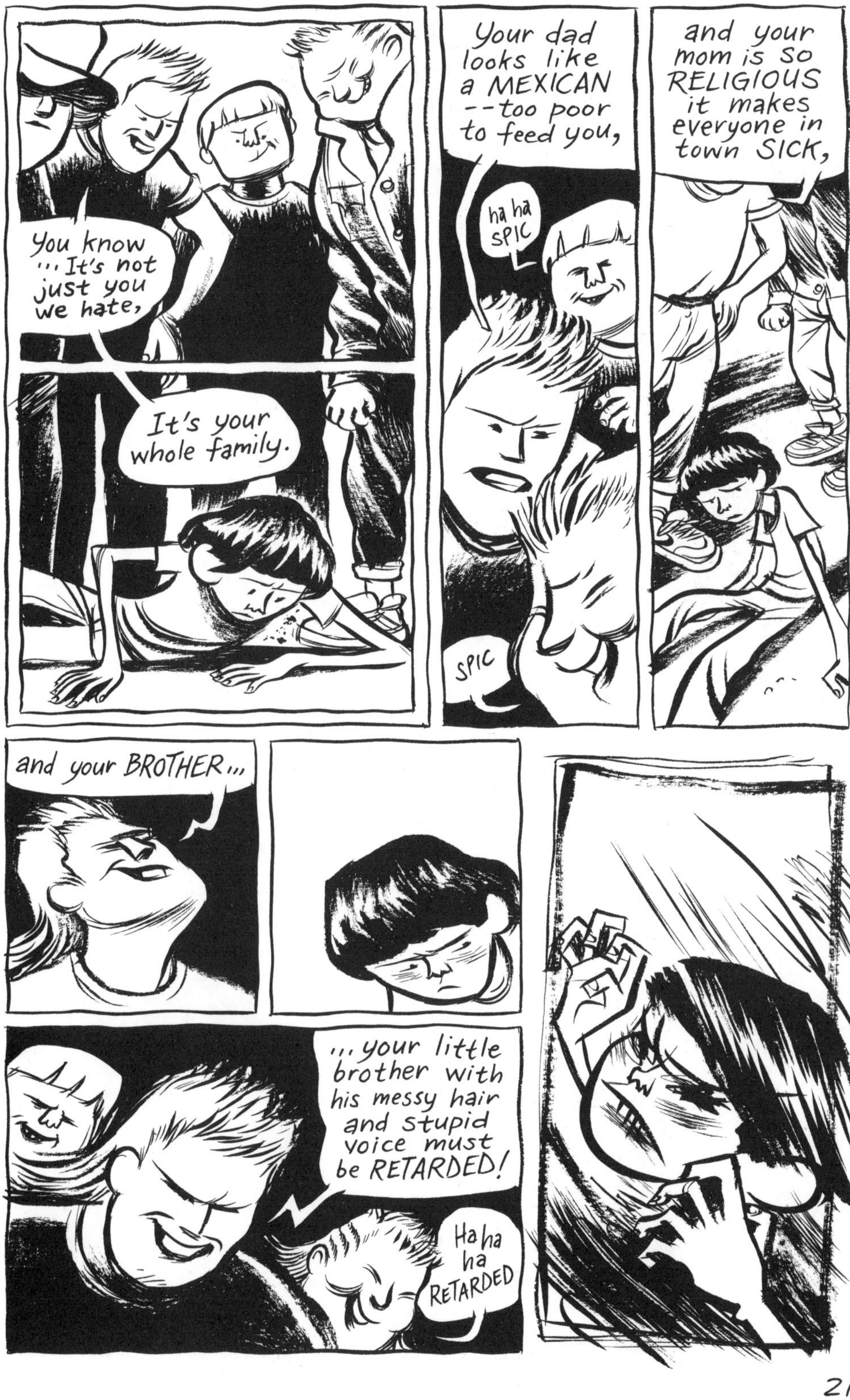
You know ... It's not just you we hate,
It's your whole family.
Your dad looks like a MEXICAN --too poor to feed you,
ha ha SPIC
SPIC
and your mom is so RELIGIOUS it makes everyone in town SICK,
and your BROTHER...
...your little brother with his messy hair and stupid voice must be RETARDED!
Ha ha ha RETARDED

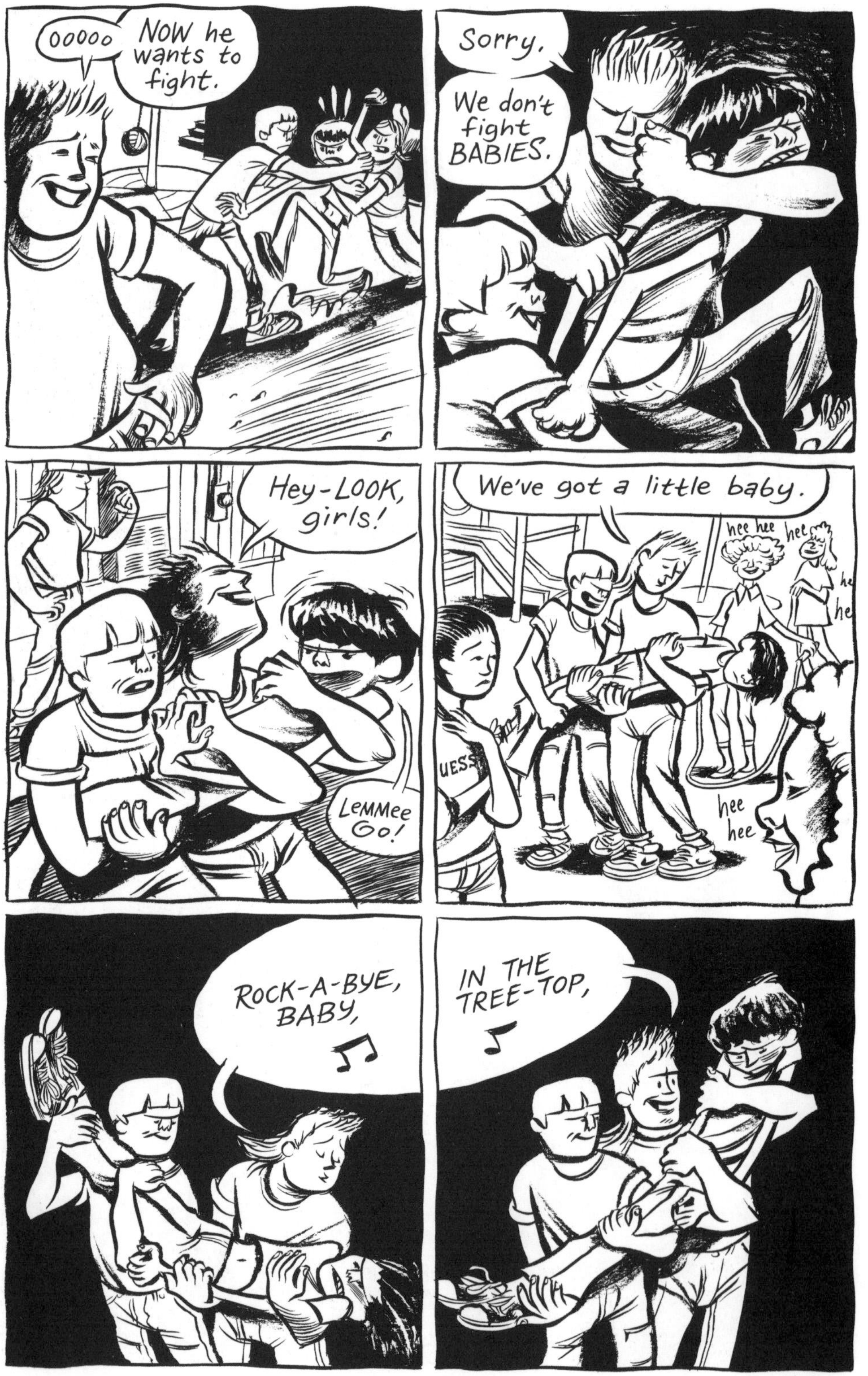
ooooo
NOW he wants to fight.
Sorry.
We don't fight BABIES.
Hey-LOOK, girls!
LemMee Go!
We've got a little baby.
hee hee
hee
hee
hee
ROCK-A-BYE, BABY,
IN THE TREE-TOP,

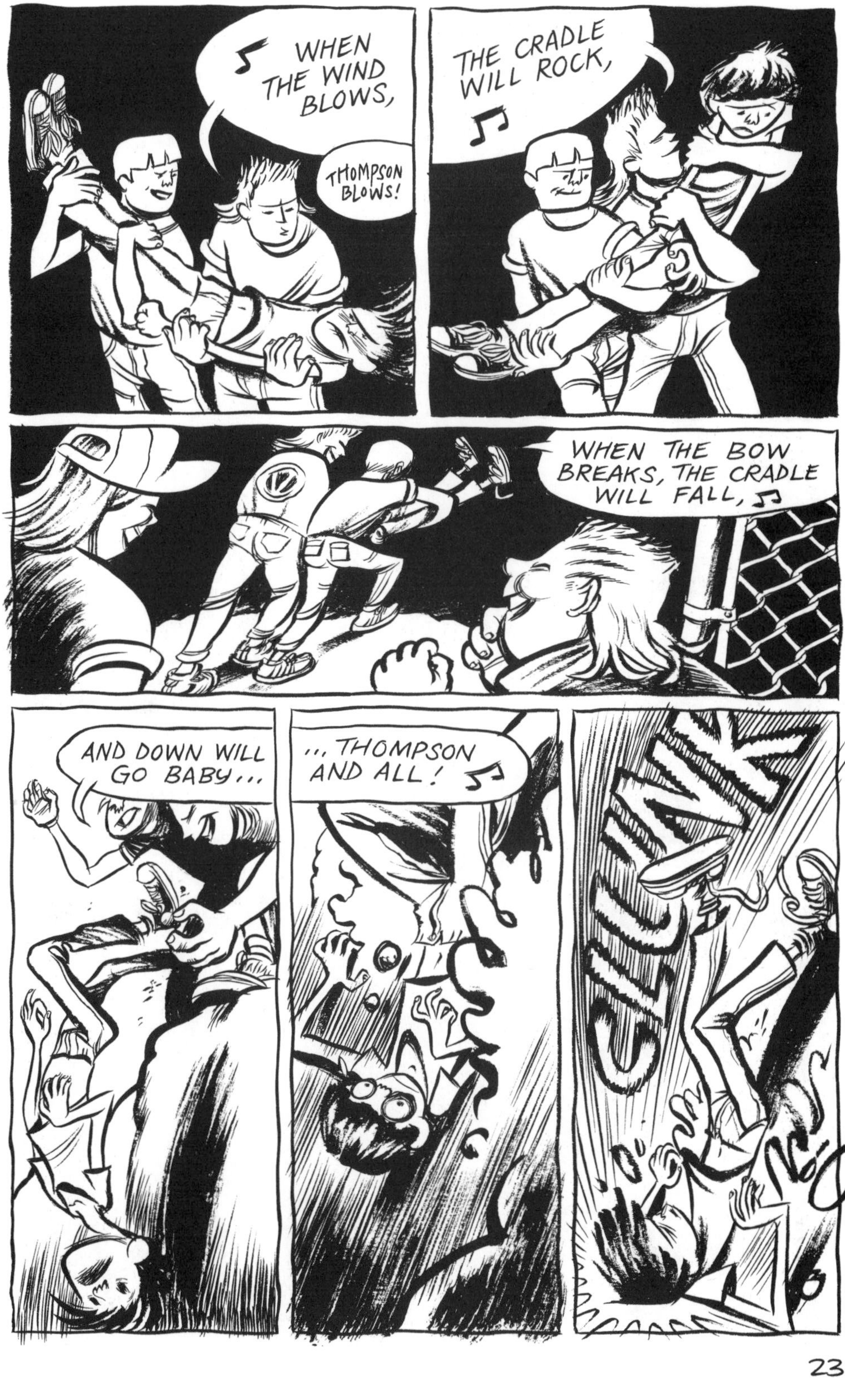
WHEN THE WIND BLOWS,
THOMPSON BLOWS!
THE CRADLE WILL ROCK,
WHEN THE BOW BREAKS, THE CRADLE WILL FALL,
AND DOWN WILL GO BABY...
..., THOMPSON AND ALL!
CLUNK

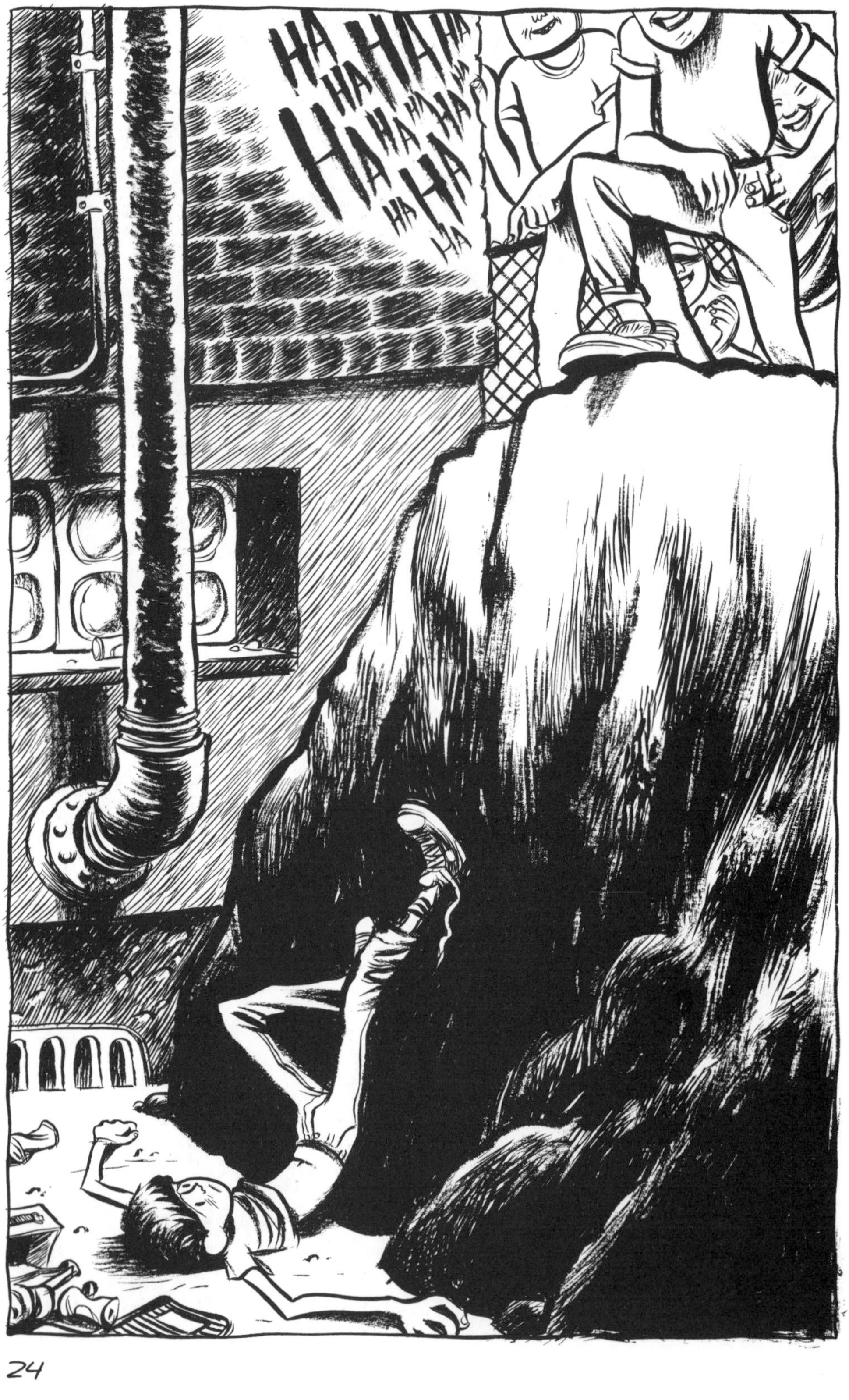
HA HA HA HA
HA HA HA HA HA
HA HA HA HA
HA HA HA

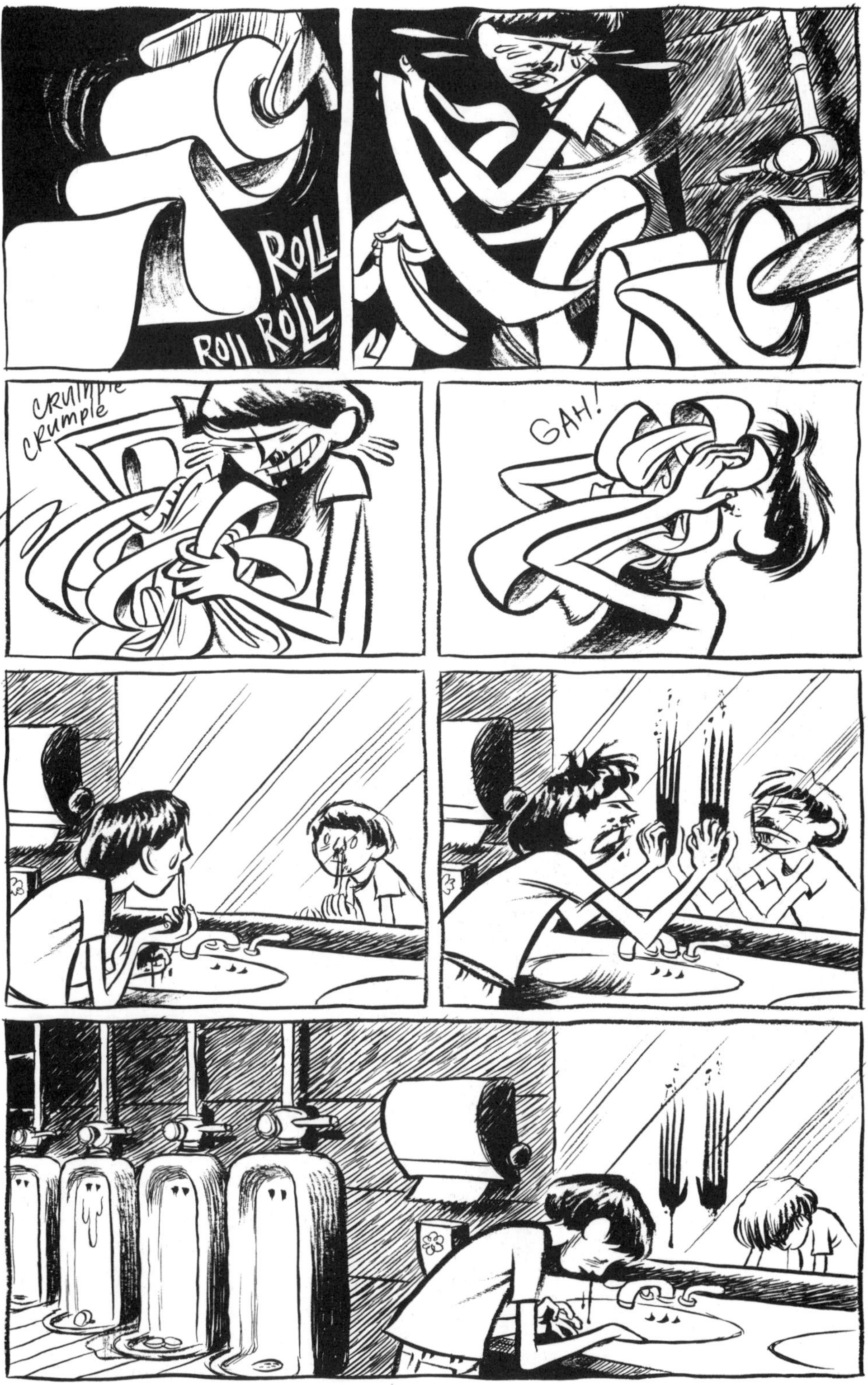
ROLL
ROLL ROLL
CRUMPLE
CRUMPLE
GAH!

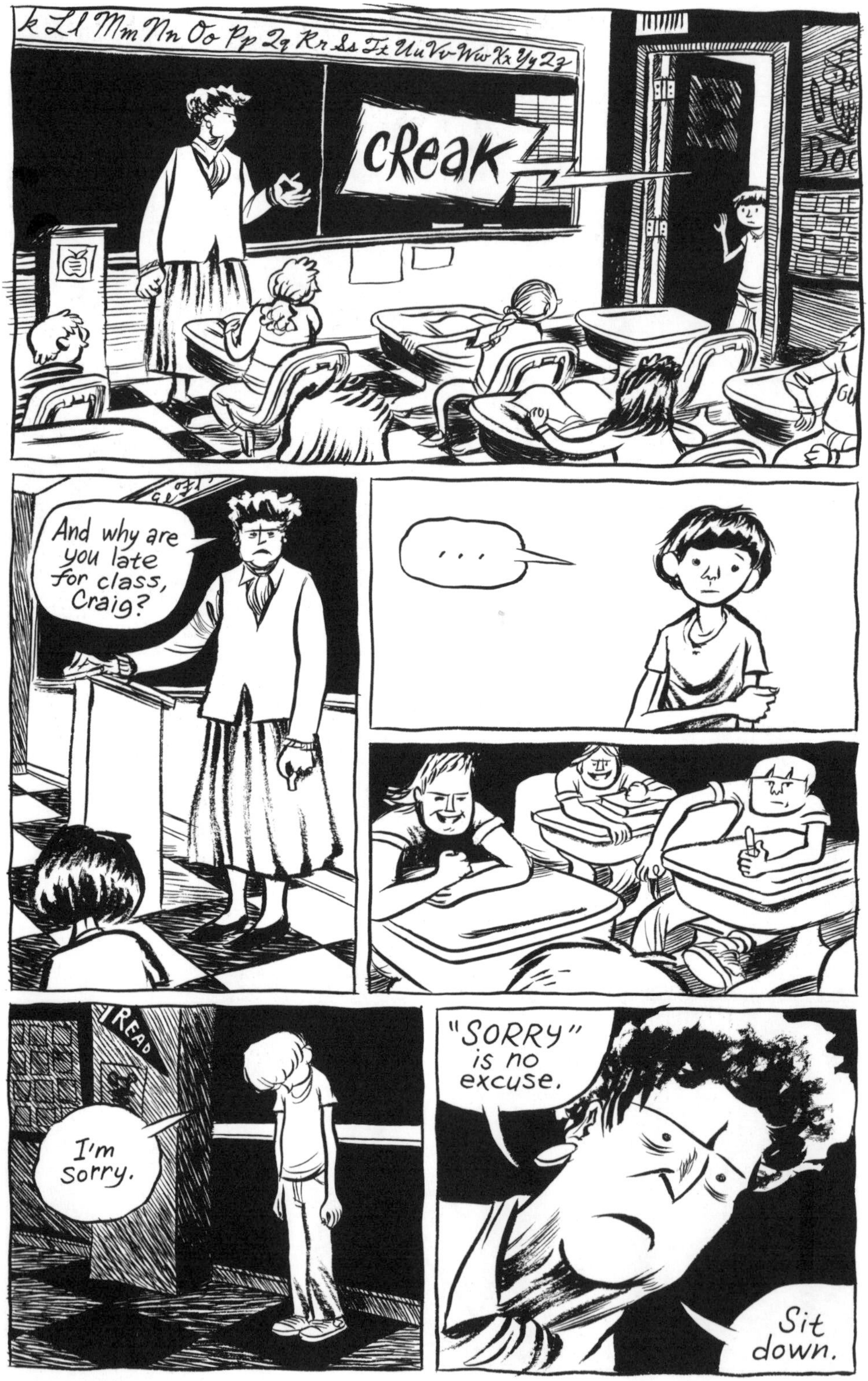

k Ll Mm Nn Oo Pp Qq Rr Ss Tt Uu Vv Ww Xx Yy Zz
CReak
And why are you late for class, Craig?
. . .
I'm sorry.
"SORRY" is no excuse.
Sit down.

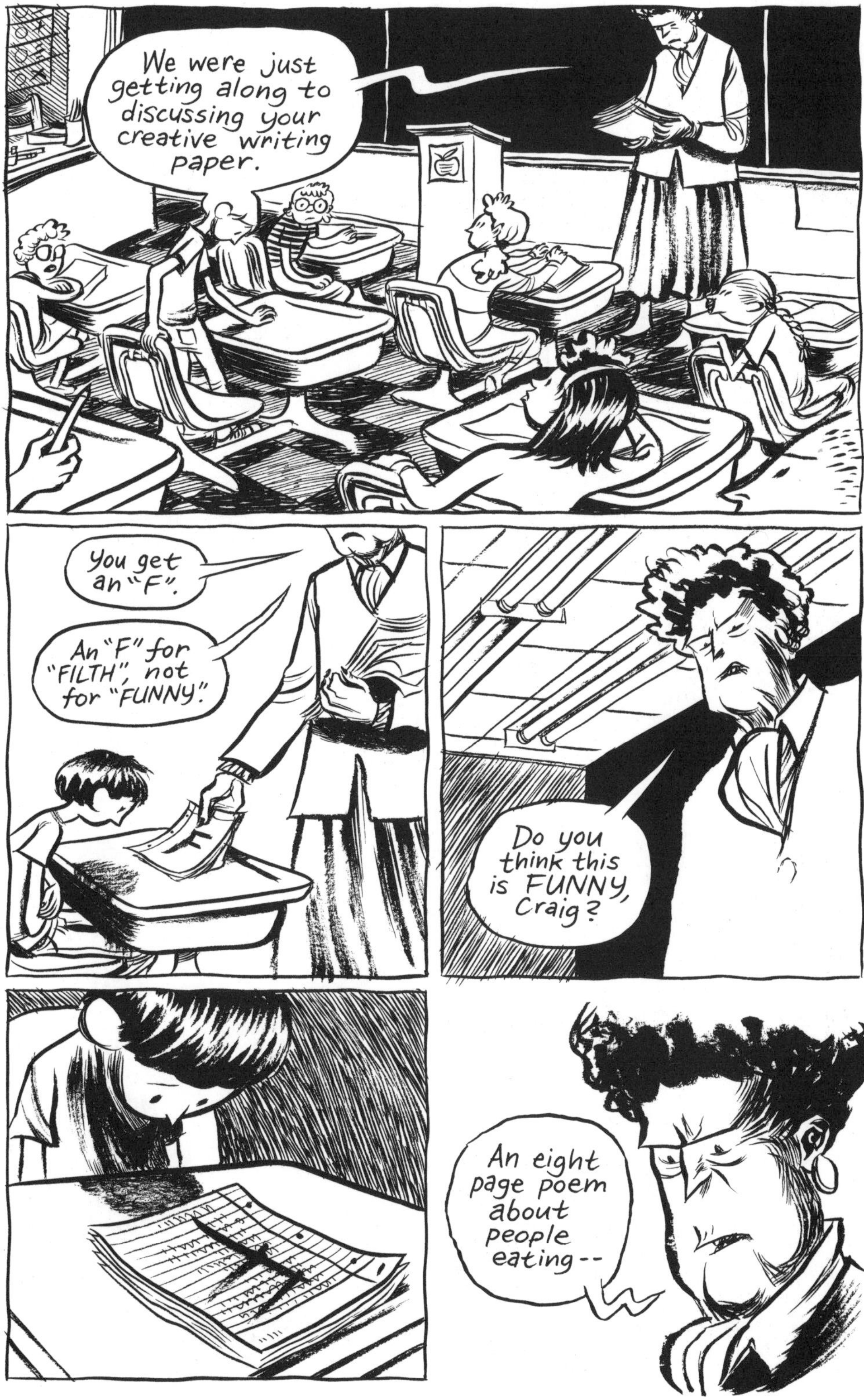
We were just getting along to discussing your creative writing paper.
You get an "F".
An "F" for "FILTH", not for "FUNNY".
Do you think this is FUNNY, Craig?
An eight page poem about people eating--

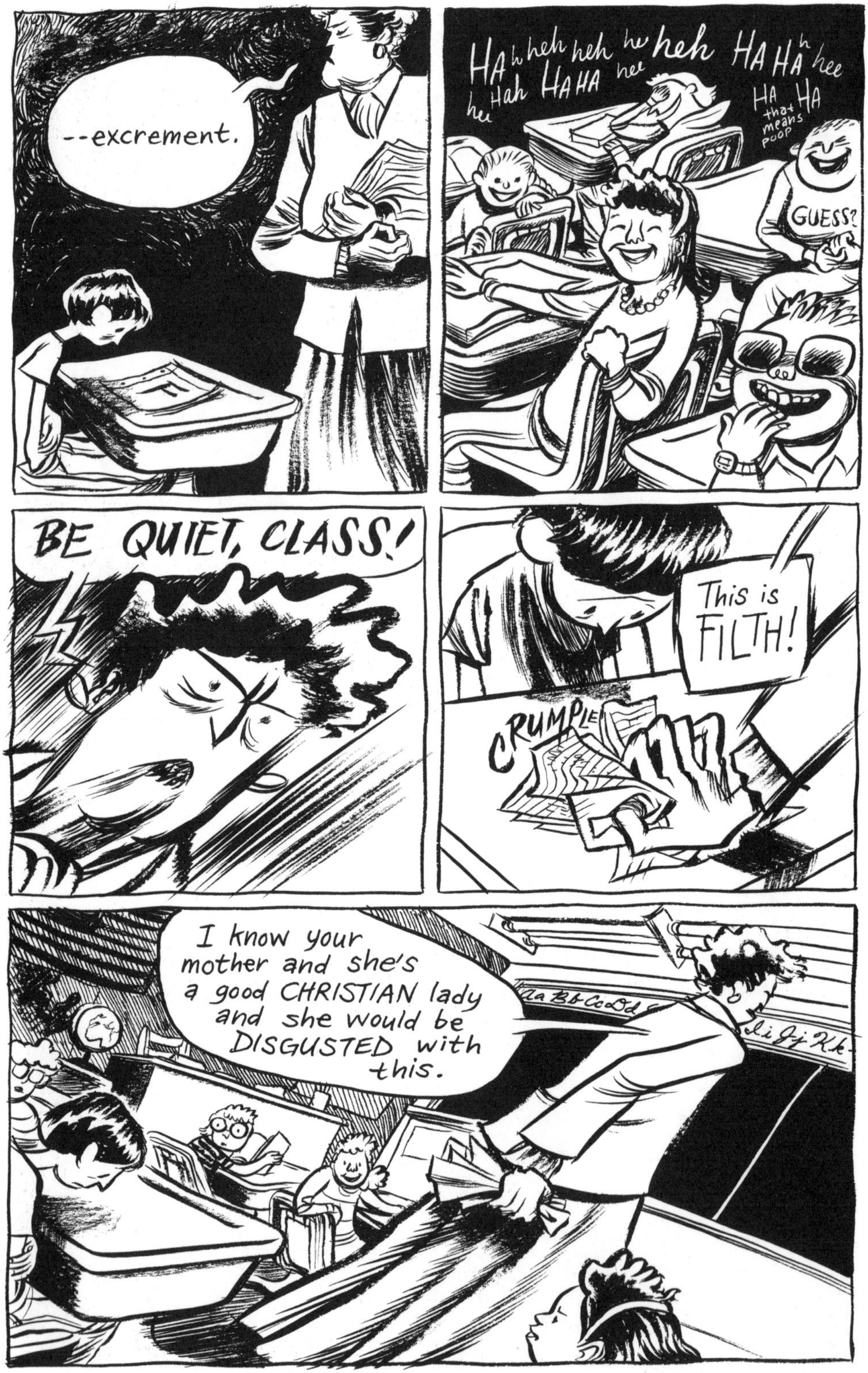
--excrement.
HA h heh heh he heh HA HA h hee
hee Hah HAHA hee
HA HA
that means poop
GUESS?
BE QUIET, CLASS!
This is FILTH!
CRUMPLE
I know your mother and she's a good CHRISTIAN lady and she would be DISGUSTED with this.
Aa Bb Cc Dd
Ii Jj Kk

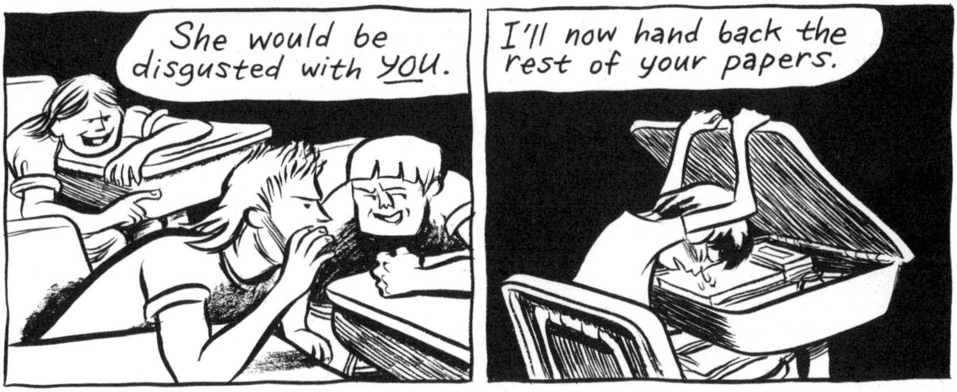
She would be disgusted with YOU.
I'll now hand back the rest of your papers.

If only God could forgive me for all the times I pictured people eating their own excrement.

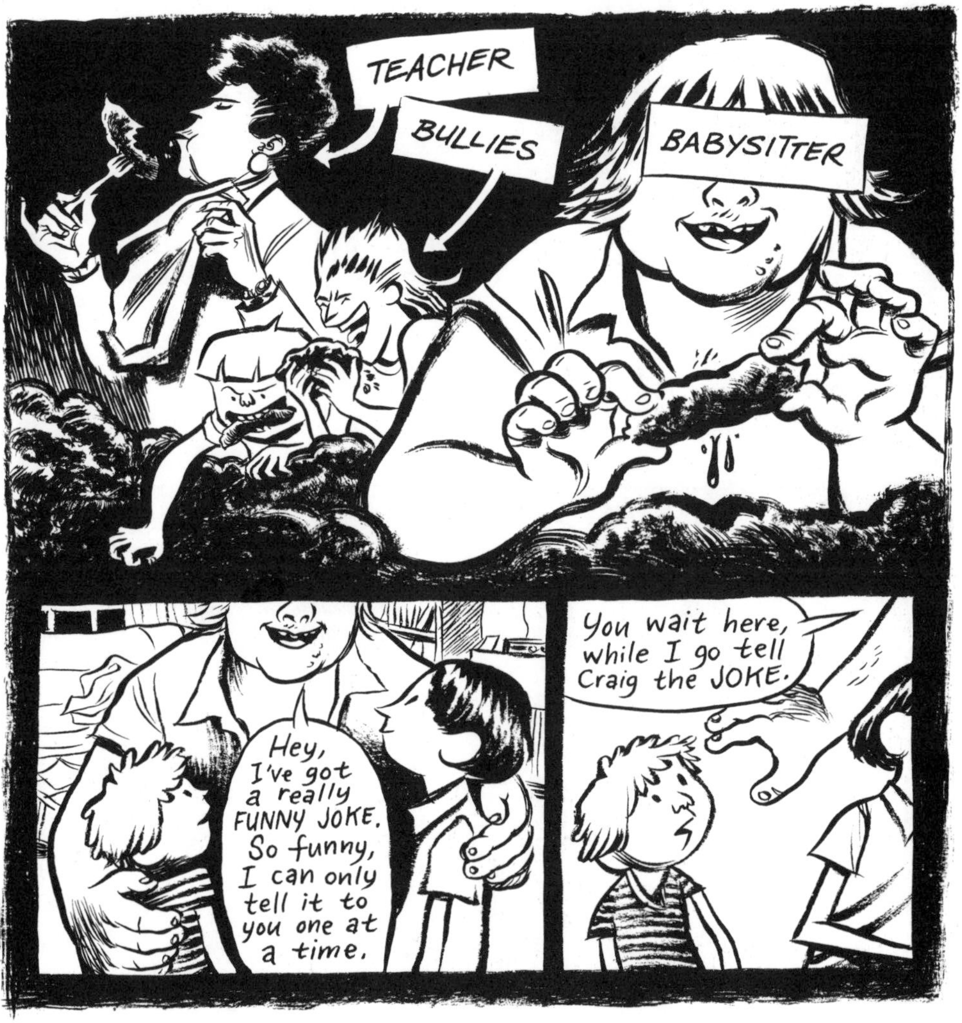
TEACHER
BULLIES
BABYSITTER
Hey, I've got a really FUNNY JOKE. So funny, I can only tell it to you one at a time.
You wait here, while I go tell Craig the JOKE.

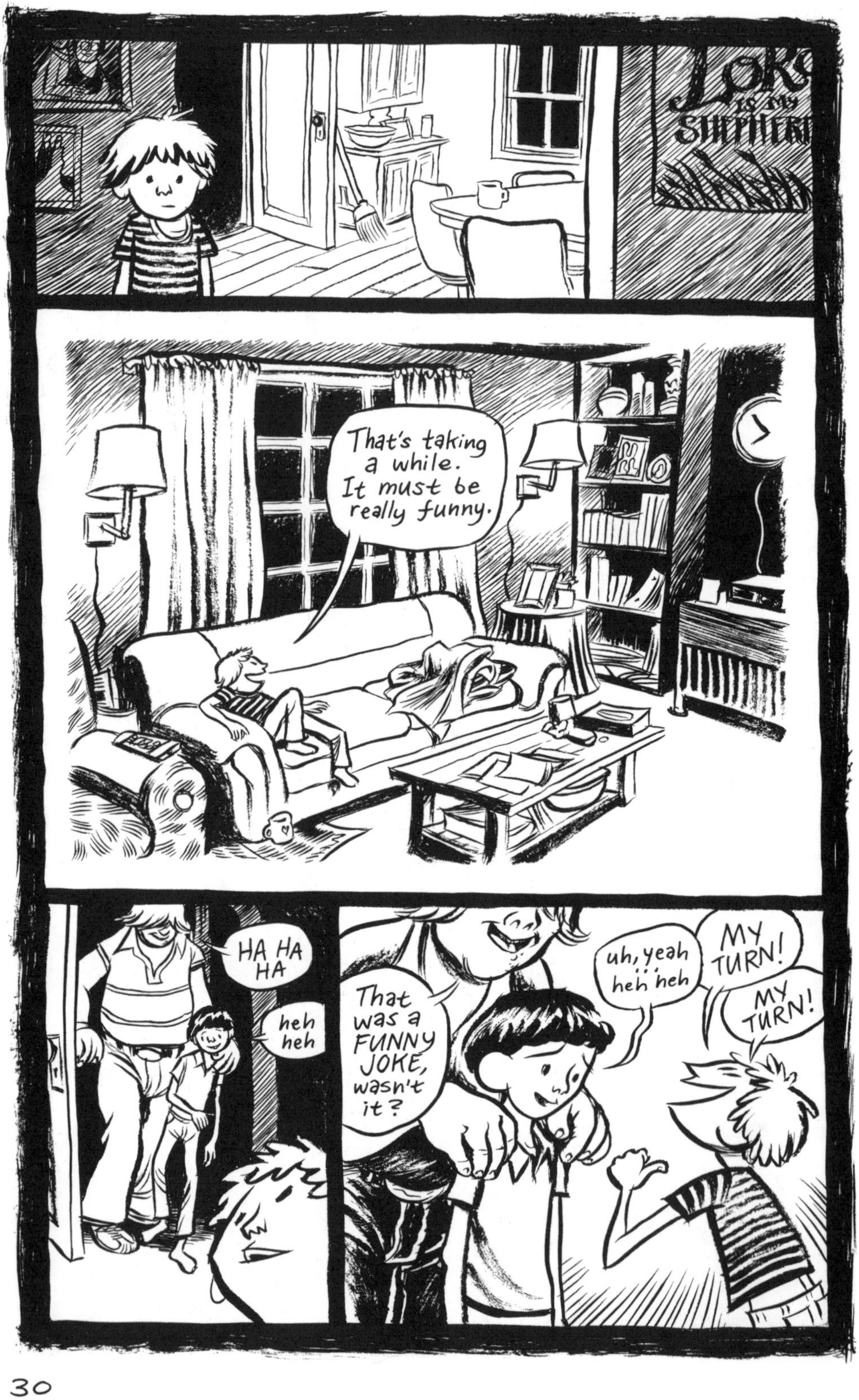

That's taking a while. It must be really funny.
HA HA HA
heh heh
That was a FUNNY JOKE, wasn't it?
uh, yeah ... heh heh
MY TURN!
MY TURN!

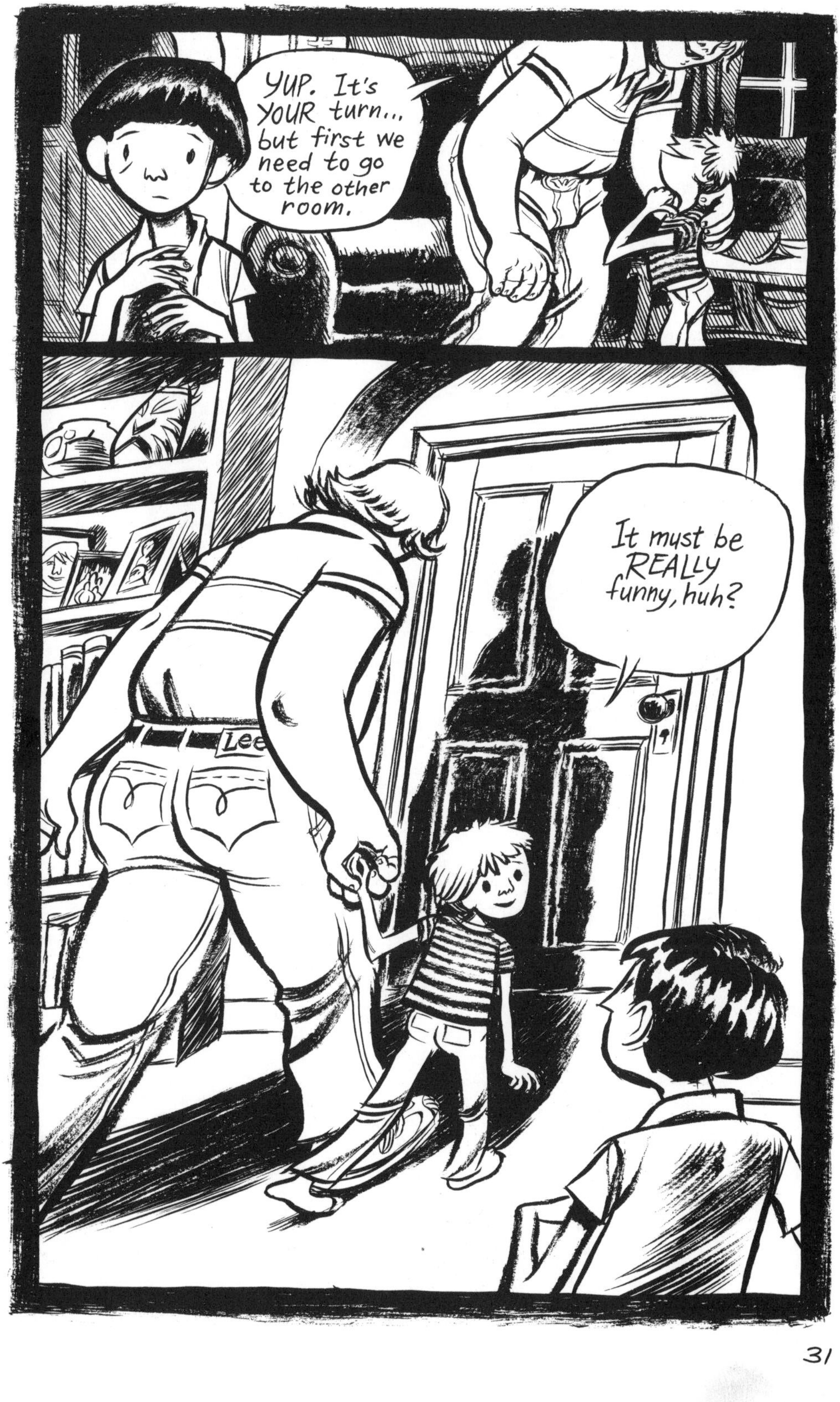
YUP. It's YOUR turn... but first we need to go to the other room.
It must be REALLY funny, huh?
Lee

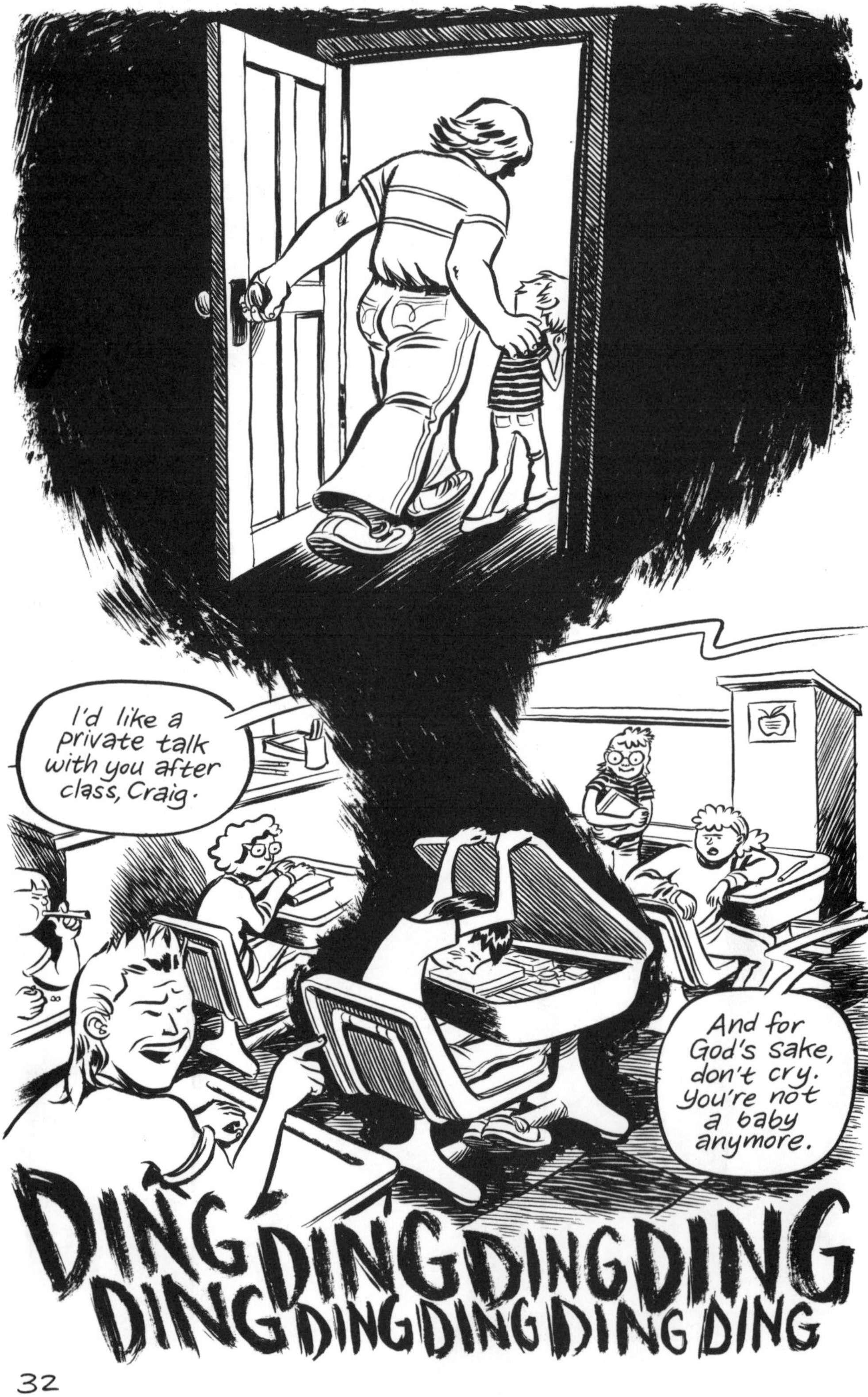
I'd like a private talk with you after class, Craig.
And for God's sake, don't cry. You're not a baby anymore.
DING DING DING DING
DING DING DING DING DING

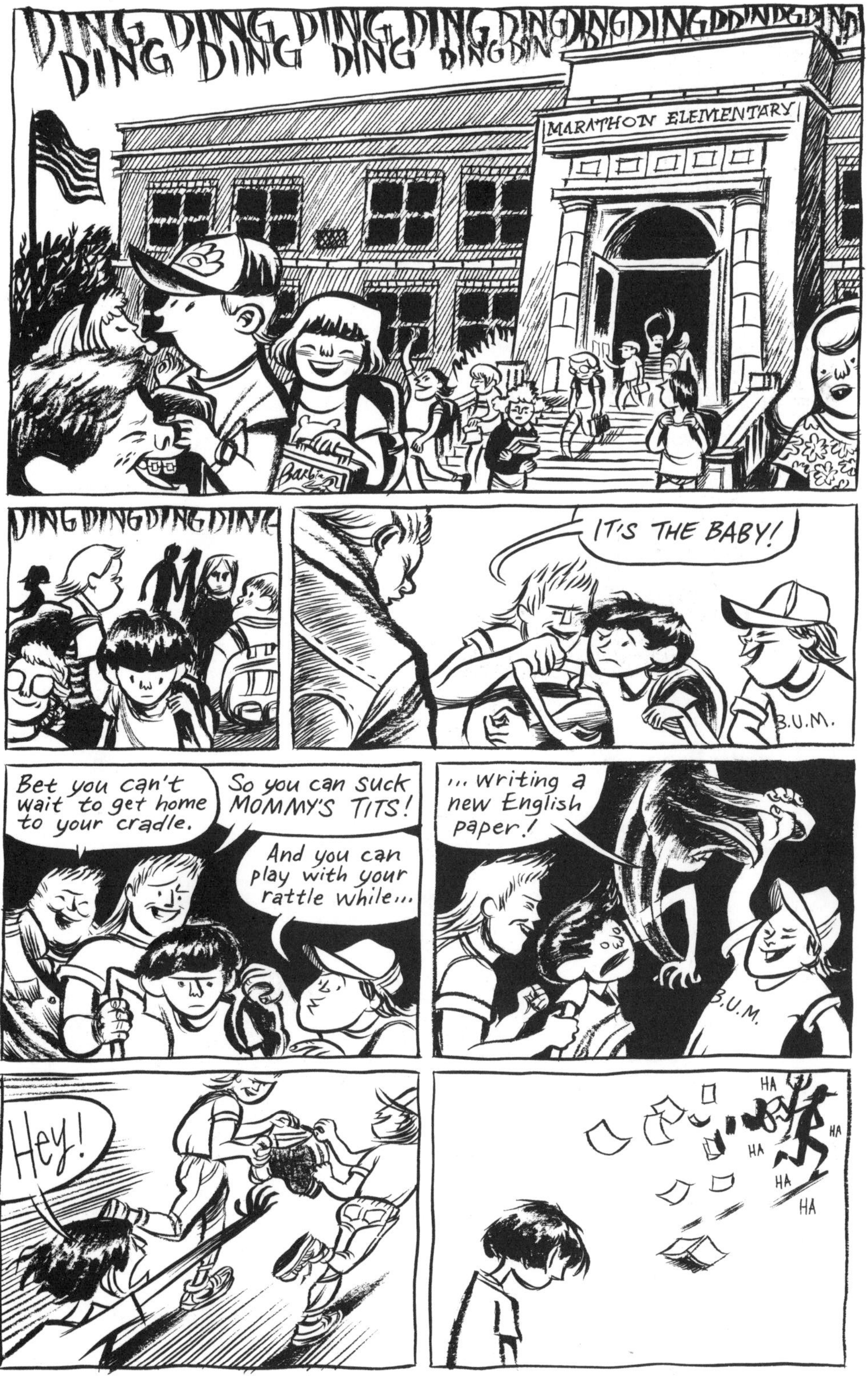
DING DING DING DING DING DING DING DING
DING DING DING DING DIN
MARATHON ELEMENTARY
DING DING DING DING
IT'S THE BABY!
B.U.M.
Bet you can't wait to get home to your cradle.
So you can suck MOMMY'S TITS!
And you can play with your rattle while...
...writing a new English paper!
B.U.M.
Hey!
HA
HA
HA
HA
HA

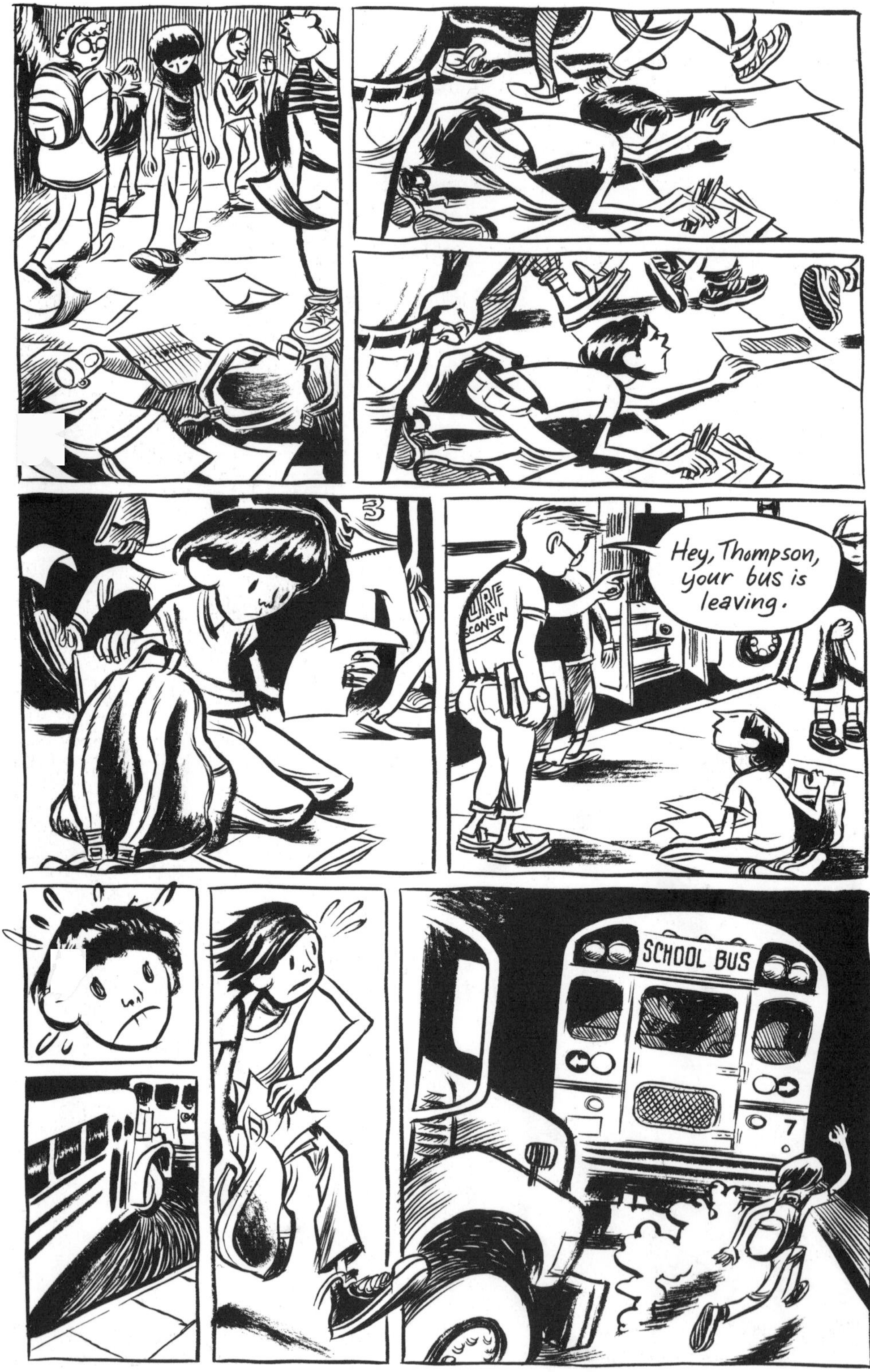

ORF
SCONSIN
3
Hey, Thompson, your bus is leaving.
SCHOOL BUS
7

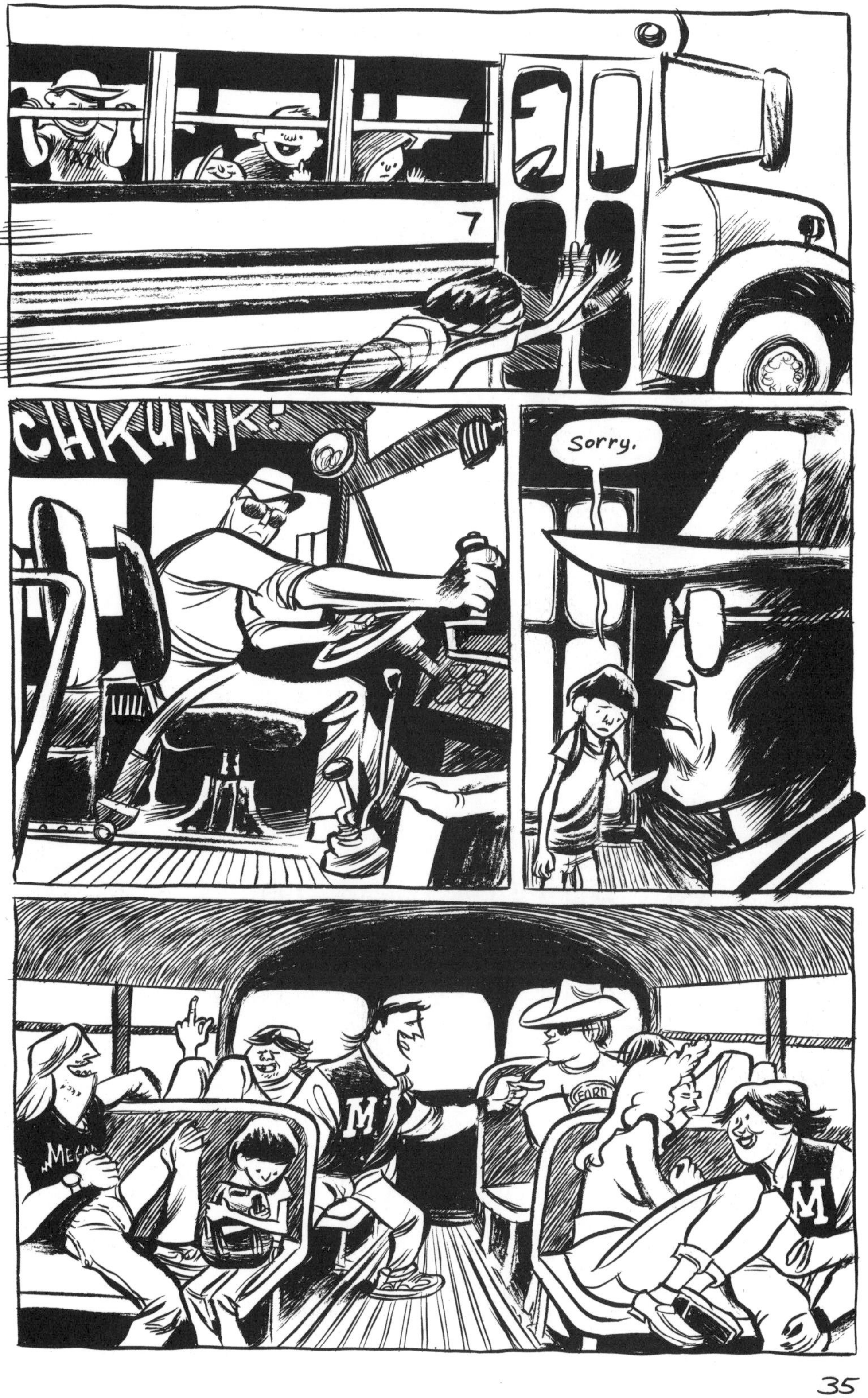
CHKUNK!
Sorry.

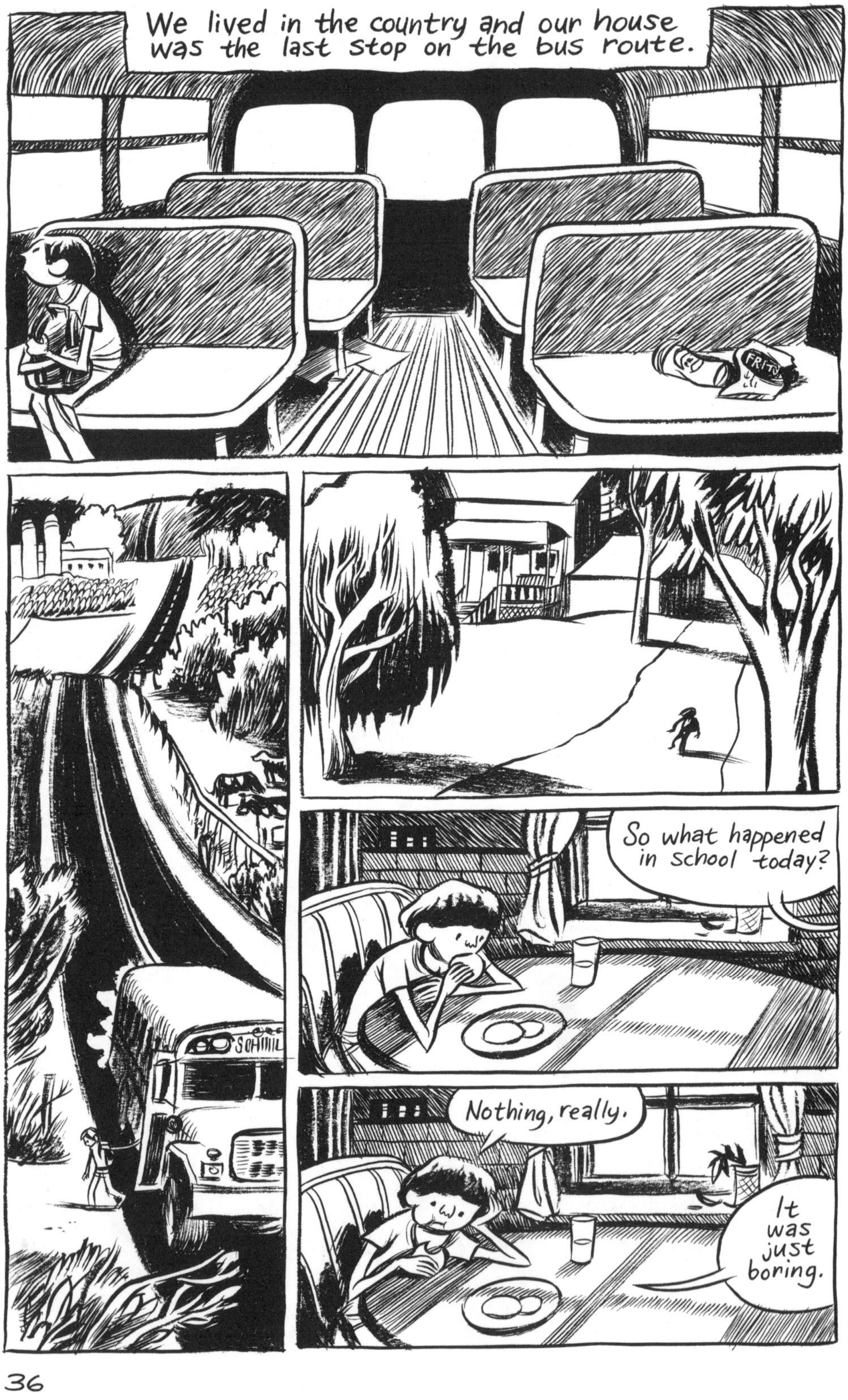
We lived in the country and our house was the last stop on the bus route.
So what happened in school today?
Nothing, really.
It was just boring.

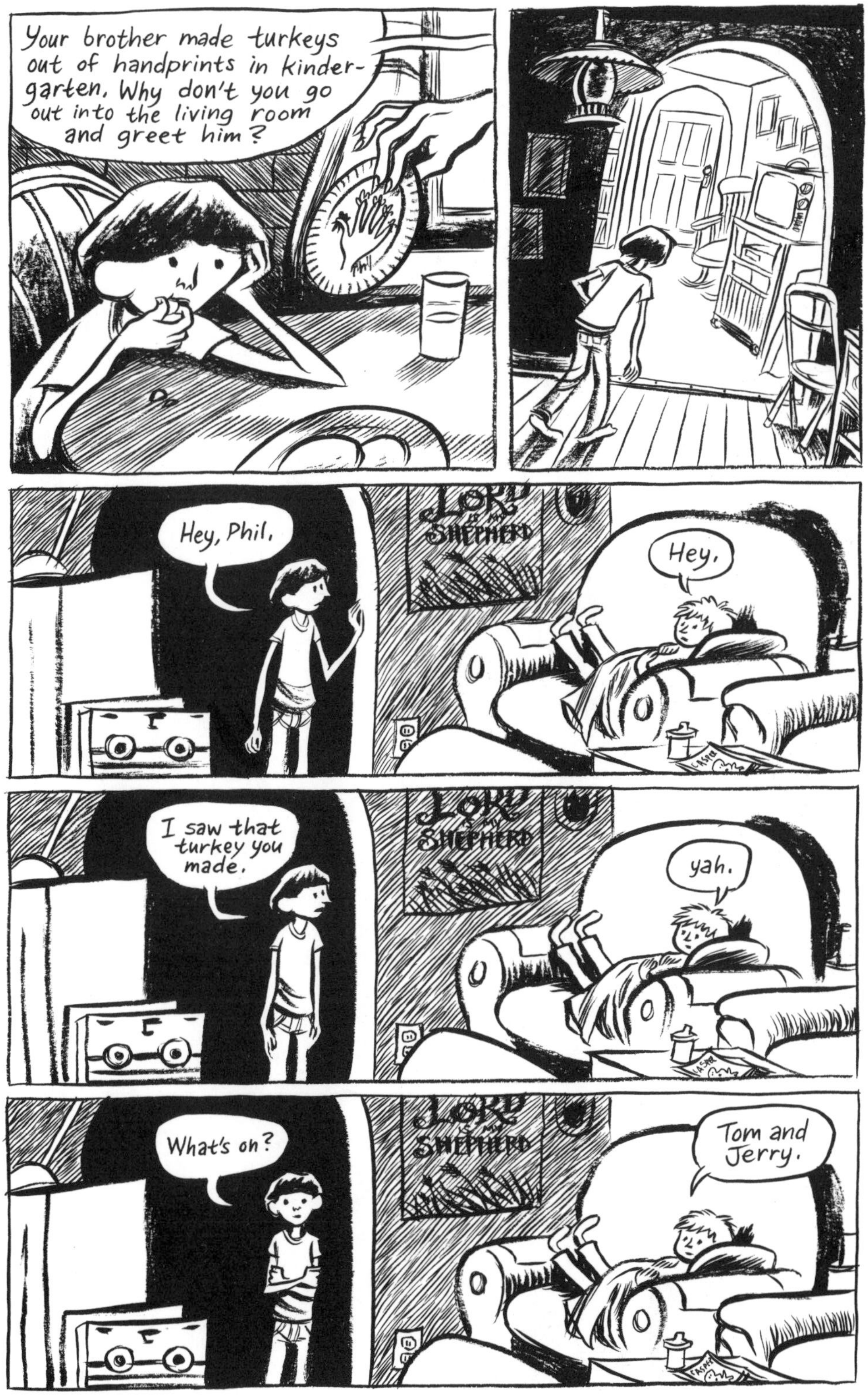
Your brother made turkeys out of handprints in kindergarten. Why don't you go out into the living room and greet him?
Hey, Phil.
Hey.
I saw that turkey you made.
yah.
What's on?
Tom and Jerry.

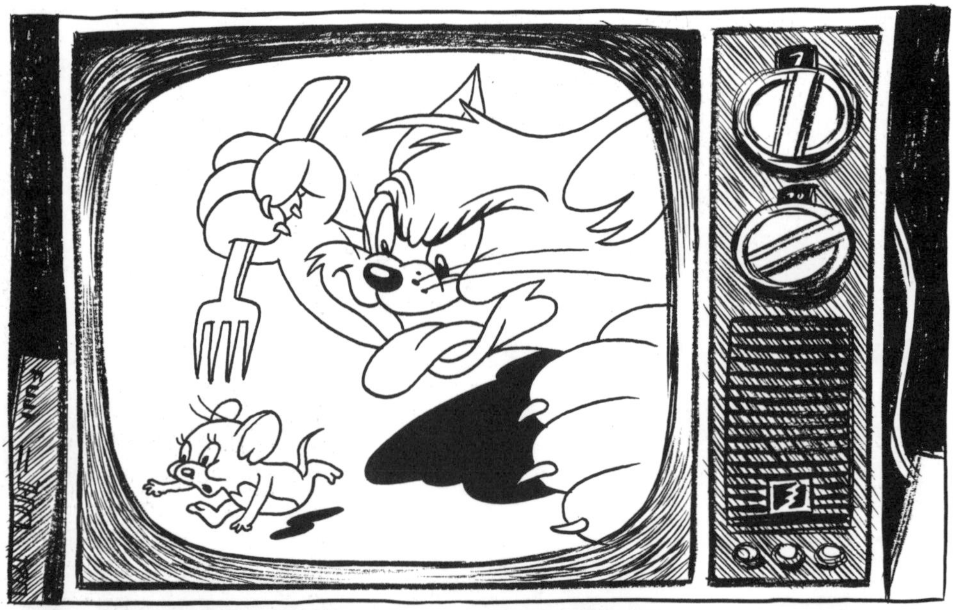

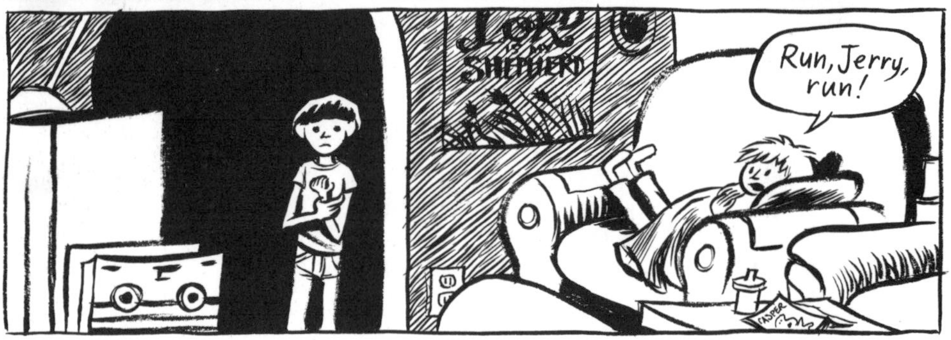
Run, Jerry, run!

As a child, I thought that life was the most horrible world anyone could ever live in, and that there HAD to be something better.

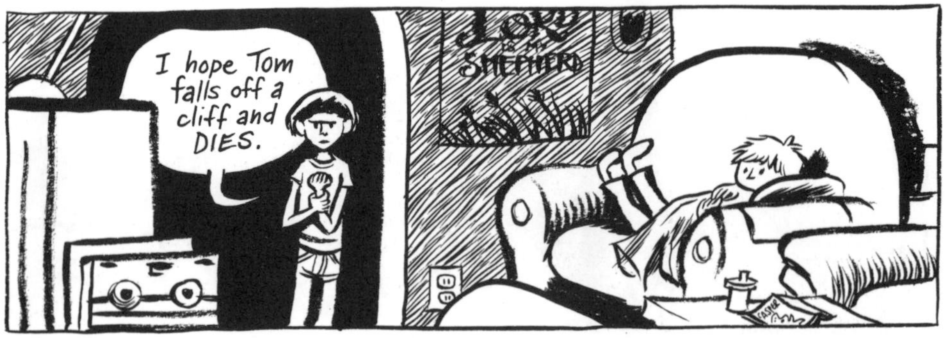
I hope Tom falls off a cliff and DIES.

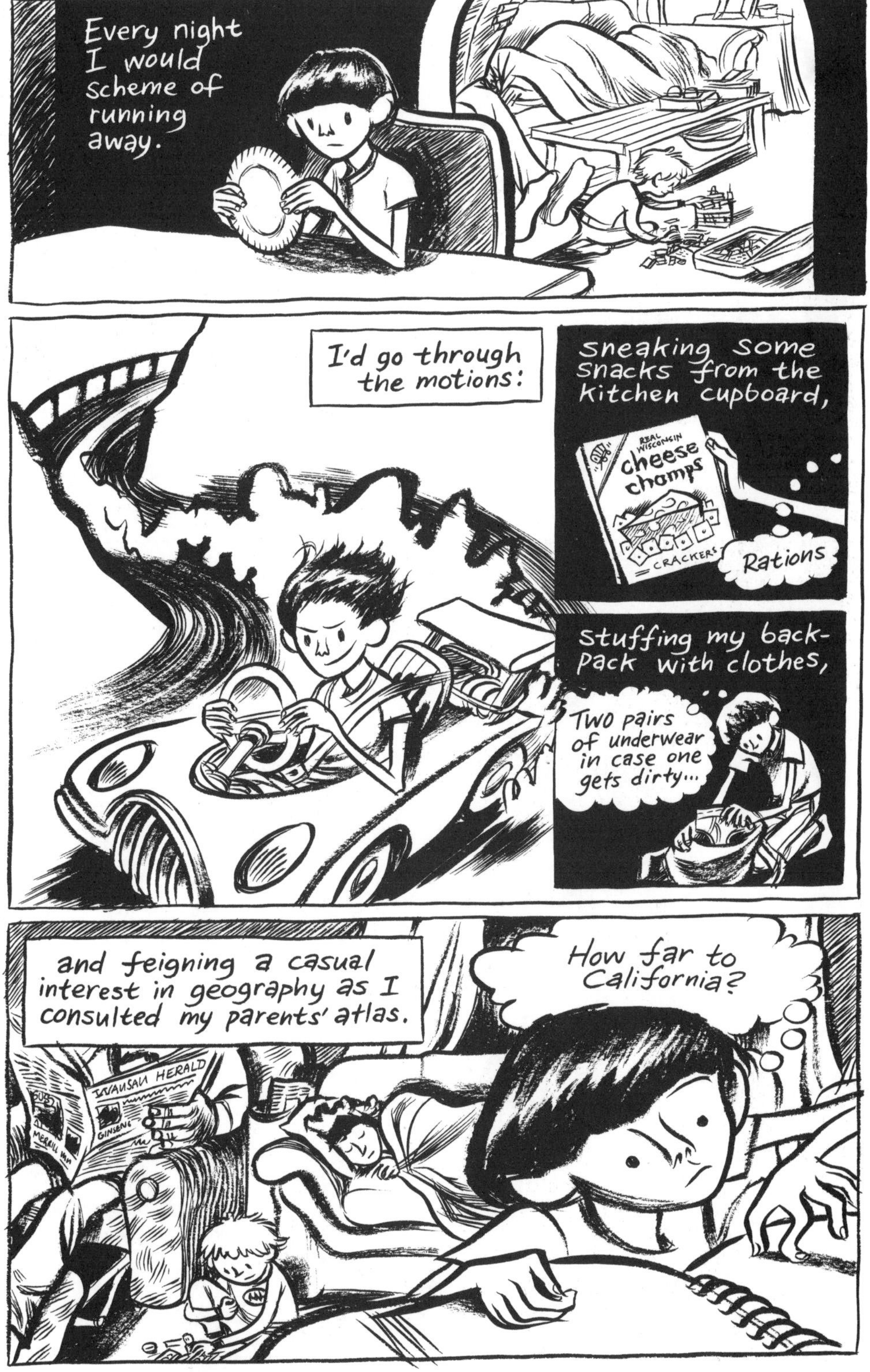
Every night I would scheme of running away.
I'd go through the motions:
sneaking some snacks from the kitchen cupboard,
REAL WISCONSIN cheese champs CRACKERS
Rations
stuffing my back-pack with clothes,
Two pairs of underwear in case one gets dirty...
and feigning a casual interest in geography as I consulted my parents' atlas.
How far to California?
WAUSAU HERALD

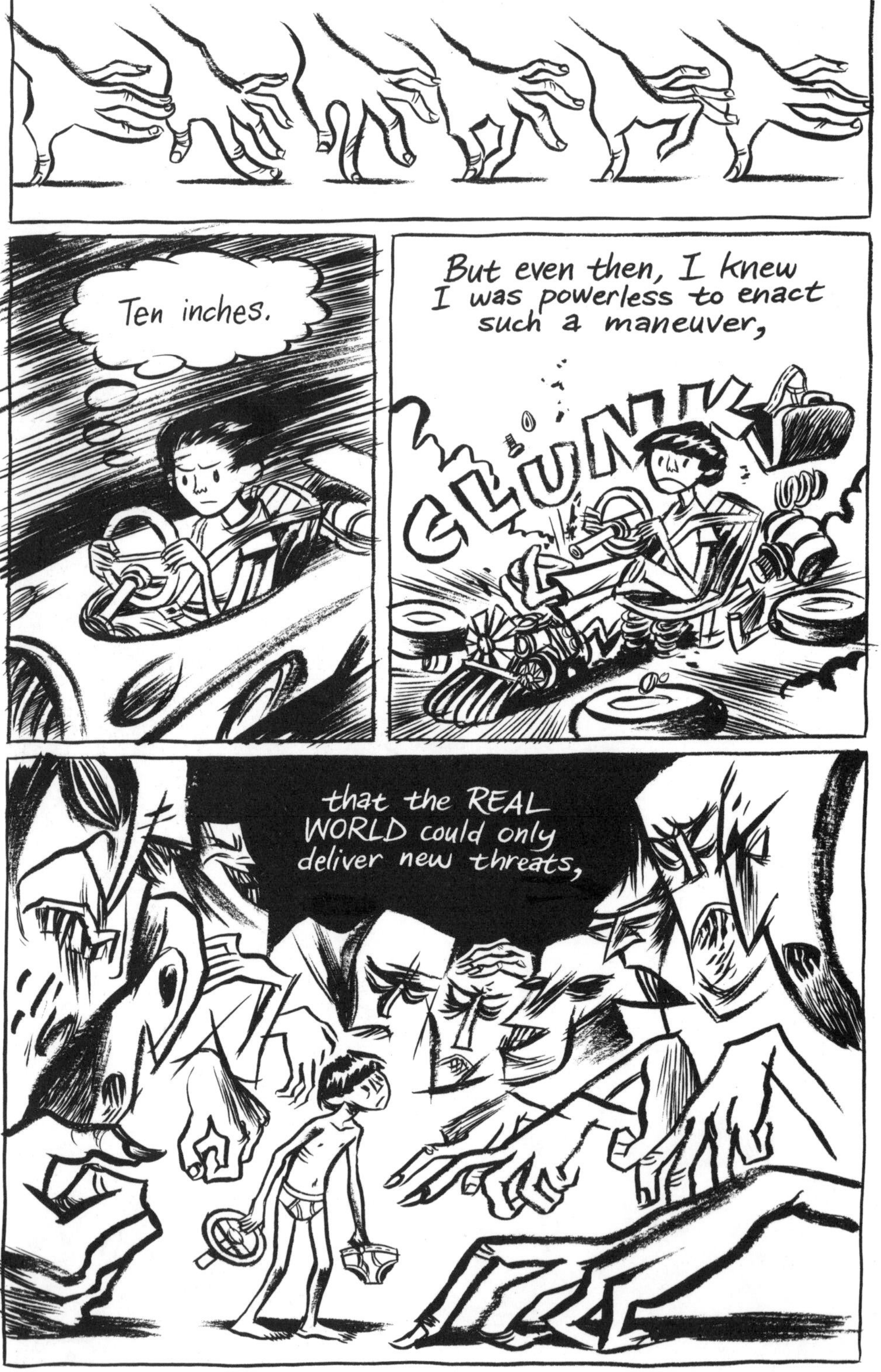
Ten inches.
But even then, I knew I was powerless to enact such a maneuver,
CLUNK
that the REAL WORLD could only deliver new threats,

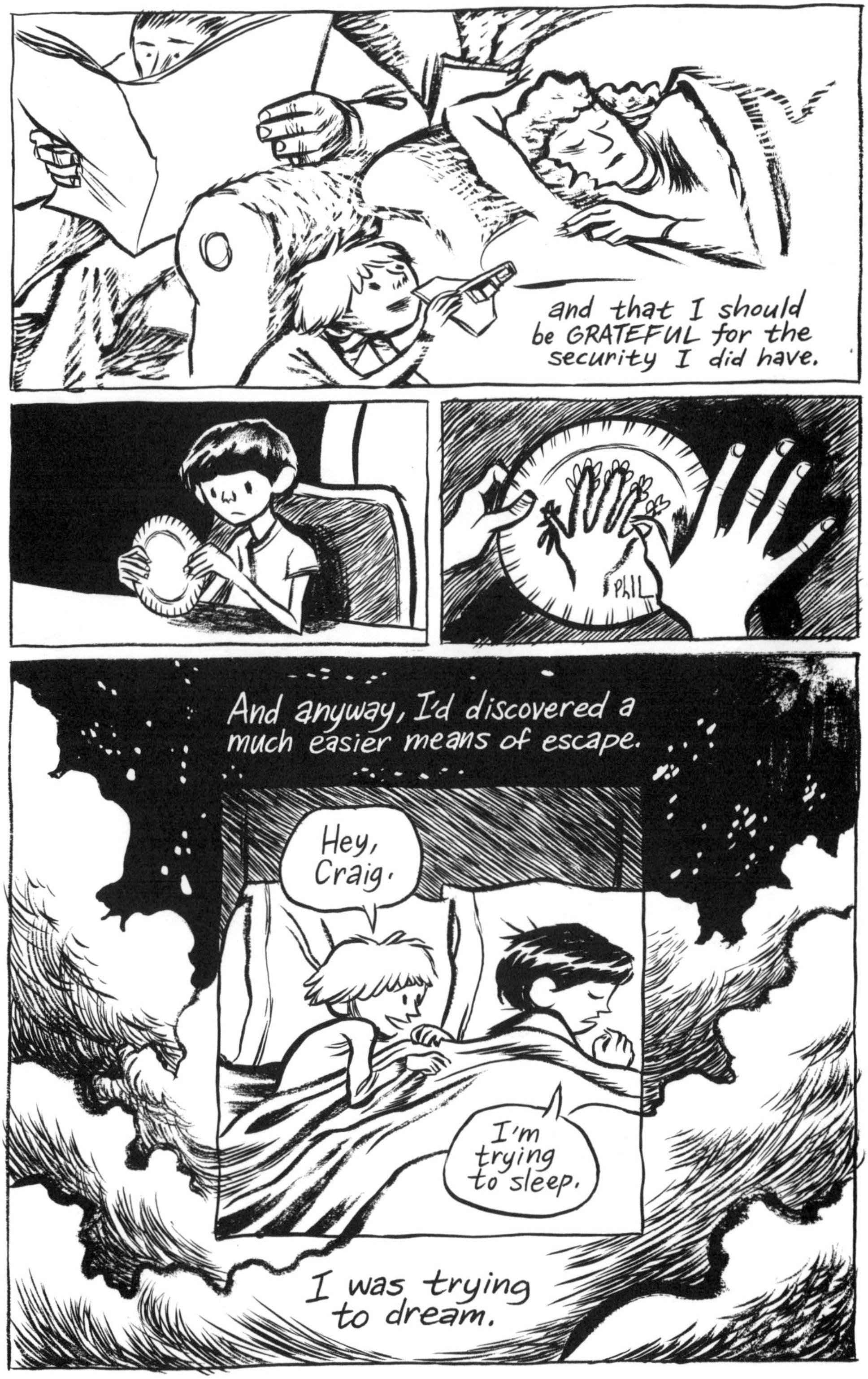
and that I should be GRATEFUL for the security I did have.
PhIL
And anyway, I'd discovered a much easier means of escape.
Hey, Craig.
I'm trying to sleep.
I was trying to dream.

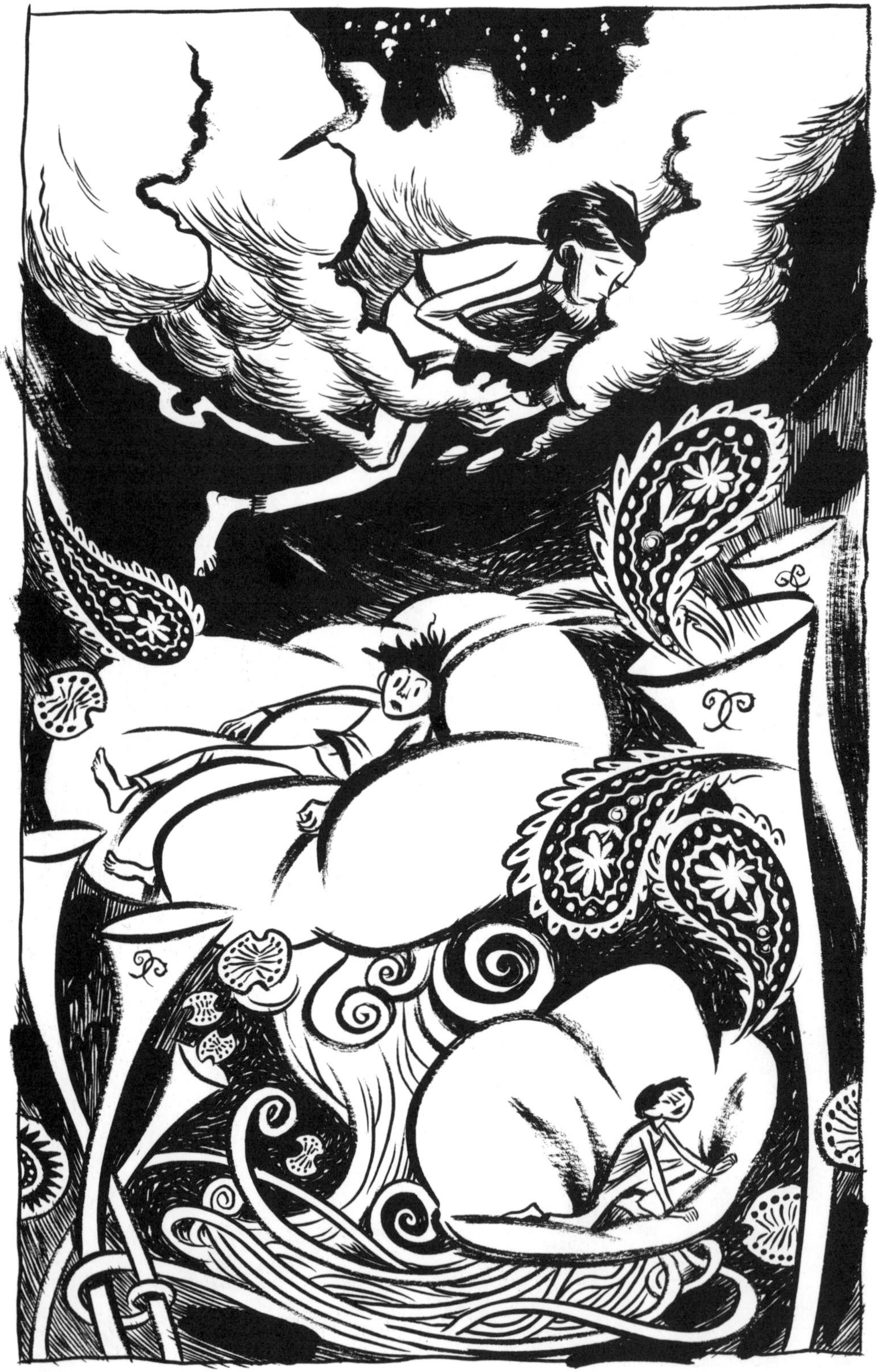

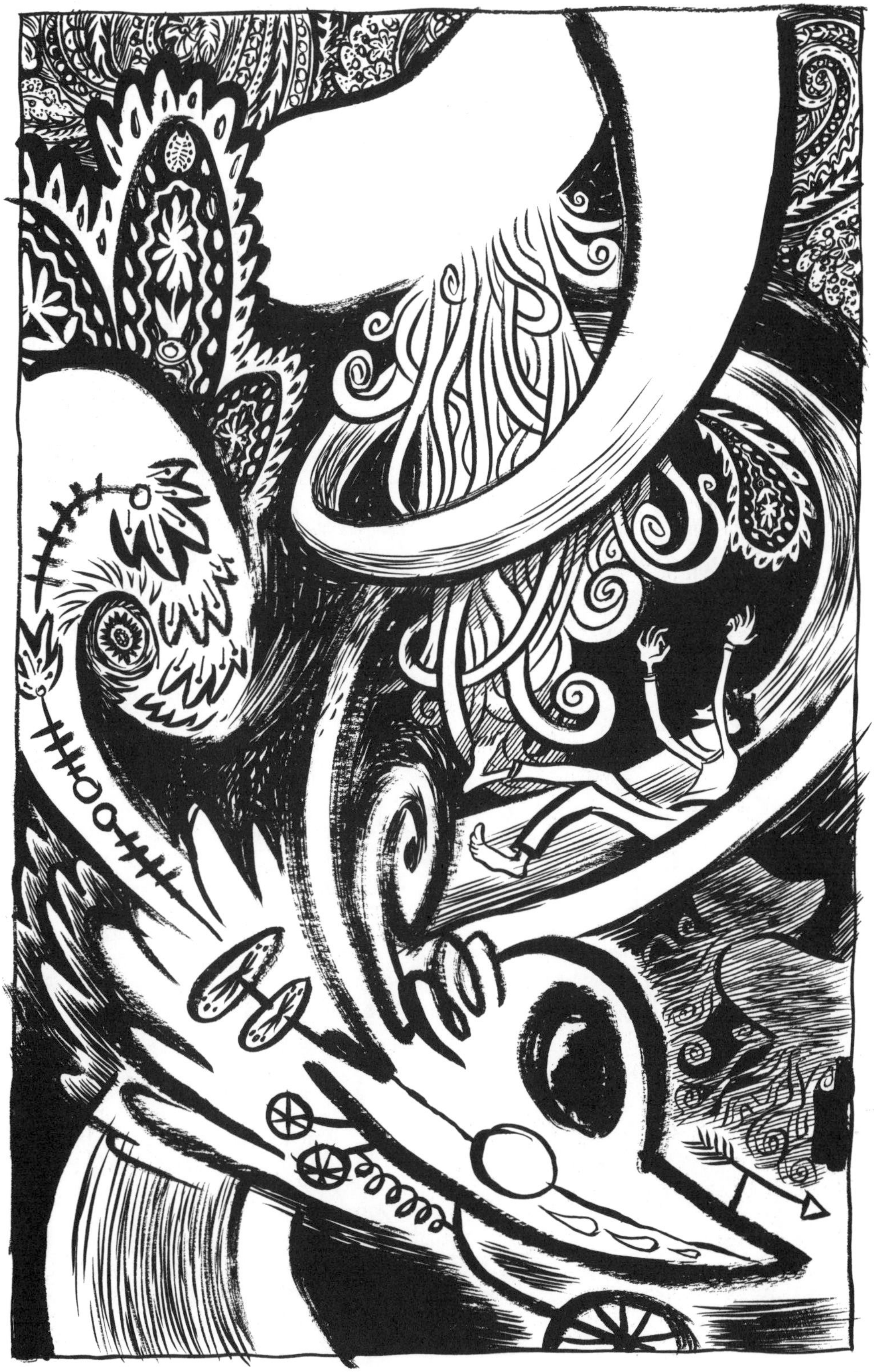

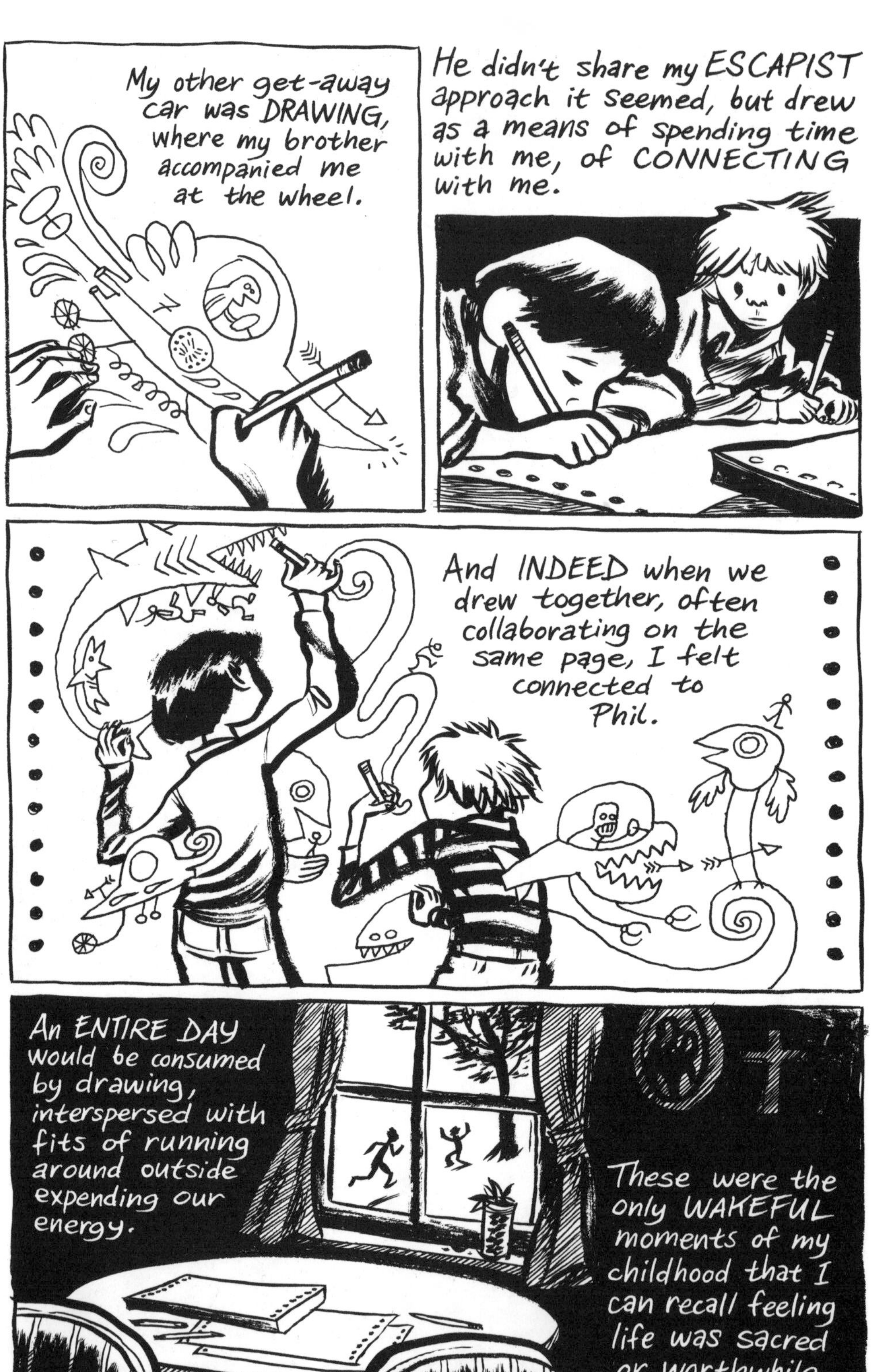
My other get-away car was DRAWING, where my brother accompanied me at the wheel.
He didn't share my ESCAPIST approach it seemed, but drew as a means of spending time with me, of CONNECTING with me.
And INDEED when we drew together, often collaborating on the same page, I felt connected to Phil.
An ENTIRE DAY would be consumed by drawing, interspersed with fits of running around outside expending our energy.
These were the only WAKEFUL moments of my childhood that I can recall feeling life was sacred or worthwhile.

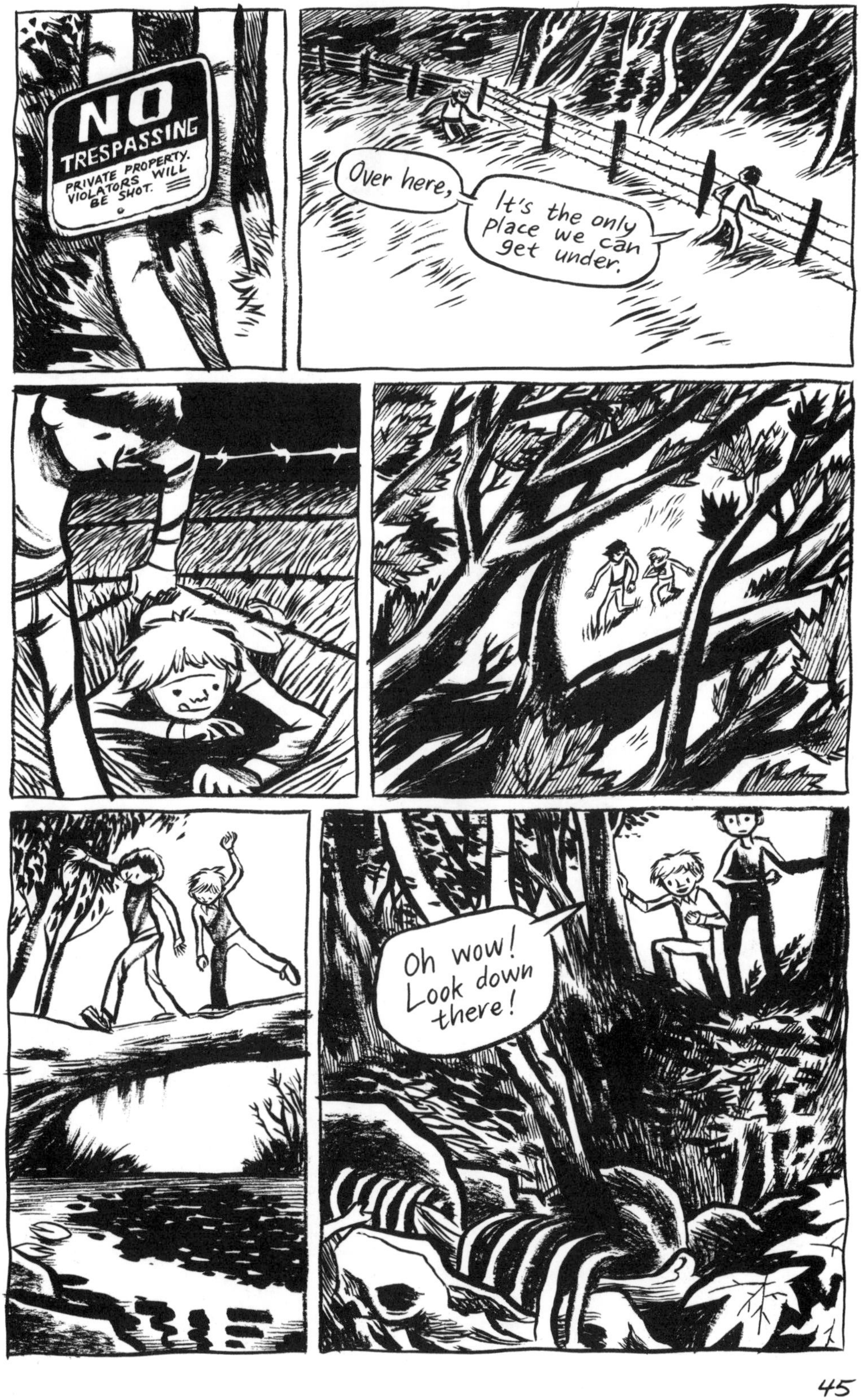
NO TRESPASSING
PRIVATE PROPERTY. VIOLATORS WILL BE SHOT.
Over here,
It's the only place we can get under.
Oh wow! Look down there!

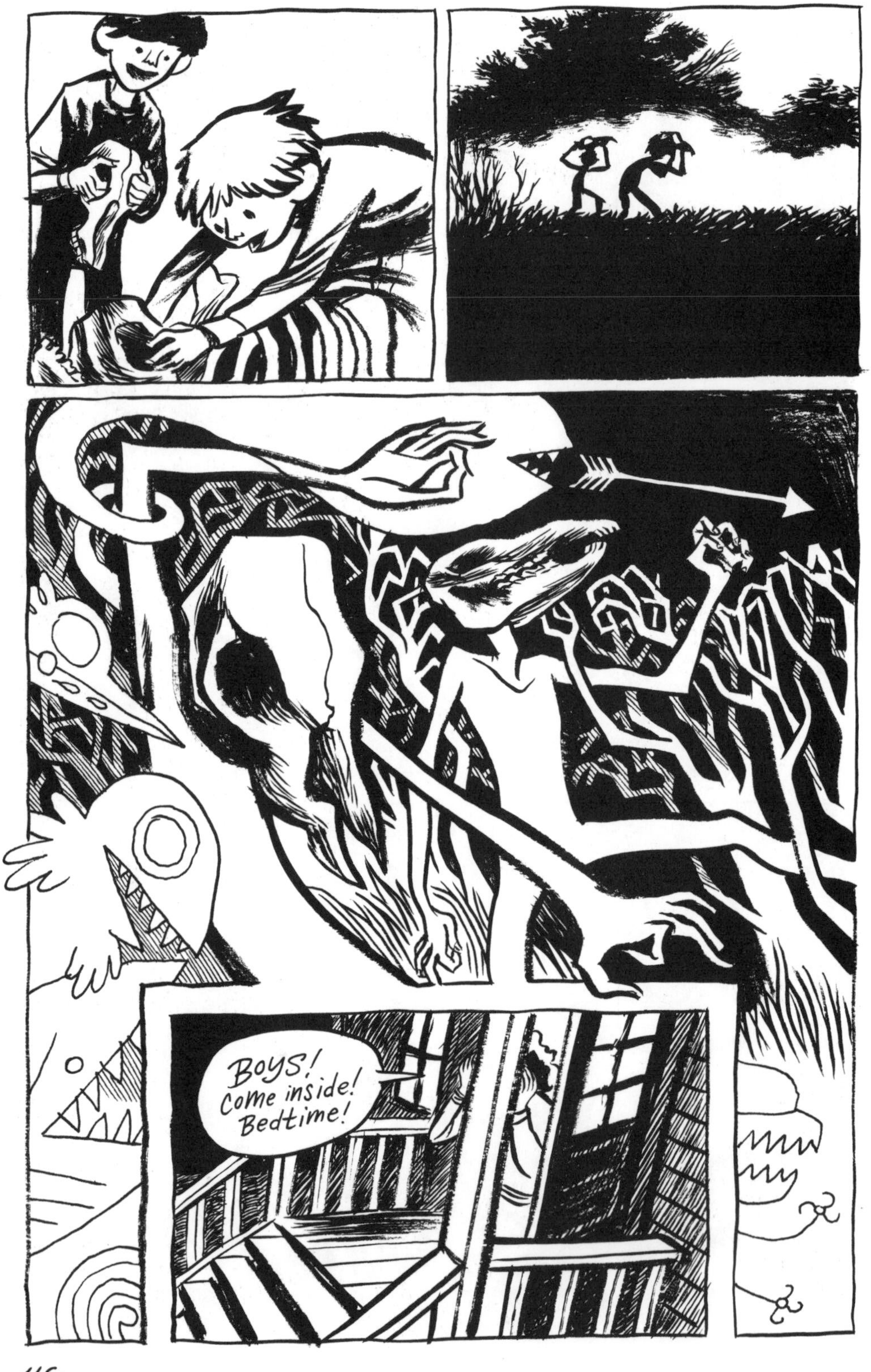
Boys!
Come inside!
Bedtime!

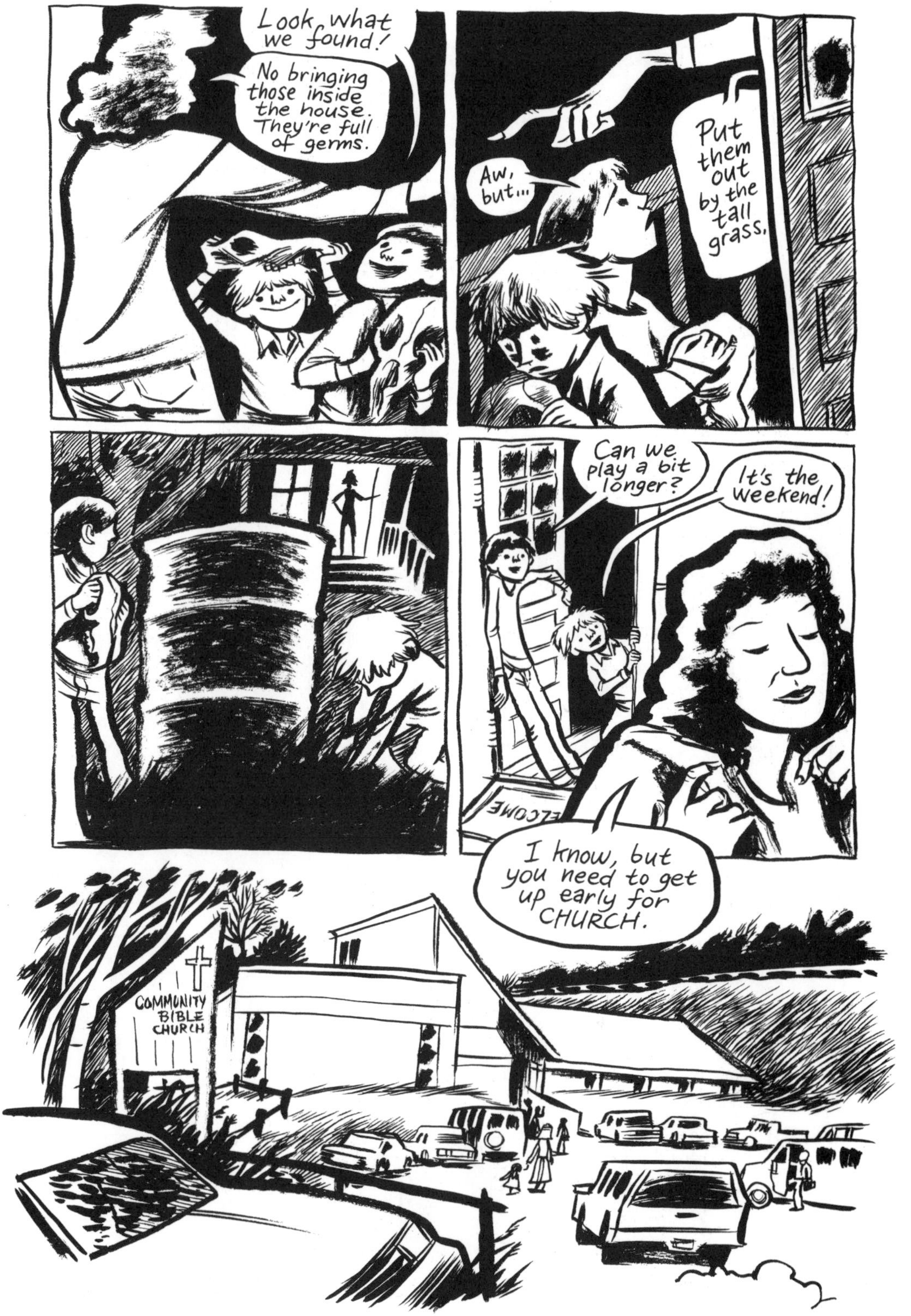

Look what we found!
No bringing those inside the house. They're full of germs.
Aw, but...
Put them out by the tall grass,
Can we play a bit longer?
It's the weekend!
I know, but you need to get up early for CHURCH.
WELCOME
COMMUNITY BIBLE CHURCH

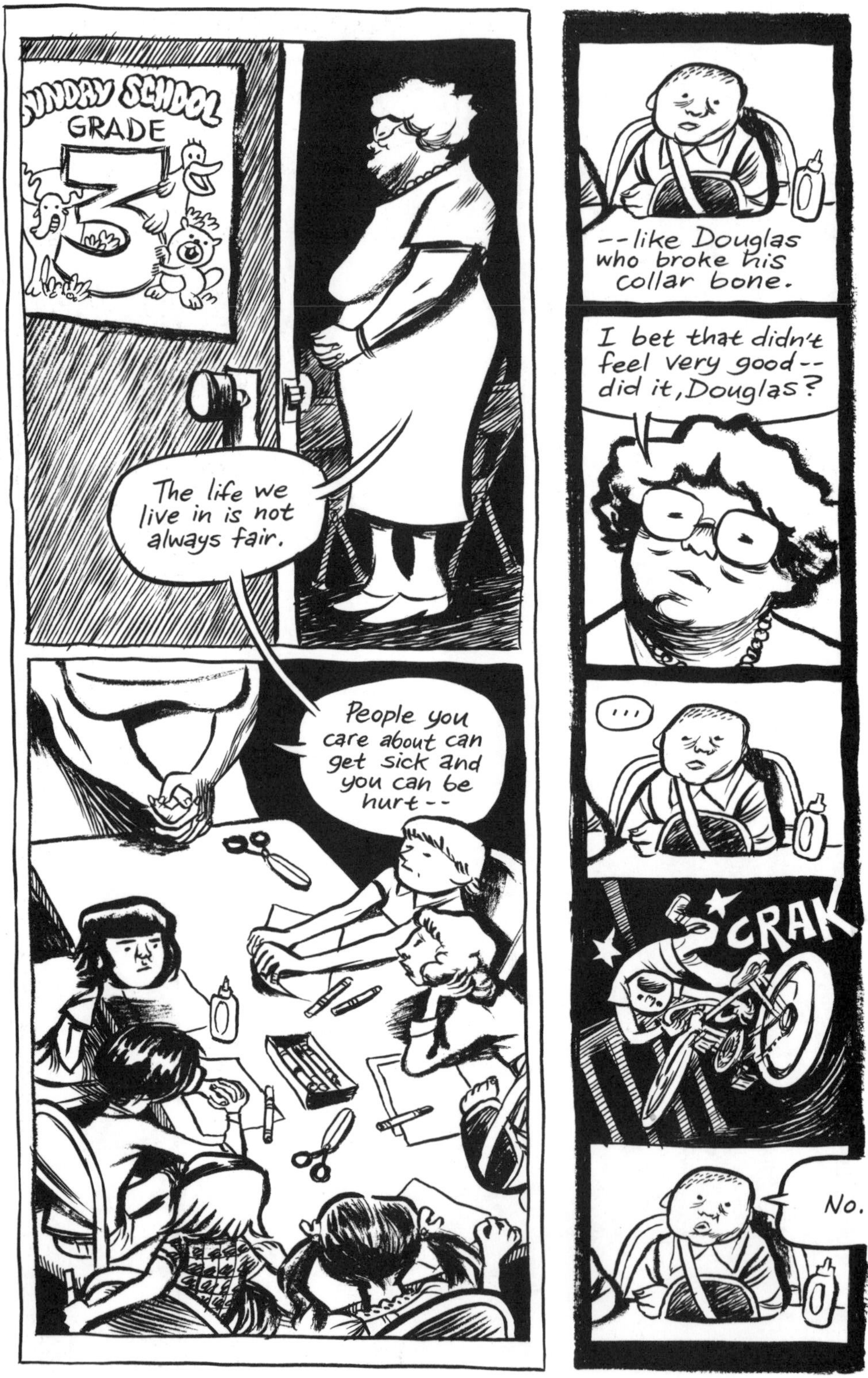
SUNDAY SCHOOL
GRADE
3
The life we live in is not always fair.
People you care about can get sick and you can be hurt--
--like Douglas who broke his collar bone.
I bet that didn't feel very good--did it, Douglas?
...
CRAK
No.

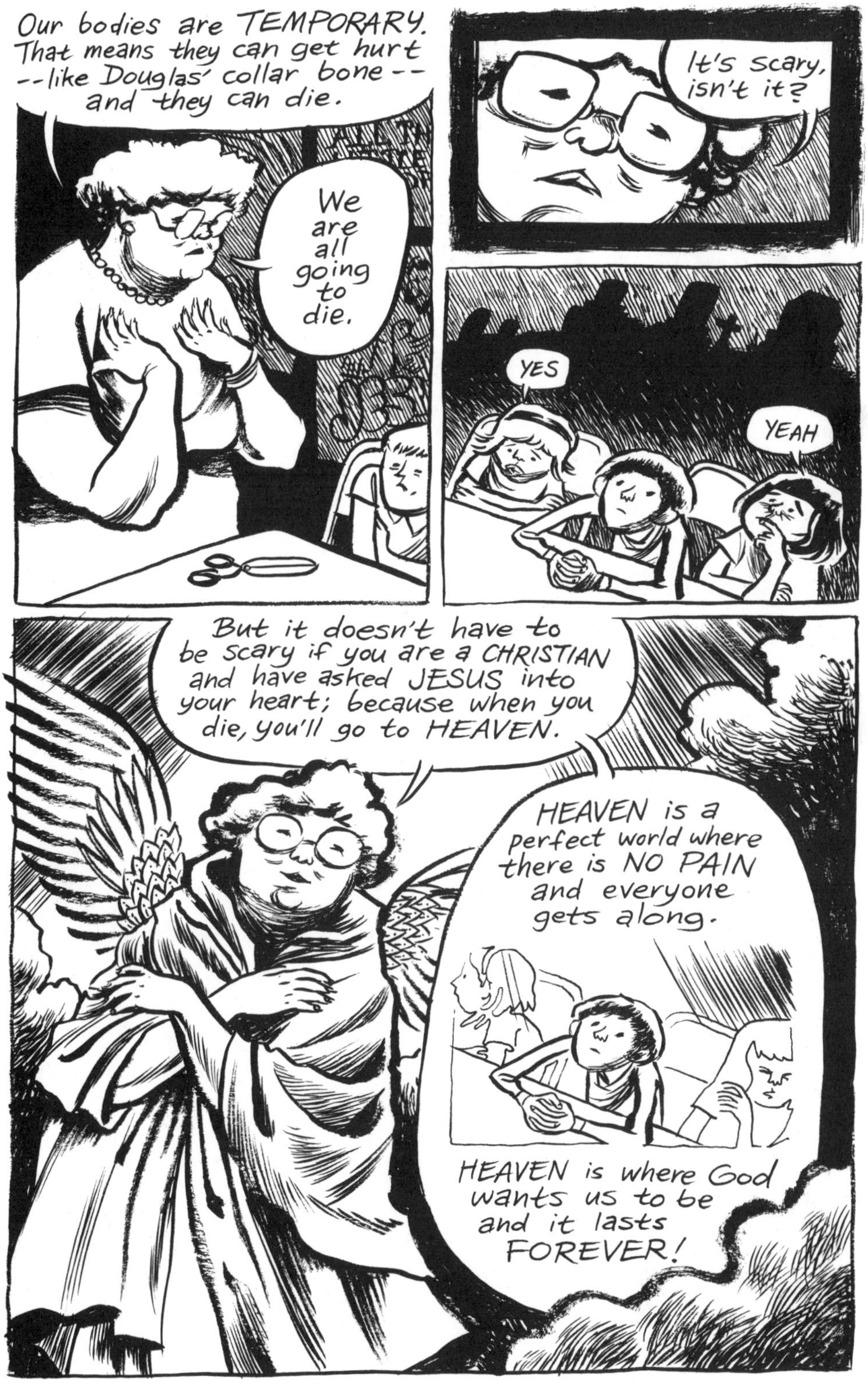
Our bodies are TEMPORARY. That means they can get hurt --like Douglas' collar bone-- and they can die.
We are all going to die.
It's scary, isn't it?
YES
YEAH
But it doesn't have to be scary if you are a CHRISTIAN and have asked JESUS into your heart; because when you die, you'll go to HEAVEN.
HEAVEN is a perfect world where there is NO PAIN and everyone gets along.
HEAVEN is where God wants us to be and it lasts FOREVER!

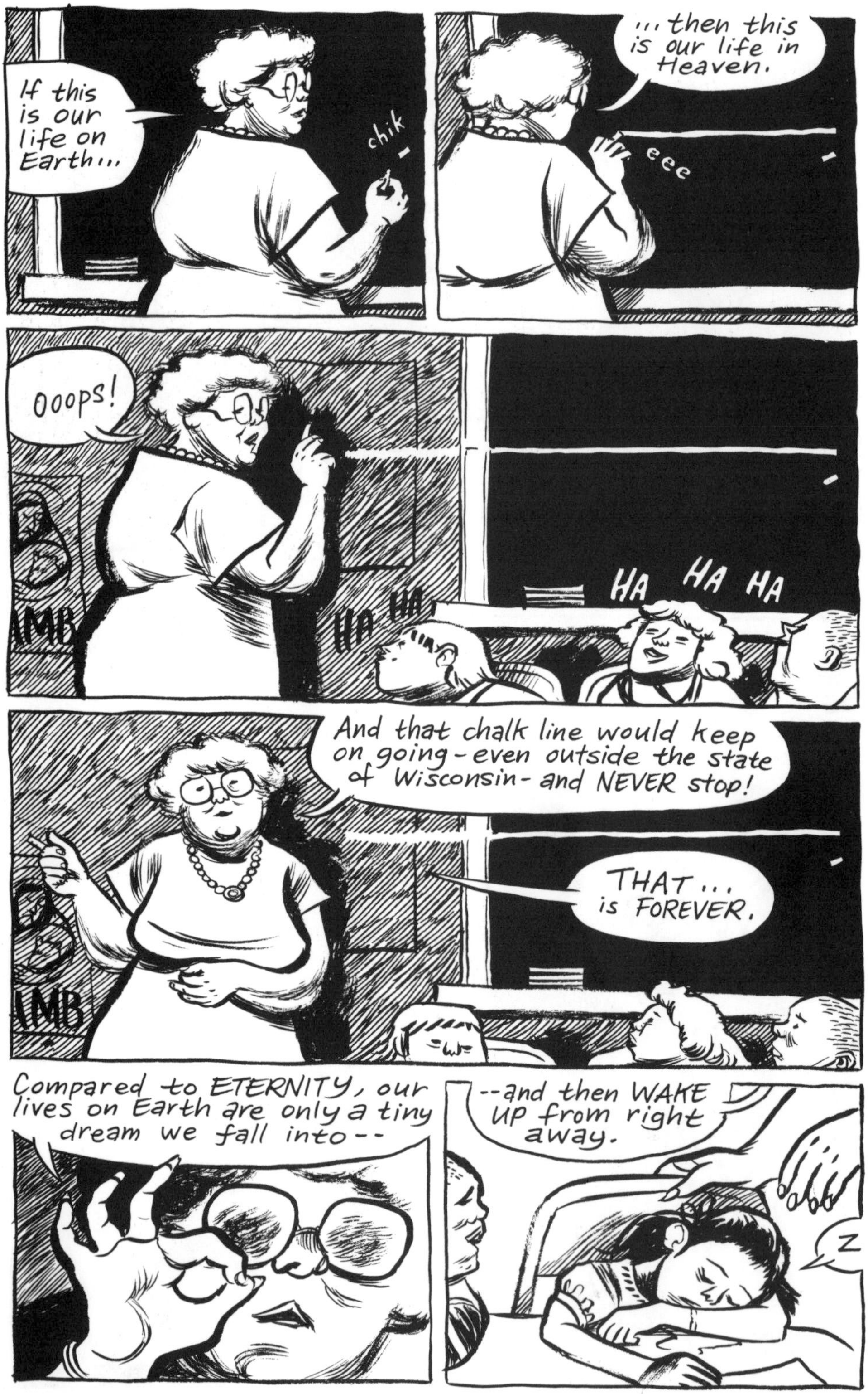
If this is our life on Earth...
chik
...then this is our life in Heaven.
eee
Ooops!
HA HA
HA HA HA
And that chalk line would keep on going - even outside the state of Wisconsin - and NEVER stop!
THAT... is FOREVER.
Compared to ETERNITY, our lives on Earth are only a tiny dream we fall into--
--and then WAKE UP from right away.
Z

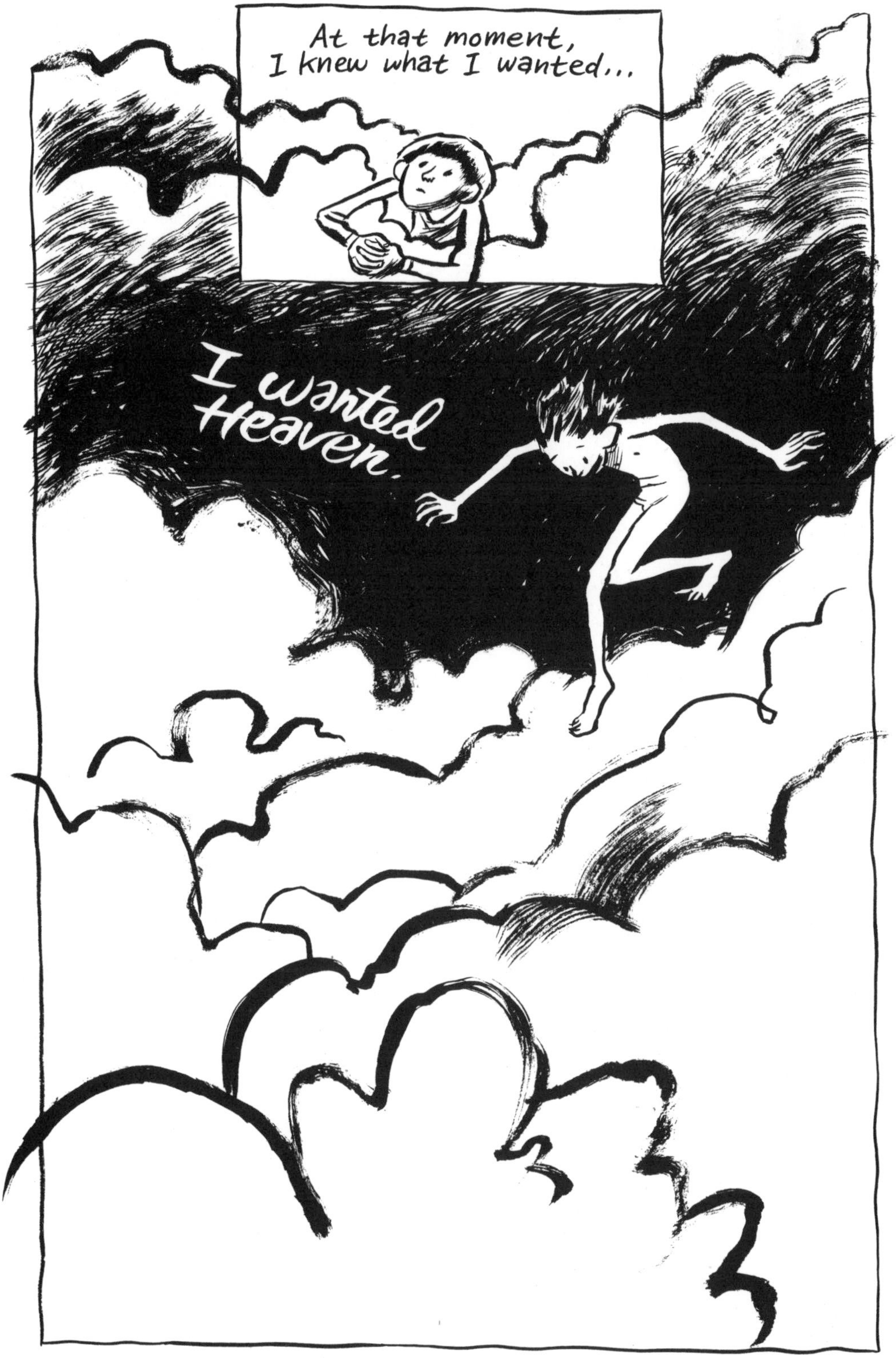
At that moment, I knew what I wanted...
I wanted Heaven.

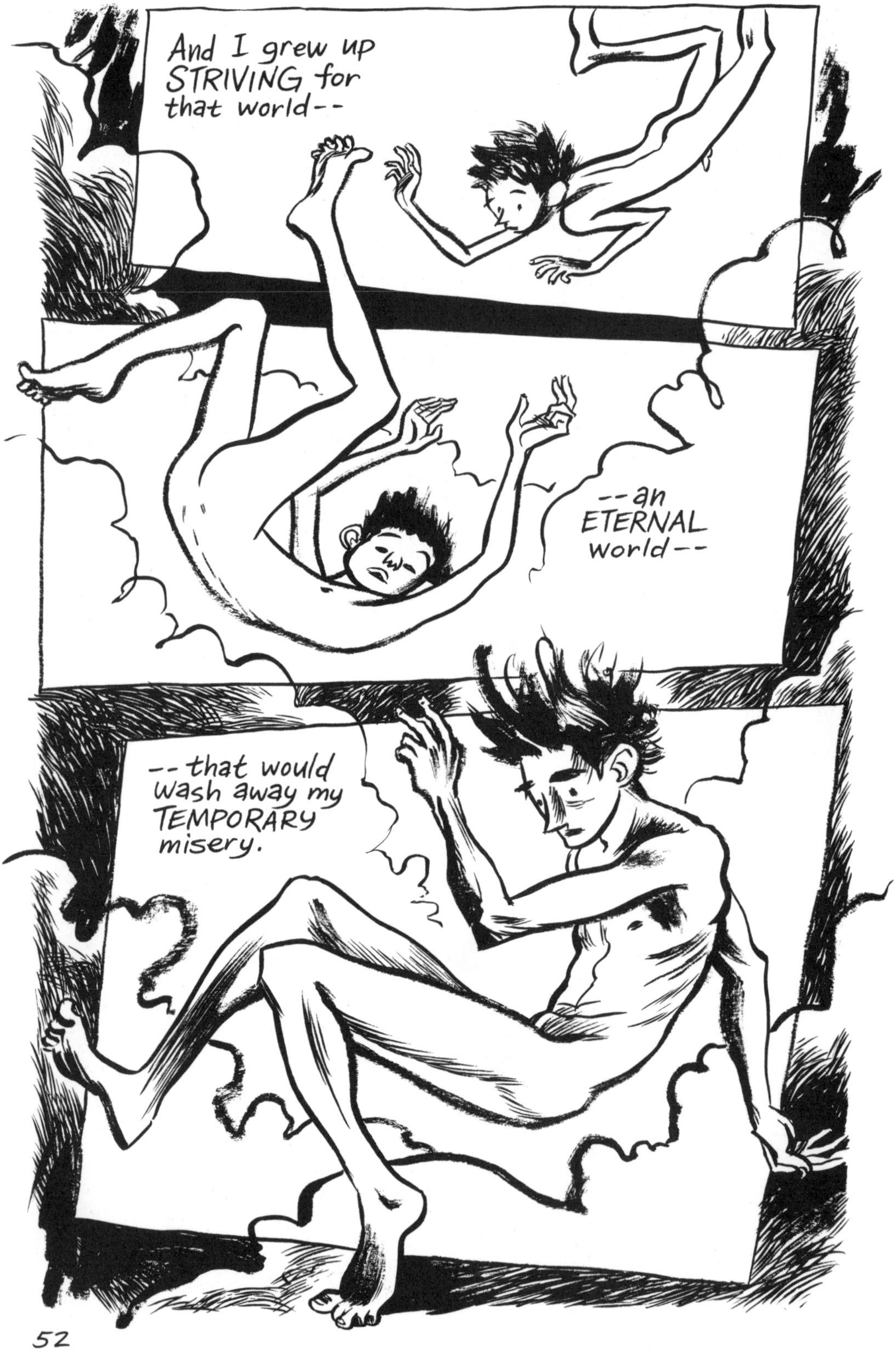
And I grew up STRIVING for that world--
--an ETERNAL world--
--that would wash away my TEMPORARY misery.

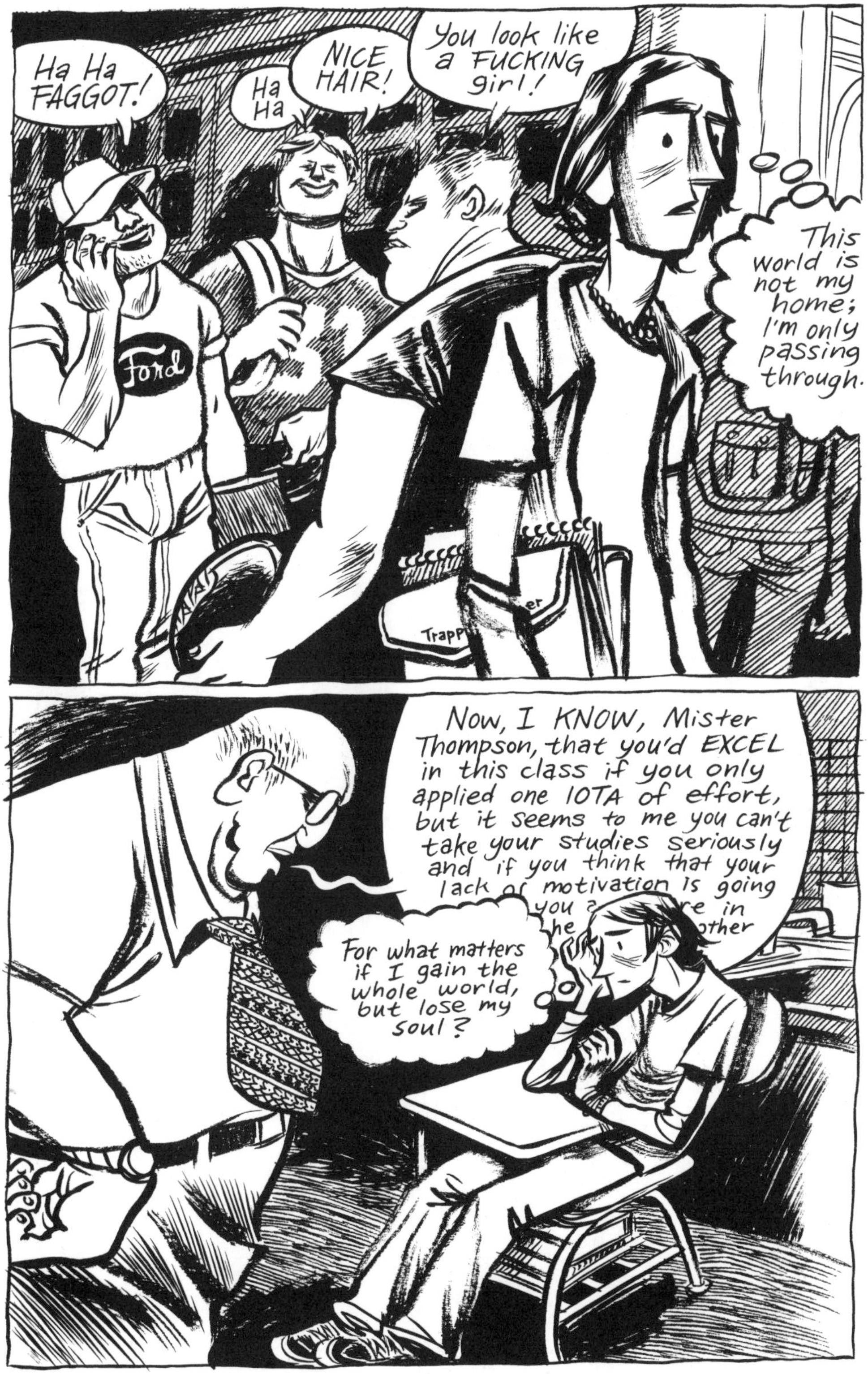
Ha Ha FAGGOT!
Ha Ha
NICE HAIR!
You look like a FUCKING girl!
This world is not my home; I'm only passing through.
Ford
Now, I KNOW, Mister Thompson, that you'd EXCEL in this class if you only applied one IOTA of effort, but it seems to me you can't take your studies seriously and if you think that your lack of motivation is going
For what matters if I gain the whole world, but lose my soul?

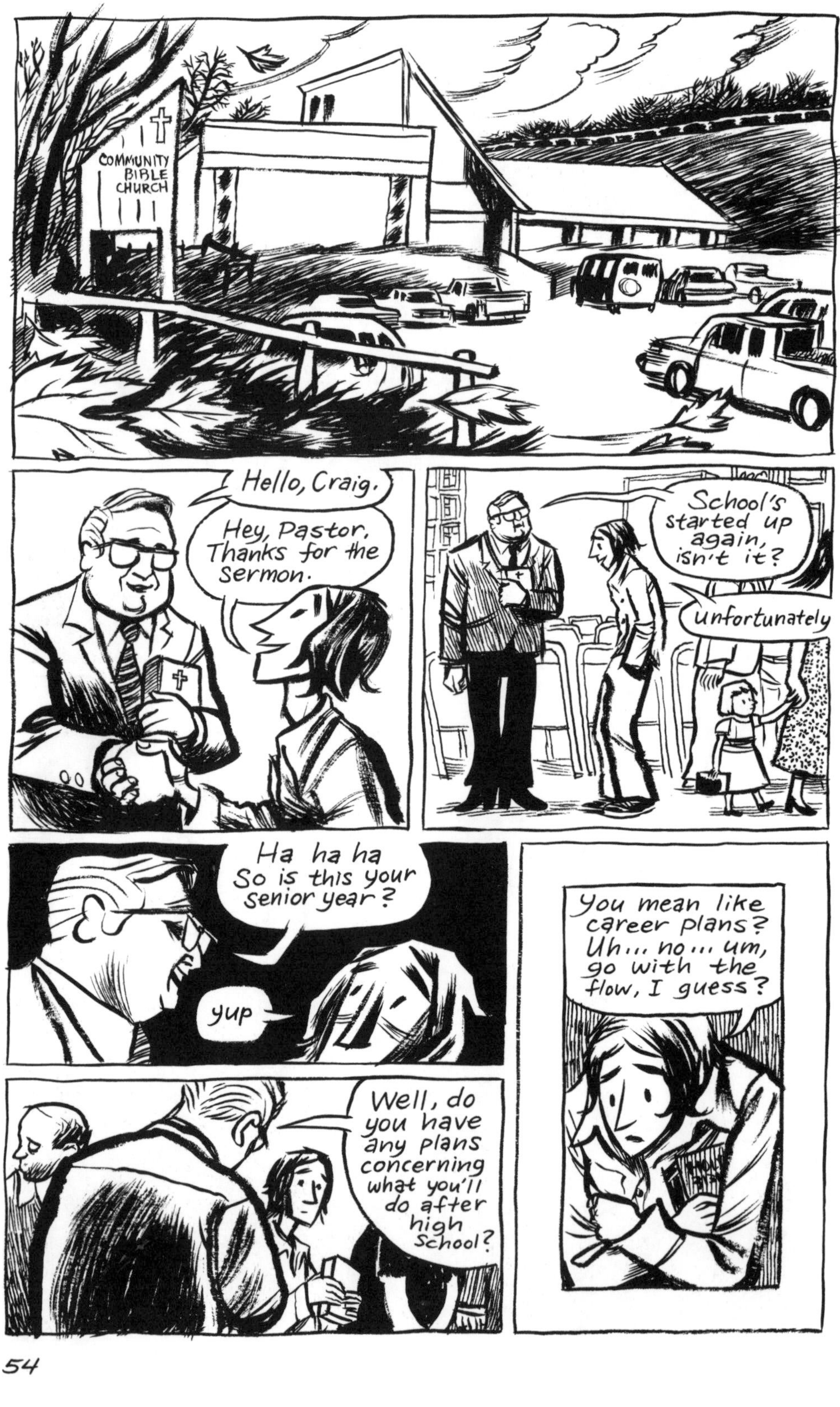
COMMUNITY BIBLE CHURCH
Hello, Craig.
Hey, Pastor, Thanks for the sermon.
School's started up again, isn't it?
unfortunately
Ha ha ha So is this your senior year?
yup
Well, do you have any plans concerning what you'll do after high school?
You mean like career plans? Uh... no... um, go with the flow, I guess?

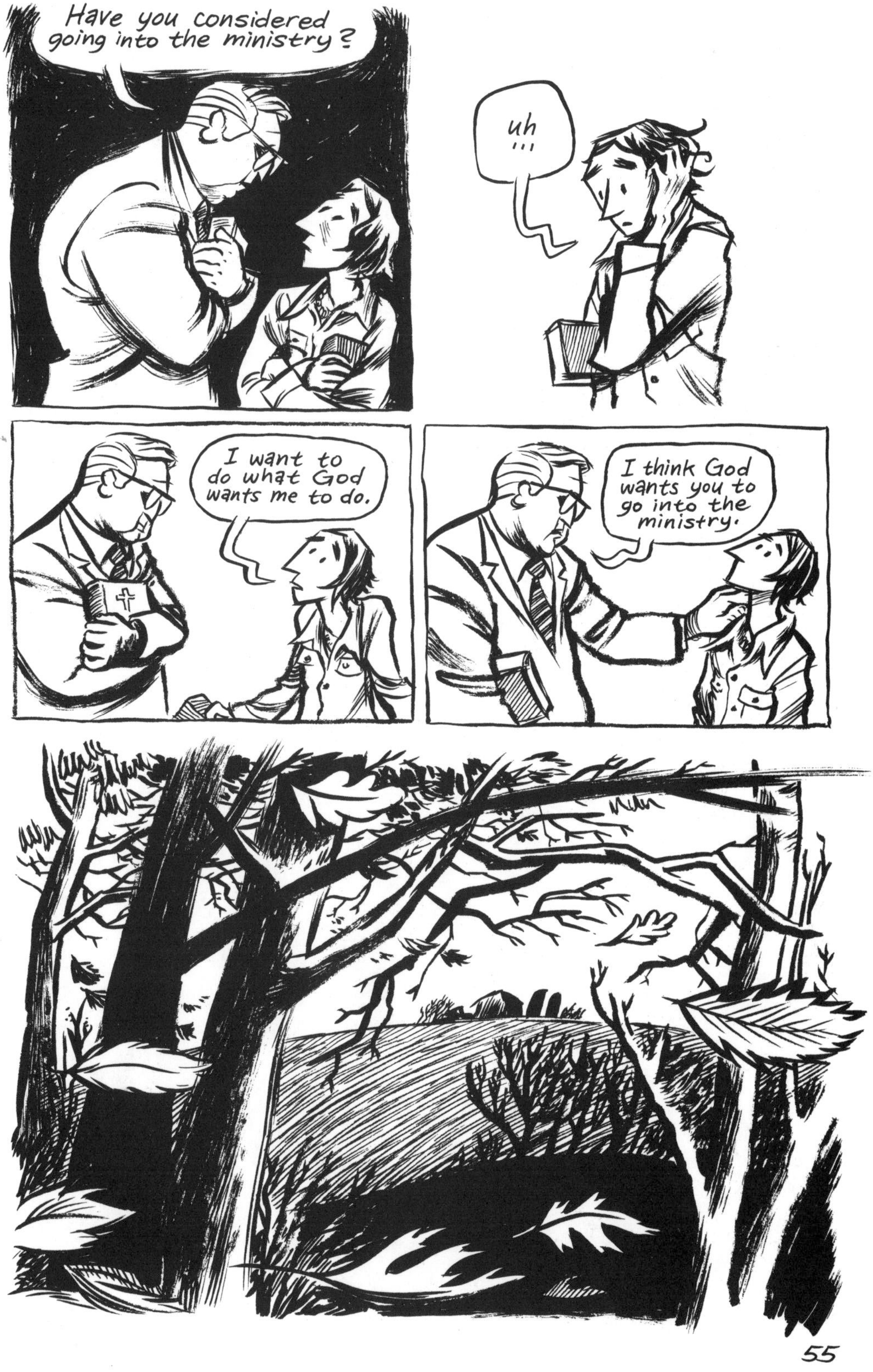
Have you considered going into the ministry?
uh ...
I want to do what God wants me to do.
I think God wants you to go into the ministry.

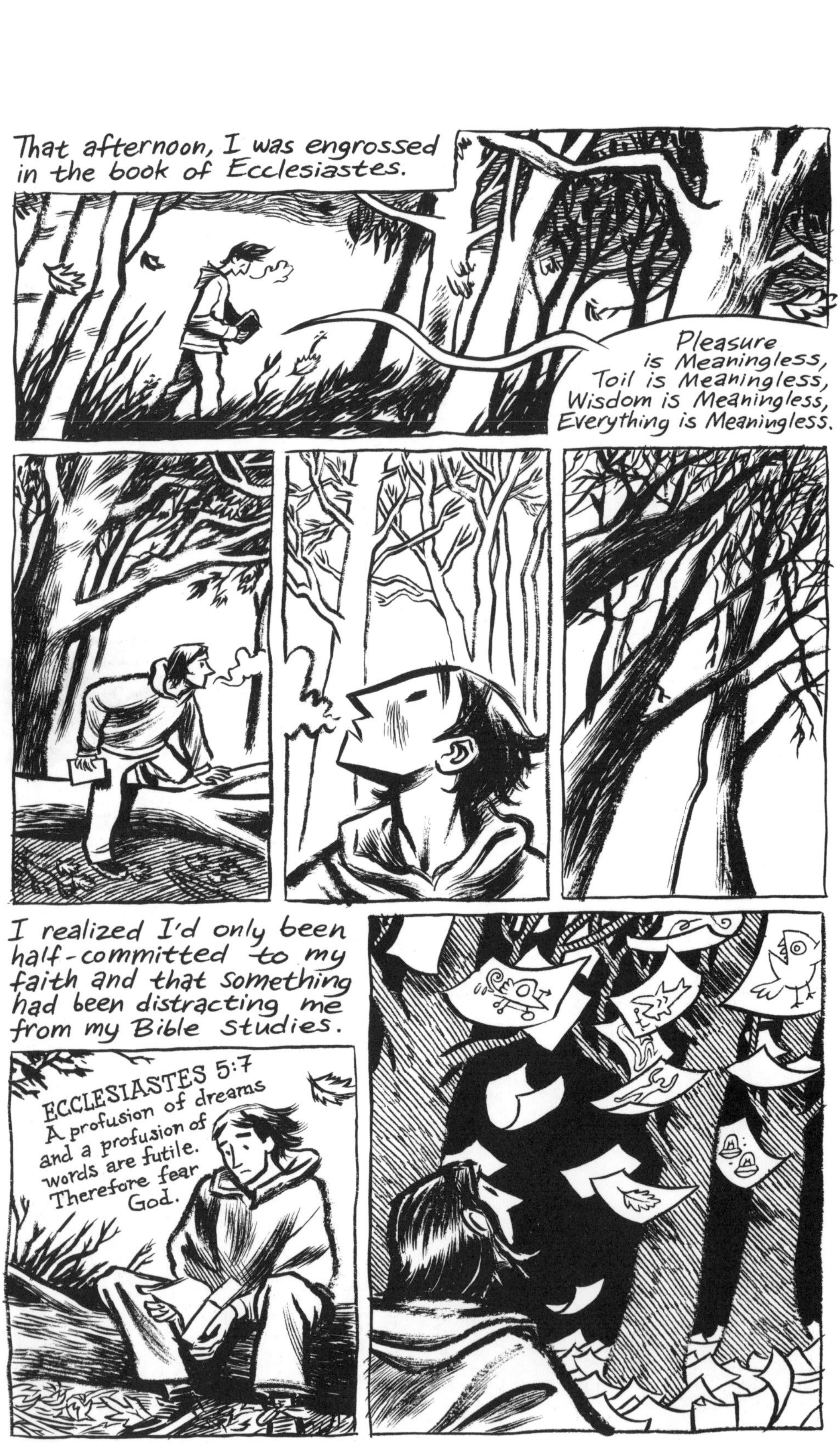
That afternoon, I was engrossed in the book of Ecclesiastes.
Pleasure is Meaningless, Toil is Meaningless, Wisdom is Meaningless, Everything is Meaningless.
I realized I'd only been half-committed to my faith and that something had been distracting me from my Bible studies.
ECCLESIASTES 5:7 A profusion of dreams and a profusion of words are futile. Therefore fear God.

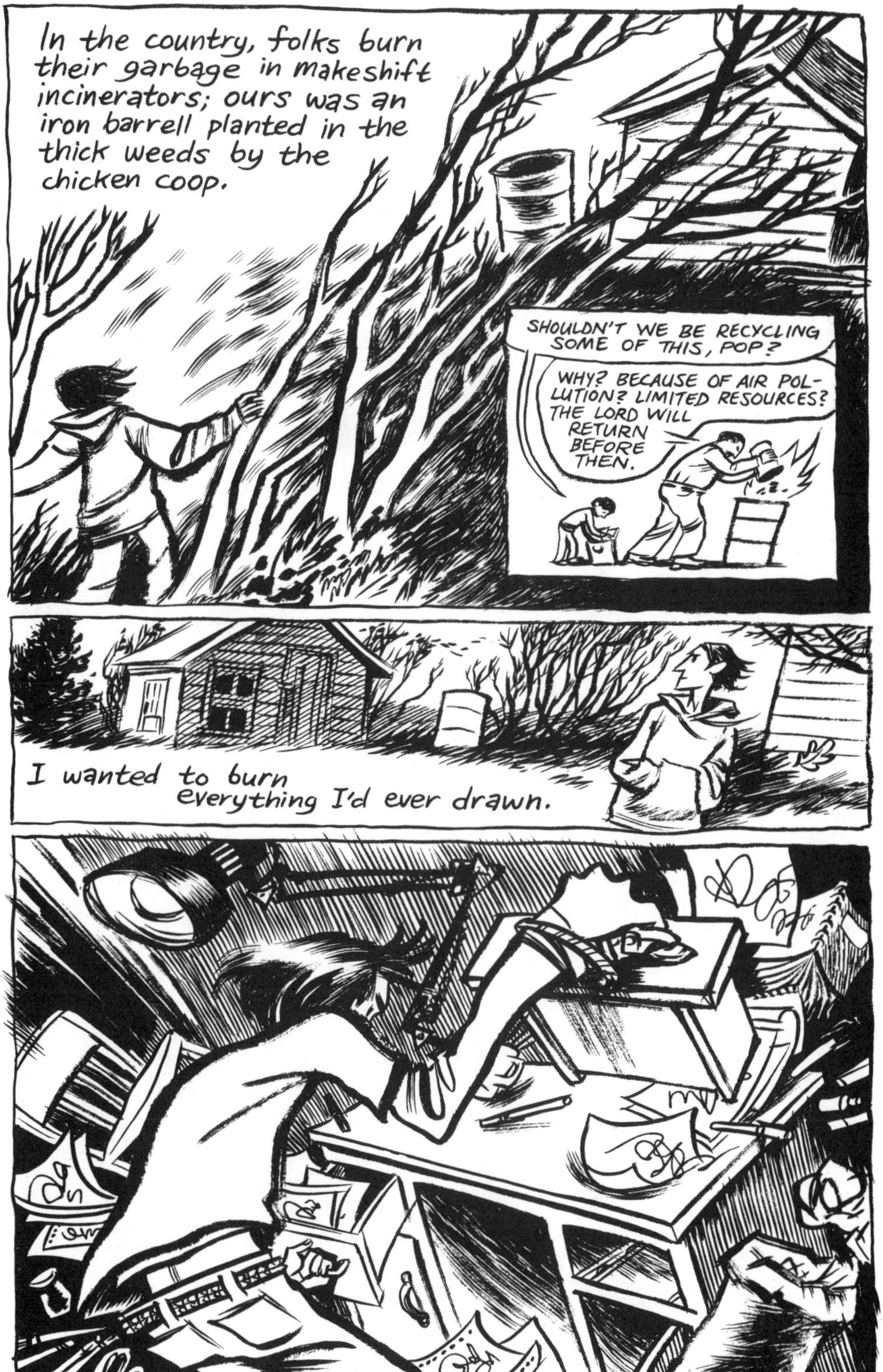
In the country, folks burn their garbage in makeshift incinerators; ours was an iron barrell planted in the thick weeds by the chicken coop.
SHOULDN'T WE BE RECYCLING SOME OF THIS, POP?
WHY? BECAUSE OF AIR POL-LUTION? LIMITED RESOURCES? THE LORD WILL RETURN BEFORE THEN.
I wanted to burn everything I'd ever drawn.

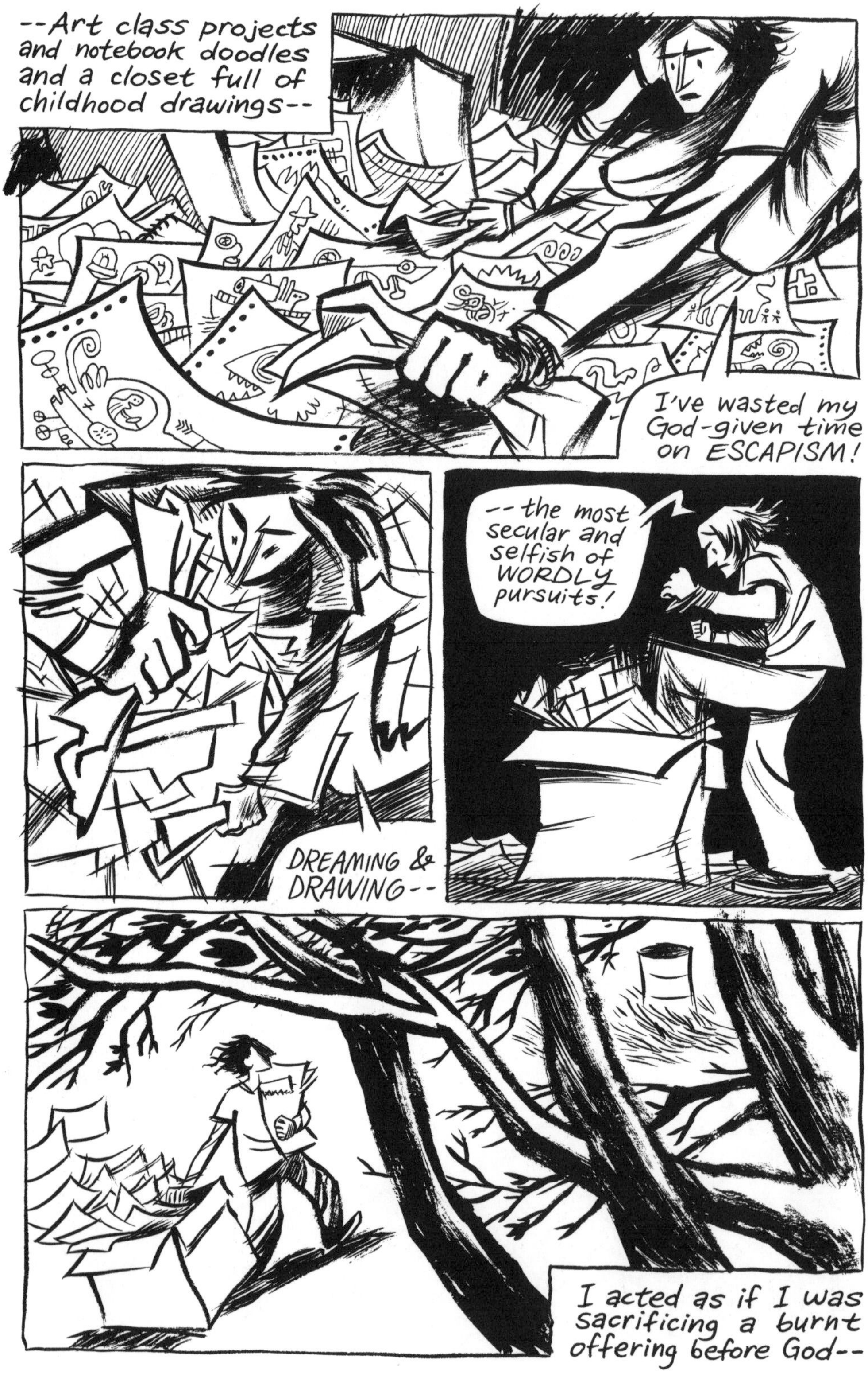
--Art class projects and notebook doodles and a closet full of childhood drawings--
I've wasted my God-given time on ESCAPISM!
DREAMING & DRAWING--
--the most secular and selfish of WORDLY pursuits!
I acted as if I was sacrificing a burnt offering before God--

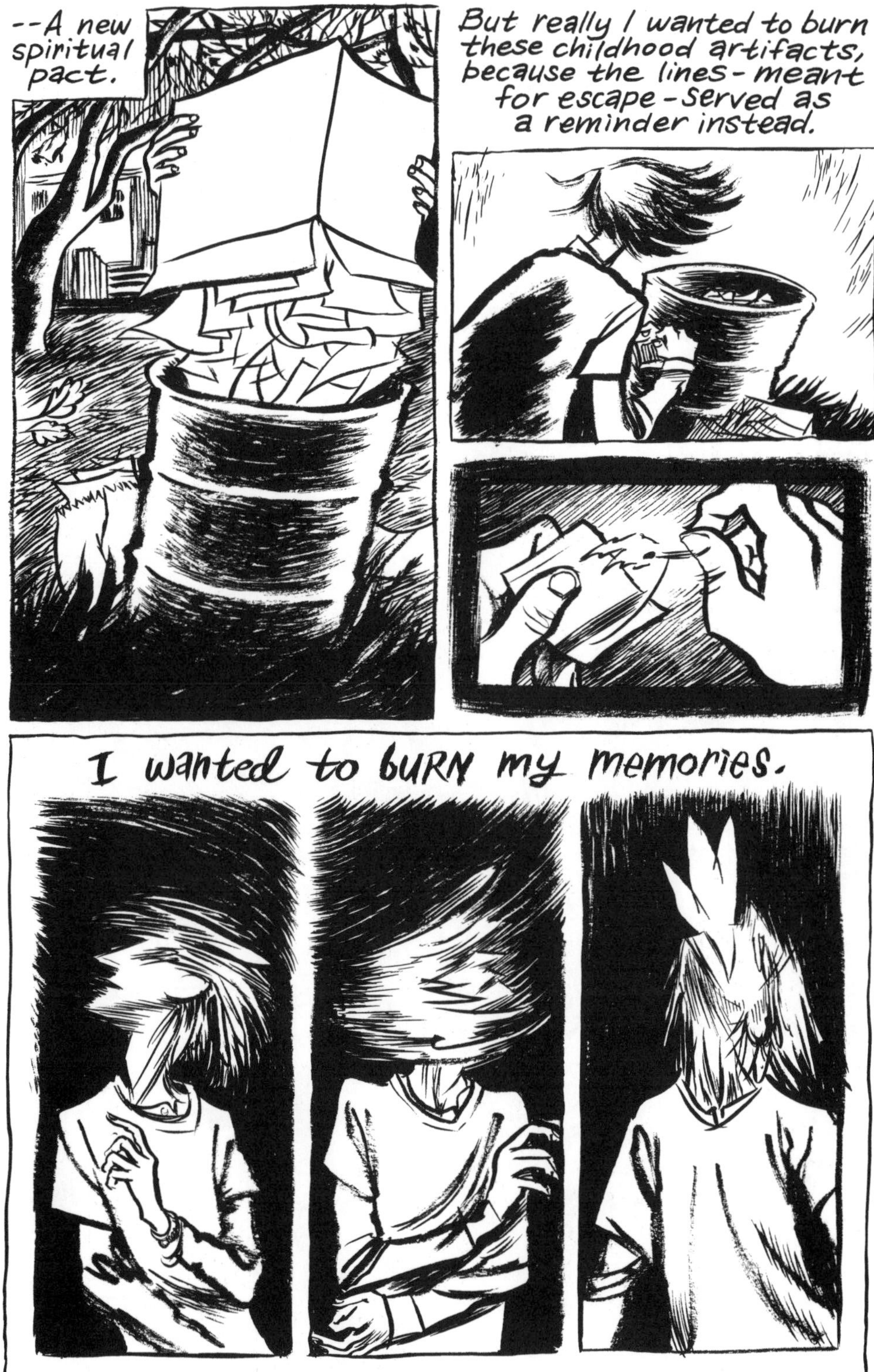
--A new spiritual pact.
But really I wanted to burn these childhood artifacts, because the lines-meant for escape-served as a reminder instead.
I wanted to burn my memories.

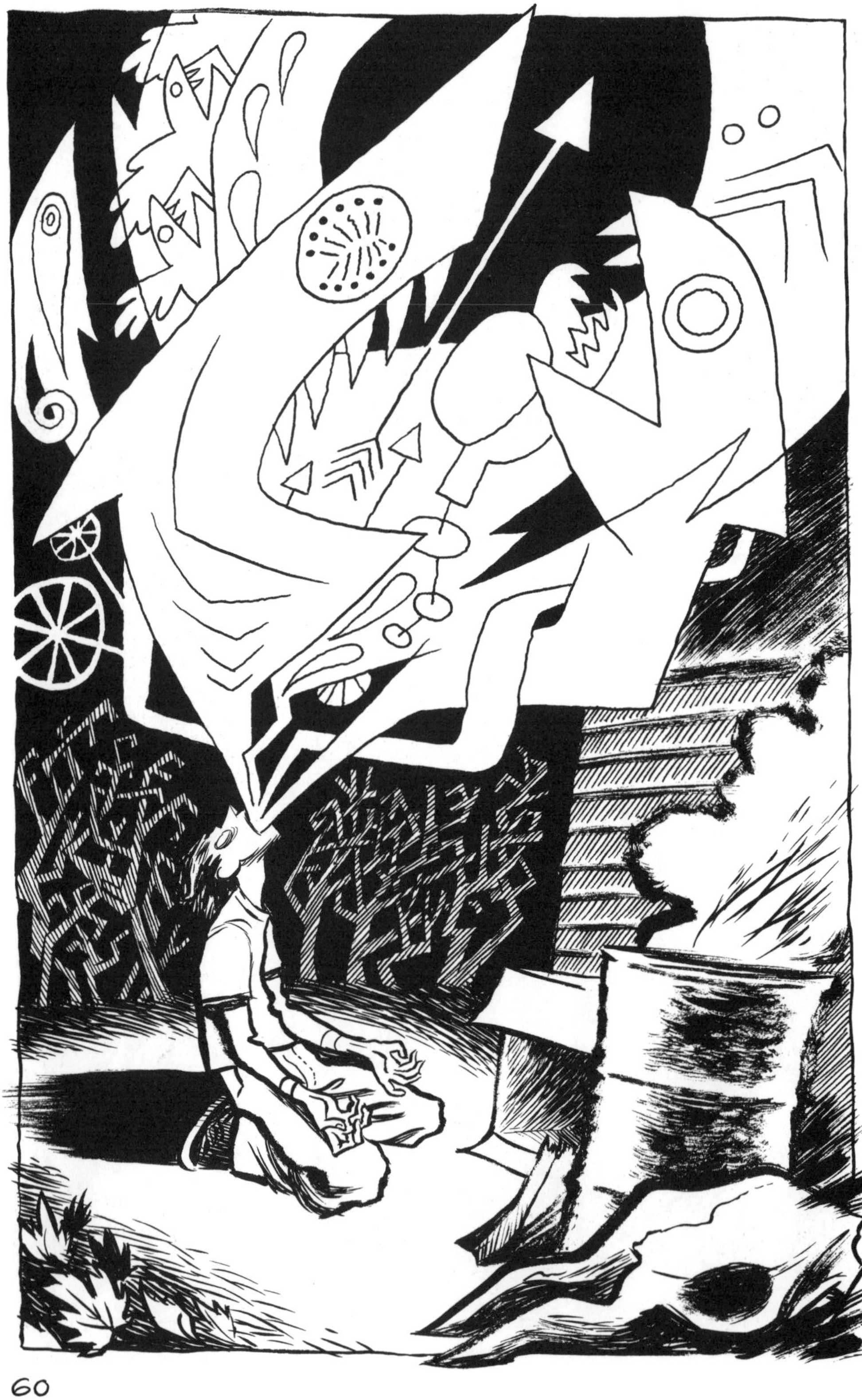

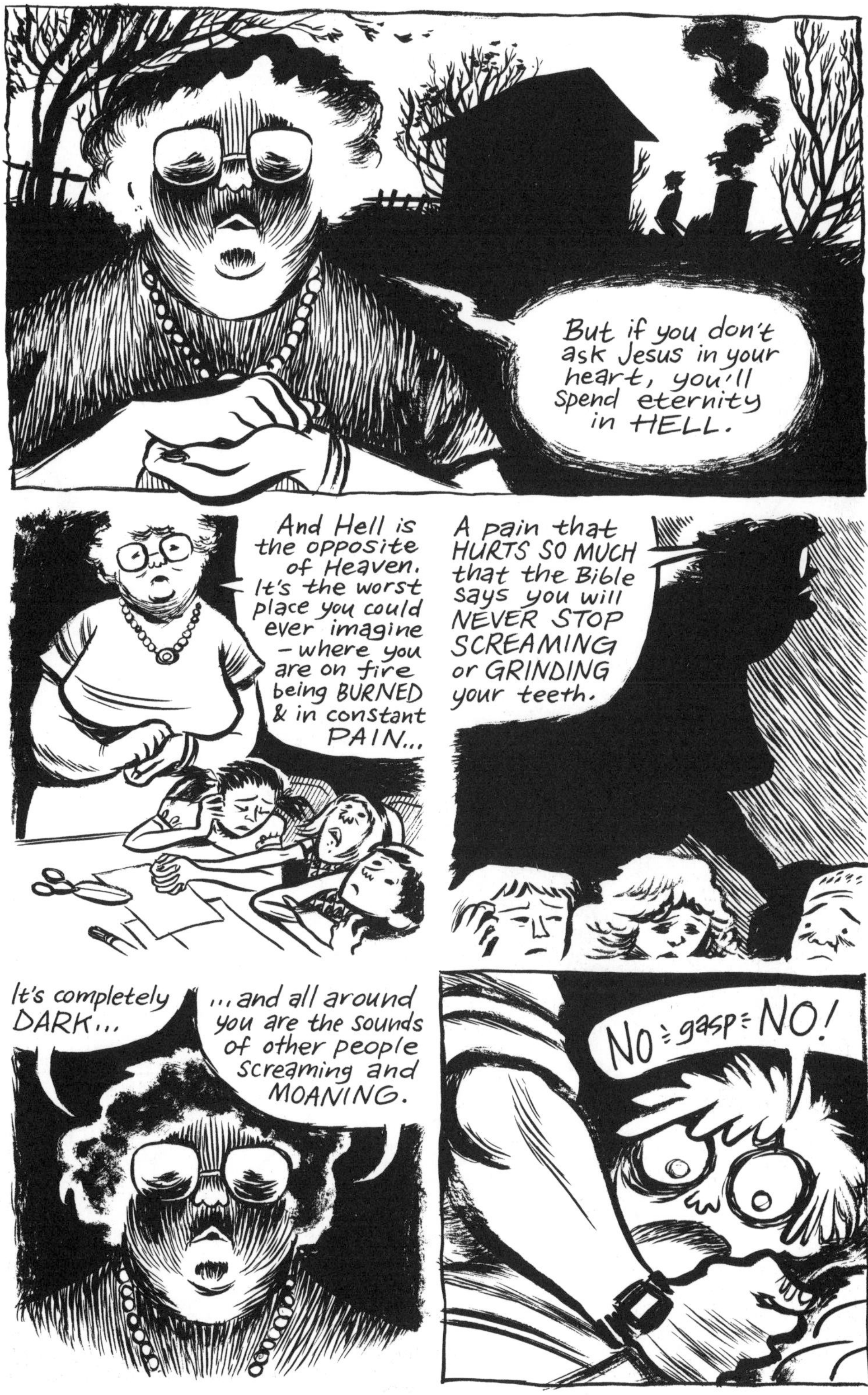
But if you don't ask Jesus in your heart, you'll spend eternity in HELL.
And Hell is the opposite of Heaven. It's the worst place you could ever imagine – where you are on fire being BURNED & in constant PAIN...
A pain that HURTS SO MUCH that the Bible says you will NEVER STOP SCREAMING or GRINDING your teeth.
It's completely DARK...
...and all around you are the sounds of other people screaming and MOANING.
NO gasp NO!

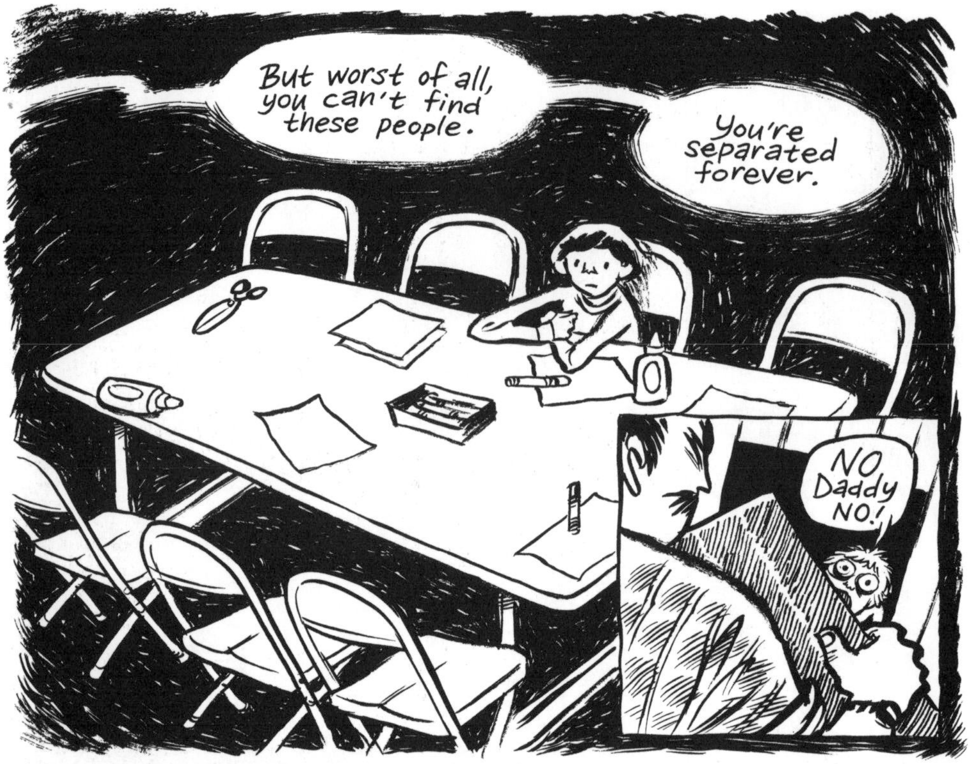

But worst of all, you can't find these people.
You're separated forever.
NO Daddy NO!

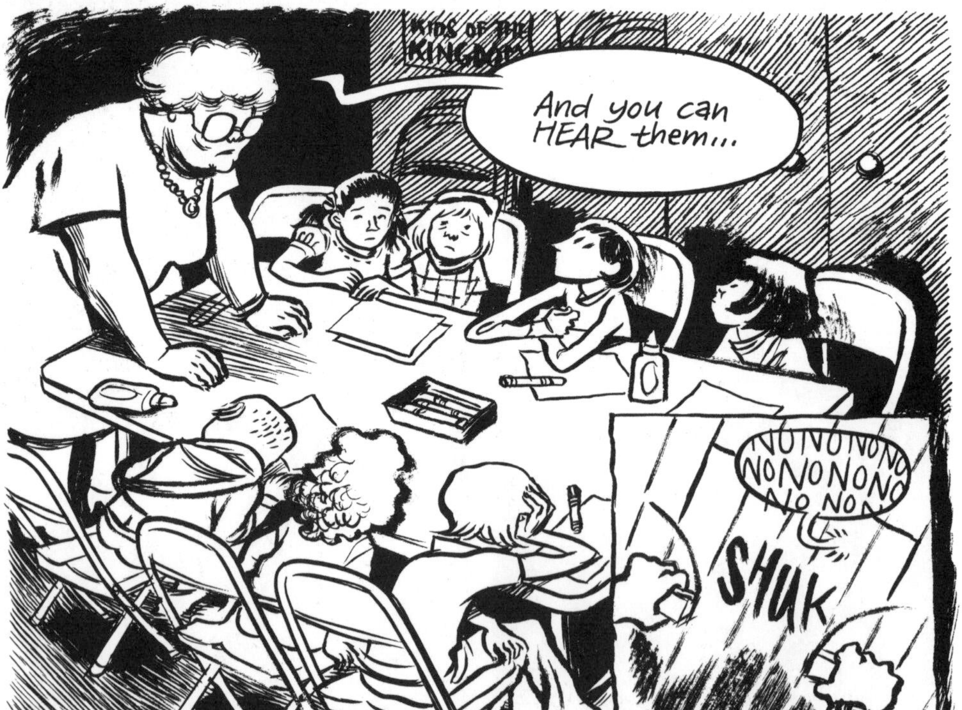

KIDS OF THE KINGDOM
And you can HEAR them...
NONONONONO
NONONONONO
NO NONONO
SHUK

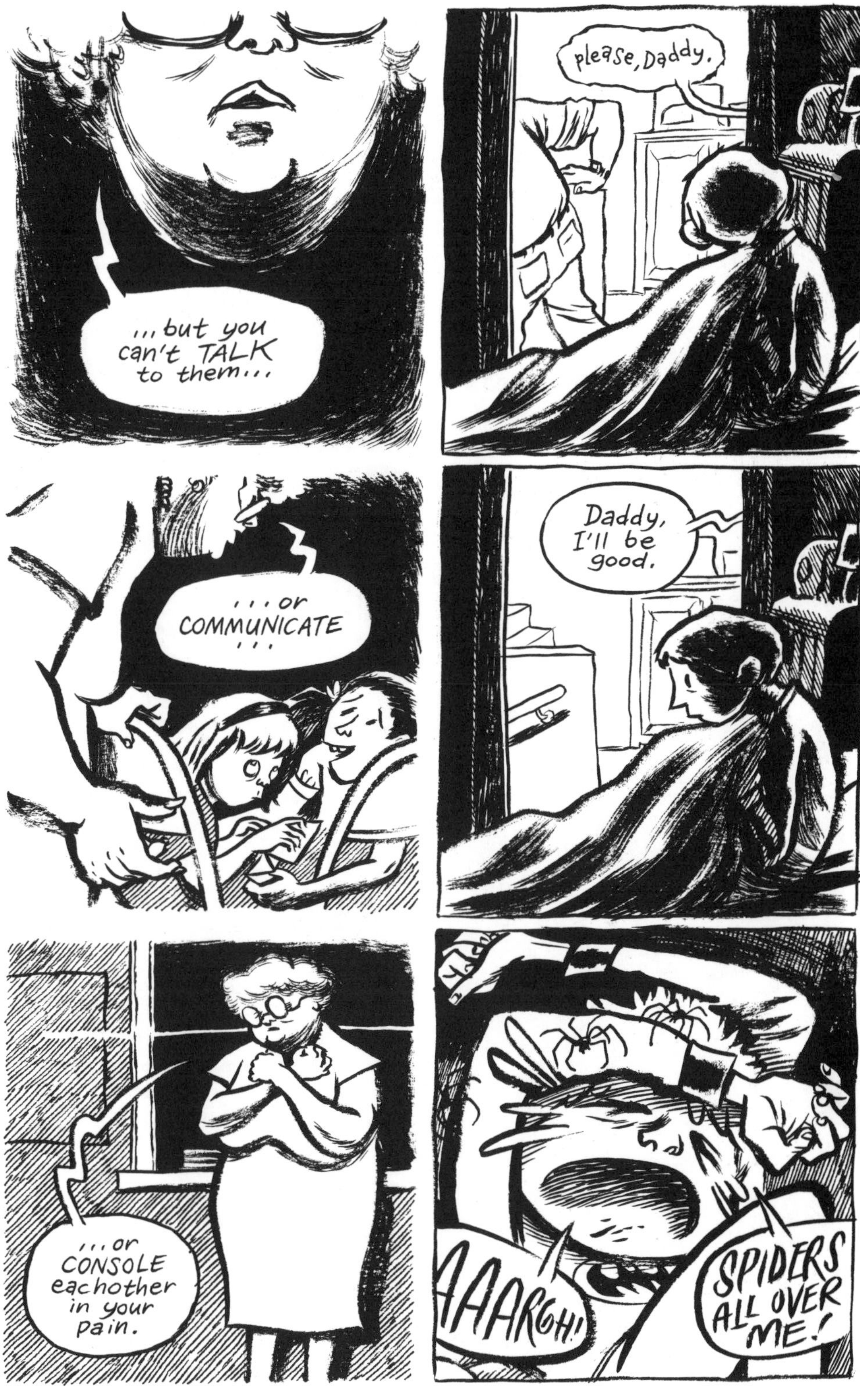
...but you can't TALK to them...
please, Daddy.
...or COMMUNICATE ...
Daddy, I'll be good.
...or CONSOLE eachother in your pain.
AAARGH!
SPIDERS ALL OVER ME!

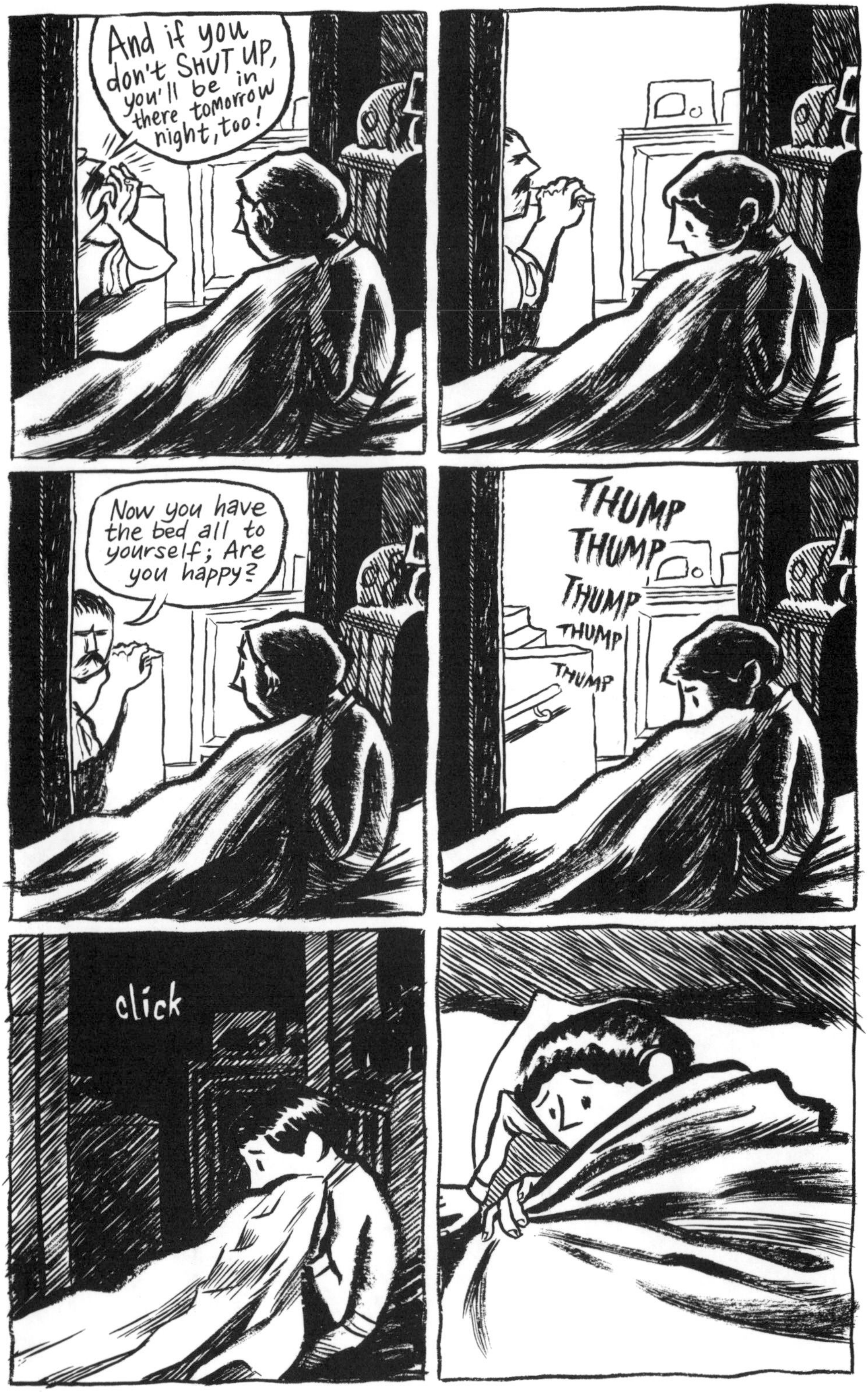
And if you don't SHUT UP, you'll be in there tomorrow night, too!
Now you have the bed all to yourself; Are you happy?
THUMP
THUMP
THUMP
THUMP
THUMP
click

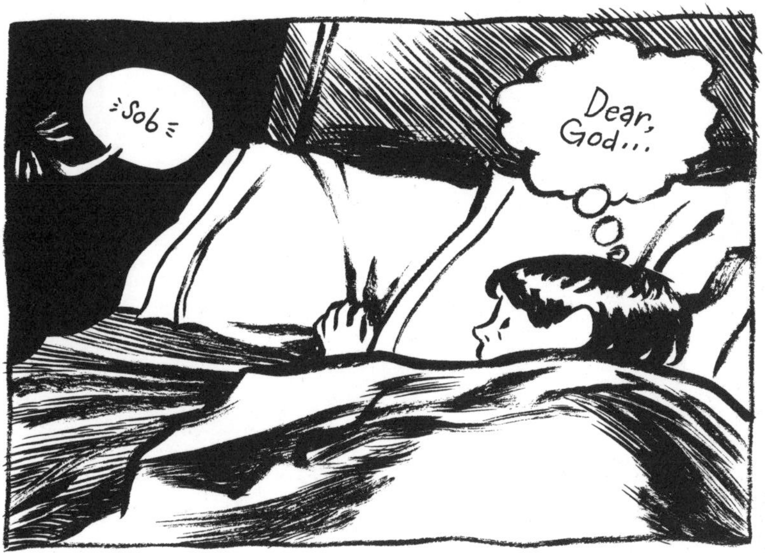
Sob
Dear, God...

II

Stirring
Furnace

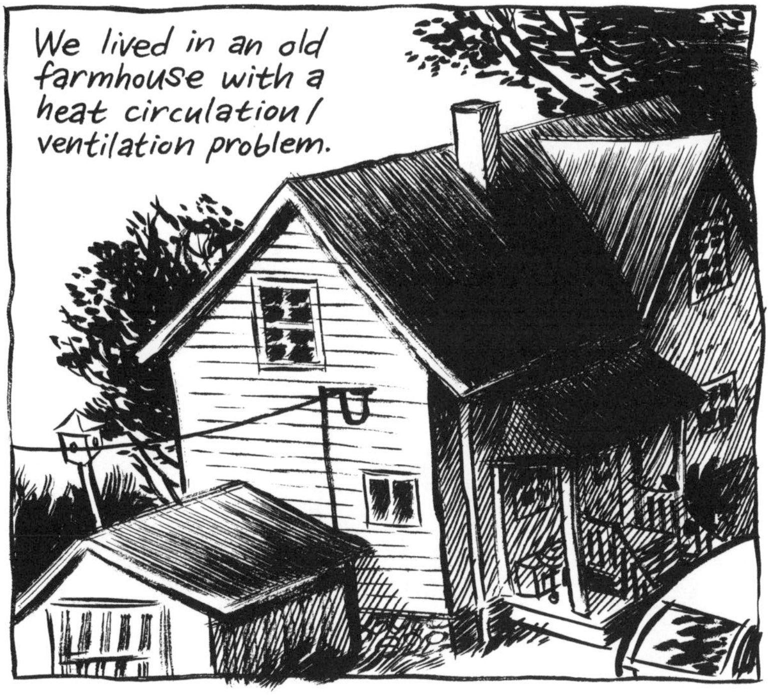
We lived in an old farmhouse with a heat circulation/ ventilation problem.

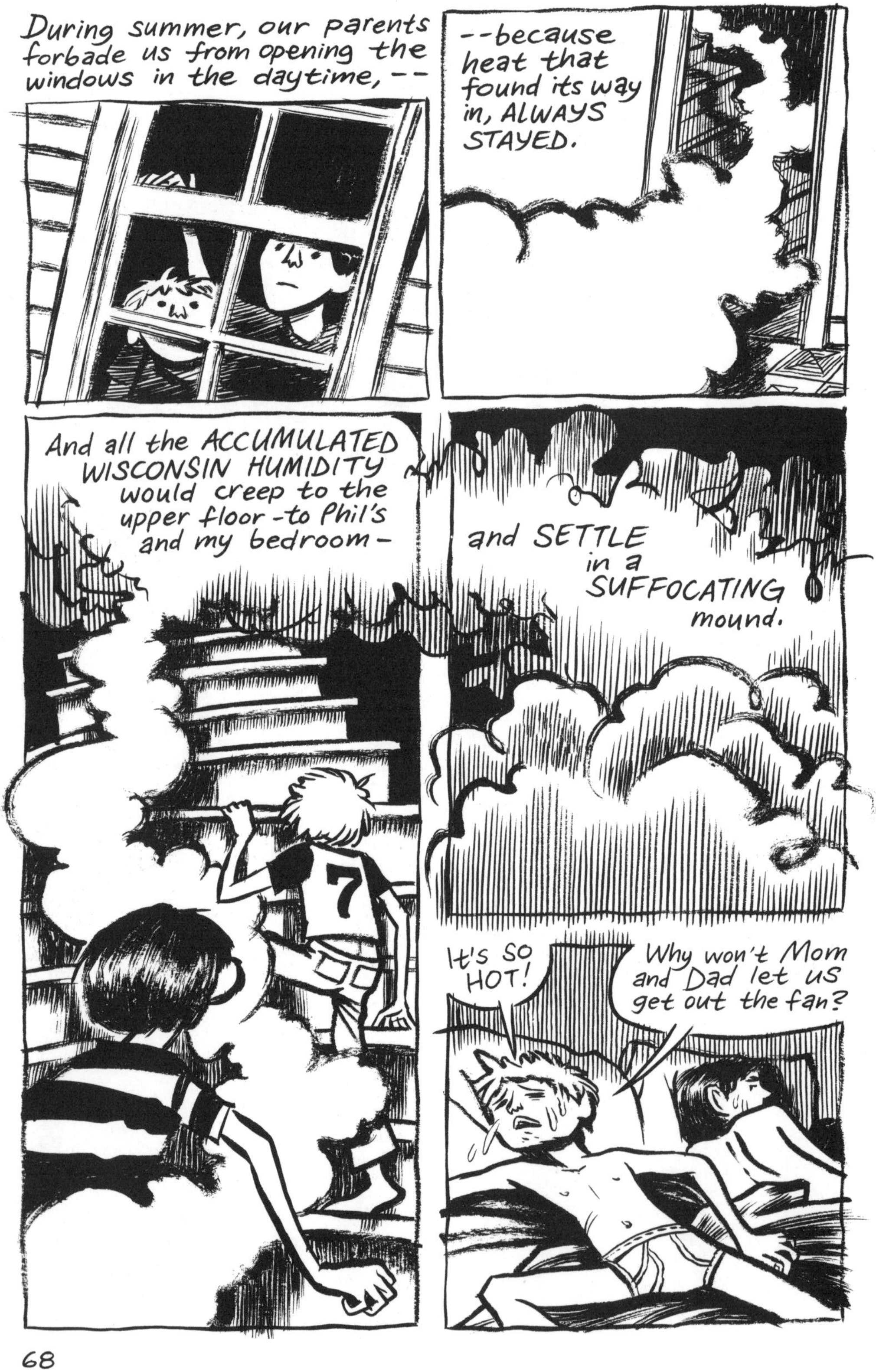
During summer, our parents forbade us from opening the windows in the daytime, --
--because heat that found its way in, ALWAYS STAYED.
And all the ACCUMULATED WISCONSIN HUMIDITY would creep to the upper floor -to Phil's and my bedroom -
and SETTLE in a SUFFOCATING mound.
7
It's SO HOT!
Why won't Mom and Dad let US get out the fan?

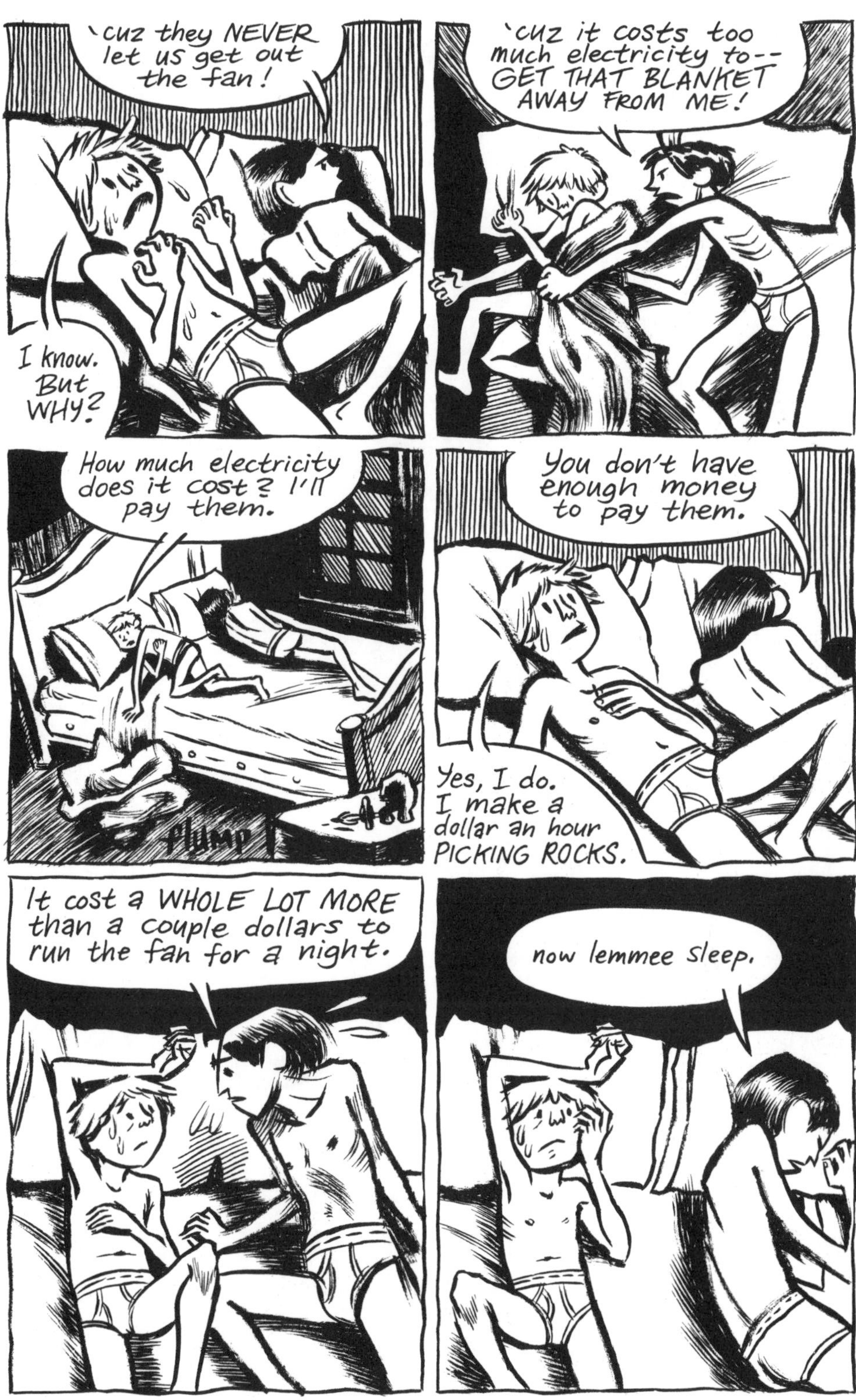
`cuz they NEVER let us get out the fan!
I know. But WHY?
`cuz it costs too much electricity to-- GET THAT BLANKET AWAY FROM ME!
How much electricity does it cost? I'll pay them.
PLUMP
You don't have enough money to pay them.
Yes, I do. I make a dollar an hour PICKING ROCKS.
It cost a WHOLE LOT MORE than a couple dollars to run the fan for a night.
now lemmee sleep.

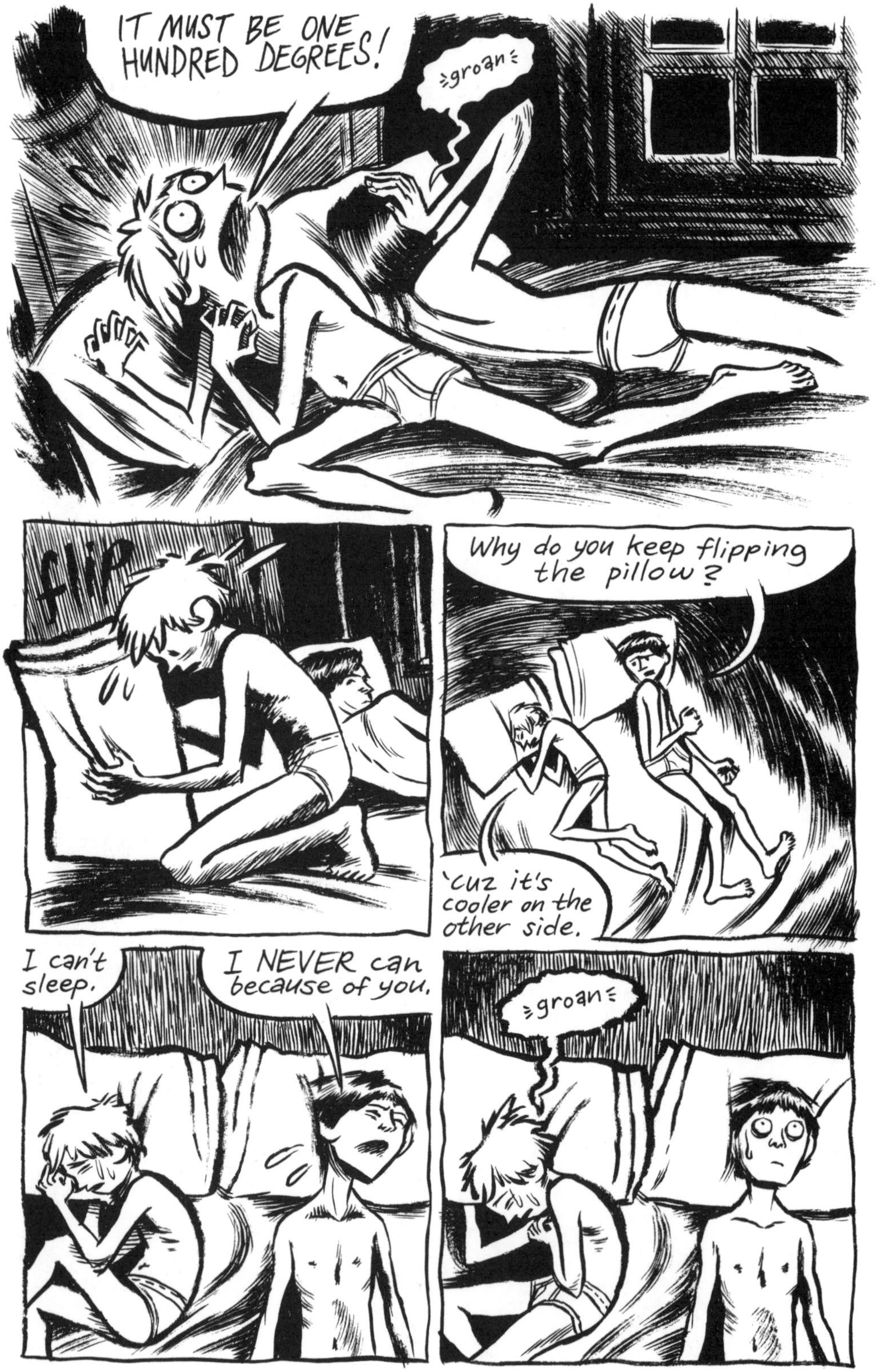
IT MUST BE ONE HUNDRED DEGREES!
groan
flip
Why do you keep flipping the pillow?
'cuz it's cooler on the other side.
I can't sleep.
I NEVER can because of you.
groan

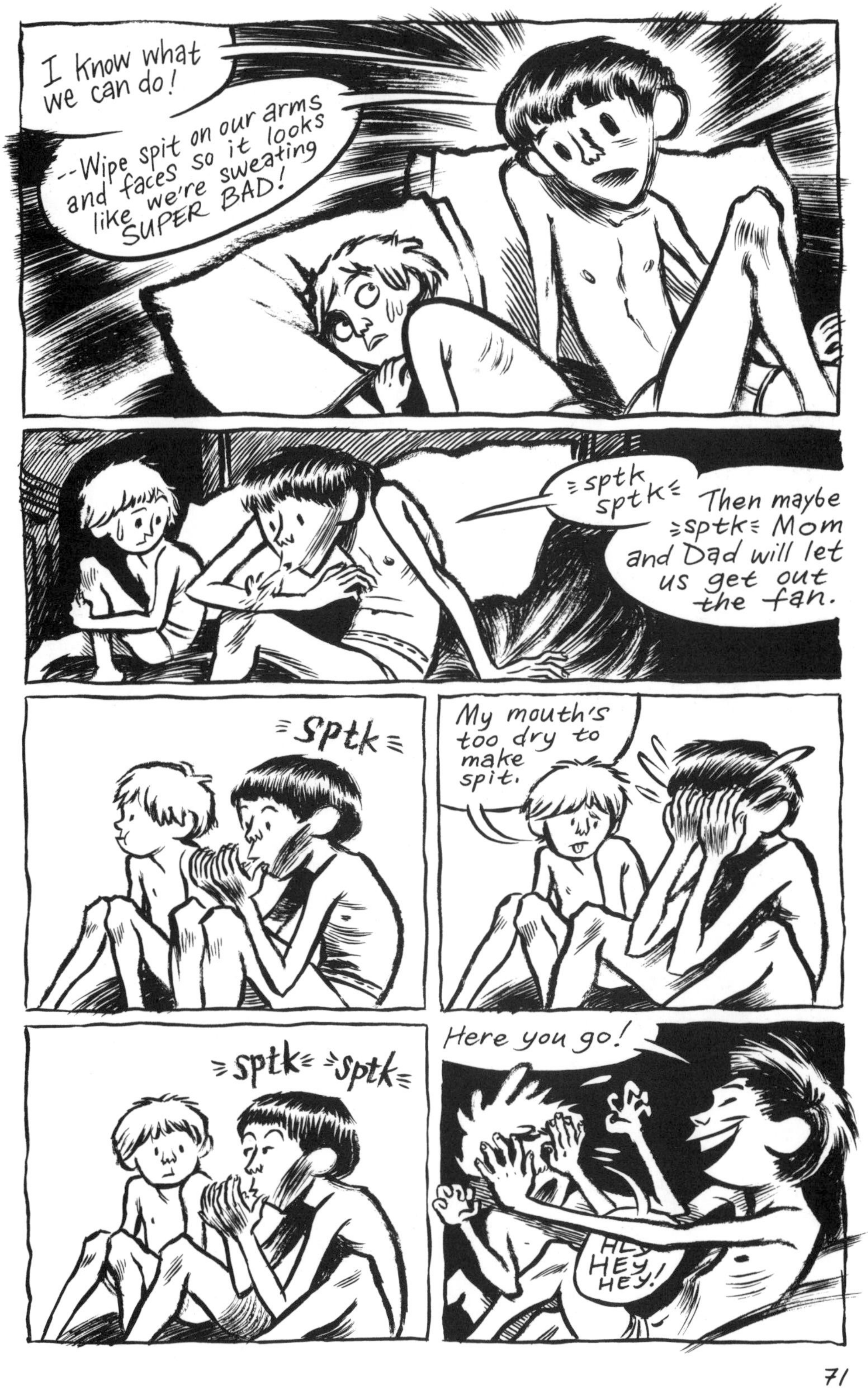
I know what we can do!
--Wipe spit on our arms and faces so it looks like we're sweating like SUPER BAD!
sptk sptk
Then maybe sptk Mom and Dad will let us get out the fan.
Sptk
My mouth's too dry to make spit.
sptk sptk
Here you go!
HEY HEY HEY!

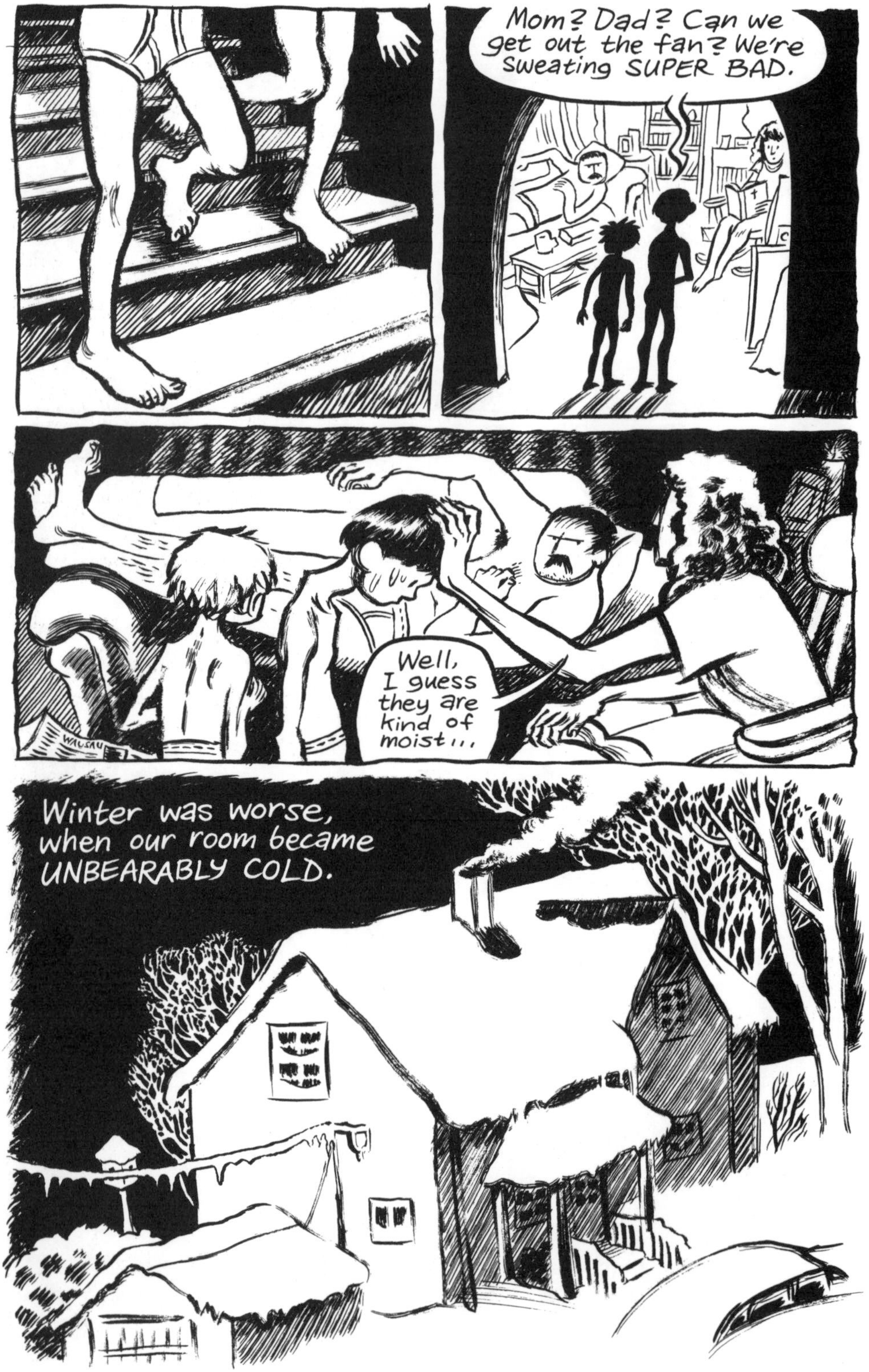
Mom? Dad? Can we get out the fan? We're sweating SUPER BAD.
Well, I guess they are kind of moist...
WAUSAU
Winter was worse, when our room became UNBEARABLY COLD.

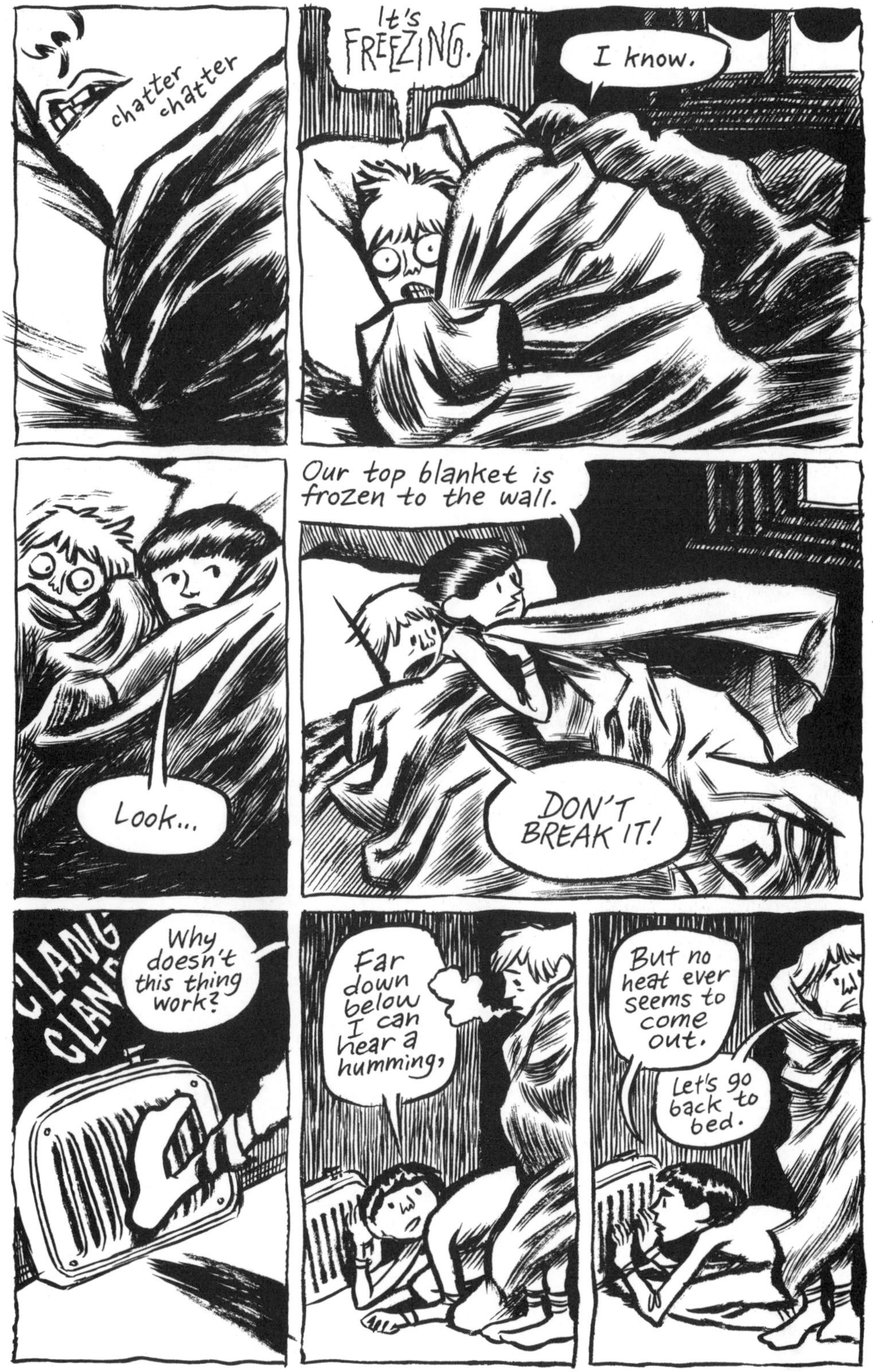
chatter chatter
It's FREEZING.
I know.
Look...
Our top blanket is frozen to the wall.
DON'T BREAK IT!
Why doesn't this thing work?
Far down below I can hear a humming,
But no heat ever seems to come out.
Let's go back to bed.

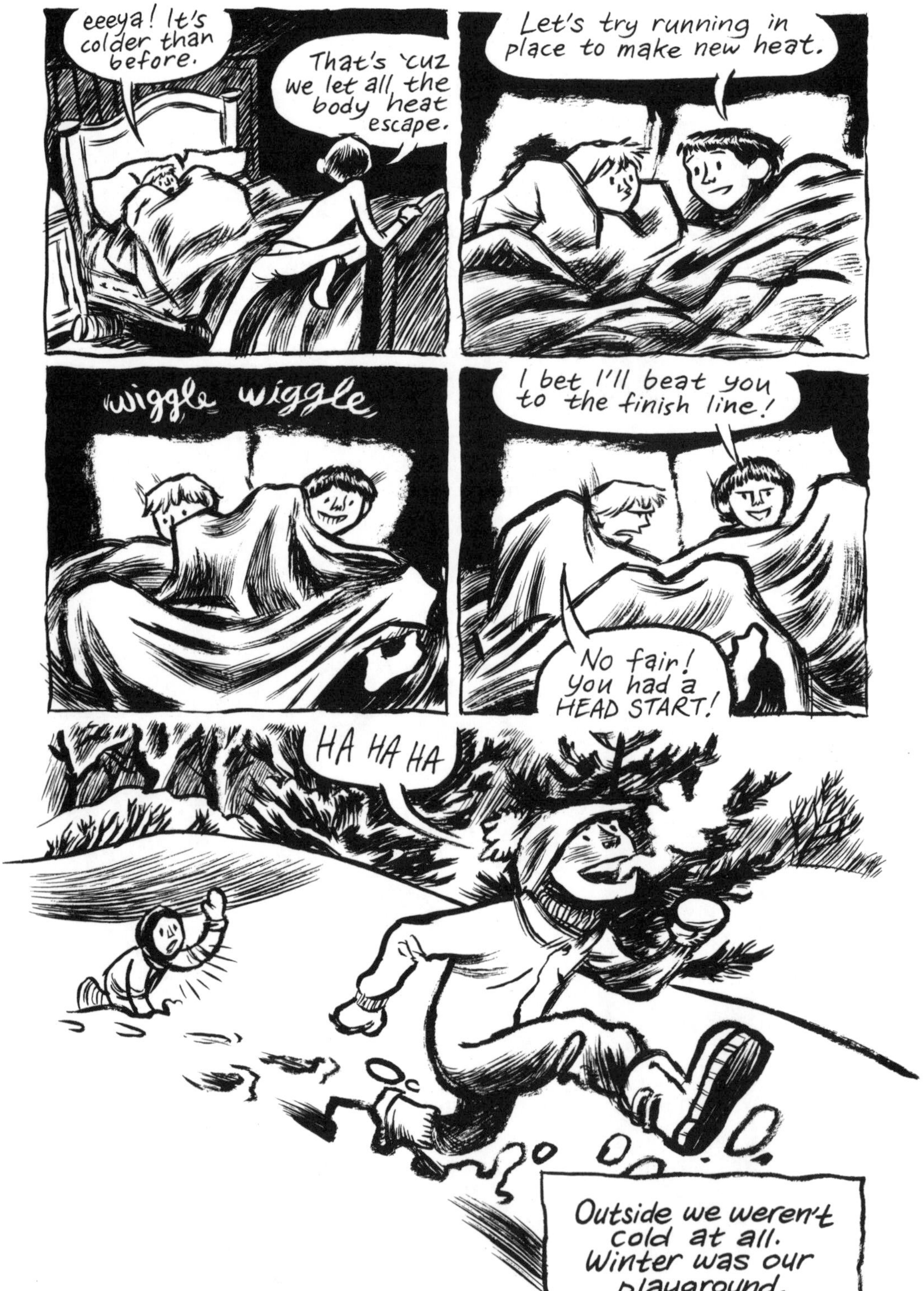
eeeya! It's colder than before.
That's 'cuz we let all the body heat escape.
Let's try running in place to make new heat.
wiggle wiggle
I bet I'll beat you to the finish line!
No fair! You had a HEAD START!
HA HA HA
Outside we weren't cold at all. Winter was our playground.

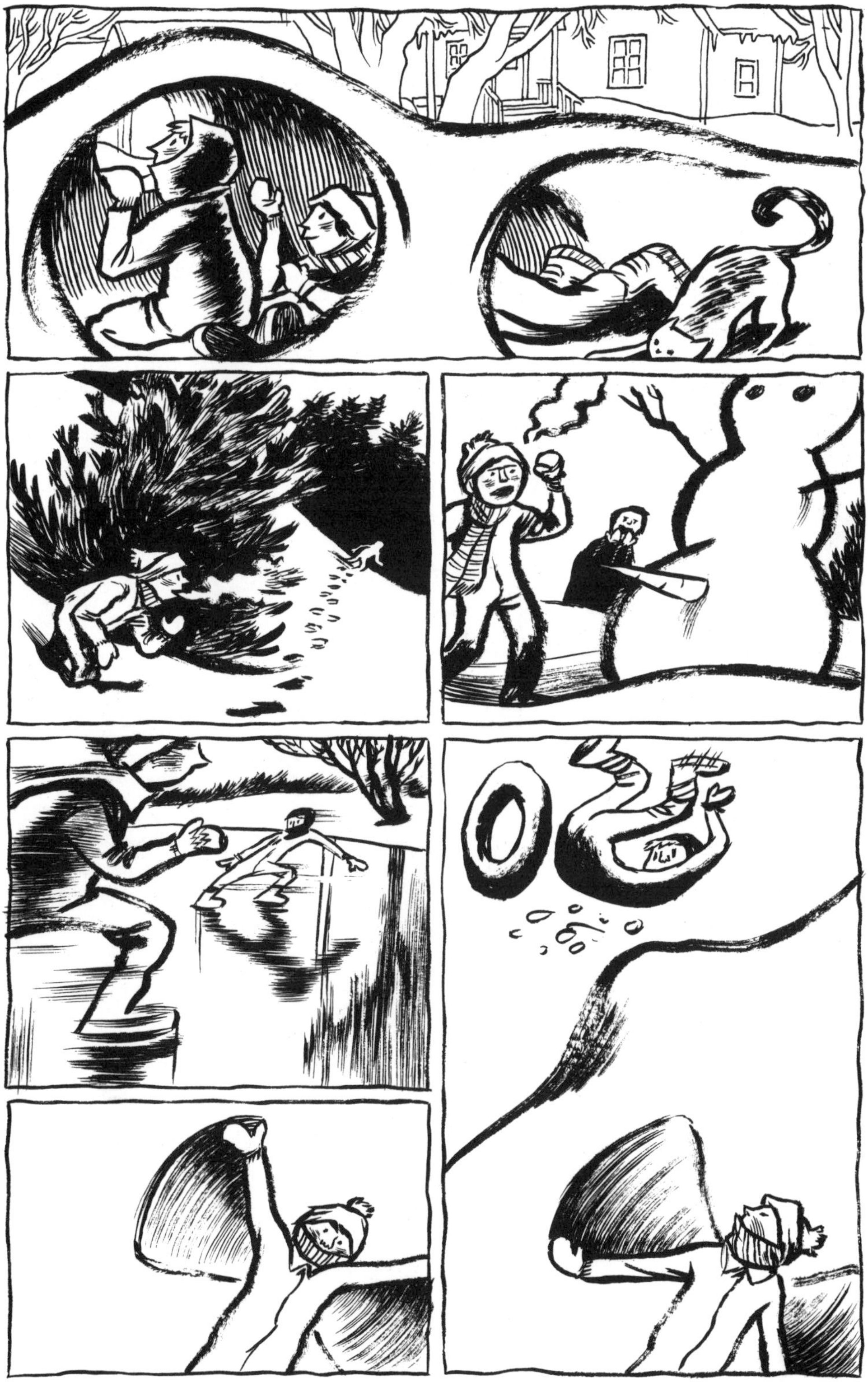

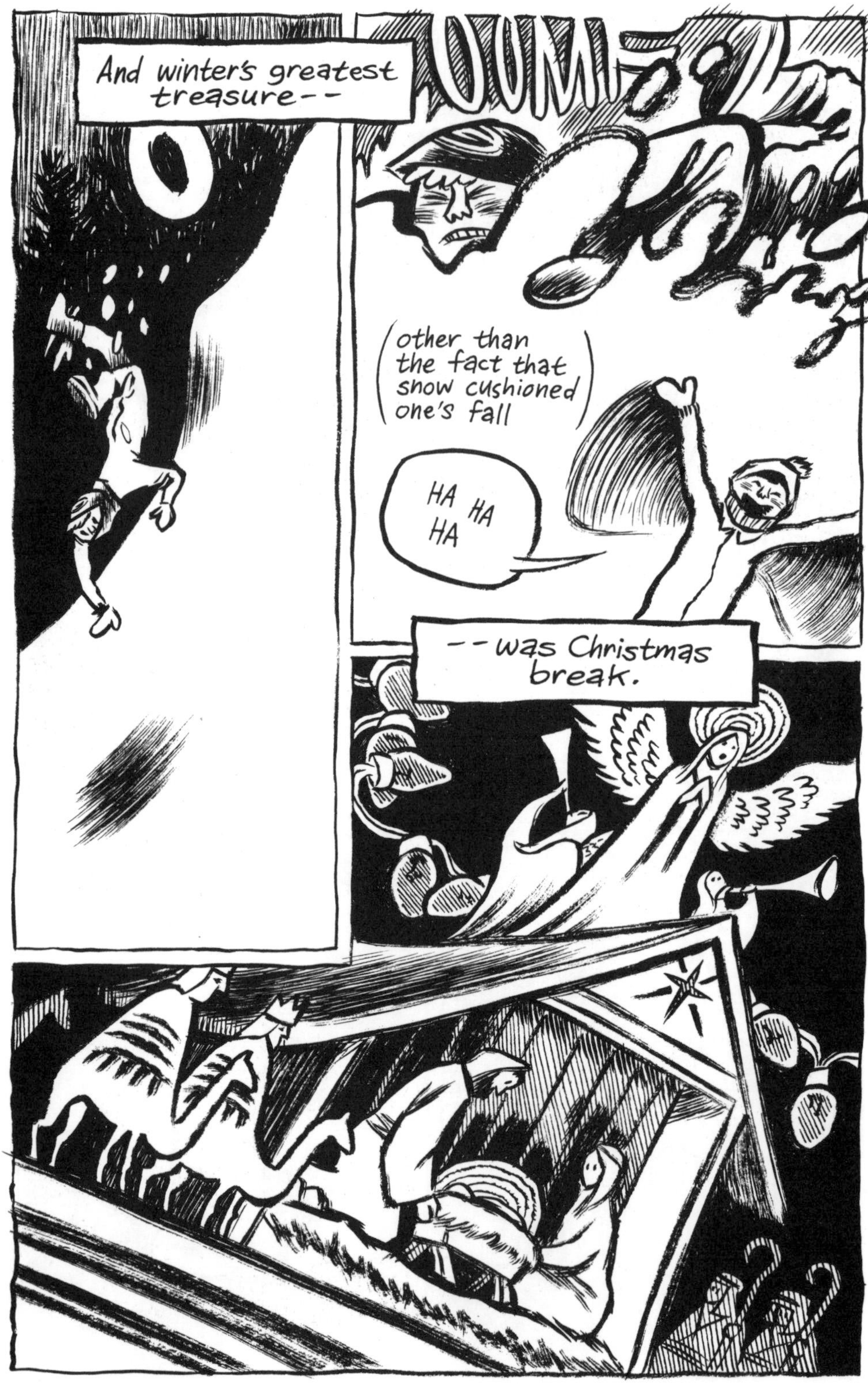
And winter's greatest treasure--
(other than the fact that snow cushioned one's fall)
HA HA HA
--was Christmas break.

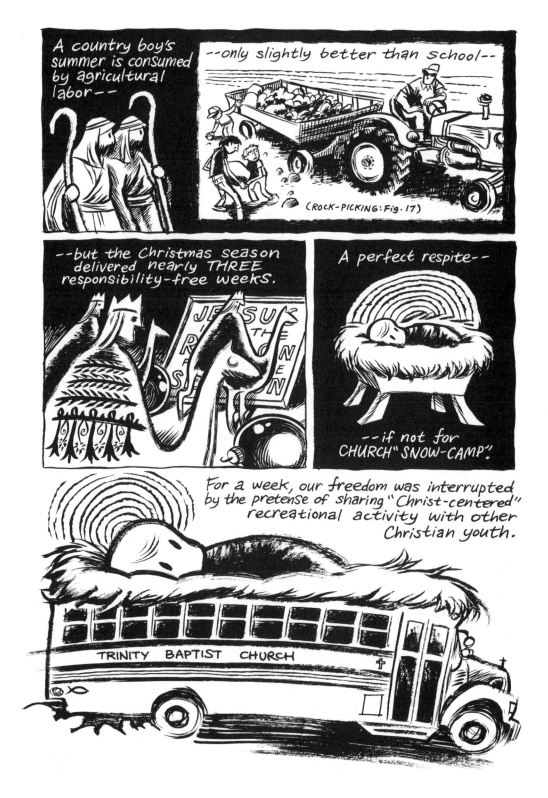

A country boy's summer is consumed by agricultural labor--

--only slightly better than school--

(ROCK-PICKING: Fig. 17)

--but the Christmas season delivered nearly THREE responsibility-free weeks.

A perfect respite--

--if not for CHURCH "SNOW-CAMP"!

For a week, our freedom was interrupted by the pretense of sharing "Christ-centered" recreational activity with other Christian youth.

TRINITY BAPTIST CHURCH

77

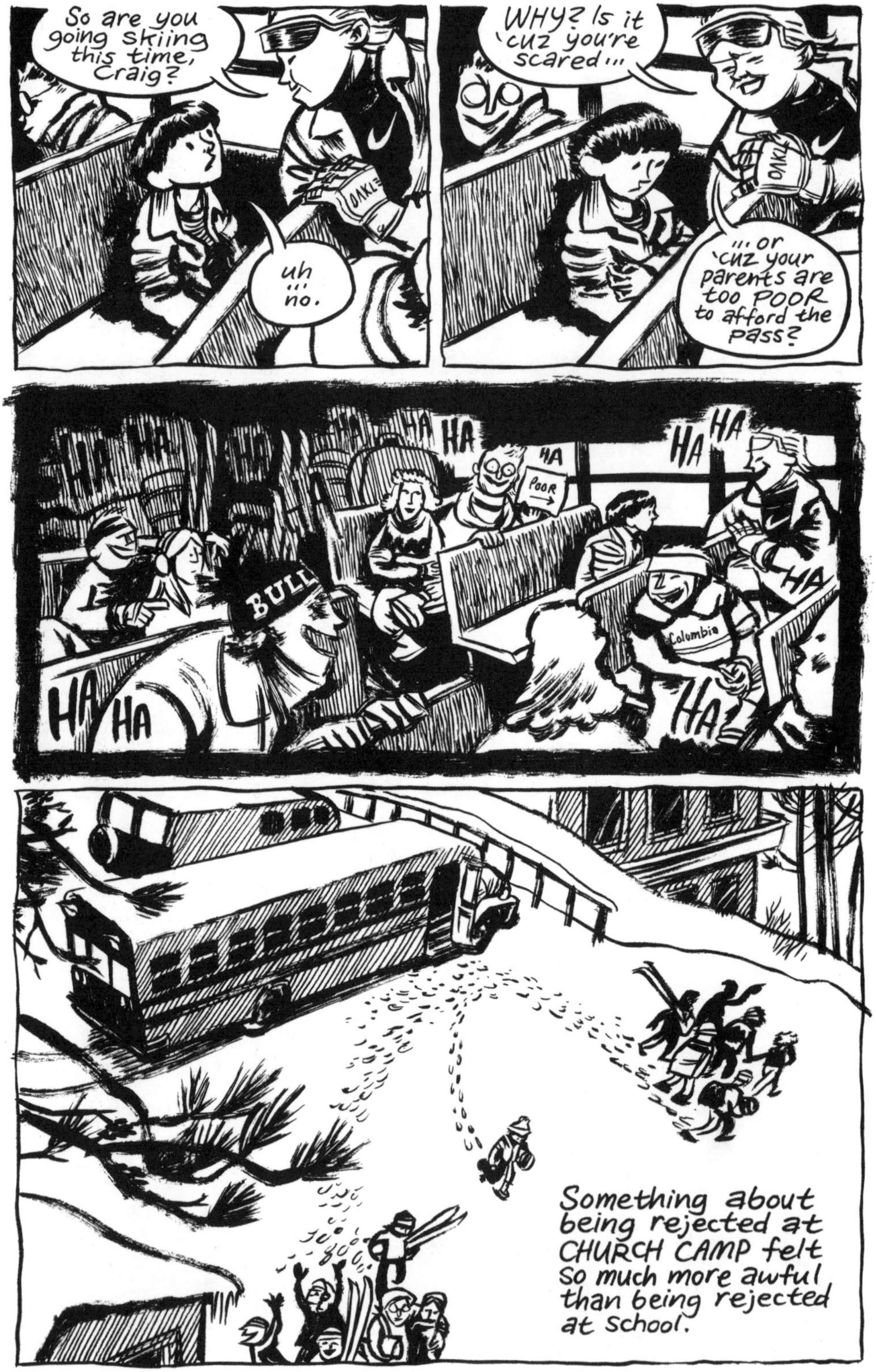
So are you going skiing this time, Craig?
uh... no.
WHY? Is it `cuz you're scared...
...or `cuz your parents are too POOR to afford the pass?
Something about being rejected at CHURCH CAMP felt so much more awful than being rejected at school.

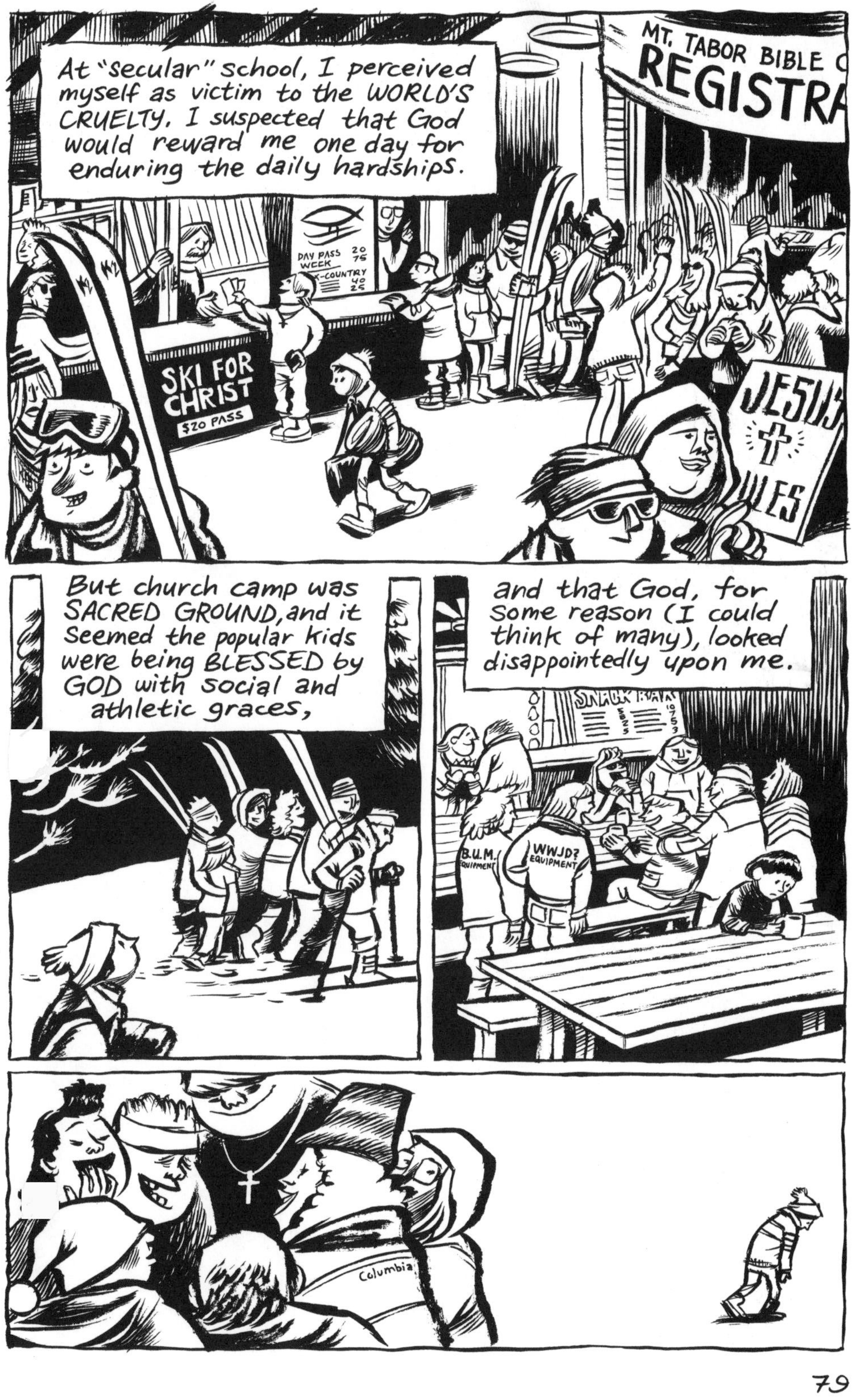
At "secular" school, I perceived myself as victim to the WORLD'S CRUELTY. I suspected that God would reward me one day for enduring the daily hardships.
MT. TABOR BIBLE C
REGISTRA
DAY PASS 20
WEEK 75
SKI FOR CHRIST
$20 PASS
But church camp was SACRED GROUND, and it seemed the popular kids were being BLESSED by GOD with social and athletic graces,
and that God, for some reason (I could think of many), looked disappointedly upon me.
B.U.M. EQUIPMENT
WWJD? EQUIPMENT
Columbia

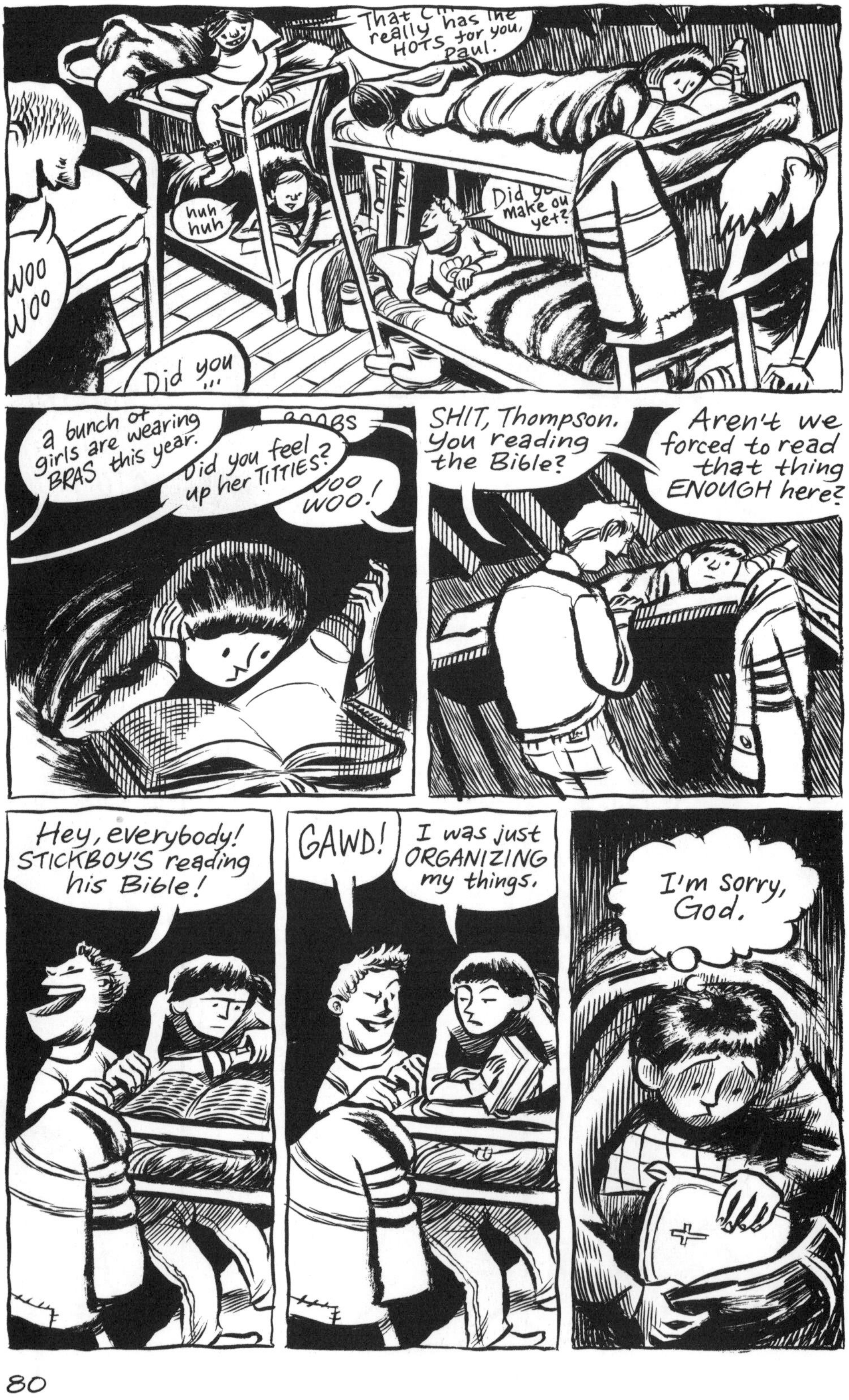
really has the HOTS for you, Paul.
huh huh
make out yet?
WOO WOO
Did you ...
a bunch of girls are wearing BRAS this year.
Did you feel up her TITTIES?
WOO!
SHIT, Thompson. You reading the Bible?
Aren't we forced to read that thing ENOUGH here?
Hey, everybody! STICKBOY'S reading his Bible!
GAWD!
I was just ORGANIZING my things.
I'm sorry, God.

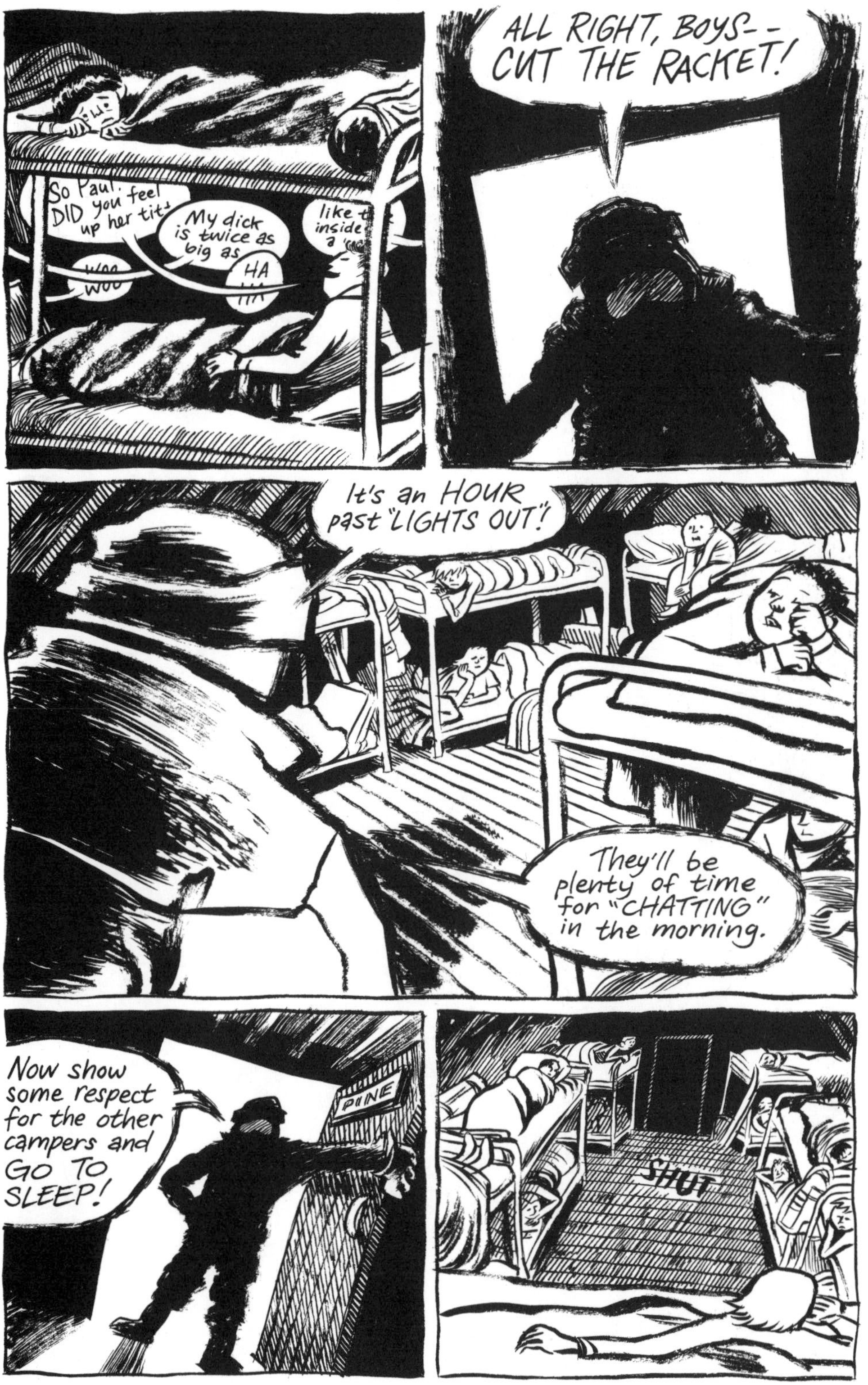
So Paul. DID you feel up her tit
My dick is twice as big as
HA
ALL RIGHT, BOYS-- CUT THE RACKET!
It's an HOUR past "LIGHTS OUT"!
They'll be plenty of time for "CHATTING" in the morning.
Now show some respect for the other campers and GO TO SLEEP!
PINE
SHUT

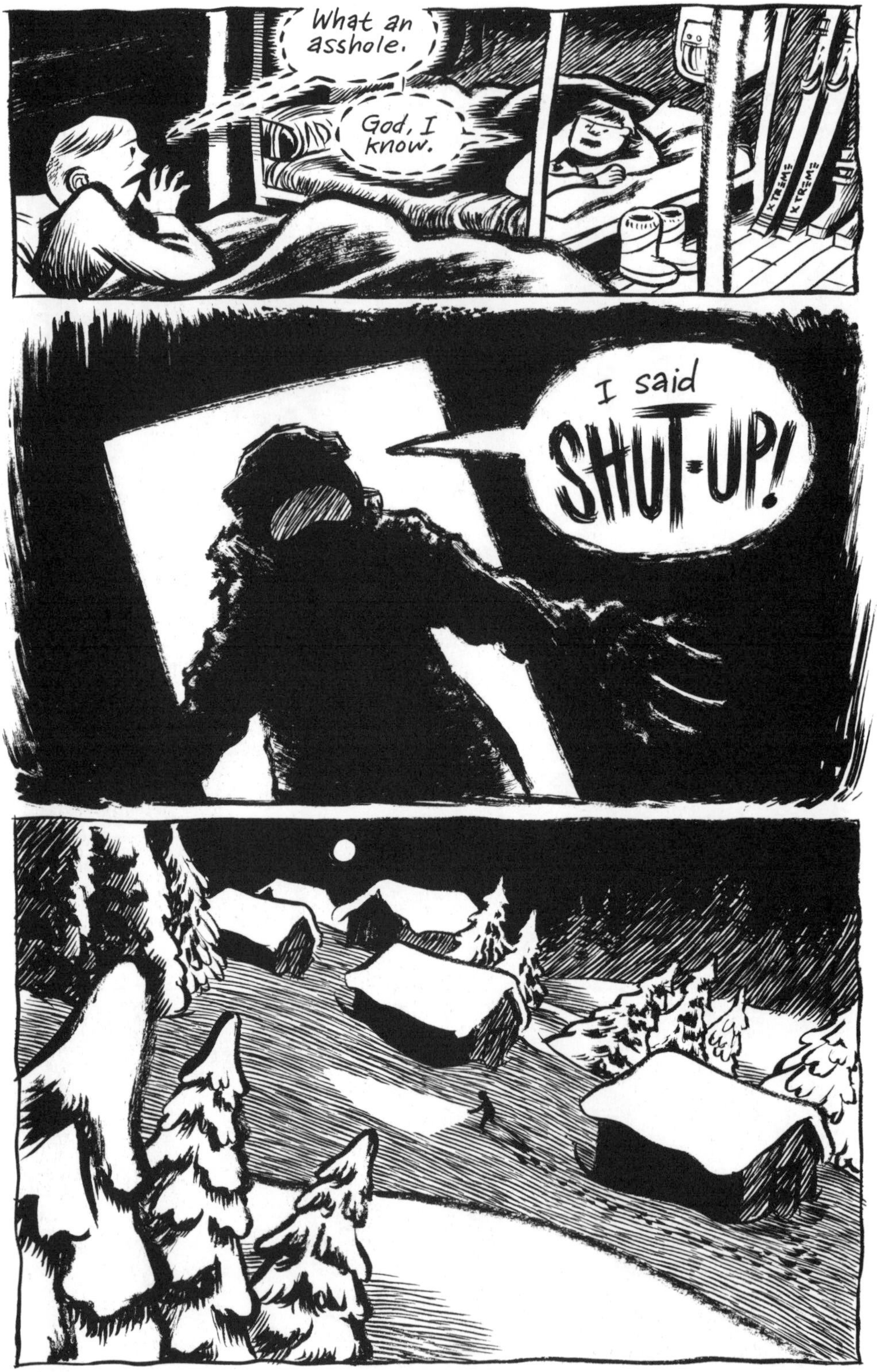
What an asshole.
God, I know.
I said SHUT-UP!

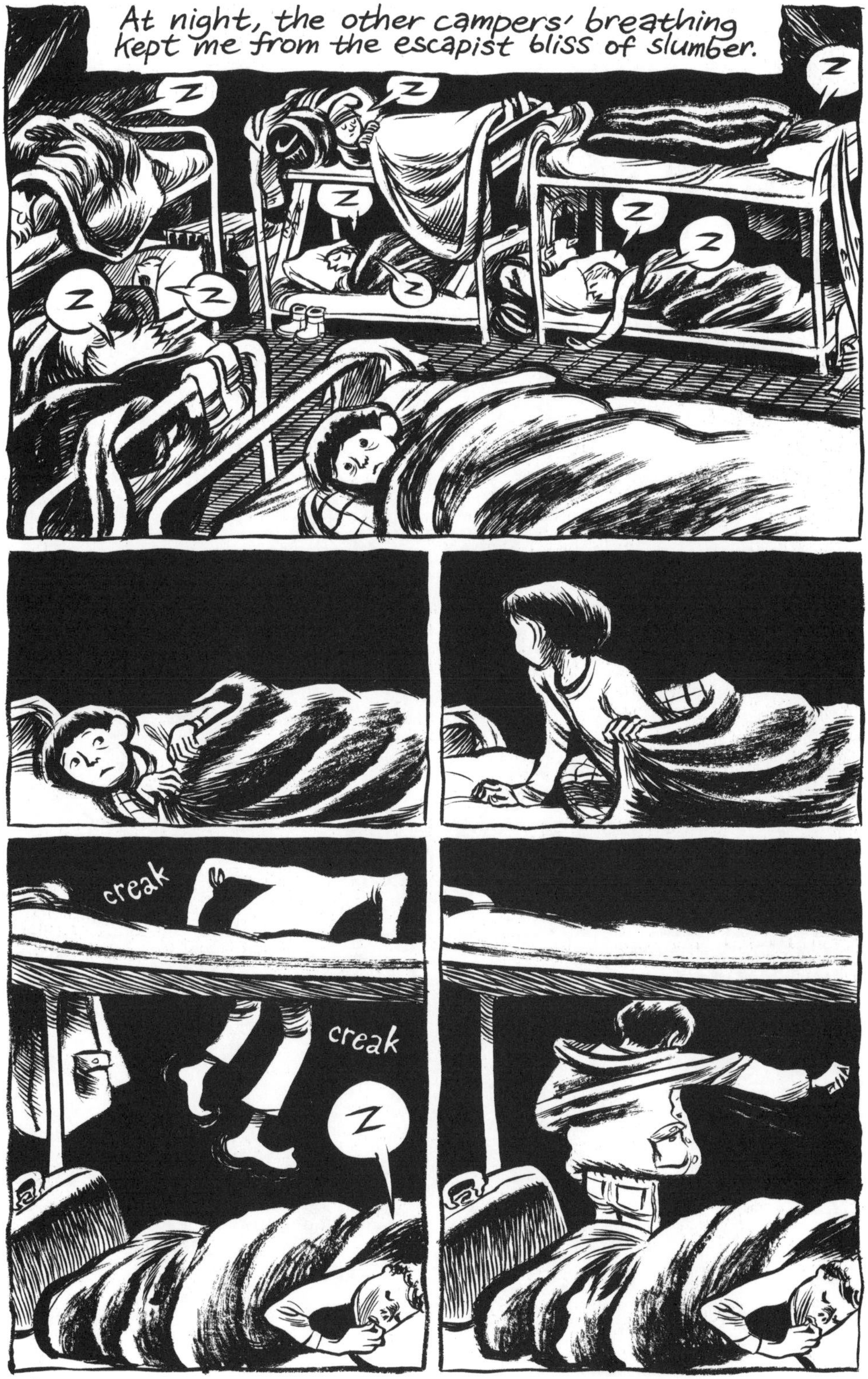
At night, the other campers' breathing kept me from the escapist bliss of slumber.
Z
Z
Z
Z
Z
Z
Z
Z
Z
creak
creak
Z

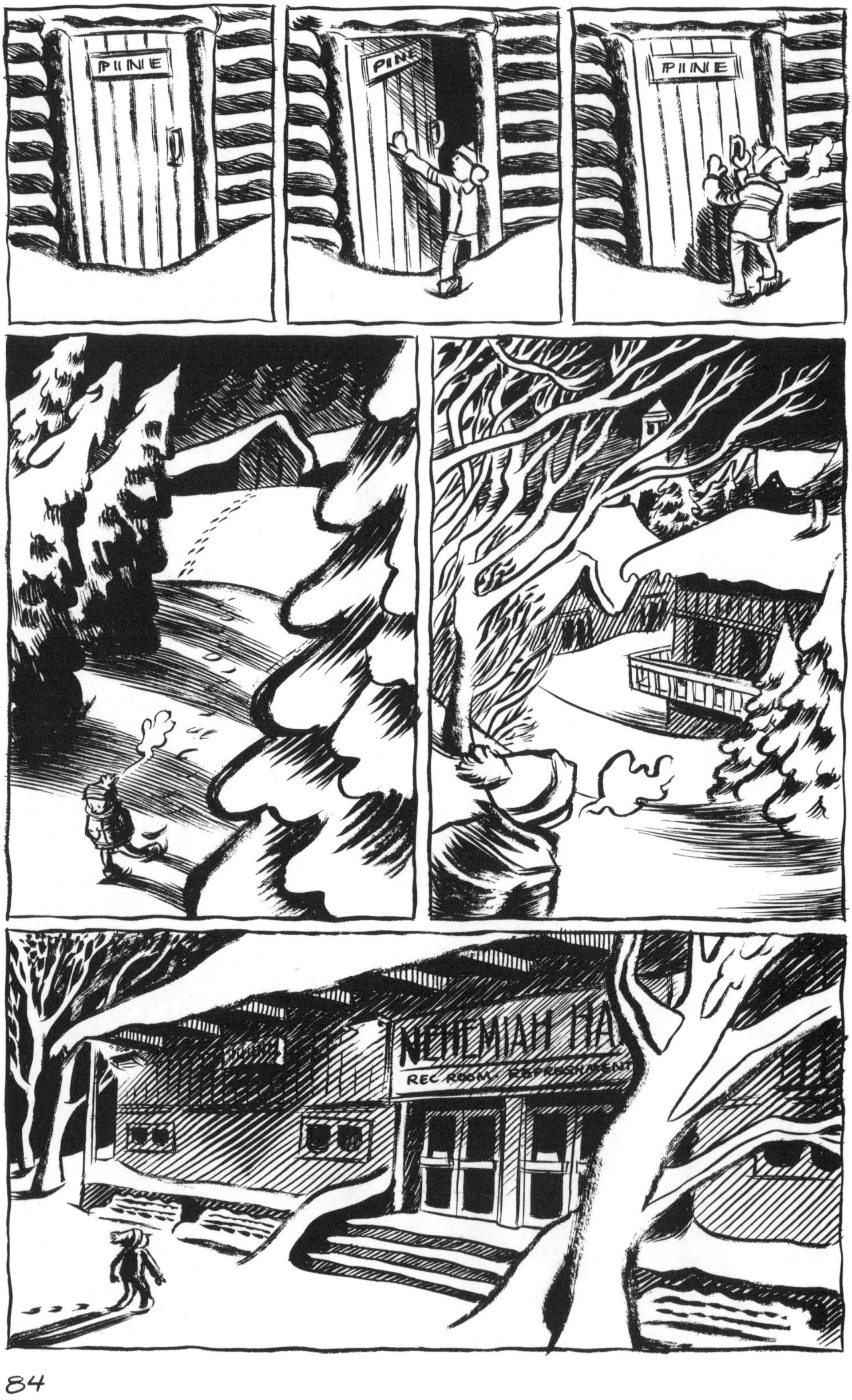
PINE
PINE
PINE
NEHEMIAH HA
REC ROOM

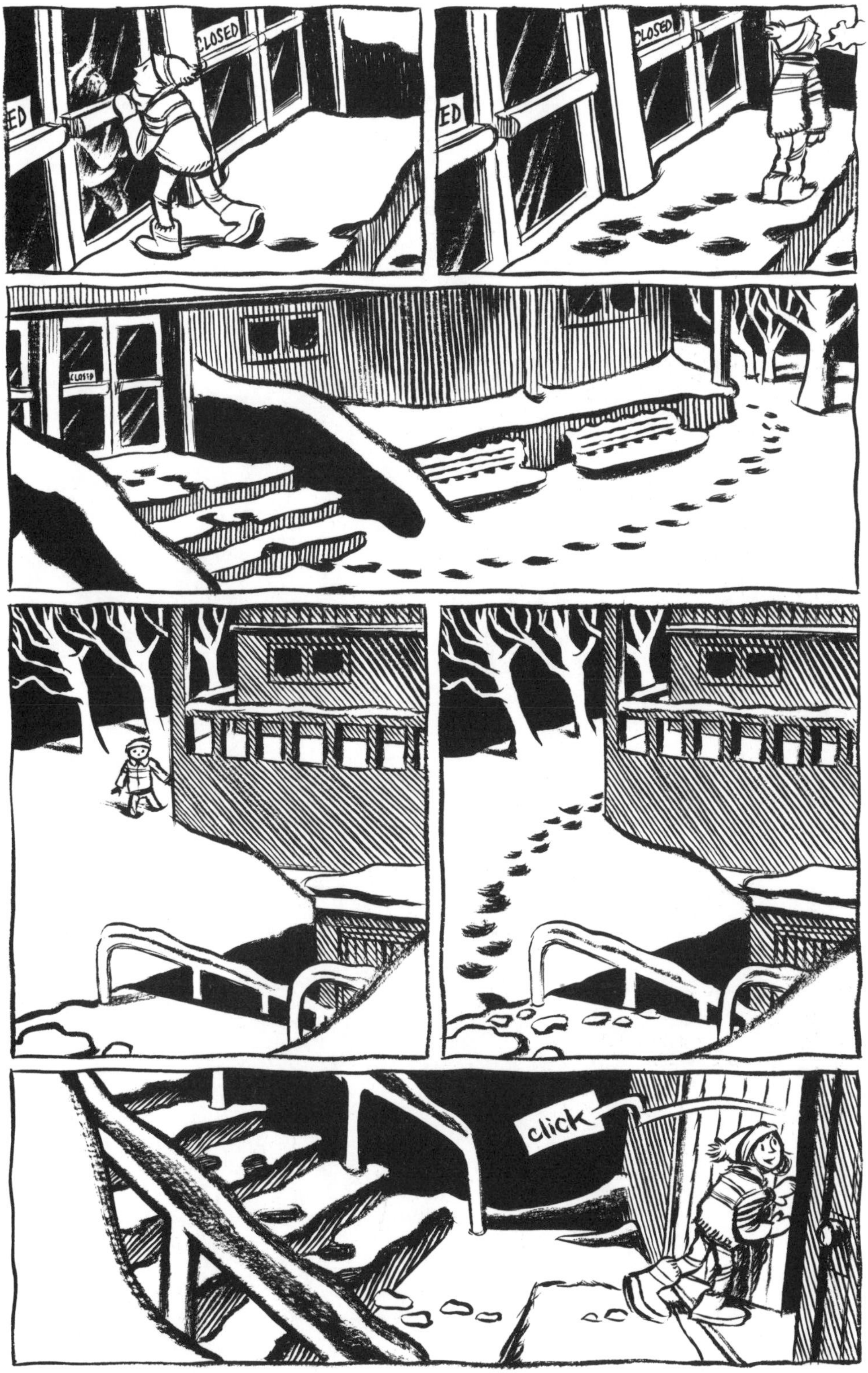
CLOSED
ED
CLOSED
ED
CLOSED
click

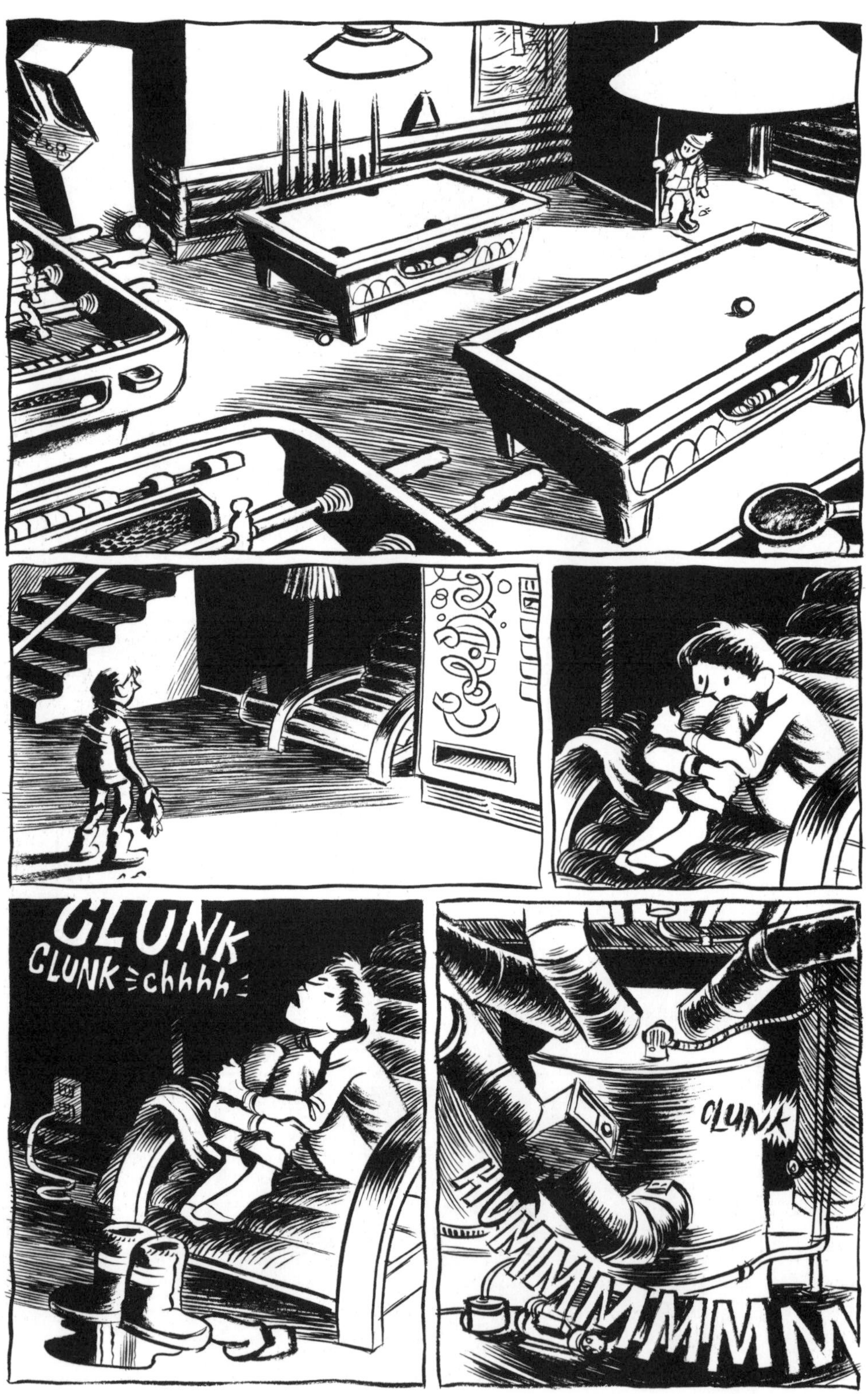
CLUNK
CLUNK chhhh
CLUNK
HUMMMMMMMM

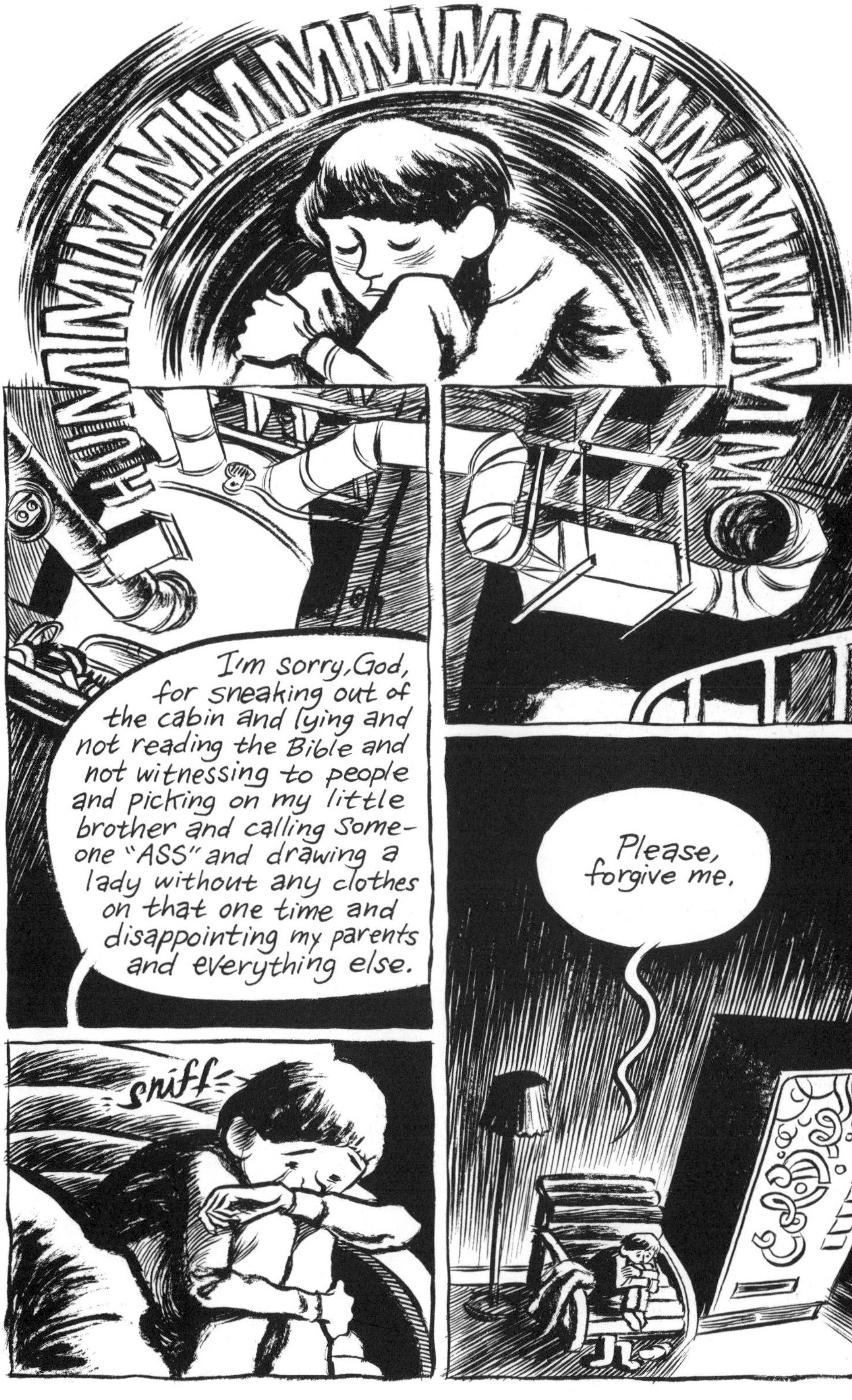
HUMMMMMMMMMMMMMMMMMMMMMMMM
I'm sorry, God, for sneaking out of the cabin and lying and not reading the Bible and not witnessing to people and picking on my little brother and calling Someone "ASS" and drawing a lady without any clothes on that one time and disappointing my parents and everything else.
Please, forgive me.
sniff

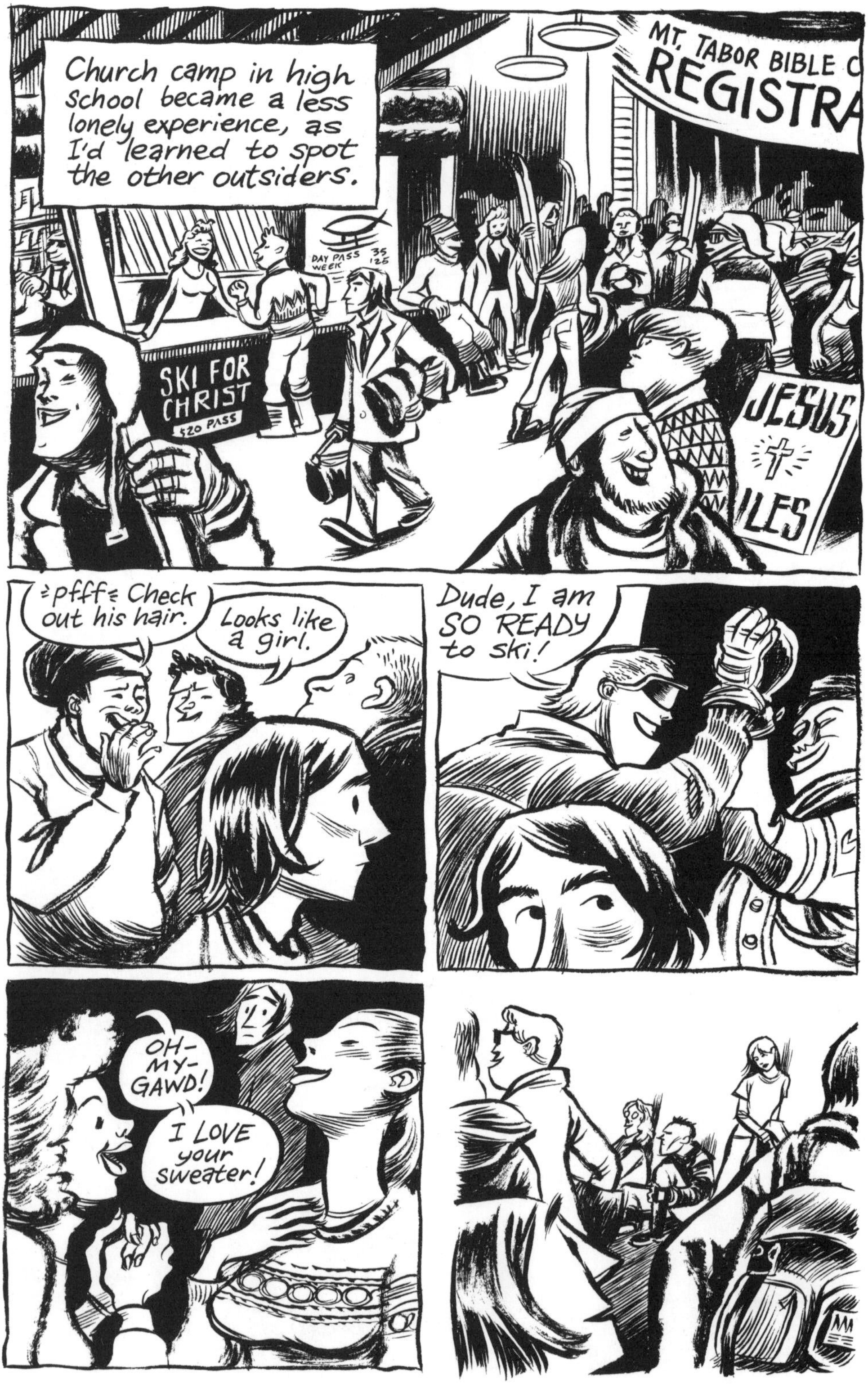
Church camp in high school became a less lonely experience, as I'd learned to spot the other outsiders.
MT. TABOR BIBLE C
REGISTRA
DAY PASS 35
WEEK 125
SKI FOR CHRIST
$20 PASS
JESUS
ILES
≈pfff≈ Check out his hair.
Looks like a girl.
Dude, I am SO READY to ski!
OH-MY-GAWD!
I LOVE your sweater!

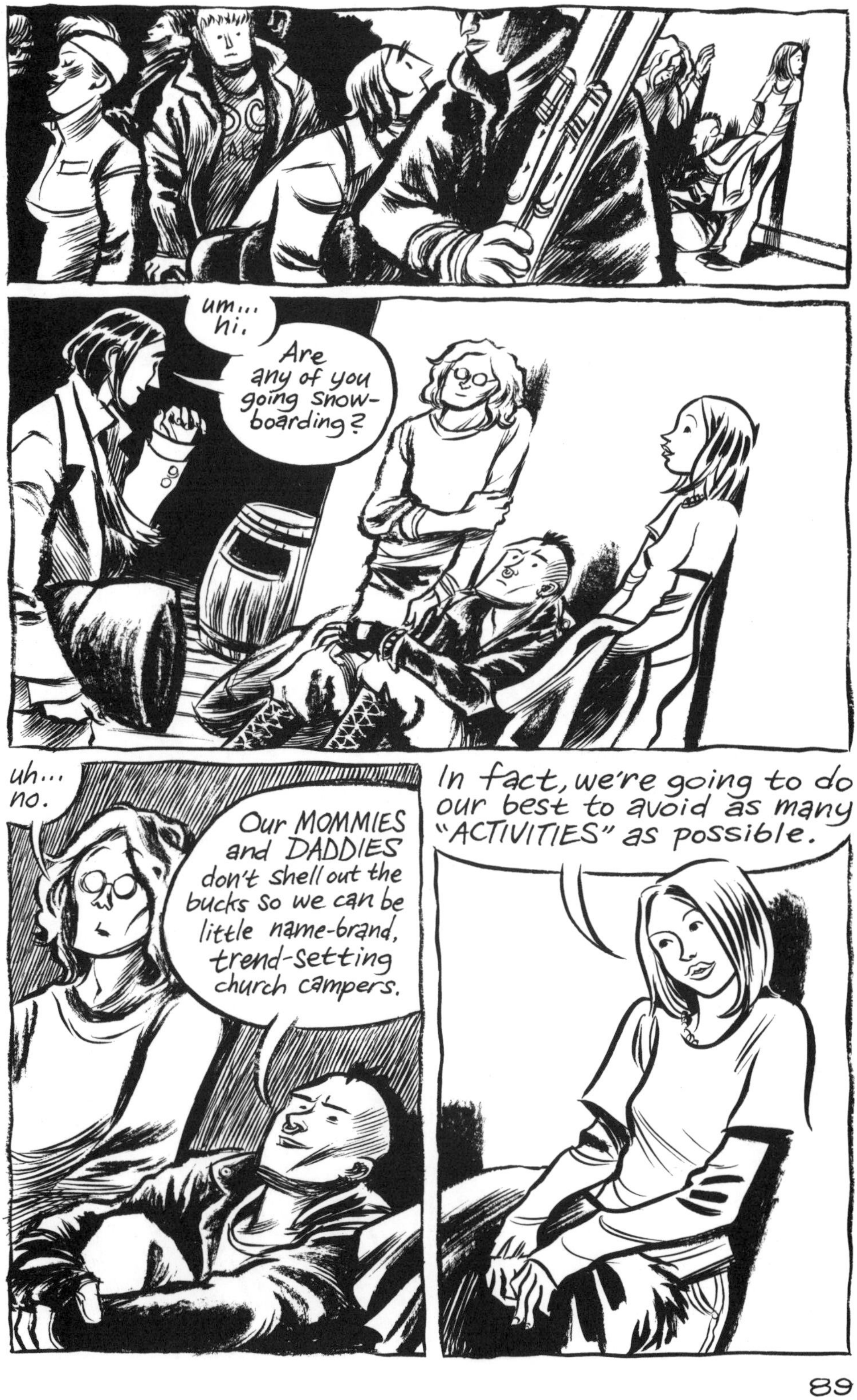

um... hi.
Are any of you going snow-boarding?
uh... no.
Our MOMMIES and DADDIES don't shell out the bucks so we can be little name-brand, trend-setting church campers.
In fact, we're going to do our best to avoid as many "ACTIVITIES" as possible.

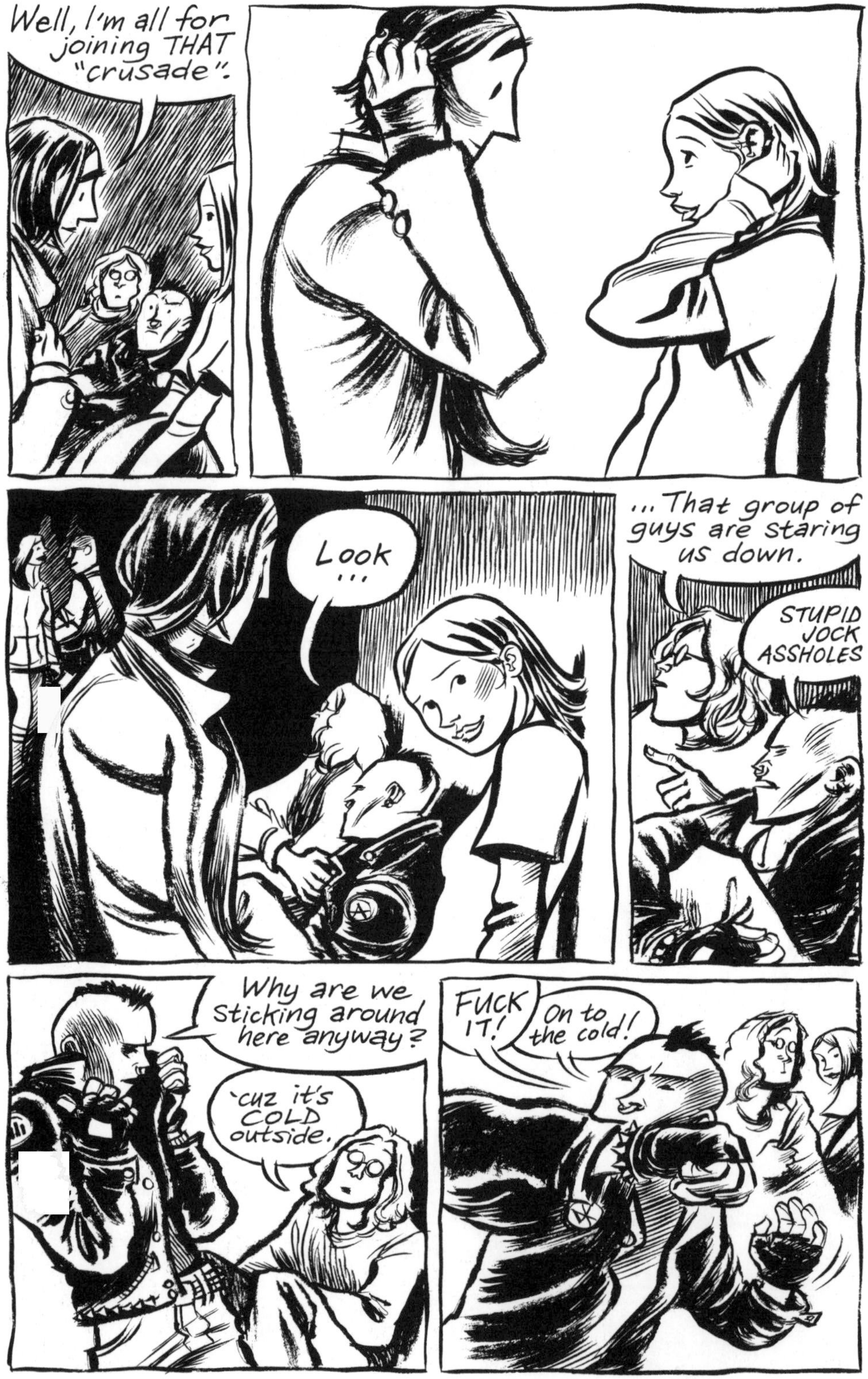

Well, I'm all for joining THAT "crusade".
Look ...
...That group of guys are staring us down.
STUPID JOCK ASSHOLES
Why are we sticking around here anyway?
'cuz it's COLD outside.
FUCK IT!
On to the cold!

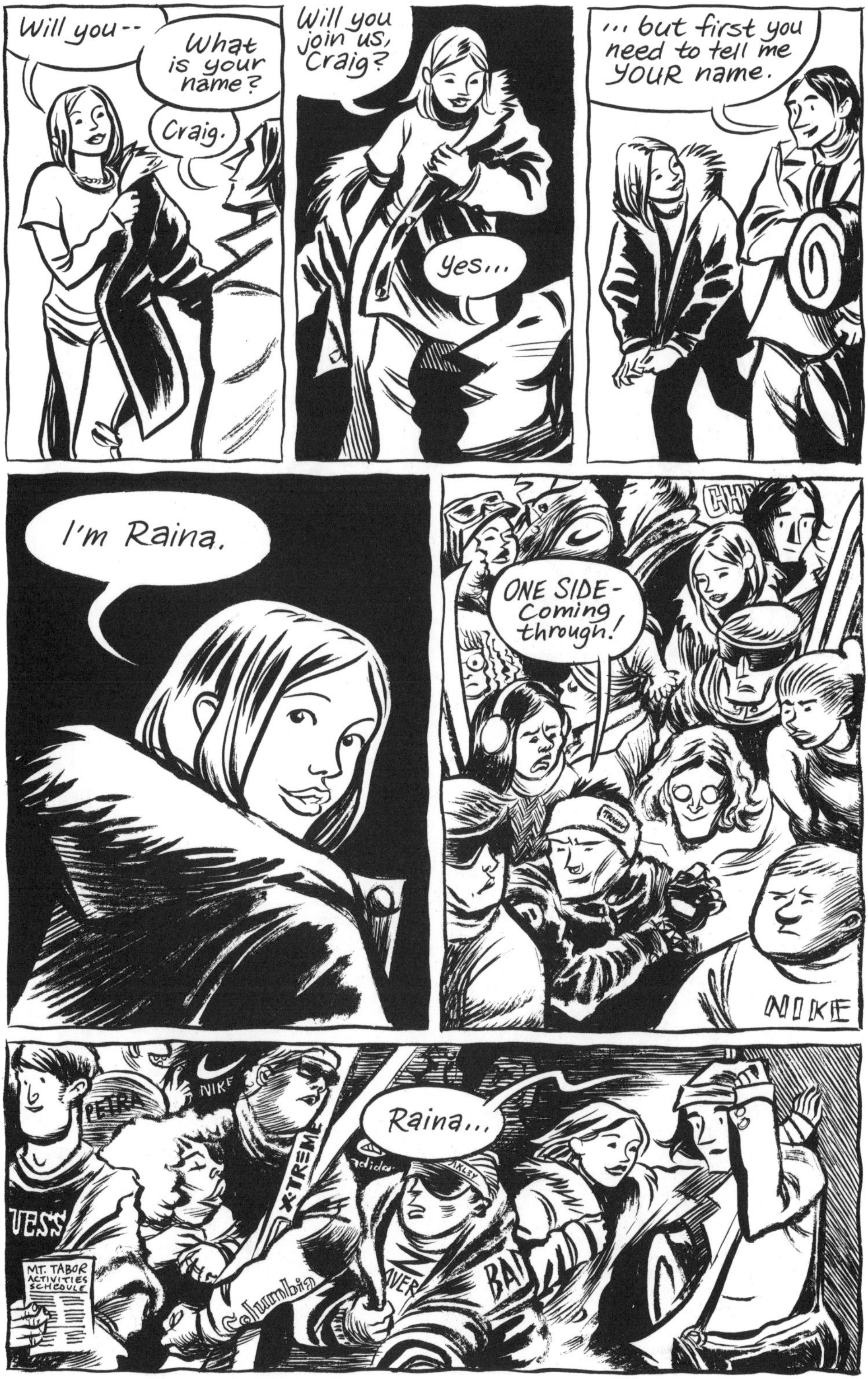
Will you--
What is your name?
Craig.
Will you join us, Craig?
Yes...
... but first you need to tell me YOUR name.
I'm Raina.
ONE SIDE- Coming through!
NIKE
NIKE
PETRA
X-TREME
Raina...
MT. TABOR ACTIVITIES SCHEDULE
columbia
BA

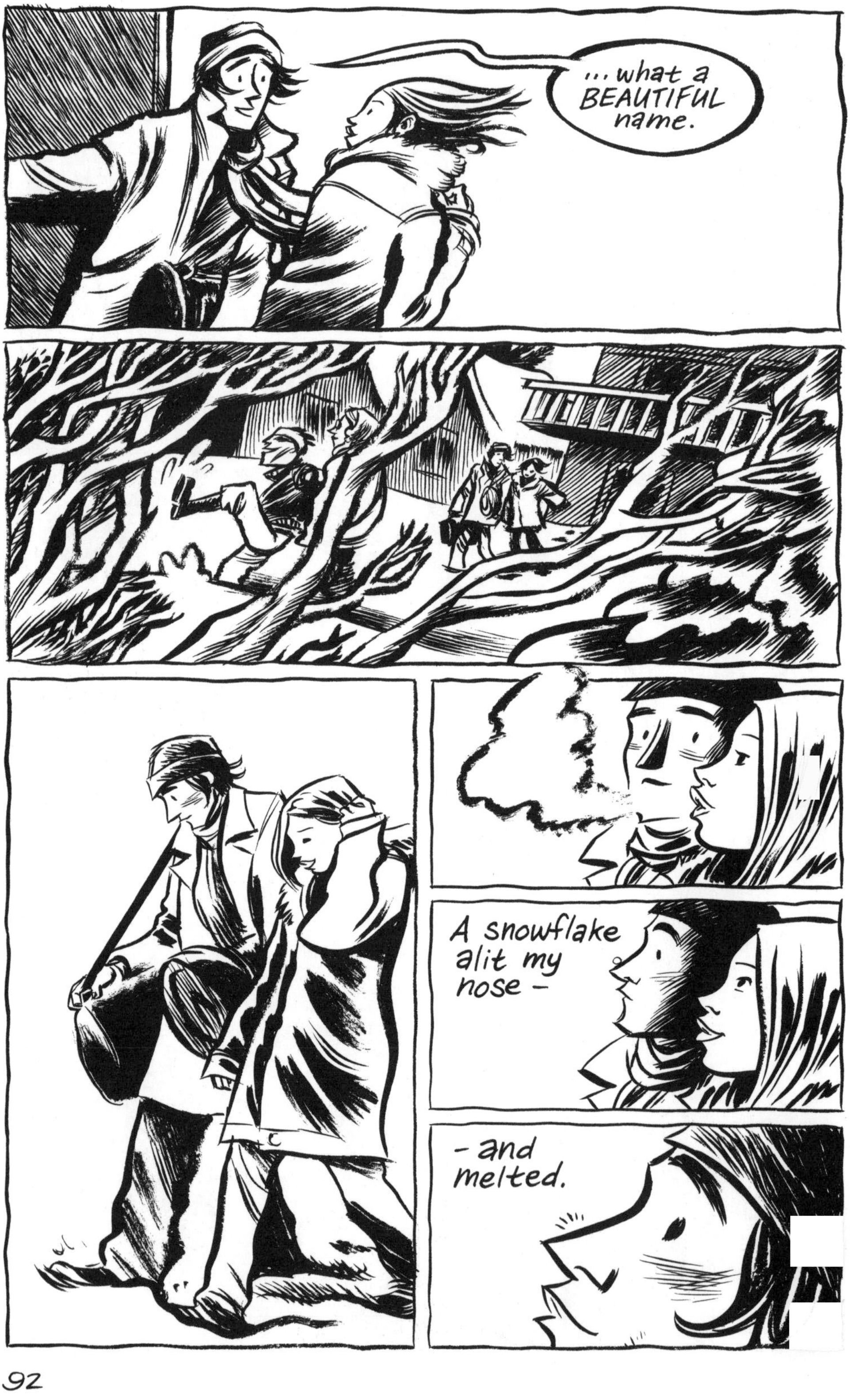
...what a BEAUTIFUL name.
A snowflake alit my nose -
- and melted.

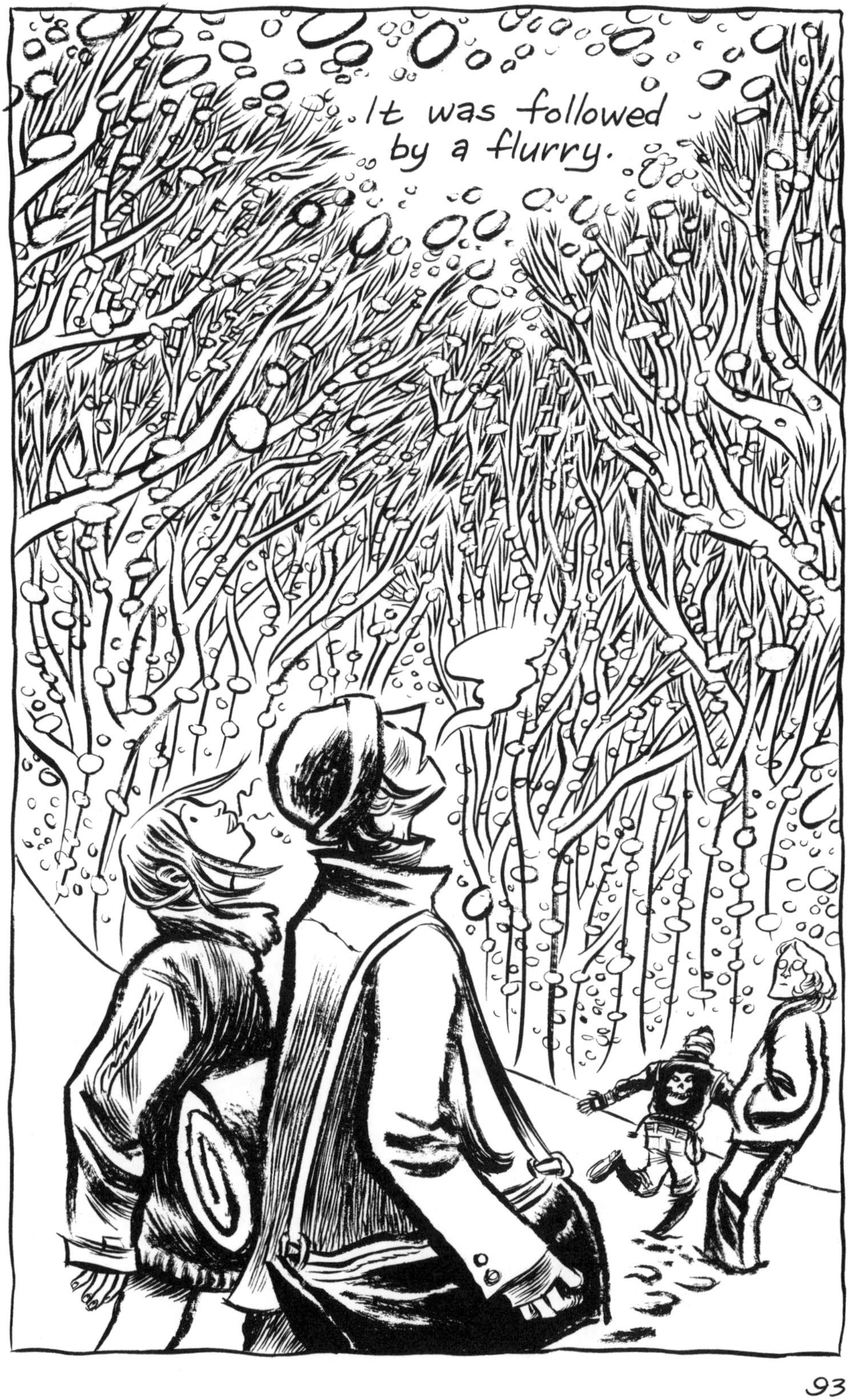
It was followed by a flurry.

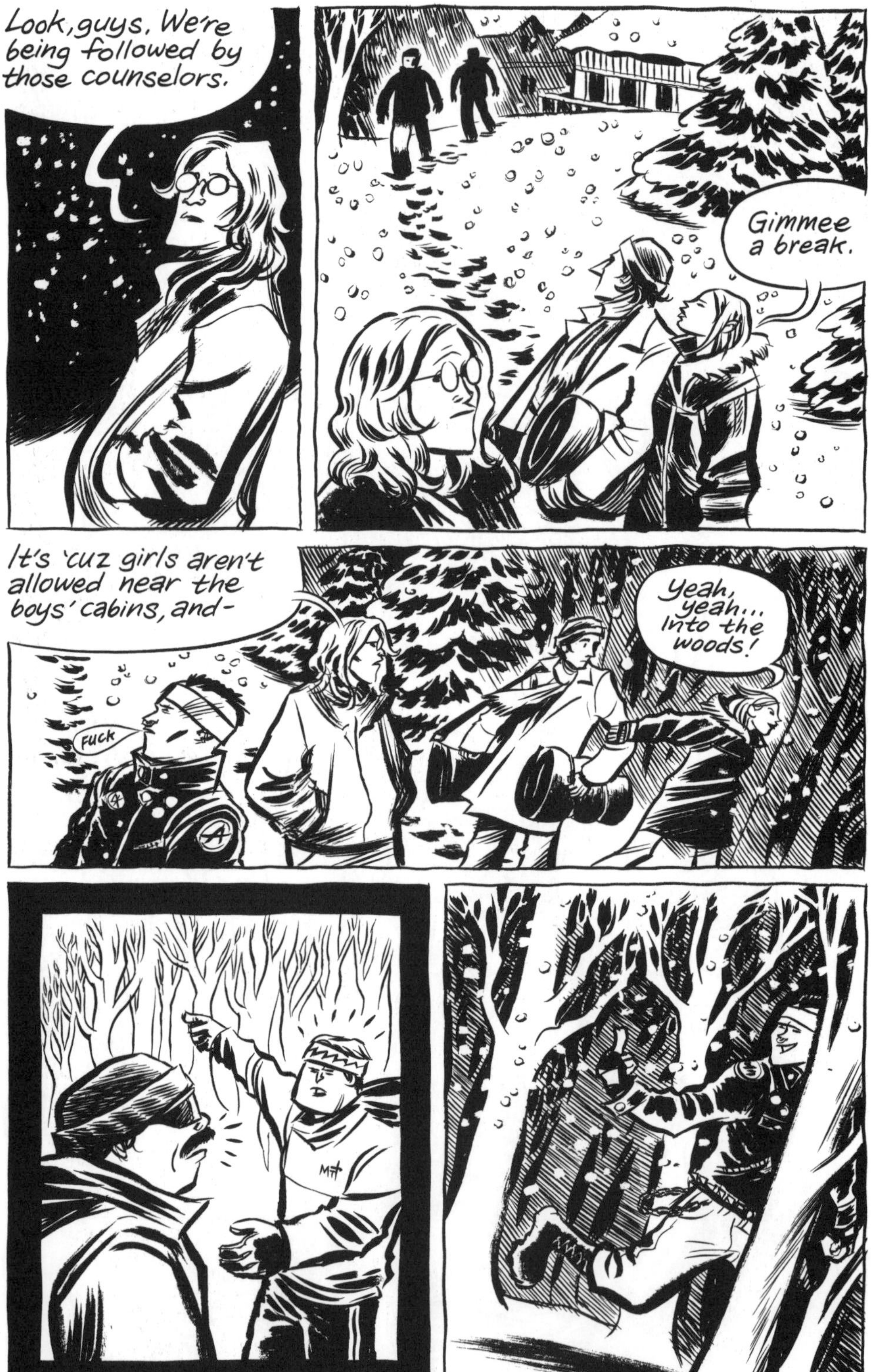
Look, guys. We're being followed by those counselors.
Gimmee a break.
It's 'cuz girls aren't allowed near the boys' cabins, and-
FUCK
Yeah, yeah... Into the woods!

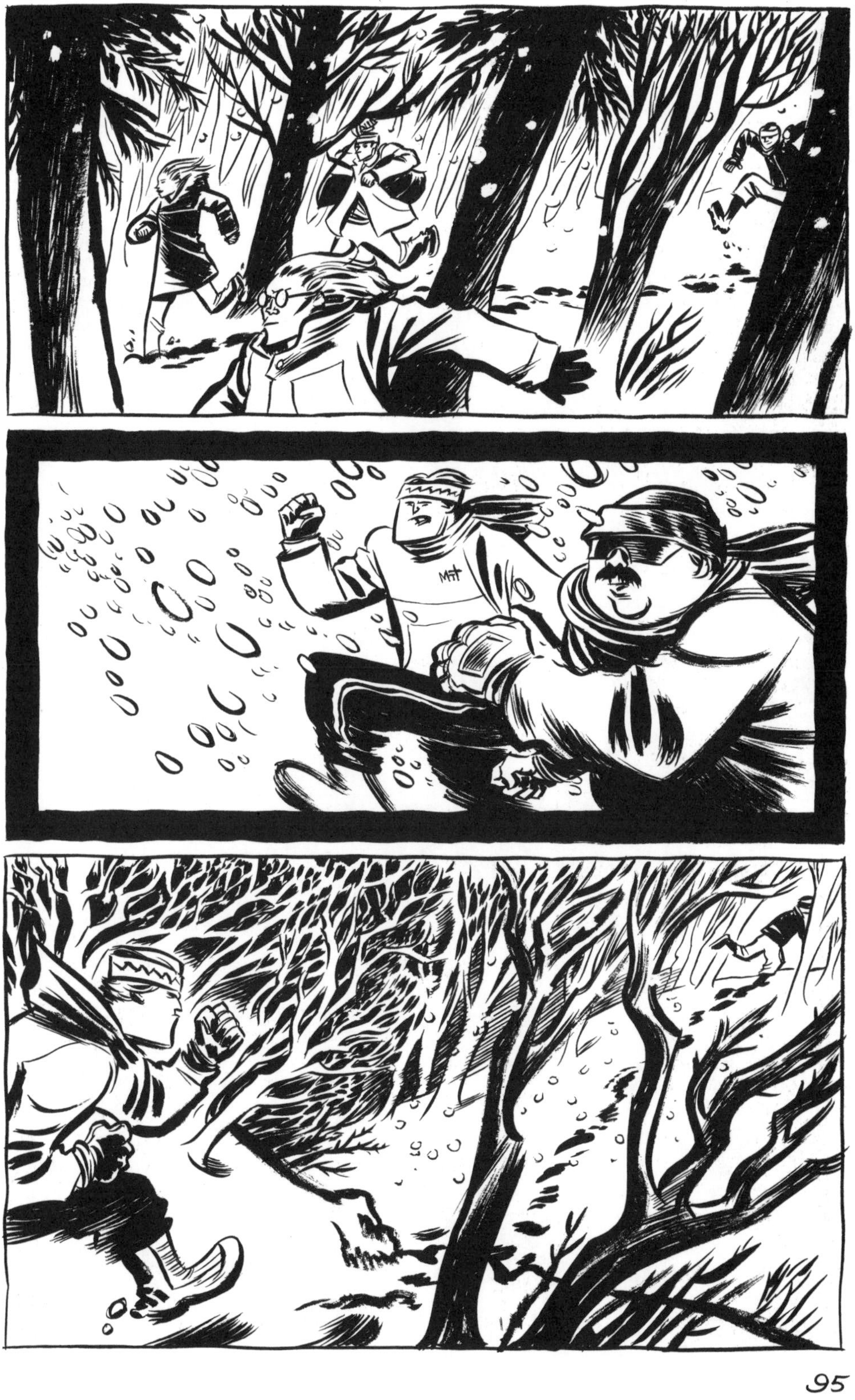

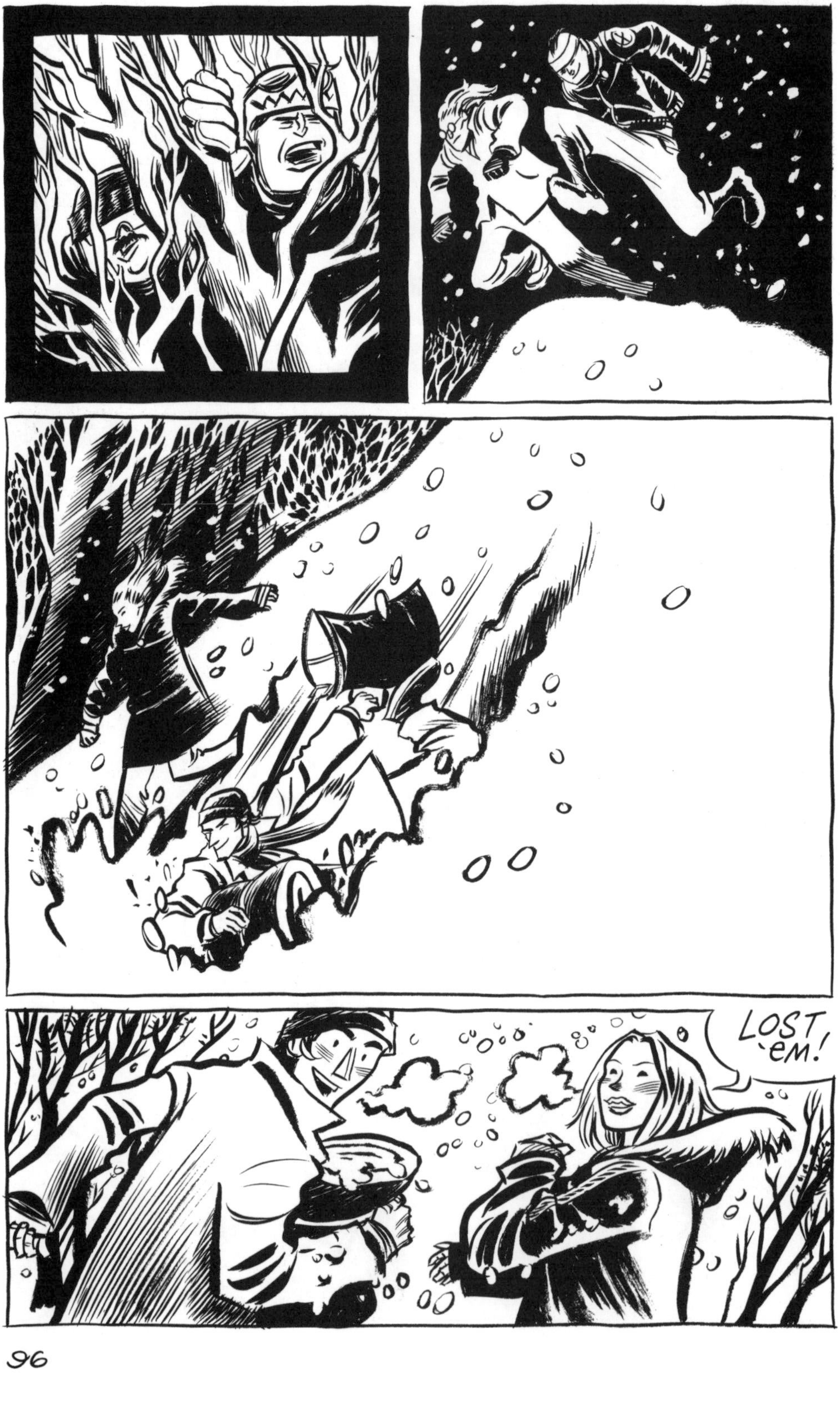
LOST 'em!

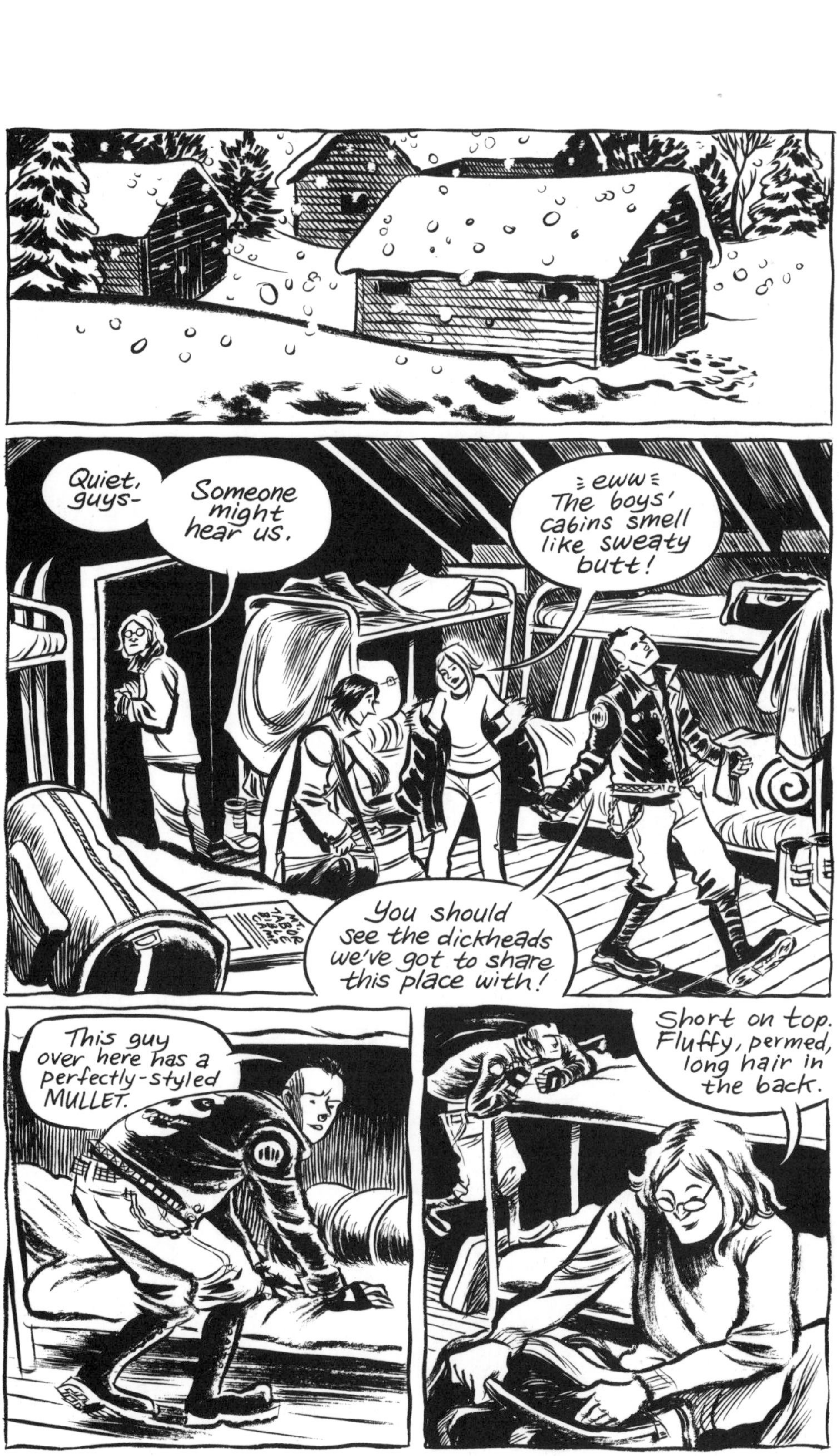

Quiet, guys-
Someone might hear us.
≡ eww ≡ The boys' cabins smell like sweaty butt!
MT. TABOR BIBLE CAMP
You should see the dickheads we've got to share this place with!
This guy over here has a perfectly-styled MULLET.
Short on top. Fluffy, permed, long hair in the back.

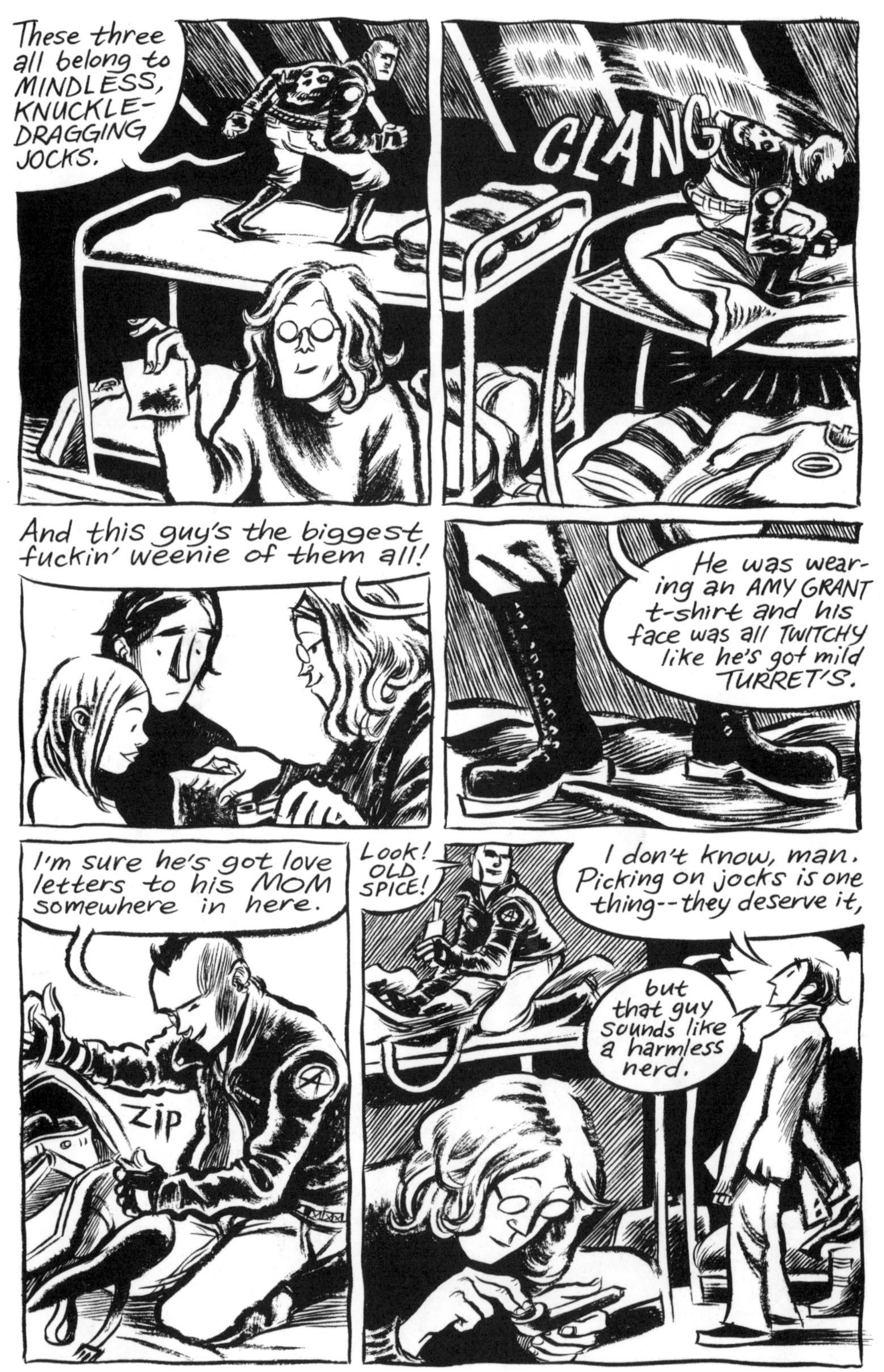
These three all belong to MINDLESS, KNUCKLE-DRAGGING JOCKS.
CLANG
And this guy's the biggest fuckin' weenie of them all!
He was wearing an AMY GRANT t-shirt and his face was all TWITCHY like he's got mild TURRET'S.
I'm sure he's got love letters to his MOM somewhere in here.
ZIP
Look! OLD SPICE!
I don't know, man. Picking on jocks is one thing--they deserve it,
but that guy sounds like a harmless nerd.

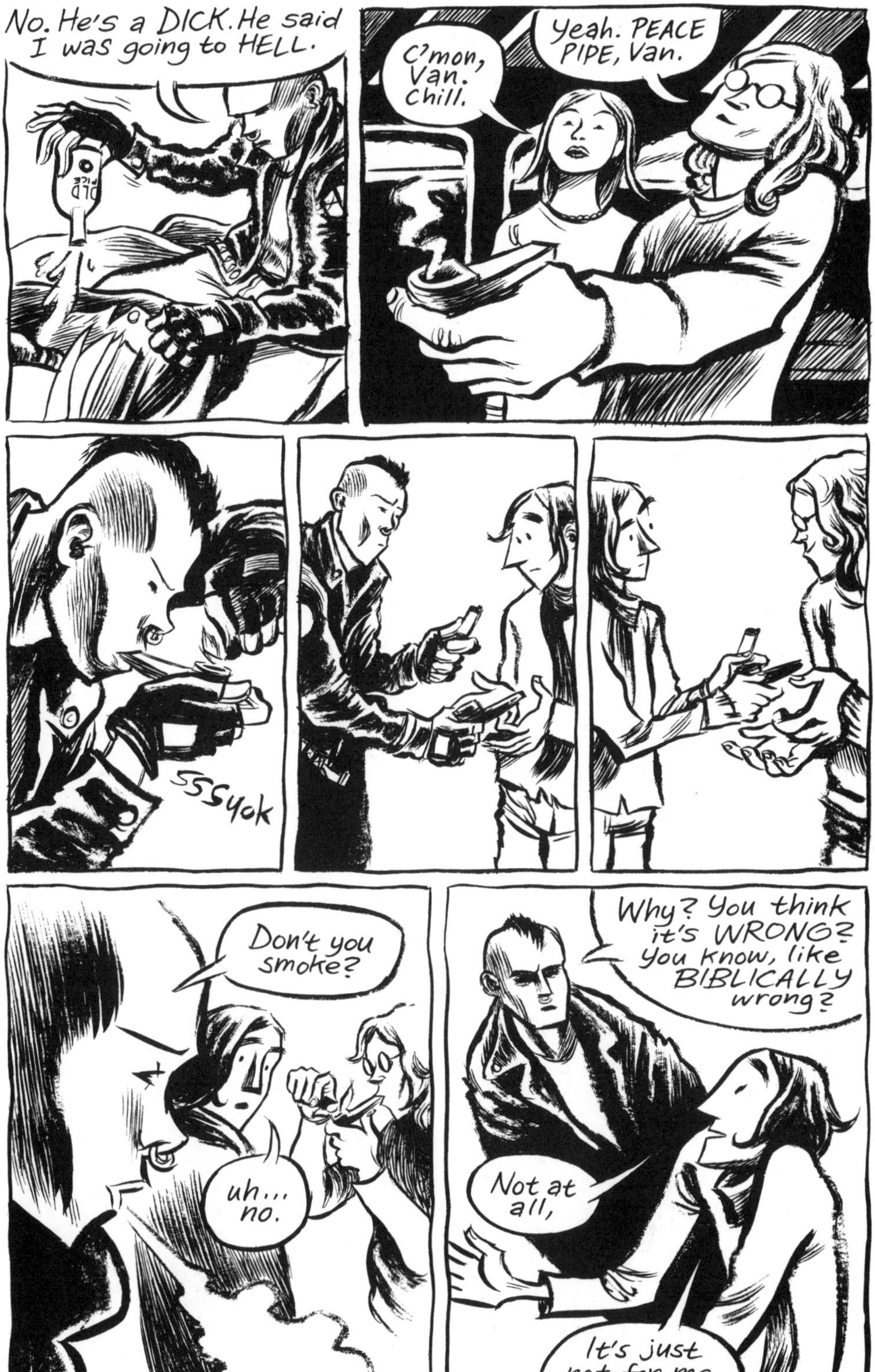
No. He's a DICK. He said I was going to HELL.
C'mon, Van. Chill.
Yeah. PEACE PIPE, Van.
SSSyok
Don't you smoke?
uh... no.
Why? You think it's WRONG? You know, like BIBLICALLY wrong?
Not at all,
It's just not for me.

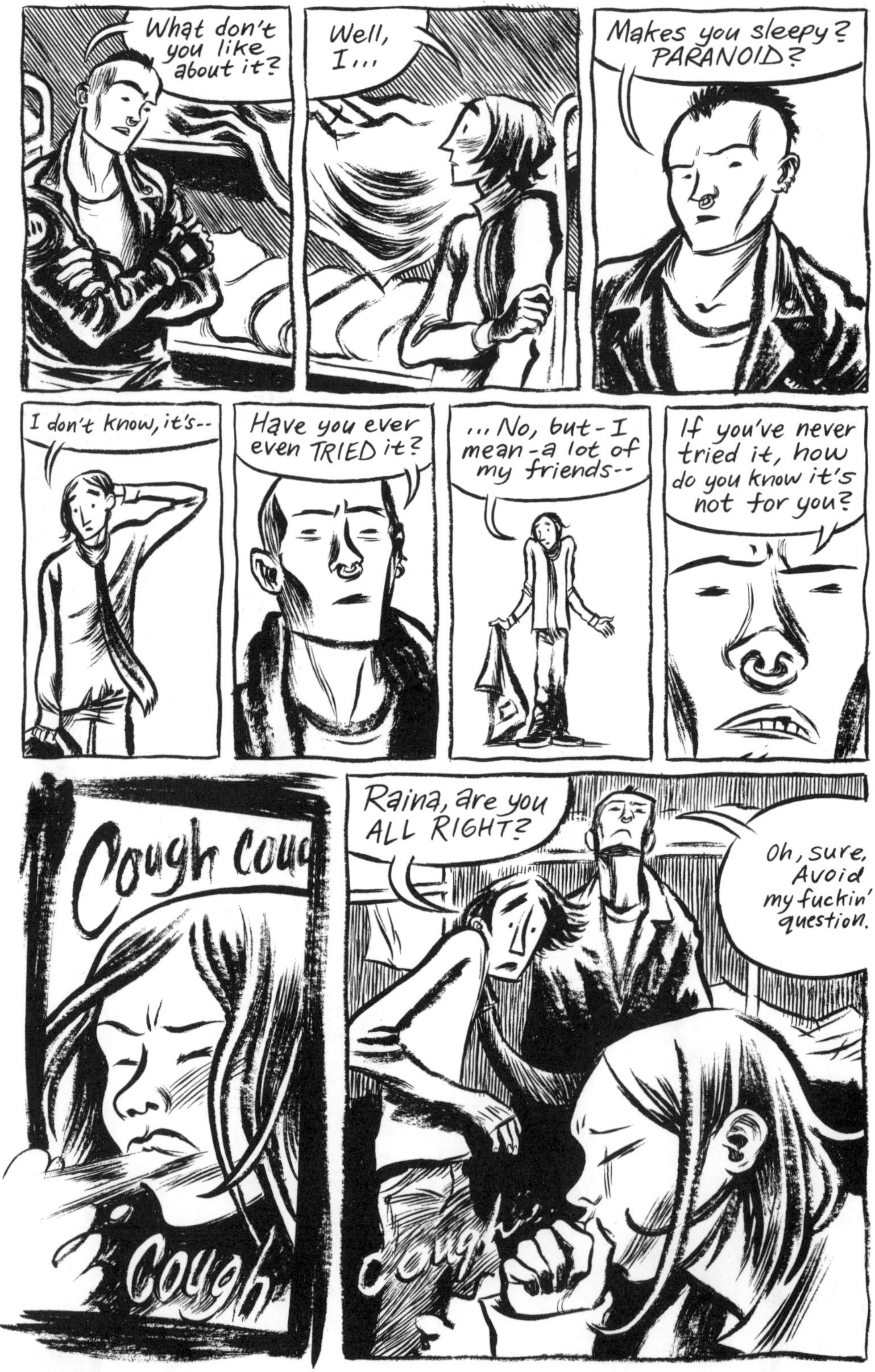
What don't you like about it?
Well, I...
Makes you sleepy? PARANOID?
I don't know, it's--
Have you ever even TRIED it?
...No, but-I mean-a lot of my friends--
If you've never tried it, how do you know it's not for you?
Cough coug
Cough
Raina, are you ALL RIGHT?
Oh, sure, Avoid my fuckin' question.
Cough

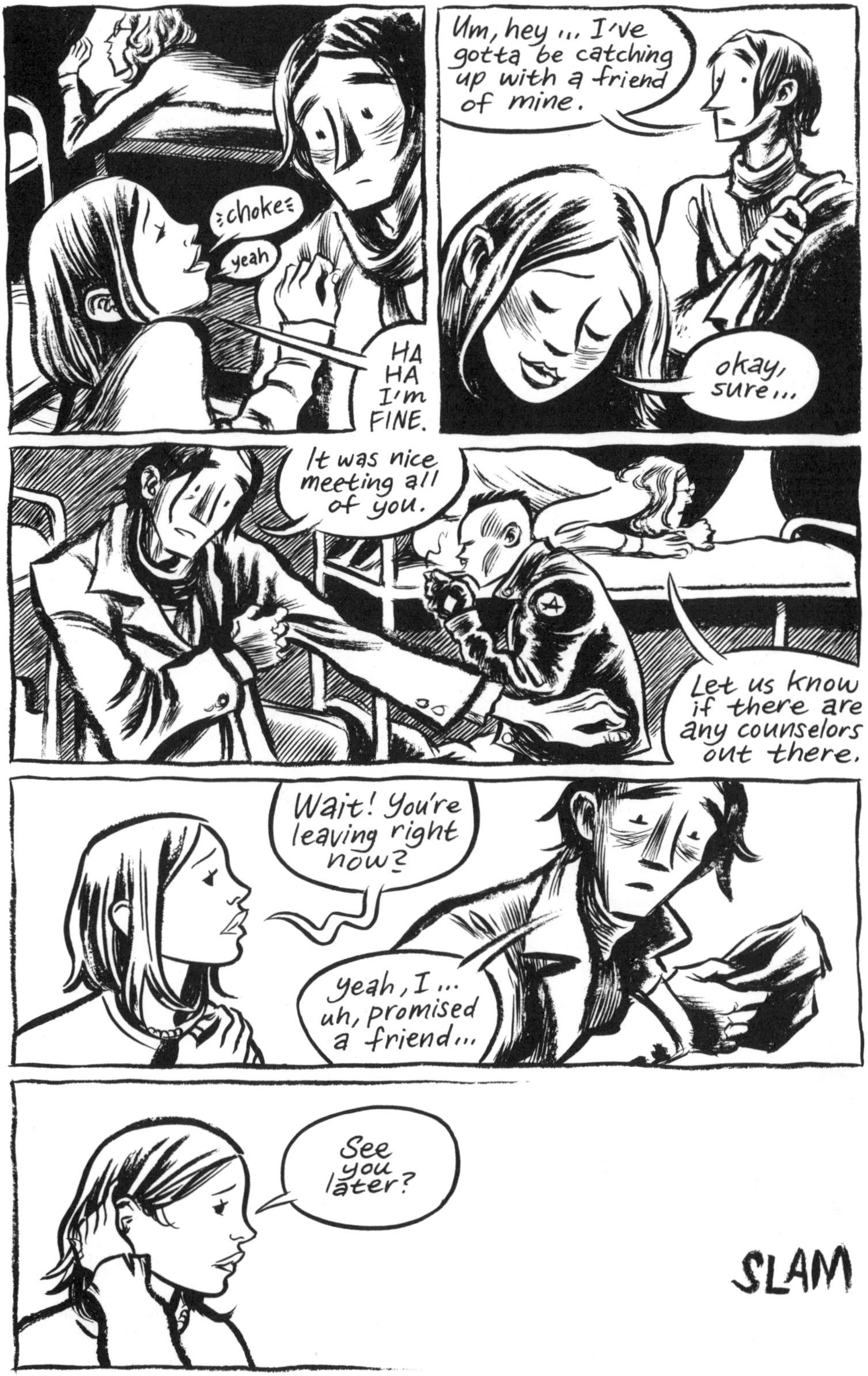
choke
yeah
HA HA I'm FINE.
Um, hey ... I've gotta be catching up with a friend of mine.
okay, sure...
It was nice meeting all of you.
Let us know if there are any counselors out there.
Wait! You're leaving right now?
yeah, I... uh, promised a friend...
See you later?
SLAM

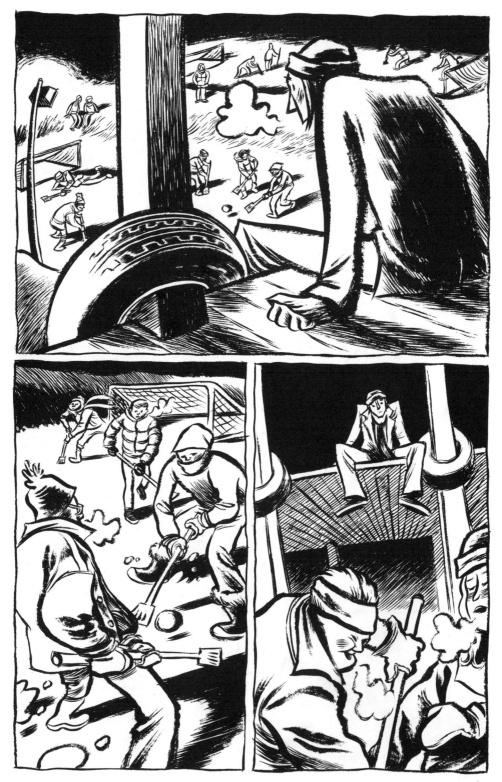

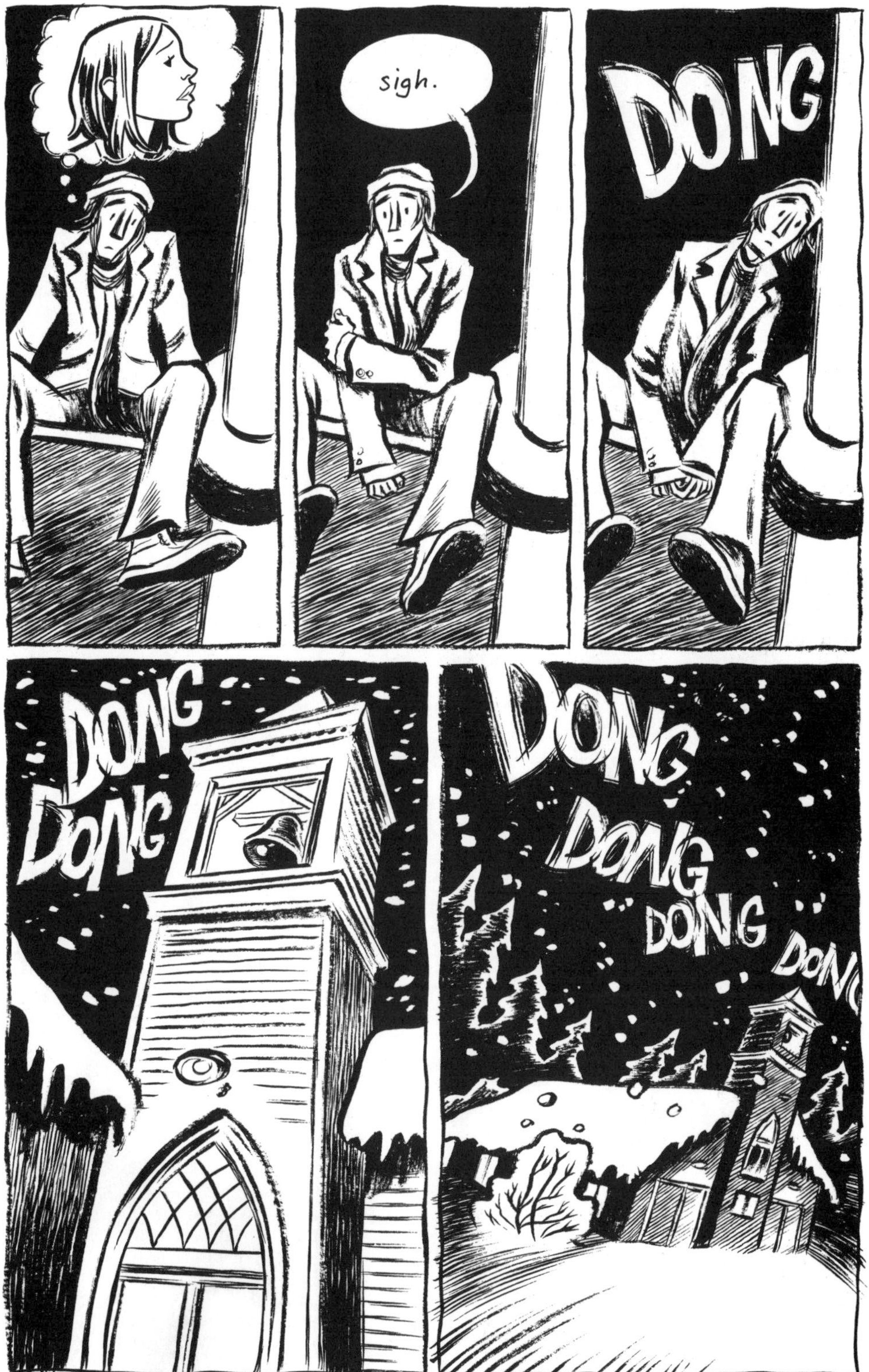
sigh.
DONG
DONG
DONG
DONG
DONG
DONG
DONG

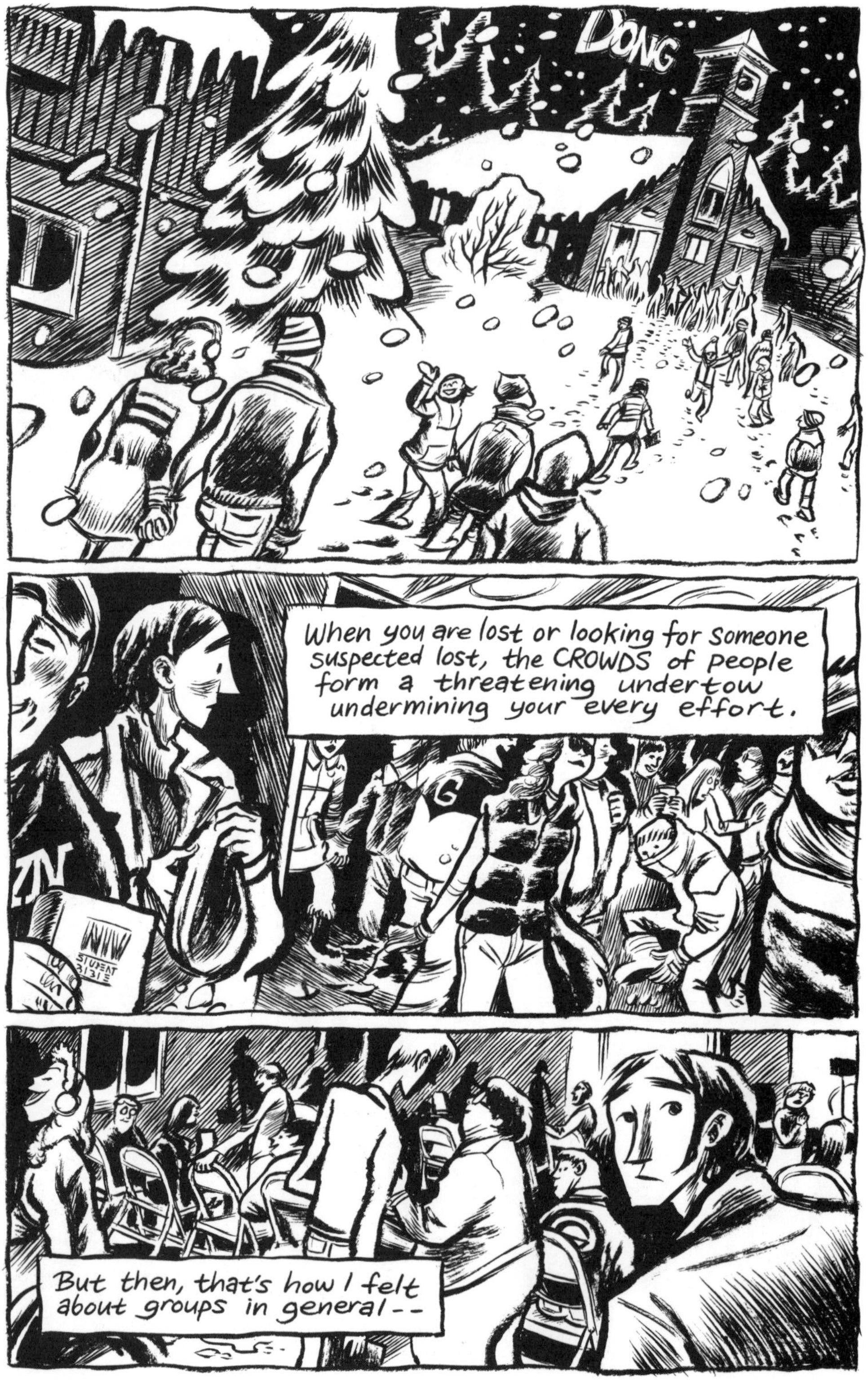
DONG
When you are lost or looking for someone suspected lost, the CROWDS of people form a threatening undertow undermining your every effort.
But then, that's how I felt about groups in general--

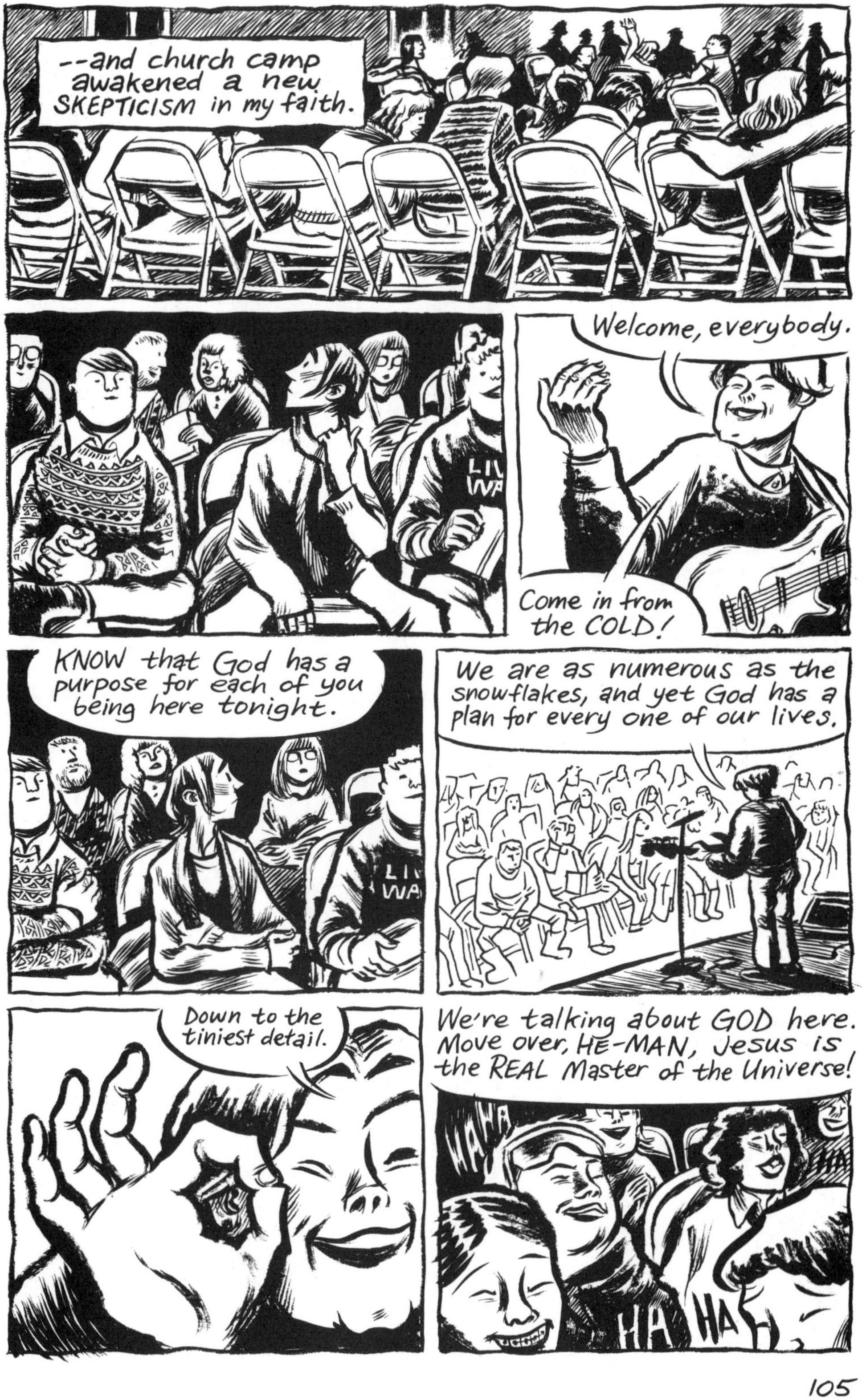
--and church camp awakened a new SKEPTICISM in my faith.
Welcome, everybody.
Come in from the COLD!
KNOW that God has a purpose for each of you being here tonight.
We are as numerous as the snowflakes, and yet God has a plan for every one of our lives.
Down to the tiniest detail.
We're talking about GOD here. Move over, HE-MAN, Jesus is the REAL Master of the Universe!
HA
HA
HA HA

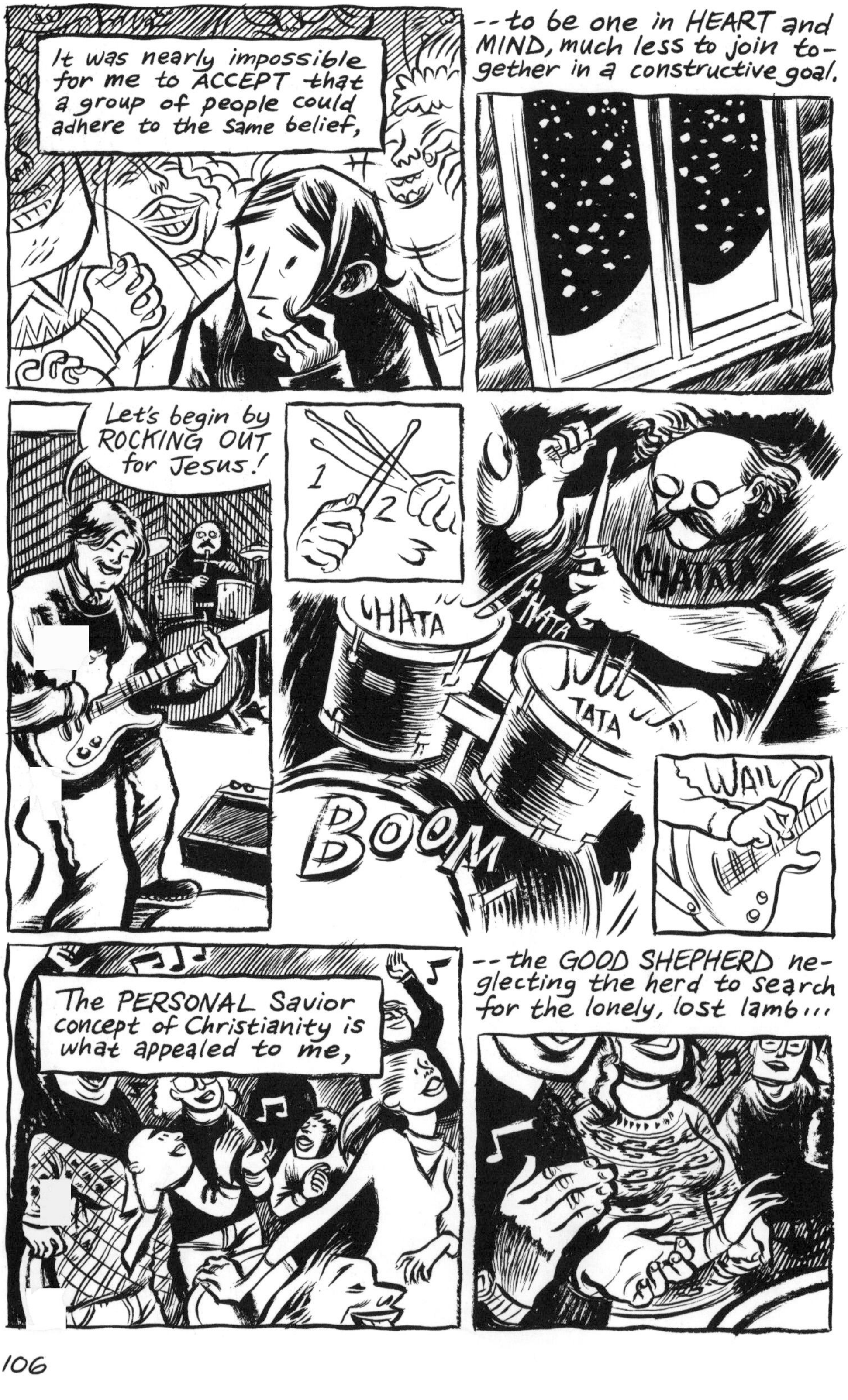

It was nearly impossible for me to ACCEPT that a group of people could adhere to the same belief,
--to be one in HEART and MIND, much less to join together in a constructive goal.
Let's begin by ROCKING OUT for Jesus!
1
2
3
CHATA
CHATA
CHATA
TATA
BOOM
WAIL
The PERSONAL Savior concept of Christianity is what appealed to me,
--the GOOD SHEPHERD neglecting the herd to search for the lonely, lost lamb...

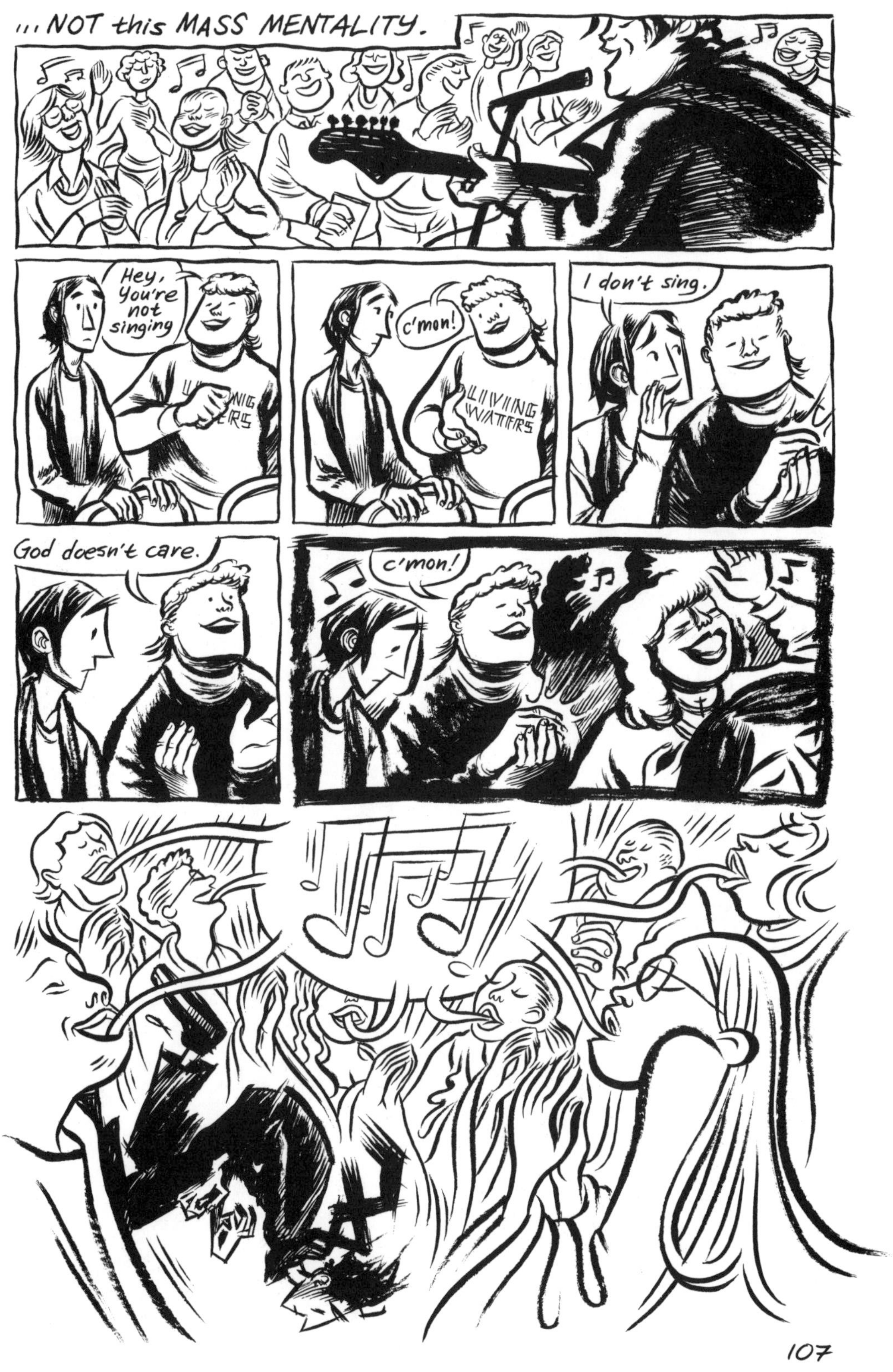
...NOT this MASS MENTALITY.
Hey, you're not singing
LIVING WATERS
c'mon!
I don't sing.
God doesn't care.
c'mon!

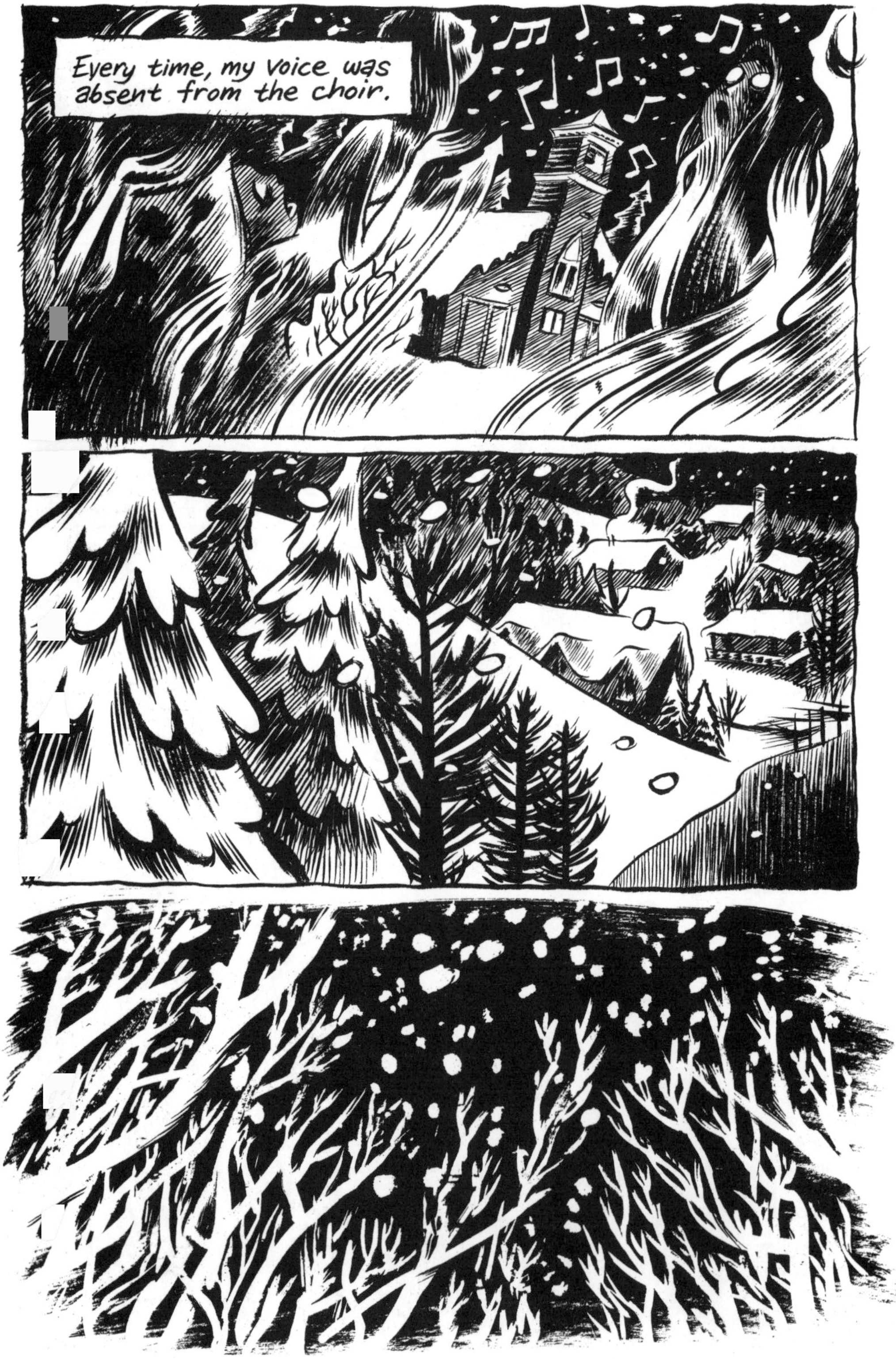
Every time, my voice was absent from the choir.

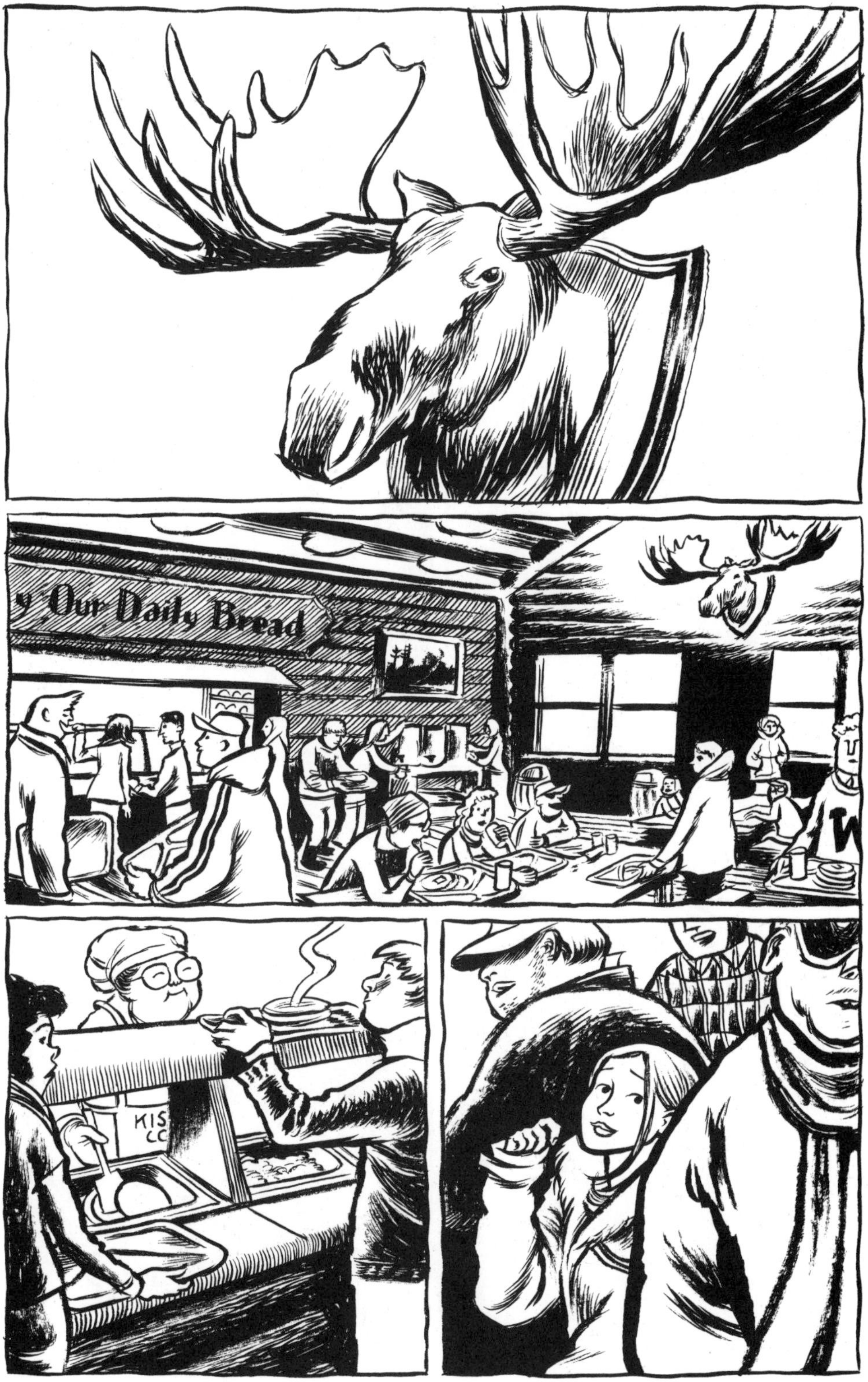
Our Daily Bread

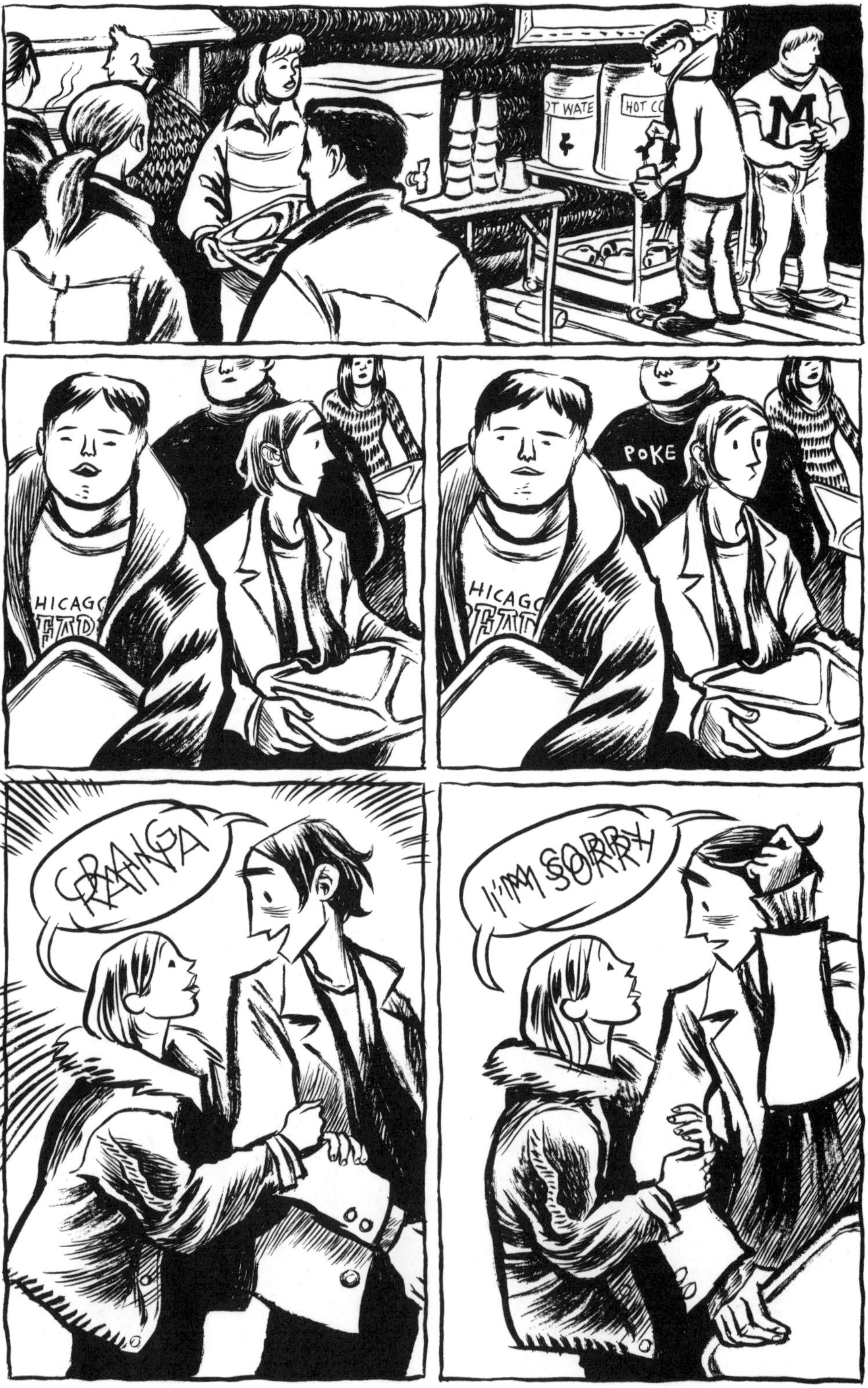

OT WATE
HOT CO
M
HICAGO
POKE
HICAGO
I'M SORRY

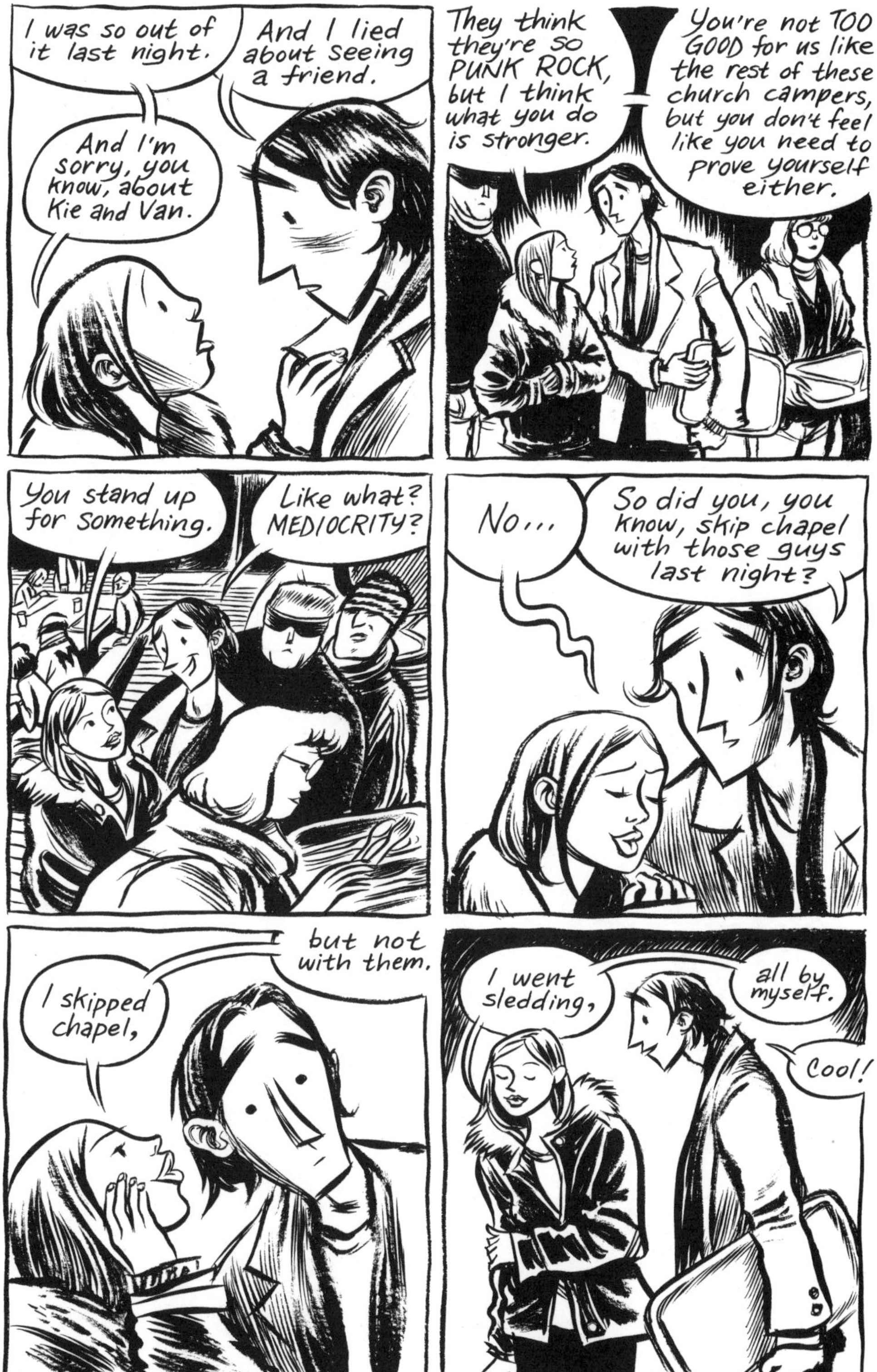
I was so out of it last night.
And I'm sorry, you know, about Kie and Van.
And I lied about seeing a friend.
They think they're so PUNK ROCK, but I think what you do is stronger.
You're not TOO GOOD for us like the rest of these church campers, but you don't feel like you need to prove yourself either.
You stand up for something.
Like what? MEDIOCRITY?
No...
So did you, you know, skip chapel with those guys last night?
I skipped chapel,
but not with them.
I went sledding,
all by myself.
Cool!

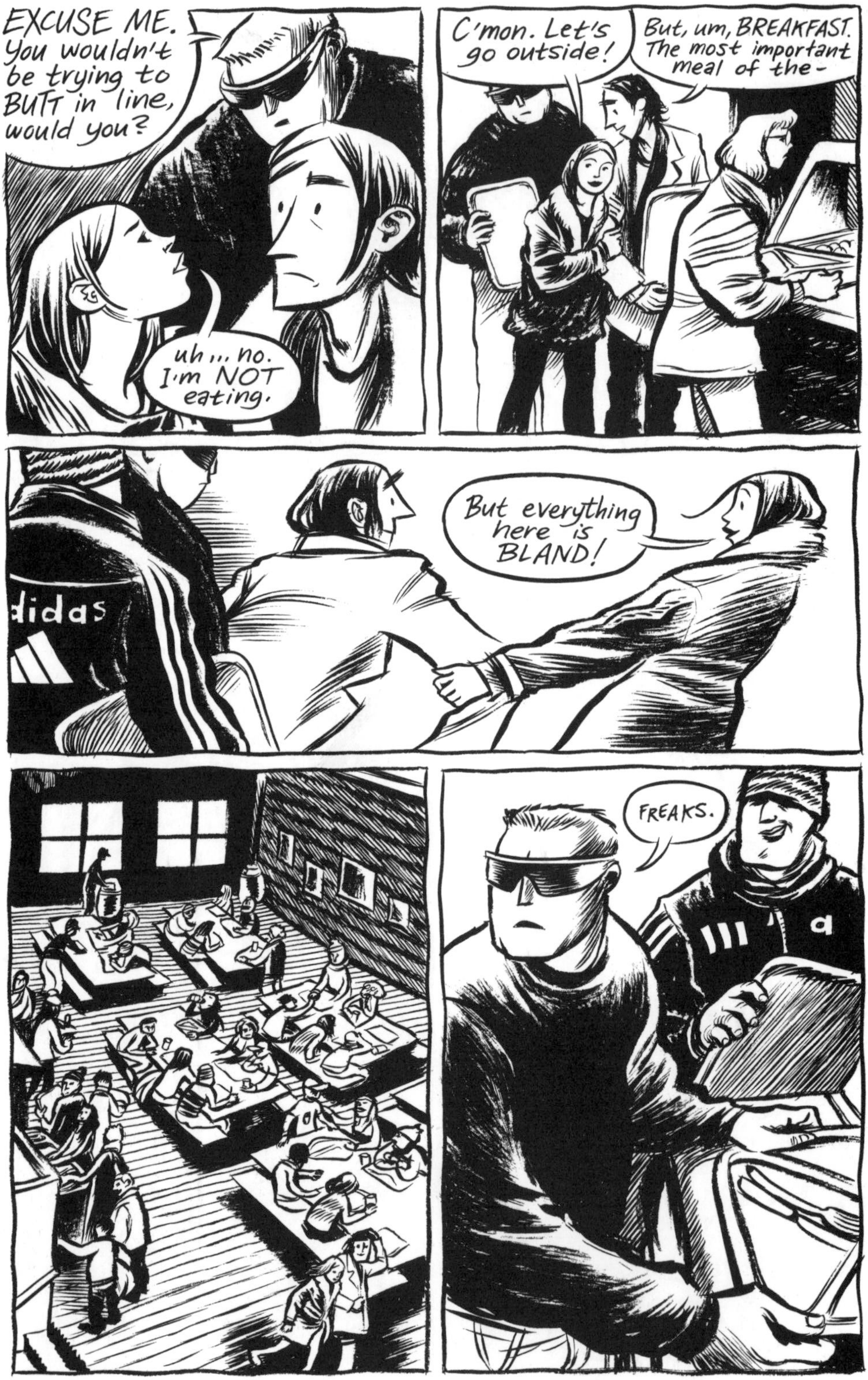
EXCUSE ME. You wouldn't be trying to BUTT in line, would you?
uh... no. I'm NOT eating.
C'mon. Let's go outside!
But, um, BREAKFAST. The most important meal of the-
But everything here is BLAND!
didas
FREAKS.

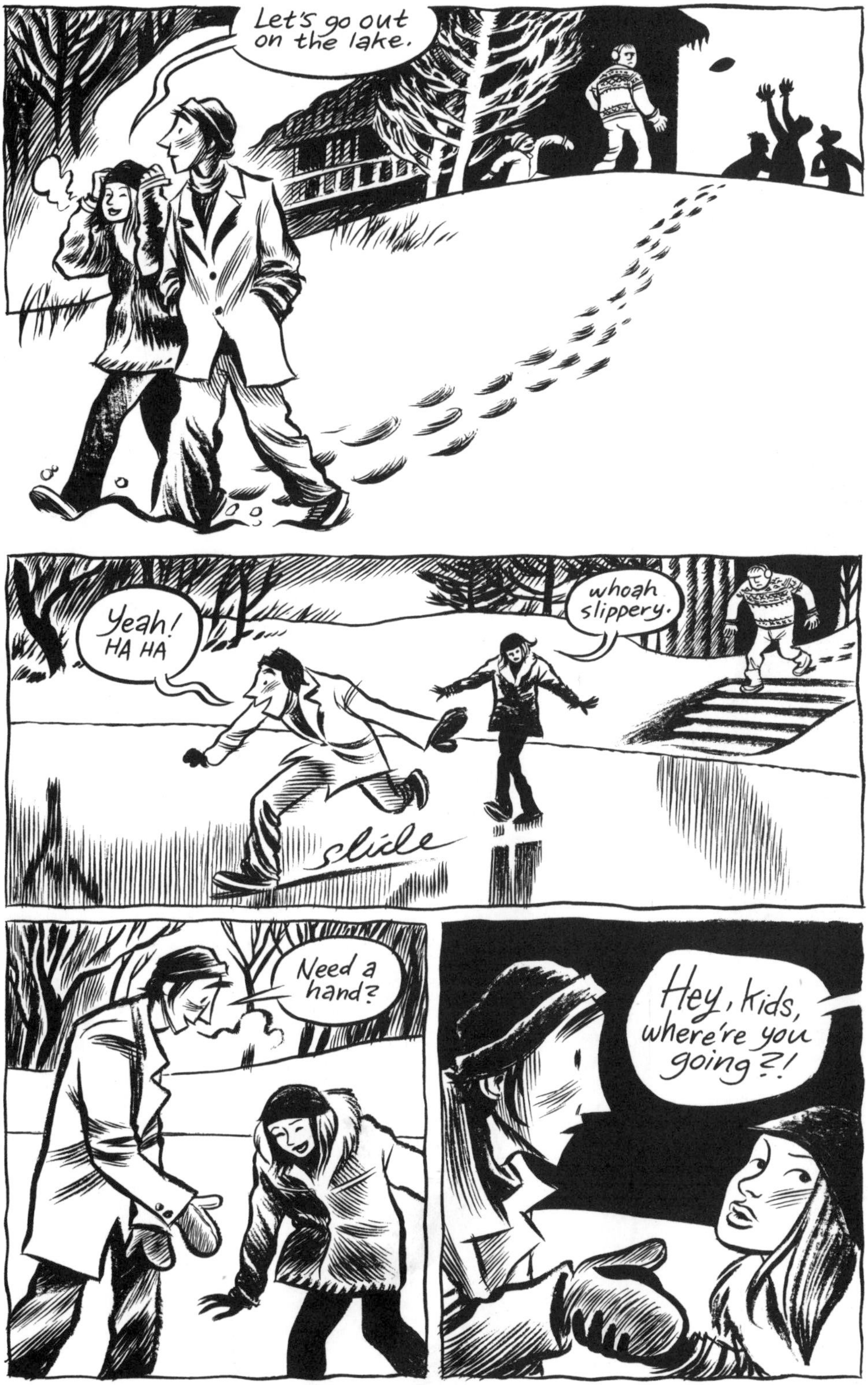
Let's go out on the lake.
Yeah! HA HA
whoah slippery.
slide
Need a hand?
Hey, kids, where're you going?!

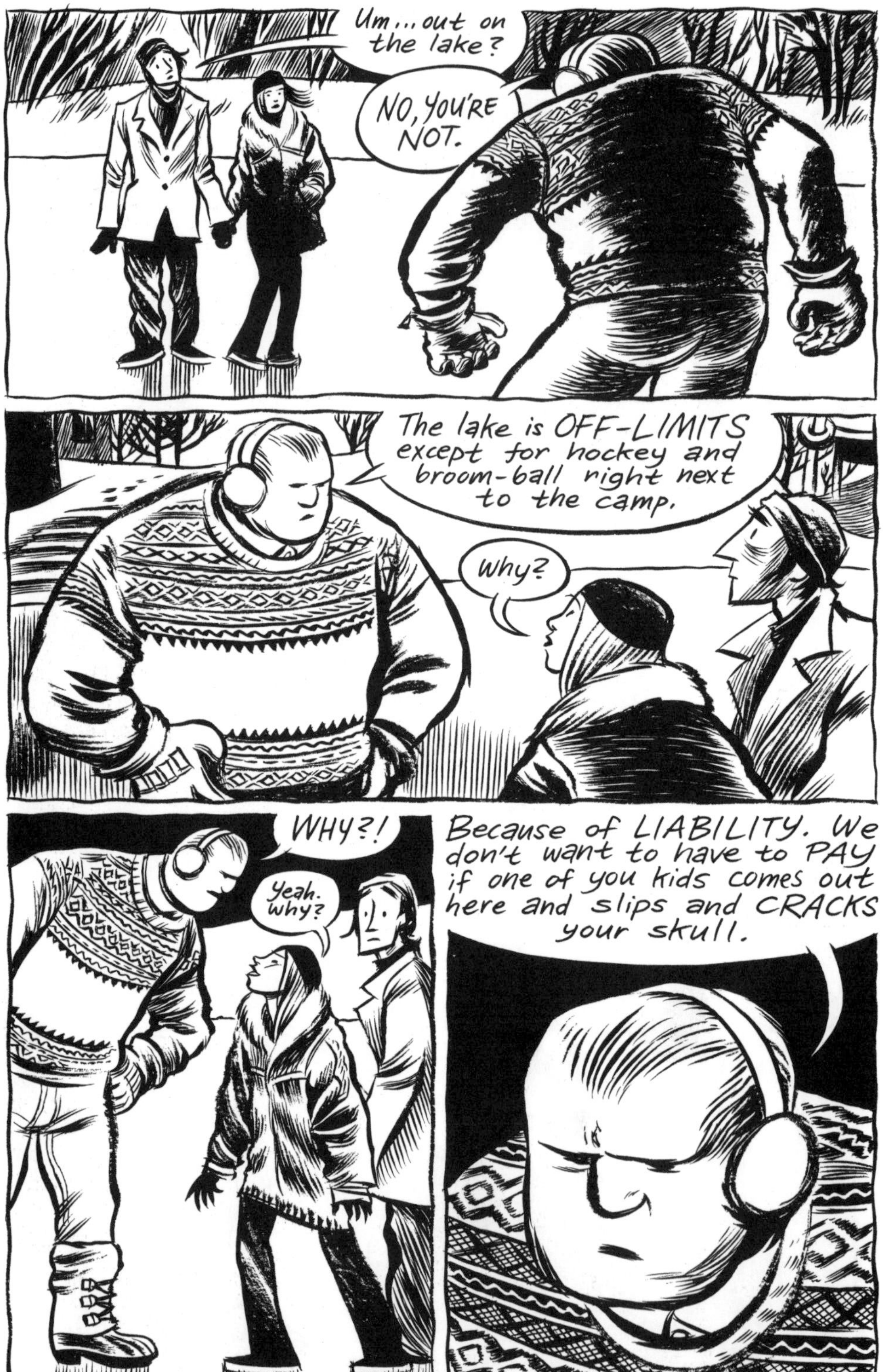
Um... out on the lake?
NO, YOU'RE NOT.
The lake is OFF-LIMITS except for hockey and broom-ball right next to the camp.
Why?
WHY?!
Yeah. Why?
Because of LIABILITY. We don't want to have to PAY if one of you kids comes out here and slips and CRACKS your skull.

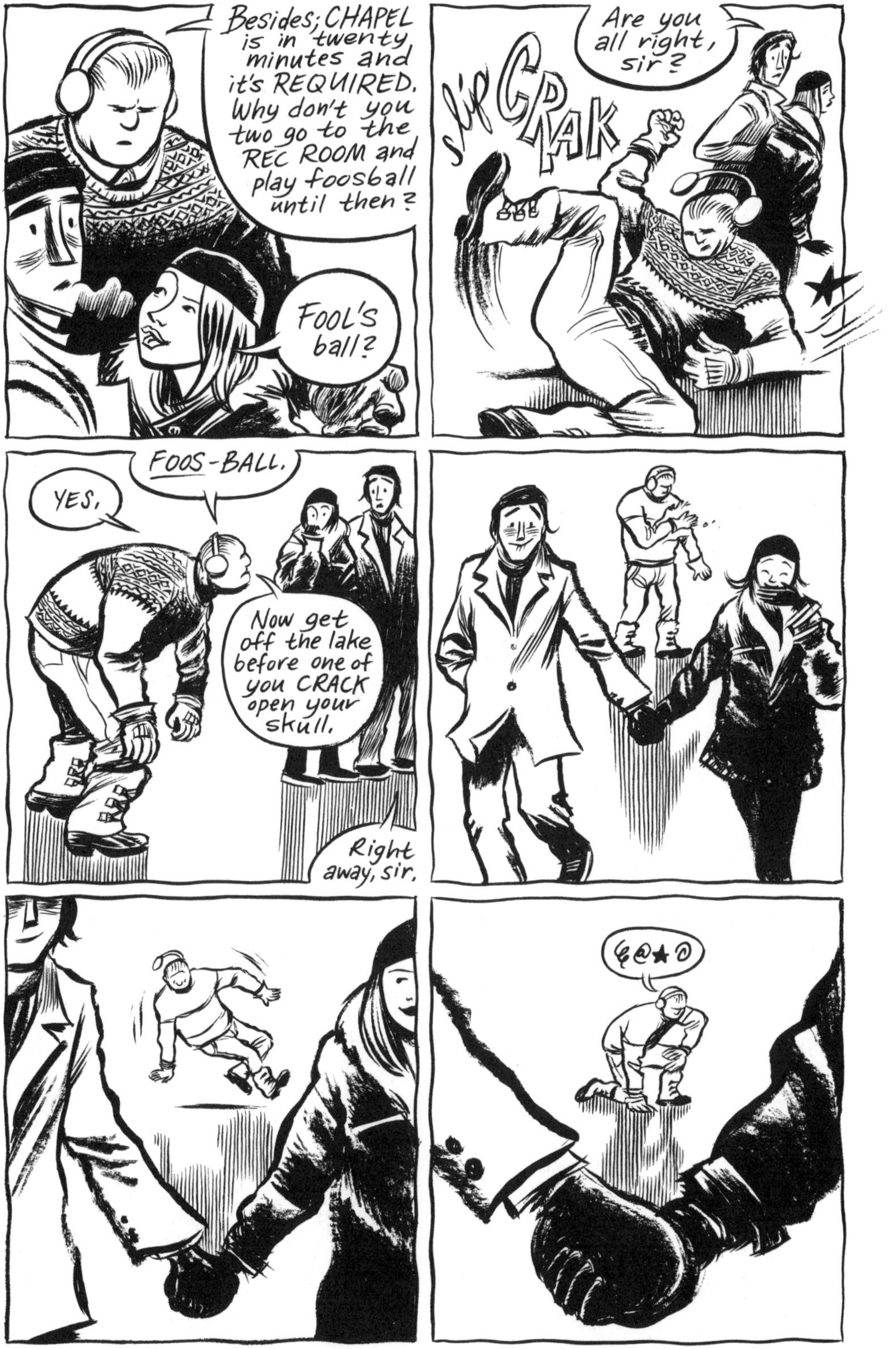
Besides; CHAPEL is in twenty minutes and it's REQUIRED. Why don't you two go to the REC ROOM and play foosball until then?
FOOL'S ball?
Are you all right, sir?
s'lip
CRAK
YES,
FOOS-BALL.
Now get off the lake before one of you CRACK open your skull.
Right away, sir.

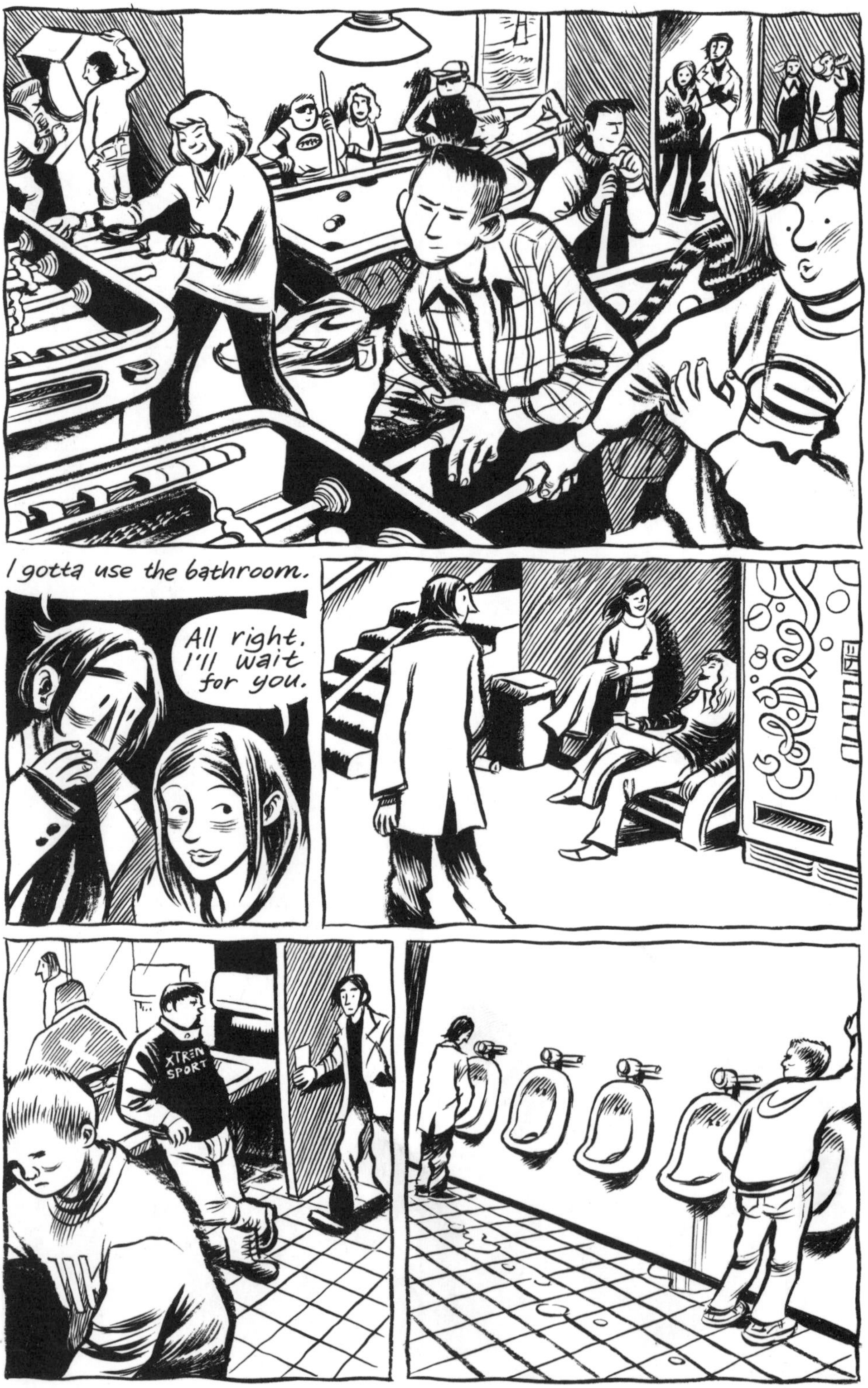

I gotta use the bathroom.
All right. I'll wait for you.
XTREM SPORT

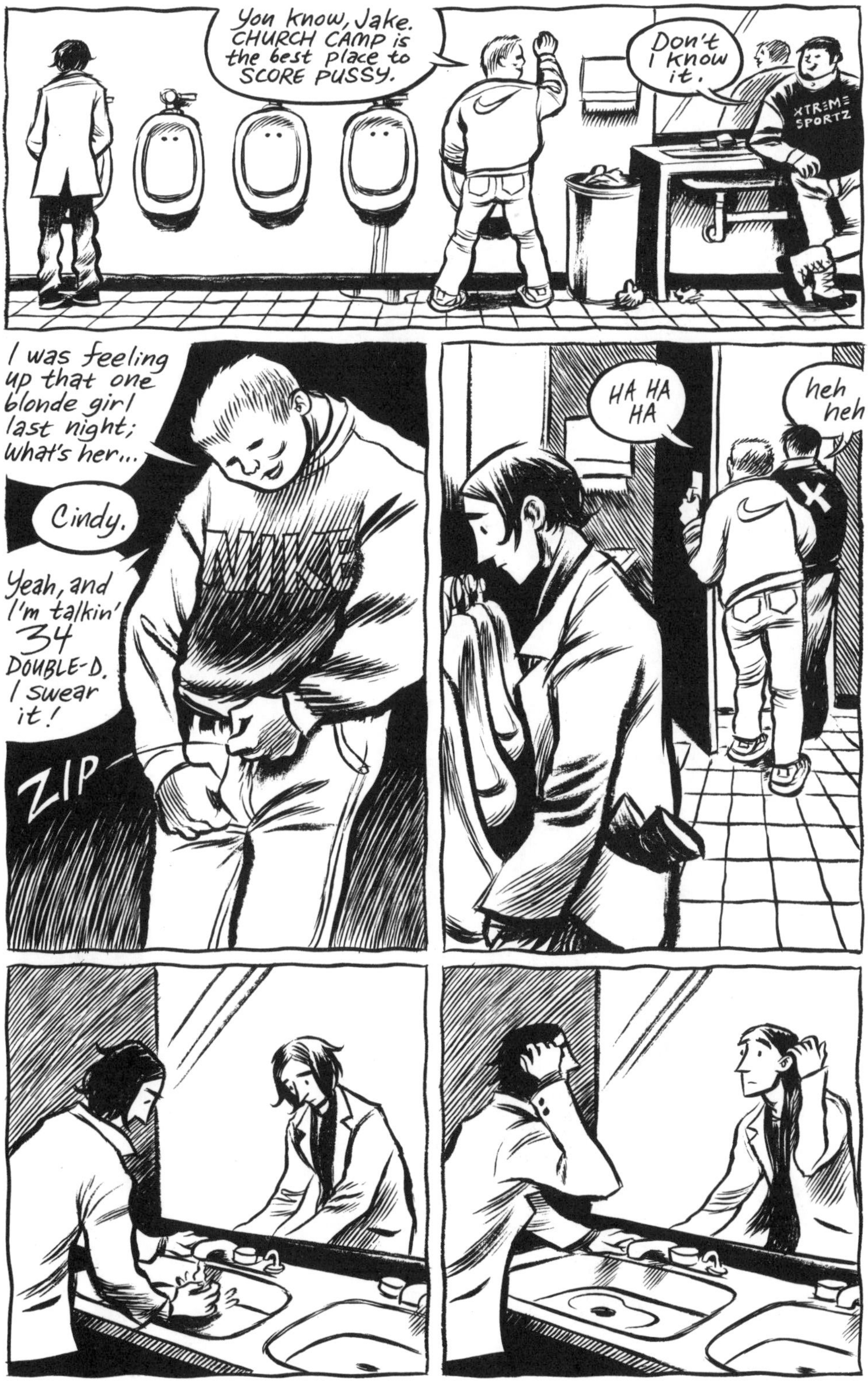
You know, Jake. CHURCH CAMP is the best place to SCORE PUSSY.
Don't I know it.
XTREME SPORTZ
I was feeling up that one blonde girl last night; what's her...
Cindy.
Yeah, and I'm talkin' 34 DOUBLE-D. I swear it!
ZIP
HA HA HA
heh heh

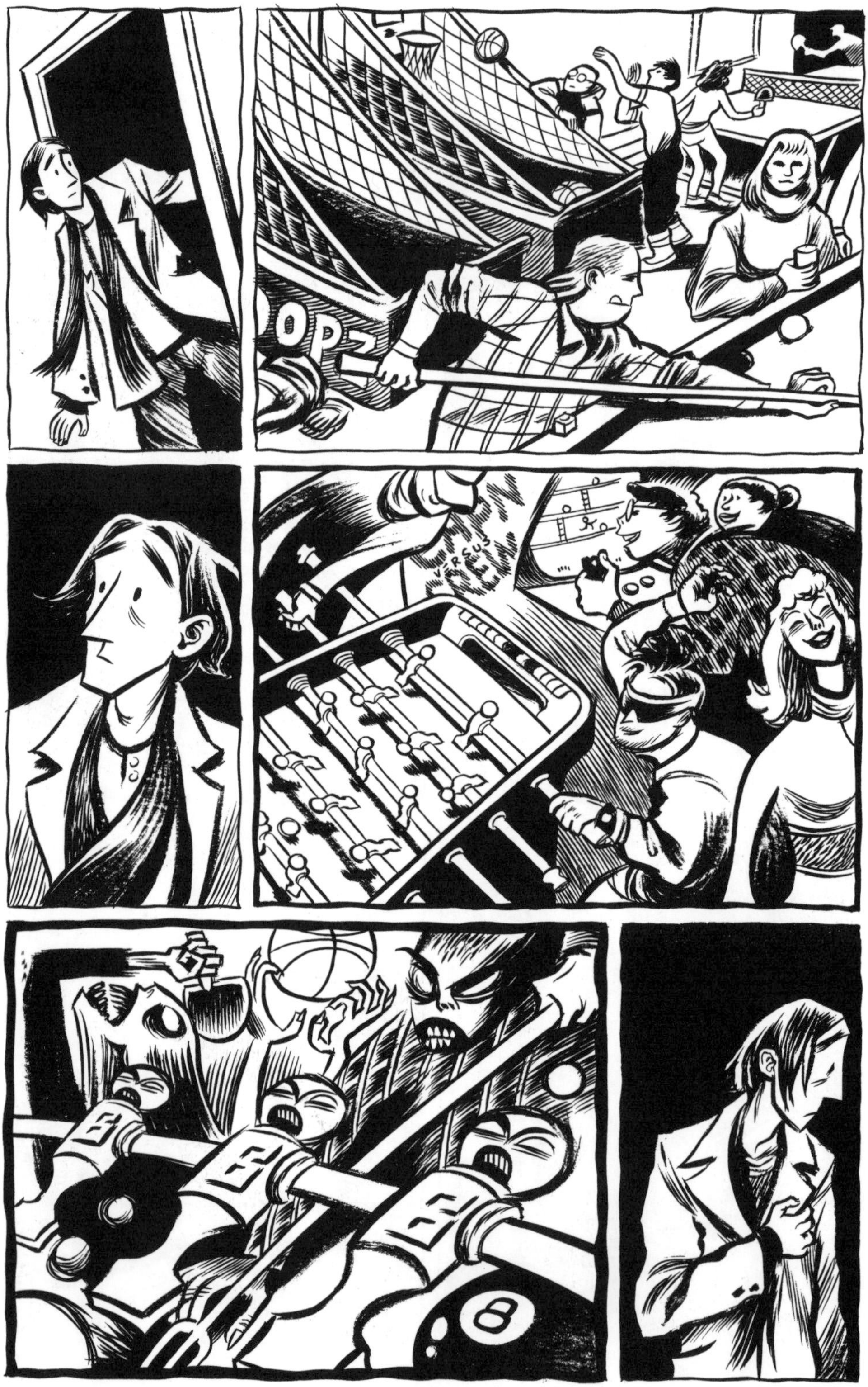

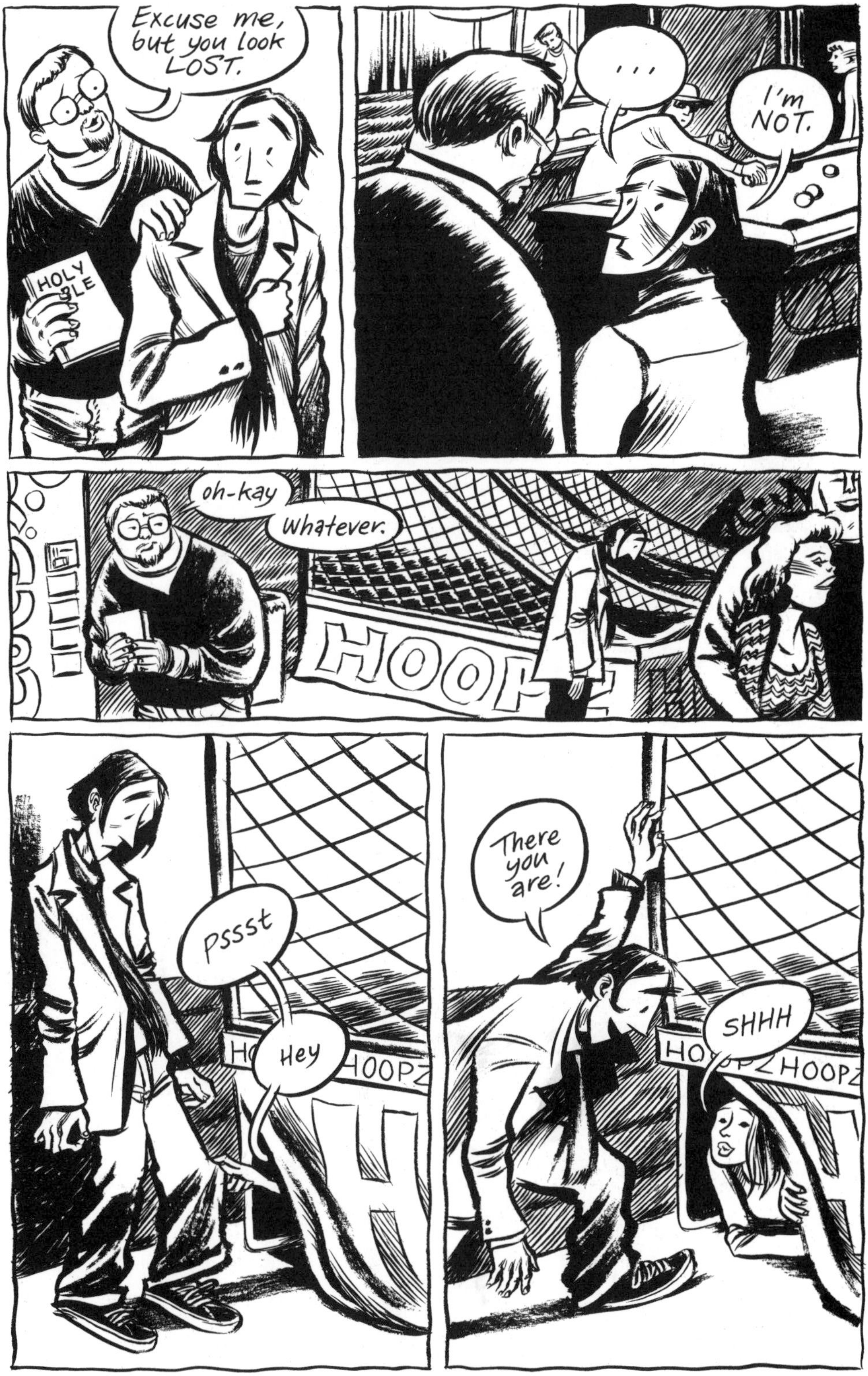
Excuse me, but you look LOST.
HOLY
...
I'm NOT.
oh-kay
whatever.
HOOP
Pssst
Hey
HOOPZ
There you are!
SHHH
HOOPZ HOOPZ

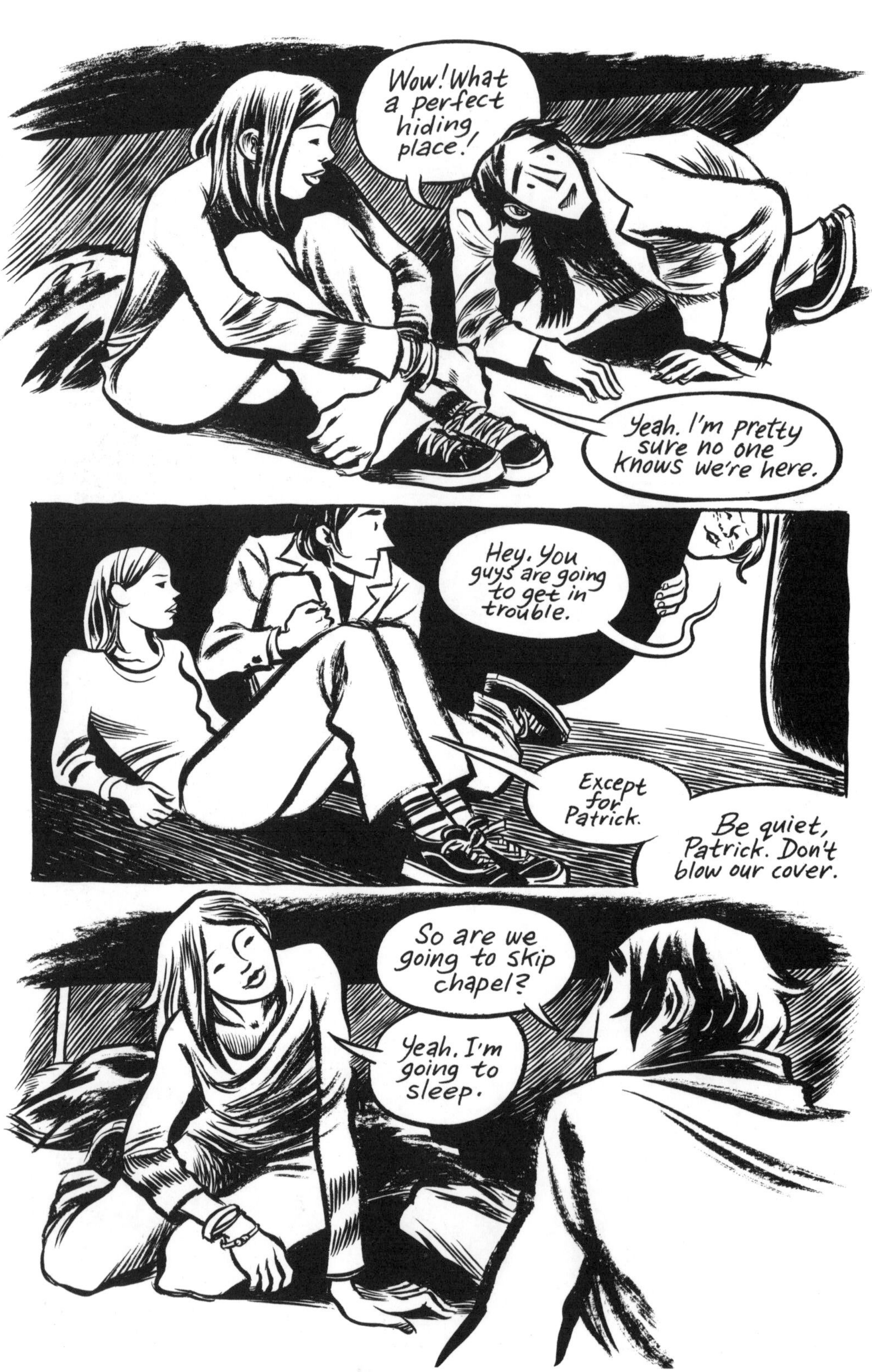
Wow! What a perfect hiding place!
Yeah. I'm pretty sure no one knows we're here.
Hey. You guys are going to get in trouble.
Except for Patrick.
Be quiet, Patrick. Don't blow our cover.
So are we going to skip chapel?
Yeah. I'm going to sleep.

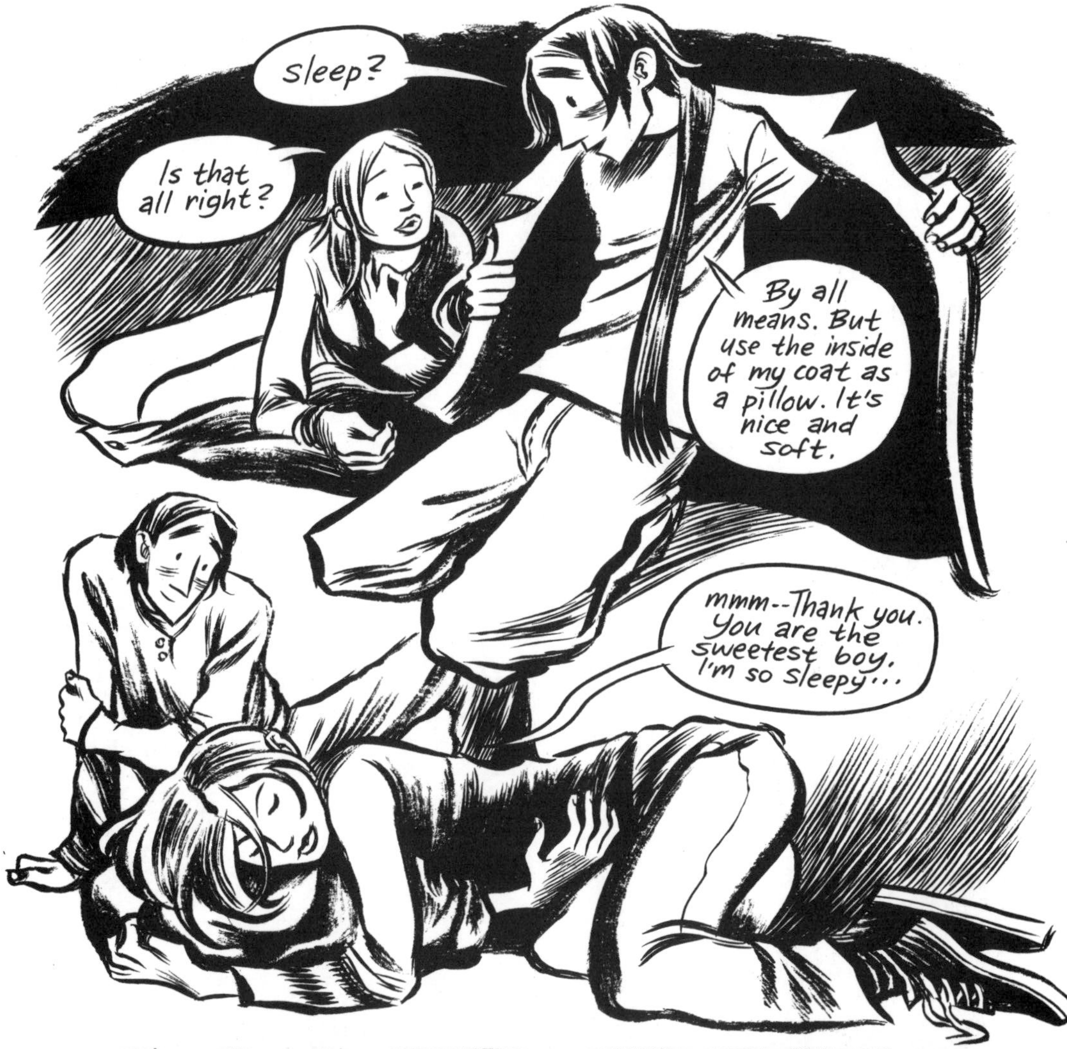
sleep?
Is that all right?
By all means. But use the inside of my coat as a pillow. It's nice and soft.
mmm--Thank you. You are the sweetest boy. I'm so sleepy...

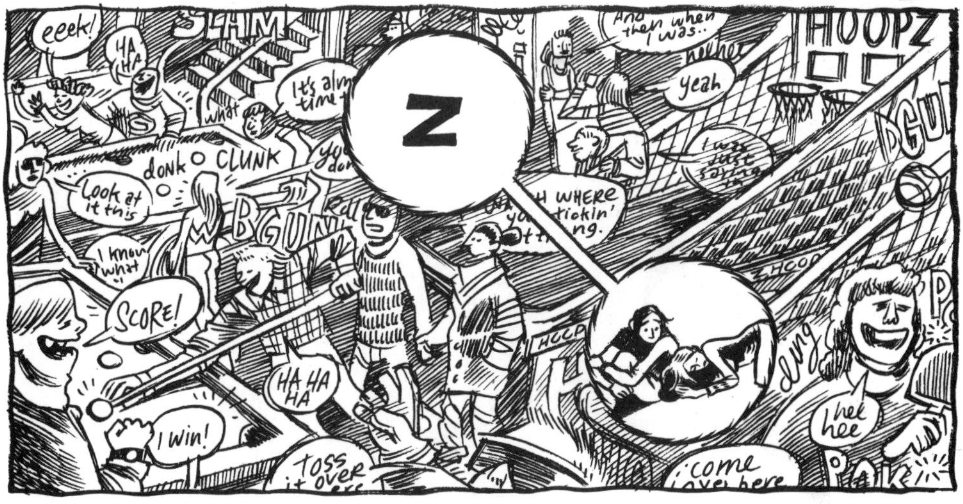
eeek!
HA HA
SLAM
HOOPZ
yeah
Z
donk
CLUNK
Look at it this
WHERE
SCORE!
HA HA HA
I win!
hee hee
come over here

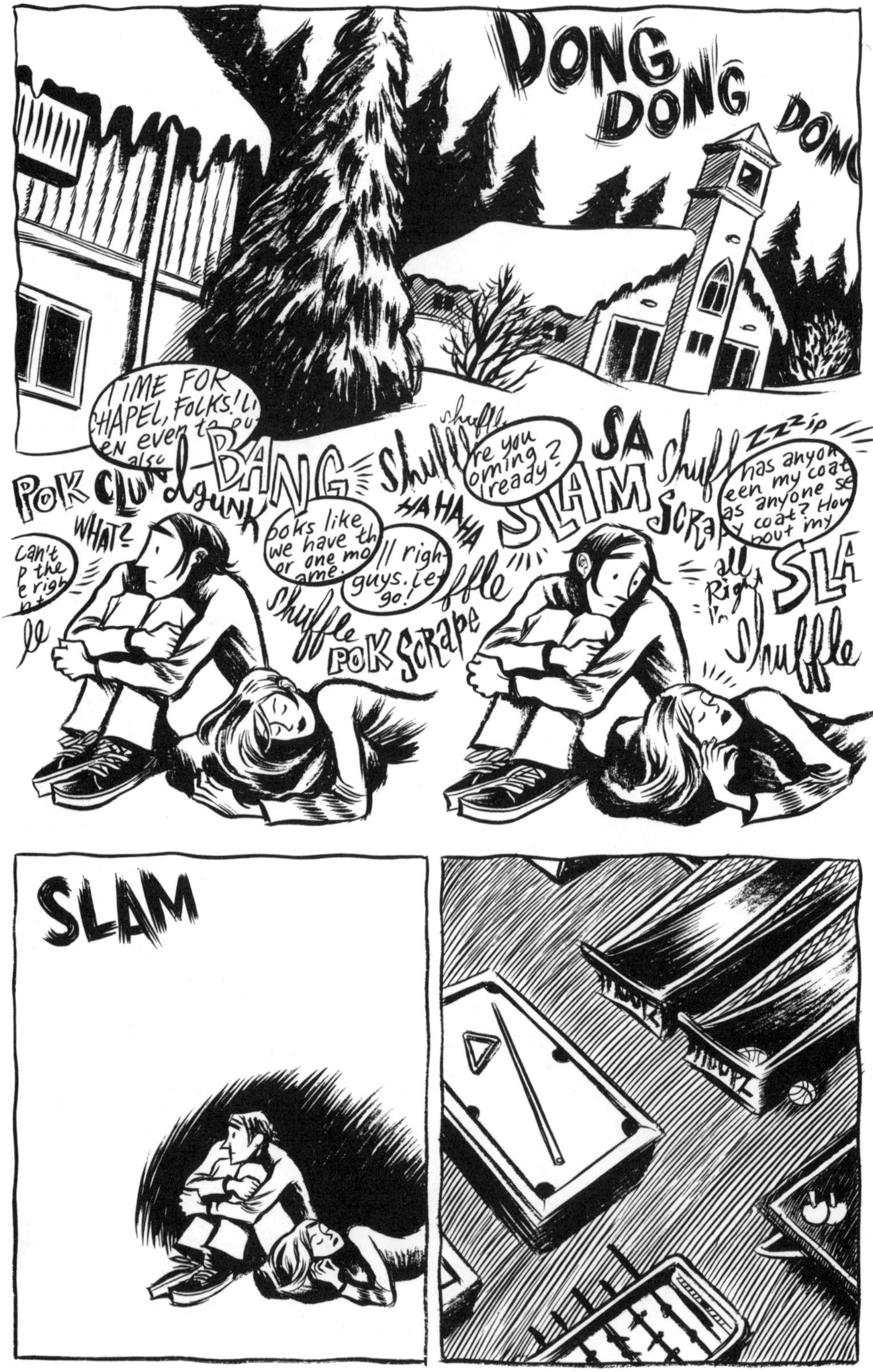
DONG
DONG
TIME FOR CHAPEL, FOLKS!
BANG
POK
WHAT?
shuffle
Shuffle
HAHAHA
SA
SLAM
Shuffle
SCRAPE
POK SCRAPE
Shuffle
SLAM

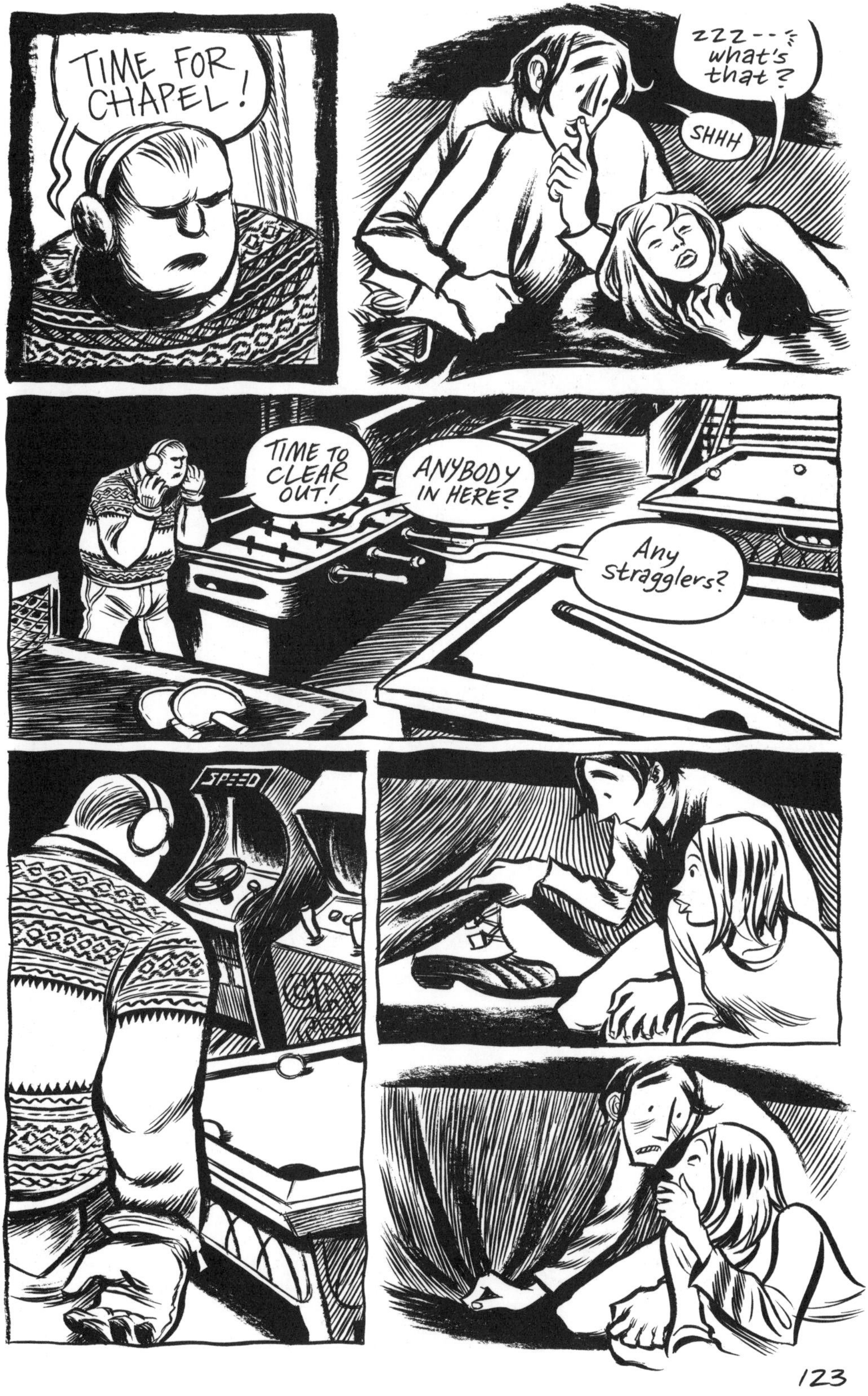
TIME FOR CHAPEL!
zzz--what's that?
SHHH
TIME TO CLEAR OUT!
ANYBODY IN HERE?
Any stragglers?
SPEED

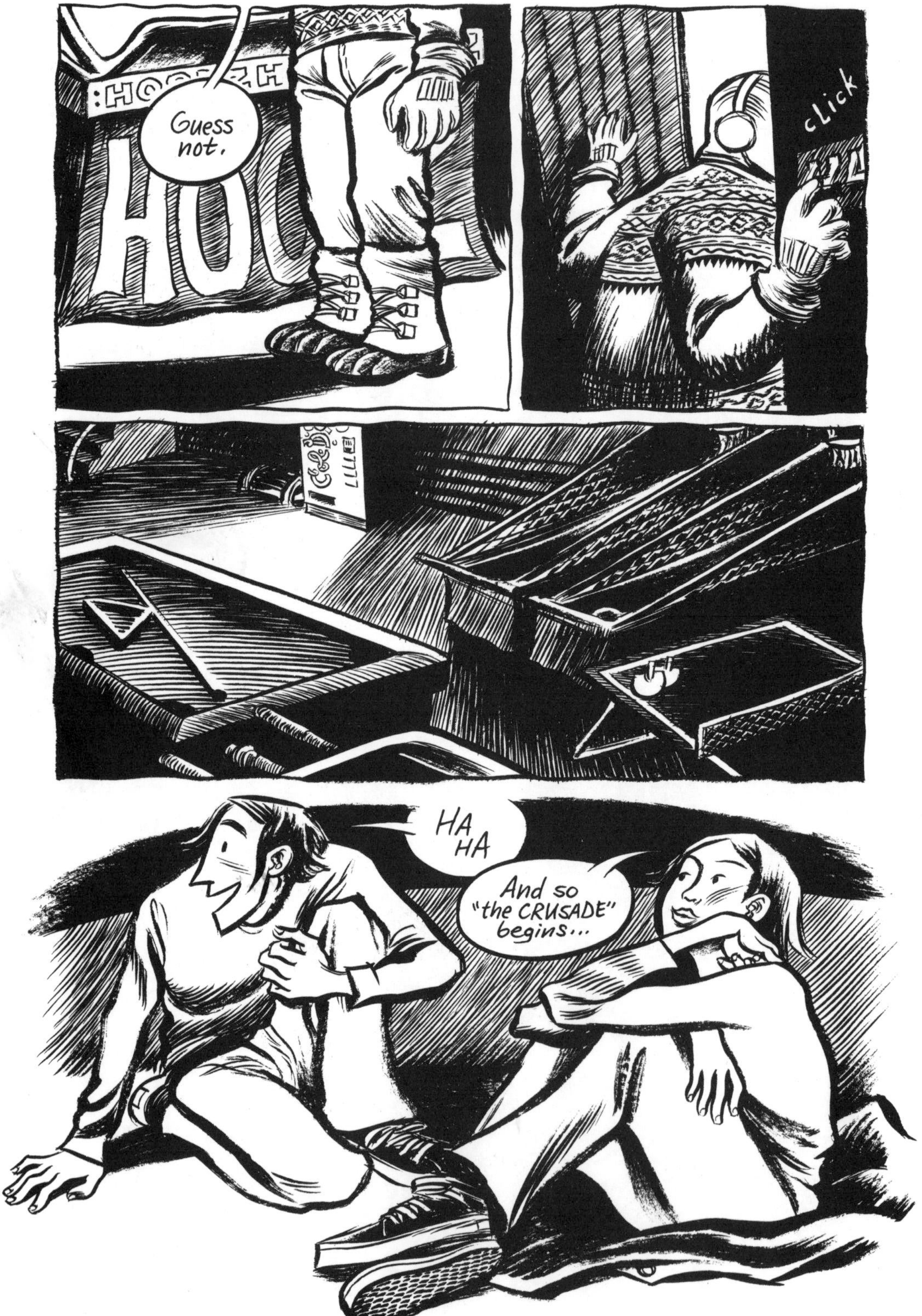
Guess not.
click
HA HA
And so "the CRUSADE" begins...

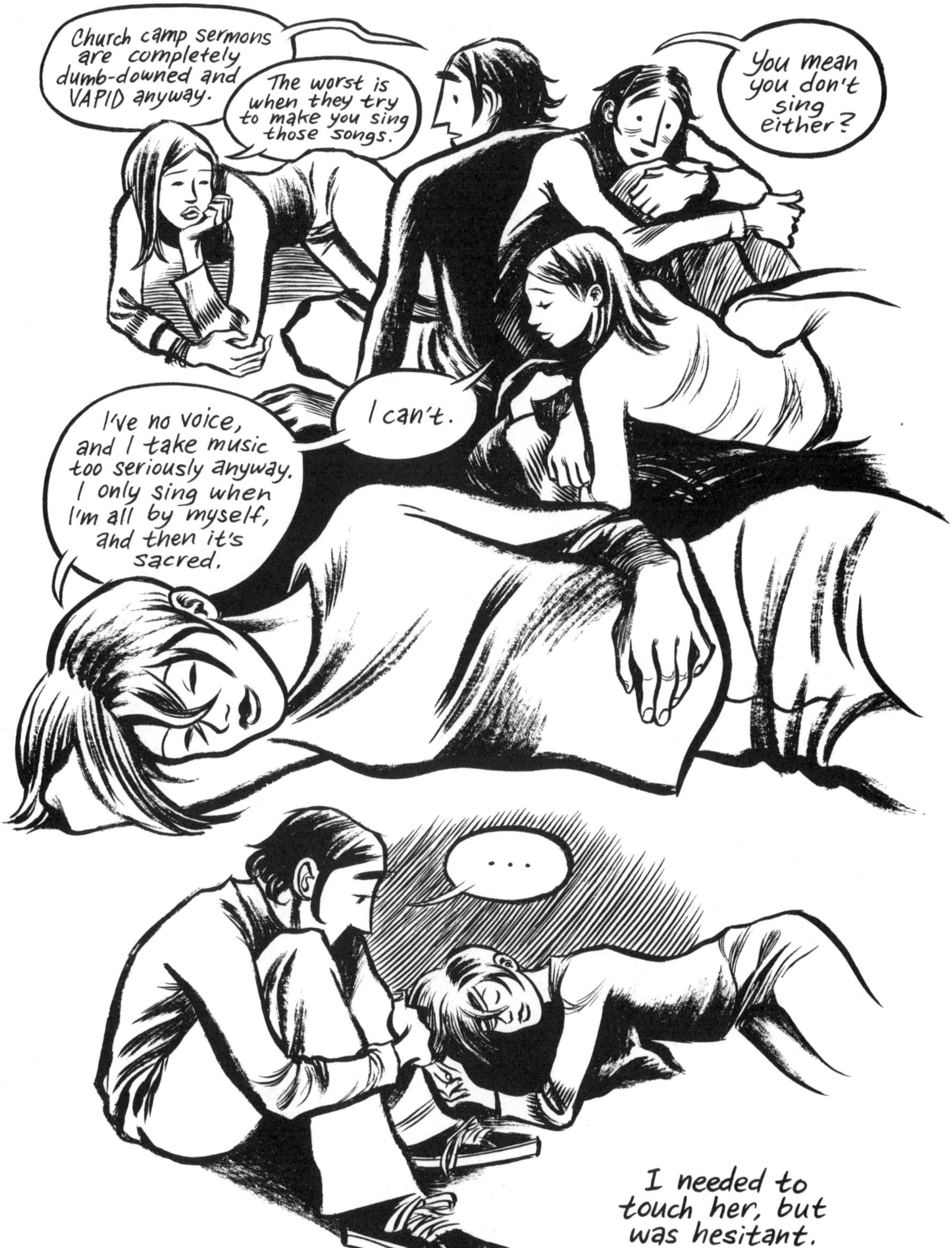
Church camp sermons are completely dumb-downed and VAPID anyway.
The worst is when they try to make you sing those songs.
You mean you don't sing either?
I can't.
I've no voice, and I take music too seriously anyway. I only sing when I'm all by myself, and then it's sacred.
...
I needed to touch her, but was hesitant.

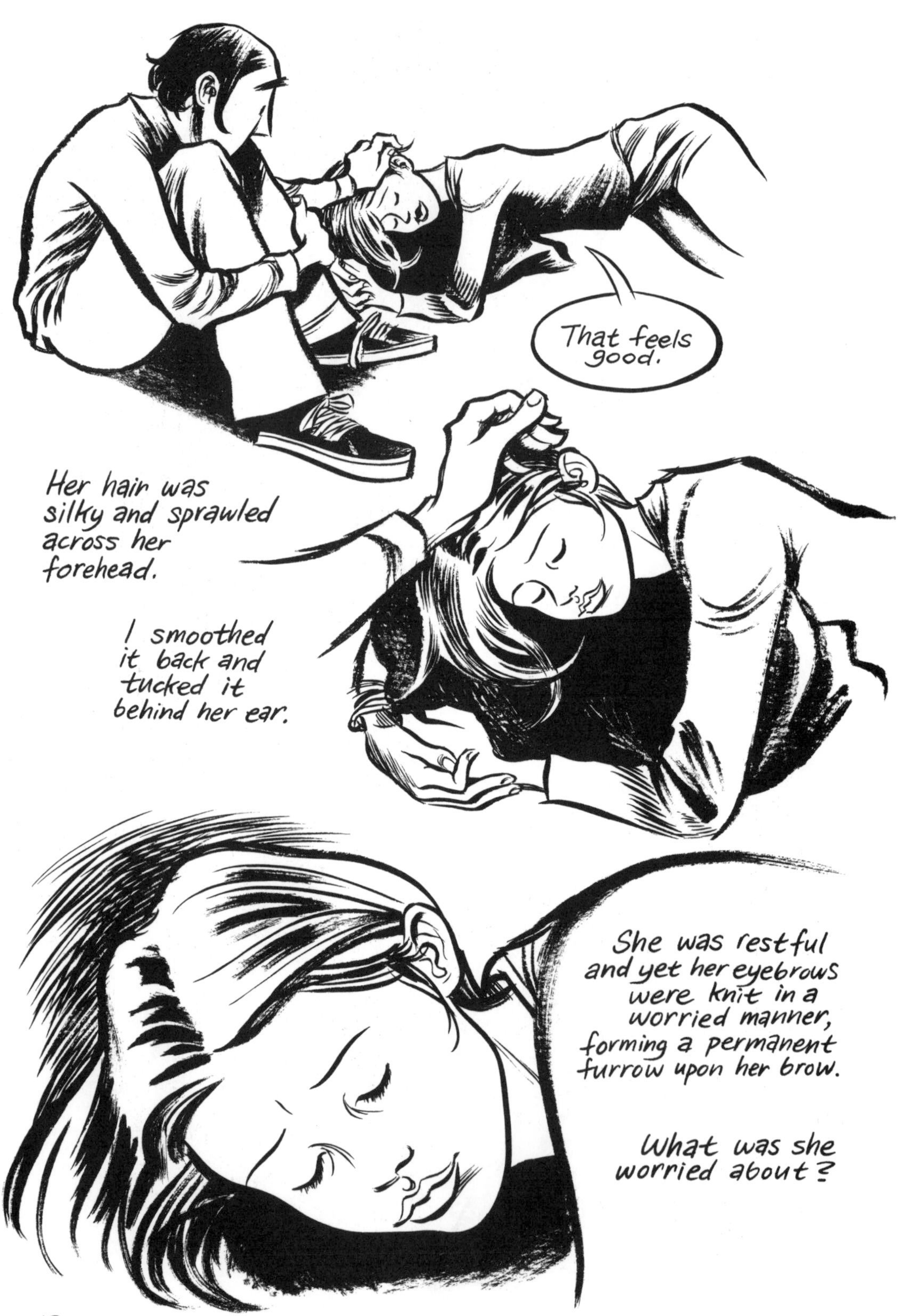
That feels good.
Her hair was silky and sprawled across her forehead.
I smoothed it back and tucked it behind her ear.
She was restful and yet her eyebrows were knit in a worried manner, forming a permanent furrow upon her brow.
What was she worried about?

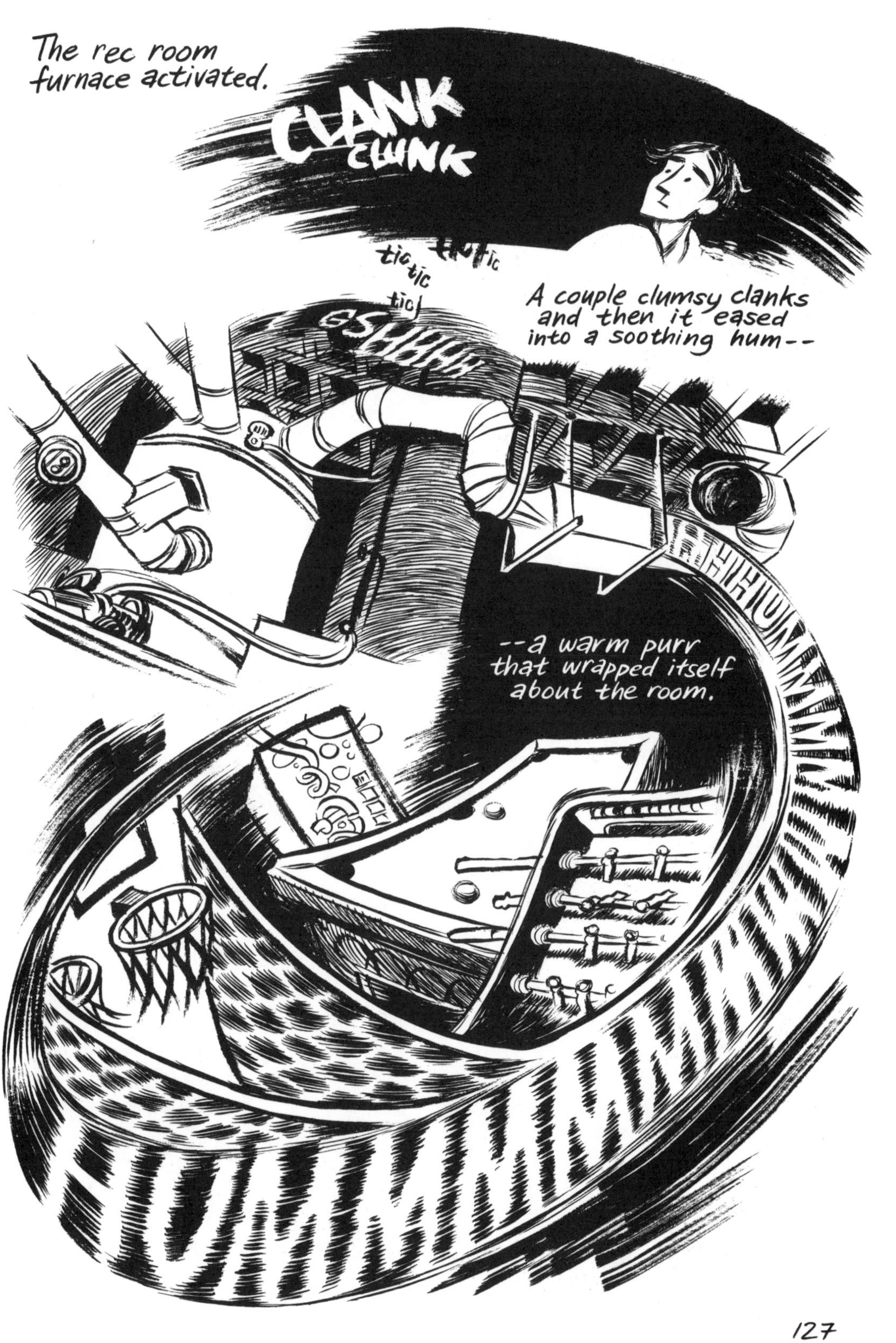

The rec room furnace activated.
CLANK
CLINK
tic tic tic
tic
tic tic
GSHHHH
A couple clumsy clanks and then it eased into a soothing hum--
--a warm purr that wrapped itself about the room.
HUMMMMMMMMMMMMMMMMMMMMMMMMMMMMM

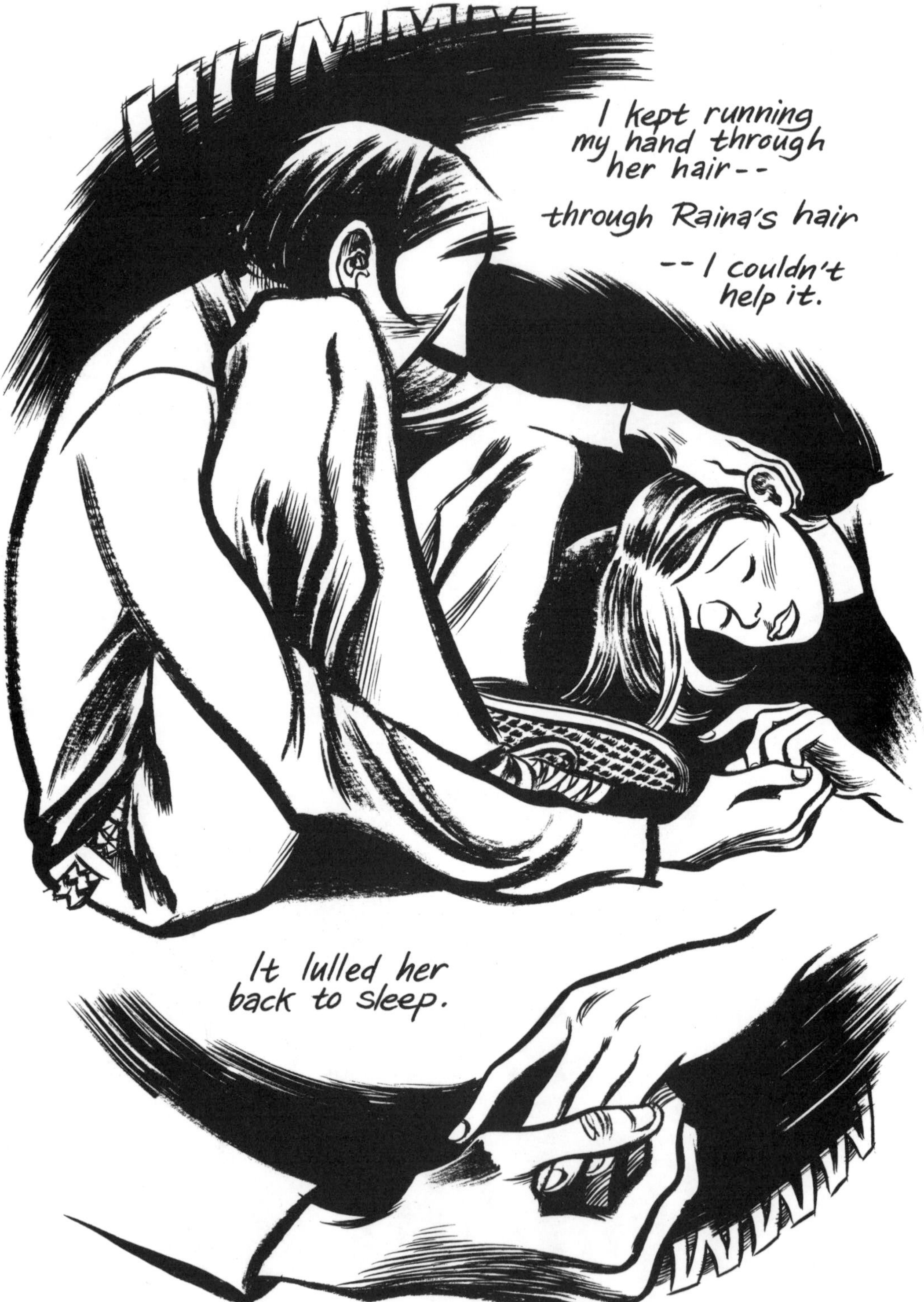
I kept running my hand through her hair--
through Raina's hair
--I couldn't help it.
It lulled her back to sleep.

III

Blank
Sheet

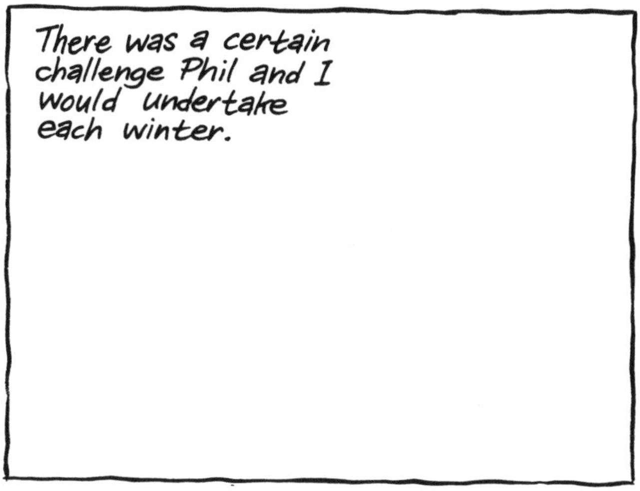
There was a certain challenge Phil and I would undertake each winter.

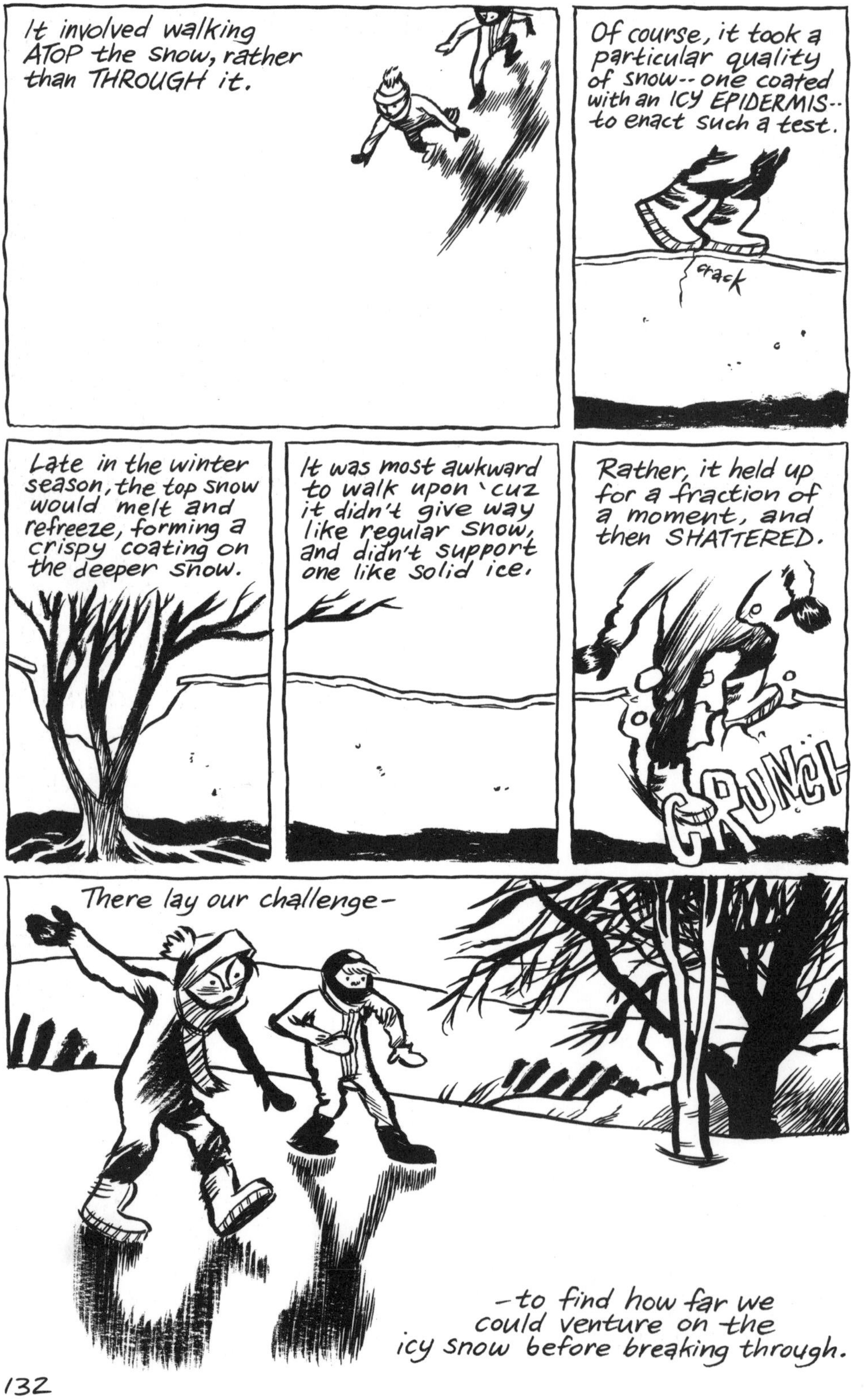
It involved walking ATOP the snow, rather than THROUGH it.
Of course, it took a particular quality of snow-- one coated with an ICY EPIDERMIS-- to enact such a test.
crack
Late in the winter season, the top snow would melt and refreeze, forming a crispy coating on the deeper snow.
It was most awkward to walk upon 'cuz it didn't give way like regular snow, and didn't support one like solid ice.
Rather, it held up for a fraction of a moment, and then SHATTERED.
CRUNCH
There lay our challenge-
-to find how far we could venture on the icy snow before breaking through.

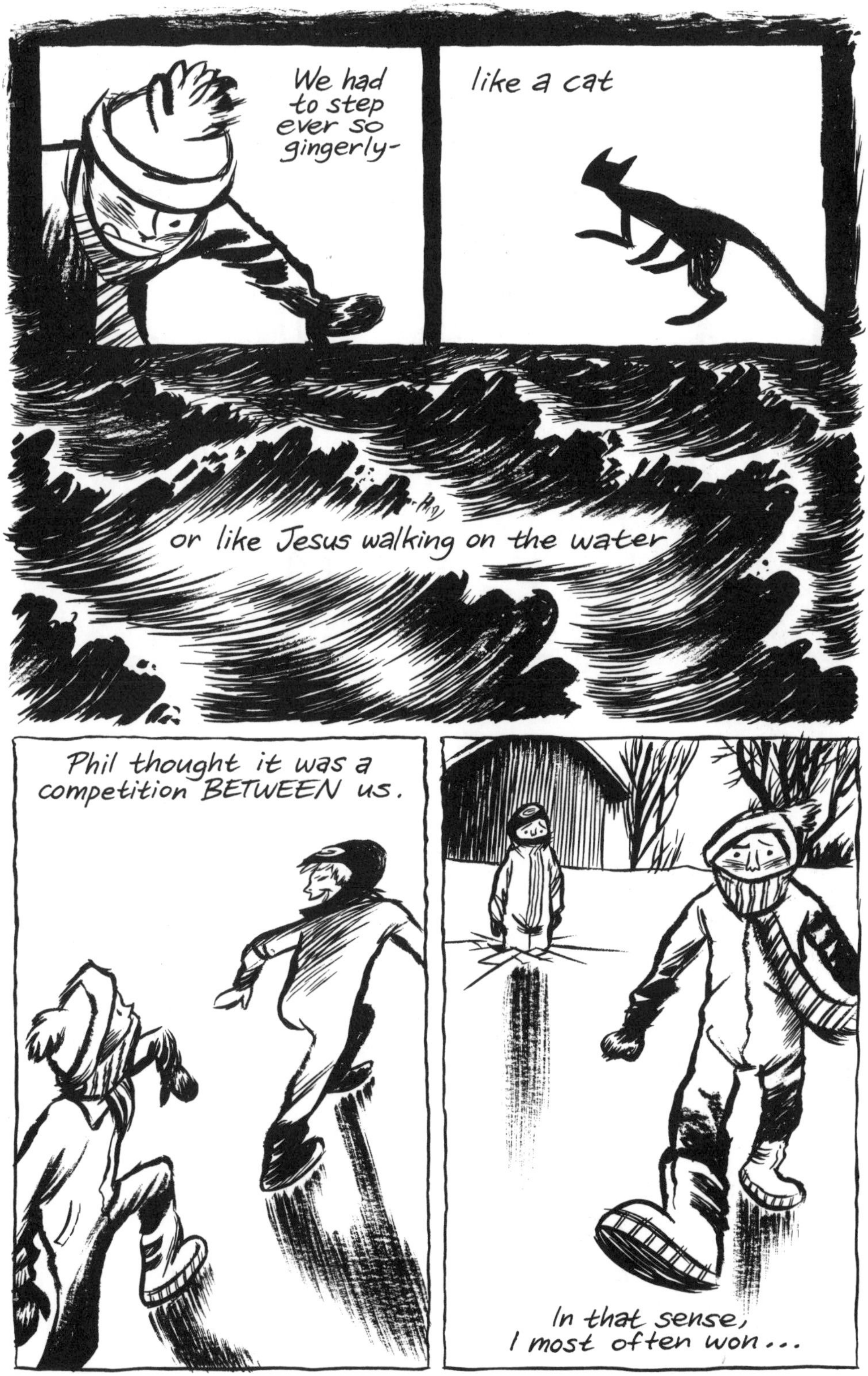
We had to step ever so gingerly-
like a cat
or like Jesus walking on the water
Phil thought it was a competition BETWEEN us.
In that sense, I most often won...

...but I knew I wasn't competing against him, but against myself-- against my own clumsy humanity that had lost synchronization with the earth.

crack

GRUNCH

In that sense,
I always lost.

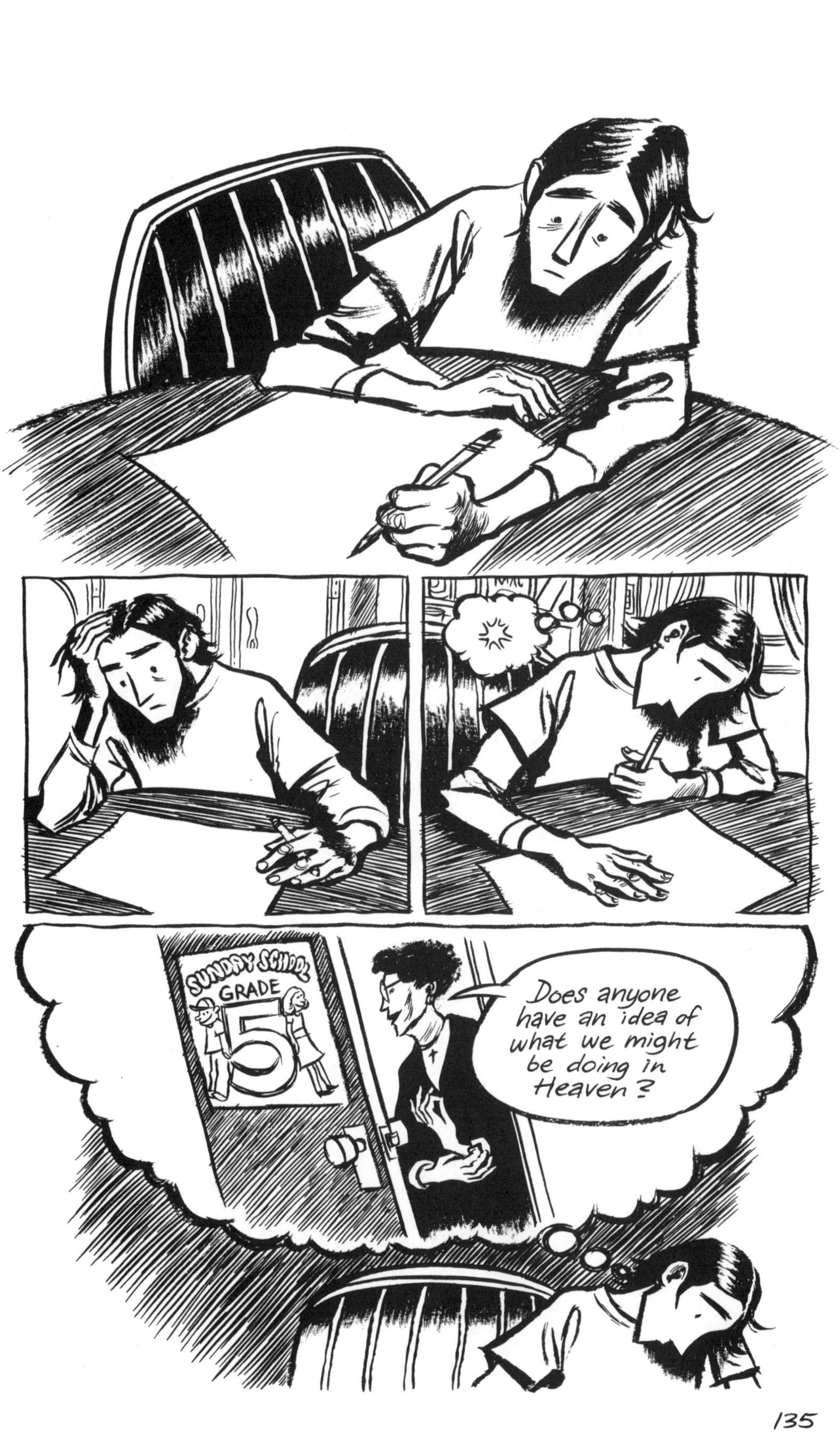
SUNDAY SCHOOL
GRADE
5
Does anyone have an idea of what we might be doing in Heaven?

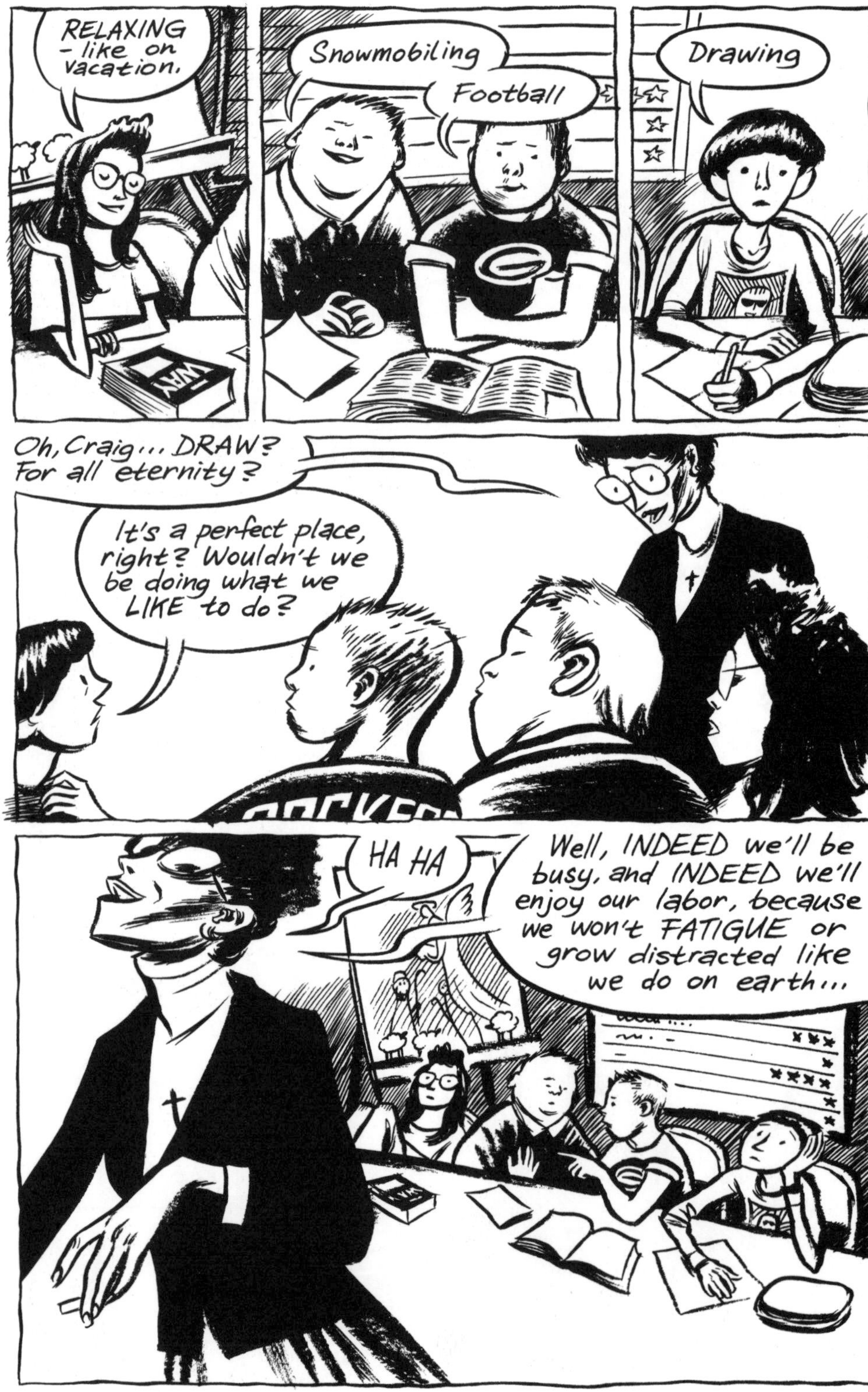

RELAXING - like on vacation.
Snowmobiling
Football
Drawing
Oh, Craig... DRAW? For all eternity?
It's a perfect place, right? Wouldn't we be doing what we LIKE to do?
HA HA
Well, INDEED we'll be busy, and INDEED we'll enjoy our labor, because we won't FATIGUE or grow distracted like we do on earth...

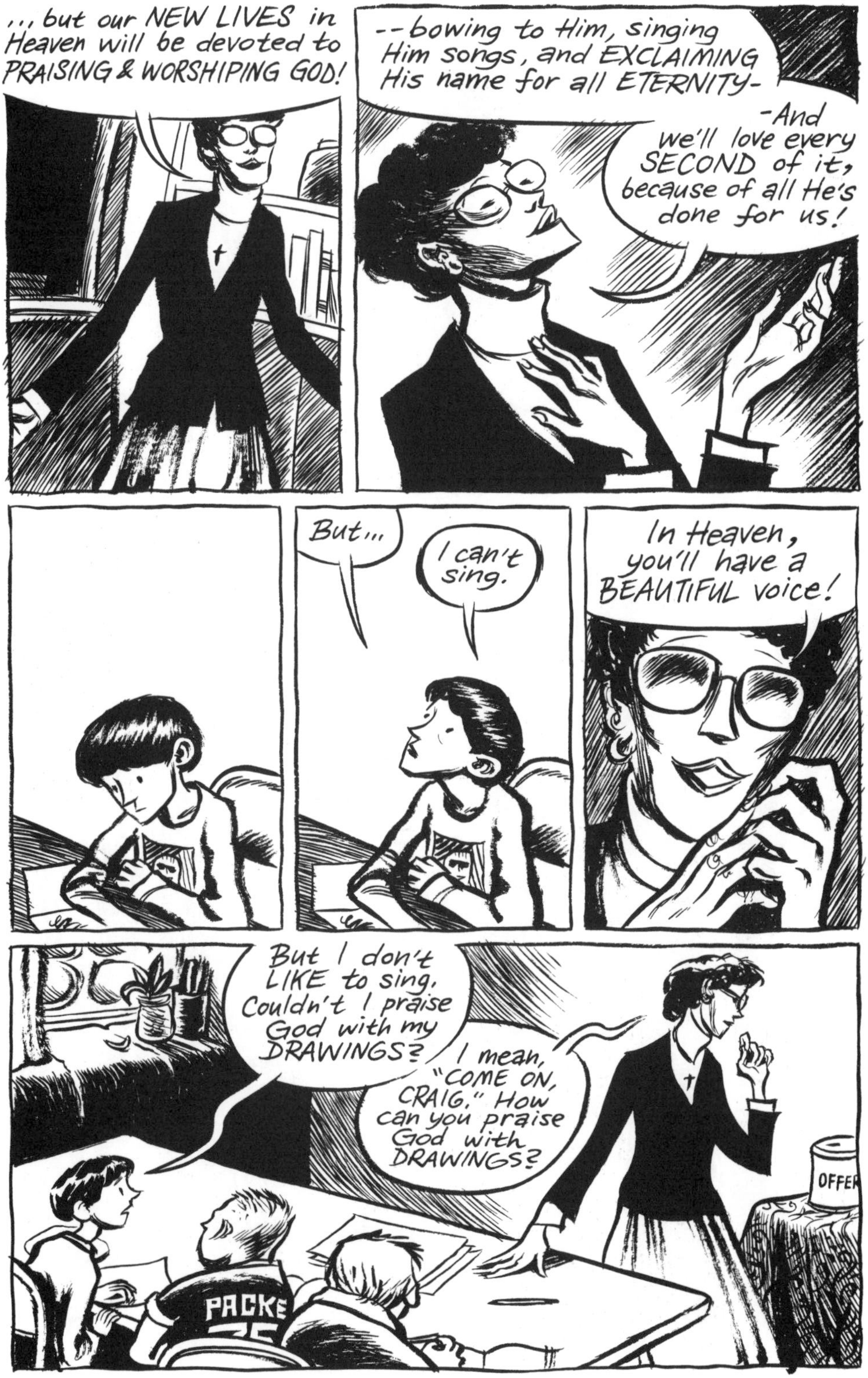

..., but our NEW LIVES in Heaven will be devoted to PRAISING & WORSHIPING GOD!
--bowing to Him, singing Him songs, and EXCLAIMING His name for all ETERNITY-
-And we'll love every SECOND of it, because of all He's done for us!
But...
I can't sing.
In Heaven, you'll have a BEAUTIFUL voice!
But I don't LIKE to sing. Couldn't I praise God with my DRAWINGS?
I mean, "COME ON, CRAIG." How can you praise God with DRAWINGS?
PACKE
OFFER

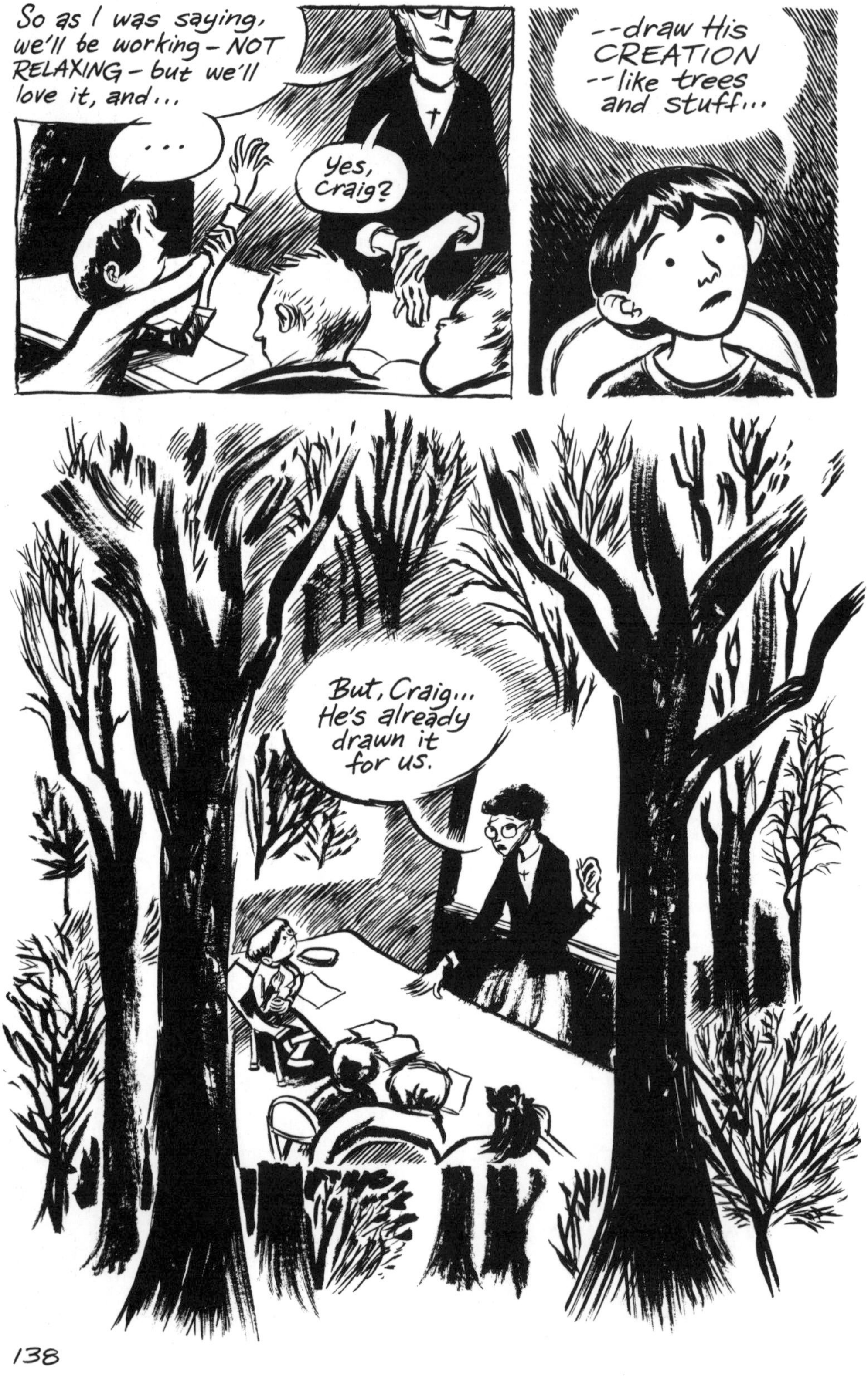
So as I was saying, we'll be working – NOT RELAXING – but we'll love it, and...
...
Yes, Craig?
--draw His CREATION --like trees and stuff...
But, Craig... He's already drawn it for us.

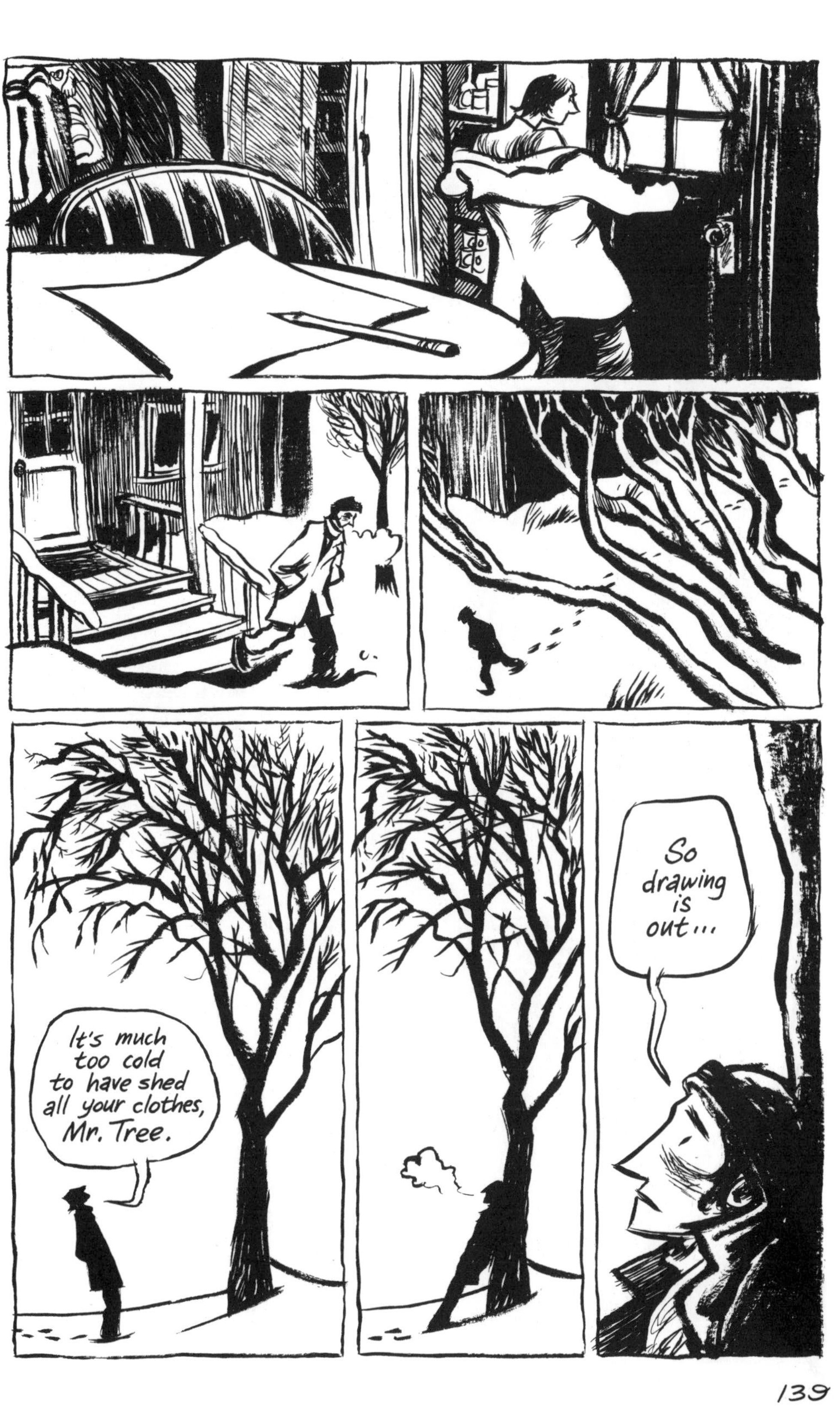
It's much too cold to have shed all your clothes, Mr. Tree.
So drawing is out...

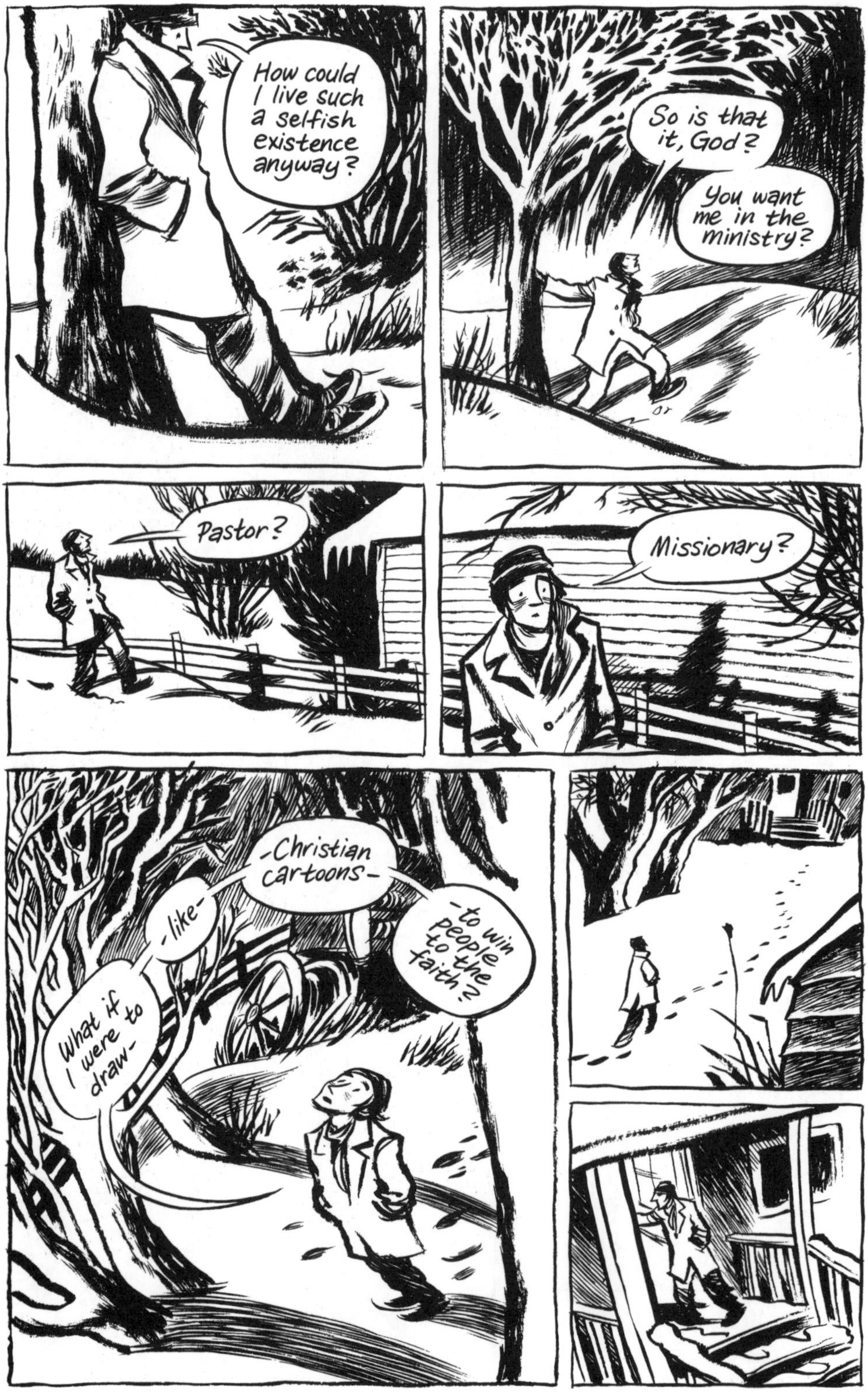
How could I live such a selfish existence anyway?
So is that it, God?
You want me in the ministry?
Pastor?
Missionary?
What if I were to draw-
-like-
-Christian cartoons-
-to win people to the faith?

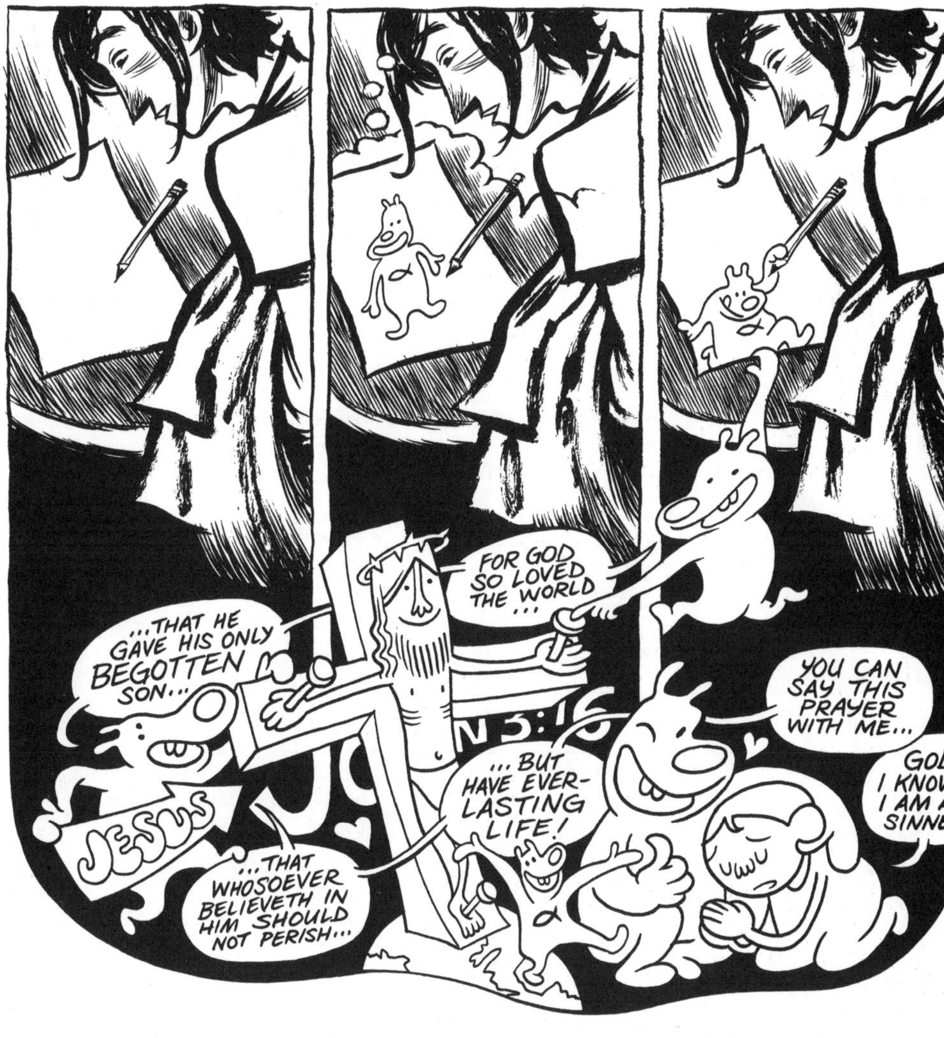
FOR GOD SO LOVED THE WORLD ...
...THAT HE GAVE HIS ONLY BEGOTTEN SON...
...THAT WHOSOEVER BELIEVETH IN HIM SHOULD NOT PERISH...
... BUT HAVE EVER-LASTING LIFE!
JESUS
YOU CAN SAY THIS PRAYER WITH ME...
GOD, I KNOW I AM A SINNER...

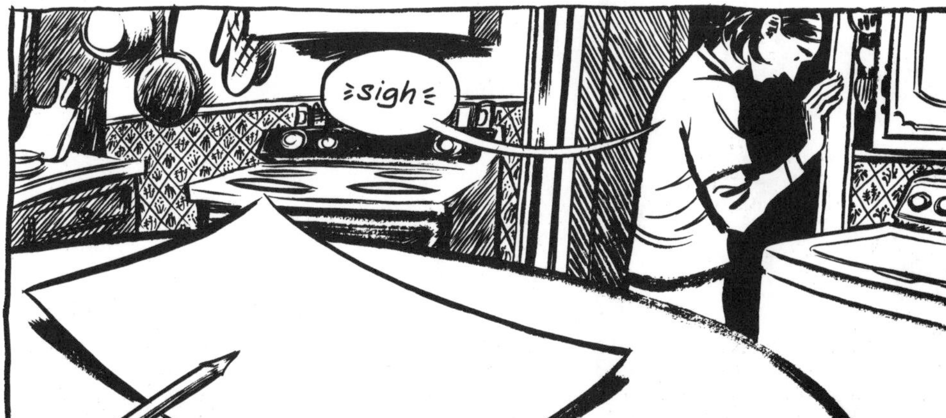
sigh

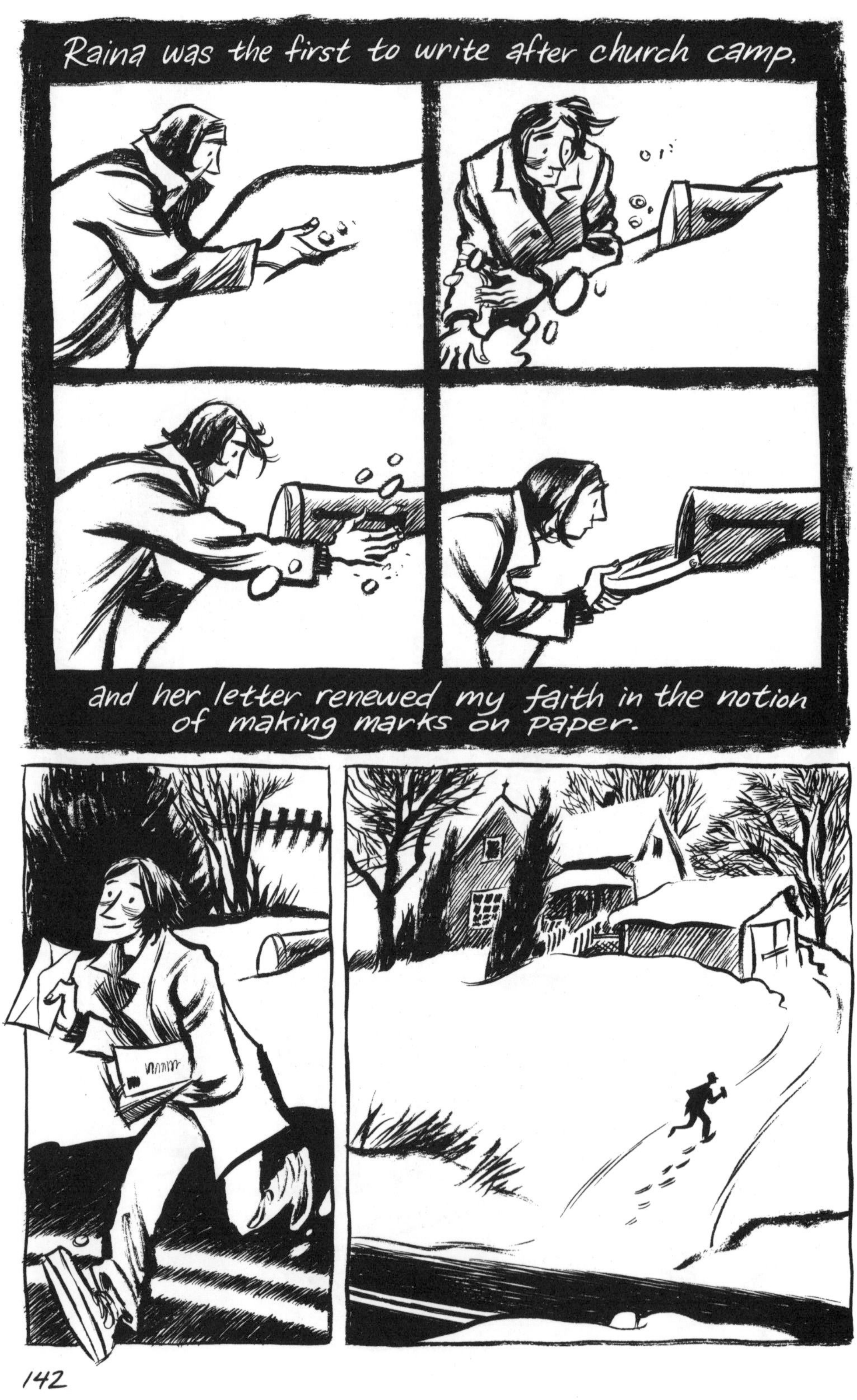
Raina was the first to write after church camp,
and her letter renewed my faith in the notion of making marks on paper.

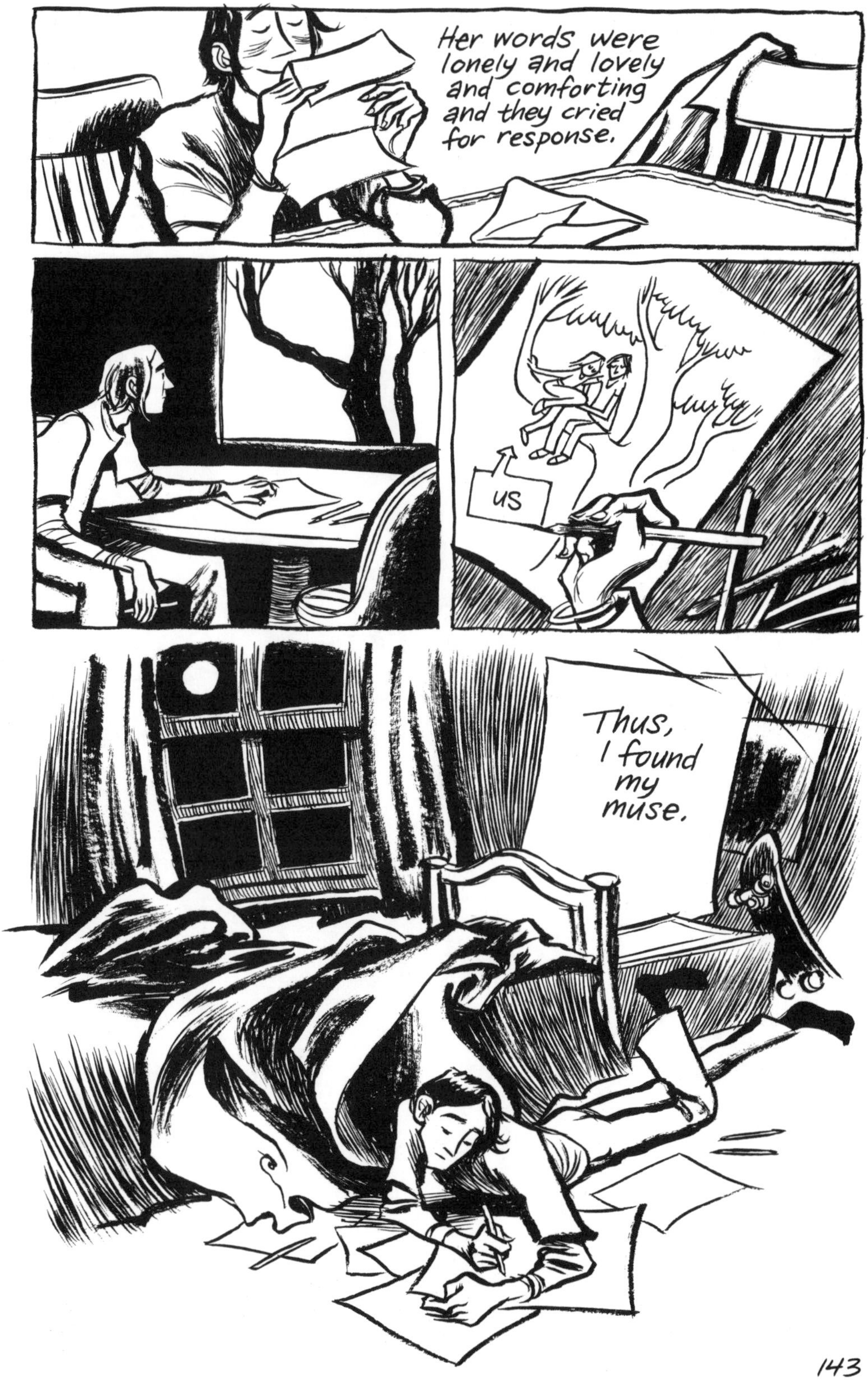
Her words were lonely and lovely and comforting and they cried for response.
US
Thus, I found my muse.

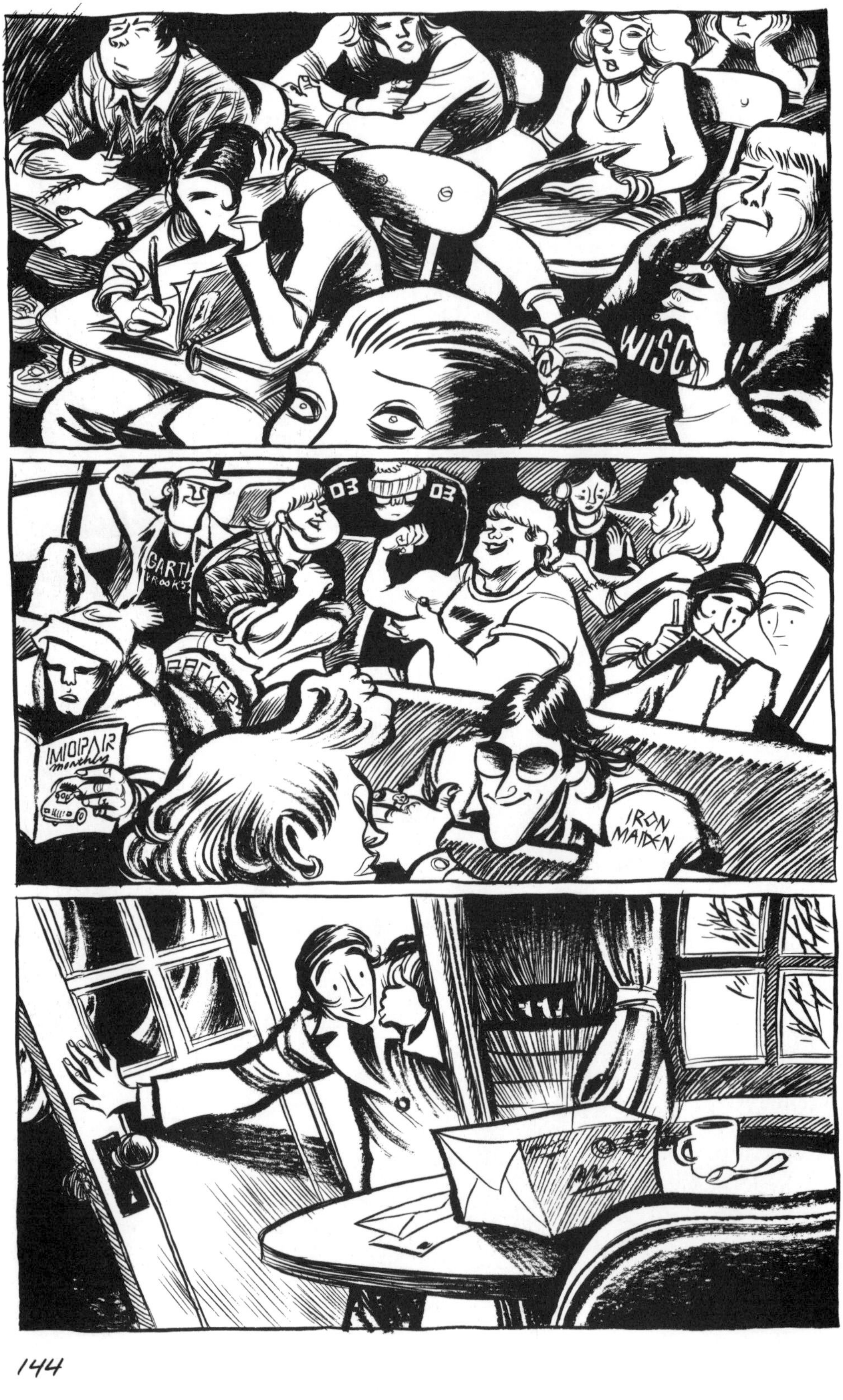
WISC
GARTH BROOKS
03
03
PACKER
MOPAR monthly
IRON MAIDEN

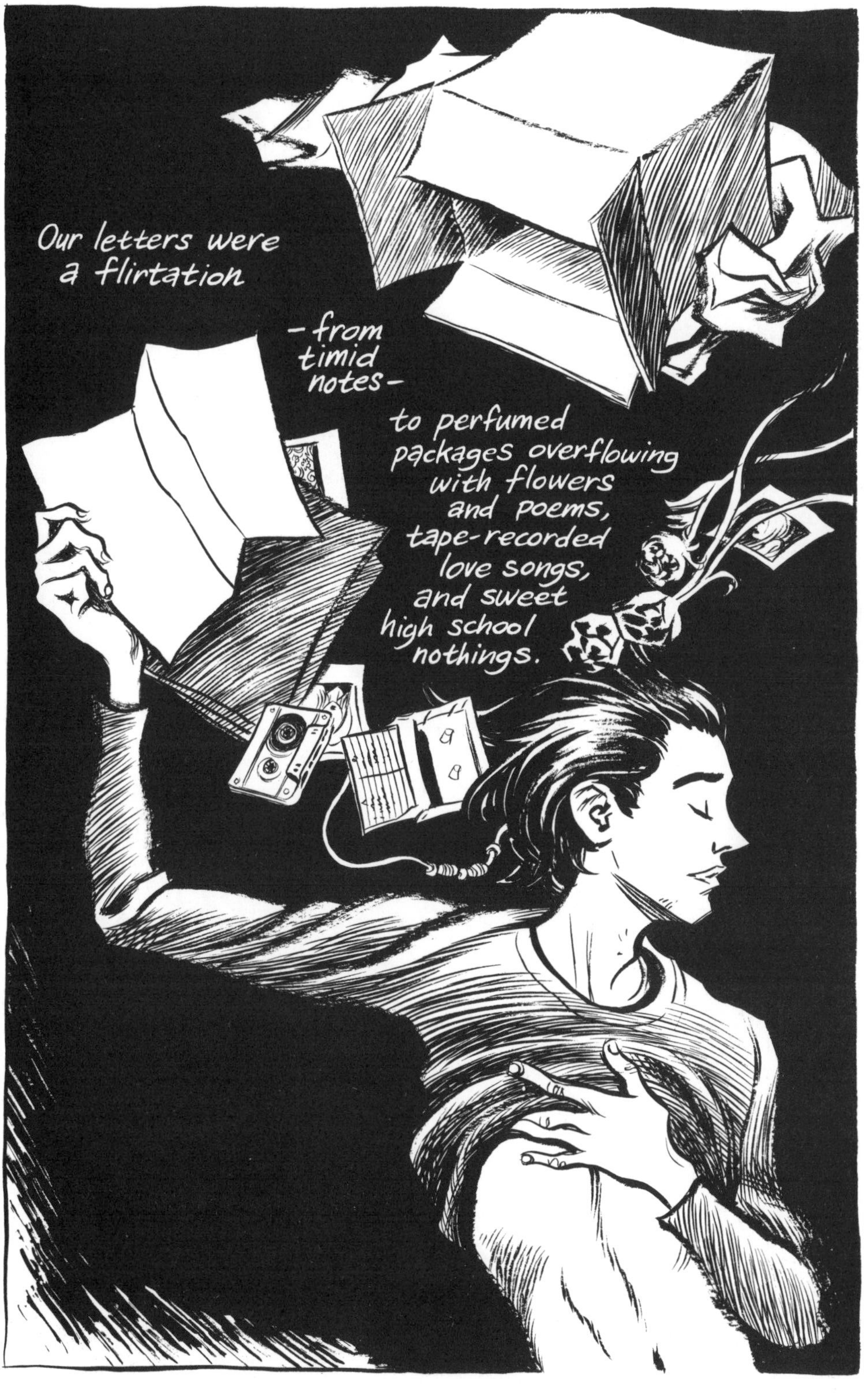
Our letters were a flirtation
-from timid notes-
to perfumed packages overflowing with flowers and poems, tape-recorded love songs, and sweet high school nothings.

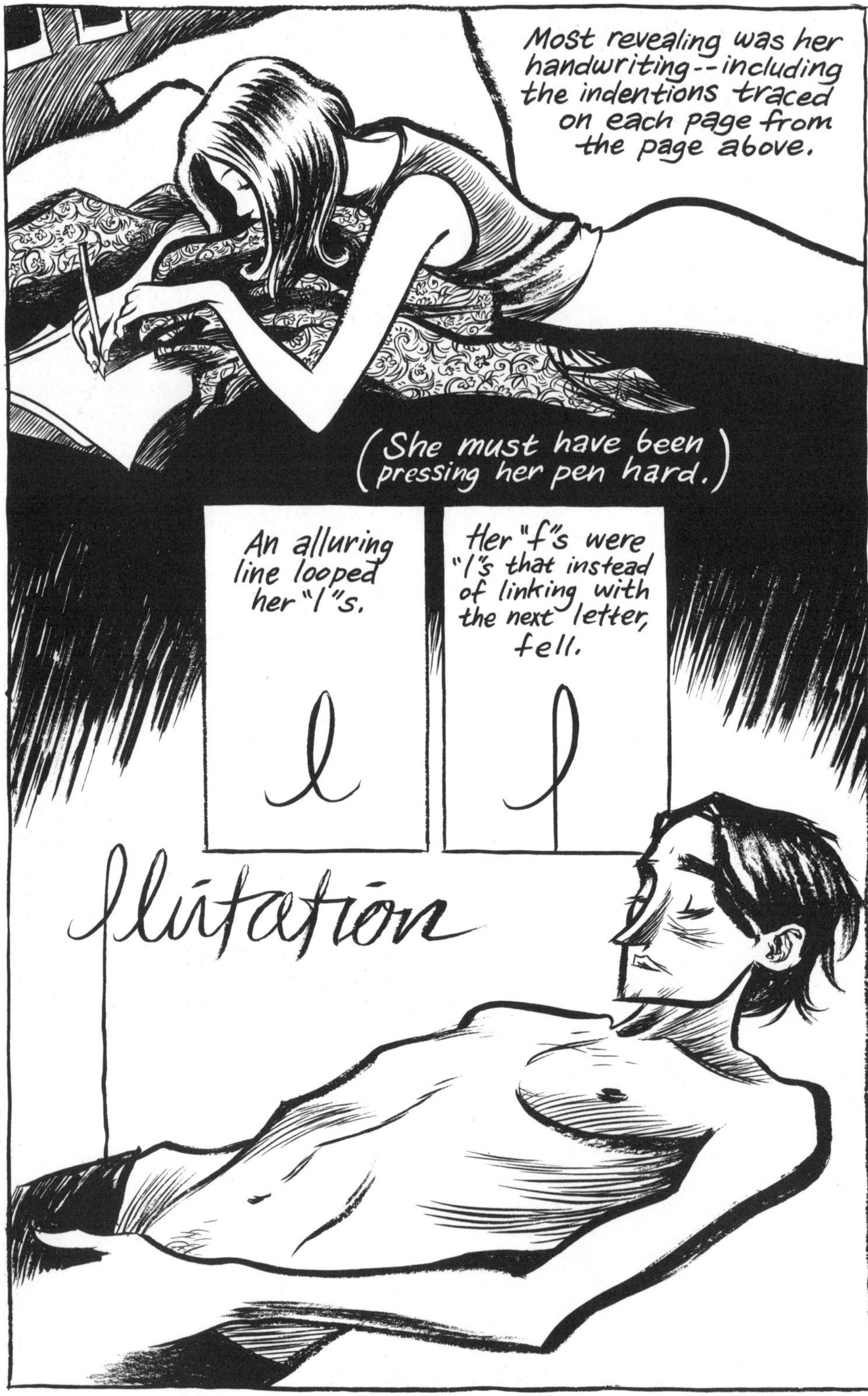
Most revealing was her handwriting--including the indentions traced on each page from the page above.
(She must have been pressing her pen hard.)
An alluring line looped her "l"s.
Her "f"s were "l"s that instead of linking with the next letter, fell.
l
f
flirtation

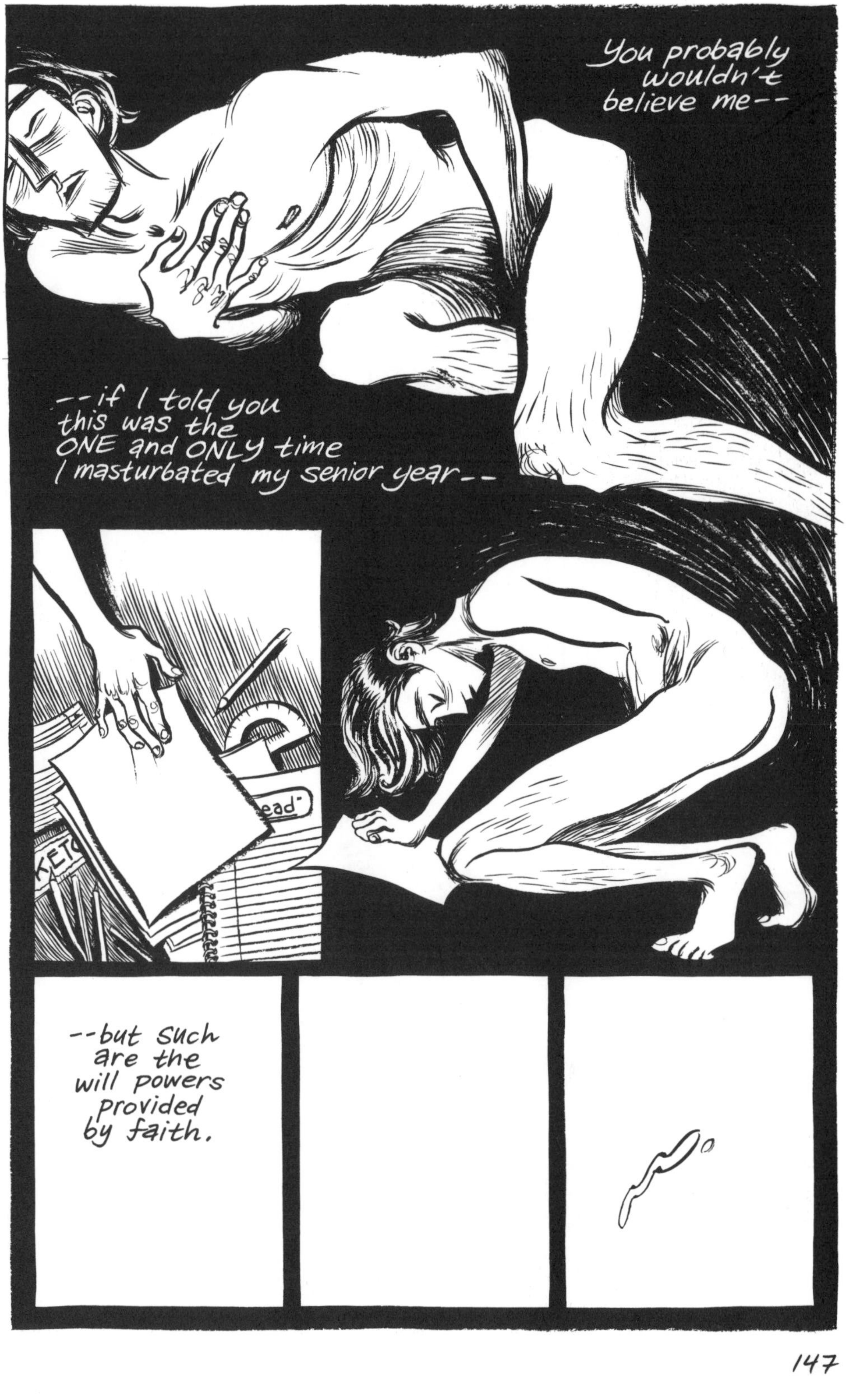
You probably wouldn't believe me--
--if I told you this was the ONE and ONLY time I masturbated my senior year--
--but such are the will powers provided by faith.

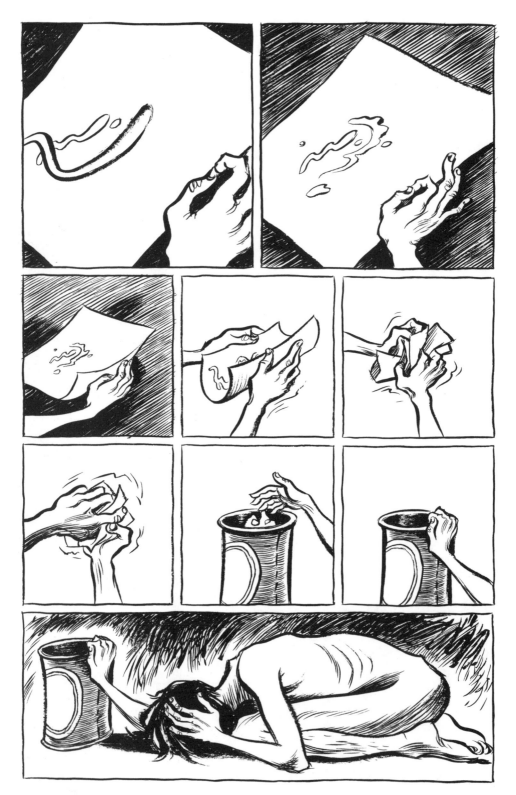

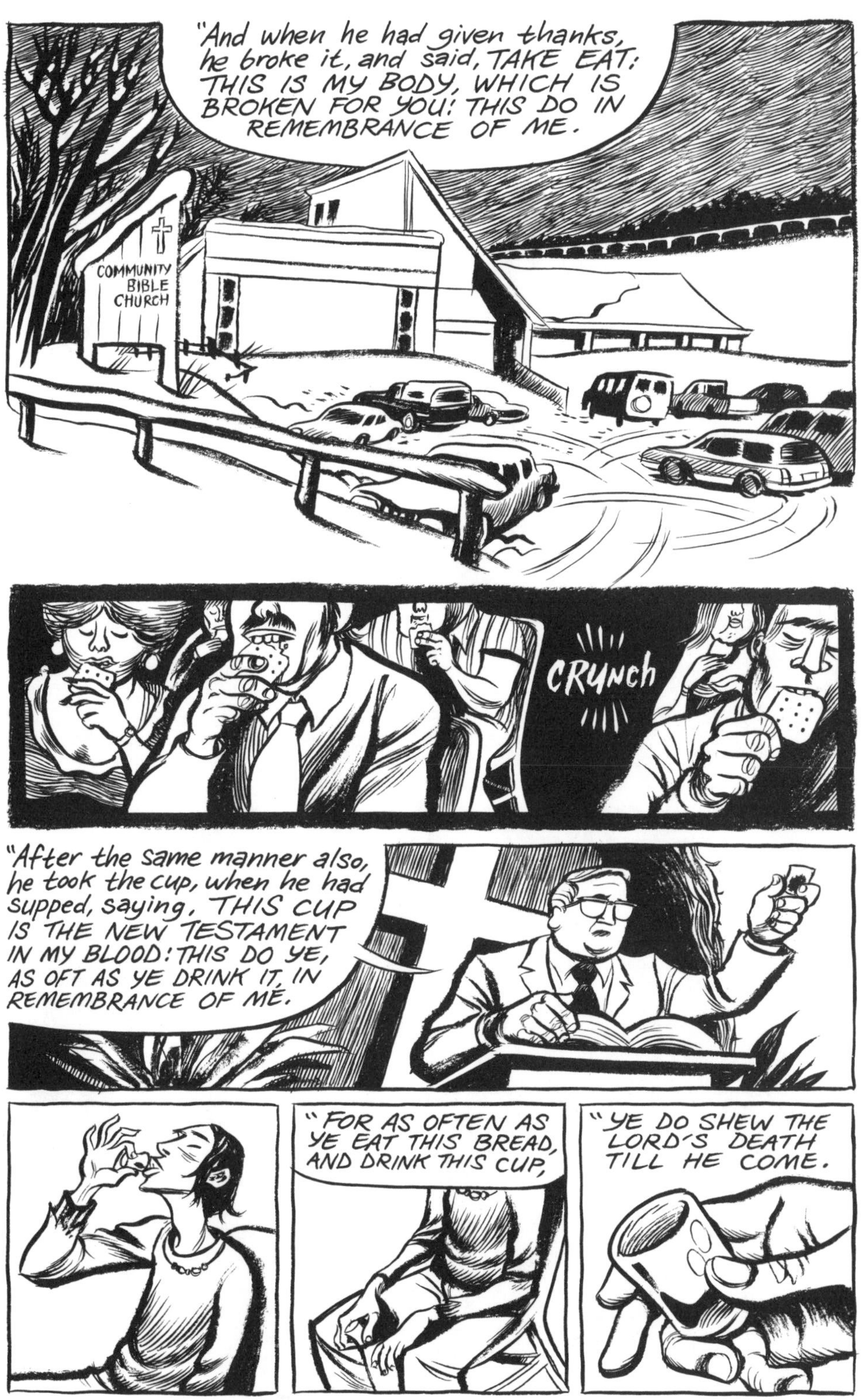
"And when he had given thanks, he broke it, and said, TAKE EAT: THIS IS MY BODY, WHICH IS BROKEN FOR YOU: THIS DO IN REMEMBRANCE OF ME.
COMMUNITY BIBLE CHURCH
CRUNCH
"After the same manner also, he took the cup, when he had supped, saying, THIS CUP IS THE NEW TESTAMENT IN MY BLOOD: THIS DO YE, AS OFT AS YE DRINK IT, IN REMEMBRANCE OF ME.
"FOR AS OFTEN AS YE EAT THIS BREAD, AND DRINK THIS CUP,
"YE DO SHEW THE LORD'S DEATH TILL HE COME.

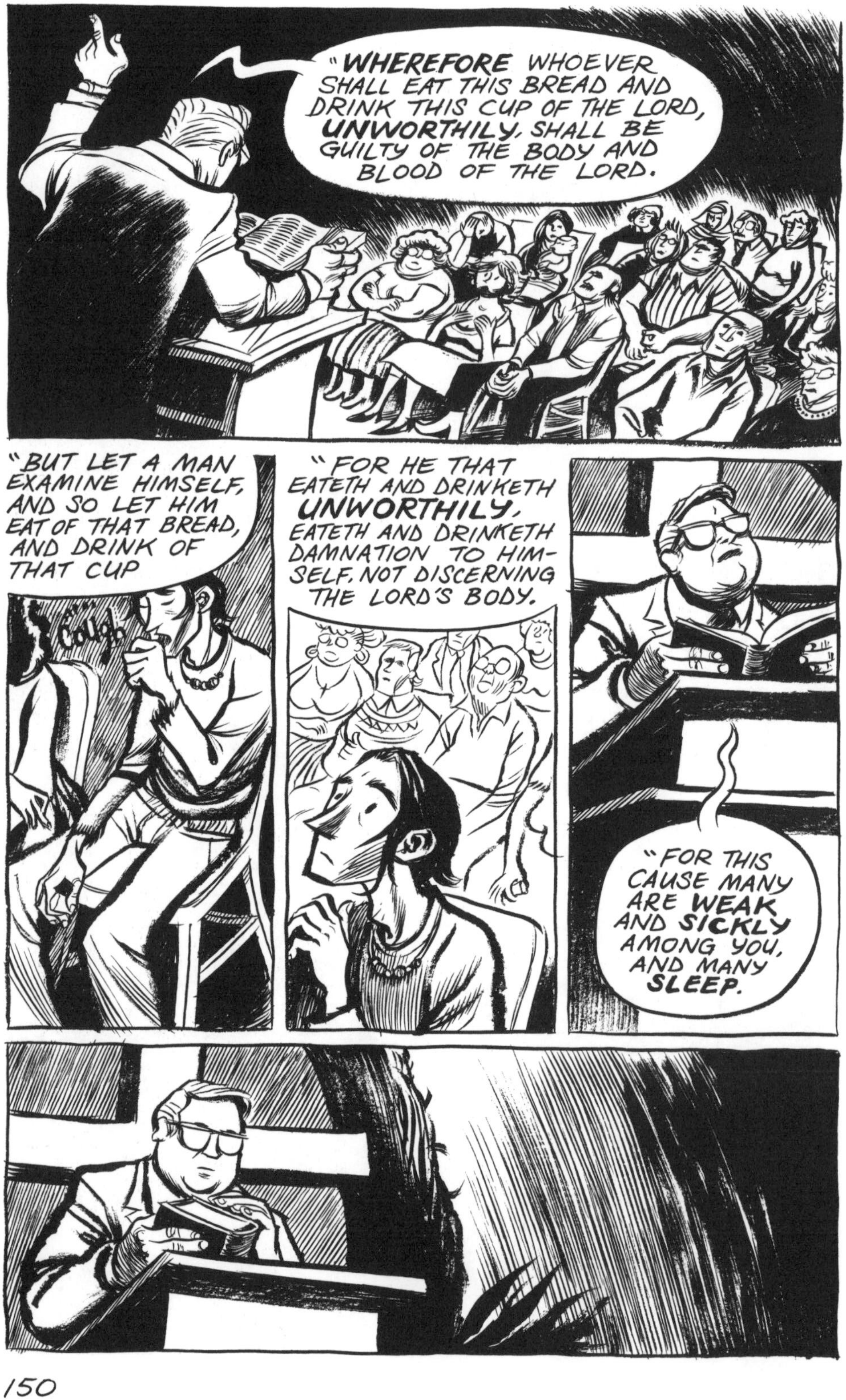
"WHEREFORE WHOEVER SHALL EAT THIS BREAD AND DRINK THIS CUP OF THE LORD, UNWORTHILY, SHALL BE GUILTY OF THE BODY AND BLOOD OF THE LORD.
"BUT LET A MAN EXAMINE HIMSELF, AND SO LET HIM EAT OF THAT BREAD, AND DRINK OF THAT CUP
COUGH
"FOR HE THAT EATETH AND DRINKETH UNWORTHILY, EATETH AND DRINKETH DAMNATION TO HIMSELF, NOT DISCERNING THE LORD'S BODY.
"FOR THIS CAUSE MANY ARE WEAK AND SICKLY AMONG YOU, AND MANY SLEEP.

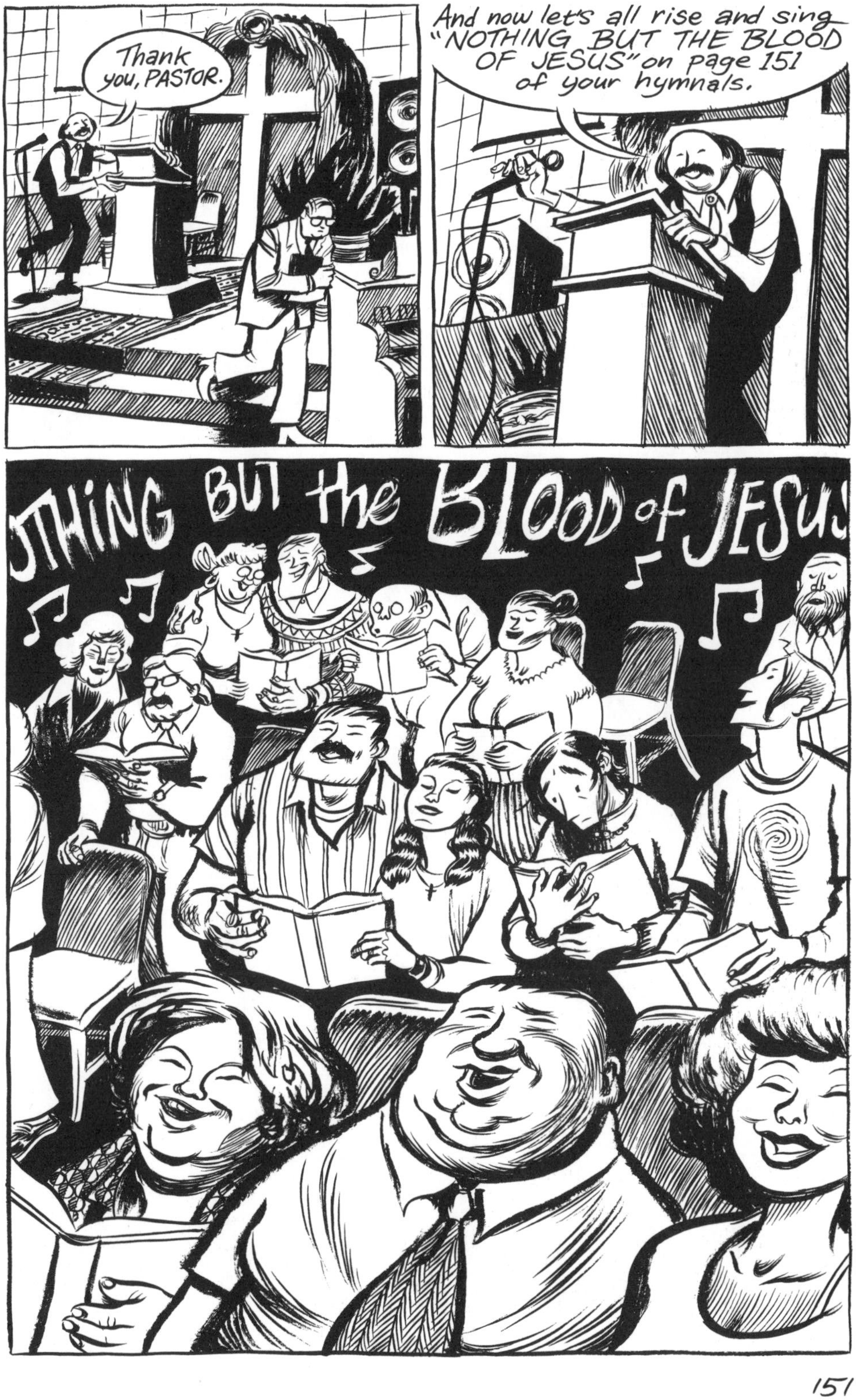
Thank you, PASTOR.
And now let's all rise and sing "NOTHING BUT THE BLOOD OF JESUS" on page 151 of your hymnals.
THING BUT the BLOOD of JESUS

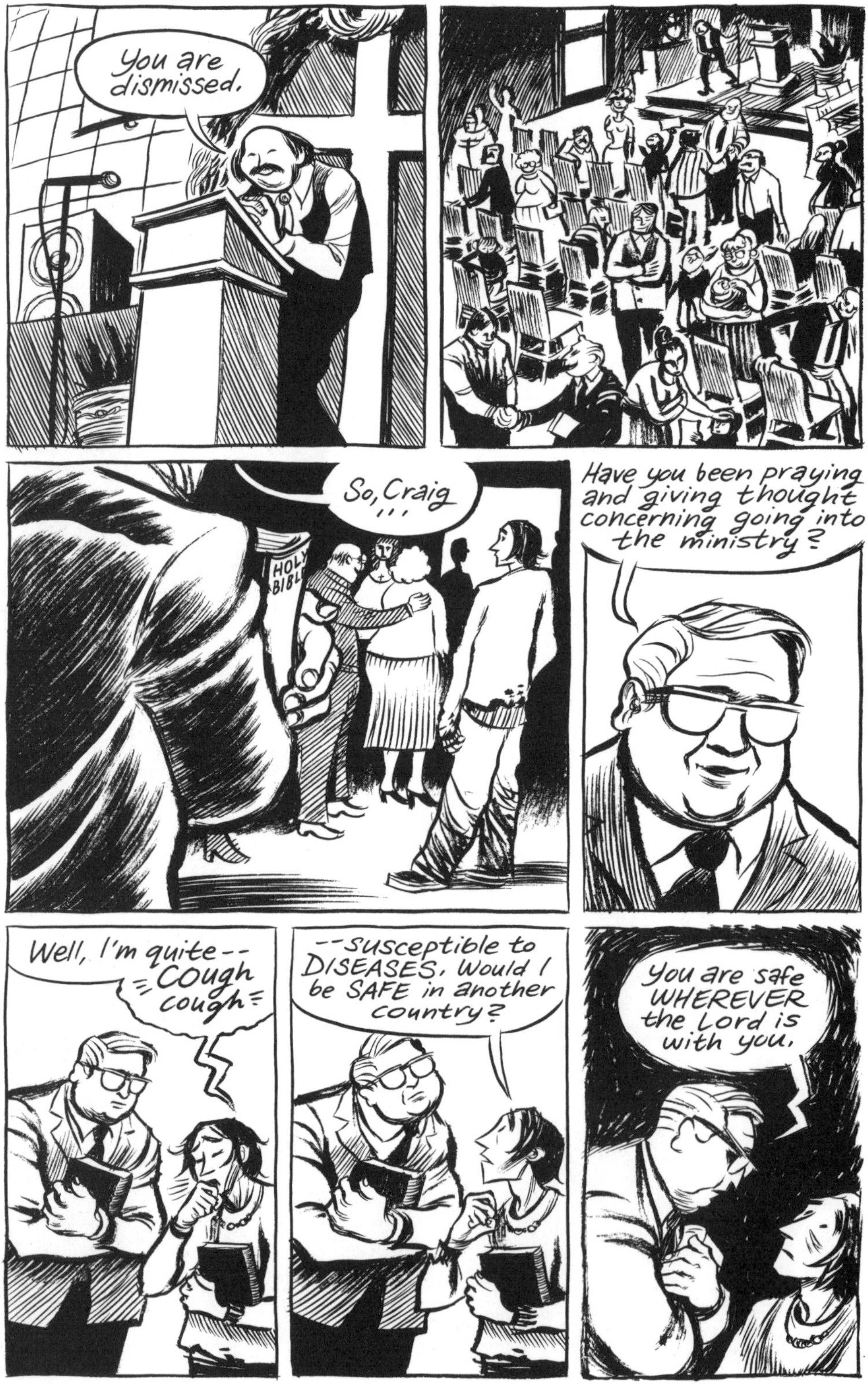

You are dismissed.
HOLY BIBLE
So, Craig ...
Have you been praying and giving thought concerning going into the ministry?
Well, I'm quite-- COUGH cough
--susceptible to DISEASES. Would I be SAFE in another country?
You are safe WHEREVER the Lord is with you.

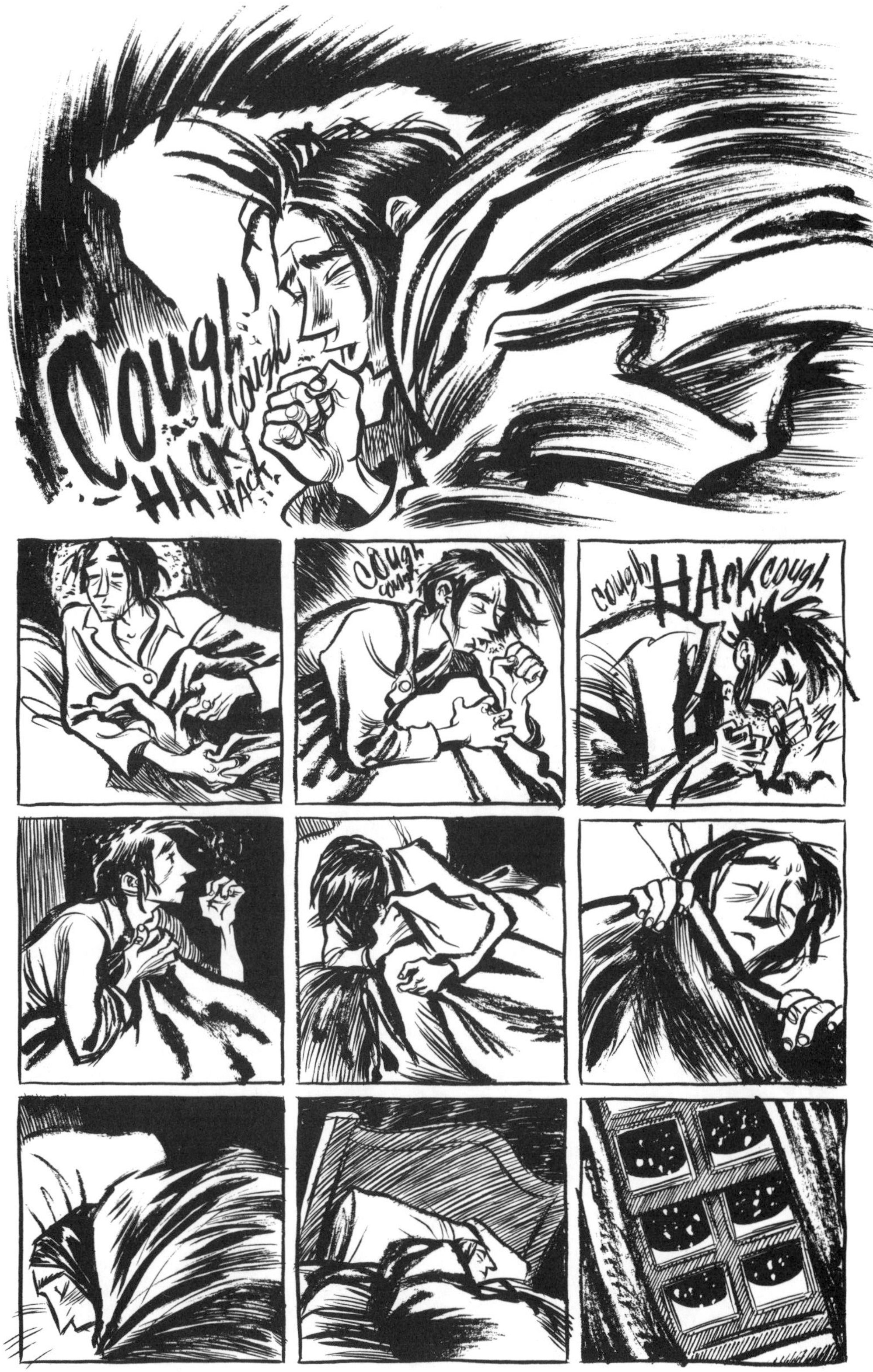
COUGH!
cough
HACK!
HACK
cough
cough
cough HACK cough

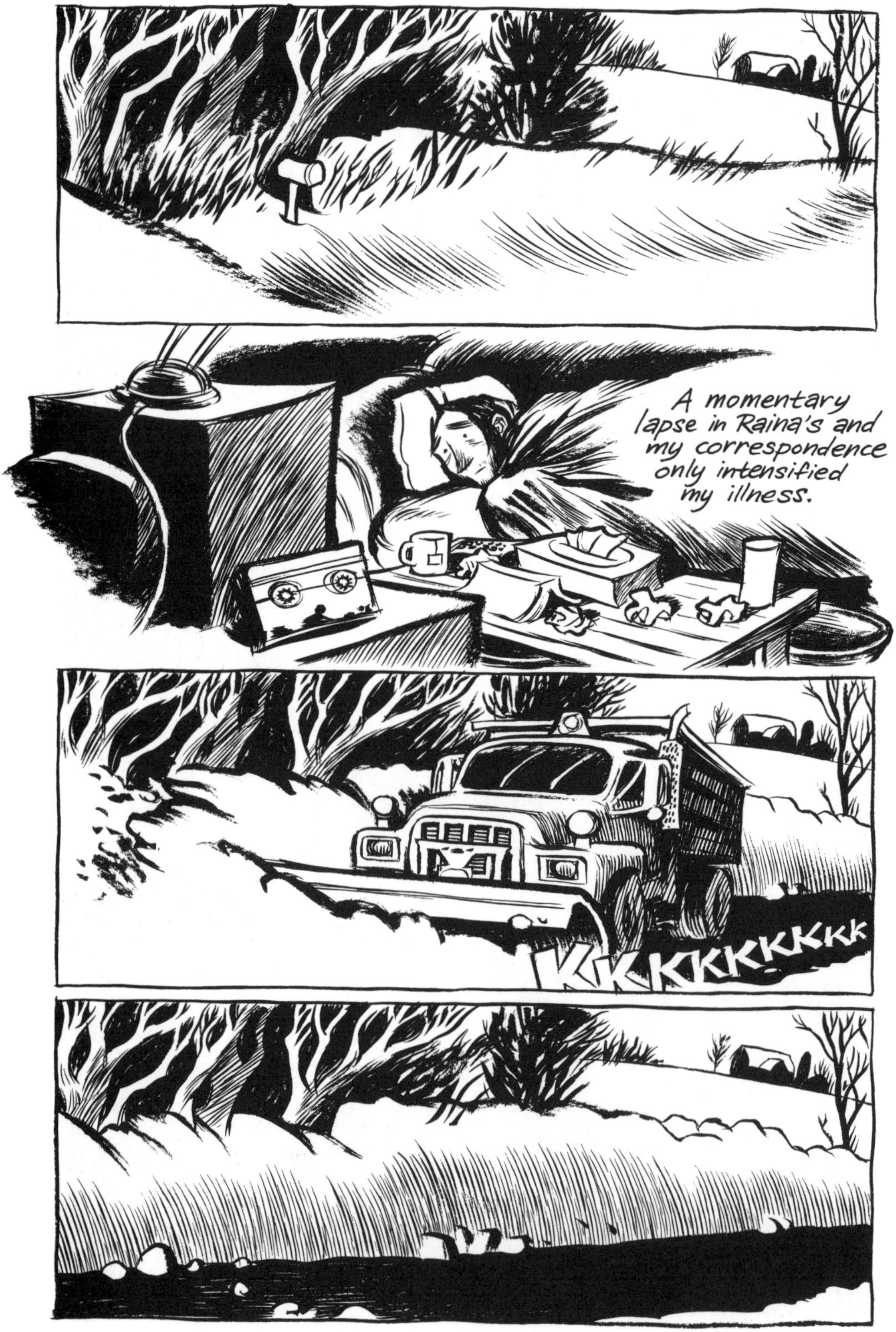
A momentary lapse in Raina's and my correspondence only intensified my illness.
KKKKKKKKK

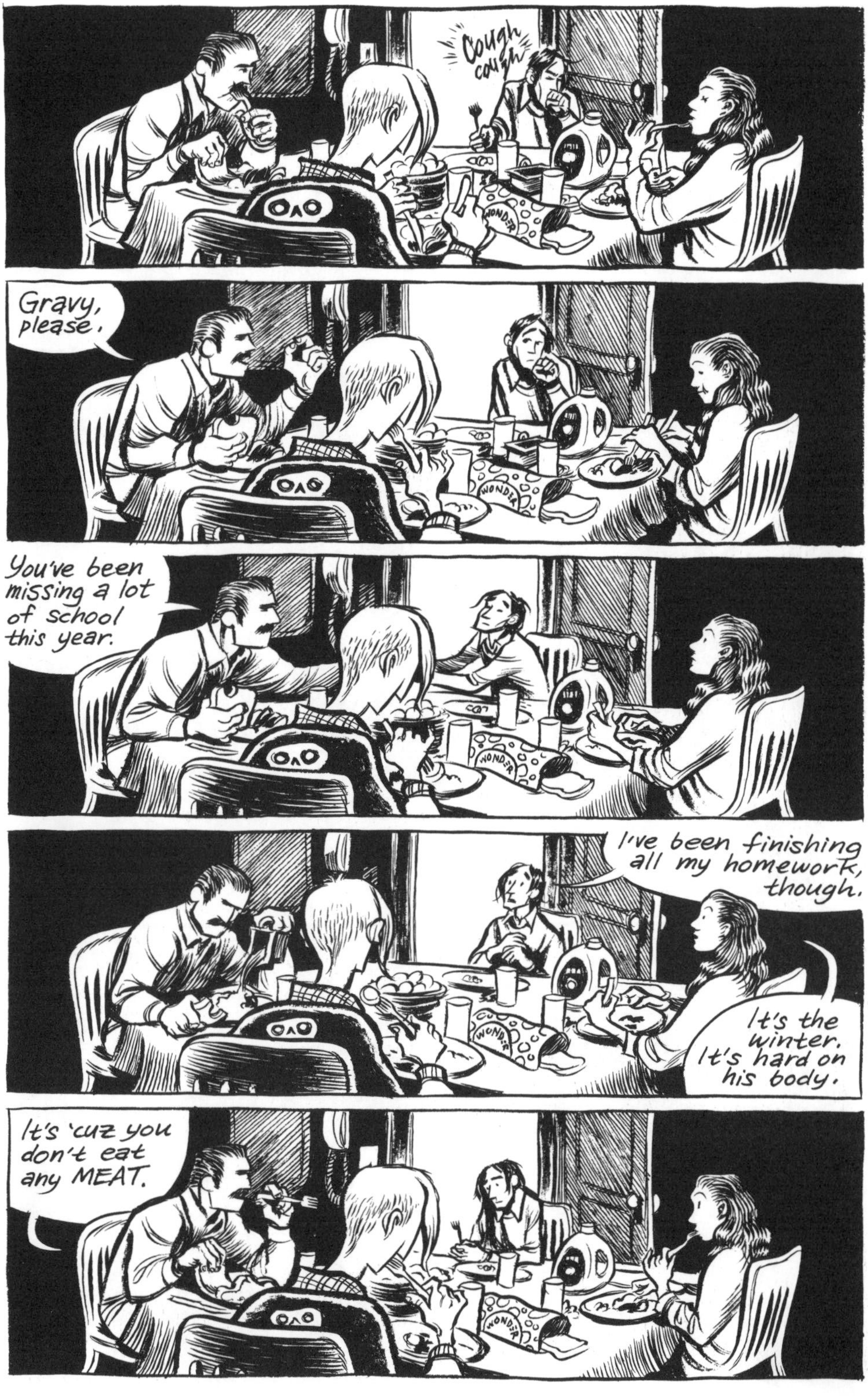
Cough cough
Gravy, please.
You've been missing a lot of school this year.
I've been finishing all my homework, though.
It's the winter. It's hard on his body.
It's 'cuz you don't eat any MEAT.
WONDER

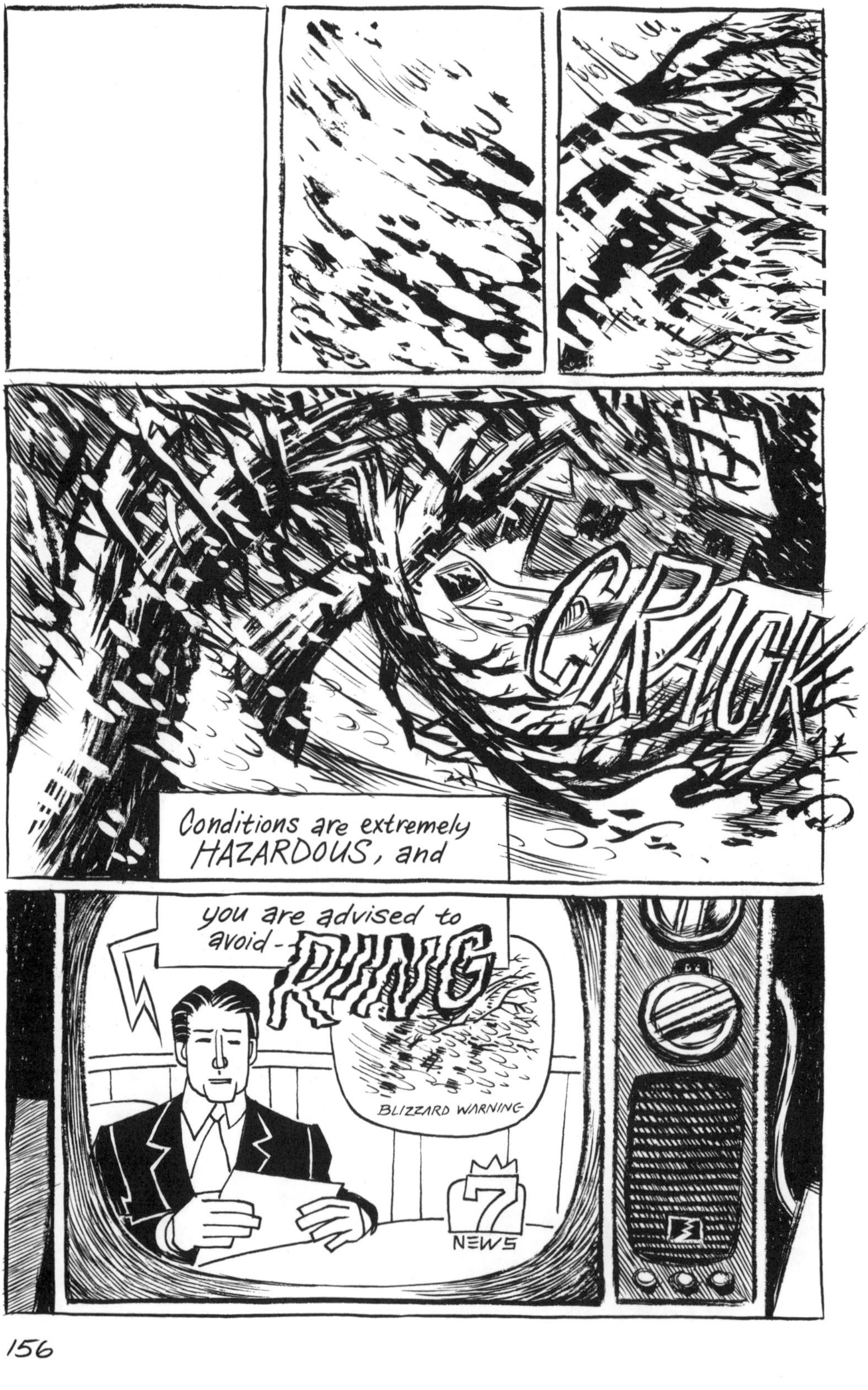

CRACK
Conditions are extremely HAZARDOUS, and
you are advised to avoid--
RING
BLIZZARD WARNING
7 NEWS

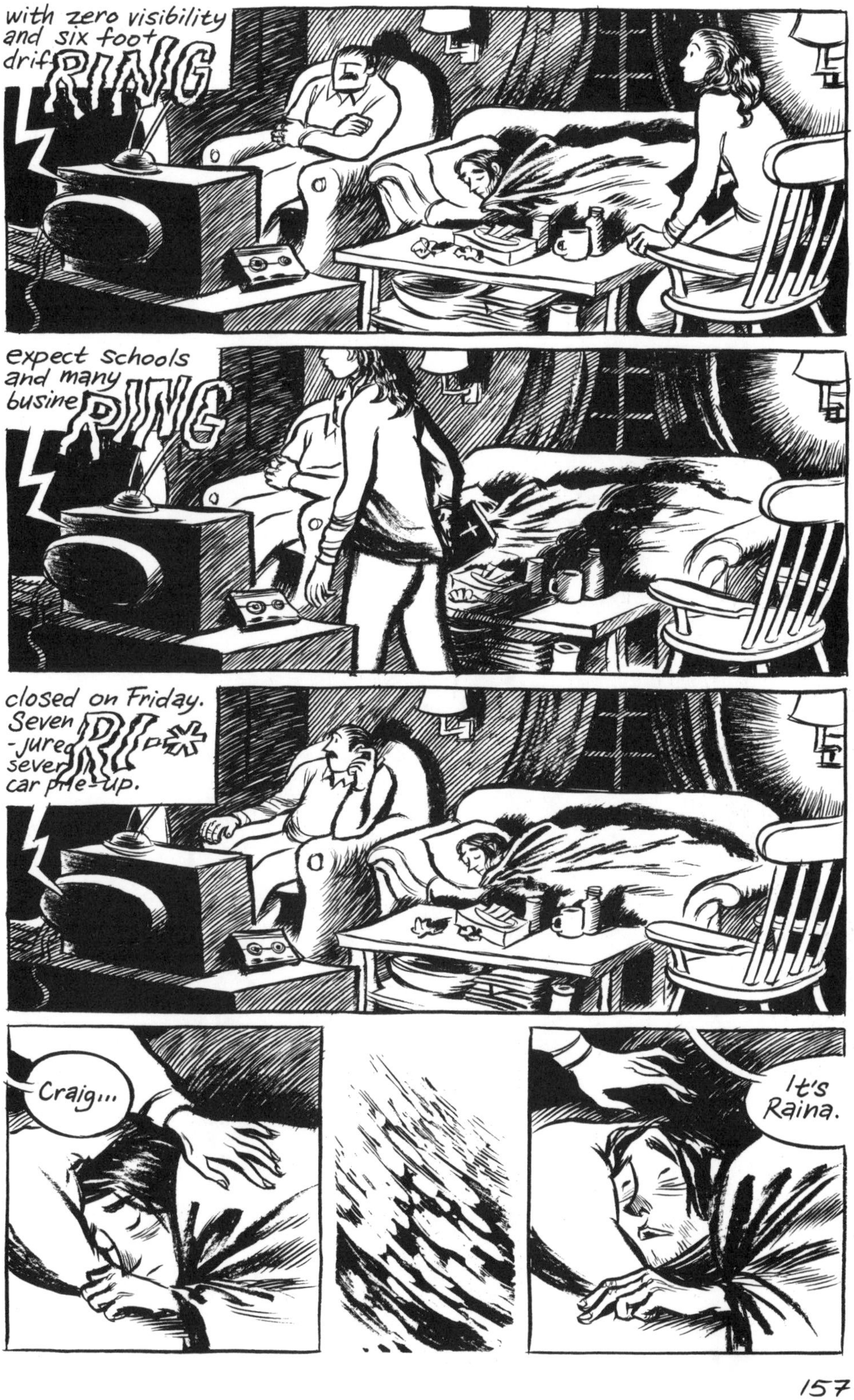
with zero visibility and six foot drif
RING
expect schools and many busine
RING
closed on Friday. Seven -jured sever car pile-up.
RI-*
Craig...
It's Raina.

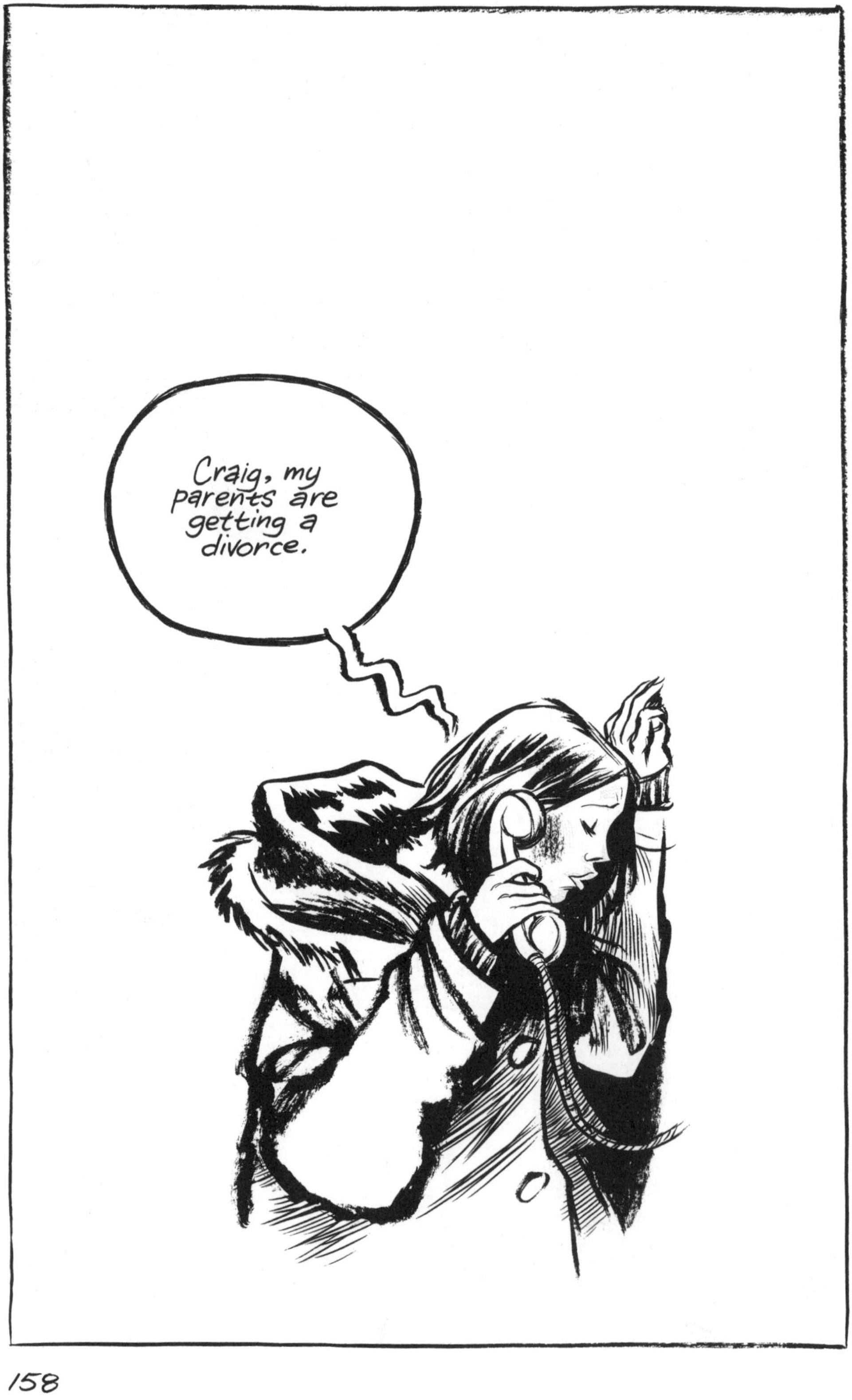
Craig, my parents are getting a divorce.

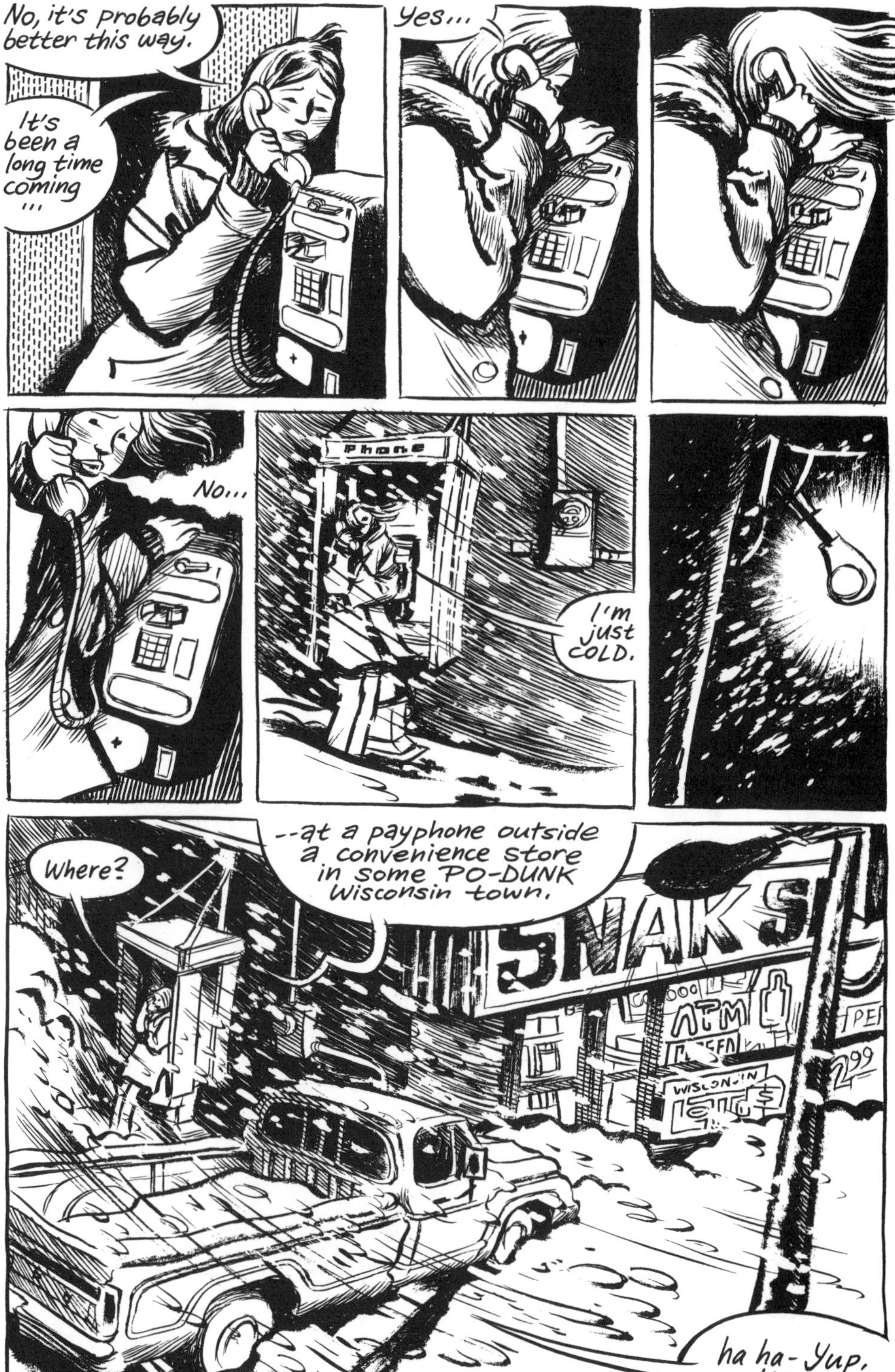
No, it's probably better this way.
It's been a long time coming ...
Yes...
No...
I'm just COLD.
Where?
--at a payphone outside a convenience store in some PO-DUNK Wisconsin town.
SNAK S
ATM
2.99
WISCONSIN
ha ha- Yup, I'm in WISCONSIN!

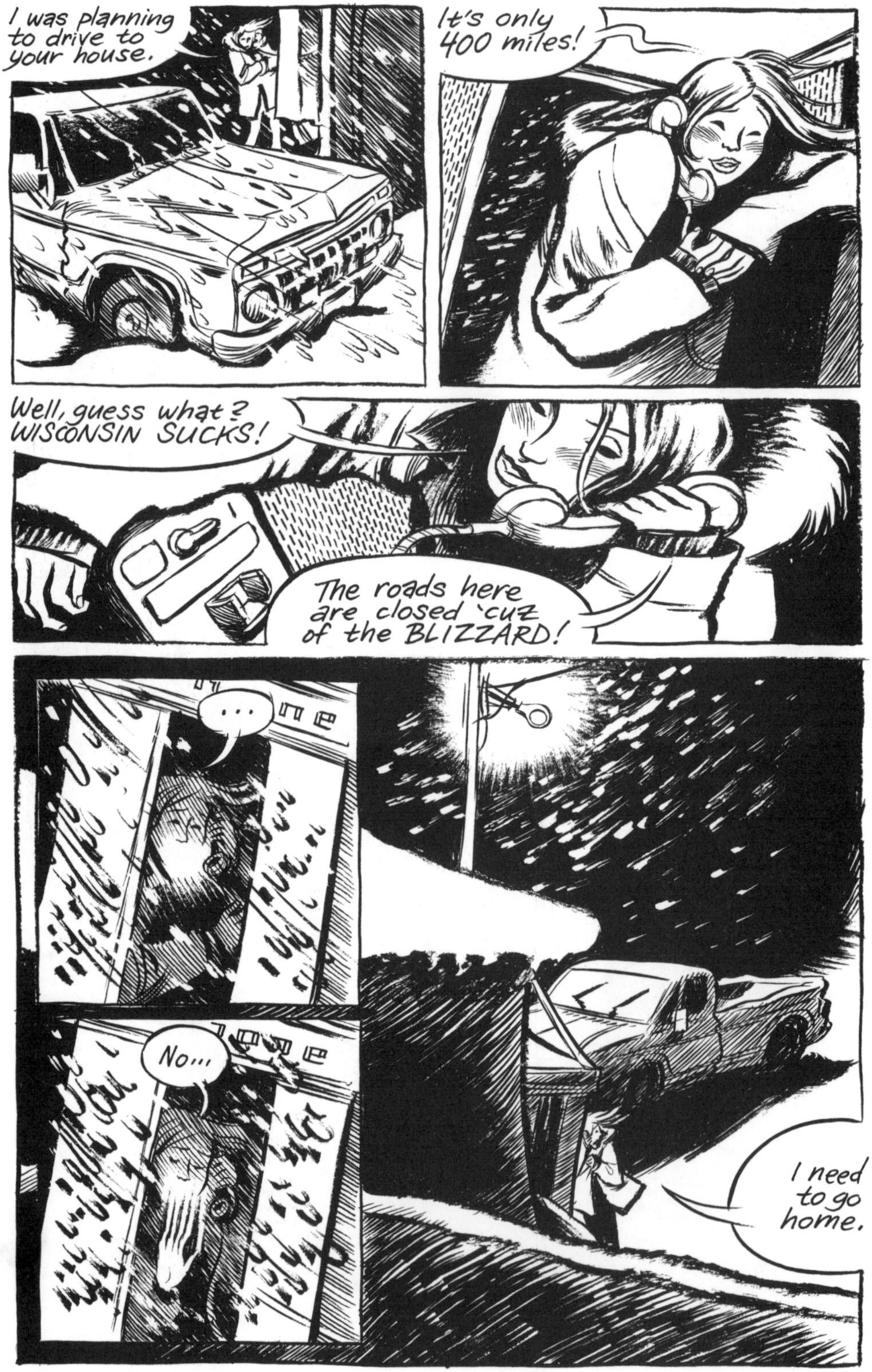
I was planning to drive to your house.
It's only 400 miles!
Well, guess what? WISCONSIN SUCKS!
The roads here are closed 'cuz of the BLIZZARD!
...
No...
I need to go home.

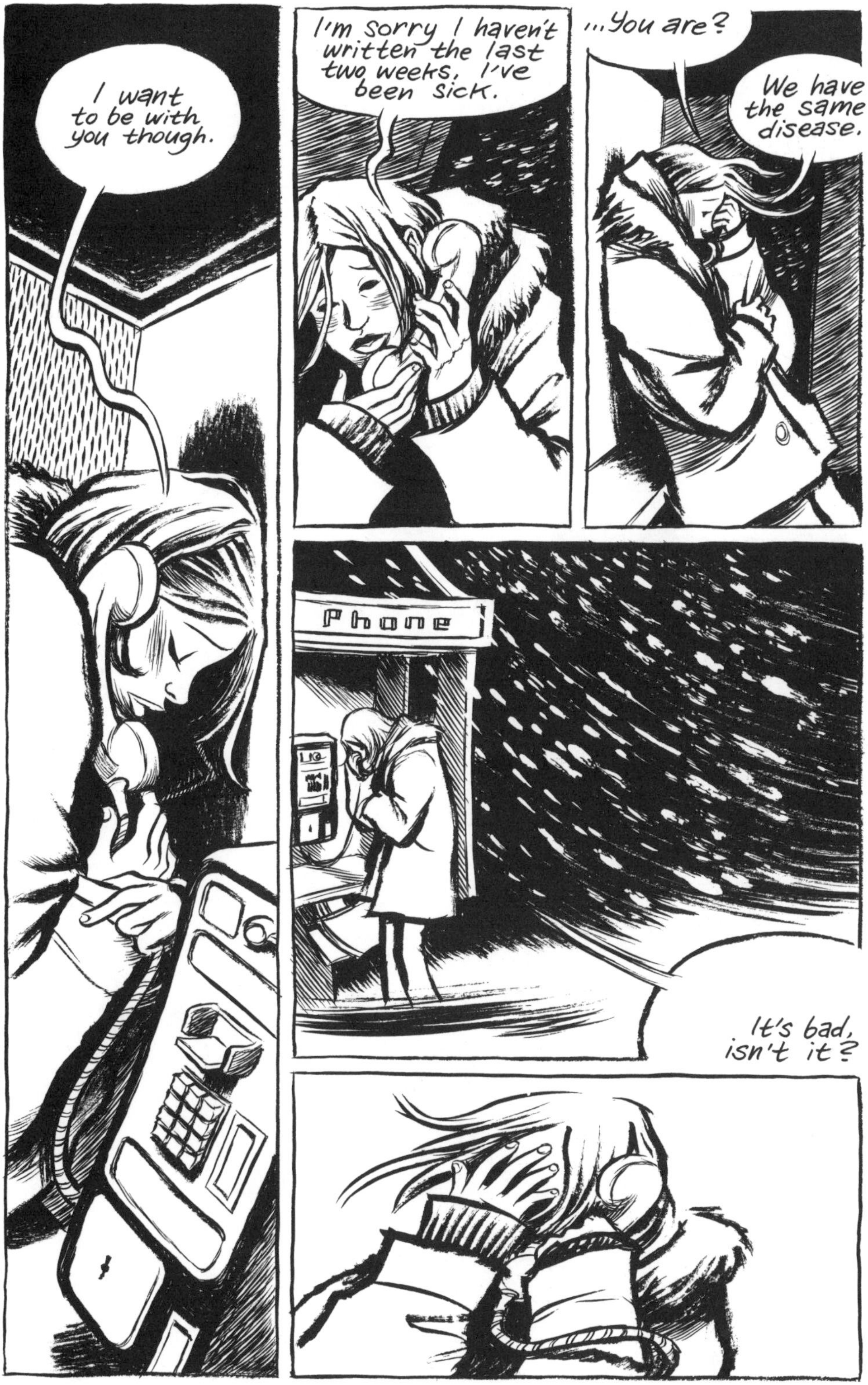
I want to be with you though.
I'm sorry I haven't written the last two weeks. I've been sick.
...You are?
We have the same disease.
Phone
It's bad, isn't it?

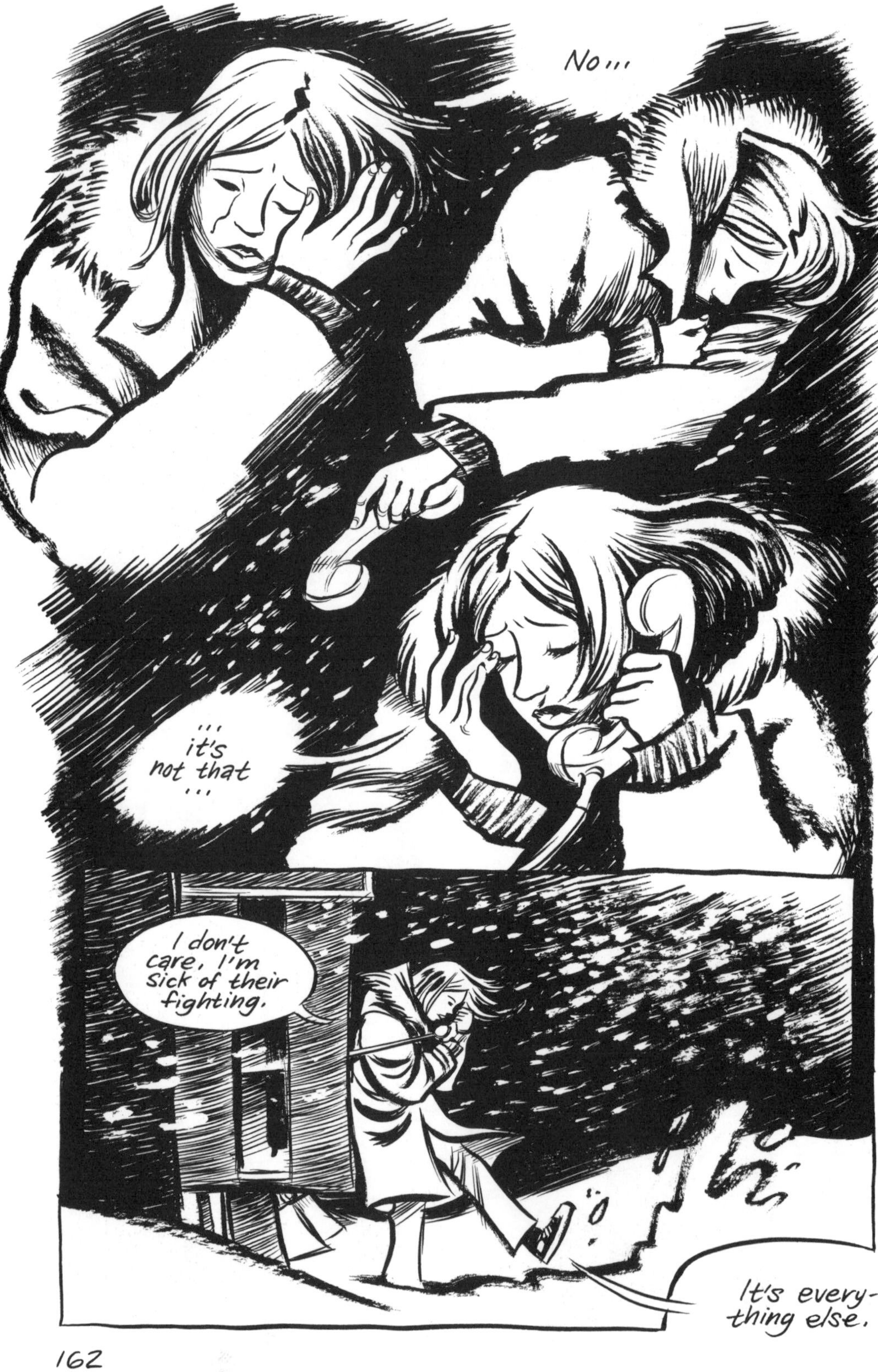
No...
... it's not that ...
I don't care, I'm sick of their fighting.
It's everything else.

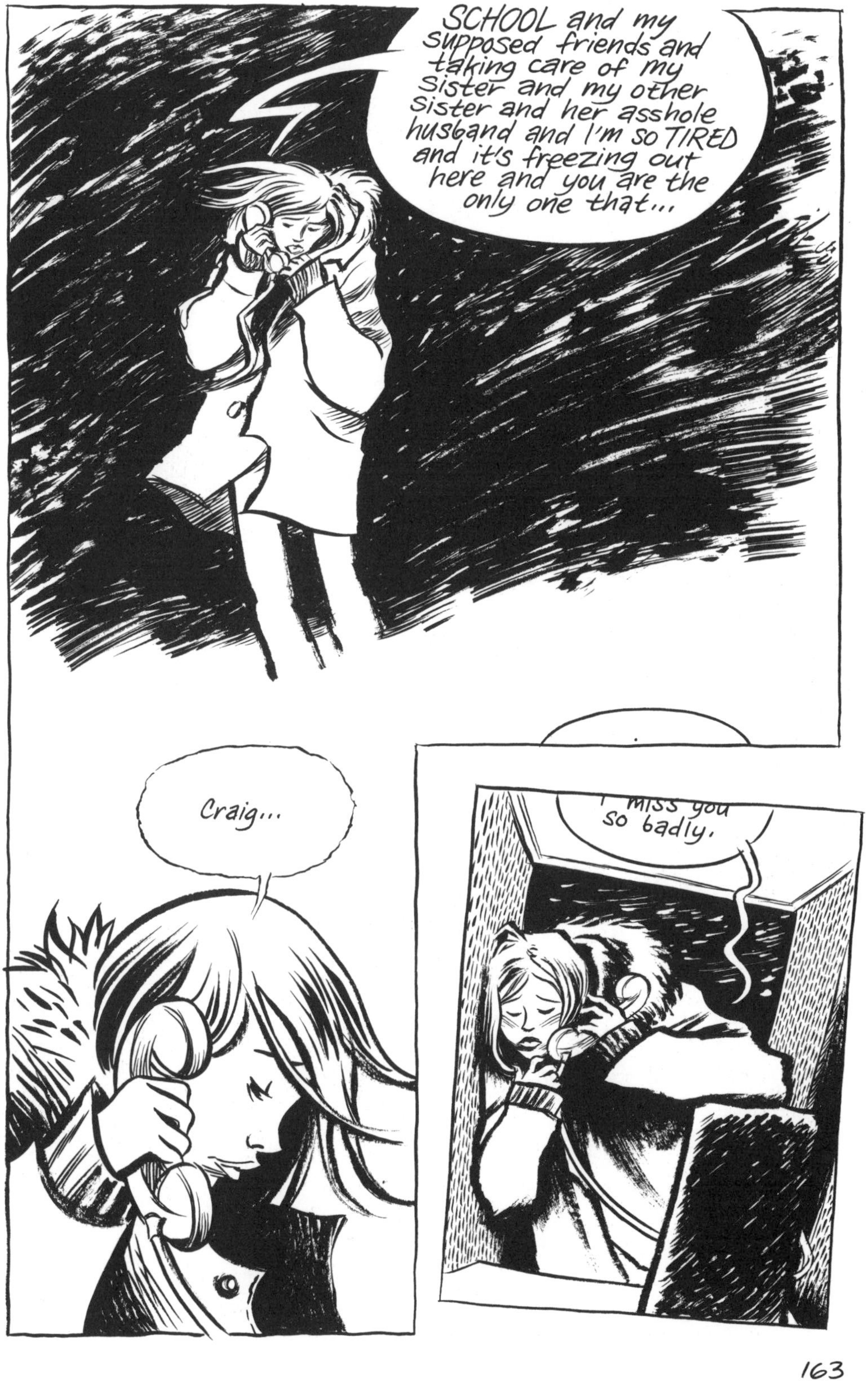
SCHOOL and my supposed friends and taking care of my sister and my other sister and her asshole husband and I'm SO TIRED and it's freezing out here and you are the only one that...
Craig...
miss you so badly.

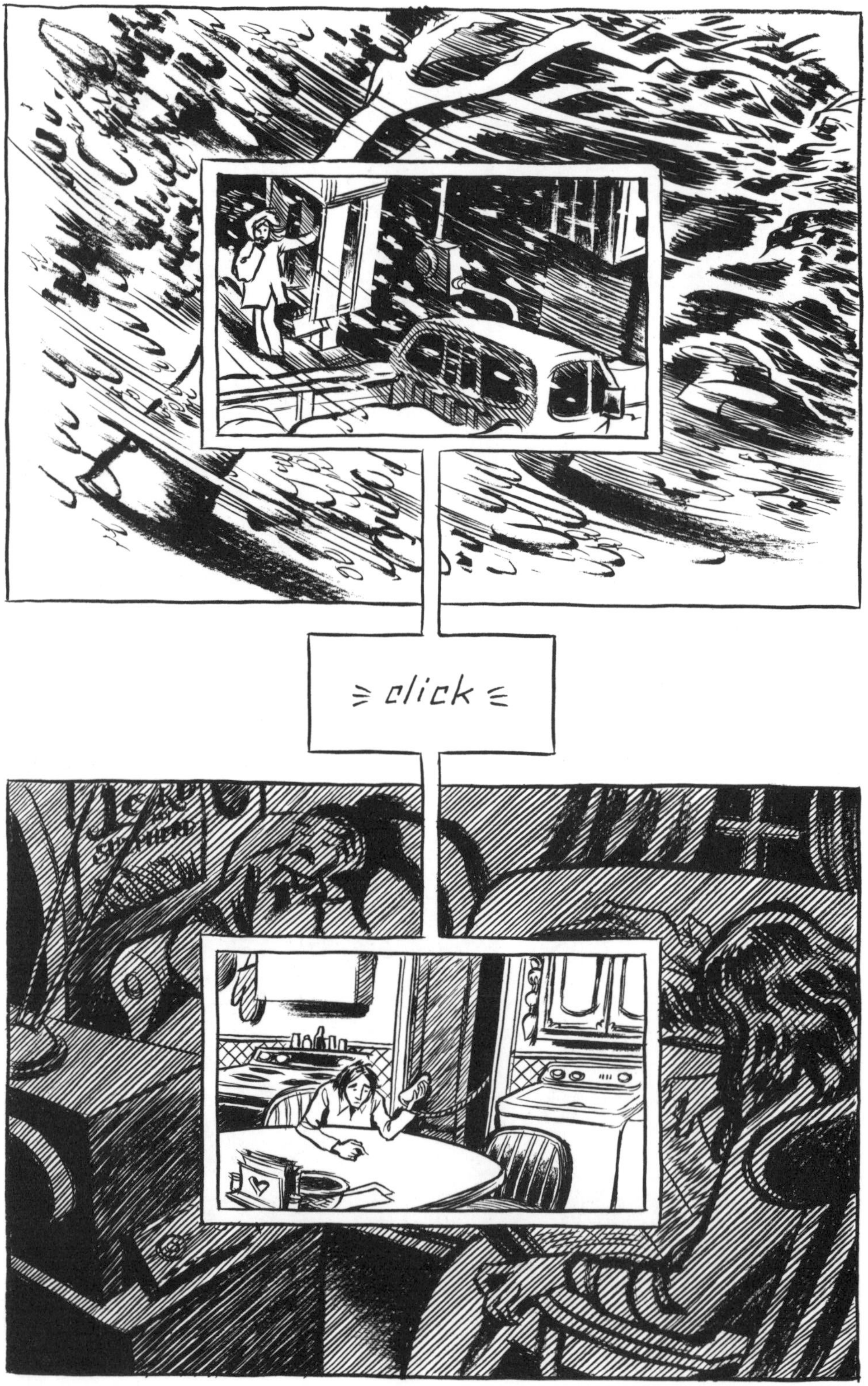
click

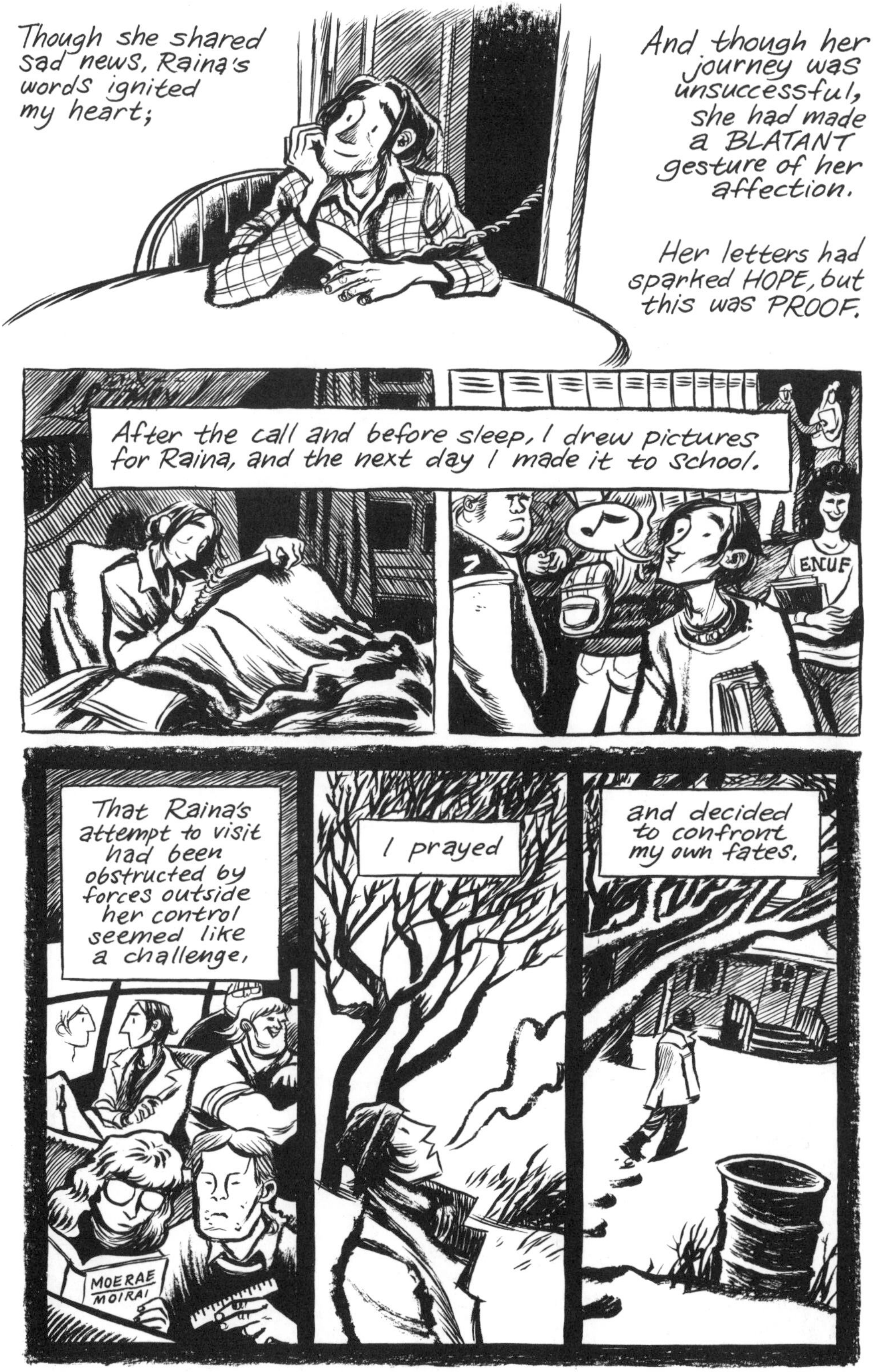
Though she shared sad news, Raina's words ignited my heart;
And though her journey was unsuccessful, she had made a BLATANT gesture of her affection.
Her letters had sparked HOPE, but this was PROOF.
After the call and before sleep, I drew pictures for Raina, and the next day I made it to school.
ENUF
That Raina's attempt to visit had been obstructed by forces outside her control seemed like a challenge,
MOERAE
MOIRAI
I prayed
and decided to confront my own fates.

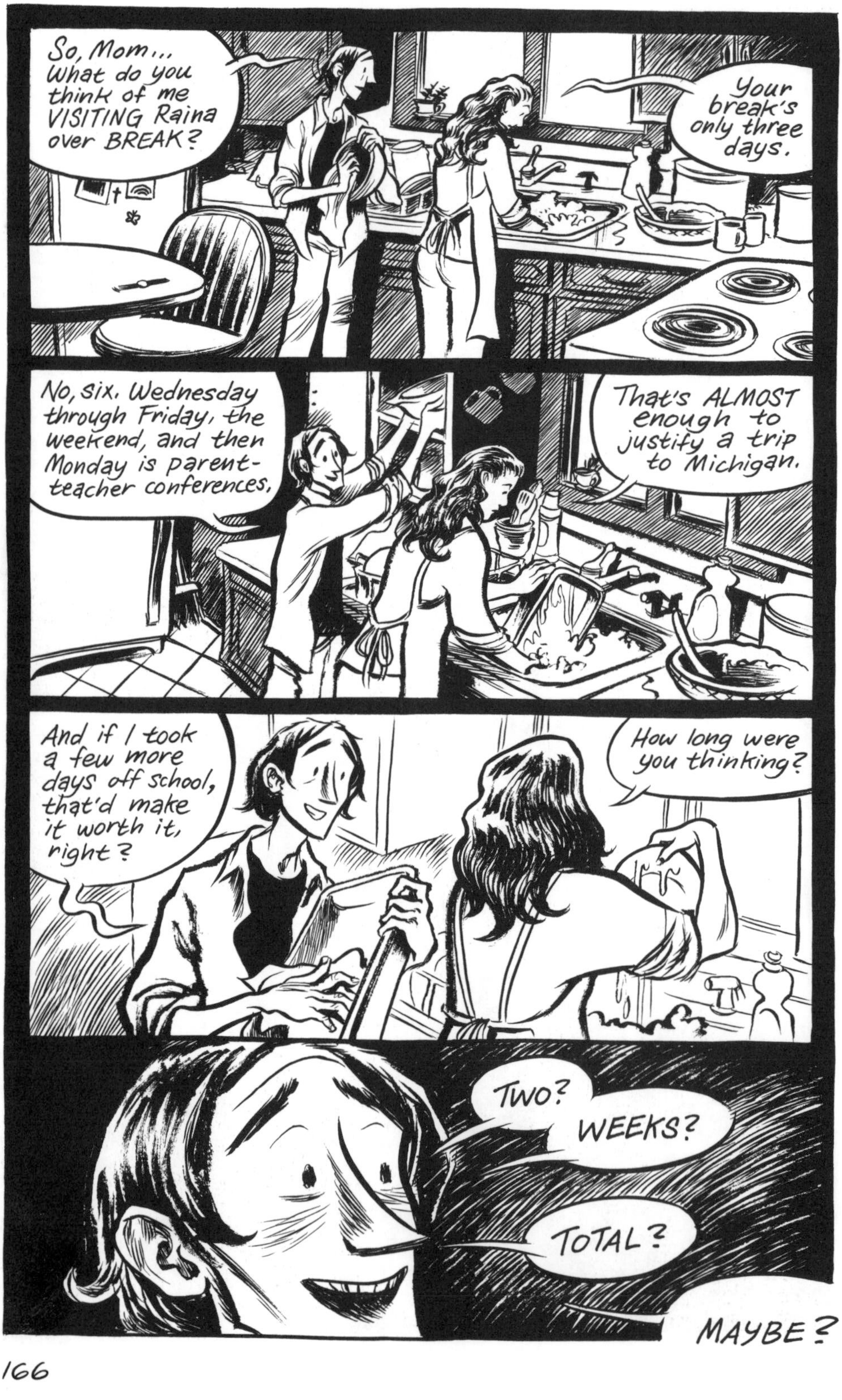
So, Mom... What do you think of me VISITING Raina over BREAK?
Your break's only three days.
No, six. Wednesday through Friday, the weekend, and then Monday is parent-teacher conferences.
That's ALMOST enough to justify a trip to Michigan.
And if I took a few more days off school, that'd make it worth it, right?
How long were you thinking?
TWO?
WEEKS?
TOTAL?
MAYBE?

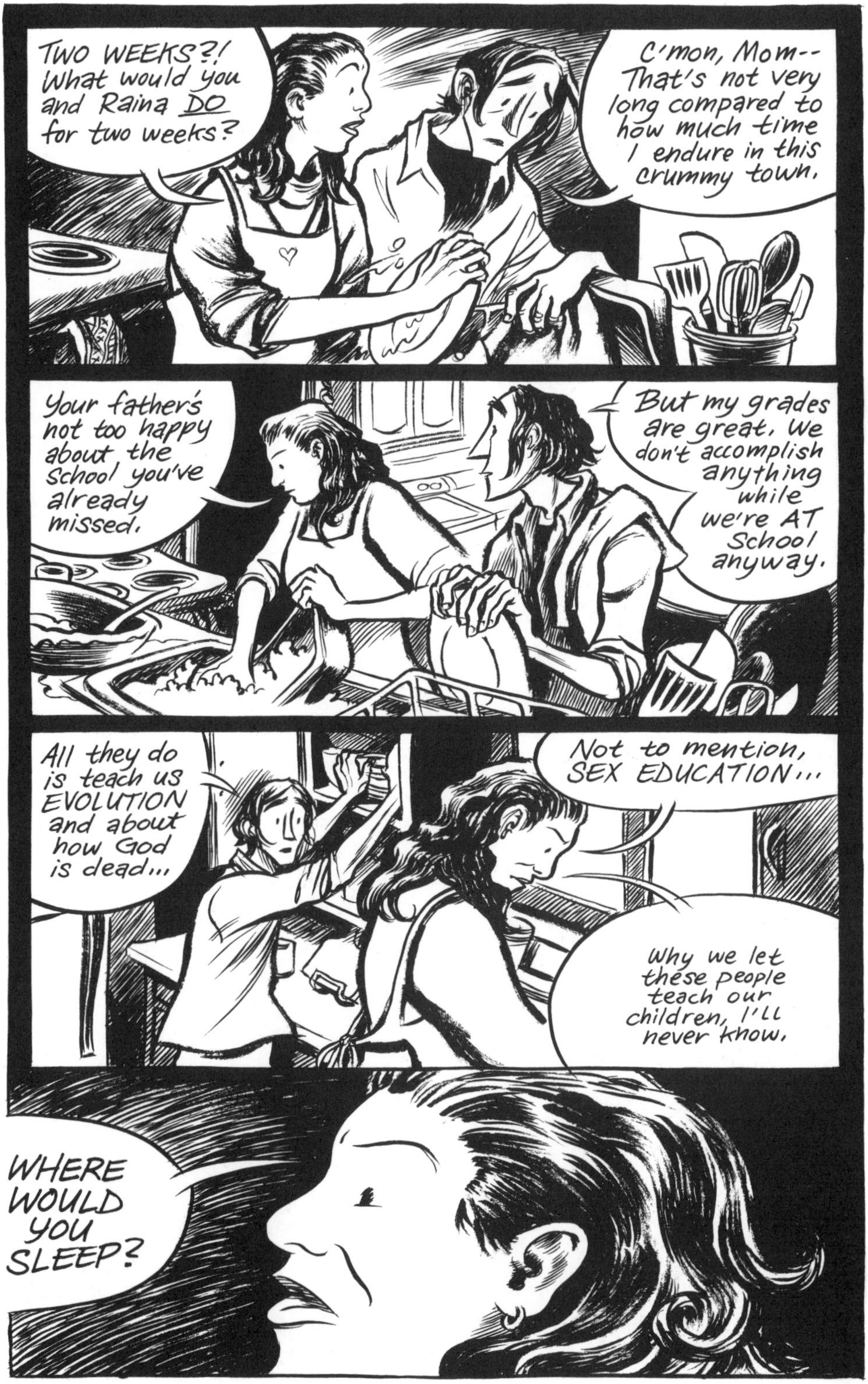
TWO WEEKS?! What would you and Raina DO for two weeks?
C'mon, Mom-- That's not very long compared to how much time I endure in this crummy town.
Your father's not too happy about the school you've already missed.
But my grades are great. We don't accomplish anything while we're AT school anyway.
All they do is teach us EVOLUTION and about how God is dead...
Not to mention, SEX EDUCATION...
Why we let these people teach our children, I'll never know.
WHERE WOULD YOU SLEEP?

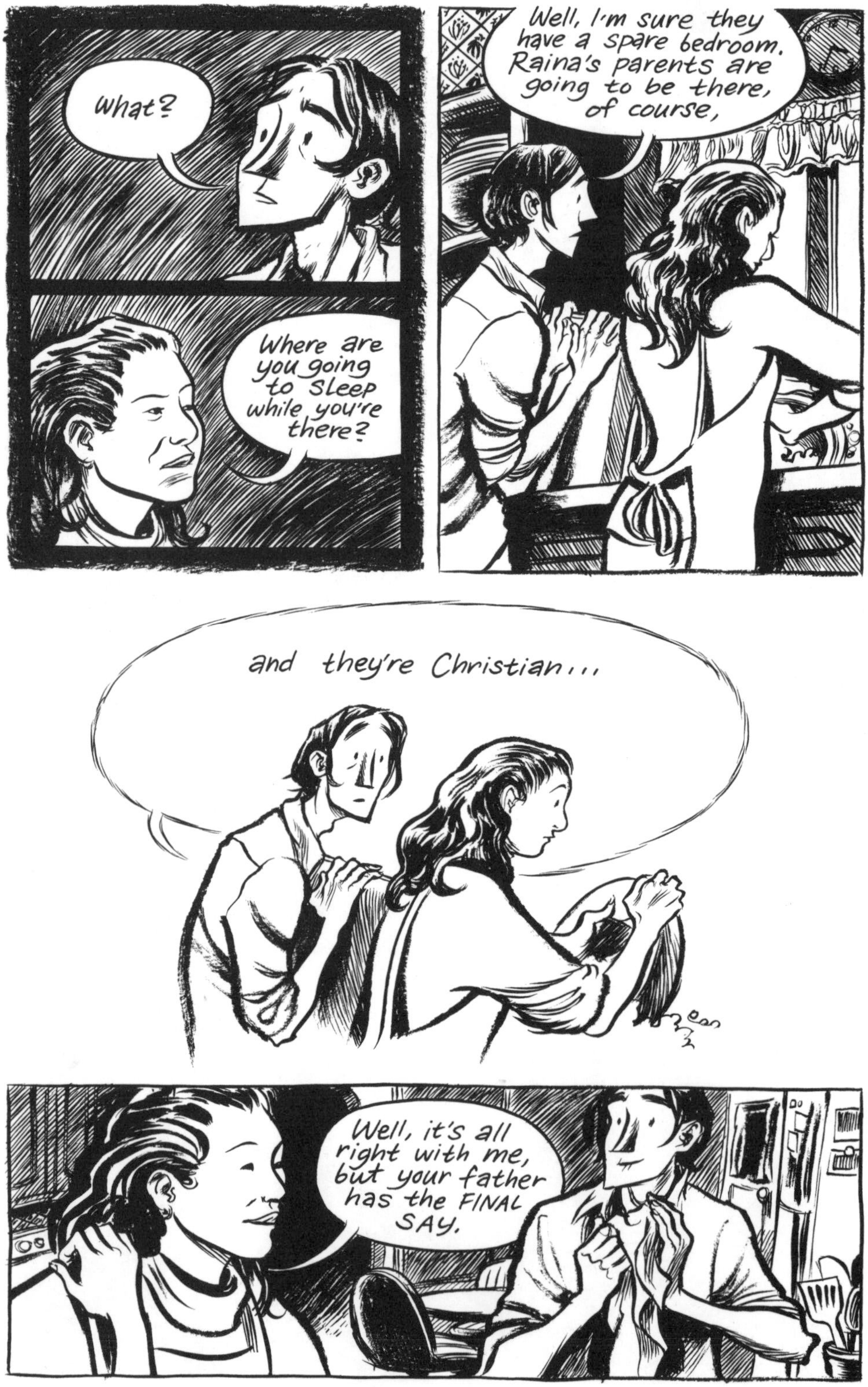
What?
Where are you going to sleep while you're there?
Well, I'm sure they have a spare bedroom. Raina's parents are going to be there, of course,
and they're Christian...
Well, it's all right with me, but your father has the FINAL SAY.

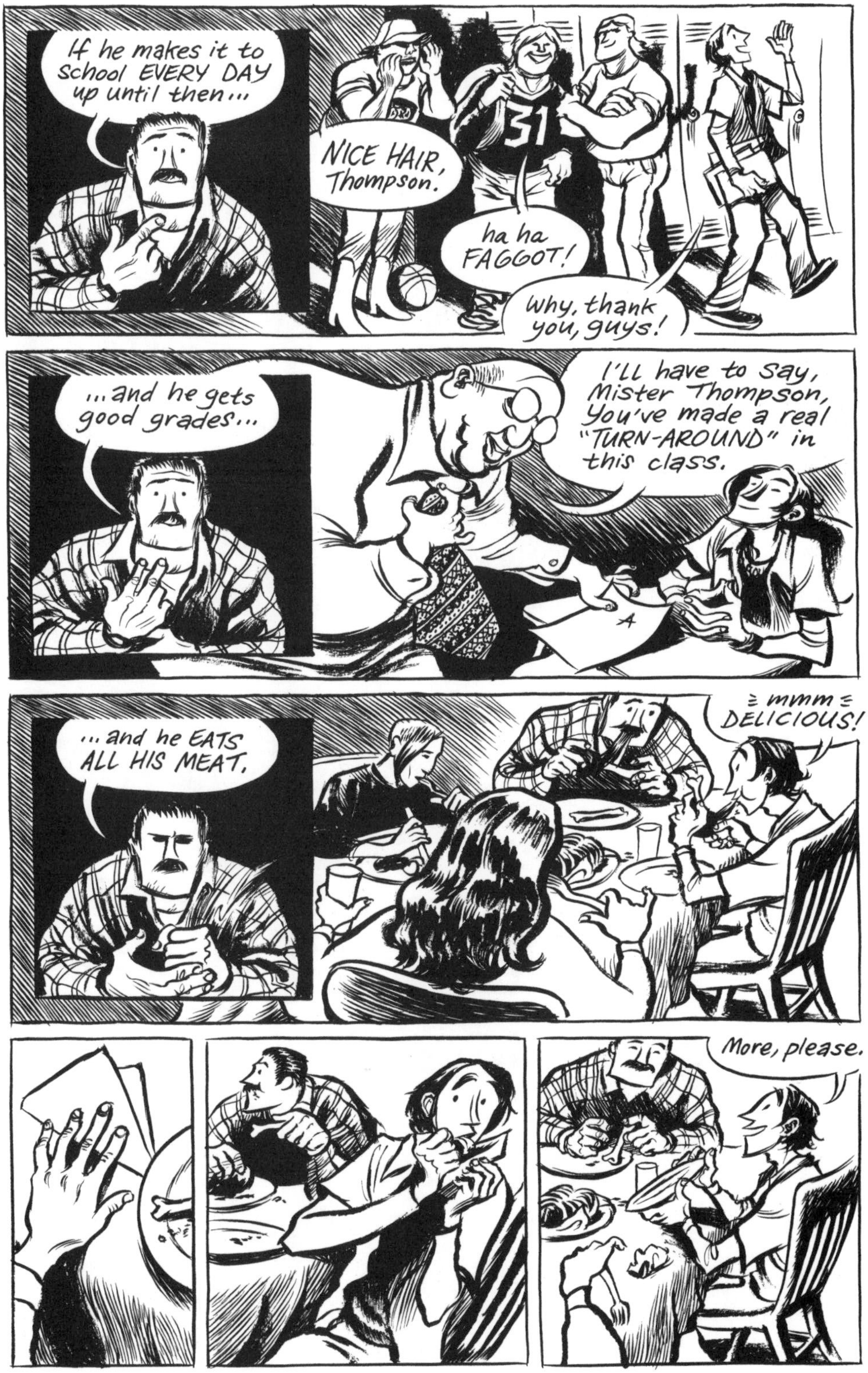
If he makes it to school EVERY DAY up until then...
NICE HAIR, Thompson.
ha ha FAGGOT!
Why, thank you, guys!
...and he gets good grades...
I'll have to say, Mister Thompson, You've made a real "TURN-AROUND" in this class.
A
...and he EATS ALL HIS MEAT.
mmm DELICIOUS!
More, please.

My mother drove me; her father drove her; and we planned to meet HALF-WAY, at the border of Wisconsin and Michigan.

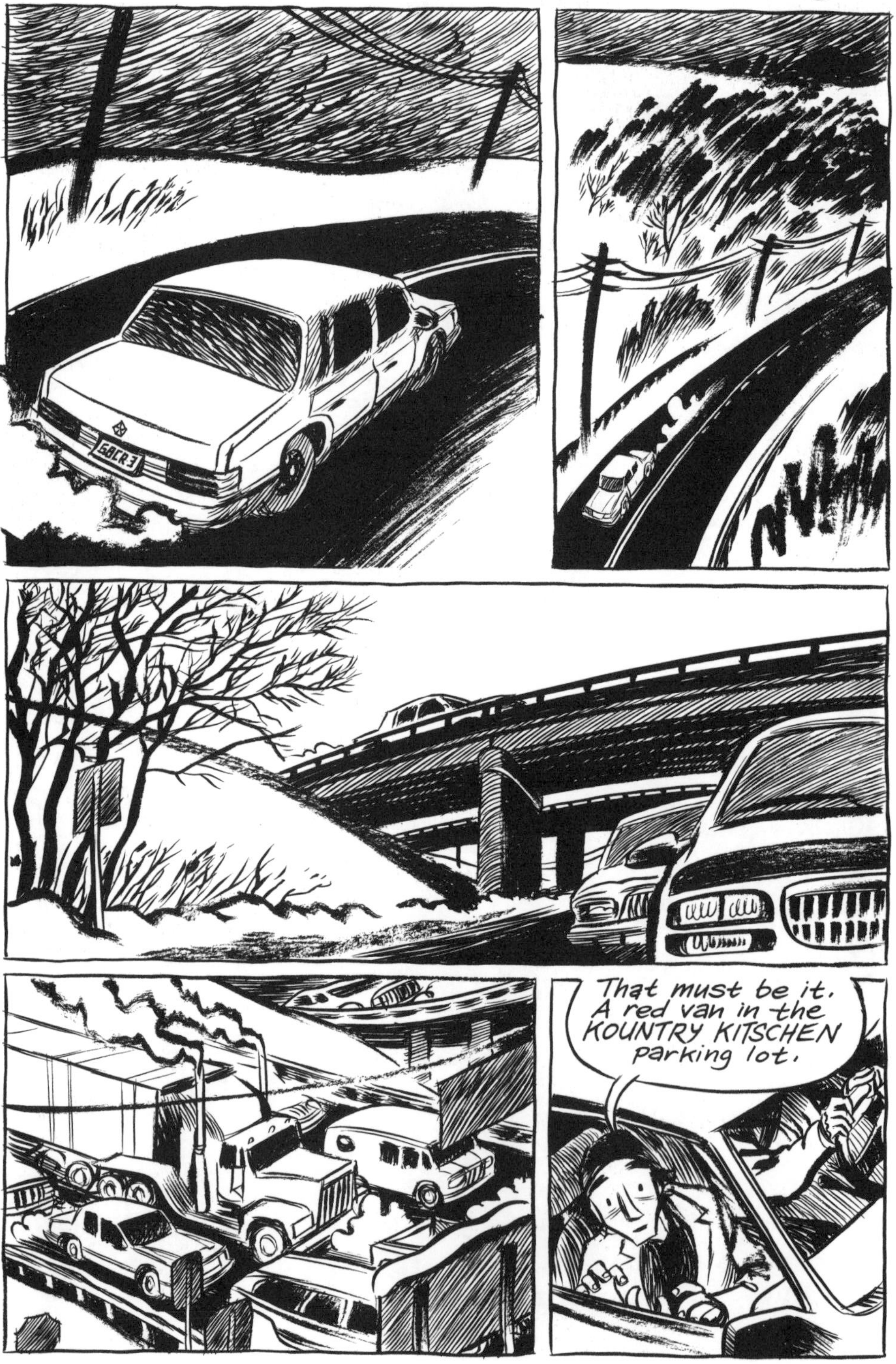
That must be it. A red van in the KOUNTRY KITSCHEN parking lot.

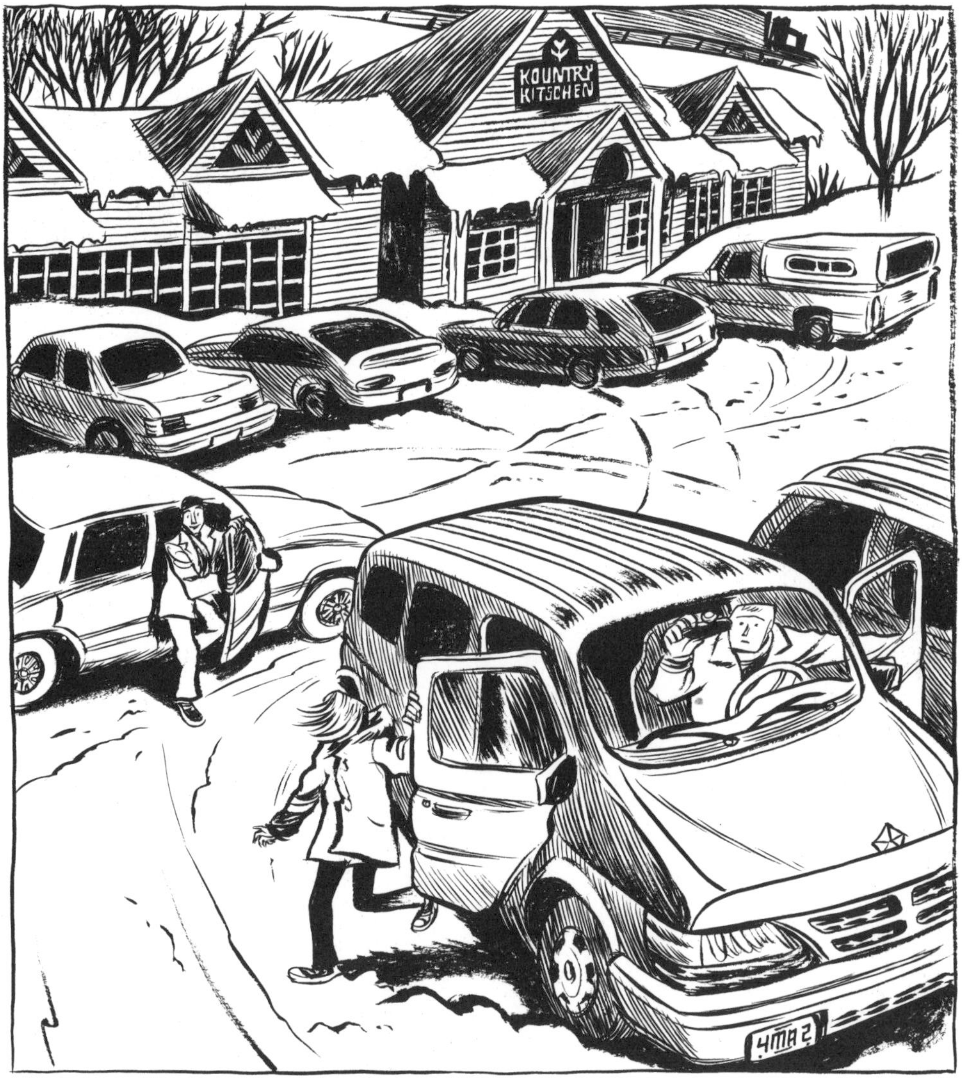
KOUNTRY
KITSCHEN
4MA2

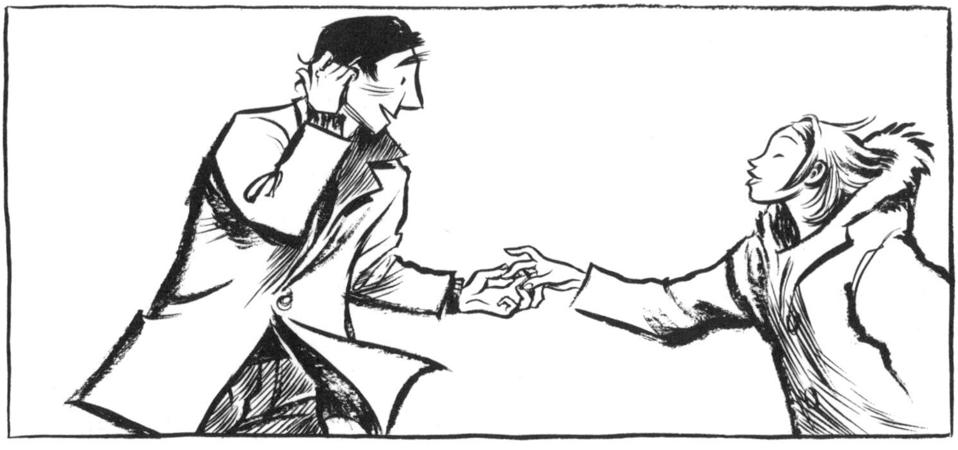

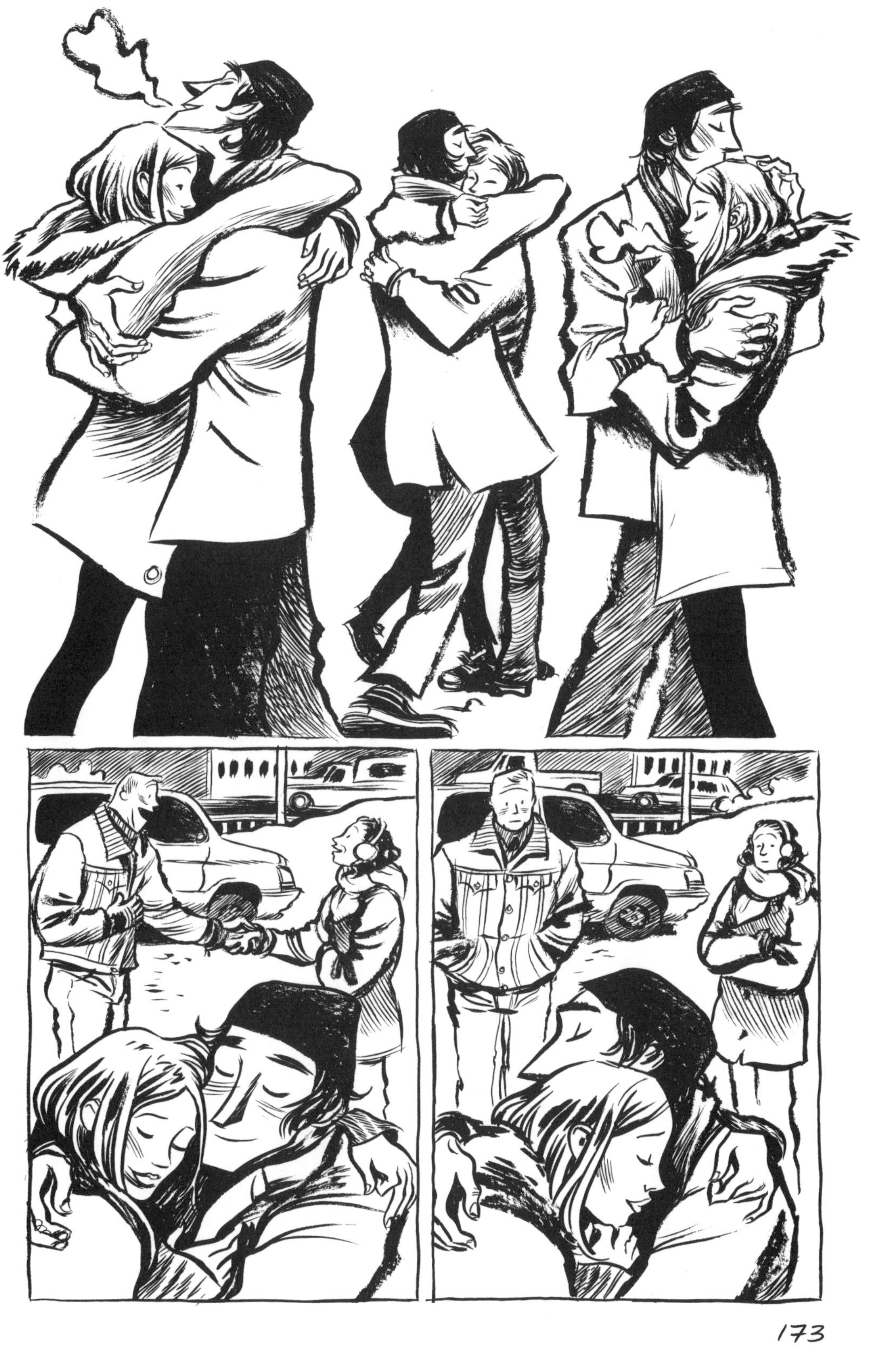

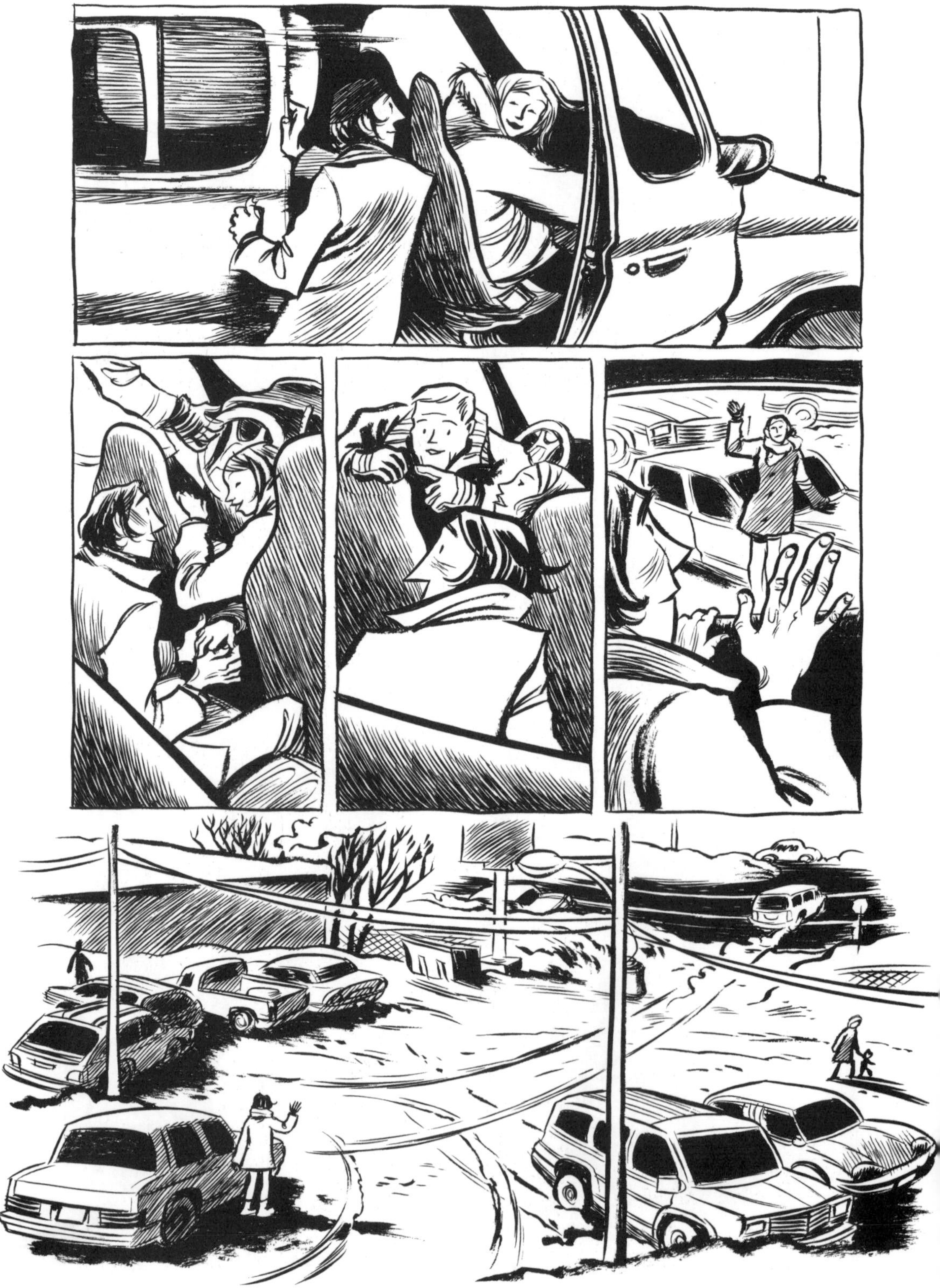

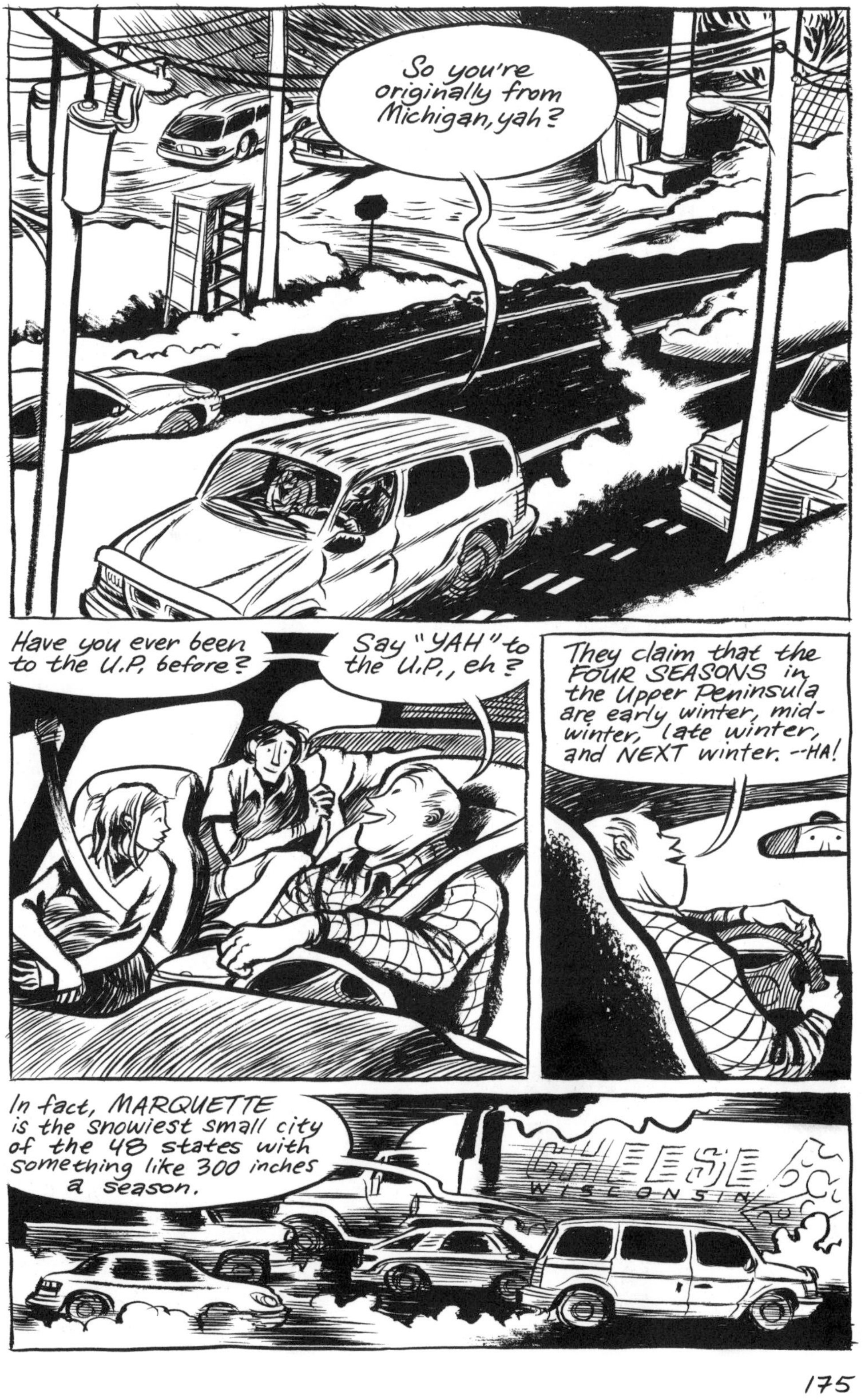
So you're originally from Michigan, yah?
Have you ever been to the U.P. before?
Say "YAH" to the U.P., eh?
They claim that the FOUR SEASONS in the Upper Peninsula are early winter, mid-winter, late winter, and NEXT winter. --HA!
In fact, MARQUETTE is the snowiest small city of the 48 states with something like 300 inches a season.
CHEESE
WISCONSIN

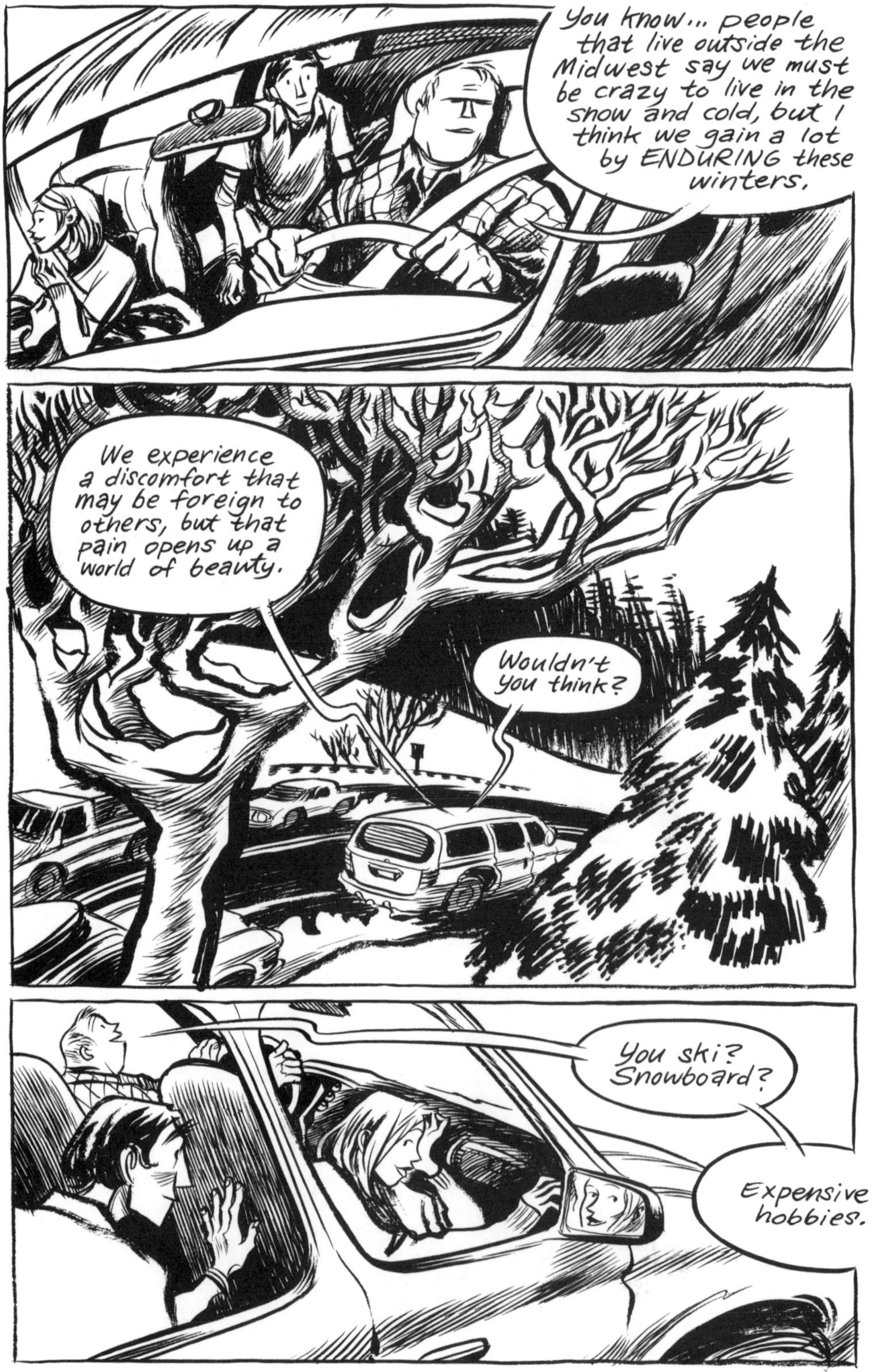
You know... people that live outside the Midwest say we must be crazy to live in the snow and cold, but I think we gain a lot by ENDURING these winters.
We experience a discomfort that may be foreign to others, but that pain opens up a world of beauty.
Wouldn't you think?
You ski? Snowboard?
Expensive hobbies.

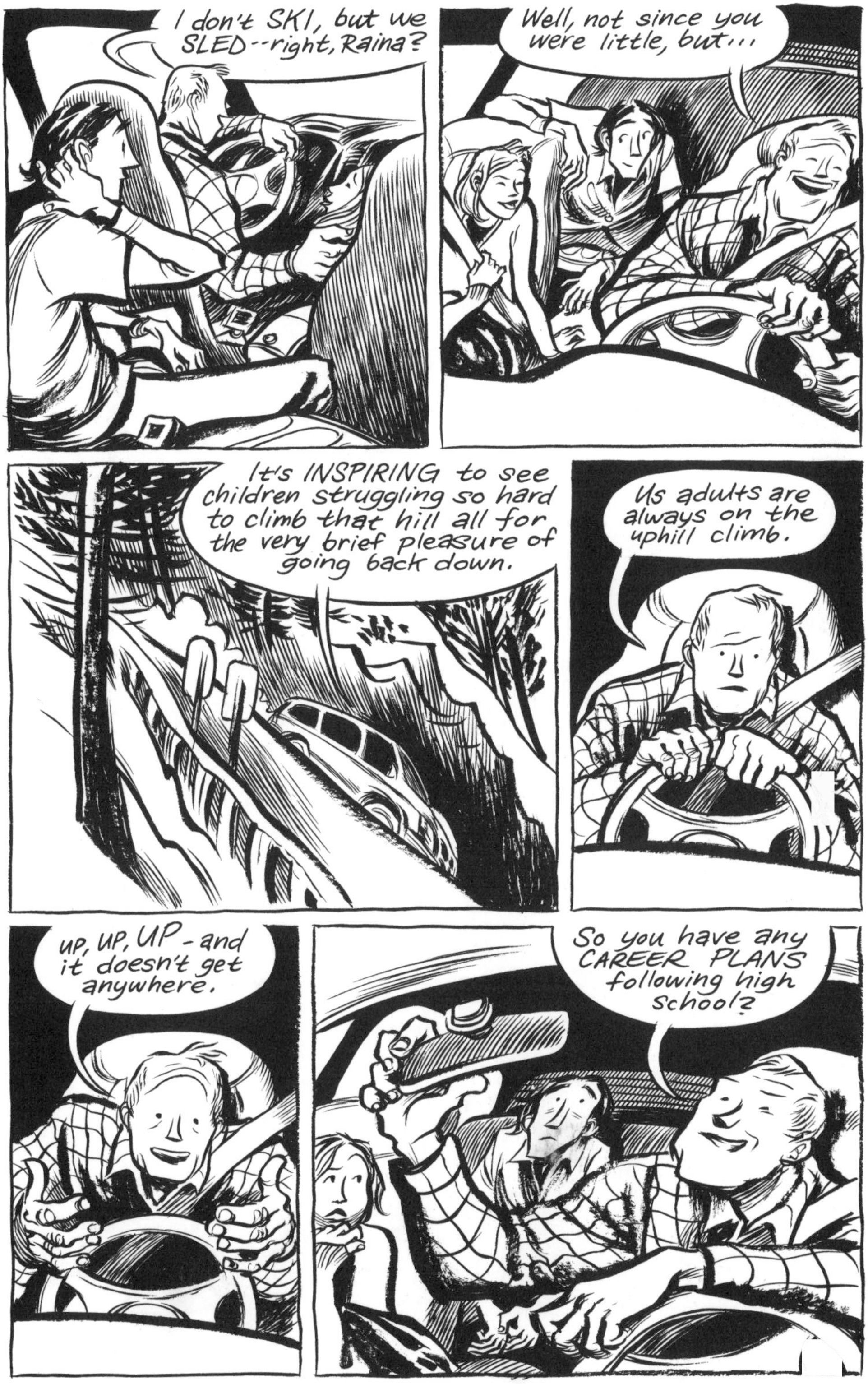
I don't SKI, but we SLED--right, Raina?
Well, not since you were little, but...
It's INSPIRING to see children struggling so hard to climb that hill all for the very brief pleasure of going back down.
Us adults are always on the uphill climb.
up, up, UP - and it doesn't get anywhere.
So you have any CAREER PLANS following high school?

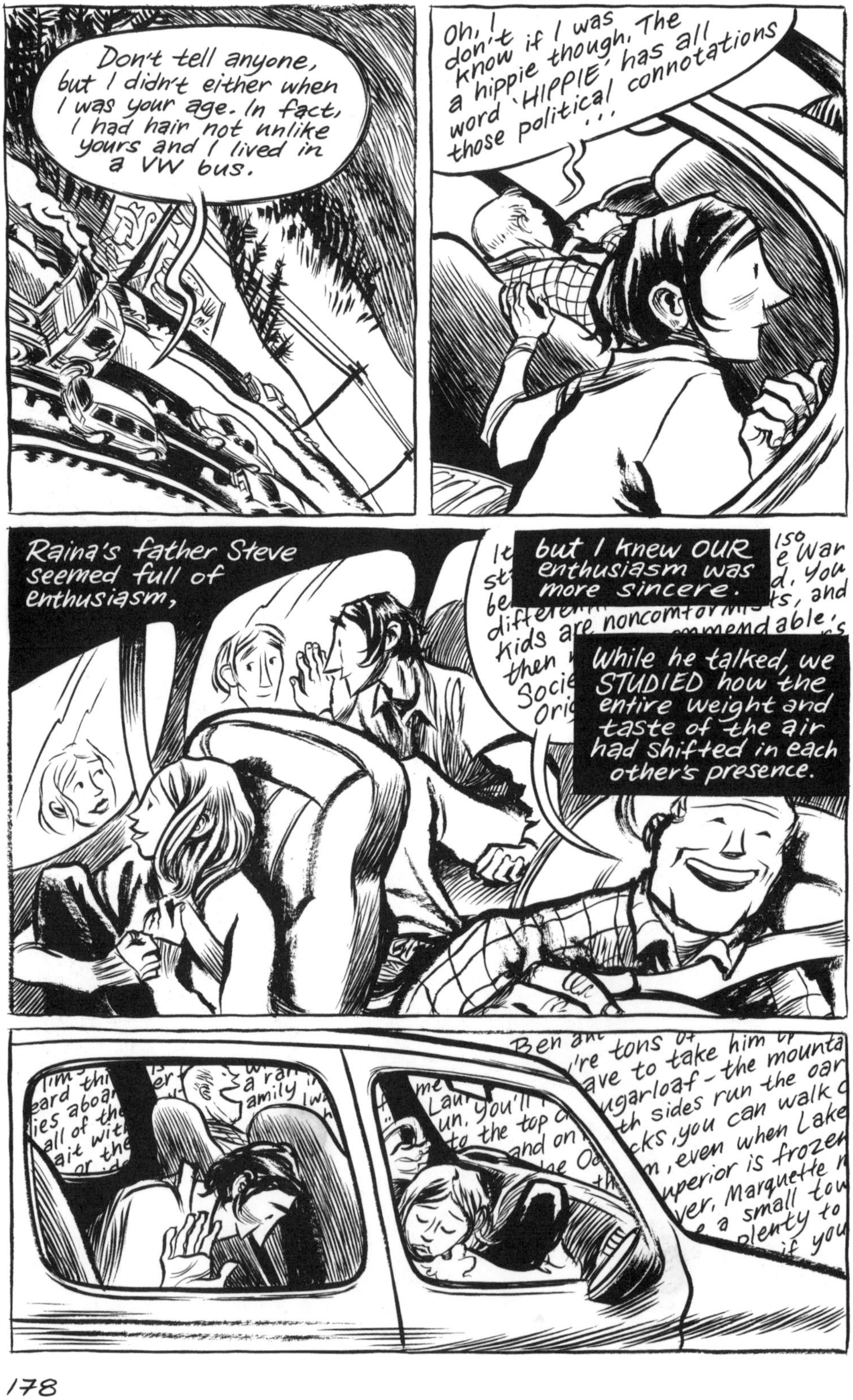
Don't tell anyone, but I didn't either when I was your age. In fact, I had hair not unlike yours and I lived in a VW bus.
Oh, I don't know if I was a hippie though. The word 'HIPPIE' has all those political connotations . . .
Raina's father Steve seemed full of enthusiasm,
but I knew OUR enthusiasm was more sincere.
While he talked, we STUDIED how the entire weight and taste of the air had shifted in each other's presence.

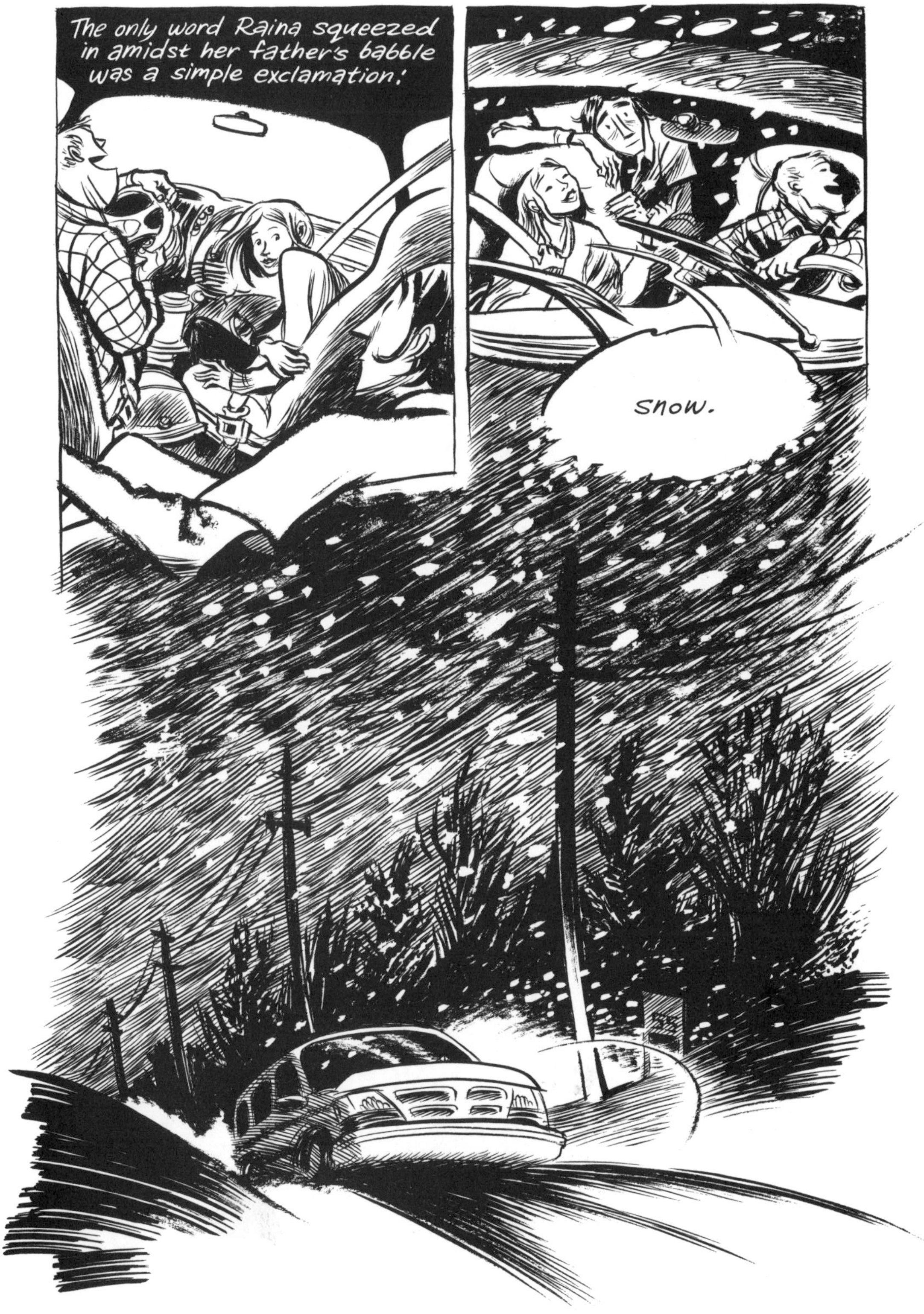
The only word Raina squeezed in amidst her father's babble was a simple exclamation:
Snow.

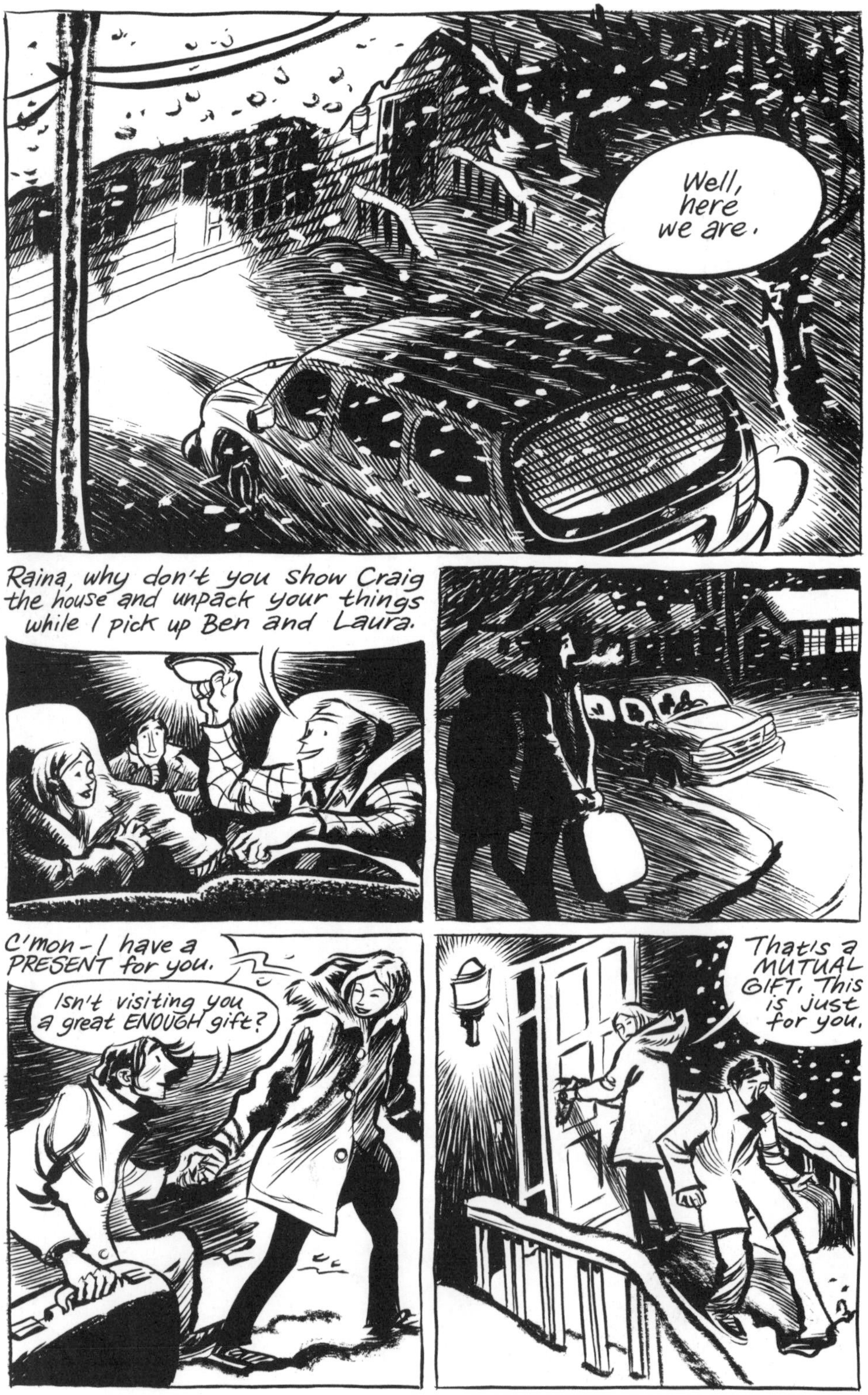
Well, here we are.
Raina, why don't you show Craig the house and unpack your things while I pick up Ben and Laura.
C'mon-I have a PRESENT for you.
Isn't visiting you a great ENOUGH gift?
That's a MUTUAL GIFT, This is just for you.

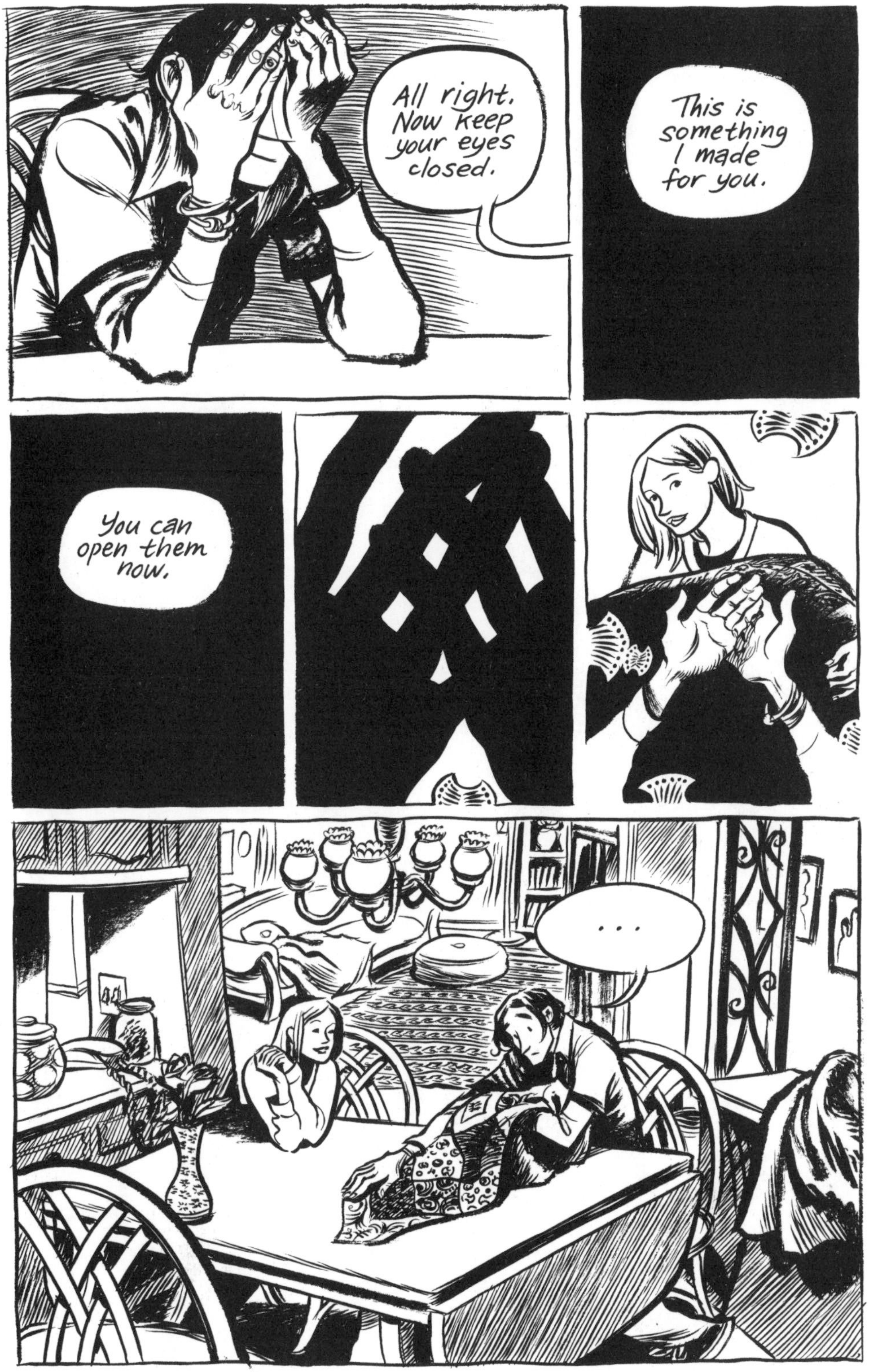
All right. Now keep your eyes closed.
This is something I made for you.
You can open them now.
. . .

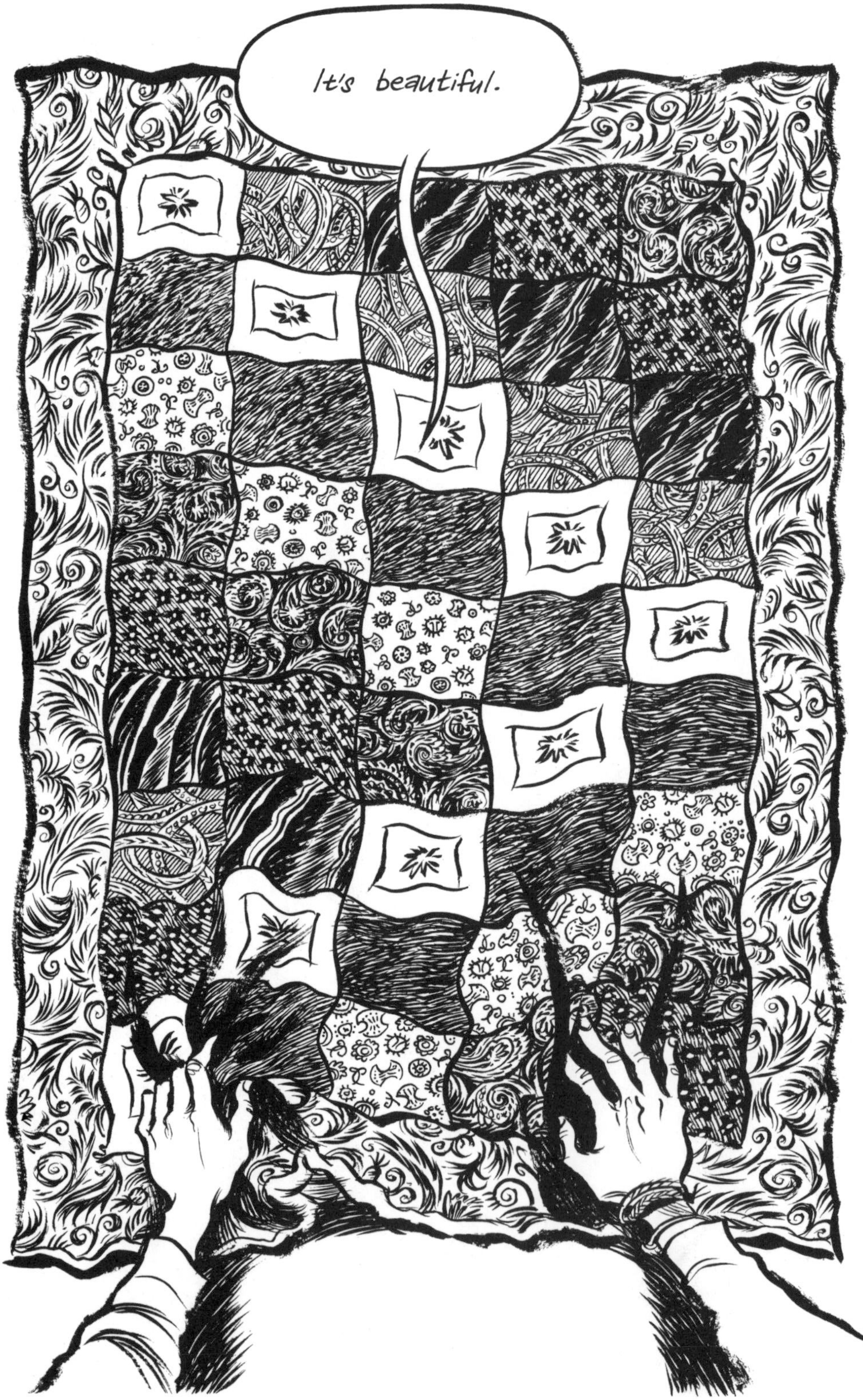
It's beautiful.

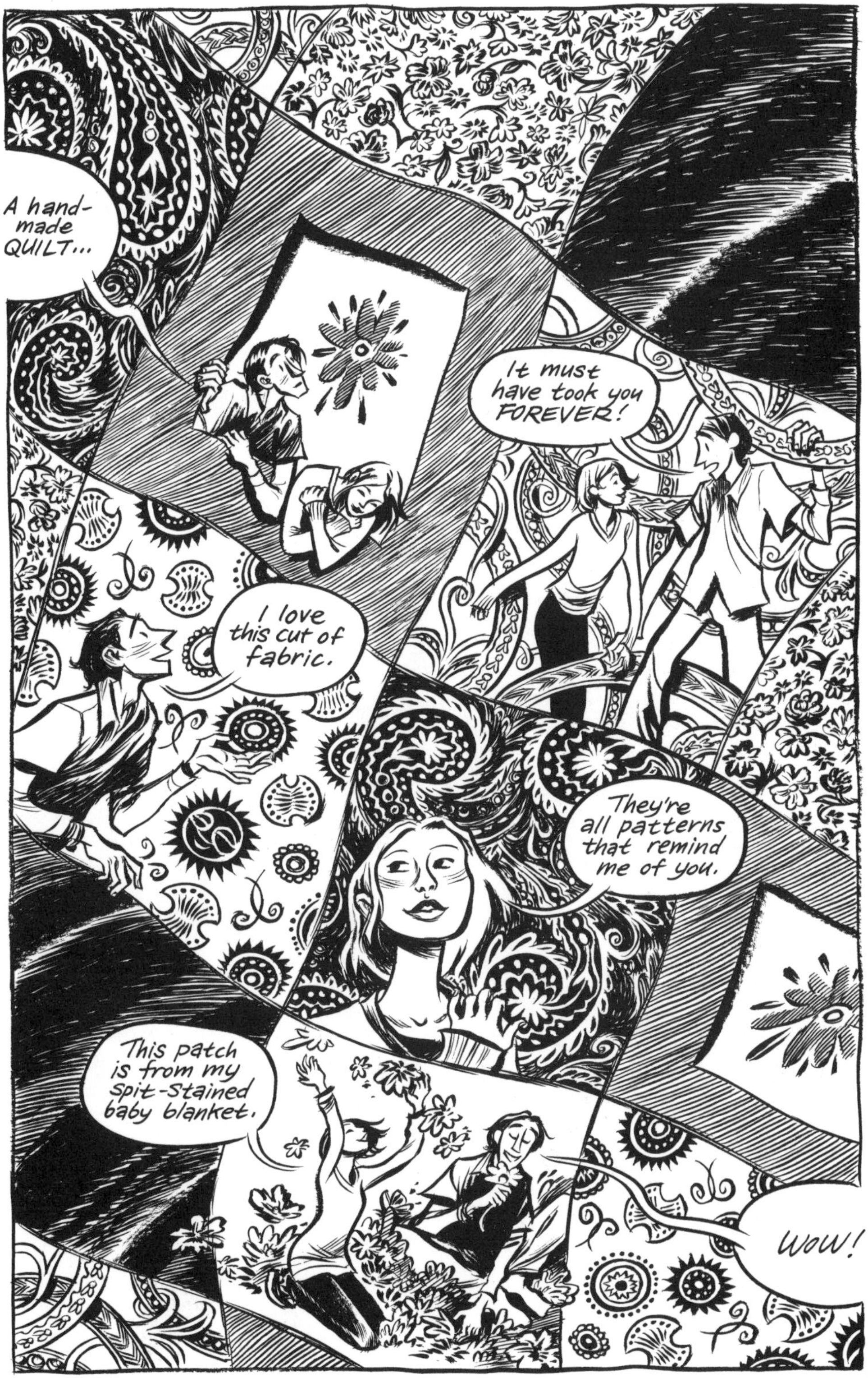
A hand-made QUILT...
It must have took you FOREVER!
I love this cut of fabric.
They're all patterns that remind me of you.
This patch is from my spit-stained baby blanket.
WOW!

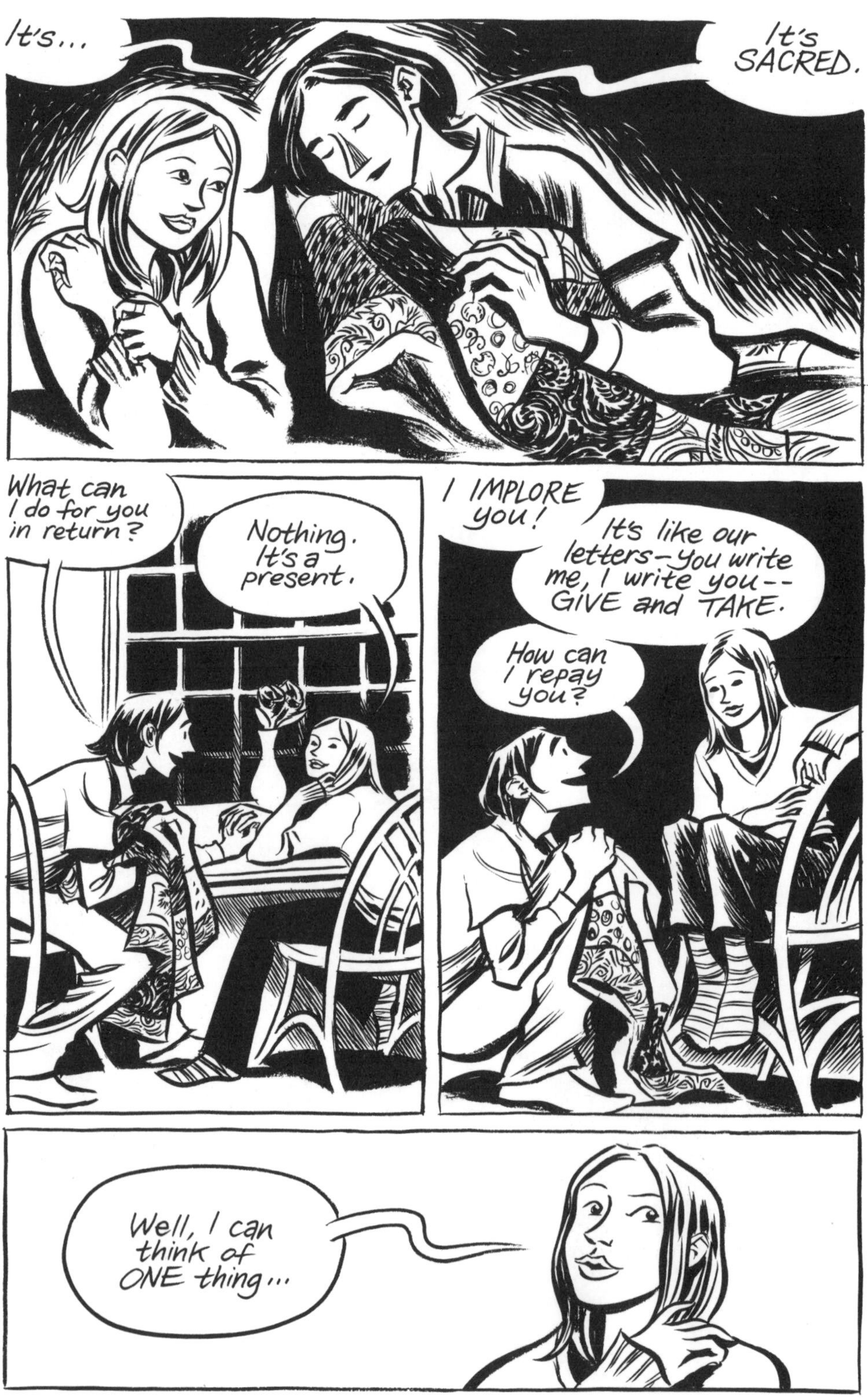
It's...
It's SACRED.
What can I do for you in return?
Nothing. It's a present.
I IMPLORE you!
It's like our letters--you write me, I write you-- GIVE and TAKE.
How can I repay you?
Well, I can think of ONE thing...

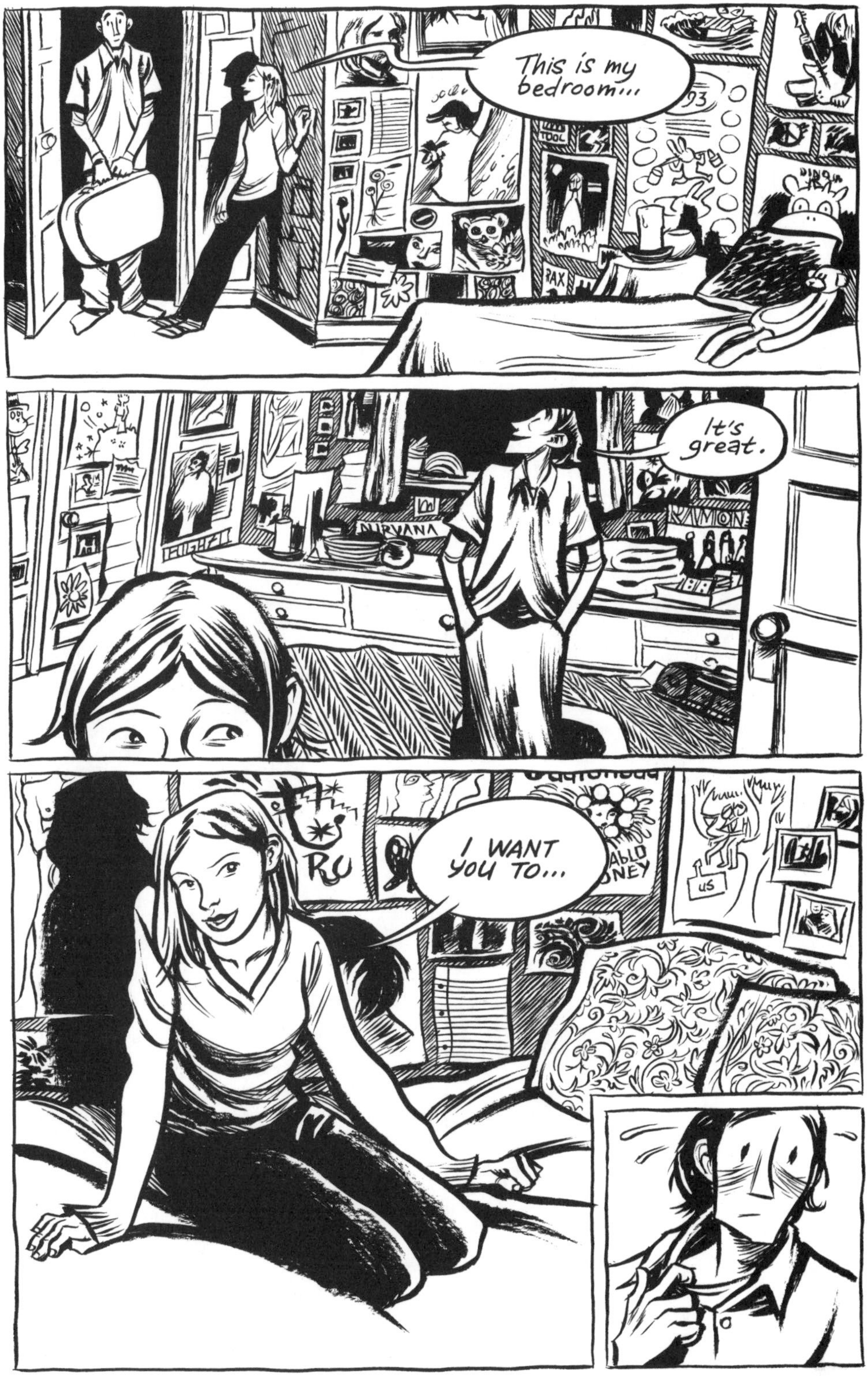
This is my bedroom...
It's great.
I WANT YOU TO...

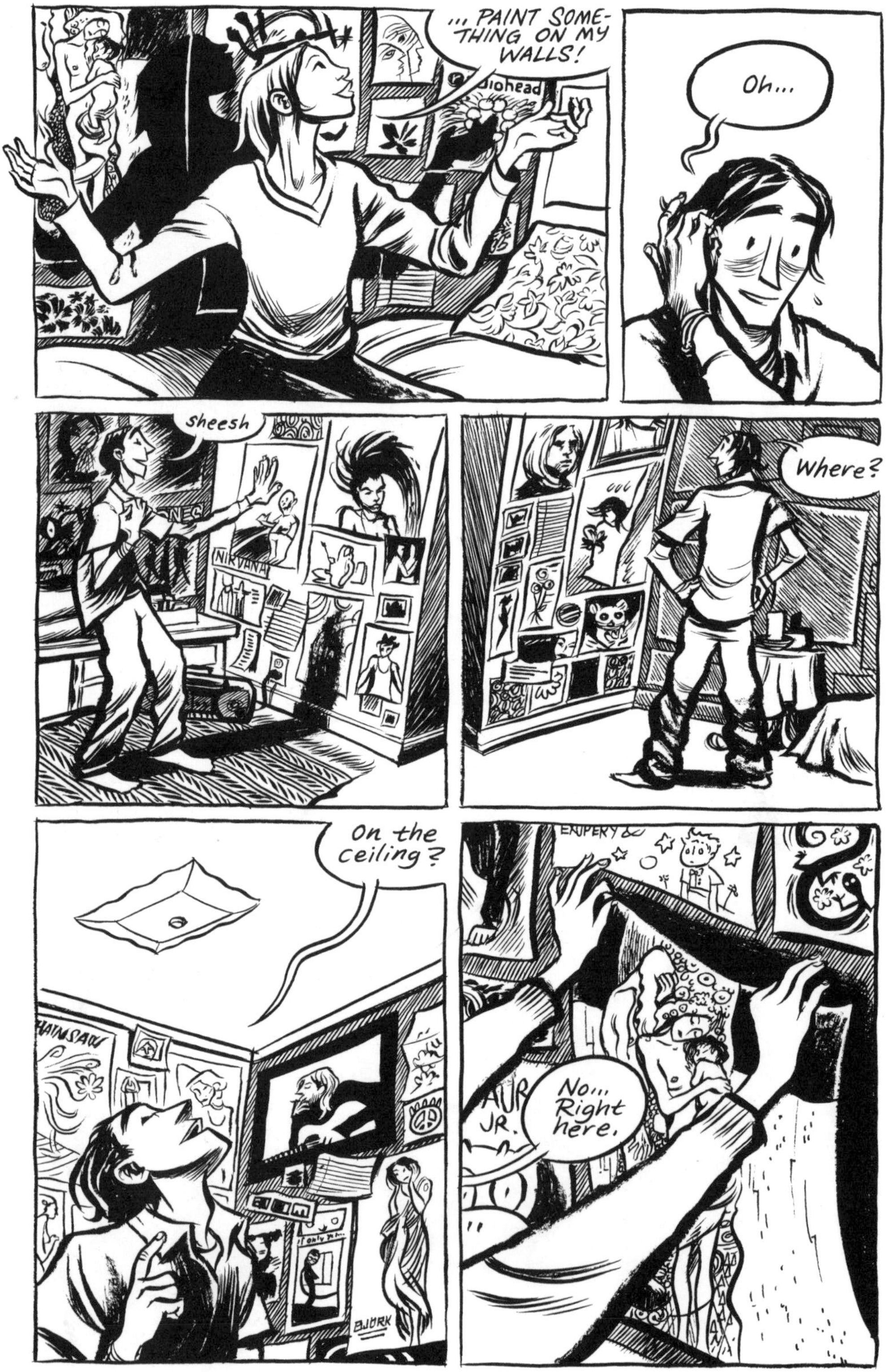
...PAINT SOME-THING ON MY WALLS!
Radiohead
Oh...
sheesh
NIRVANA
Where?
On the ceiling?
CHAINSAW
BJÖRK
EXUPERY
No... Right here.
DINOSAUR JR.

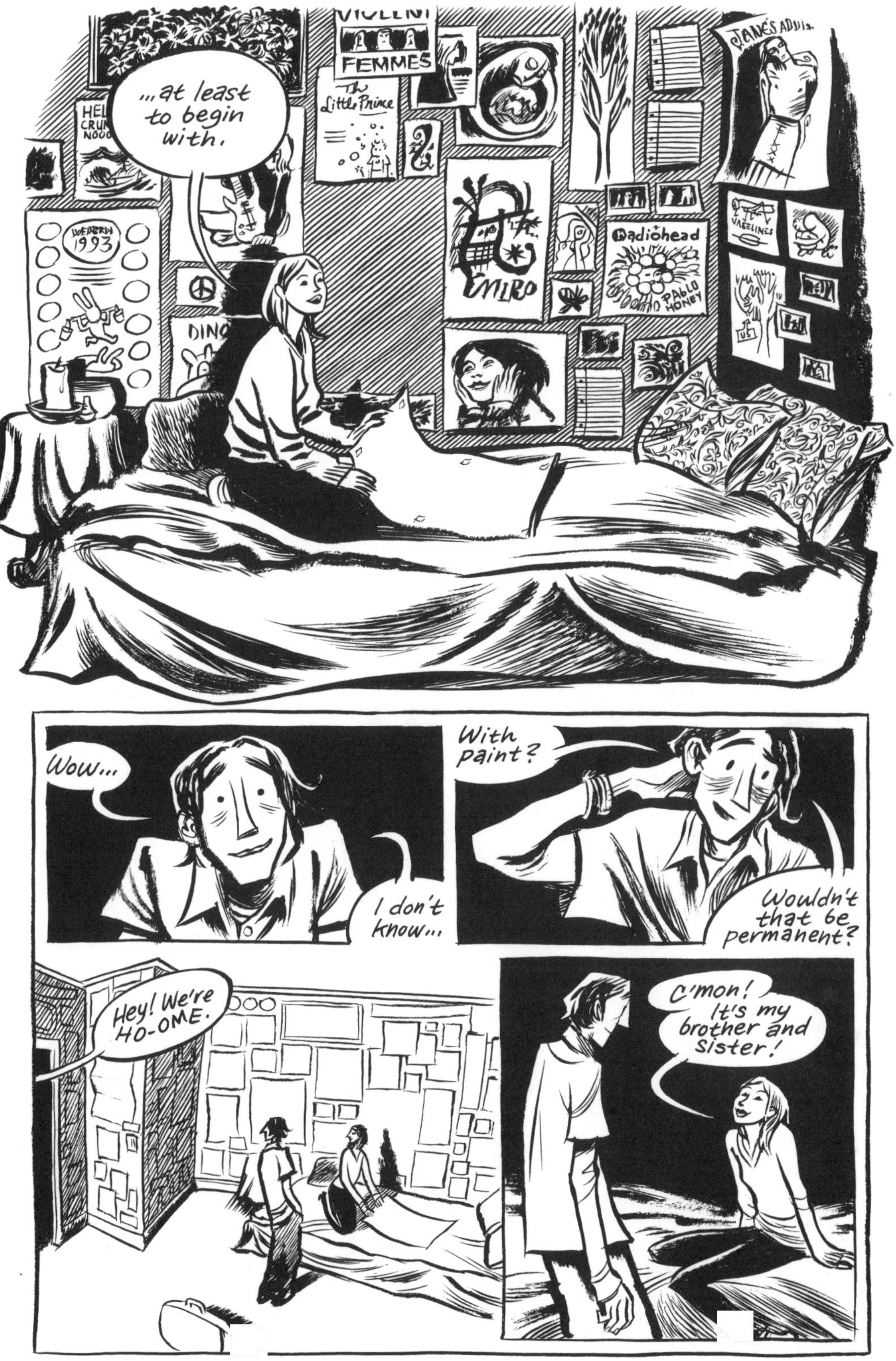
FEMMES
The Little Prince
MIRO
Radiohead
PABLO HONEY
1993
...at least to begin with.
Wow...
I don't know...
With paint?
Wouldn't that be permanent?
Hey! We're HO-OME.
C'mon! It's my brother and sister!

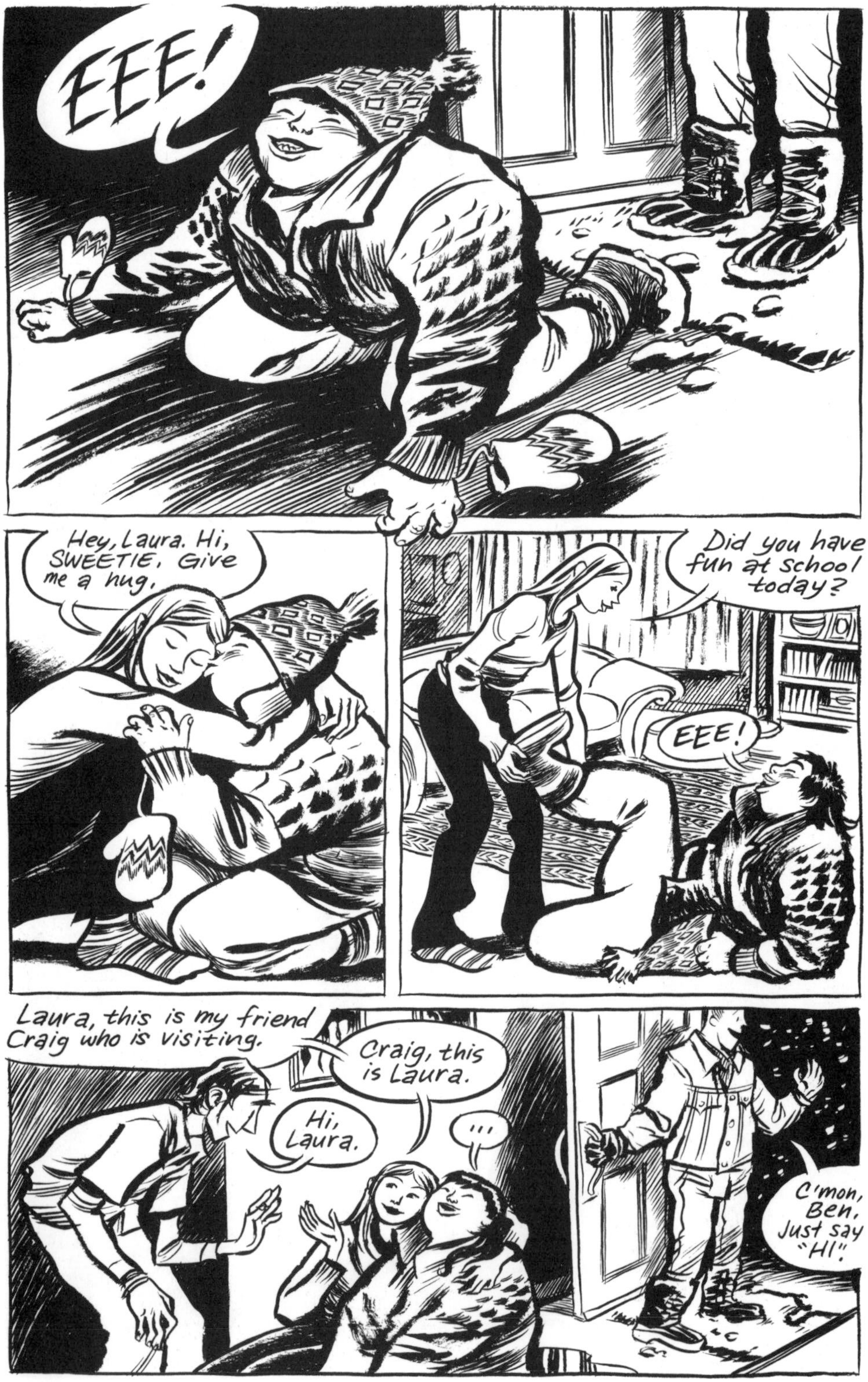
EEE!
Hey, Laura. Hi, SWEETIE, Give me a hug.
Did you have fun at school today?
EEE!
Laura, this is my friend Craig who is visiting.
Craig, this is Laura.
Hi, Laura.
...
C'mon, Ben, Just say "HI".

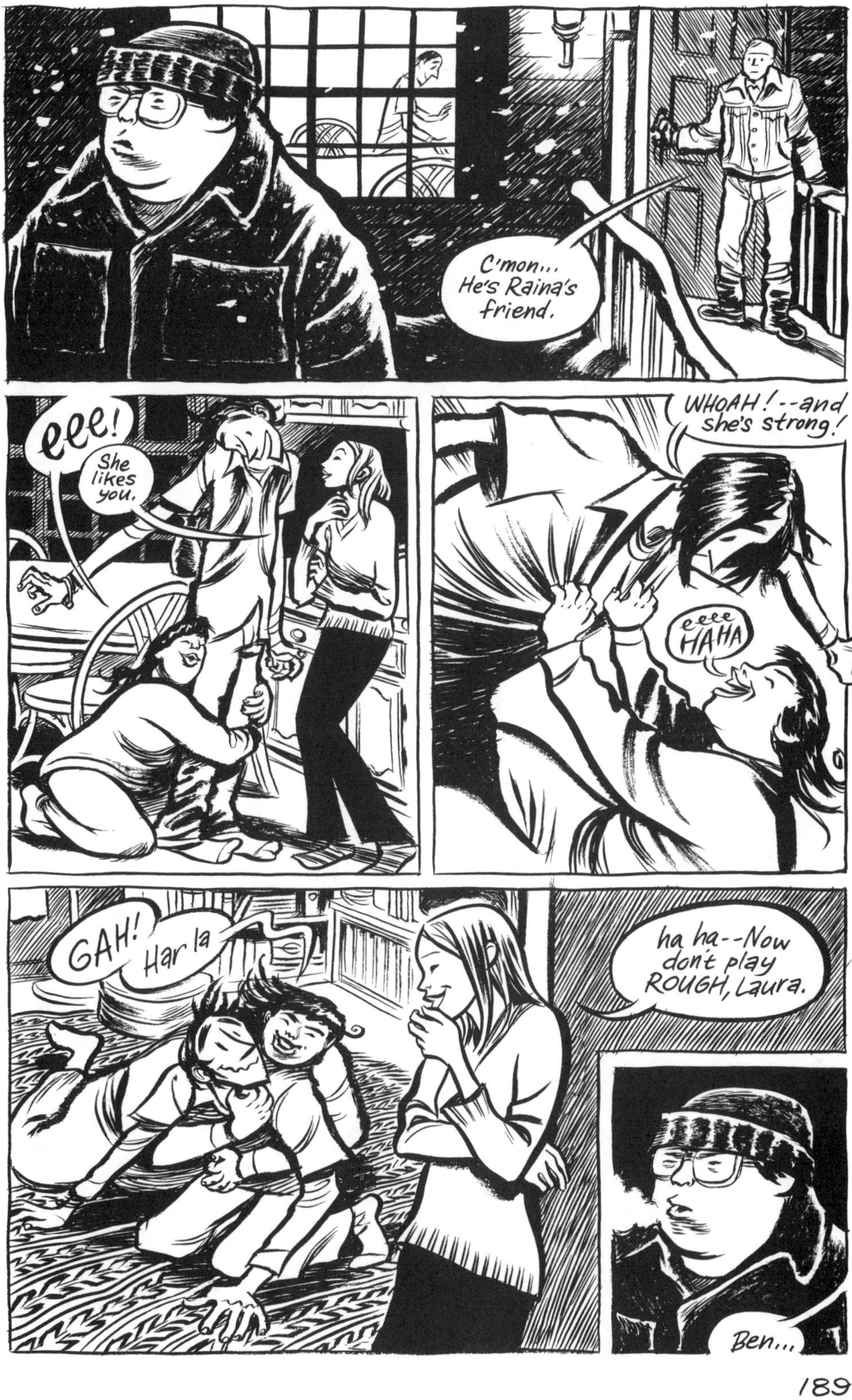
C'mon... He's Raina's friend.
eee!
She likes you.
WHOAH! --and she's strong!
eeee HAHA
GAH!
Har la
ha ha--Now don't play ROUGH, Laura.
Ben...

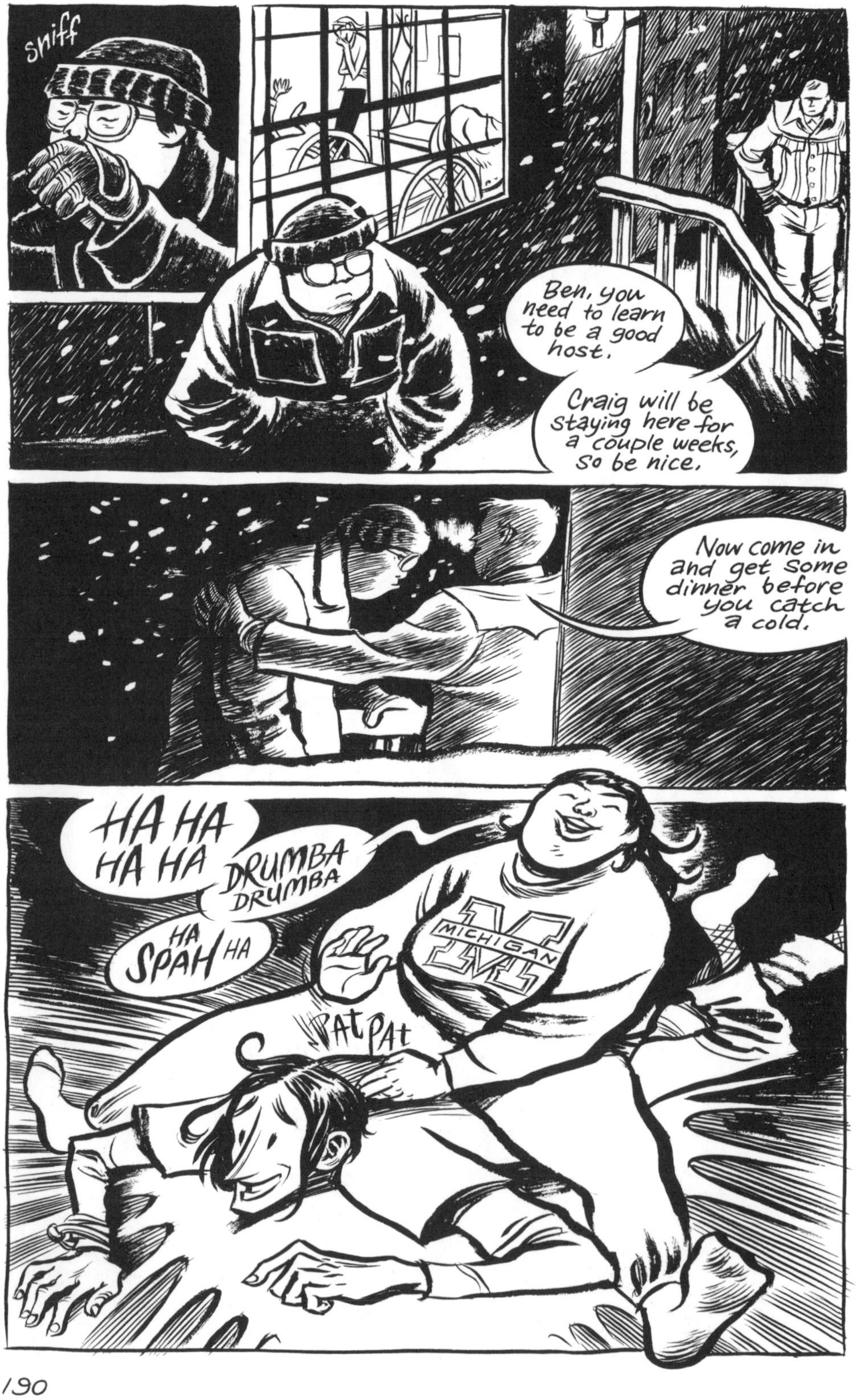

sniff
Ben, you need to learn to be a good host.
Craig will be staying here for a couple weeks, so be nice.
Now come in and get some dinner before you catch a cold.
HA HA HA HA
DRUMBA DRUMBA
HA SPAH HA
PAT PAT
MICHIGAN

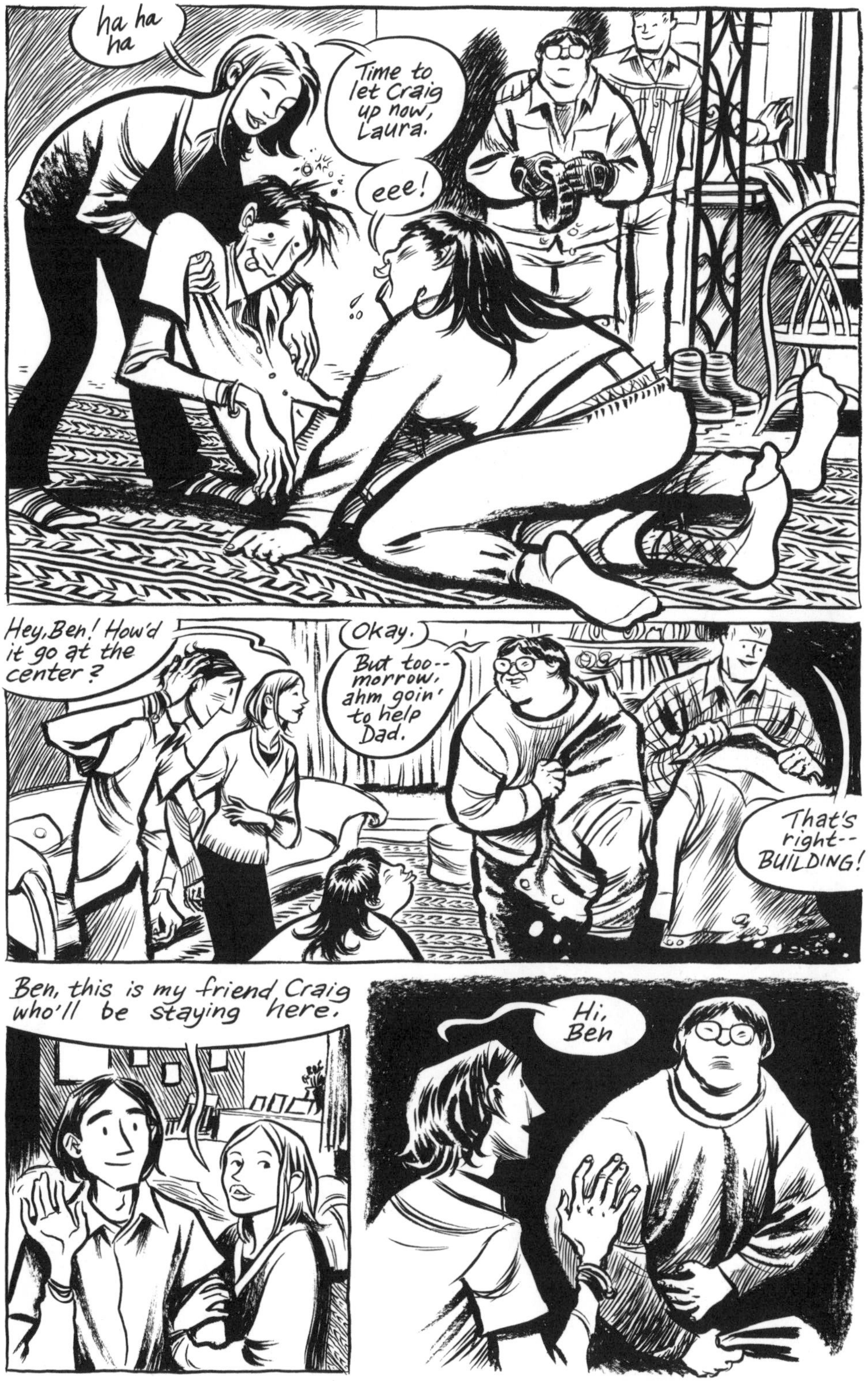
ha ha ha
Time to let Craig up now, Laura.
eee!
Hey, Ben! How'd it go at the center?
Okay.
But too-- morrow, ahm goin' to help Dad.
That's right-- BUILDING!
Ben, this is my friend Craig who'll be staying here.
Hi, Ben

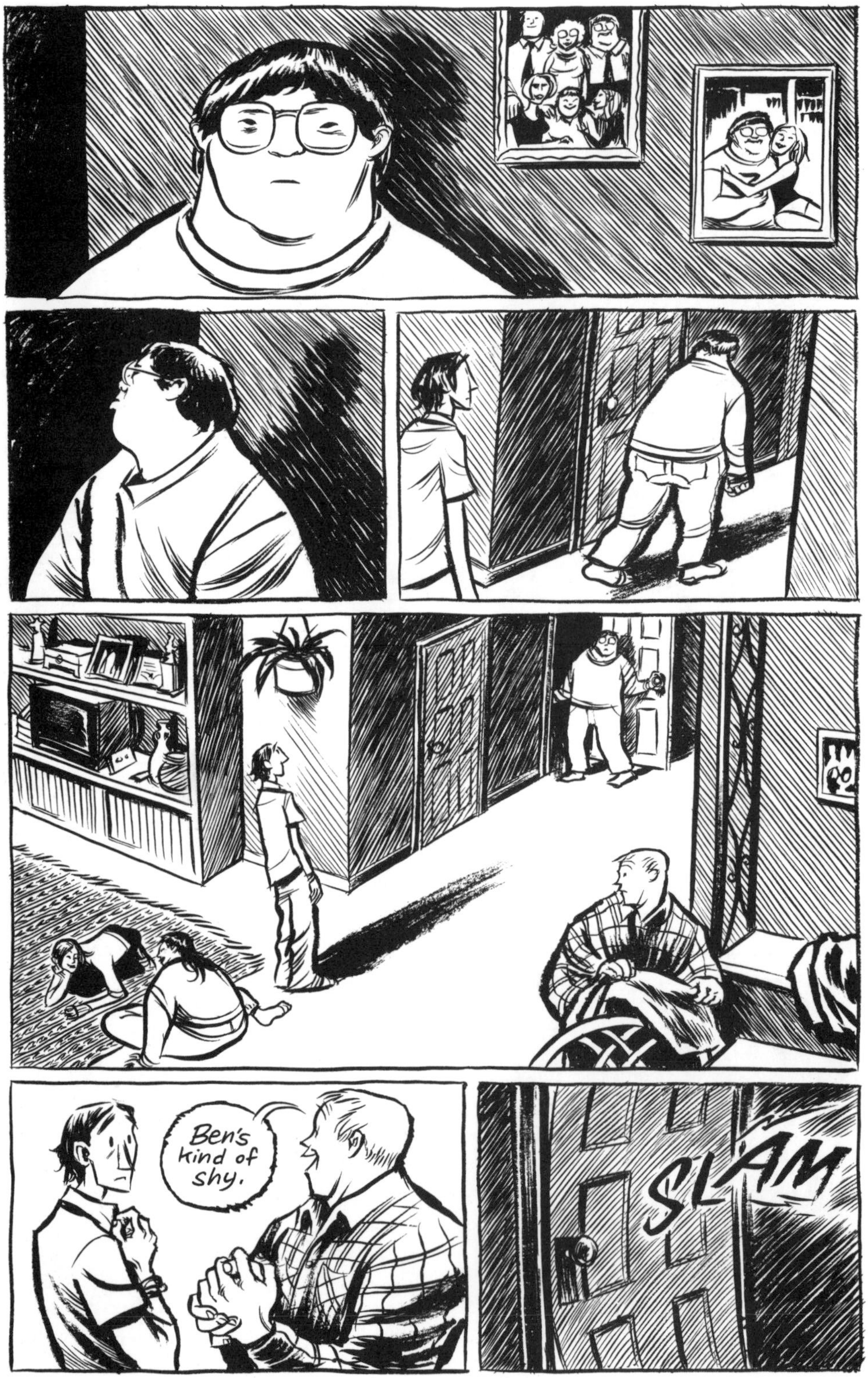
Ben's kind of shy.
SLAM

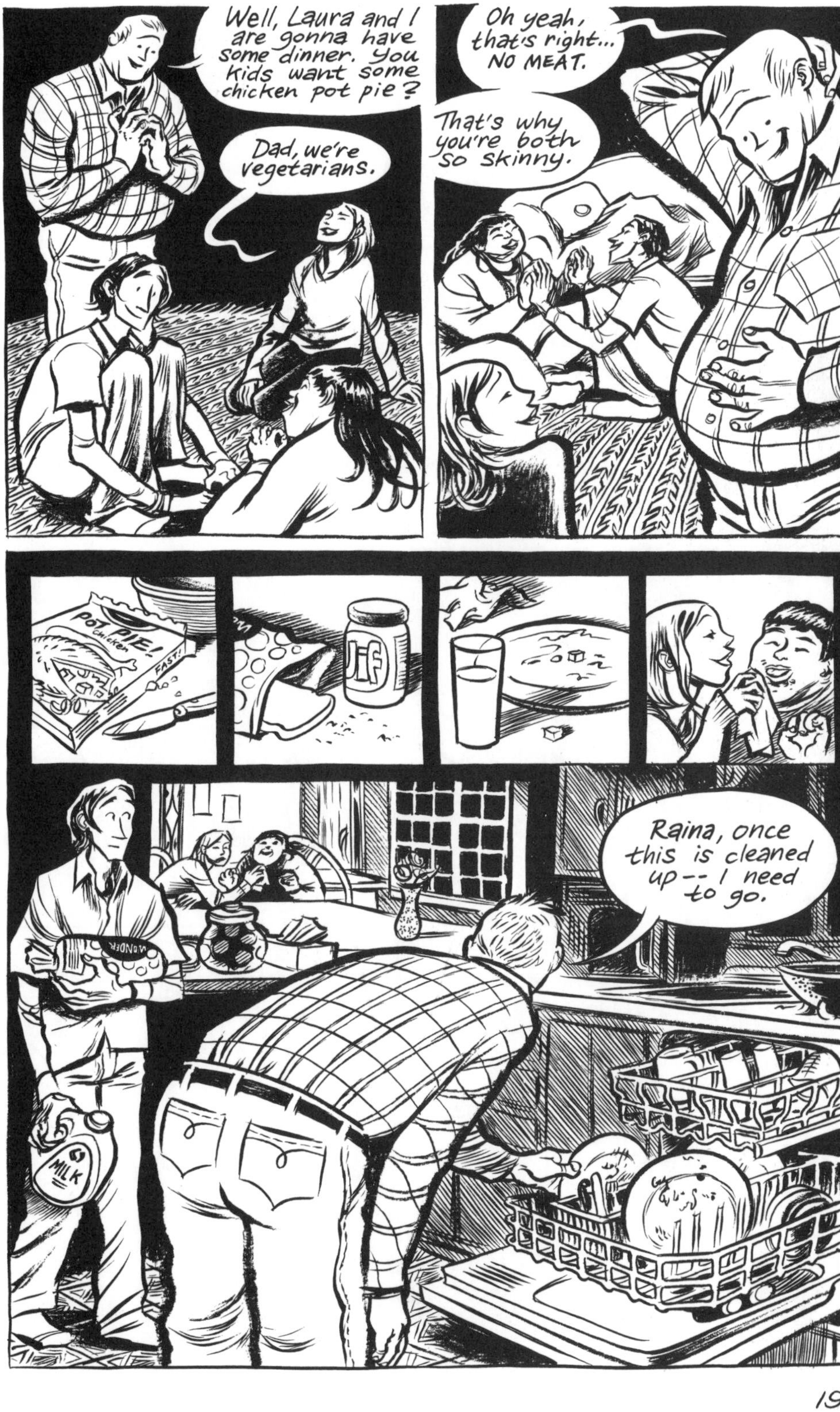
Well, Laura and I are gonna have some dinner. You kids want some chicken pot pie?
Dad, we're vegetarians.
Oh yeah, that's right... NO MEAT.
That's why you're both so skinny.
POT PIE! Chicken
FAST!
JIF
WONDER
MILK
Raina, once this is cleaned up -- I need to go.

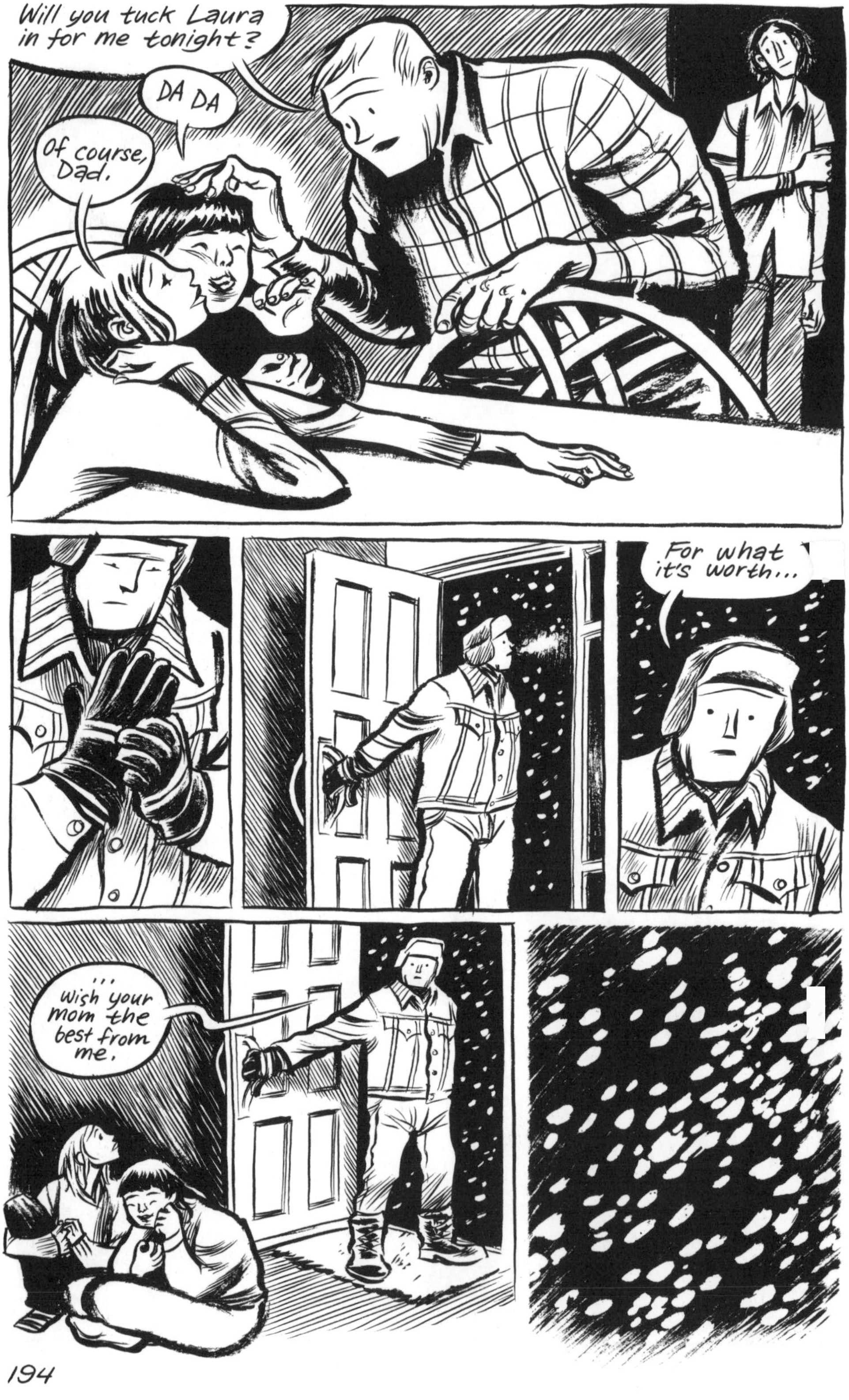
Will you tuck Laura in for me tonight?
DA DA
Of course, Dad.
For what it's worth...
... wish your mom the best from me.

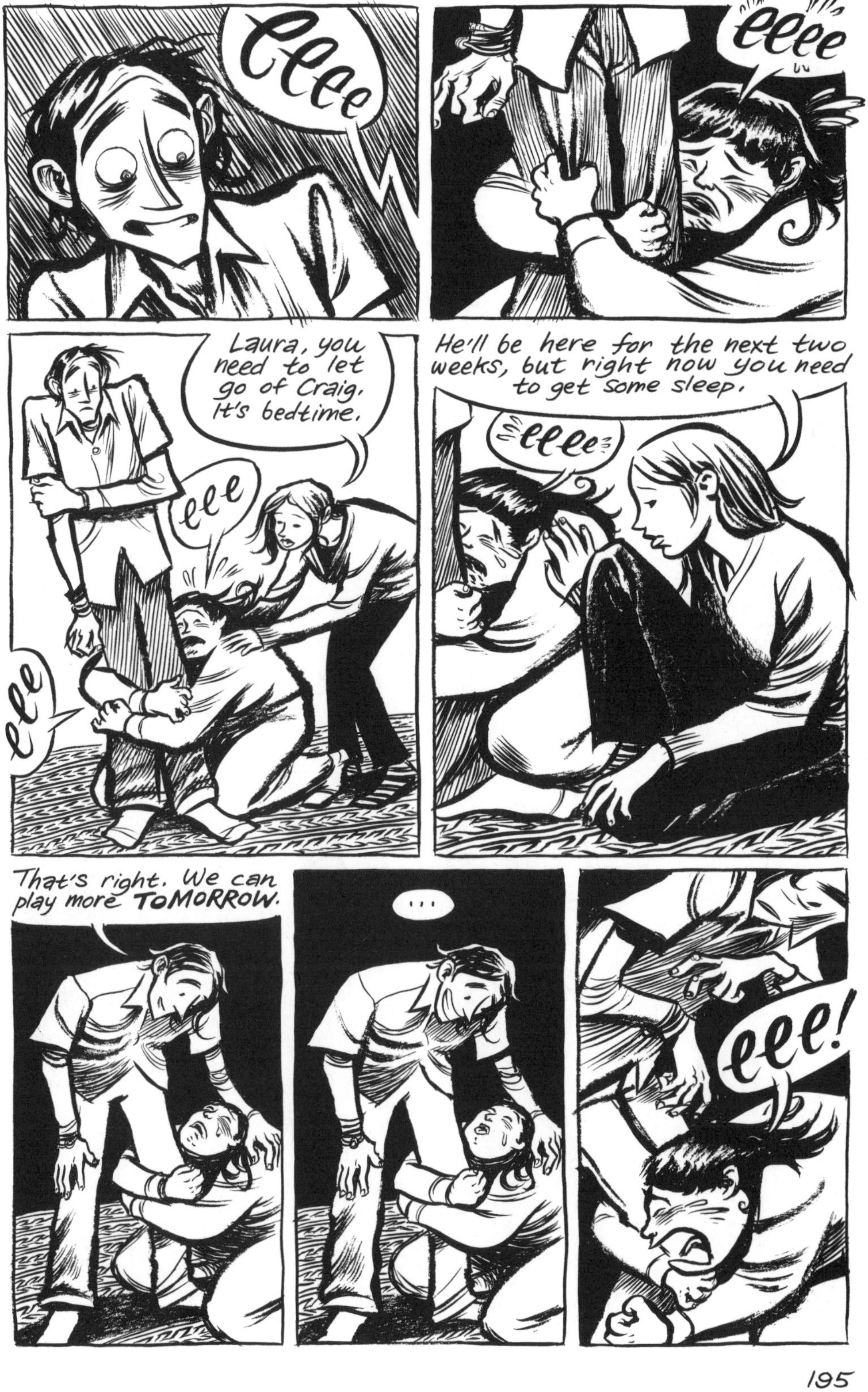
eeee
eeee
Laura, you need to let go of Craig. It's bedtime.
eee
eee
He'll be here for the next two weeks, but right now you need to get some sleep.
eeee
That's right. We can play more TOMORROW.
...
eee!

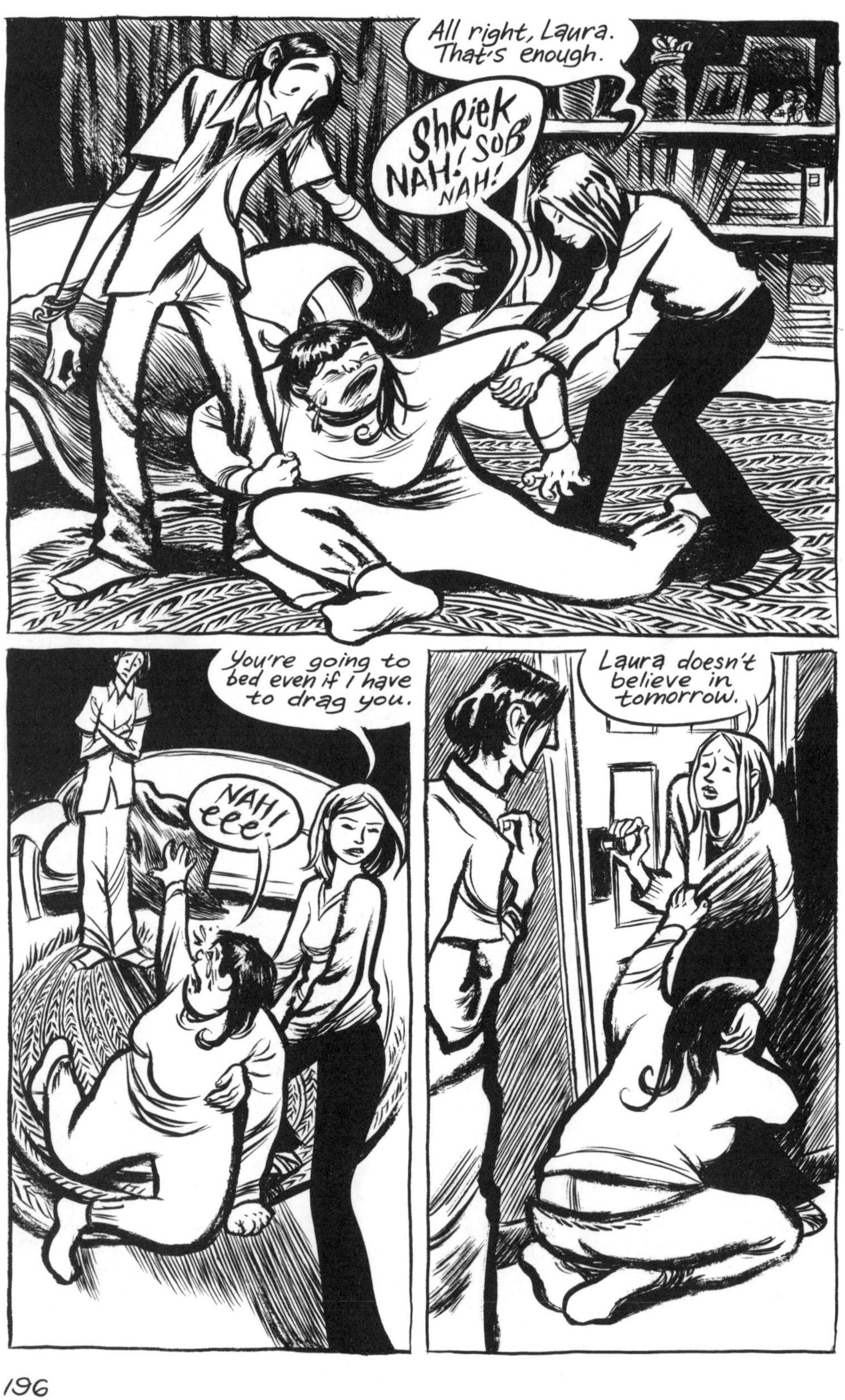
All right, Laura. That's enough.
SHRIEK SOB NAH! NAH!
You're going to bed even if I have to drag you.
NAH! EEE!
Laura doesn't believe in tomorrow.

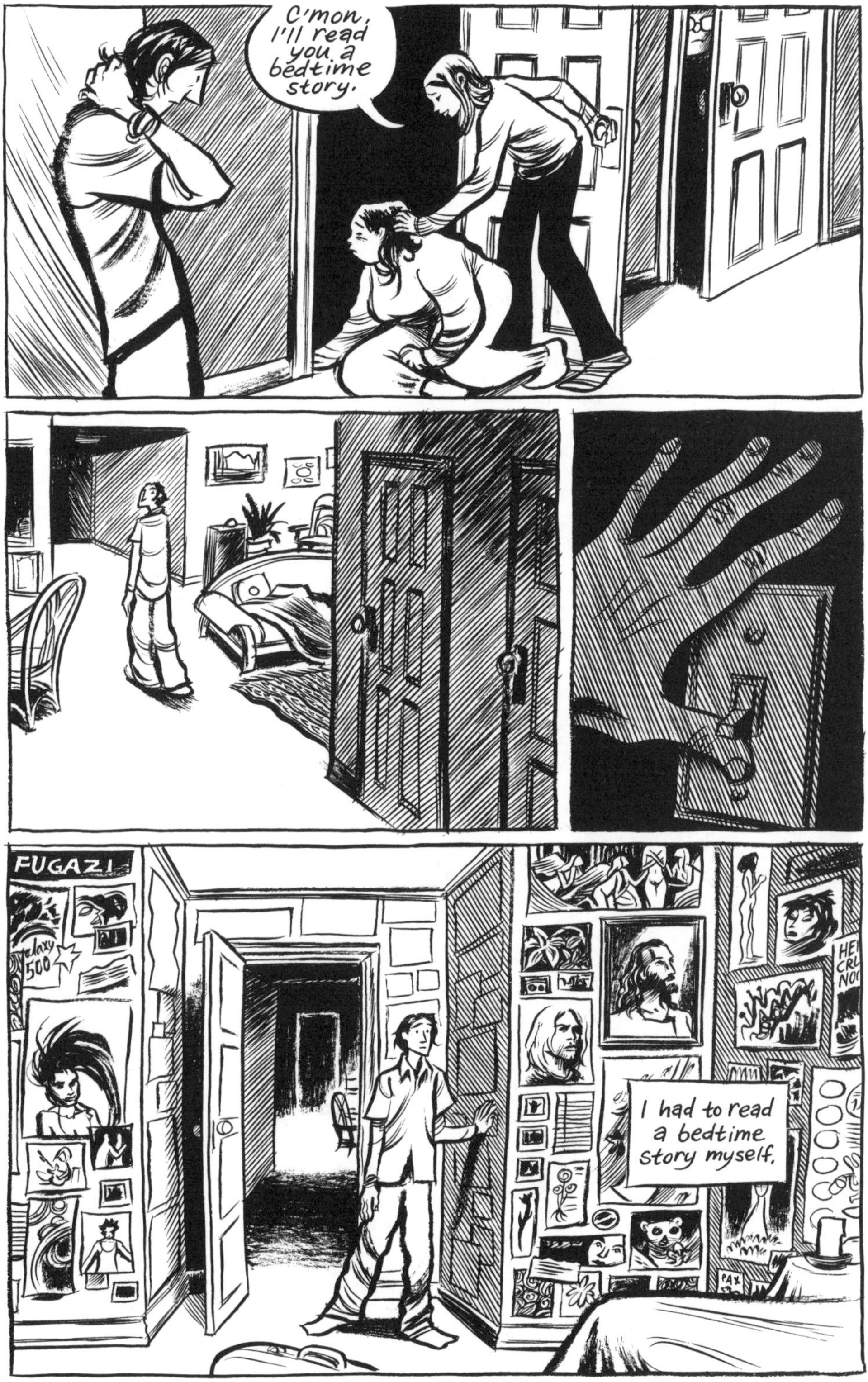
C'mon, I'll read you a bedtime story.
FUGAZI
I had to read a bedtime story myself.

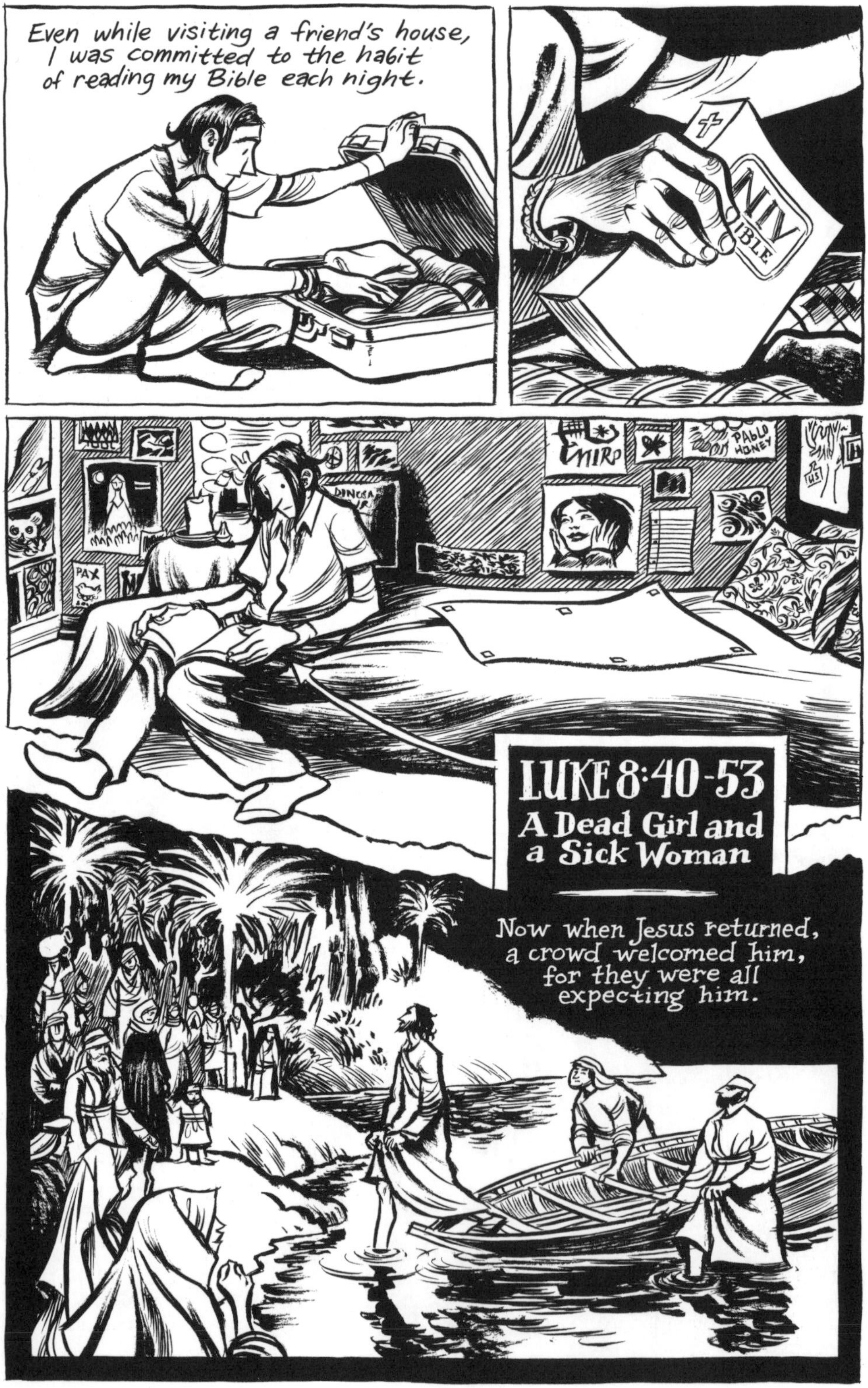
Even while visiting a friend's house, I was committed to the habit of reading my Bible each night.
NIV BIBLE
PABLO HONEY
PAX
LUKE 8:40-53
A Dead Girl and a Sick Woman
Now when Jesus returned, a crowd welcomed him, for they were all expecting him.

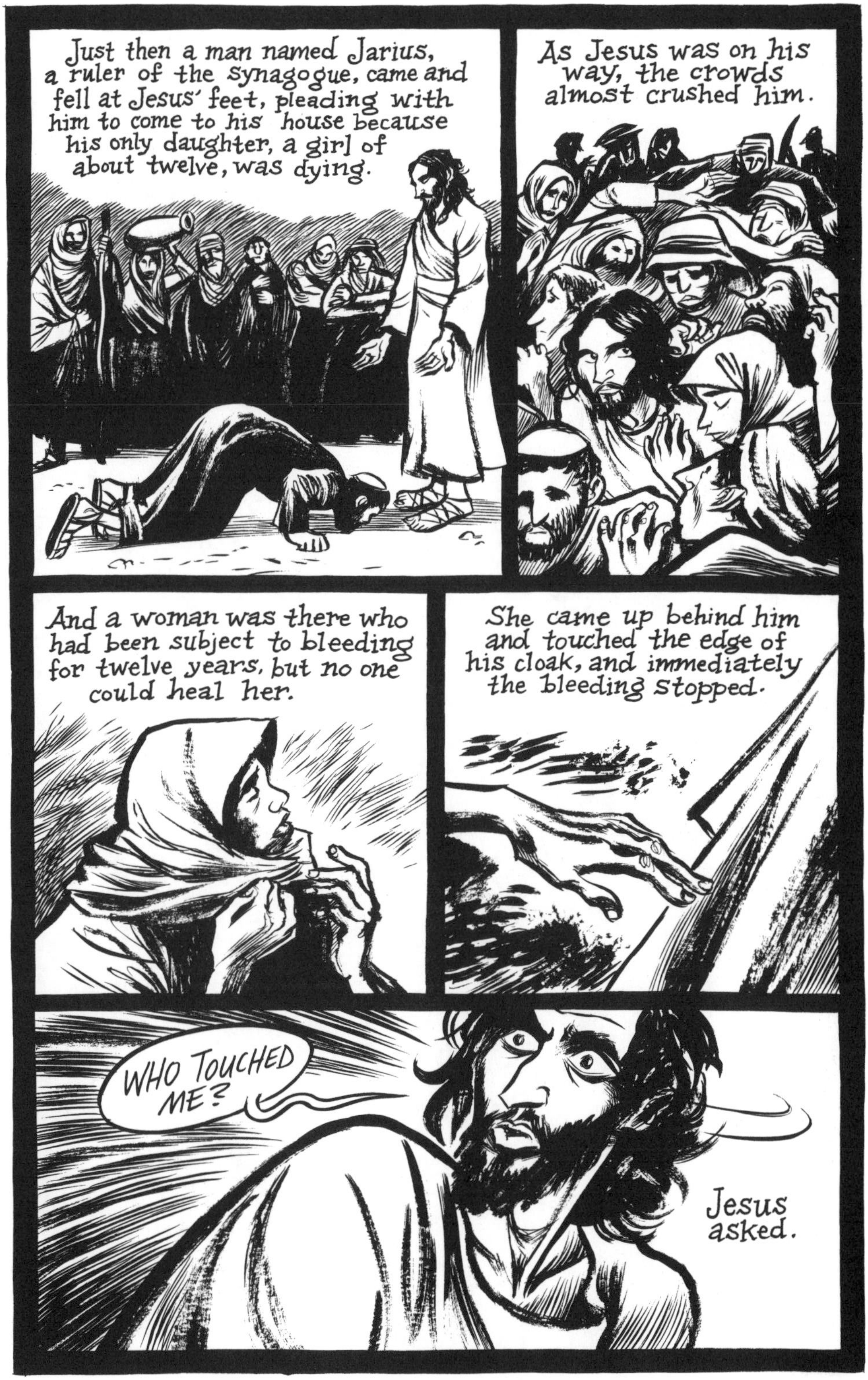
Just then a man named Jarius, a ruler of the synagogue, came and fell at Jesus' feet, pleading with him to come to his house because his only daughter, a girl of about twelve, was dying.
As Jesus was on his way, the crowds almost crushed him.
And a woman was there who had been subject to bleeding for twelve years, but no one could heal her.
She came up behind him and touched the edge of his cloak, and immediately the bleeding stopped.
WHO TOUCHED ME?
Jesus asked.

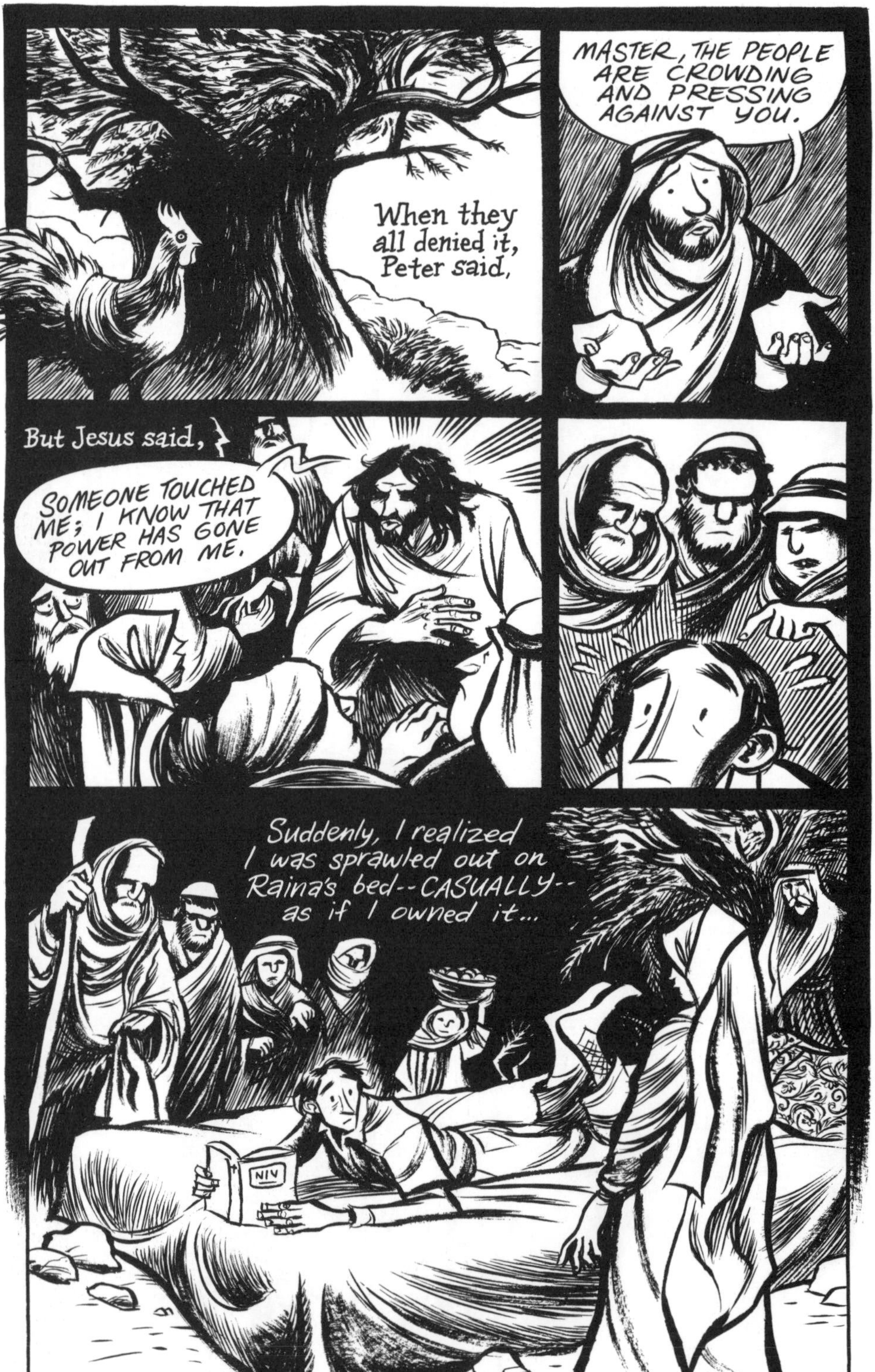
When they all denied it, Peter said,
MASTER, THE PEOPLE ARE CROWDING AND PRESSING AGAINST YOU.
But Jesus said,
SOMEONE TOUCHED ME; I KNOW THAT POWER HAS GONE OUT FROM ME.
Suddenly, I realized I was sprawled out on Raina's bed--CASUALLY--as if I owned it...
NIV

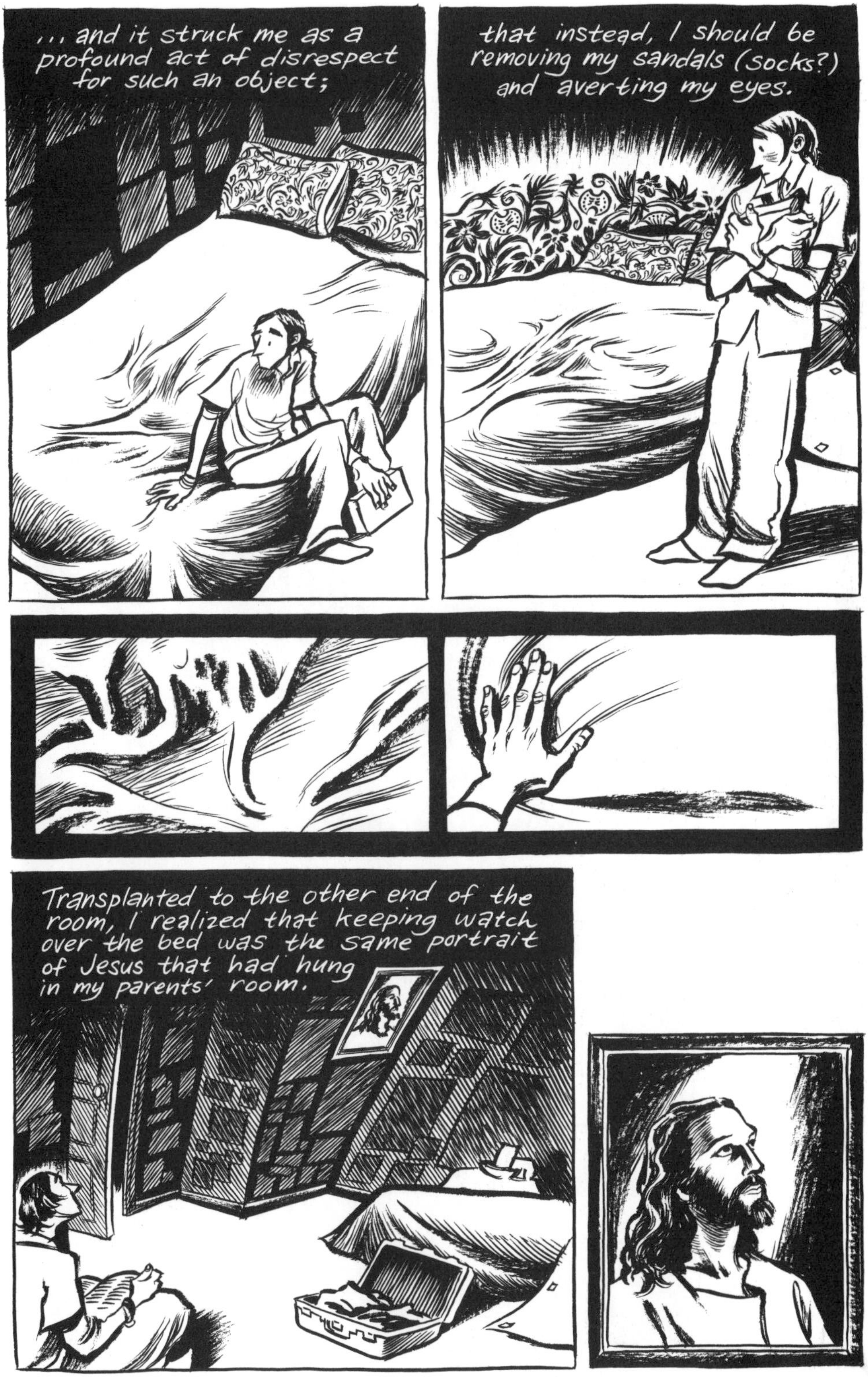
...and it struck me as a profound act of disrespect for such an object;
that instead, I should be removing my sandals (socks?) and averting my eyes.
Transplanted to the other end of the room, I realized that keeping watch over the bed was the same portrait of Jesus that had hung in my parents' room.

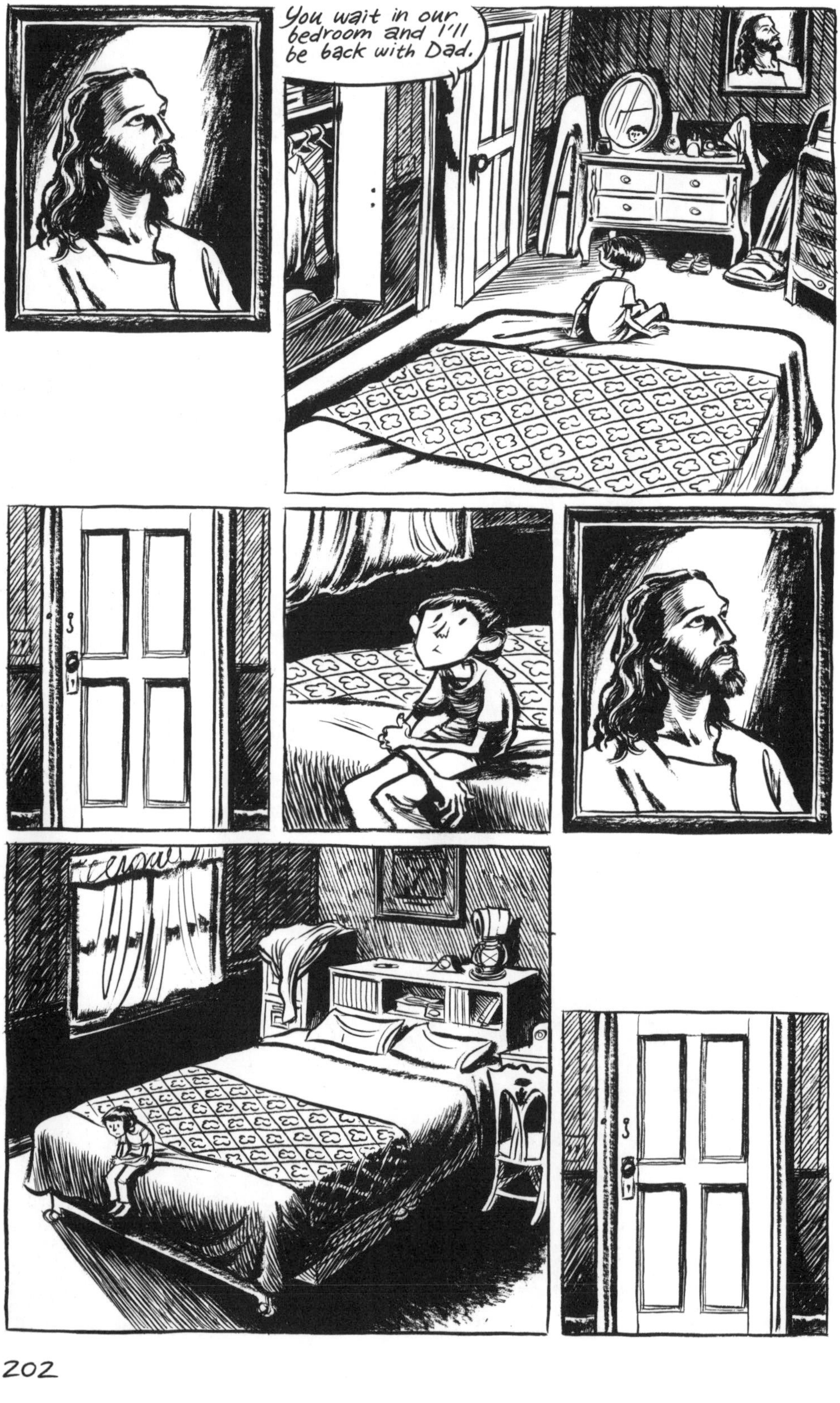
You wait in our bedroom and I'll be back with Dad.

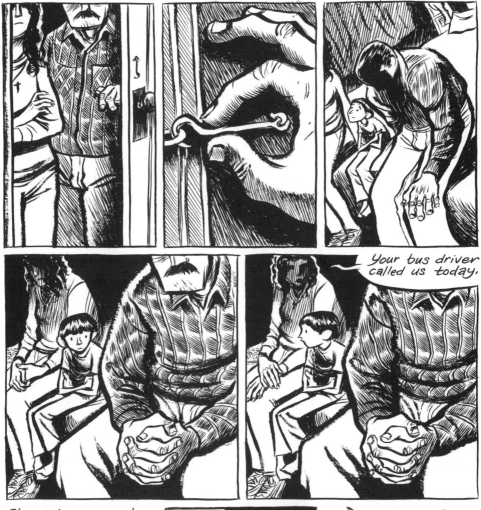

Your bus driver called us today.

She said you were drawing on the bus and you threw something in the waste basket.

Do you remember what it was?

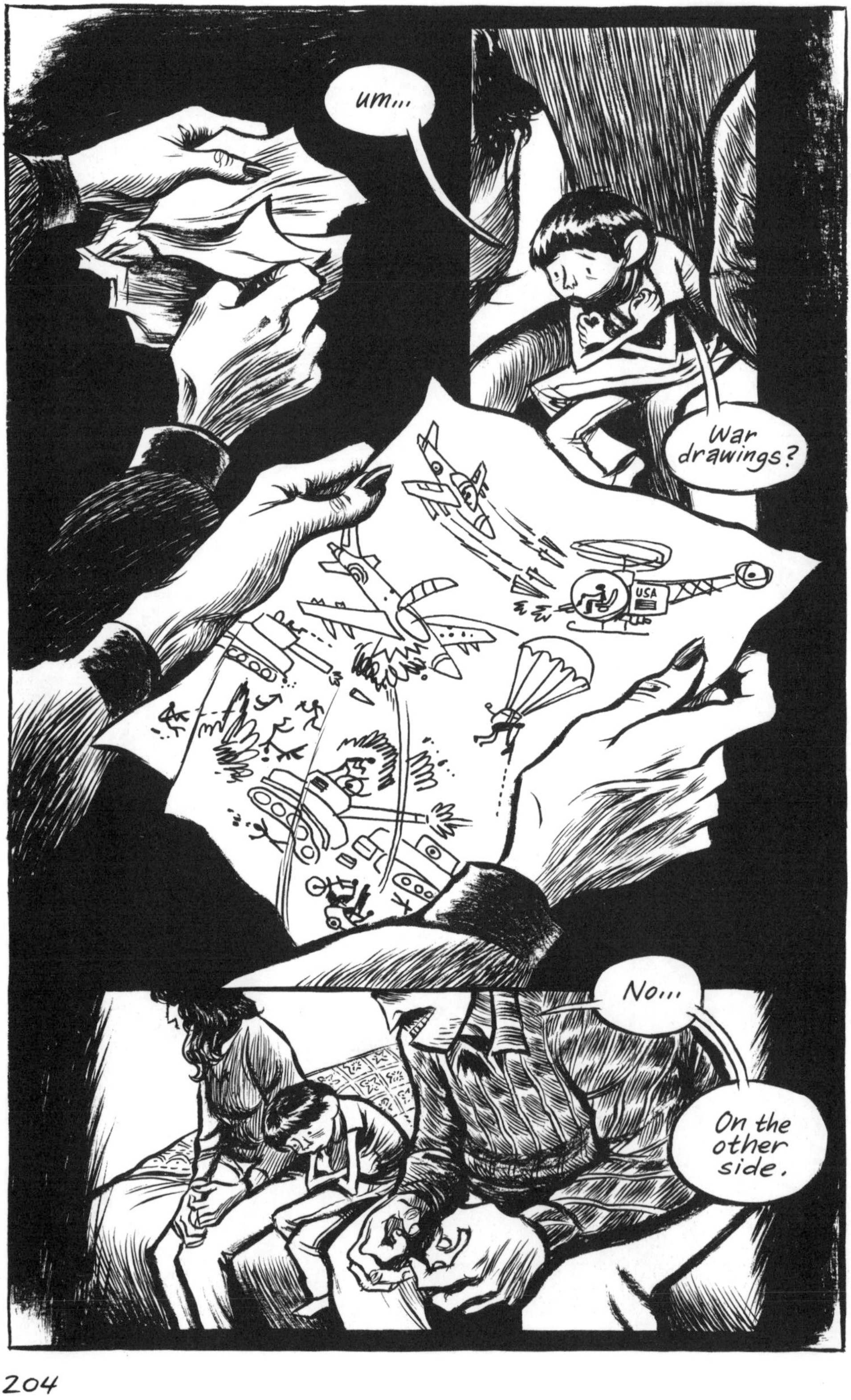
um...
War drawings?
USA
No...
On the other side.

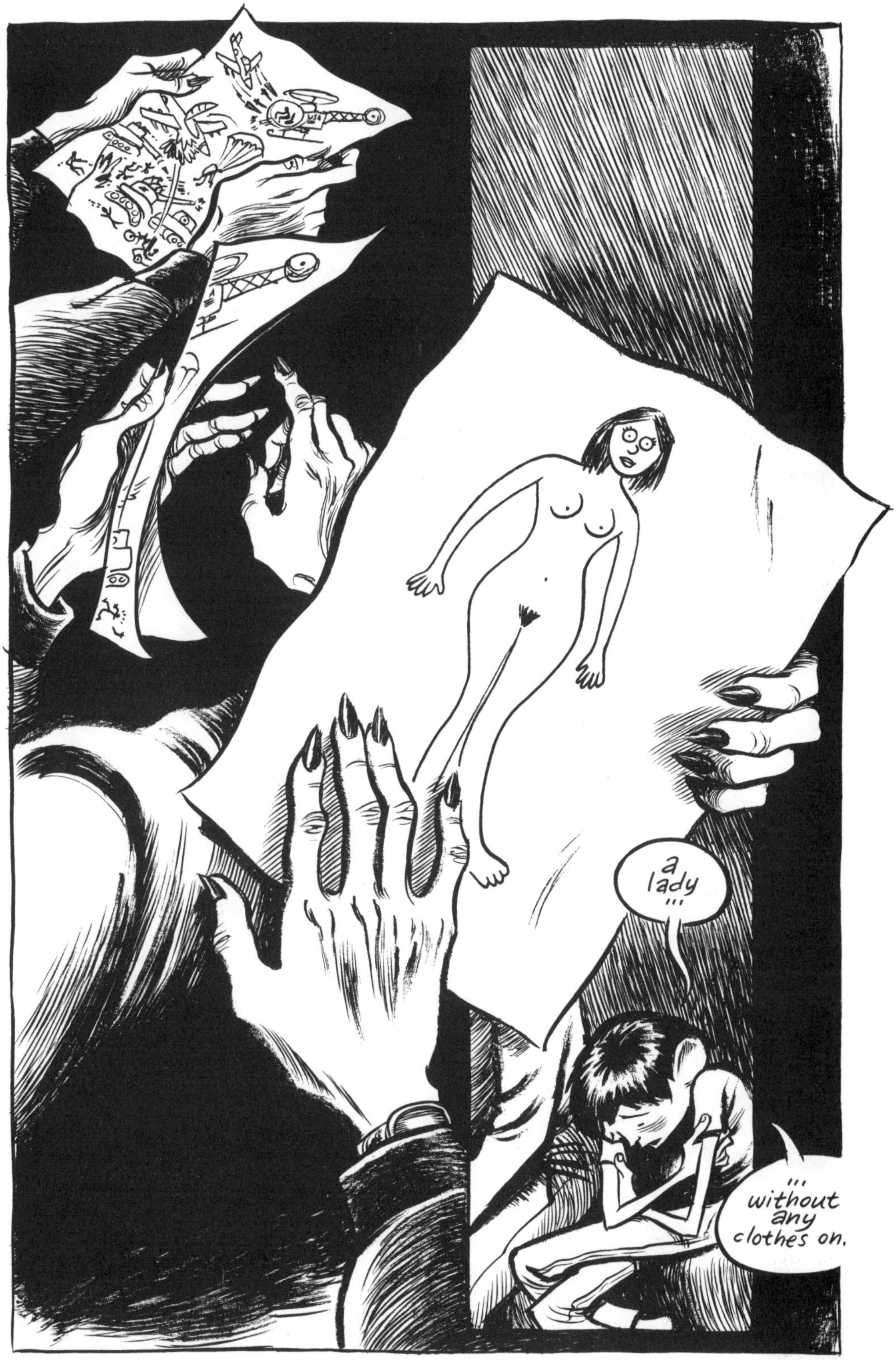
a lady ...
... without any clothes on.

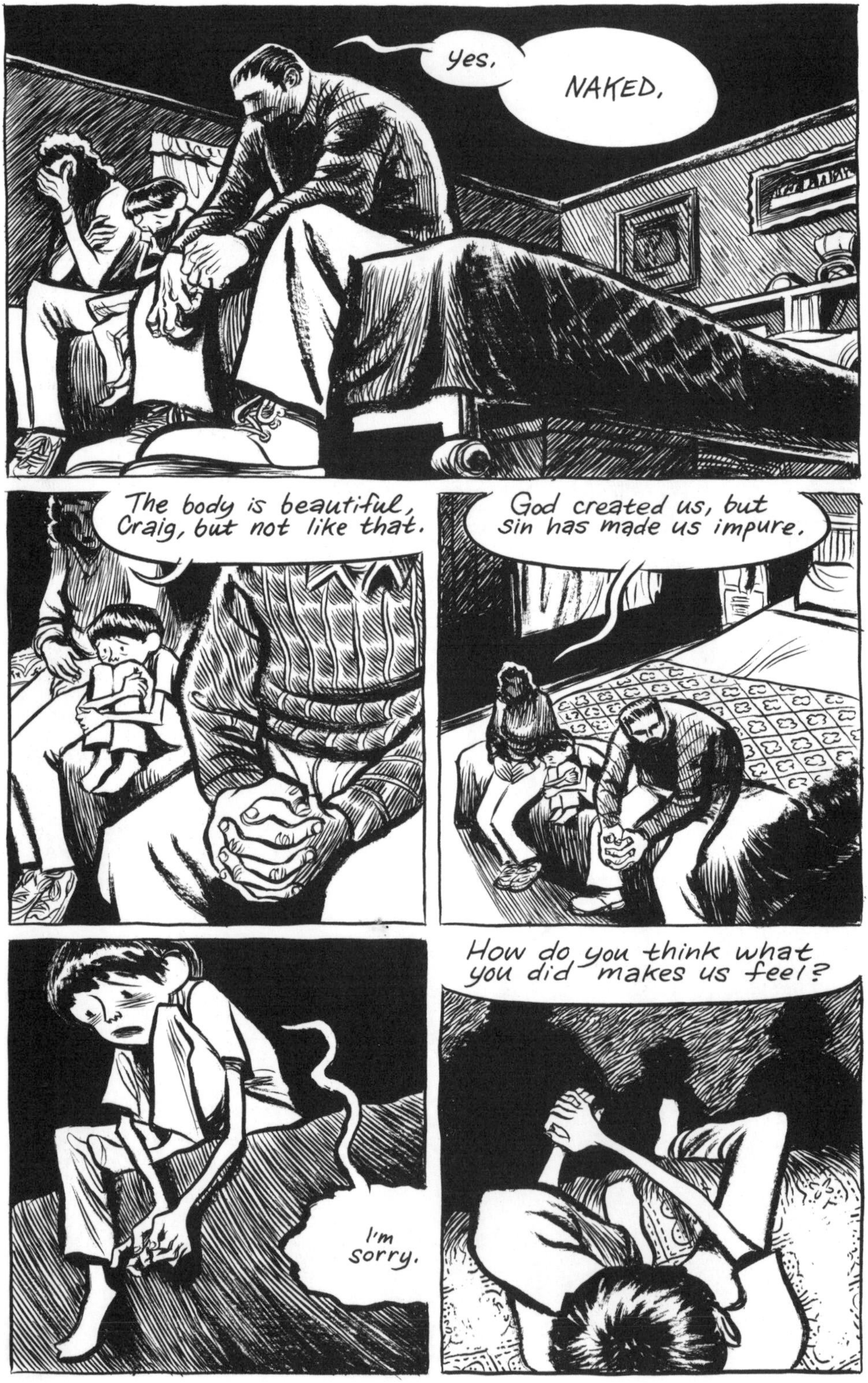
yes,
NAKED,
The body is beautiful, Craig, but not like that.
God created us, but sin has made us impure.
How do you think what you did makes us feel?
I'm sorry.

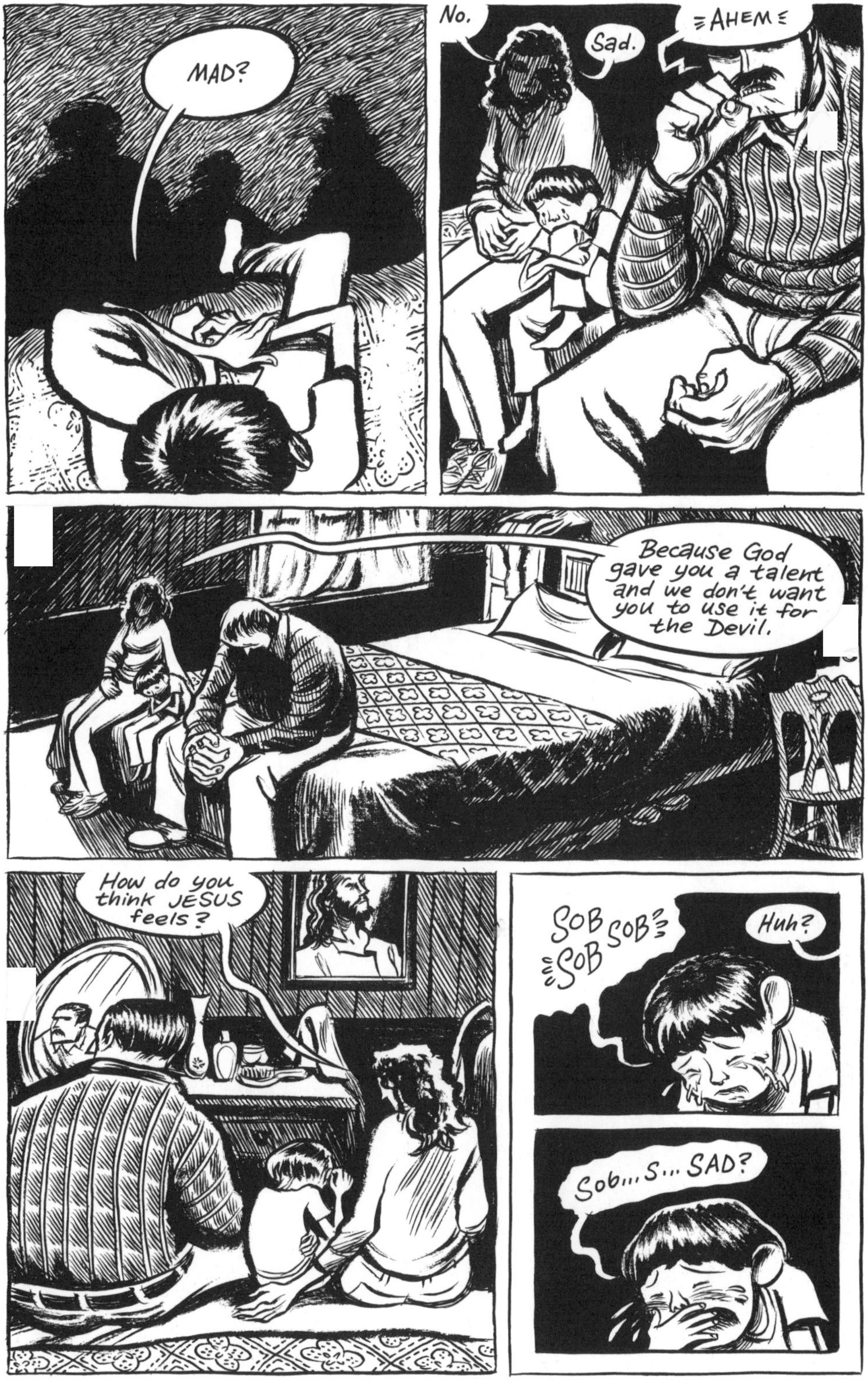
MAD?
No.
Sad.
AHEM
Because God gave you a talent and we don't want you to use it for the Devil.
How do you think JESUS feels?
SOB SOB SOB SOB
Huh?
Sob... S... SAD?

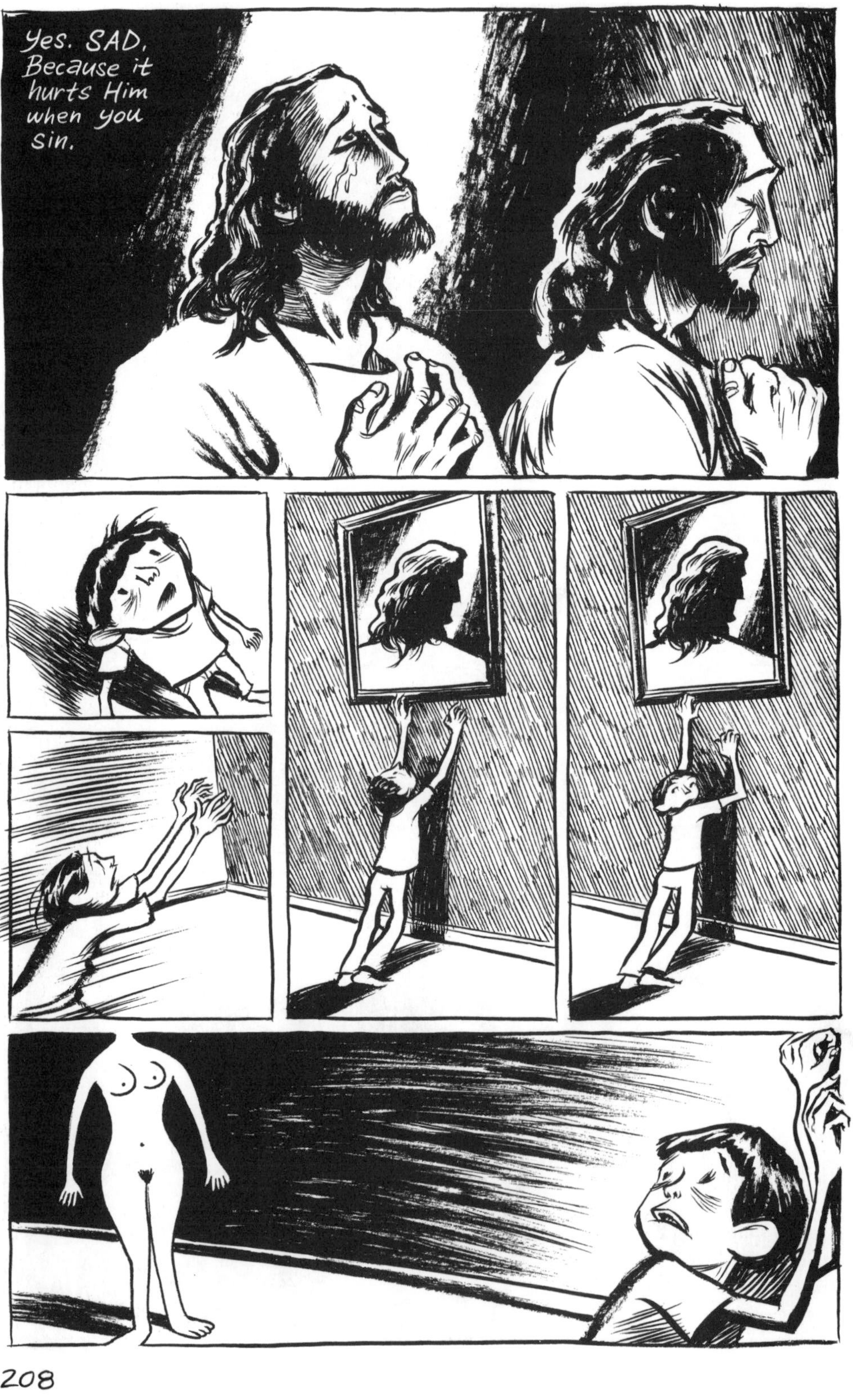
Yes. SAD. Because it hurts Him when you sin.

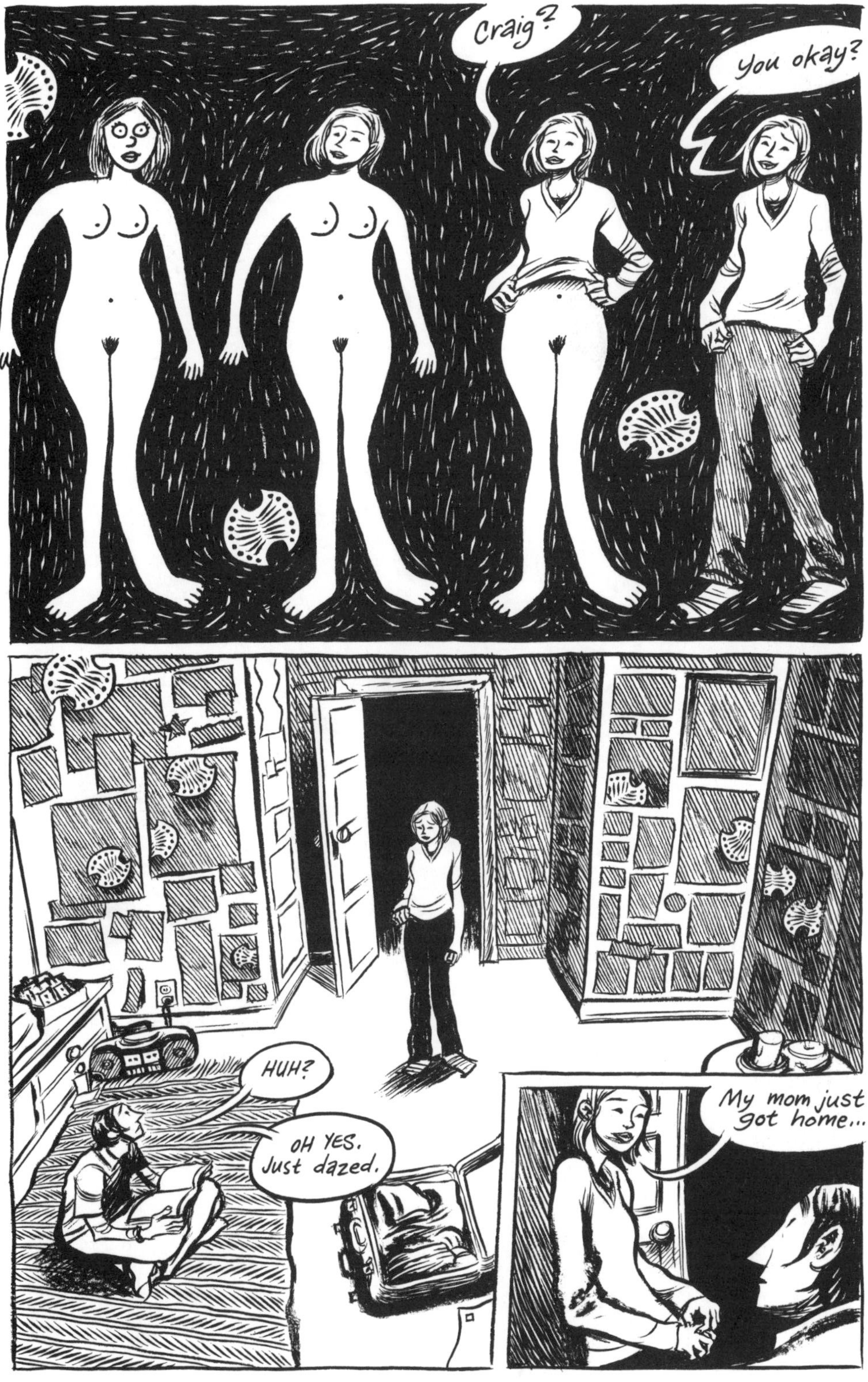

Craig?
You okay?
HUH?
OH YES. Just dazed.
My mom just got home...

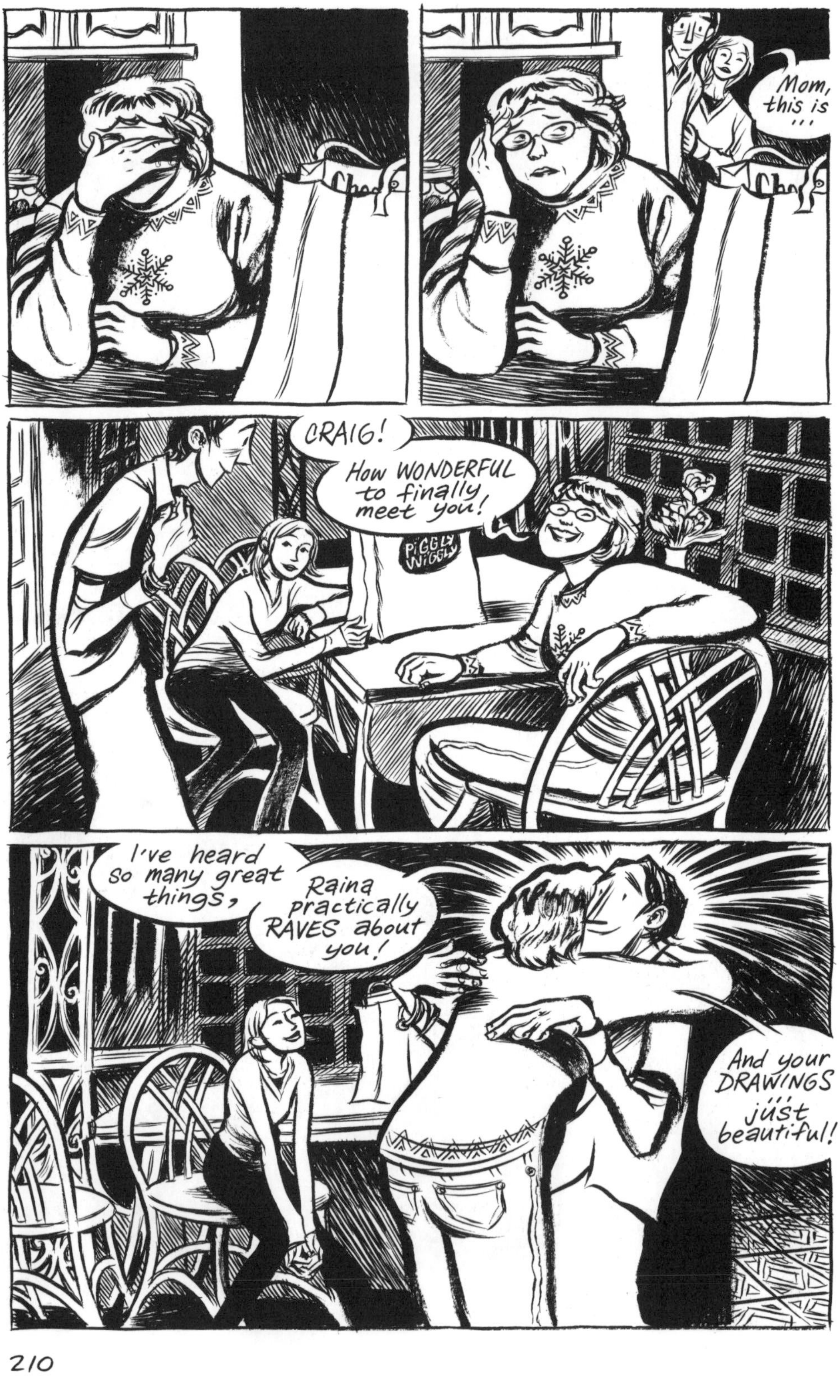
Mom, this is ...
CRAIG!
How WONDERFUL to finally meet you!
PIGGLY WIGGLY
I've heard so many great things,
Raina practically RAVES about you!
And your DRAWINGS ... just beautiful!

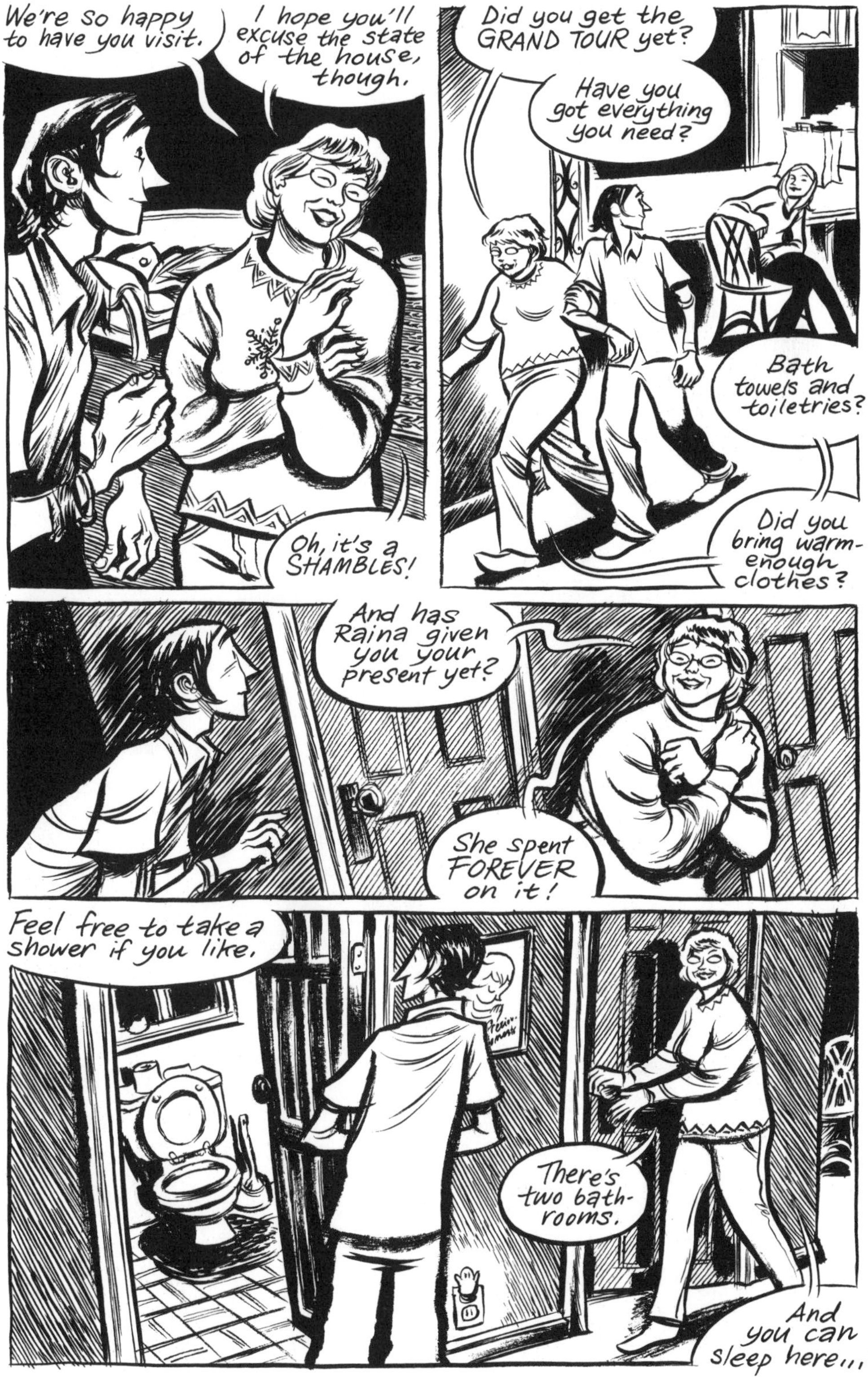
We're so happy to have you visit.
I hope you'll excuse the state of the house, though.
Oh, it's a SHAMBLES!
Did you get the GRAND TOUR yet?
Have you got everything you need?
Bath towels and toiletries?
Did you bring warm-enough clothes?
And has Raina given you your present yet?
She spent FOREVER on it!
Feel free to take a shower if you like.
There's two bathrooms.
And you can sleep here...

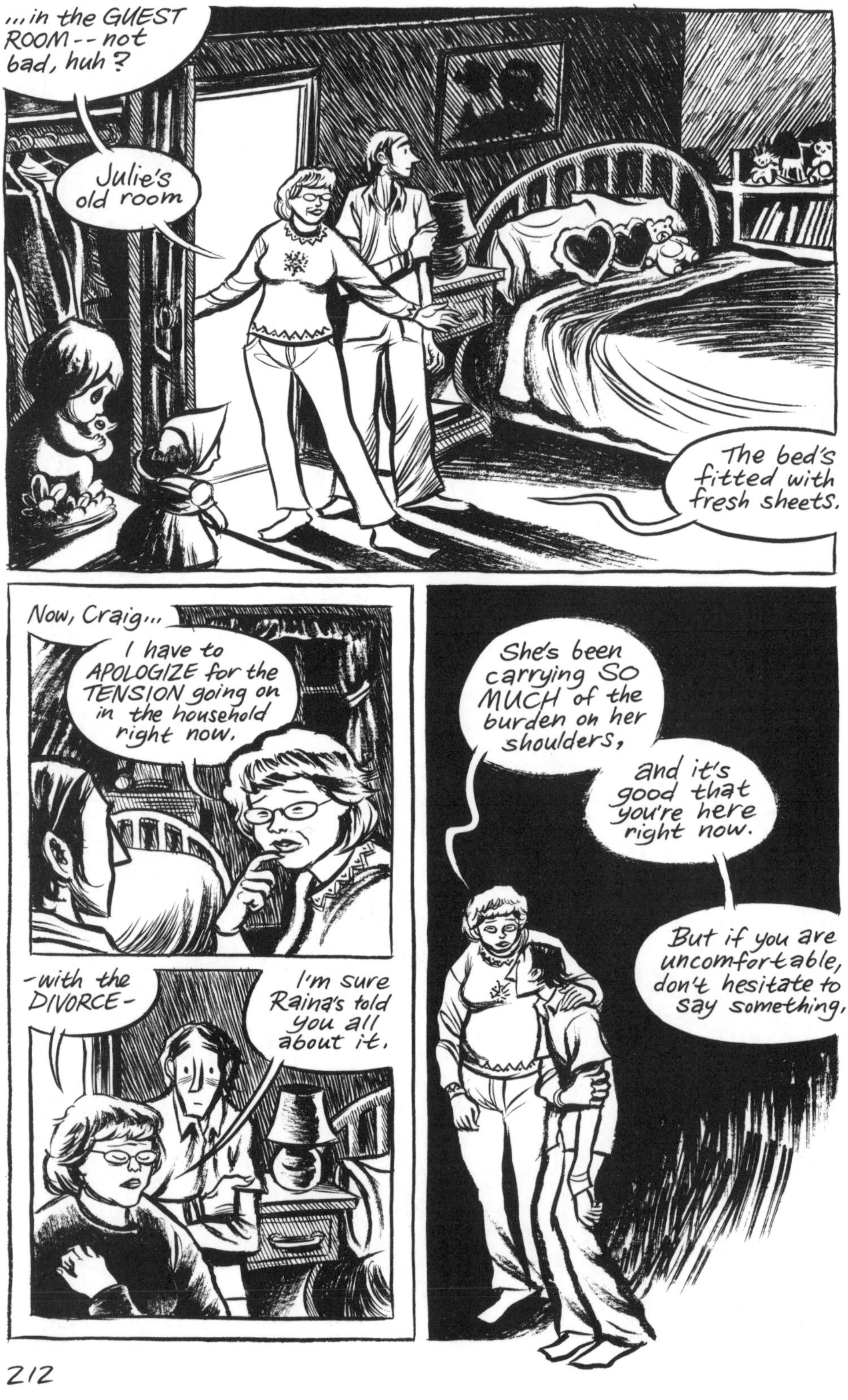
...in the GUEST ROOM -- not bad, huh?
Julie's old room
The bed's fitted with fresh sheets.
Now, Craig...
I have to APOLOGIZE for the TENSION going on in the household right now.
-with the DIVORCE-
I'm sure Raina's told you all about it.
She's been carrying SO MUCH of the burden on her shoulders,
and it's good that you're here right now.
But if you are uncomfortable, don't hesitate to say something.

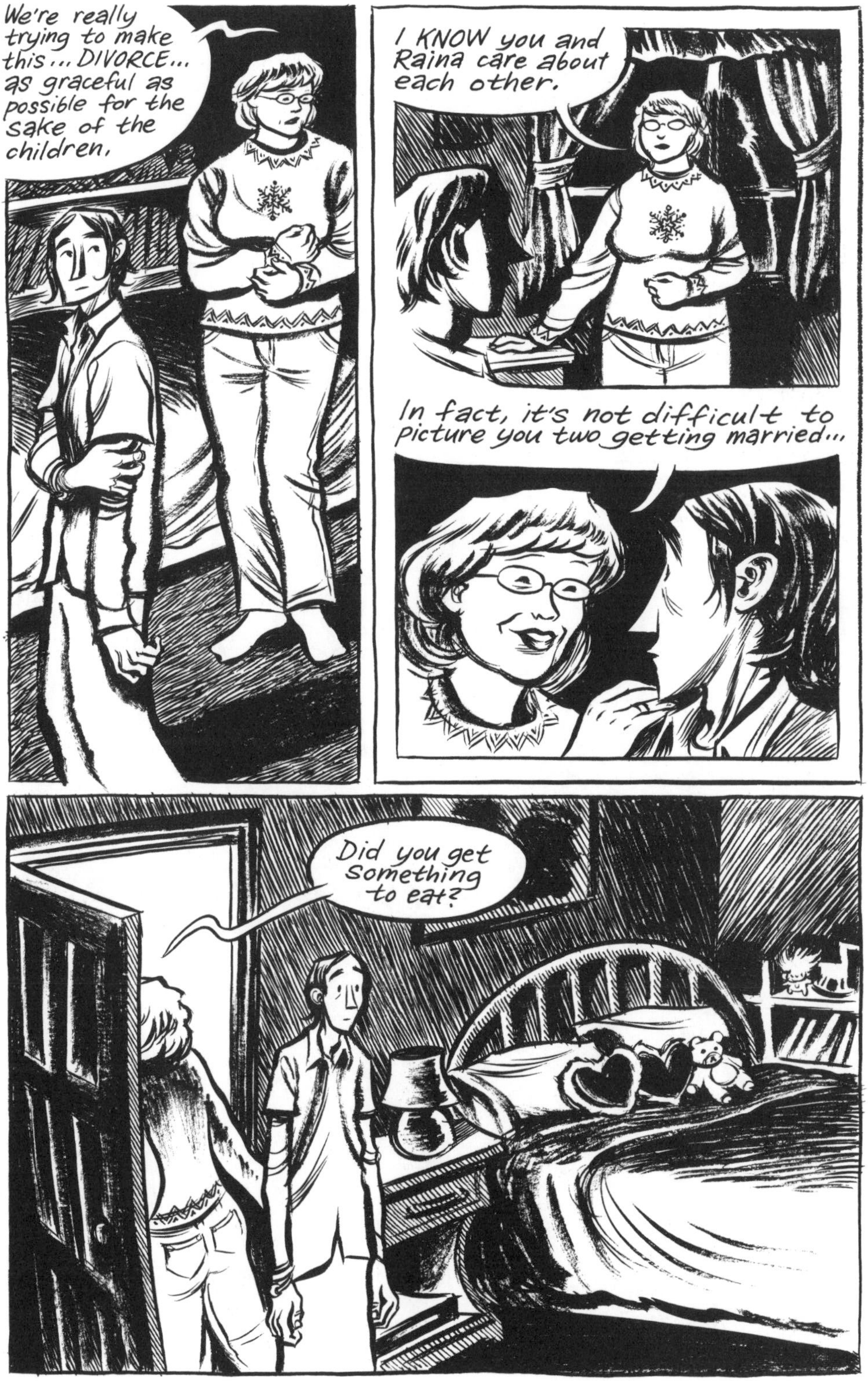
We're really trying to make this... DIVORCE... as graceful as possible for the sake of the children.
I KNOW you and Raina care about each other.
In fact, it's not difficult to picture you two getting married...
Did you get something to eat?

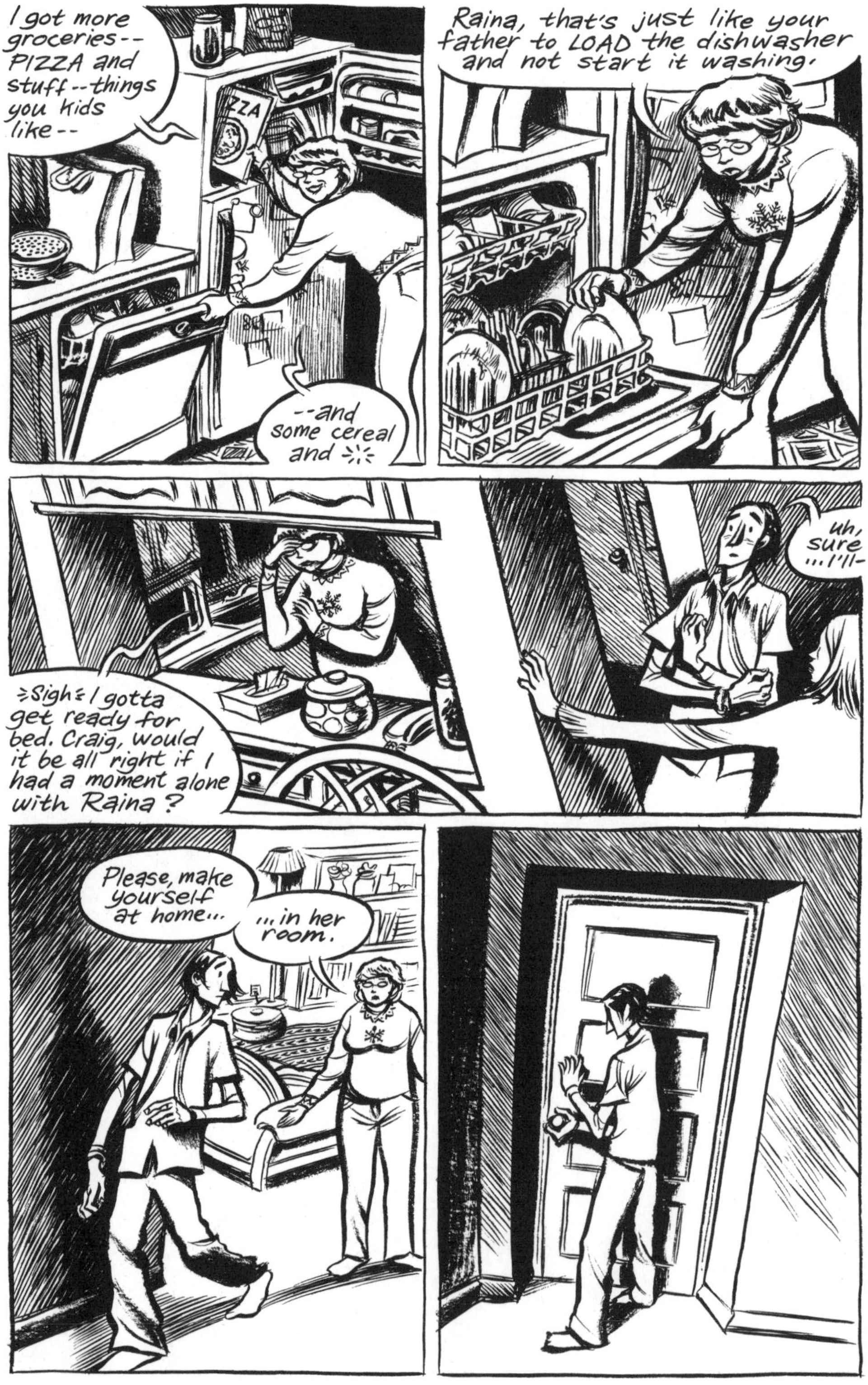
I got more groceries-- PIZZA and stuff--things you kids like--
--and some cereal and ⁑
Raina, that's just like your father to LOAD the dishwasher and not start it washing.
⁑Sigh⁑ I gotta get ready for bed. Craig, would it be all right if I had a moment alone with Raina?
uh, sure ...I'll-
Please, make yourself at home...
...in her room.

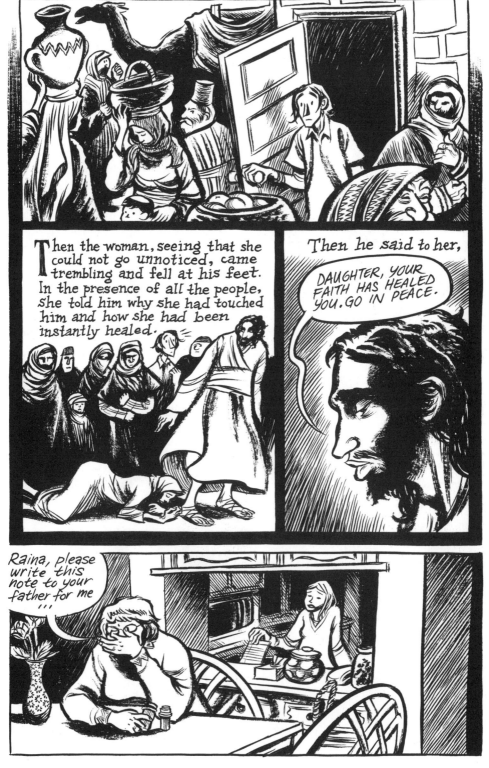

Then the woman, seeing that she could not go unnoticed, came trembling and fell at his feet. In the presence of all the people, she told him why she had touched him and how she had been instantly healed.

Then he said to her,

DAUGHTER, YOUR FAITH HAS HEALED YOU. GO IN PEACE.

Raina, please write this note to your father for me...

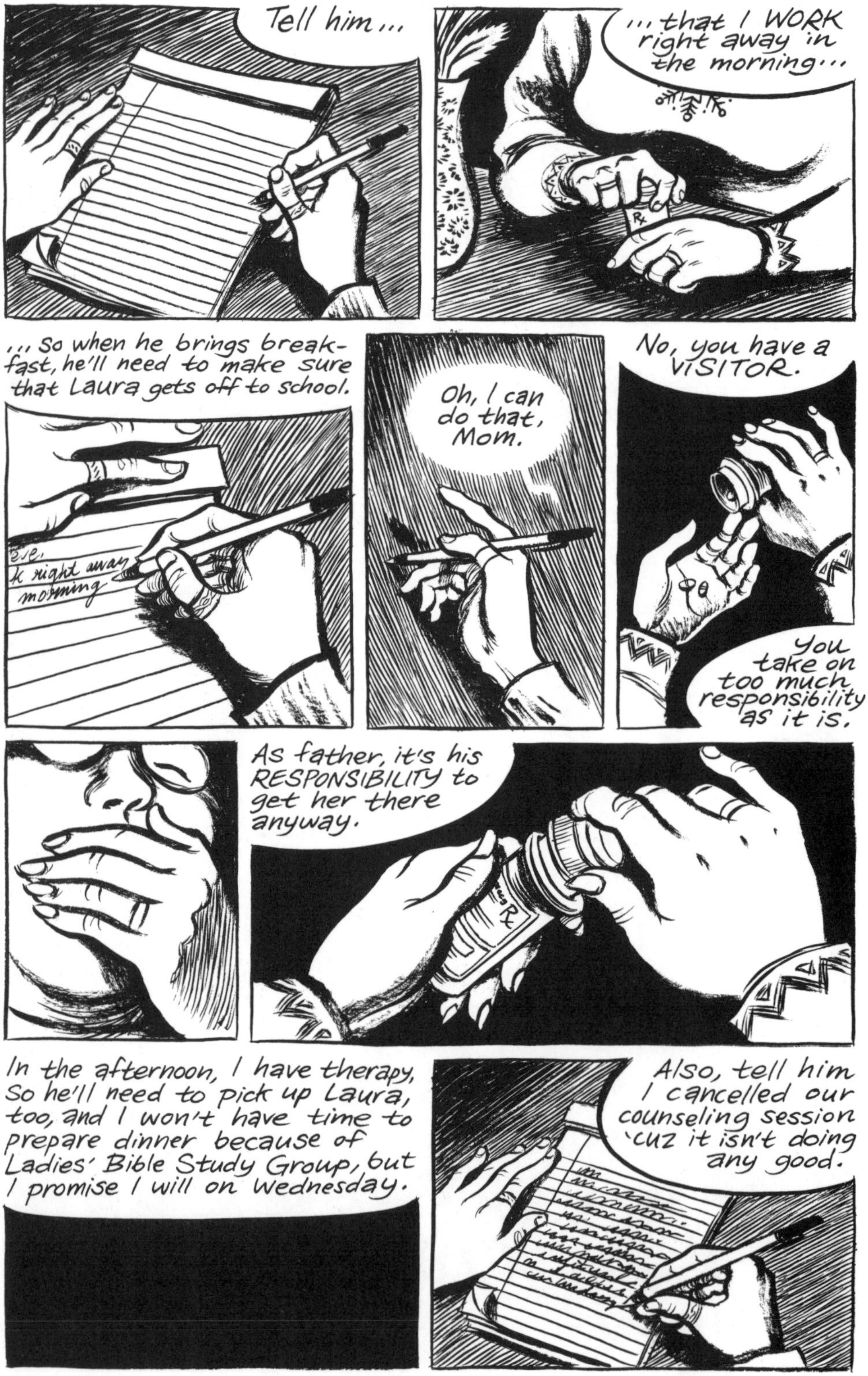
Tell him...
...that I WORK right away in the morning...
...so when he brings breakfast, he'll need to make sure that Laura gets off to school.
Oh, I can do that, Mom.
No, you have a VISITOR.
You take on too much responsibility as it is.
As father, it's his RESPONSIBILITY to get her there anyway.
In the afternoon, I have therapy, so he'll need to pick up Laura, too, and I won't have time to prepare dinner because of Ladies' Bible Study Group, but I promise I will on Wednesday.
Also, tell him I cancelled our counseling session 'cuz it isn't doing any good.

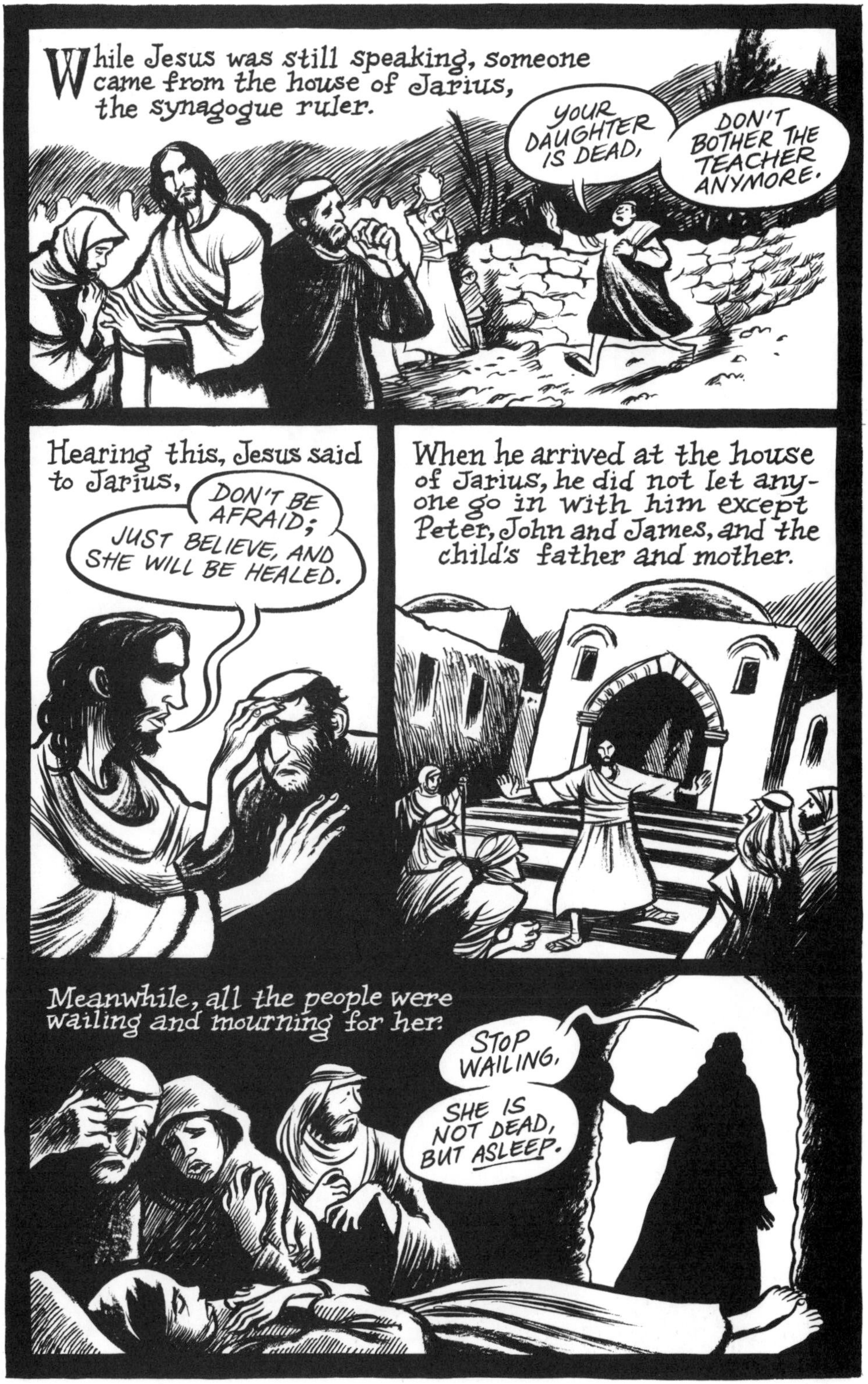
While Jesus was still speaking, someone came from the house of Jarius, the synagogue ruler.
YOUR DAUGHTER IS DEAD,
DON'T BOTHER THE TEACHER ANYMORE.
Hearing this, Jesus said to Jarius,
DON'T BE AFRAID;
JUST BELIEVE, AND SHE WILL BE HEALED.
When he arrived at the house of Jarius, he did not let anyone go in with him except Peter, John and James, and the child's father and mother.
Meanwhile, all the people were wailing and mourning for her.
STOP WAILING,
SHE IS NOT DEAD, BUT ASLEEP.

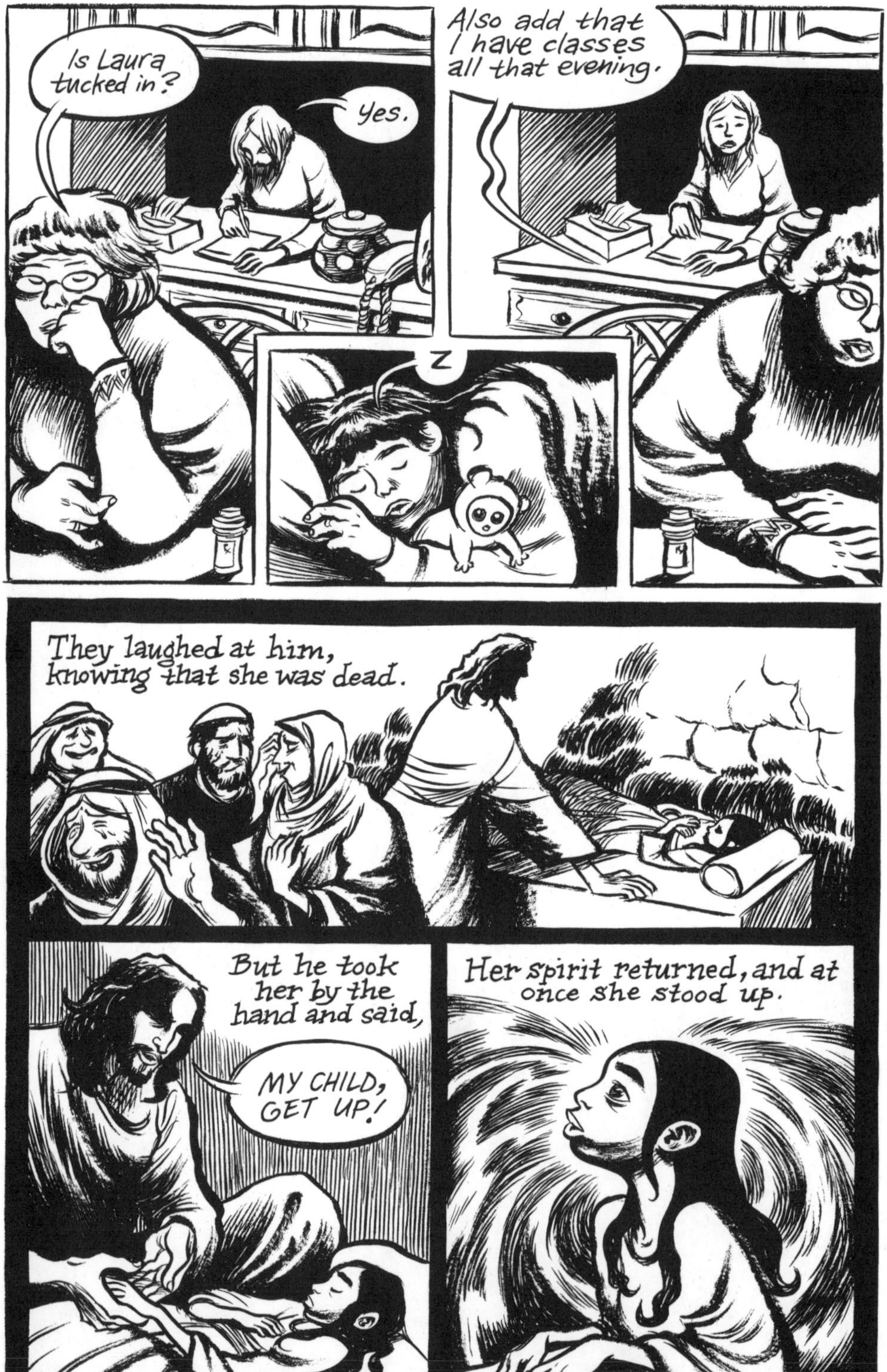

Is Laura tucked in?
Yes.
Z
Also add that I have classes all that evening.
They laughed at him, knowing that she was dead.
But he took her by the hand and said,
MY CHILD, GET UP!
Her spirit returned, and at once she stood up.

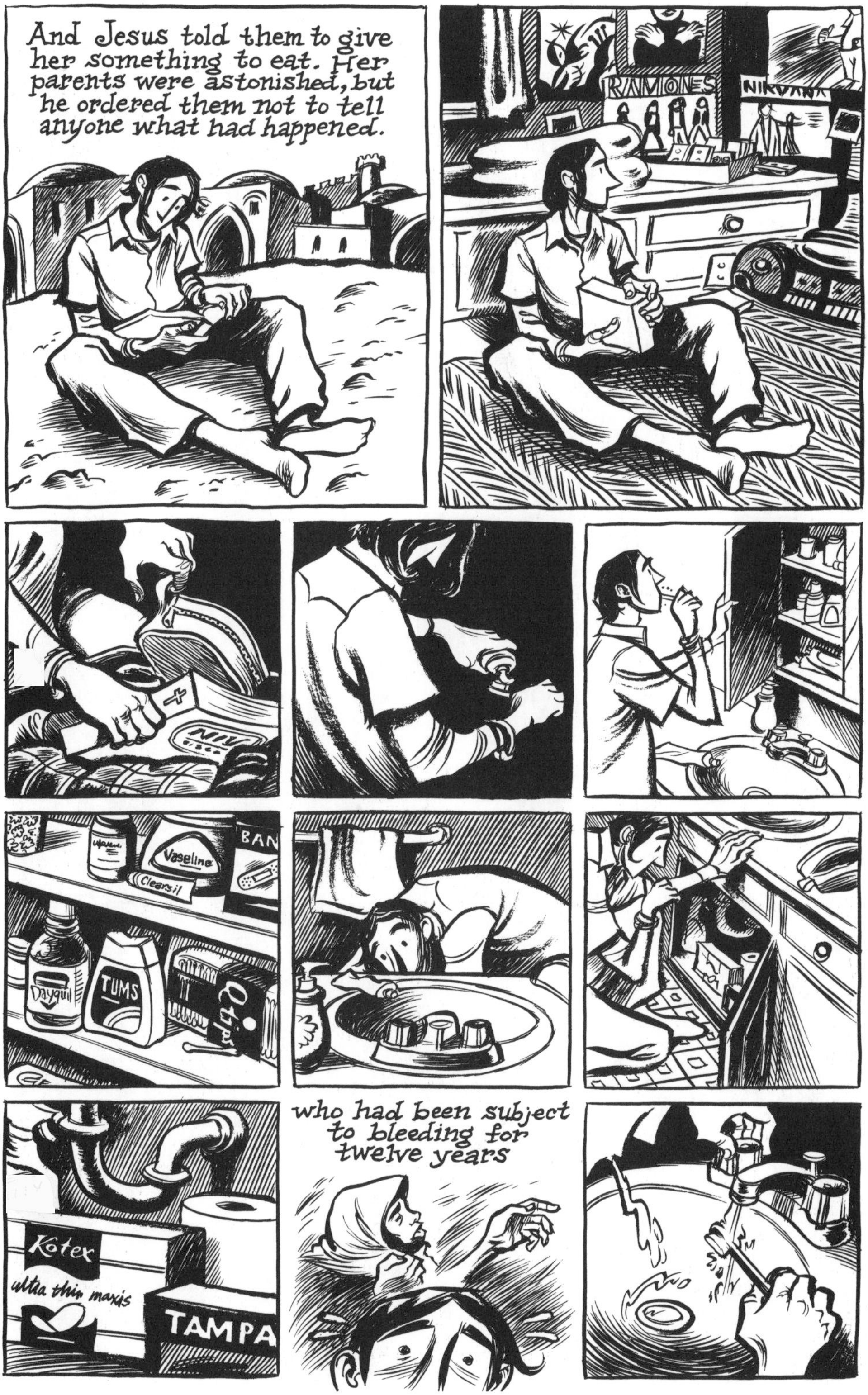
And Jesus told them to give her something to eat. Her parents were astonished, but he ordered them not to tell anyone what had happened.
RAMONES
NIRVANA
Vaseline
Clearsil
BAN
Dayquil
TUMS
Kotex
ultra thin maxis
TAMPA
who had been subject to bleeding for twelve years

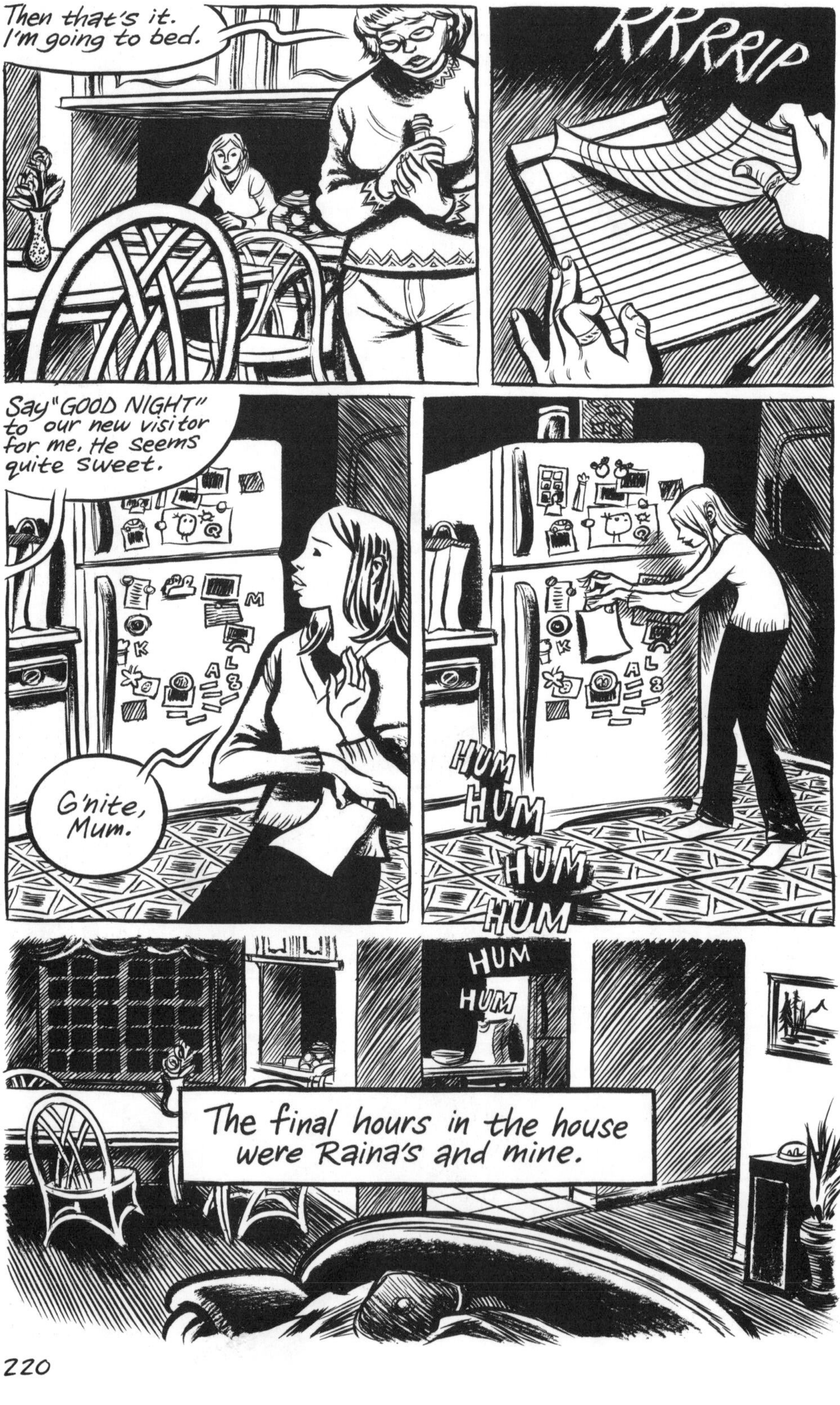
Then that's it. I'm going to bed.
RRRRIP
Say "GOOD NIGHT" to our new visitor for me. He seems quite sweet.
G'nite, Mum.
HUM HUM HUM HUM
HUM HUM
The final hours in the house were Raina's and mine.

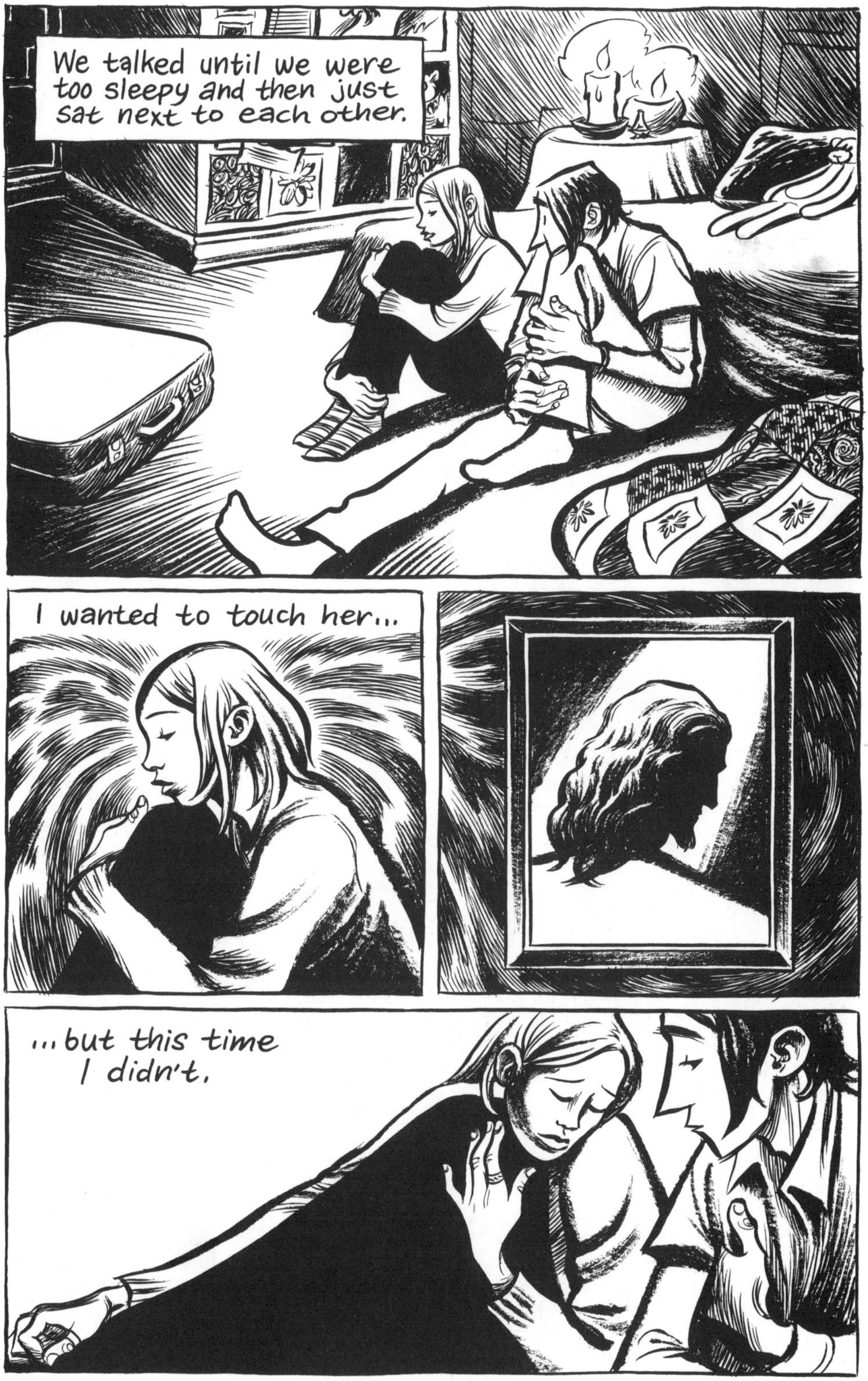
We talked until we were too sleepy and then just sat next to each other.
I wanted to touch her...
...but this time I didn't.

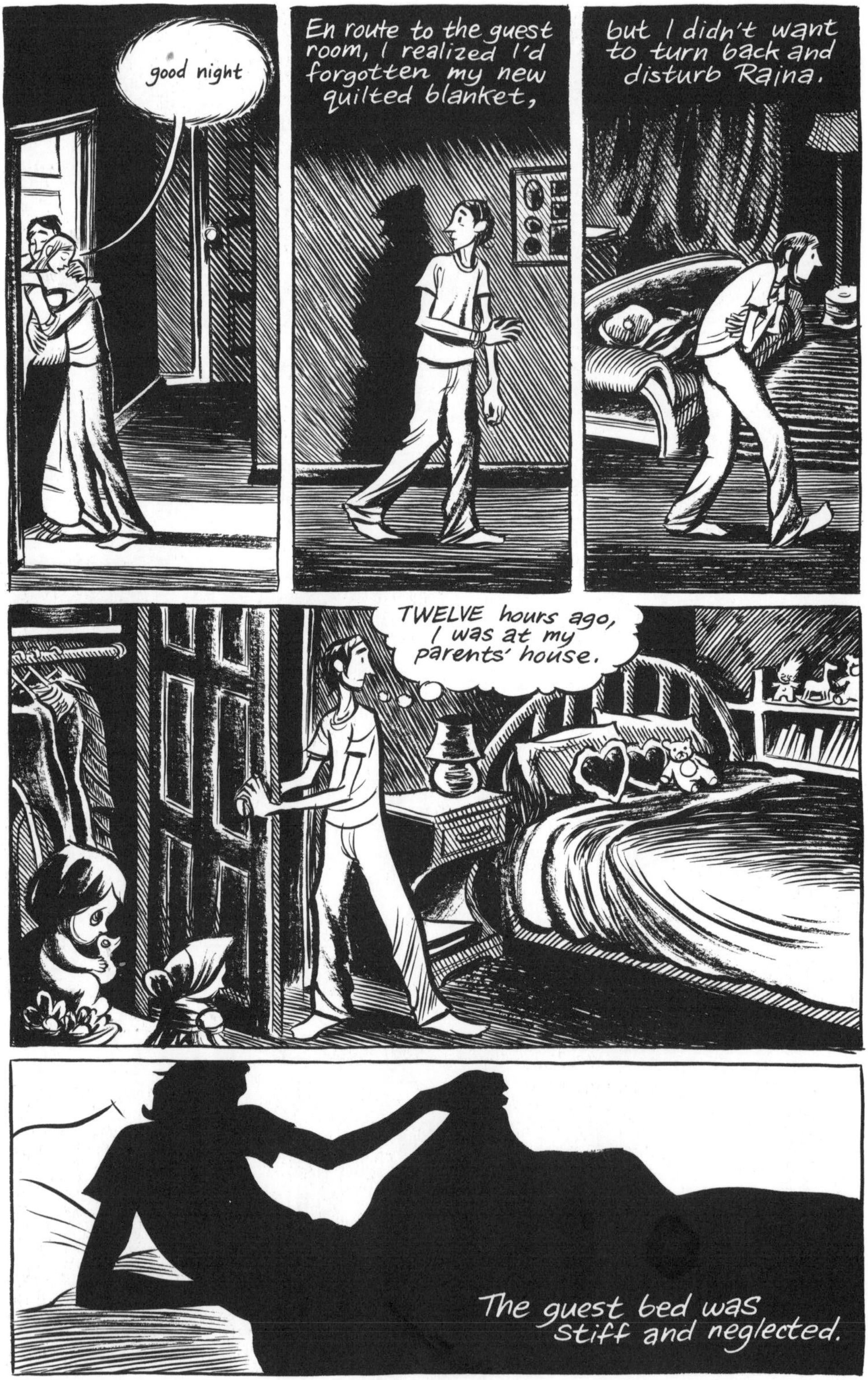
good night
En route to the guest room, I realized I'd forgotten my new quilted blanket,
but I didn't want to turn back and disturb Raina.
TWELVE hours ago, I was at my parents' house.
The guest bed was stiff and neglected.

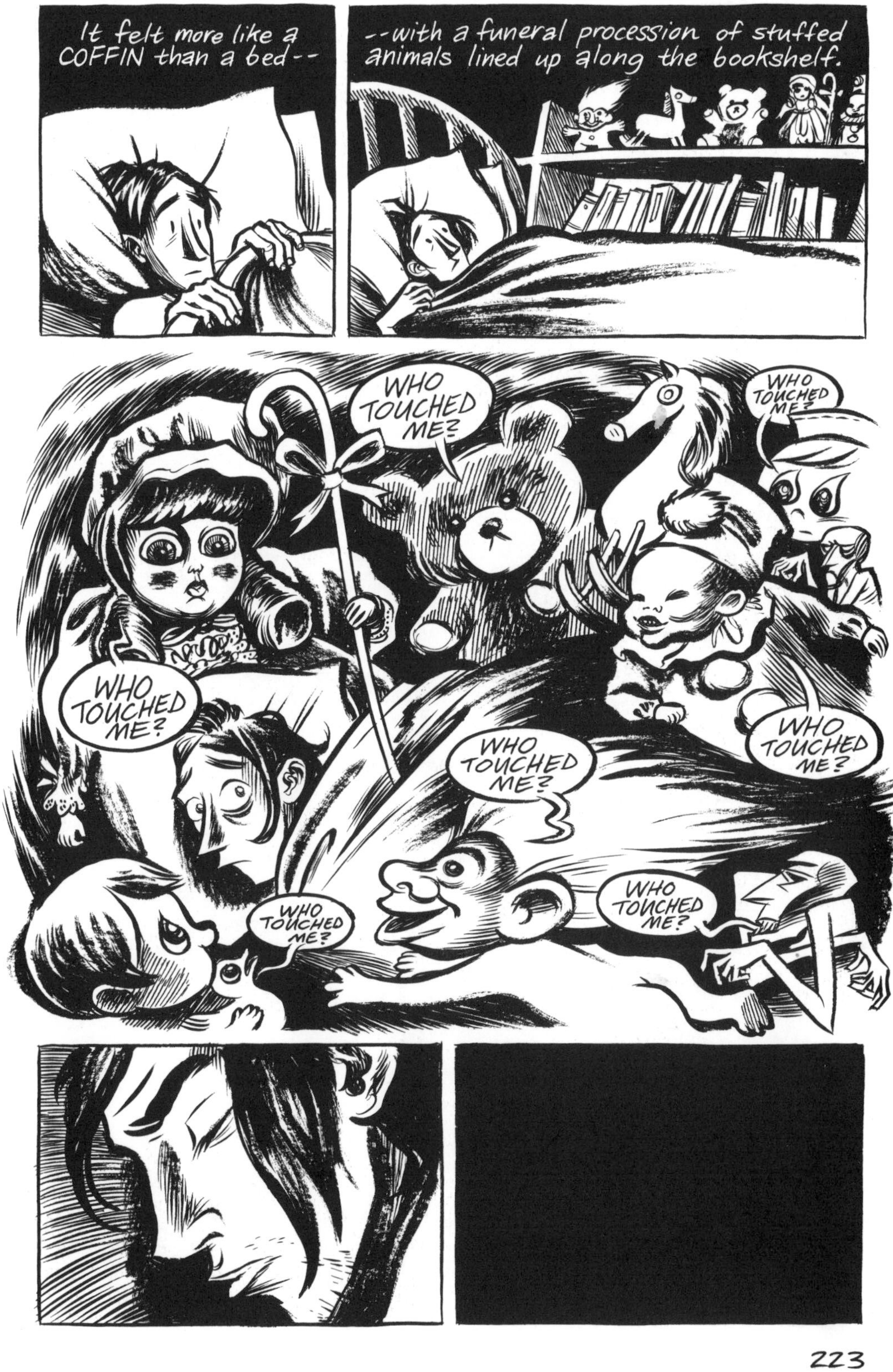
It felt more like a COFFIN than a bed--
--with a funeral procession of stuffed animals lined up along the bookshelf.
WHO TOUCHED ME?
WHO TOUCHED ME?
WHO TOUCHED ME?
WHO TOUCHED ME?
WHO TOUCHED ME?
WHO TOUCHED ME?
WHO TOUCHED ME?

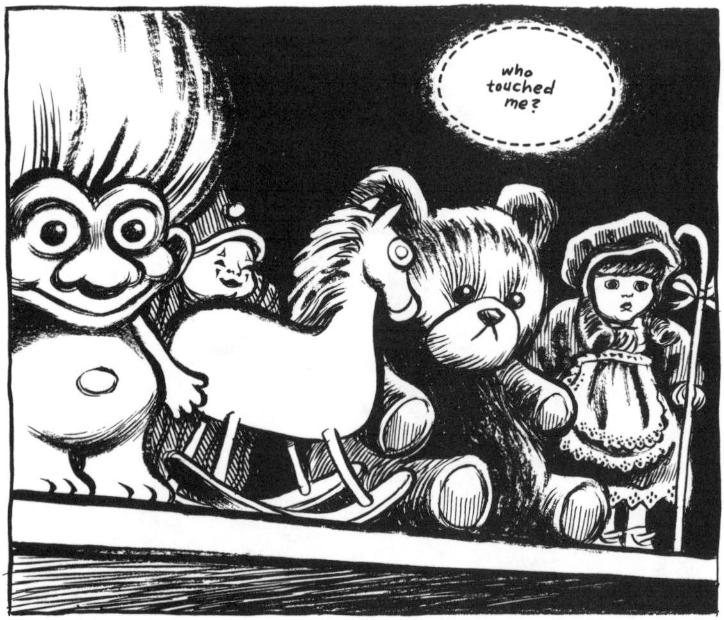
who touched me?

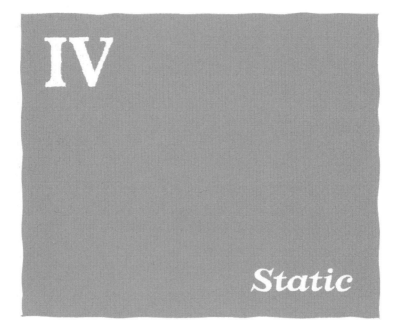

IV

Static

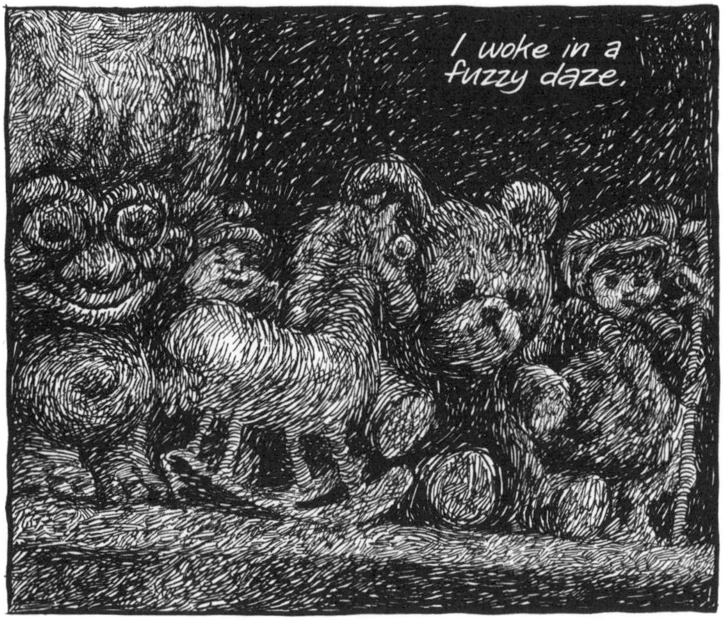
I woke in a fuzzy daze.

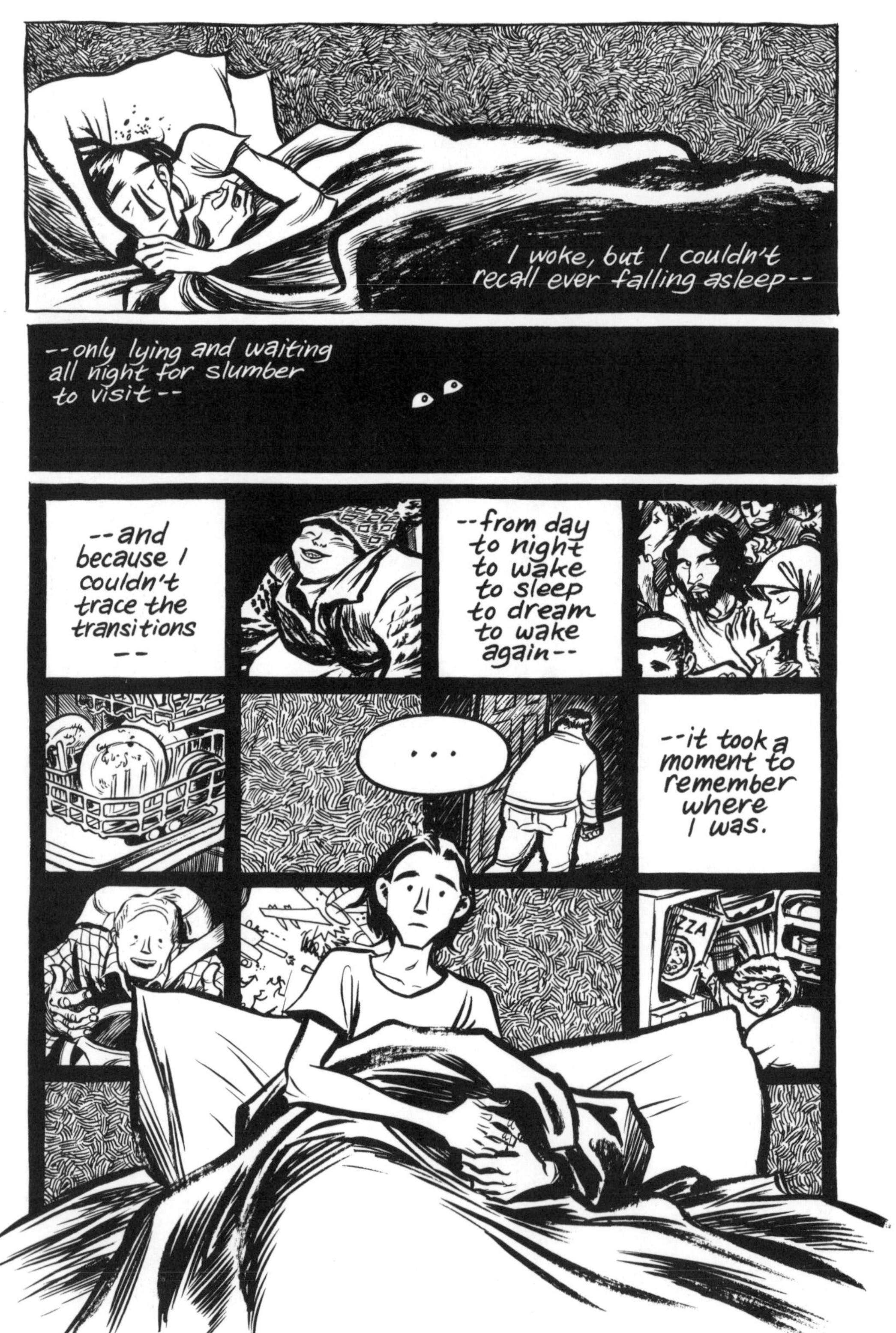
I woke, but I couldn't recall ever falling asleep--
--only lying and waiting all night for slumber to visit--
--and because I couldn't trace the transitions --
--from day to night to wake to sleep to dream to wake again--
...
--it took a moment to remember where I was.
ZZA

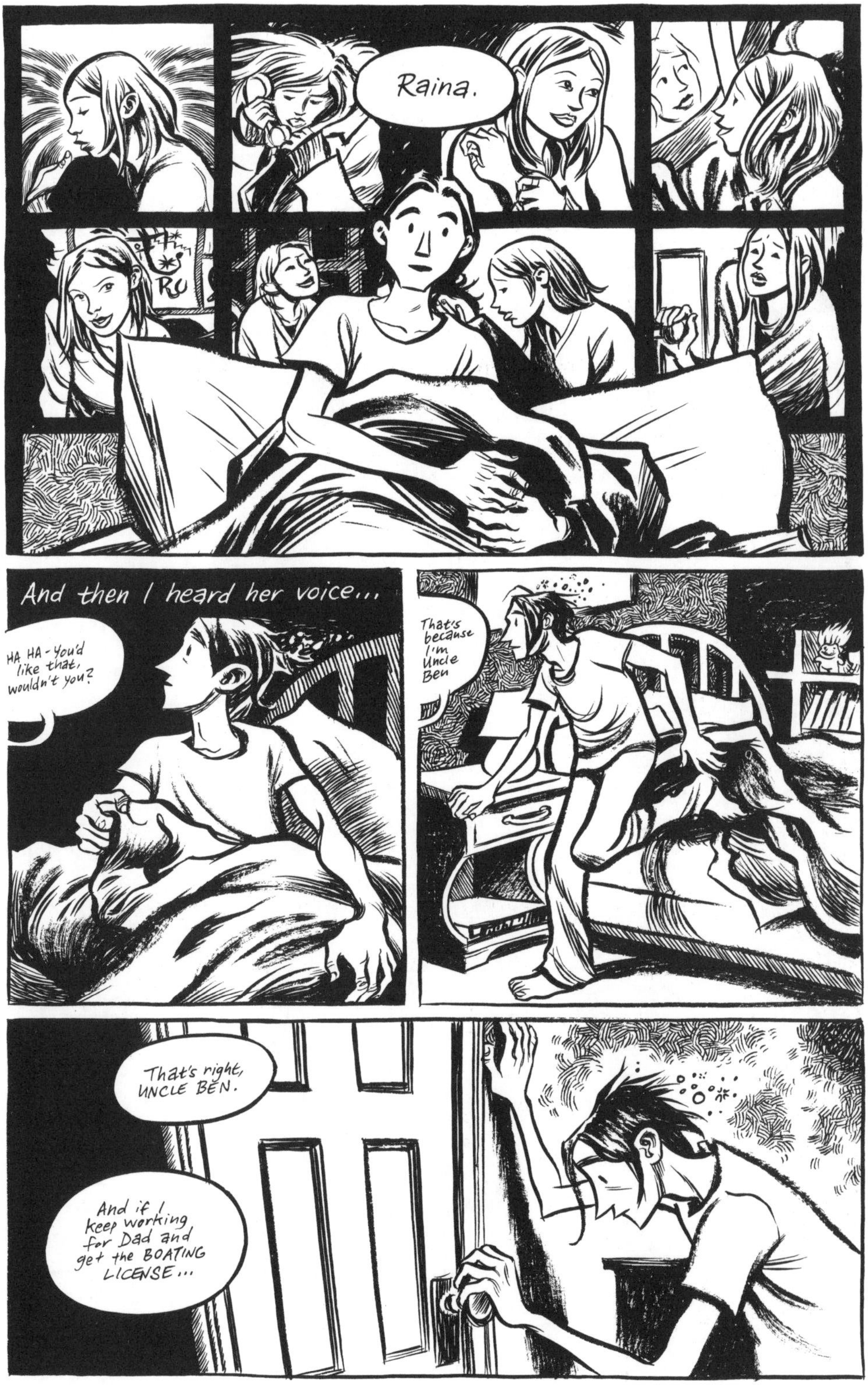
Raina.
And then I heard her voice...
HA HA - You'd like that, wouldn't you?
That's because I'm Uncle Ben
That's right, UNCLE BEN.
And if I keep working for Dad and get the BOATING LICENSE...

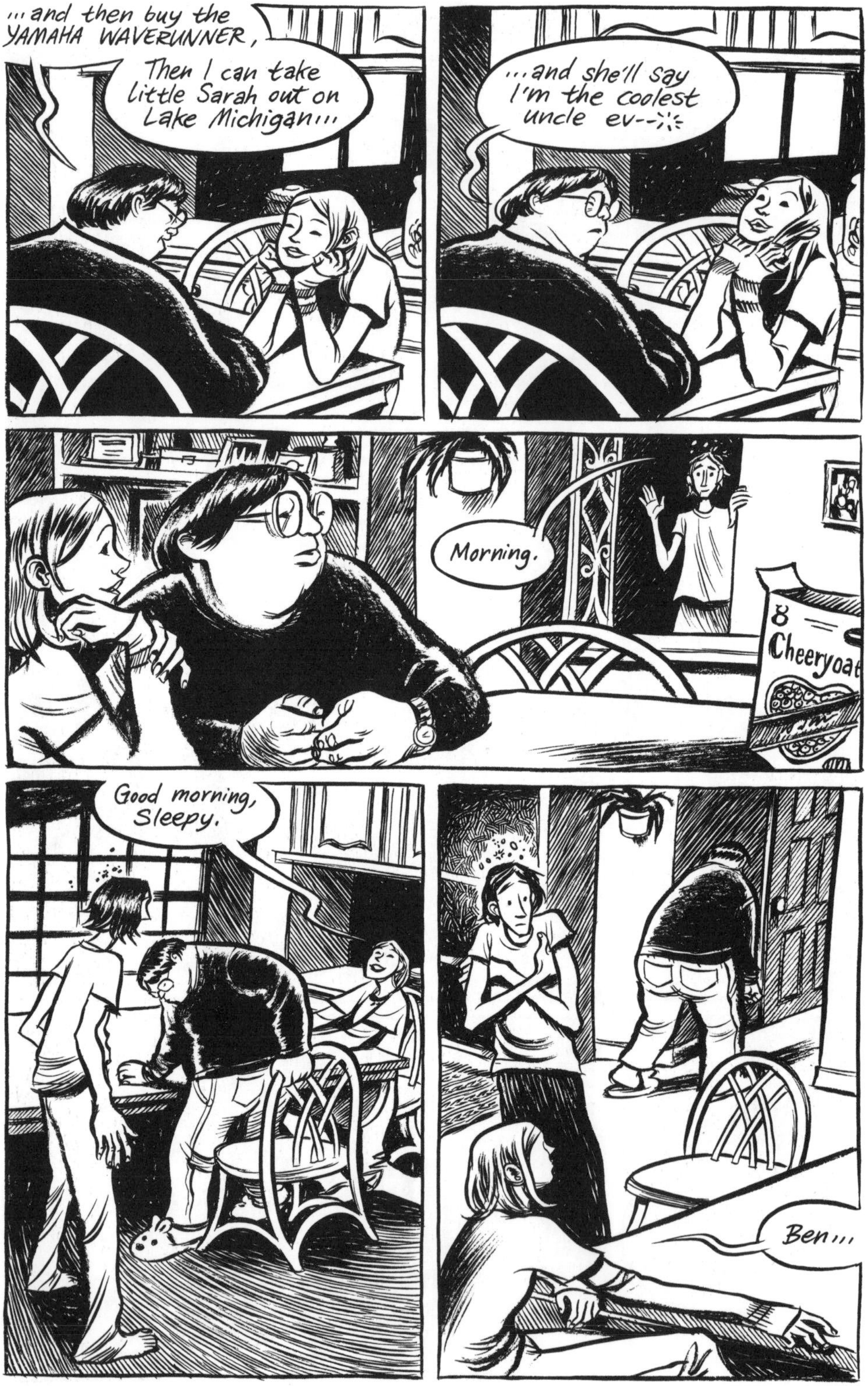
...and then buy the YAMAHA WAVERUNNER,
Then I can take little Sarah out on Lake Michigan...
...and she'll say I'm the coolest uncle ev--
Morning.
Cheeryoat
Good morning, Sleepy.
Ben...

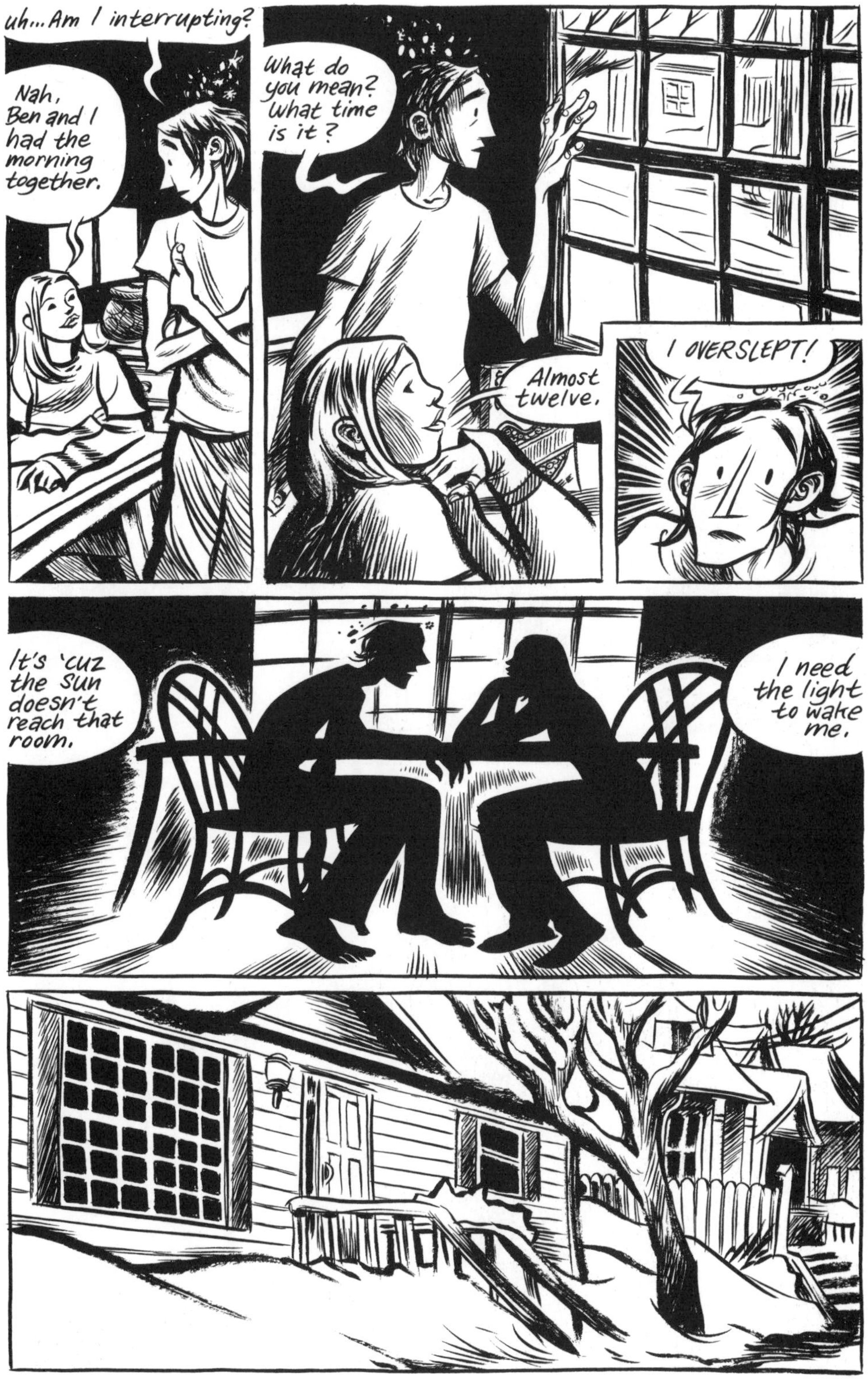

uh... Am I interrupting?
Nah, Ben and I had the morning together.
What do you mean? What time is it?
Almost twelve.
I OVERSLEPT!
It's 'cuz the sun doesn't reach that room.
I need the light to wake me.

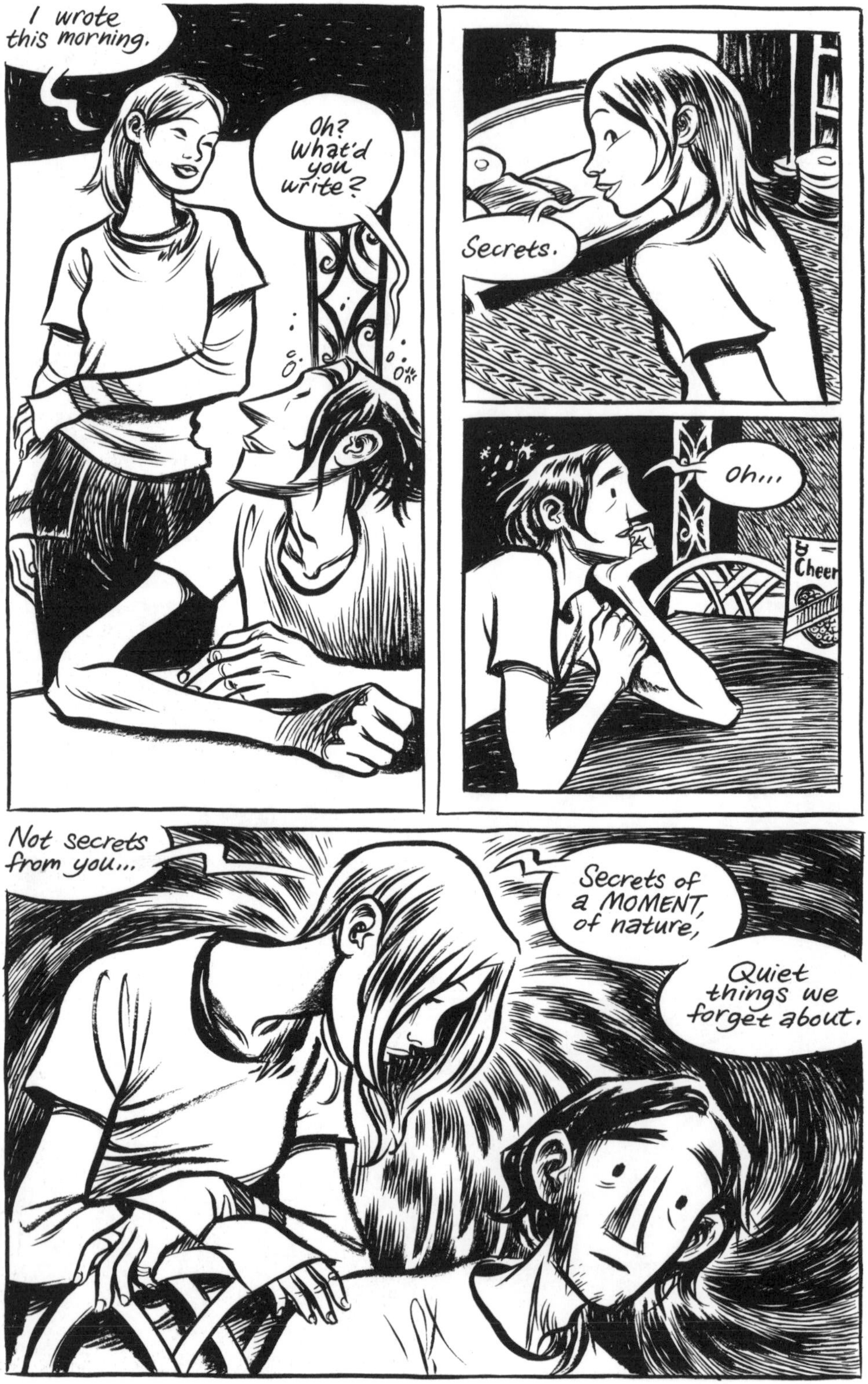

I wrote this morning.
Oh? What'd you write?
Secrets.
Oh...
Cheer
Not secrets from you...
Secrets of a MOMENT, of nature,
Quiet things we forget about.

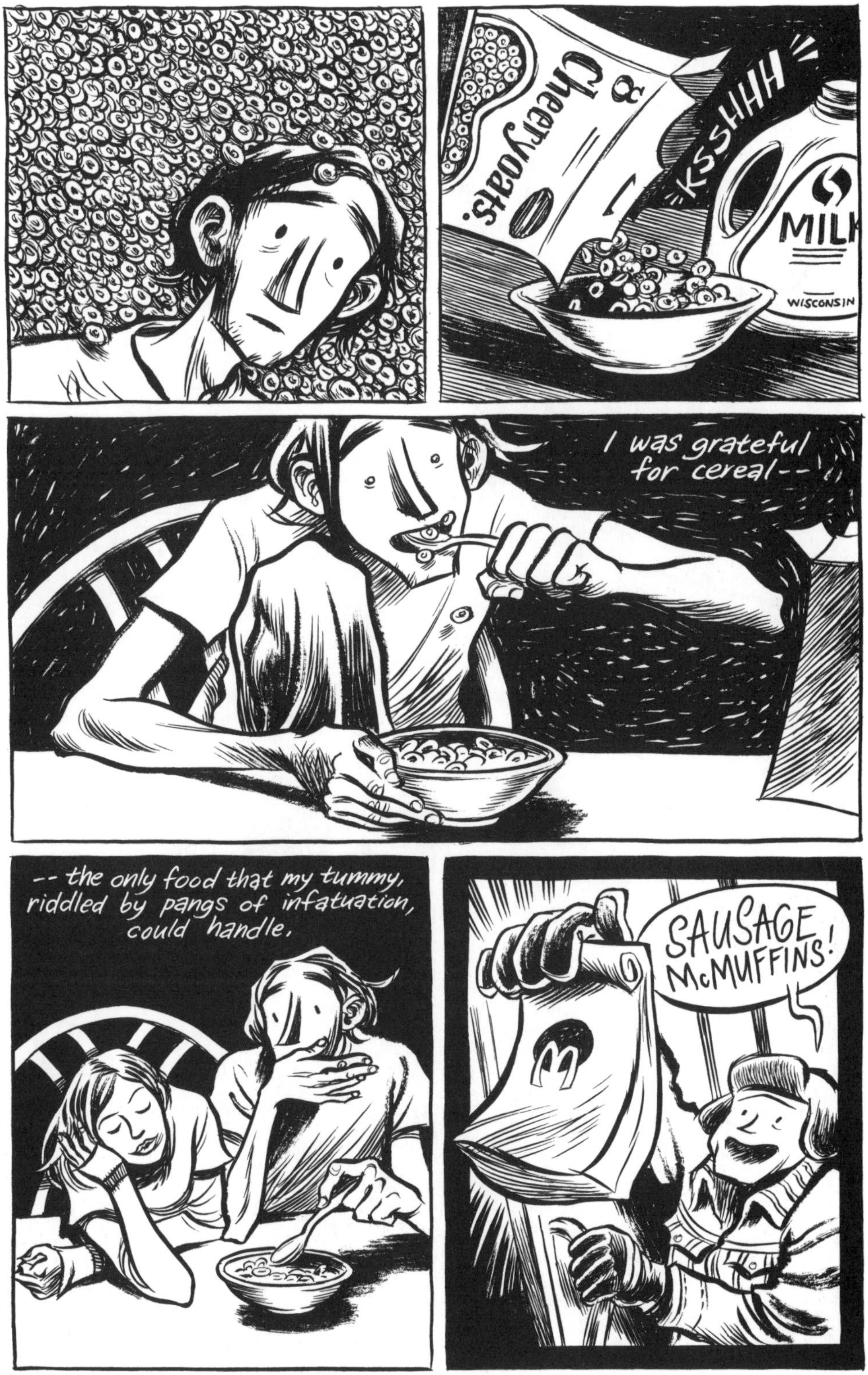
Cheeryoats
KSSHHH
MILK
WISCONSIN
I was grateful for cereal--
-- the only food that my tummy, riddled by pangs of infatuation, could handle.
SAUSAGE McMUFFINS!

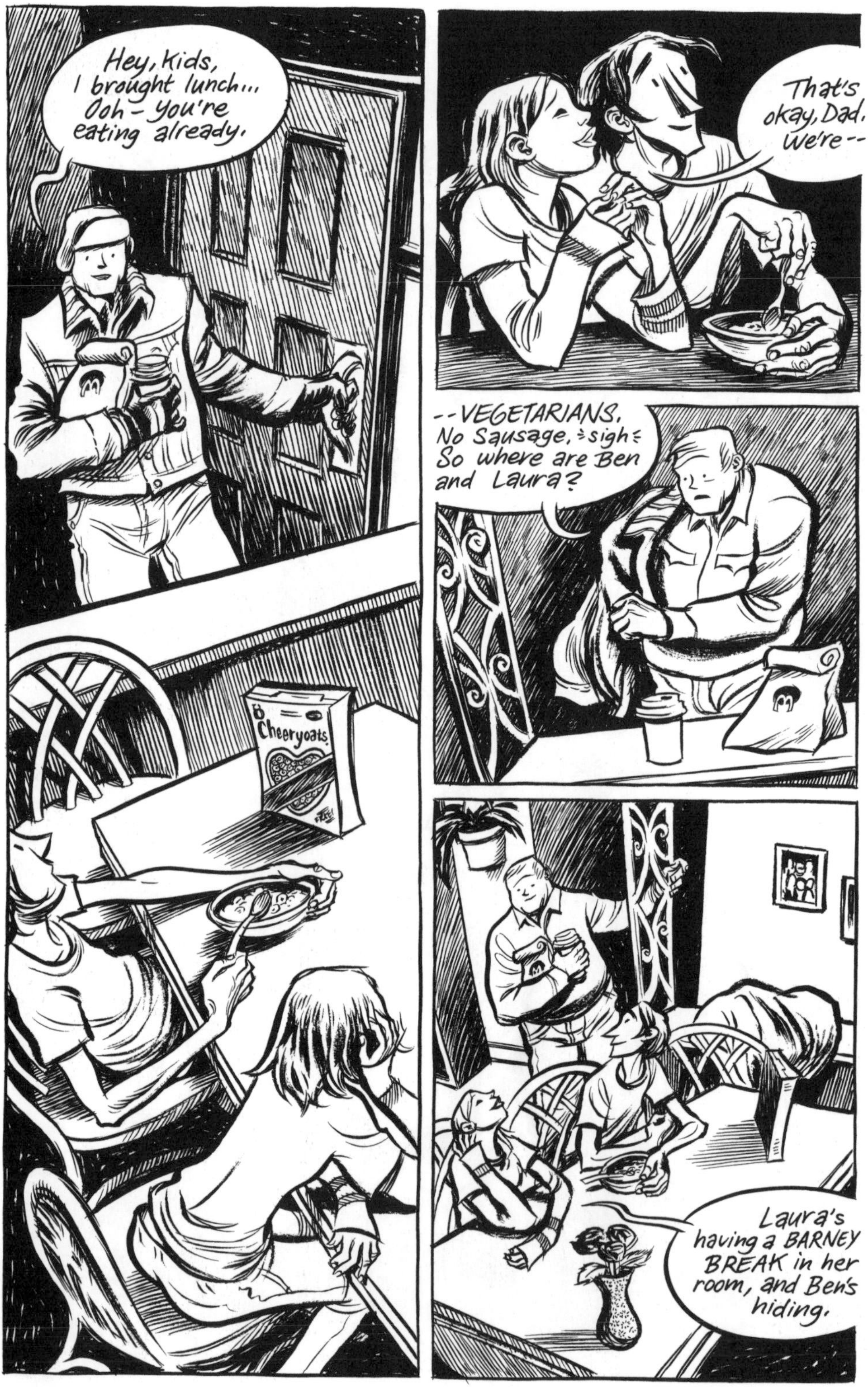
Hey, Kids, I brought lunch... Ooh - You're eating already.
That's okay, Dad. We're--
--VEGETARIANS. No Sausage. sigh So where are Ben and Laura?
Cheeryoats
Laura's having a BARNEY BREAK in her room, and Ben's hiding.

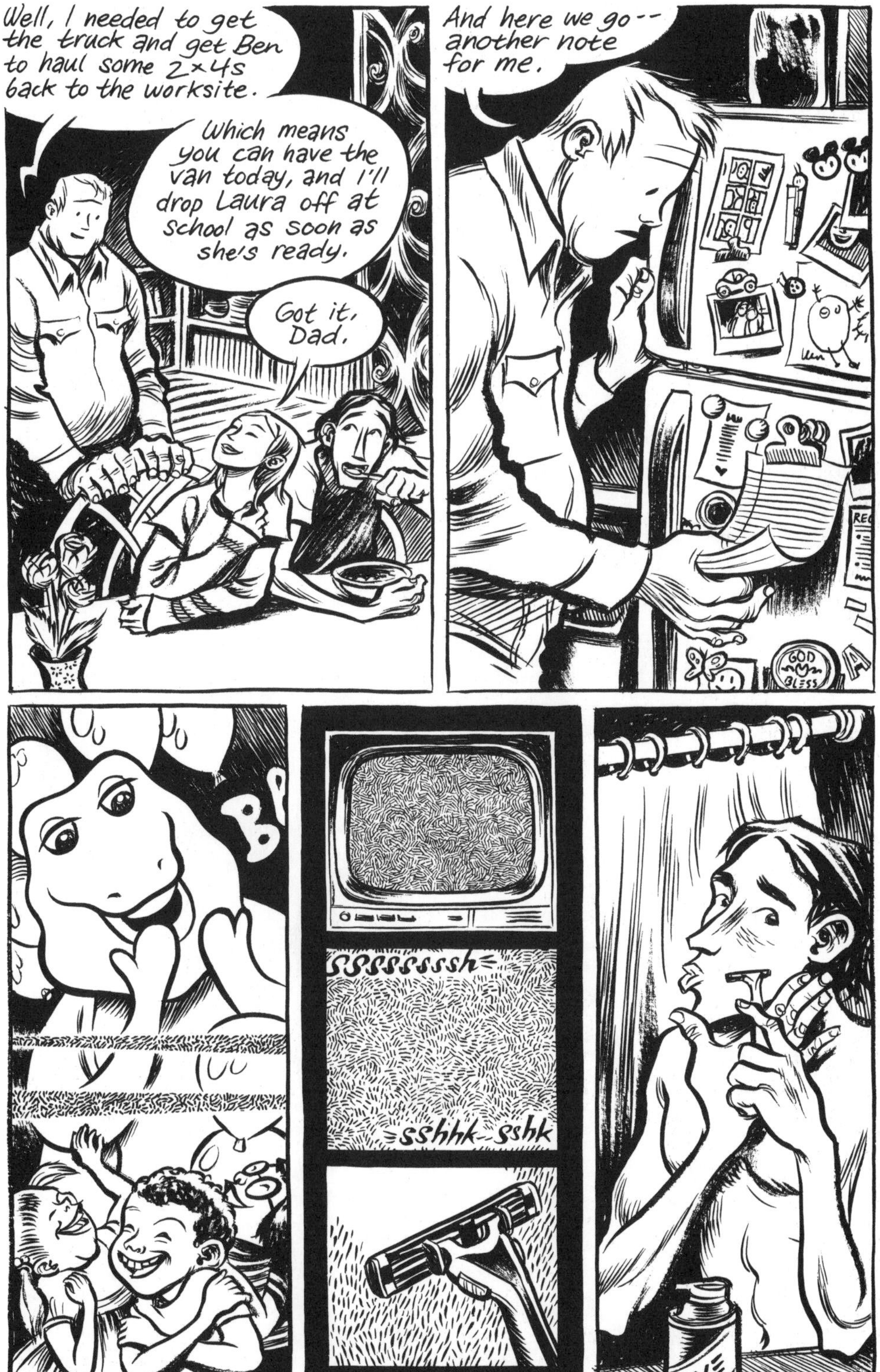
Well, I needed to get the truck and get Ben to haul some 2×4s back to the worksite.
Which means you can have the van today, and I'll drop Laura off at school as soon as she's ready.
Got it, Dad.
And here we go -- another note for me.
GOD BLESS
SSSSSSSSh
sshhk-sshk

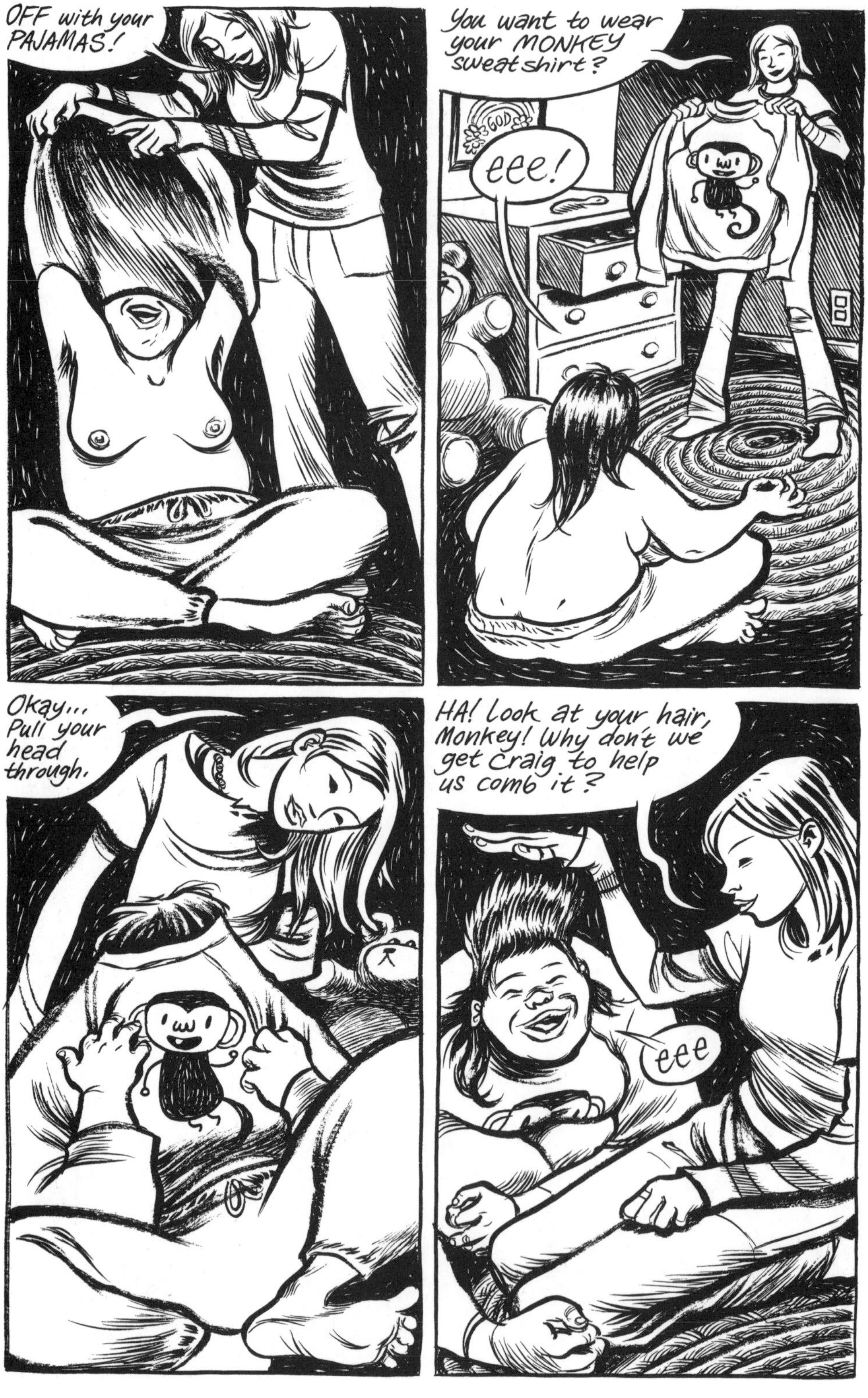
OFF with your PAJAMAS!
You want to wear your MONKEY sweatshirt?
GOD
eee!
Okay... Pull your head through.
HA! Look at your hair, Monkey! Why don't we get Craig to help us comb it?
eee

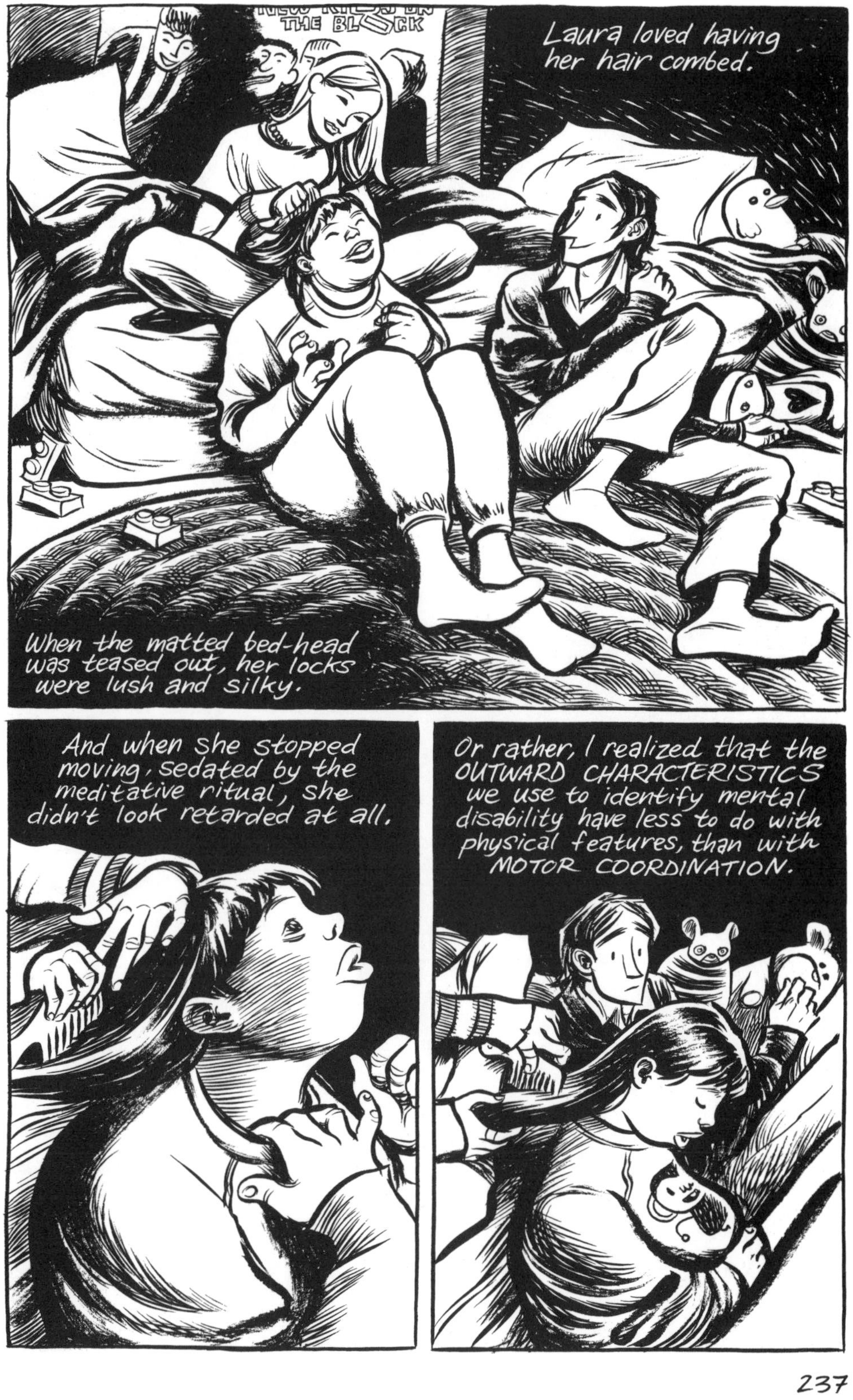
Laura loved having her hair combed.
When the matted bed-head was teased out, her locks were lush and silky.
And when she stopped moving, sedated by the meditative ritual, she didn't look retarded at all.
Or rather, I realized that the OUTWARD CHARACTERISTICS we use to identify mental disability have less to do with physical features, than with MOTOR COORDINATION.

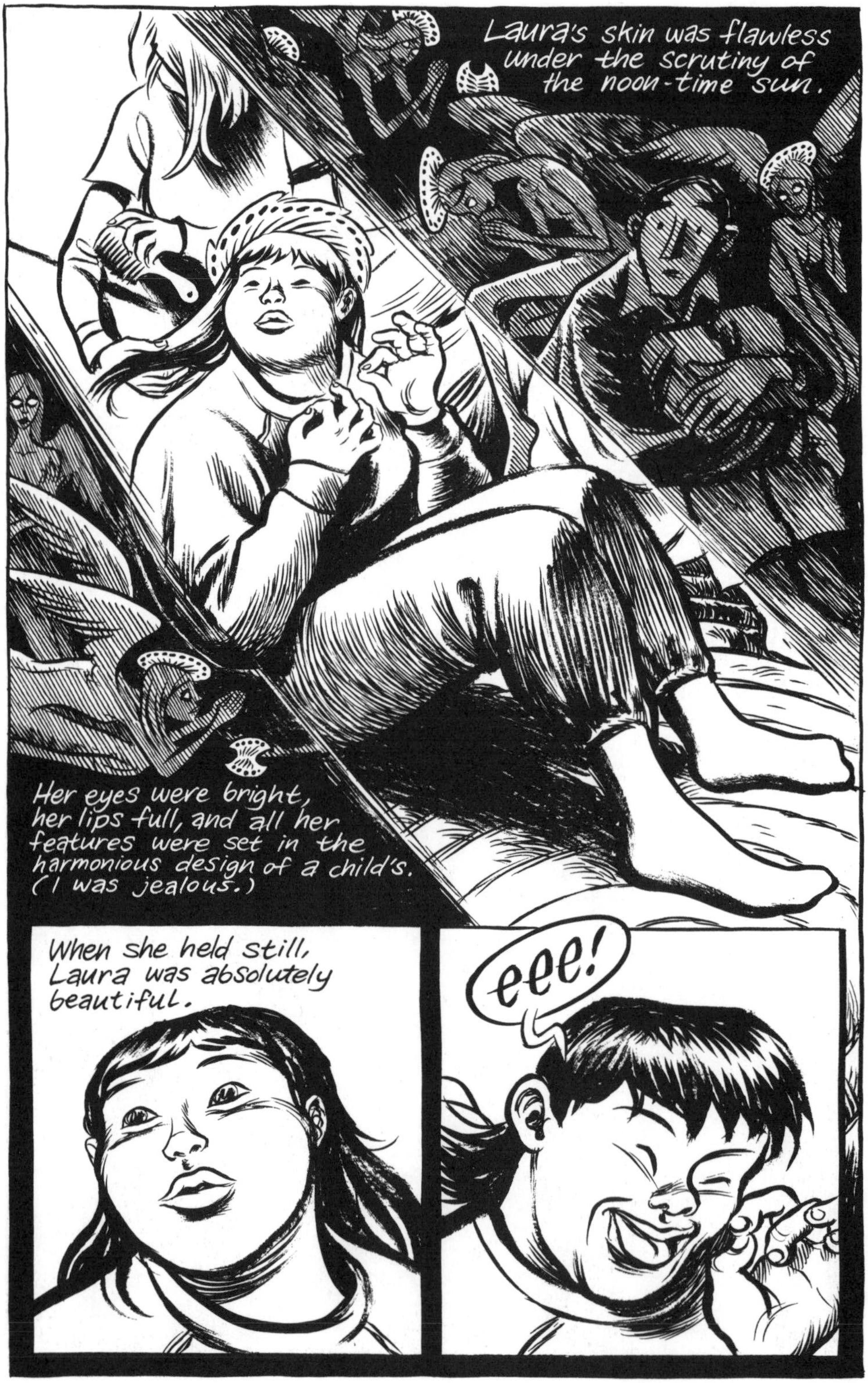
Laura's skin was flawless under the scrutiny of the noon-time sun.
Her eyes were bright, her lips full, and all her features were set in the harmonious design of a child's. (I was jealous.)
When she held still, Laura was absolutely beautiful.
eee!

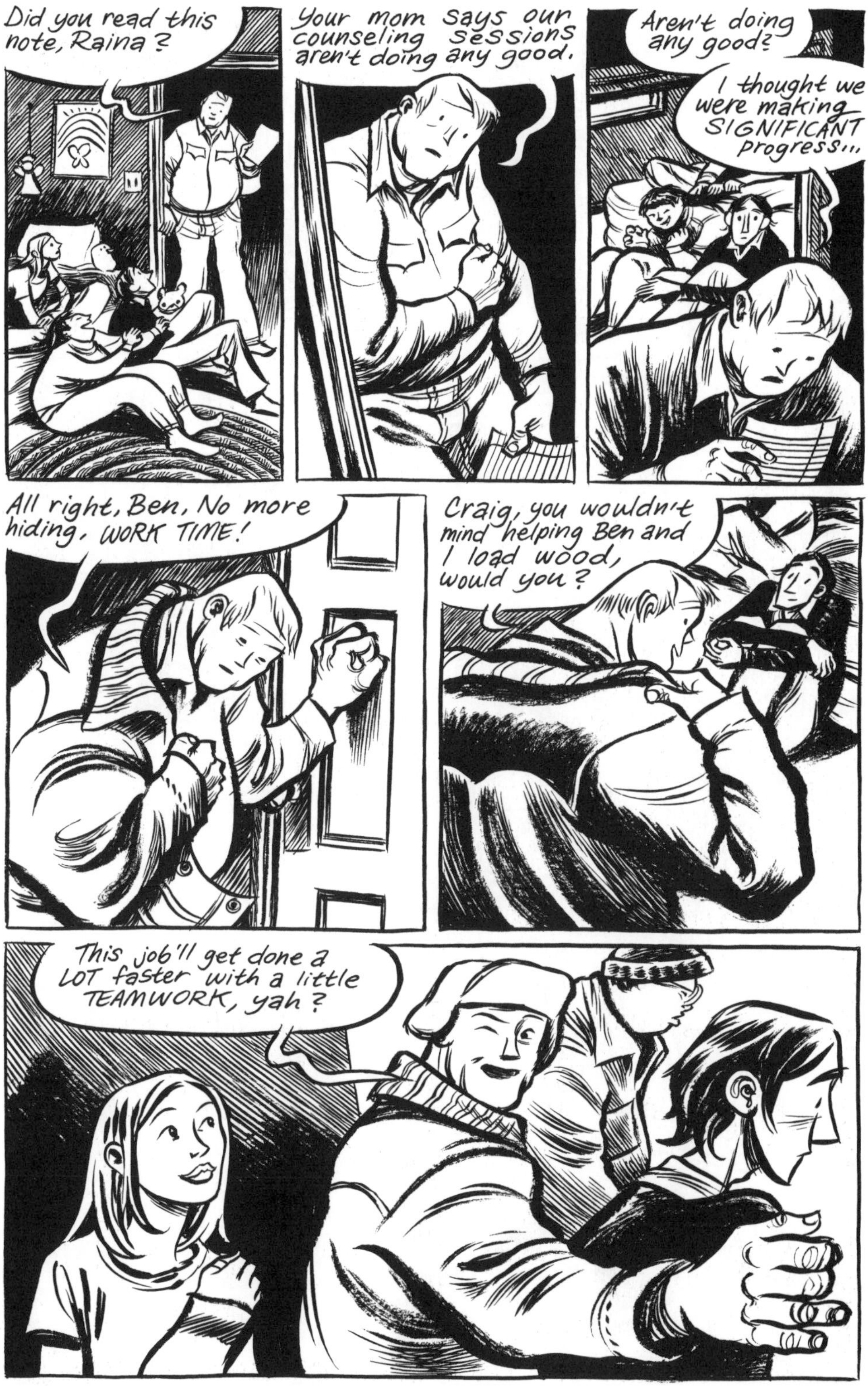
Did you read this note, Raina?
Your mom says our counseling sessions aren't doing any good.
Aren't doing any good?
I thought we were making SIGNIFICANT progress...
All right, Ben, No more hiding, WORK TIME!
Craig, you wouldn't mind helping Ben and I load wood, would you?
This job'll get done a LOT faster with a little TEAMWORK, yah?

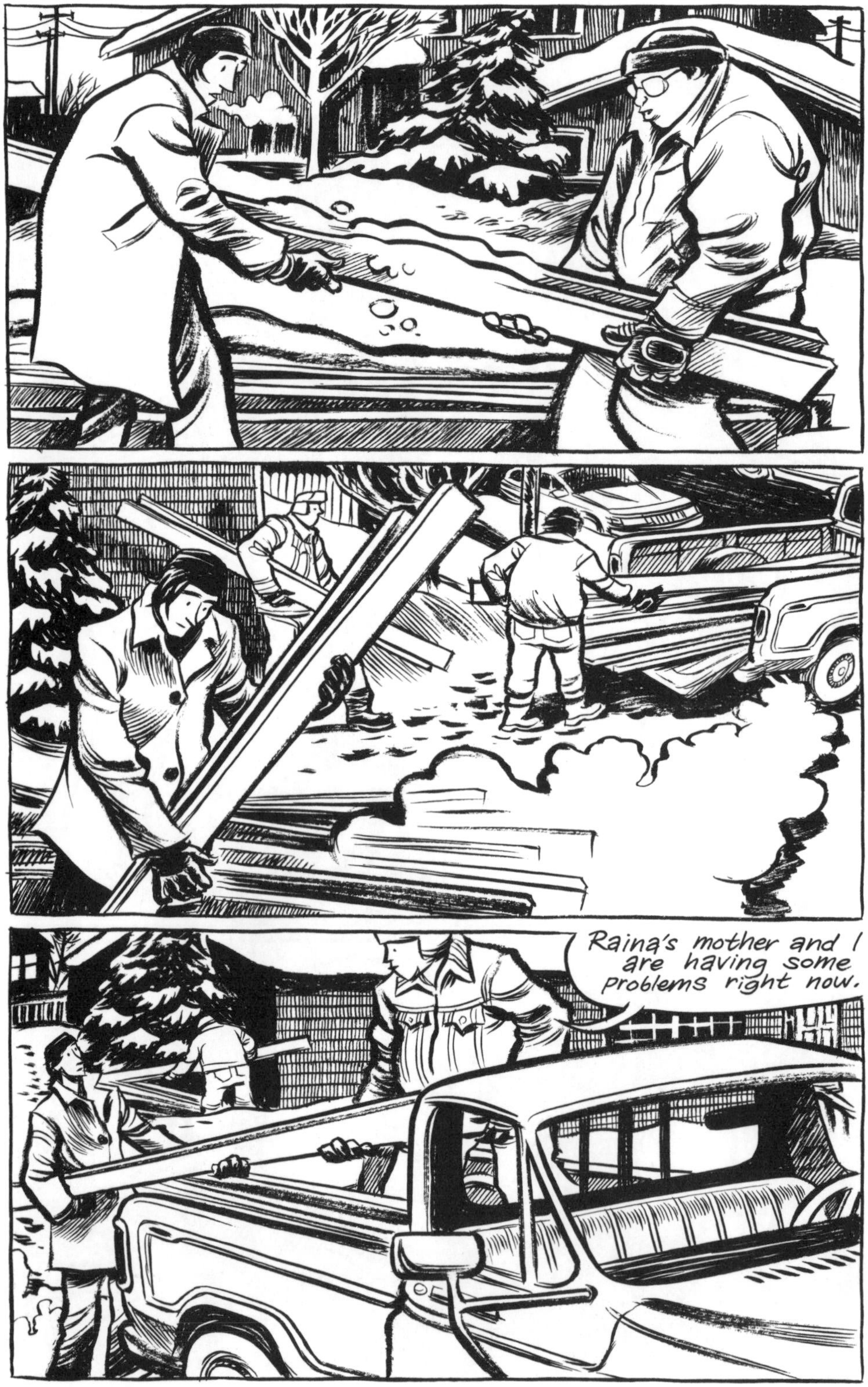
Raina's mother and I are having some problems right now.

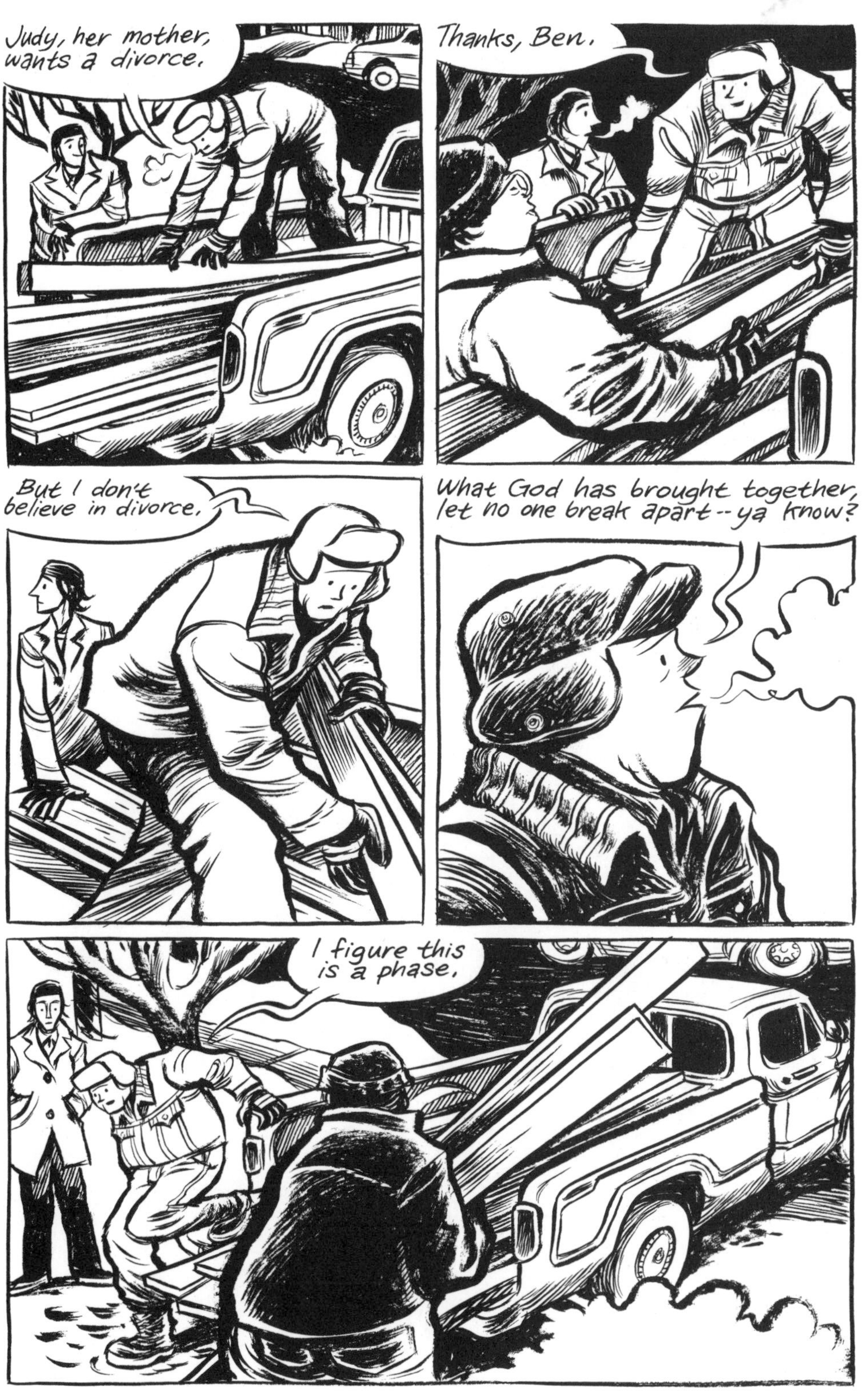
Judy, her mother, wants a divorce.
Thanks, Ben.
But I don't believe in divorce.
What God has brought together, let no one break apart--ya know?
I figure this is a phase.

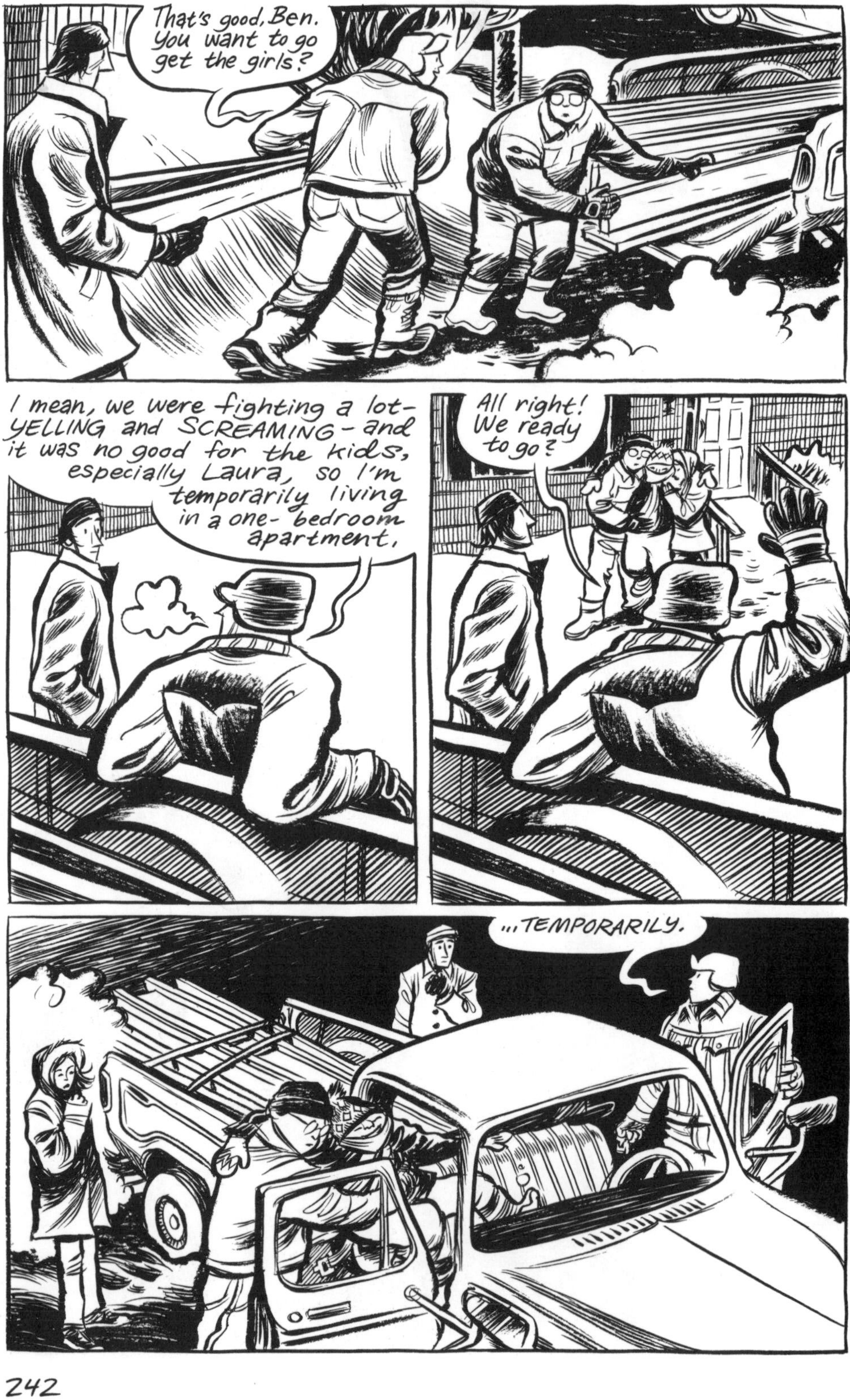
That's good, Ben. You want to go get the girls?
I mean, we were fighting a lot- YELLING and SCREAMING - and it was no good for the kids, especially Laura, so I'm temporarily living in a one-bedroom apartment.
All right! We ready to go?
...TEMPORARILY.

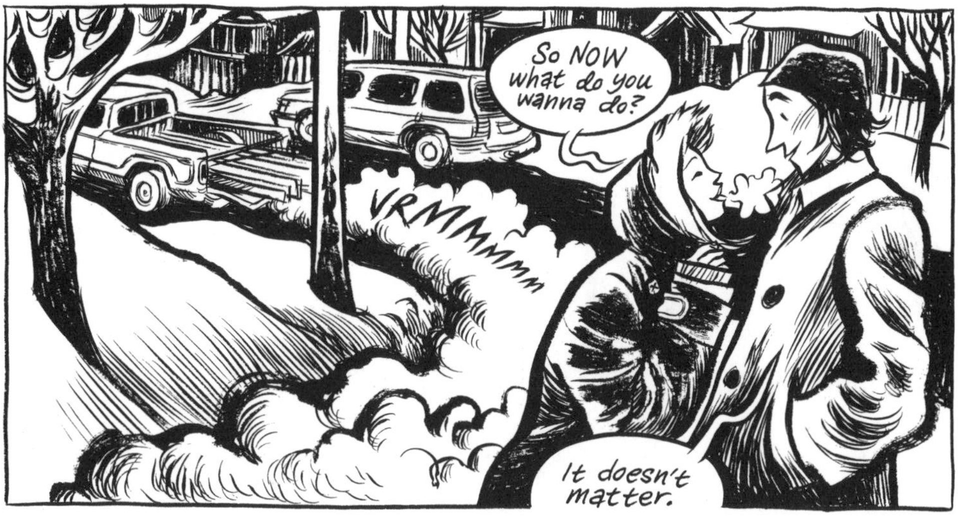
So NOW what do you wanna do?
VRMMMMMMM
It doesn't matter.

And so we drove about town.

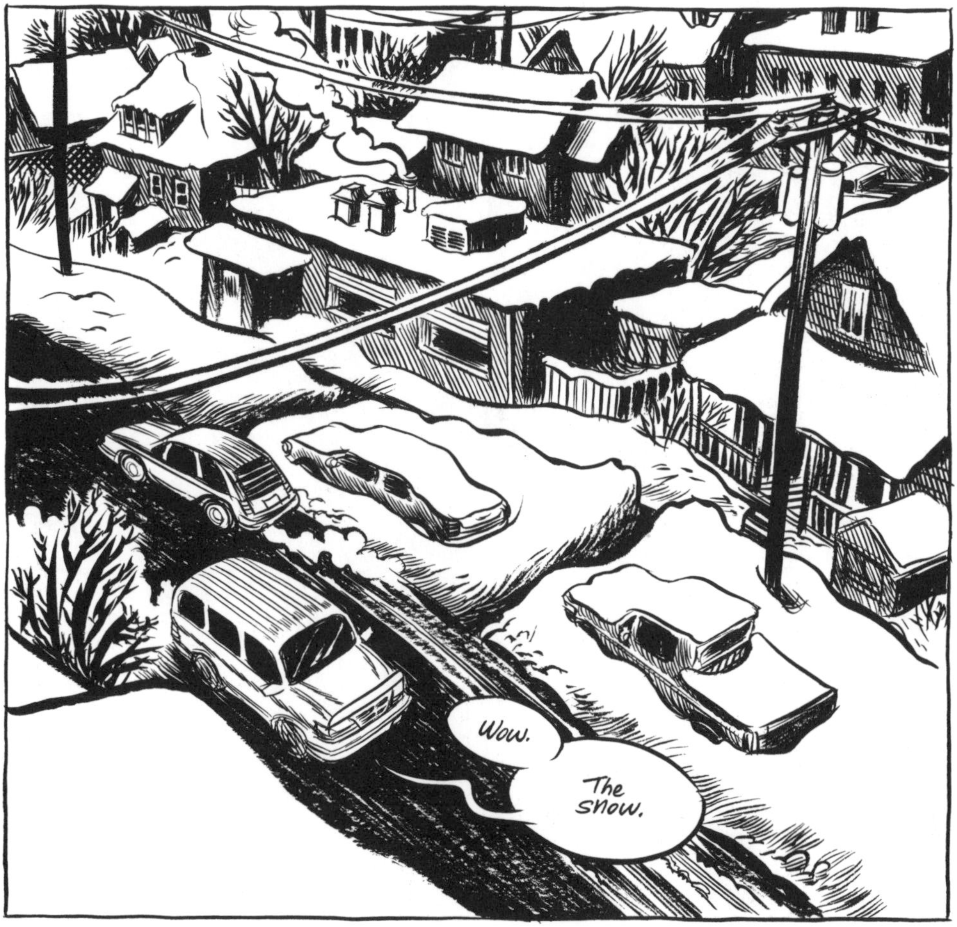
Wow.
The snow.

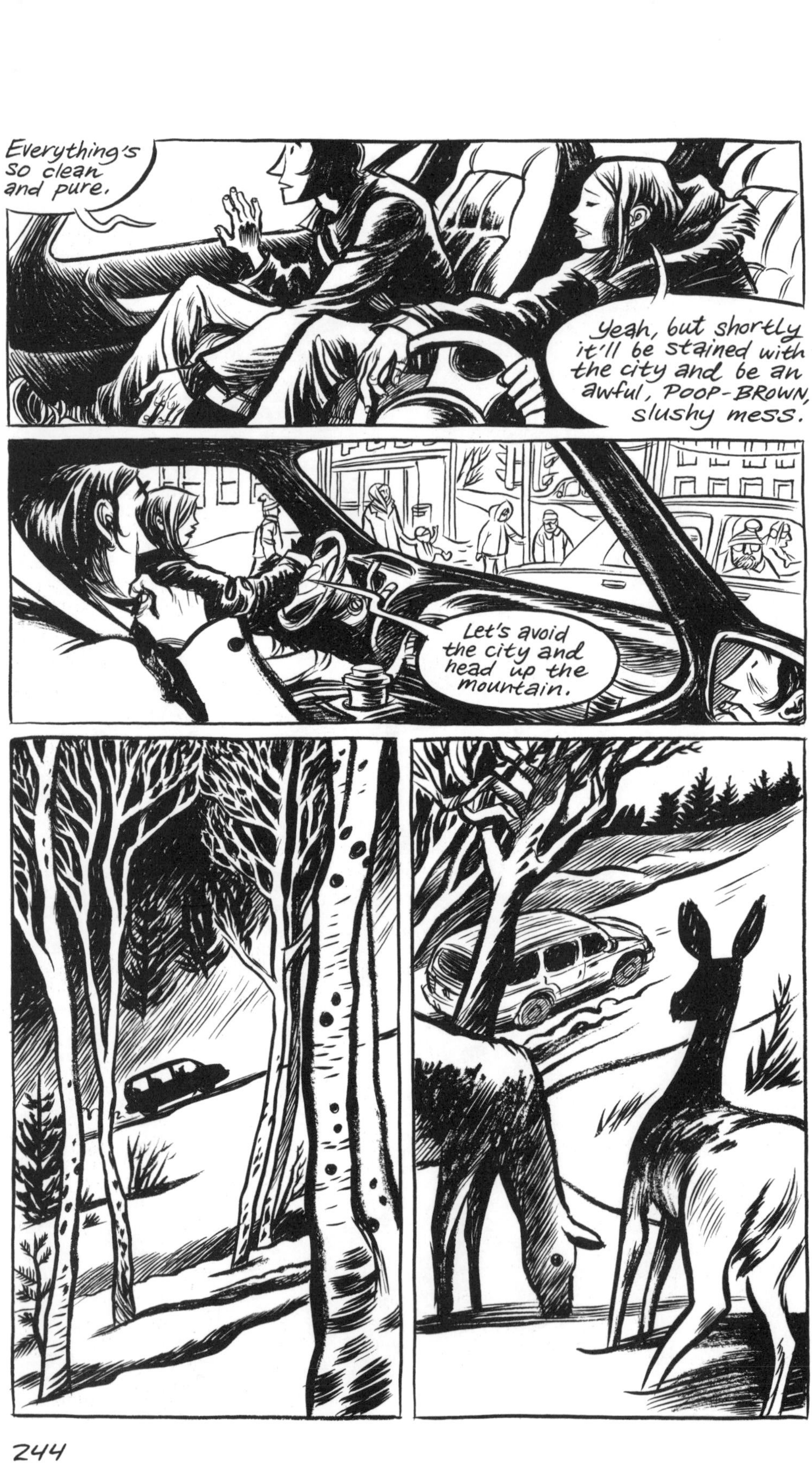
Everything's so clean and pure.
Yeah, but shortly it'll be stained with the city and be an awful, POOP-BROWN, slushy mess.
Let's avoid the city and head up the mountain.

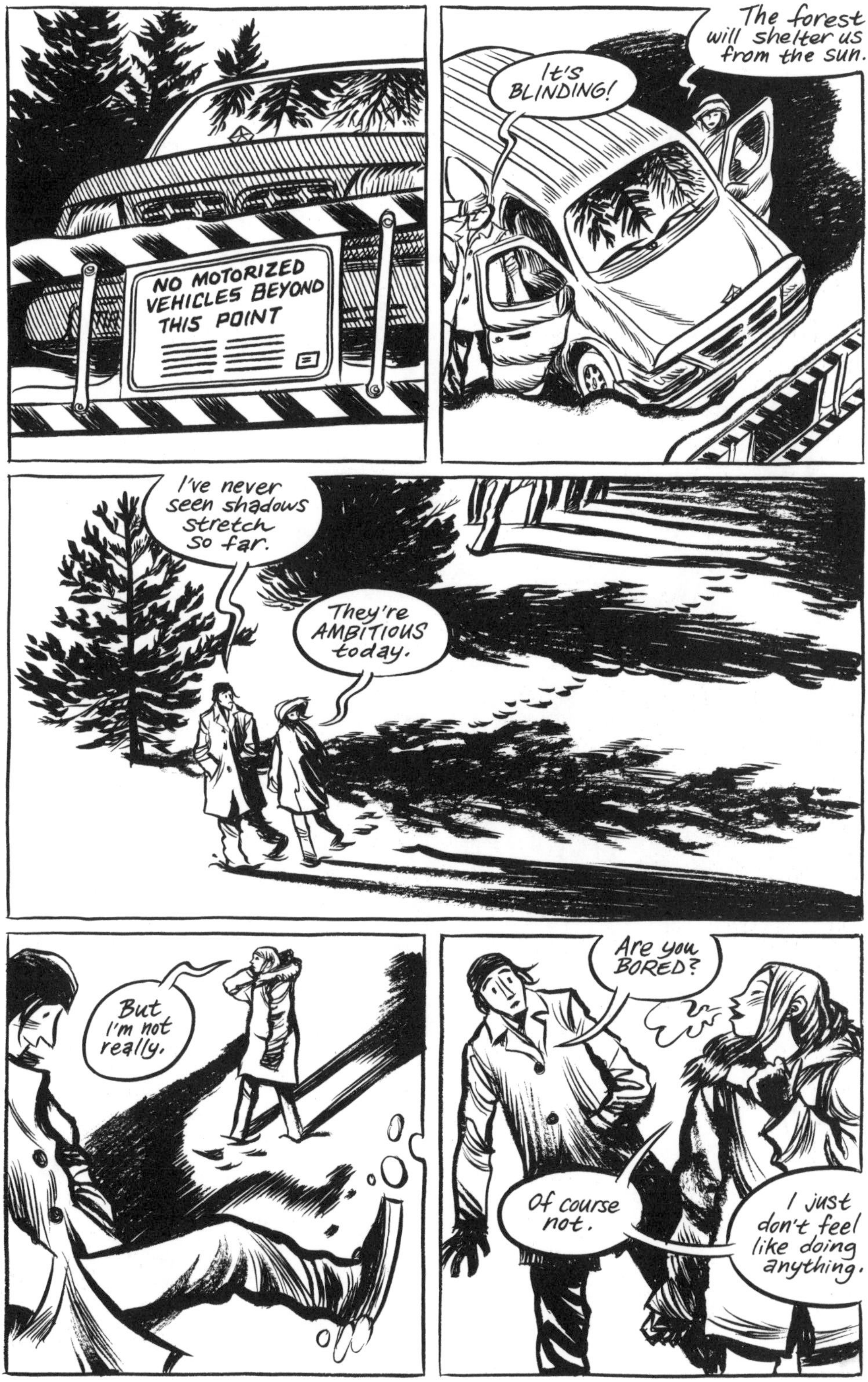
NO MOTORIZED VEHICLES BEYOND THIS POINT
It's BLINDING!
The forest will shelter us from the sun.
I've never seen shadows stretch so far.
They're AMBITIOUS today.
But I'm not really.
Are you BORED?
Of course not.
I just don't feel like doing anything.

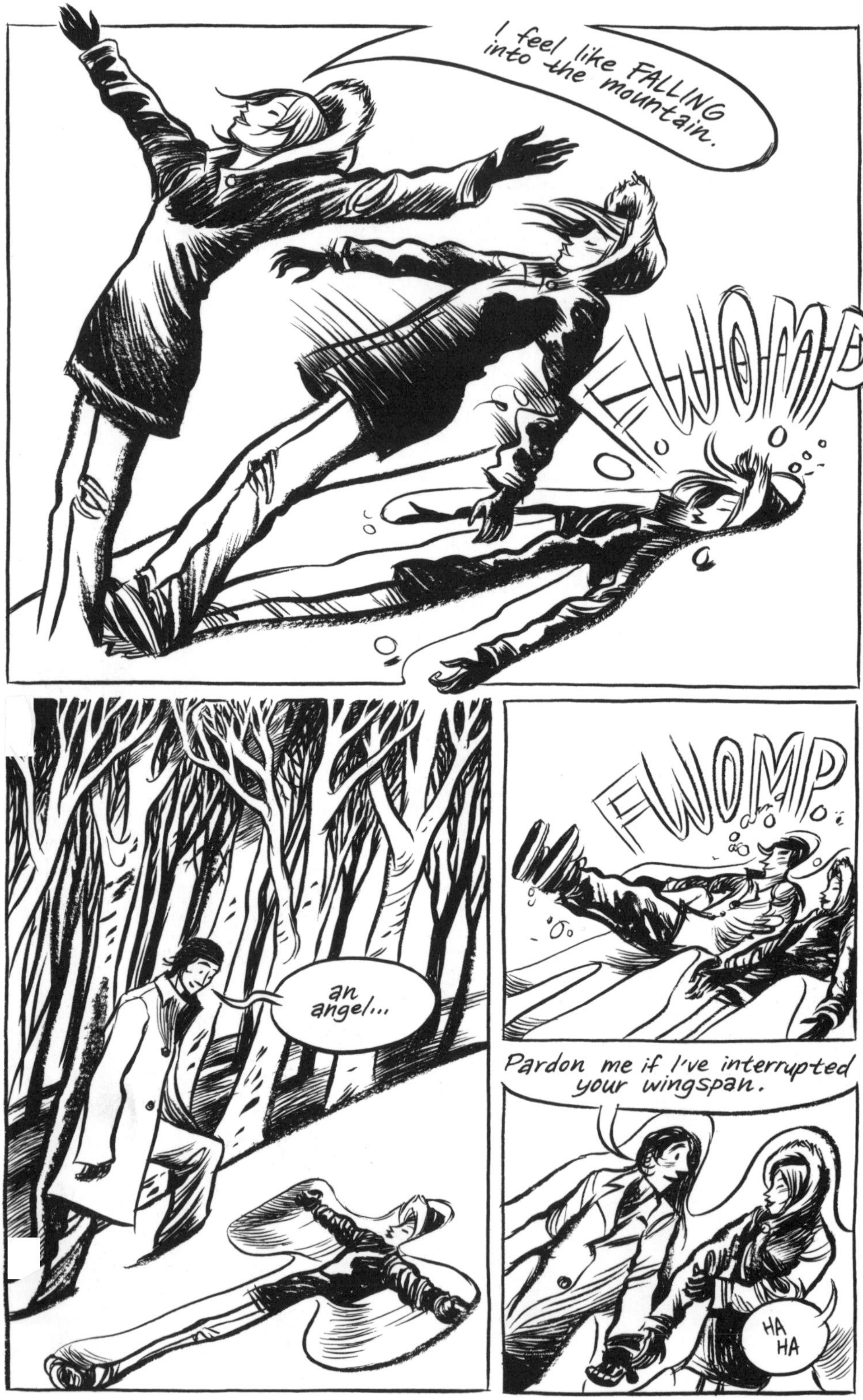
I feel like FALLING into the mountain.
FWOMP
FWOMP
an angel...
Pardon me if I've interrupted your wingspan.
HA HA

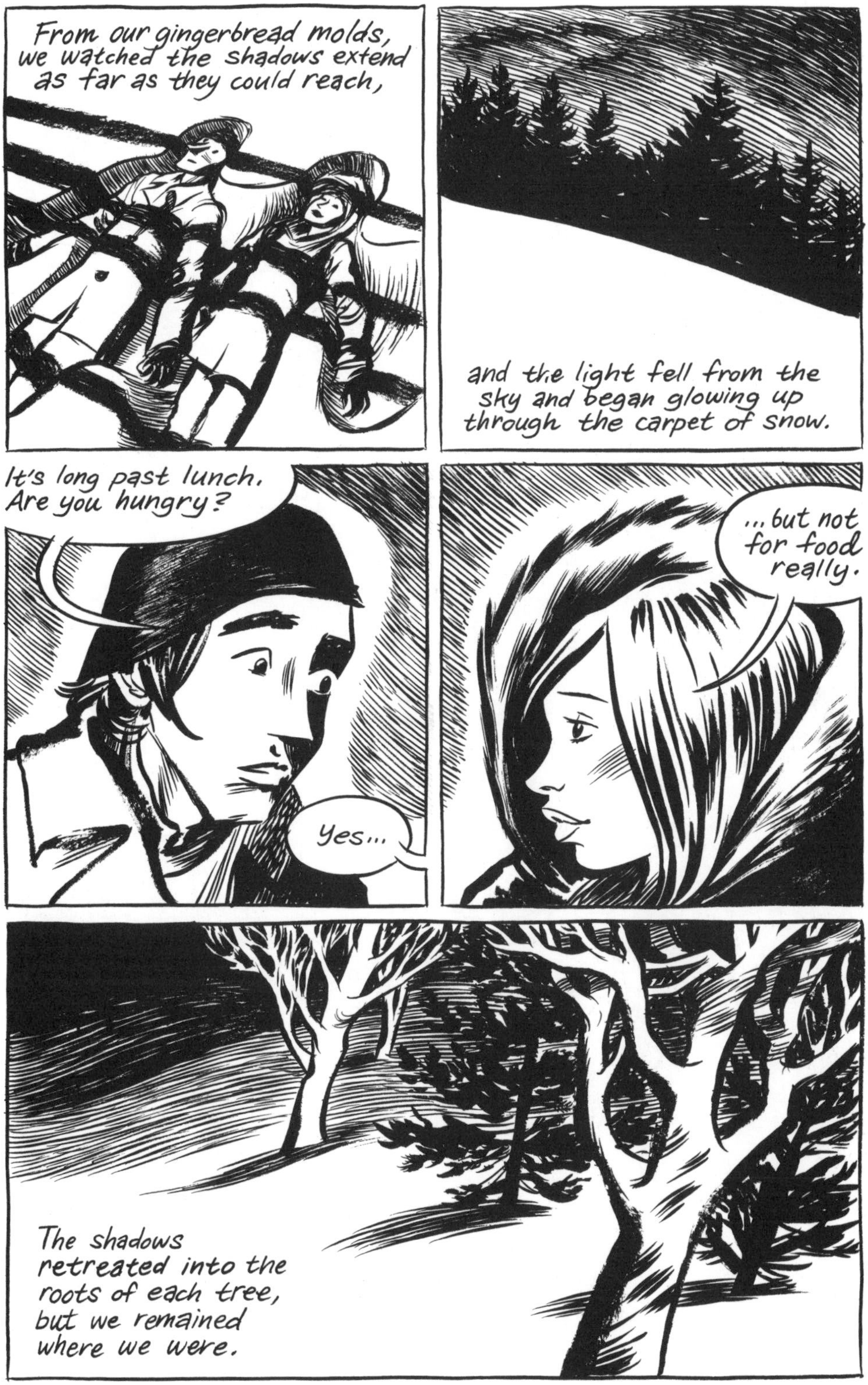
From our gingerbread molds, we watched the shadows extend as far as they could reach,
and the light fell from the sky and began glowing up through the carpet of snow.
It's long past lunch. Are you hungry?
Yes...
...but not for food really.
The shadows retreated into the roots of each tree, but we remained where we were.

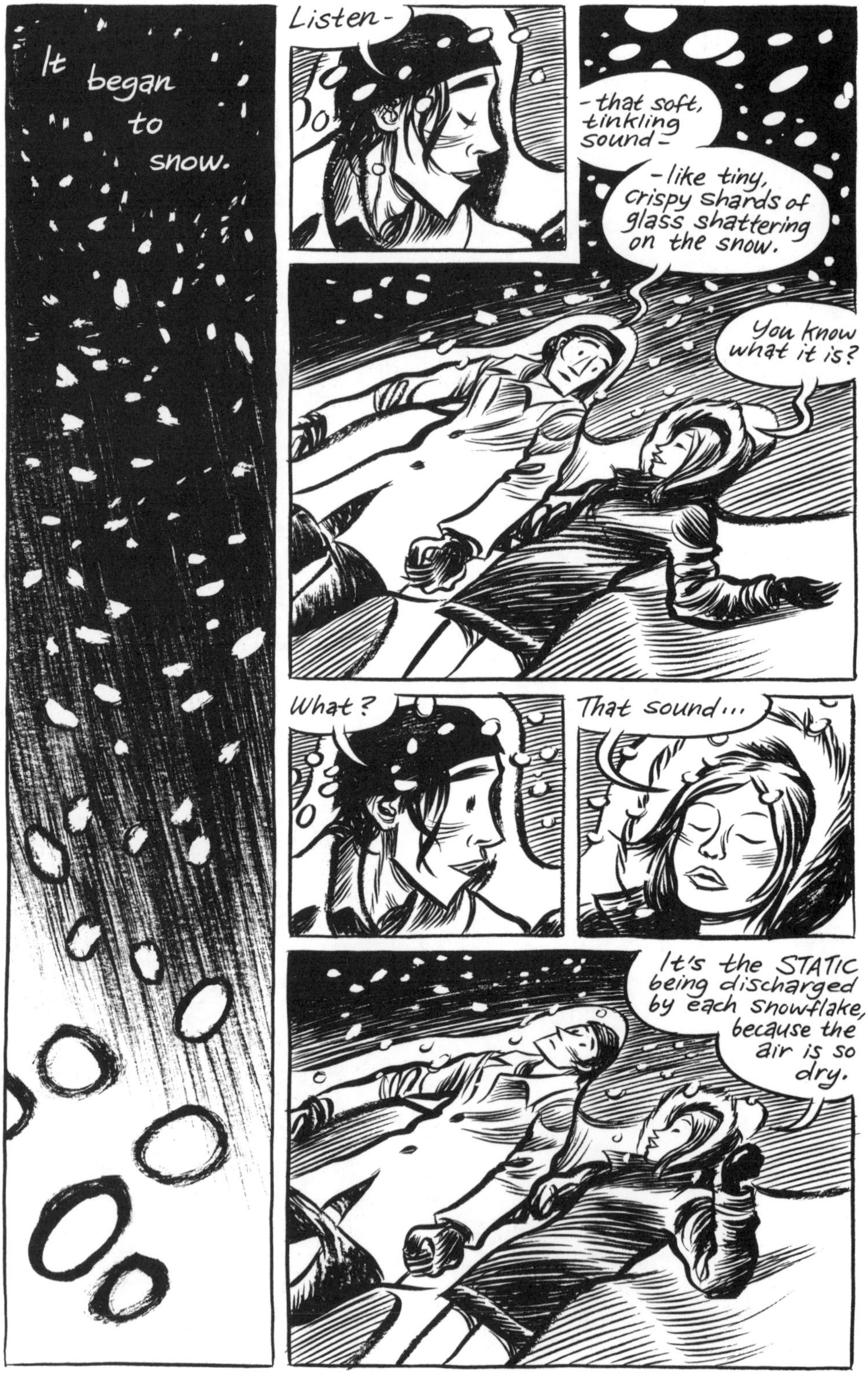
It began to snow.
Listen-
-that soft, tinkling sound-
-like tiny, crispy shards of glass shattering on the snow.
You know what it is?
What?
That sound...
It's the STATIC being discharged by each snowflake, because the air is so dry.

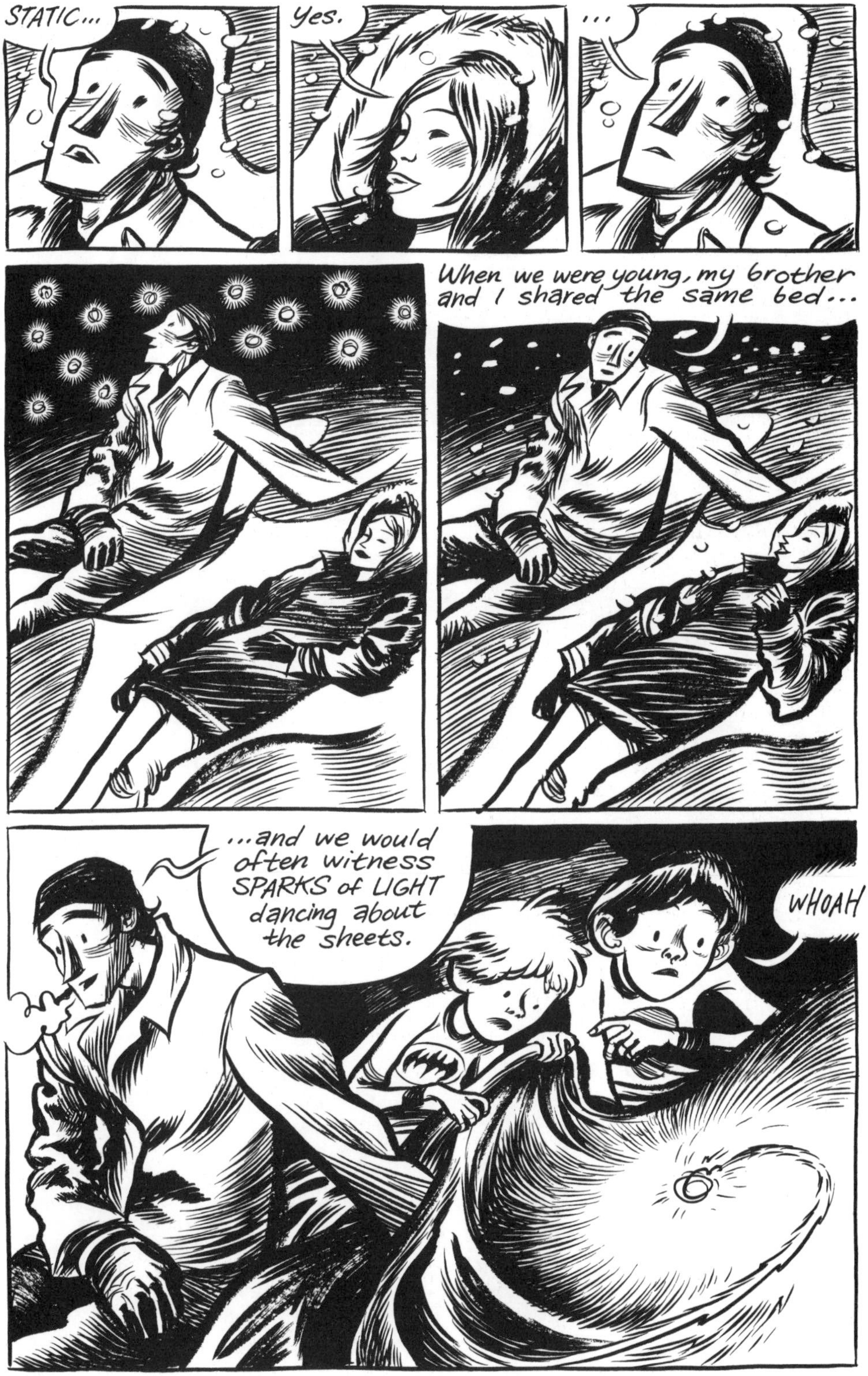
STATIC...
Yes.
...
When we were young, my brother and I shared the same bed...
...and we would often witness SPARKS of LIGHT dancing about the sheets.
WHOAH

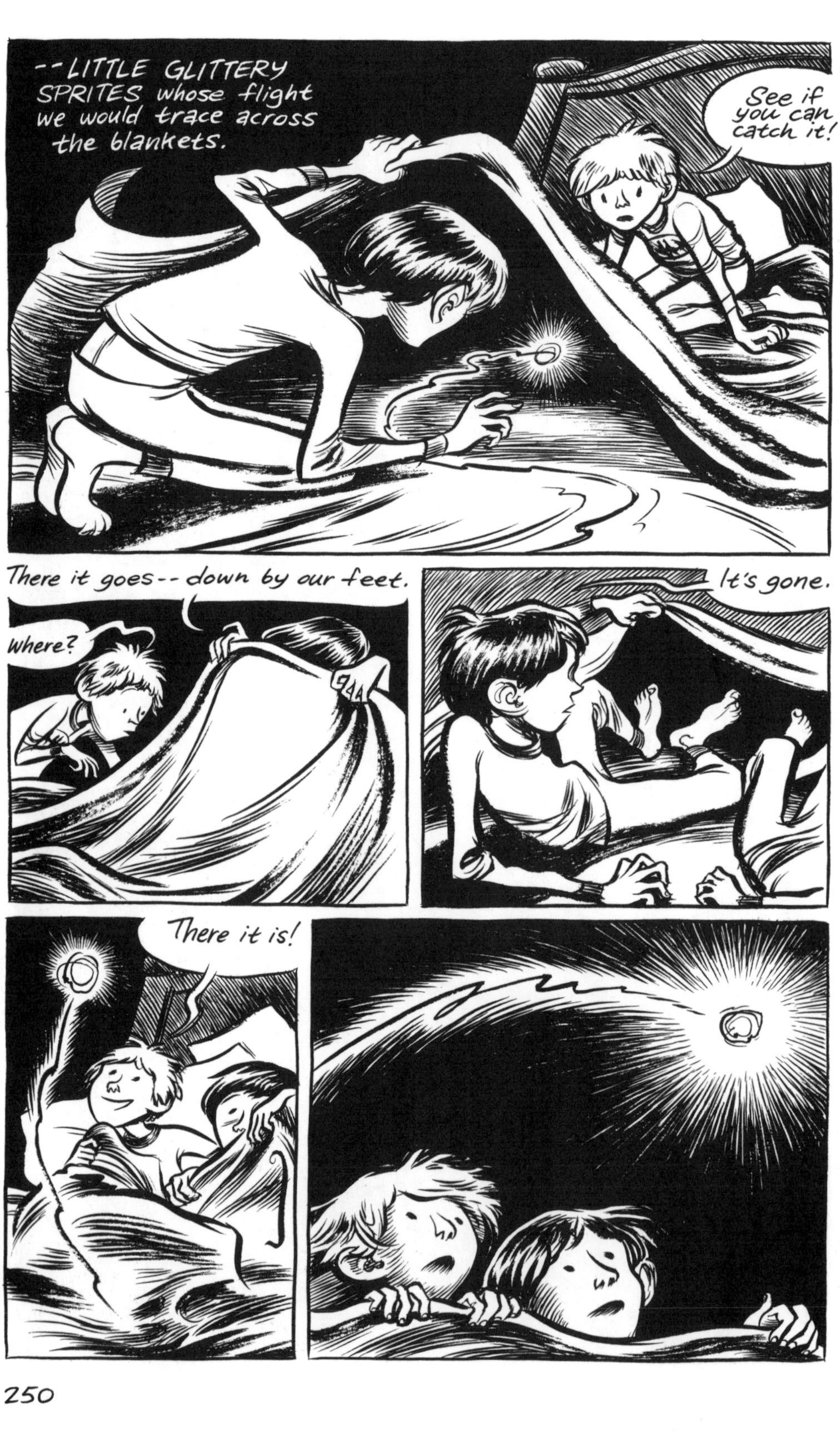

--LITTLE GLITTERY SPRITES whose flight we would trace across the blankets.
See if you can catch it!
There it goes--down by our feet.
Where?
It's gone.
There it is!

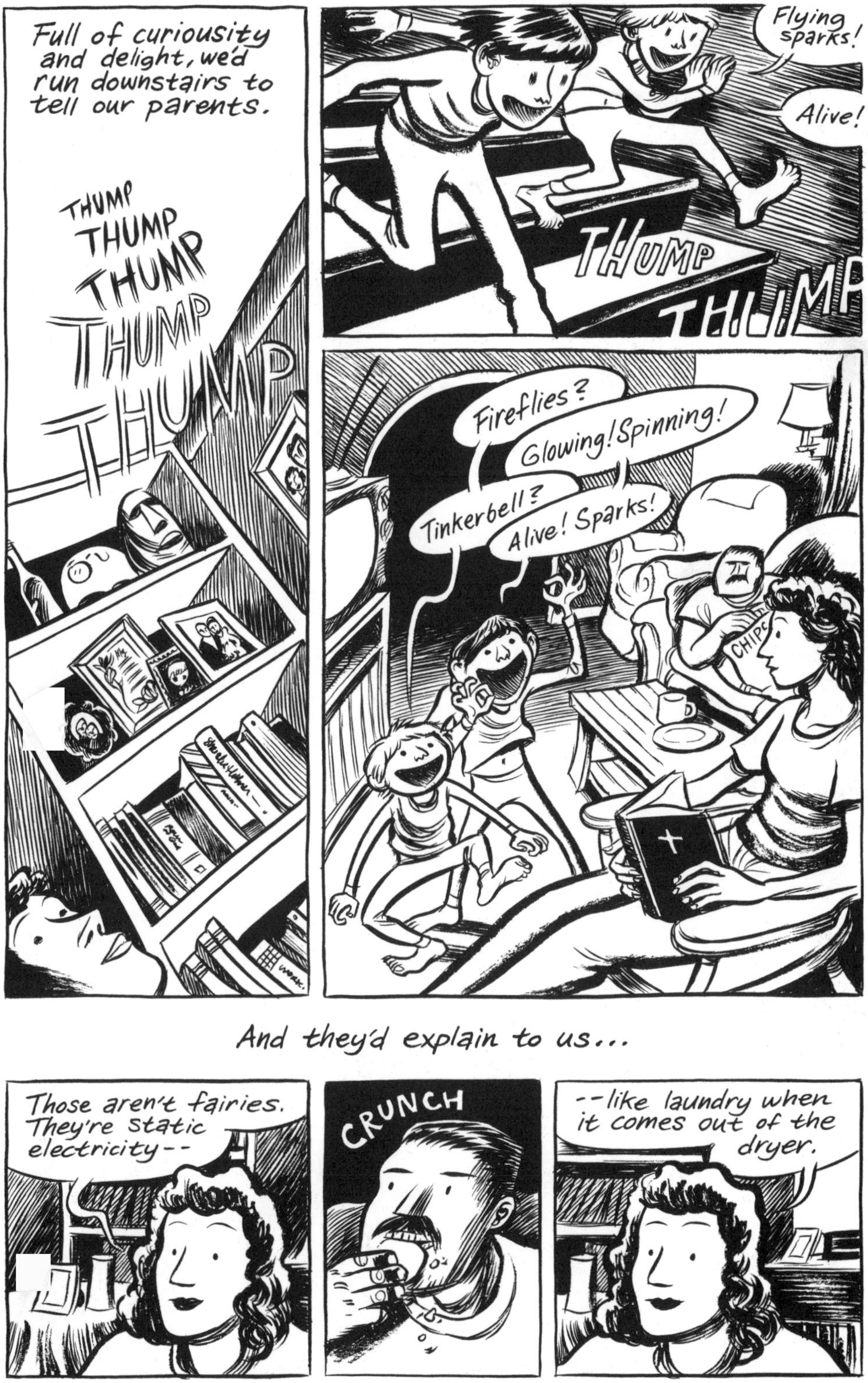
Full of curiousity and delight, we'd run downstairs to tell our parents.
THUMP THUMP THUMP THUMP THUMP
Flying sparks!
Alive!
THUMP THUMP
Fireflies?
Glowing! Spinning!
Tinkerbell?
Alive! Sparks!
CHIPS
And they'd explain to us...
Those aren't fairies. They're static electricity--
CRUNCH
--like laundry when it comes out of the dryer.

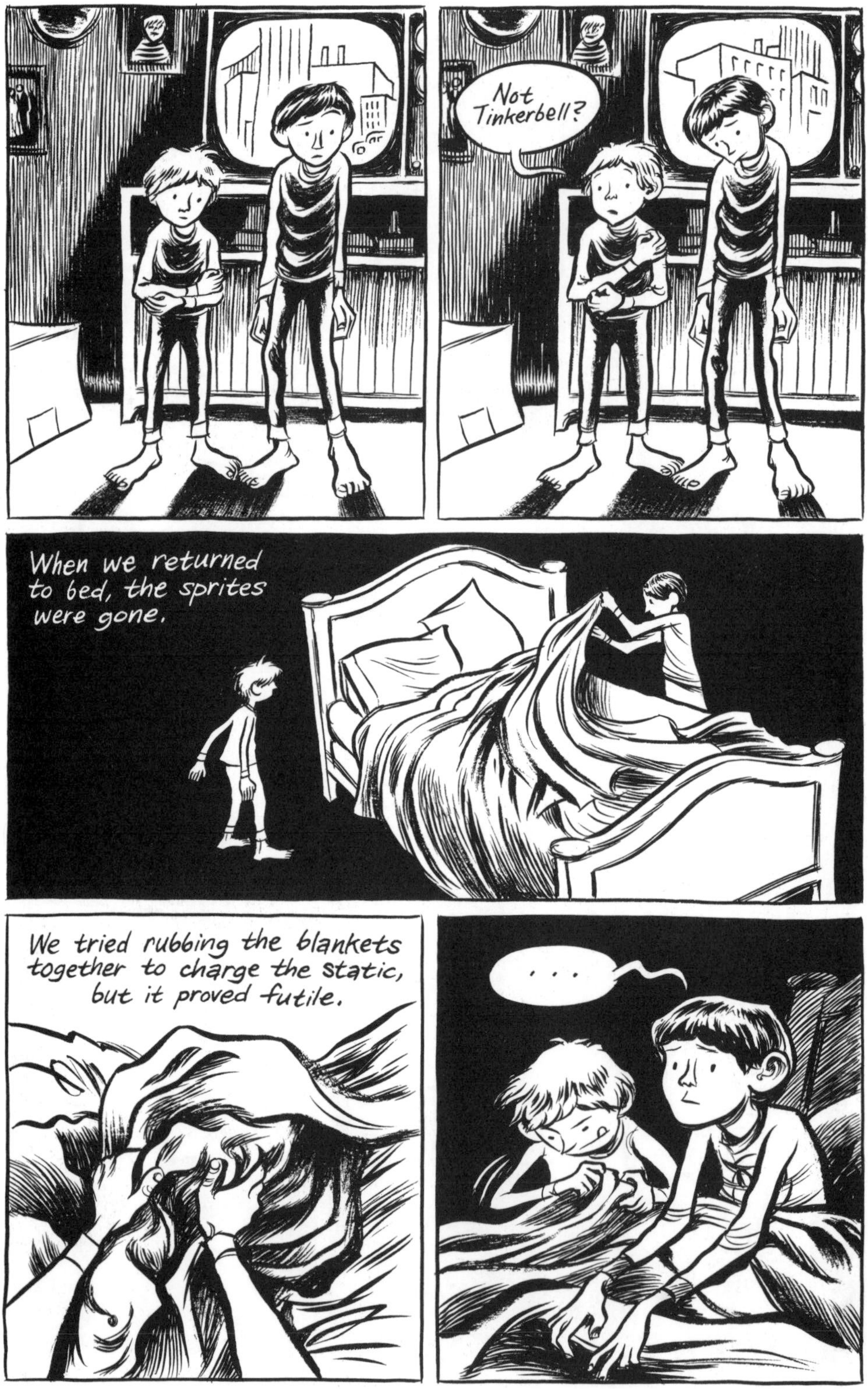
Not Tinkerbell?
When we returned to bed, the sprites were gone.
We tried rubbing the blankets together to charge the static, but it proved futile.
. . .

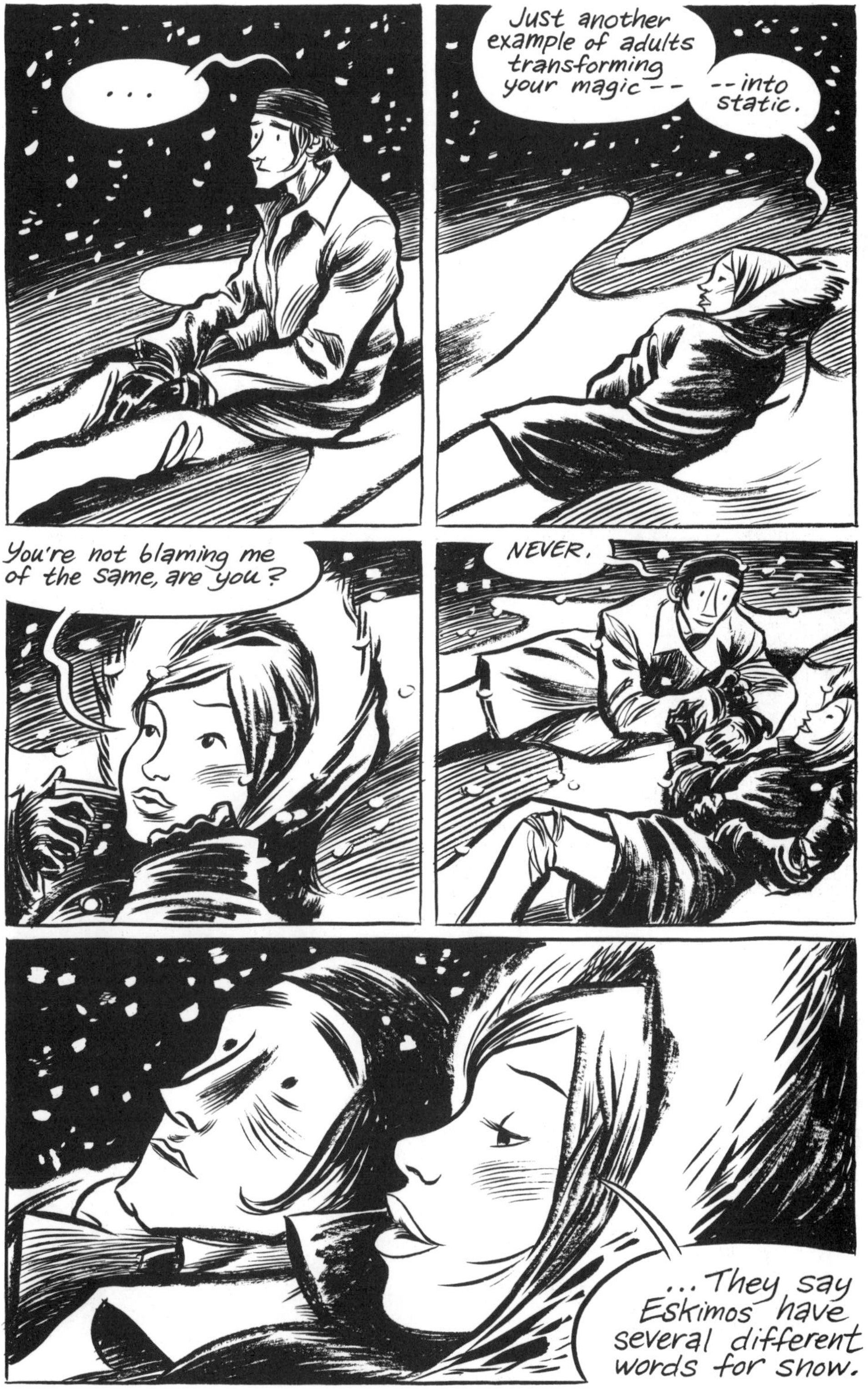
...
Just another example of adults transforming your magic--
--into static.
You're not blaming me of the same, are you?
NEVER.
...They say Eskimos have several different words for snow.

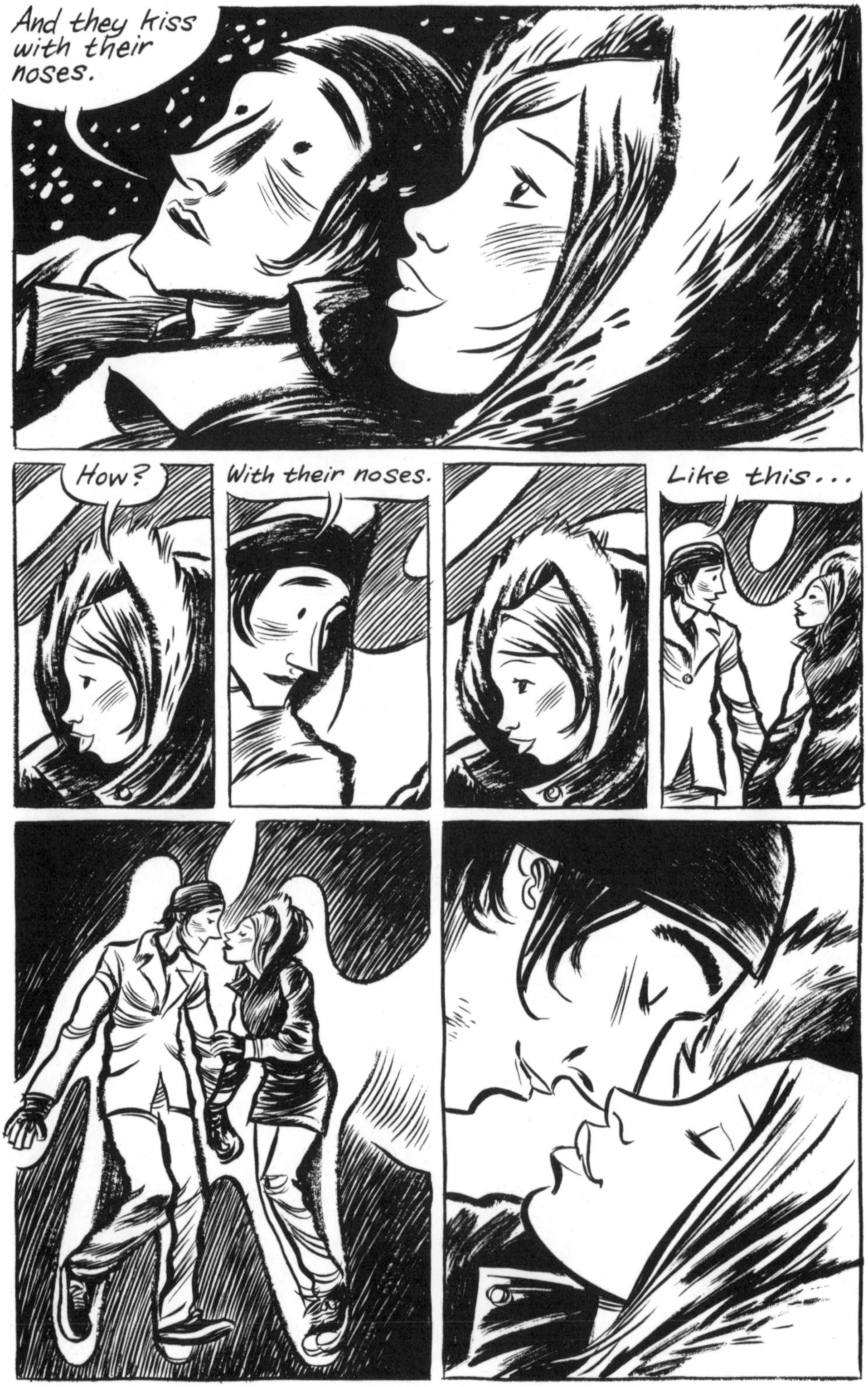
And they kiss with their noses.
How?
With their noses.
Like this...

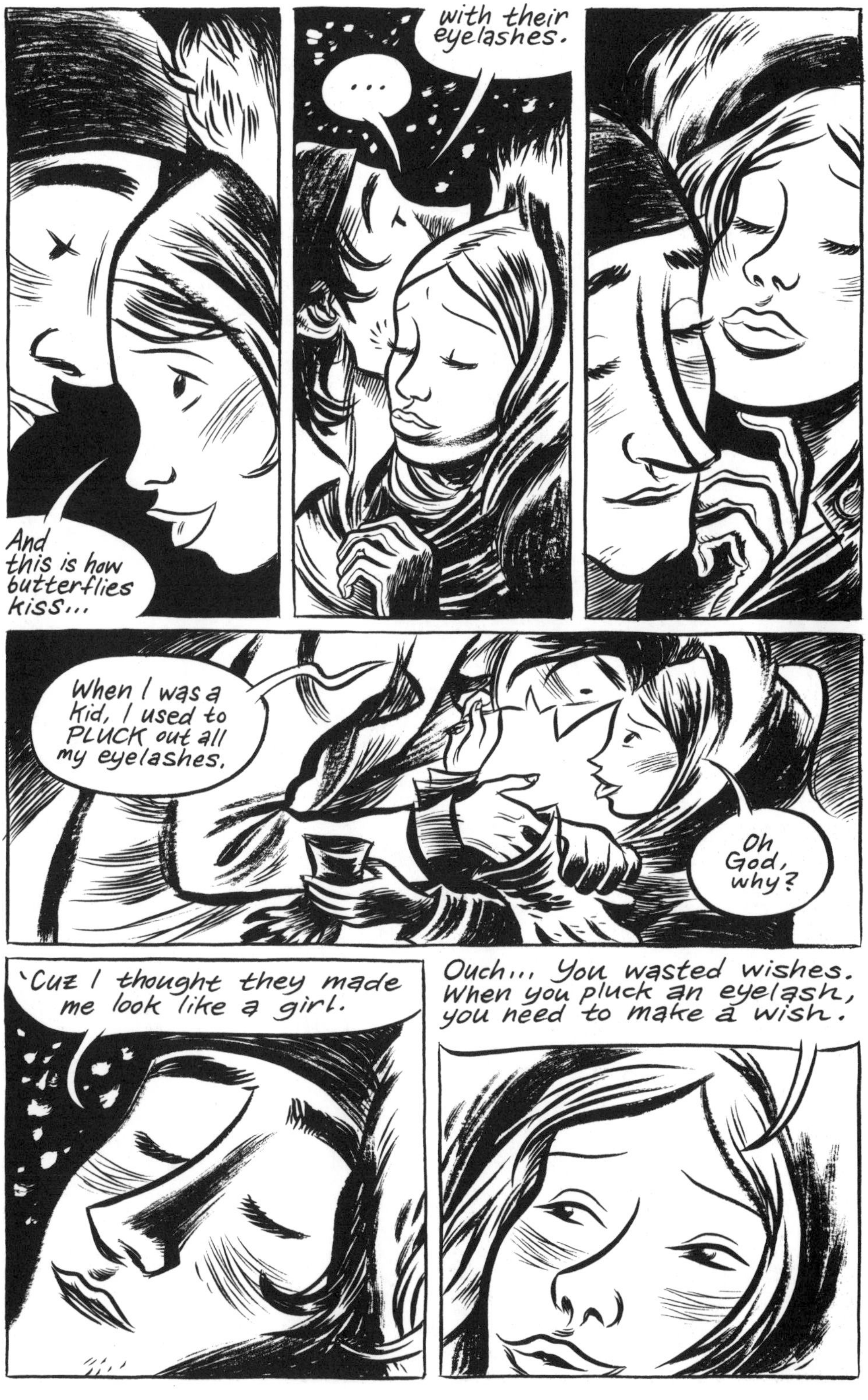
And this is how butterflies kiss...
...
with their eyelashes.
When I was a kid, I used to PLUCK out all my eyelashes.
Oh God, why?
'Cuz I thought they made me look like a girl.
Ouch... You wasted wishes. When you pluck an eyelash, you need to make a wish.

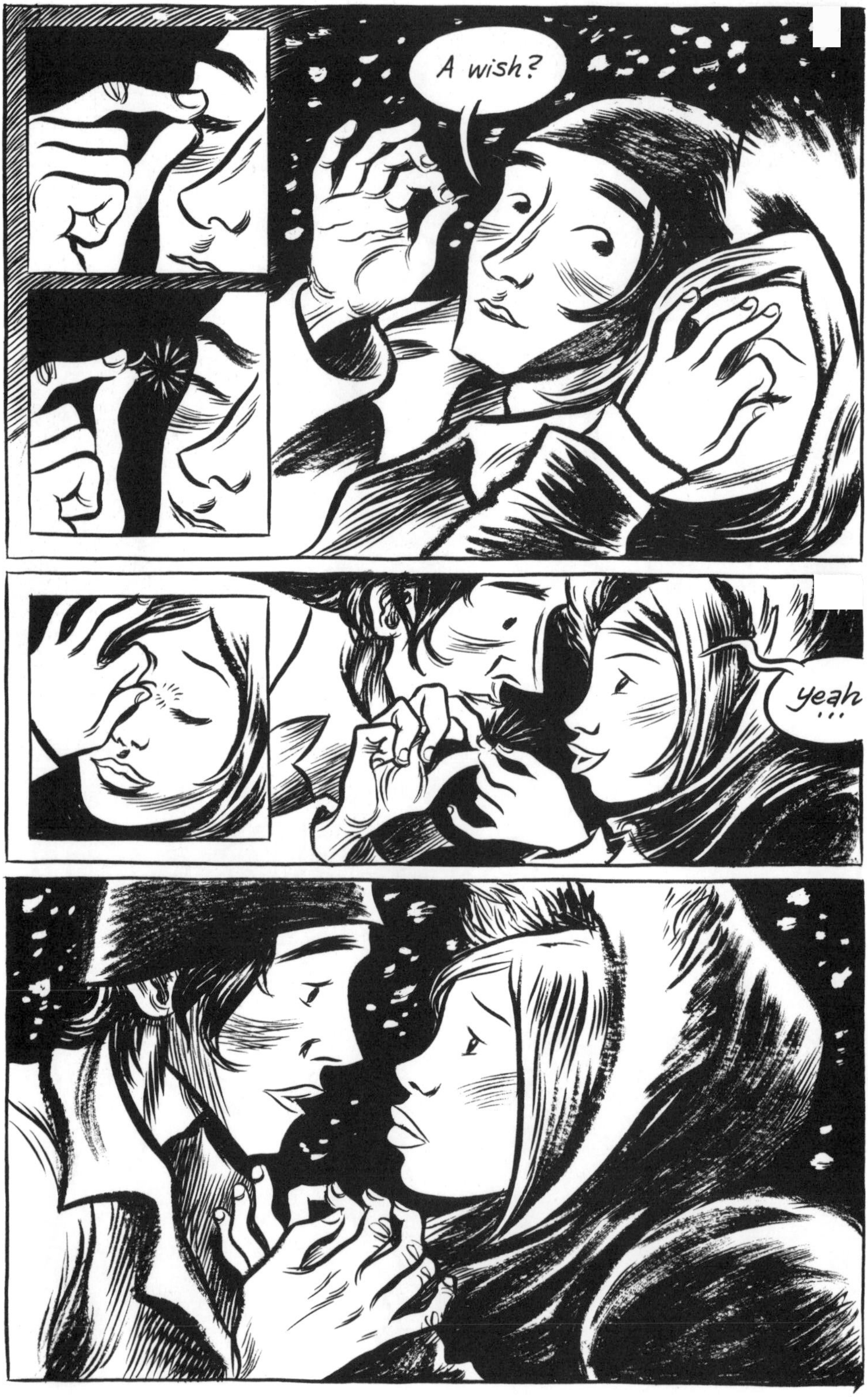
A wish?
yeah
...

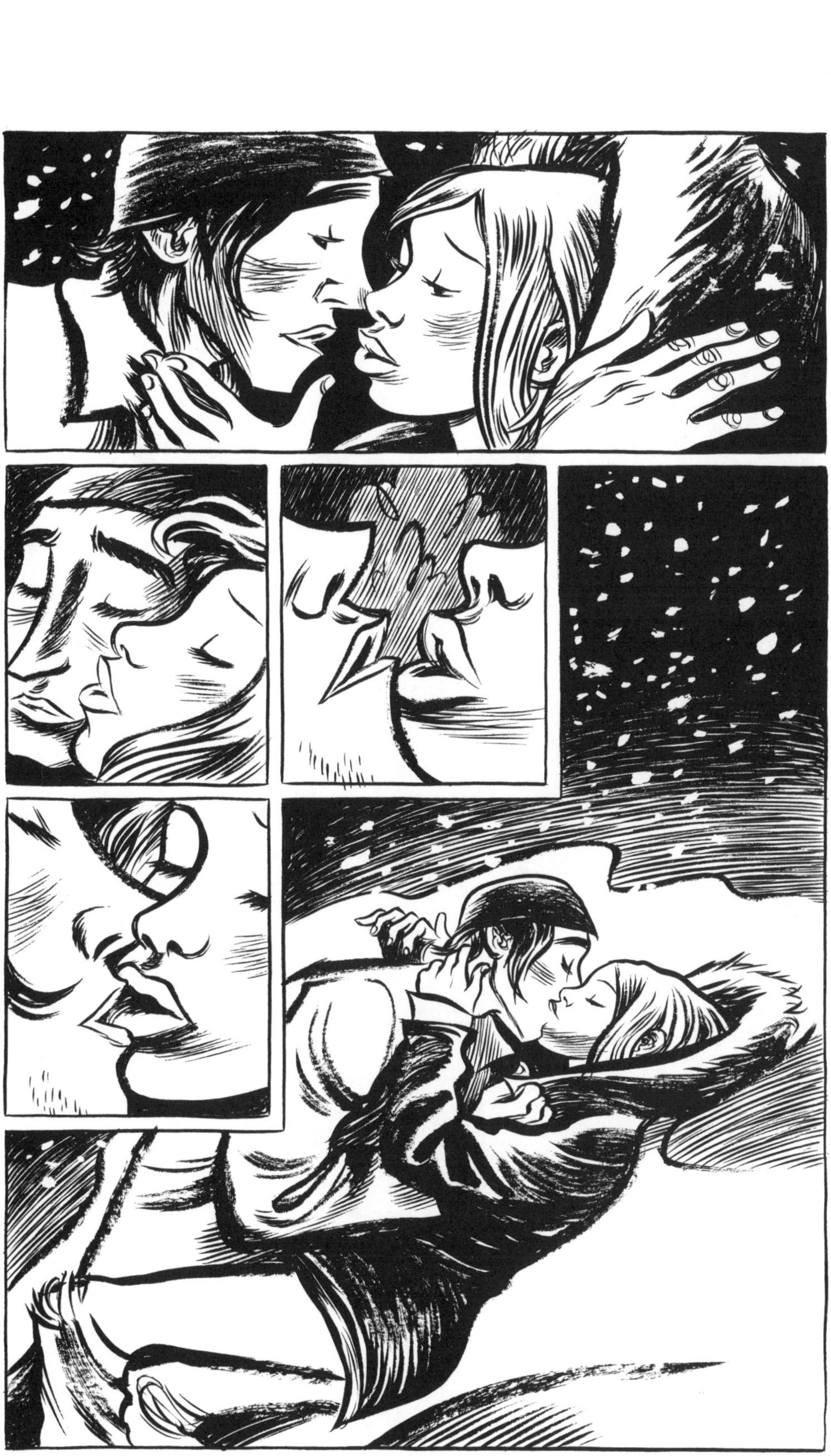

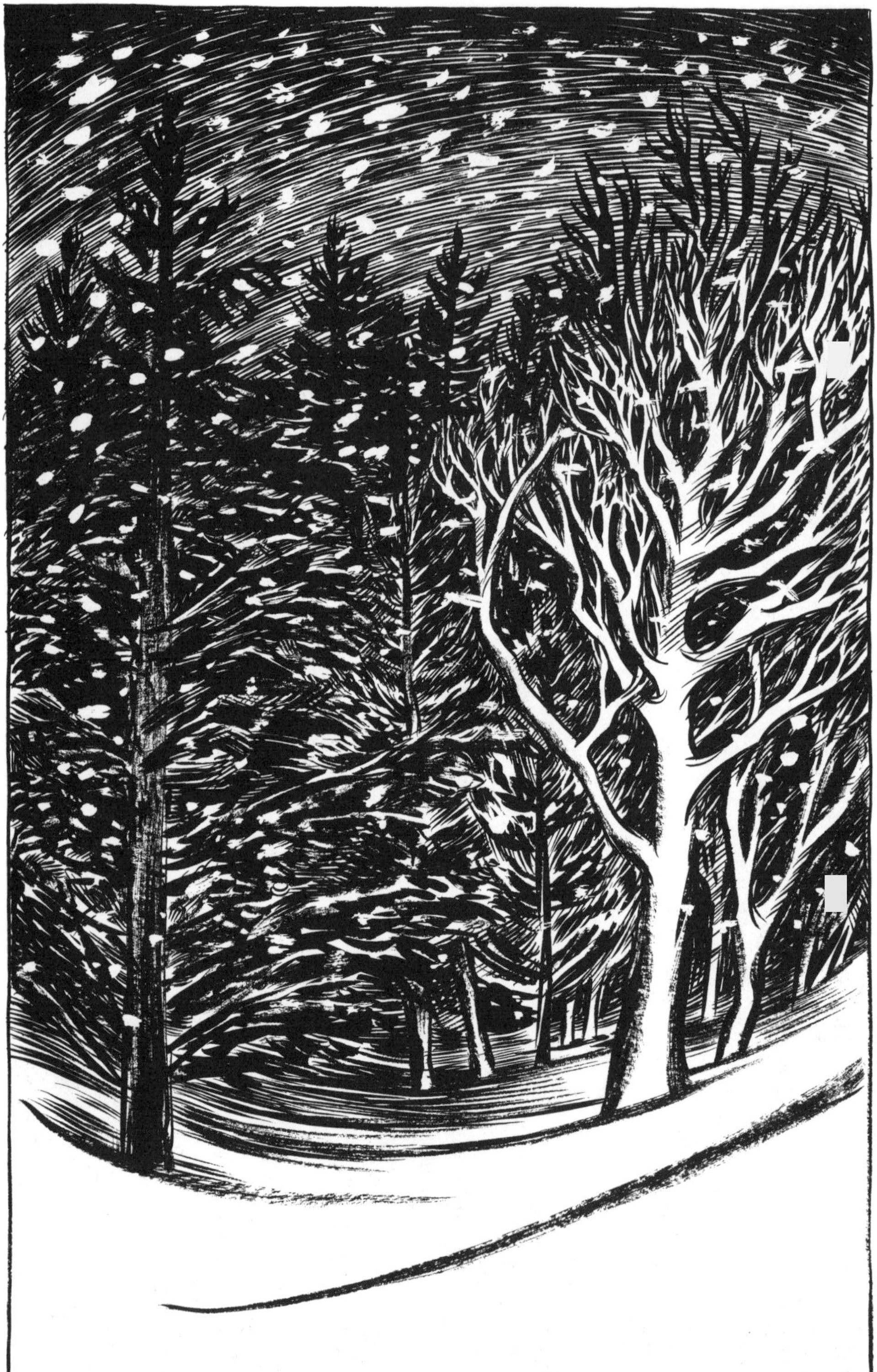

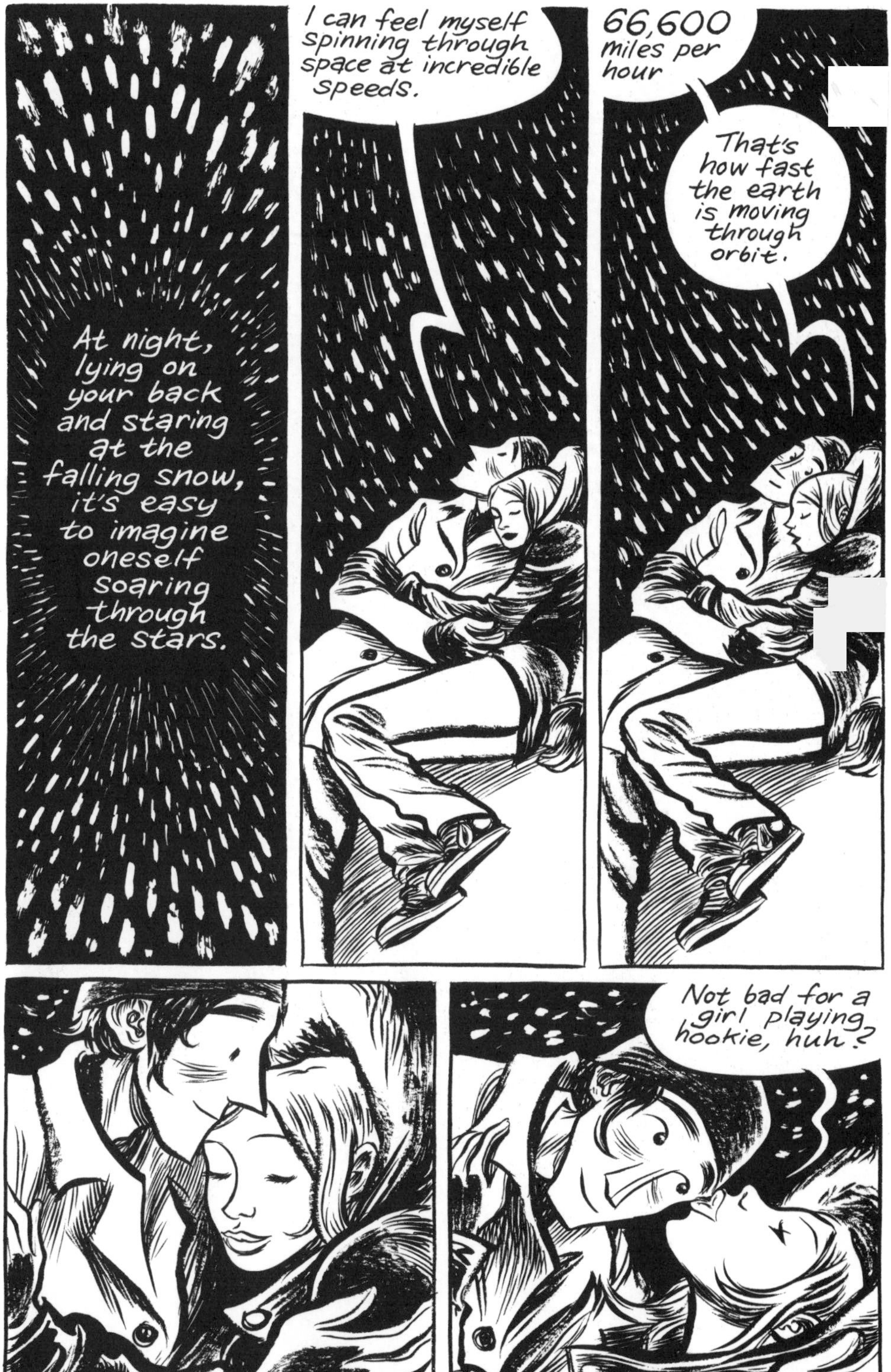
At night, lying on your back and staring at the falling snow, it's easy to imagine oneself soaring through the stars.
I can feel myself spinning through space at incredible speeds.
66,600 miles per hour
That's how fast the earth is moving through orbit.
Not bad for a girl playing hookie, huh?

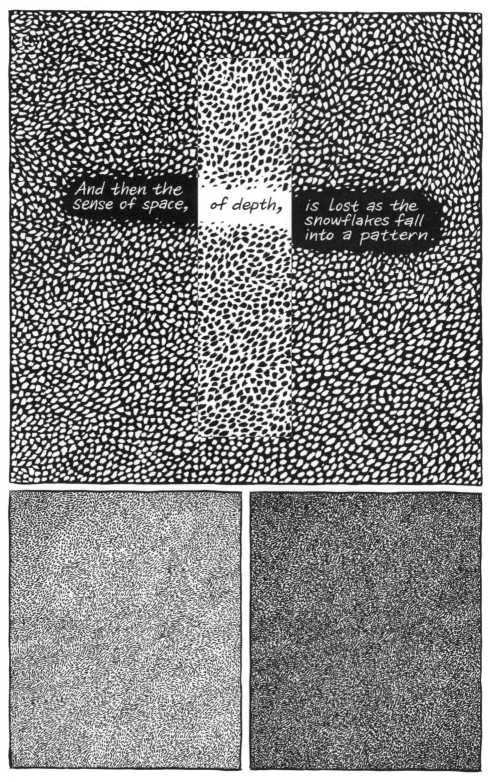

And then the sense of space, of depth, is lost as the snowflakes fall into a pattern.

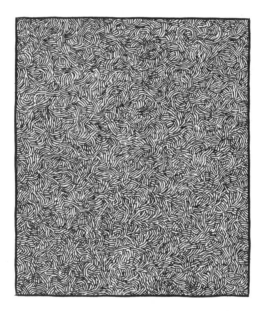

261

V

*I Don't
Wanna
Grow
Up*

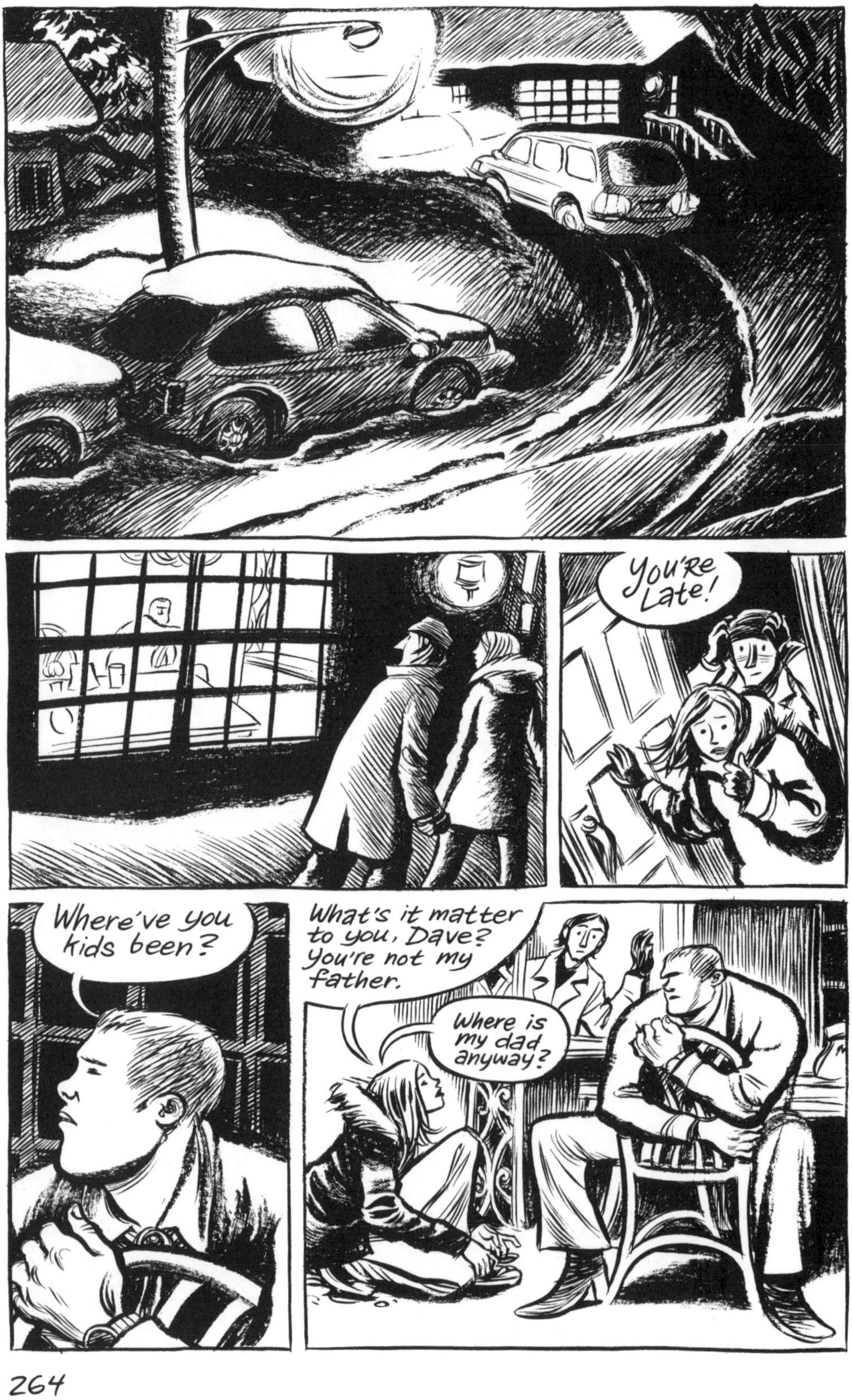
You're Late!
Where've you kids been?
What's it matter to you, Dave? You're not my father.
Where is my dad anyway?

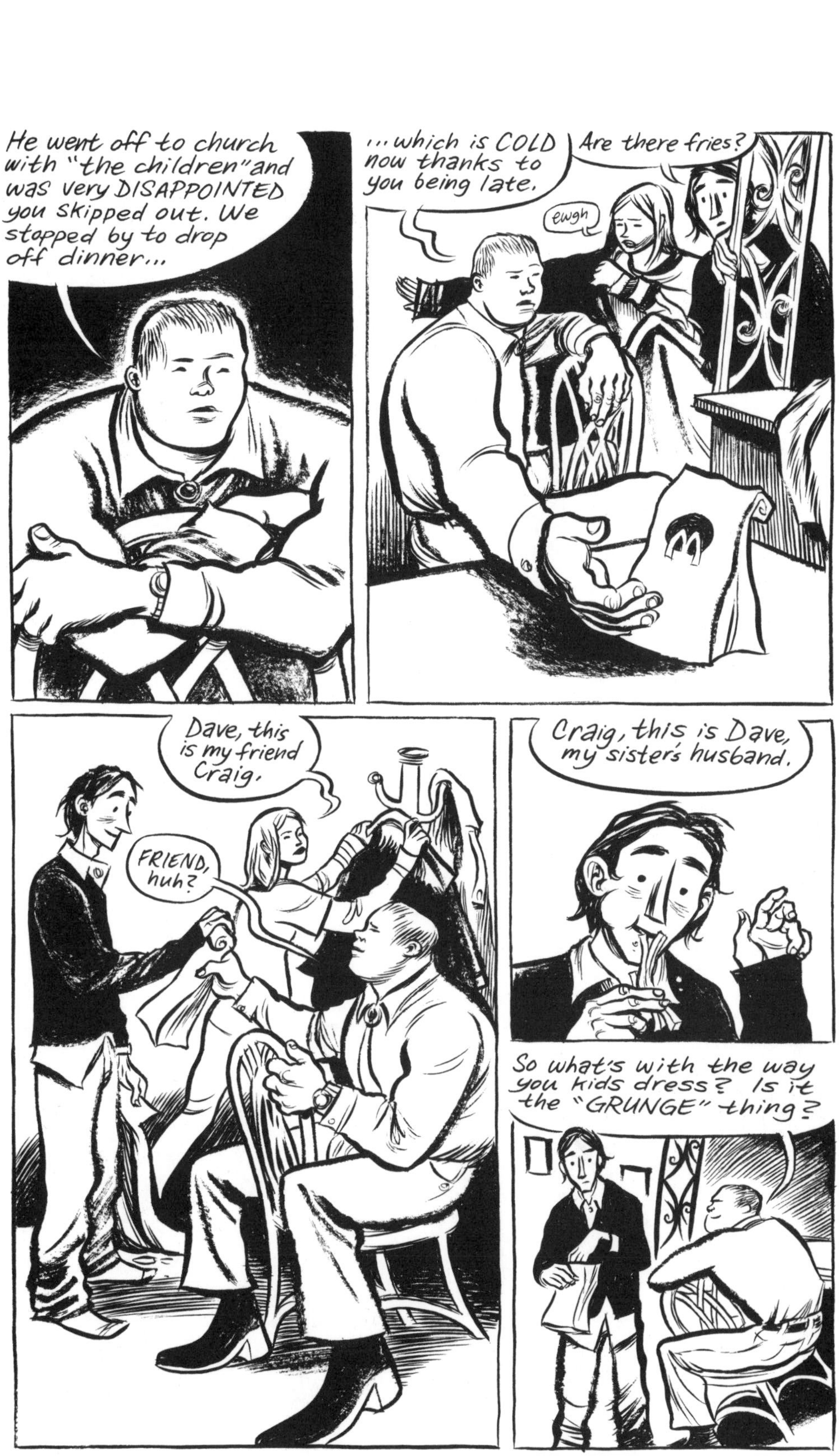
He went off to church with "the children" and was very DISAPPOINTED you skipped out. We stopped by to drop off dinner...
...which is COLD now thanks to you being late.
Are there fries?
ewgh
Dave, this is my friend Craig.
FRIEND, huh?
Craig, this is Dave, my sister's husband.
So what's with the way you kids dress? Is it the "GRUNGE" thing?

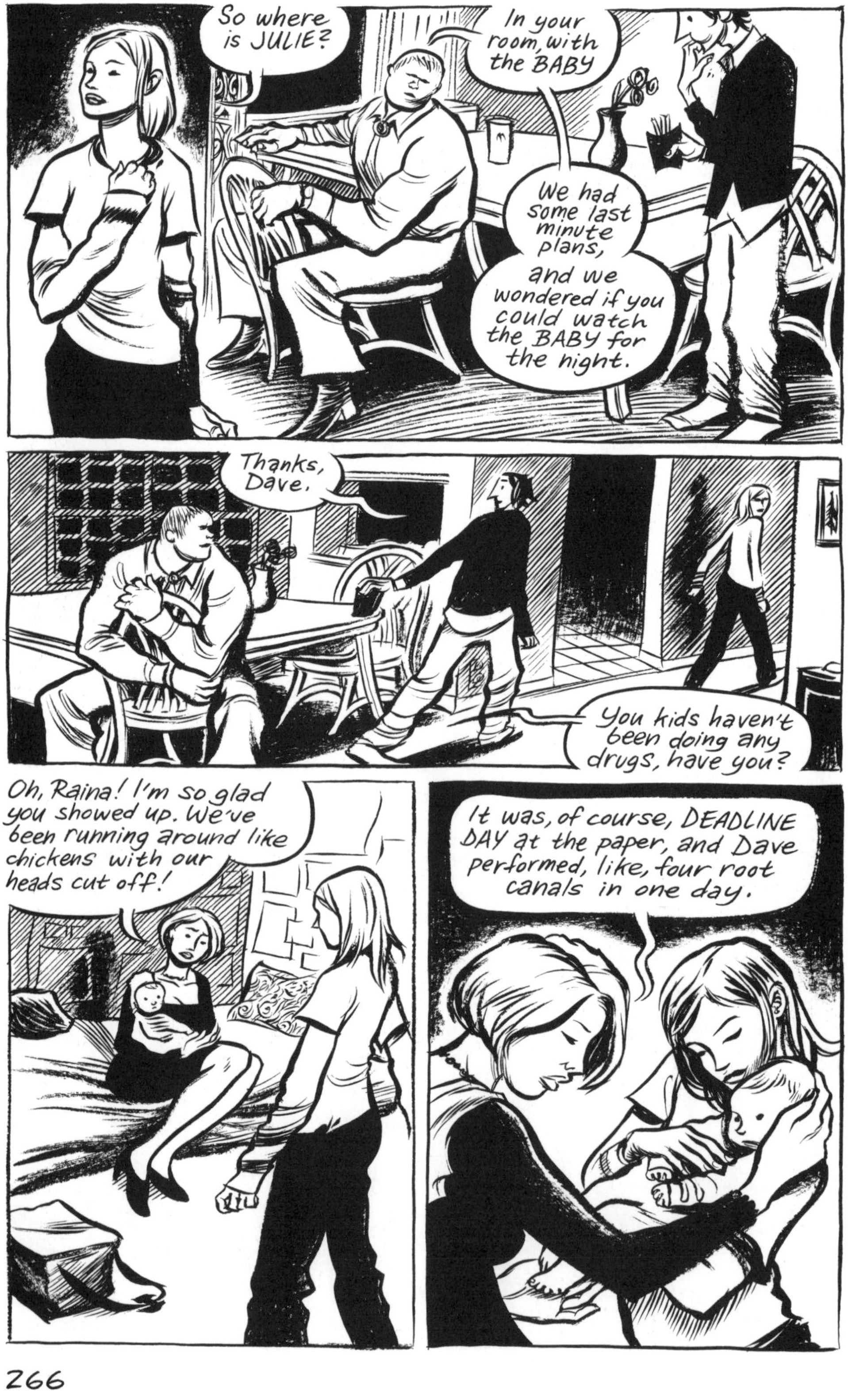
So where is JULIE?
In your room, with the BABY
We had some last minute plans,
and we wondered if you could watch the BABY for the night.
Thanks, Dave.
You kids haven't been doing any drugs, have you?
Oh, Raina! I'm so glad you showed up. We've been running around like chickens with our heads cut off!
It was, of course, DEADLINE DAY at the paper, and Dave performed, like, four root canals in one day.

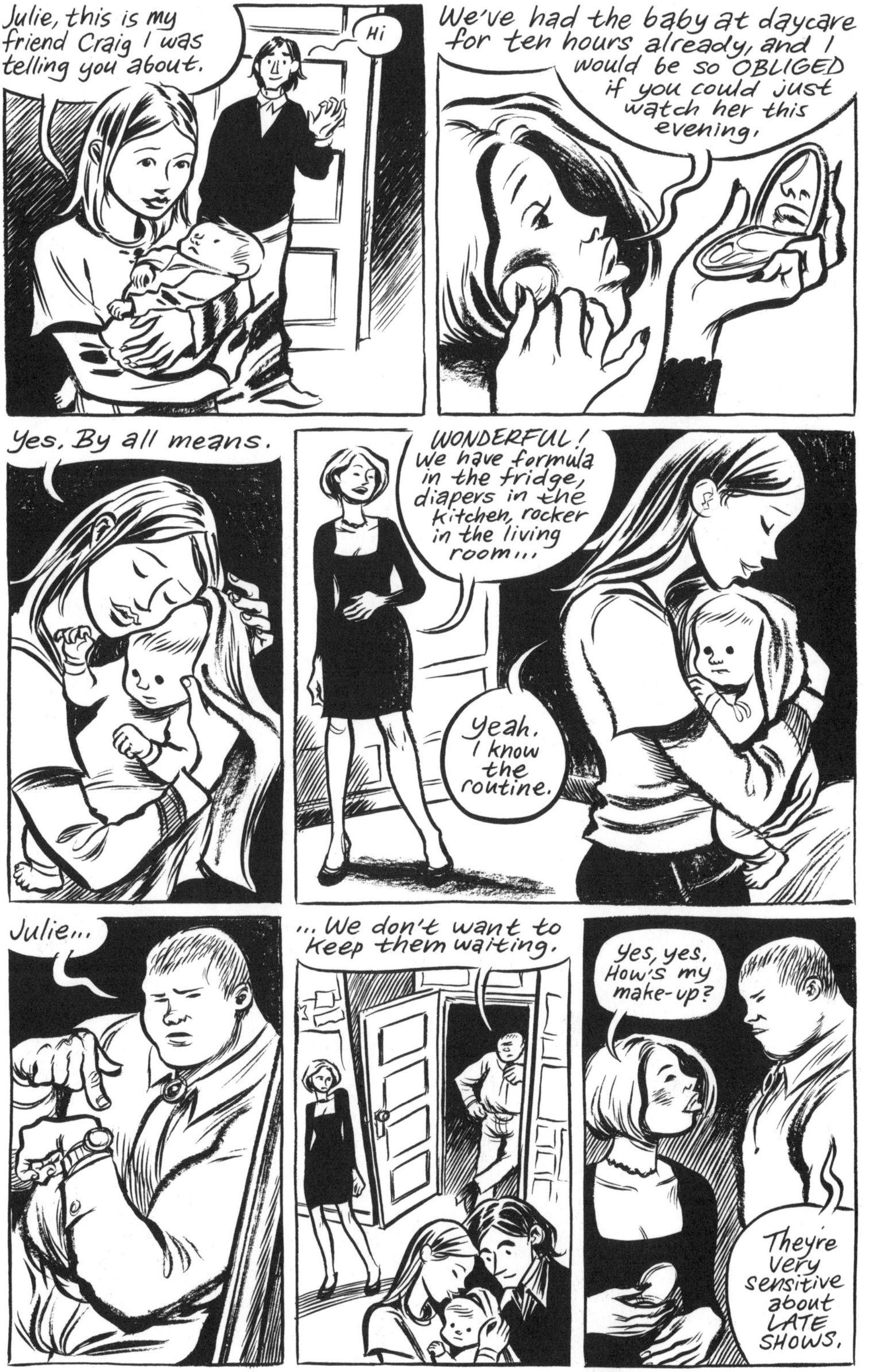
Julie, this is my friend Craig I was telling you about.
Hi
We've had the baby at daycare for ten hours already, and I would be so OBLIGED if you could just watch her this evening.
Yes. By all means.
WONDERFUL! We have formula in the fridge, diapers in the kitchen, rocker in the living room...
Yeah. I know the routine.
Julie...
...We don't want to keep them waiting.
Yes, yes. How's my make-up?
Theyre very sensitive about LATE SHOWS.

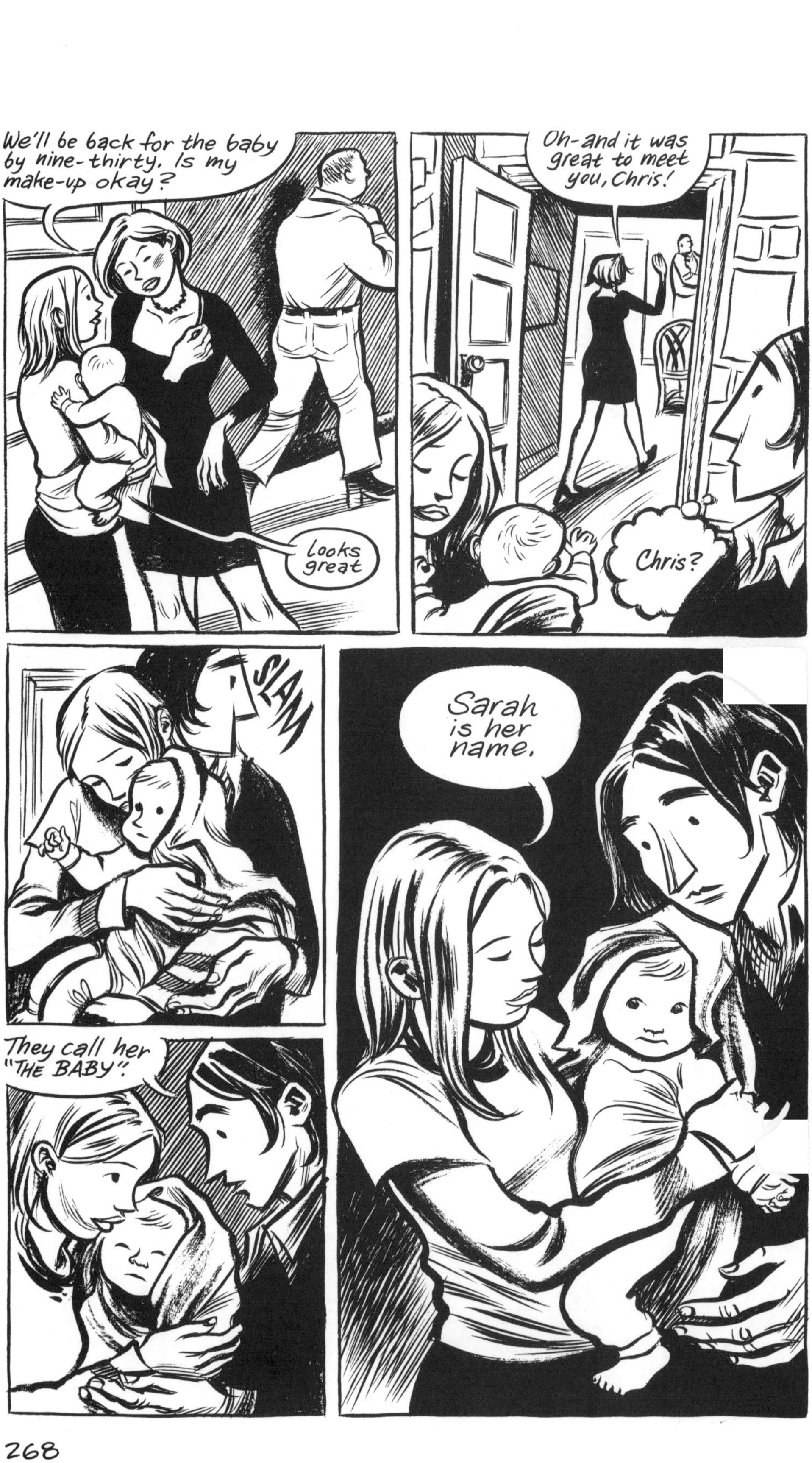
We'll be back for the baby by nine-thirty. Is my make-up okay?
Looks great
Oh- and it was great to meet you, Chris!
Chris?
SLAM
They call her "THE BABY".
Sarah is her name.

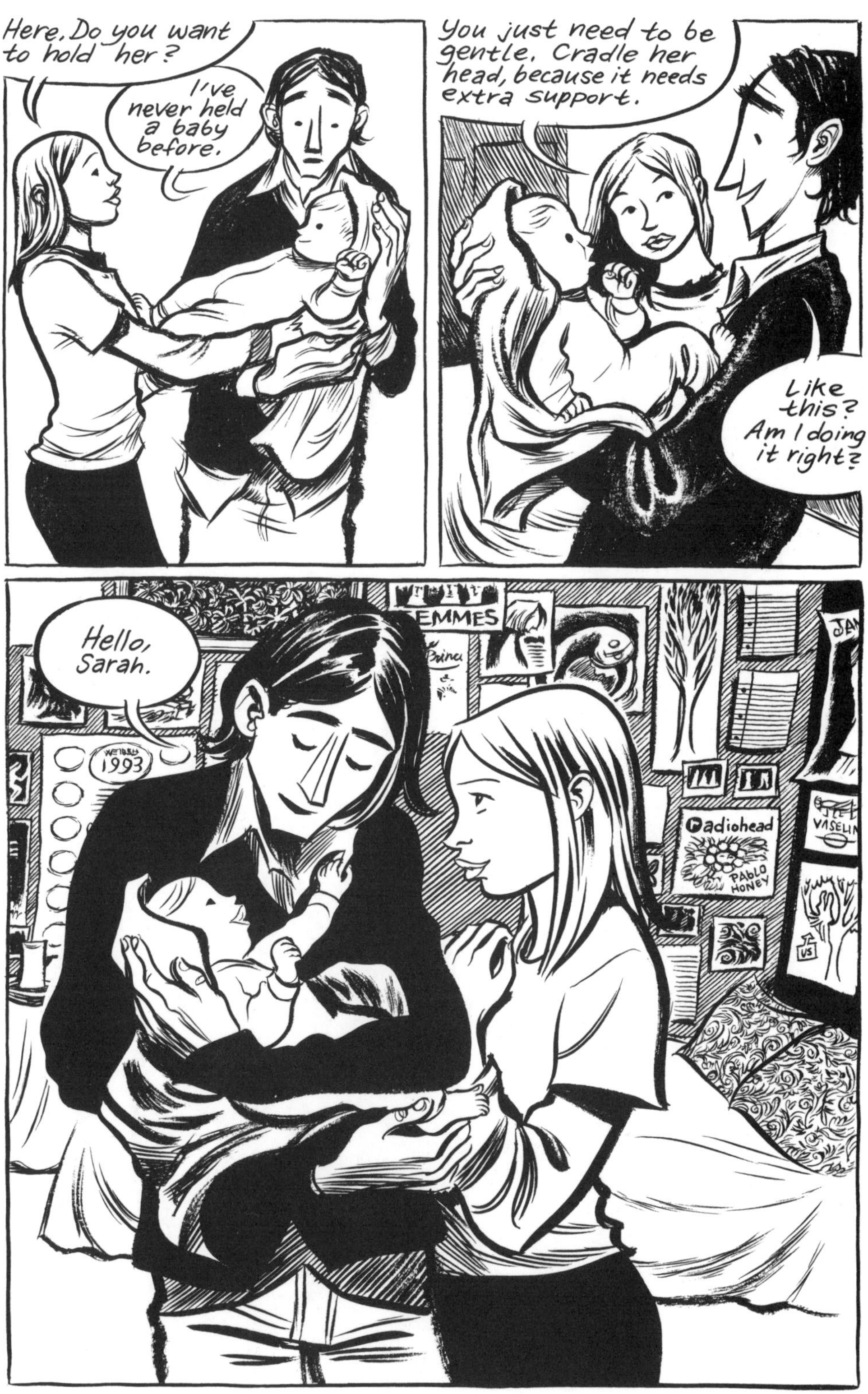
Here. Do you want to hold her?
I've never held a baby before.
You just need to be gentle. Cradle her head, because it needs extra support.
Like this? Am I doing it right?
Hello, Sarah.
FEMMES
1993
Radiohead
PABLO HONEY
VASELIN

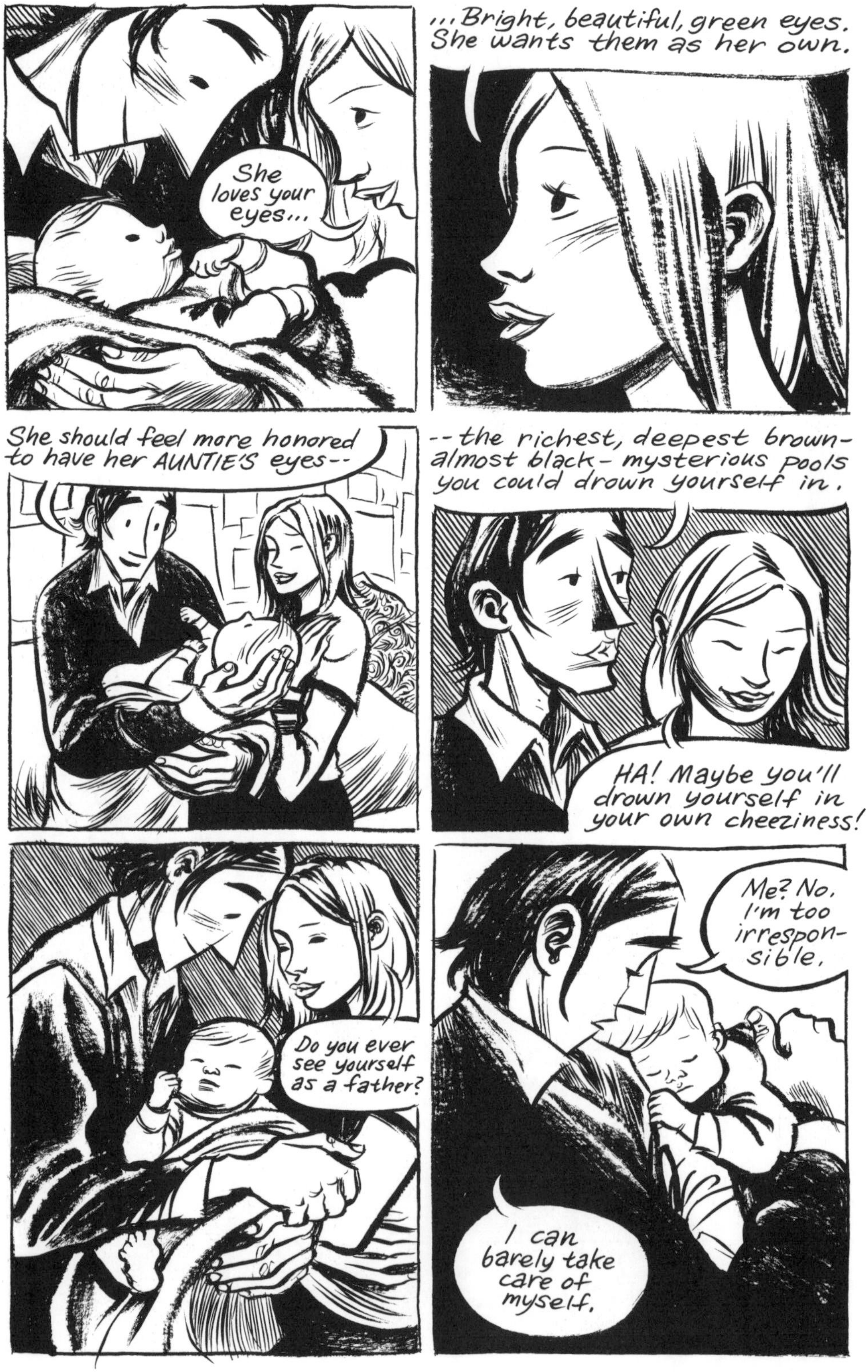
She loves your eyes...
...Bright, beautiful, green eyes. She wants them as her own.
She should feel more honored to have her AUNTIE'S eyes--
--the richest, deepest brown-almost black- mysterious pools you could drown yourself in.
HA! Maybe you'll drown yourself in your own cheeziness!
Do you ever see yourself as a father?
Me? No. I'm too irrespon-sible.
I can barely take care of myself.

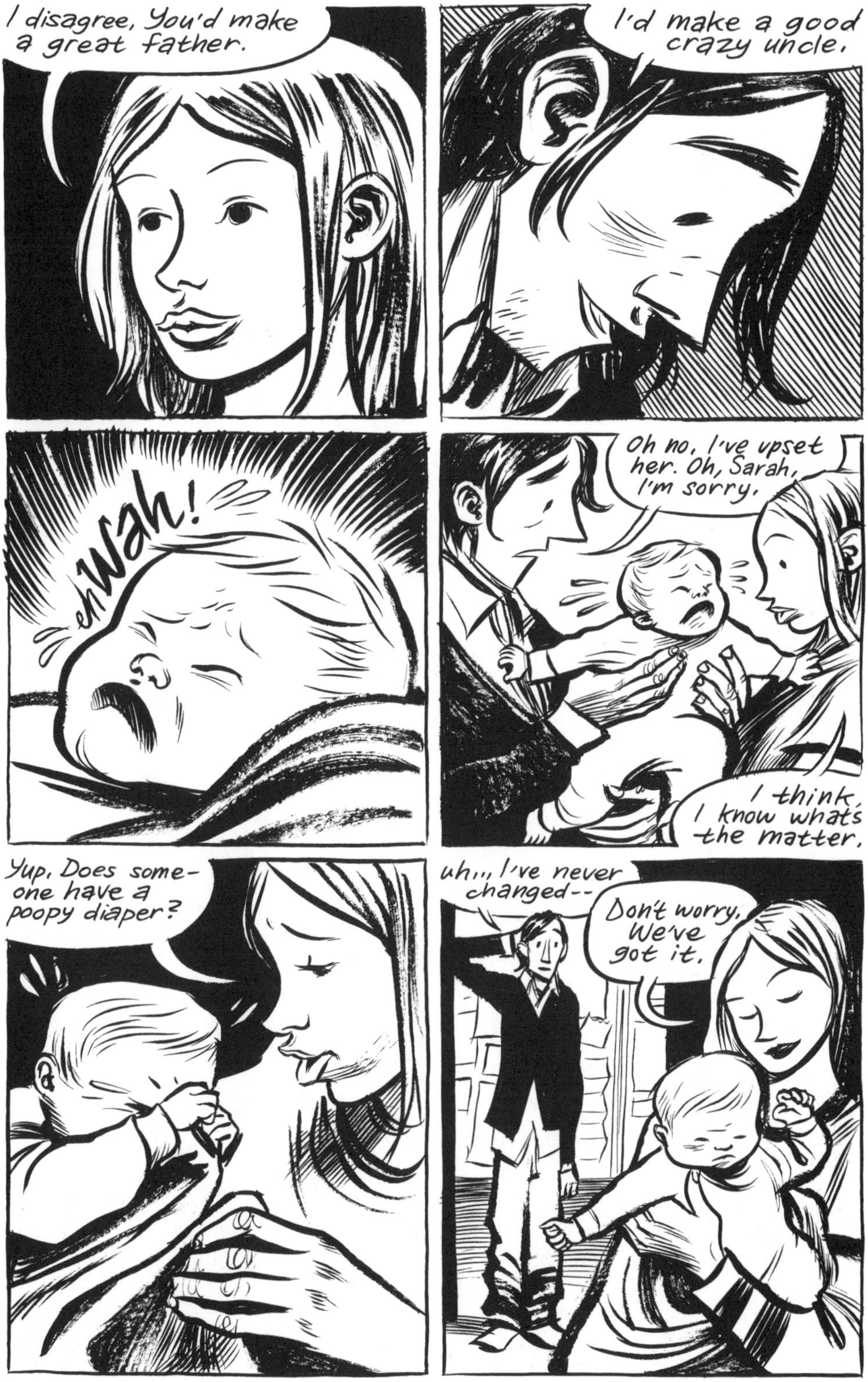
I disagree, You'd make a great father.
I'd make a good crazy uncle.
ehWAH!
Oh no, I've upset her. Oh, Sarah, I'm sorry.
I think I know what's the matter.
Yup, Does someone have a poopy diaper?
uh.., I've never changed--
Don't worry, We've got it.

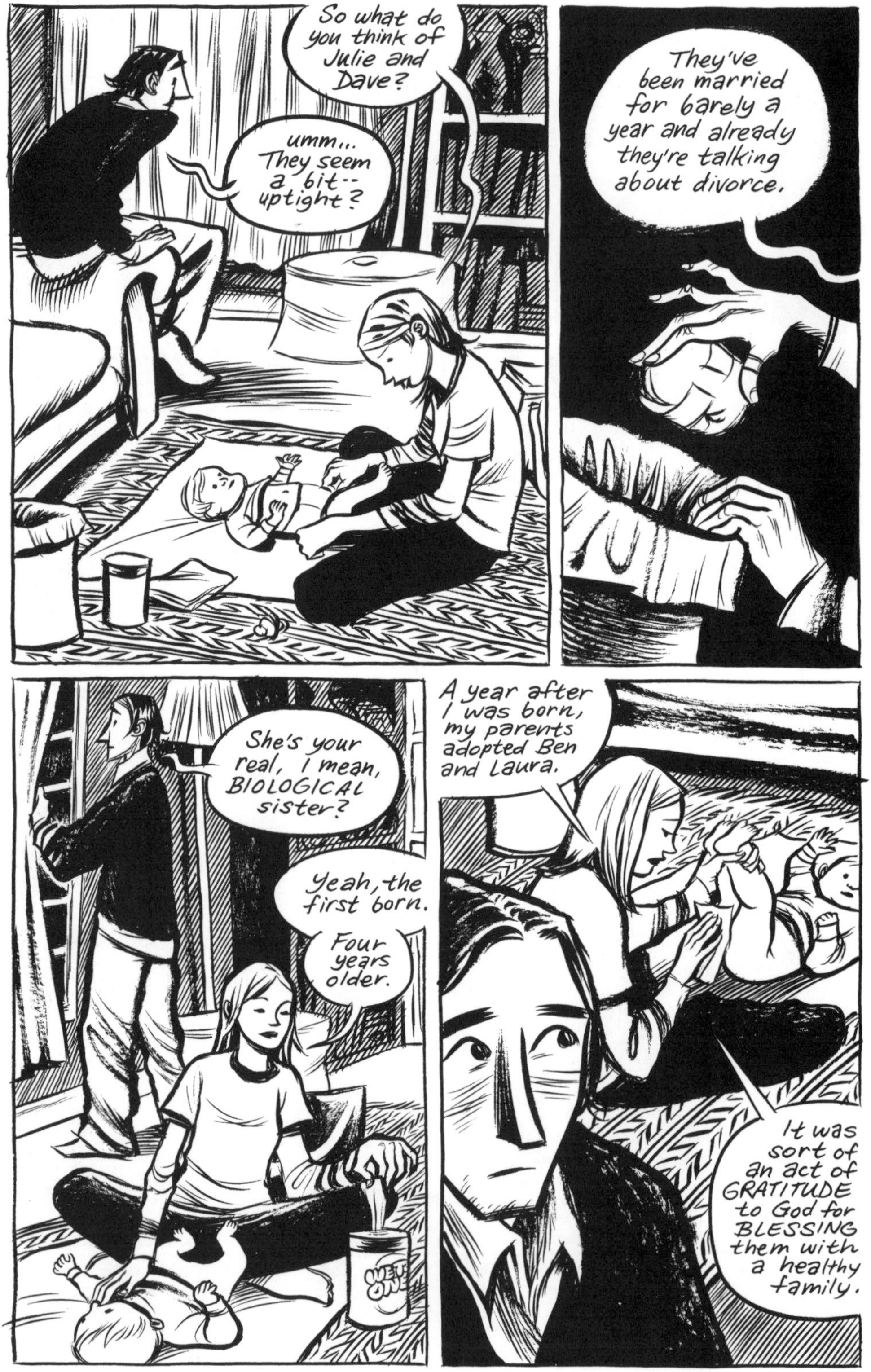
So what do you think of Julie and Dave?
umm... They seem a bit-- uptight?
They've been married for barely a year and already they're talking about divorce.
She's your real, I mean, BIOLOGICAL sister?
Yeah, the first born.
Four years older.
WET ONES
A year after I was born, my parents adopted Ben and Laura.
It was sort of an act of GRATITUDE to God for BLESSING them with a healthy family.

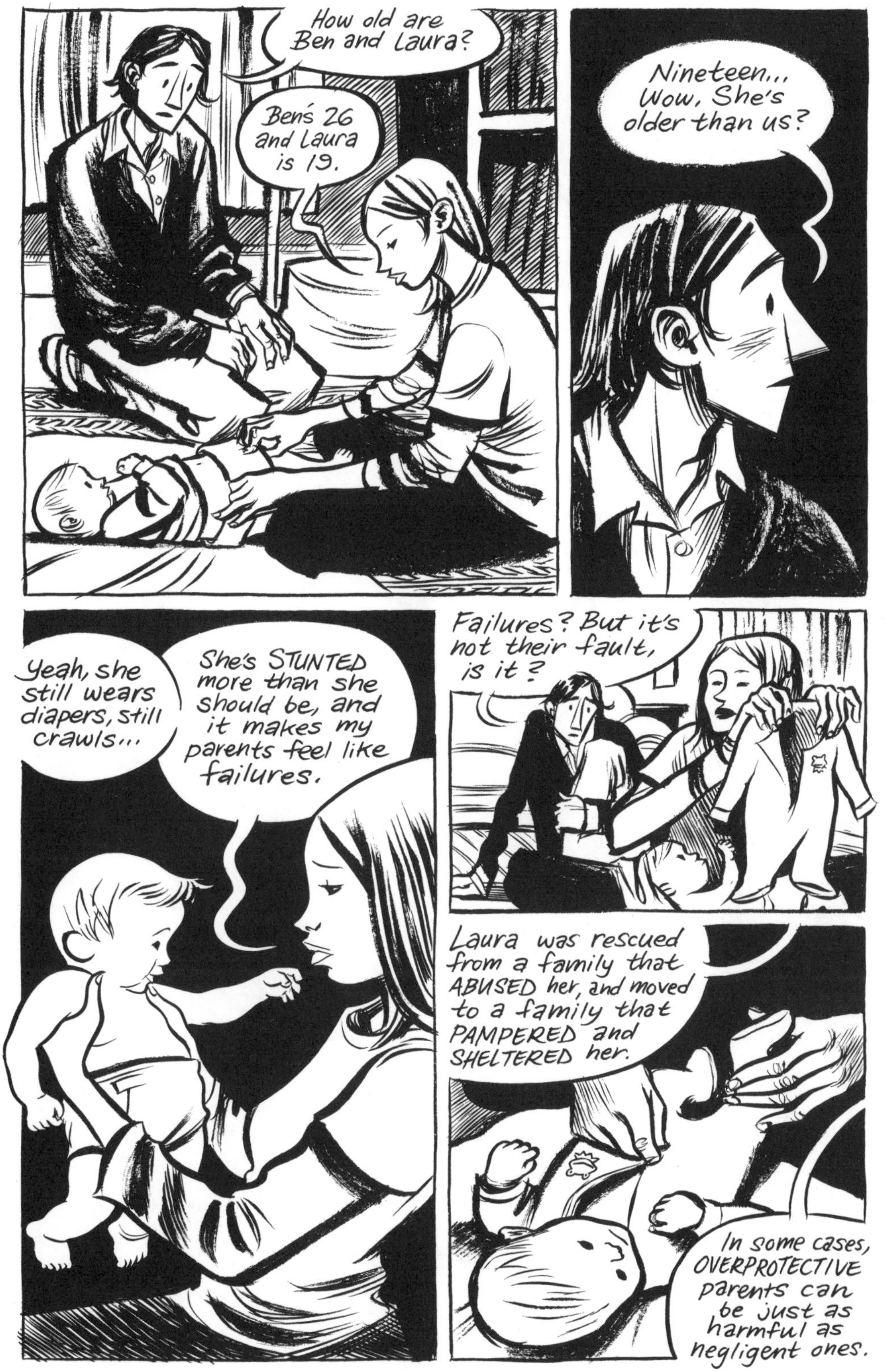
How old are Ben and Laura?
Ben's 26 and Laura is 19.
Nineteen... Wow, She's older than us?
Yeah, she still wears diapers, still crawls...
She's STUNTED more than she should be, and it makes my parents feel like failures.
Failures? But it's not their fault, is it?
Laura was rescued from a family that ABUSED her, and moved to a family that PAMPERED and SHELTERED her.
In some cases, OVERPROTECTIVE parents can be just as harmful as negligent ones.

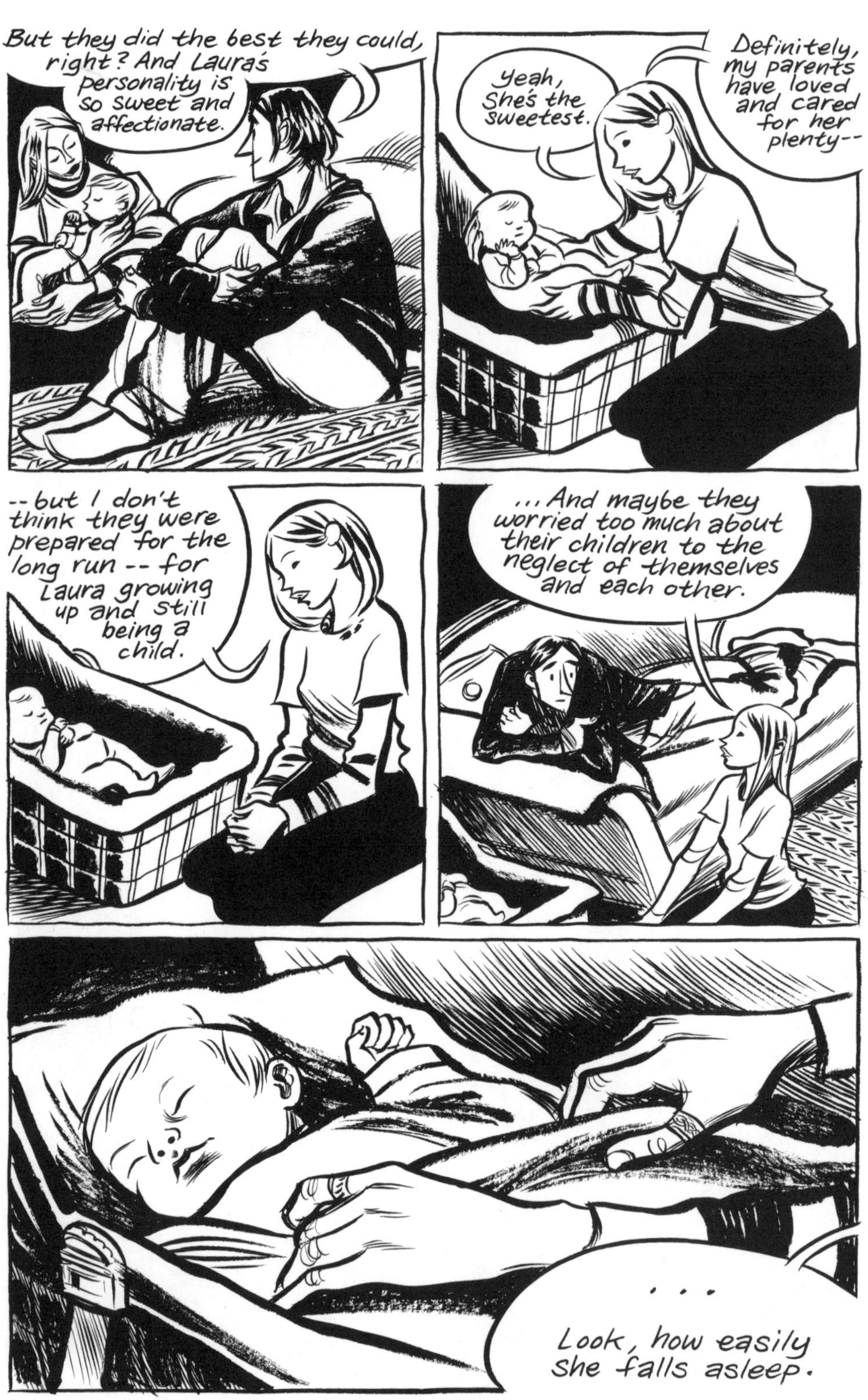
But they did the best they could, right? And Laura's personality is so sweet and affectionate.
Yeah, She's the sweetest.
Definitely, my parents have loved and cared for her plenty--
--but I don't think they were prepared for the long run -- for Laura growing up and still being a child.
...And maybe they worried too much about their children to the neglect of themselves and each other.
. . .
Look, how easily she falls asleep.

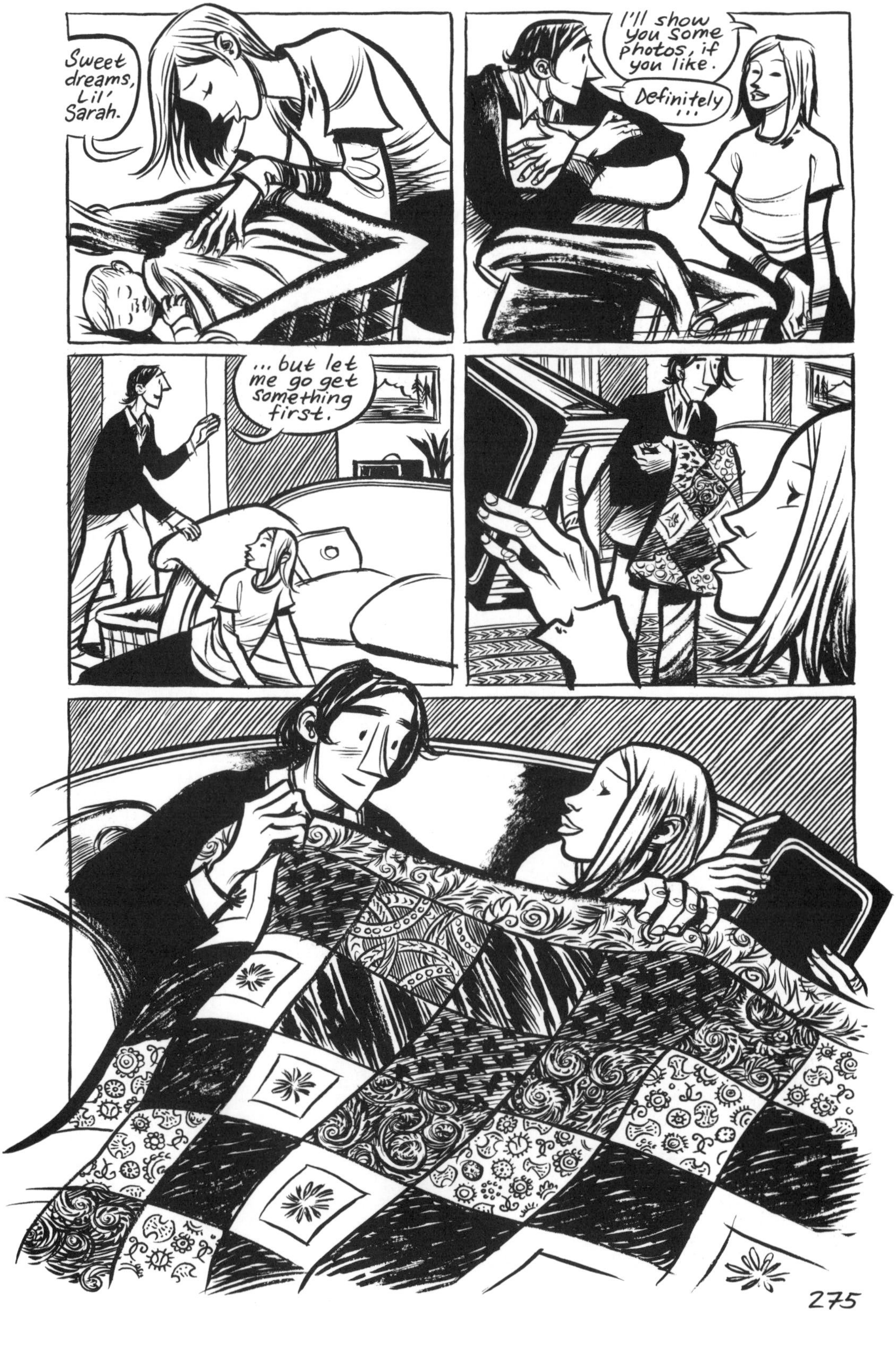
Sweet dreams, Lil' Sarah.
I'll show you some photos, if you like.
Definitely ...
... but let me go get something first.

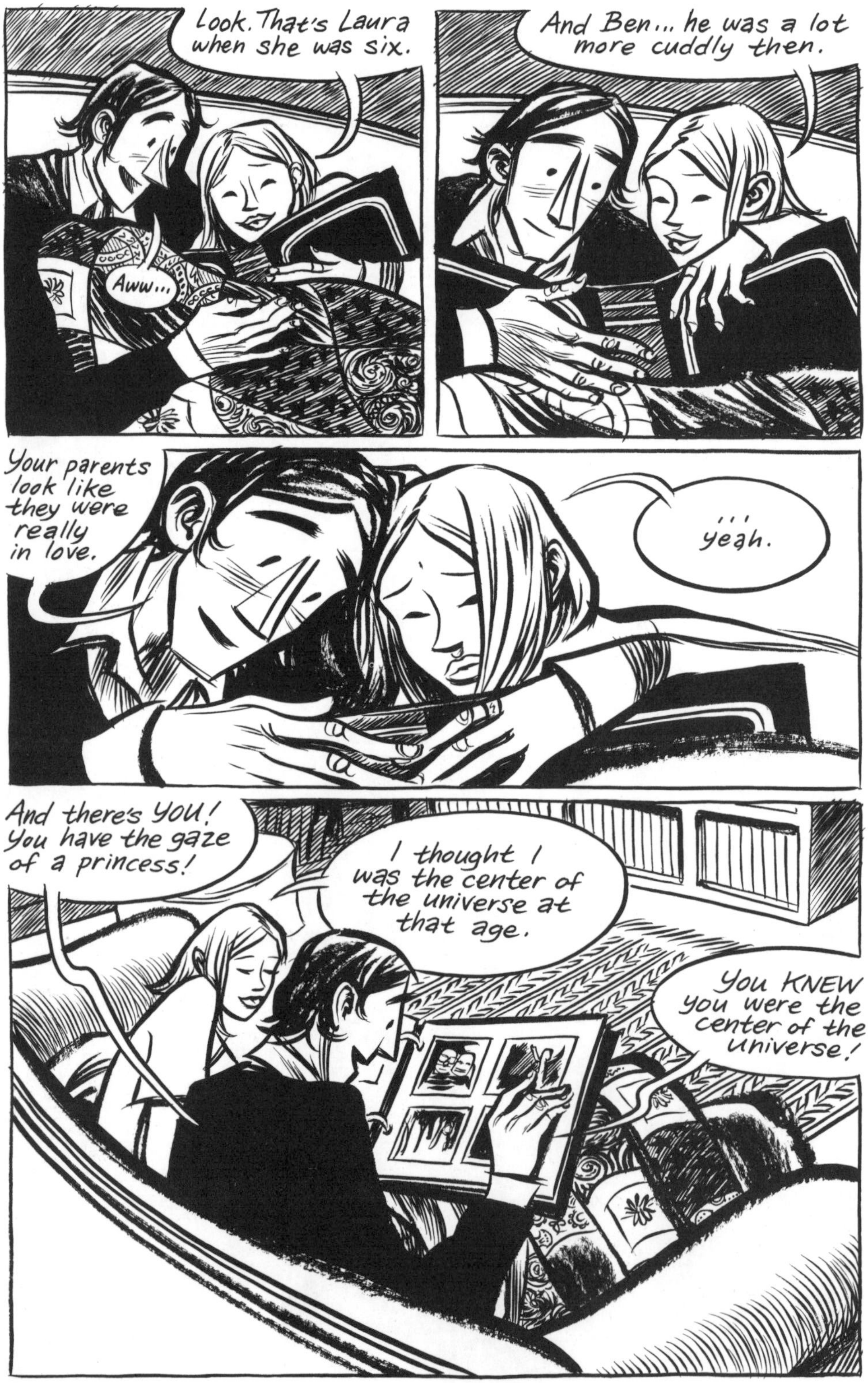
Look. That's Laura when she was six.
Aww...
And Ben... he was a lot more cuddly then.
Your parents look like they were really in love.
... yeah.
And there's YOU! You have the gaze of a princess!
I thought I was the center of the universe at that age.
You KNEW you were the center of the universe!

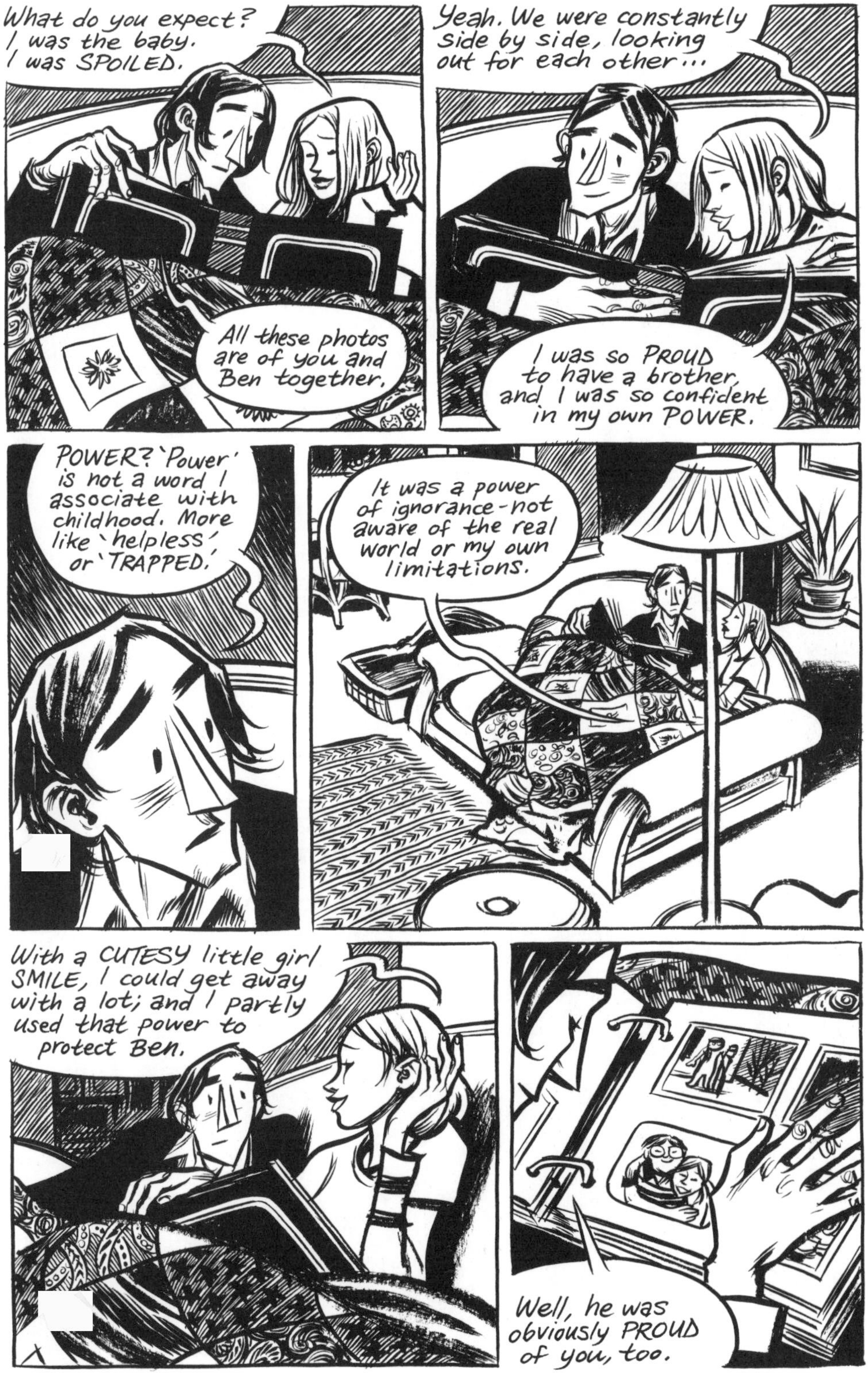
What do you expect? I was the baby. I was SPOILED.
All these photos are of you and Ben together.
Yeah. We were constantly side by side, looking out for each other...
I was so PROUD to have a brother, and I was so confident in my own POWER.
POWER? 'Power' is not a word I associate with childhood. More like 'helpless,' or 'TRAPPED.'
It was a power of ignorance-not aware of the real world or my own limitations.
With a CUTESY little girl SMILE, I could get away with a lot; and I partly used that power to protect Ben.
Well, he was obviously PROUD of you, too.

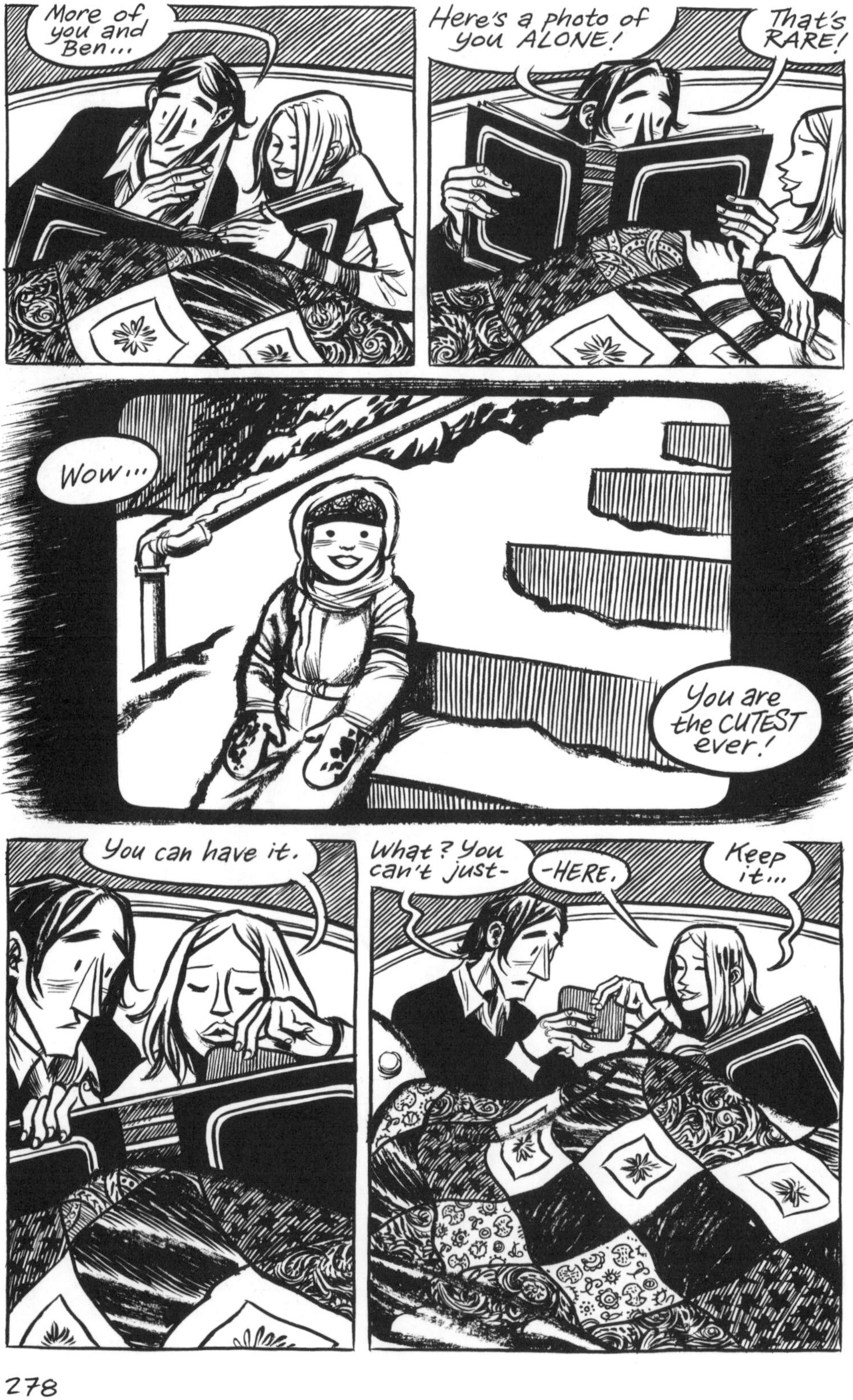
More of you and Ben...
Here's a photo of you ALONE!
That's RARE!
Wow...
You are the CUTEST ever!
You can have it.
What? You can't just-
-HERE.
Keep it...

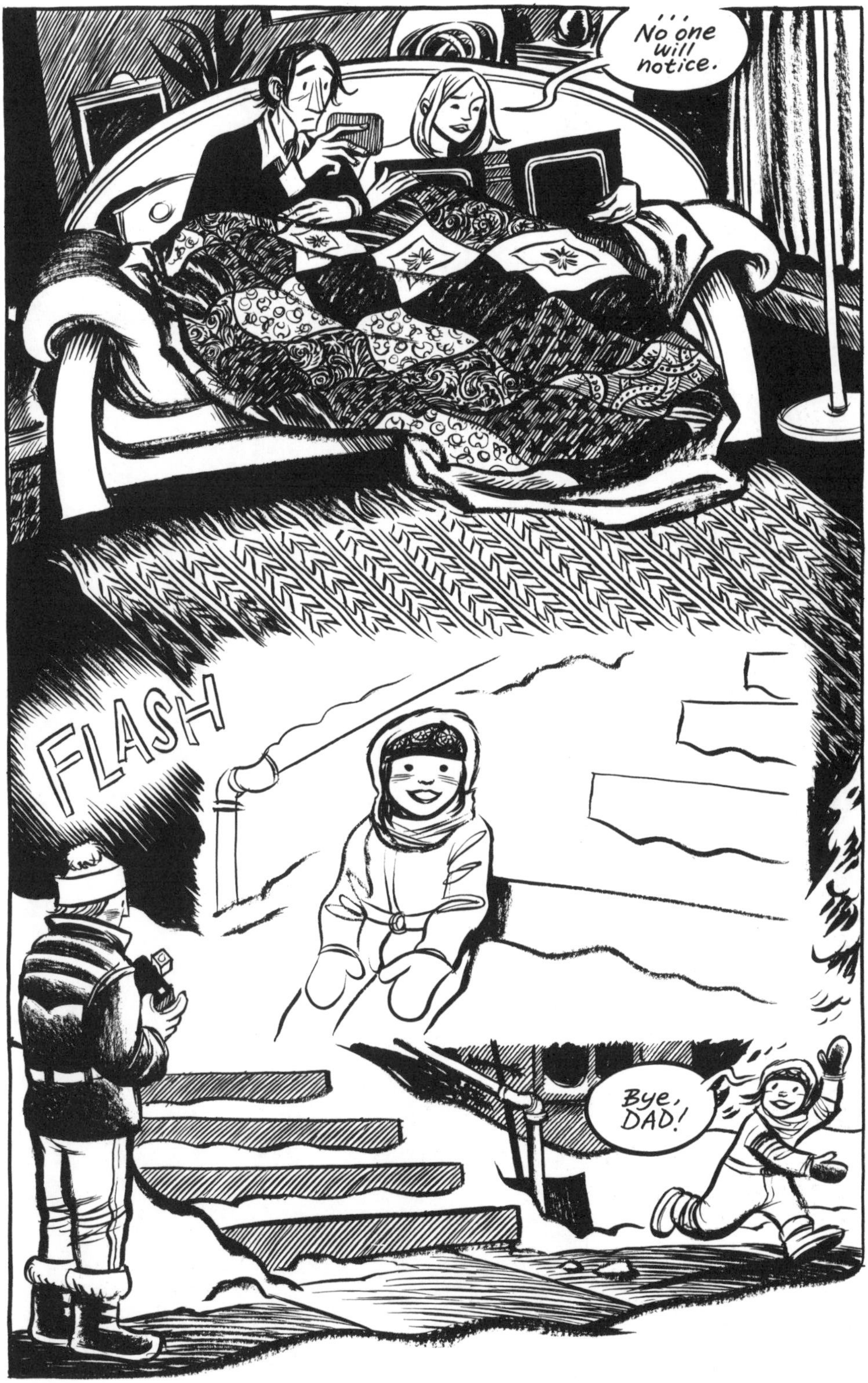
... No one will notice.
FLASH
Bye, DAD!

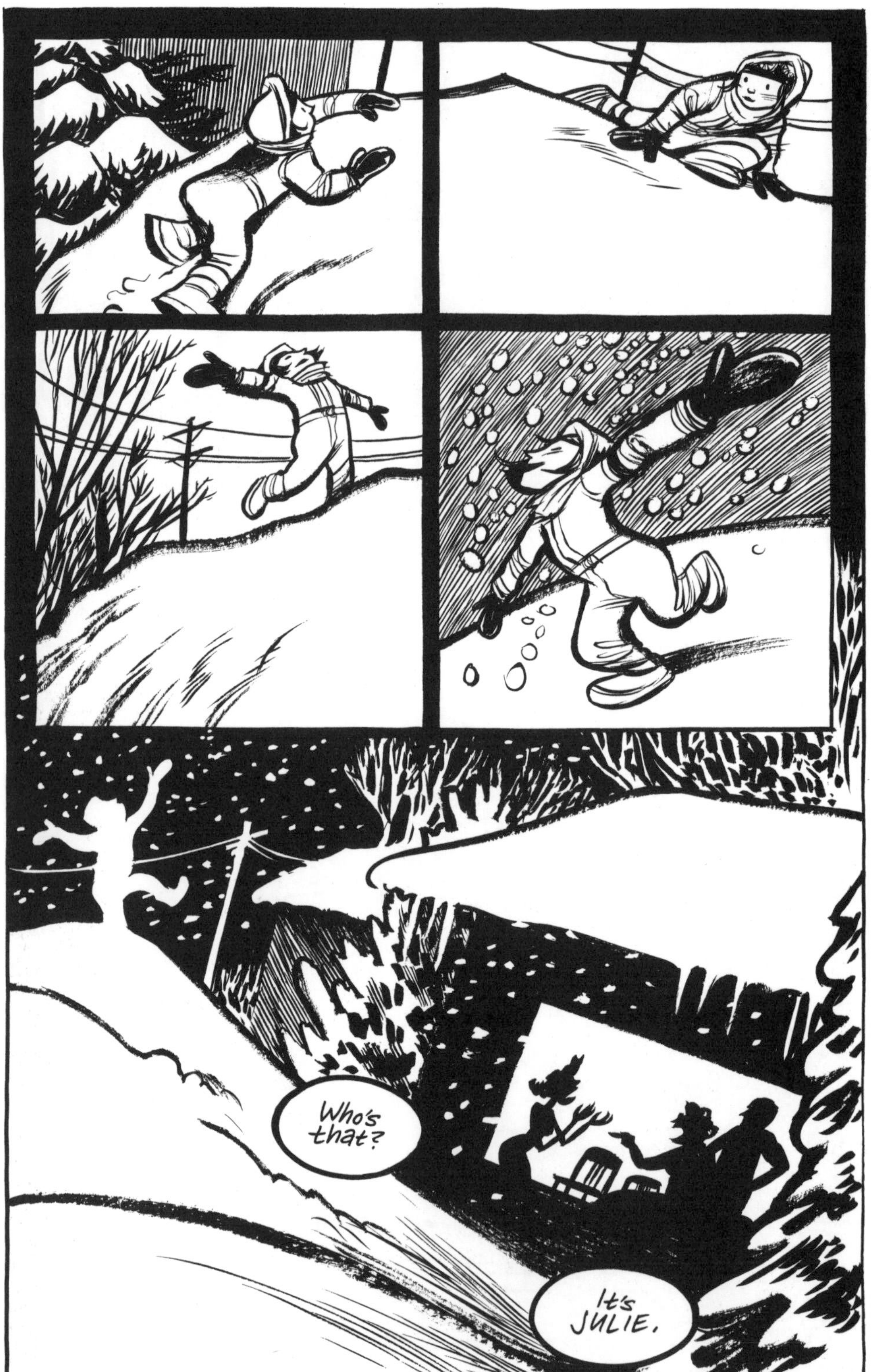

Who's that?
It's JULIE.

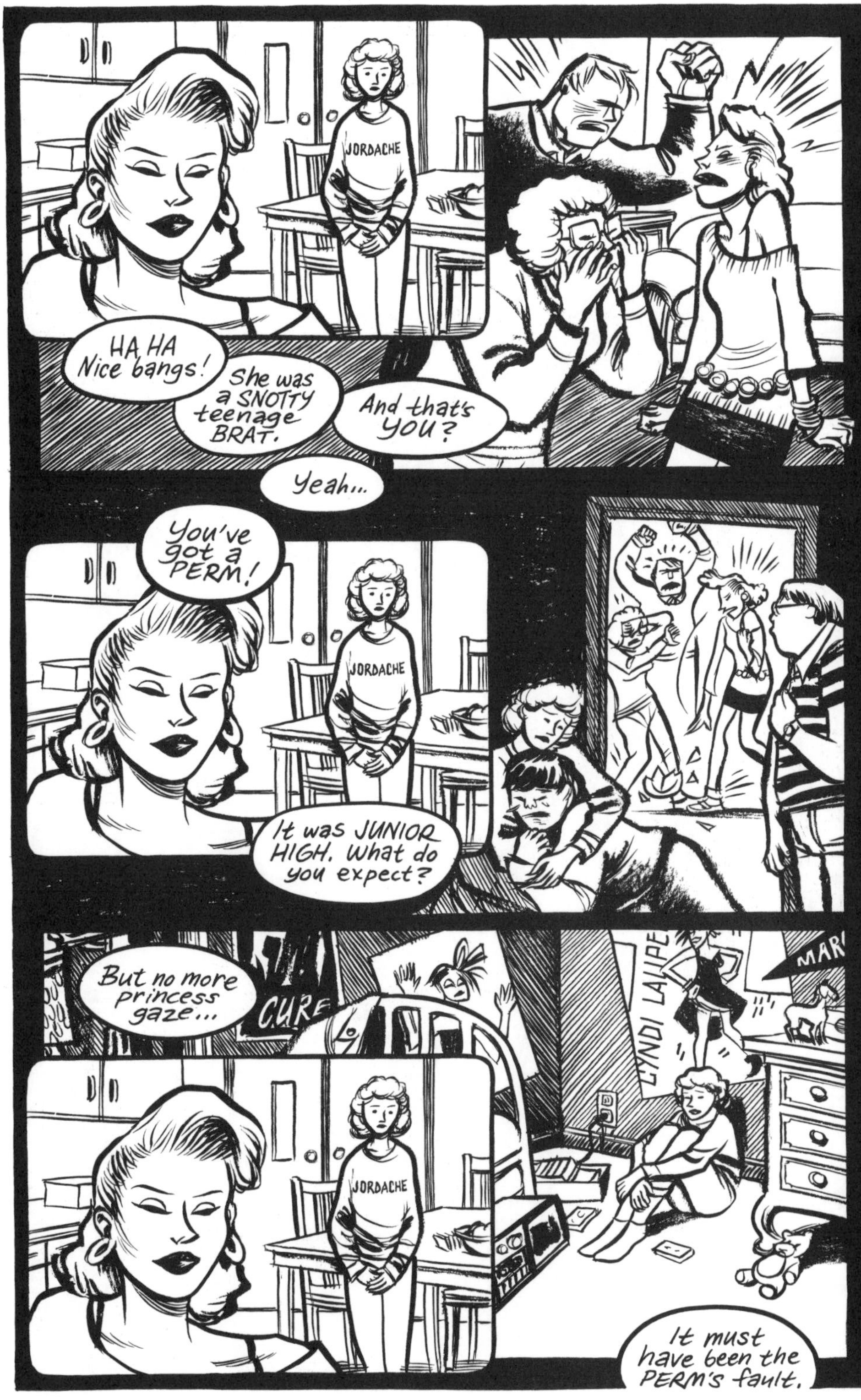
HA HA Nice bangs!
She was a SNOTTY teenage BRAT.
And that's YOU?
JORDACHE
Yeah...
You've got a PERM!
It was JUNIOR HIGH. What do you expect?
JORDACHE
But no more princess gaze...
CURE
CYNDI LAUPE
JORDACHE
It must have been the PERM's fault.

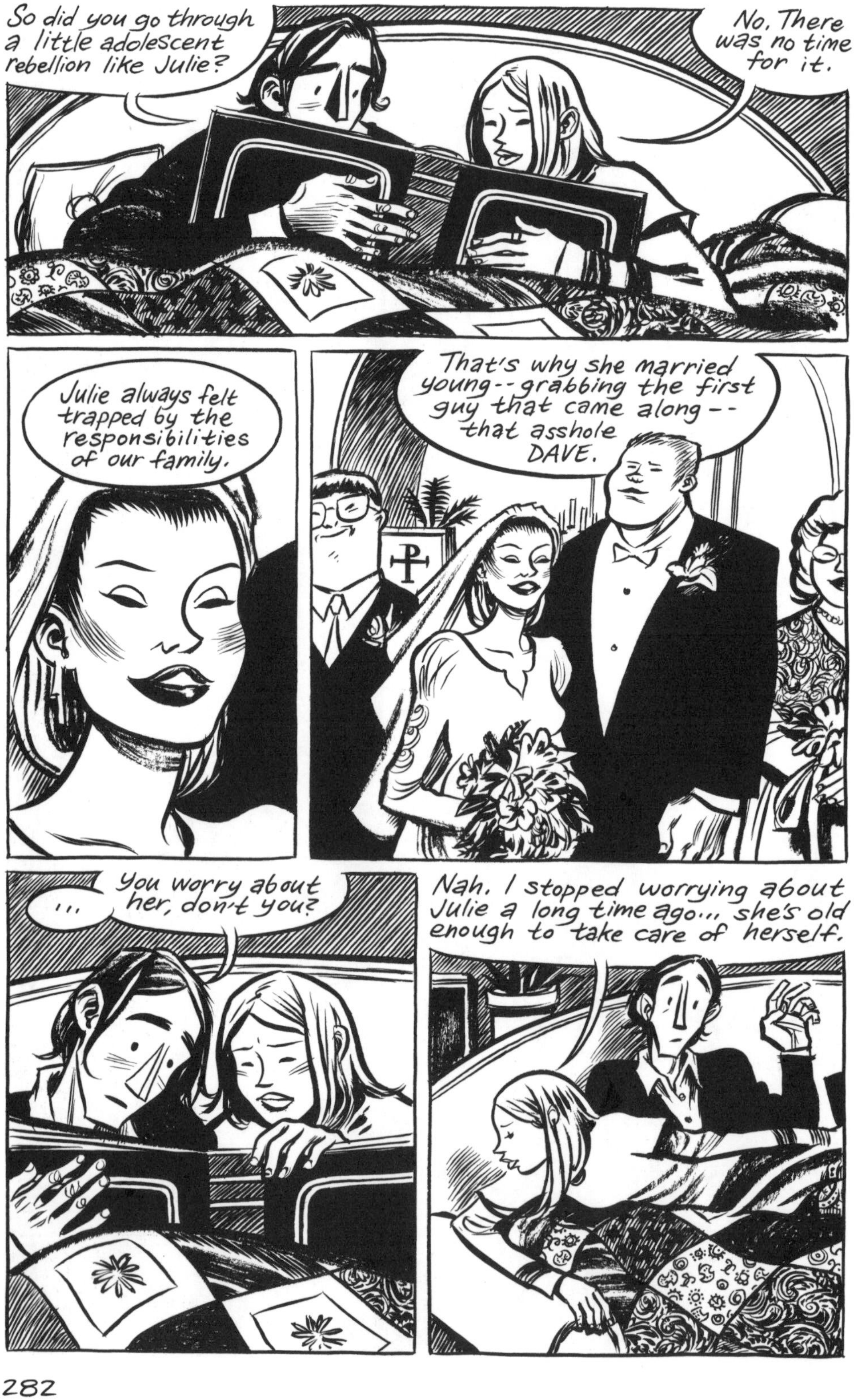
So did you go through a little adolescent rebellion like Julie?
No. There was no time for it.
Julie always felt trapped by the responsibilities of our family.
That's why she married young--grabbing the first guy that came along--that asshole DAVE.
...
You worry about her, don't you?
Nah. I stopped worrying about Julie a long time ago.., she's old enough to take care of herself.

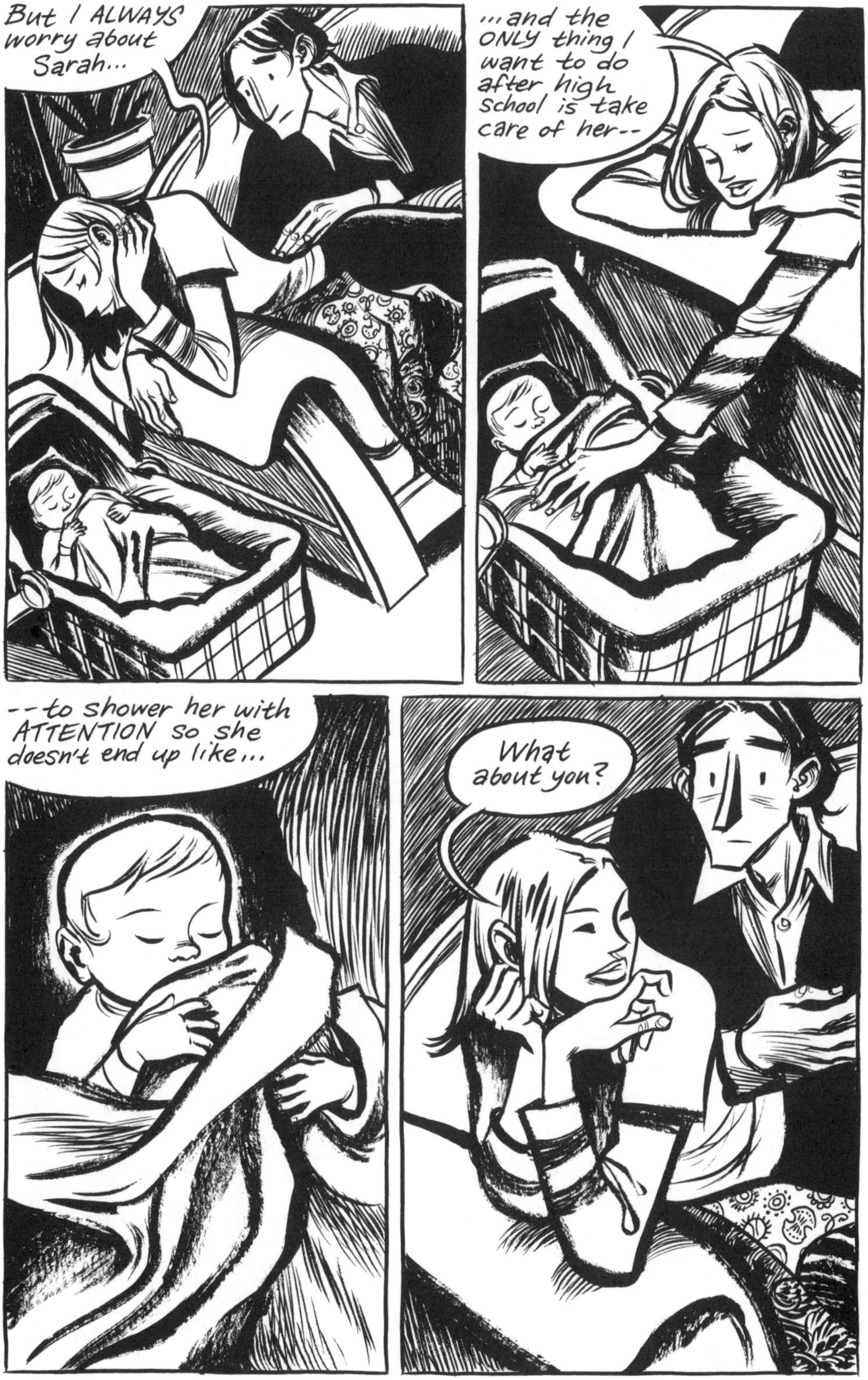
But I ALWAYS worry about Sarah...
...and the ONLY thing I want to do after high school is take care of her--
--to shower her with ATTENTION so she doesn't end up like...
What about you?

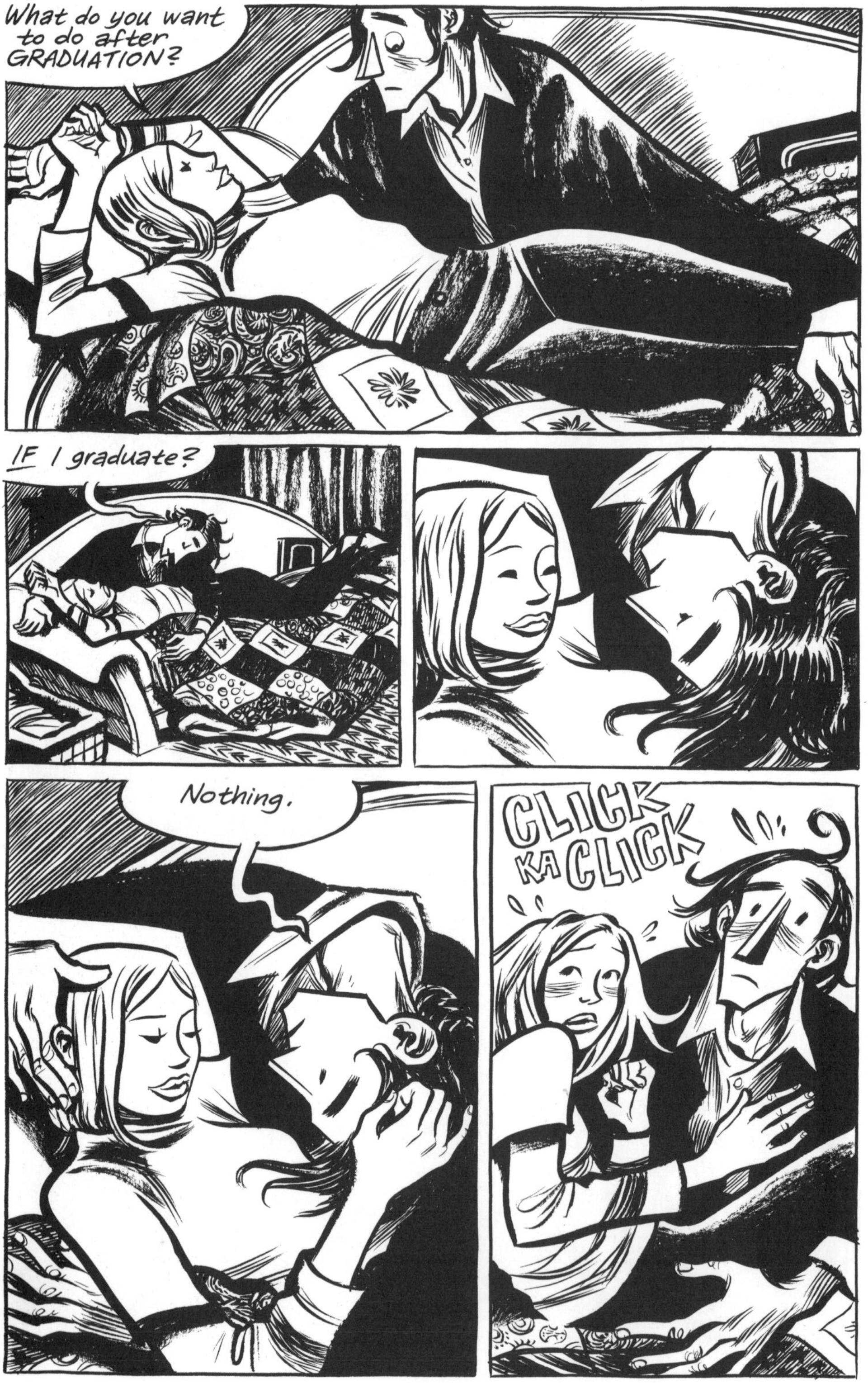

What do you want to do after GRADUATION?
IF I graduate?
Nothing.
CLICK KA CLICK

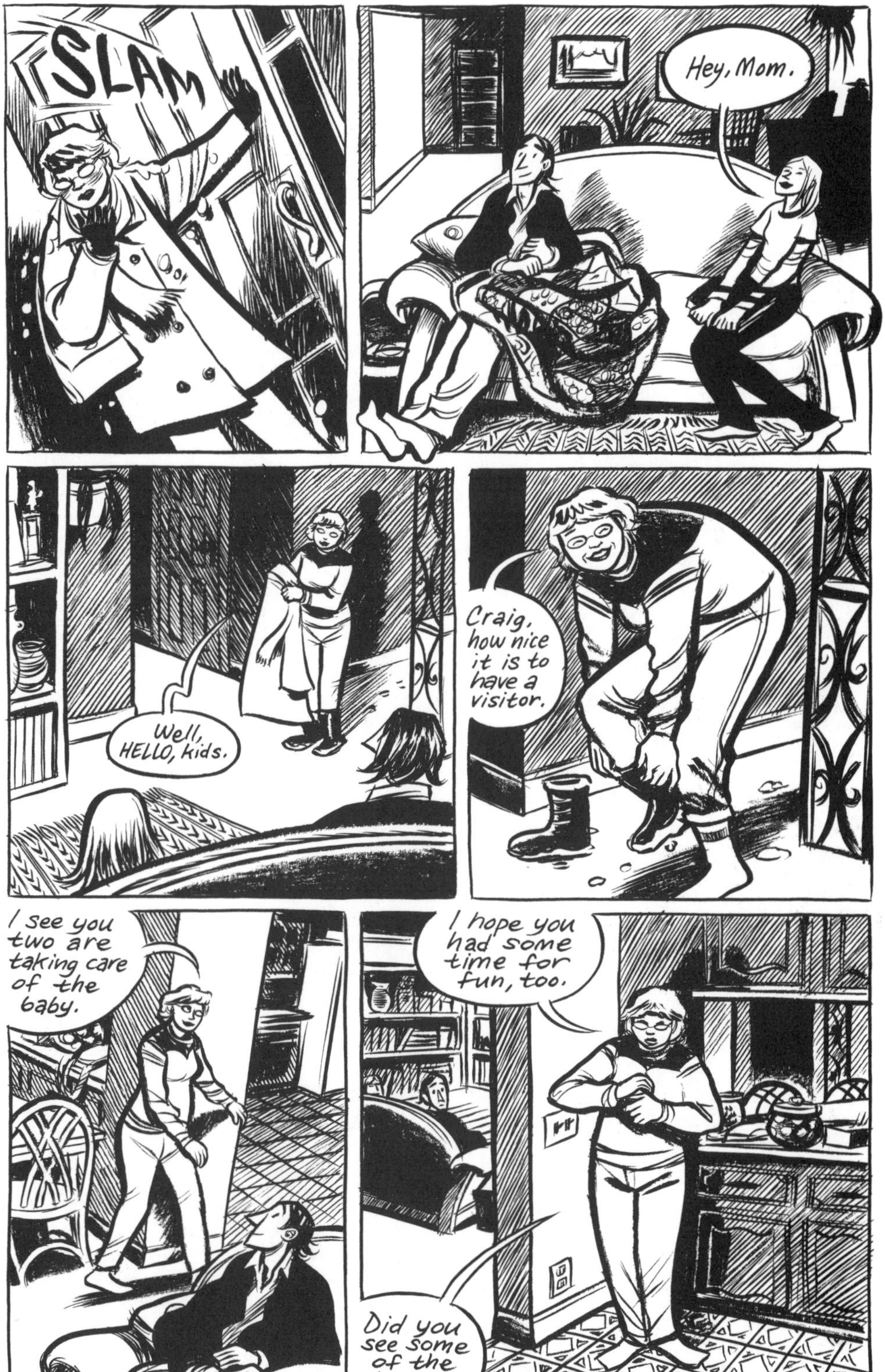
SLAM
Hey, Mom.
Well, HELLO, kids.
Craig, how nice it is to have a visitor.
I see you two are taking care of the baby.
I hope you had some time for fun, too.
Did you see some of the town?

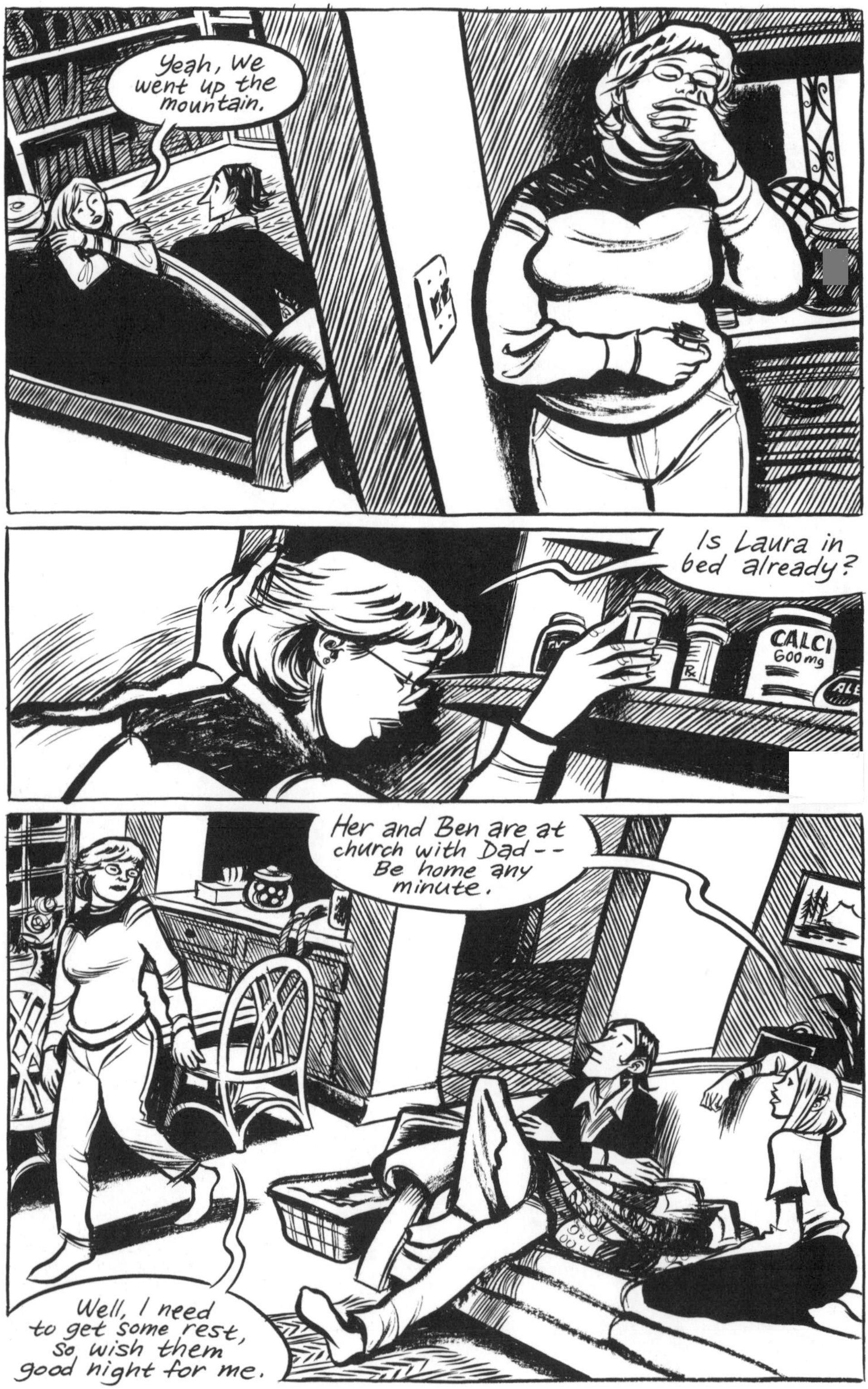
Yeah, we went up the mountain.
Is Laura in bed already?
CALCI 600mg
Her and Ben are at church with Dad-- Be home any minute.
Well, I need to get some rest, so wish them good night for me.

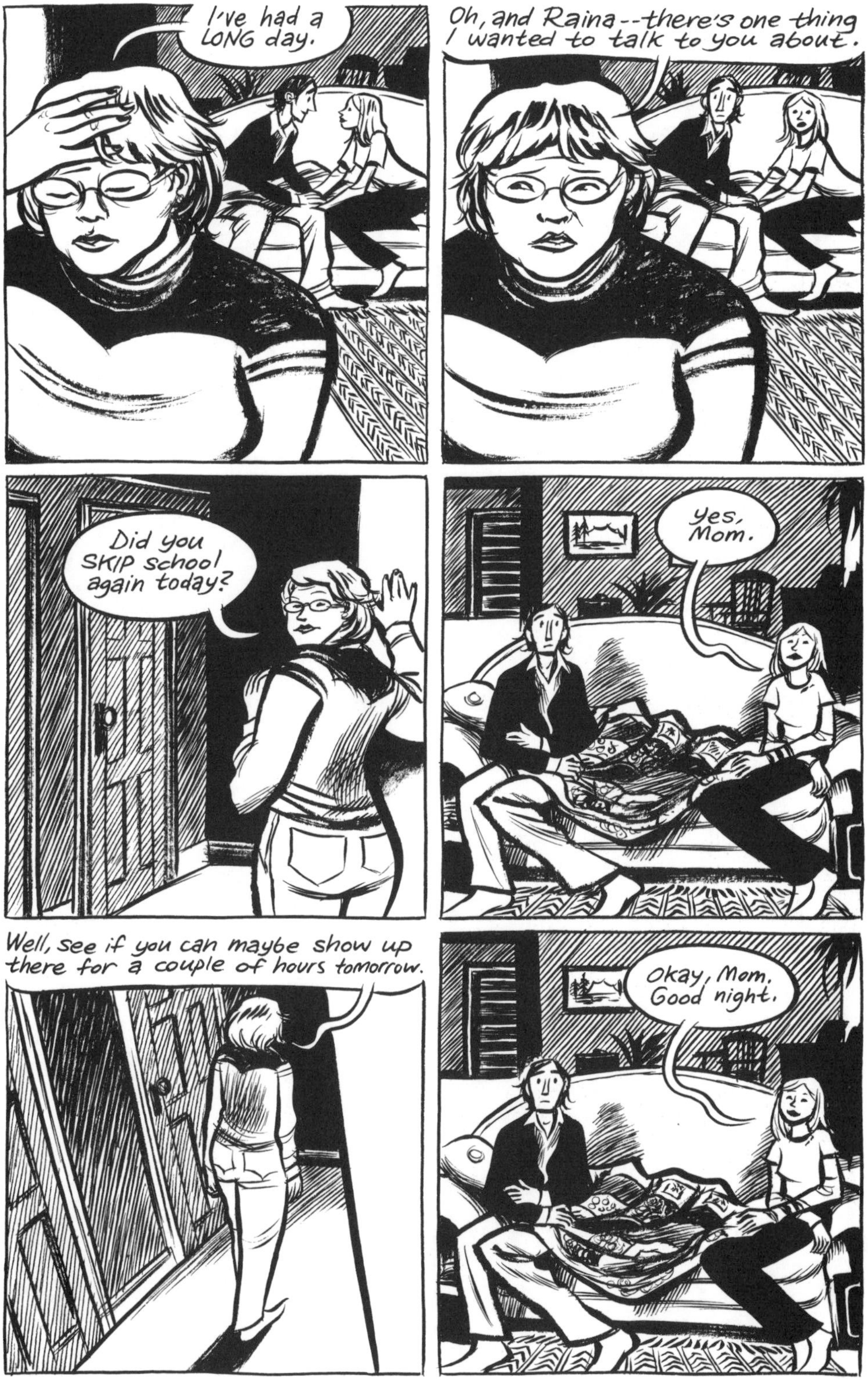
I've had a LONG day.
Oh, and Raina--there's one thing I wanted to talk to you about.
Did you SKIP school again today?
Yes, Mom.
Well, see if you can maybe show up there for a couple of hours tomorrow.
Okay, Mom. Good night.

Soon after, Steve, Laura, and Ben returned, and–nearly simultaneously– Julie and Dave. The kitchen was a jungle of jangling car keys and awkward conversation.

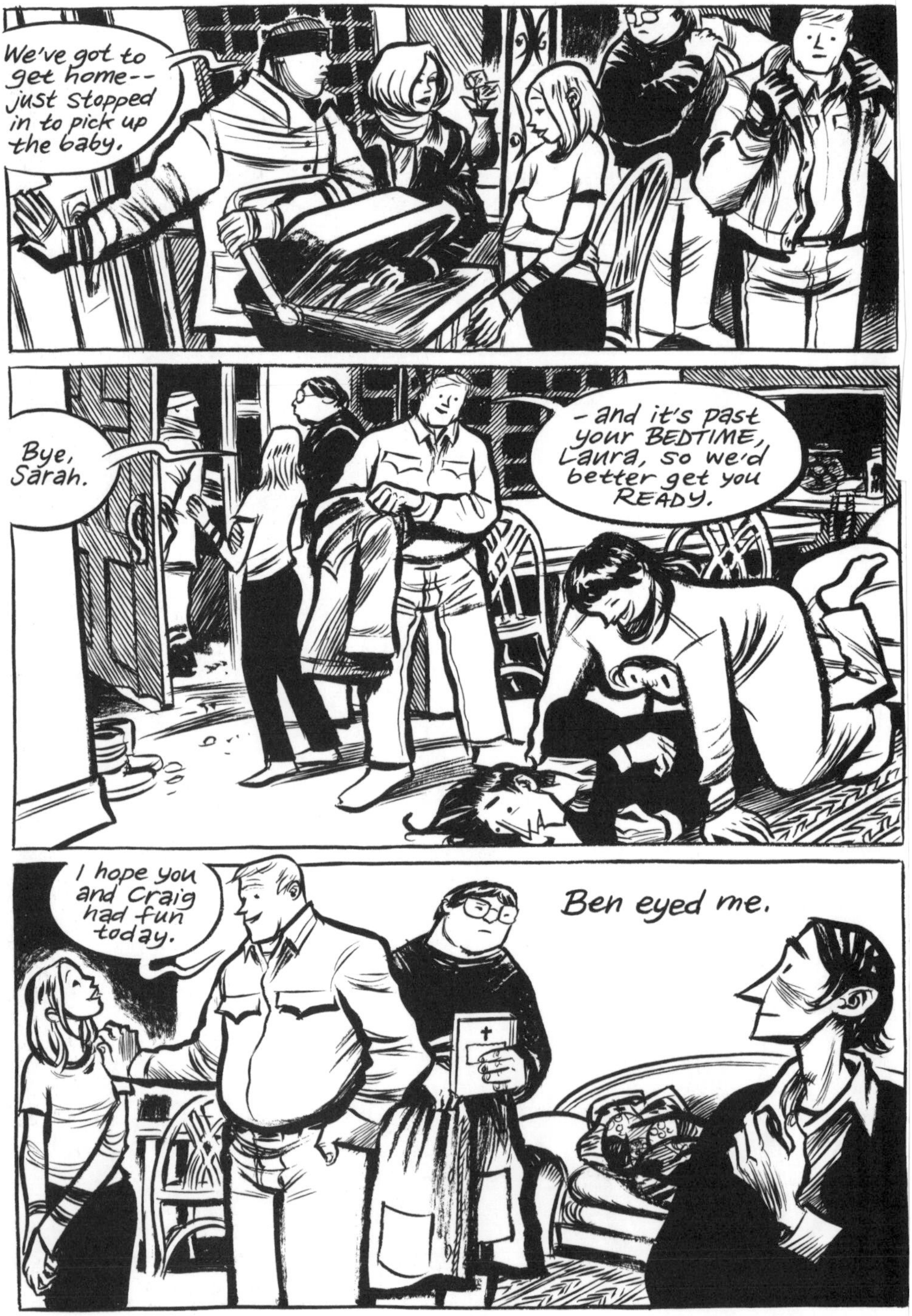
We've got to get home-- just stopped in to pick up the baby.
Bye, Sarah.
–and it's past your BEDTIME, Laura, so we'd better get you READY.
I hope you and Craig had fun today.
Ben eyed me.

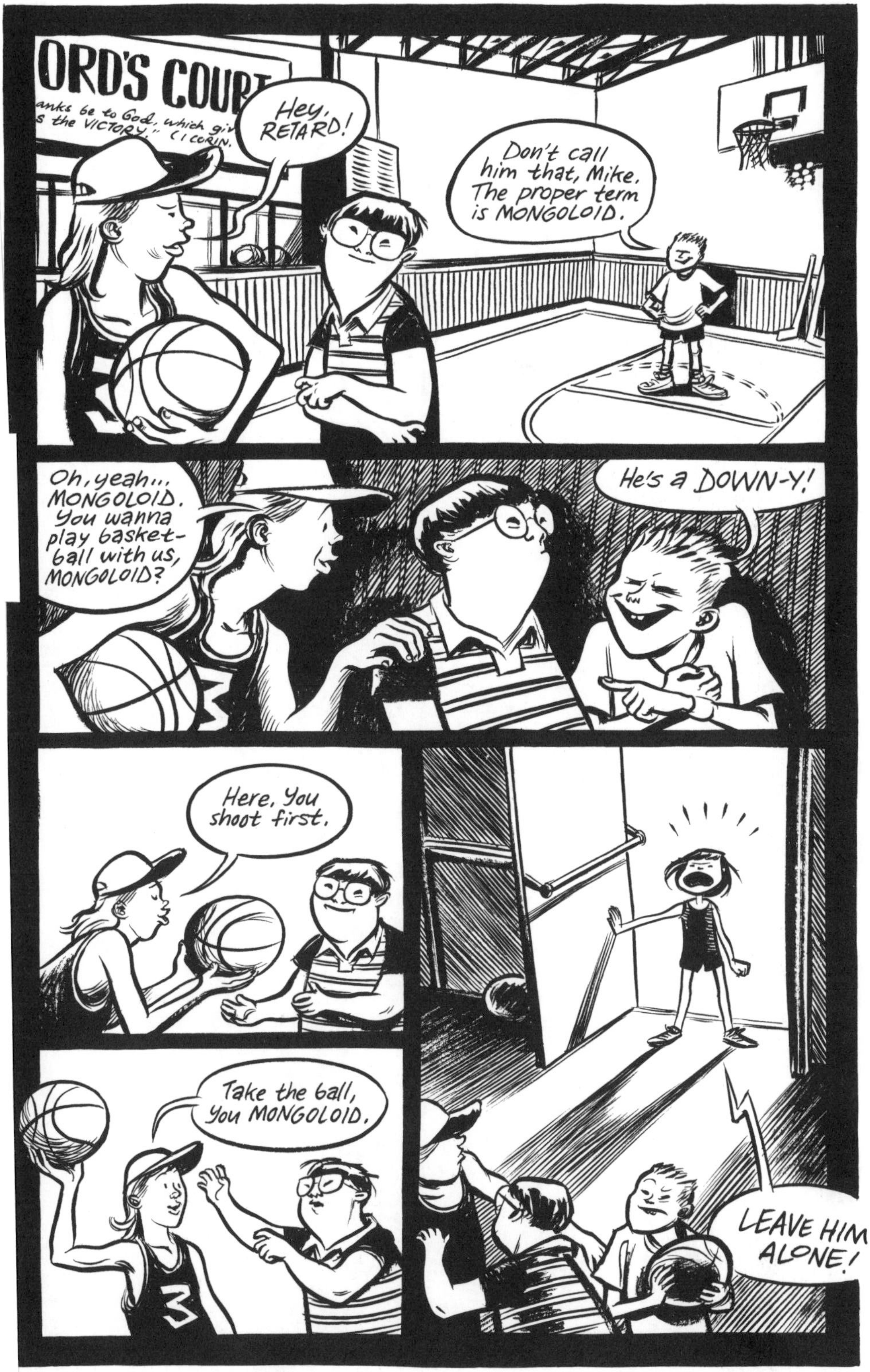
ORD'S COURT
anks be to God, which giv
s the VICTORY." I CORIN.
Hey, RETARD!
Don't call him that, Mike. The proper term is MONGOLOID.
Oh, yeah... MONGOLOID. You wanna play basket-ball with us, MONGOLOID?
He's a DOWN-Y!
Here, You shoot first.
Take the ball, You MONGOLOID.
LEAVE HIM ALONE!

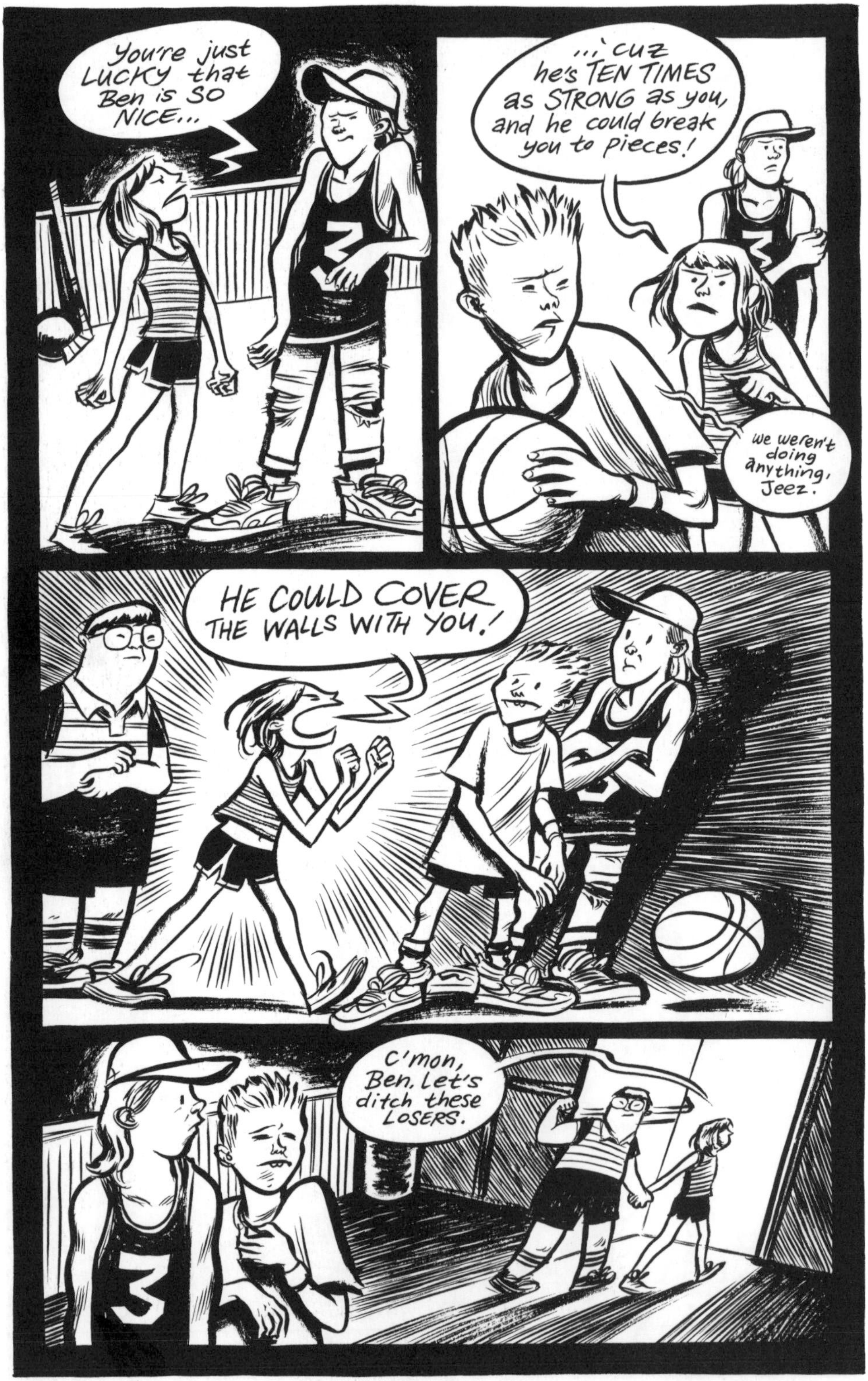

You're just LUCKY that Ben is SO NICE...
...'cuz he's TEN TIMES as STRONG as you, and he could break you to pieces!
we weren't doing anything, Jeez.
HE COULD COVER THE WALLS WITH YOU!
C'mon, Ben, let's ditch these LOSERS.

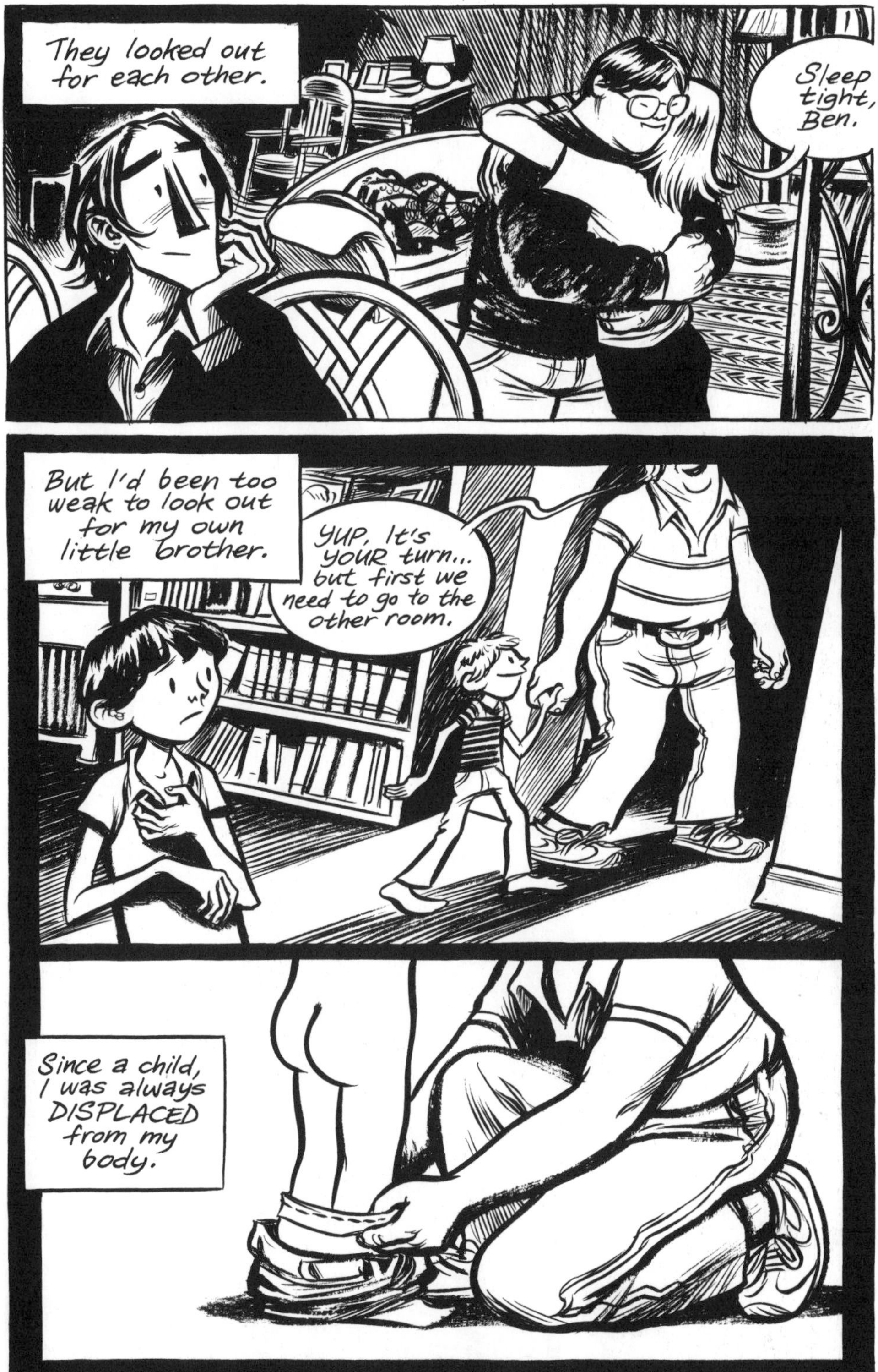
They looked out for each other.
Sleep tight, Ben.
But I'd been too weak to look out for my own little brother.
YUP, It's YOUR turn... but first we need to go to the other room.
Since a child, I was always DISPLACED from my body.

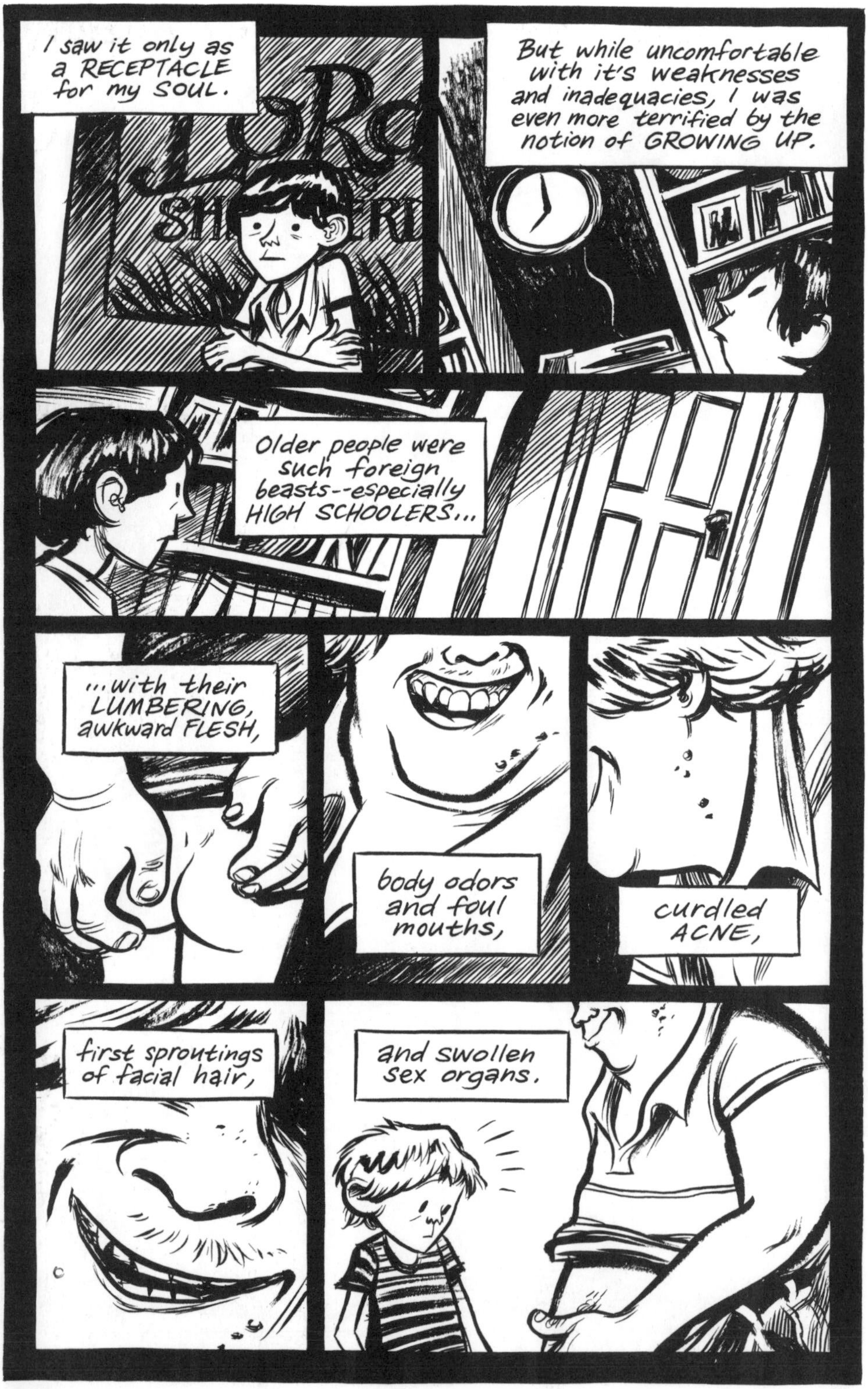
I saw it only as a RECEPTACLE for my SOUL.
But while uncomfortable with it's weaknesses and inadequacies, I was even more terrified by the notion of GROWING UP.
Older people were such foreign beasts--especially HIGH SCHOOLERS...
...with their LUMBERING, awkward FLESH,
body odors and foul mouths,
curdled ACNE,
first sproutings of facial hair,
and swollen sex organs.

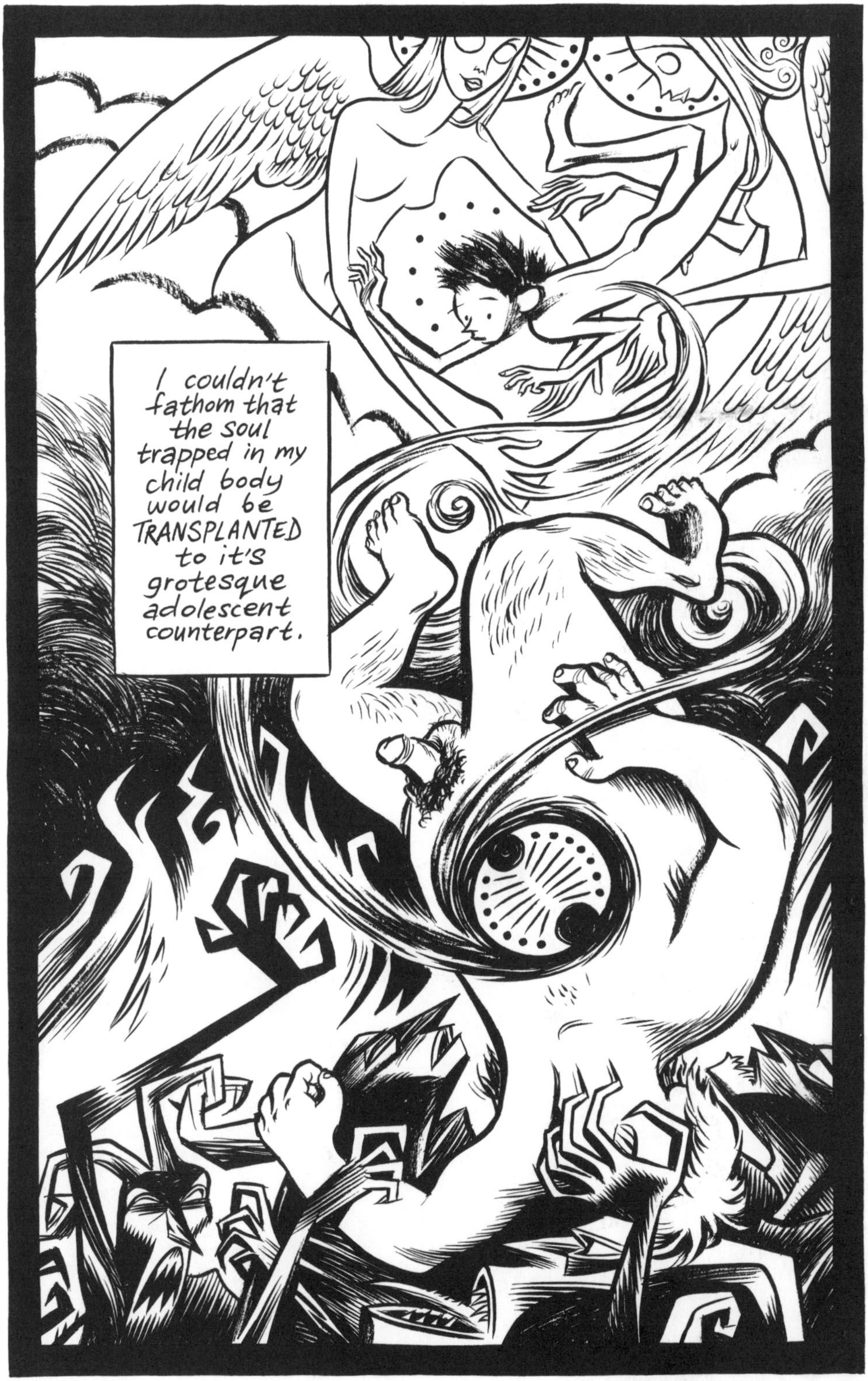
I couldn't fathom that the soul trapped in my child body would be TRANSPLANTED to it's grotesque adolescent counterpart.

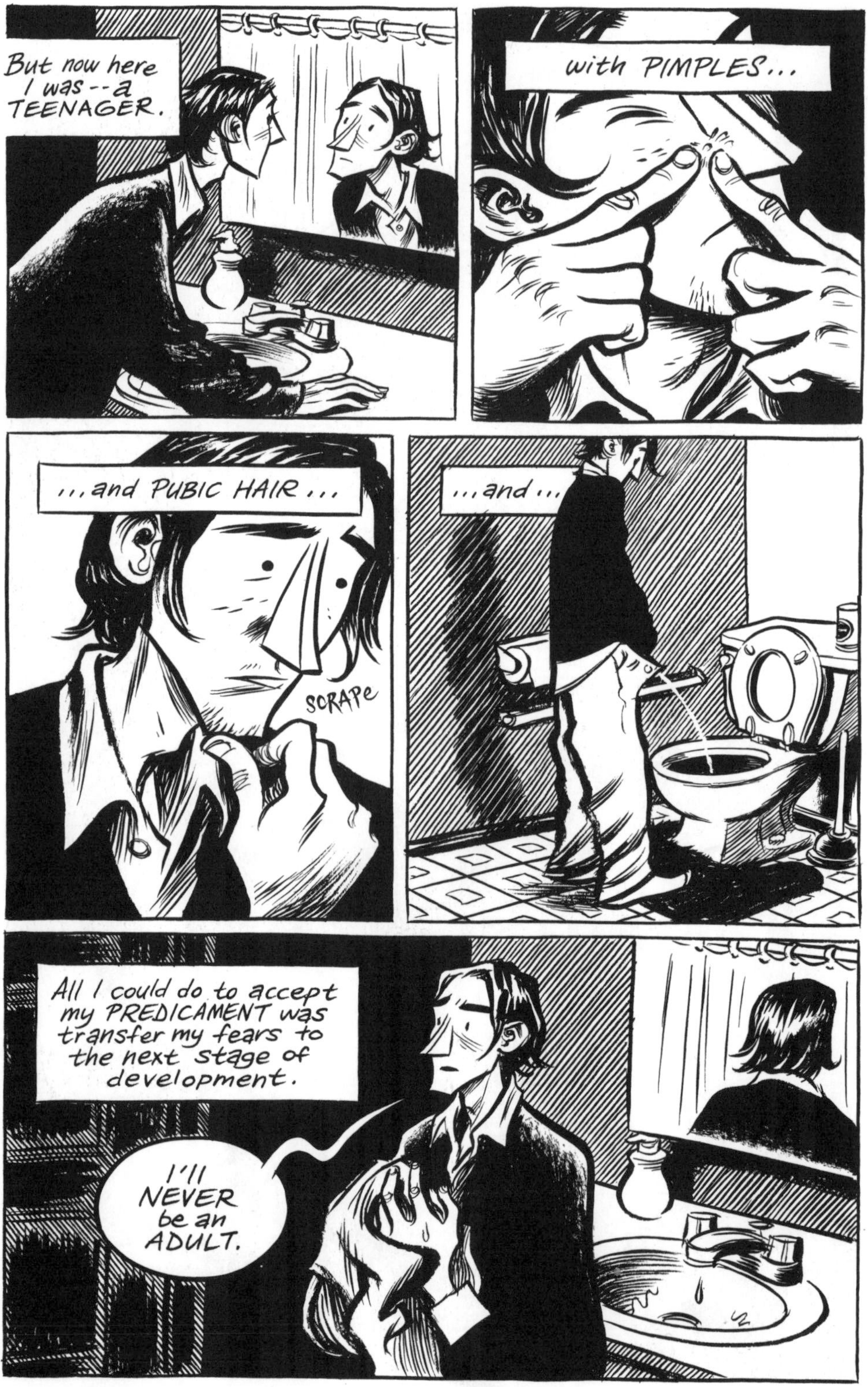

But now here I was--a TEENAGER.
with PIMPLES...
...and PUBIC HAIR...
SCRAPE
...and...
All I could do to accept my PREDICAMENT was transfer my fears to the next stage of development.
I'll NEVER be an ADULT.

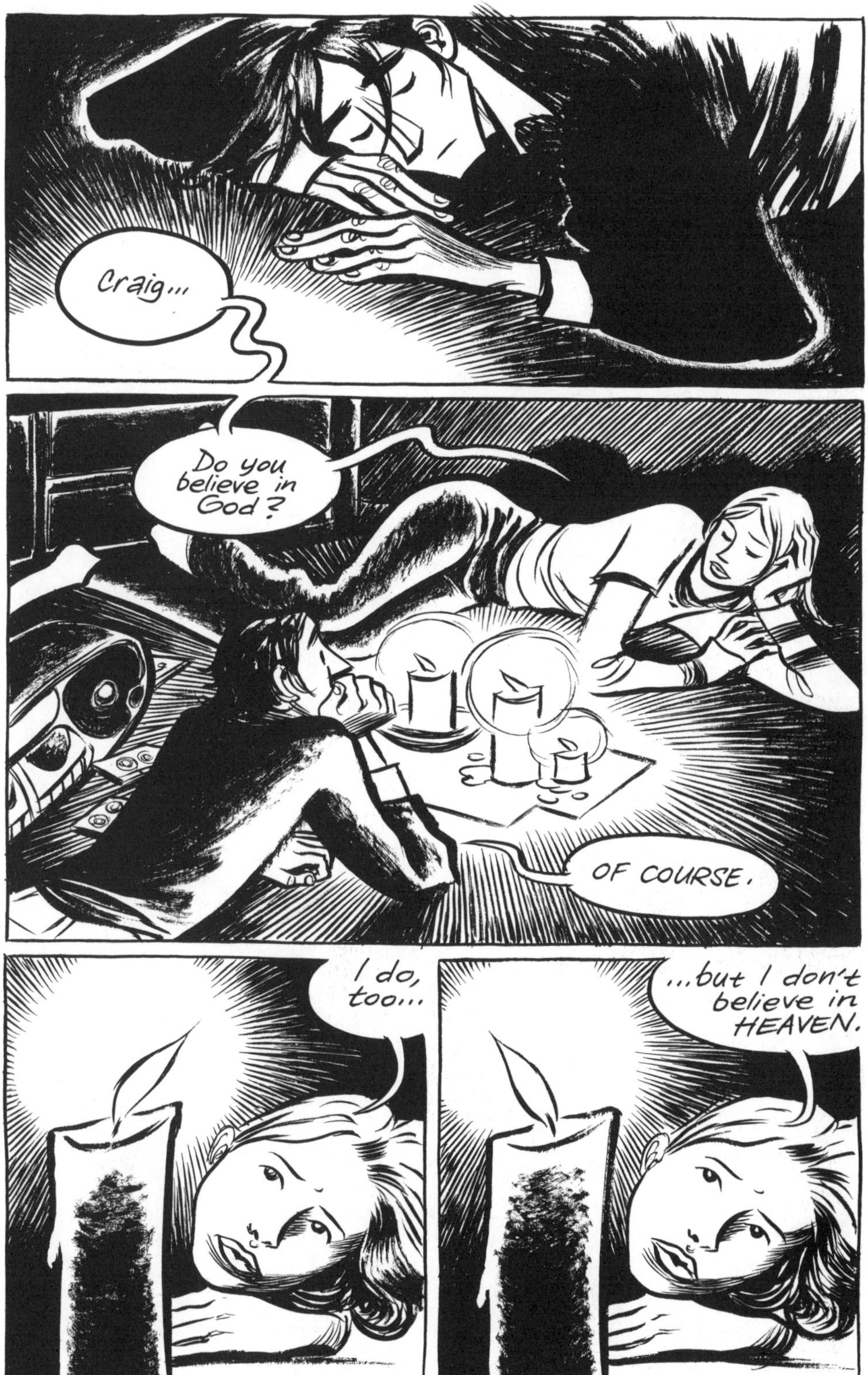
Craig...
Do you believe in God?
OF COURSE.
I do, too...
...but I don't believe in HEAVEN.

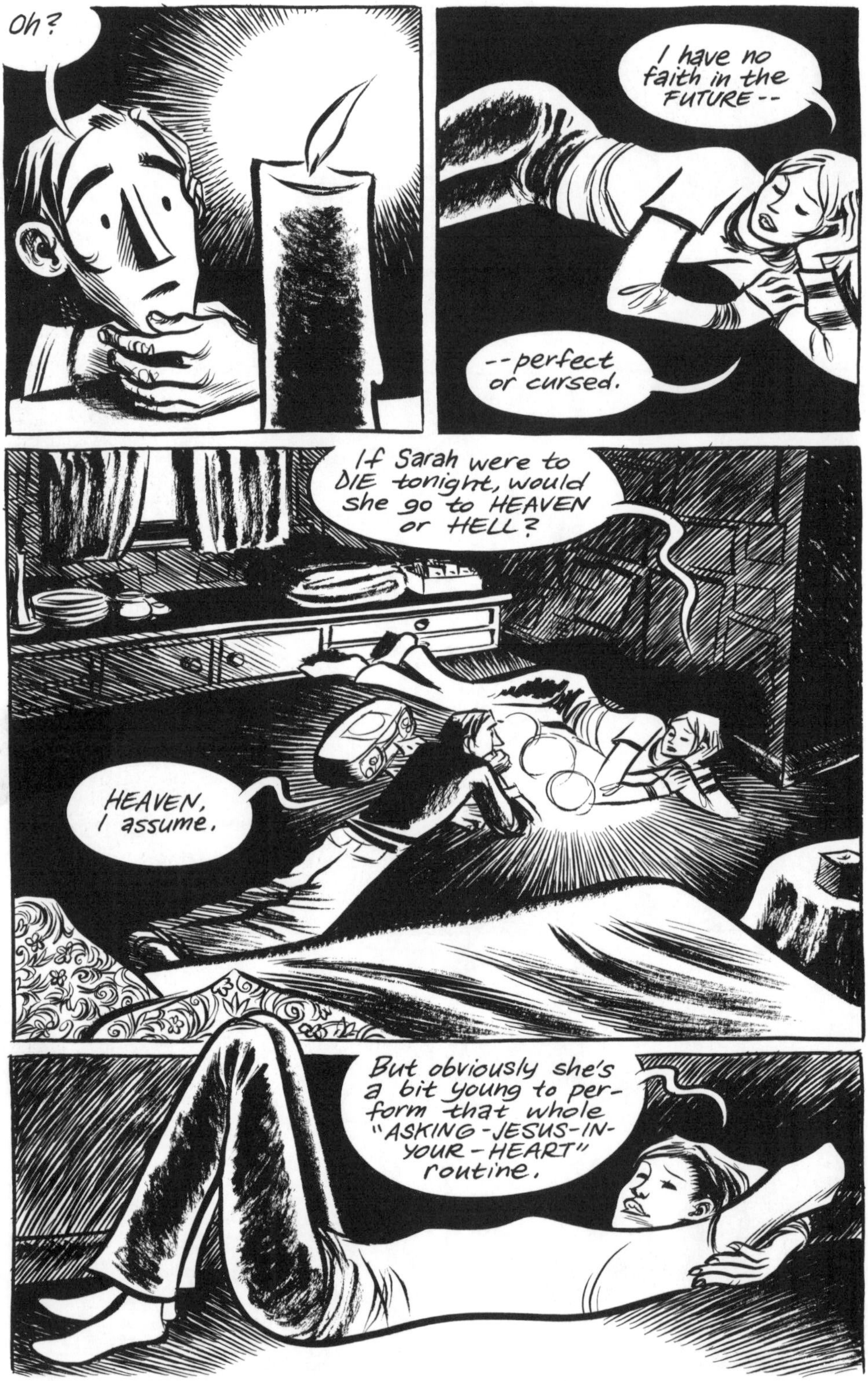
Oh?
I have no faith in the FUTURE--
--perfect or cursed.
If Sarah were to DIE tonight, would she go to HEAVEN or HELL?
HEAVEN, I assume.
But obviously she's a bit young to perform that whole "ASKING-JESUS-IN-YOUR-HEART" routine.

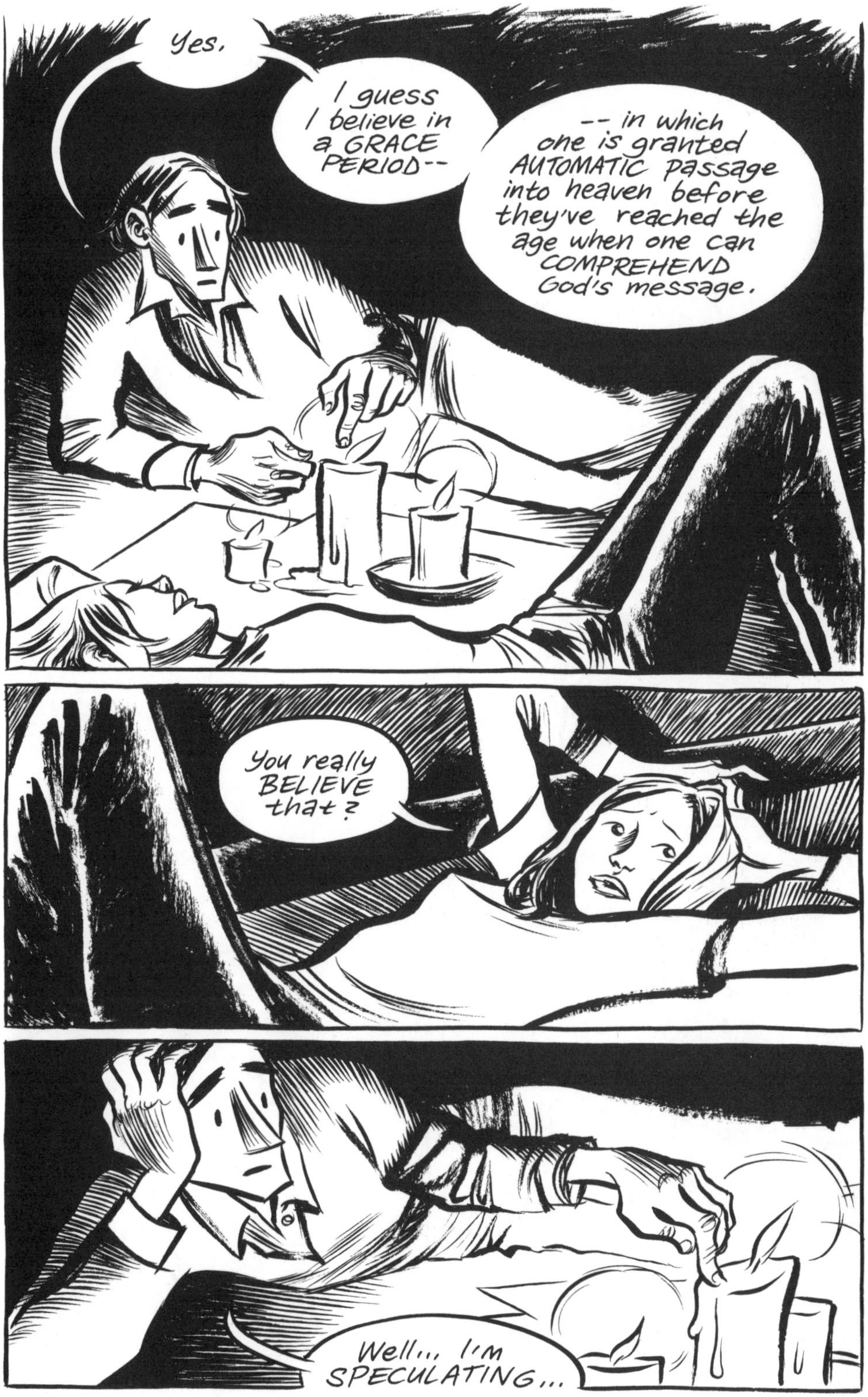
Yes.
I guess I believe in a GRACE PERIOD--
-- in which one is granted AUTOMATIC passage into heaven before they've reached the age when one can COMPREHEND God's message.
You really BELIEVE that?
Well... I'm SPECULATING...

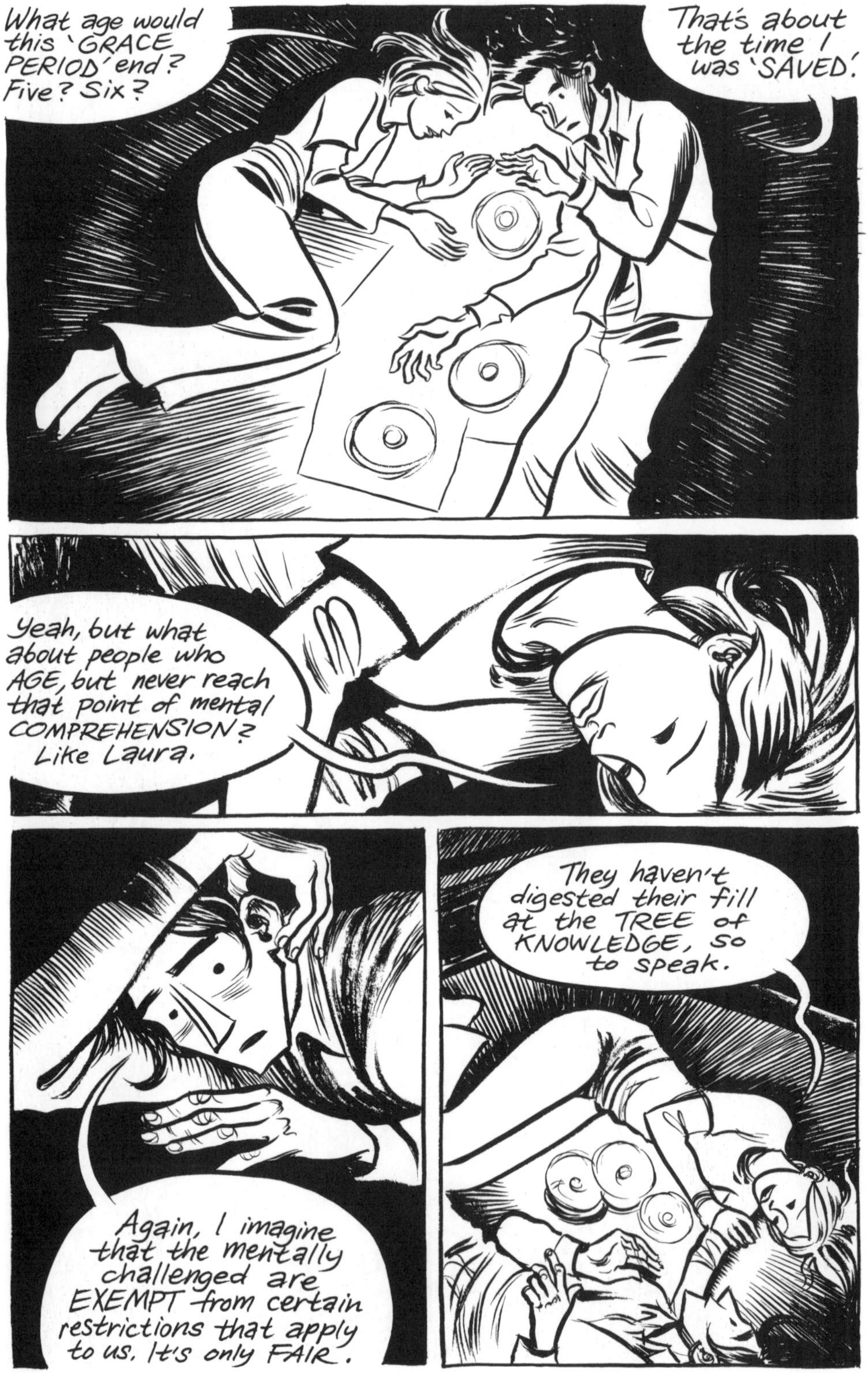
What age would this 'GRACE PERIOD' end? Five? Six?
That's about the time I was 'SAVED'.
Yeah, but what about people who AGE, but never reach that point of mental COMPREHENSION? Like Laura.
Again, I imagine that the mentally challenged are EXEMPT from certain restrictions that apply to us. It's only FAIR.
They haven't digested their fill at the TREE of KNOWLEDGE, so to speak.

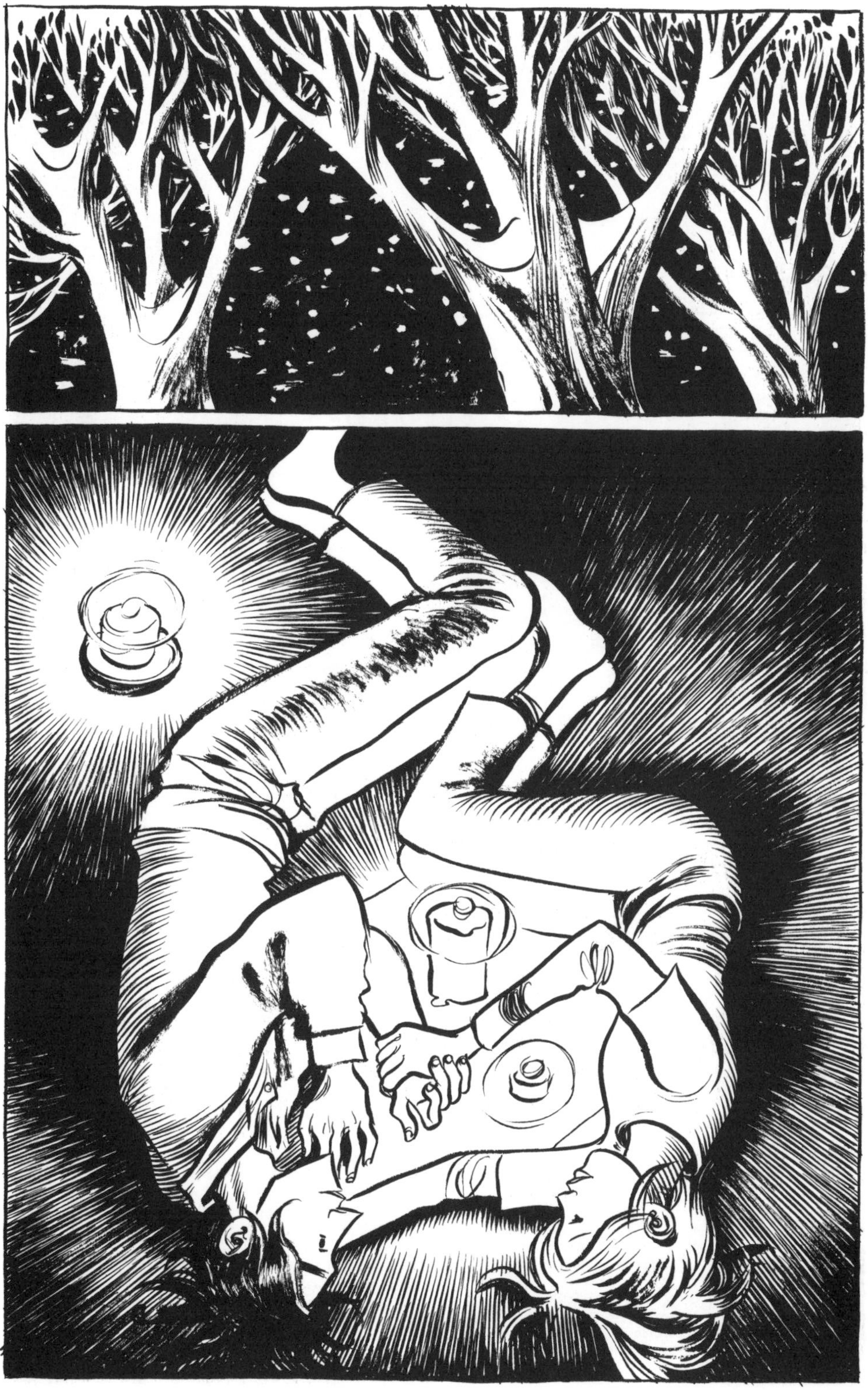

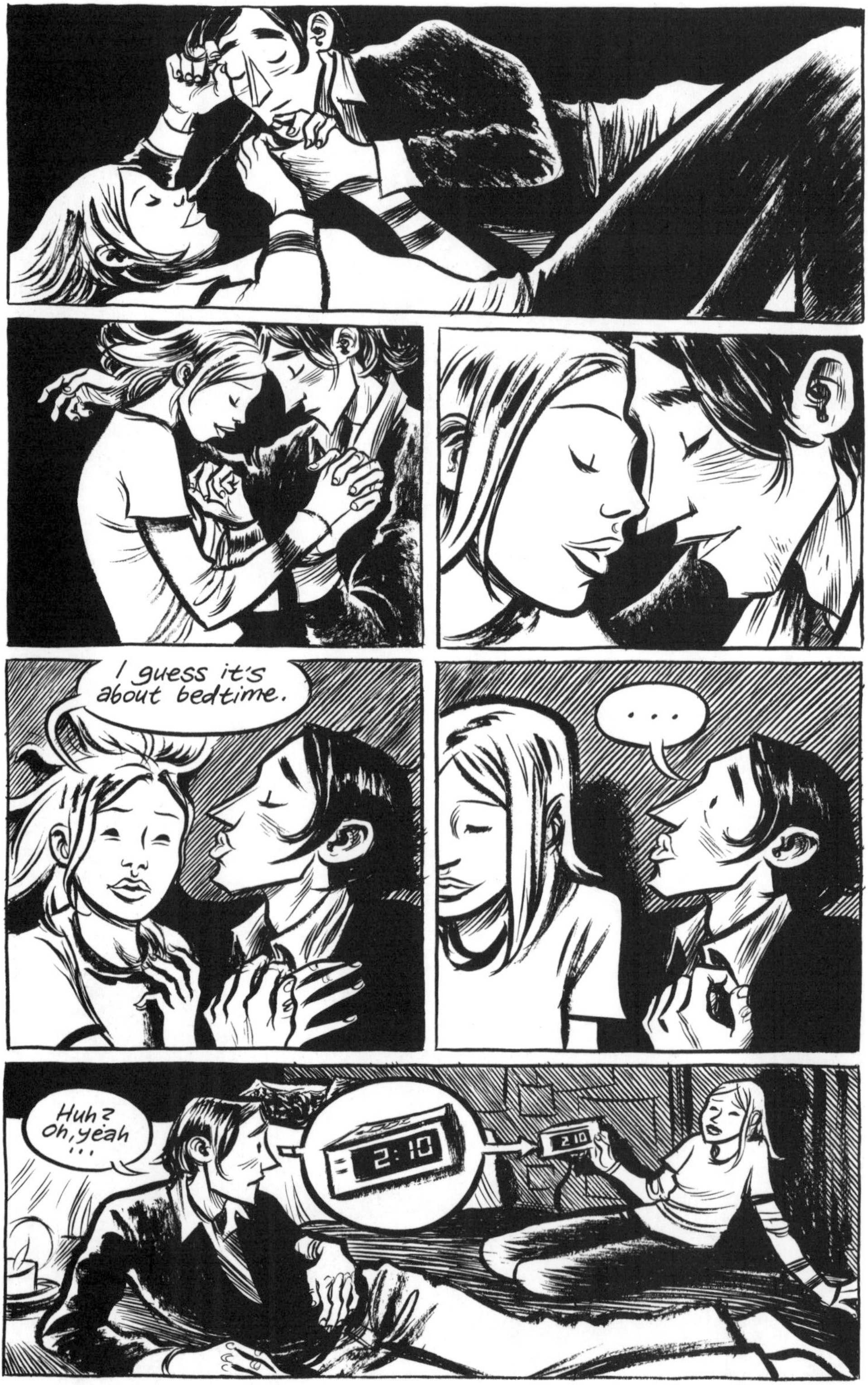
I guess it's about bedtime.
. . .
Huh? Oh, yeah . . .
2:10
2:10

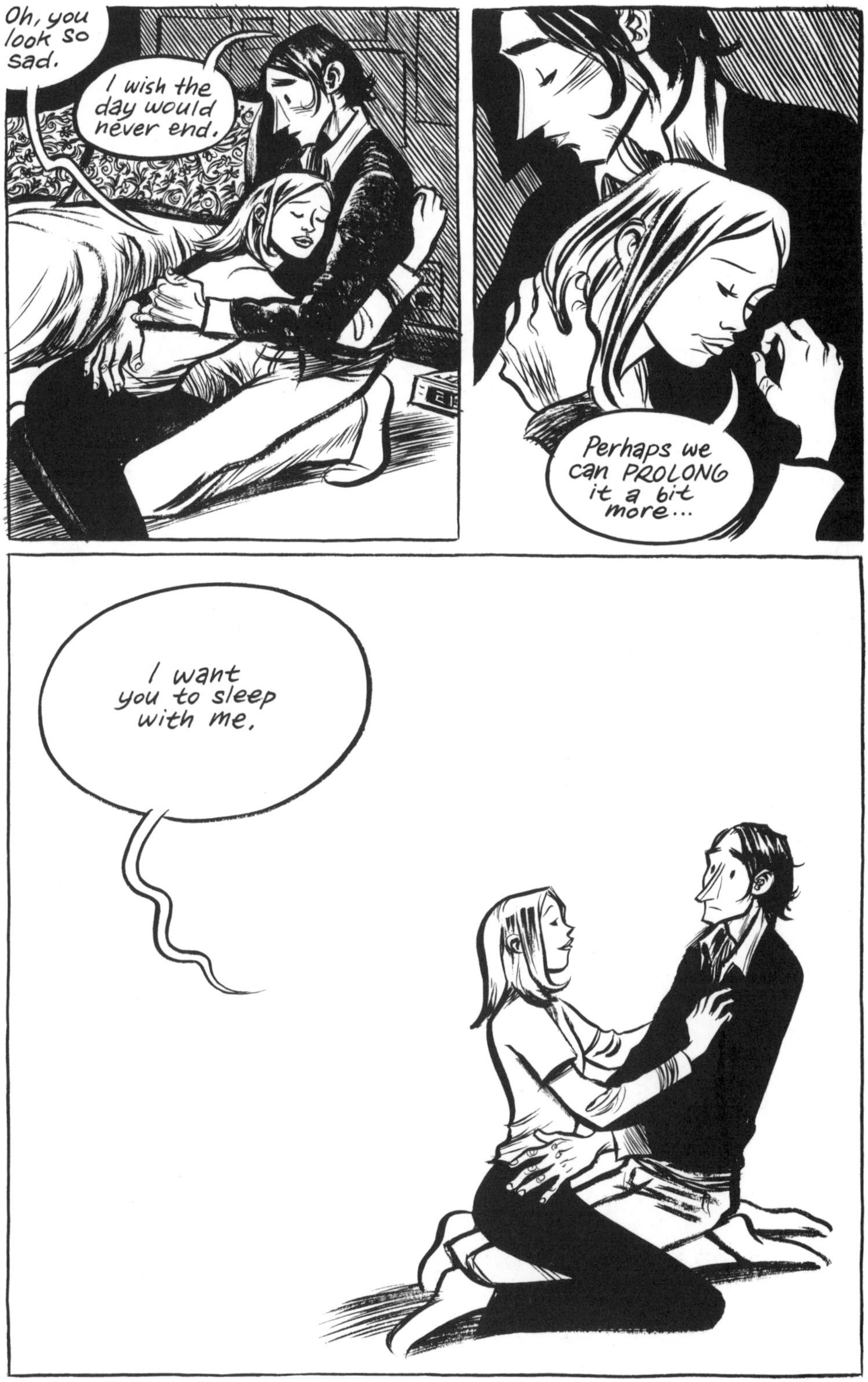
Oh, you look so sad.
I wish the day would never end.
Perhaps we can PROLONG it a bit more...
I want you to sleep with me.

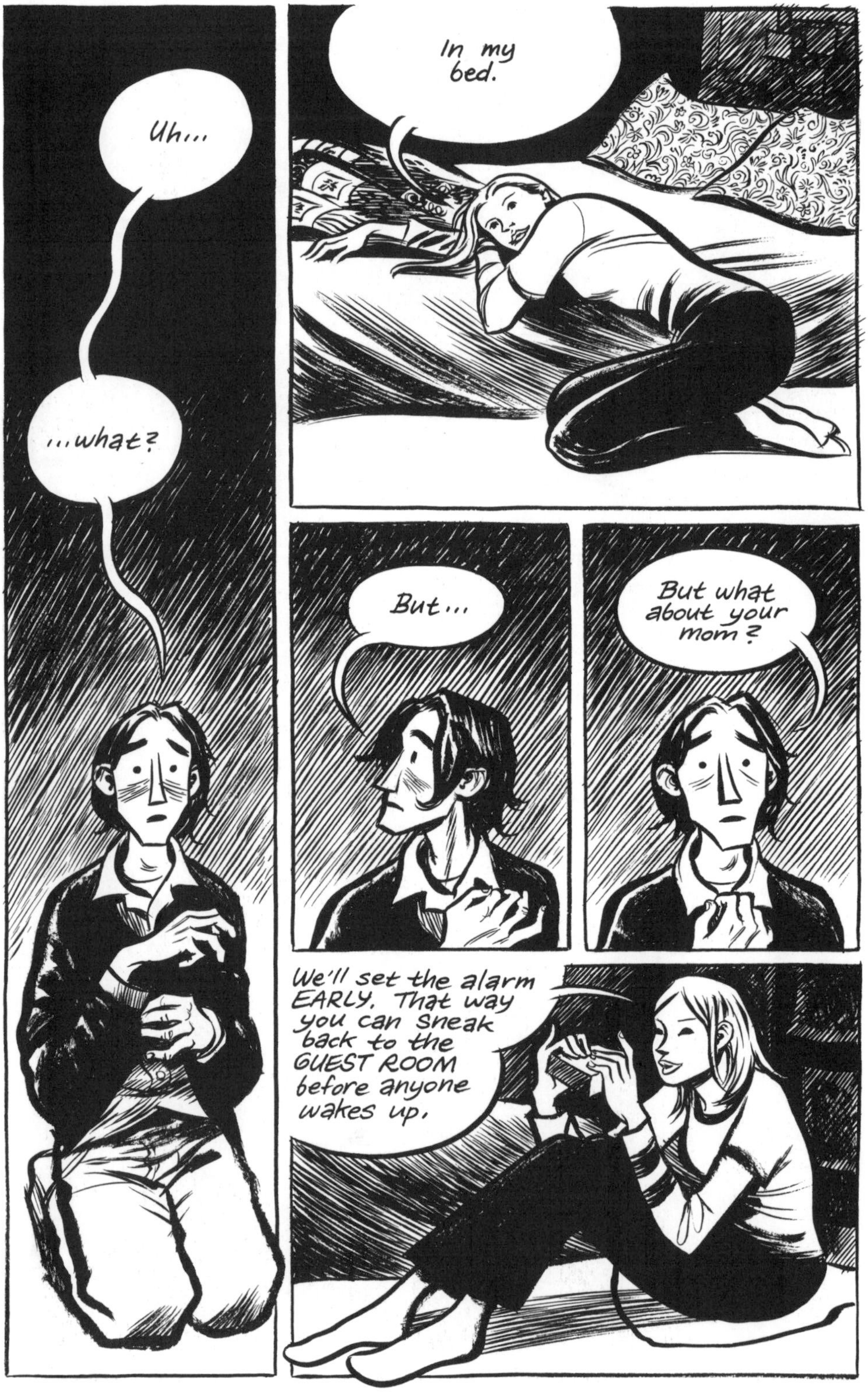
In my bed.
Uh...
...what?
But...
But what about your mom?
We'll set the alarm EARLY. That way you can sneak back to the GUEST ROOM before anyone wakes up.

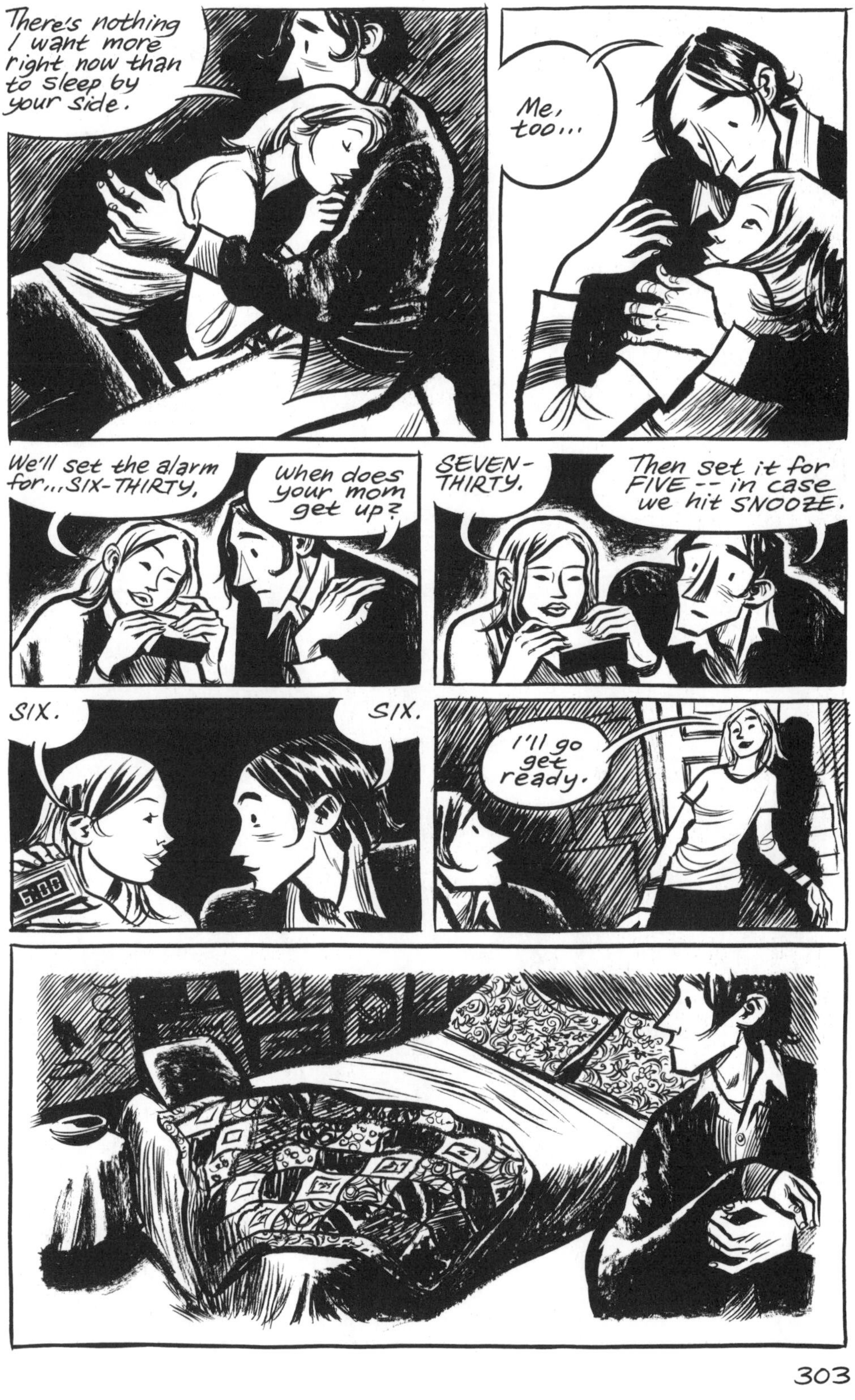
There's nothing I want more right now than to sleep by your side.
Me, too...
We'll set the alarm for... SIX-THIRTY.
When does your mom get up?
SEVEN-THIRTY.
Then set it for FIVE -- in case we hit SNOOZE.
SIX.
SIX.
I'll go get ready.

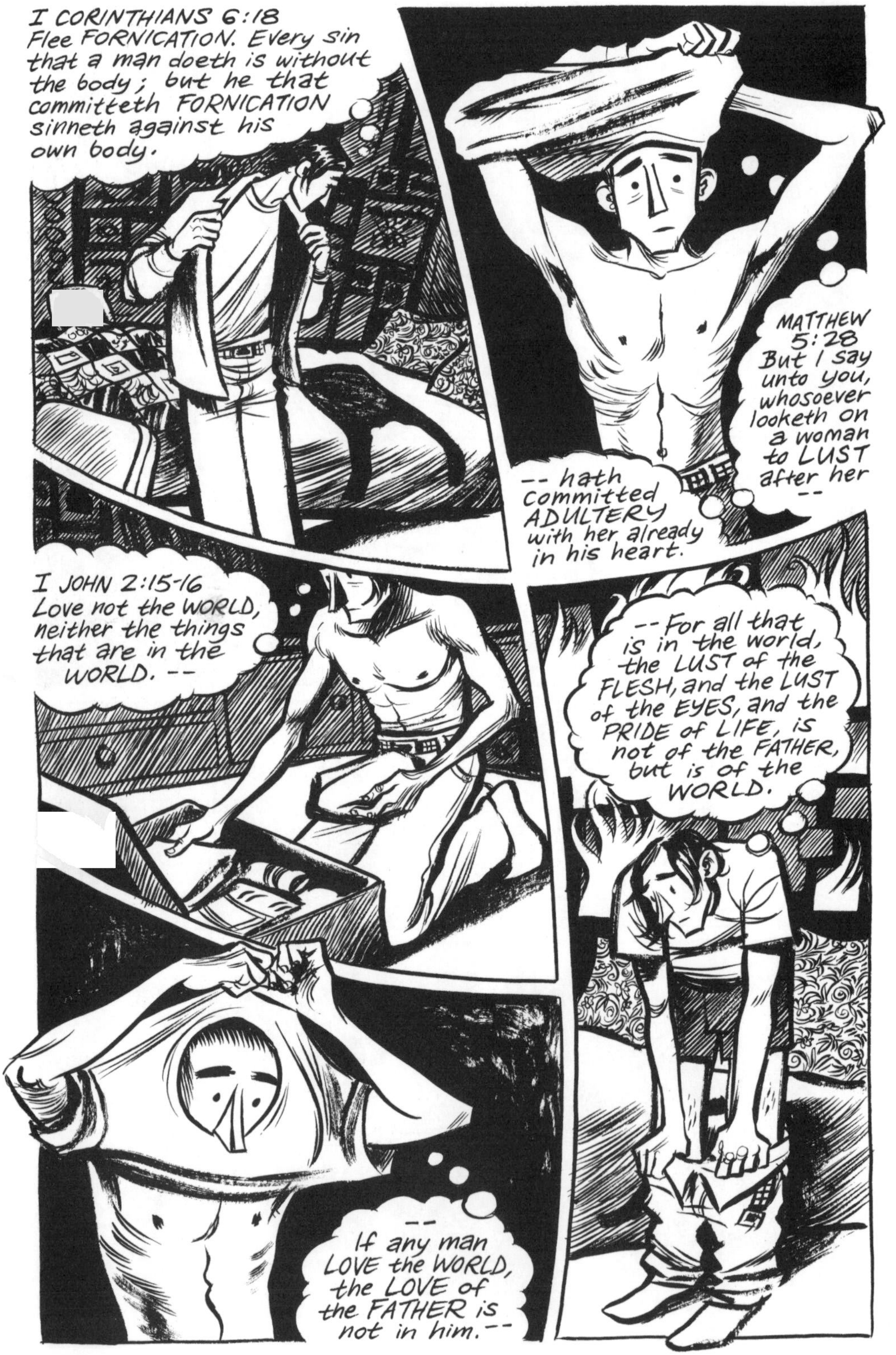
I CORINTHIANS 6:18 Flee FORNICATION. Every sin that a man doeth is without the body; but he that committeth FORNICATION sinneth against his own body.
MATTHEW 5:28 But I say unto you, whosoever looketh on a woman to LUST after her --
-- hath committed ADULTERY with her already in his heart.
I JOHN 2:15-16 Love not the WORLD, neither the things that are in the WORLD. --
-- For all that is in the world, the LUST of the FLESH, and the LUST of the EYES, and the PRIDE of LIFE, is not of the FATHER, but is of the WORLD.
-- If any man LOVE the WORLD, the LOVE of the FATHER is not in him. --

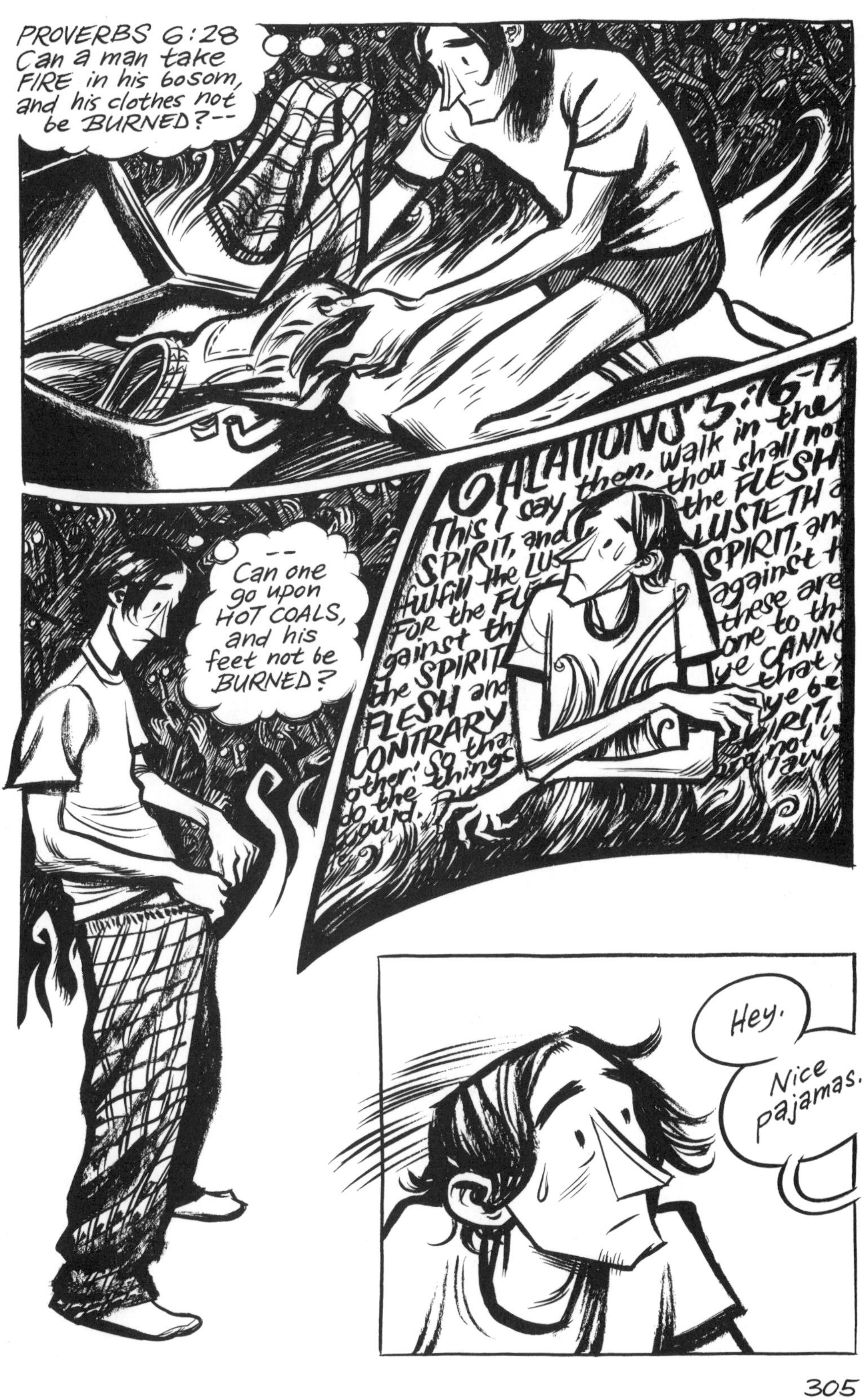

PROVERBS 6:28 Can a man take FIRE in his bosom, and his clothes not be BURNED?--
-- Can one go upon HOT COALS, and his feet not be BURNED?
GALATIONS 5:16-17
This I say then, walk in the
SPIRIT, and thou shall not
fulfill the LUS the FLESH
FOR the FL LUSTETH a
gainst th SPIRIT, and
the SPIRIT against t
FLESH and these are
CONTRARY one to th
other: So that ye CANNO
do the things that
would. ye be
SPIRIT,
not
law
Hey.
Nice pajamas.

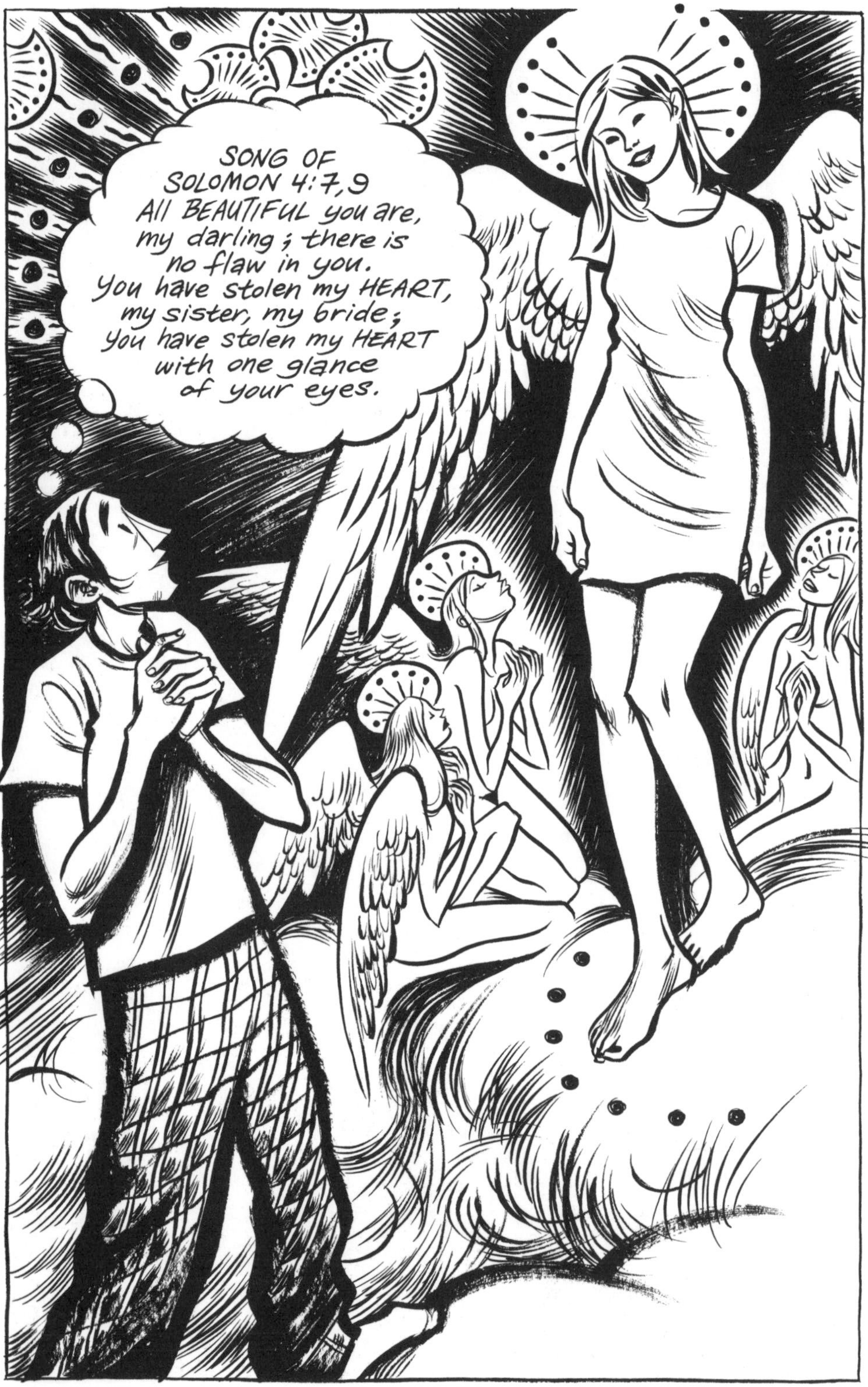
SONG OF SOLOMON 4:7,9 All BEAUTIFUL you are, my darling; there is no flaw in you. You have stolen my HEART, my sister, my bride; You have stolen my HEART with one glance of your eyes.

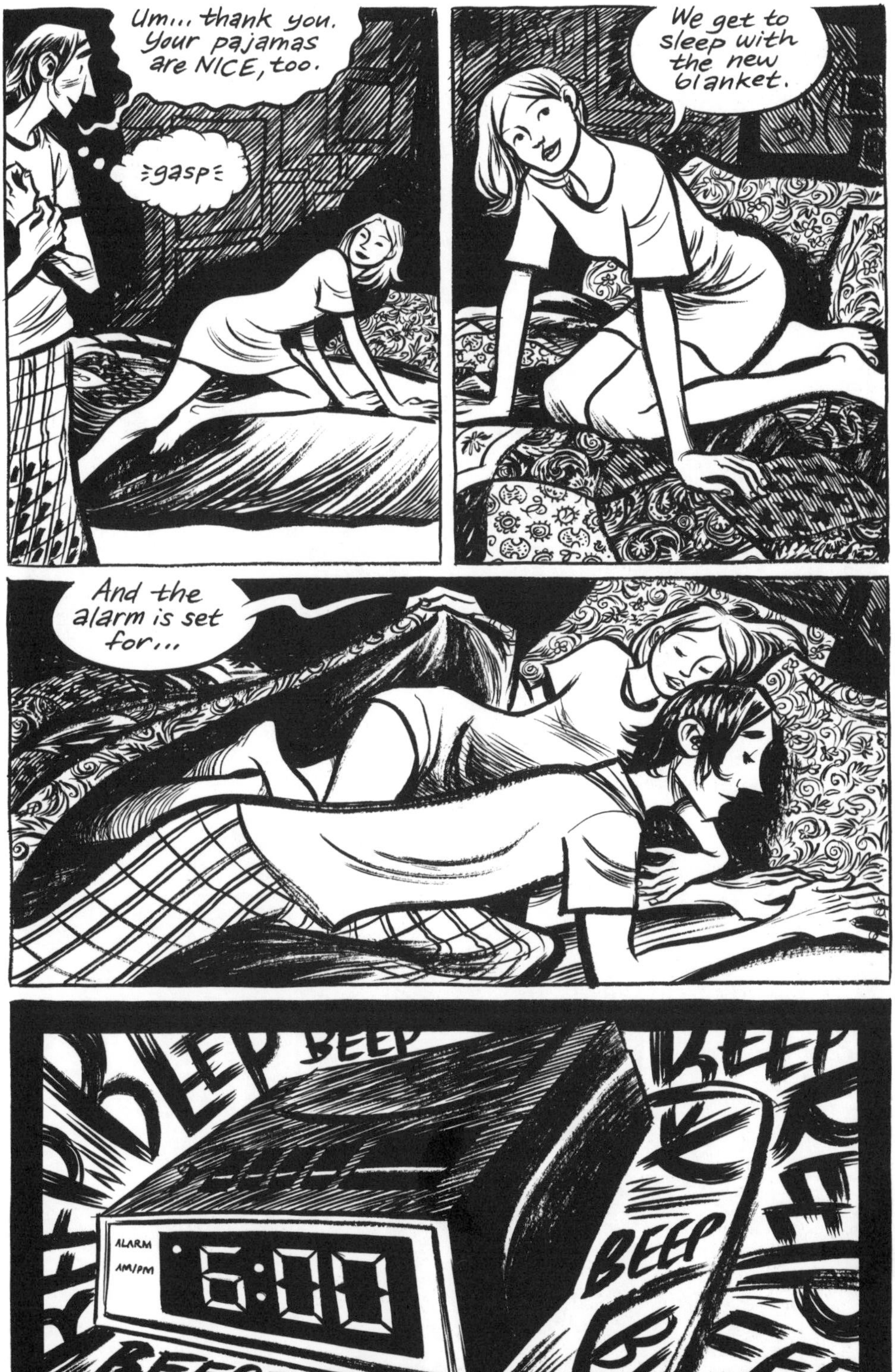
Um... thank you. Your pajamas are NICE, too.
gasp
We get to sleep with the new blanket.
And the alarm is set for...
BEEP BEEP
BEEP
BEEP
BEEP
ALARM
AM/PM
6:00

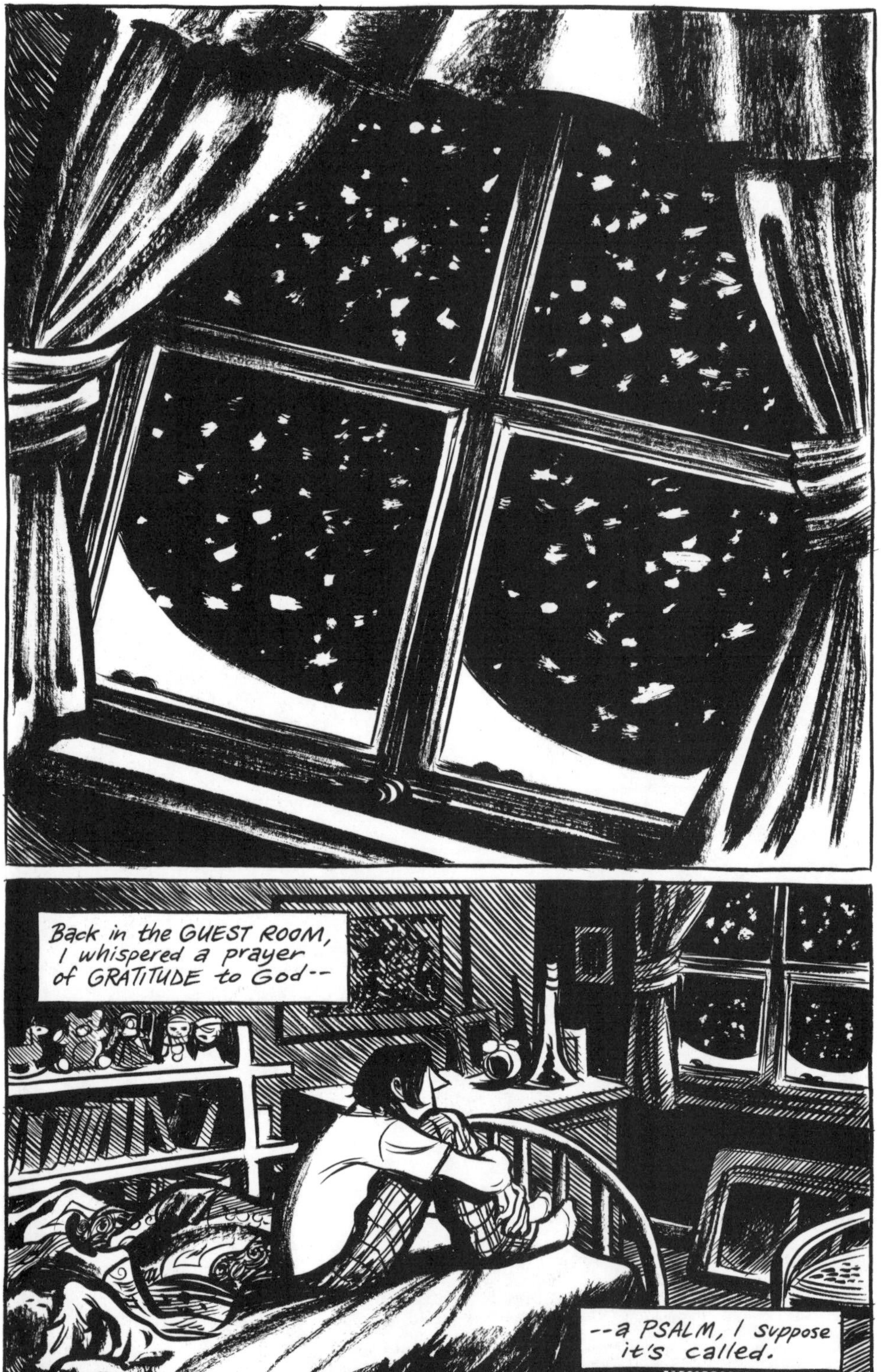
Back in the GUEST ROOM, I whispered a prayer of GRATITUDE to God--
--a PSALM, I suppose it's called.

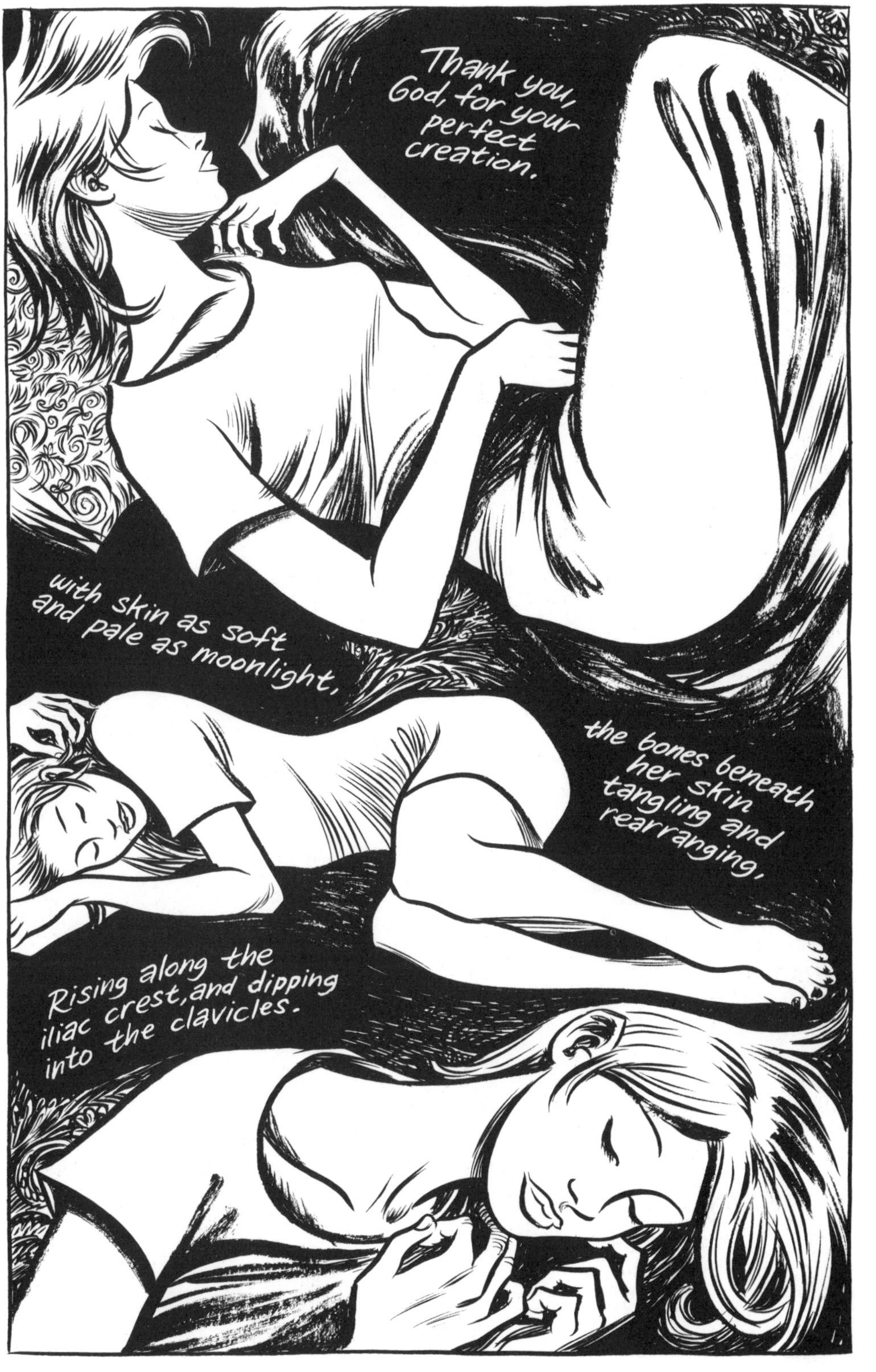
Thank you, God, for your perfect creation.
with skin as soft and pale as moonlight,
the bones beneath her skin tangling and rearranging.
Rising along the iliac crest, and dipping into the clavicles.

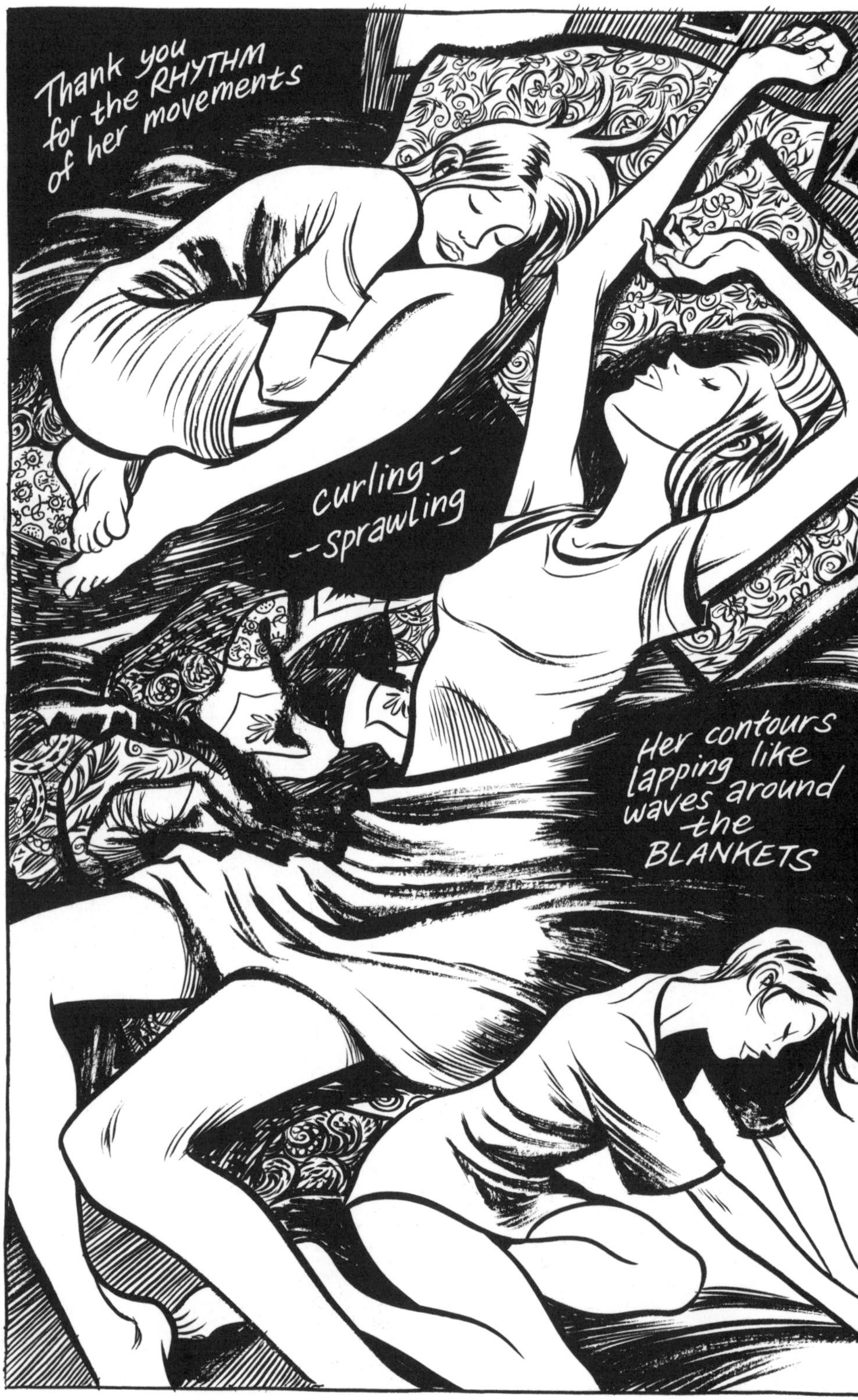
Thank you for the RHYTHM of her movements
curling-- --sprawling
Her contours lapping like waves around the BLANKETS

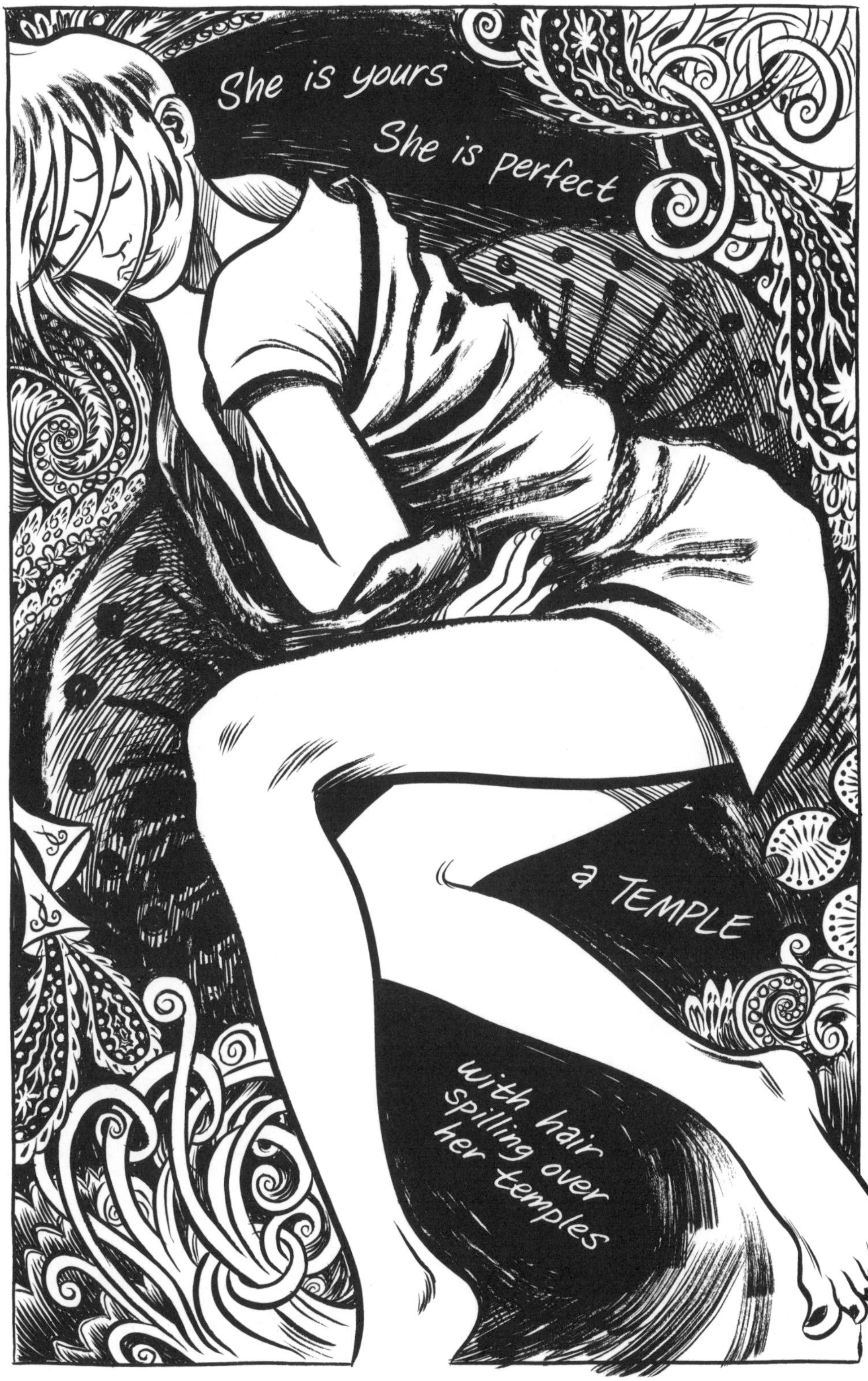
She is yours
She is perfect
a TEMPLE
with hair spilling over her temples

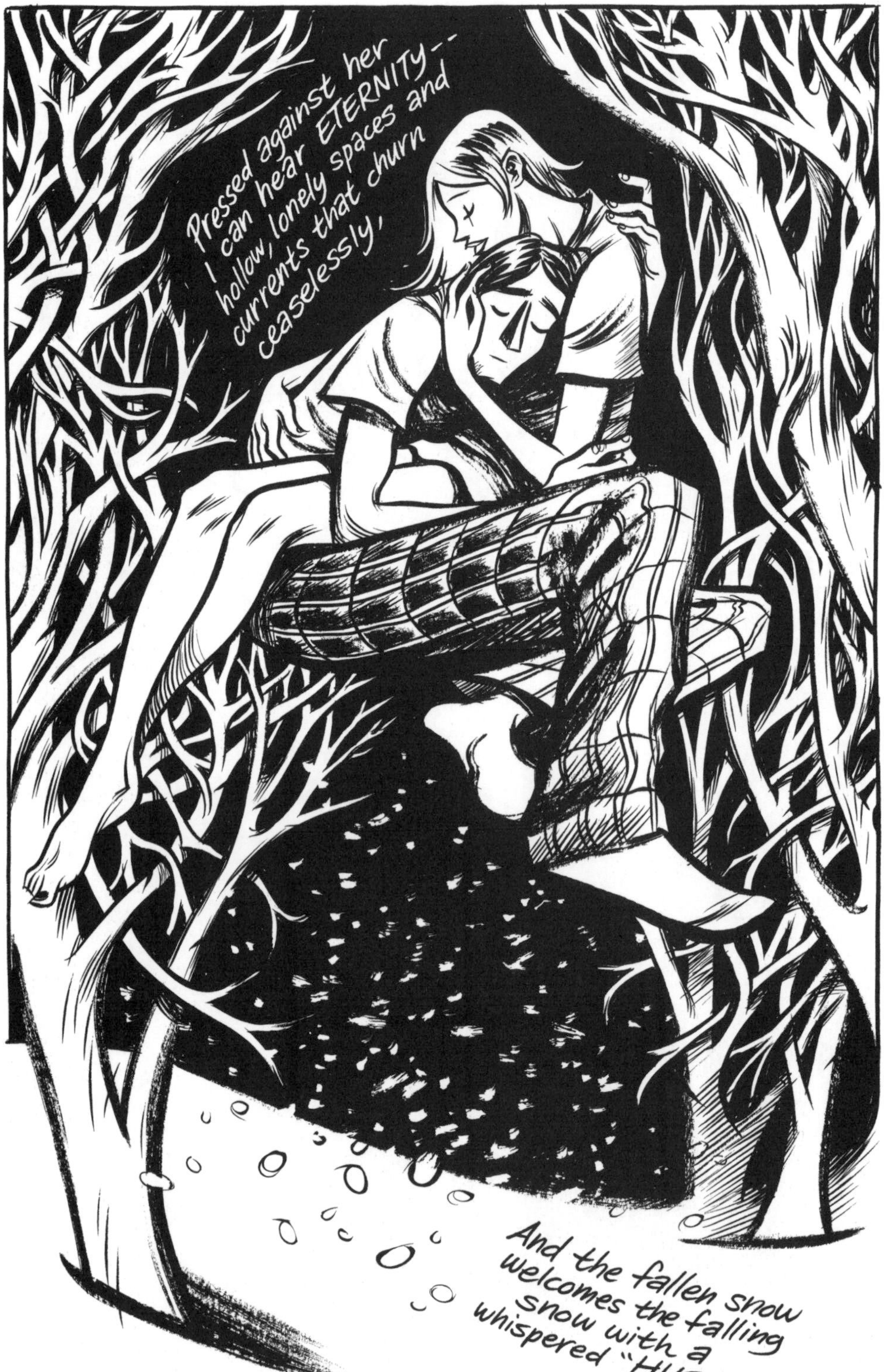
Pressed against her I can hear ETERNITY-- hollow, lonely spaces and currents that churn ceaselessly,
And the fallen snow welcomes the falling snow with a whispered "HUSH."

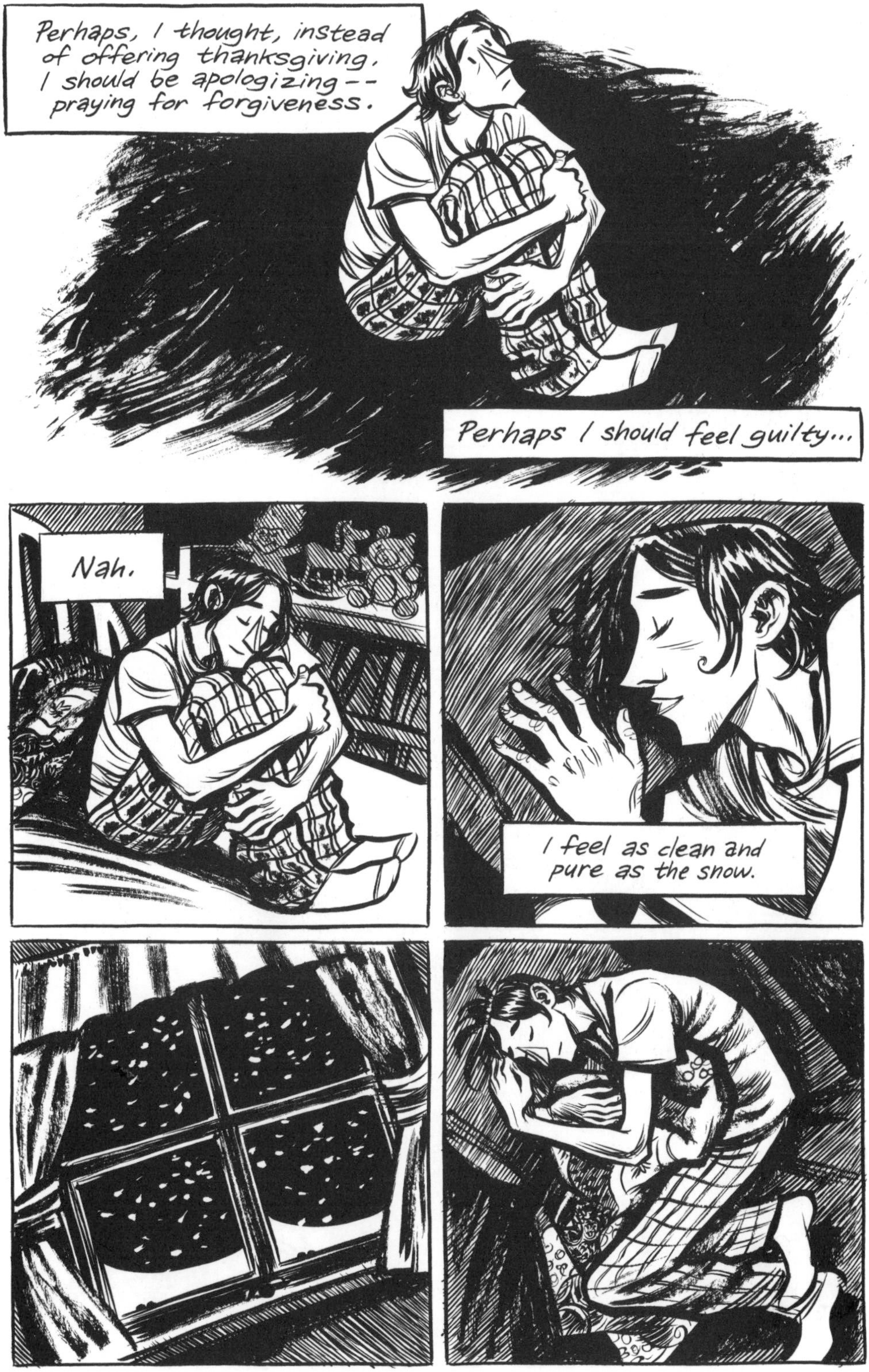
Perhaps, I thought, instead of offering thanksgiving, I should be apologizing-- praying for forgiveness.
Perhaps I should feel guilty...
Nah.
I feel as clean and pure as the snow.

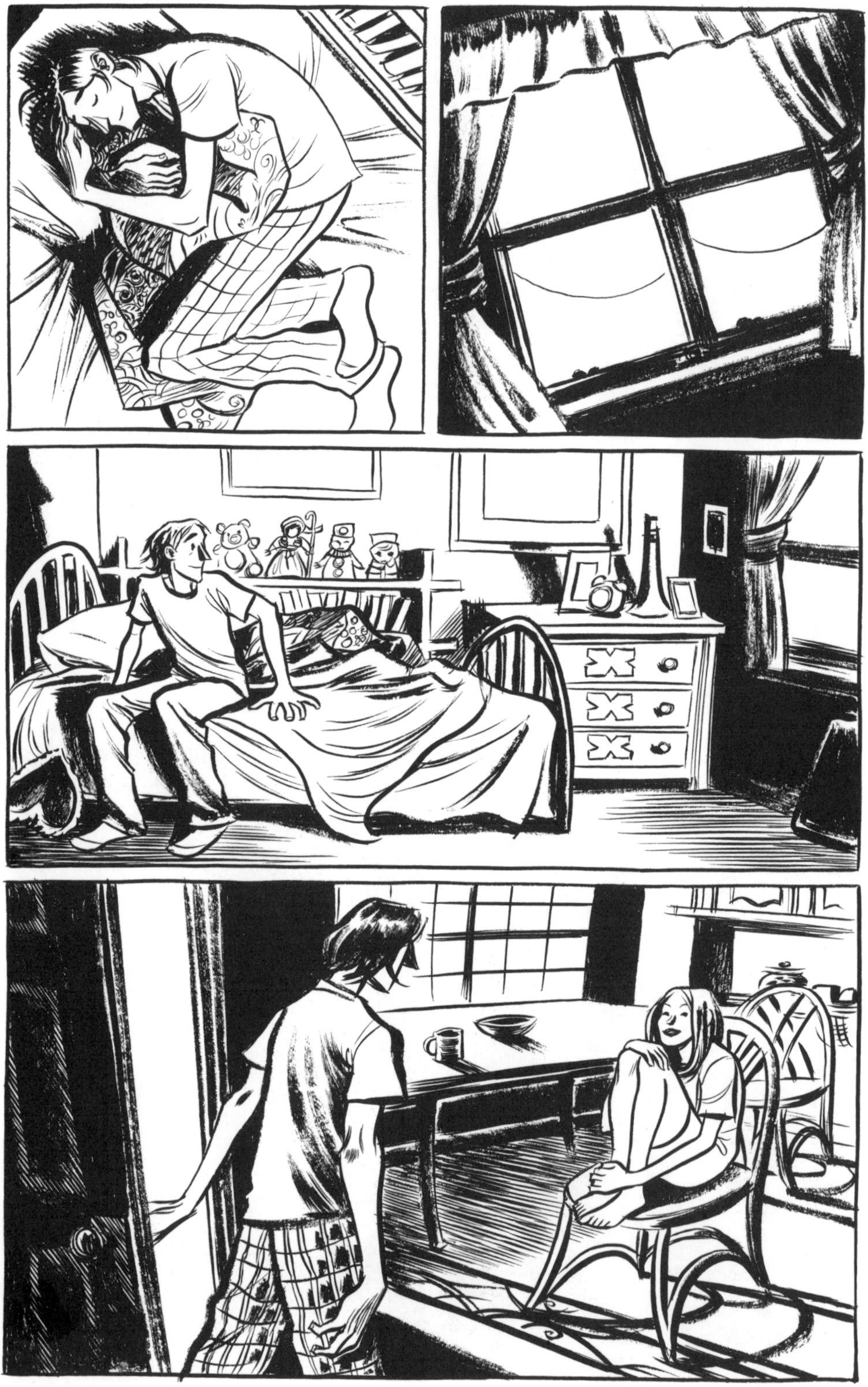

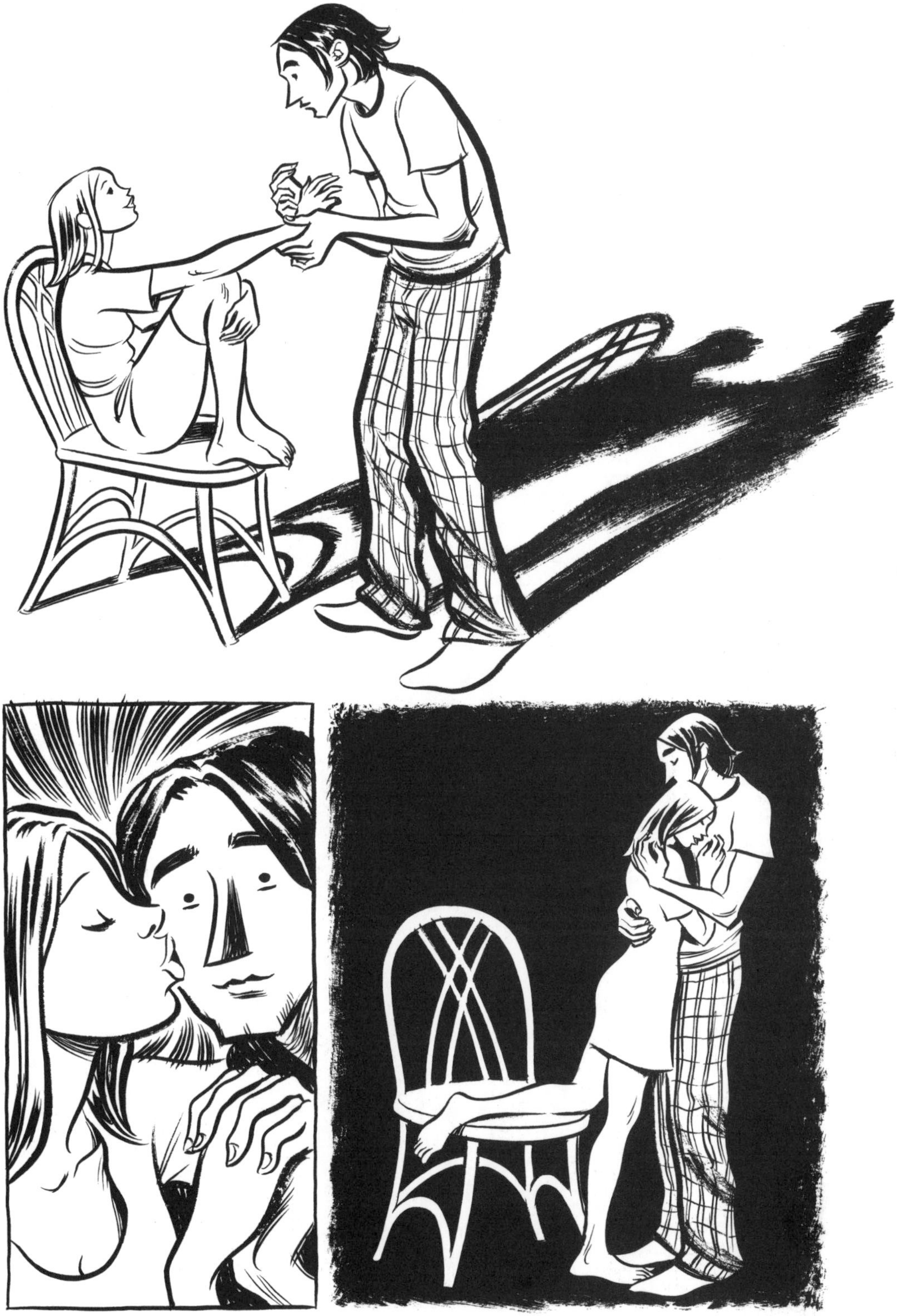

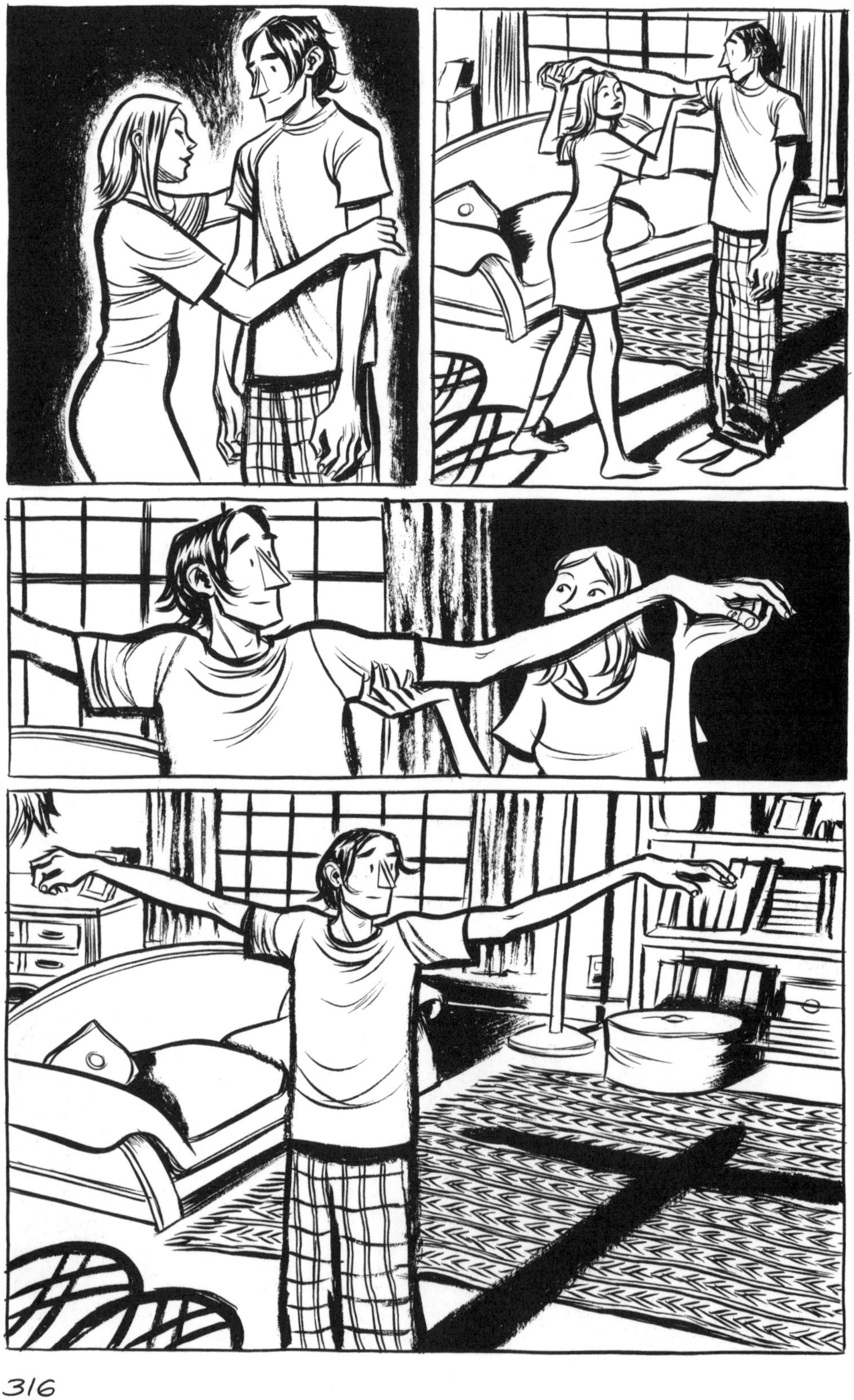

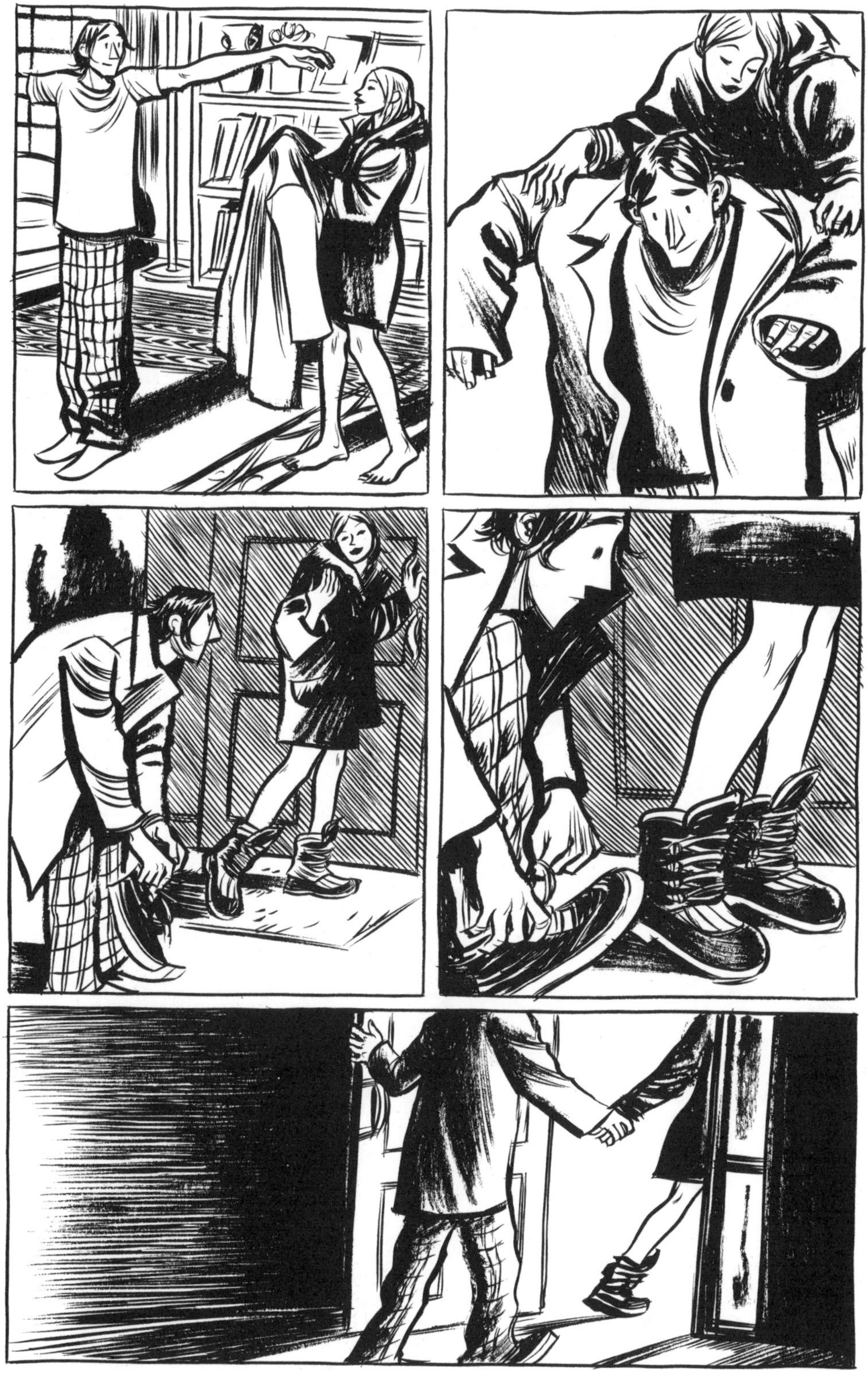

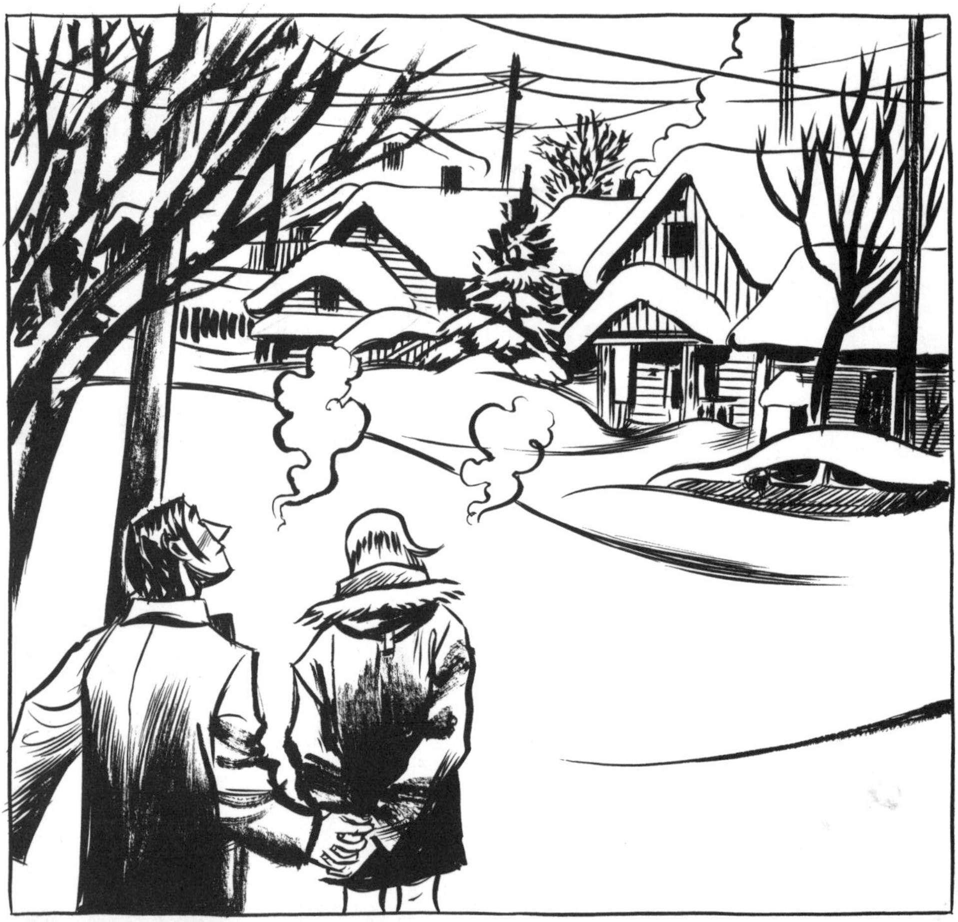

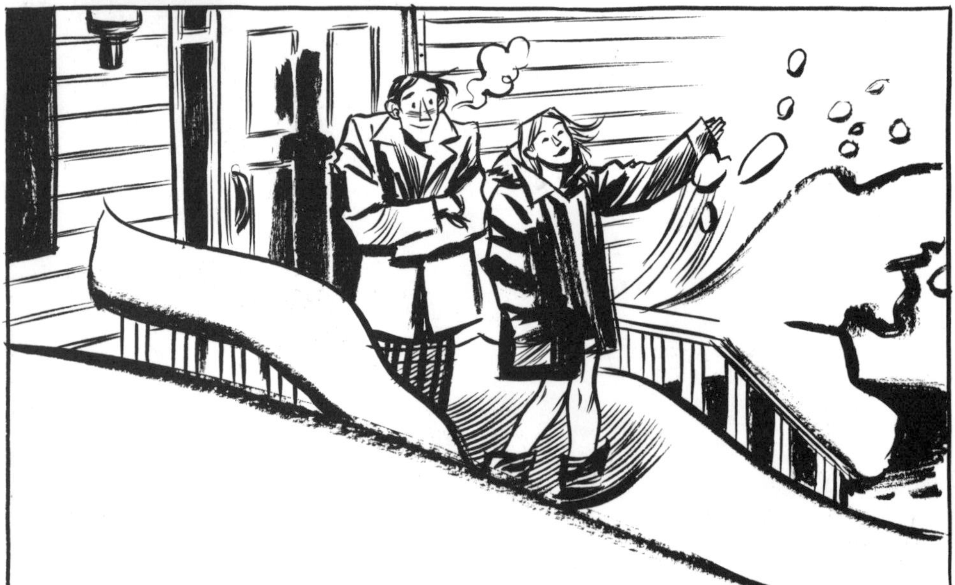

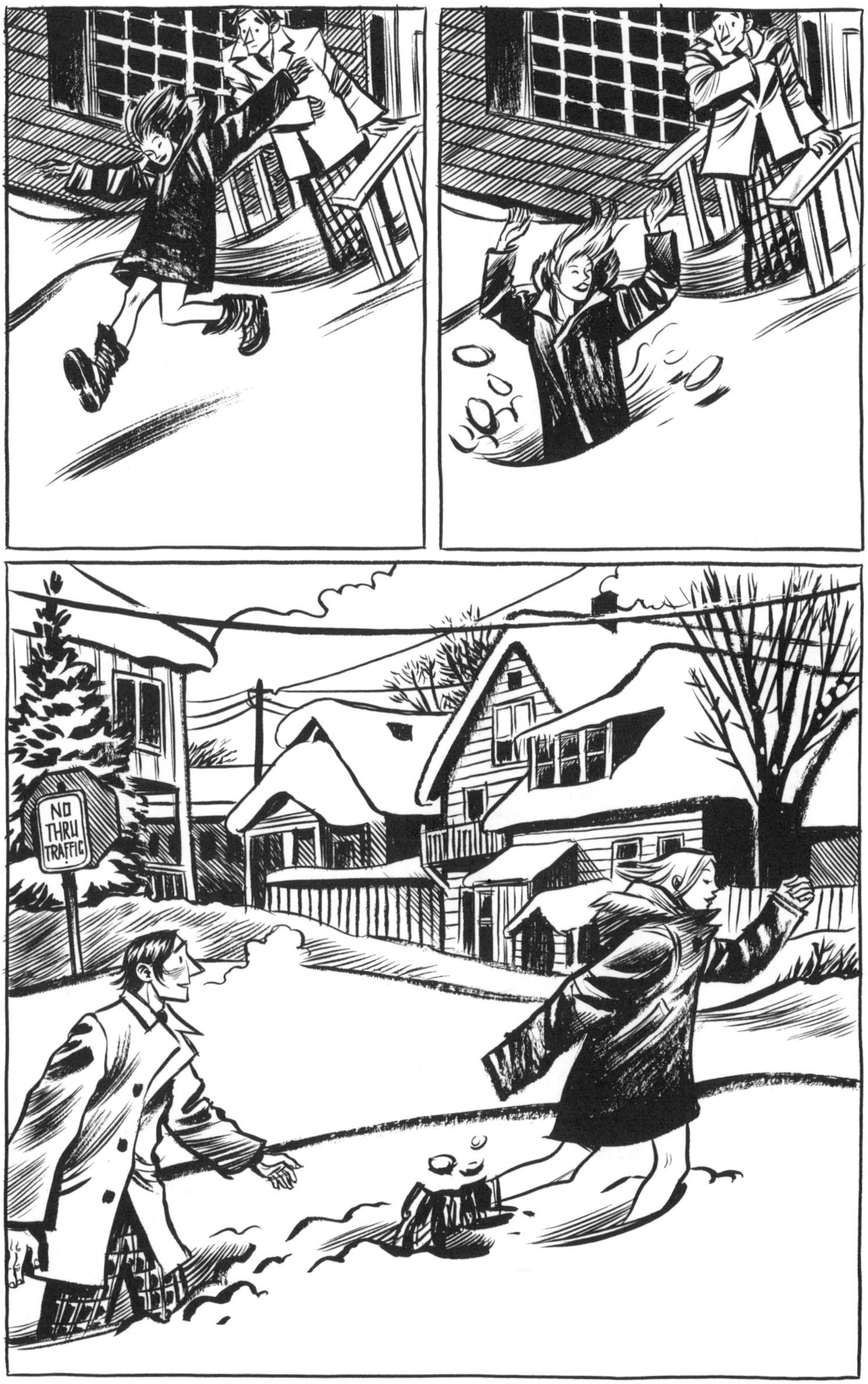
NO THRU TRAFFIC

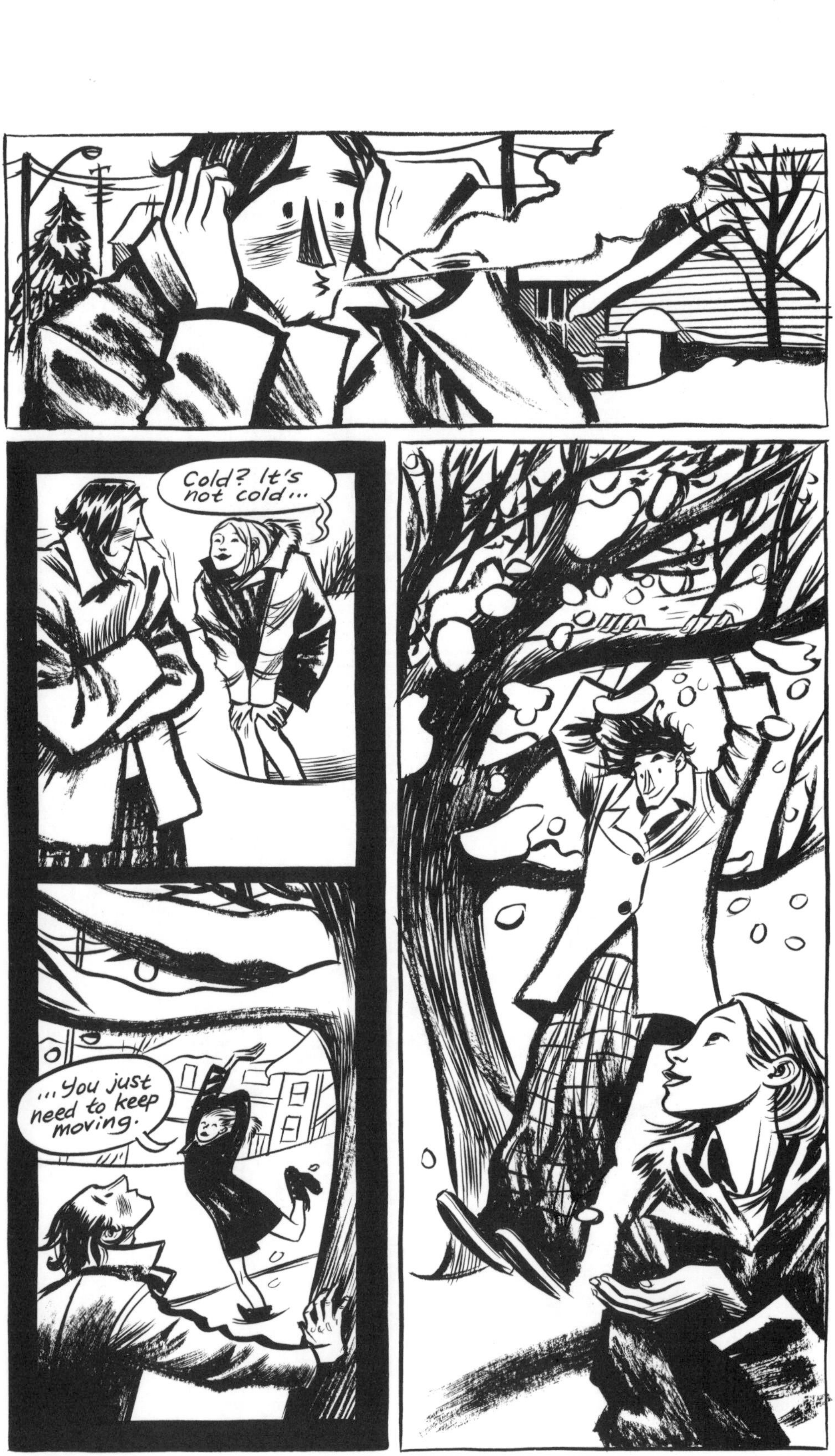
Cold? It's not cold...
...You just need to keep moving.

VI

Teen Spirit

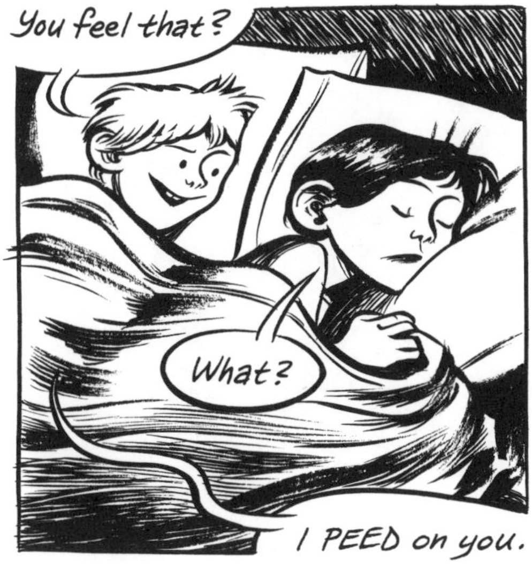
You feel that?
What?
I PEED on you.

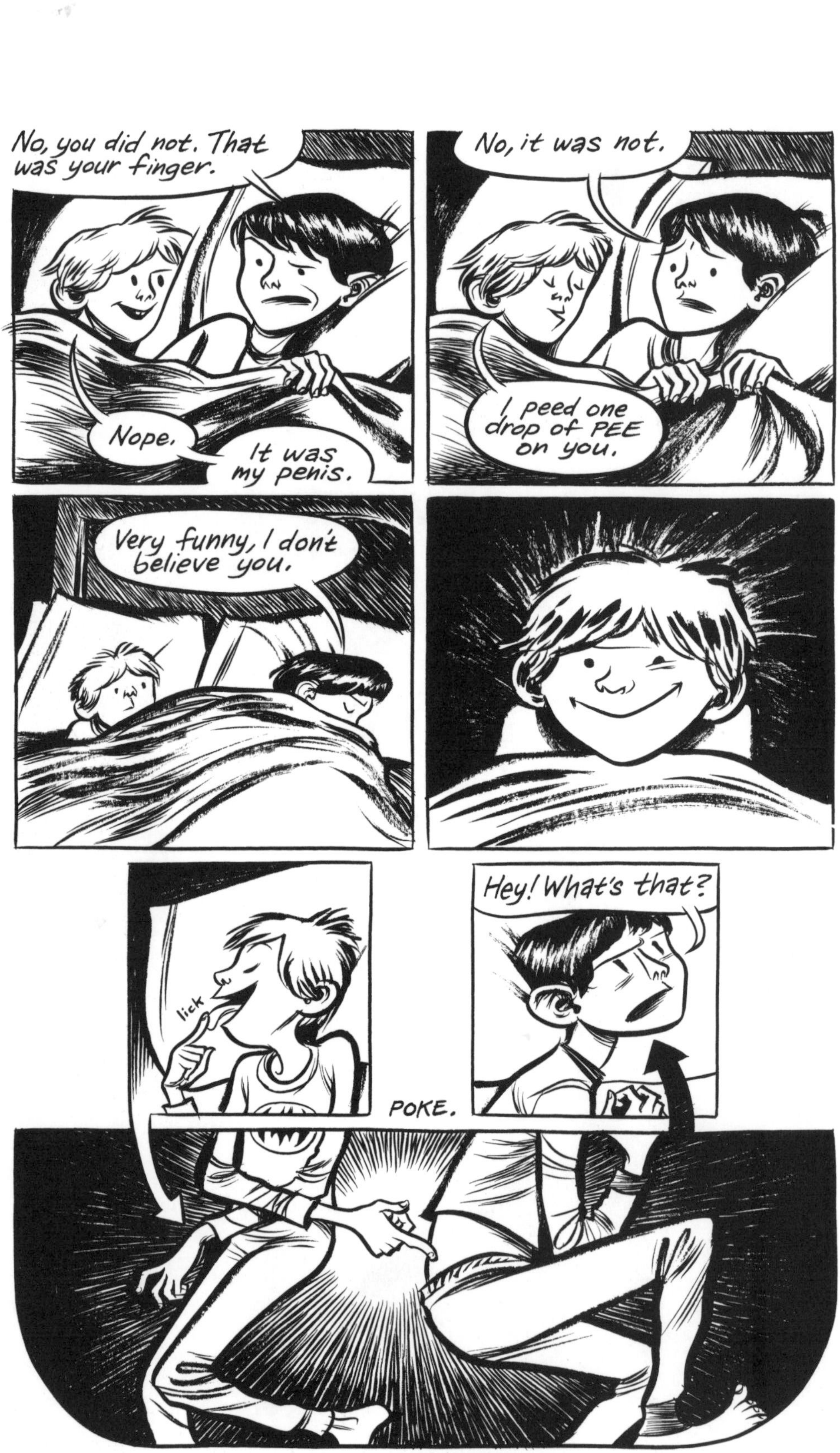
No, you did not. That was your finger.
Nope.
It was my penis.
No, it was not.
I peed one drop of PEE on you.
Very funny, I don't believe you.
lick
Hey! What's that?
POKE.

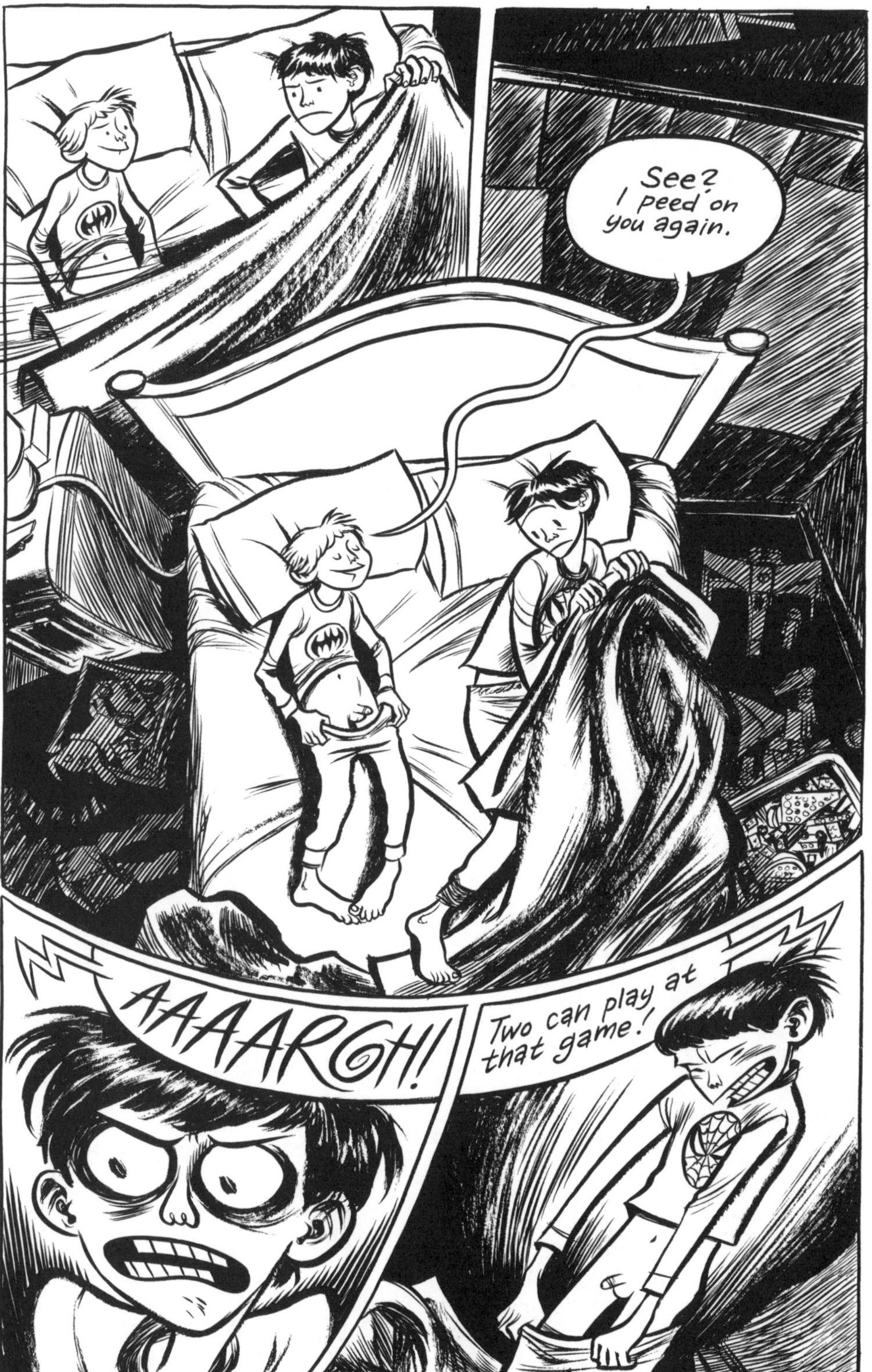
See? I peed on you again.
AAAARGH!
Two can play at that game!

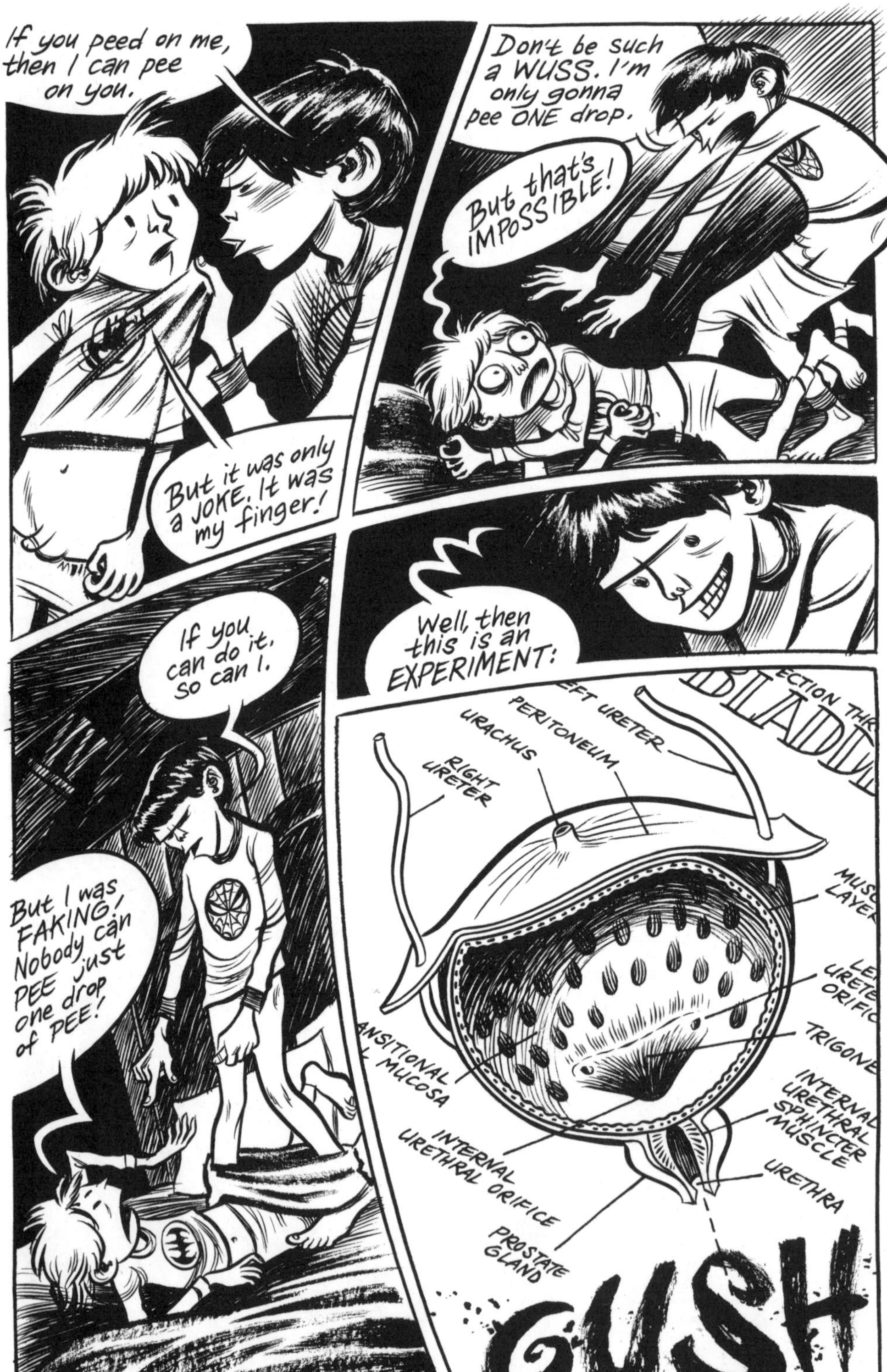
If you peed on me, then I can pee on you.
But it was only a JOKE. It was my finger!
Don't be such a WUSS. I'm only gonna pee ONE drop.
But that's IMPOSSIBLE!
Well, then this is an EXPERIMENT:
If you can do it, so can I.
But I was FAKING! Nobody can PEE just one drop of PEE!
PERITONEUM
URACHUS
RIGHT URETER
TRIGONE
INTERNAL URETHRAL SPHINCTER MUSCLE
URETHRA
INTERNAL URETHRAL ORIFICE
PROSTATE GLAND
GUSH

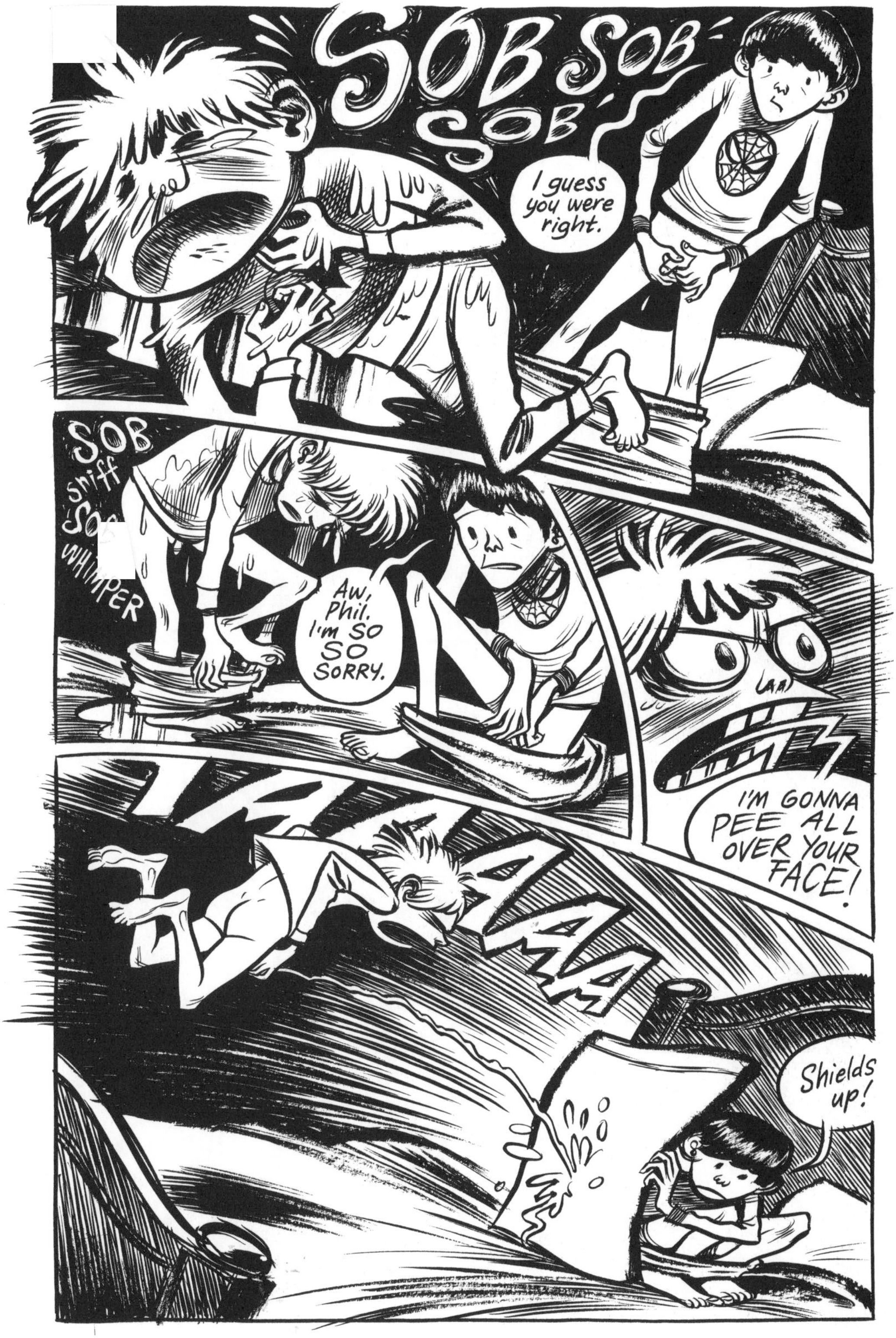
SOB SOB
SOB
I guess you were right.
SOB
sniff
Aw, Phil. I'm SO SO SORRY.
I'M GONNA PEE ALL OVER YOUR FACE!
Shields up!

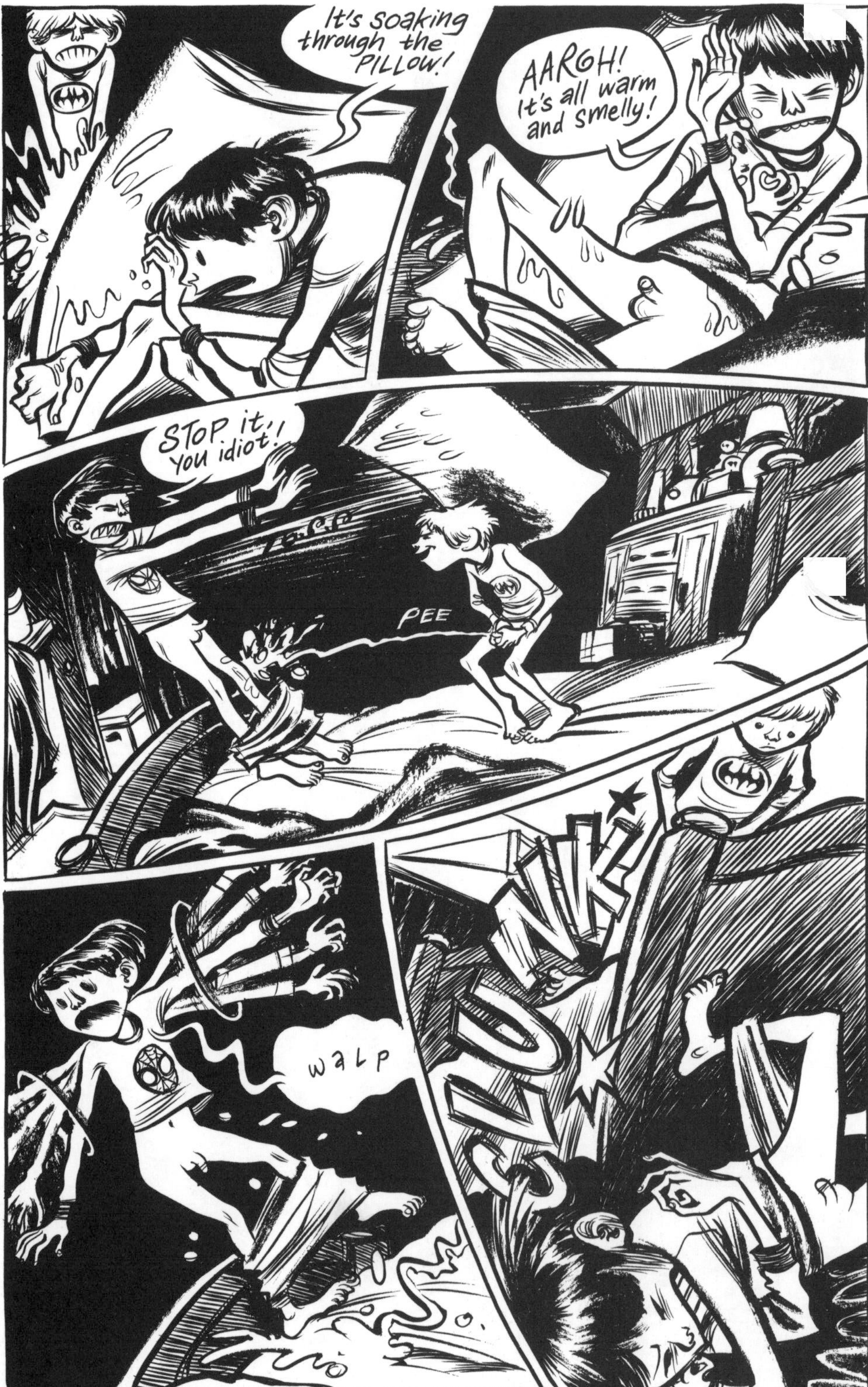
It's soaking through the PILLOW!
AARGH! It's all warm and smelly!
STOP it, you idiot!
PEE
walp
CLUNK!

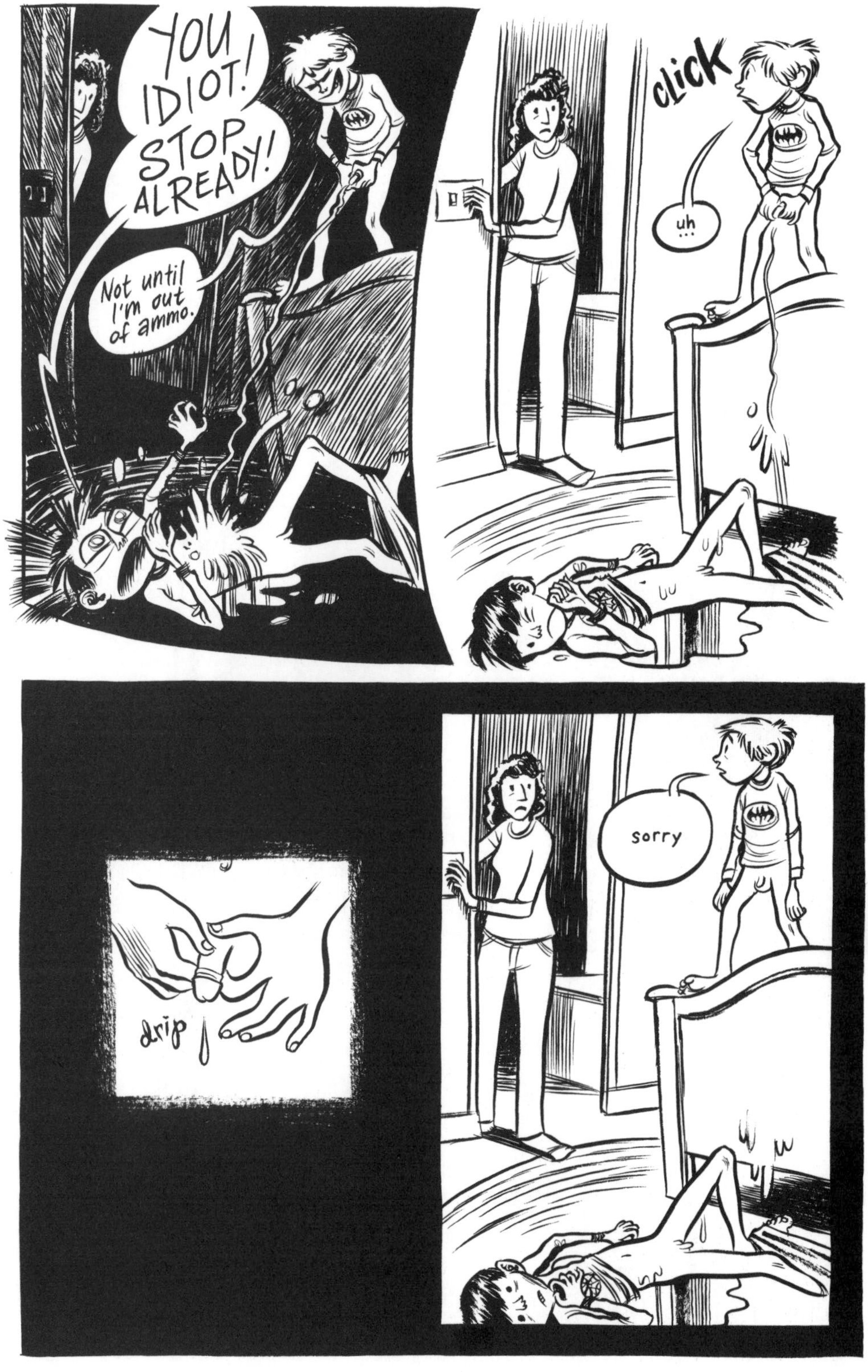
YOU IDIOT! STOP ALREADY!
Not until I'm out of ammo.
click
uh ...
drip
sorry

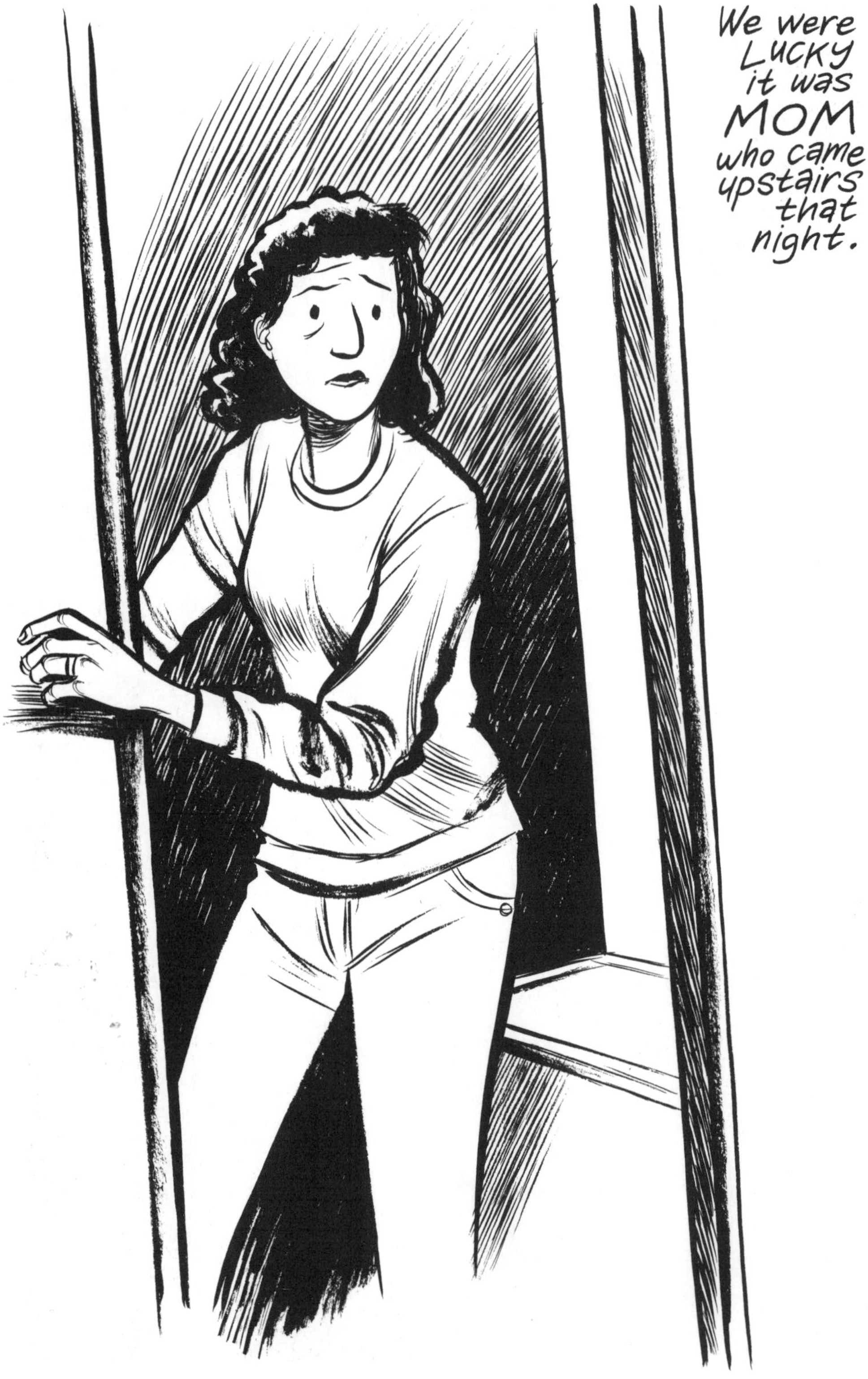
We were LUCKY it was MOM who came upstairs that night.

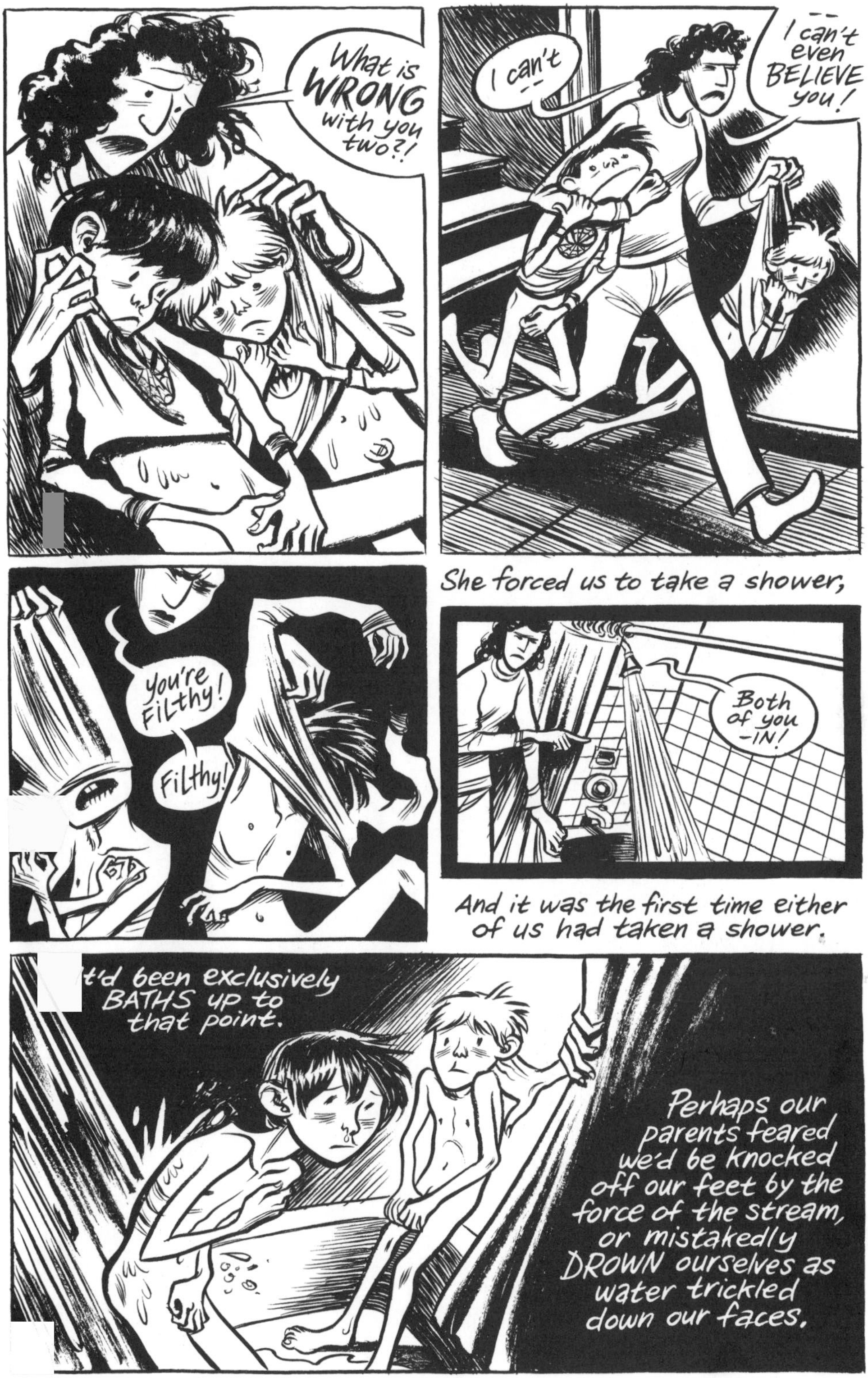
What is WRONG with you two?!
I can't --
-- I can't even BELIEVE you!
You're FiLthy!
FiLthy!
She forced us to take a shower,
Both of you -IN!
And it was the first time either of us had taken a shower.
t'd been exclusively BATHS up to that point.
Perhaps our parents feared we'd be knocked off our feet by the force of the stream, or mistakedly DROWN ourselves as water trickled down our faces.

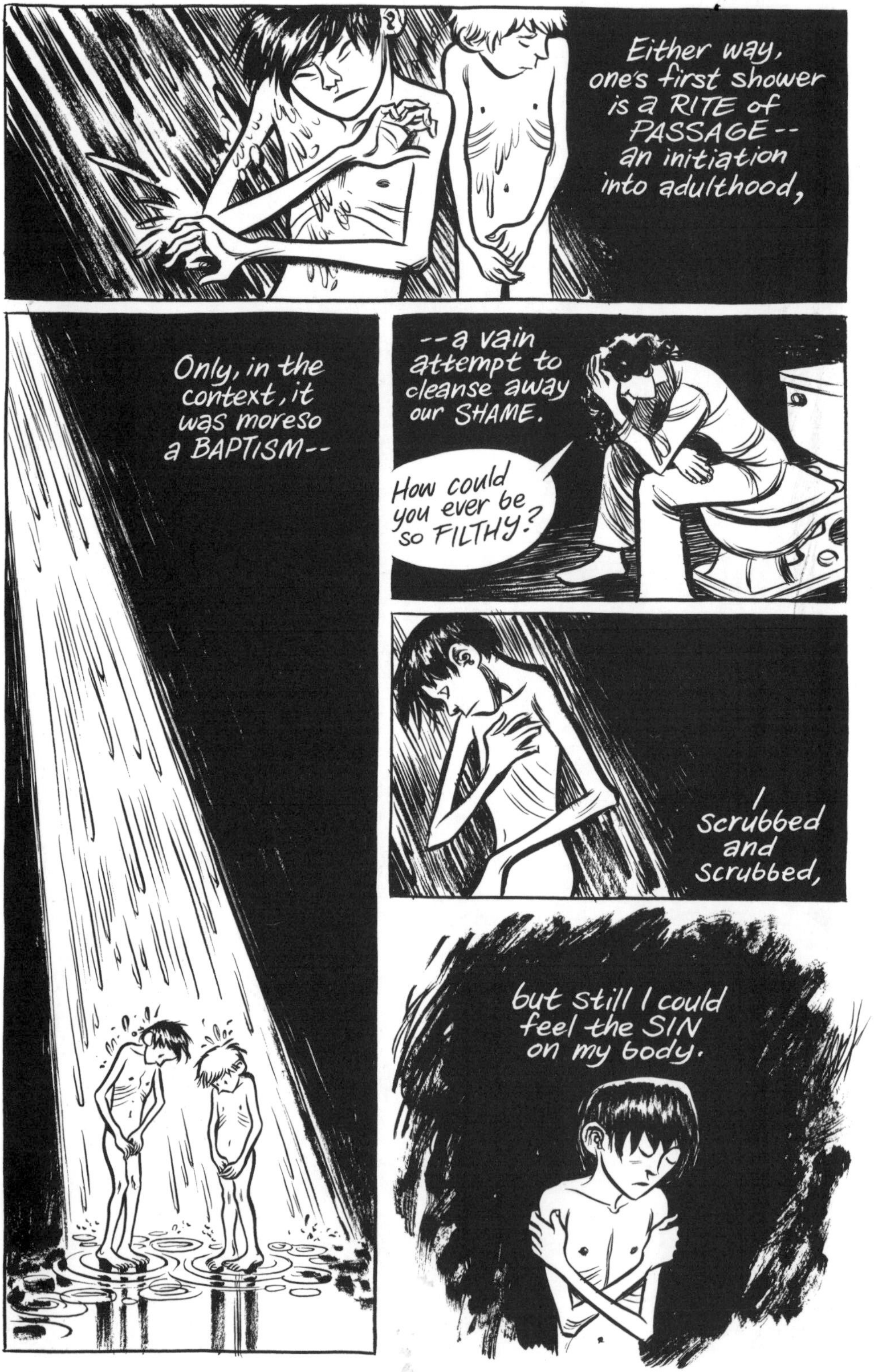
Either way, one's first shower is a RITE of PASSAGE-- an initiation into adulthood,
Only, in the context, it was moreso a BAPTISM--
--a vain attempt to cleanse away our SHAME.
How could you ever be so FILTHY?
I scrubbed and scrubbed,
but still I could feel the SIN on my body.

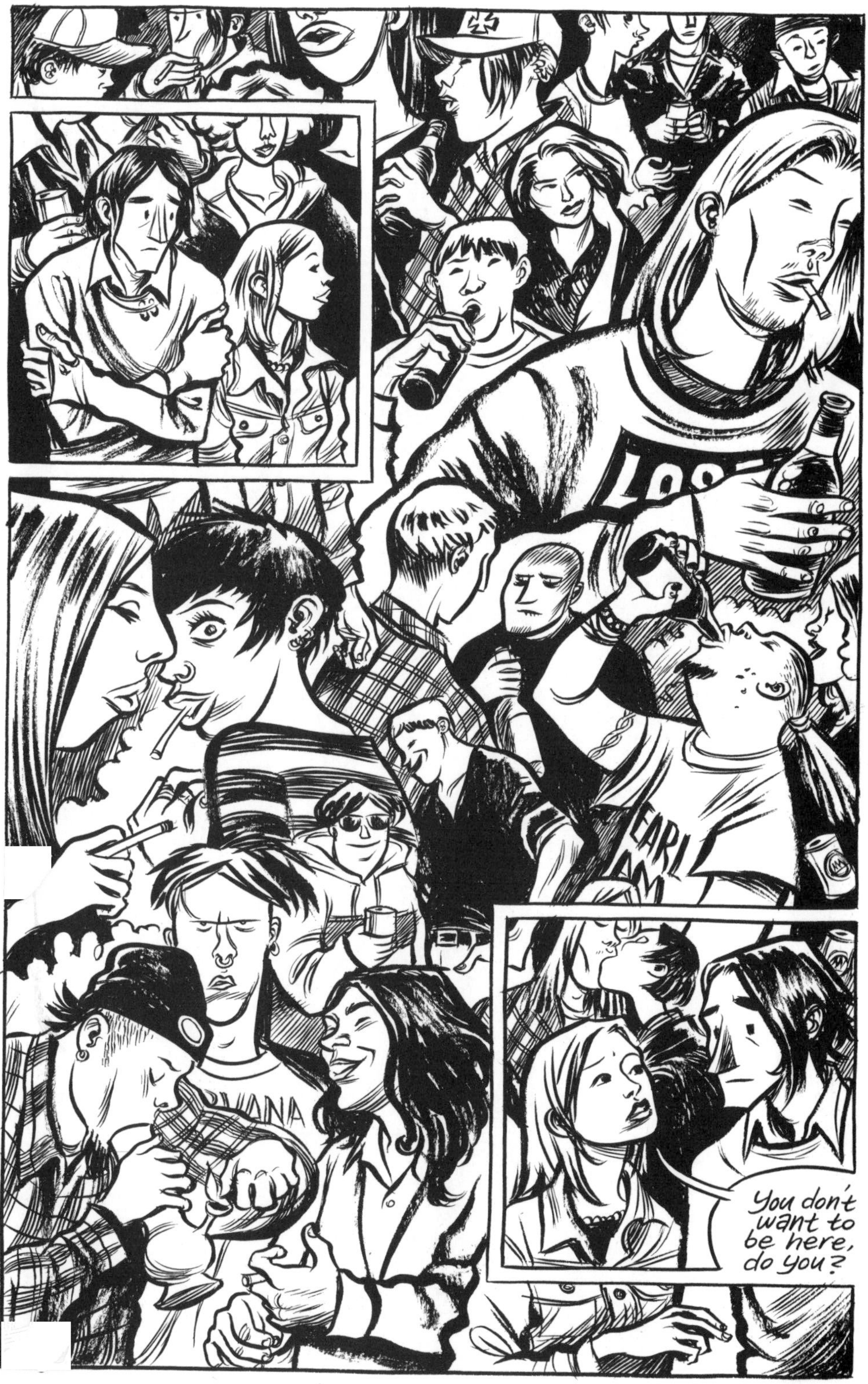
You don't want to be here, do you?

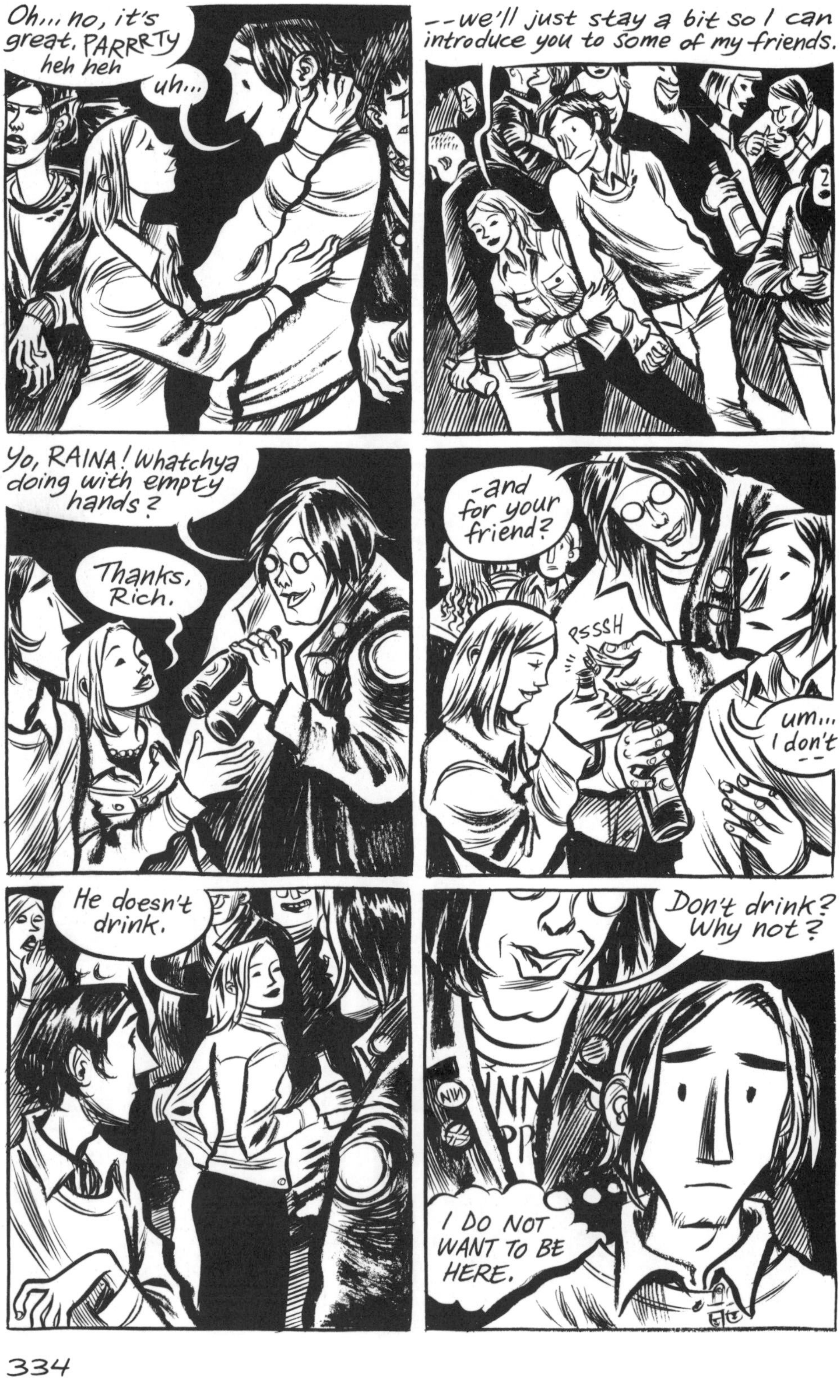
Oh... no, it's great. PARRRTY heh heh
uh...
--we'll just stay a bit so I can introduce you to some of my friends.
Yo, RAINA! Whatchya doing with empty hands?
Thanks, Rich.
-and for your friend?
PSSSH
um... I don't --
He doesn't drink.
Don't drink? Why not?
I DO NOT WANT TO BE HERE.

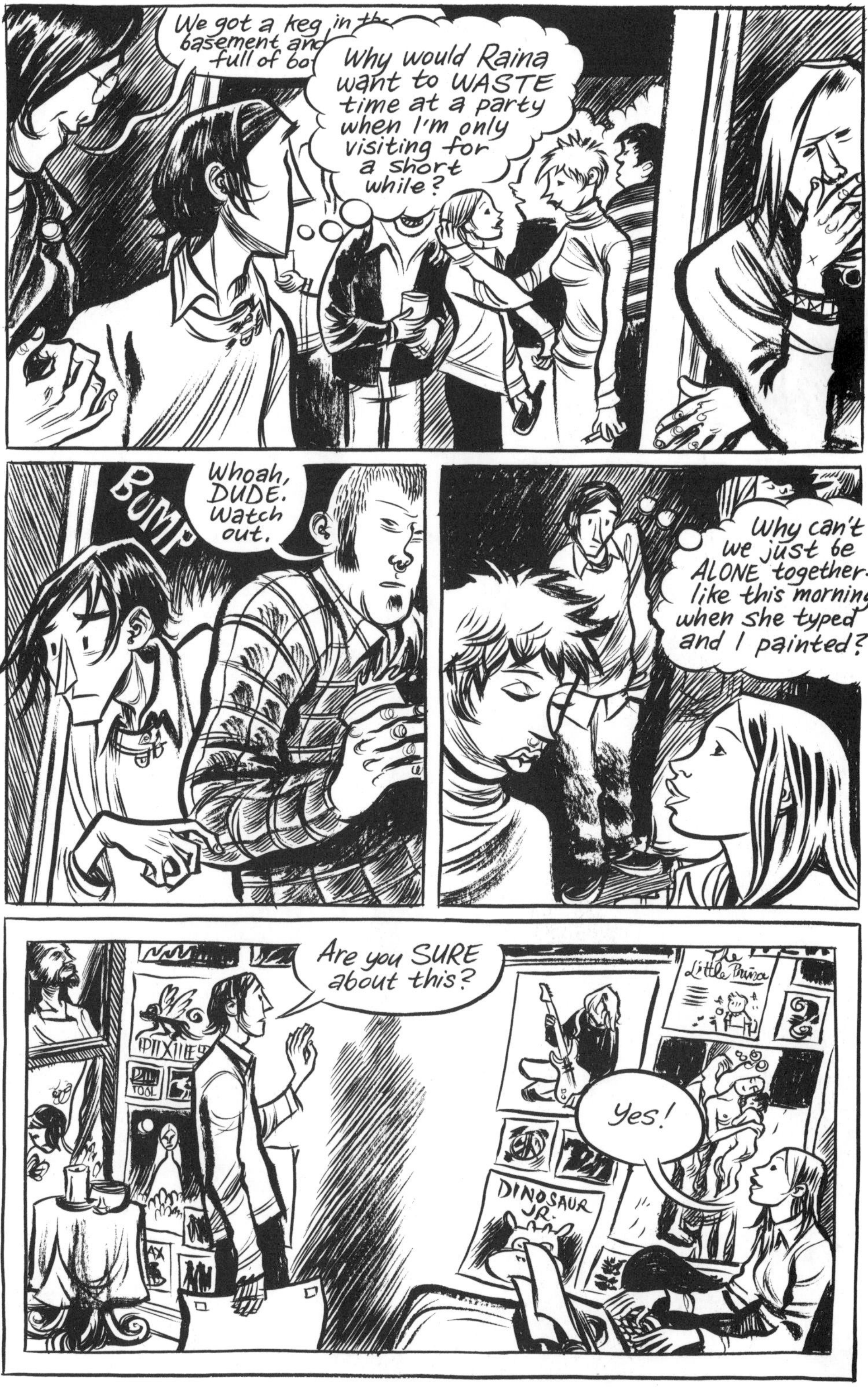

We got a keg in the basement and full of bo
Why would Raina want to WASTE time at a party when I'm only visiting for a short while?
BUMP
Whoah, DUDE. Watch out.
Why can't we just be ALONE together- like this morning, when she typed and I painted?
Are you SURE about this?
Yes!
PIXIES
TOOL
DINOSAUR JR.
The Little Raina

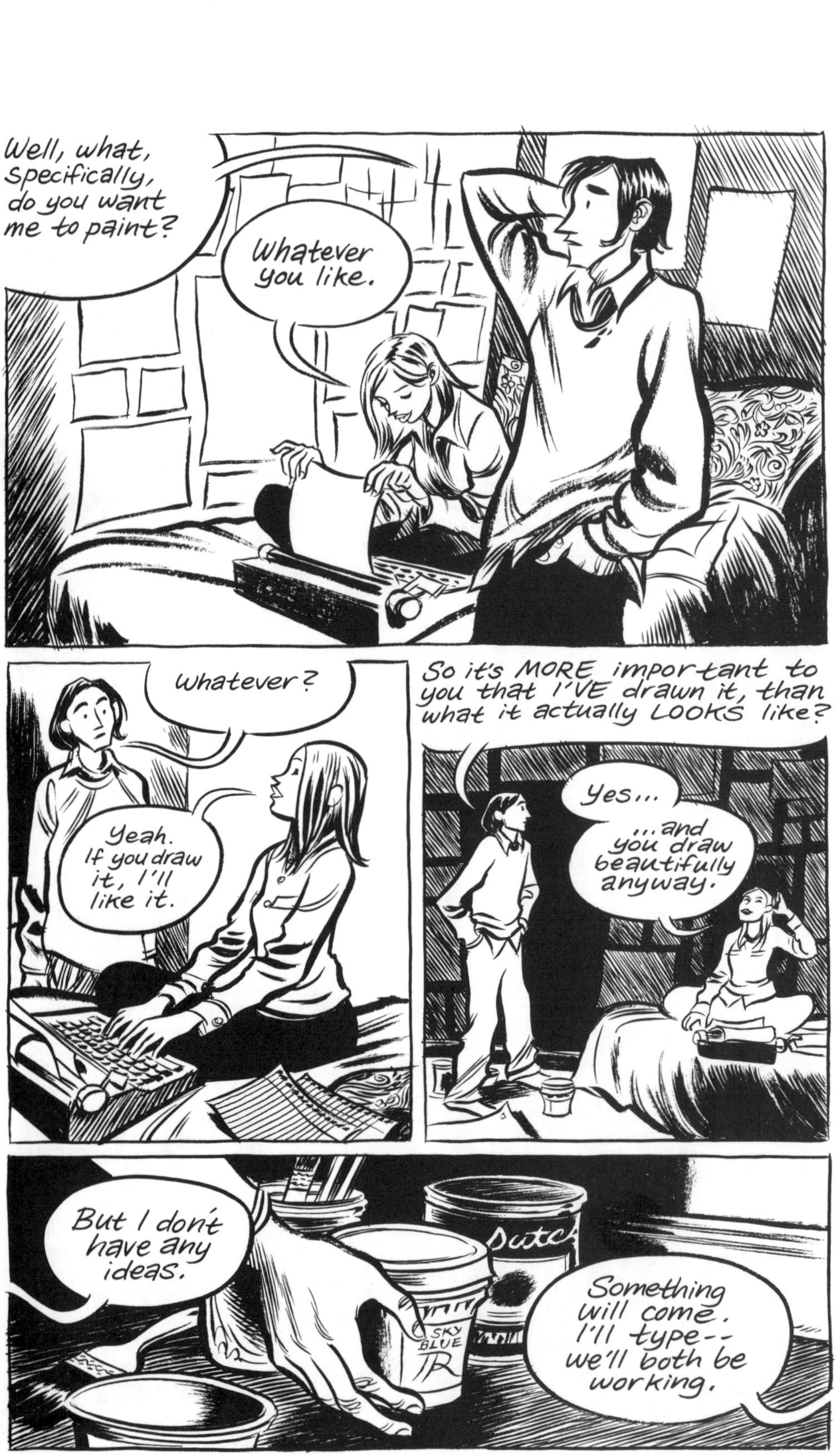
Well, what, specifically, do you want me to paint?
Whatever you like.
Whatever?
Yeah. If you draw it, I'll like it.
So it's MORE important to you that I'VE drawn it, than what it actually LOOKS like?
Yes...
...and you draw beautifully anyway.
But I don't have any ideas.
Dutc
SKY BLUE
Something will come. I'll type-- we'll both be working.

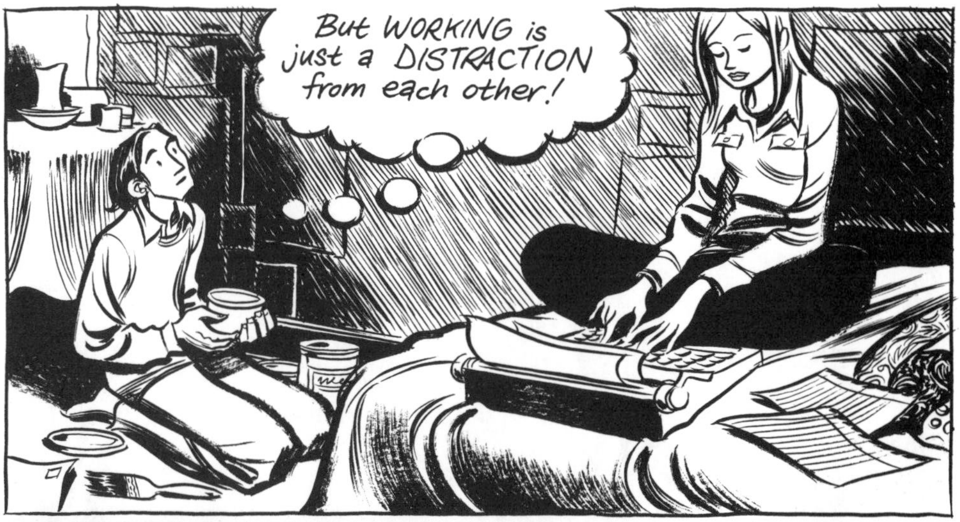
But WORKING is just a DISTRACTION from each other!

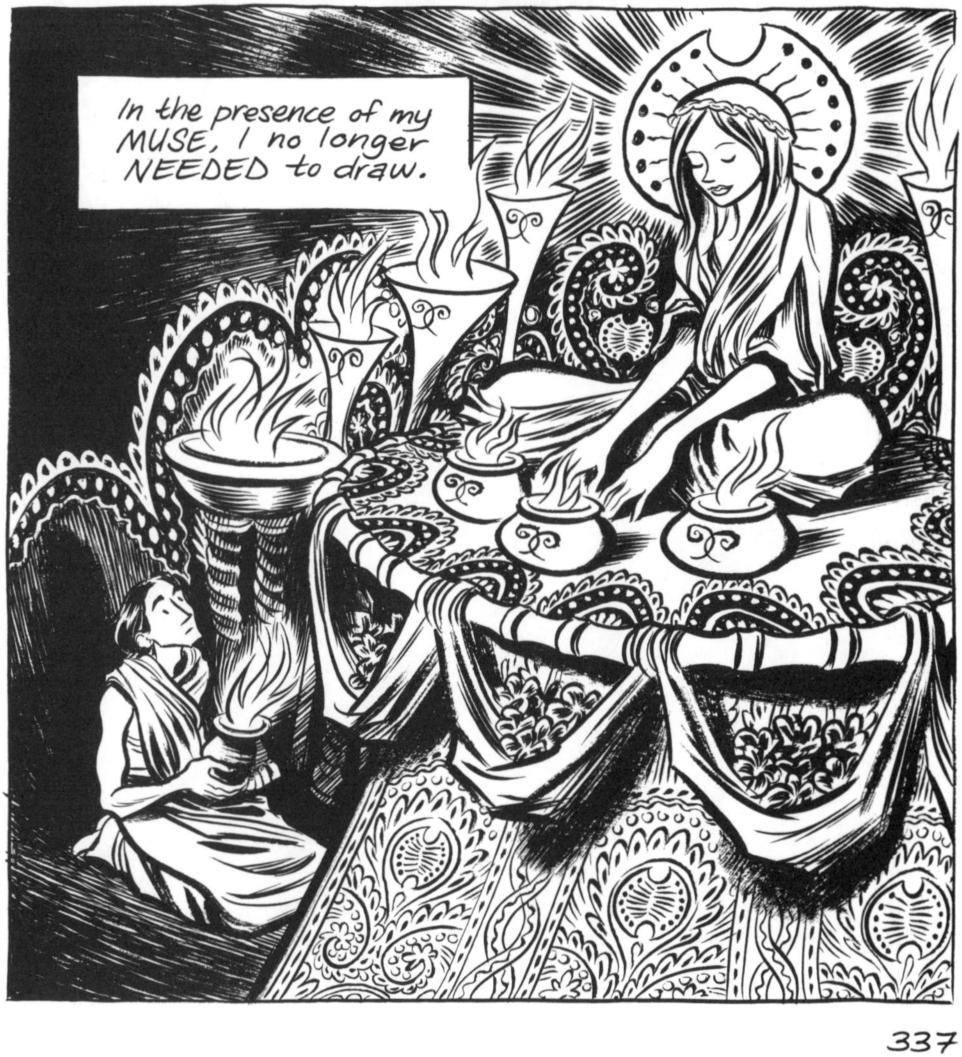
In the presence of my MUSE, I no longer NEEDED to draw.

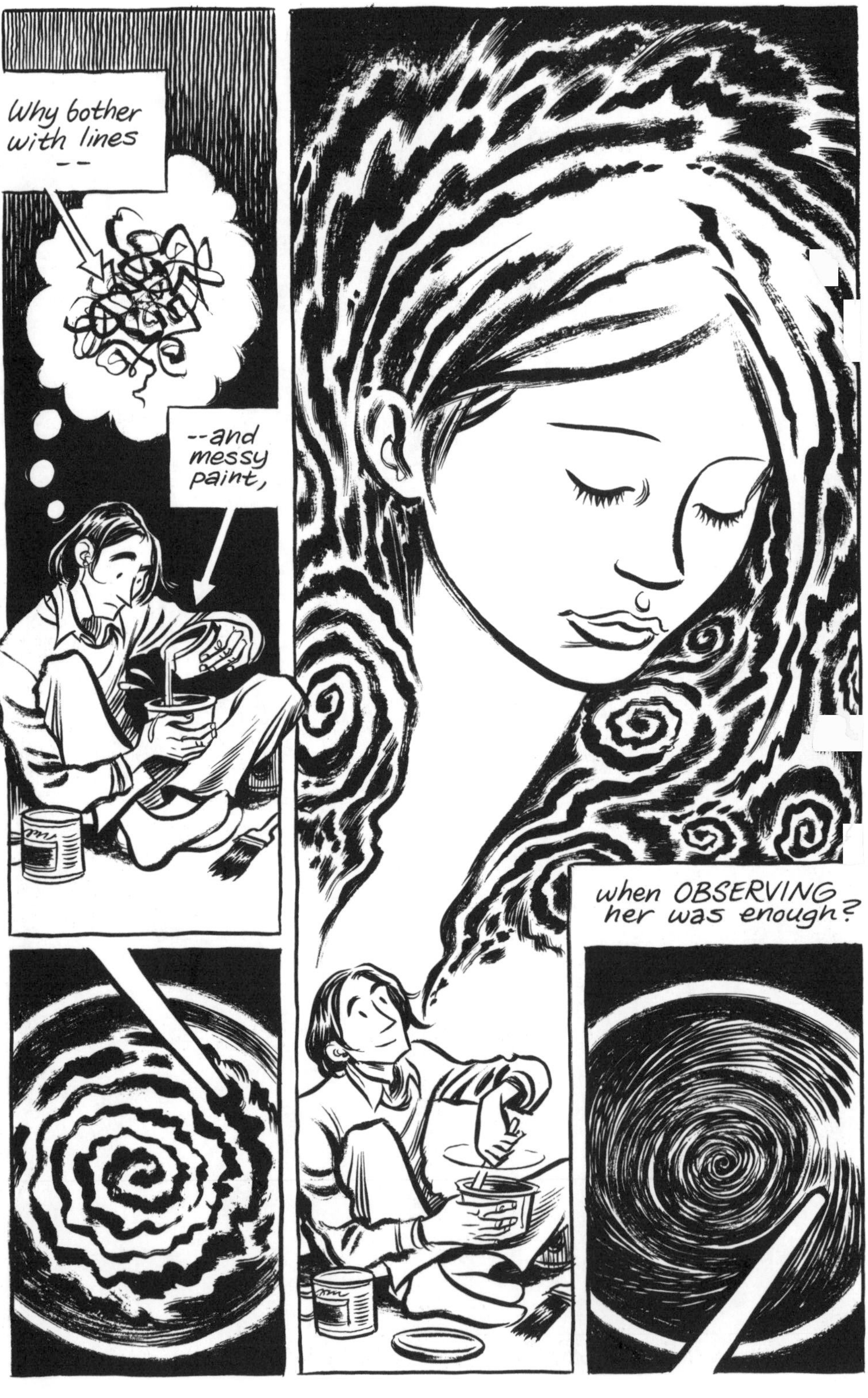
Why bother with lines --
--and messy paint,
when OBSERVING her was enough?

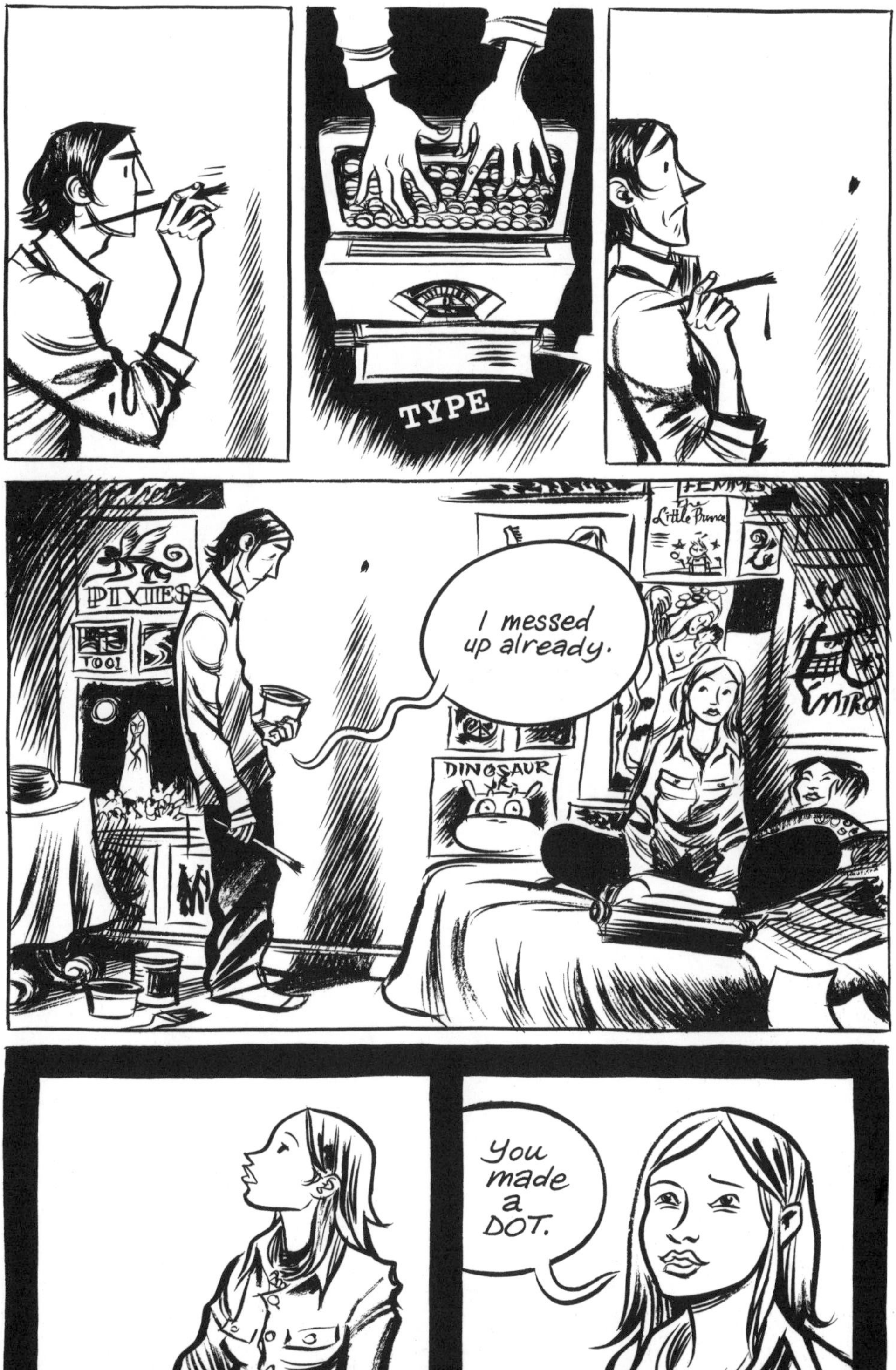
TYPE
PIXIES
TOOL
DINOSAUR JR
The Little Prince
MIRO
I messed up already.
You made a DOT.

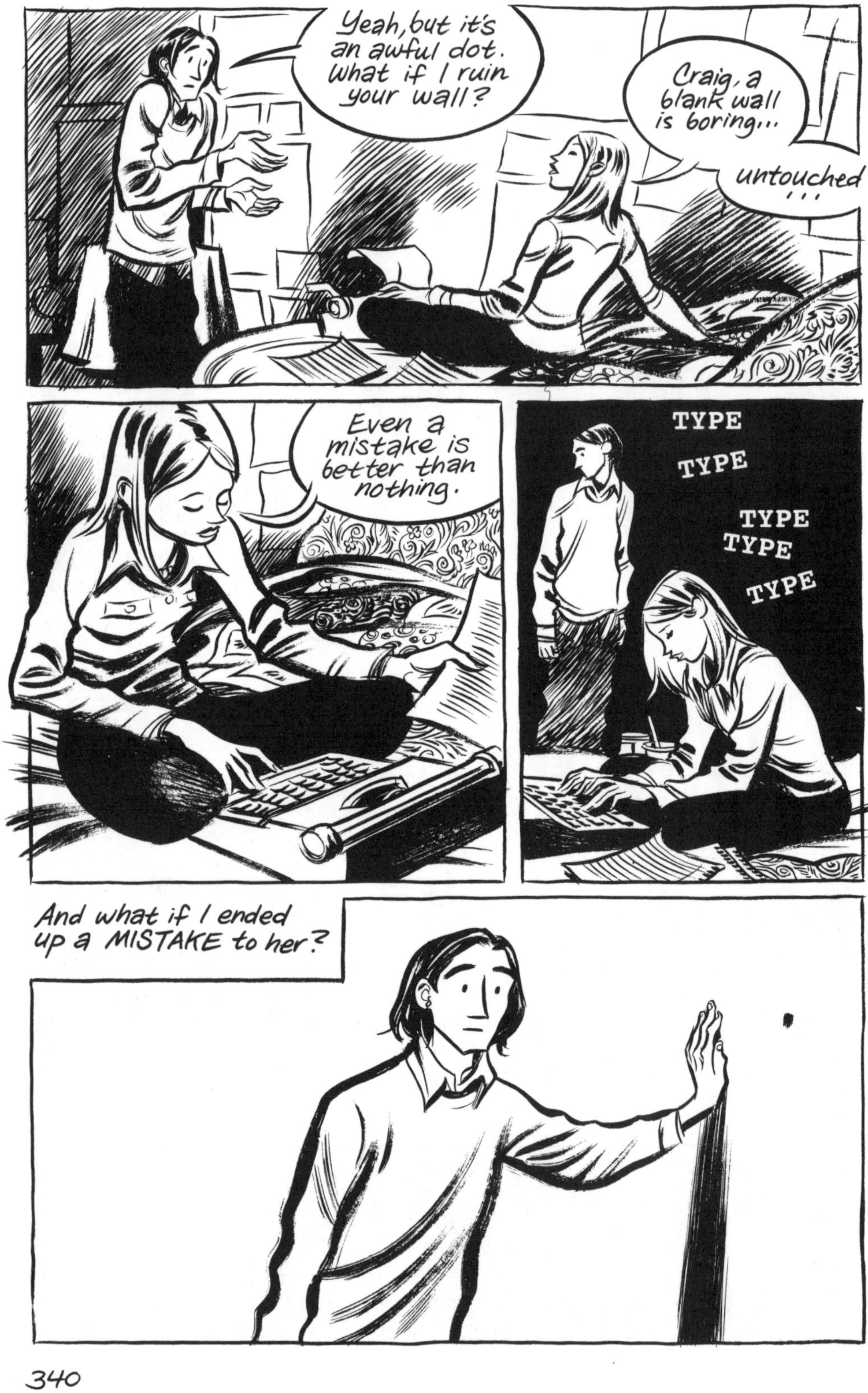
Yeah, but it's an awful dot. What if I ruin your wall?
Craig, a blank wall is boring...
untouched...
Even a mistake is better than nothing.
TYPE
TYPE
TYPE
TYPE
TYPE
And what if I ended up a MISTAKE to her?

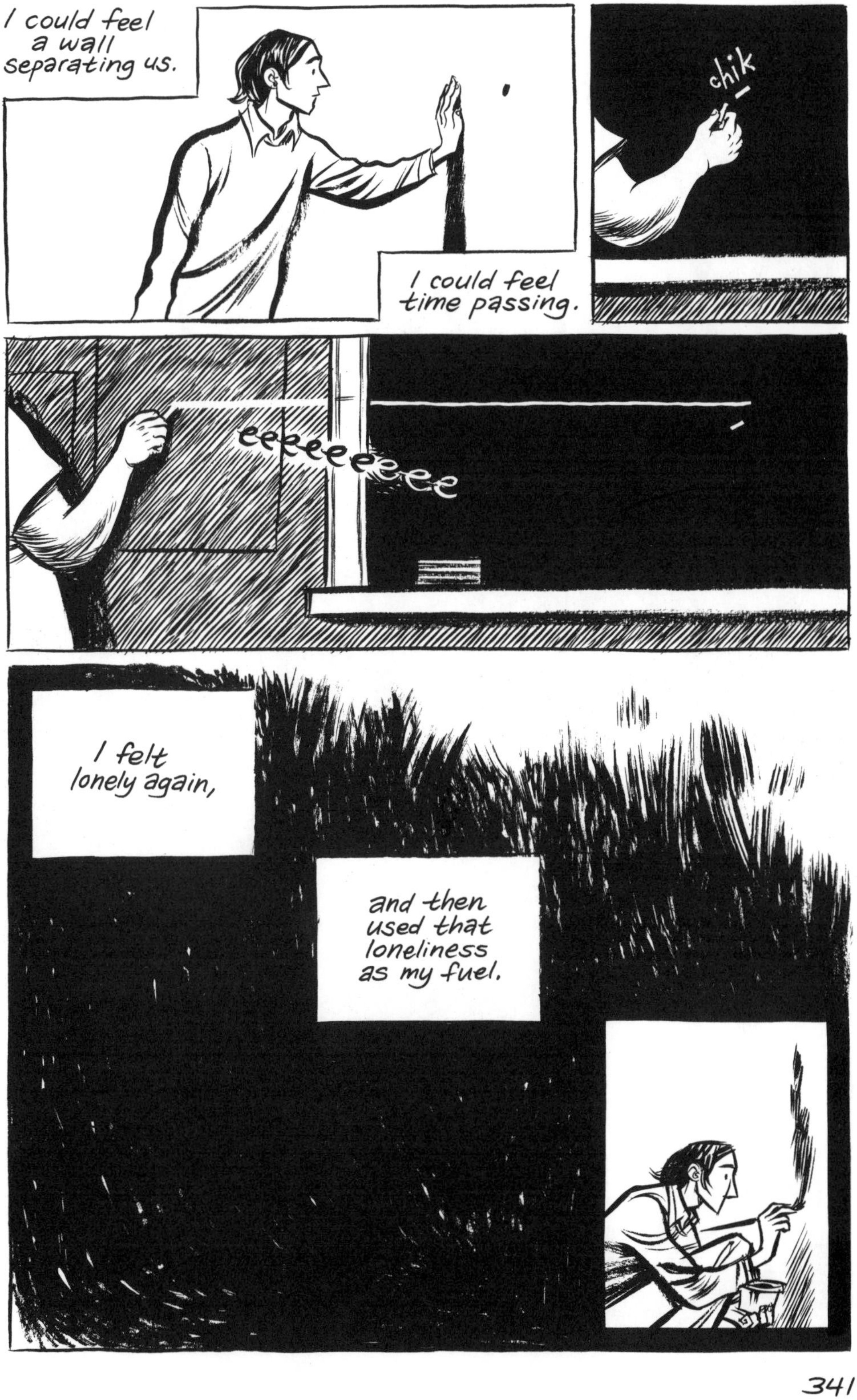
I could feel a wall separating us.
I could feel time passing.
chik
eeeeeeeeeee
I felt lonely again,
and then used that loneliness as my fuel.

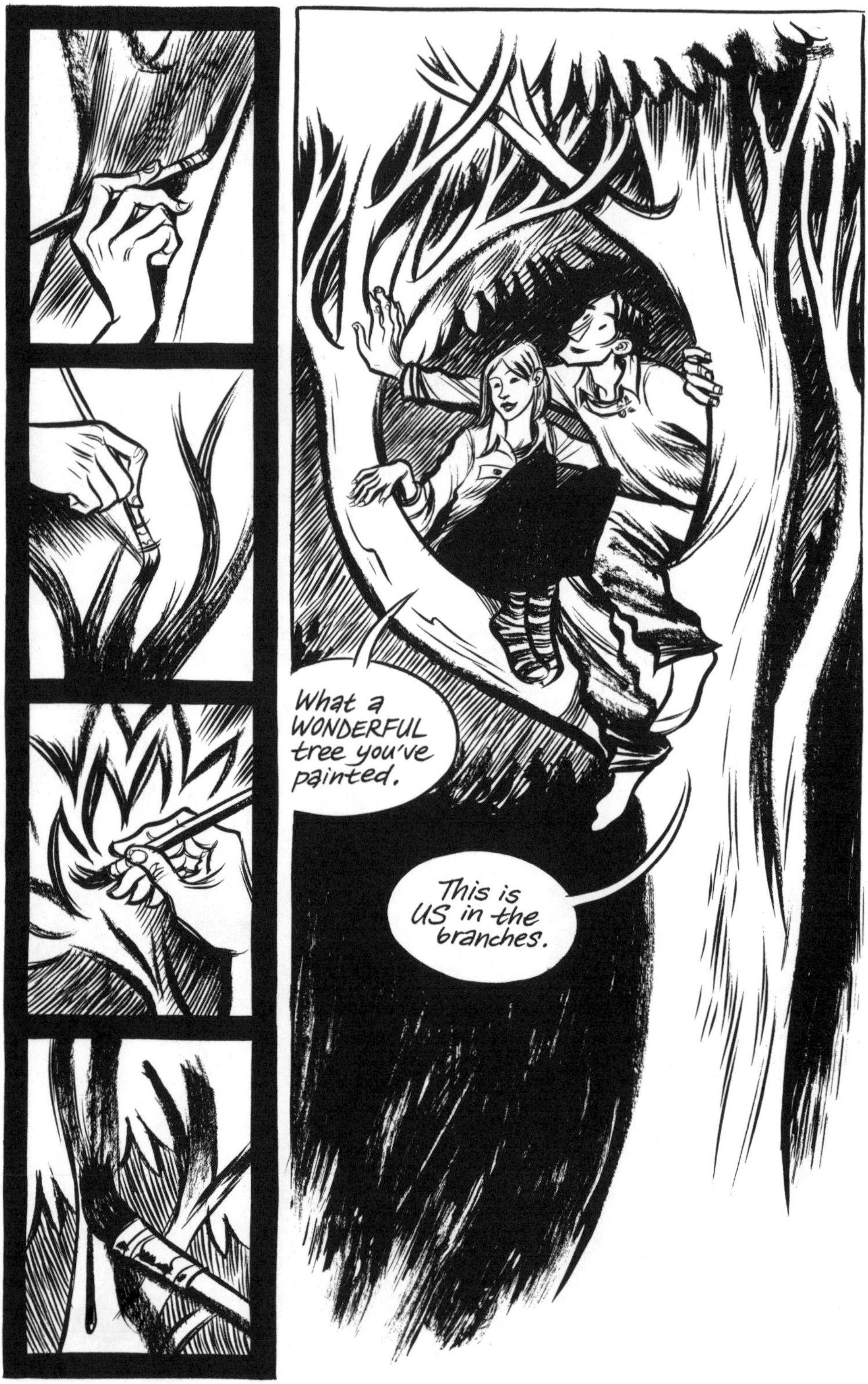
What a WONDERFUL tree you've painted.
This is US in the branches.

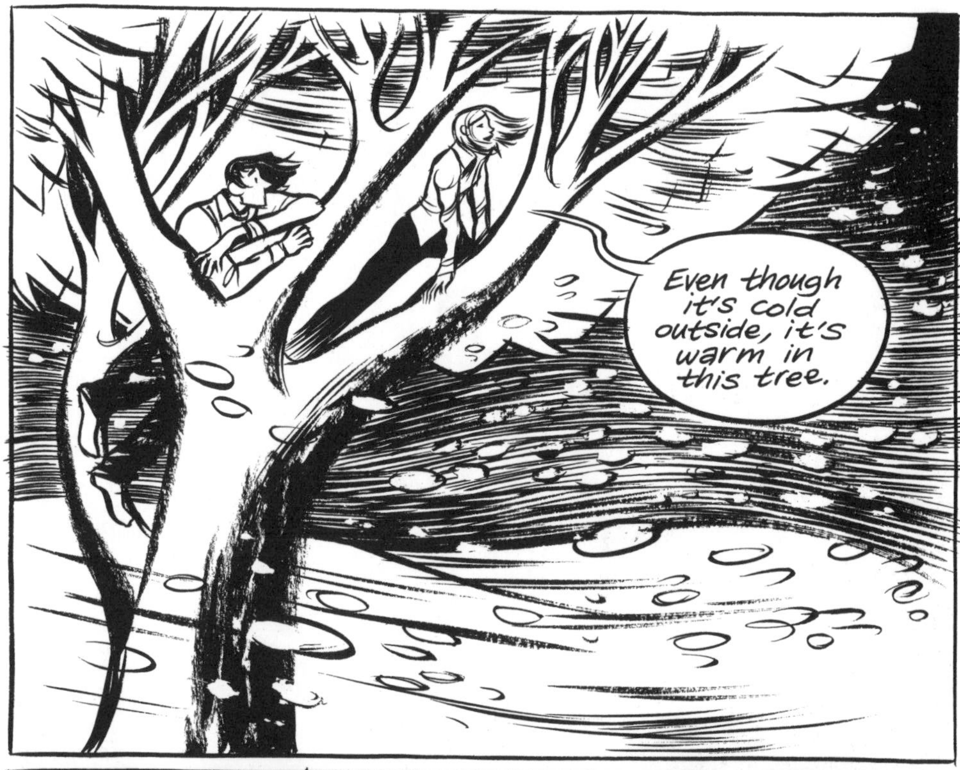
Even though it's cold outside, it's warm in this tree.

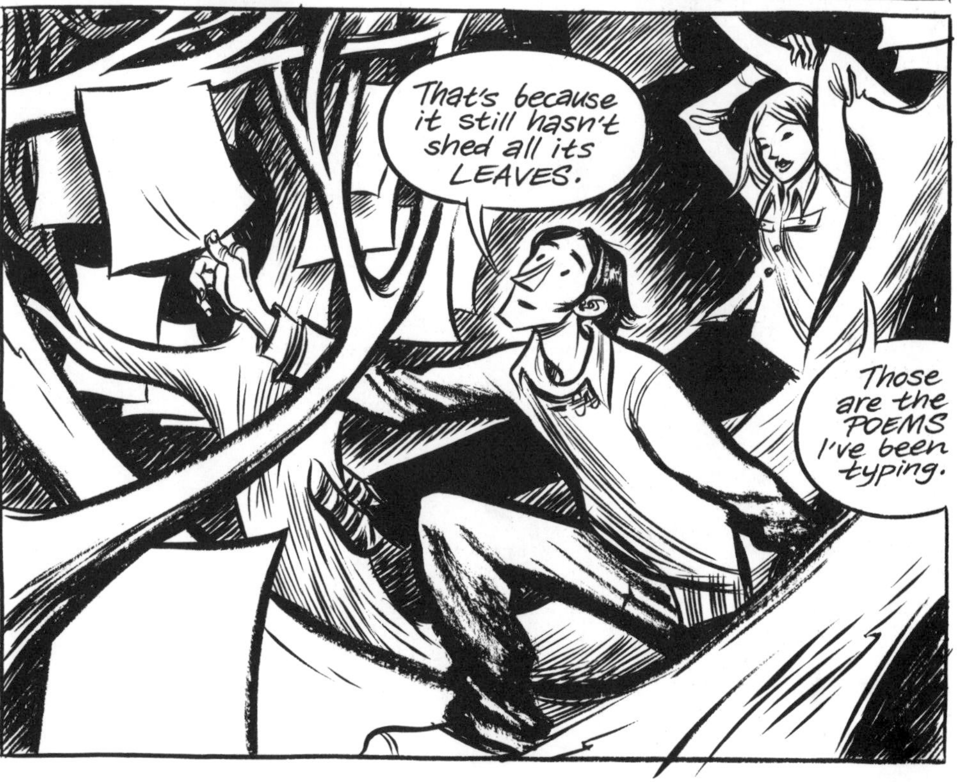
That's because it still hasn't shed all its LEAVES.
Those are the POEMS I've been typing.

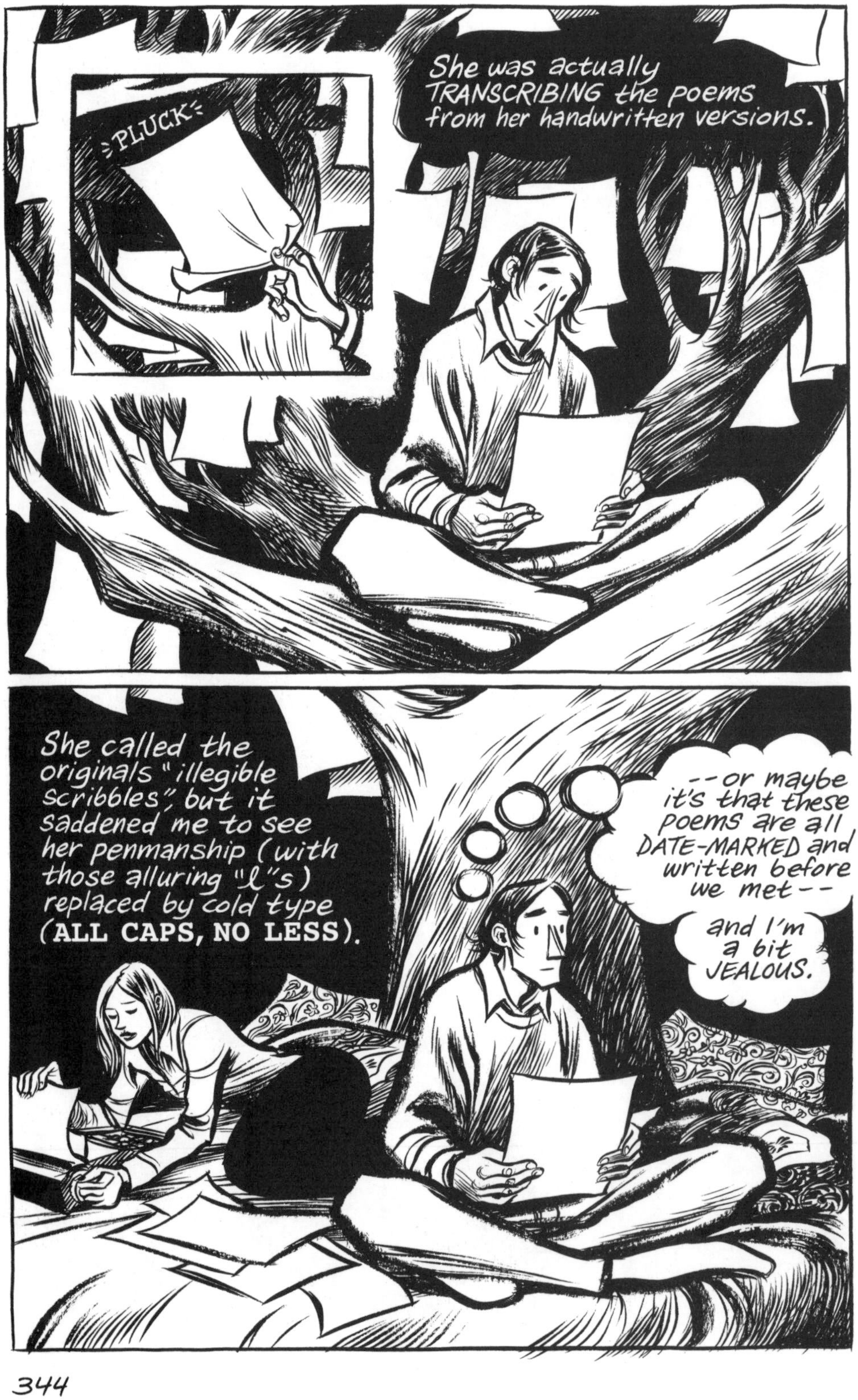

PLUCK
She was actually TRANSCRIBING the poems from her handwritten versions.
She called the originals "illegible scribbles", but it saddened me to see her penmanship (with those alluring "ℓ"s) replaced by cold type (ALL CAPS, NO LESS).
--or maybe it's that these poems are all DATE-MARKED and written before we met--
and I'm a bit JEALOUS.

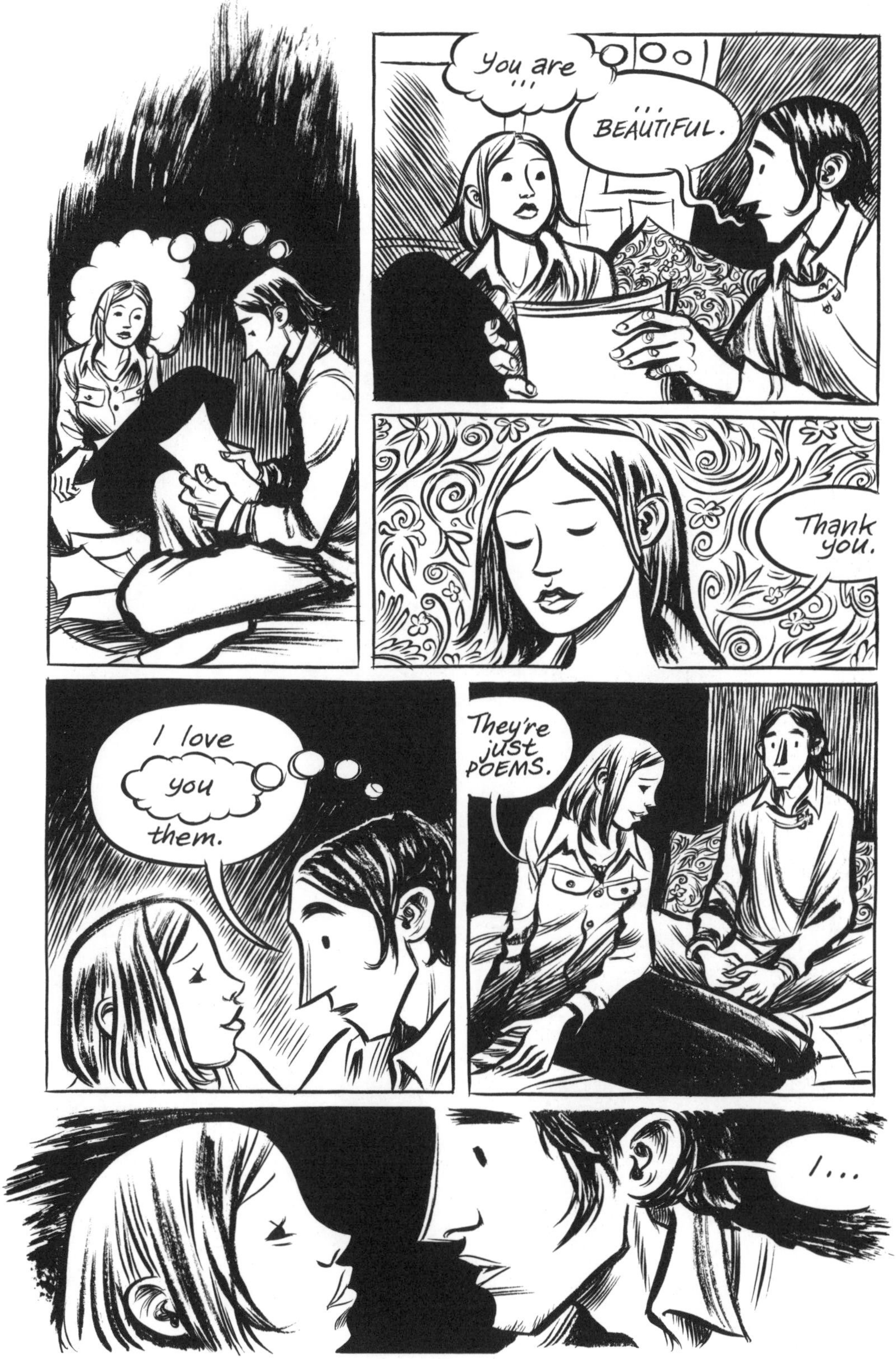
You are ...
... BEAUTIFUL.
Thank you.
I love you them.
They're just POEMS.
I...

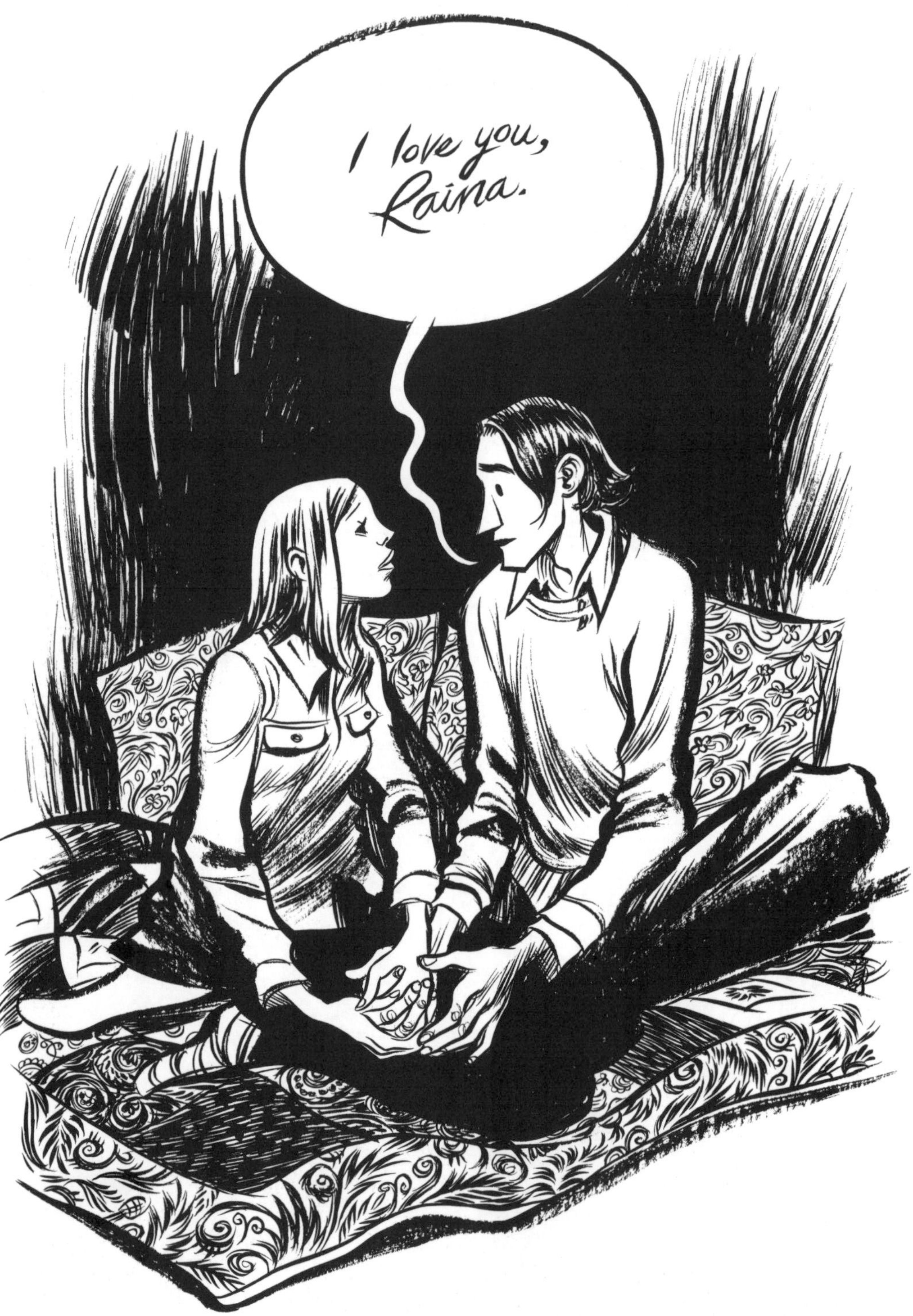
I love you, Raina.

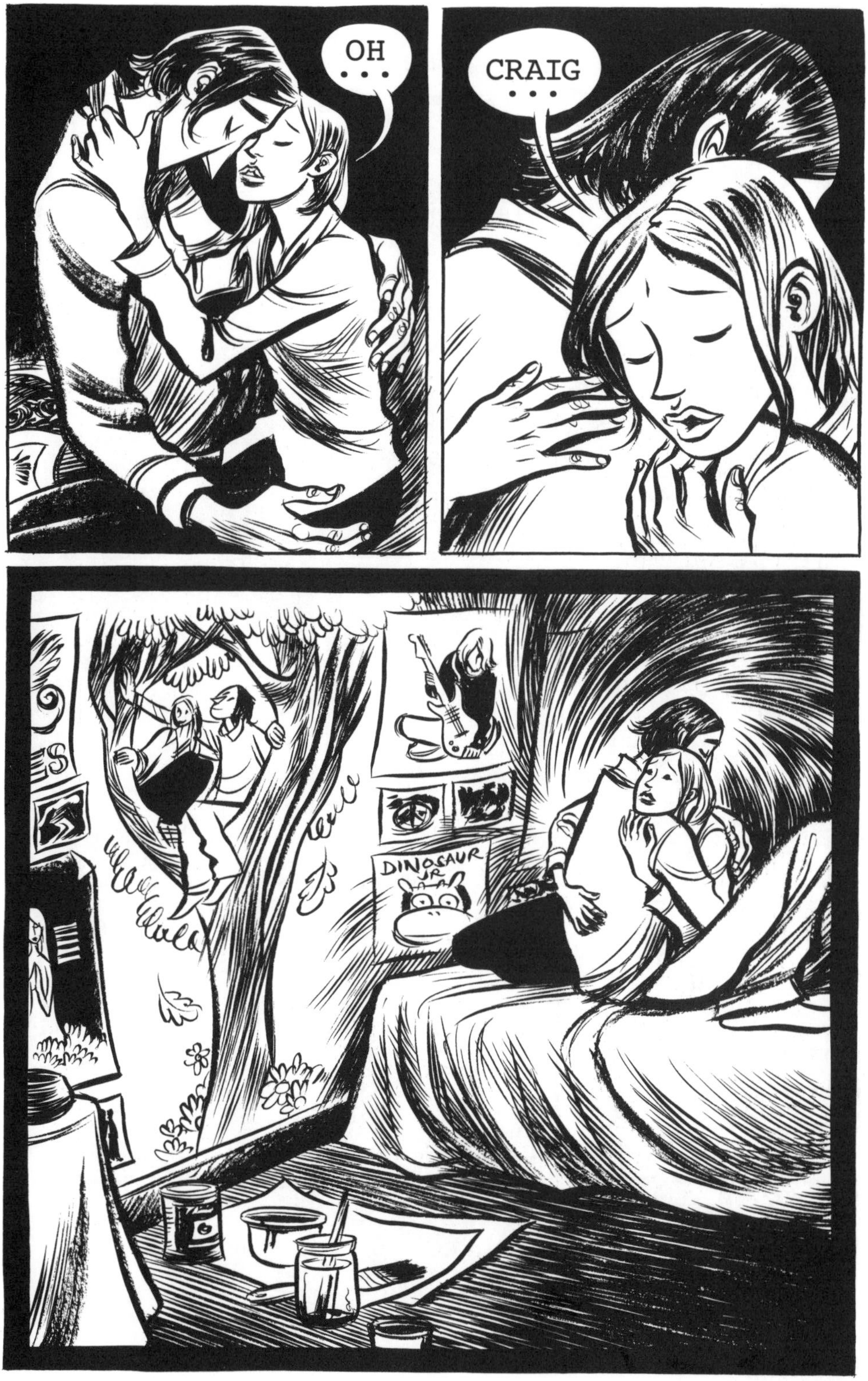
OH ...
CRAIG ...
DINOSAUR JR

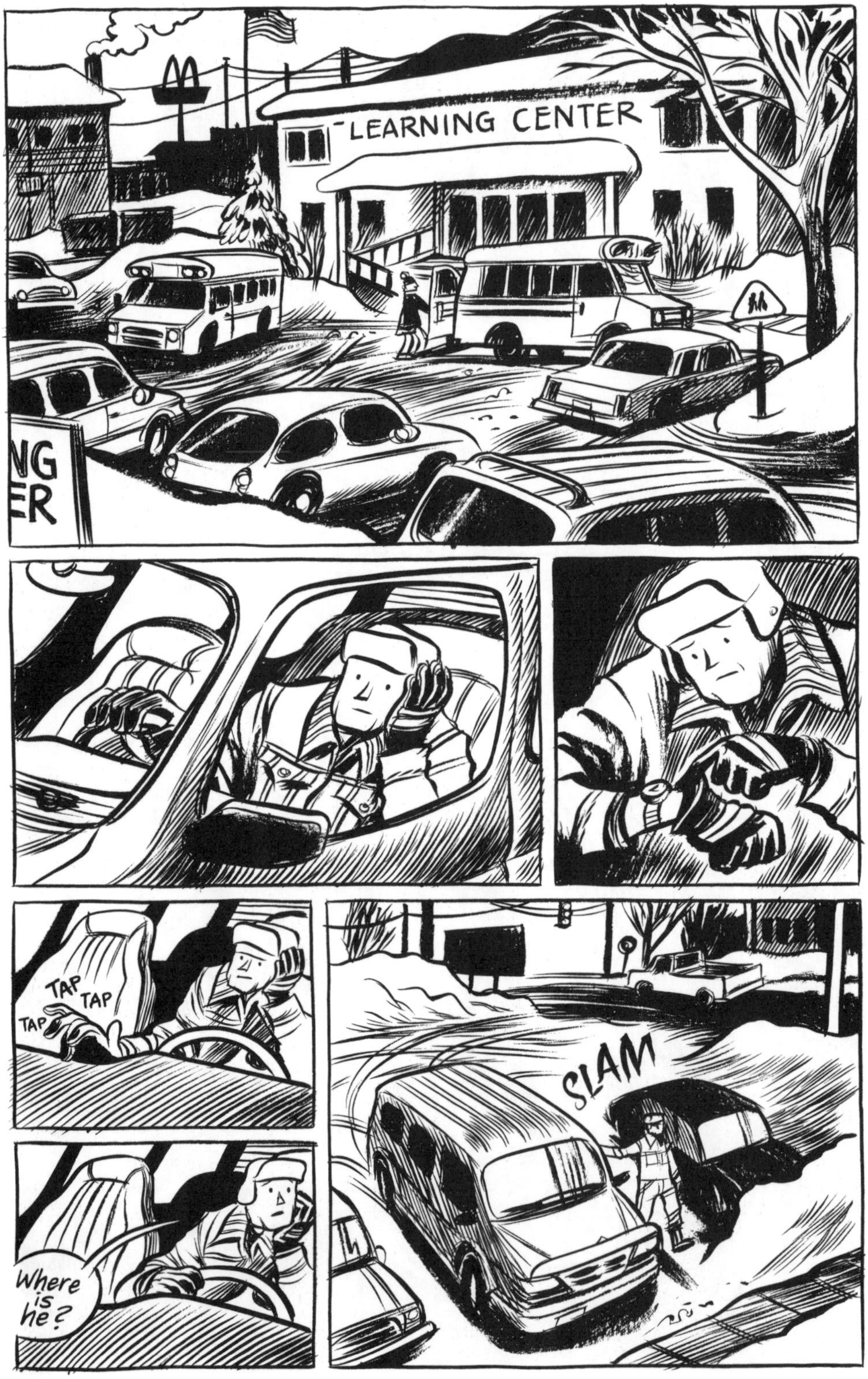
LEARNING CENTER
NG
ER
TAP TAP TAP
Where is he?
SLAM

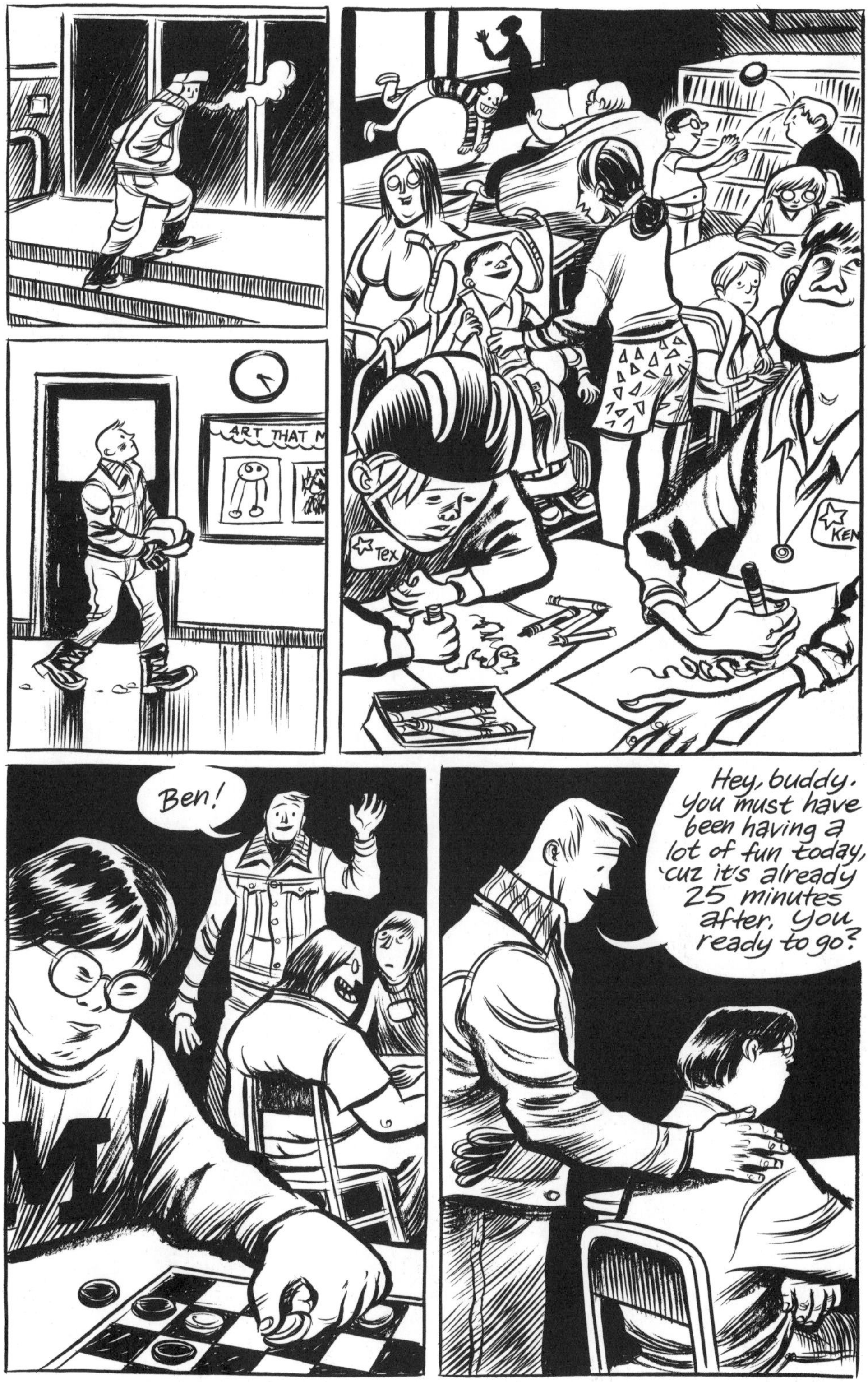
ART THAT M
TEX
KEN
Ben!
Hey, buddy. You must have been having a lot of fun today, 'cuz it's already 25 minutes after. You ready to go?

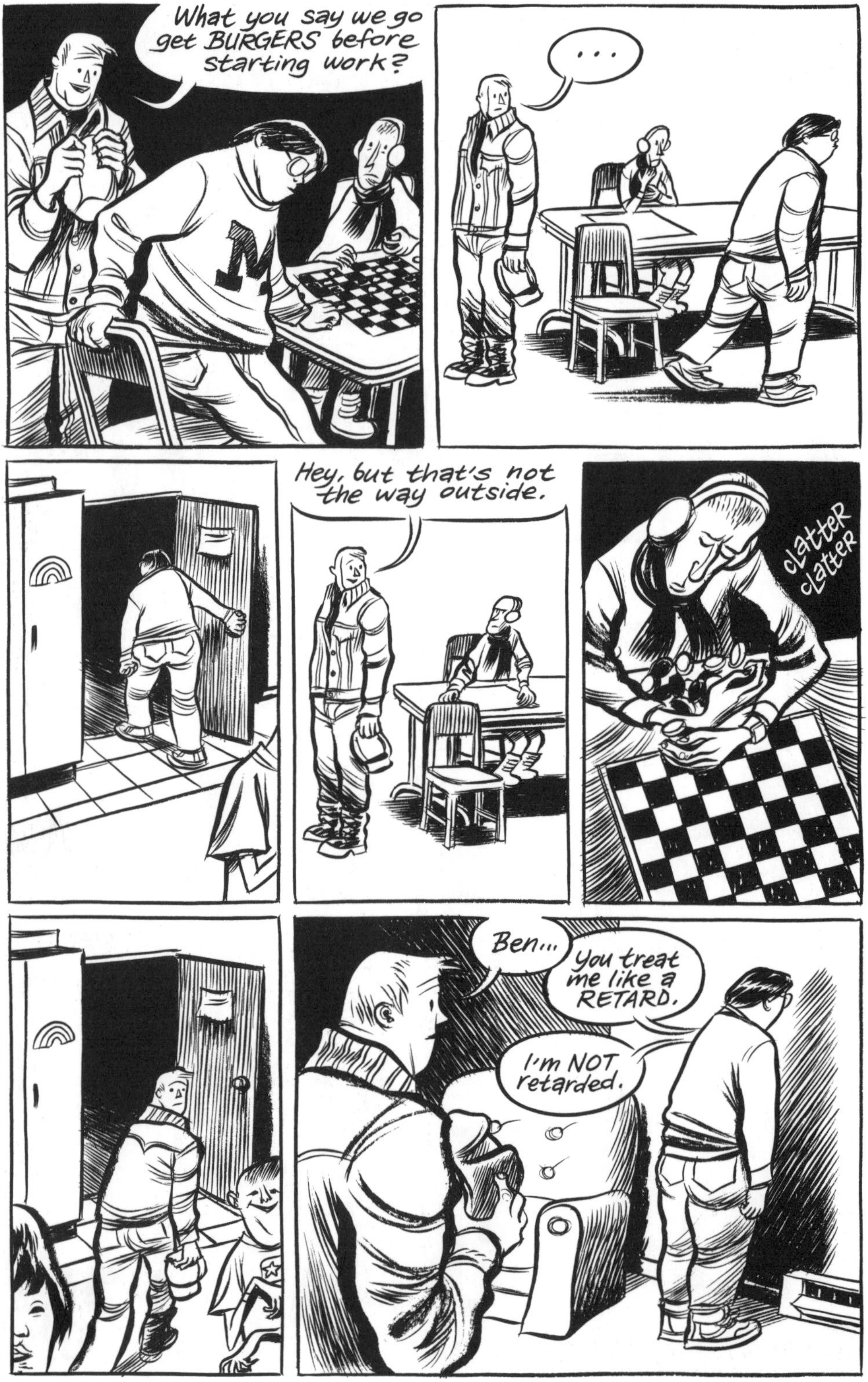
What you say we go get BURGERS before starting work?
...
Hey, but that's not the way outside.
clatter clatter
Ben...
You treat me like a RETARD.
I'm NOT retarded.

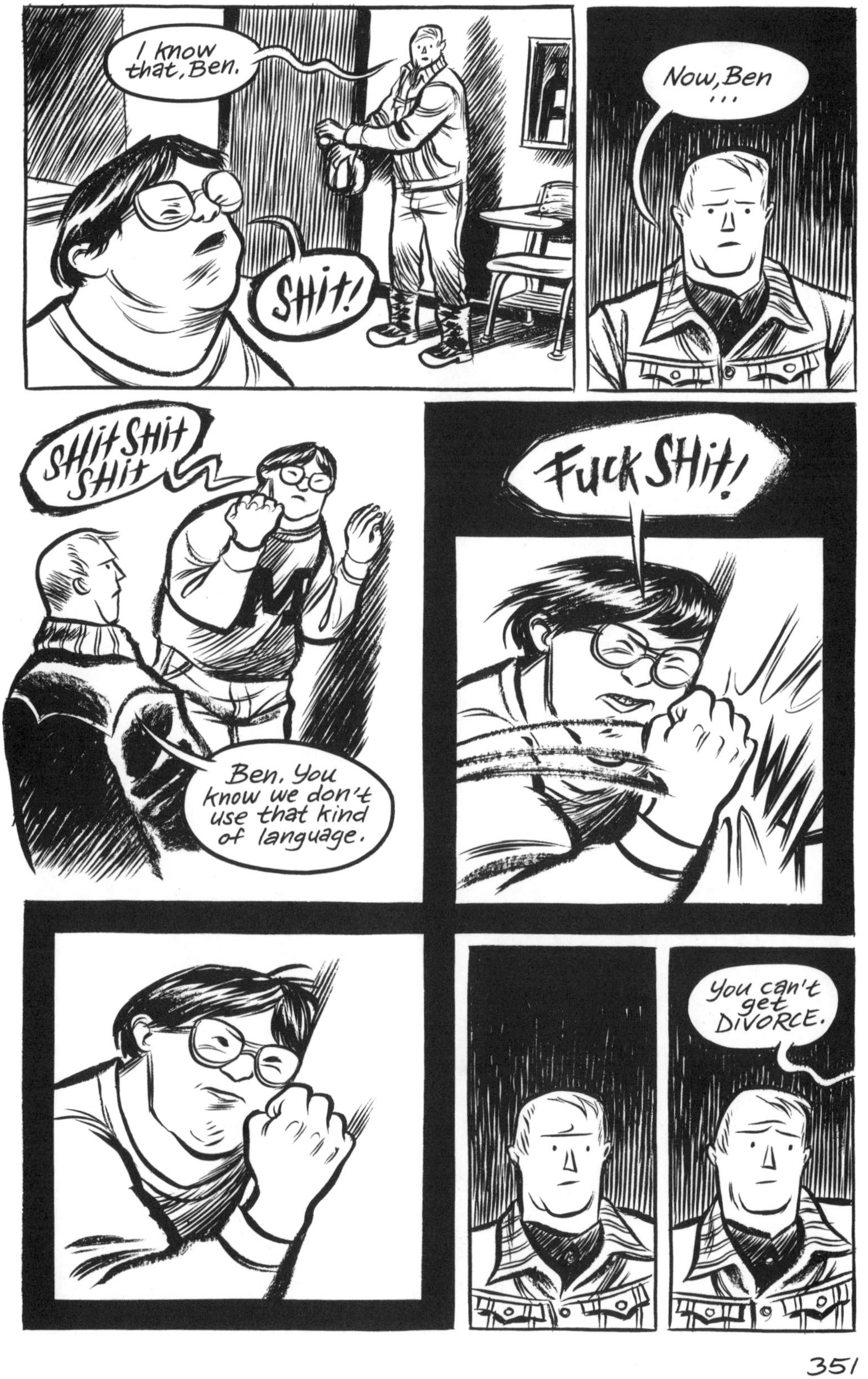
I know that, Ben.
SHIT!
Now, Ben ...
SHIT SHIT SHIT
Ben. You know we don't use that kind of language.
FUCK SHIT!
WAK
You can't get DIVORCE.

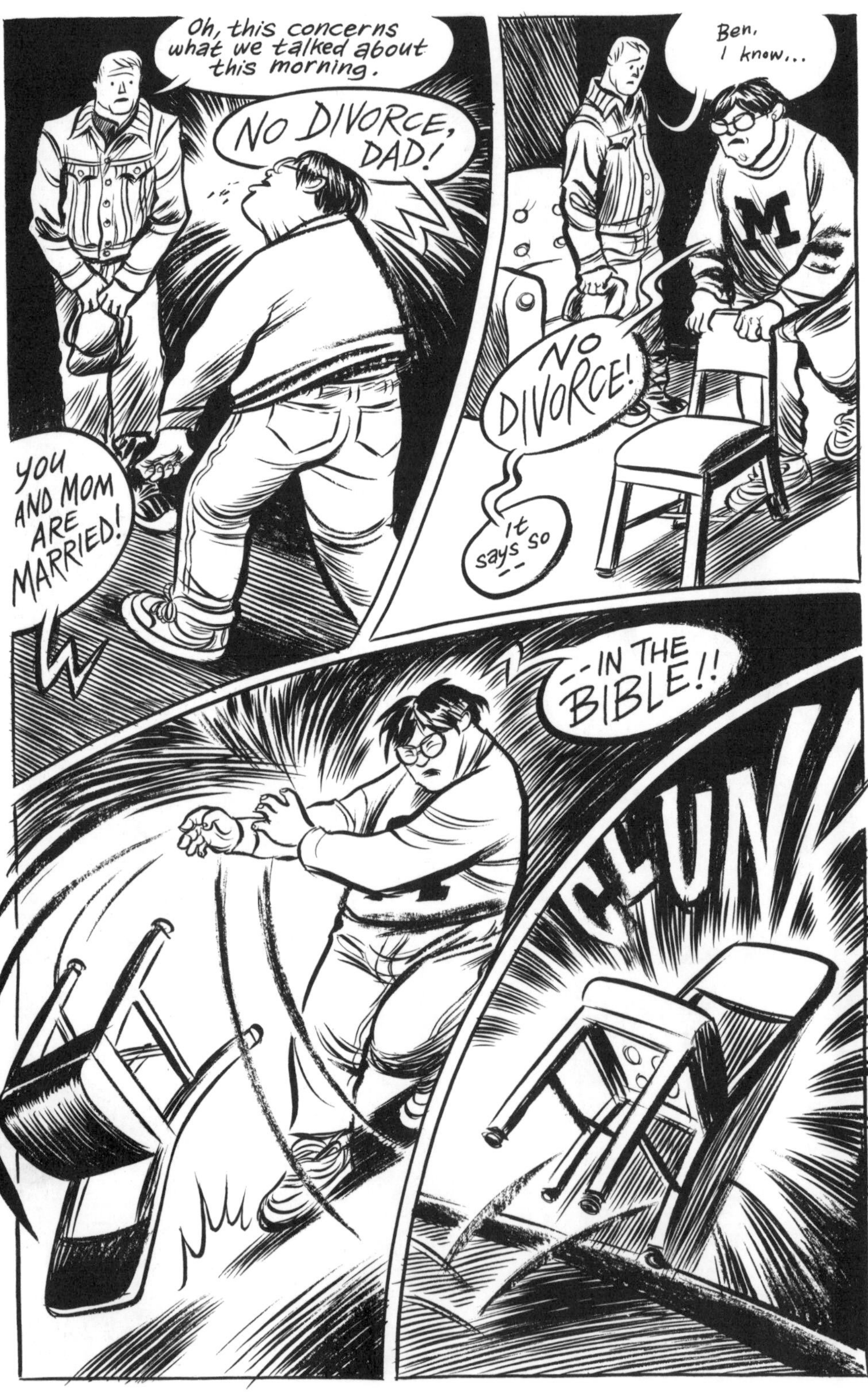
Oh, this concerns what we talked about this morning.
NO DIVORCE, DAD!
YOU AND MOM ARE MARRIED!
Ben, I know...
NO DIVORCE!
It says so --
--IN THE BIBLE!!
CLUNK

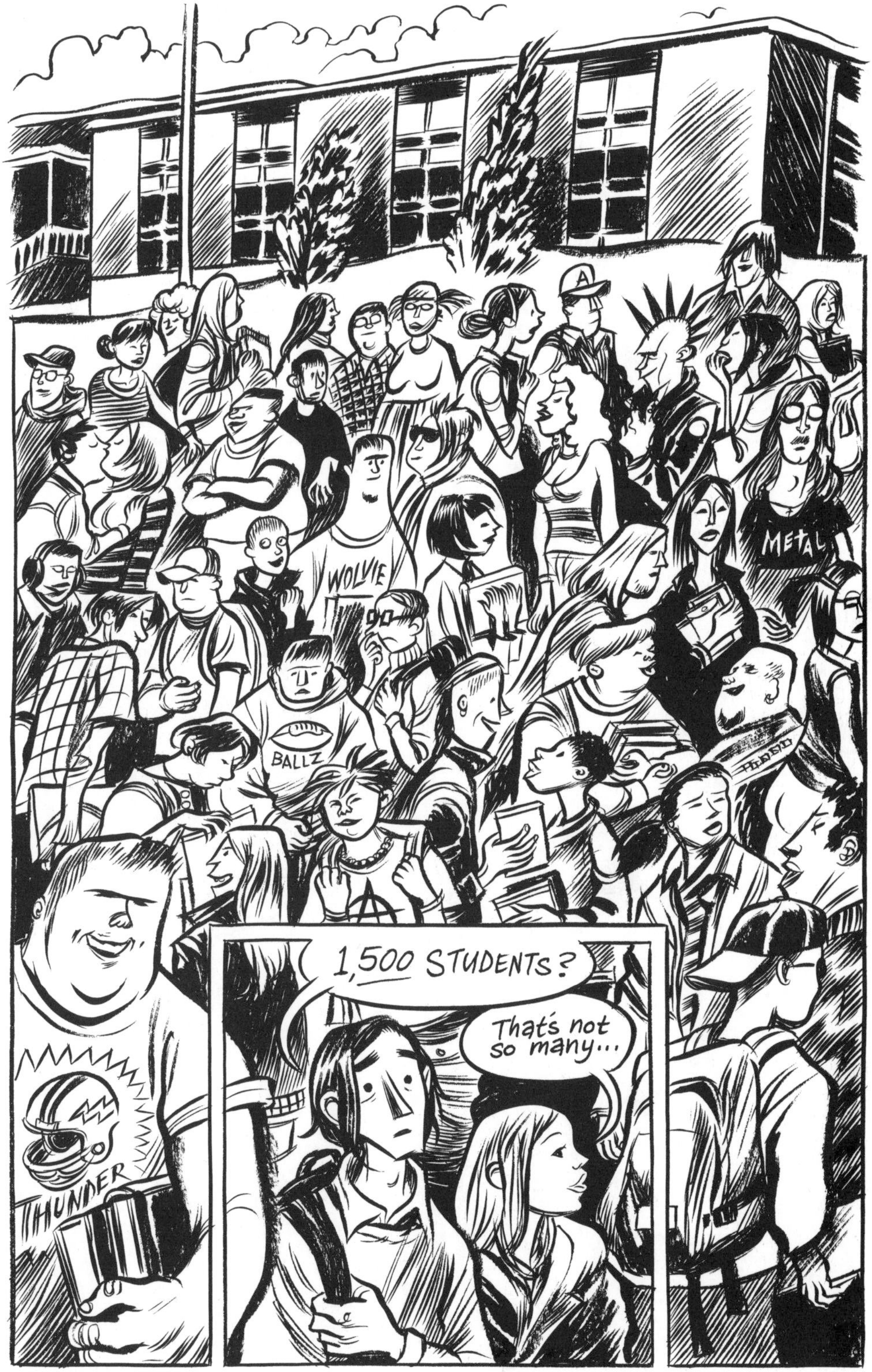
WOLVIE
METAL
BALLZ
THUNDER
1,500 STUDENTS?
That's not so many...

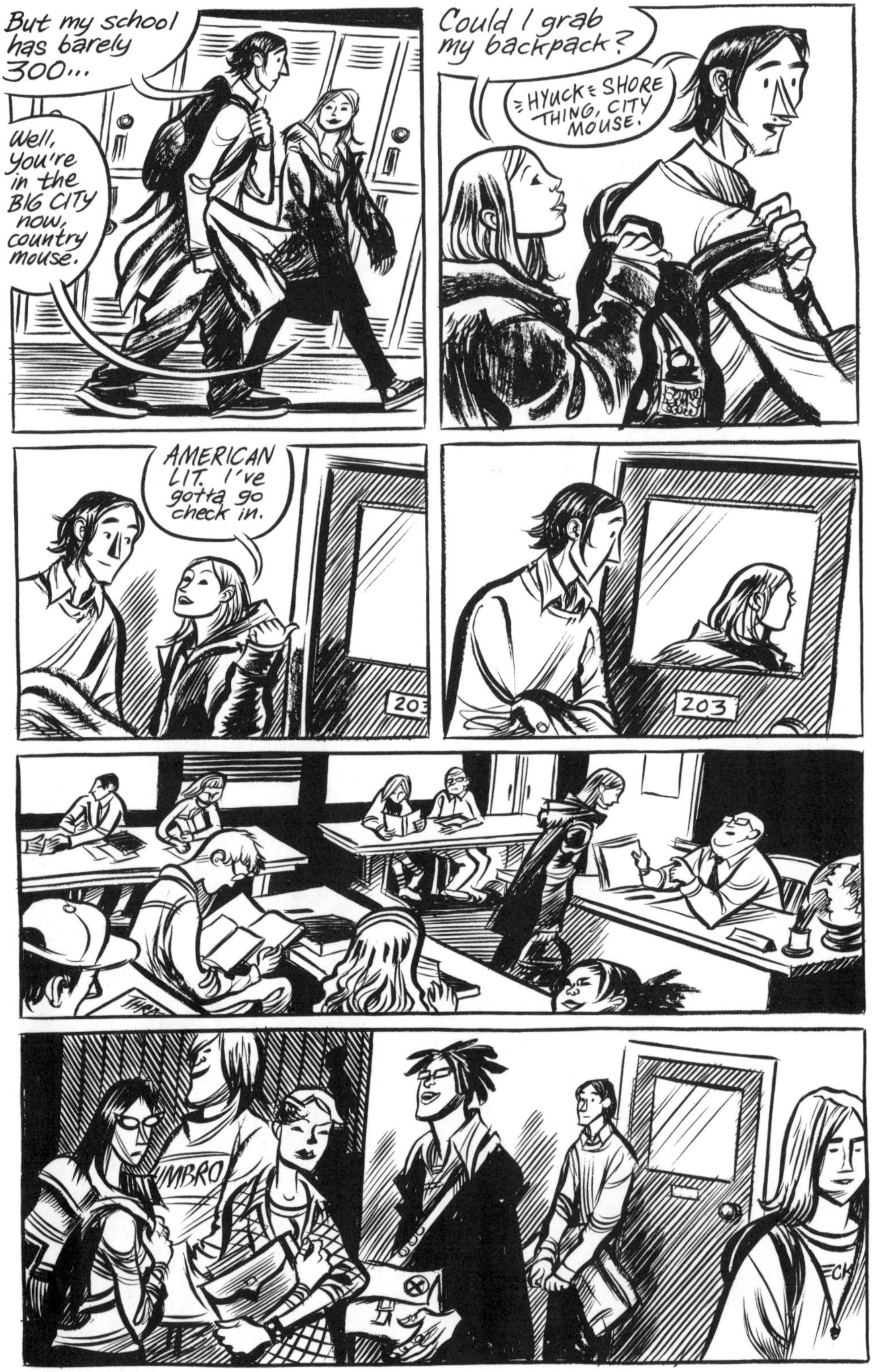
But my school has barely 300...
Well, you're in the BIG CITY now, country mouse.
Could I grab my backpack?
HYUCK SHORE THING, CITY MOUSE.
AMERICAN LIT. I've gotta go check in.
203
203
UMBRO

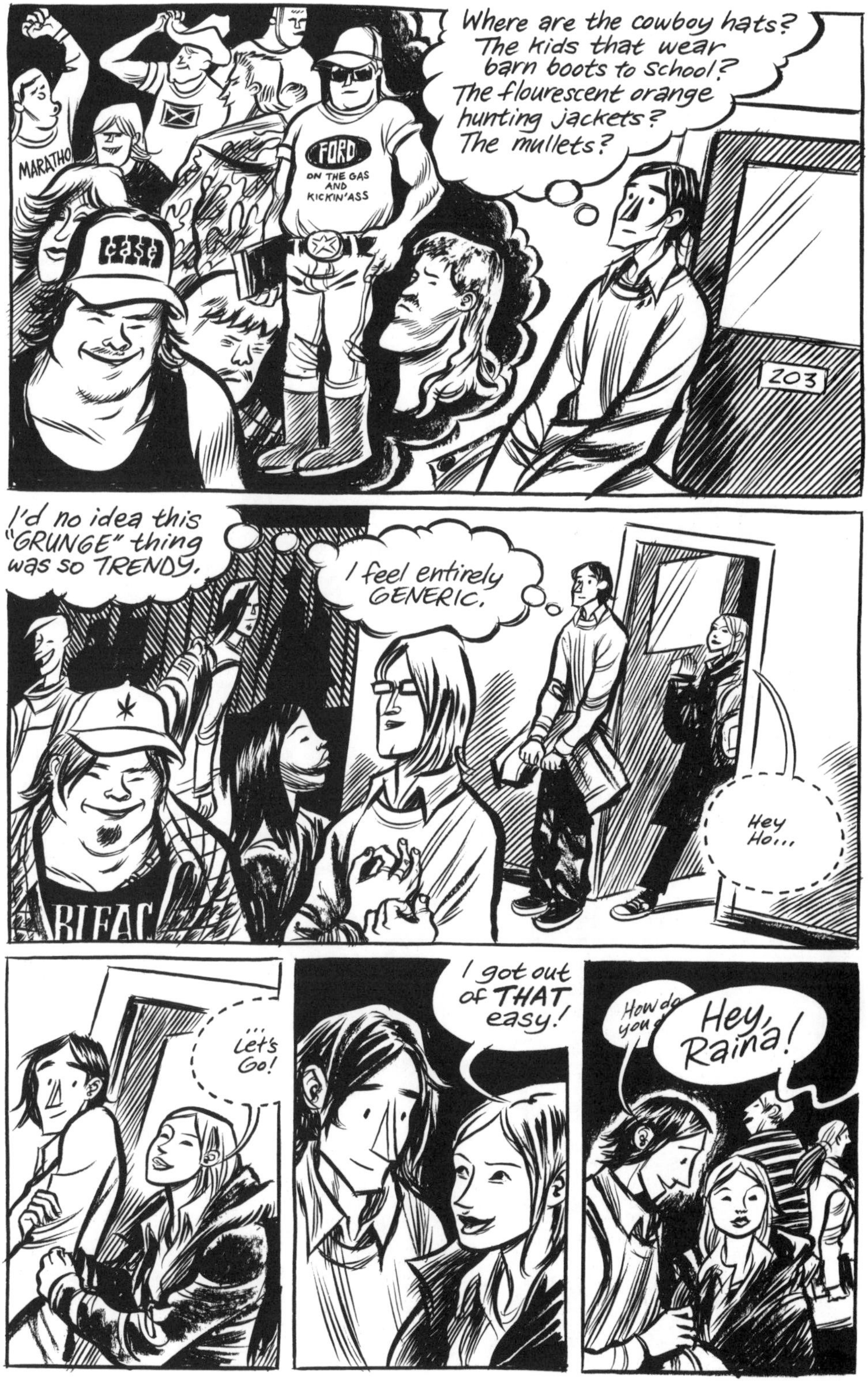
MARATHO
FORD
ON THE GAS AND KICKIN'ASS
case
Where are the cowboy hats? The kids that wear barn boots to school? The flourescent orange hunting jackets? The mullets?
203
I'd no idea this "GRUNGE" thing was so TRENDY.
I feel entirely GENERIC.
Hey Ho...
...Let's Go!
I got out of THAT easy!
Hey, Raina!

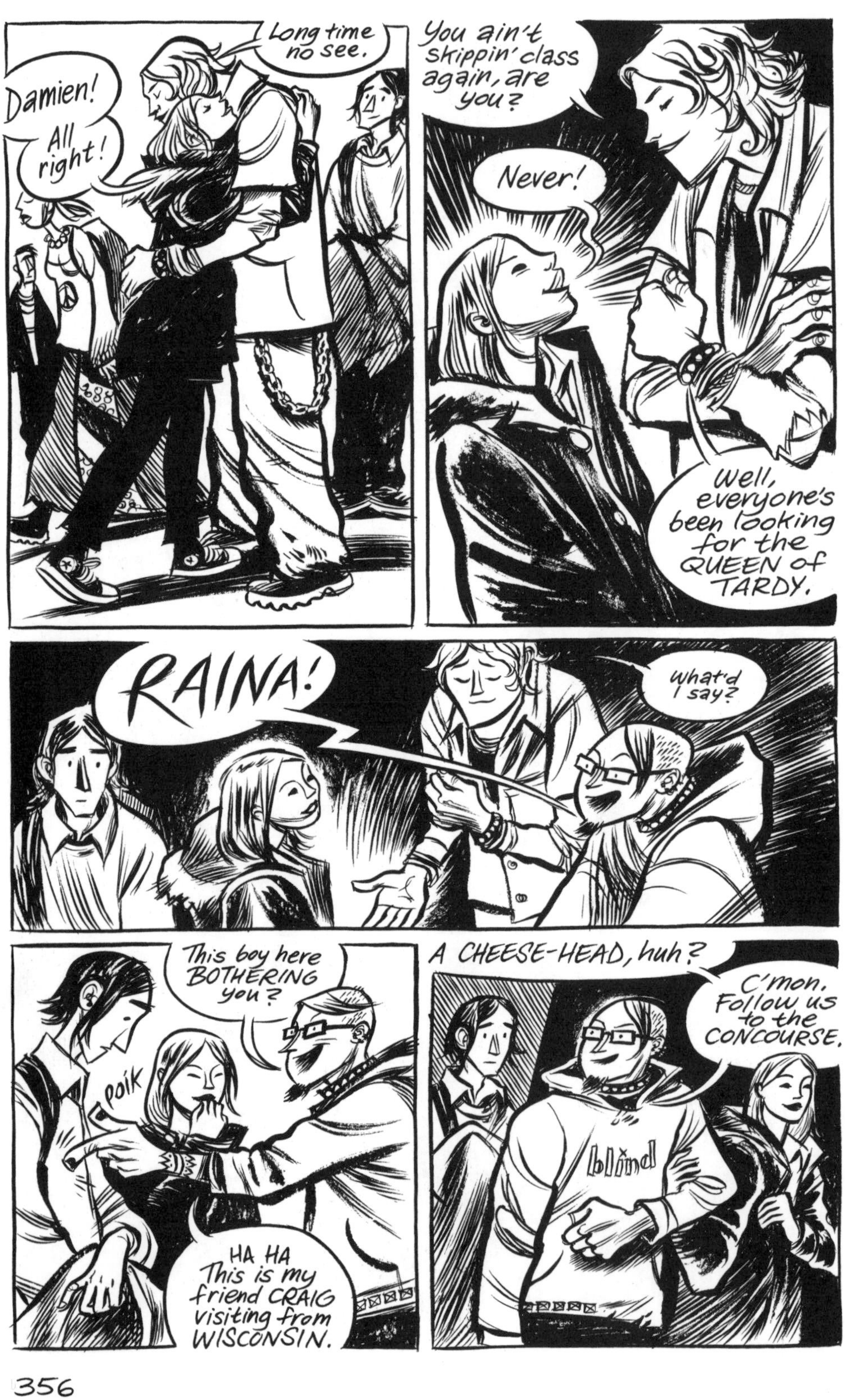
Damien!
Long time no see.
All right!
You ain't skippin' class again, are you?
Never!
Well, everyone's been looking for the QUEEN of TARDY.
RAINA!
what'd I say?
This boy here BOTHERING you?
poik
HA HA This is my friend CRAIG visiting from WISCONSIN.
A CHEESE-HEAD, huh?
C'mon. Follow us to the CONCOURSE.
blind

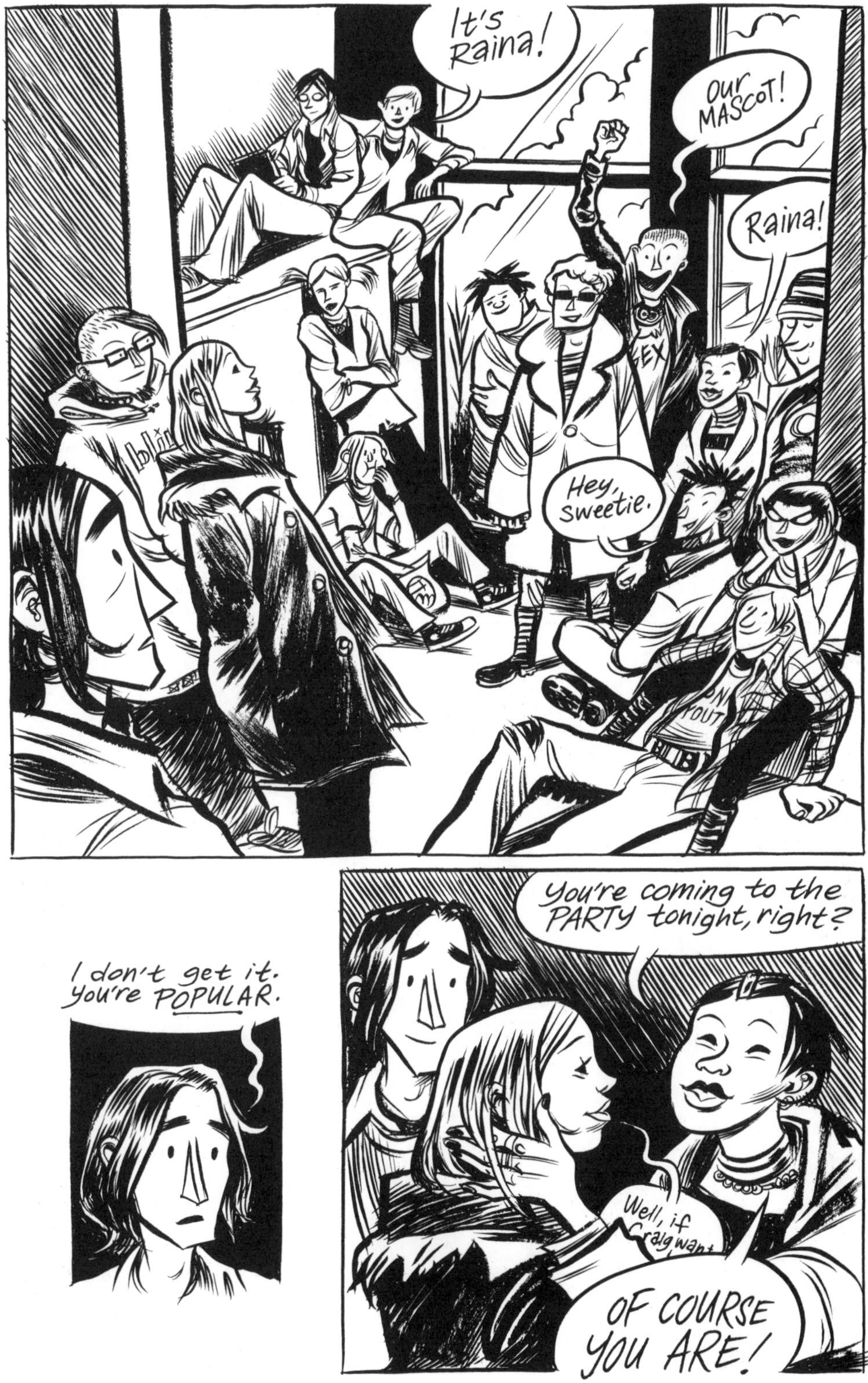
It's Raina!
Our MASCOT!
Raina!
Hey, sweetie.
I don't get it. You're POPULAR.
You're coming to the PARTY tonight, right?
Well, if Craig want
OF COURSE YOU ARE!

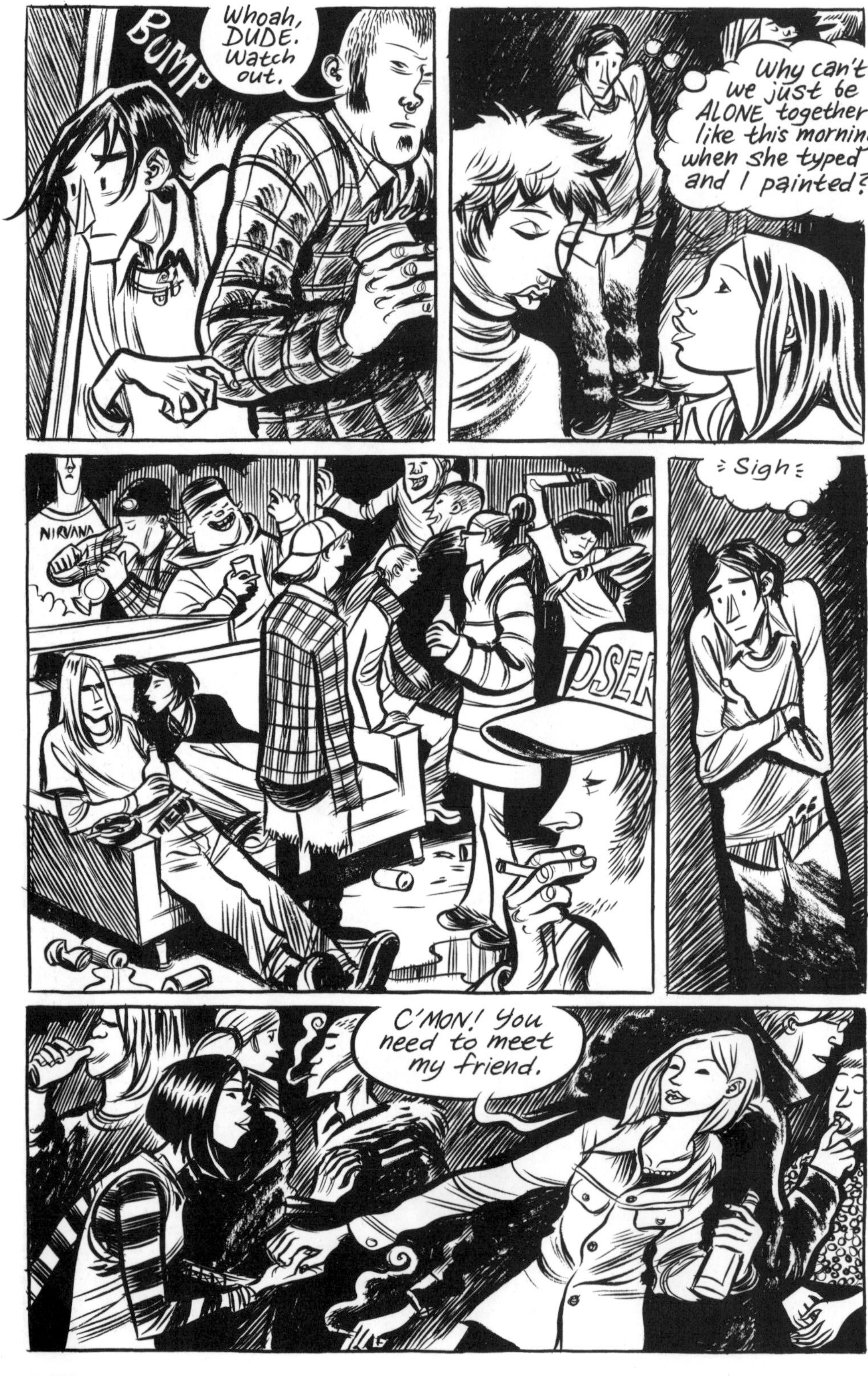
BUMP
Whoah, DUDE. Watch out.
Why can't we just be ALONE together- like this morning, when she typed and I painted?
NIRVANA
OSER
Sigh
C'MON! You need to meet my friend.

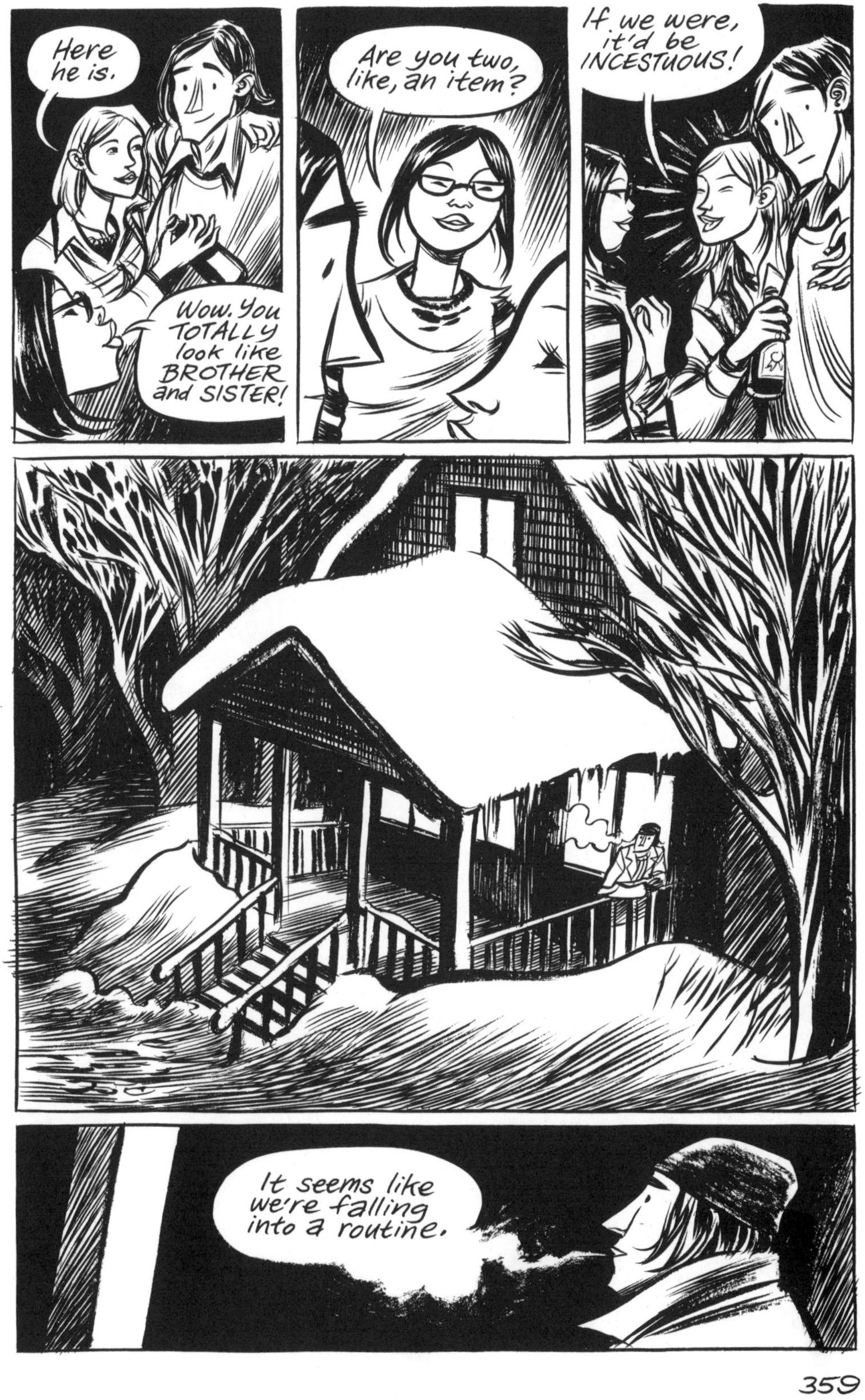
Here he is.
Wow. You TOTALLY look like BROTHER and SISTER!
Are you two, like, an item?
If we were, it'd be INCESTUOUS!
It seems like we're falling into a routine.

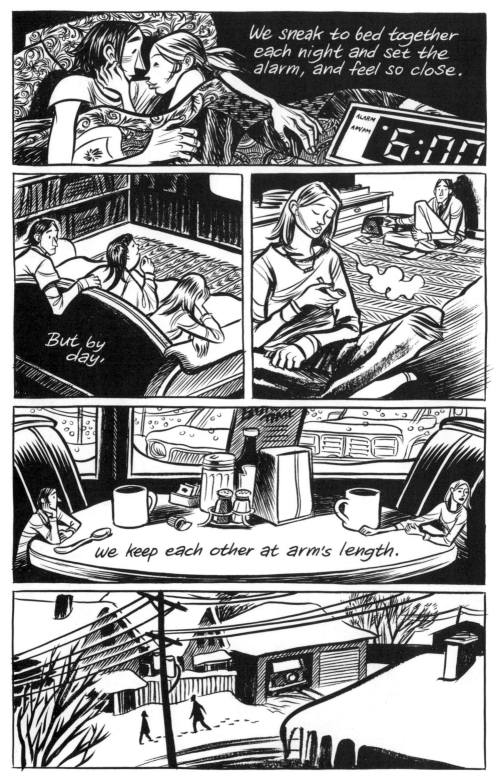

We sneak to bed together each night and set the alarm, and feel so close.

But by day.

we keep each other at arm's length.

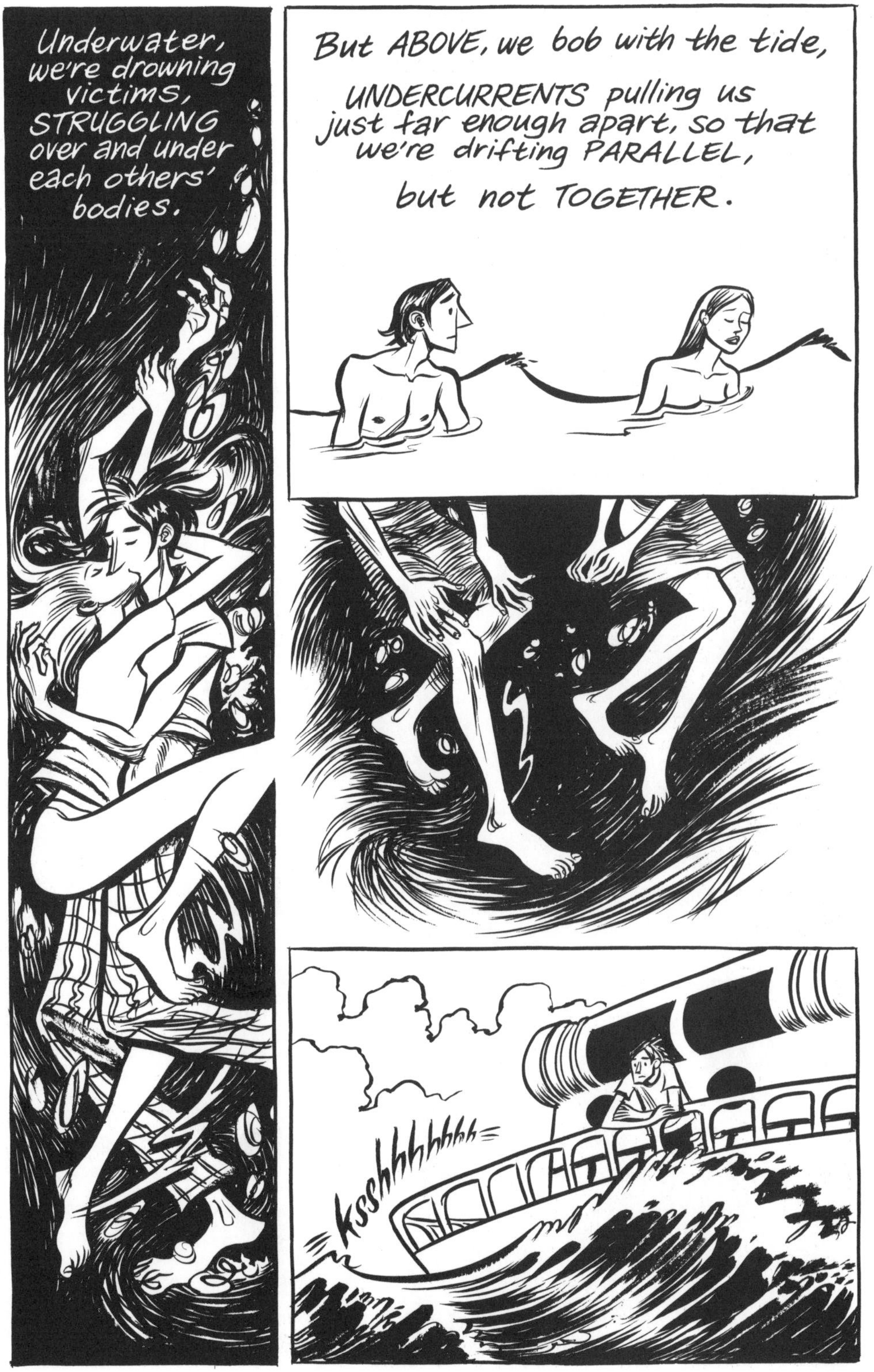
Underwater, we're drowning victims, STRUGGLING over and under each others' bodies.
But ABOVE, we bob with the tide,
UNDERCURRENTS pulling us just far enough apart, so that we're drifting PARALLEL,
but not TOGETHER.
ksshhhhhhhh

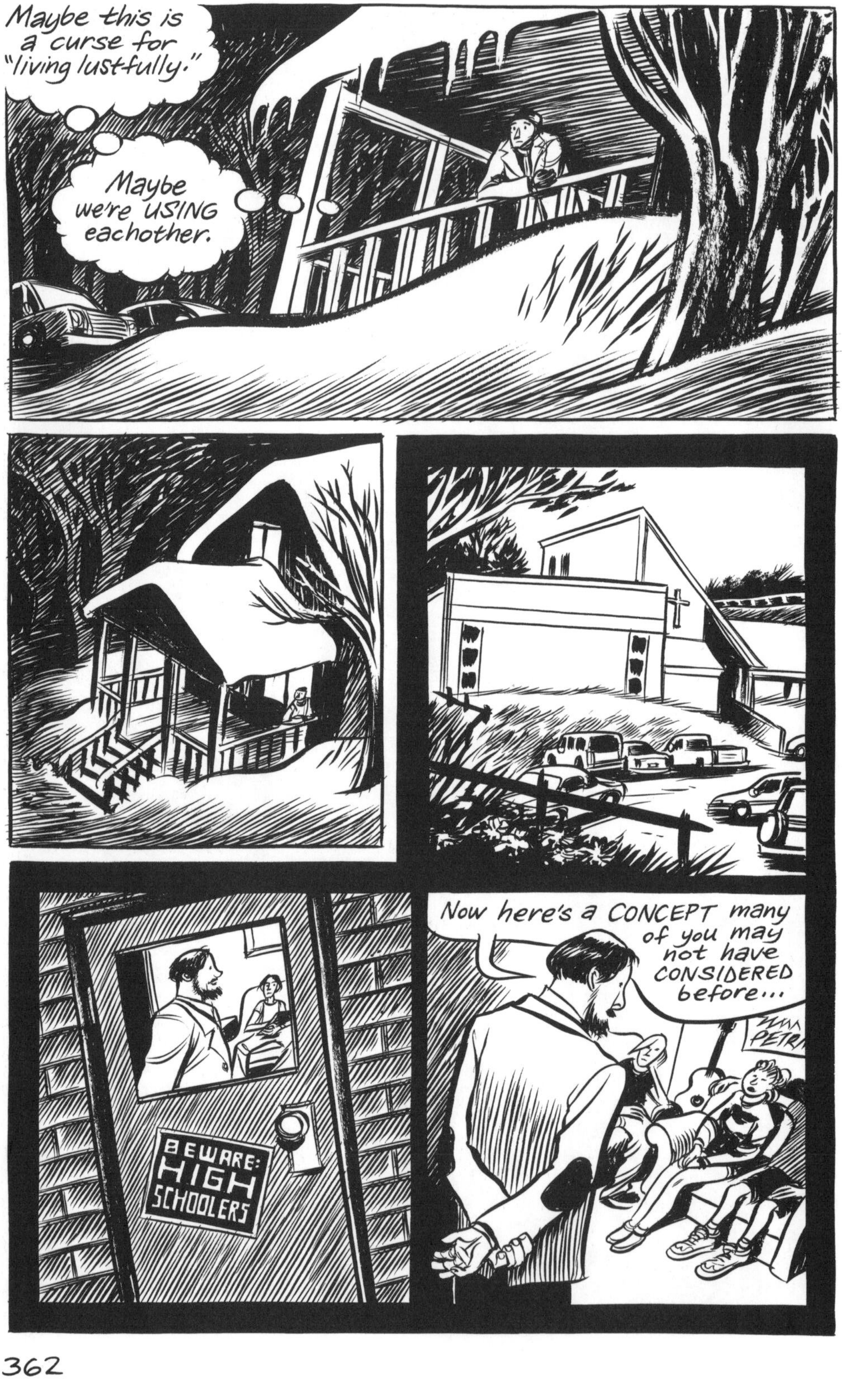
Maybe this is a curse for "living lustfully."
Maybe we're USING eachother.
BEWARE: HIGH SCHOOLERS
Now here's a CONCEPT many of you may not have CONSIDERED before...

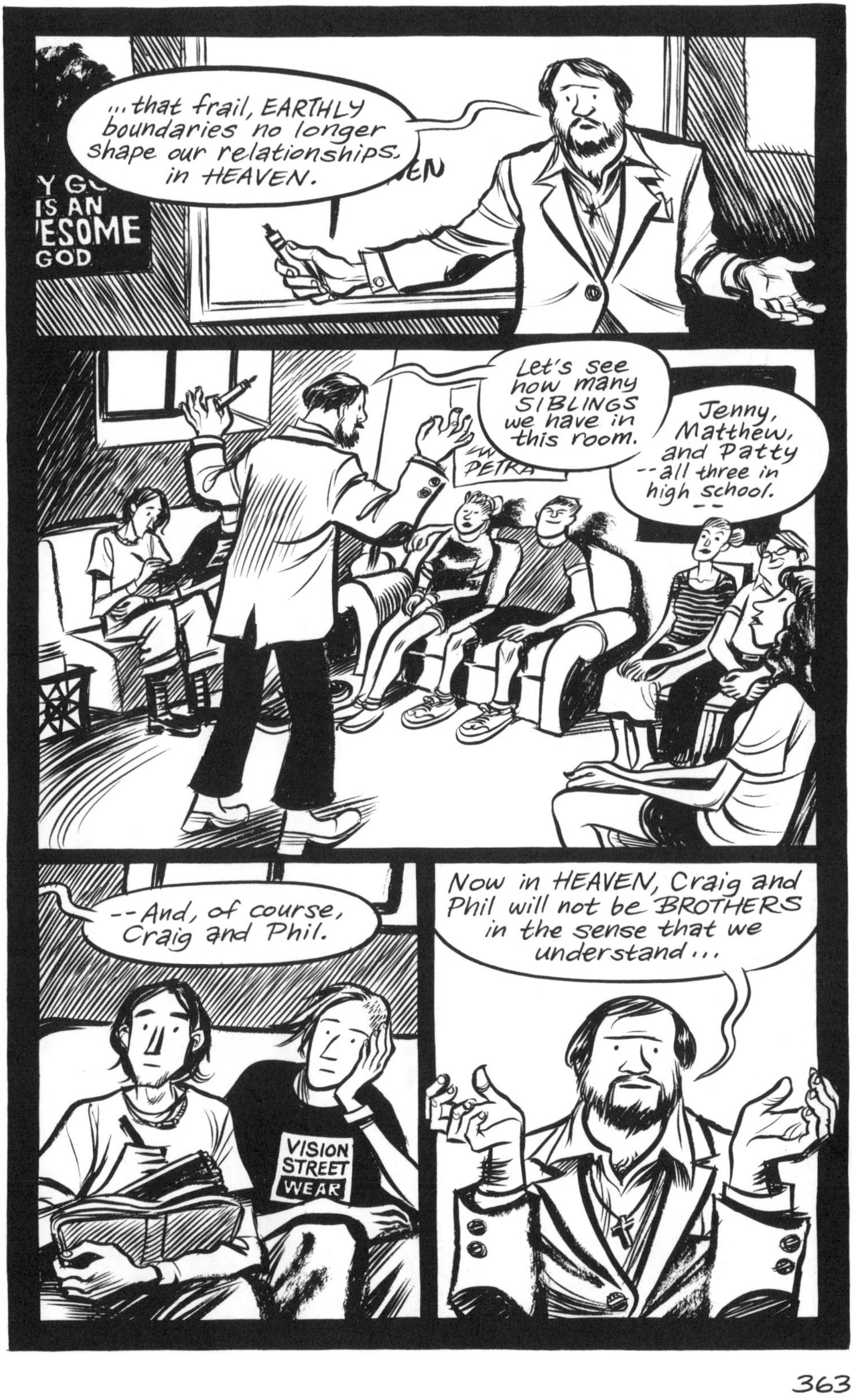
...that frail, EARTHLY boundaries no longer shape our relationships in HEAVEN.
Let's see how many SIBLINGS we have in this room.
Jenny, Matthew, and Patty --all three in high school--
--And, of course, Craig and Phil.
VISION STREET WEAR
Now in HEAVEN, Craig and Phil will not be BROTHERS in the sense that we understand...

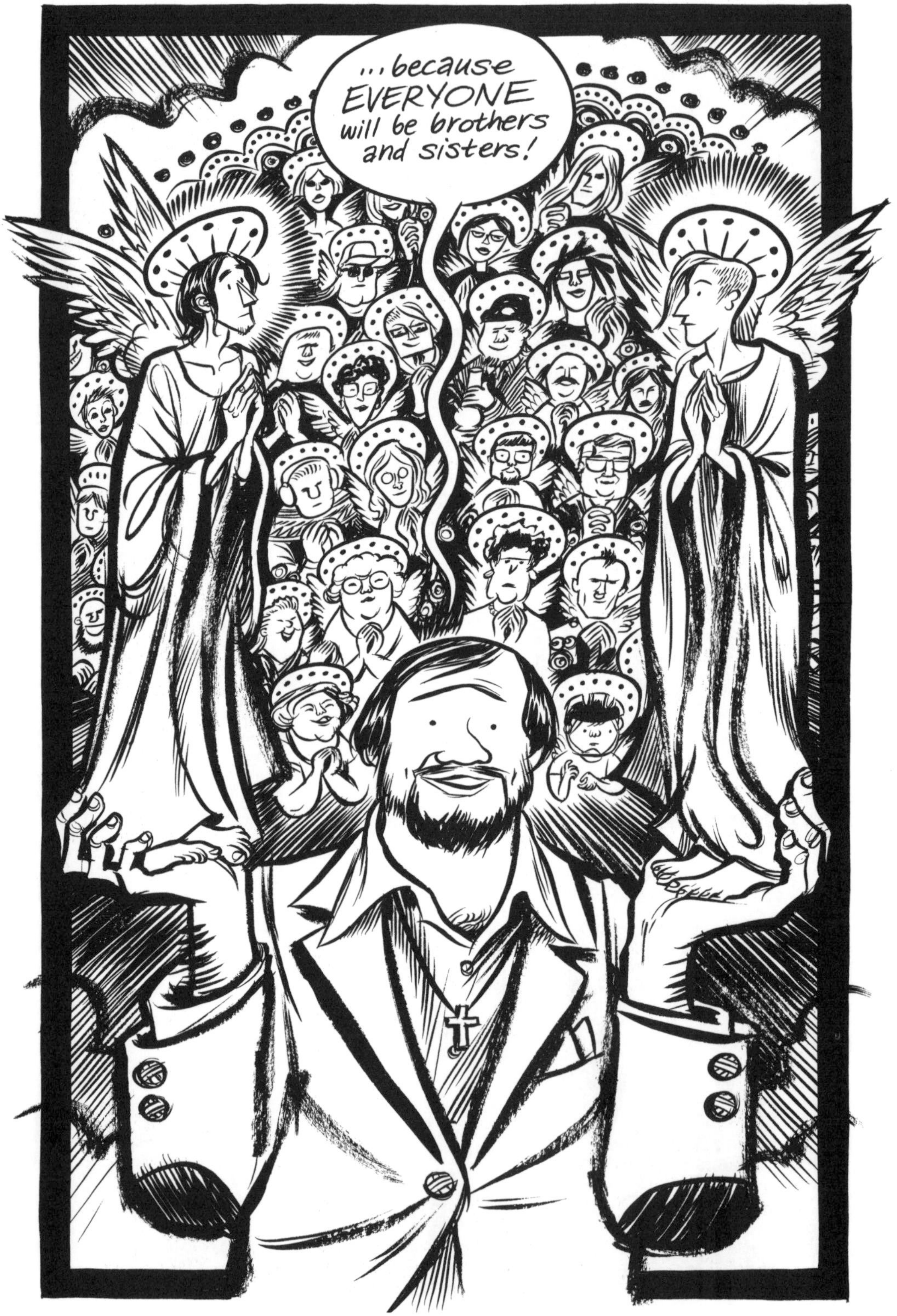
...because EVERYONE will be brothers and sisters!

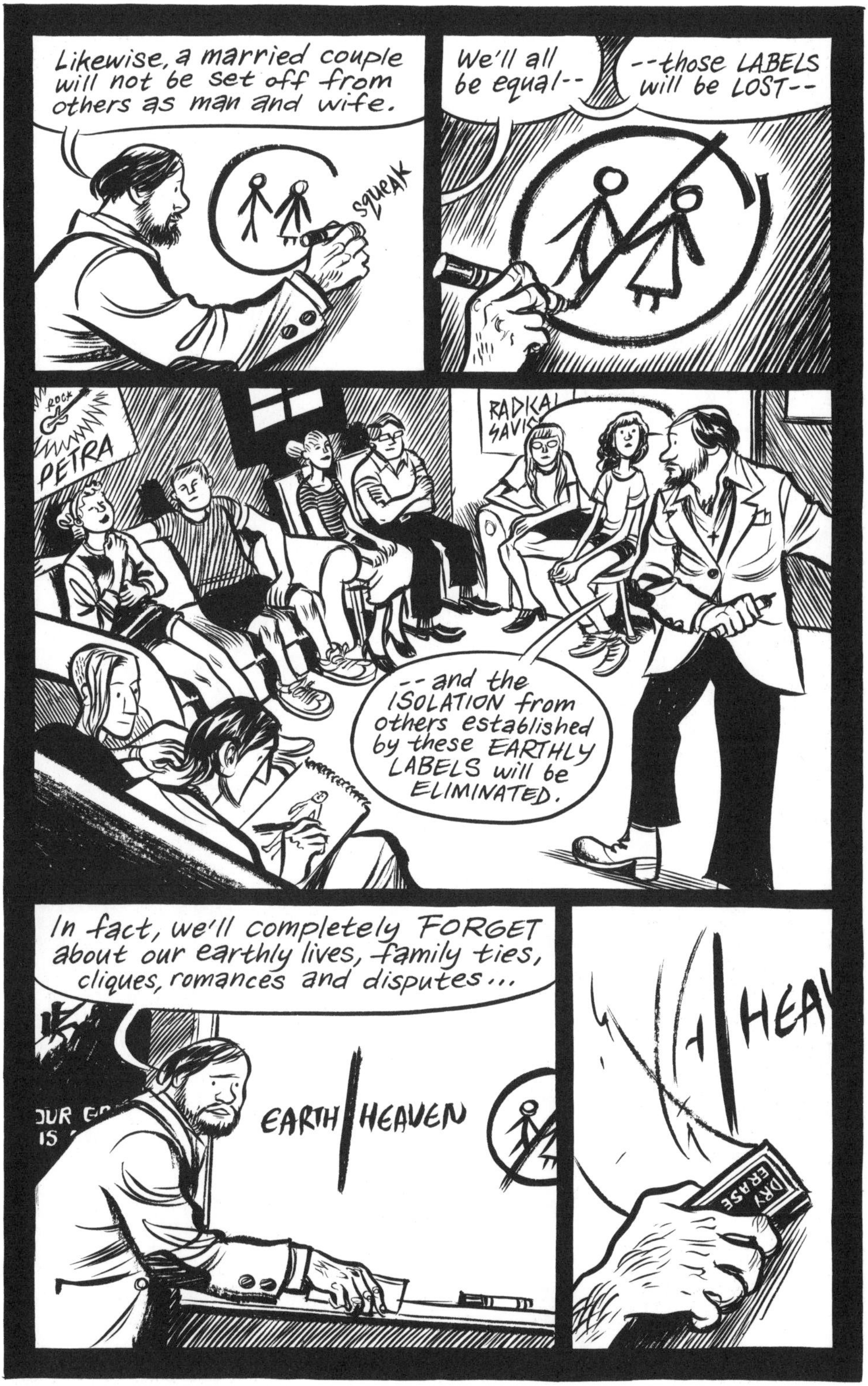
Likewise, a married couple will not be set off from others as man and wife.
SQUEAK
We'll all be equal--
--those LABELS will be LOST--
ROCK
PETRA
RADICAL SAVIO
--and the ISOLATION from others established by these EARTHLY LABELS will be ELIMINATED.
In fact, we'll completely FORGET about our earthly lives, family ties, cliques, romances and disputes...
EARTH HEAVEN
HEA
DRY ERASE

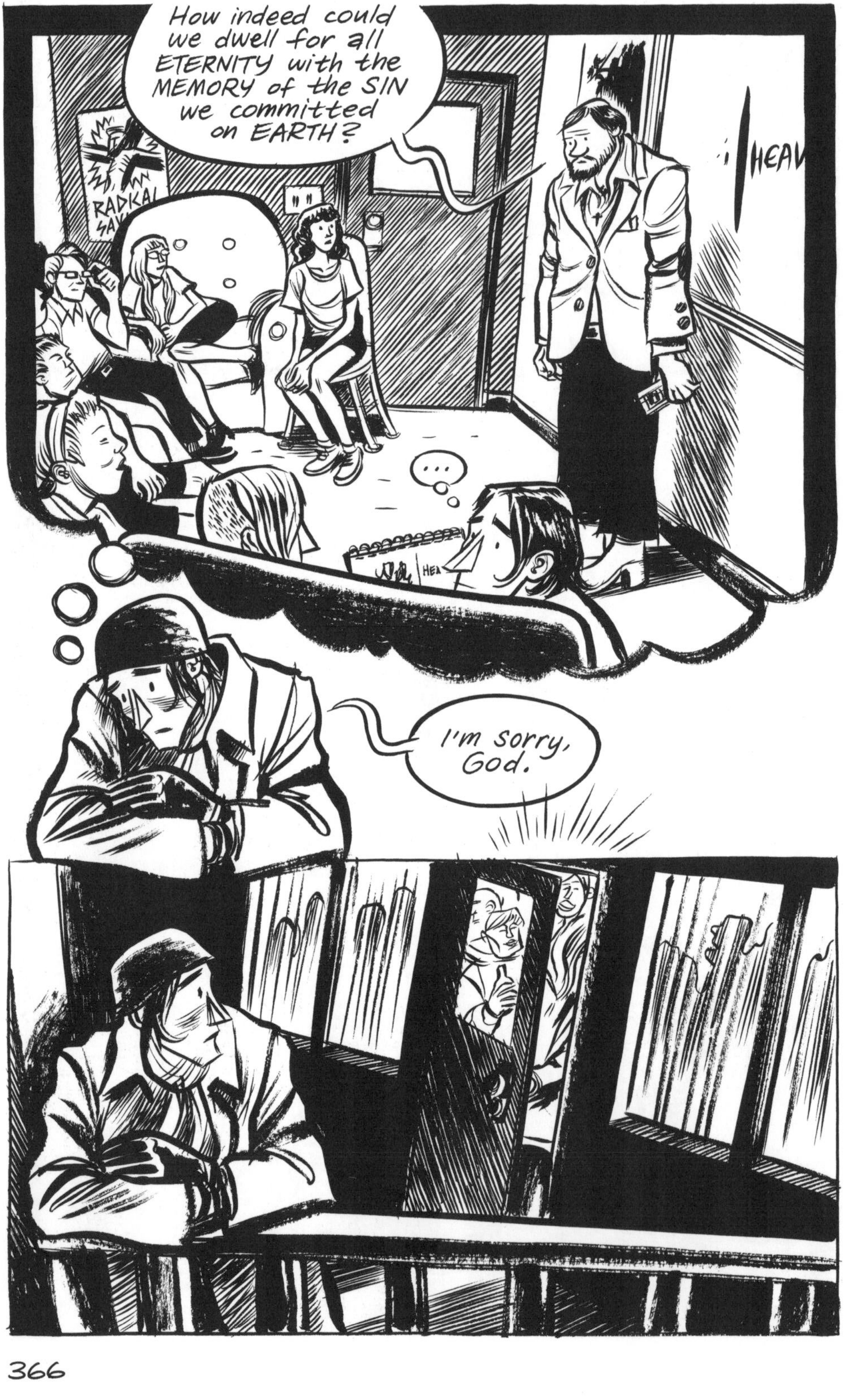
How indeed could we dwell for all ETERNITY with the MEMORY of the SIN we committed on EARTH?
HEAV
RADKAL SAV
...
HEA
I'm sorry, God.

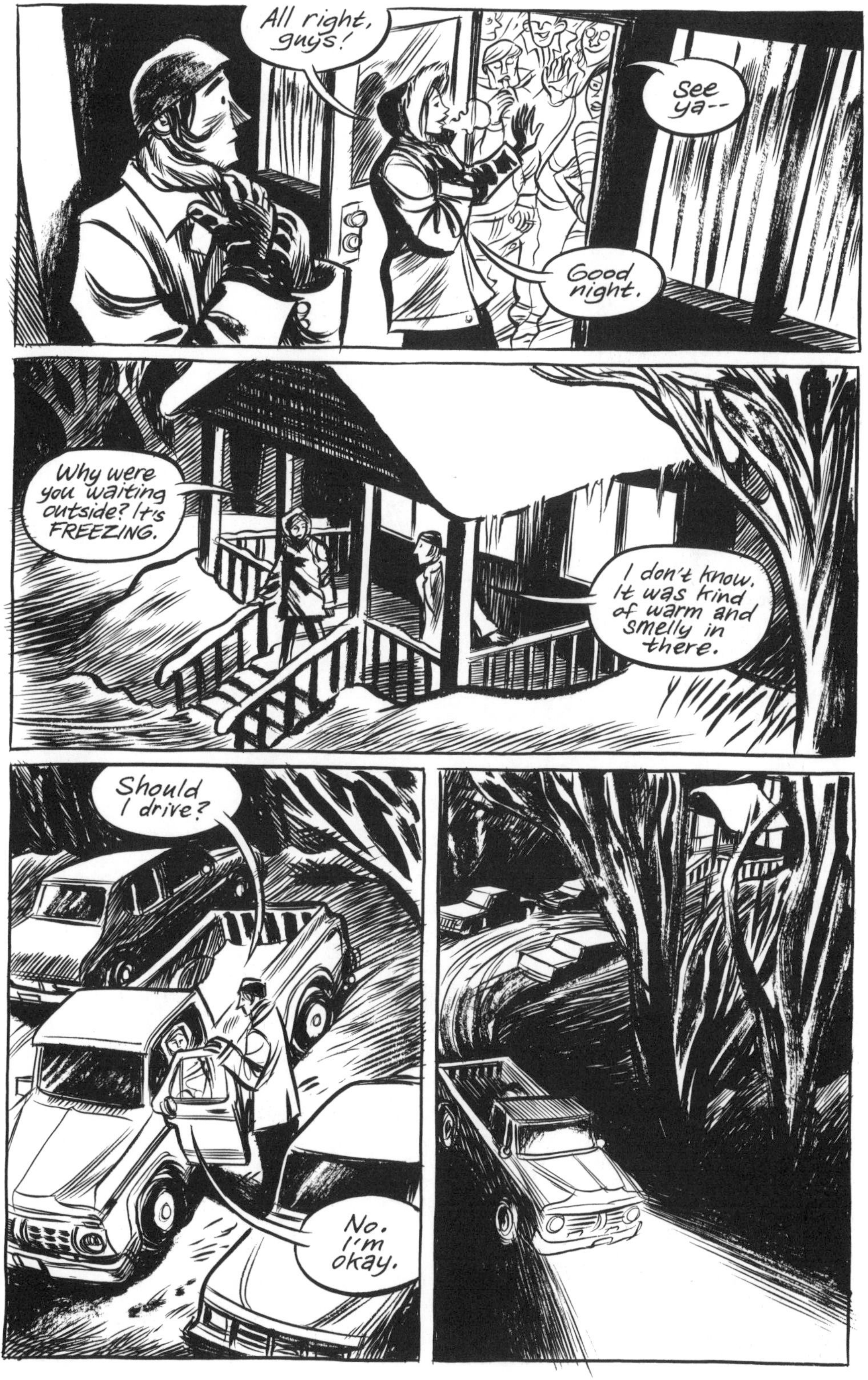
All right, guys!
See ya--
Good night.
Why were you waiting outside? It's FREEZING.
I don't know. It was kind of warm and smelly in there.
Should I drive?
No. I'm okay.

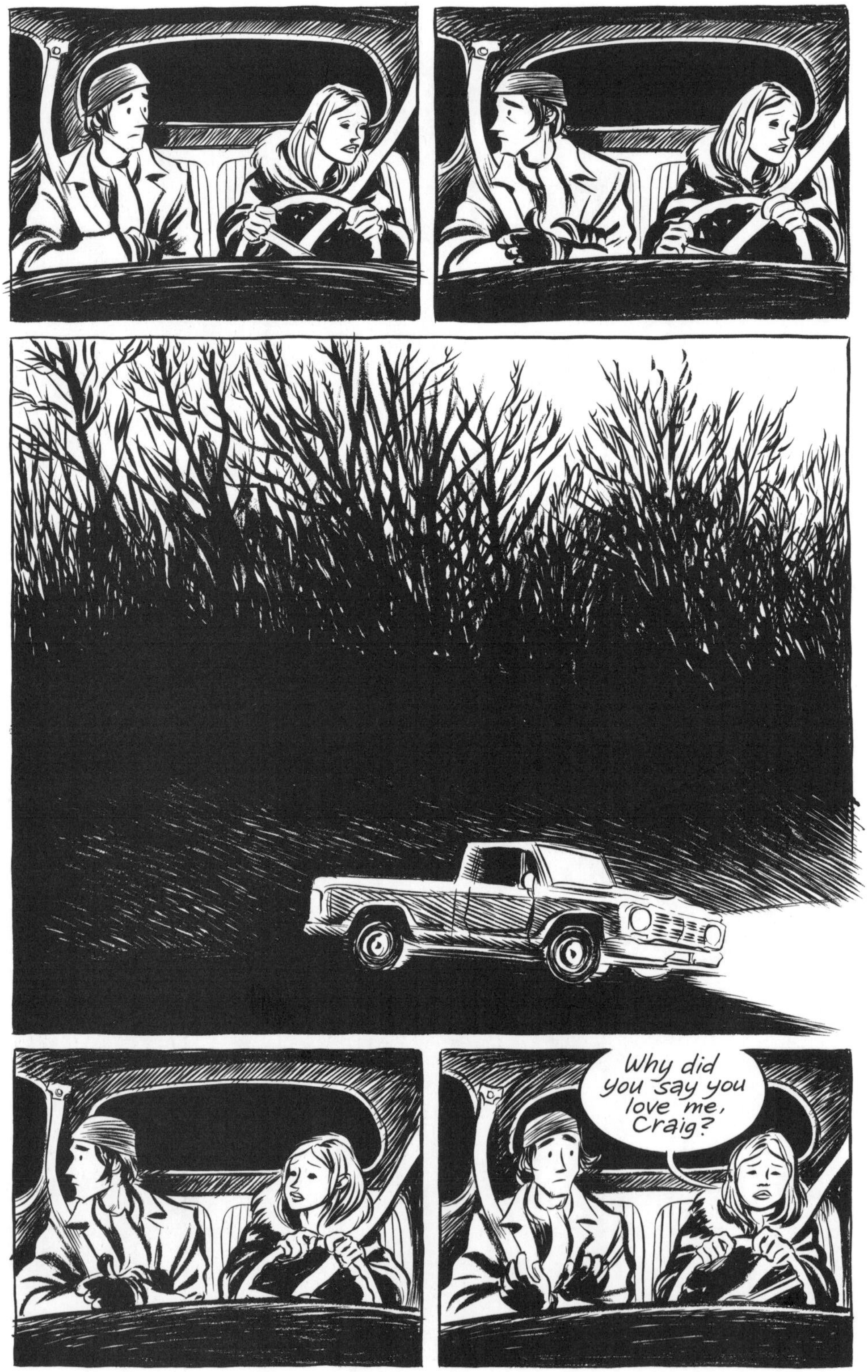
Why did you say you love me, Craig?

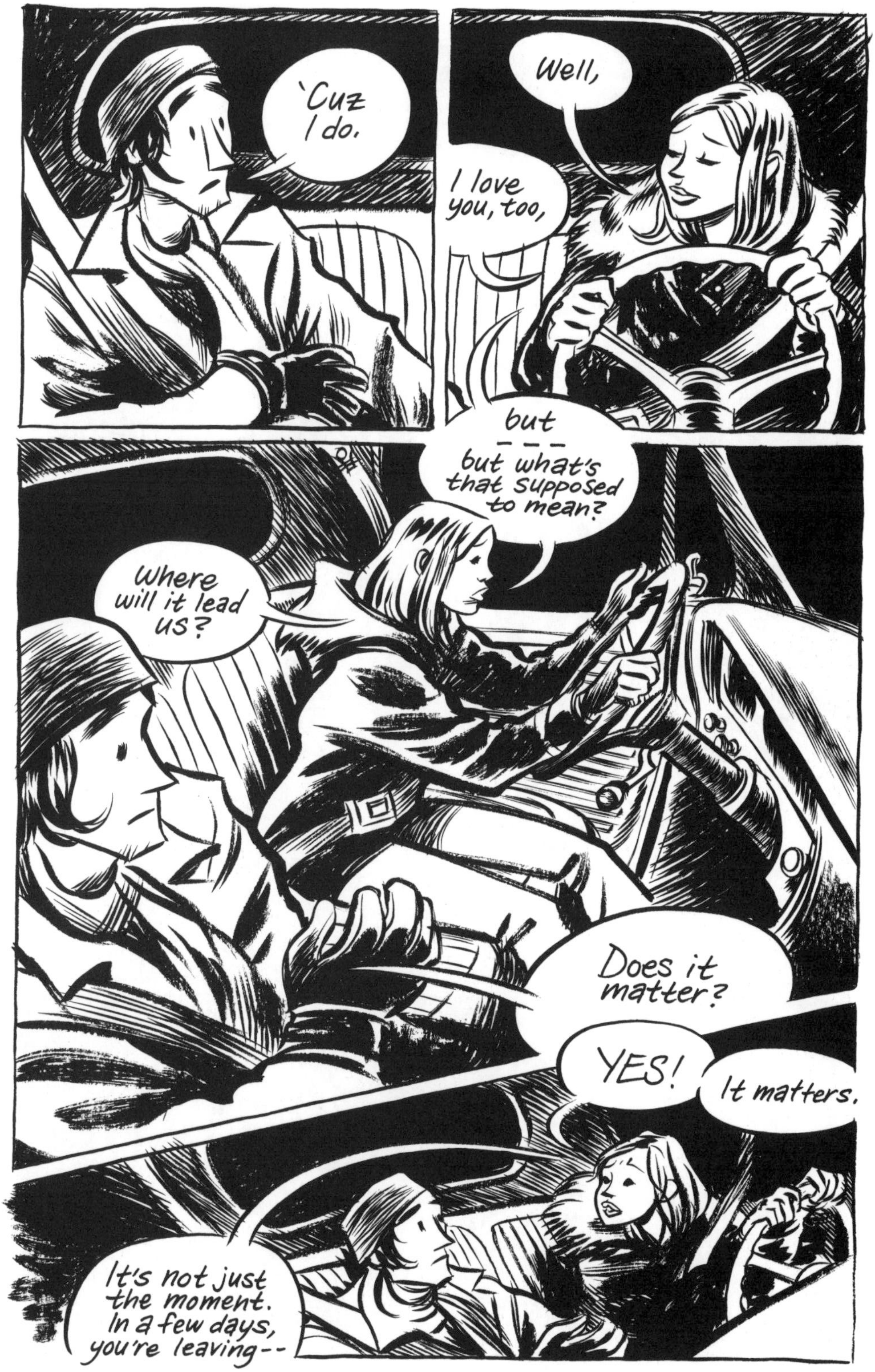
`Cuz I do.
Well,
I love you, too,
but --- but what's that supposed to mean?
Where will it lead us?
Does it matter?
YES!
It matters.
It's not just the moment. In a few days, you're leaving--

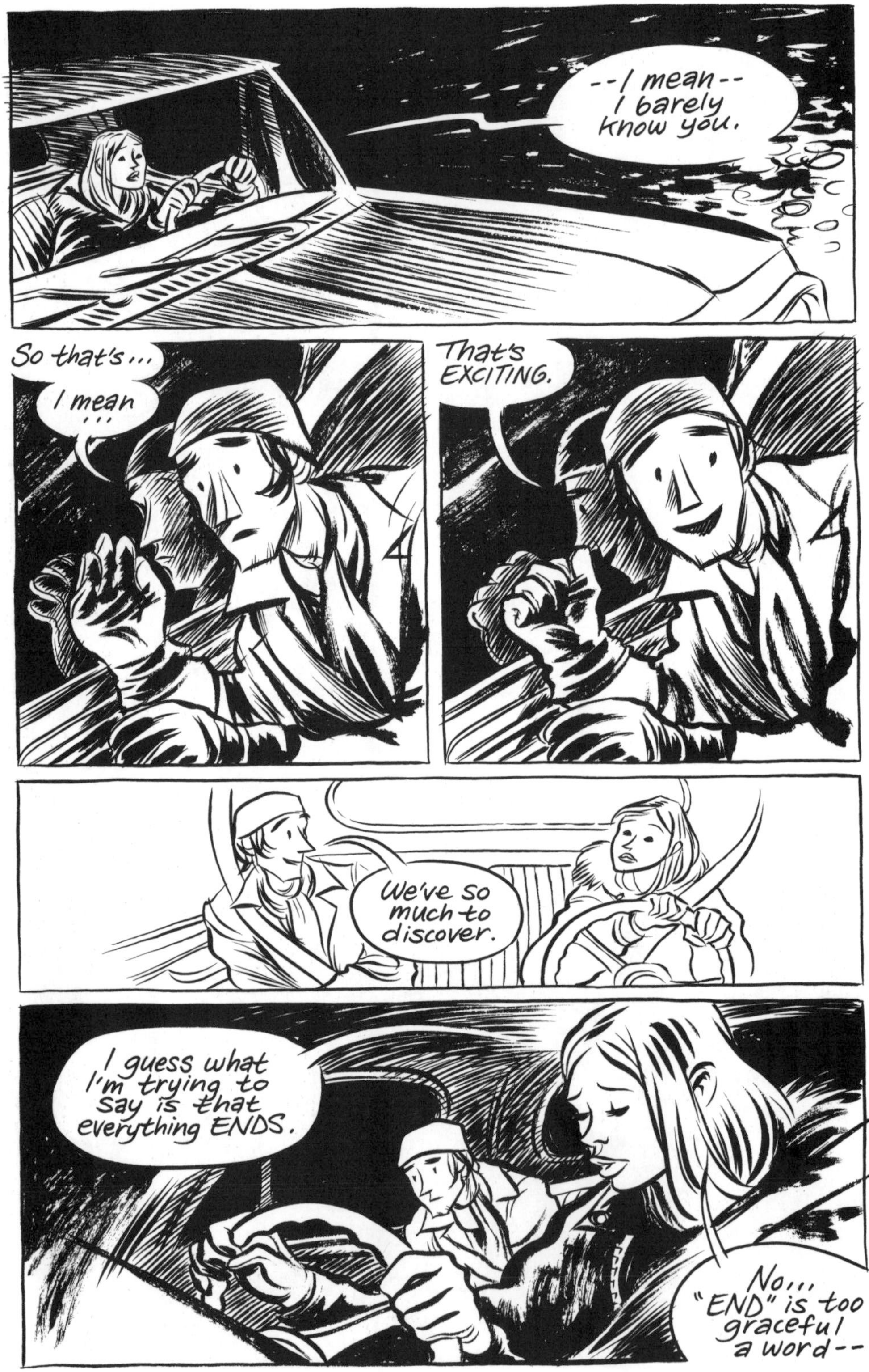
--I mean--
I barely know you.
So that's...
I mean
...
That's EXCITING.
We've so much to discover.
I guess what I'm trying to say is that everything ENDS.
No... "END" is too graceful a word--

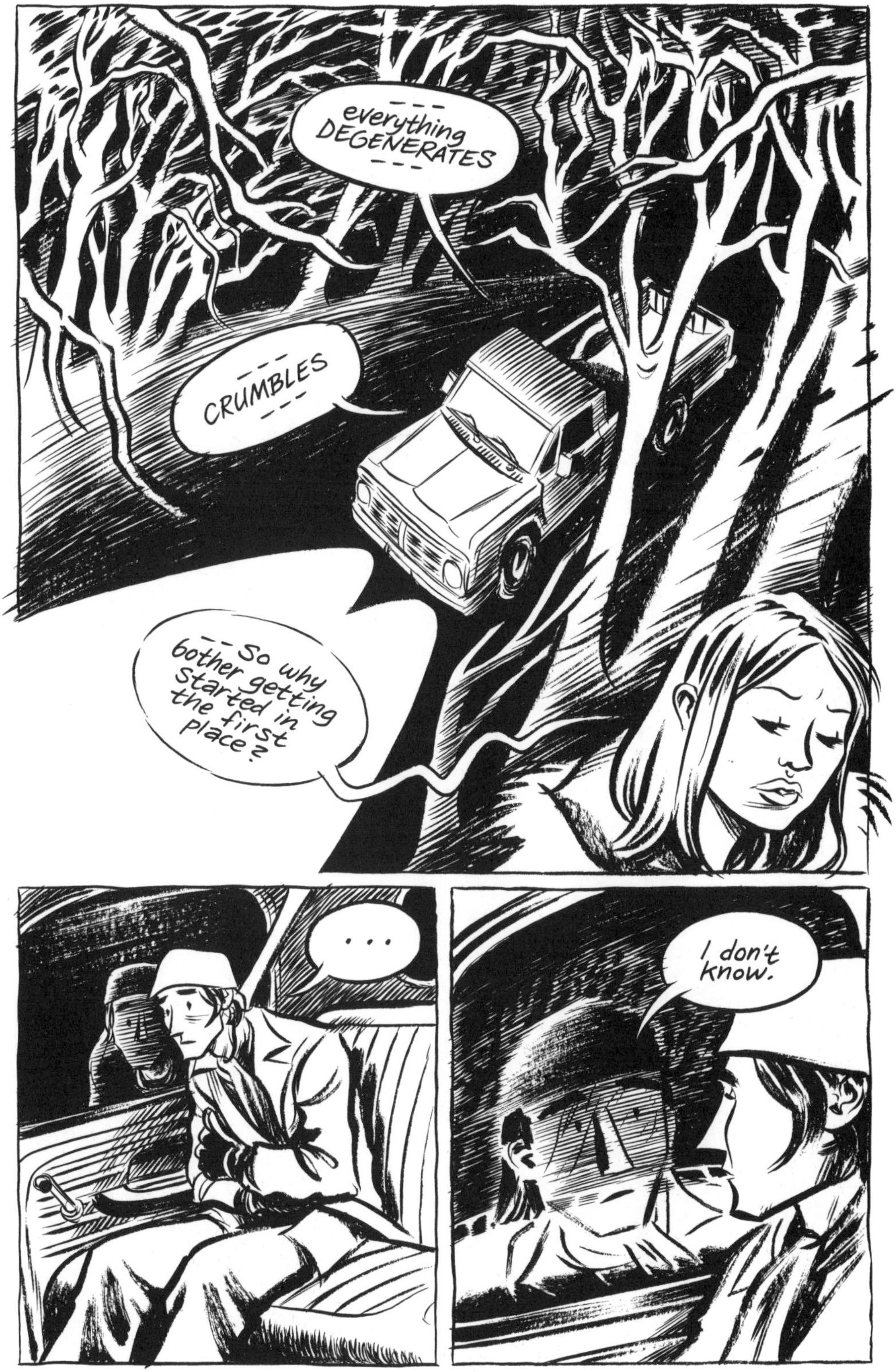
--- everything DEGENERATES ---
--- CRUMBLES ---
--- So why bother getting started in the first place?
...
I don't know.

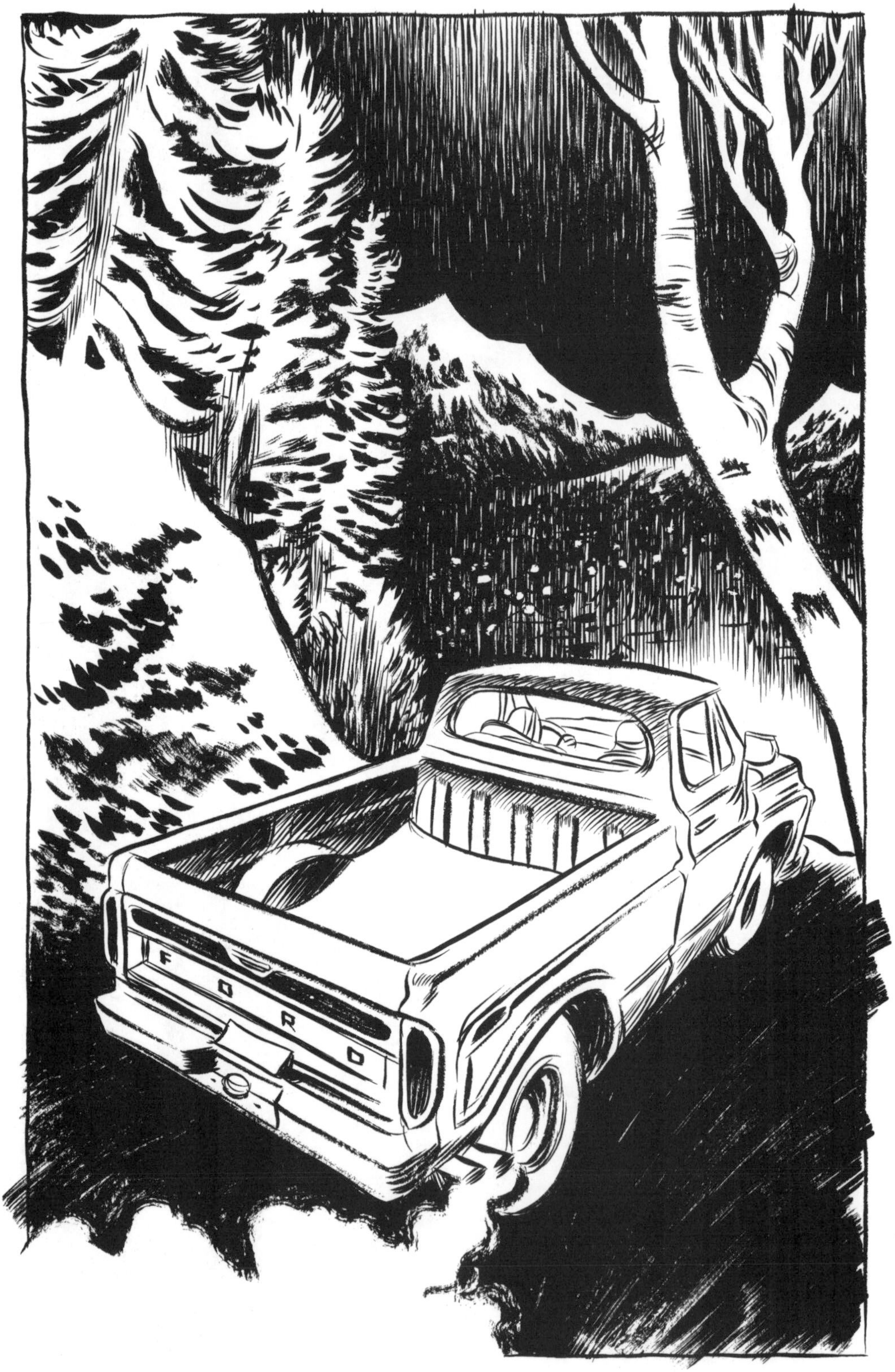
FORD

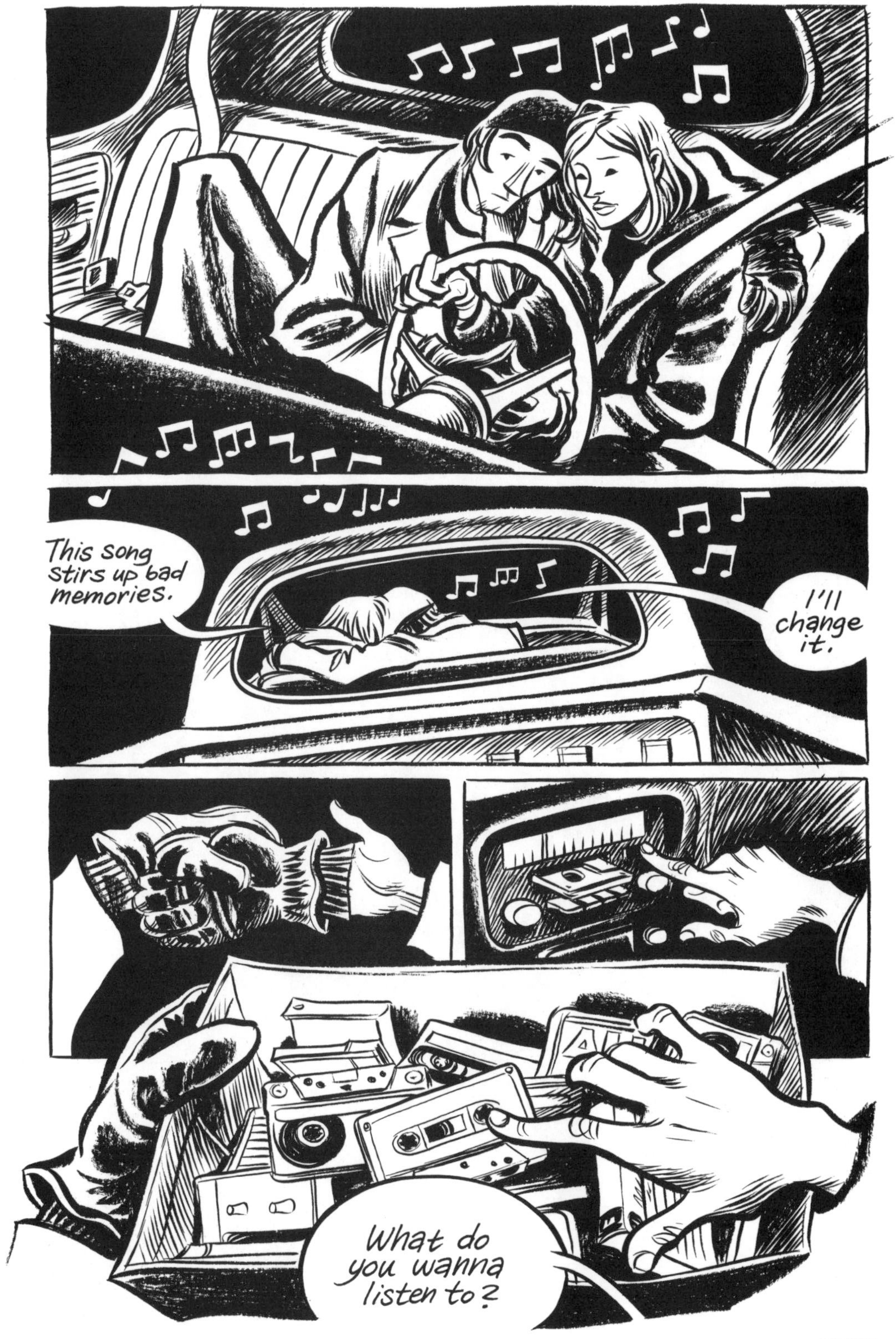
This song stirs up bad memories.
I'll change it.
What do you wanna listen to?

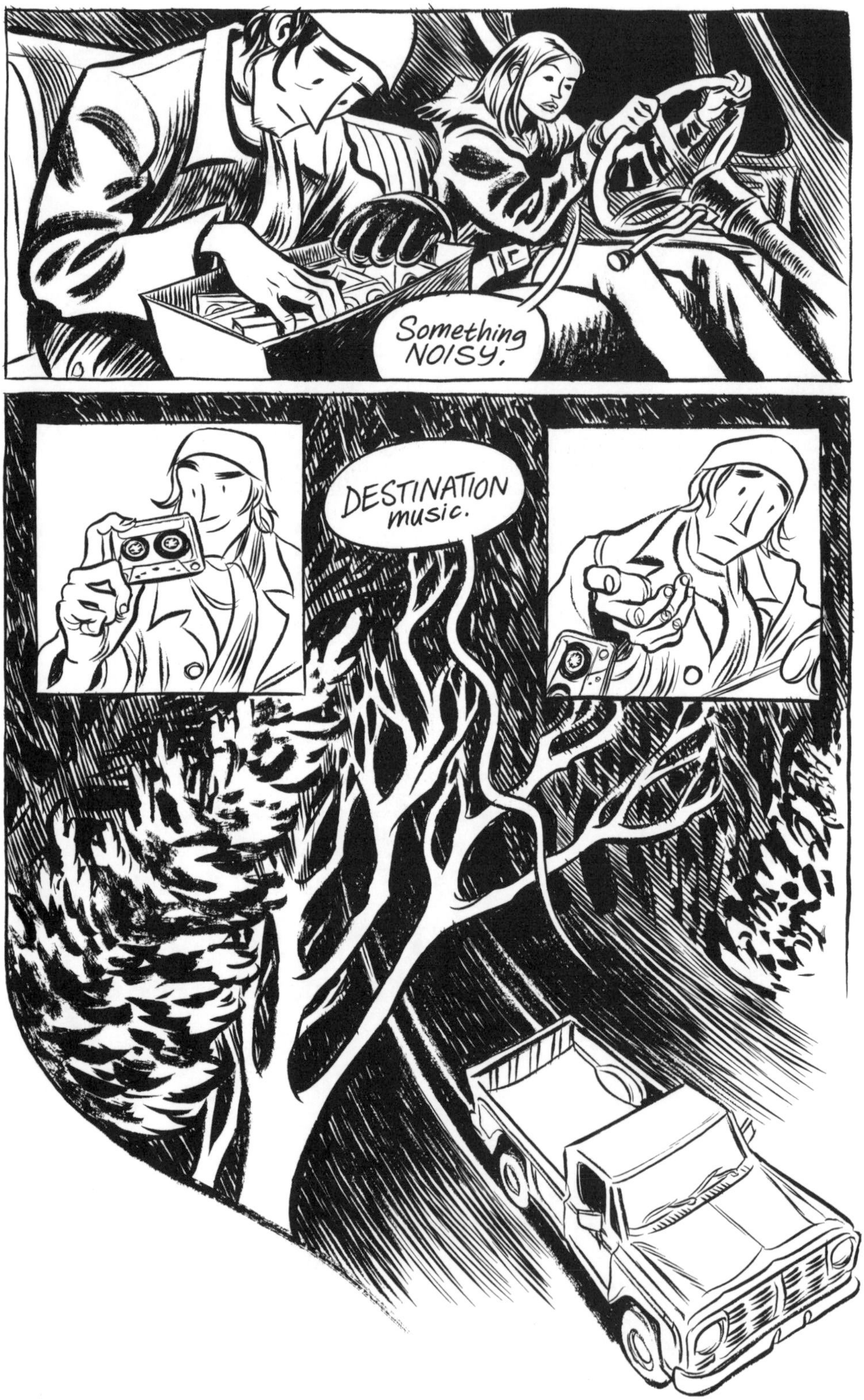
Something NOISY.
DESTINATION music.

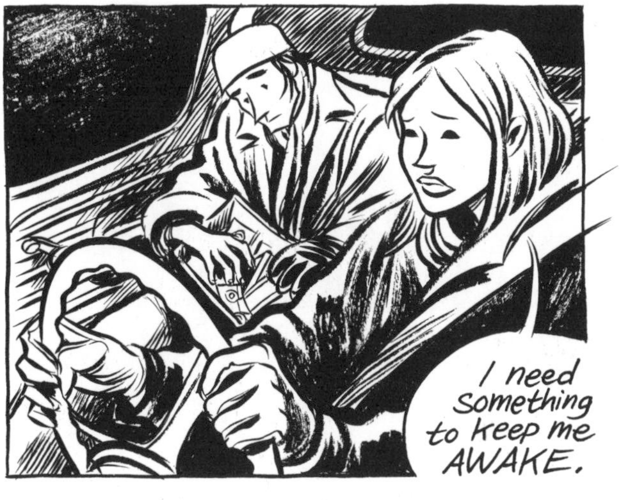
I need something to keep me AWAKE.

VII

Just Like Heaven

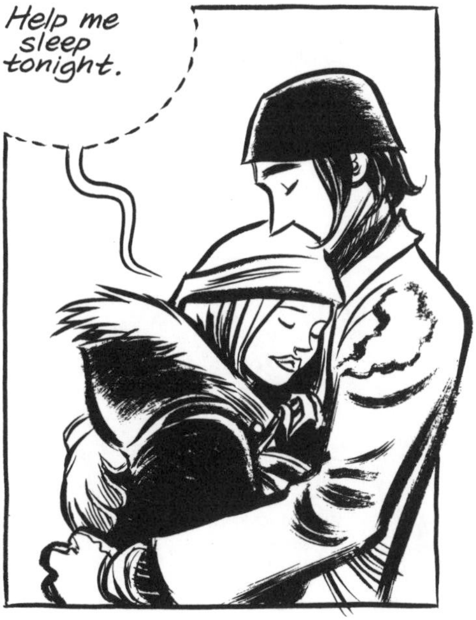
Help me sleep tonight.

That's what she asked of me the day we returned to the mountain.

Clouds of breath lingered at her chapped lips.

VASELINE

It was overcast--

--chillier than before--

--much too cold to lay all day in the snow.

The plants and trees were LACQUERED with an icy coating that made them BRITTLE to the touch.

SNAP

I'm sorry, tree.

More than the weather had changed, however.

378

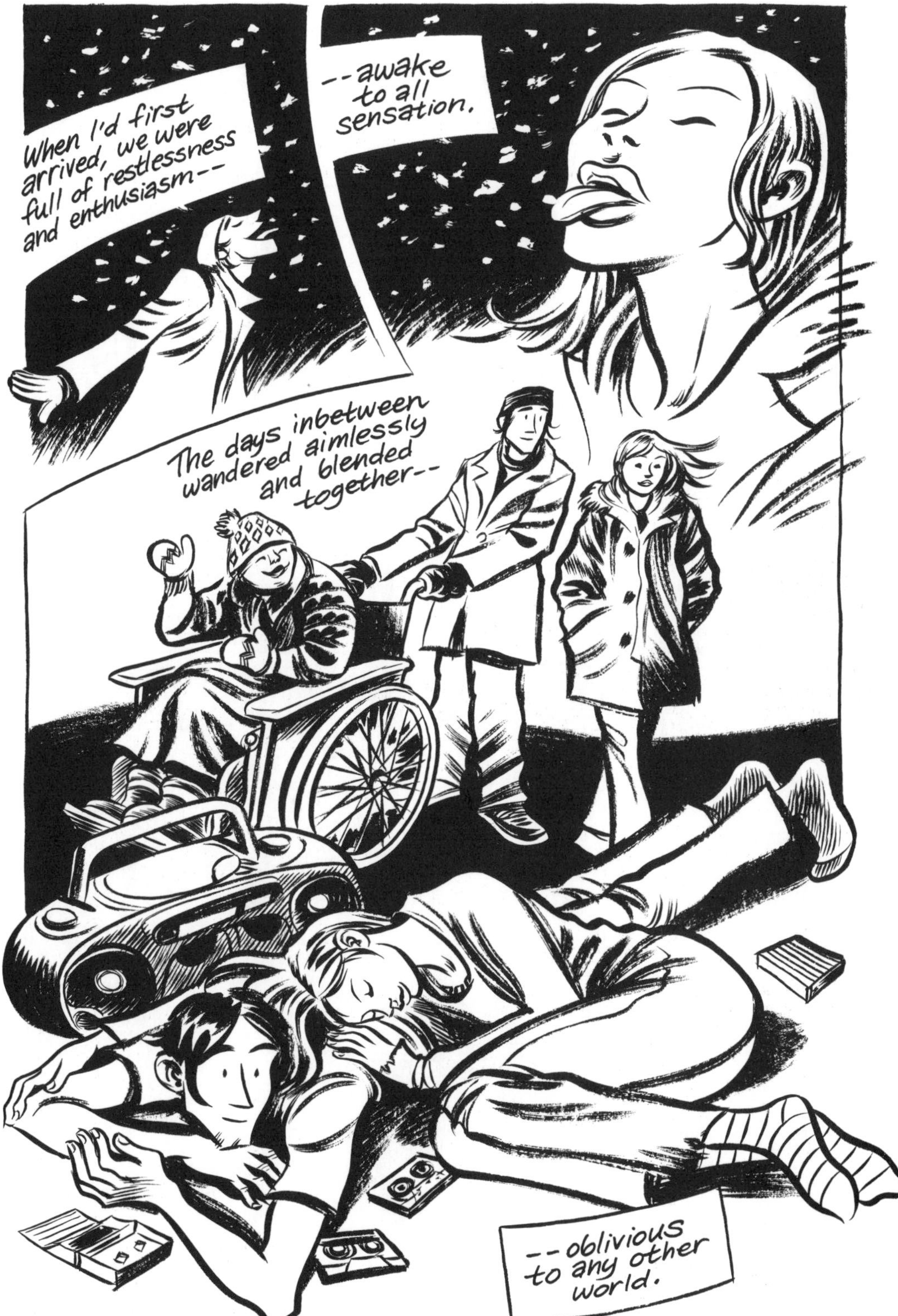

When I'd first arrived, we were full of restlessness and enthusiasm--
--awake to all sensation.
The days inbetween wandered aimlessly and blended together--
--oblivious to any other world.

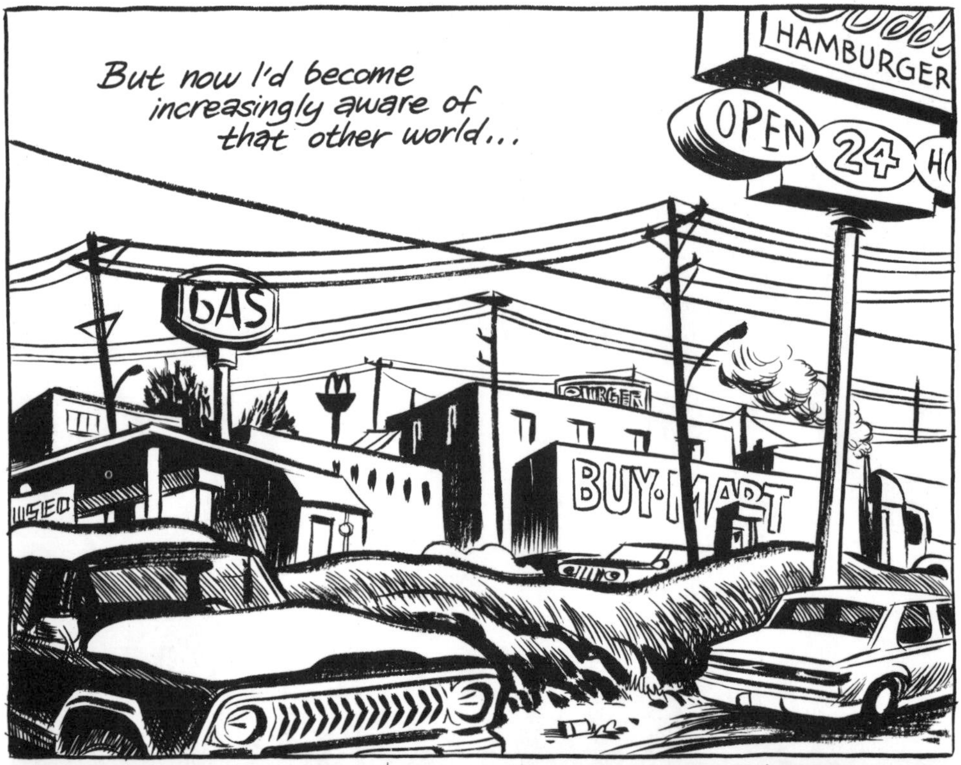
But now I'd become increasingly aware of that other world...
HAMBURGER
OPEN
24
GAS
BUY·MART

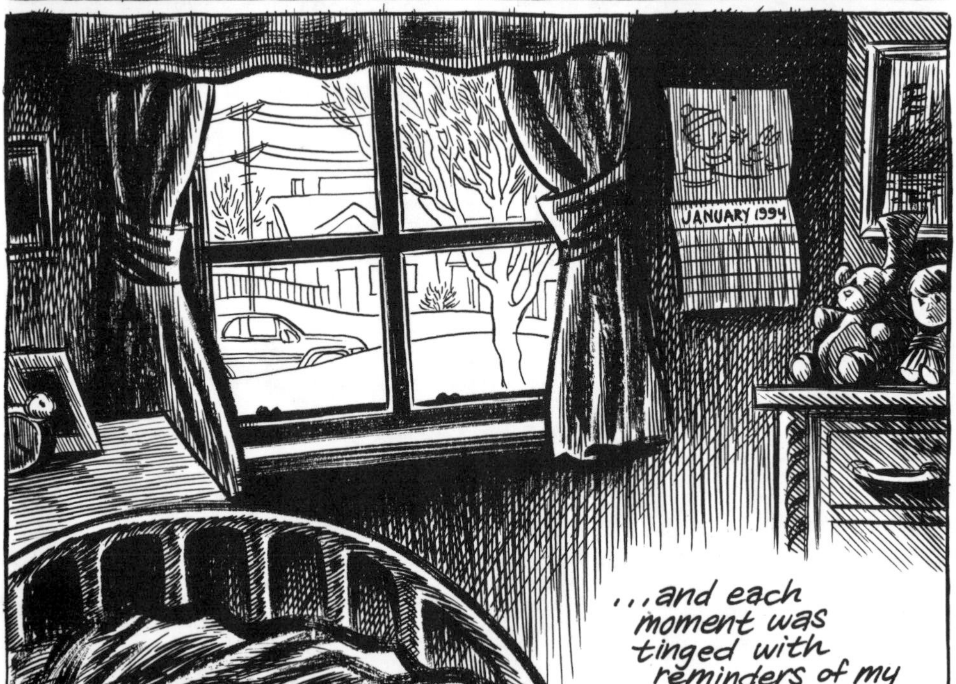
JANUARY 1994
...and each moment was tinged with reminders of my return home.

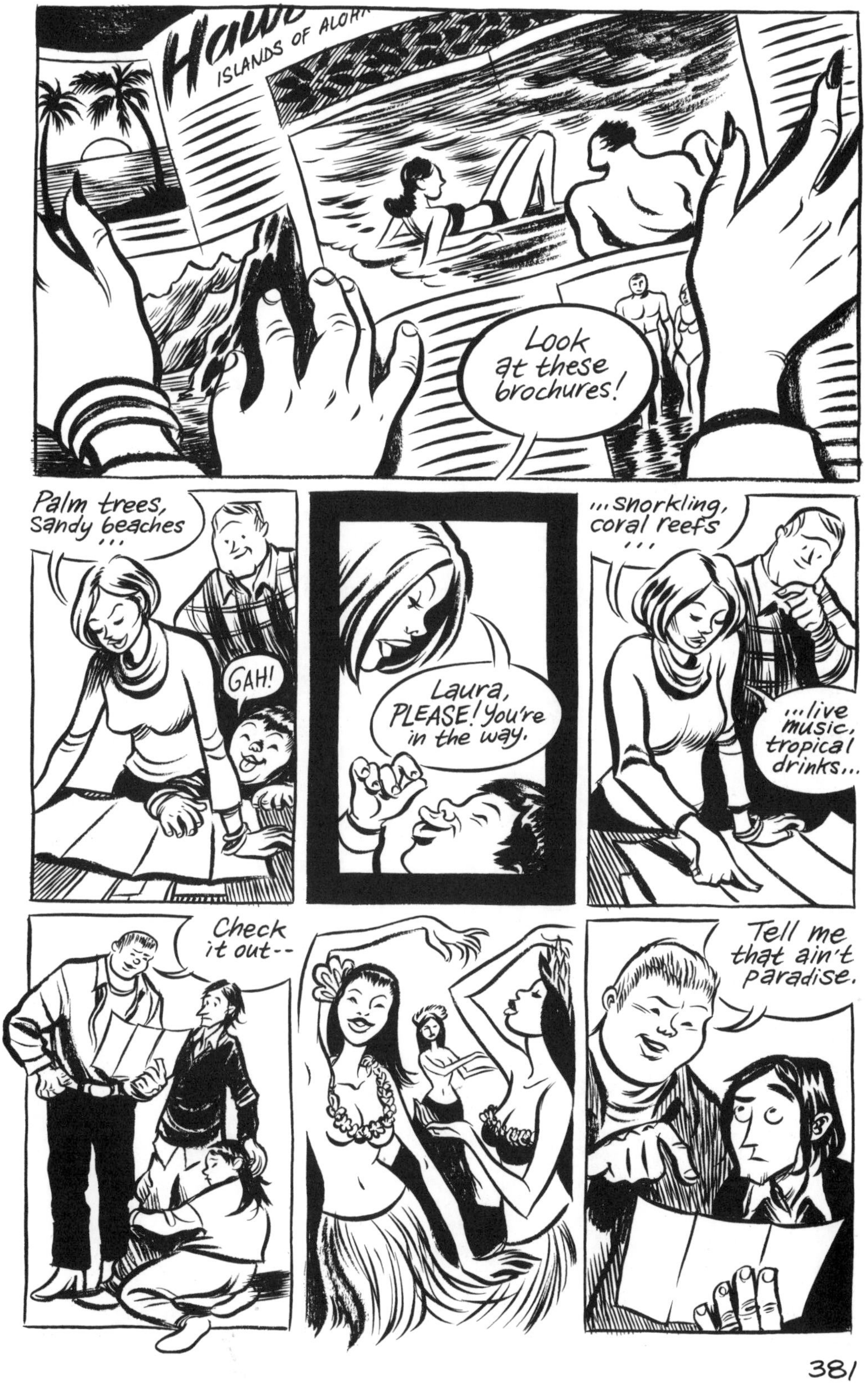

HAWAII
ISLANDS OF ALOHA
Look at these brochures!
Palm trees, sandy beaches . . .
GAH!
Laura, PLEASE! You're in the way.
...snorkling, coral reefs . . .
...live music, tropical drinks...
Check it out--
Tell me that ain't paradise.

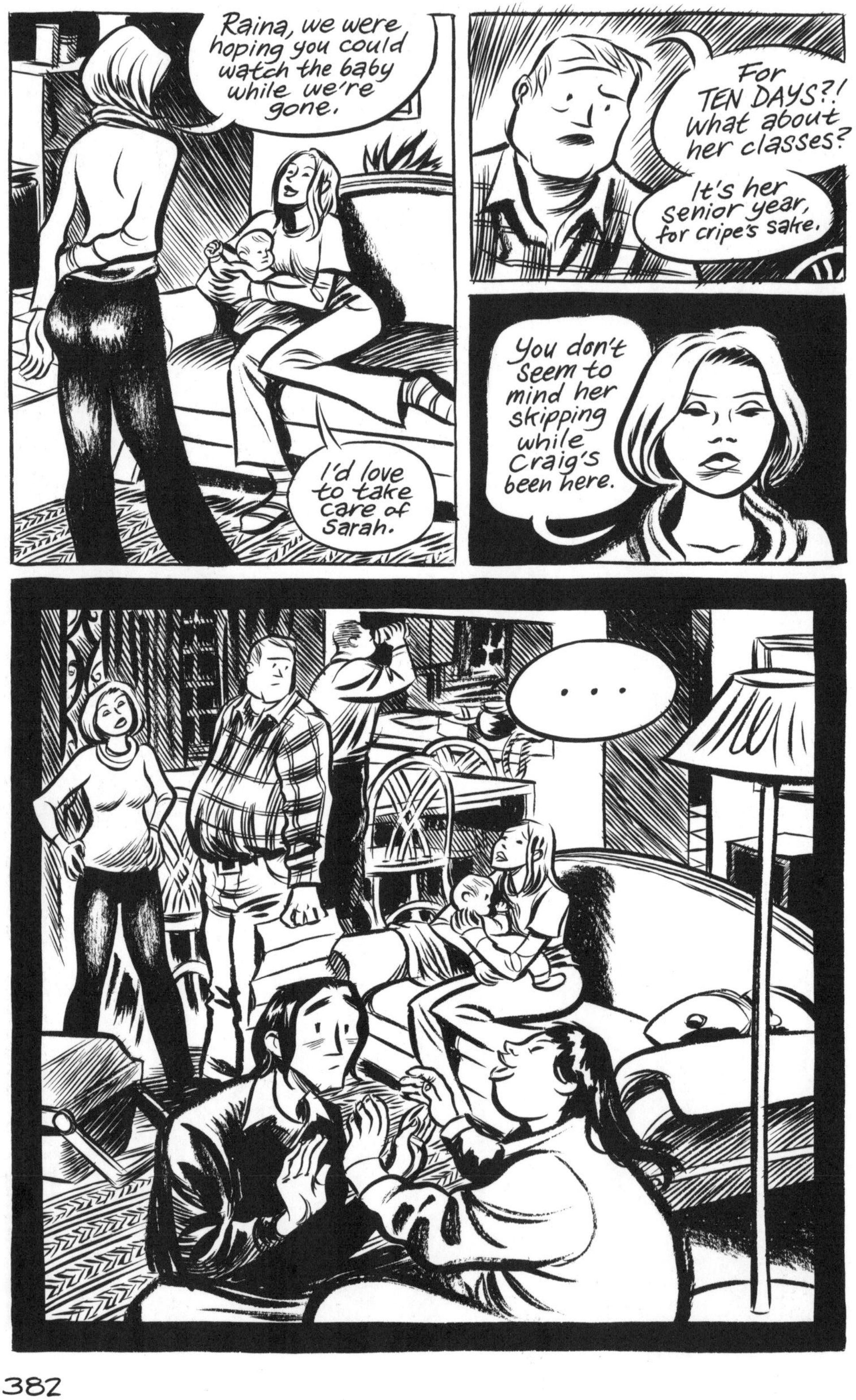
Raina, we were hoping you could watch the baby while we're gone.
I'd love to take care of Sarah.
For TEN DAYS?! what about her classes?
It's her senior year, for cripe's sake.
You don't seem to mind her skipping while Craig's been here.
. . .

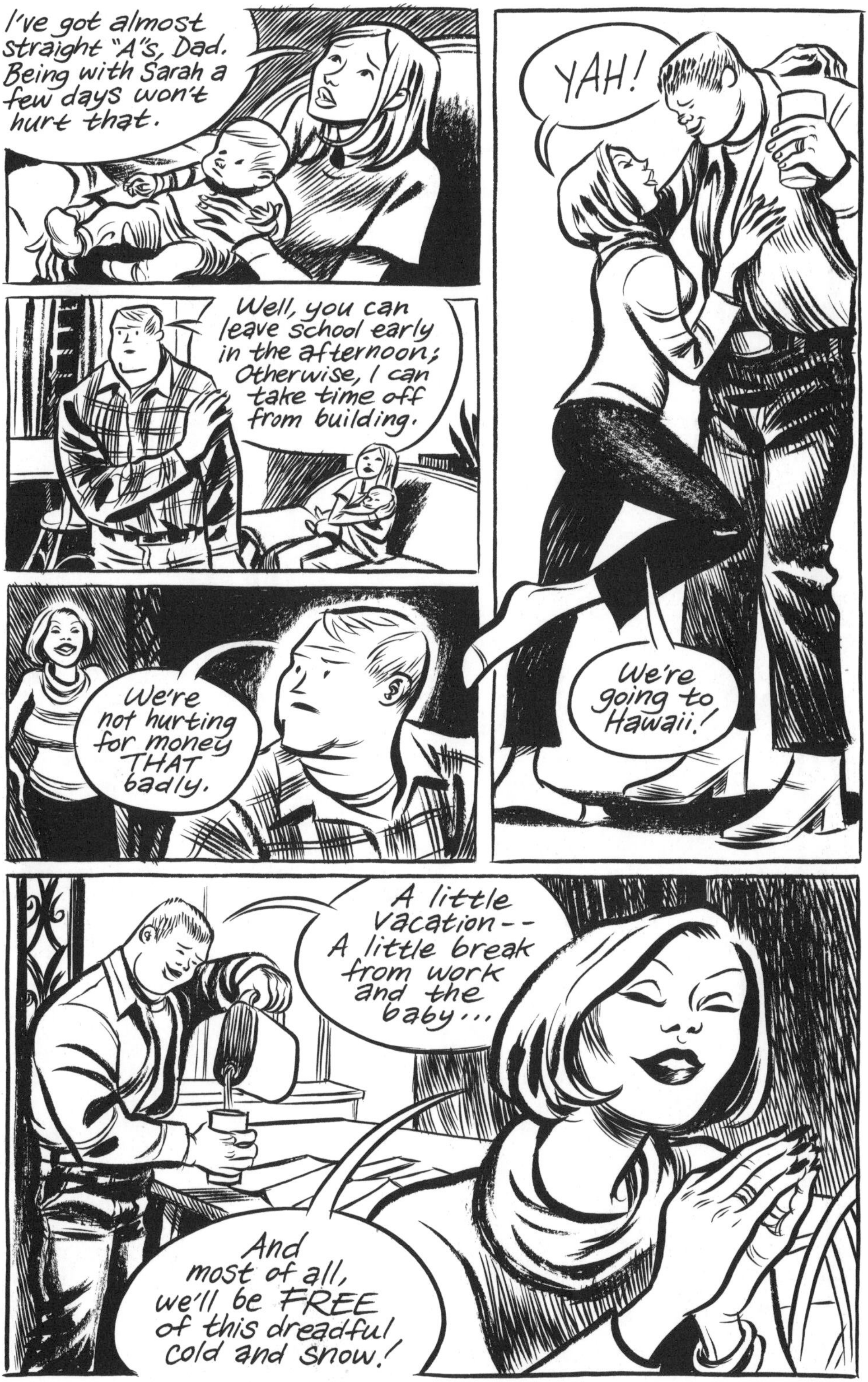
I've got almost straight "A's, Dad. Being with Sarah a few days won't hurt that.
Well, you can leave school early in the afternoon; Otherwise, I can take time off from building.
We're not hurting for money THAT badly.
YAH!
We're going to Hawaii!
A little vacation-- A little break from work and the baby...
And most of all, we'll be FREE of this dreadful cold and snow!

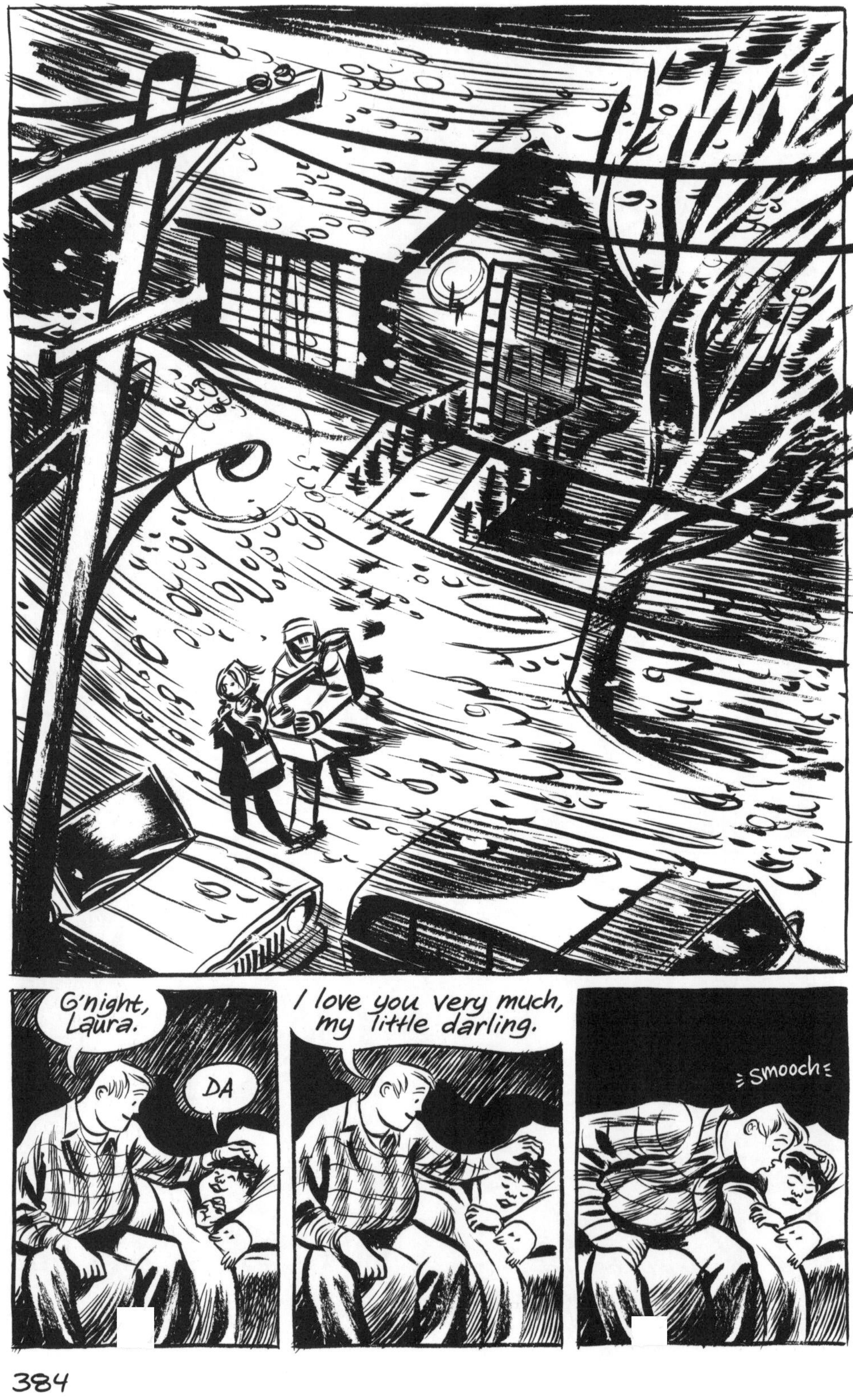
G'night, Laura.
DA
I love you very much, my little darling.
SMOOCH

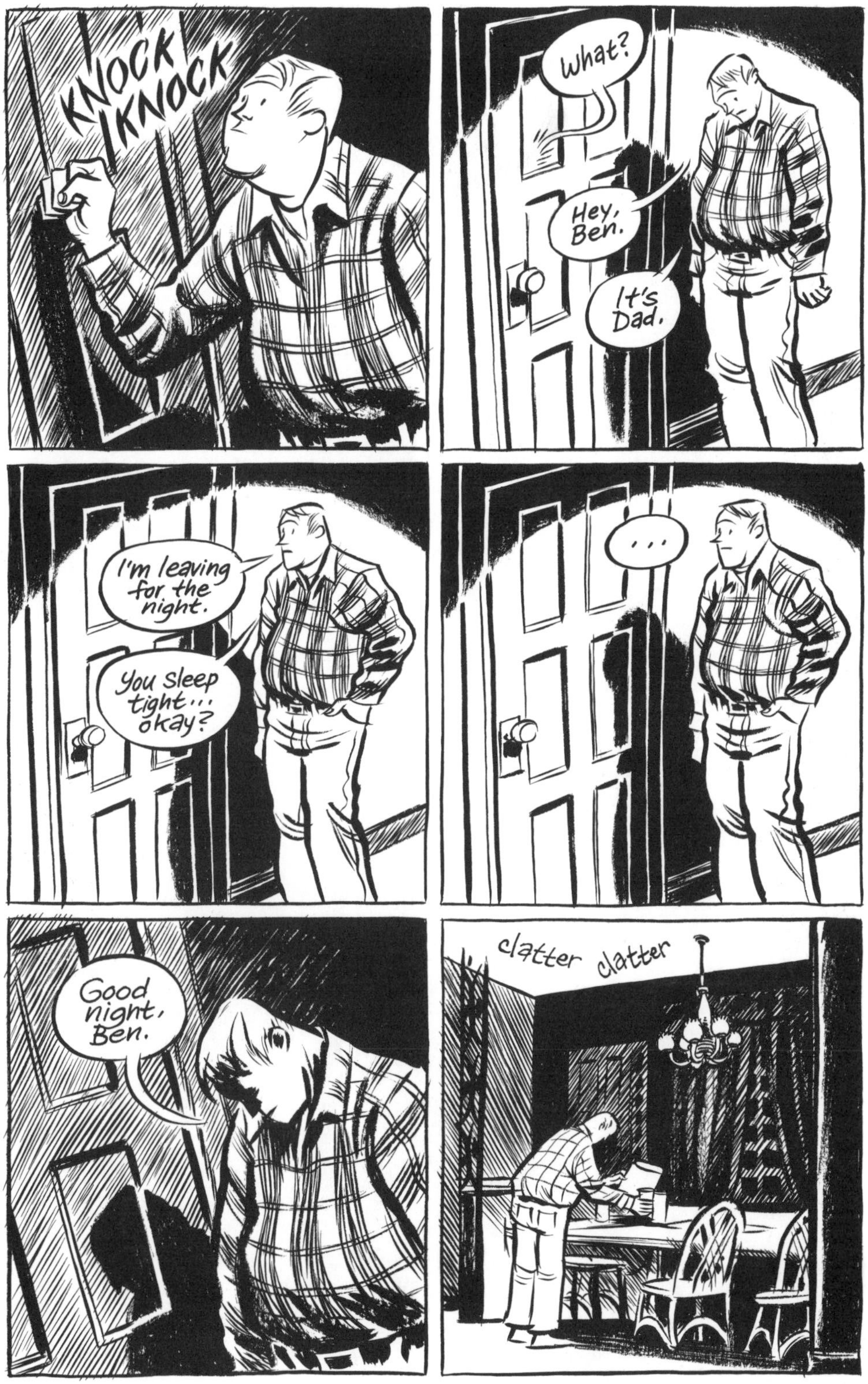
KNOCK KNOCK
What?
Hey, Ben.
It's Dad.
I'm leaving for the night.
You sleep tight... okay?
...
Good night, Ben.
clatter clatter

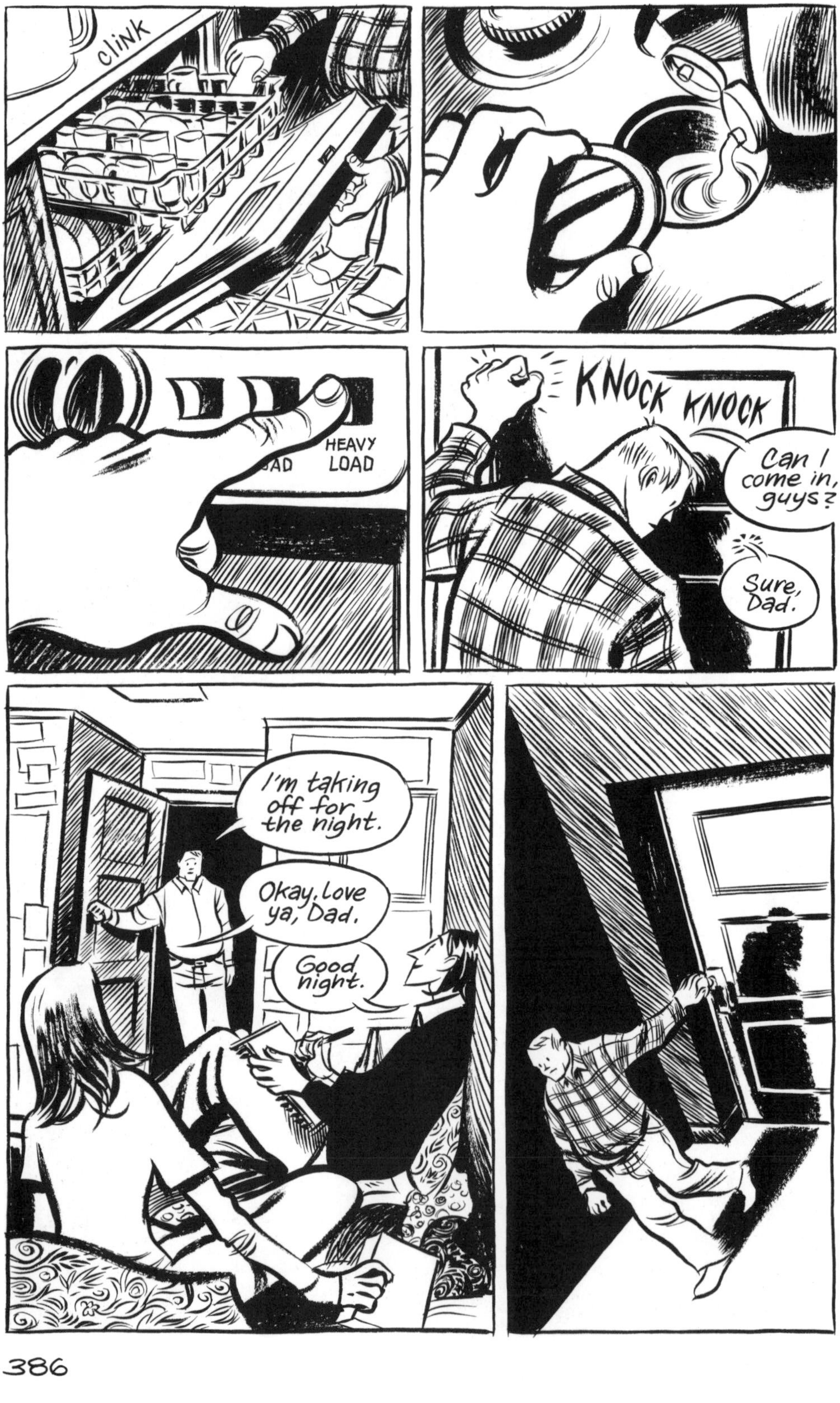
CLINK
HEAVY LOAD
KNOCK KNOCK
Can I come in, guys?
Sure, Dad.
I'm taking off for the night.
Okay, love ya, Dad.
Good night.

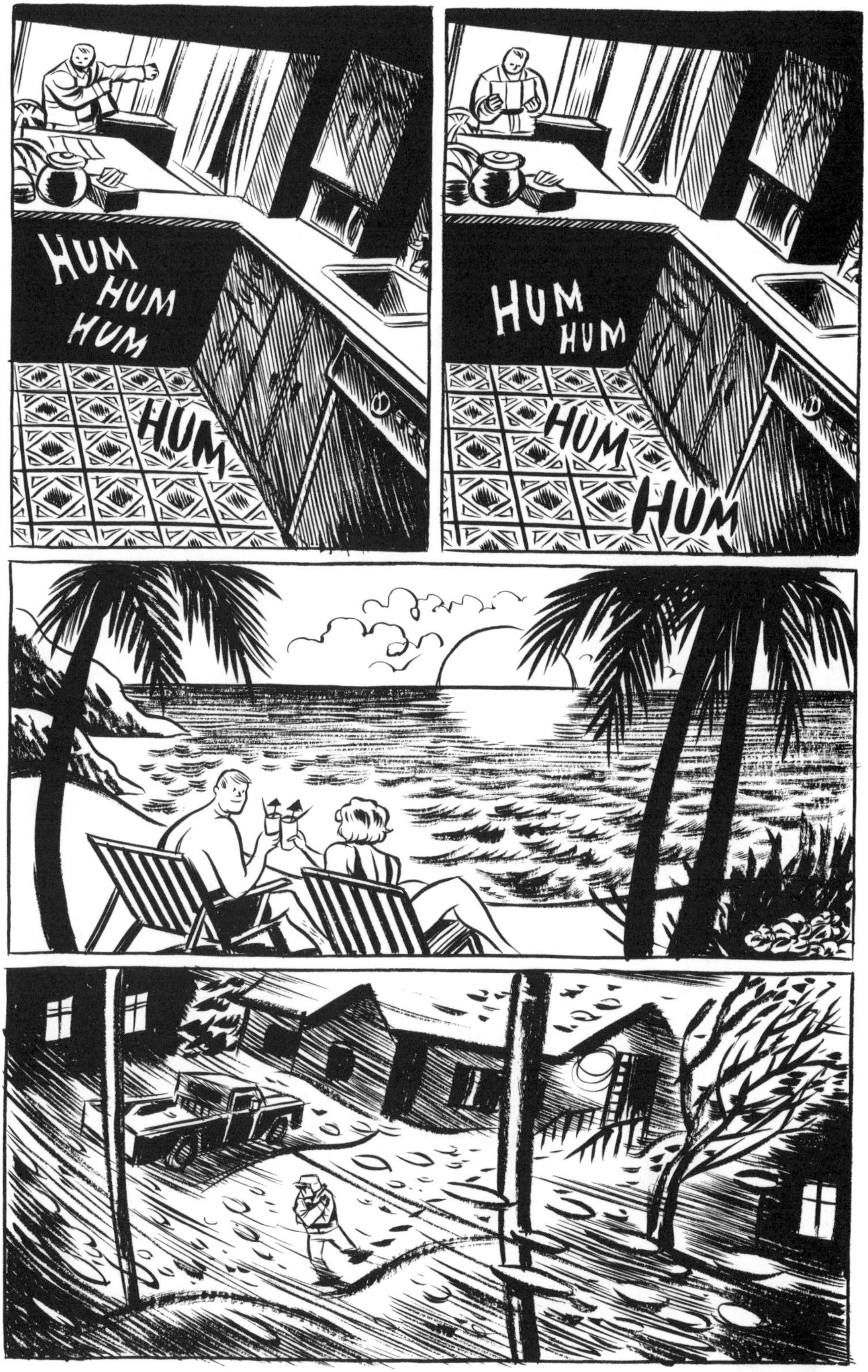
HUM
HUM
HUM
HUM
HUM
HUM
HUM
HUM

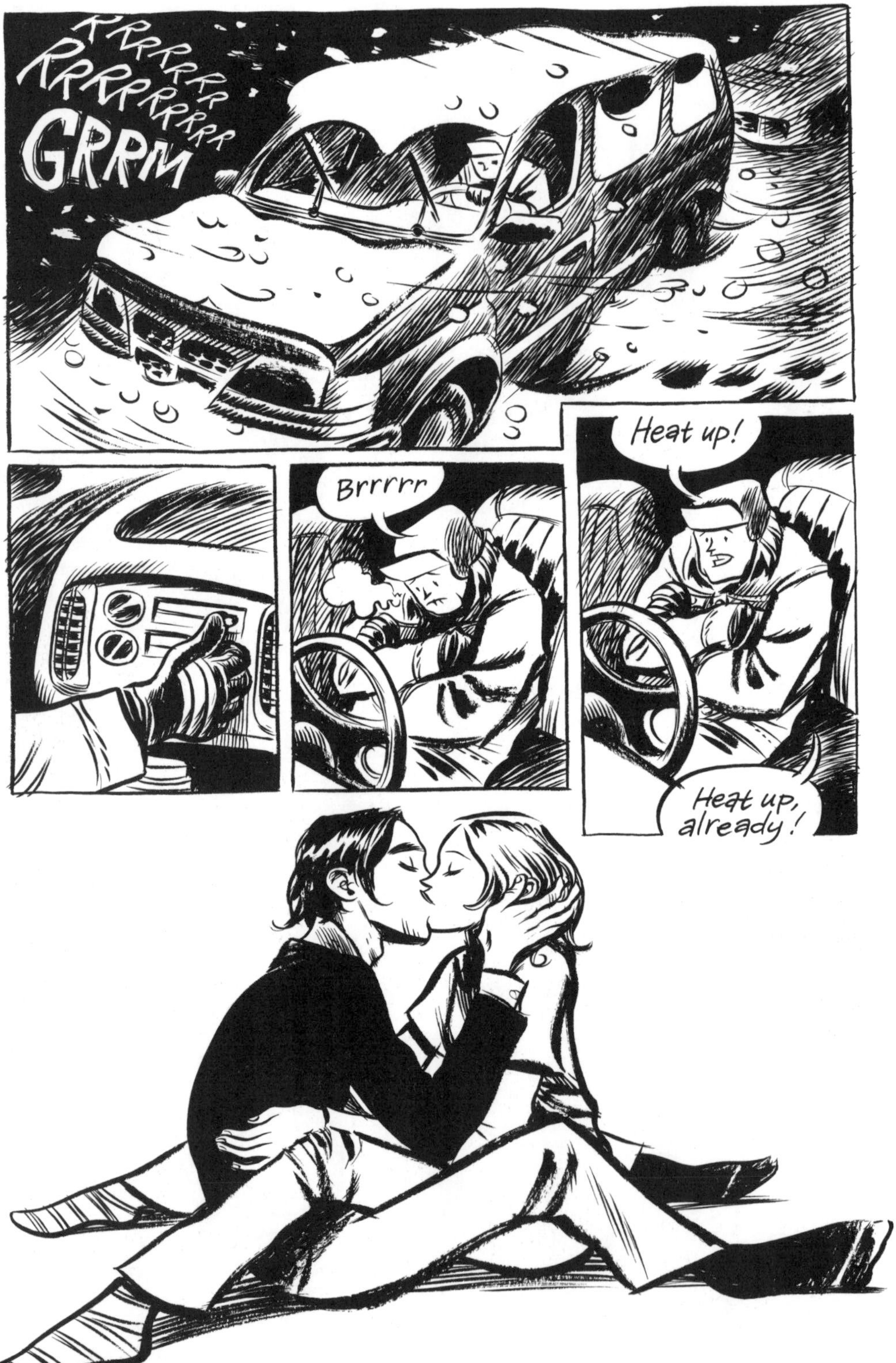
RRRRRRRR
RRRRRRRRRR
RRRRRRRRRRRR
GRRRM
Brrrrr
Heat up!
Heat up, already!

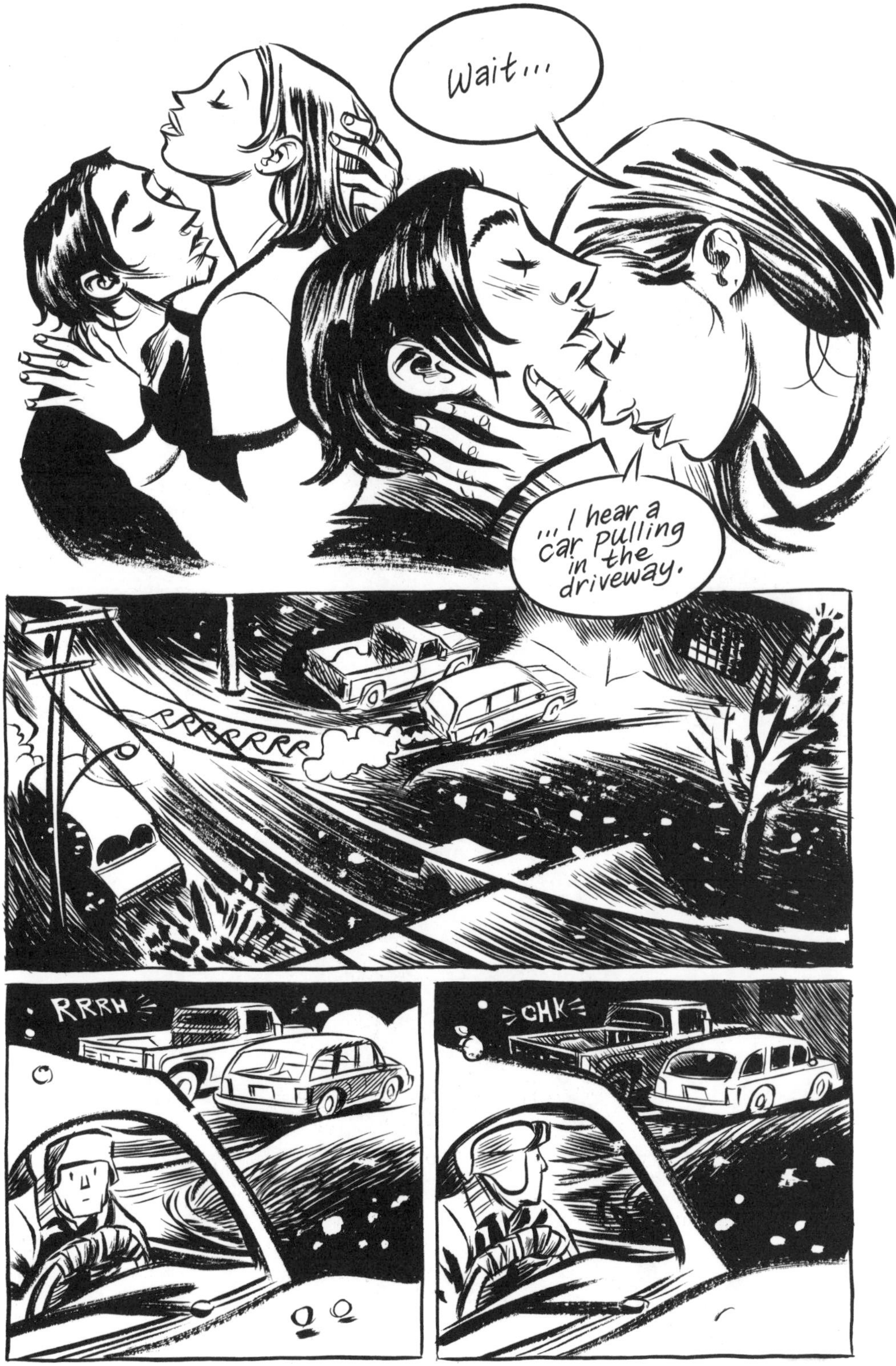
Wait...
...I hear a car pulling in the driveway.
RRRRRRRR
RRRH
CHK

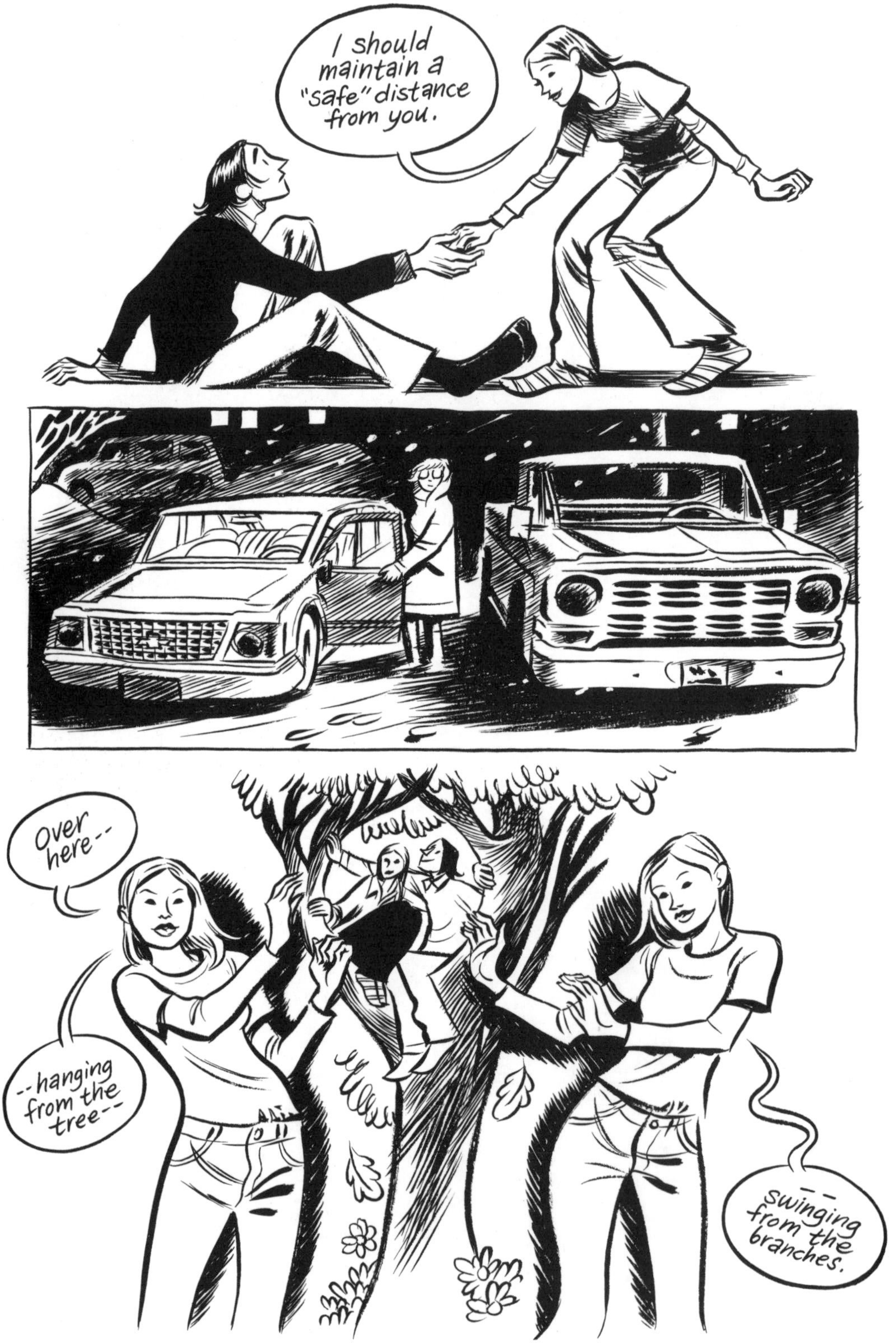
I should maintain a "safe" distance from you.
Over here--
--hanging from the tree--
--swinging from the branches.

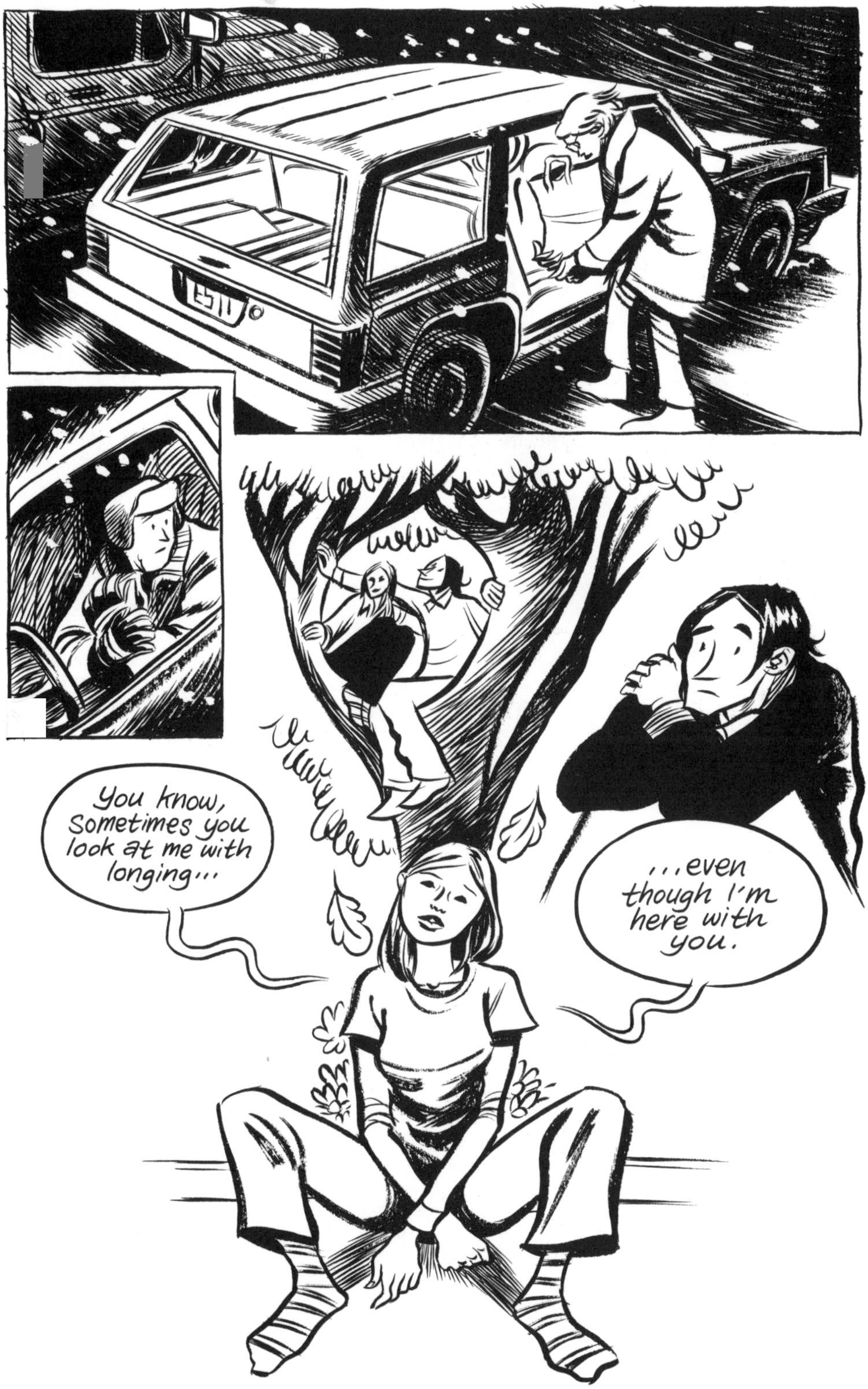
You know, sometimes you look at me with longing...
...even though I'm here with you.

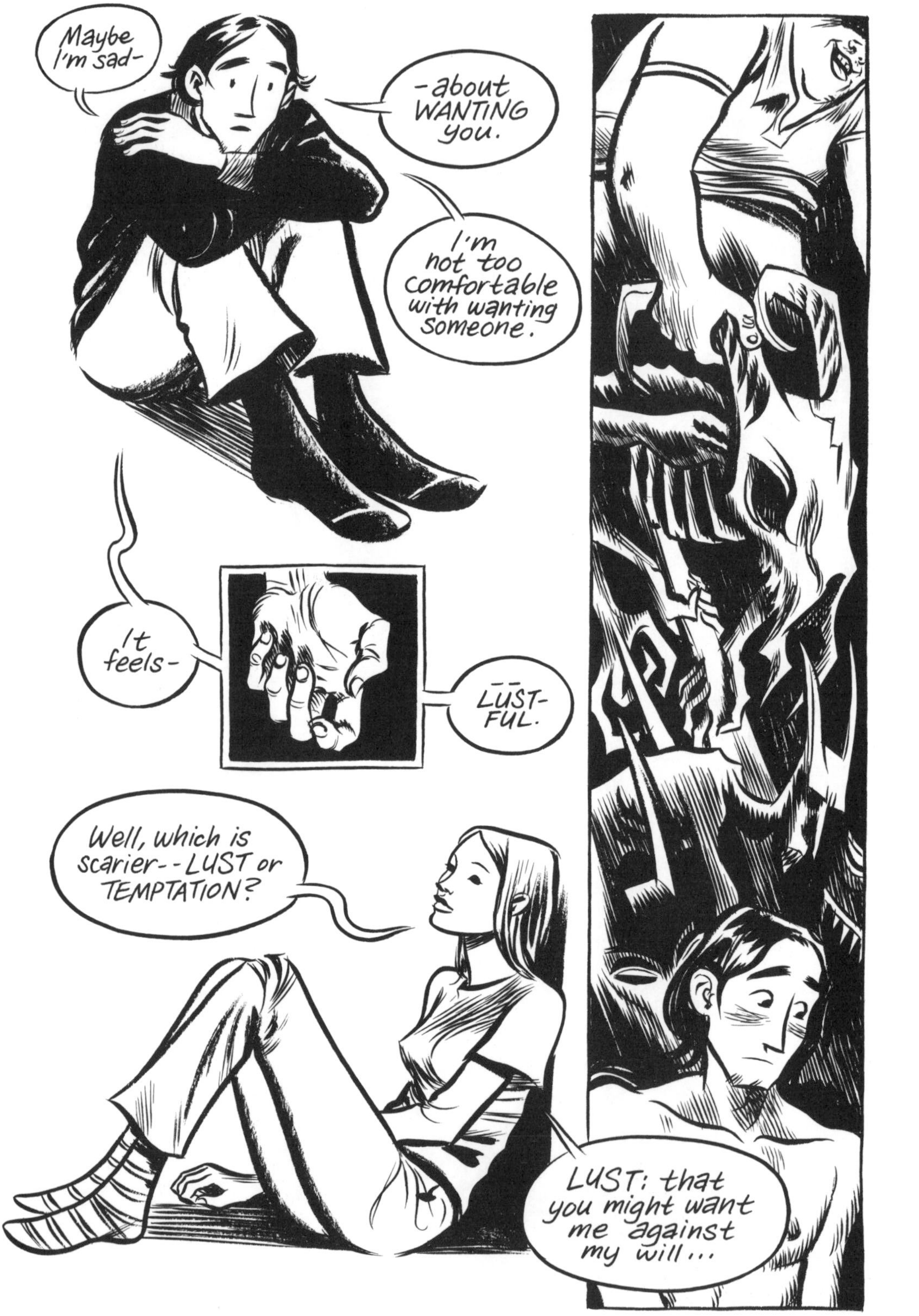
Maybe I'm sad-
-about WANTING you.
I'm not too comfortable with wanting someone.
It feels-
--LUST-FUL.
Well, which is scarier--LUST or TEMPTATION?
LUST: that you might want me against my will...

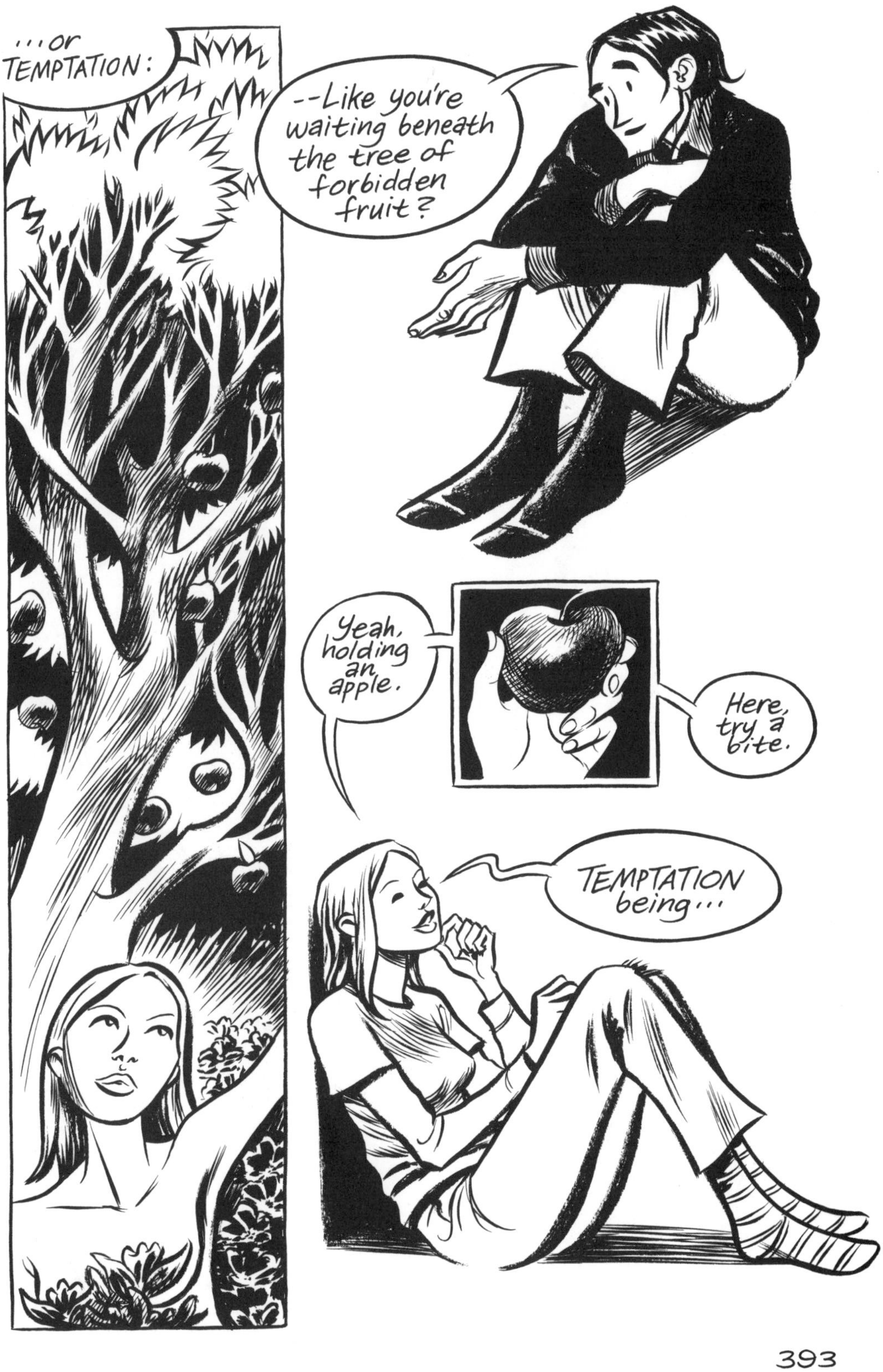
...or TEMPTATION:
--Like you're waiting beneath the tree of forbidden fruit?
Yeah, holding an apple.
Here, try a bite.
TEMPTATION being...

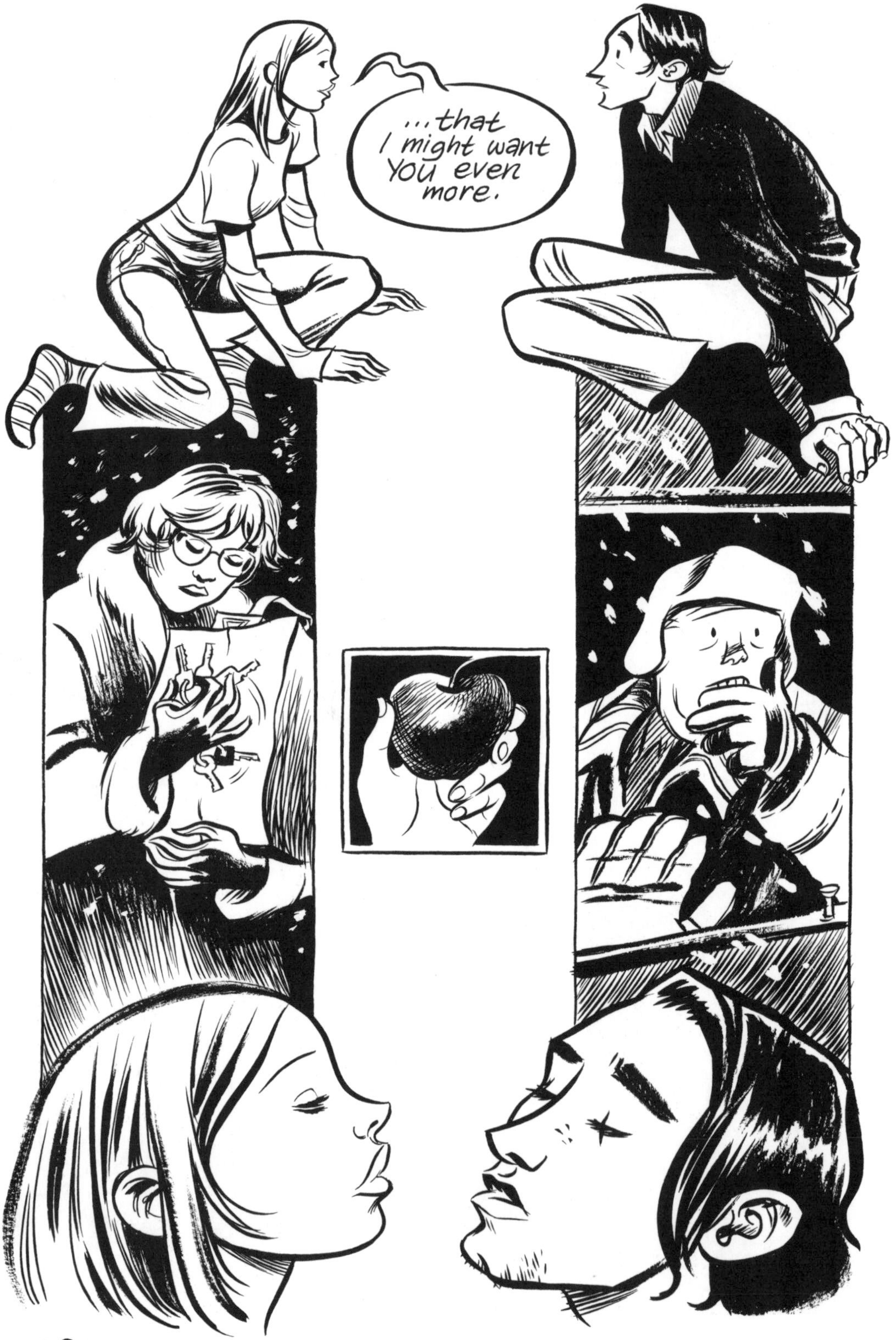
...that I might want You even more.

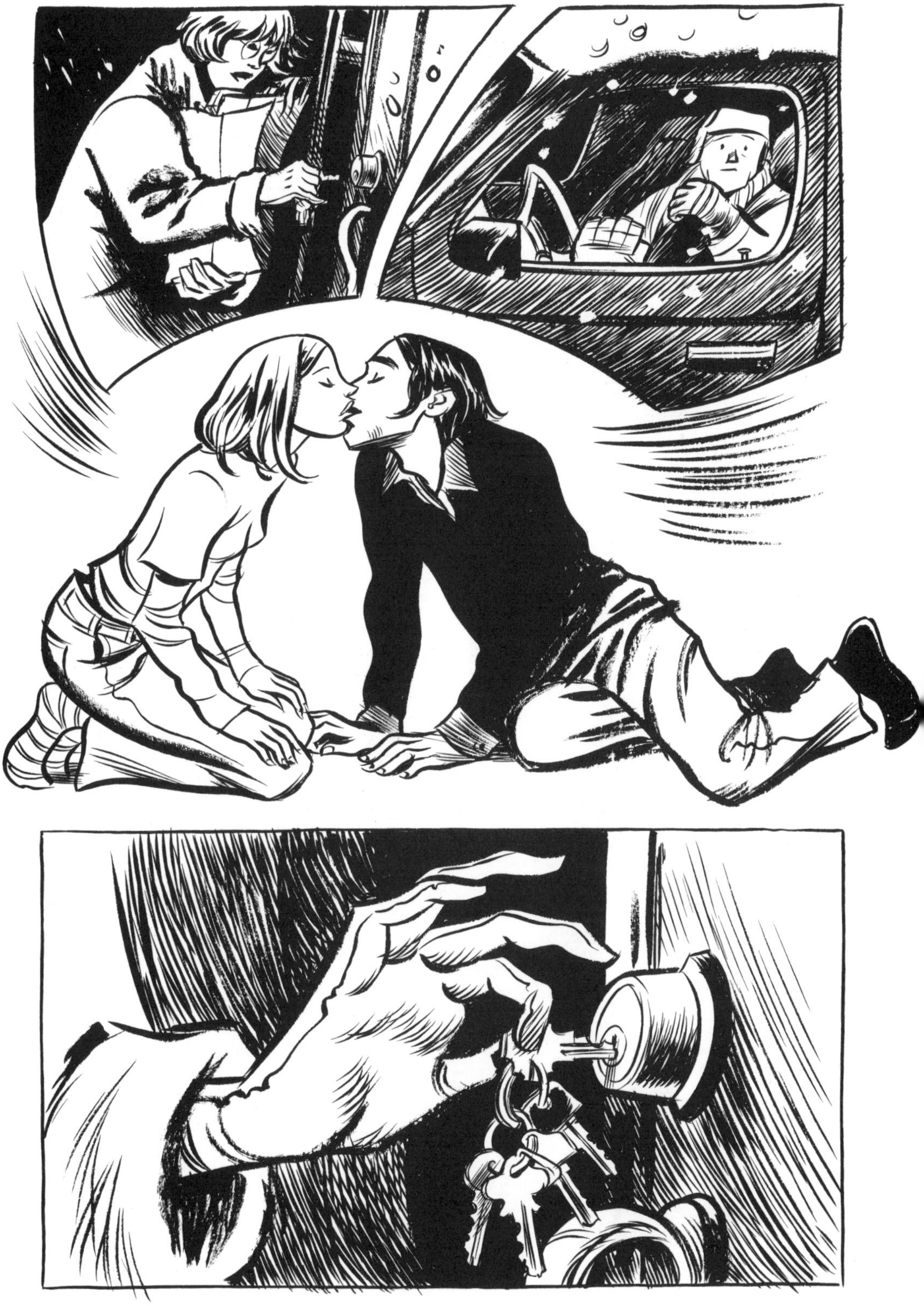

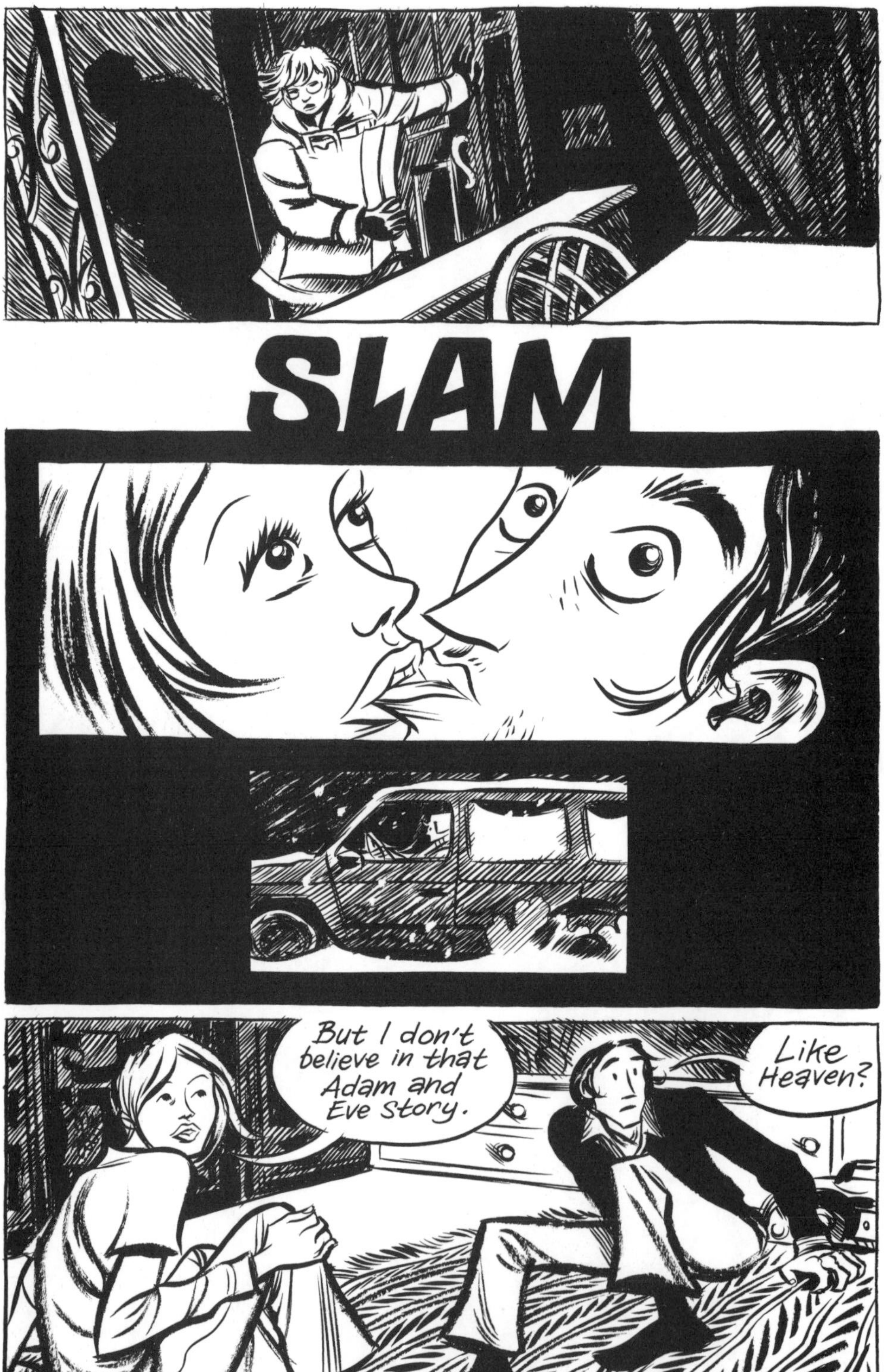
SLAM
But I don't believe in that Adam and Eve story.
Like Heaven?

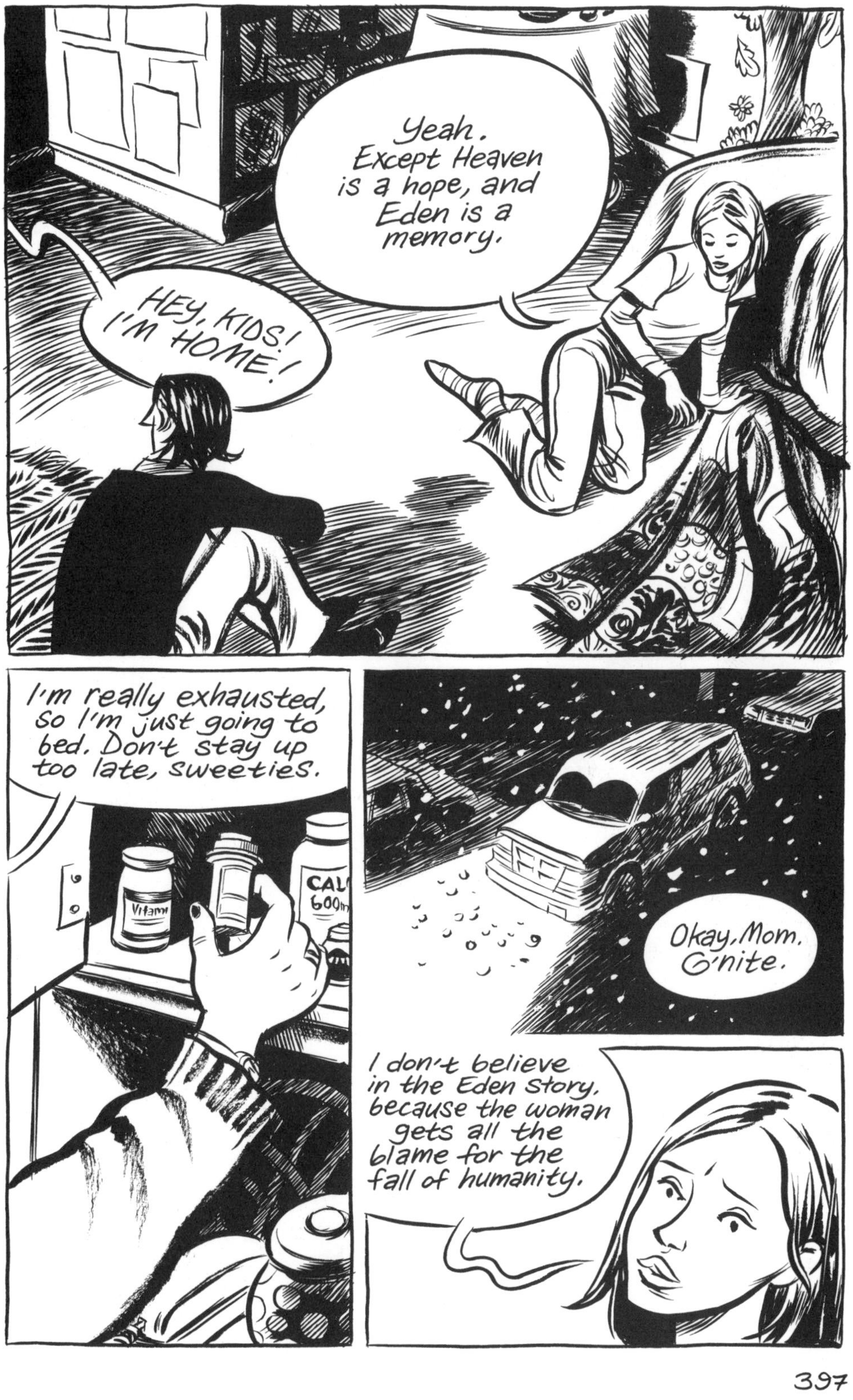
Yeah. Except Heaven is a hope, and Eden is a memory.
HEY, KIDS! I'M HOME!
I'm really exhausted, so I'm just going to bed. Don't stay up too late, sweeties.
Vitami
CAL 600m
Okay, Mom. G'nite.
I don't believe in the Eden story, because the woman gets all the blame for the fall of humanity.

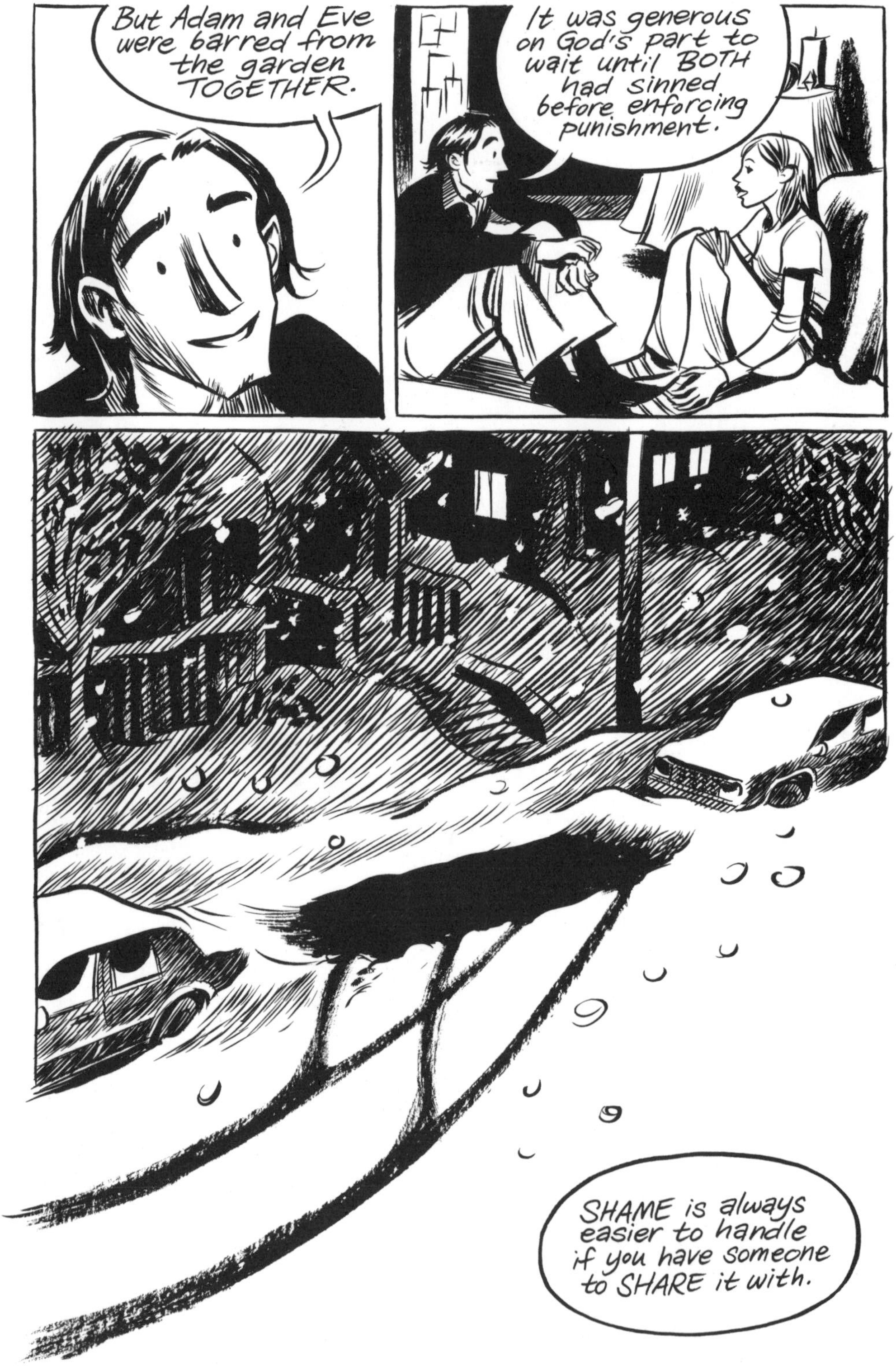
But Adam and Eve were barred from the garden TOGETHER.
It was generous on God's part to wait until BOTH had sinned before enforcing punishment.
SHAME is always easier to handle if you have someone to SHARE it with.

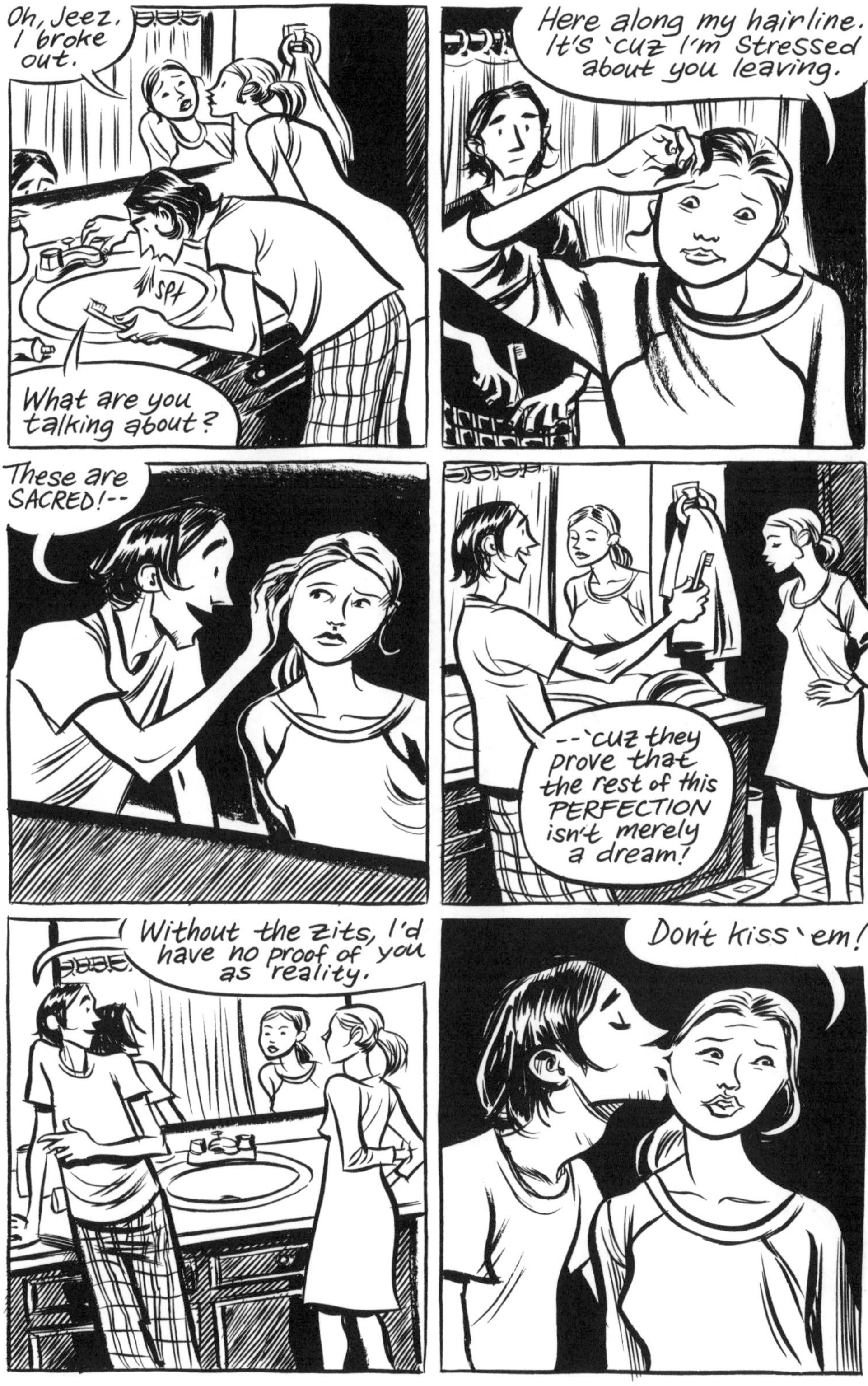
Oh, Jeez. I broke out.
spt
What are you talking about?
Here along my hairline. It's 'cuz I'm stressed about you leaving.
These are SACRED!--
--'cuz they prove that the rest of this PERFECTION isn't merely a dream!
Without the zits, I'd have no proof of you as reality.
Don't kiss 'em!

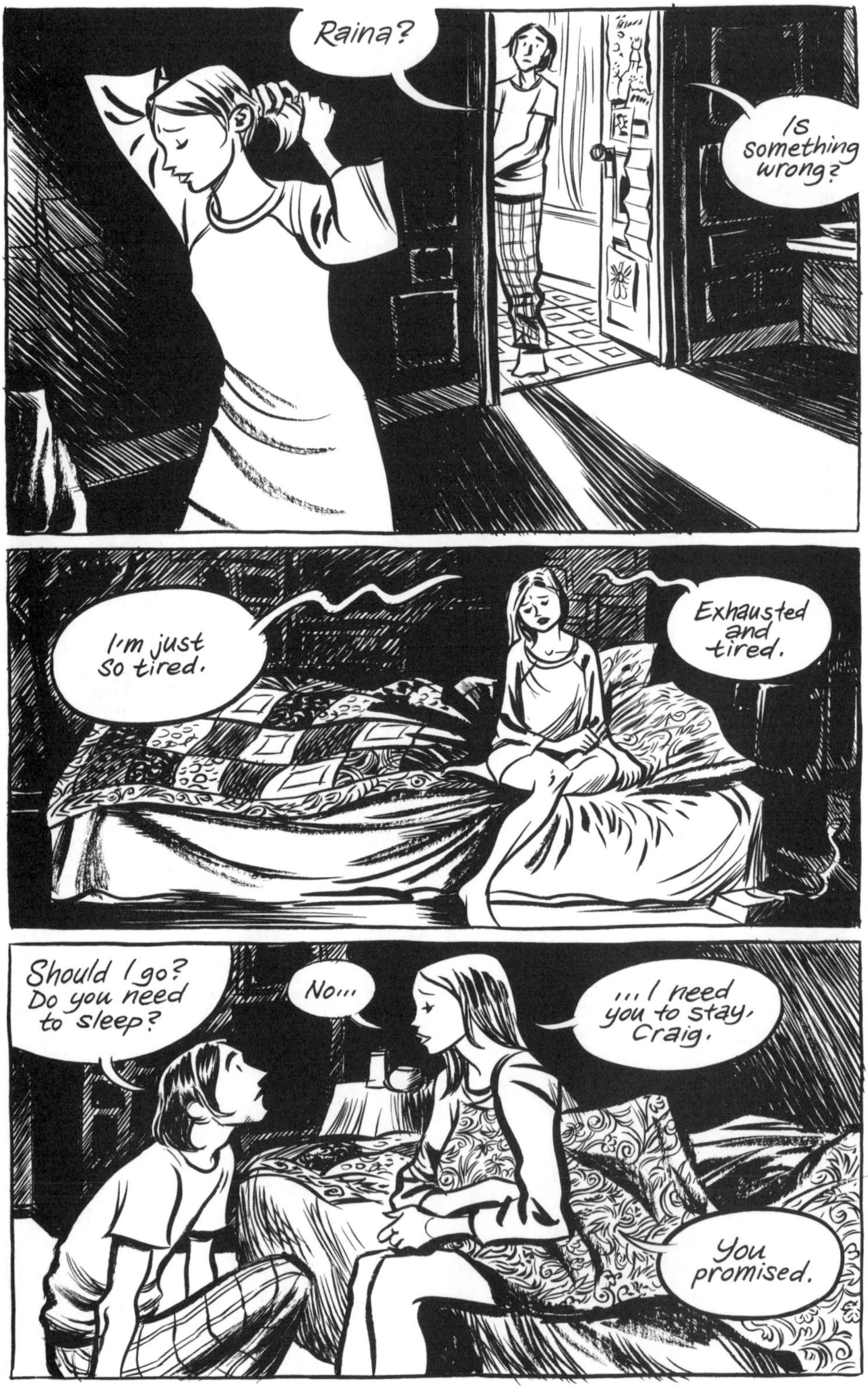
Raina?
Is something wrong?
I'm just so tired.
Exhausted and tired.
Should I go? Do you need to sleep?
No...
...I need you to stay, Craig.
You promised.

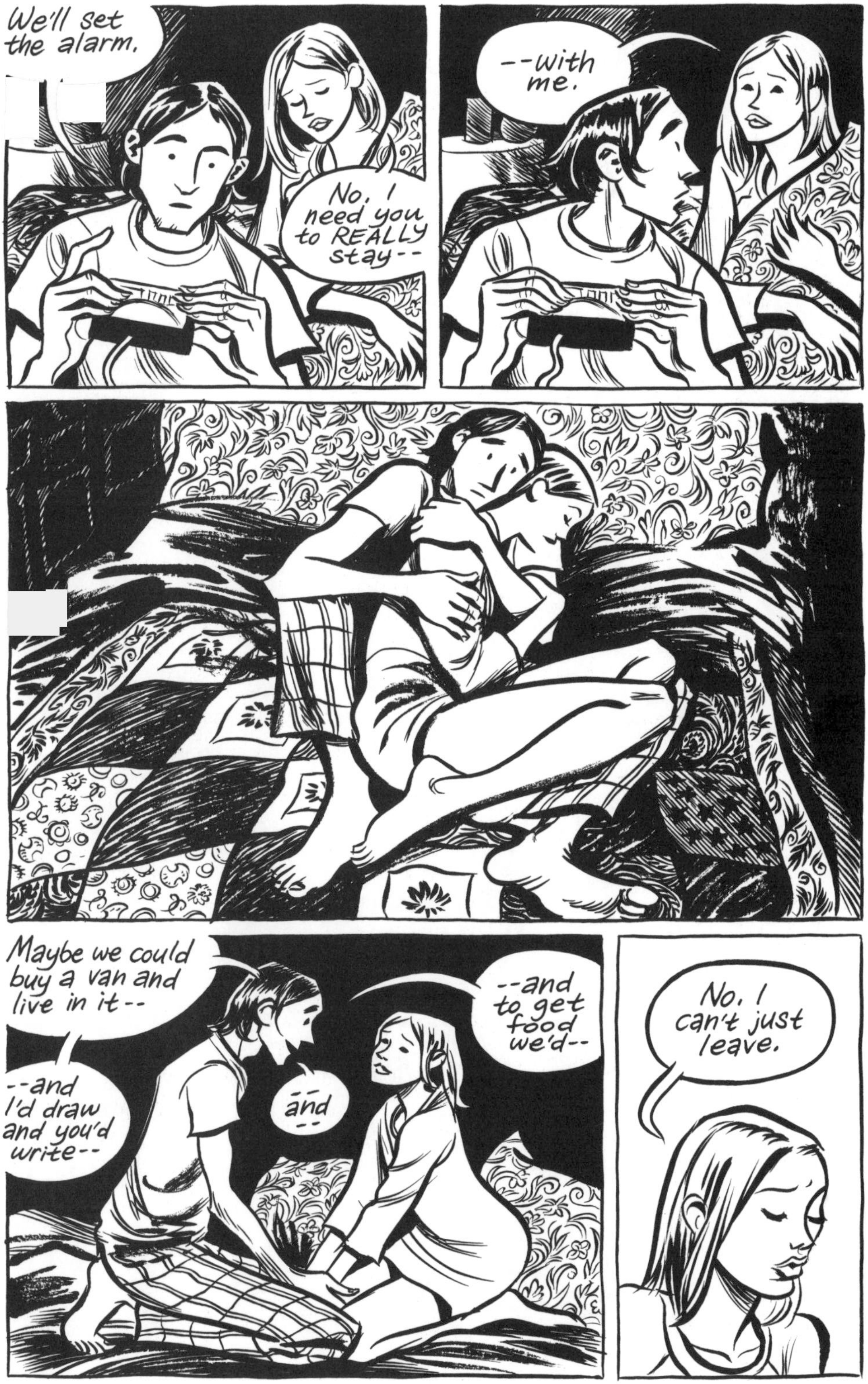
We'll set the alarm.
No. I need you to REALLY stay--
--with me.
Maybe we could buy a van and live in it--
--and I'd draw and you'd write--
--and--
--and to get food we'd--
No. I can't just leave.

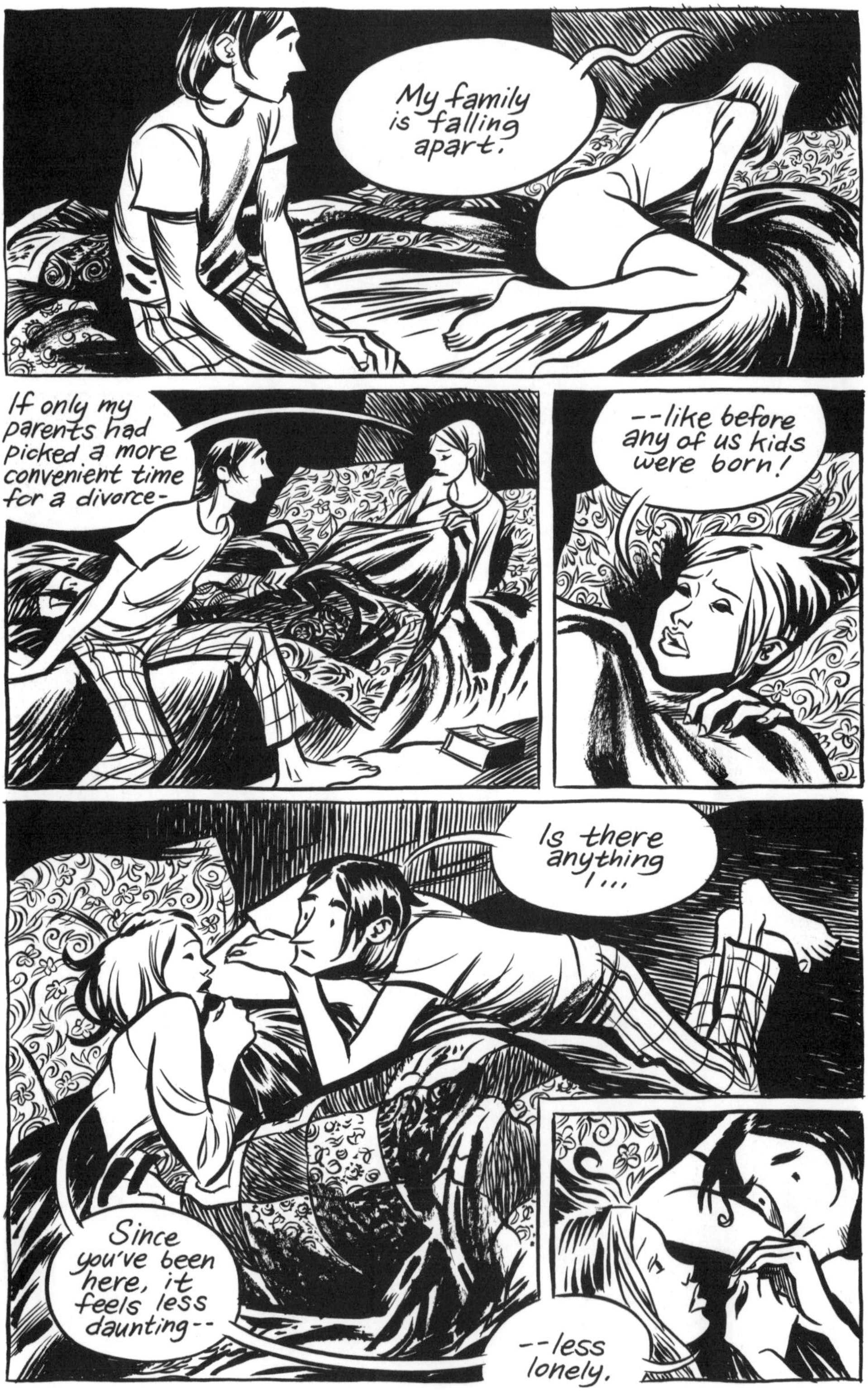
My family is falling apart.
If only my parents had picked a more convenient time for a divorce-
--like before any of us kids were born!
Is there anything I...
Since you've been here, it feels less daunting--
--less lonely.

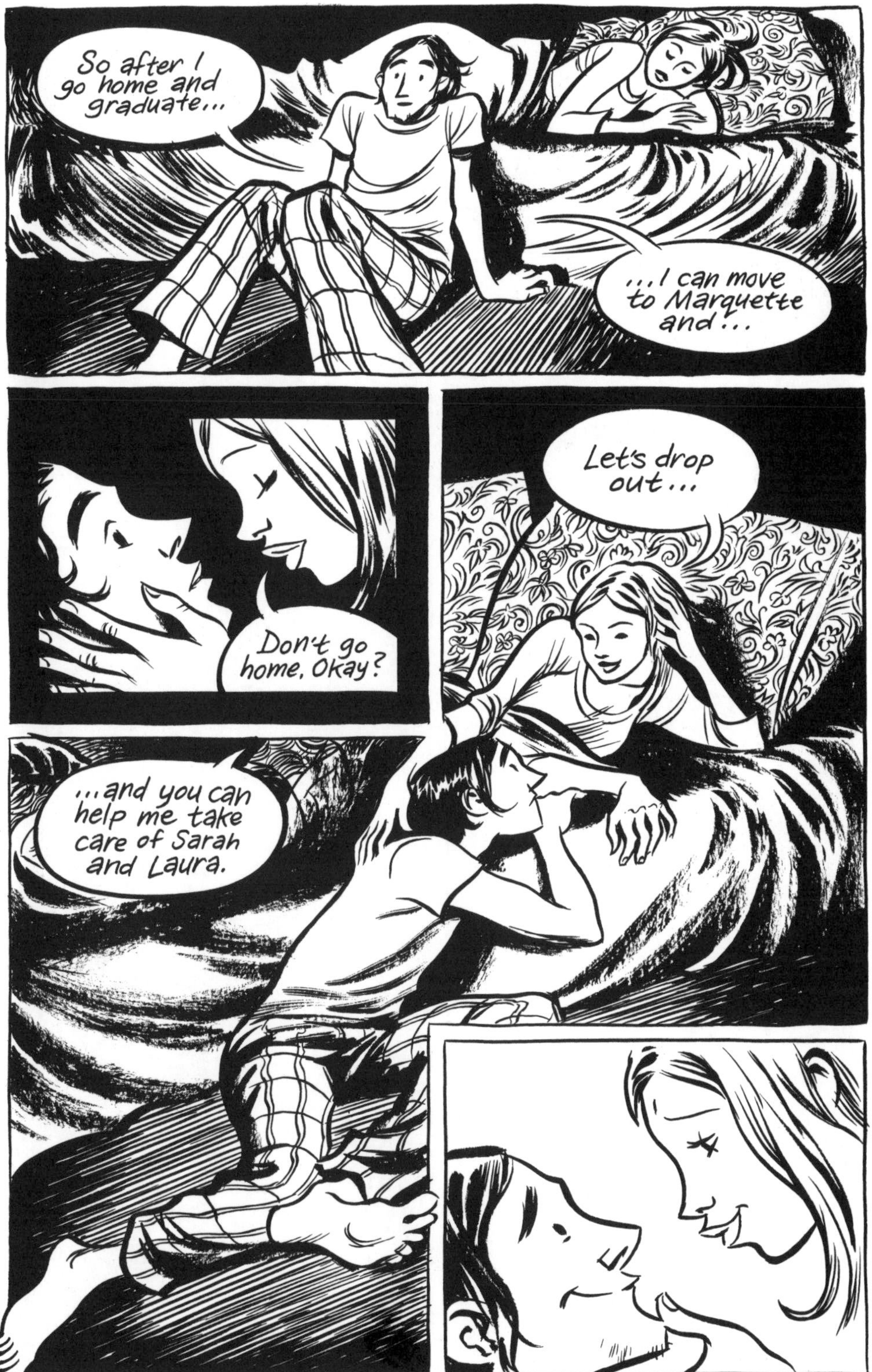
So after I go home and graduate...
...I can move to Marquette and...
Don't go home, Okay?
Let's drop out...
...and you can help me take care of Sarah and Laura.

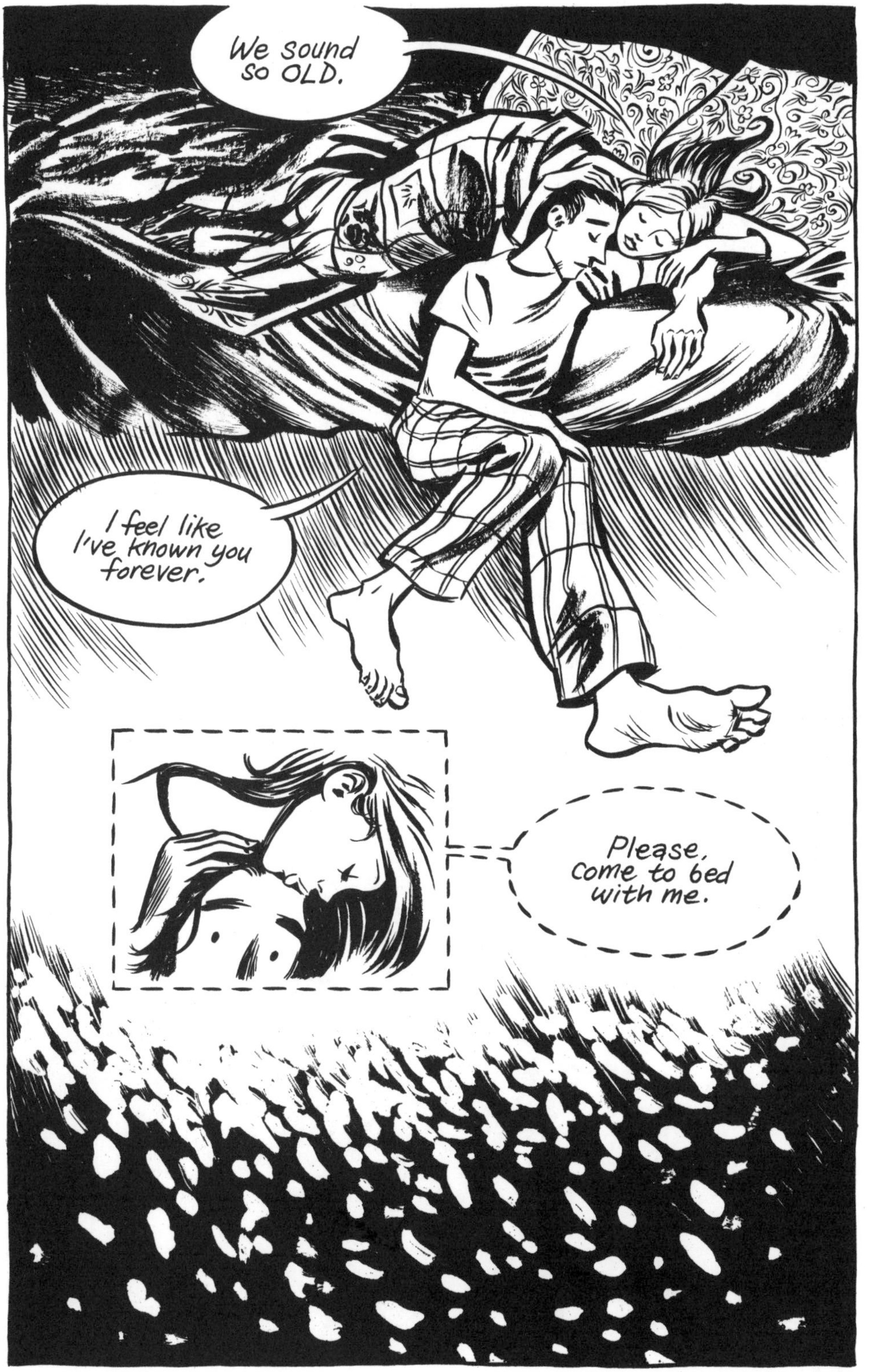
We sound so OLD.
I feel like I've known you forever.
Please, come to bed with me.

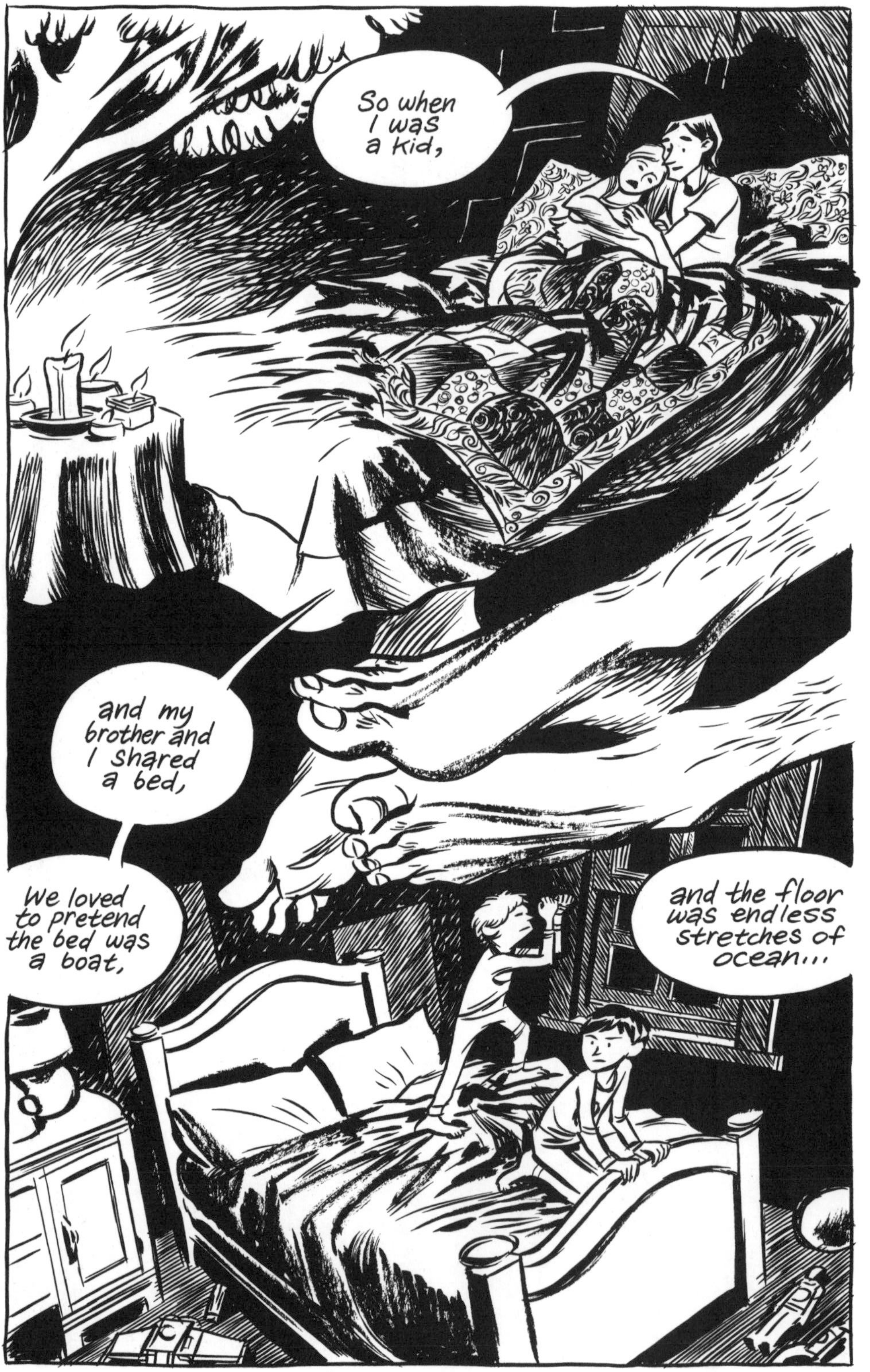
So when I was a kid,
and my brother and I shared a bed,
We loved to pretend the bed was a boat,
and the floor was endless stretches of ocean...

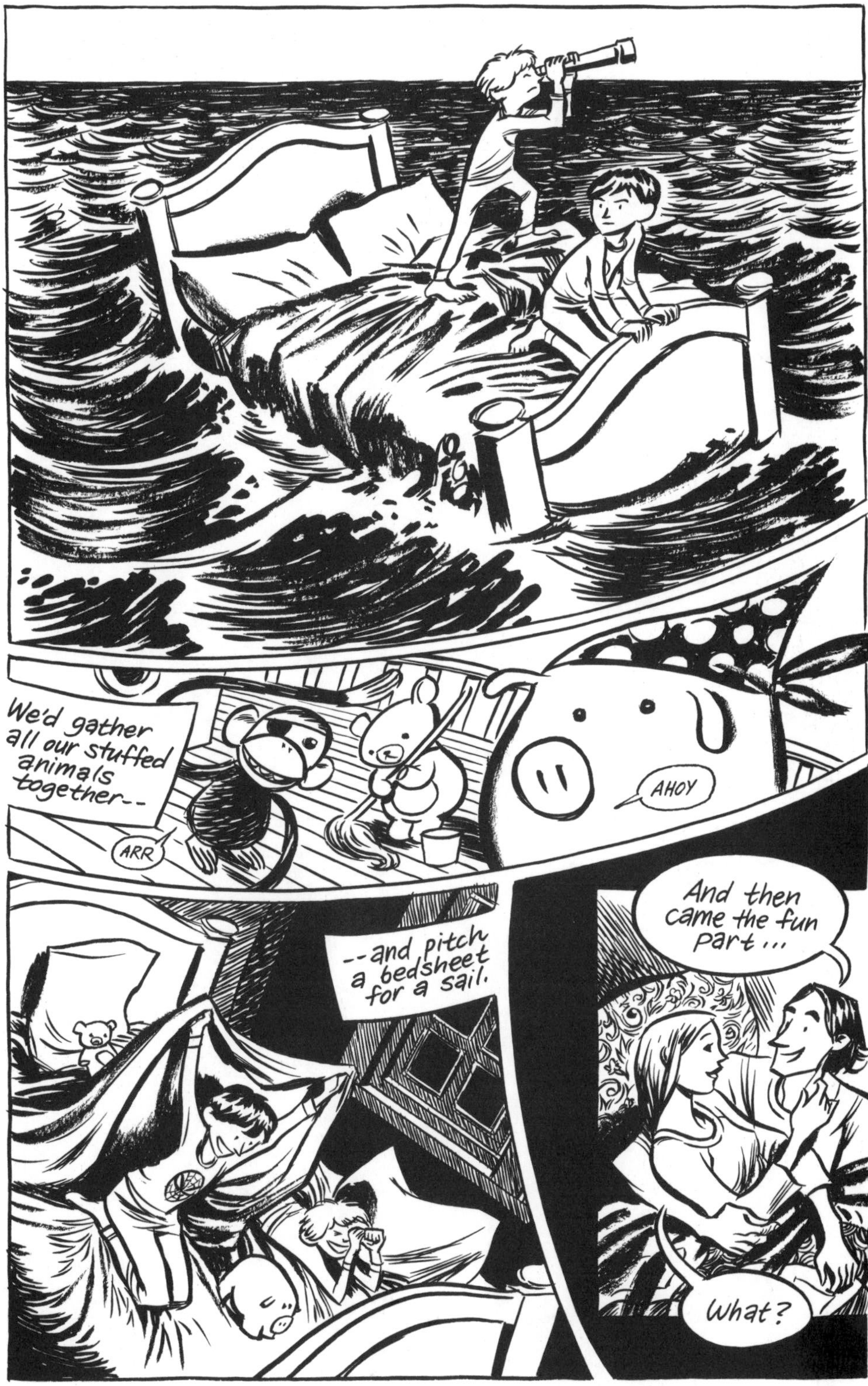
We'd gather all our stuffed animals together--
ARR
AHOY
--and pitch a bedsheet for a sail.
And then came the fun part...
What?

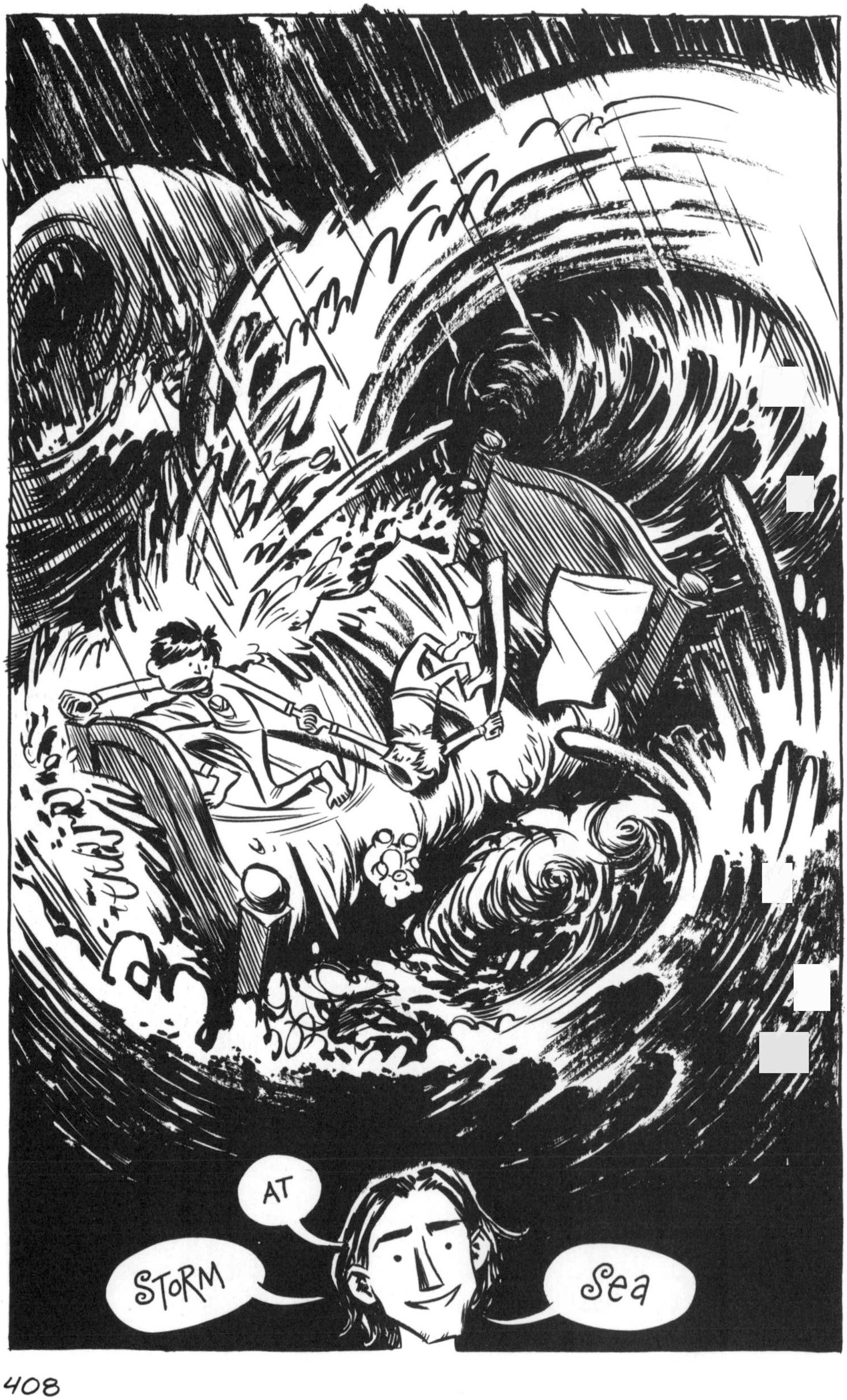
STORM
AT
Sea

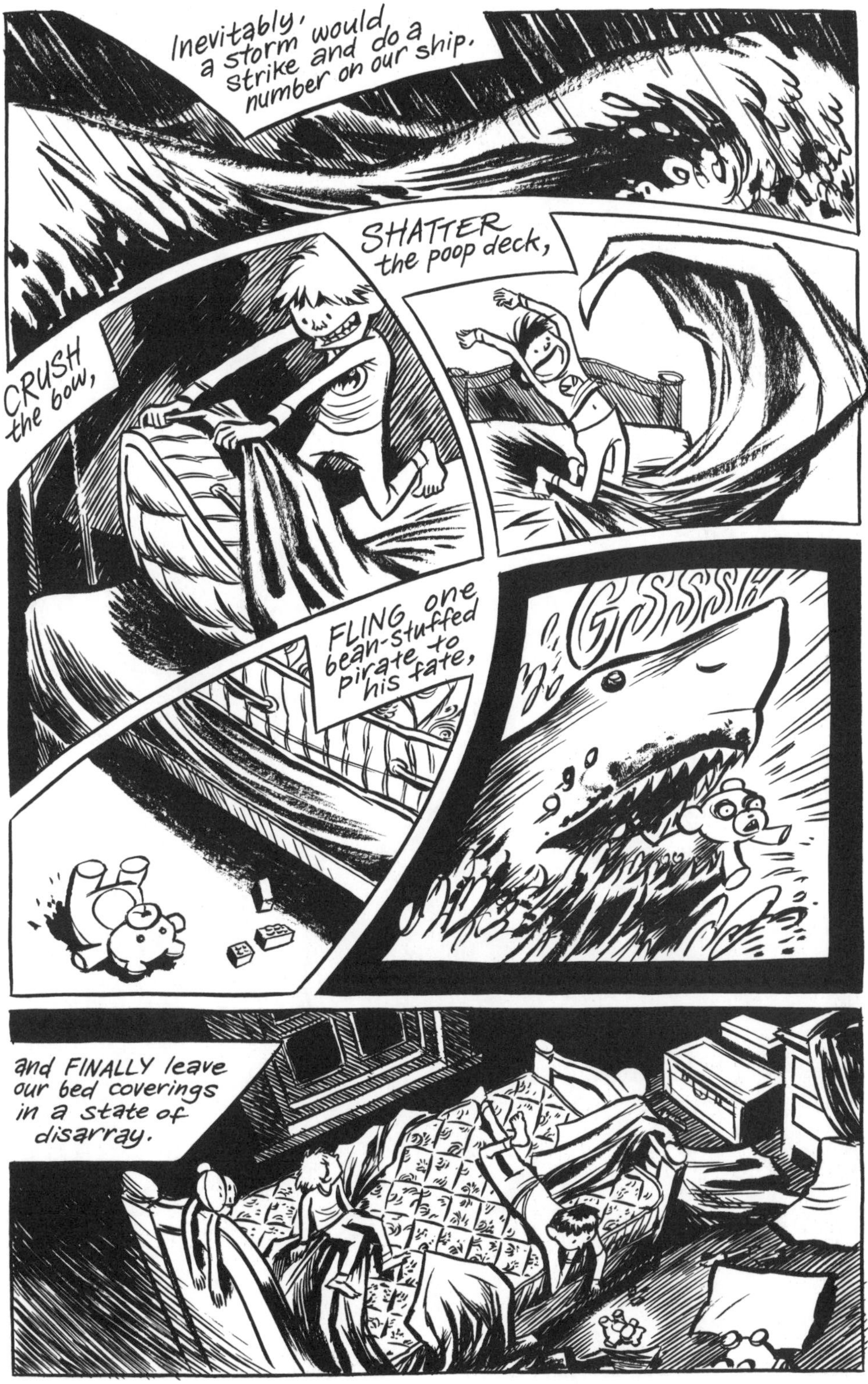
Inevitably, a storm would strike and do a number on our ship.
CRUSH the bow,
SHATTER the poop deck,
FLING one bean-stuffed pirate to his fate,
GSSSH
and FINALLY leave our bed coverings in a state of disarray.

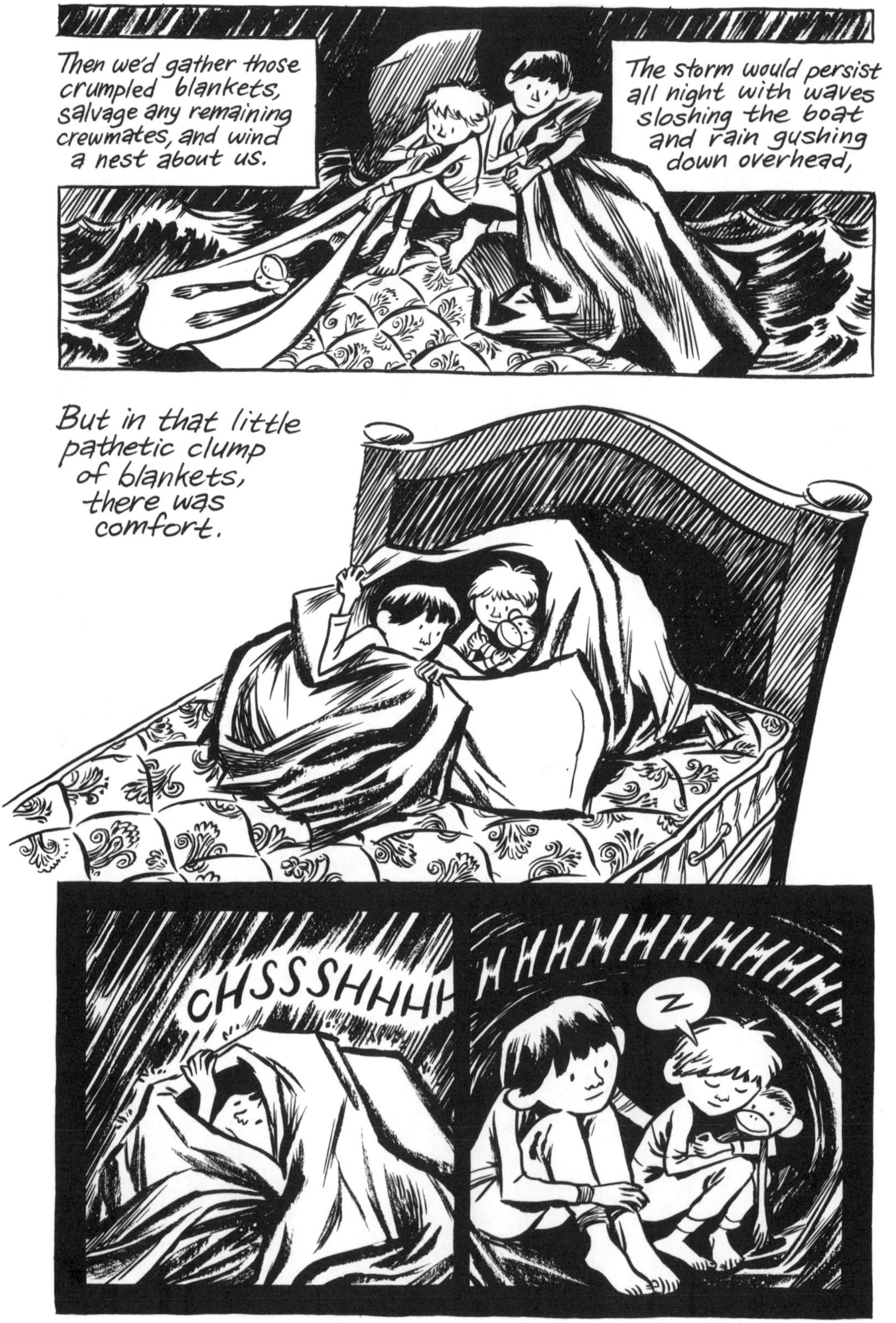
Then we'd gather those crumpled blankets, salvage any remaining crewmates, and wind a nest about us.
The storm would persist all night with waves sloshing the boat and rain gushing down overhead,
But in that little pathetic clump of blankets, there was comfort.
CHSSSHHHHHHHHHHHHHHHHH
Z

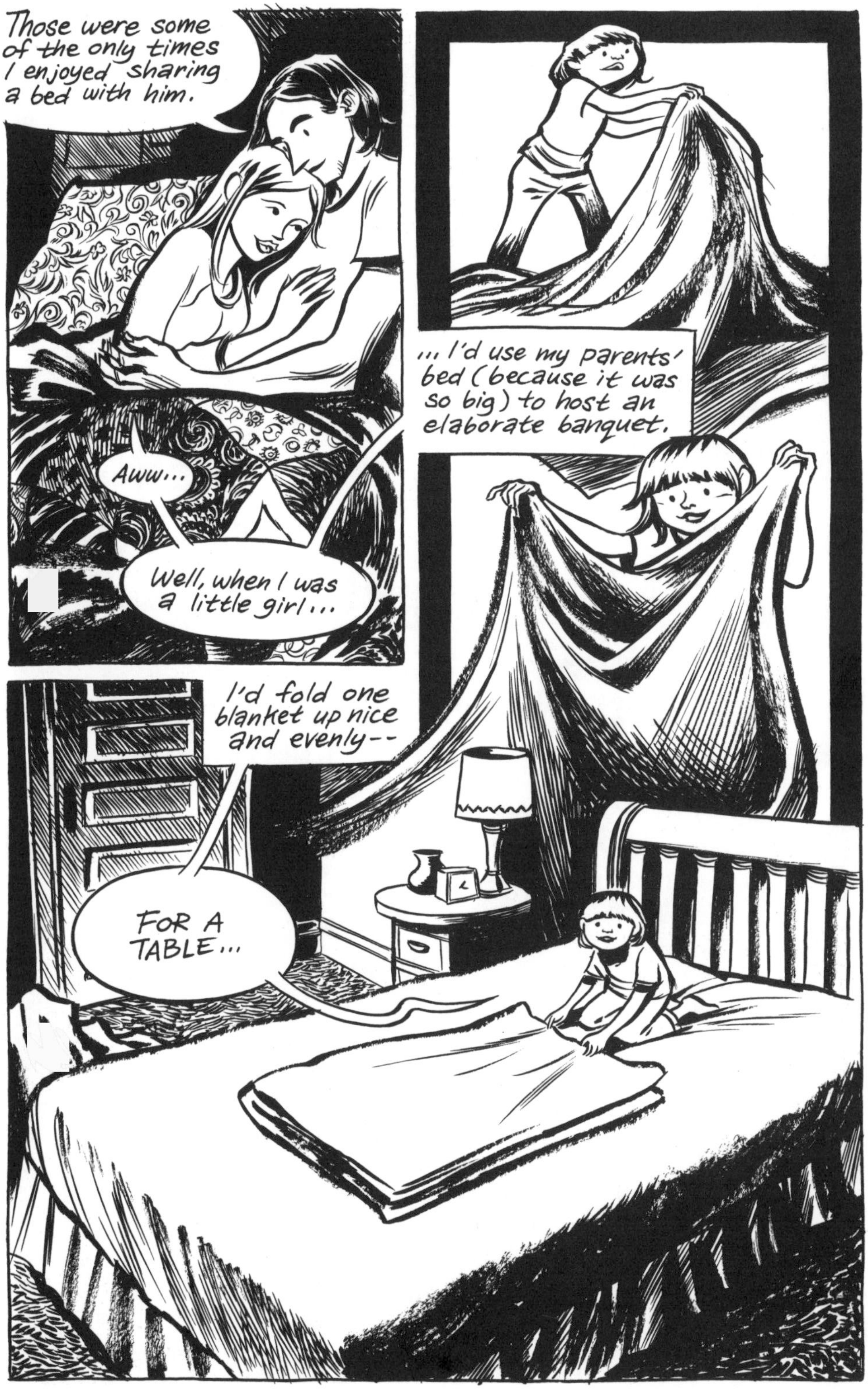
Those were some of the only times I enjoyed sharing a bed with him.
Aww...
Well, when I was a little girl...
...I'd use my parents' bed (because it was so big) to host an elaborate banquet.
I'd fold one blanket up nice and evenly--
FOR A TABLE...

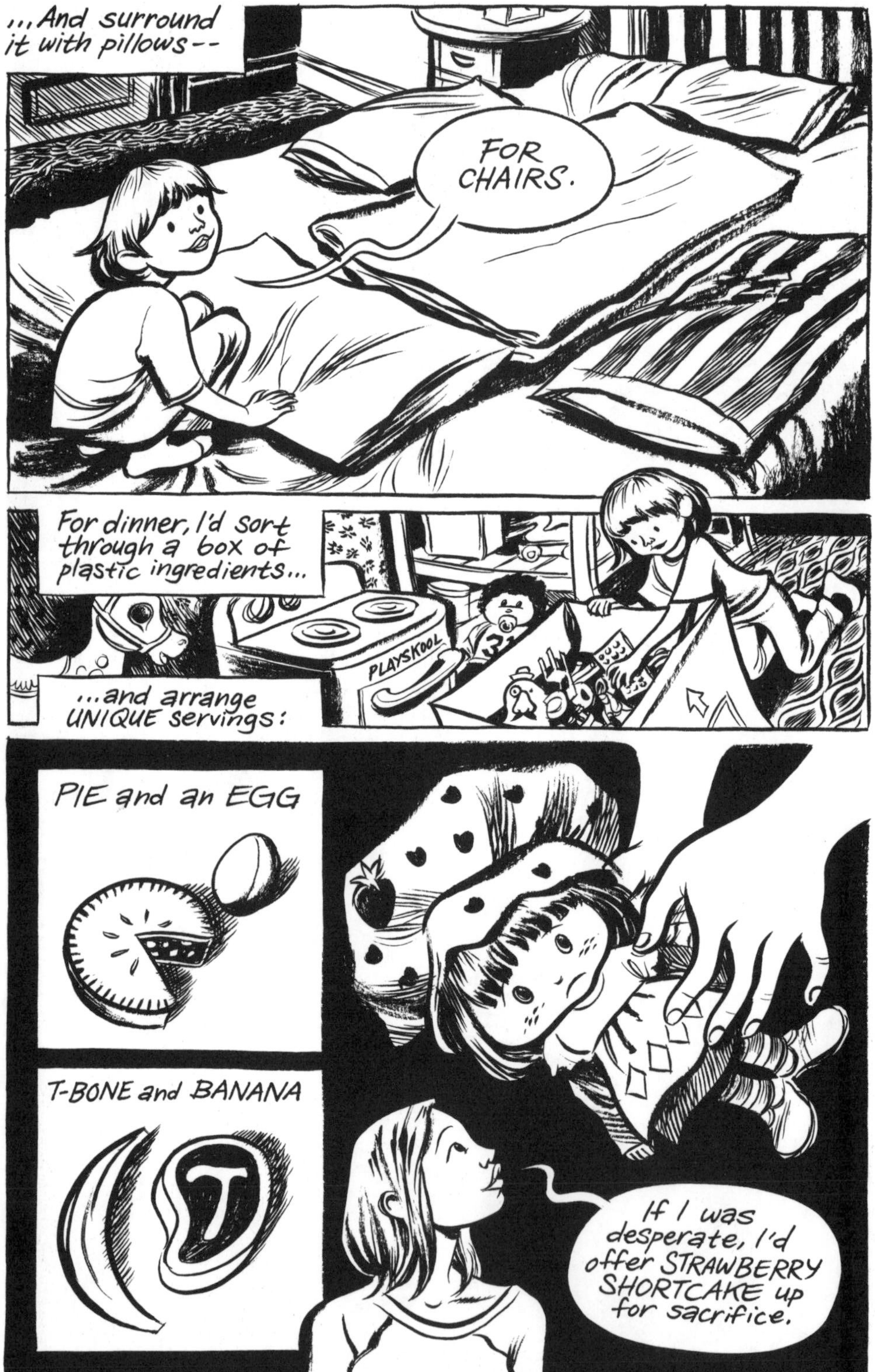
...And surround it with pillows--
FOR CHAIRS.
For dinner, I'd sort through a box of plastic ingredients...
PLAYSKOOL
...and arrange UNIQUE servings:
PIE and an EGG
T-BONE and BANANA
If I was desperate, I'd offer STRAWBERRY SHORTCAKE up for sacrifice.

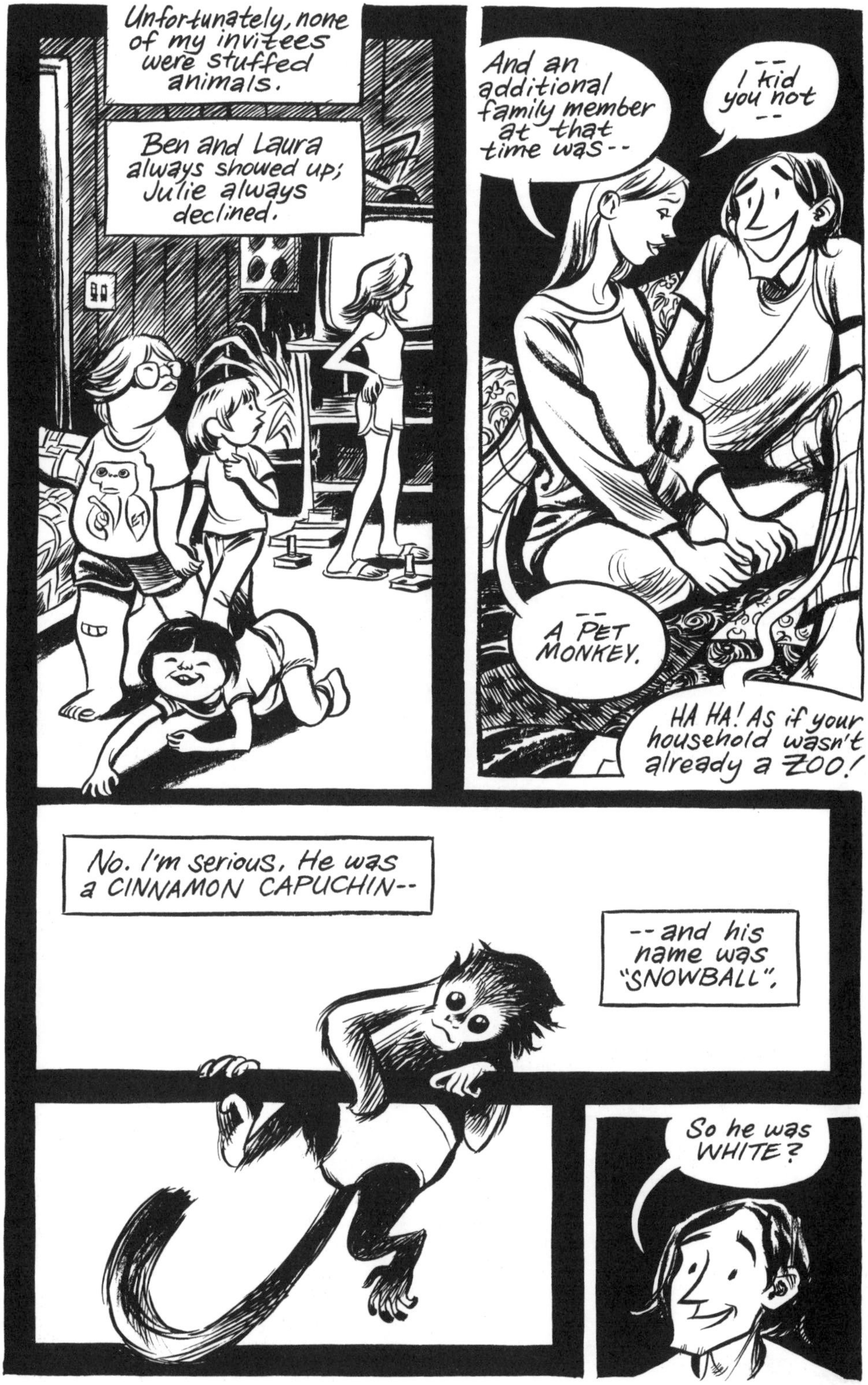
Unfortunately, none of my invitees were stuffed animals.
Ben and Laura always showed up; Julie always declined.
And an additional family member at that time was--
--I kid you not--
--A PET MONKEY.
HA HA! As if your household wasn't already a ZOO!
No. I'm serious. He was a CINNAMON CAPUCHIN--
--and his name was "SNOWBALL".
So he was WHITE?

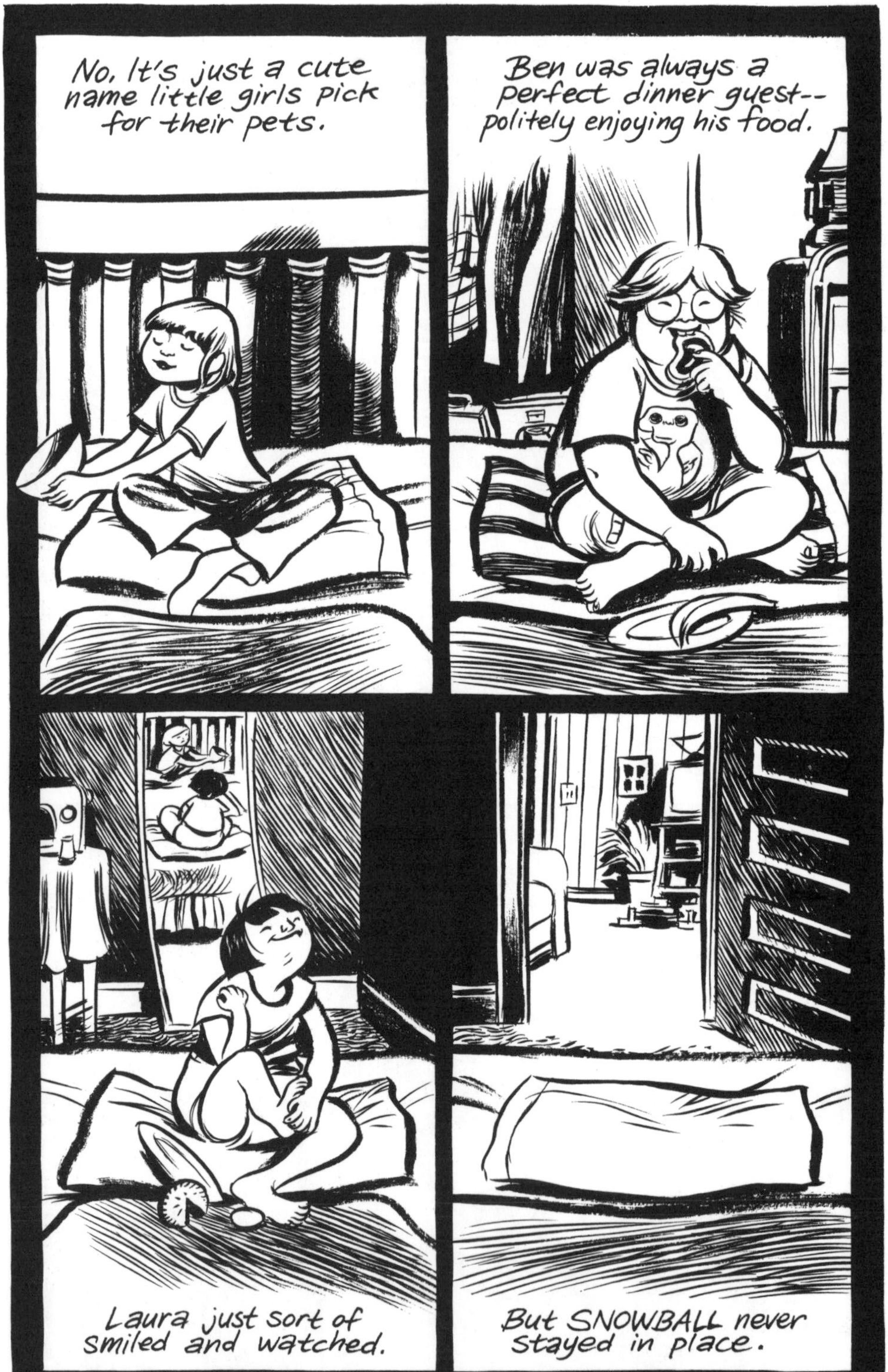
No, It's just a cute name little girls pick for their pets.
Ben was always a perfect dinner guest-- politely enjoying his food.
Laura just sort of smiled and watched.
But SNOWBALL never stayed in place.

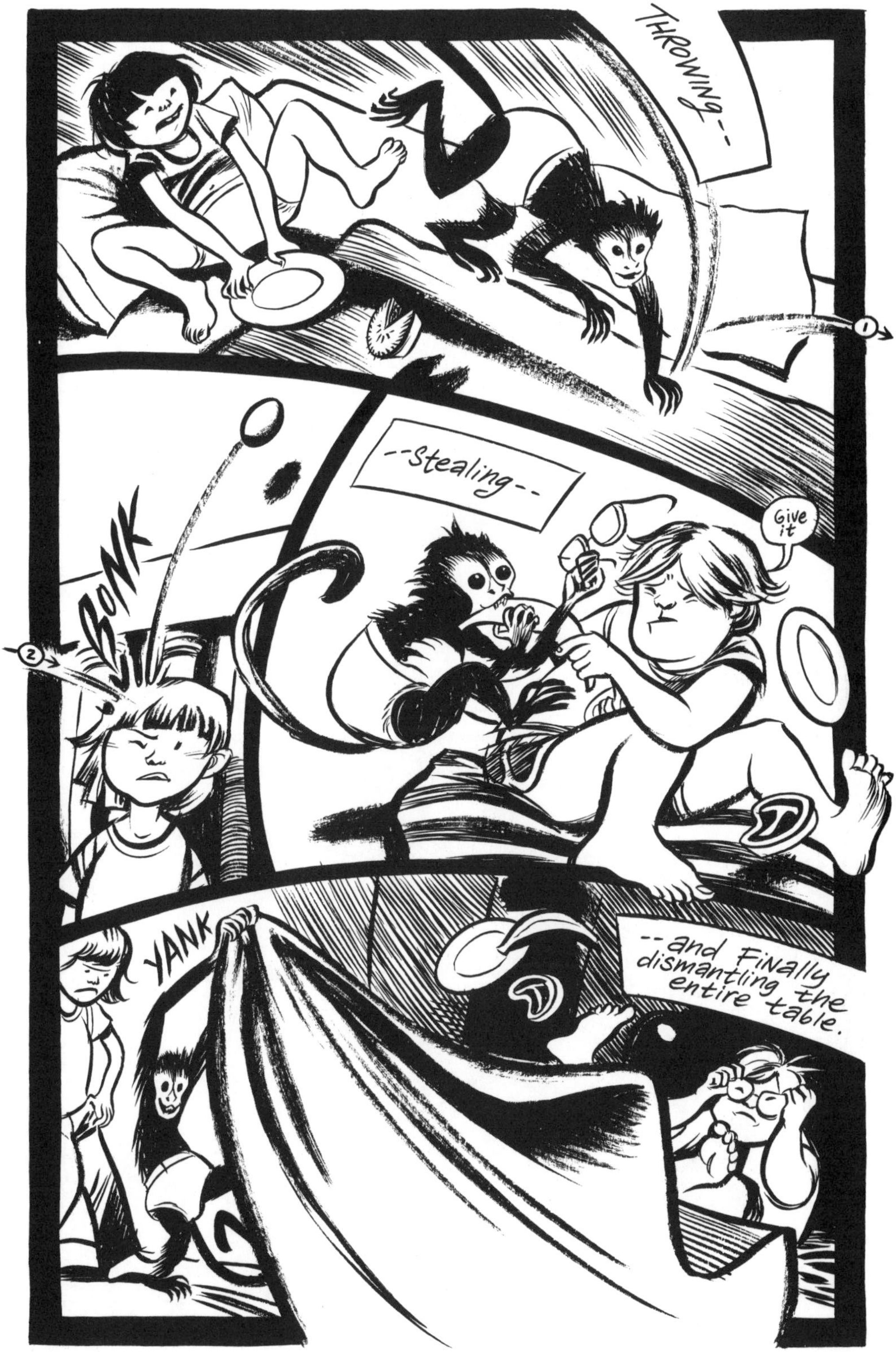
THROWING--
--Stealing--
Give it
BONK
YANK
--and Finally dismantling the entire table.

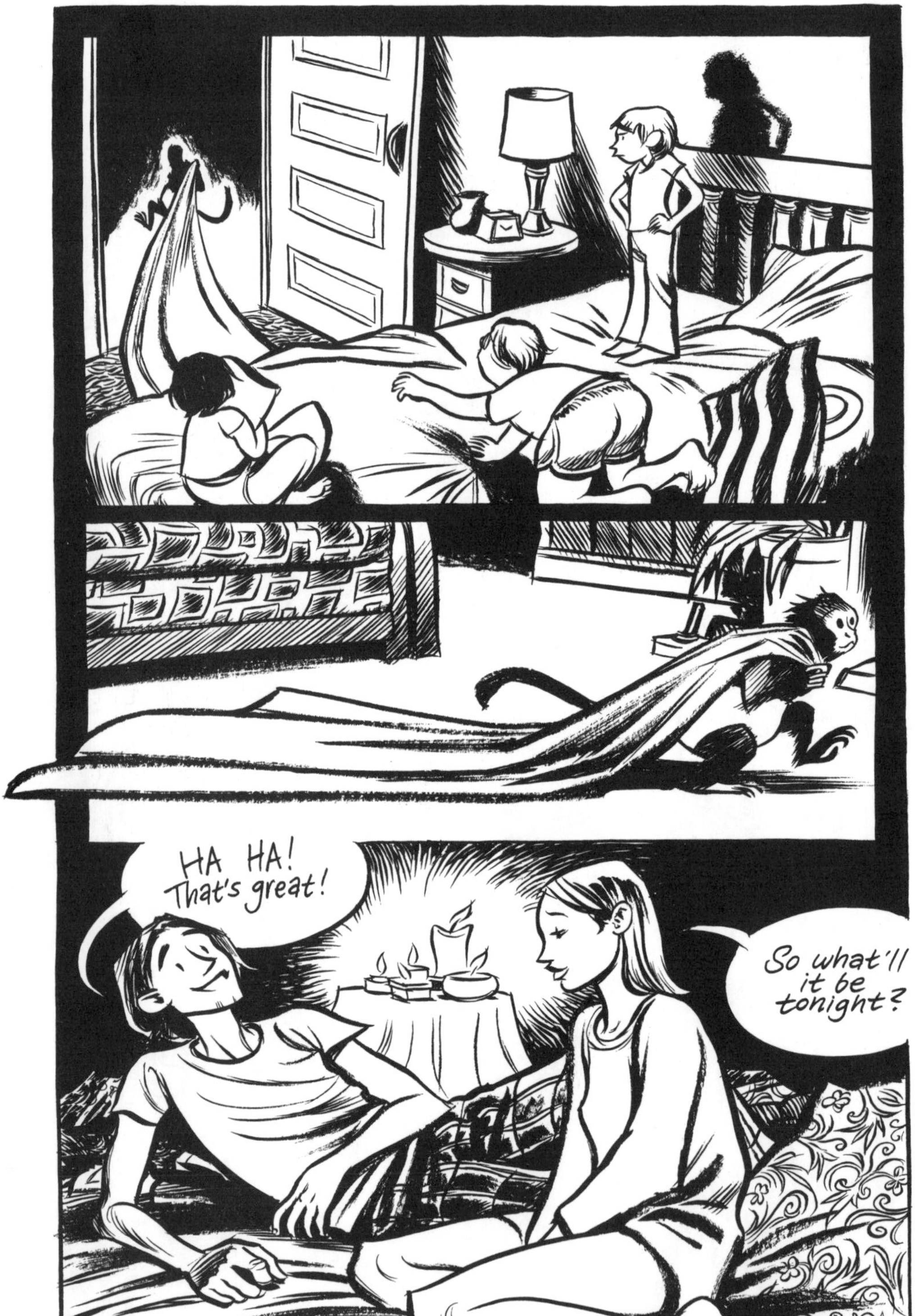
HA HA! That's great!
So what'll it be tonight?

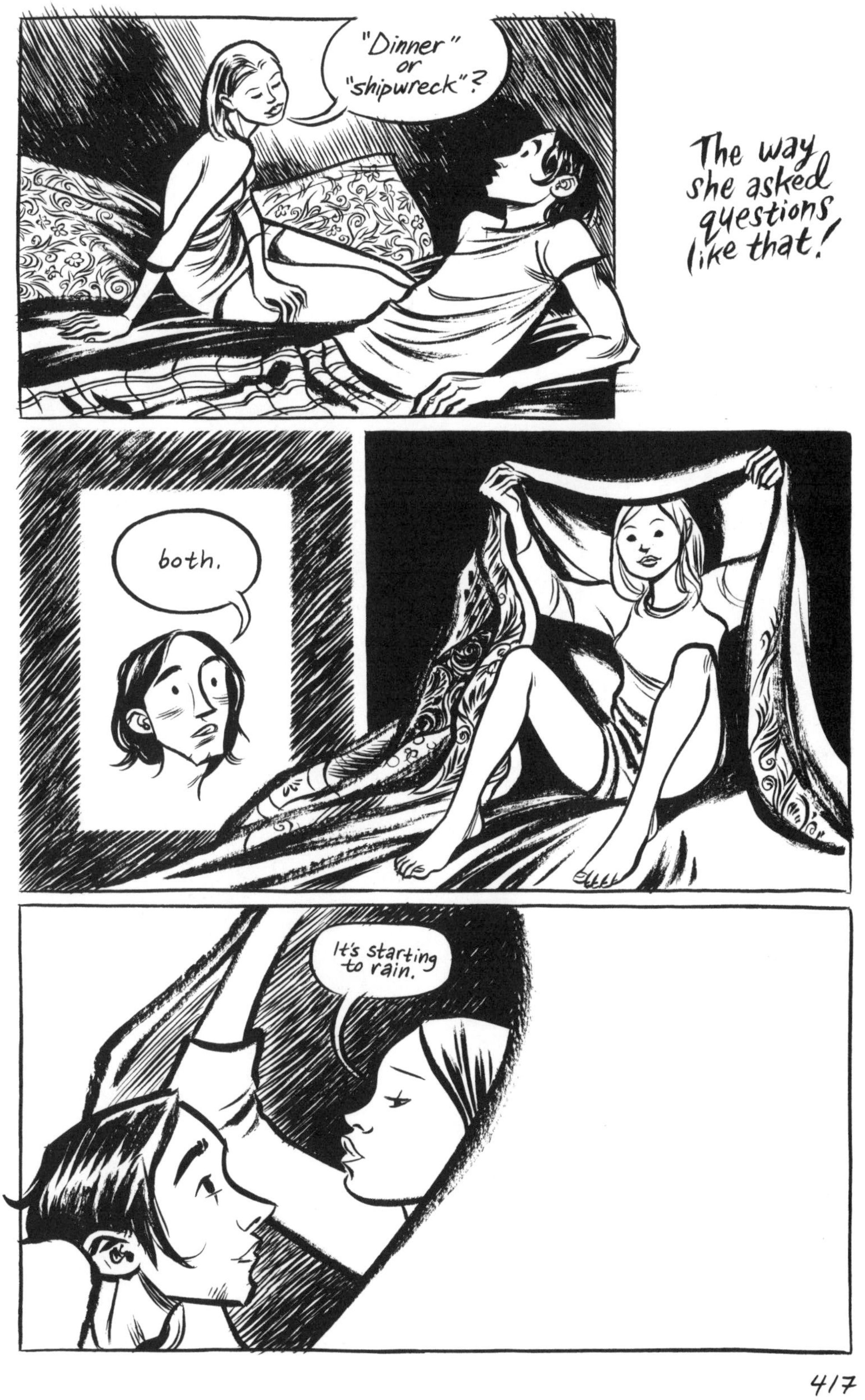
"Dinner" or "shipwreck"?
The way she asked questions like that!
both.
It's starting to rain.

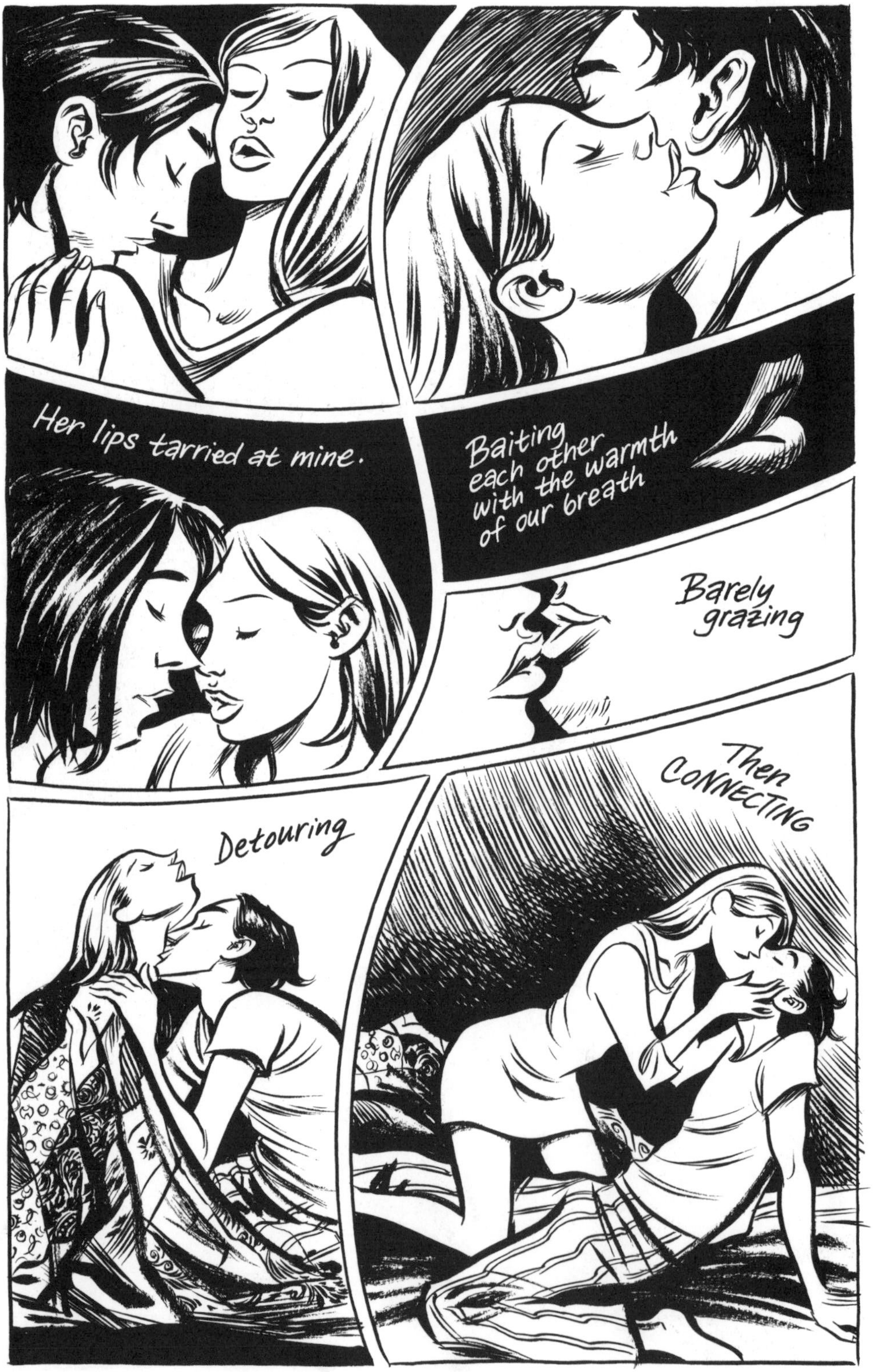
Her lips tarried at mine.
Baiting each other with the warmth of our breath
Barely grazing
Detouring
Then CONNECTING

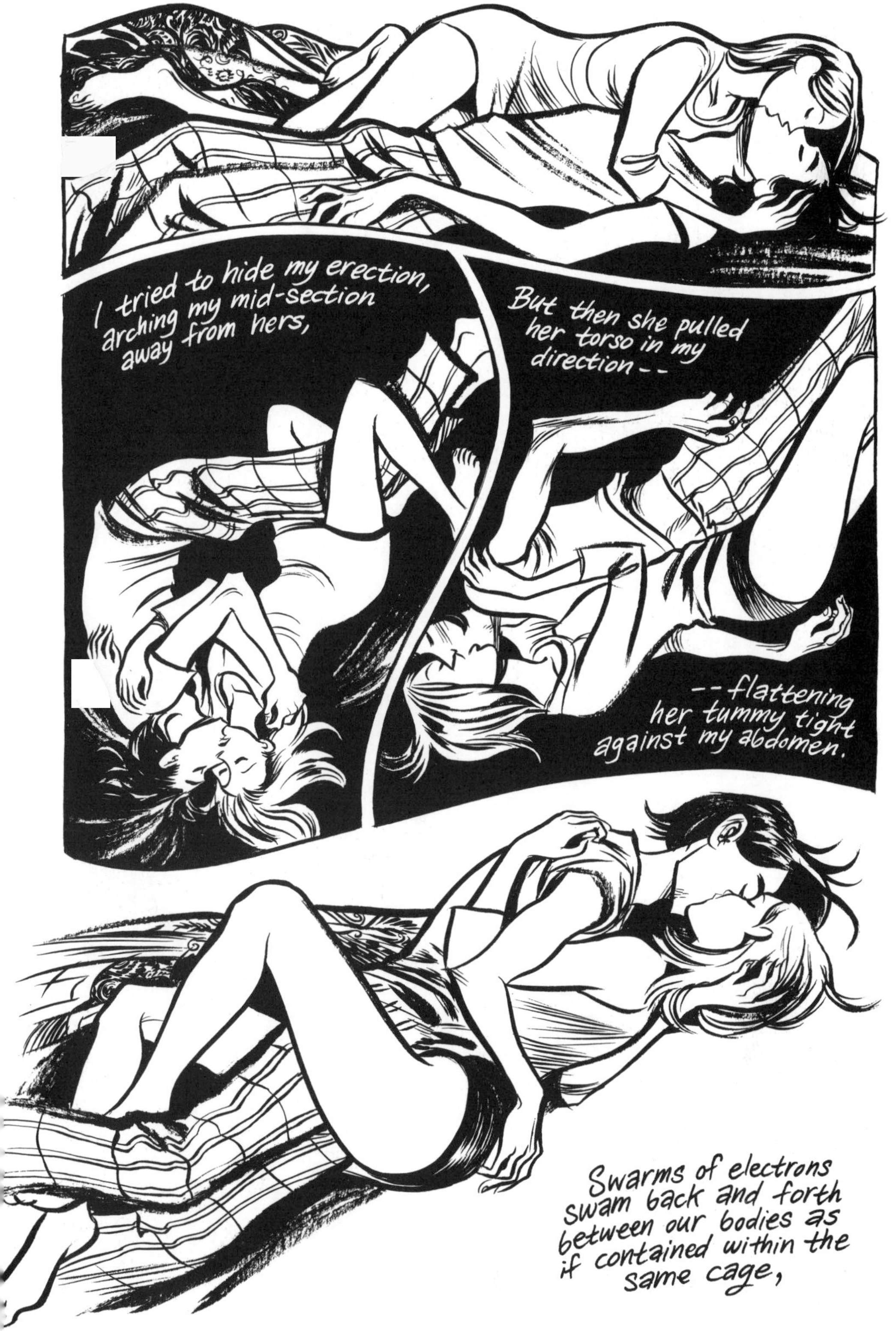
I tried to hide my erection, arching my mid-section away from hers,
But then she pulled her torso in my direction--
--flattening her tummy tight against my abdomen.
Swarms of electrons swam back and forth between our bodies as if contained within the same cage,

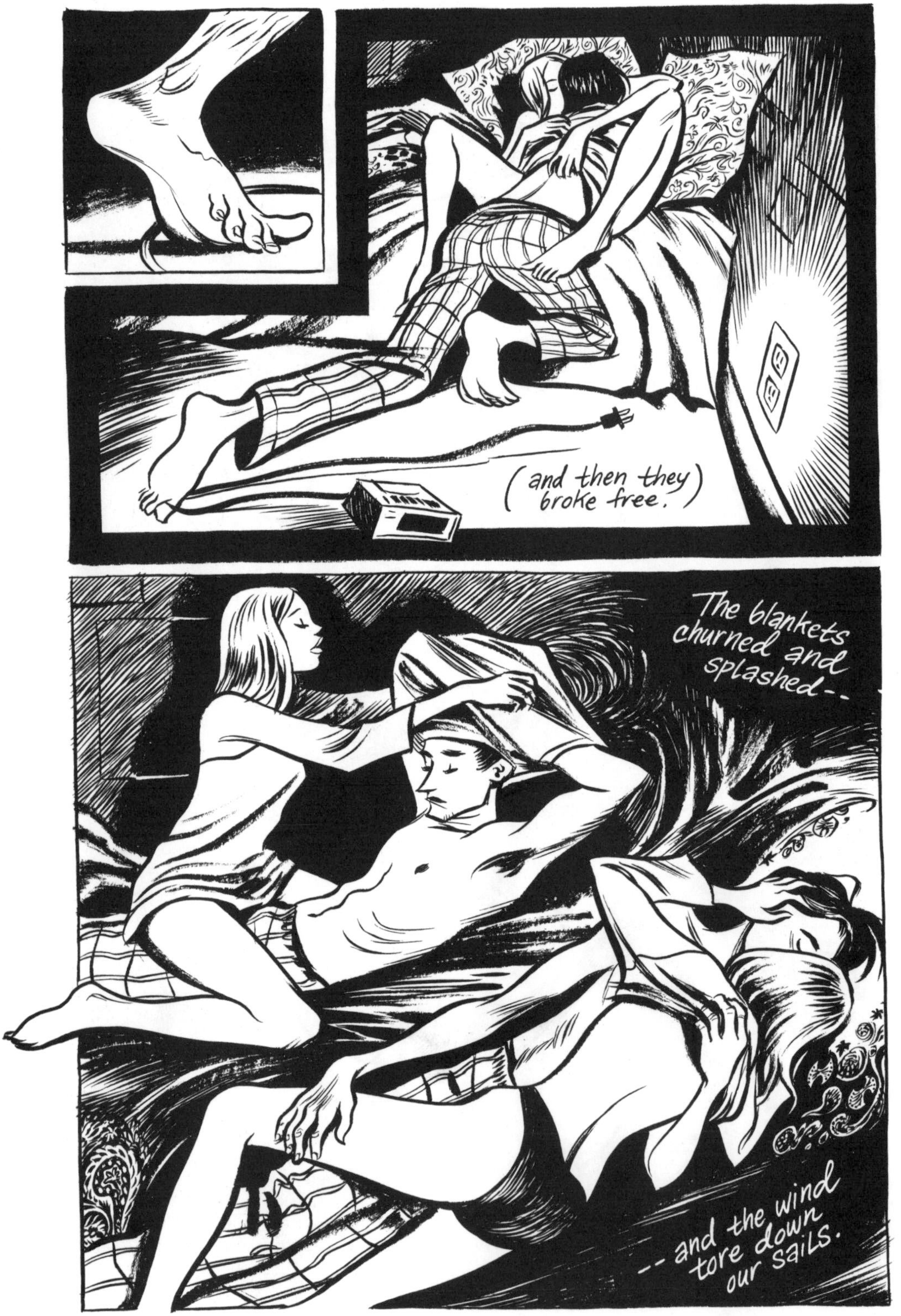
(and then they broke free.)
The blankets churned and splashed--
--and the wind tore down our sails.

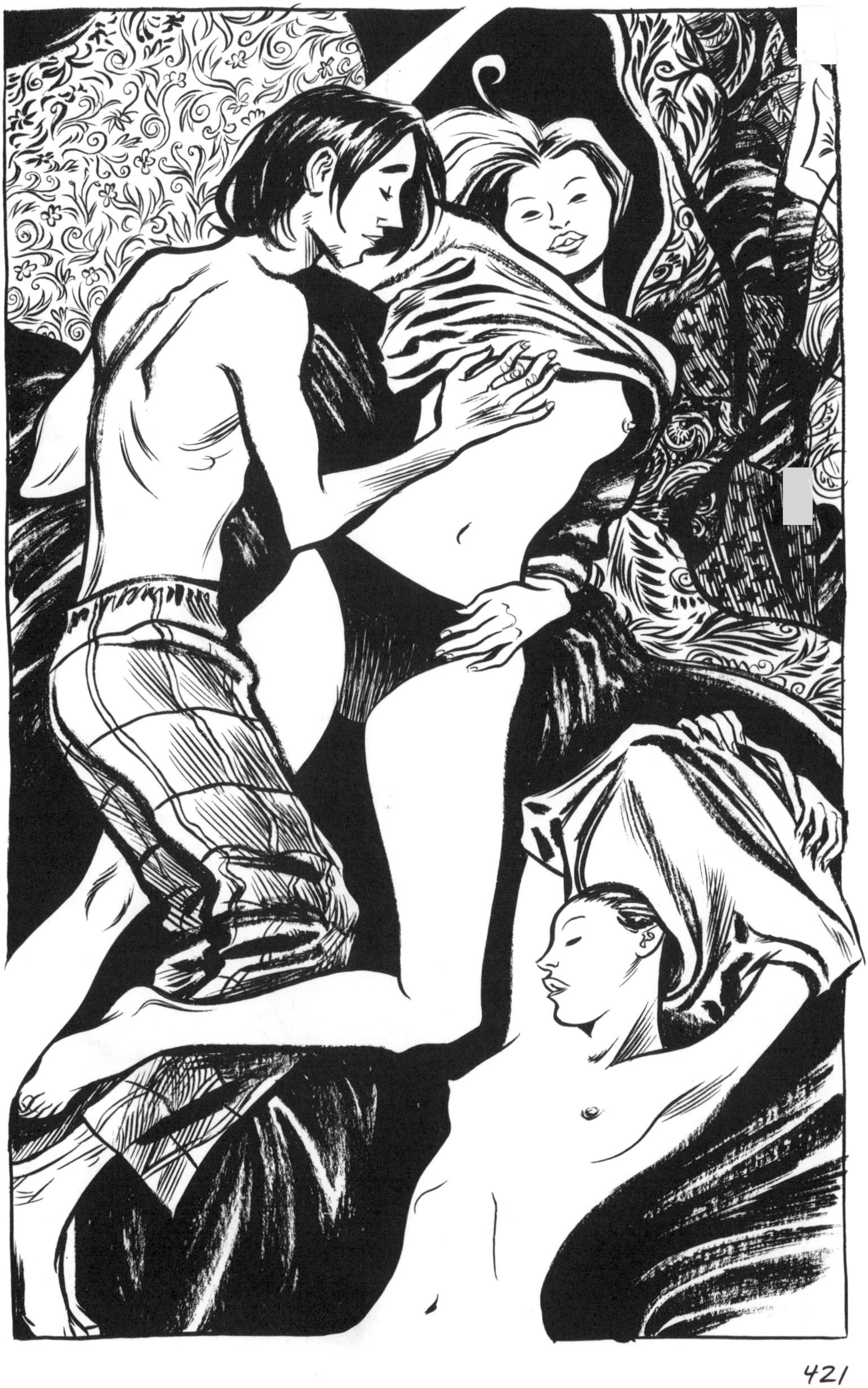

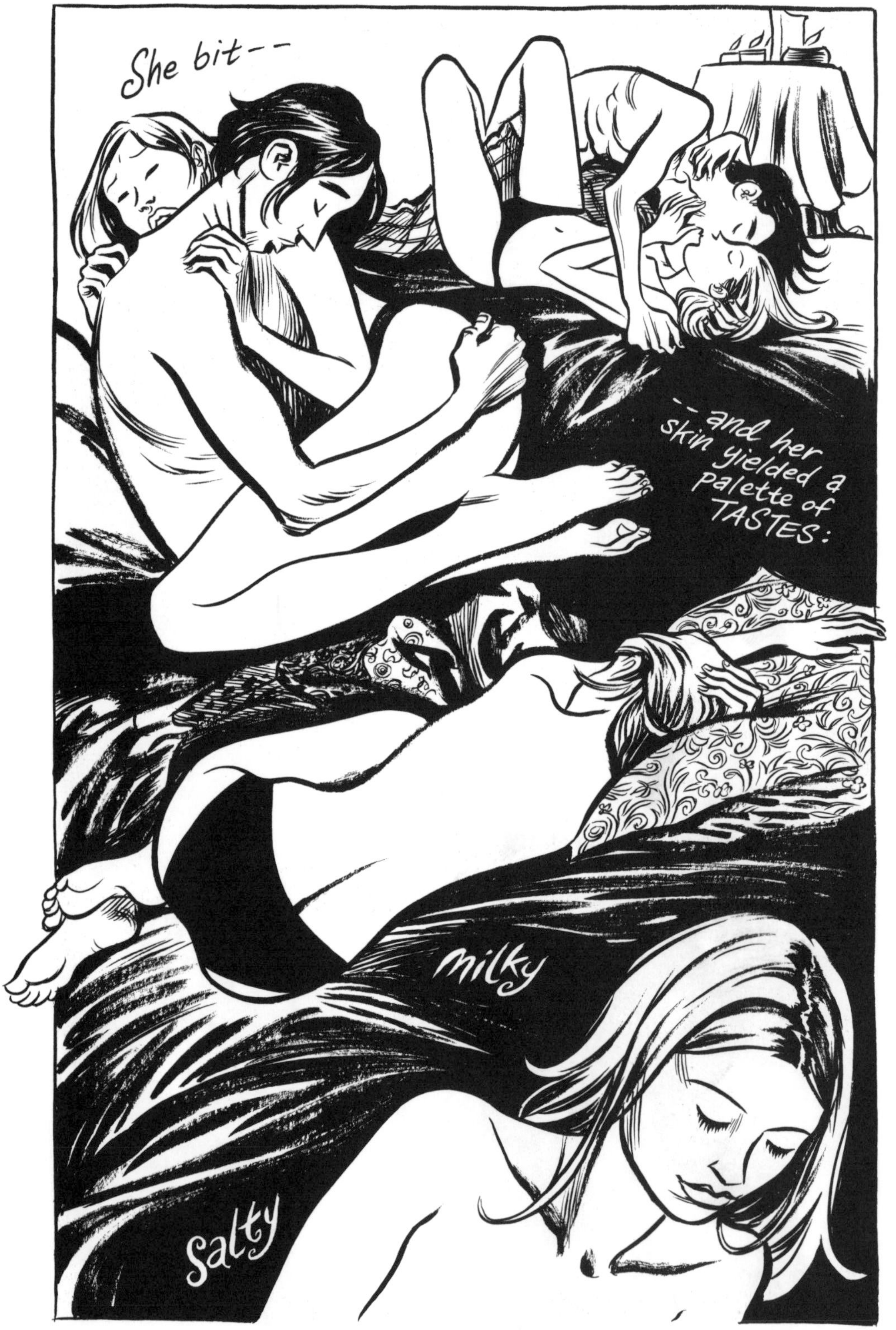
She bit--
--and her skin yielded a palette of TASTES:
milky
salty

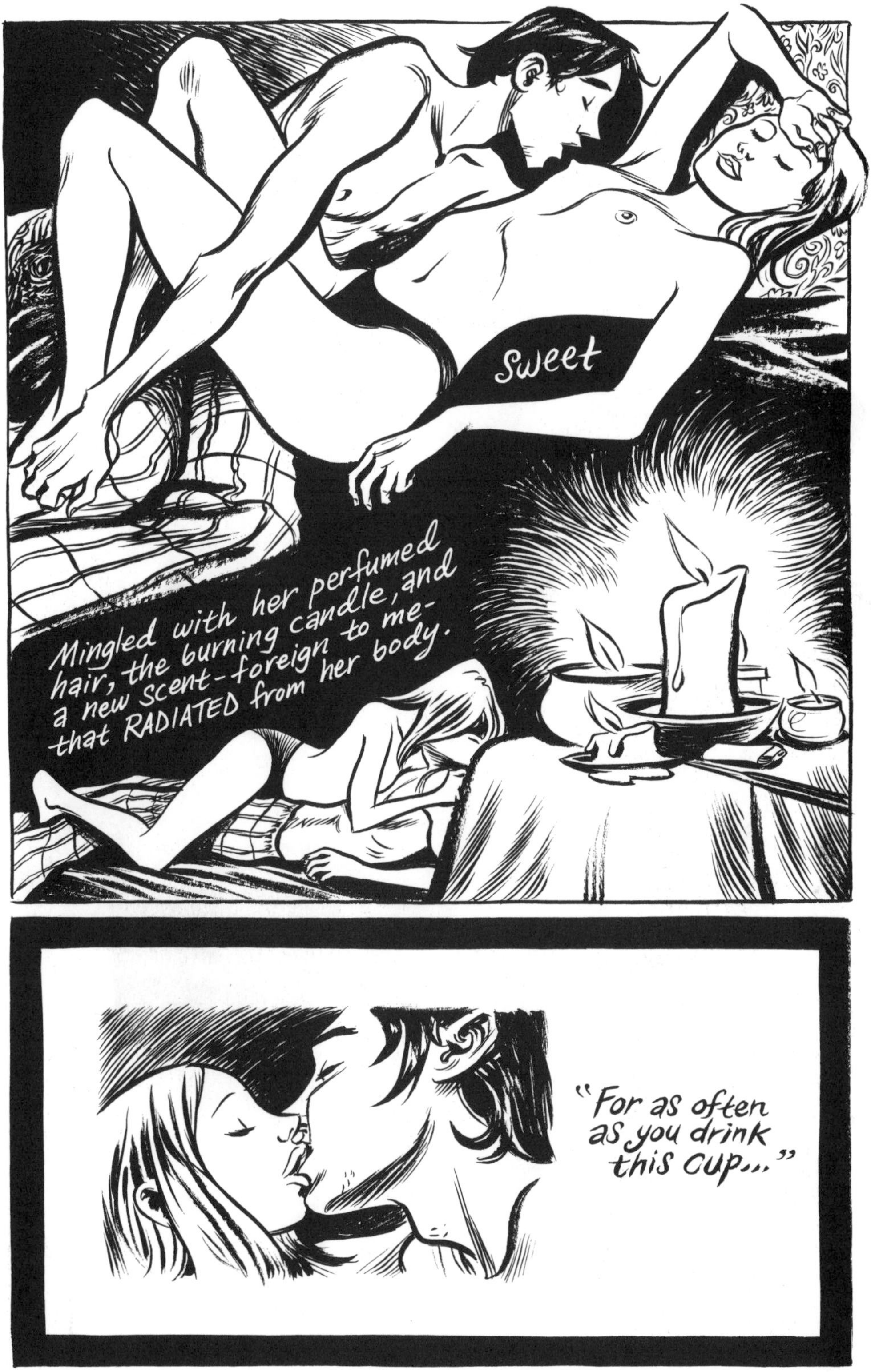
sweet
Mingled with her perfumed hair, the burning candle, and a new scent-foreign to me-that RADIATED from her body.
"For as often as you drink this cup..."

... it is never enough.

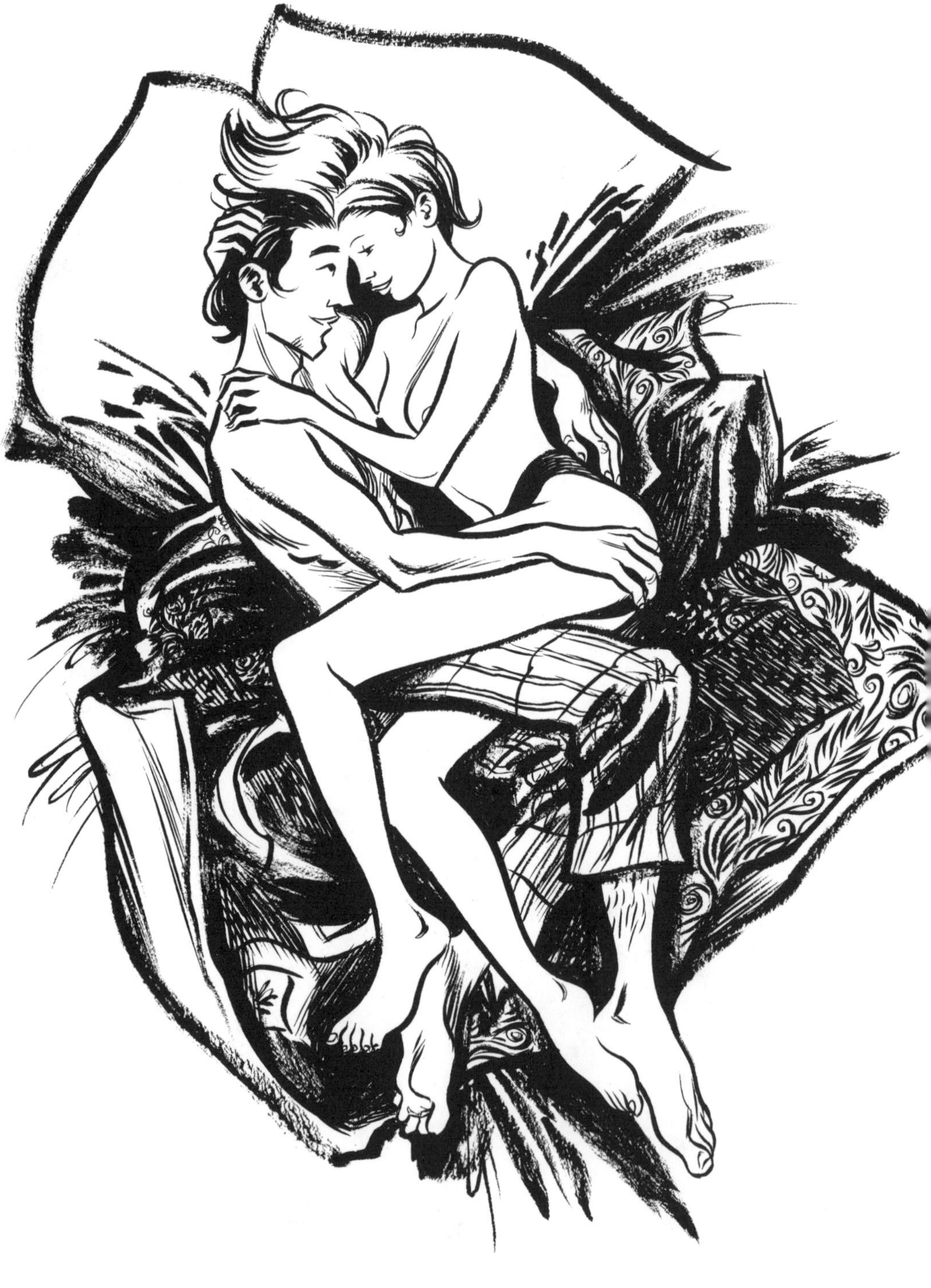

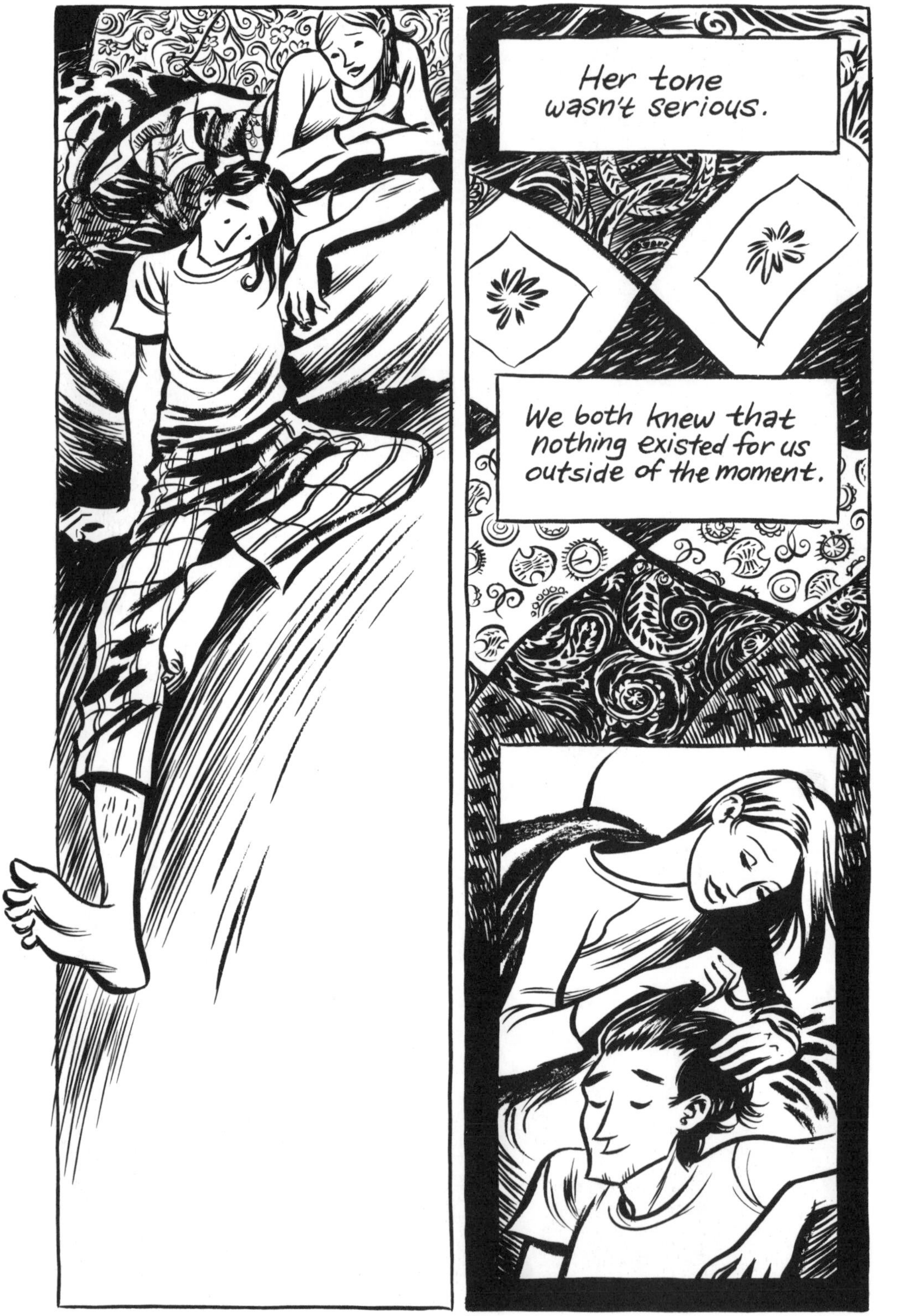
Her tone wasn't serious.
We both knew that nothing existed for us outside of the moment.

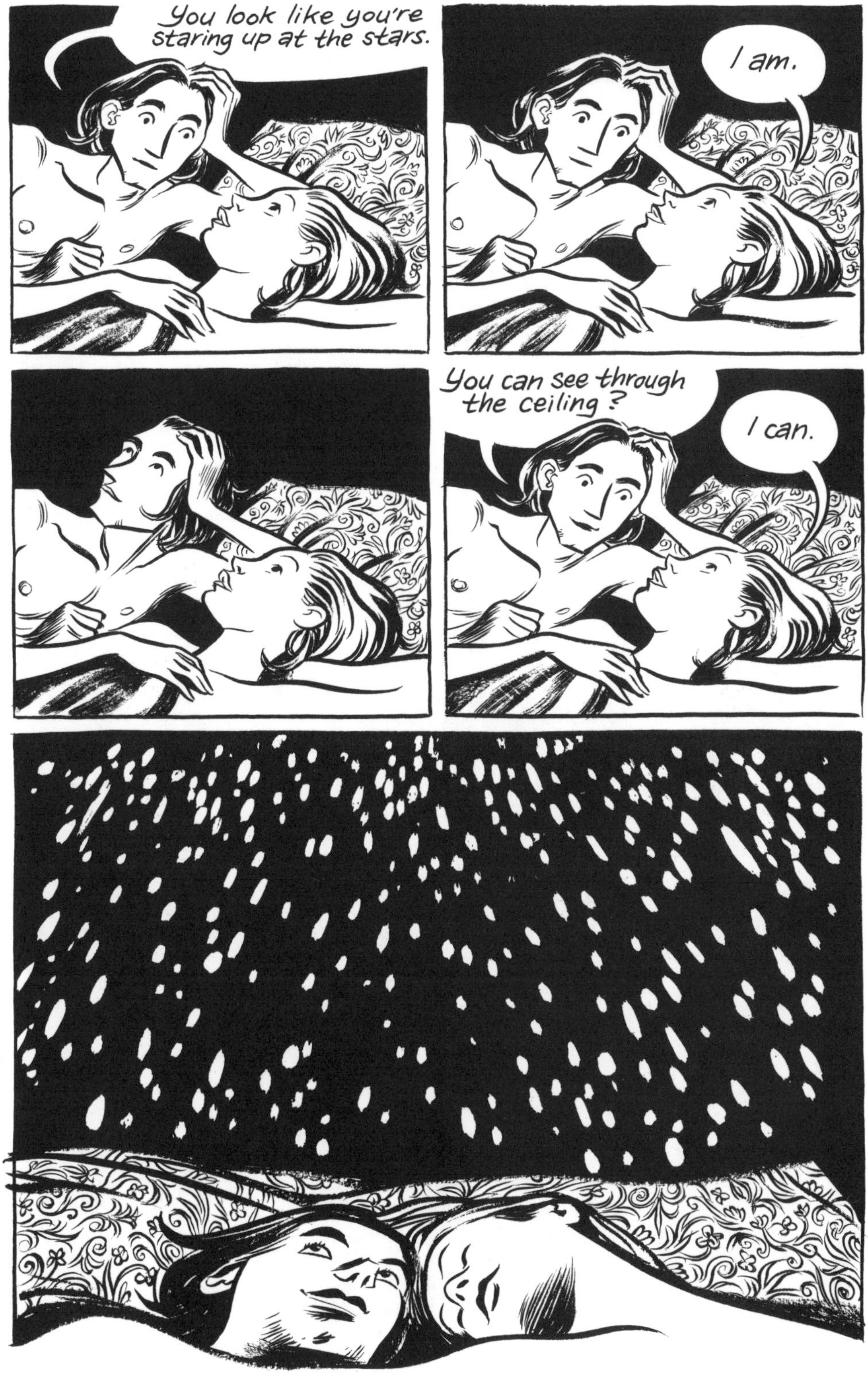
You look like you're staring up at the stars.
I am.
You can see through the ceiling?
I can.

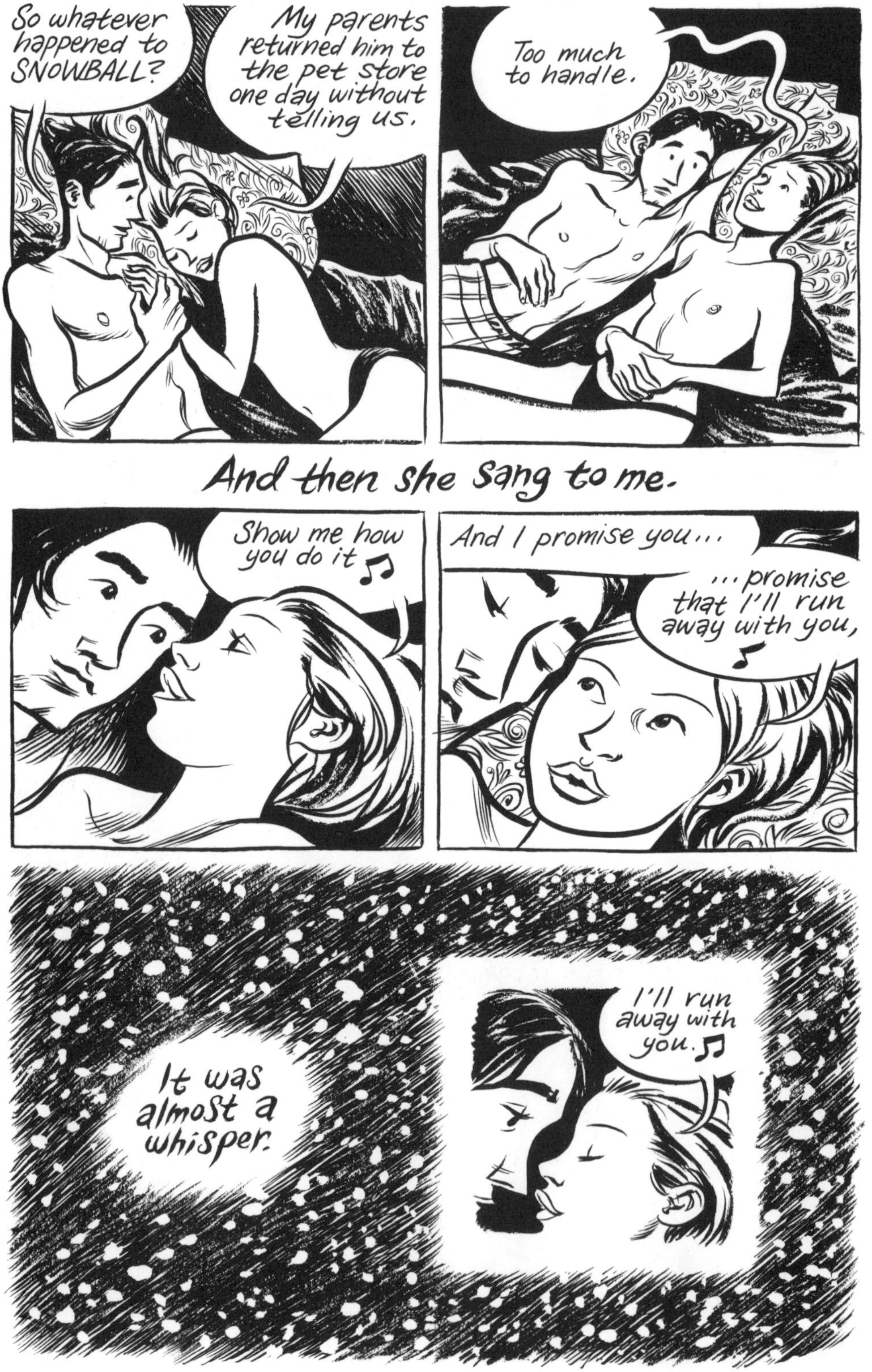

So whatever happened to SNOWBALL?
My parents returned him to the pet store one day without telling us.
Too much to handle.
And then she sang to me.
Show me how you do it ♫
And I promise you...
...promise that I'll run away with you,
It was almost a whisper.
I'll run away with you. ♫

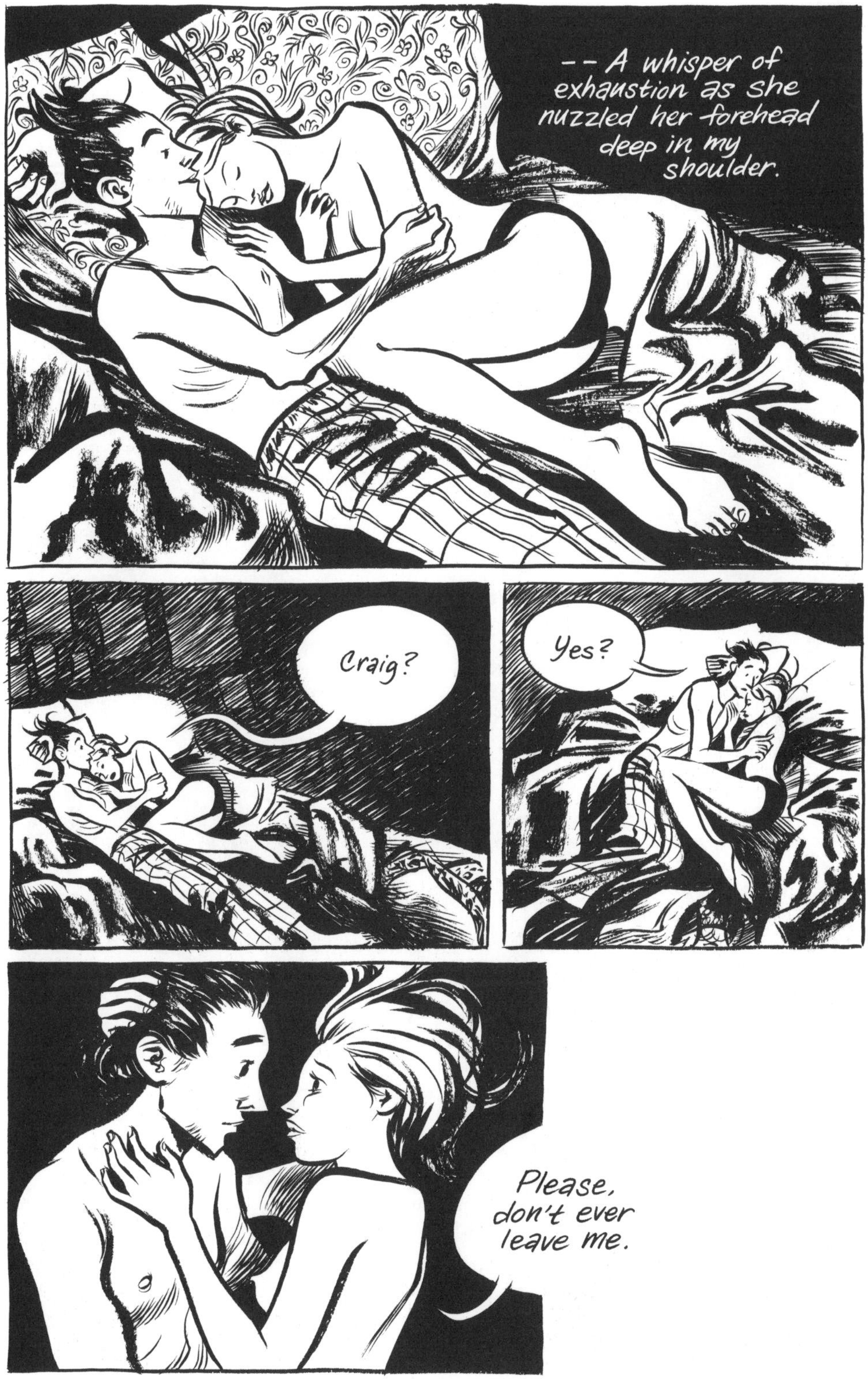
-- A whisper of exhaustion as she nuzzled her forehead deep in my shoulder.
Craig?
Yes?
Please, don't ever leave me.

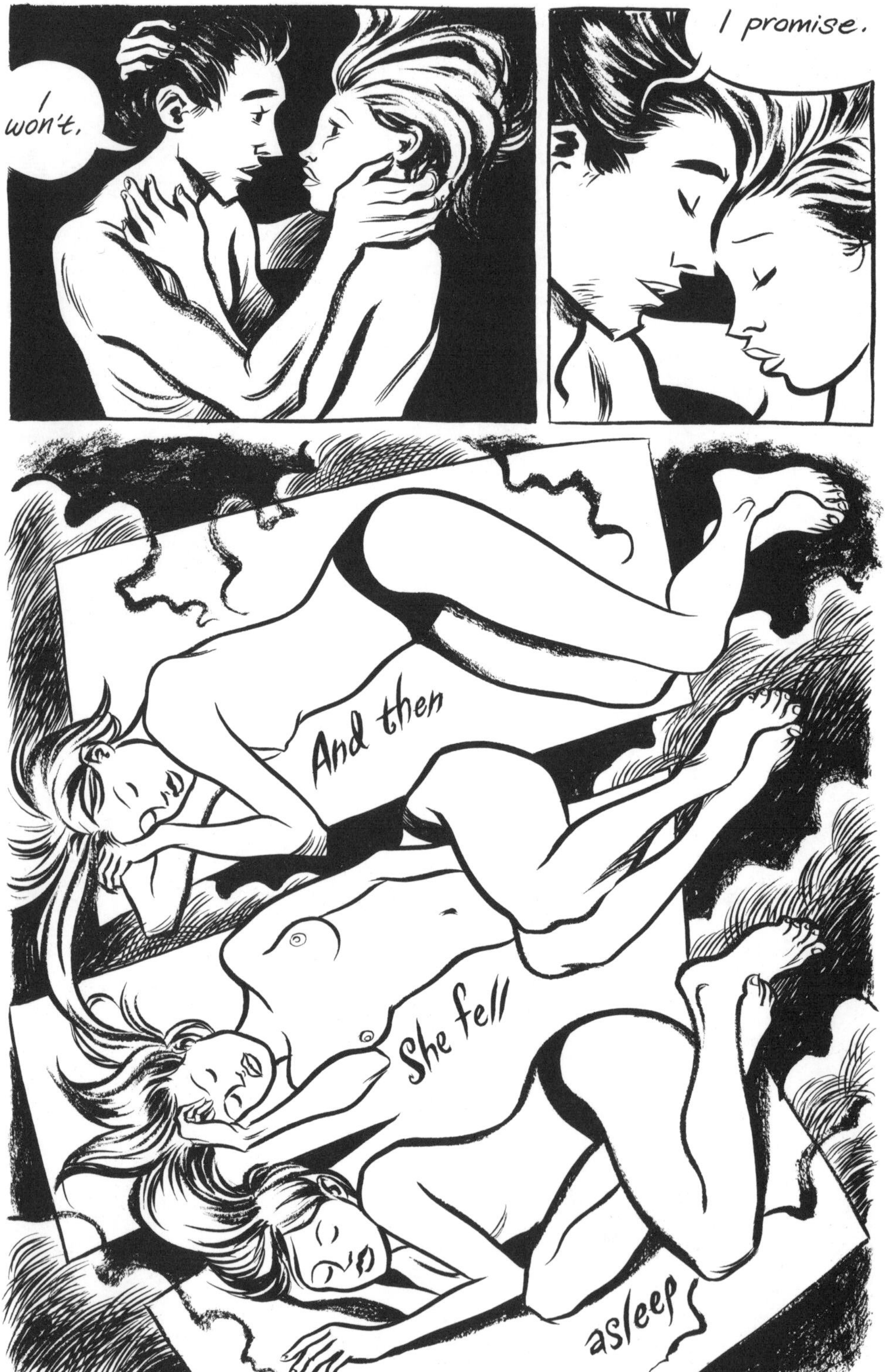
I won't.
I promise.
And then
She fell
asleep

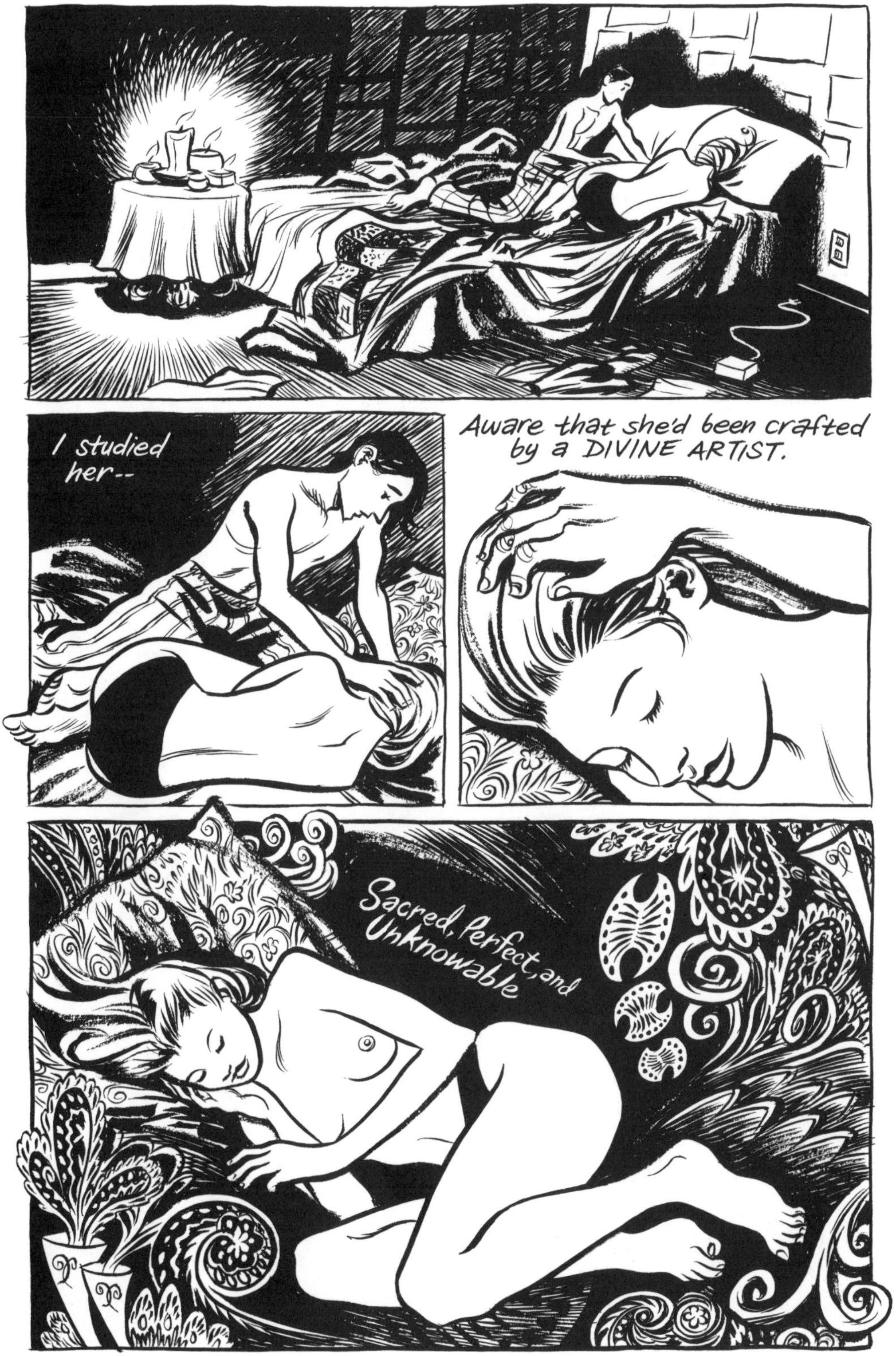
I studied her--
Aware that she'd been crafted by a DIVINE ARTIST.
Sacred, Perfect, and Unknowable

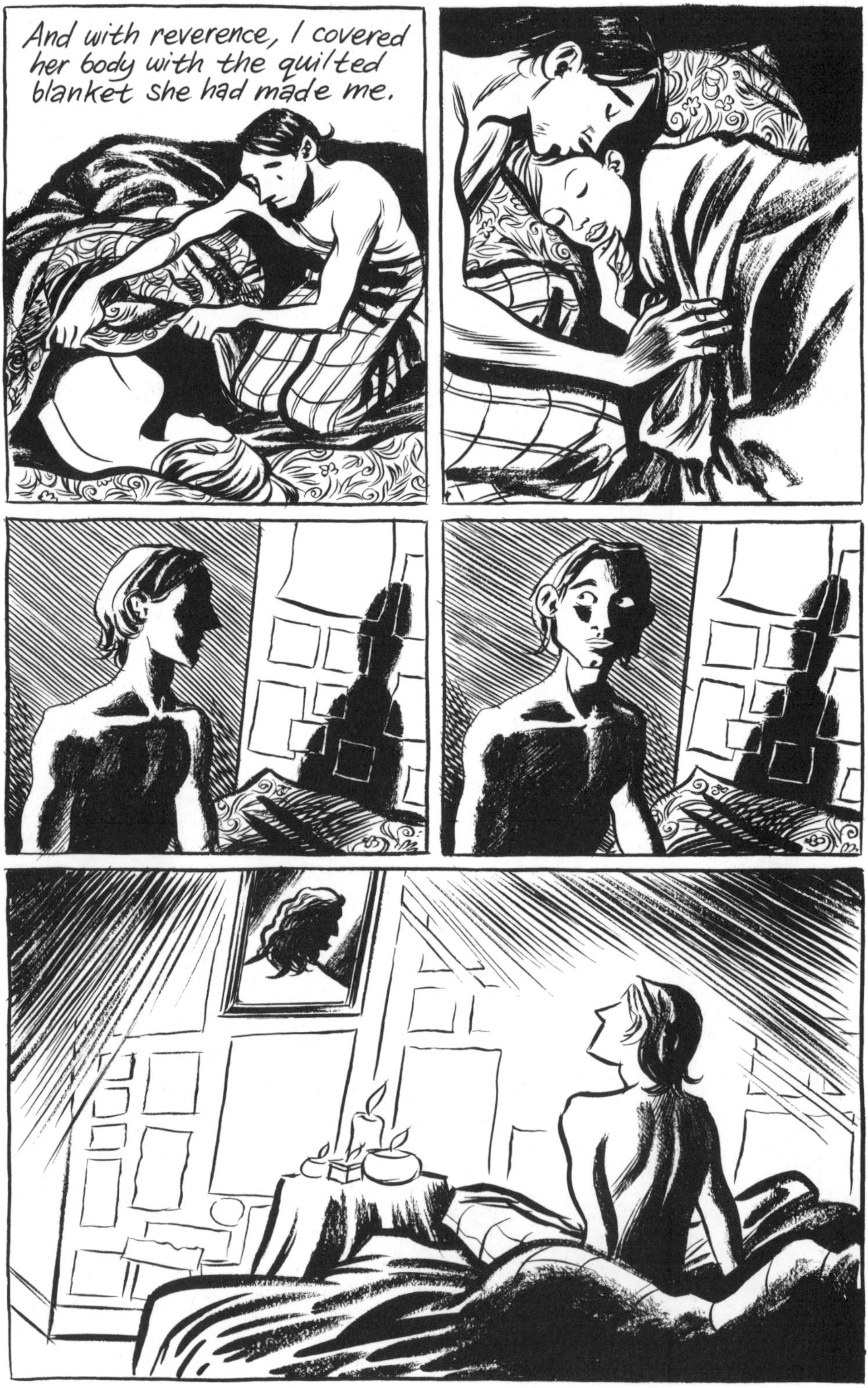
And with reverence, I covered her body with the quilted blanket she had made me.

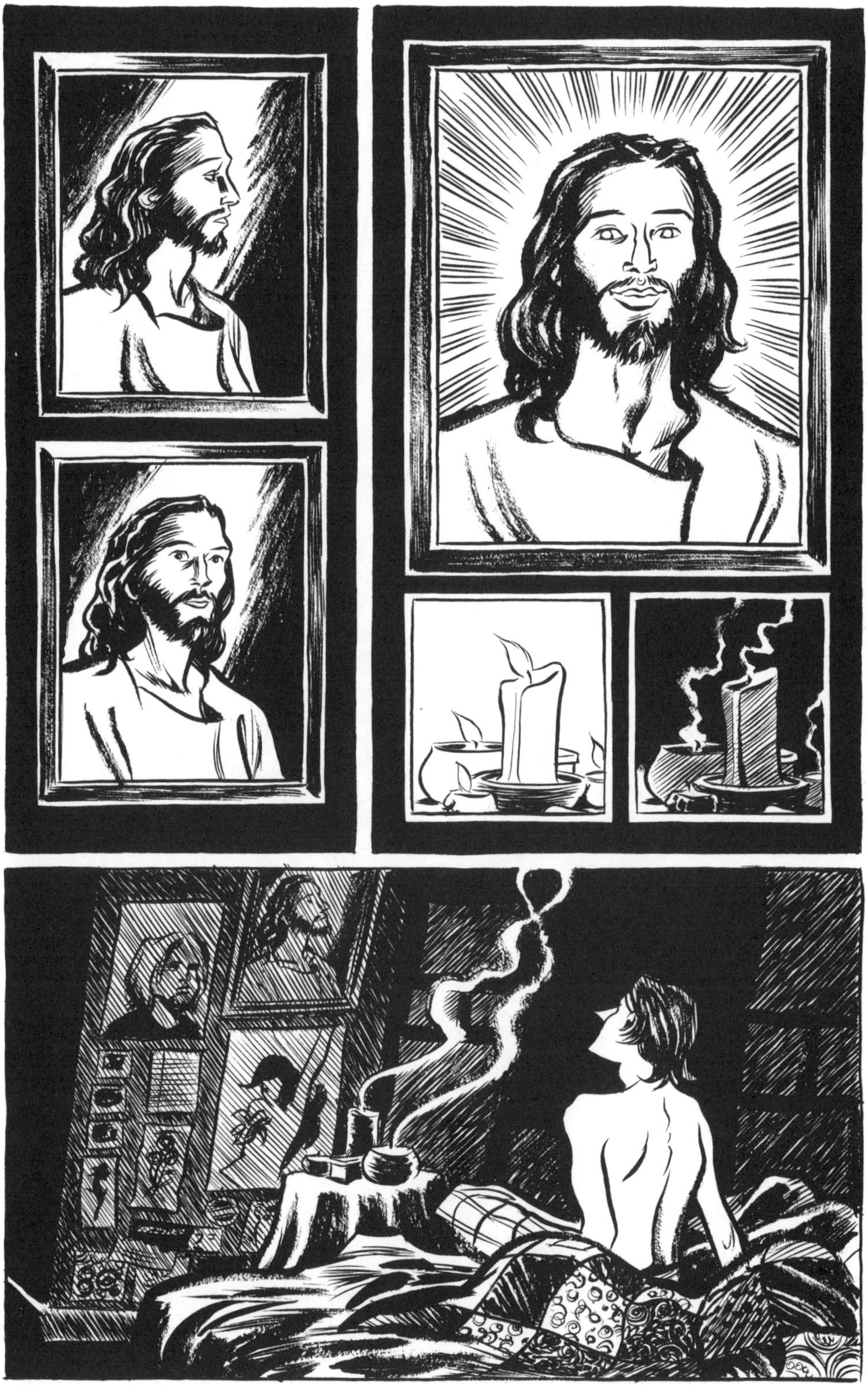

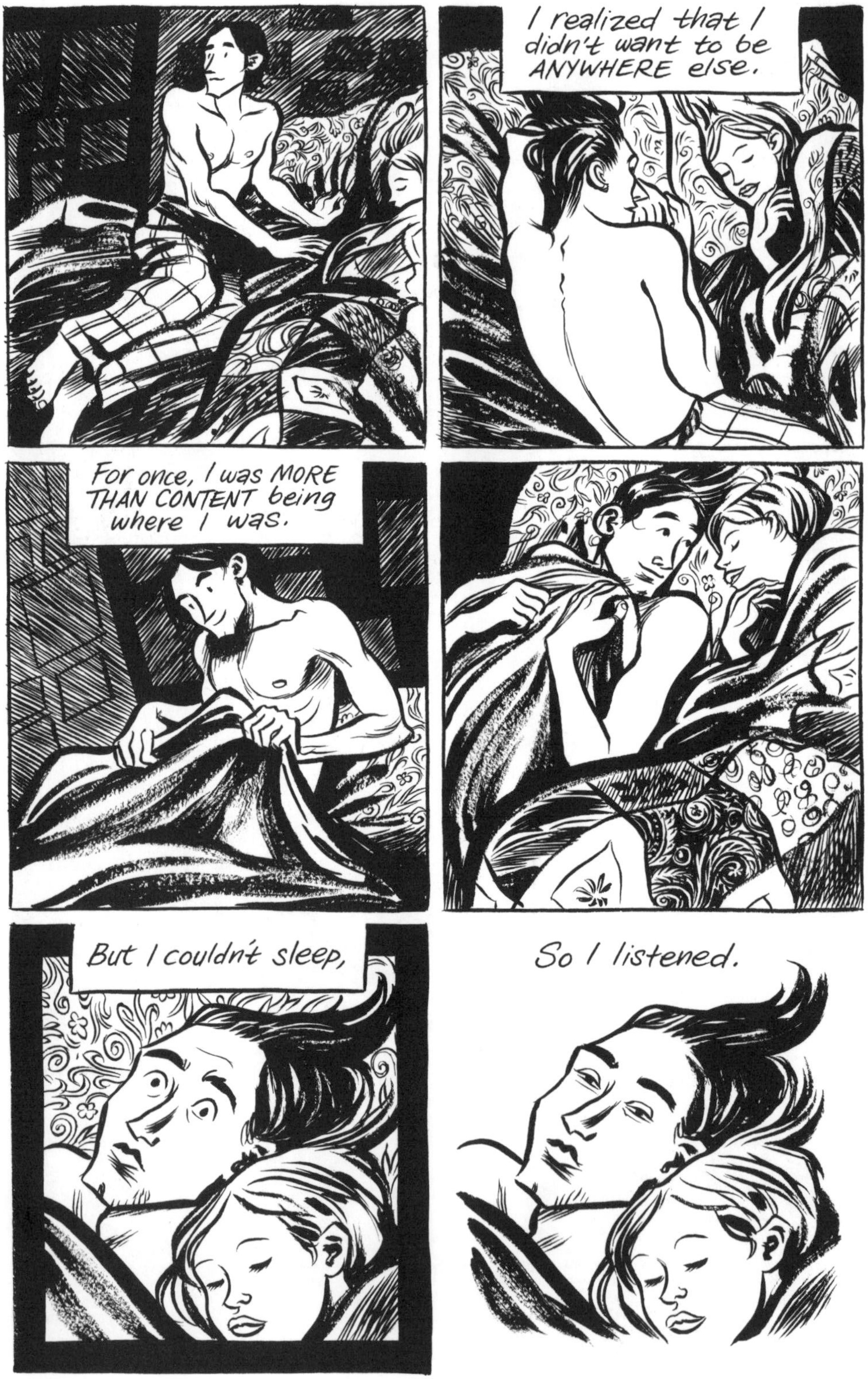

I realized that I didn't want to be ANYWHERE else.
For once, I was MORE THAN CONTENT being where I was.
But I couldn't sleep,
So I listened.

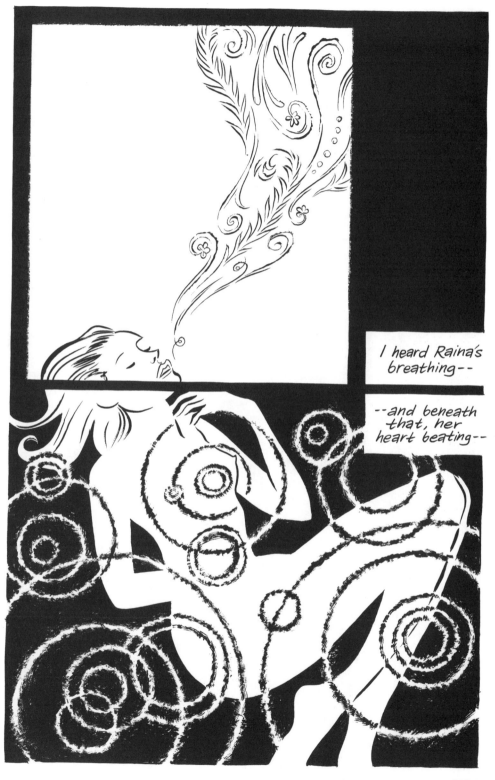

I heard Raina's breathing--

--and beneath that, her heart beating--

433

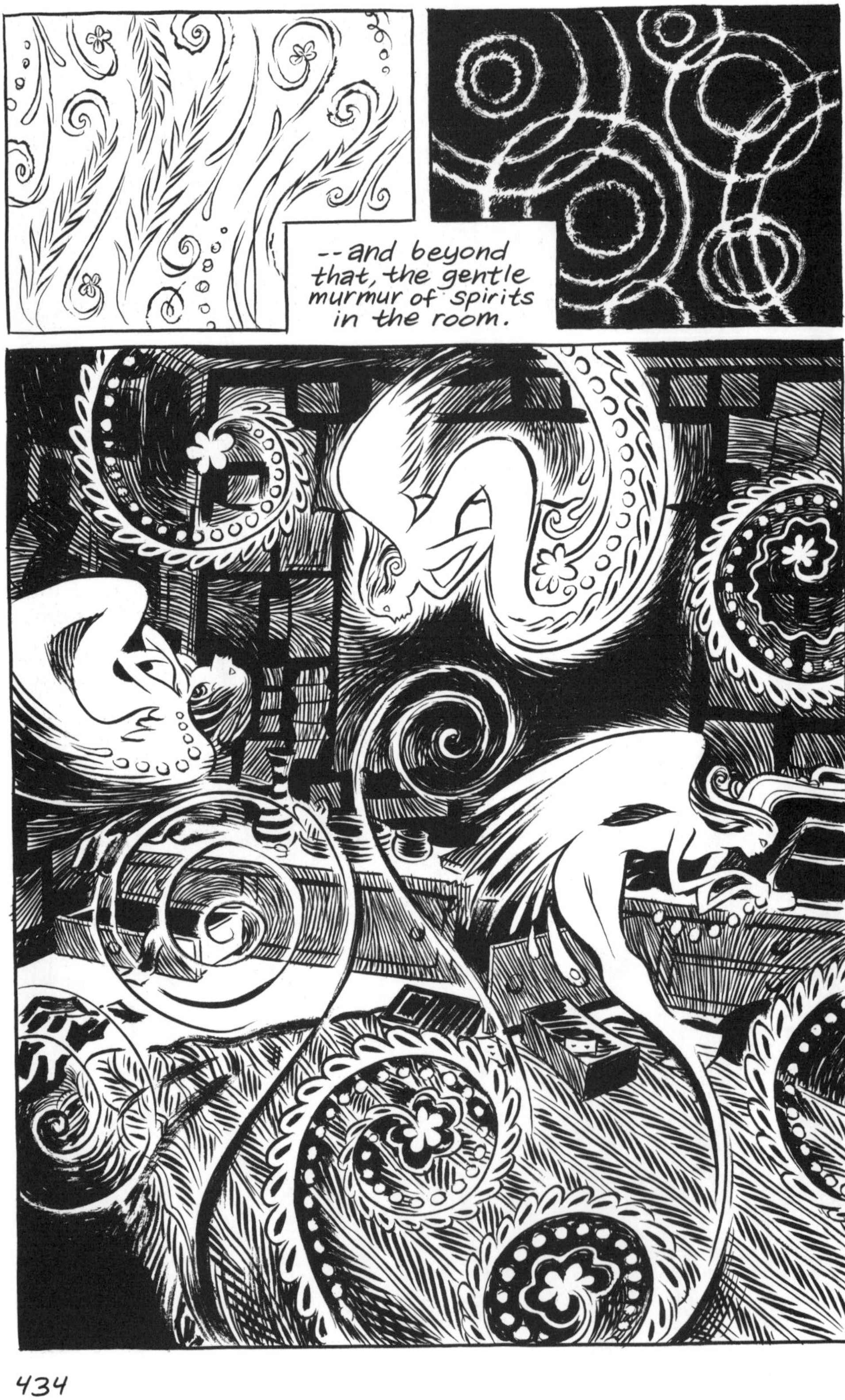
--and beyond that, the gentle murmur of spirits in the room.

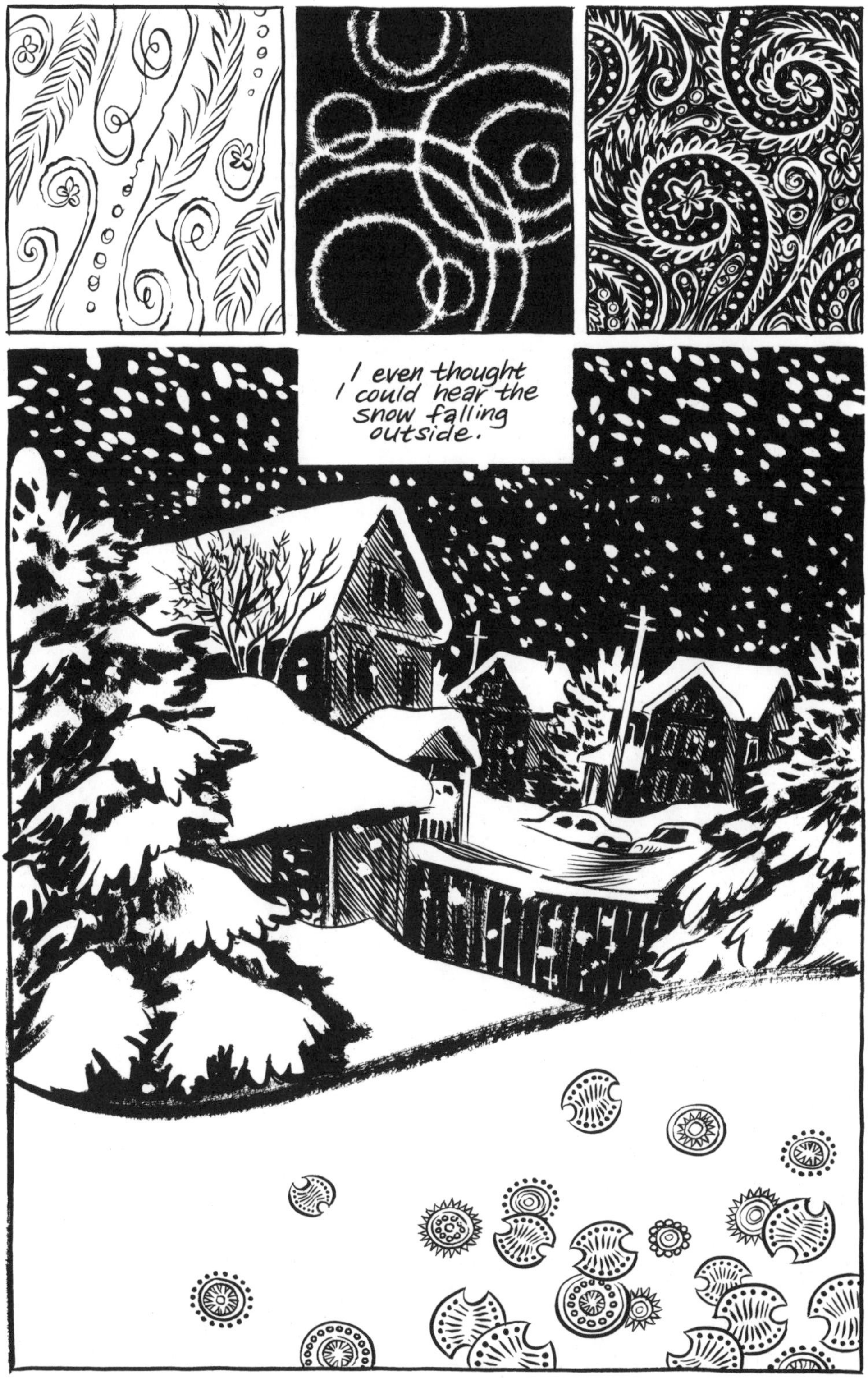
I even thought I could hear the snow falling outside.

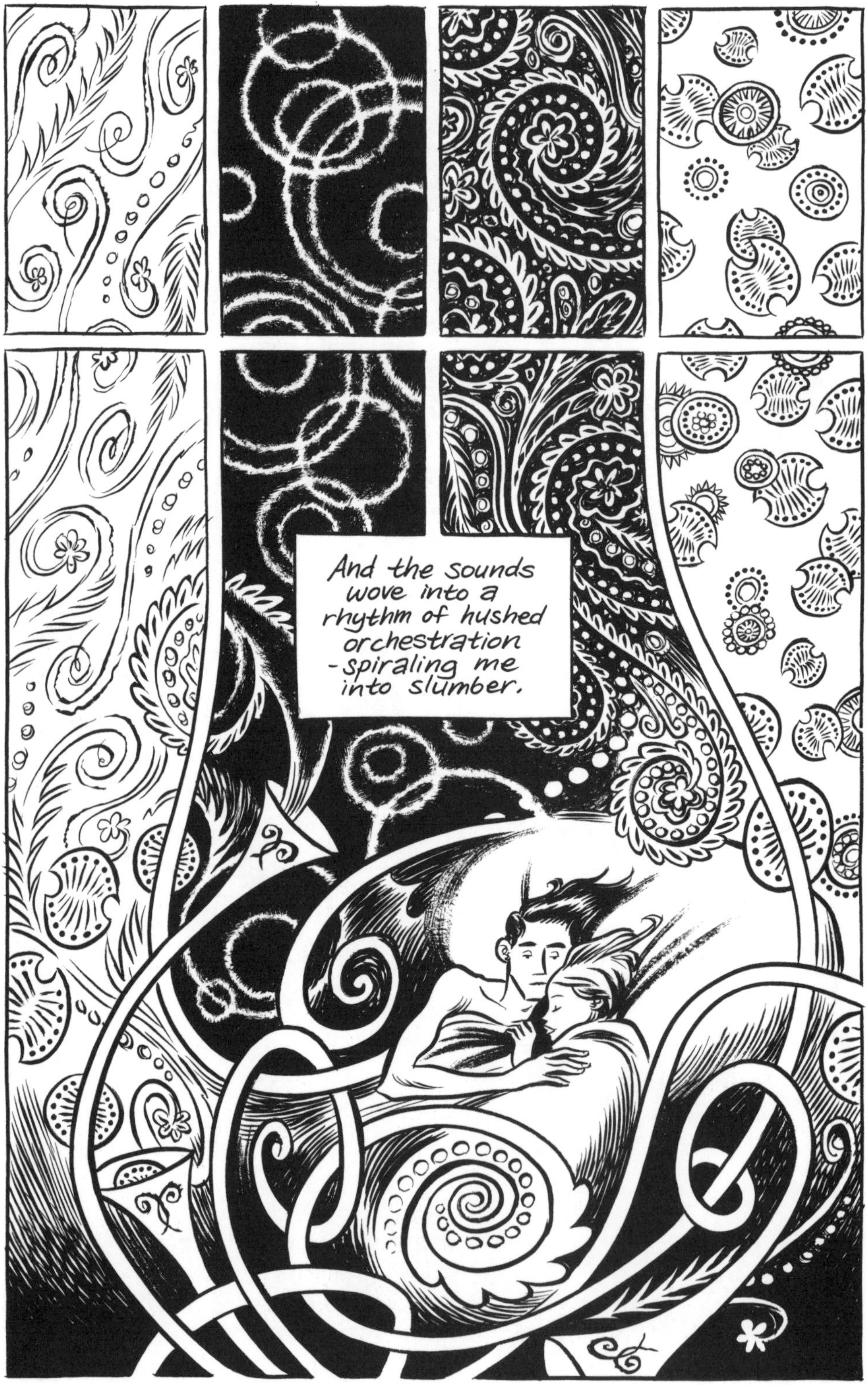
And the sounds wove into a rhythm of hushed orchestration -spiraling me into slumber.

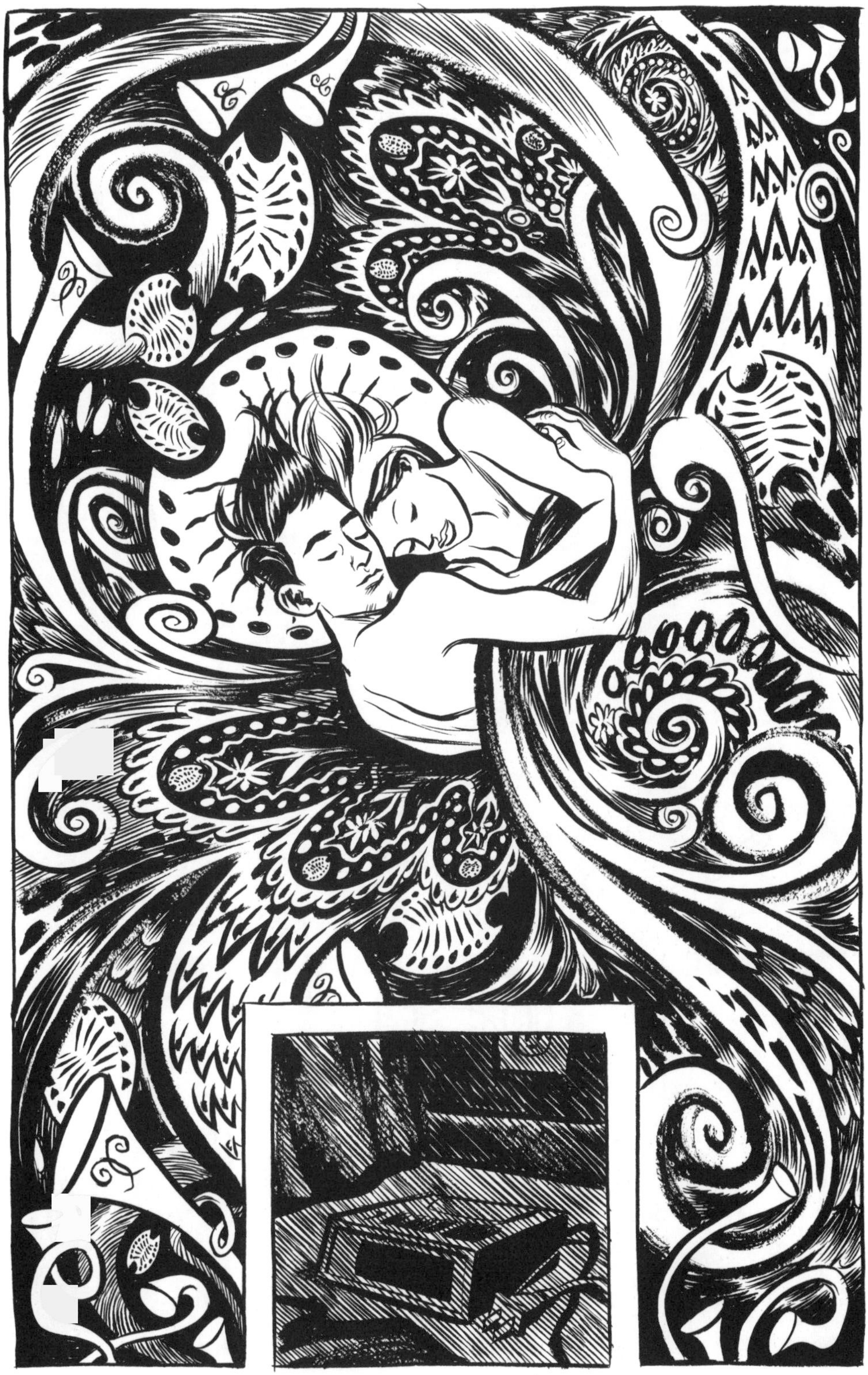

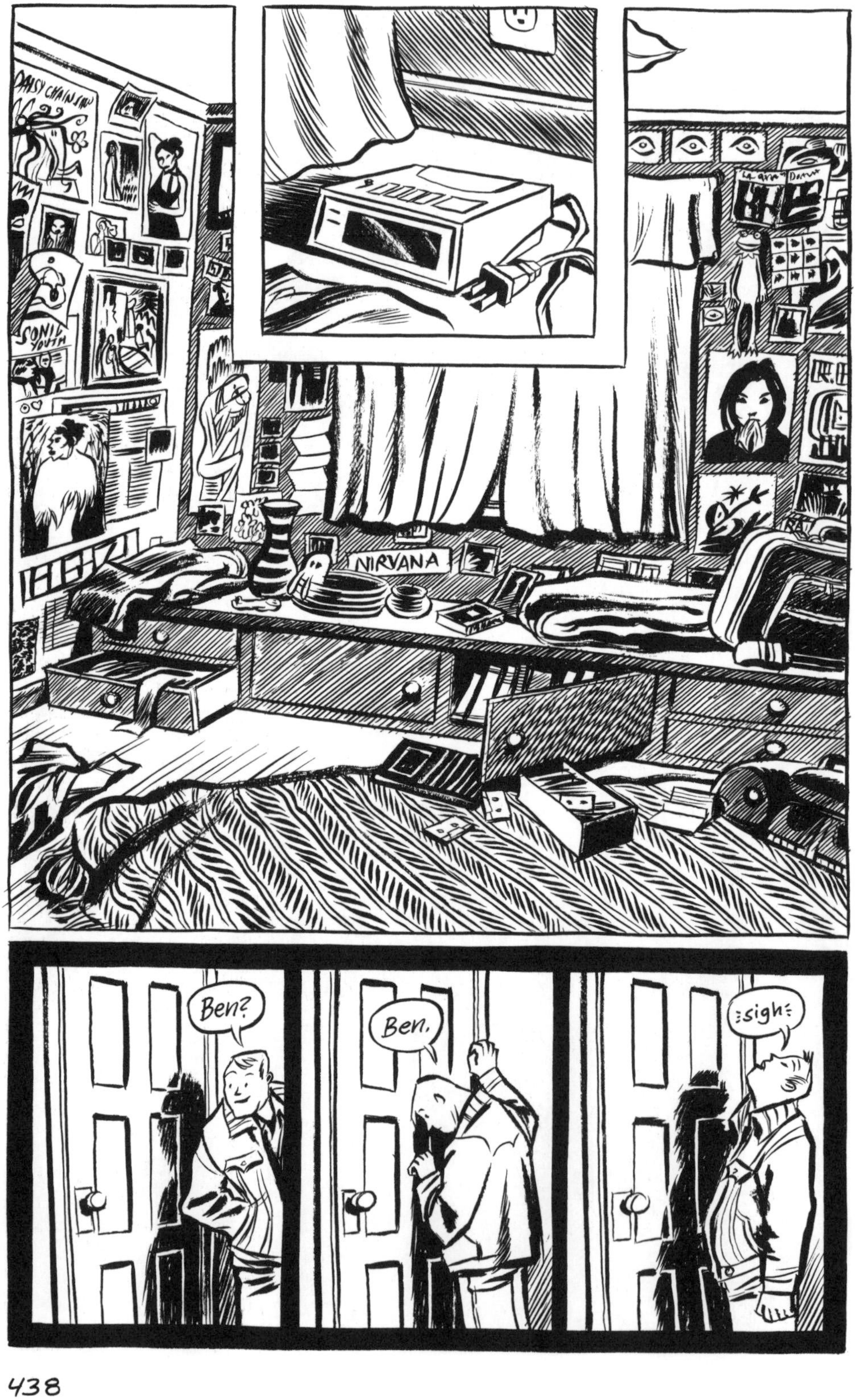
DAISY CHAINSAW
SONIC YOUTH
NIRVANA
Ben?
Ben.
:sigh:

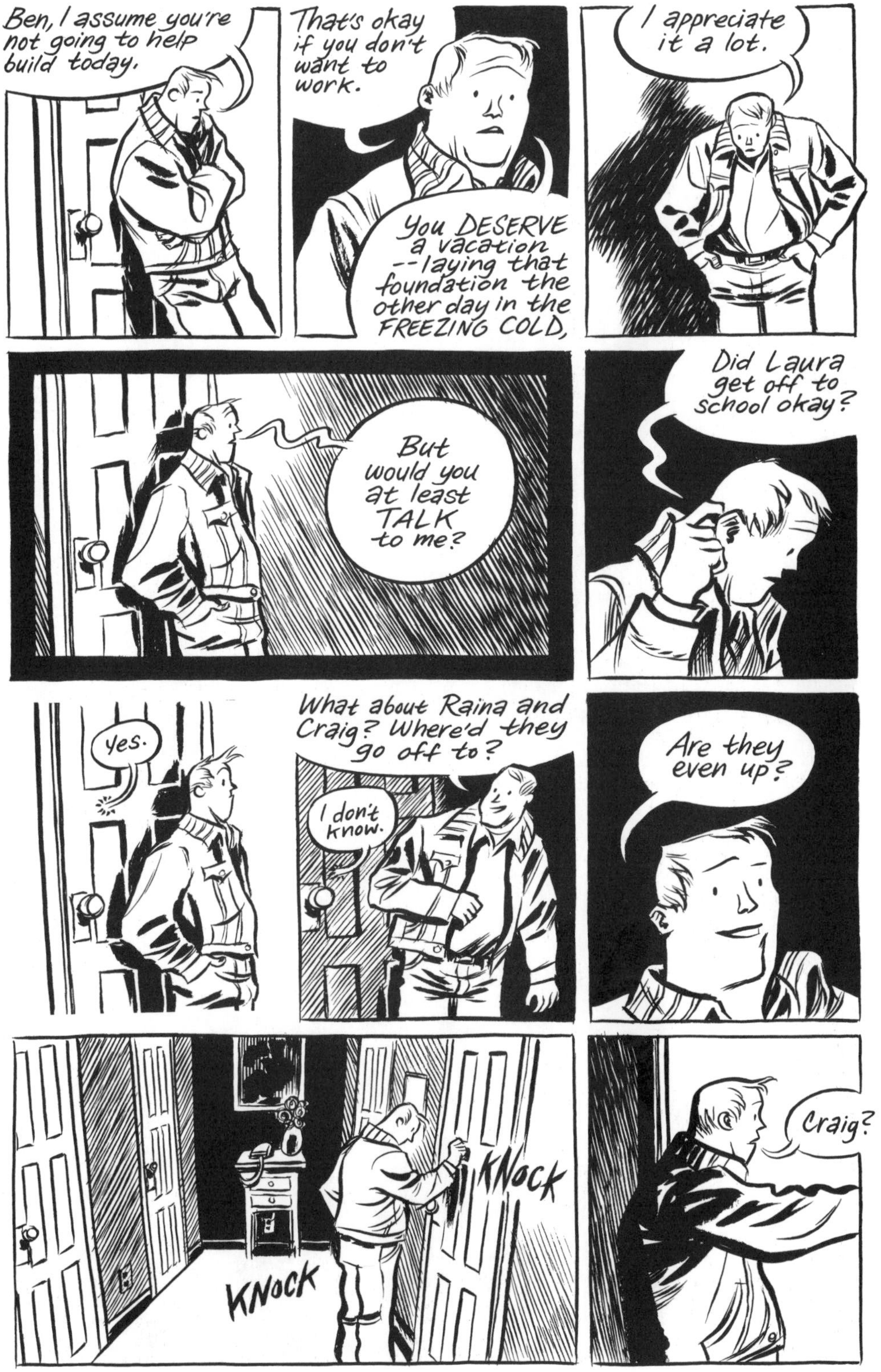
Ben, I assume you're not going to help build today.
That's okay if you don't want to work.
You DESERVE a vacation --laying that foundation the other day in the FREEZING COLD.
I appreciate it a lot.
But would you at least TALK to me?
Did Laura get off to school okay?
yes.
What about Raina and Craig? Where'd they go off to?
I don't know.
Are they even up?
KNOCK
KNOCK
Craig?

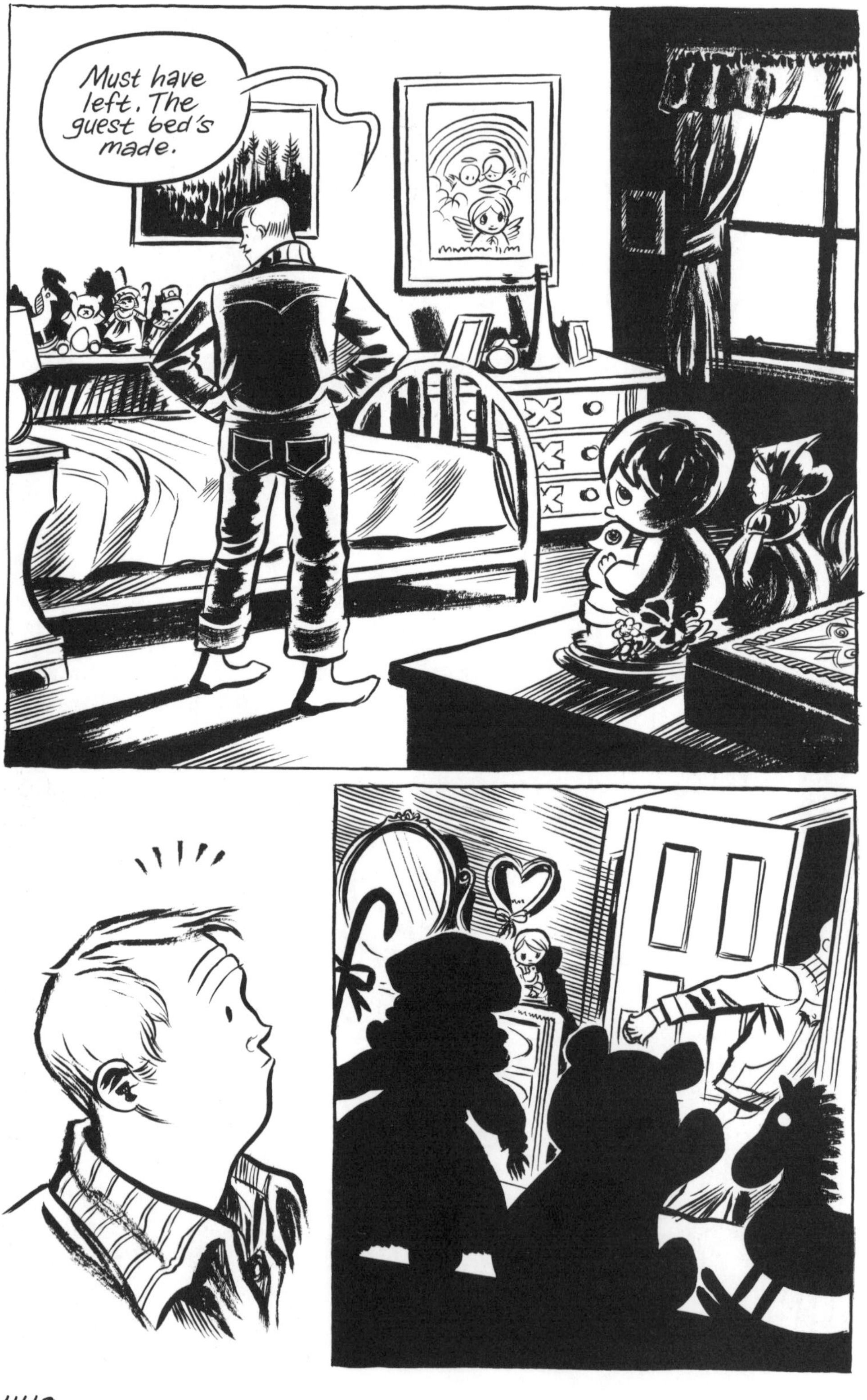
Must have left. The guest bed's made.

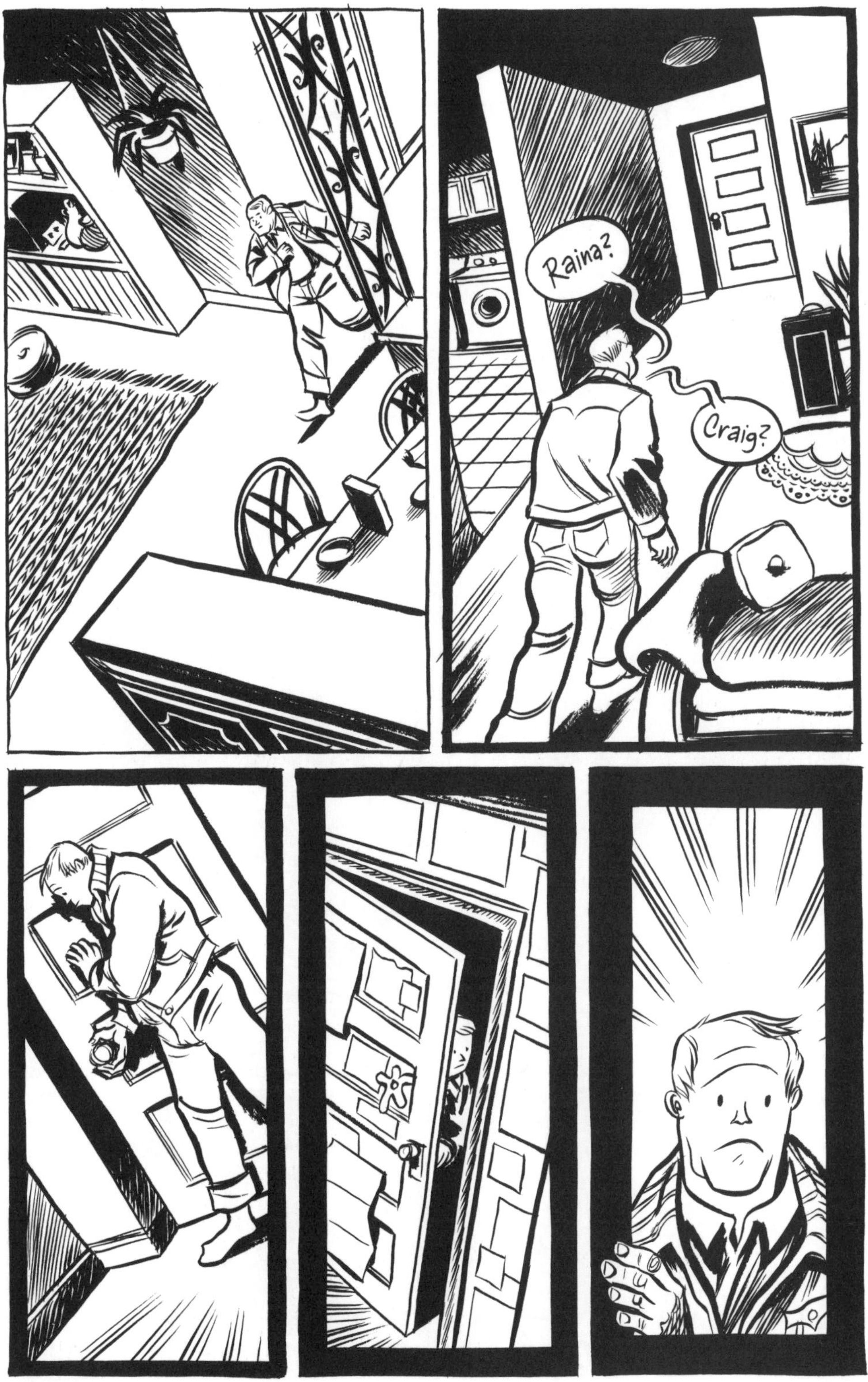
Raina?
Craig?

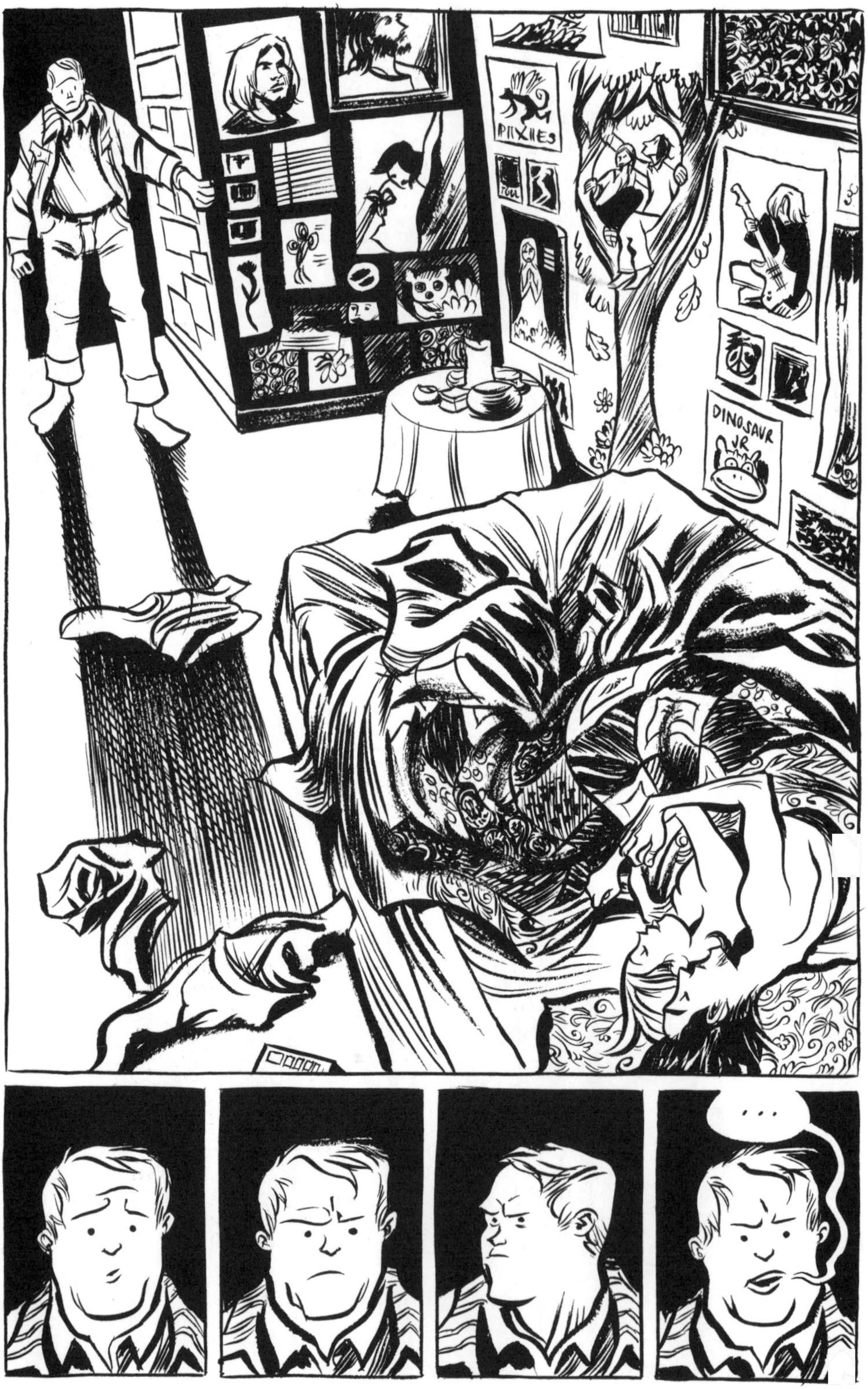
PIXIES
DINOSAUR JR
...

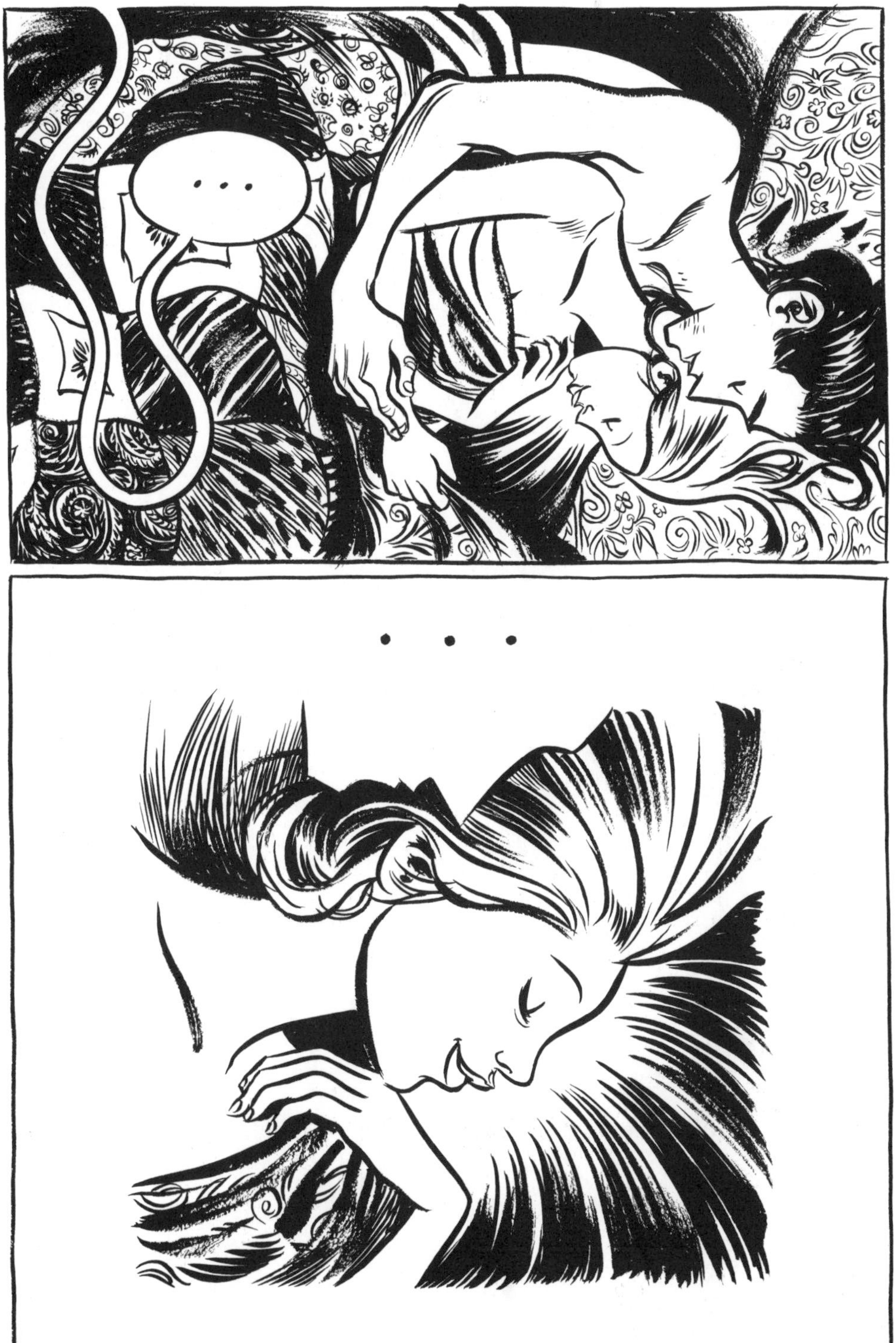
...
...

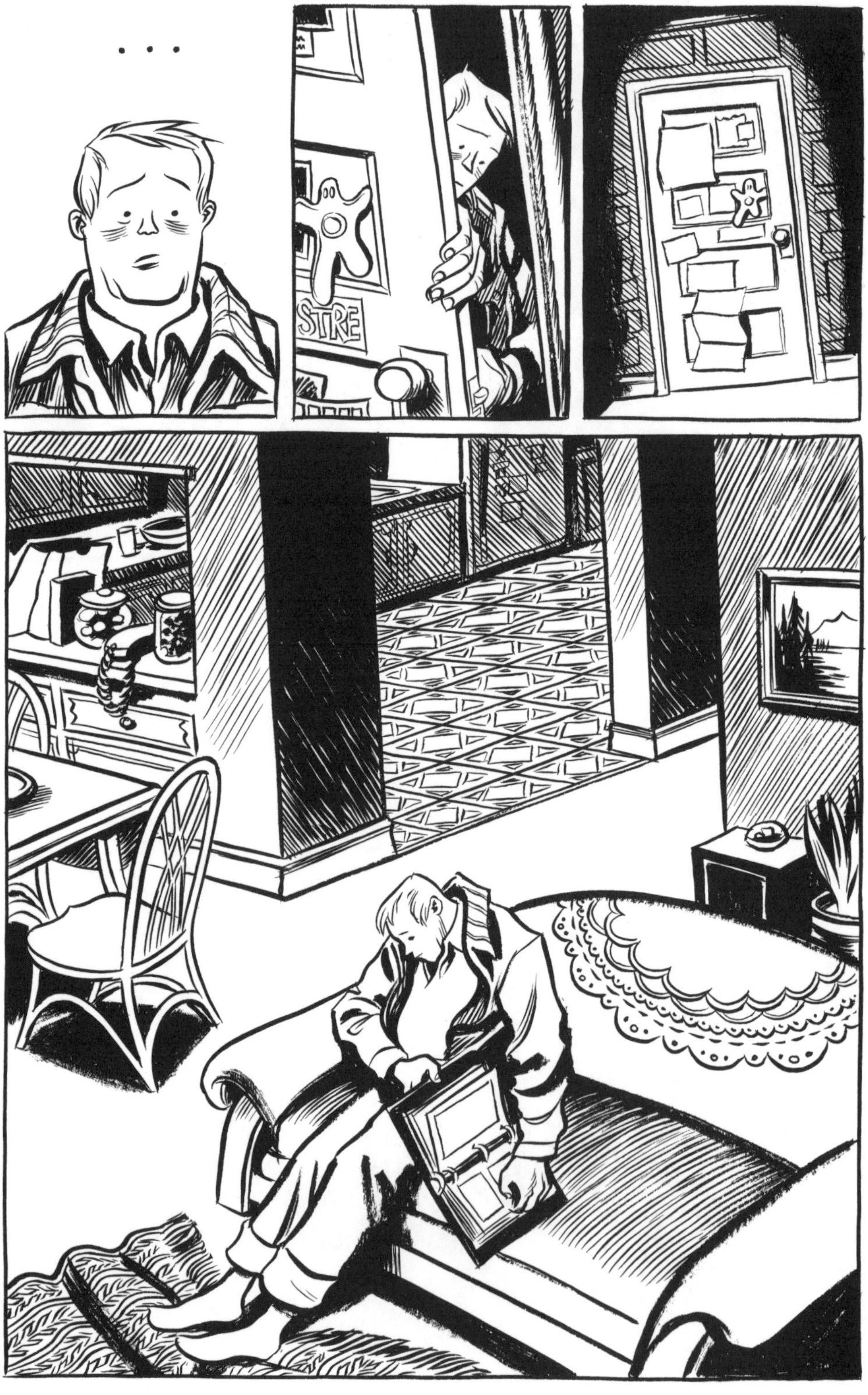
. . .
STRE

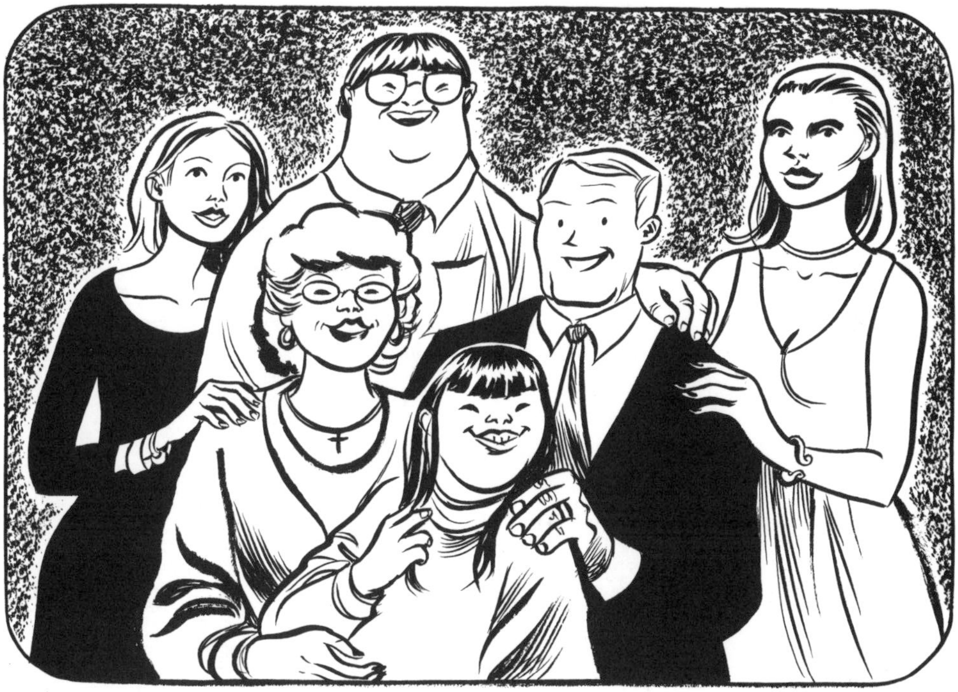

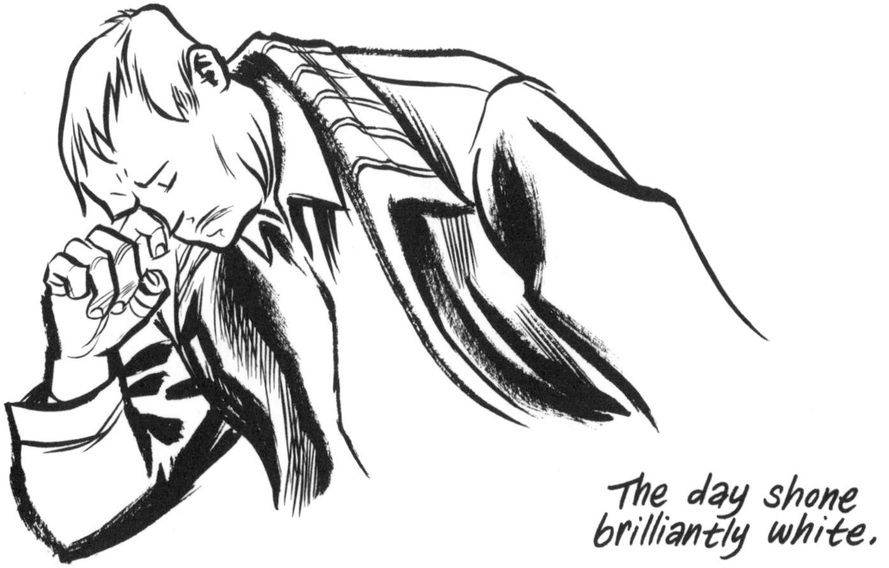
The day shone brilliantly white.

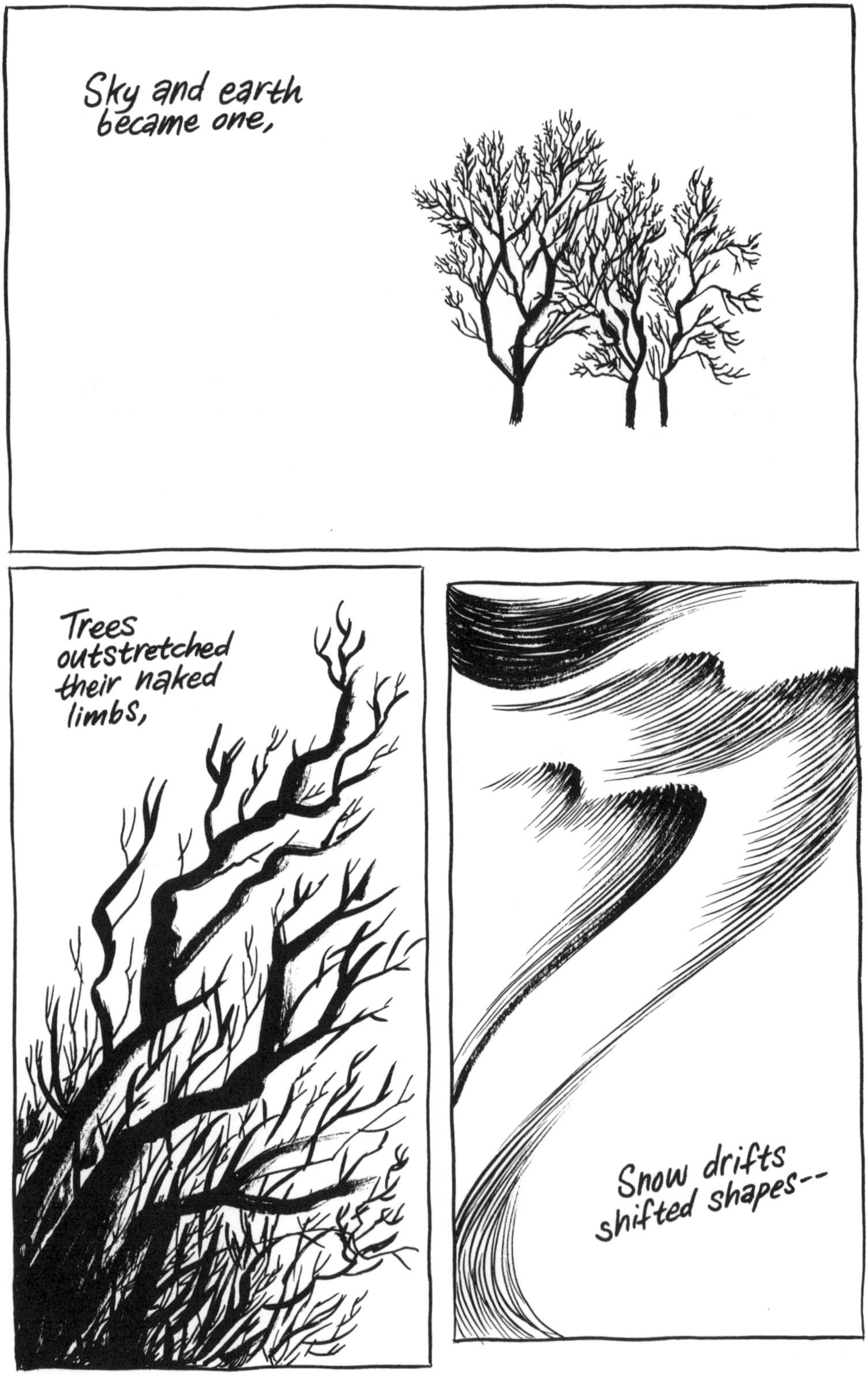
Sky and earth became one,
Trees outstretched their naked limbs,
Snow drifts shifted shapes--

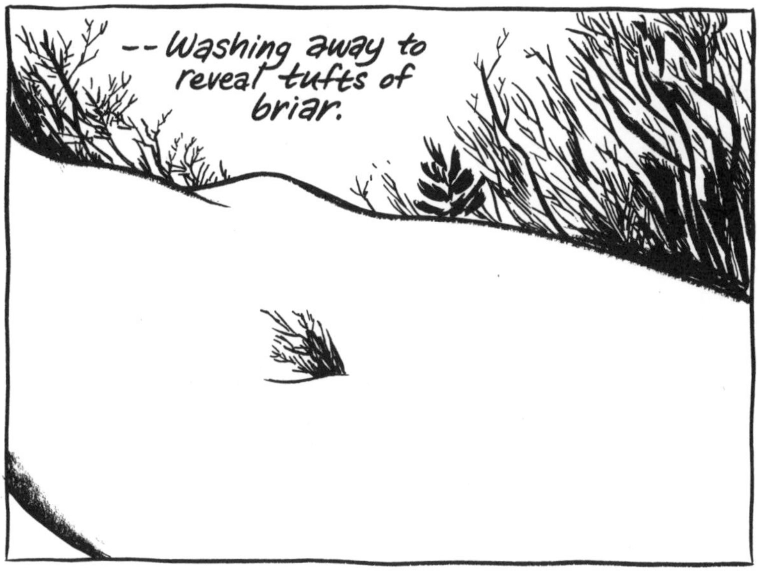
--Washing away to reveal tufts of briar.

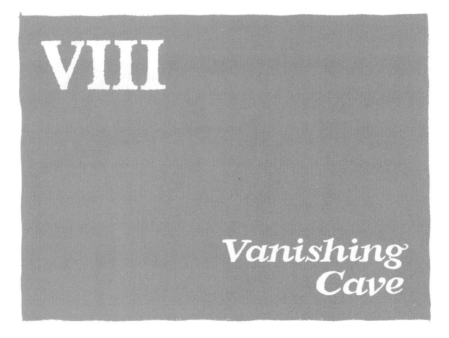

VIII

Vanishing Cave

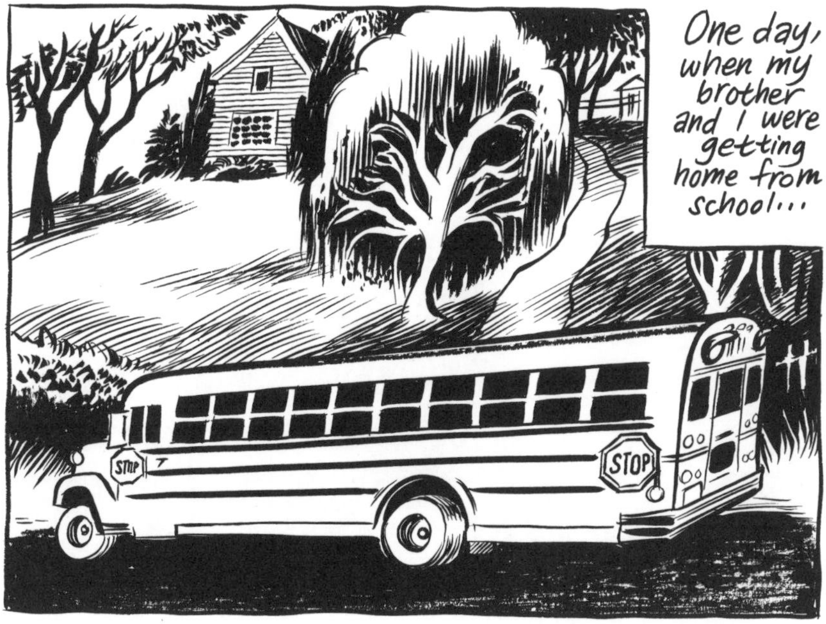
One day, when my brother and I were getting home from school...
STOP
STOP

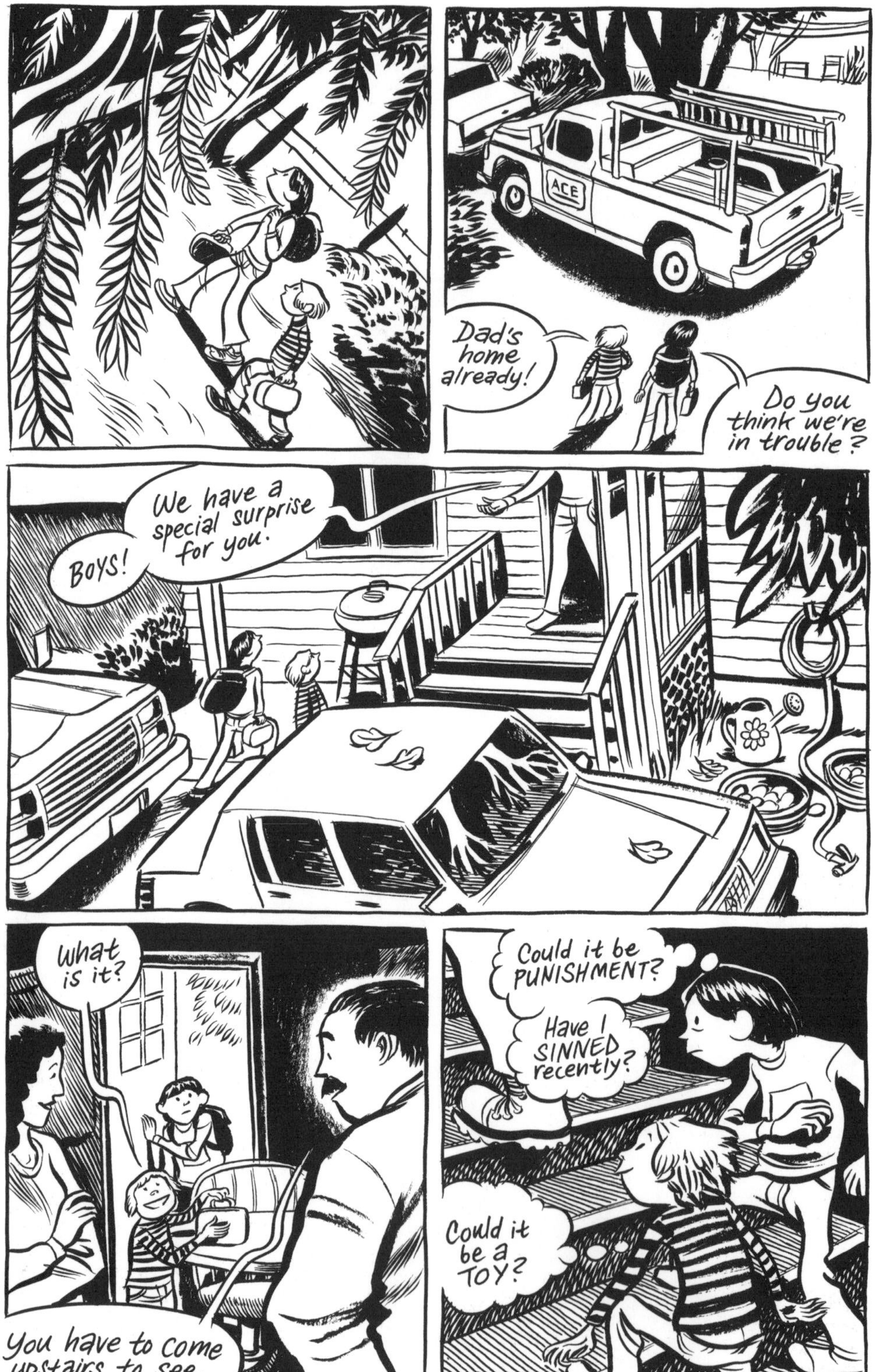

Dad's home already!
Do you think we're in trouble?
Boys!
We have a special surprise for you.
What is it?
You have to come upstairs to see.
Could it be PUNISHMENT?
Have I SINNED recently?
Could it be a TOY?

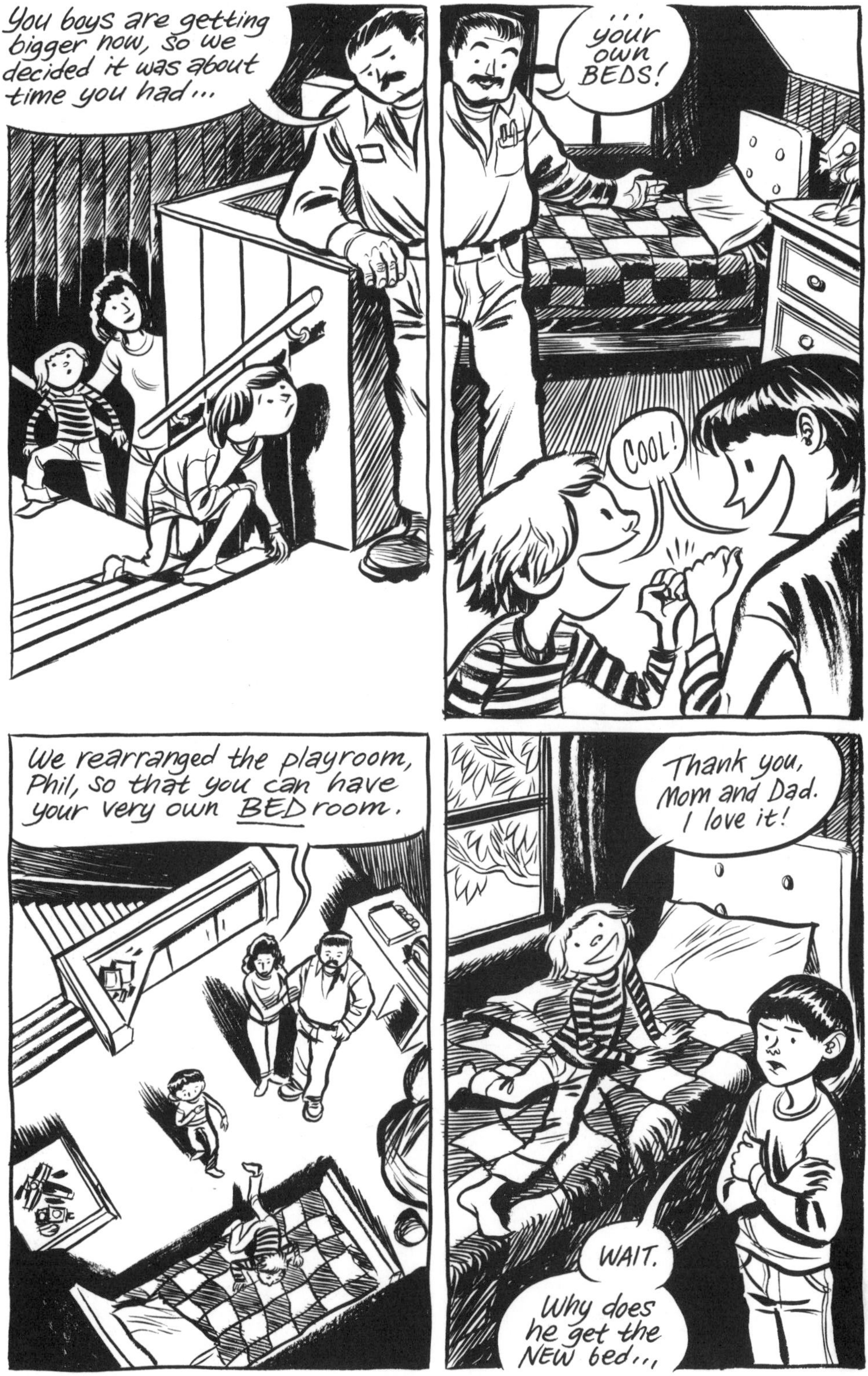
You boys are getting bigger now, so we decided it was about time you had...
... your own BEDS!
COOL!
We rearranged the playroom, Phil, so that you can have your very own BEDroom.
Thank you, Mom and Dad. I love it!
WAIT.
Why does he get the NEW bed...

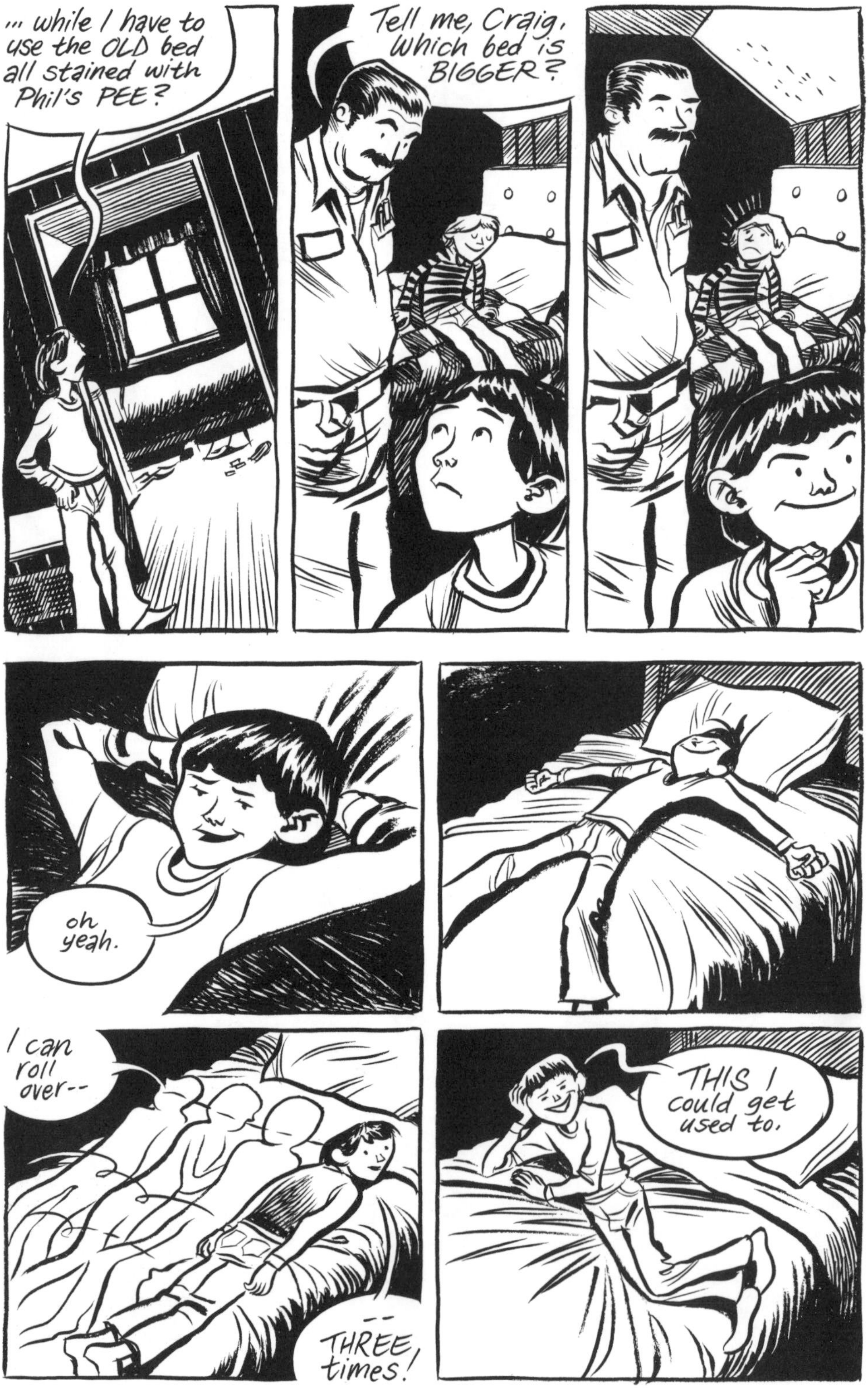
... while I have to use the OLD bed all stained with Phil's PEE?
Tell me, Craig, Which bed is BIGGER?
oh yeah.
I can roll over--
--THREE times!
THIS I could get used to.

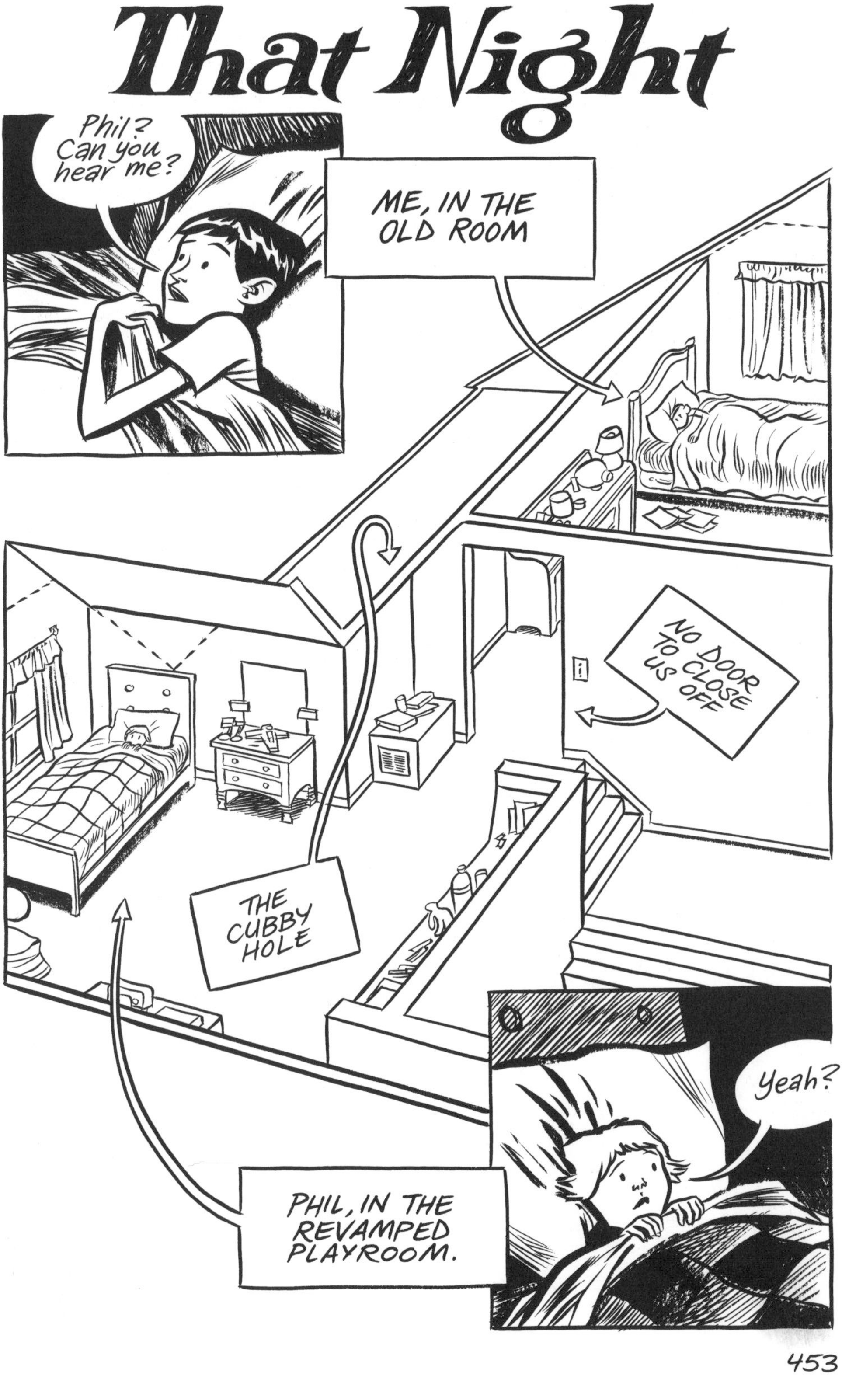
That Night
Phil? Can you hear me?
ME, IN THE OLD ROOM
NO DOOR TO CLOSE US OFF
THE CUBBY HOLE
PHIL, IN THE REVAMPED PLAYROOM.
Yeah?

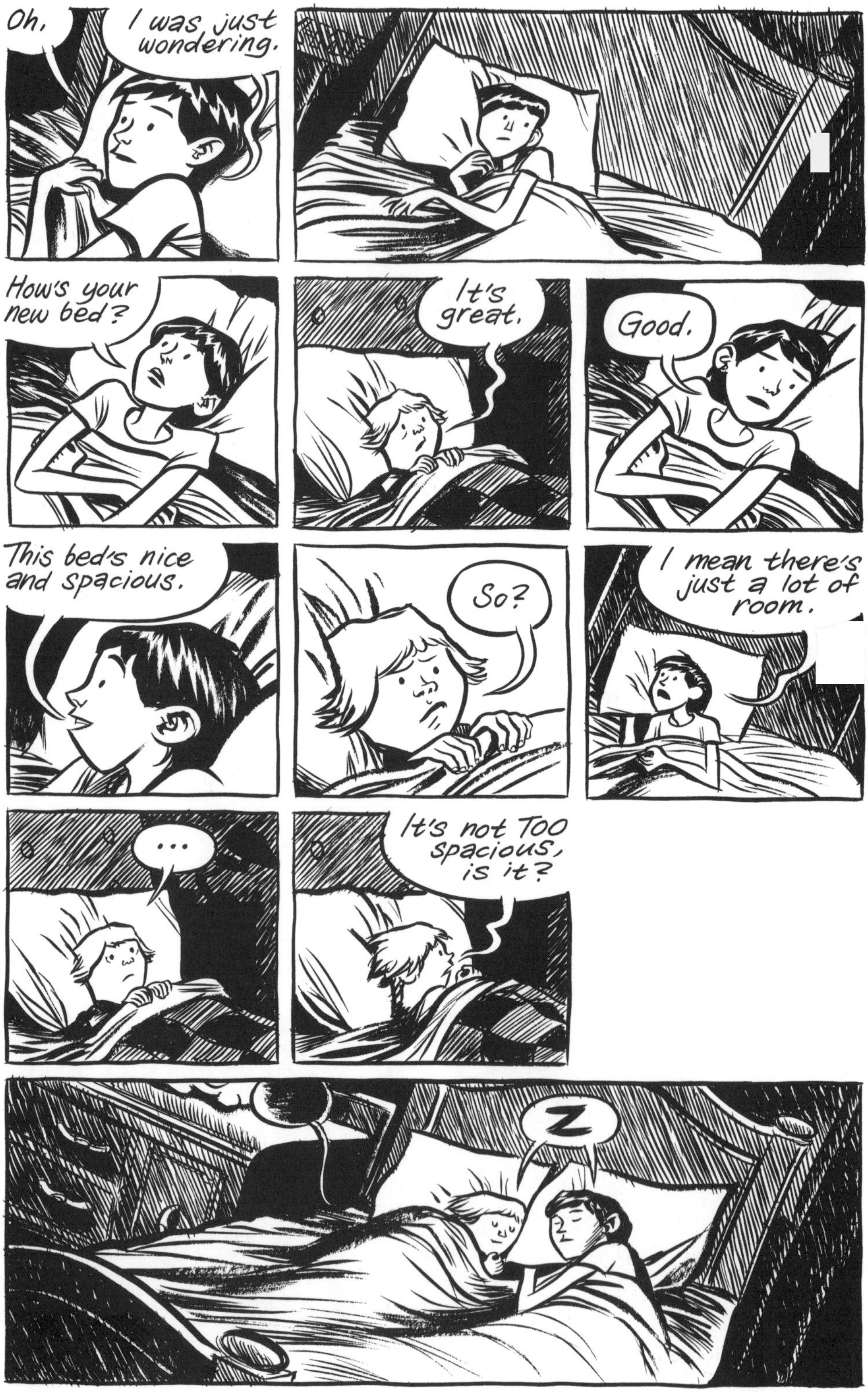
Oh,
I was just wondering.
How's your new bed?
It's great.
Good.
This bed's nice and spacious.
So?
I mean there's just a lot of room.
...
It's not TOO spacious, is it?
Z

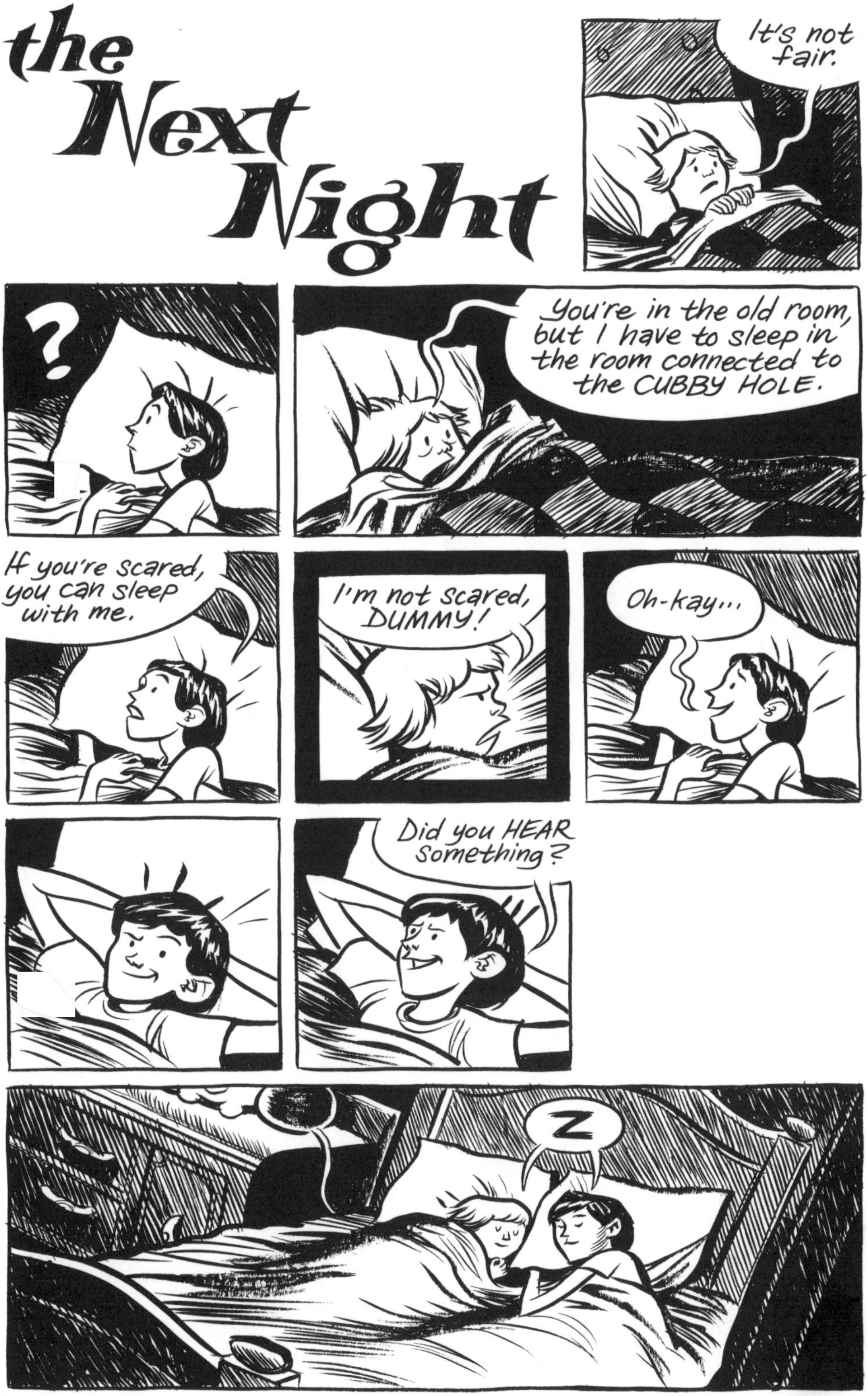
the Next Night
It's not fair.
?
You're in the old room, but I have to sleep in the room connected to the CUBBY HOLE.
If you're scared, you can sleep with me.
I'm not scared, DUMMY!
Oh-kay...
Did you HEAR something?
Z

and the Night After that

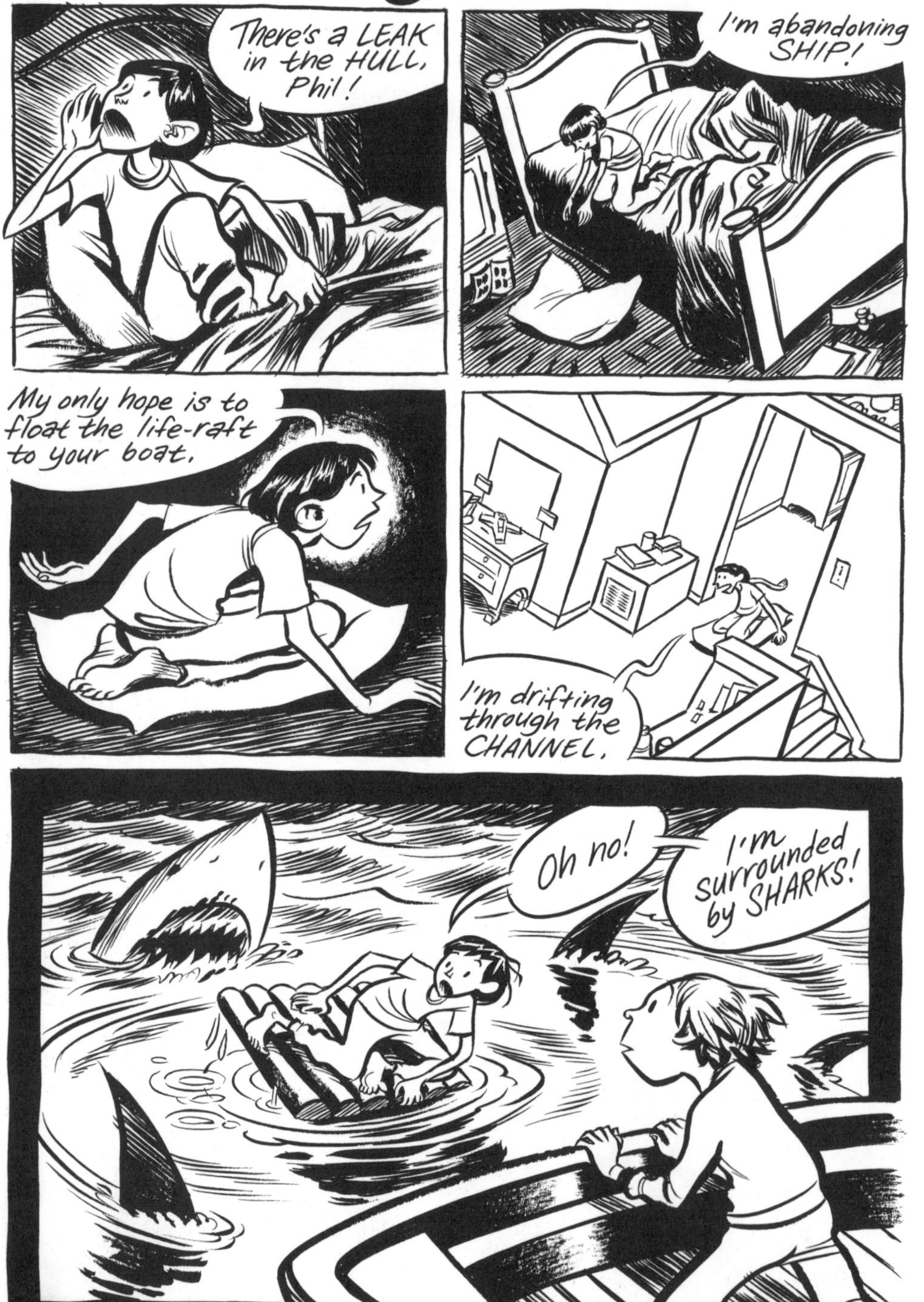
There's a LEAK in the HULL, Phil!
I'm abandoning SHIP!
My only hope is to float the life-raft to your boat.
I'm drifting through the CHANNEL.
Oh no!
I'm surrounded by SHARKS!

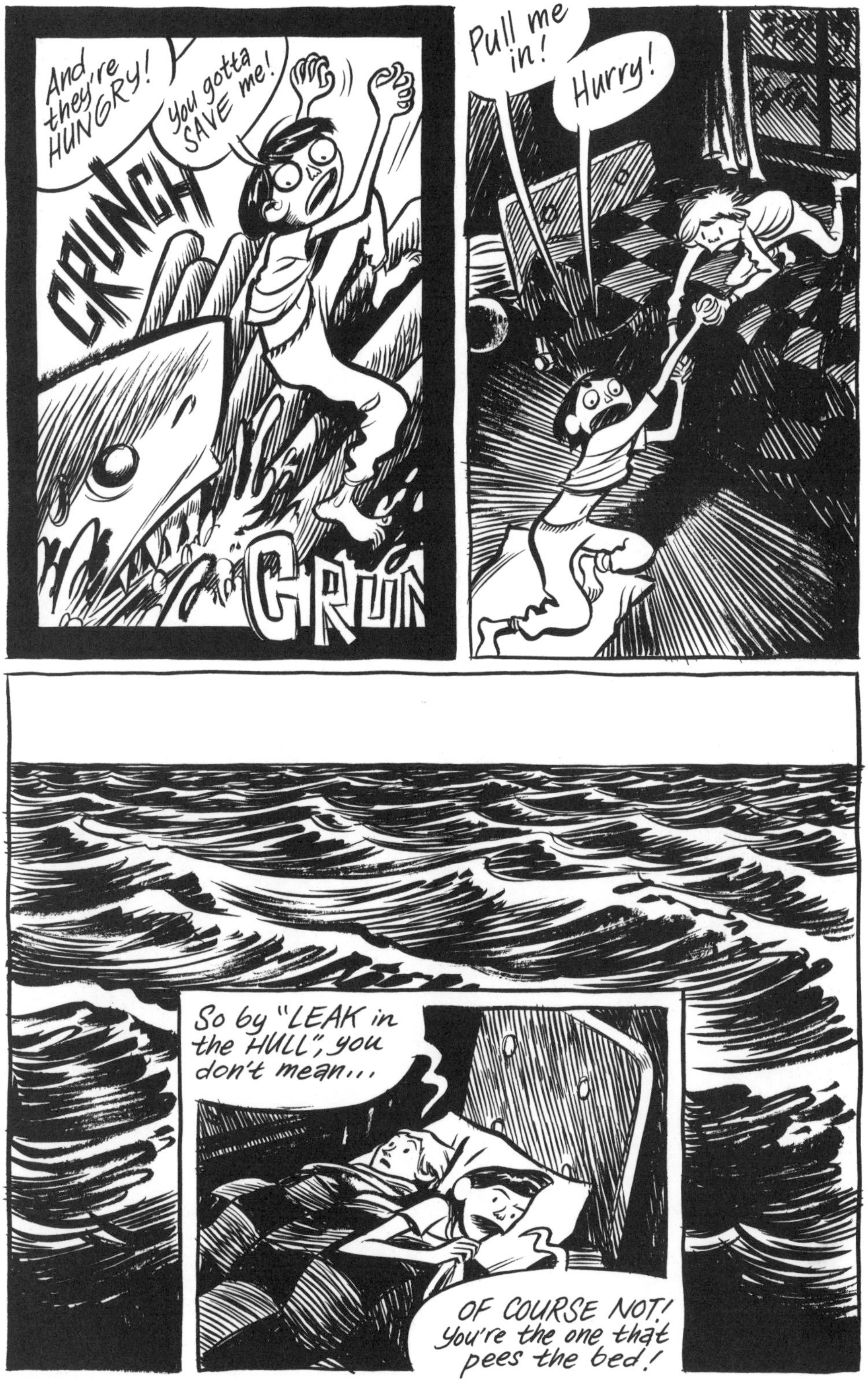
And they're HUNGRY!
You gotta SAVE me!
CRUNCH
CRUN
Pull me in!
Hurry!
So by "LEAK in the HULL", you don't mean...
OF COURSE NOT! You're the one that pees the bed!

and in Winter

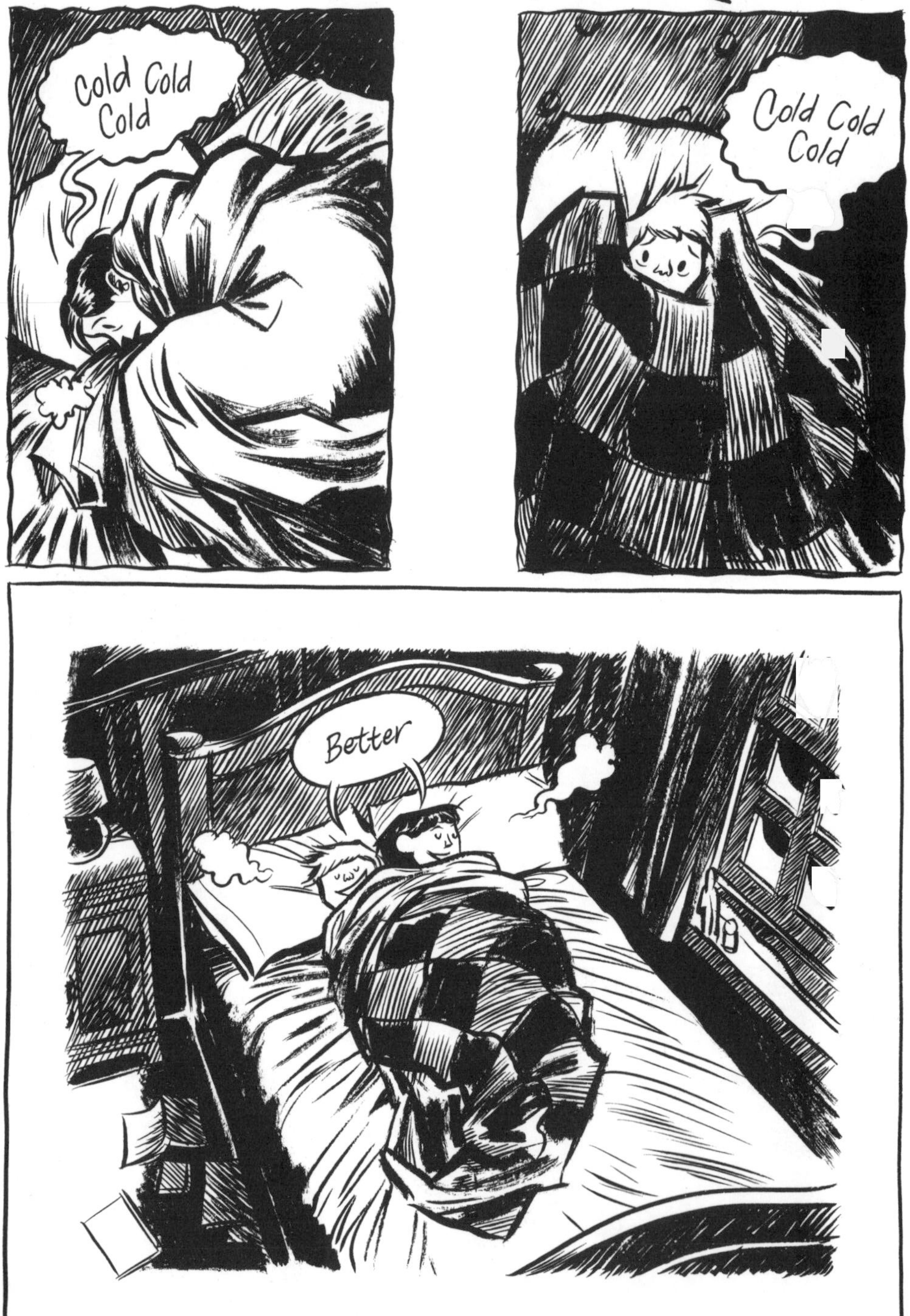
Cold Cold Cold
Cold Cold Cold
Better

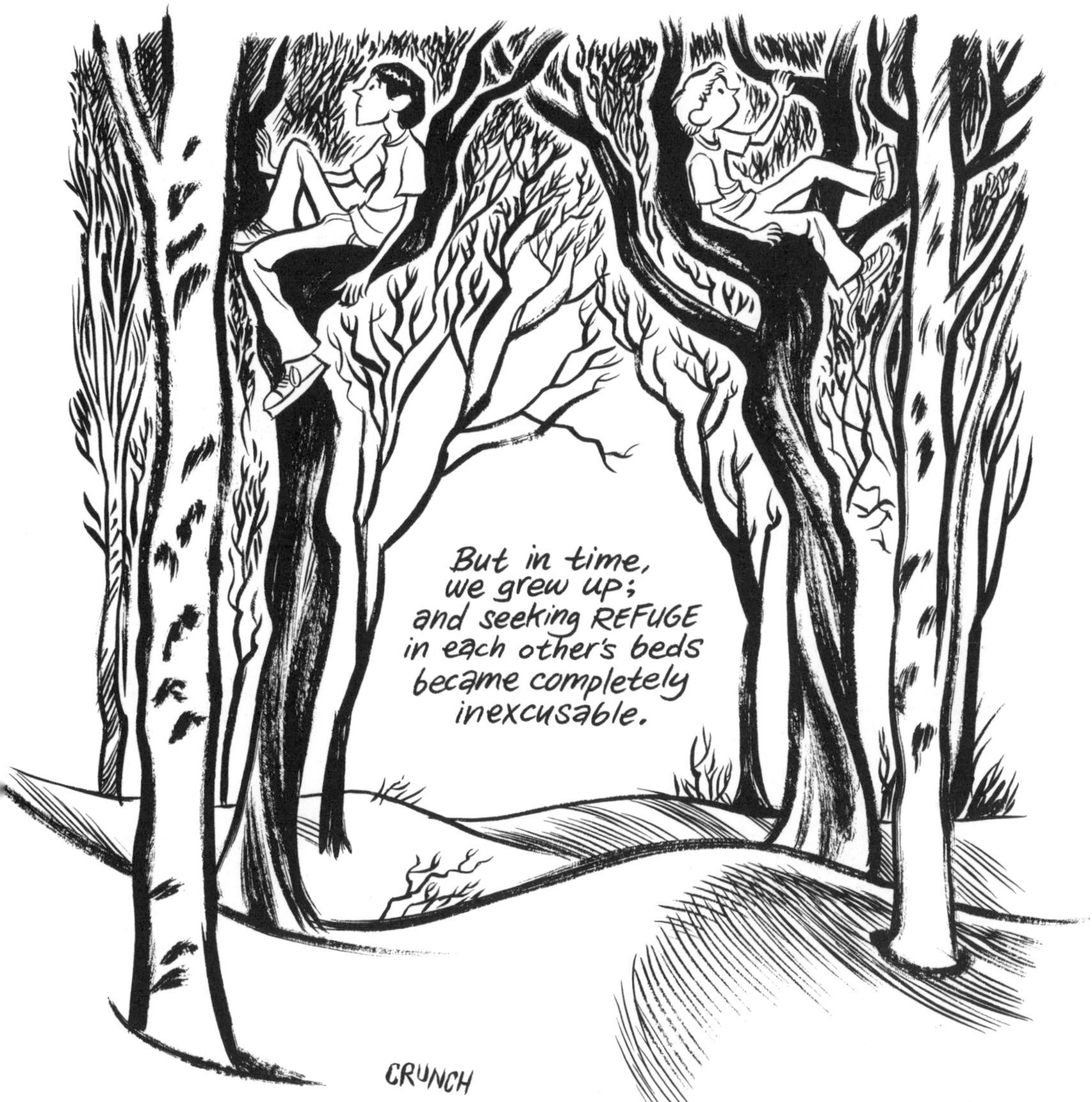
But in time, we grew up; and seeking REFUGE in each other's beds became completely inexcusable.
CRUNCH

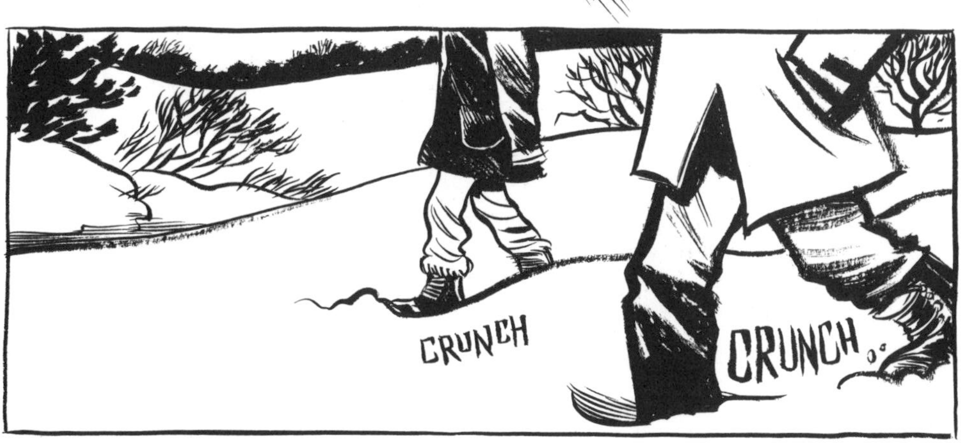
CRUNCH
CRUNCH

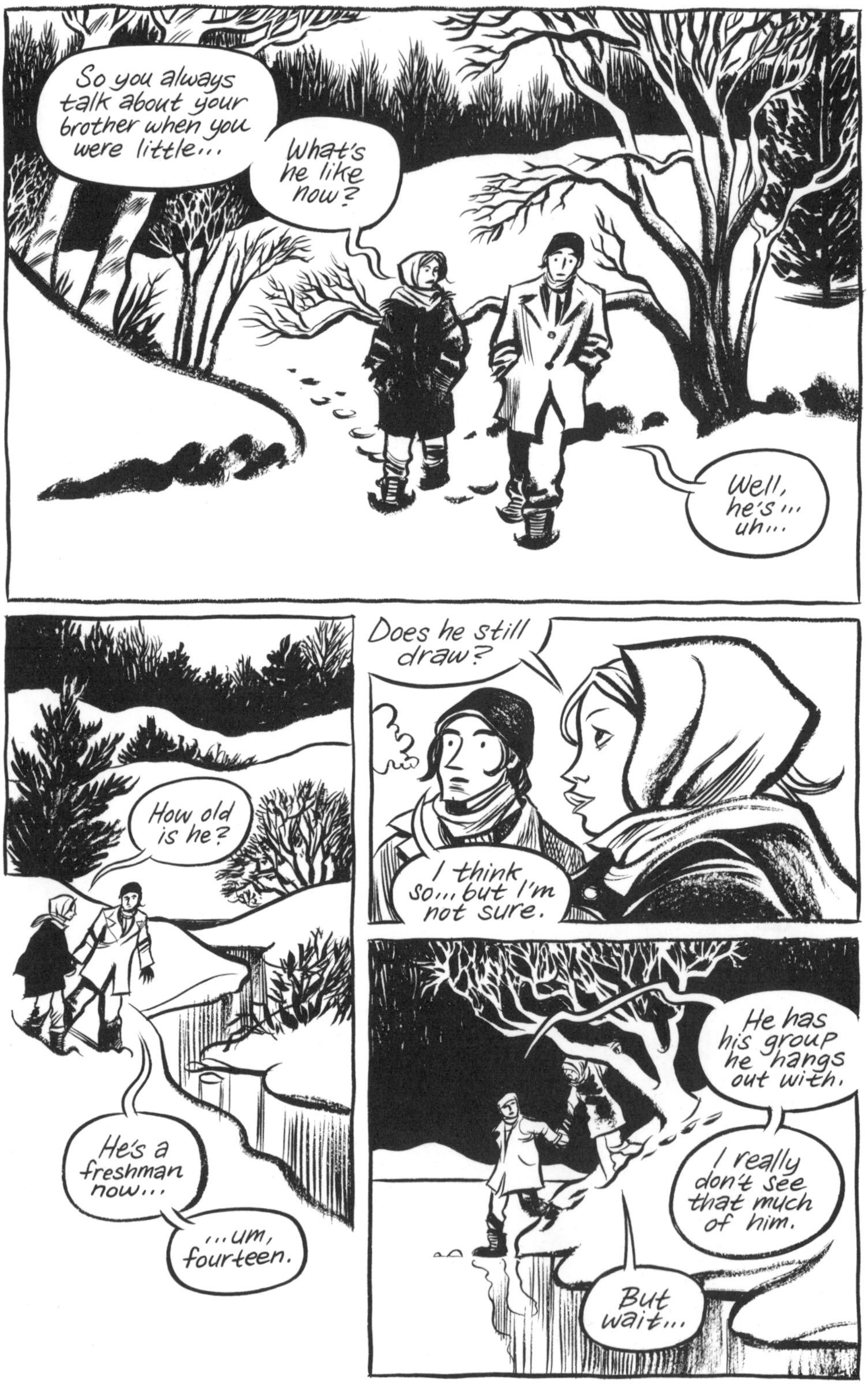

So you always talk about your brother when you were little...
What's he like now?
Well, he's... uh...
How old is he?
He's a freshman now...
...um, fourteen.
Does he still draw?
I think so... but I'm not sure.
He has his group he hangs out with.
I really don't see that much of him.
But wait...

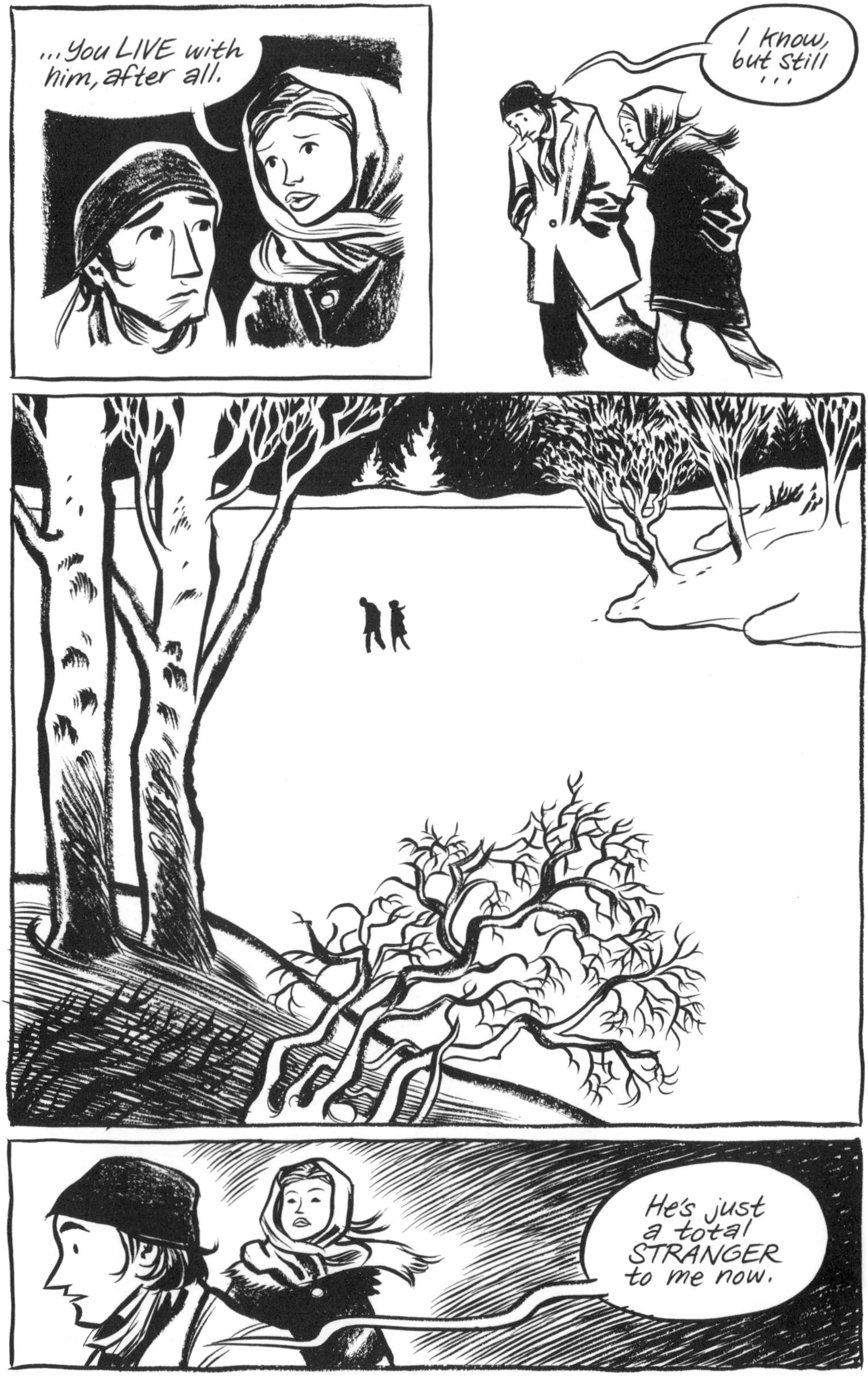
...You LIVE with him, after all.
I know, but still . . .
He's just a total STRANGER to me now.

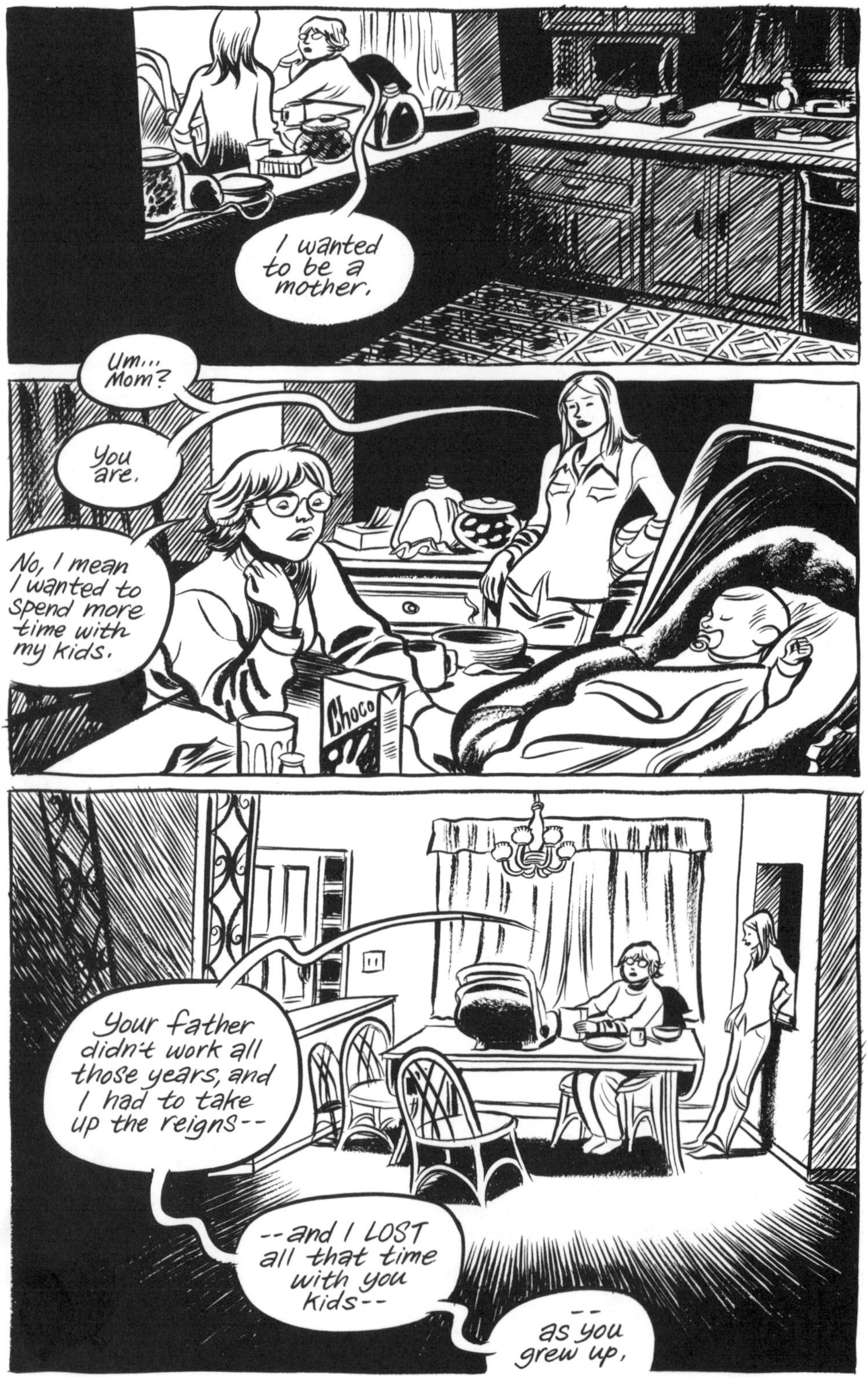
I wanted to be a mother.
Um... Mom?
You are.
No, I mean I wanted to spend more time with my kids.
Choco
Your father didn't work all those years, and I had to take up the reigns--
--and I LOST all that time with you kids--
--as you grew up.

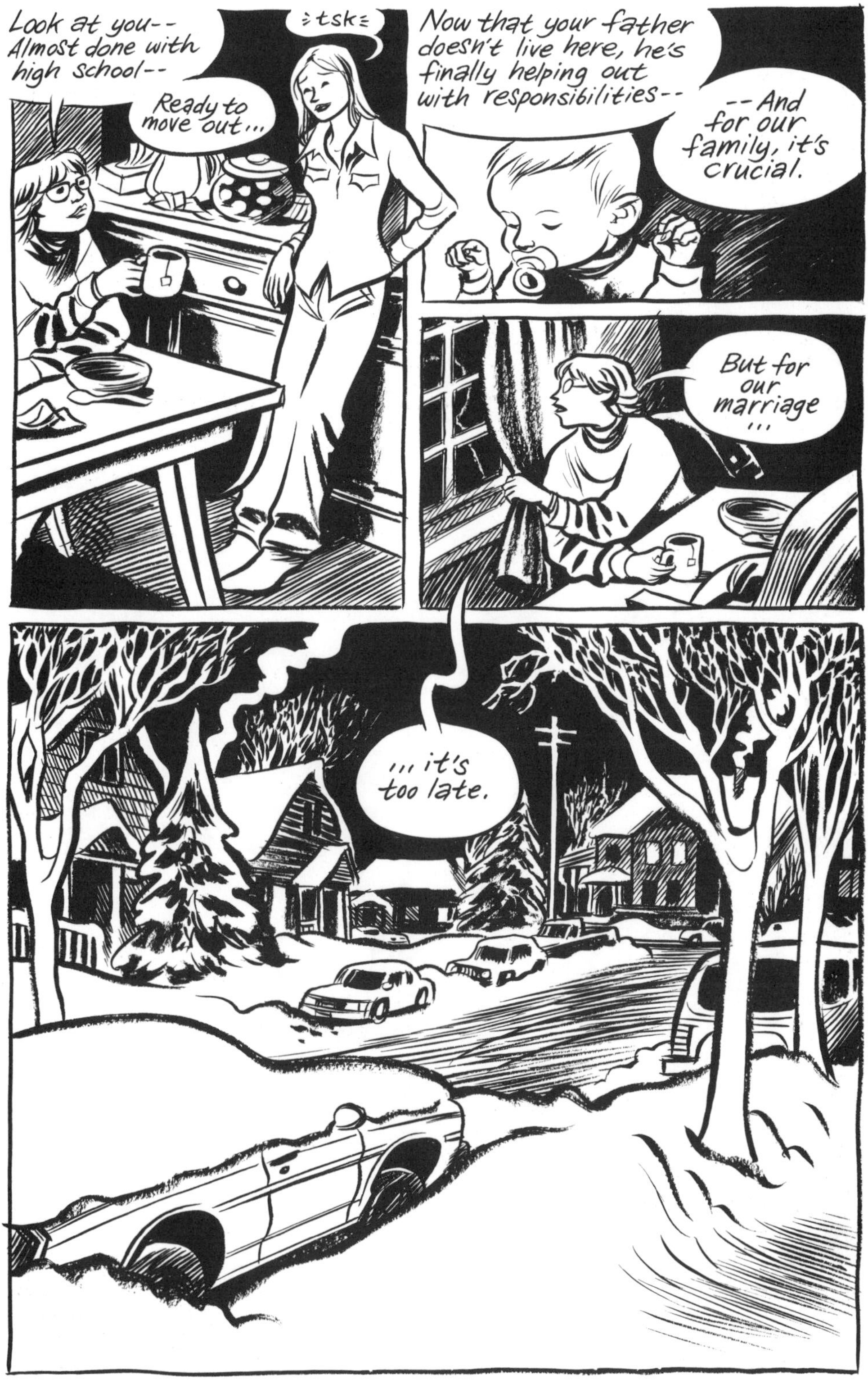
Look at you-- Almost done with high school--
:tsk:
Ready to move out...
Now that your father doesn't live here, he's finally helping out with responsibilities--
--And for our family, it's crucial.
But for our marriage ...
... it's too late.

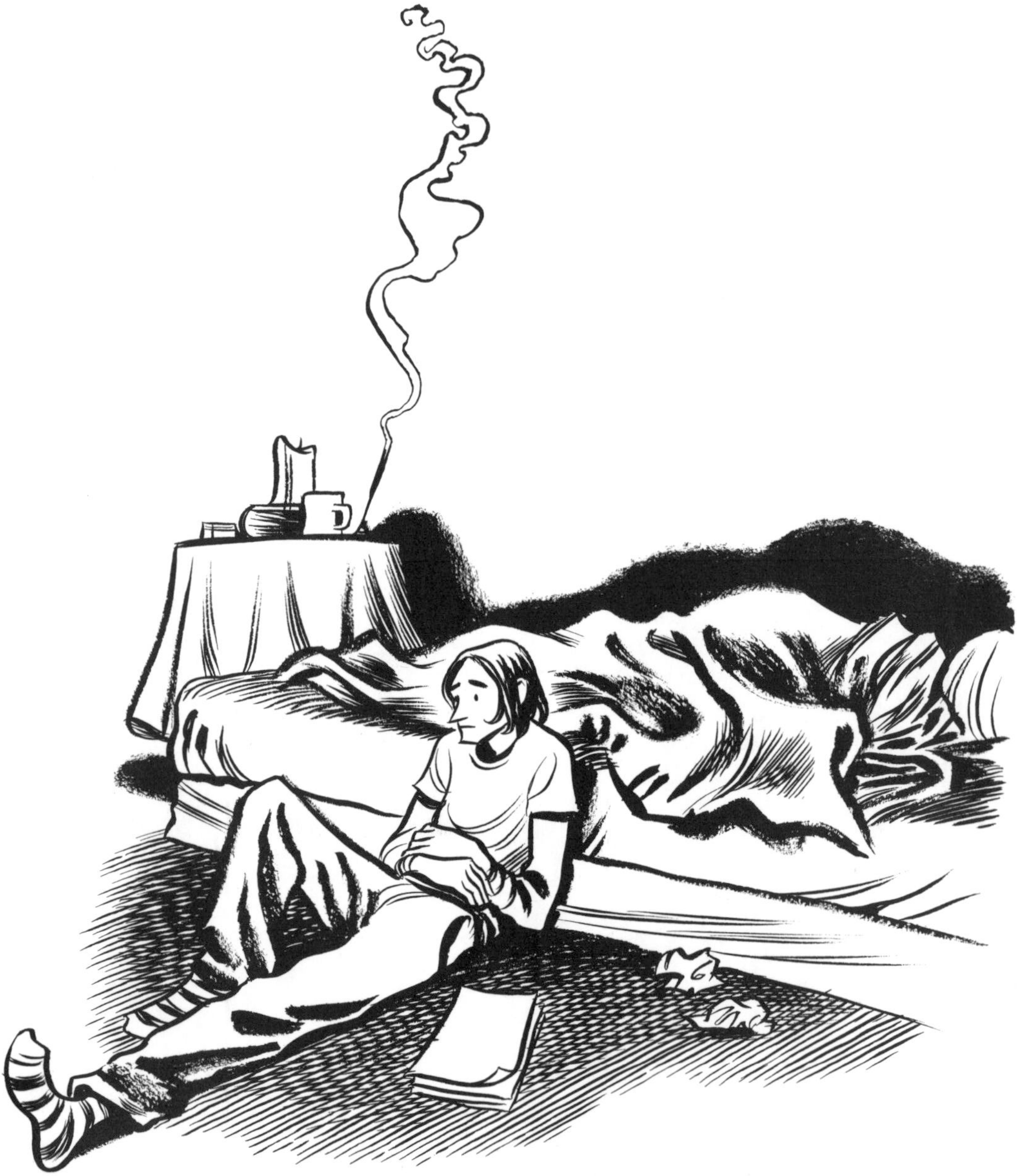
On our last day together, Raina was sick.

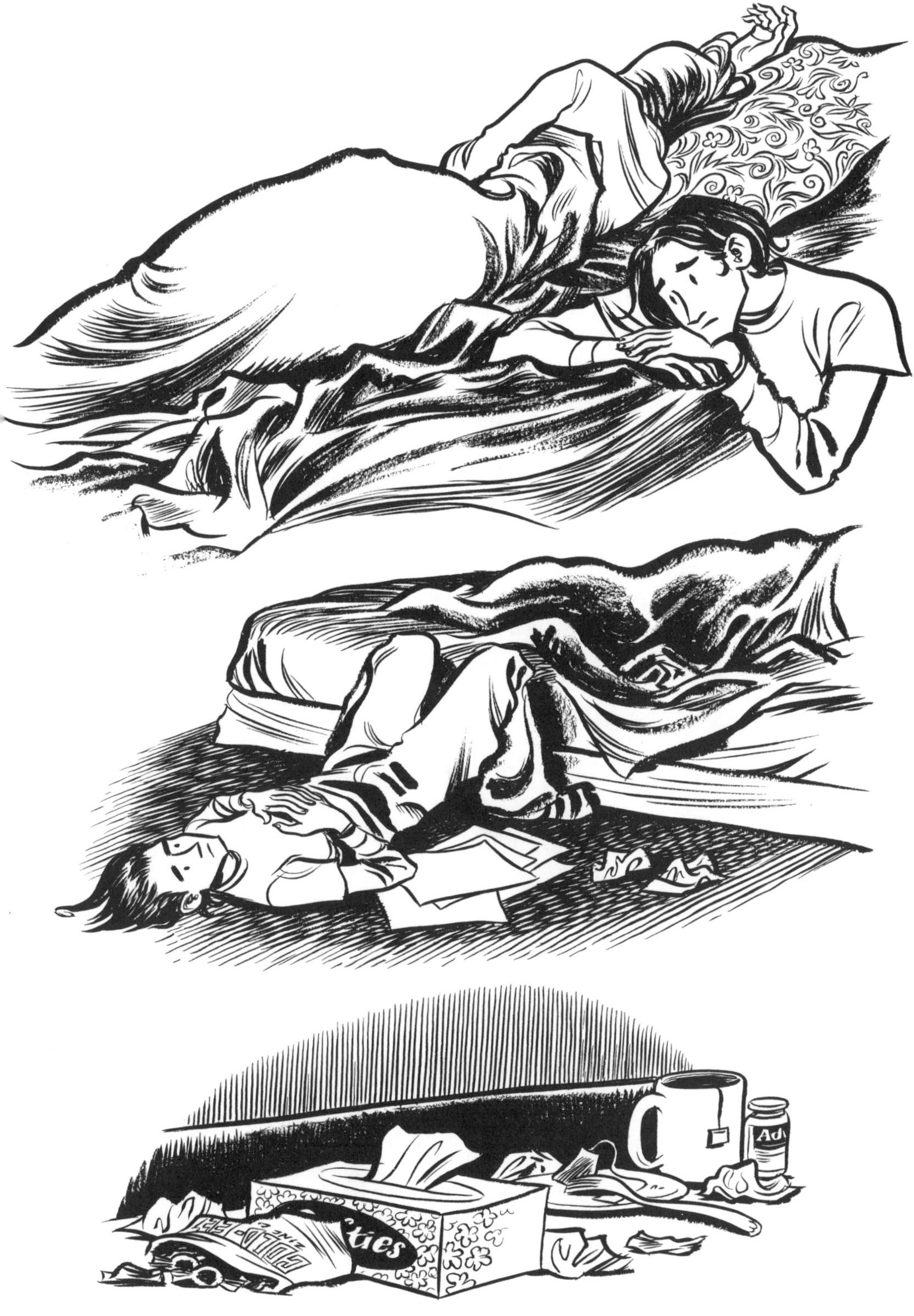

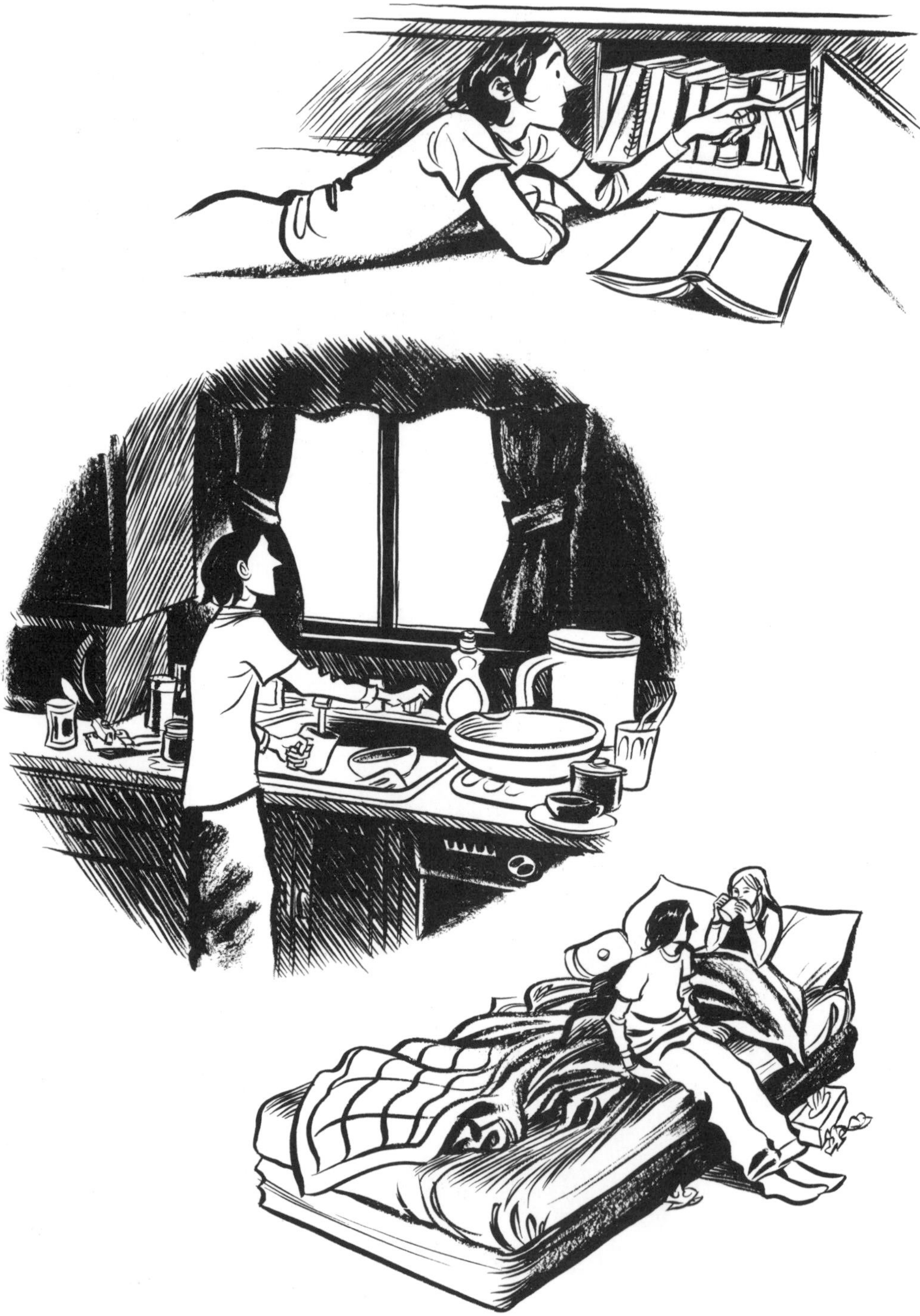

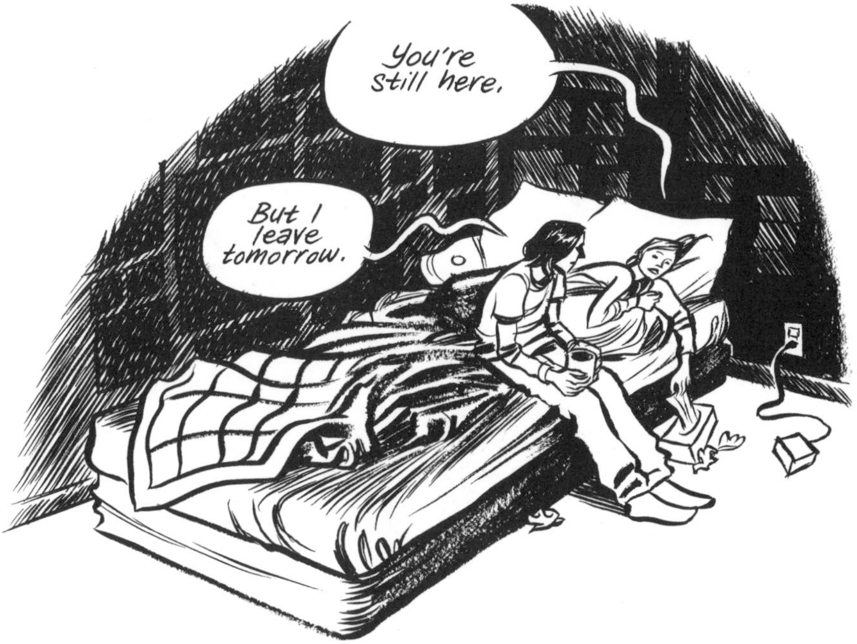
You're still here.
But I leave tomorrow.

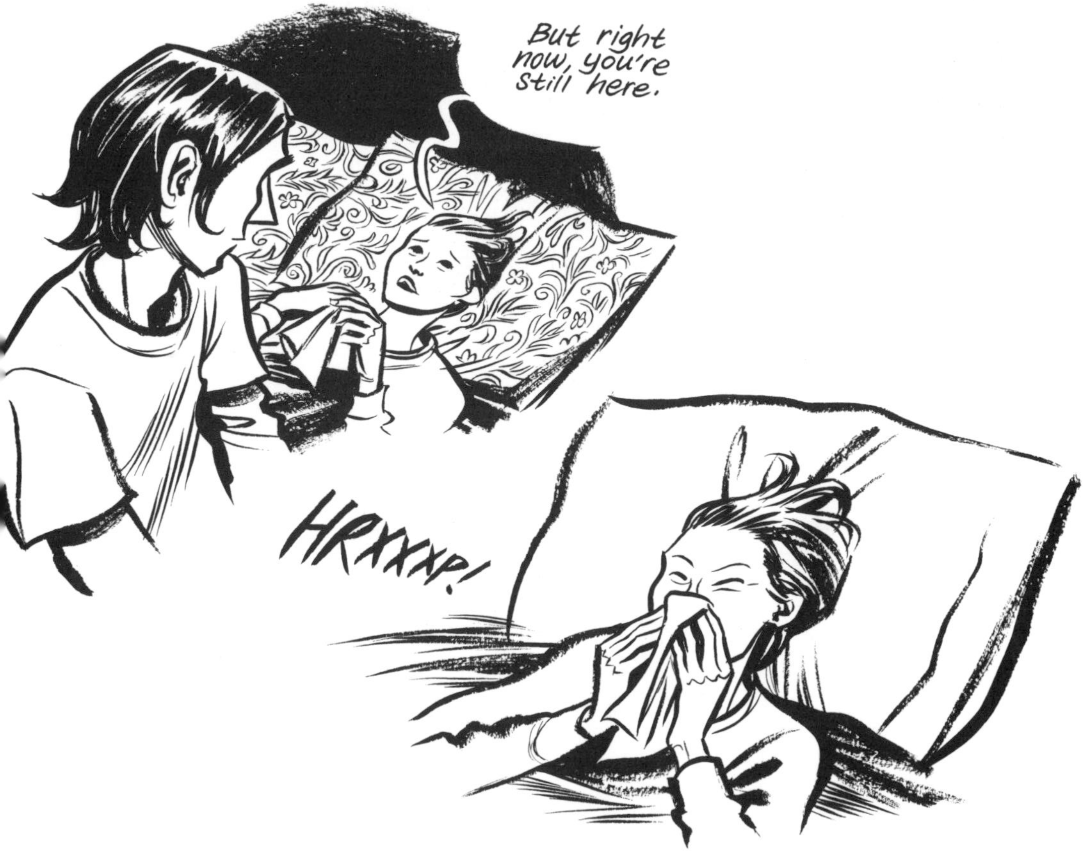
But right now, you're still here.
HRXXXP!

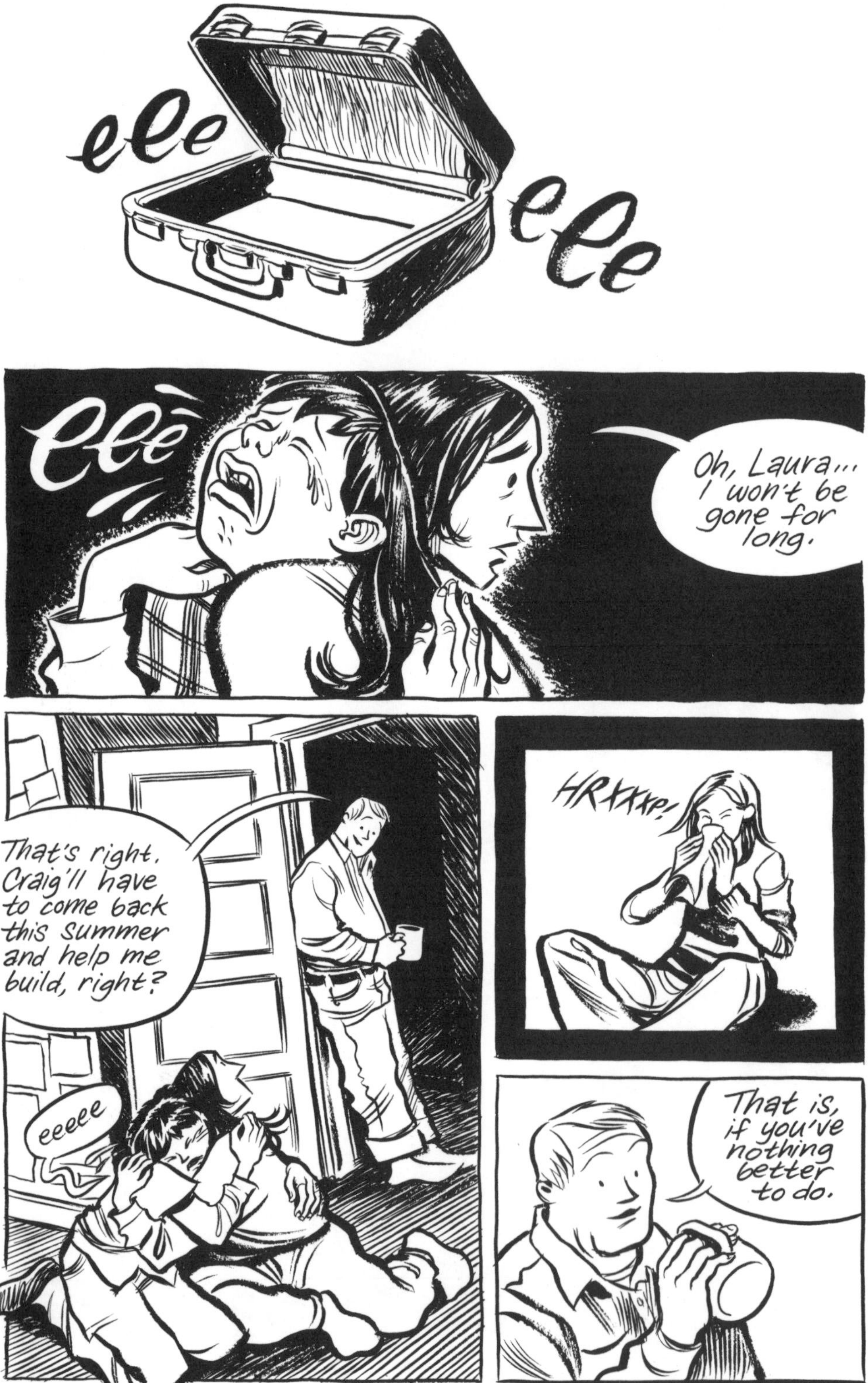

elle
elle
elle
Oh, Laura... I won't be gone for long.
That's right. Craig'll have to come back this summer and help me build, right?
eeeee
HRXXXP!
That is, if you've nothing better to do.

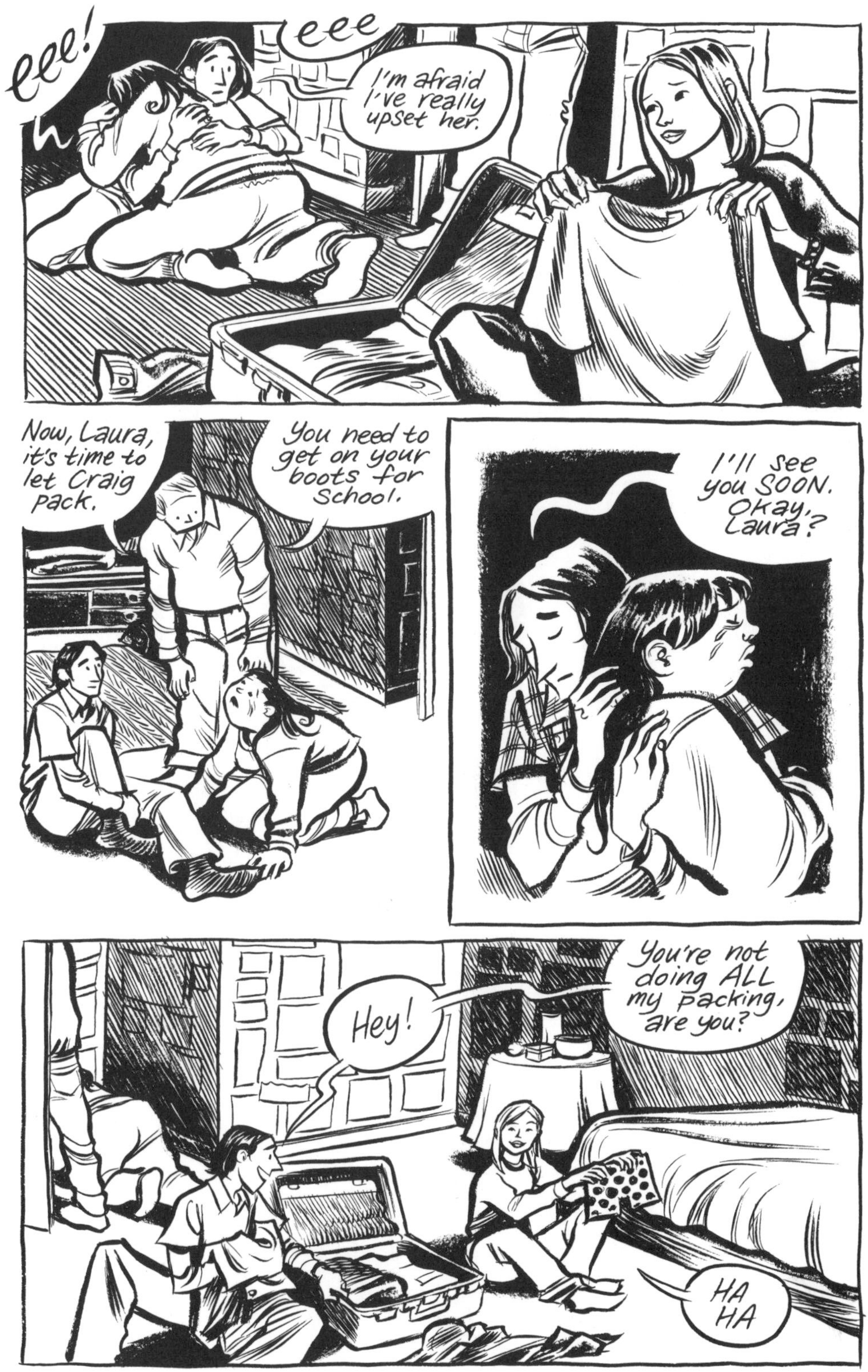
eee!
eee
I'm afraid I've really upset her.
Now, Laura, it's time to let Craig pack.
You need to get on your boots for school.
I'll see you SOON. Okay, Laura?
Hey!
You're not doing ALL my packing, are you?
HA HA

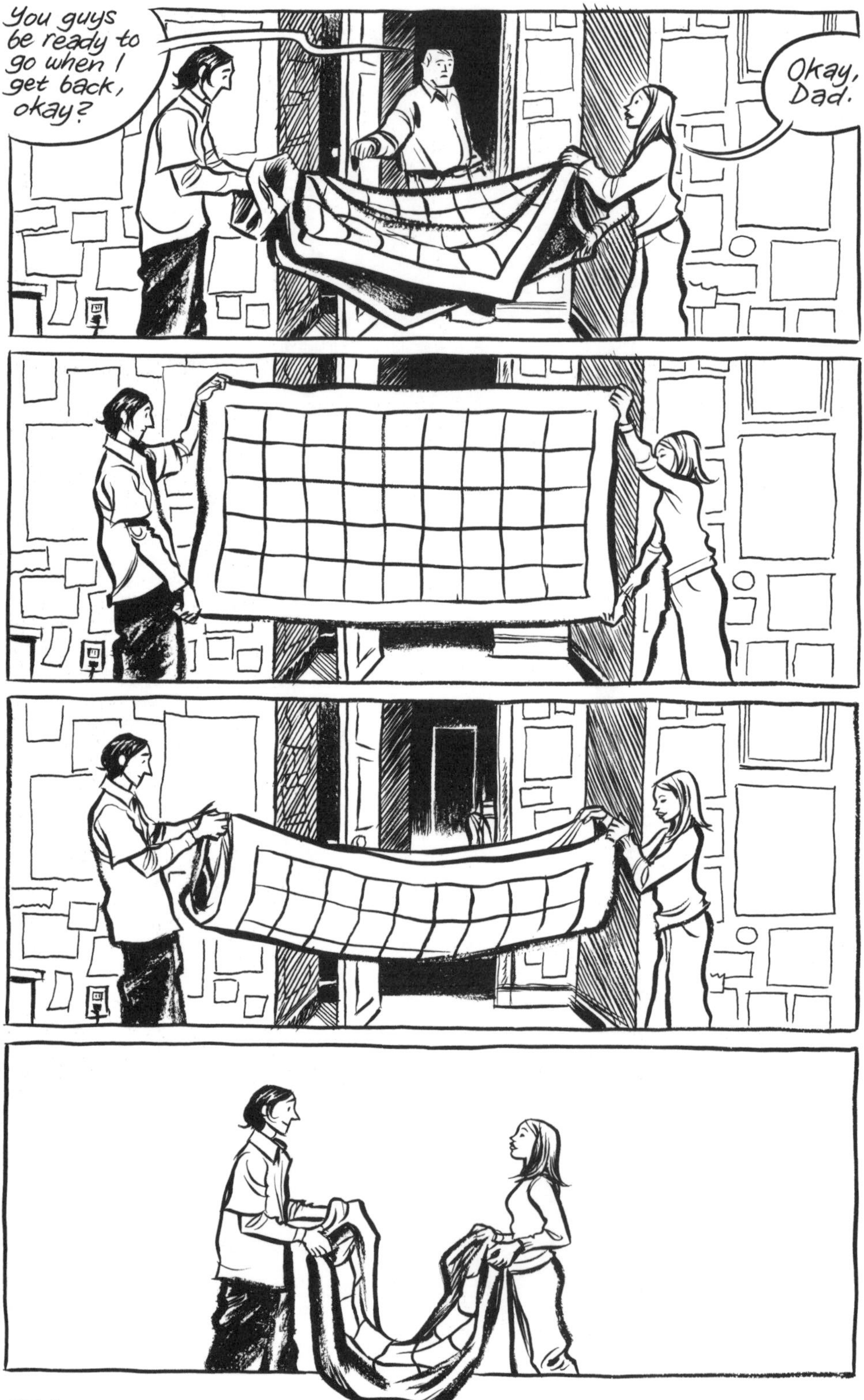
You guys be ready to go when I get back, okay?
Okay, Dad.

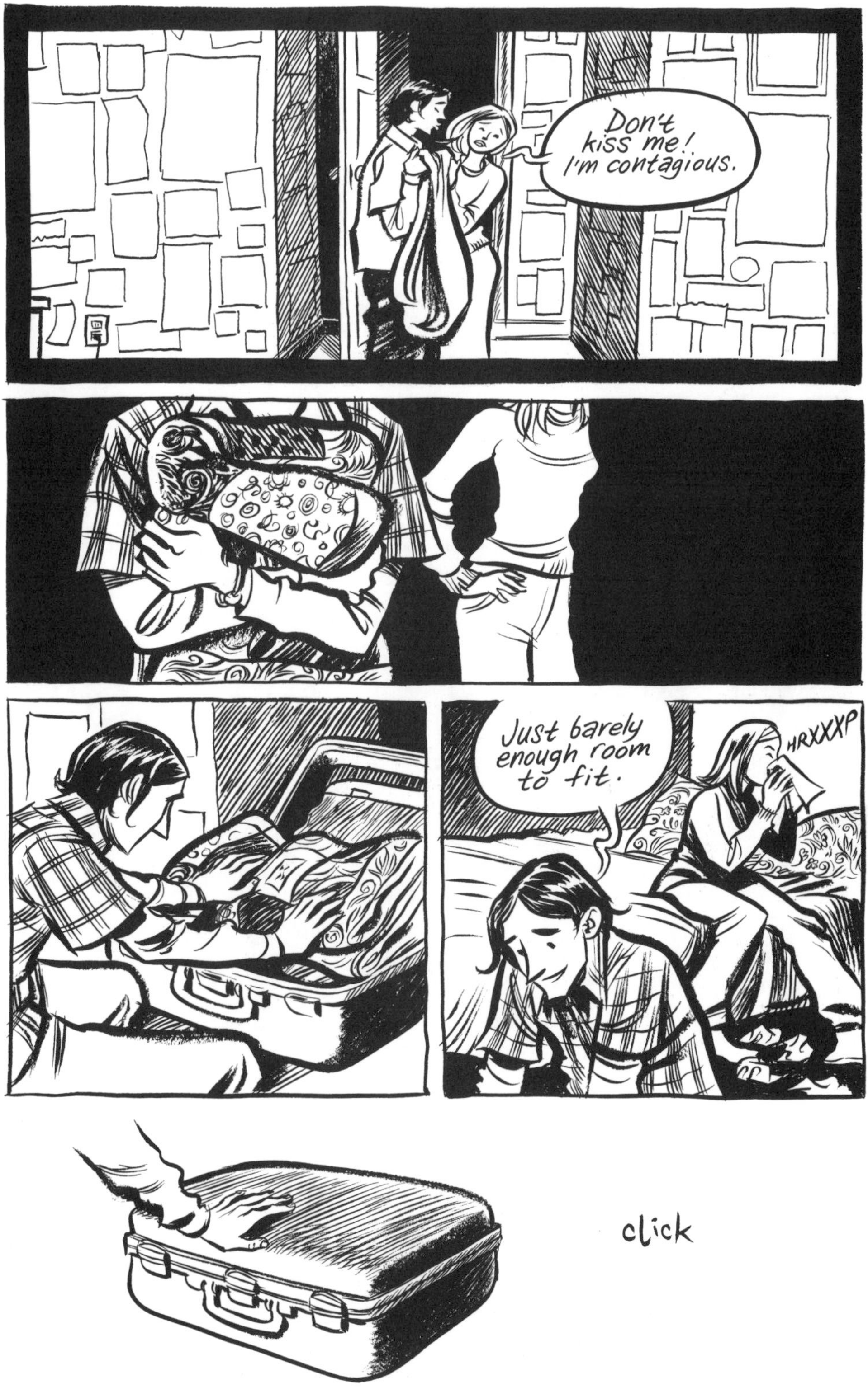
Don't kiss me! I'm contagious.
Just barely enough room to fit.
HRXXXP
click

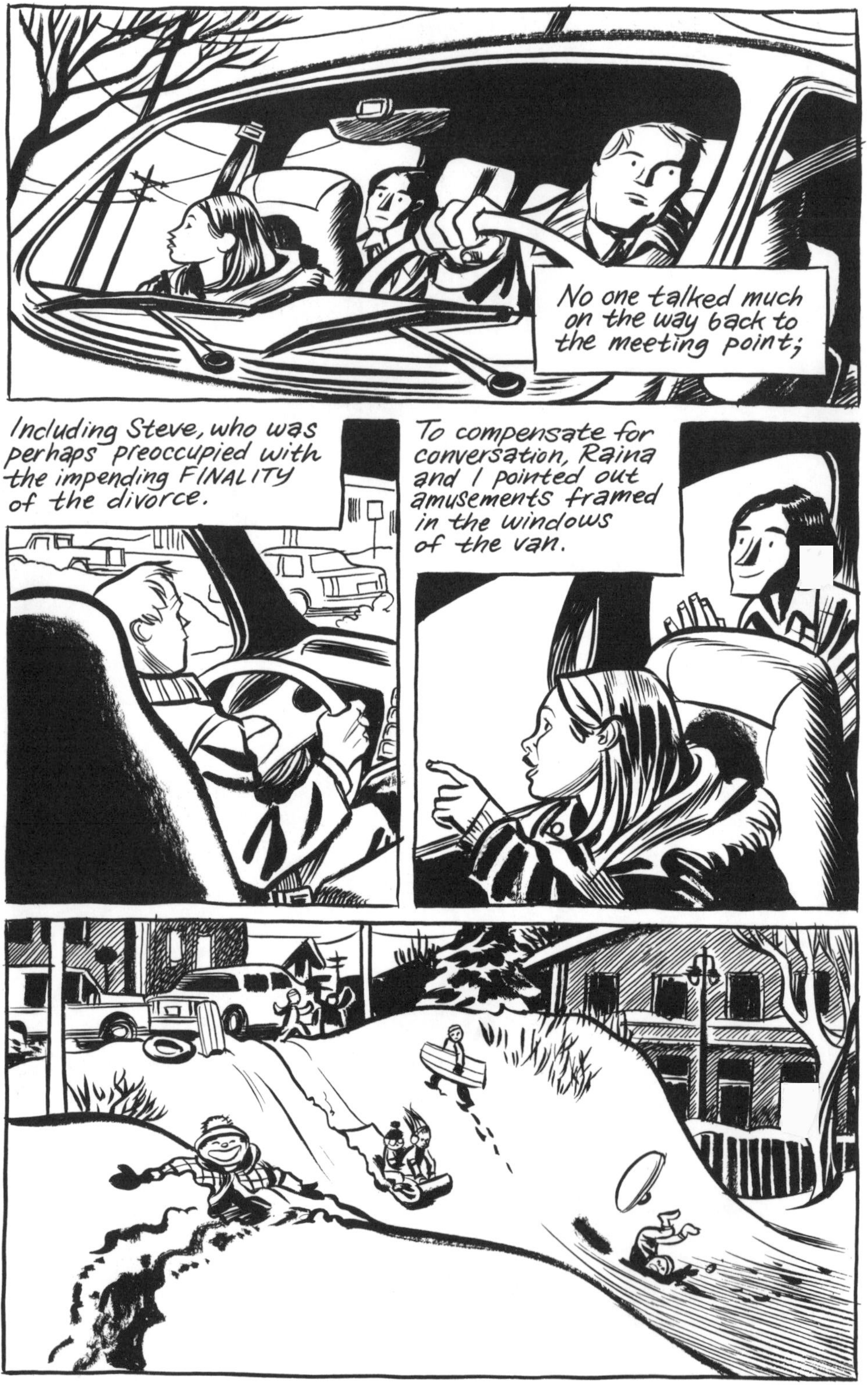
No one talked much on the way back to the meeting point;
Including Steve, who was perhaps preoccupied with the impending FINALITY of the divorce.
To compensate for conversation, Raina and I pointed out amusements framed in the windows of the van.

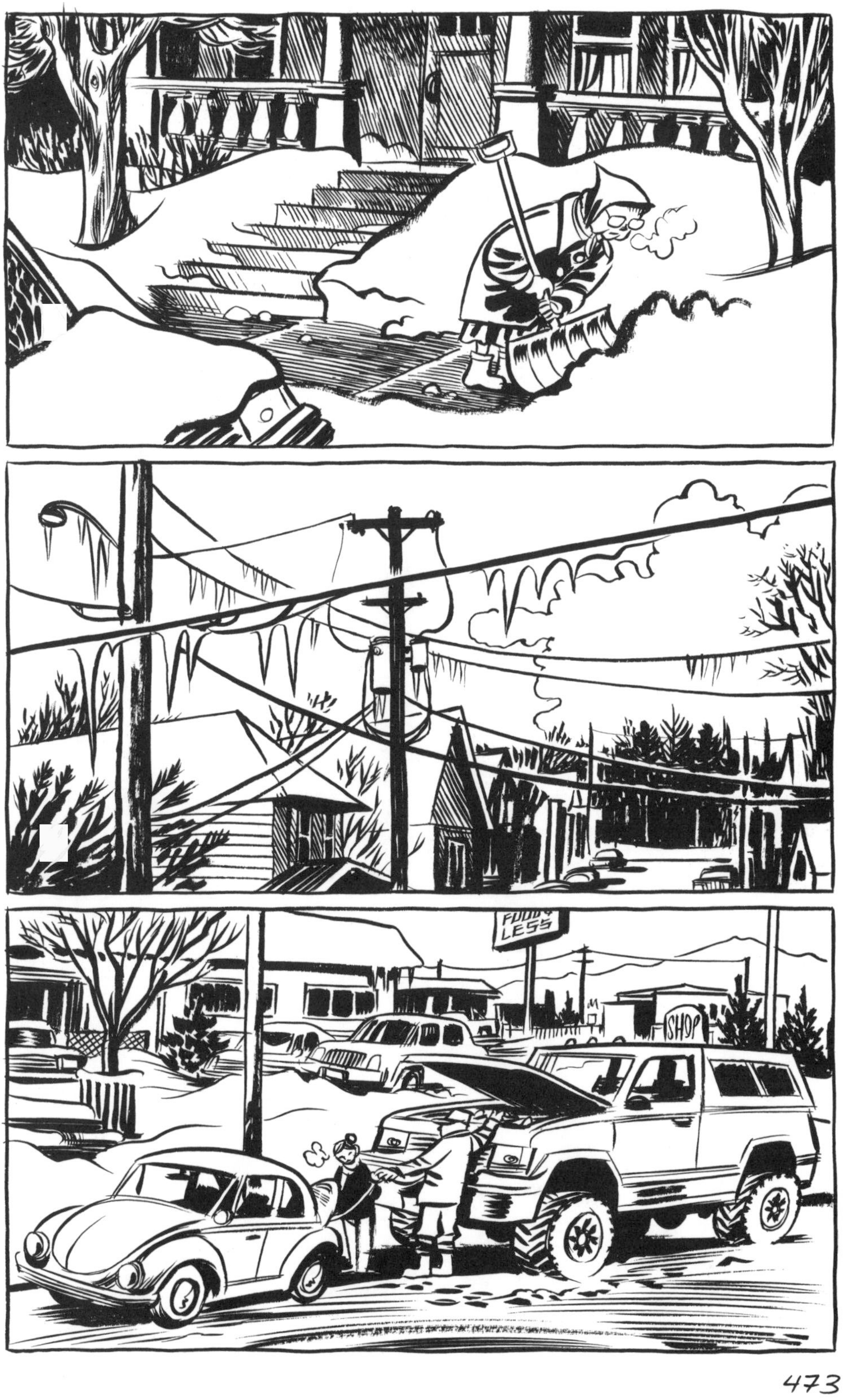
LESS
SHOP

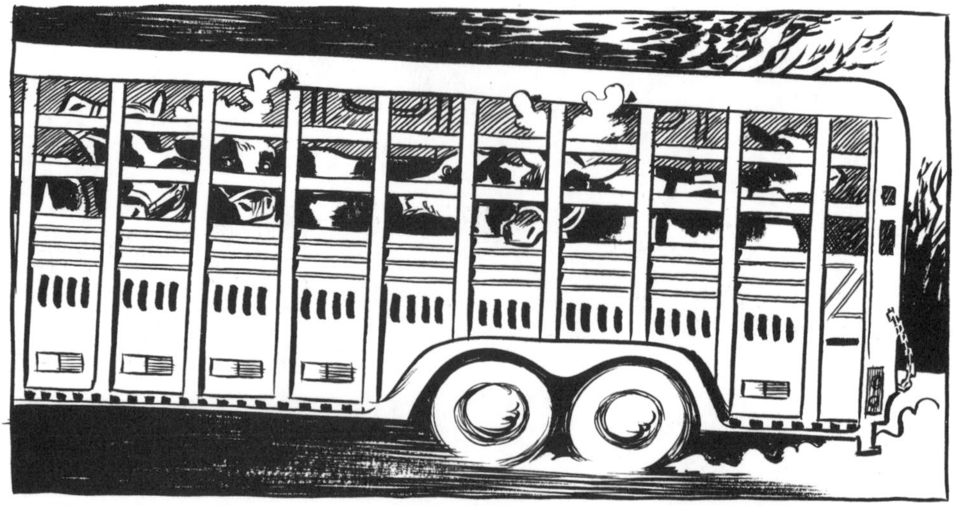

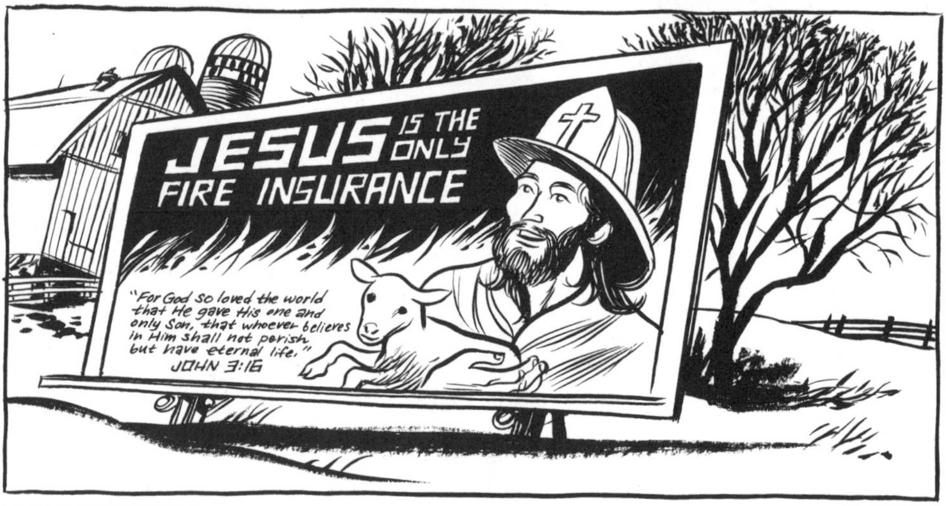
JESUS IS THE ONLY FIRE INSURANCE
"For God so loved the world that He gave His one and only Son, that whoever believes in Him shall not perish but have eternal life."
JOHN 3:16

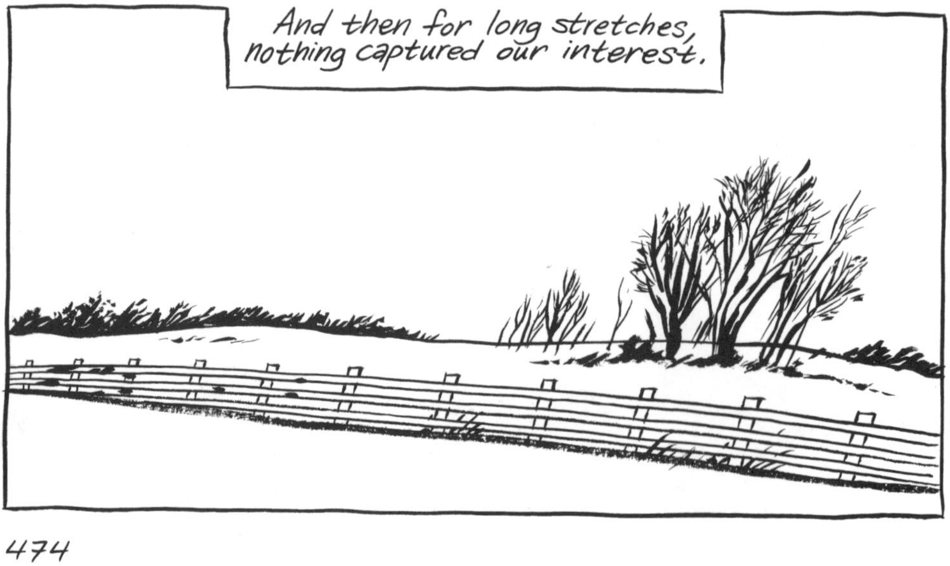
And then for long stretches, nothing captured our interest.

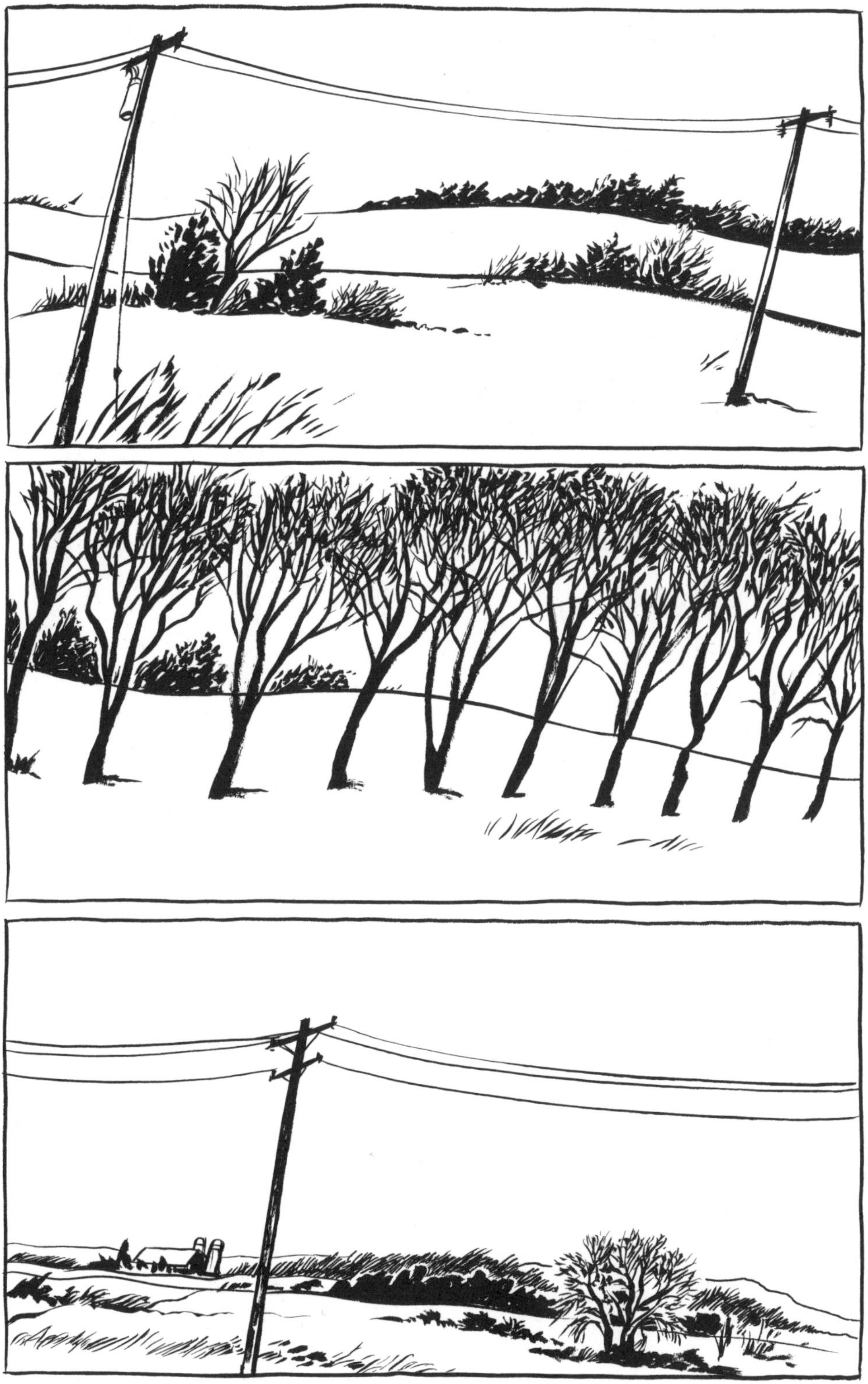

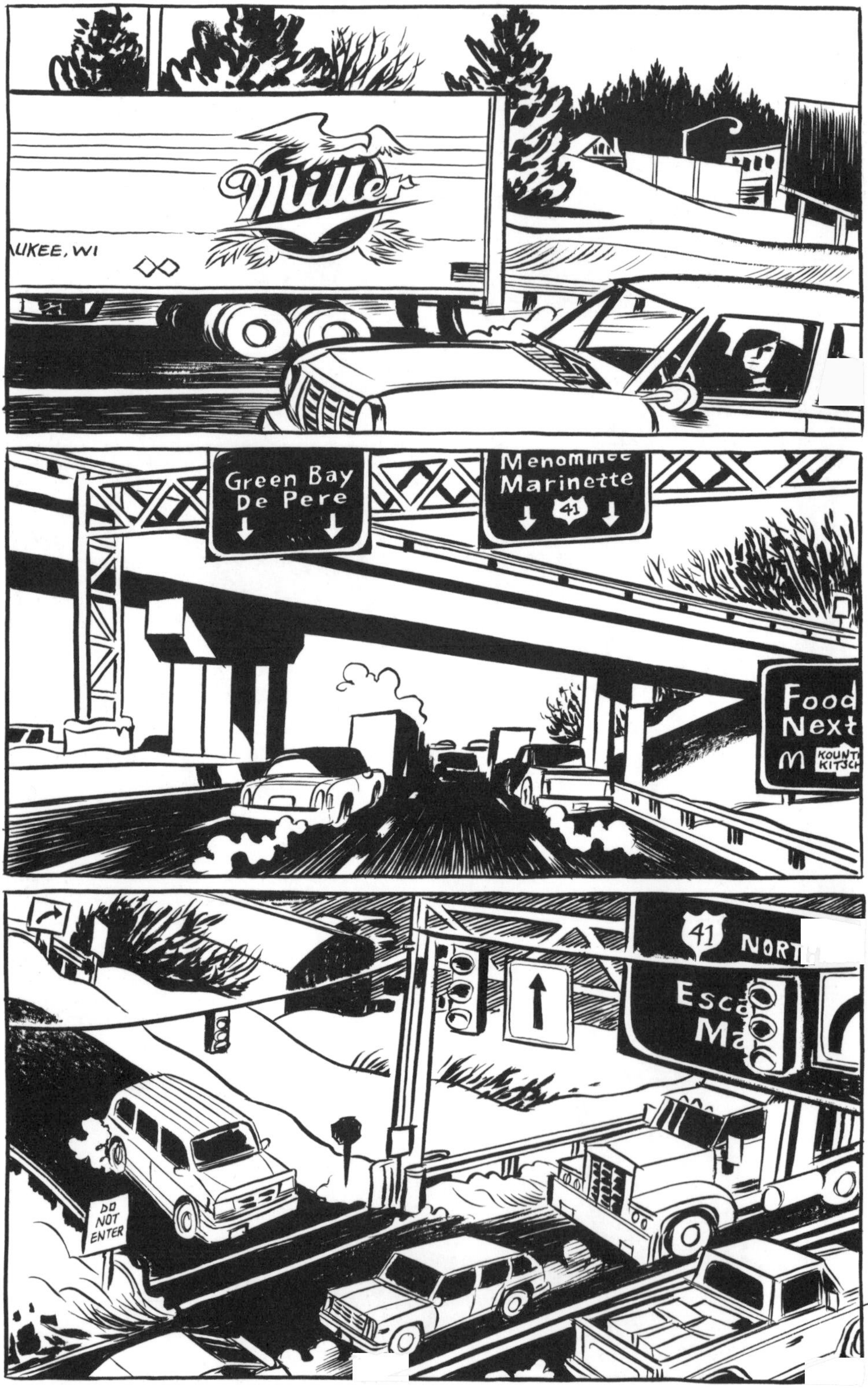
Miller
UKEE, WI
Green Bay
De Pere
Menominee
Marinette
41
Food
Next
KOUNT
KITSCH
41 NORT
Esca
Ma
DO NOT ENTER

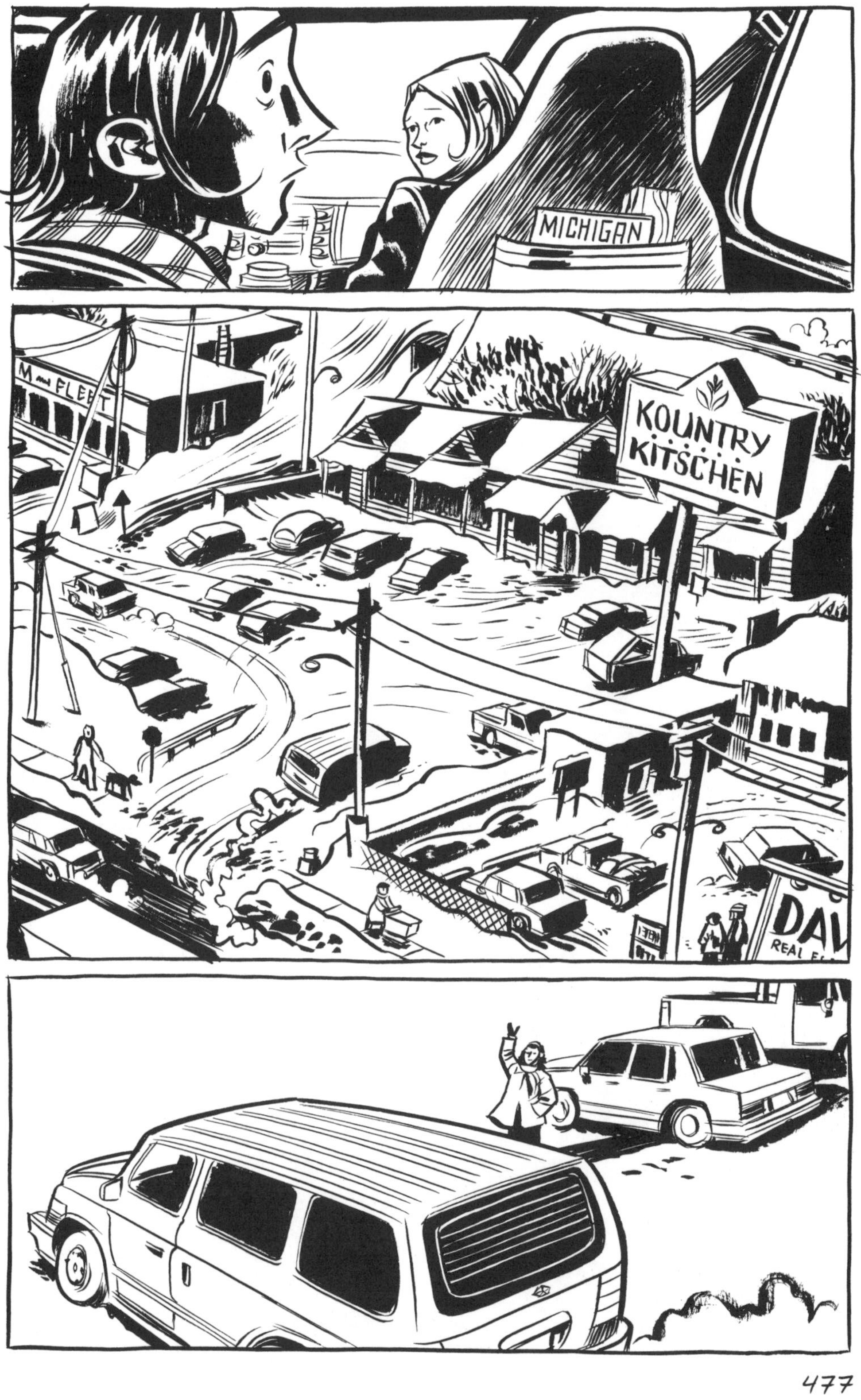
MICHIGAN
KOUNTRY KITSCHEN

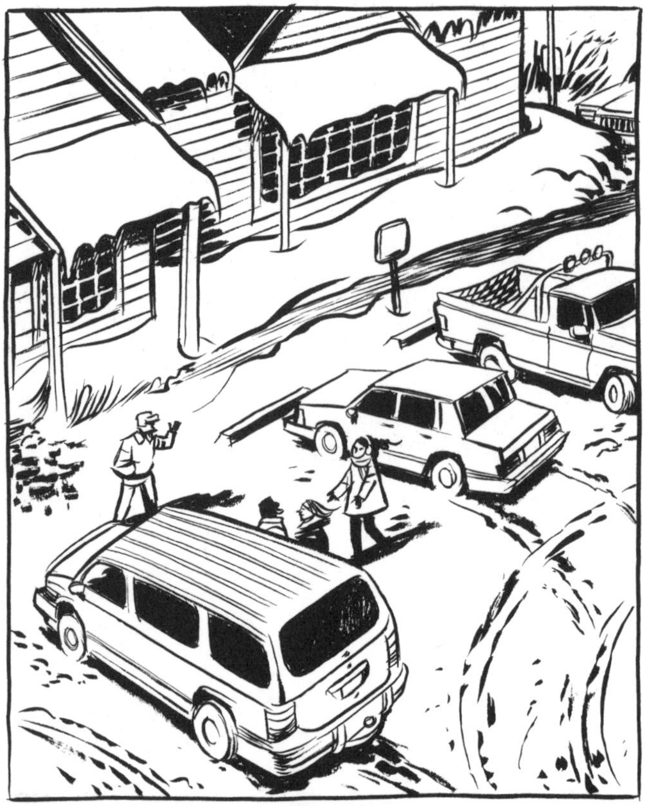

At the moment, parental small-talk was practically unbearable --

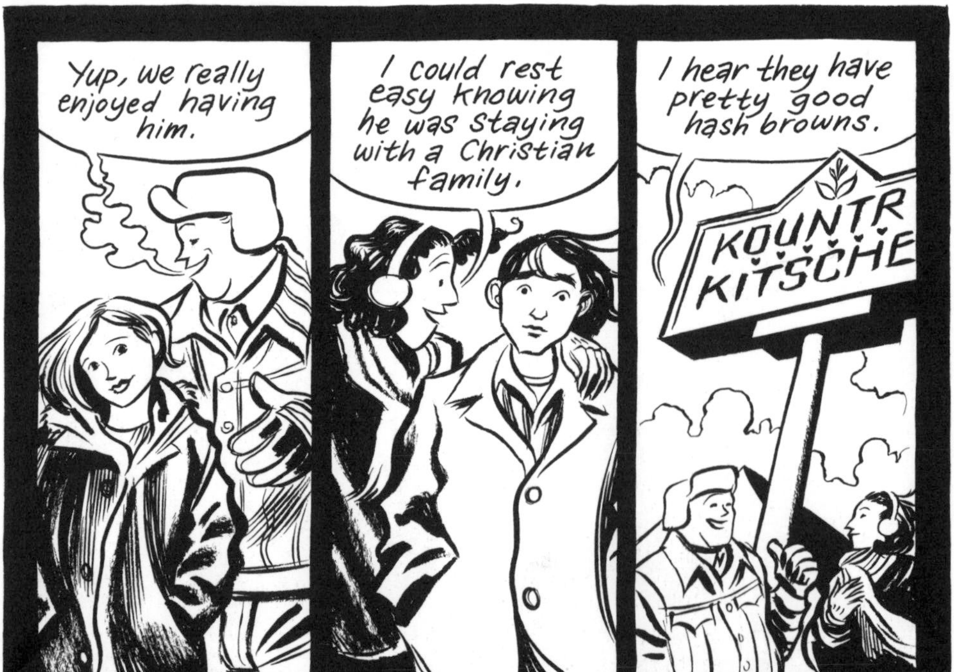

Yup, we really enjoyed having him.
I could rest easy knowing he was staying with a Christian family.
I hear they have pretty good hash browns.
KOUNTR
KITSCHE

--except that it constructed a pretense for Raina and I to exchange glances a moment longer.

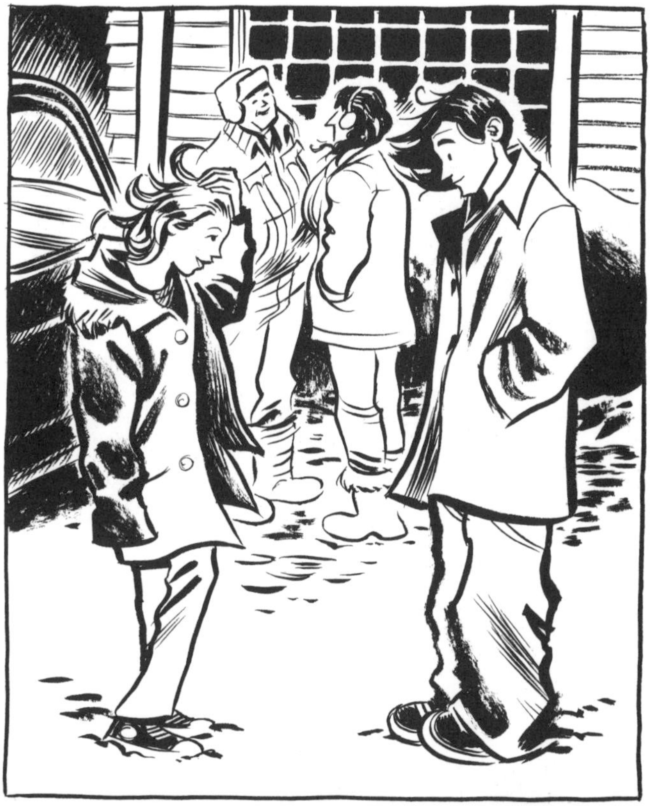

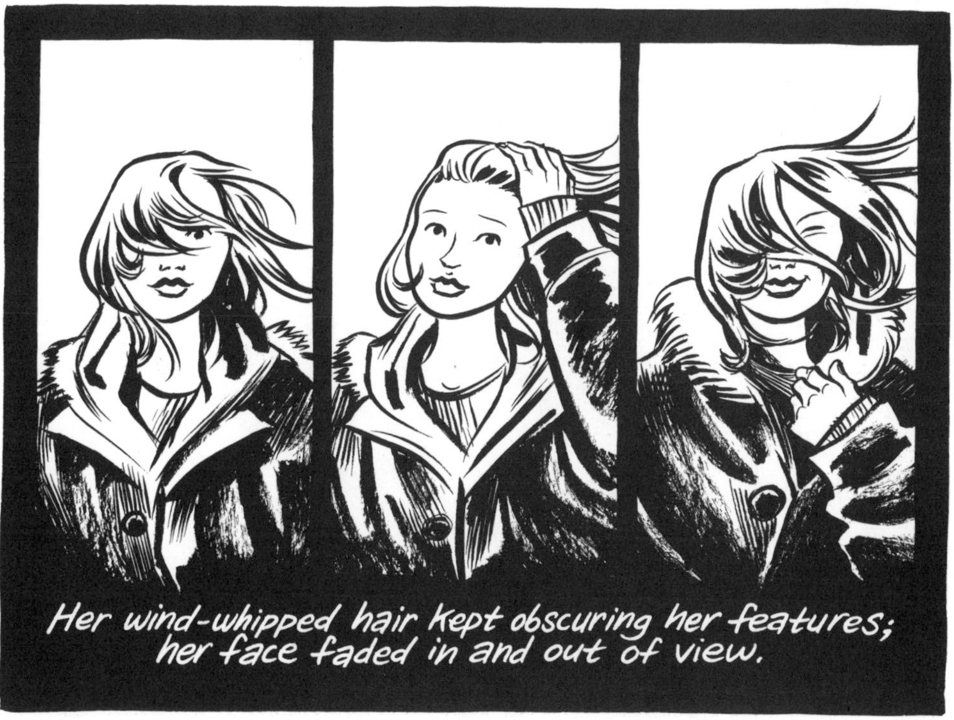
Her wind-whipped hair kept obscuring her features; her face faded in and out of view.

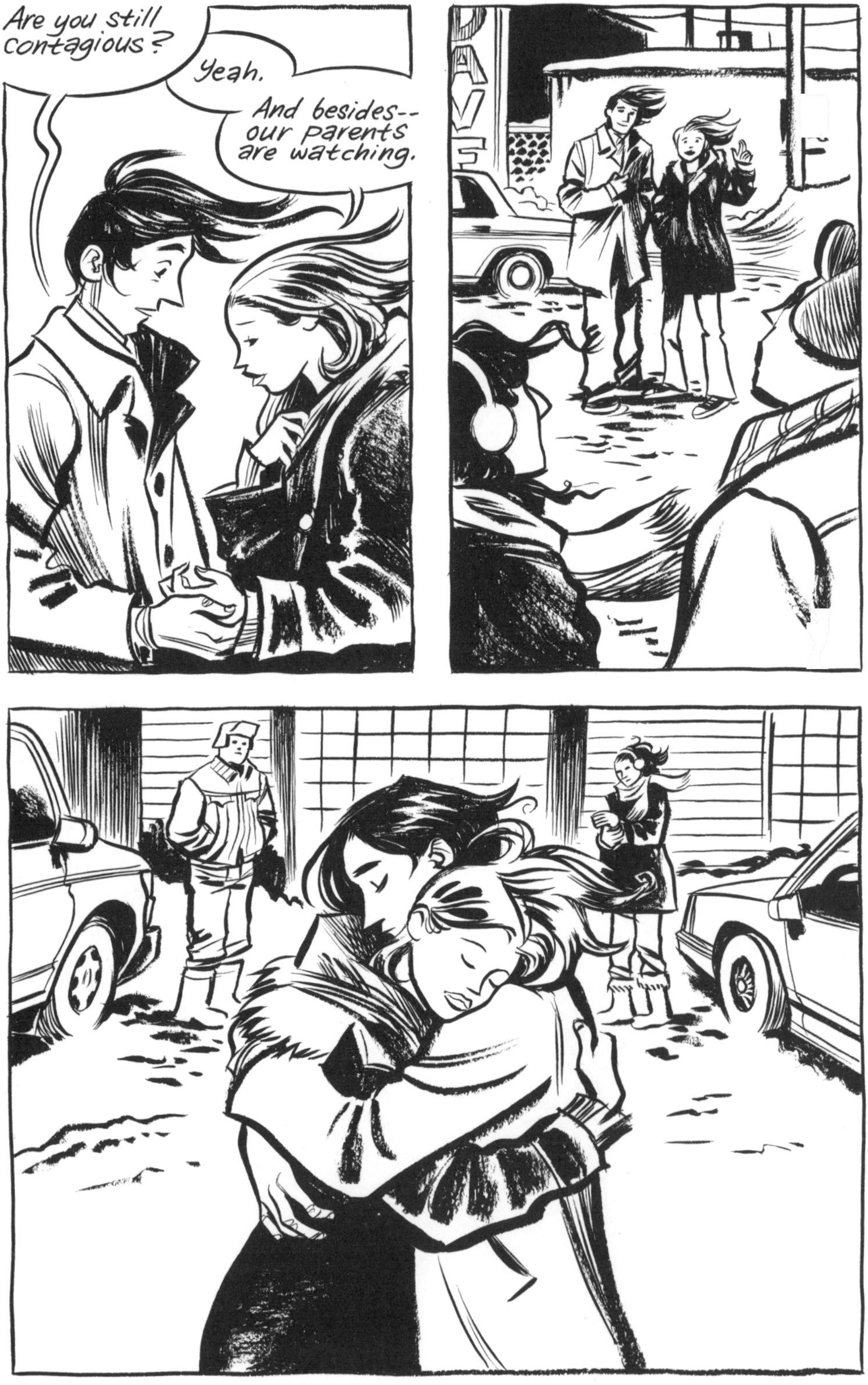
Are you still contagious?
Yeah.
And besides-- our parents are watching.

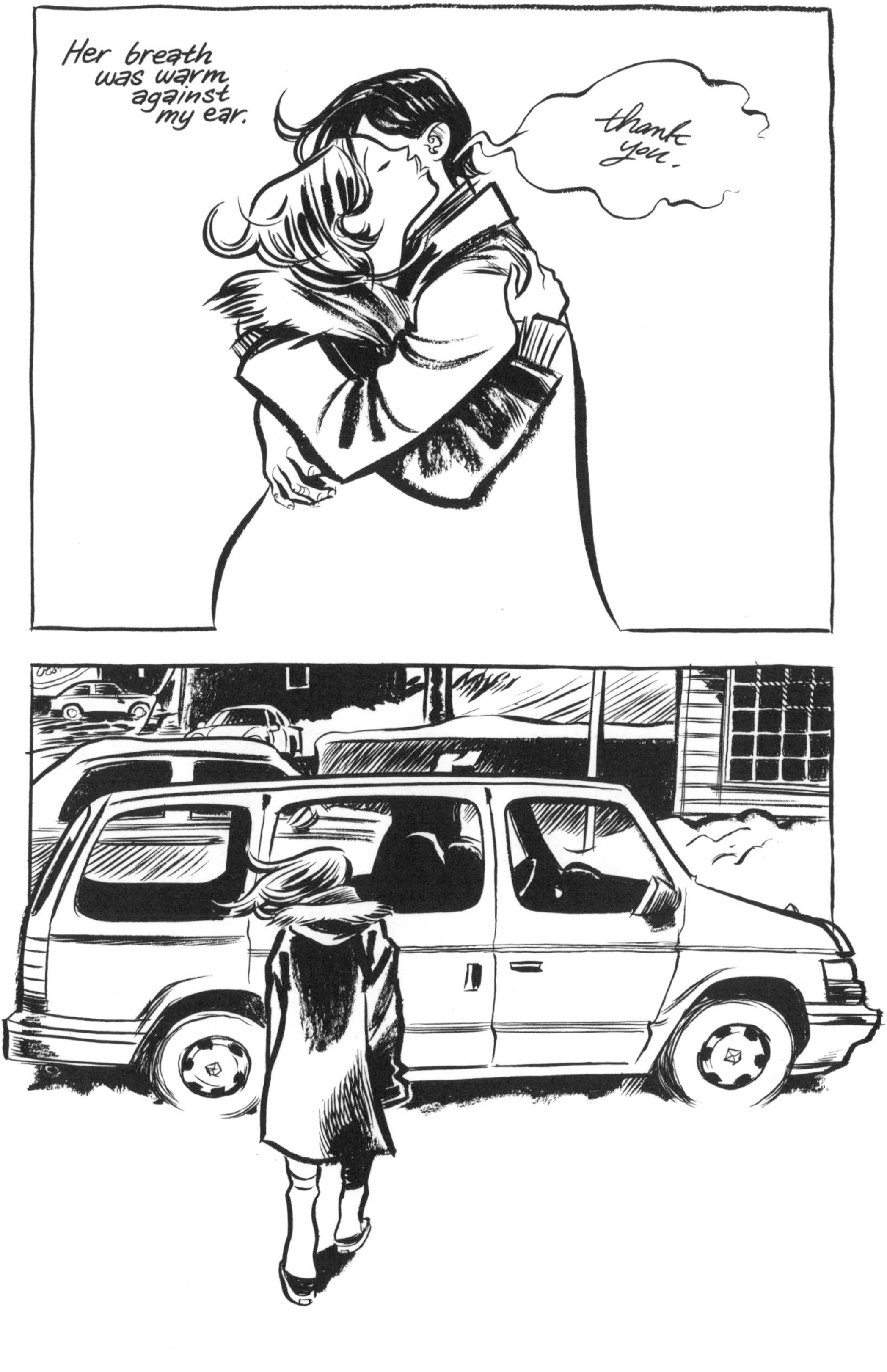
Her breath was warm against my ear.
thank you.

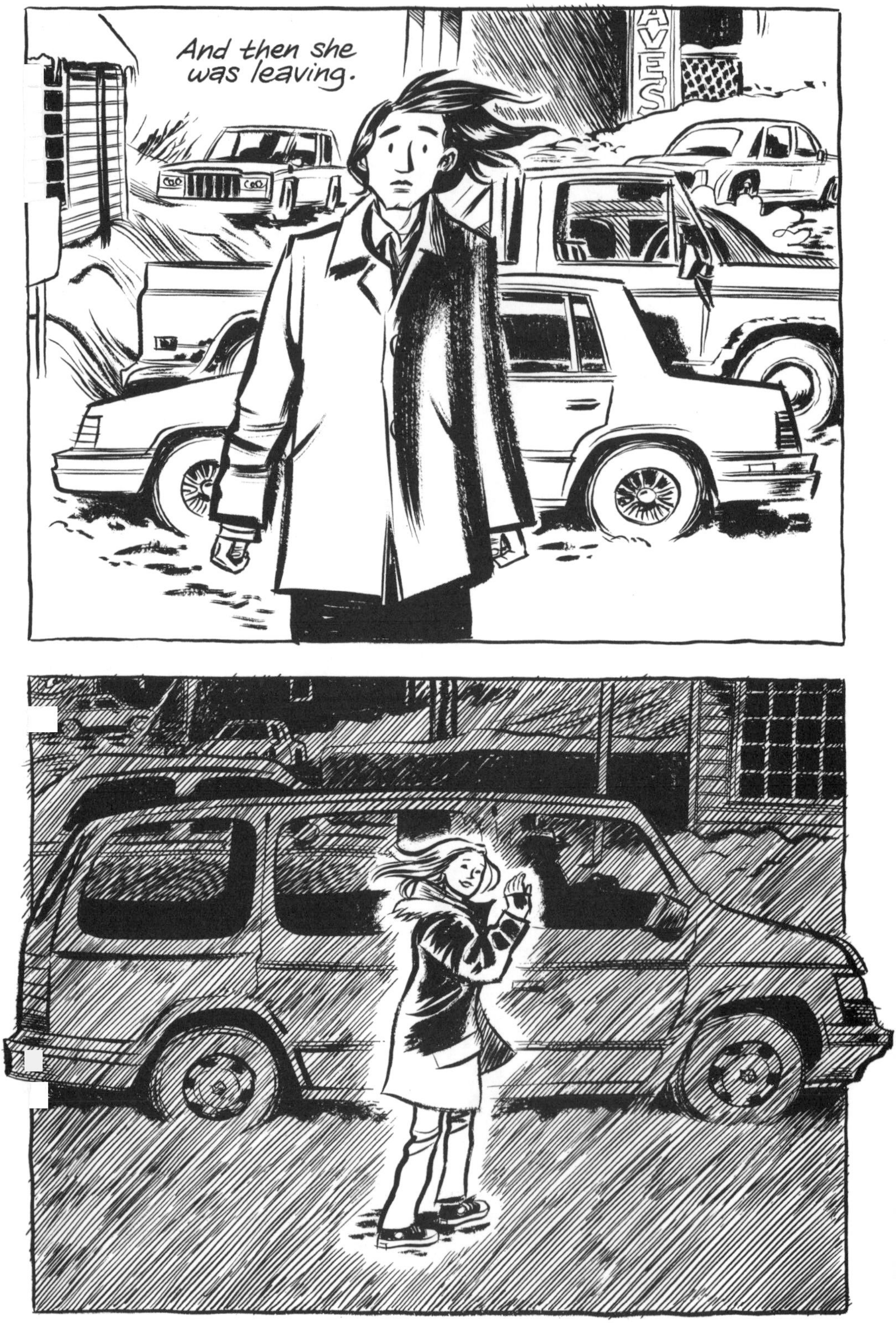
And then she was leaving.

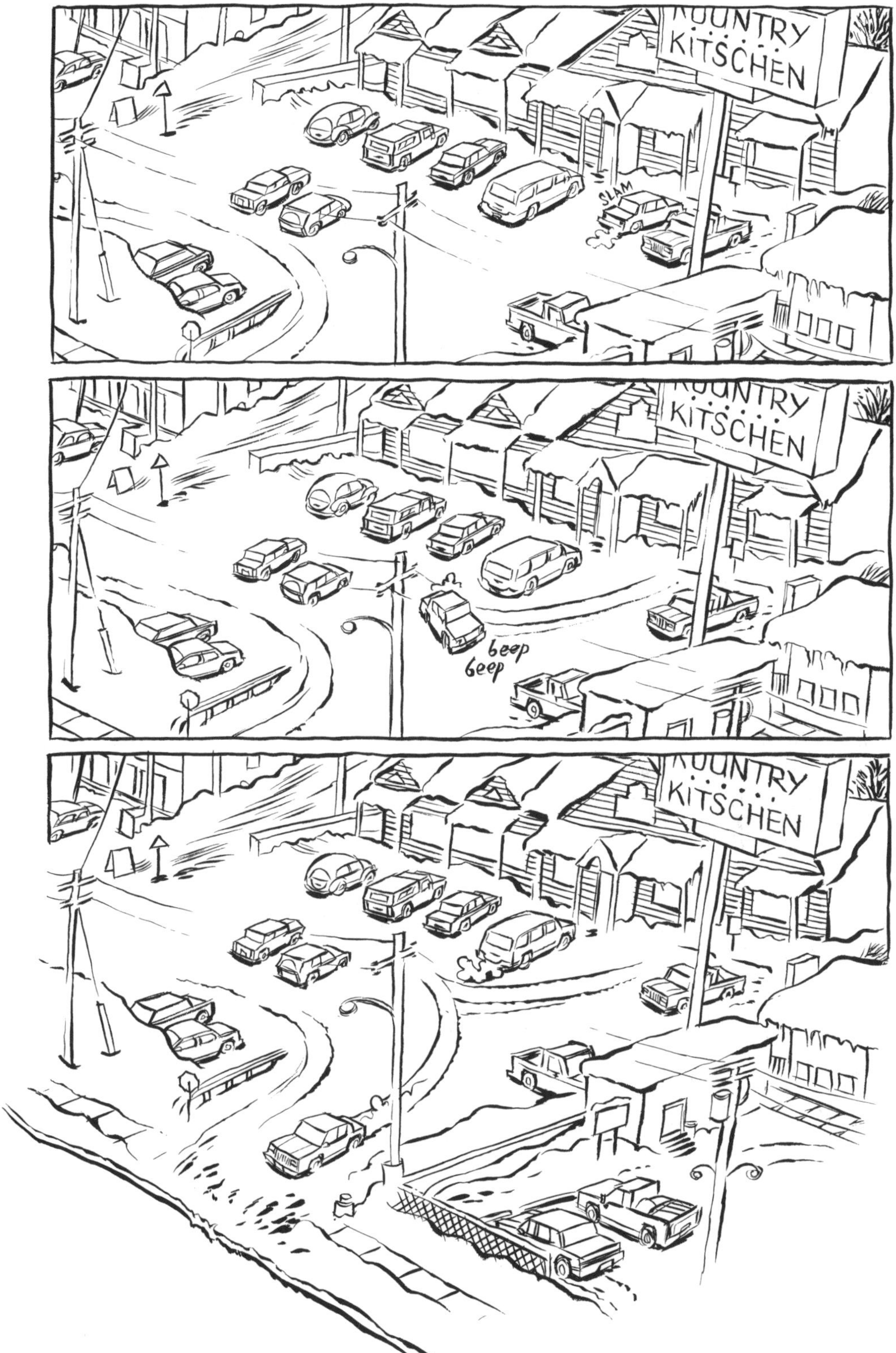
KOUNTRY KITSCHEN
SLAM
KOUNTRY KITSCHEN
beep
beep
KOUNTRY KITSCHEN

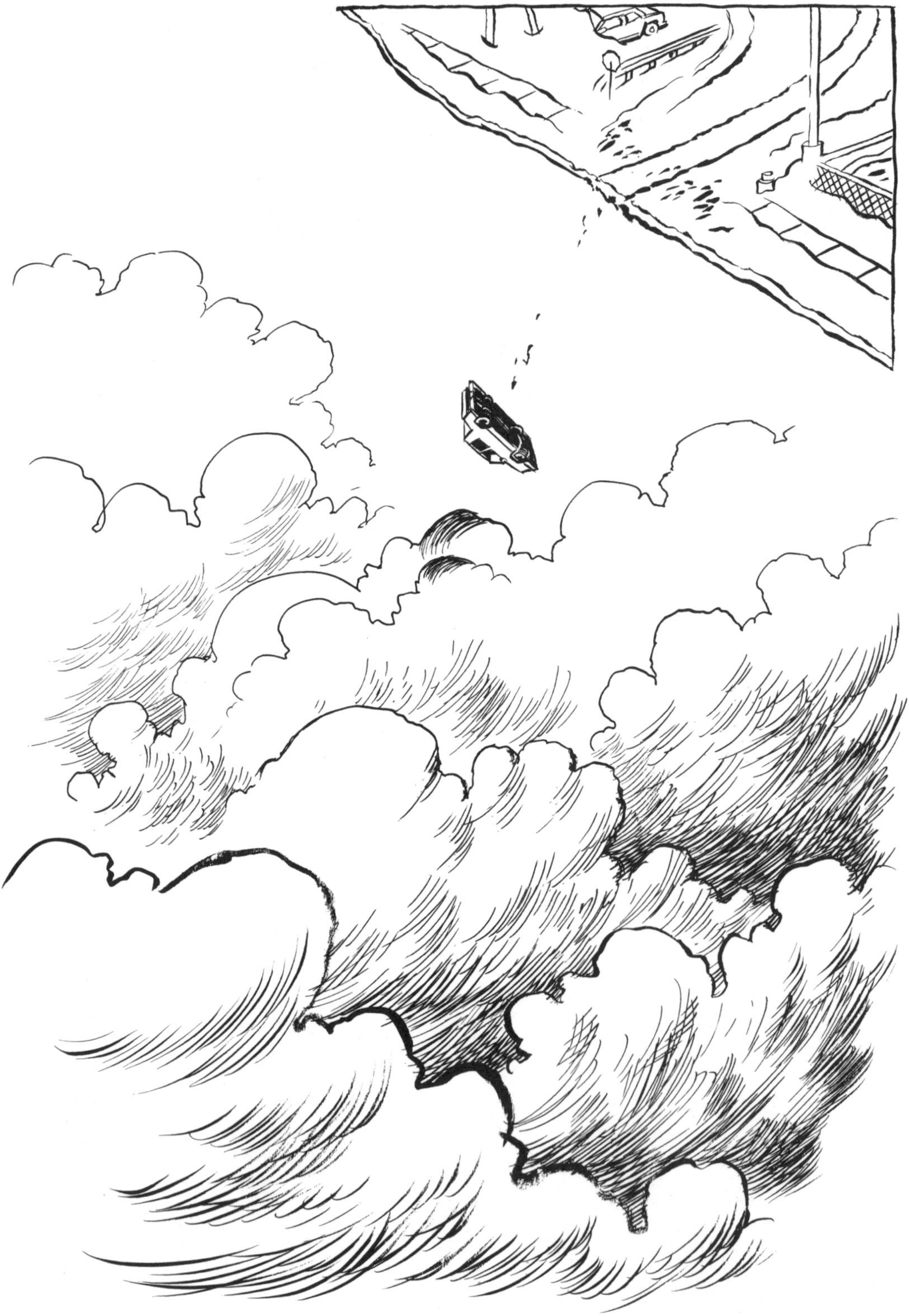

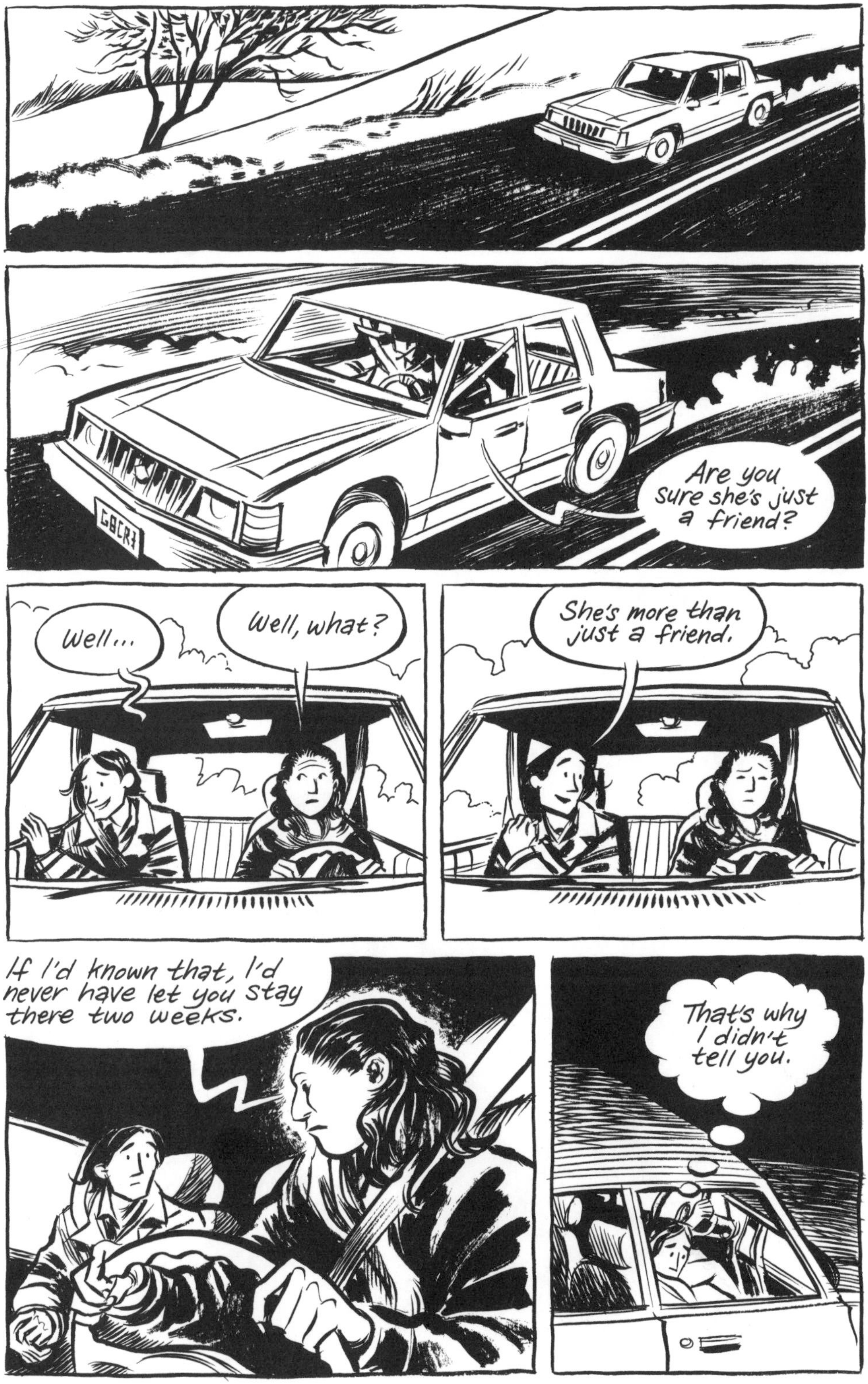
Are you sure she's just a friend?
Well...
Well, what?
She's more than just a friend.
If I'd known that, I'd never have let you stay there two weeks.
That's why I didn't tell you.

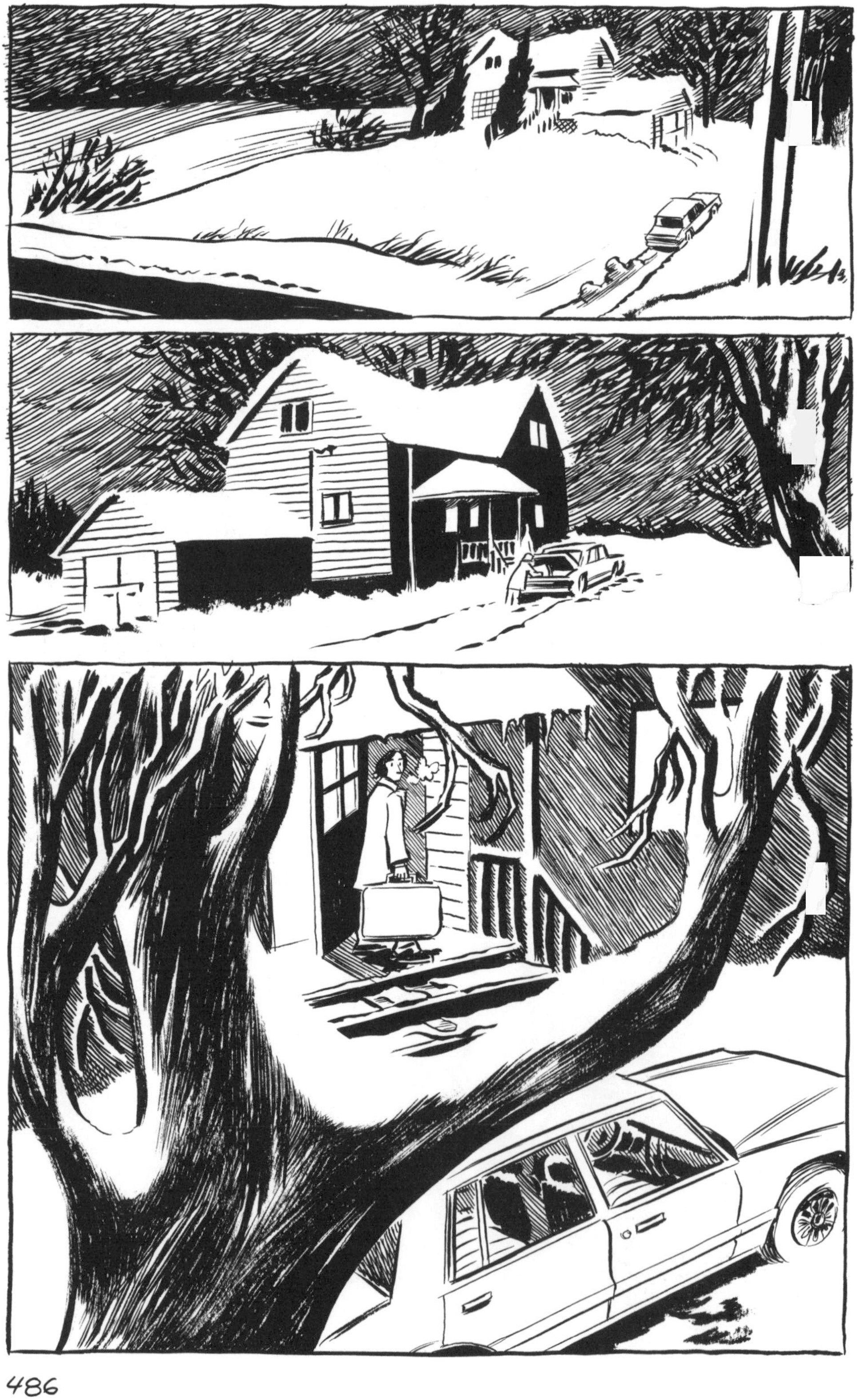

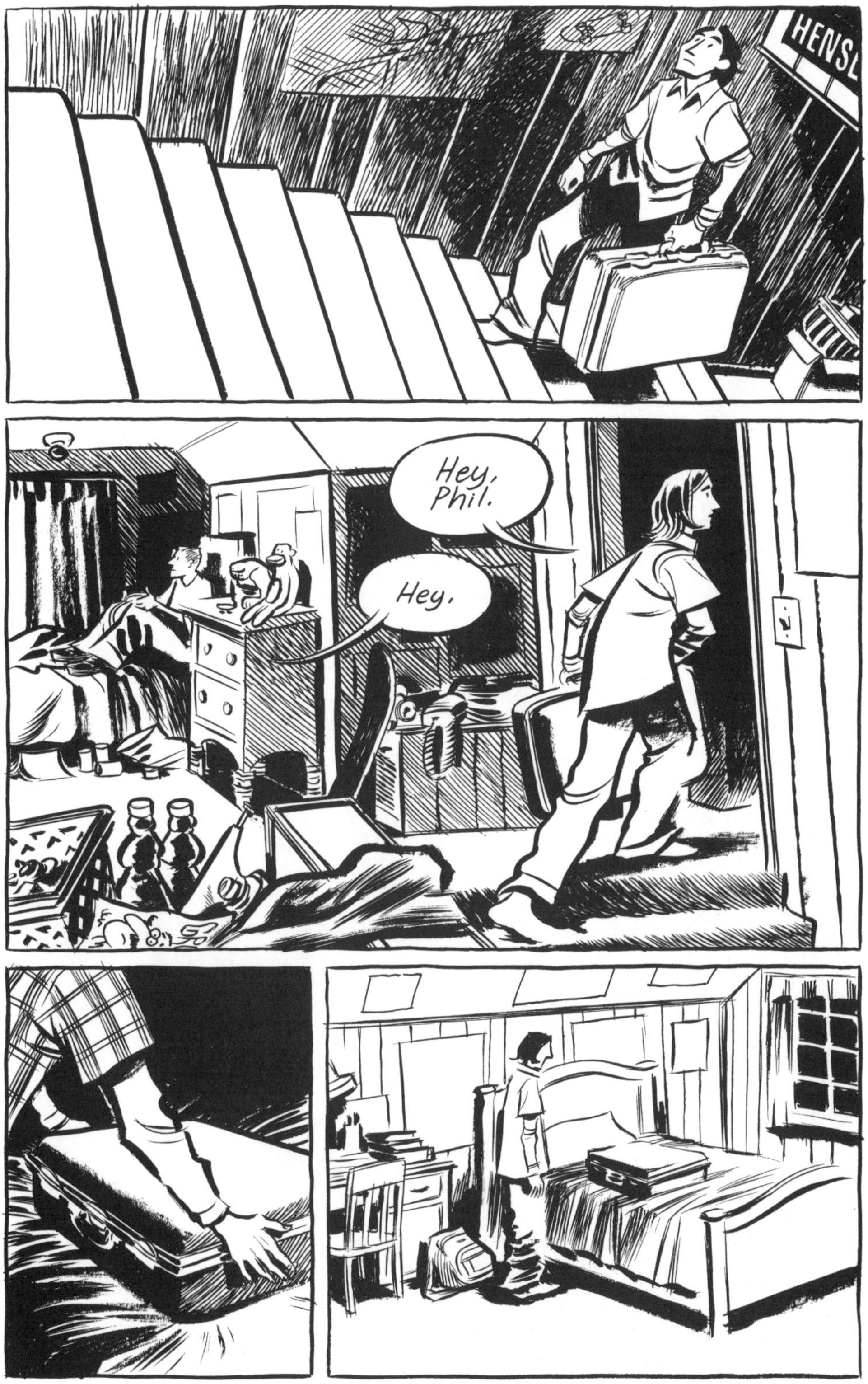
Hey, Phil.
Hey.

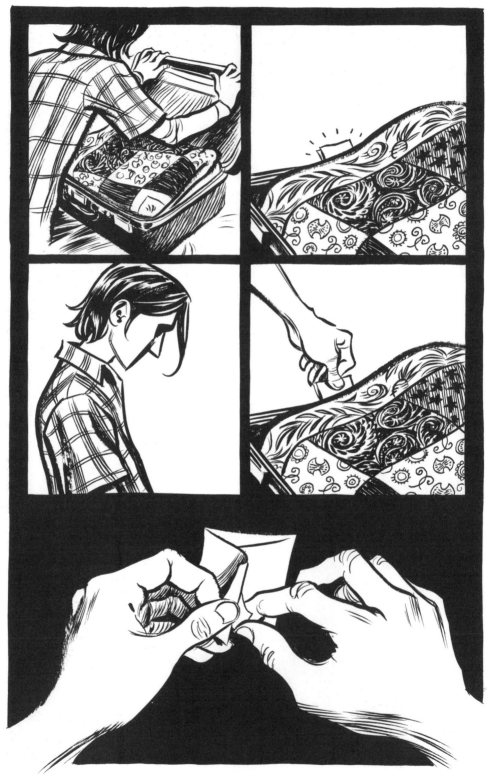

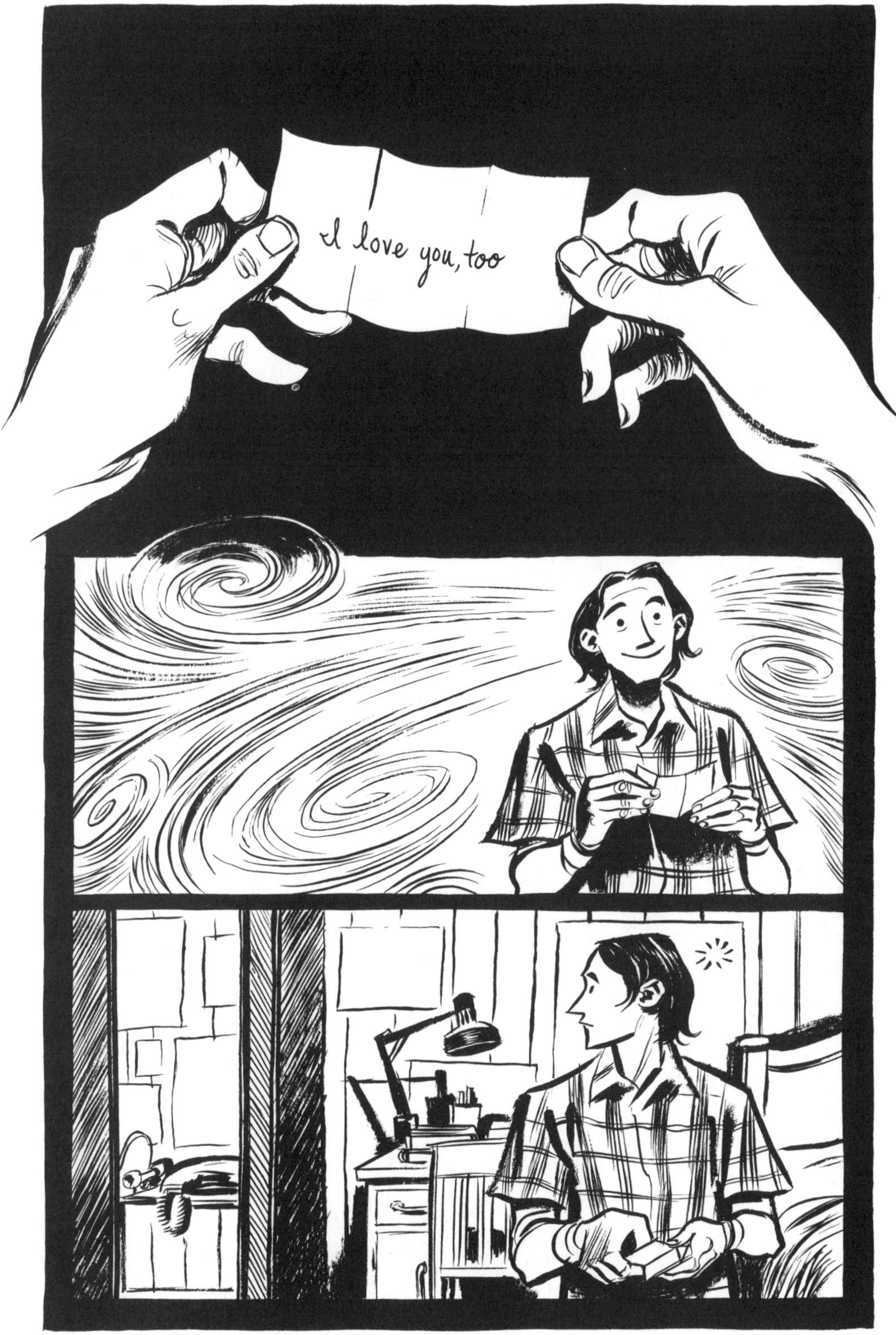
I love you, too

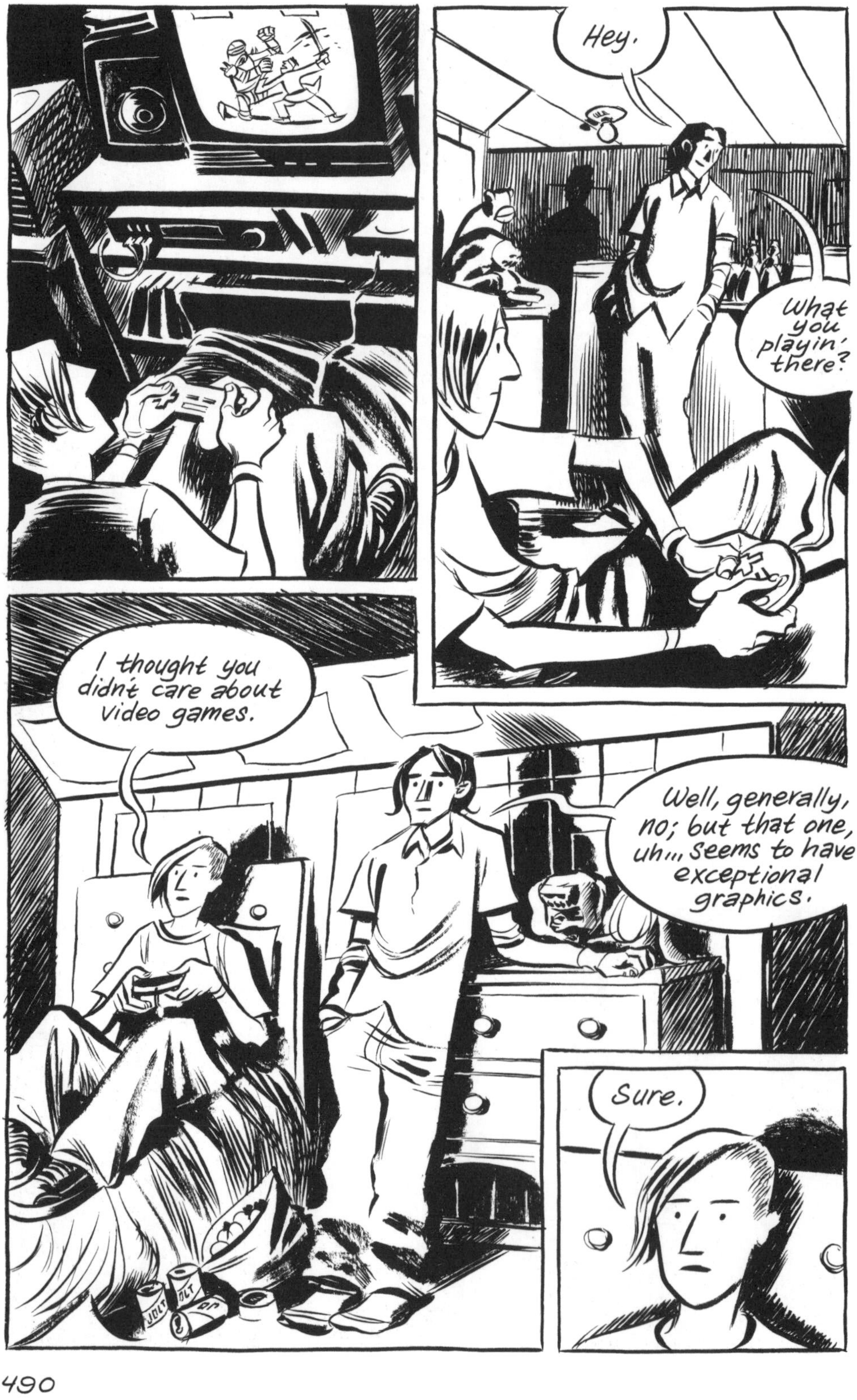
Hey.
What you playin' there?
I thought you didn't care about video games.
Well, generally, no; but that one, uh... seems to have exceptional graphics.
Sure.

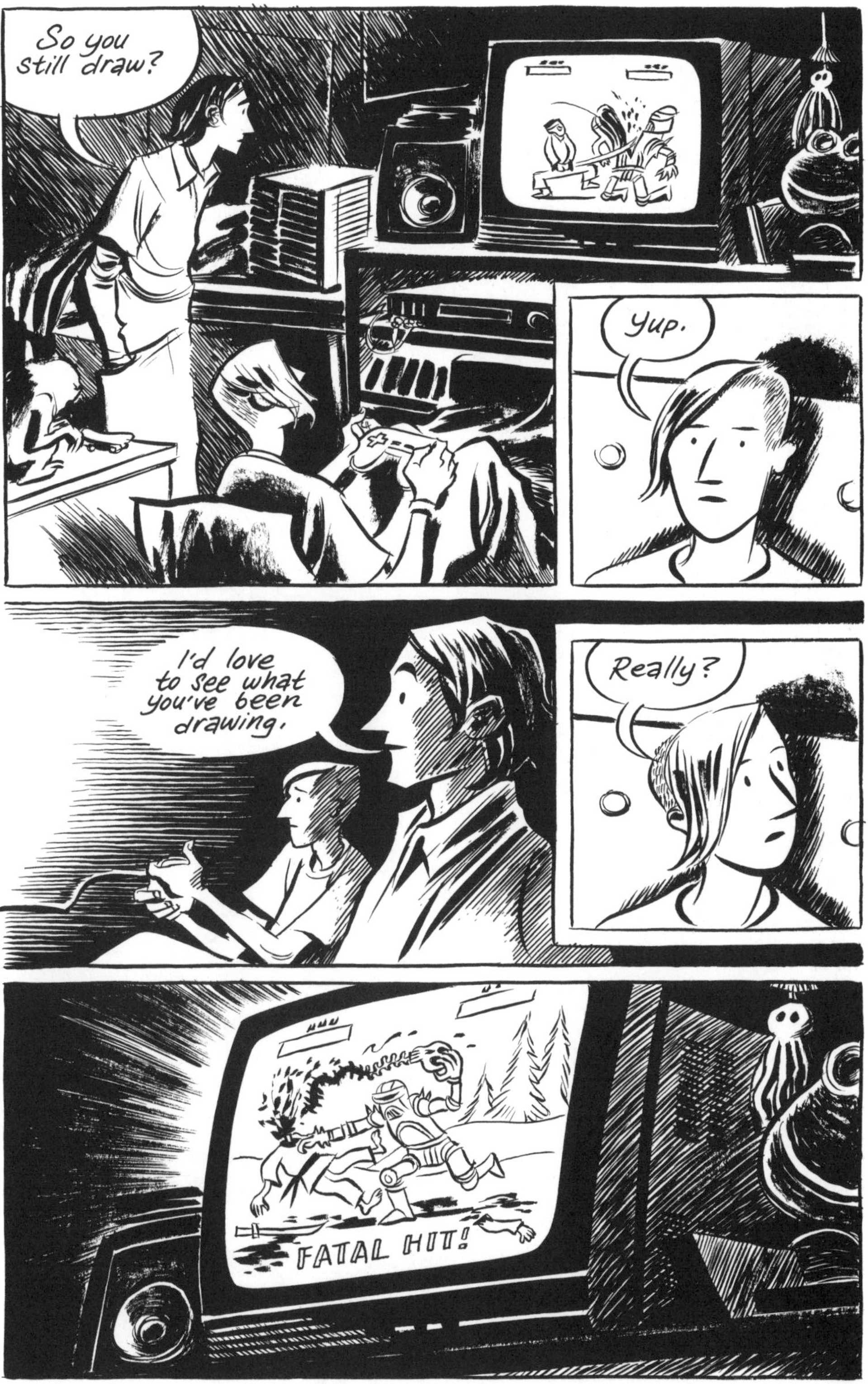
So you still draw?
Yup.
I'd love to see what you've been drawing.
Really?
FATAL HIT!

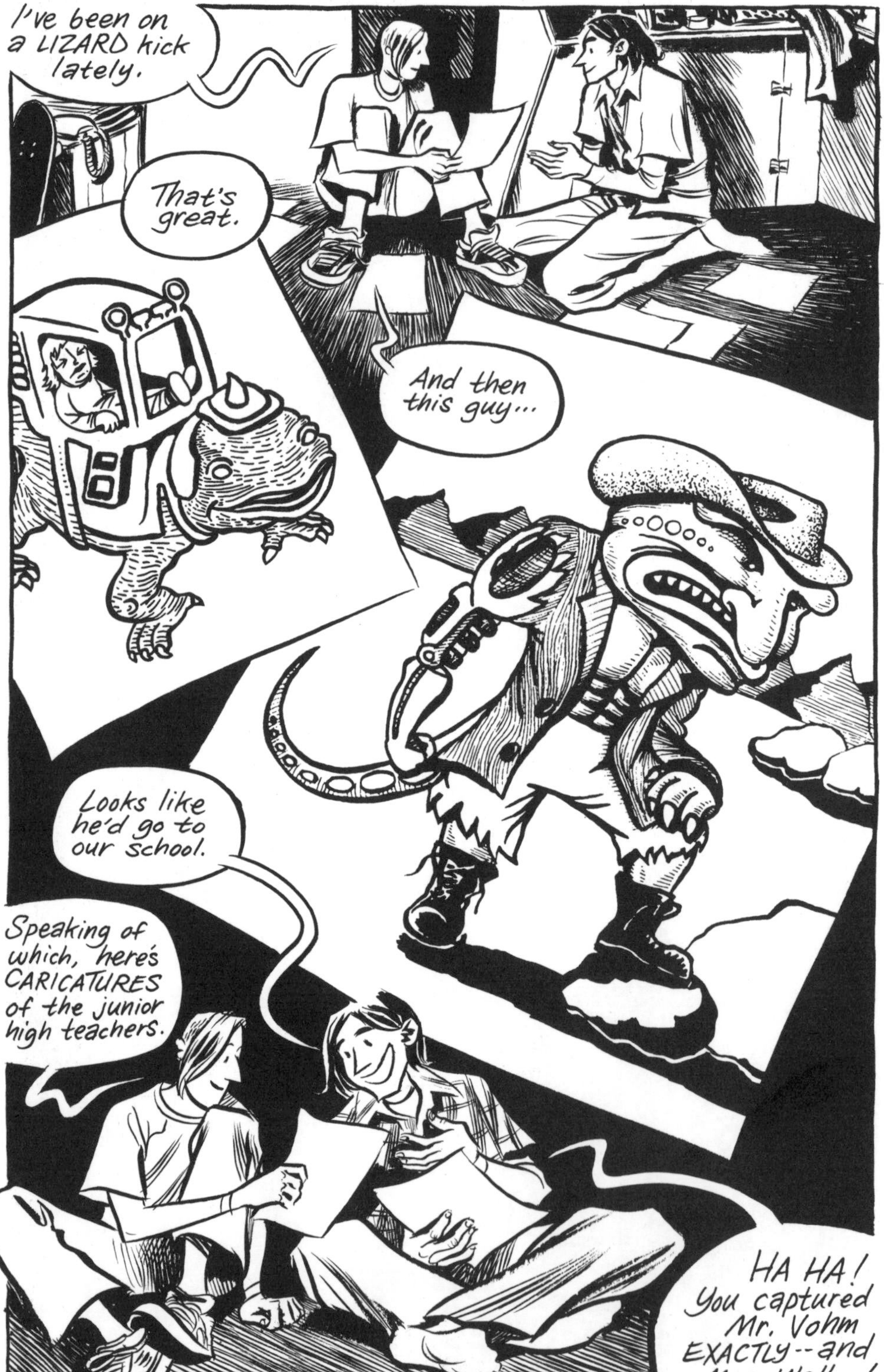
I've been on a LIZARD kick lately.
That's great.
And then this guy...
Looks like he'd go to our school.
Speaking of which, here's CARICATURES of the junior high teachers.
HA HA! You captured Mr. Vohm EXACTLY--and Mrs. Weller!

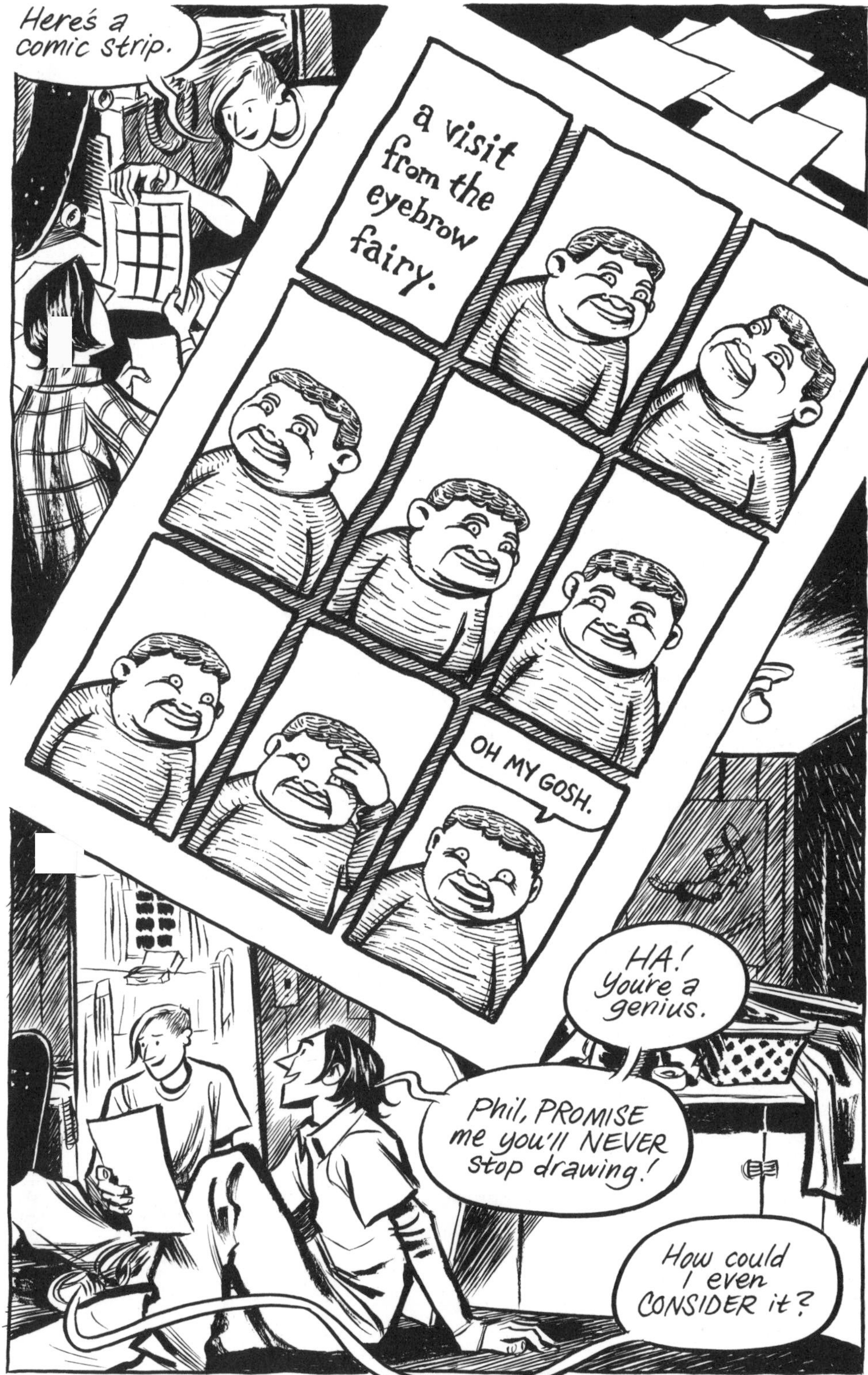

Here's a comic strip.
a visit from the eyebrow fairy.
OH MY GOSH.
HA! You're a genius.
Phil, PROMISE me you'll NEVER stop drawing!
How could I even CONSIDER it?

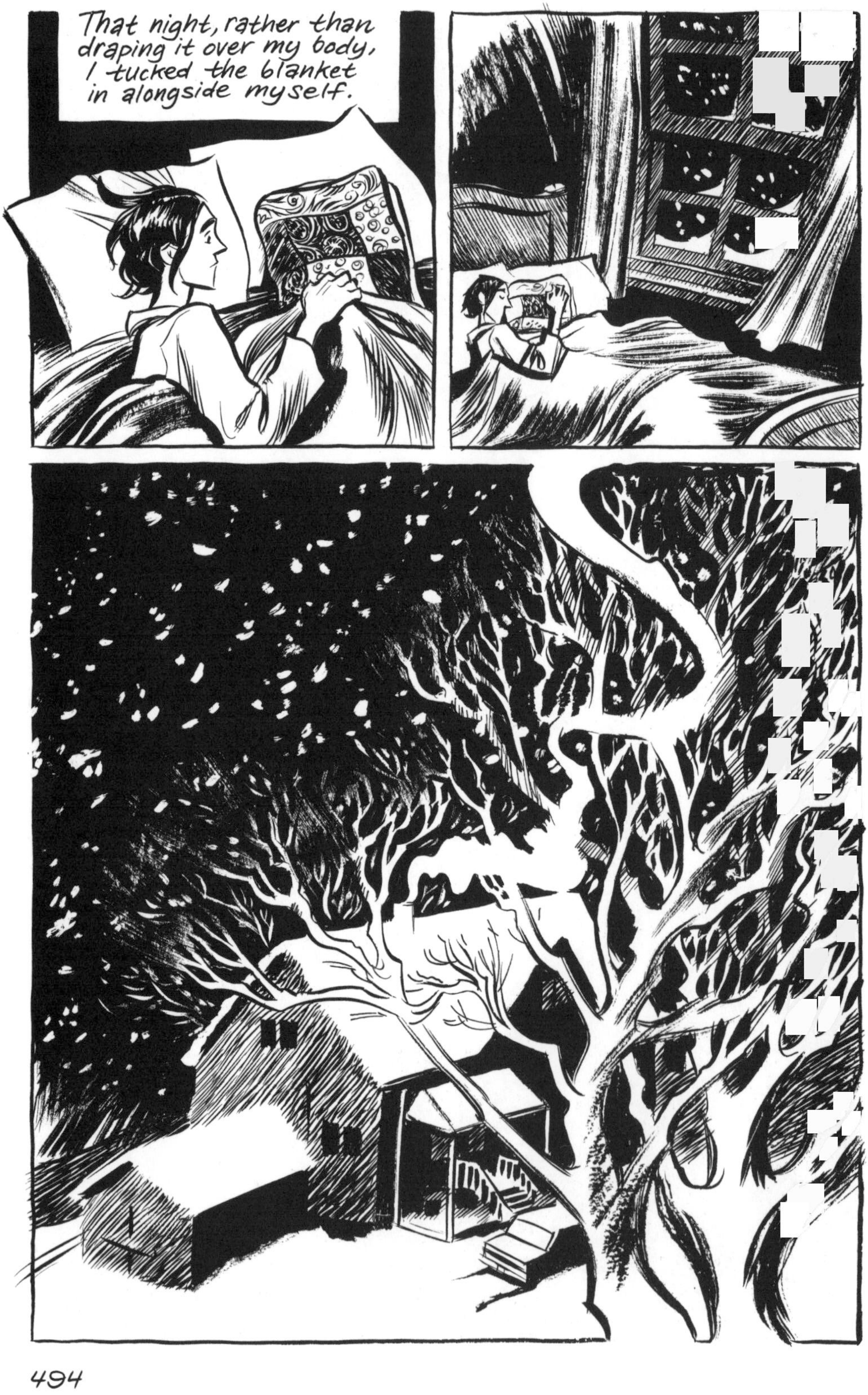
That night, rather than draping it over my body, I tucked the blanket in alongside myself.

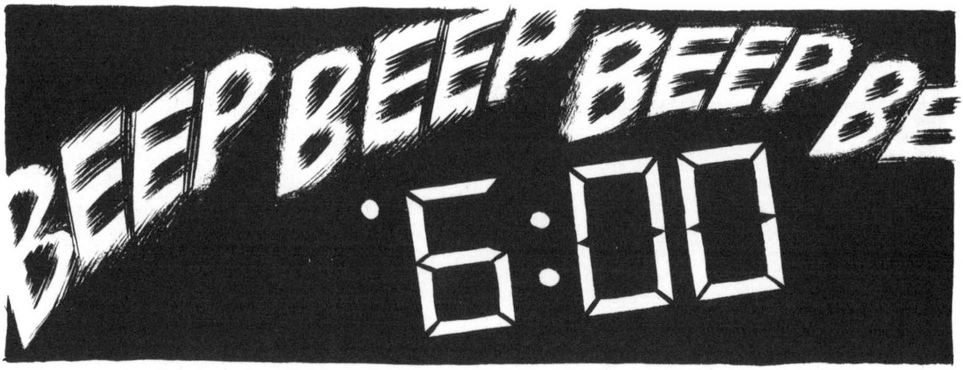
BEEP BEEP BEEP BEEP BE
6:00

SOCRATES ASKS HIS DISCIPLE GLAUCON TO IMAGINE HUMAN BEINGS LIVING WITHIN A DARK CAVERN.

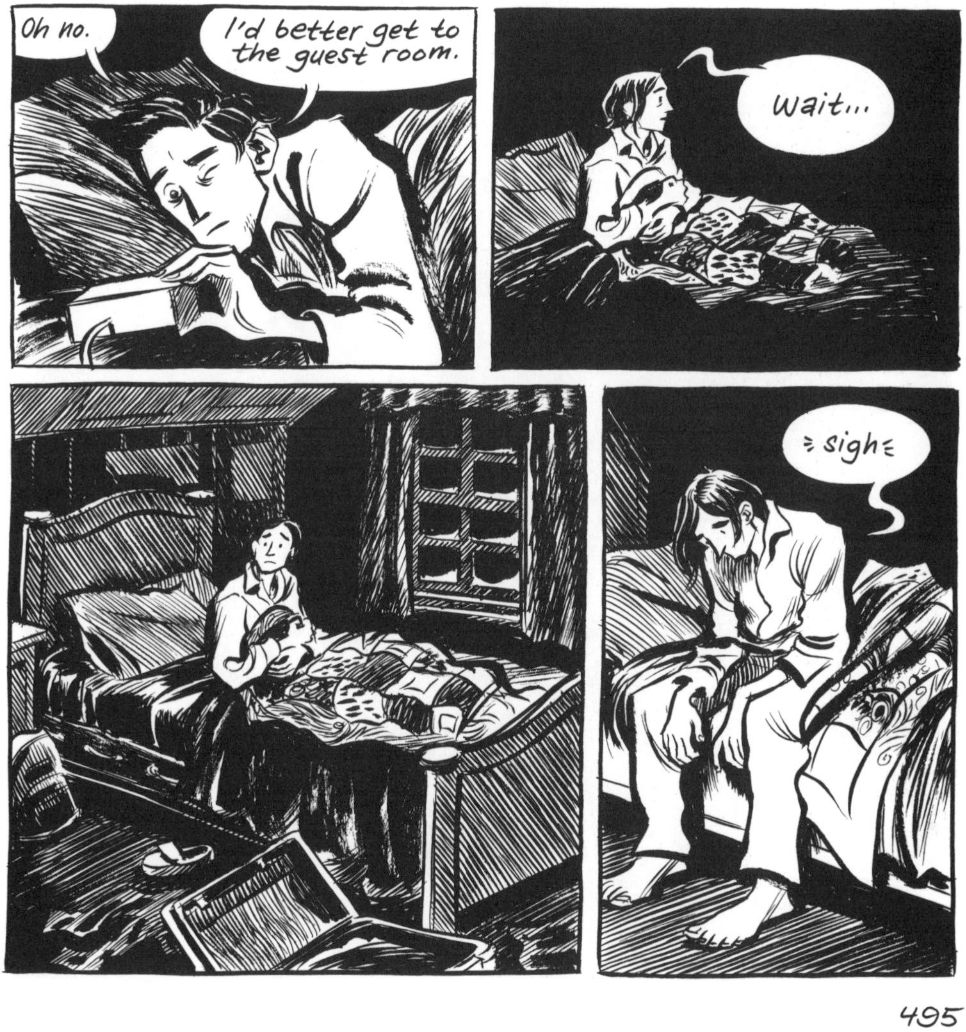
Oh no.
I'd better get to the guest room.
wait...
sigh

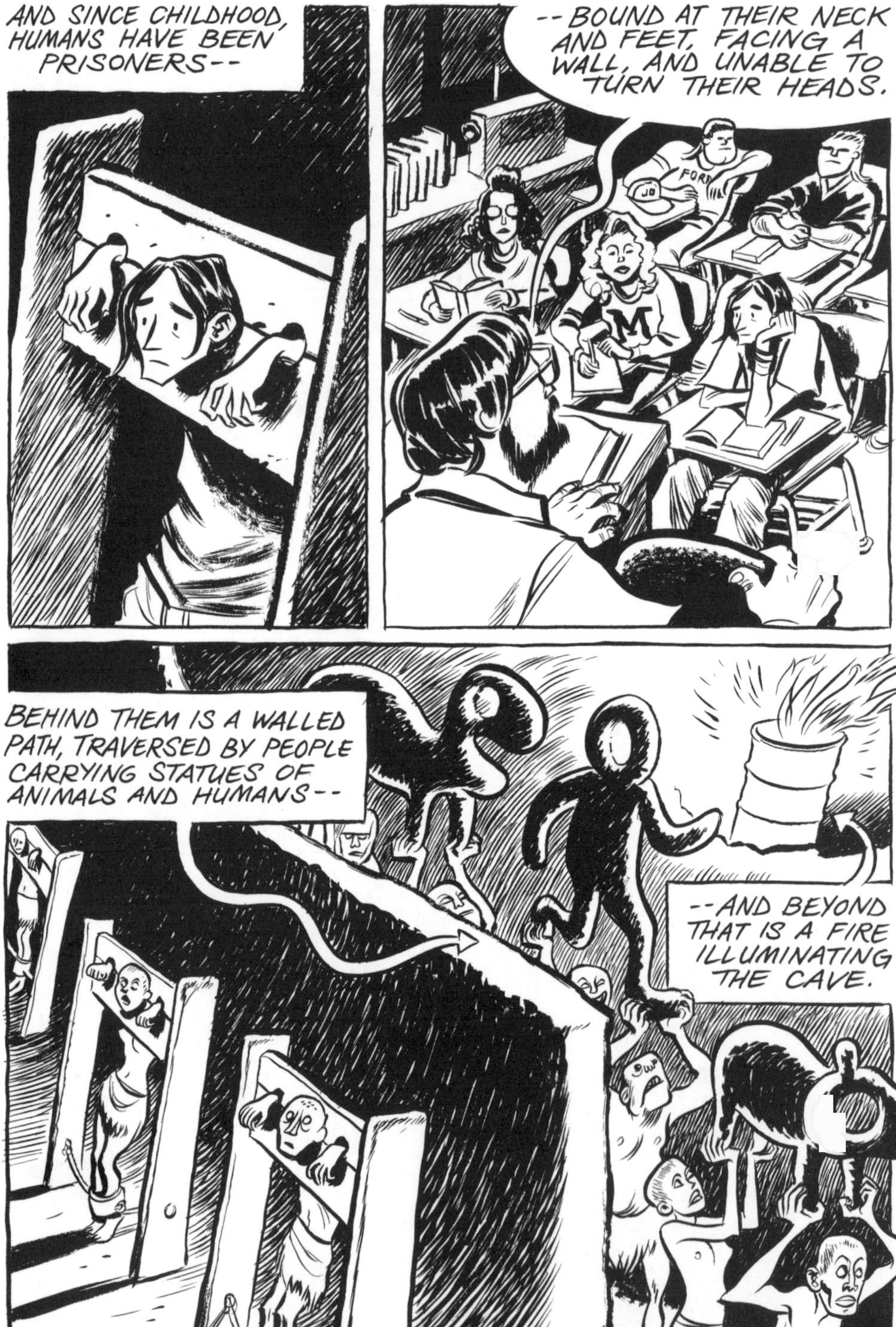
AND SINCE CHILDHOOD, HUMANS HAVE BEEN PRISONERS--
--BOUND AT THEIR NECK AND FEET, FACING A WALL, AND UNABLE TO TURN THEIR HEADS.
FORD
JD
M
BEHIND THEM IS A WALLED PATH, TRAVERSED BY PEOPLE CARRYING STATUES OF ANIMALS AND HUMANS--
--AND BEYOND THAT IS A FIRE ILLUMINATING THE CAVE.

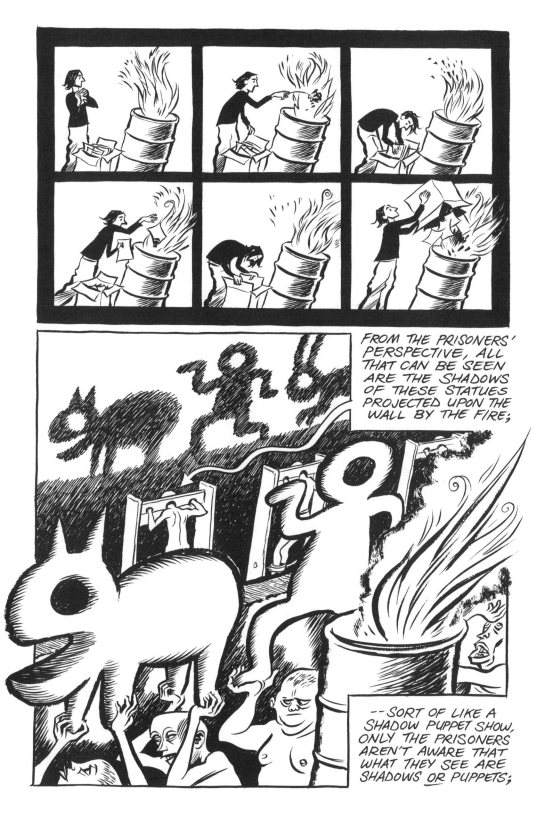

FROM THE PRISONERS' PERSPECTIVE, ALL THAT CAN BE SEEN ARE THE SHADOWS OF THESE STATUES PROJECTED UPON THE WALL BY THE FIRE;

--SORT OF LIKE A SHADOW PUPPET SHOW, ONLY THE PRISONERS AREN'T AWARE THAT WHAT THEY SEE ARE SHADOWS OR PUPPETS;

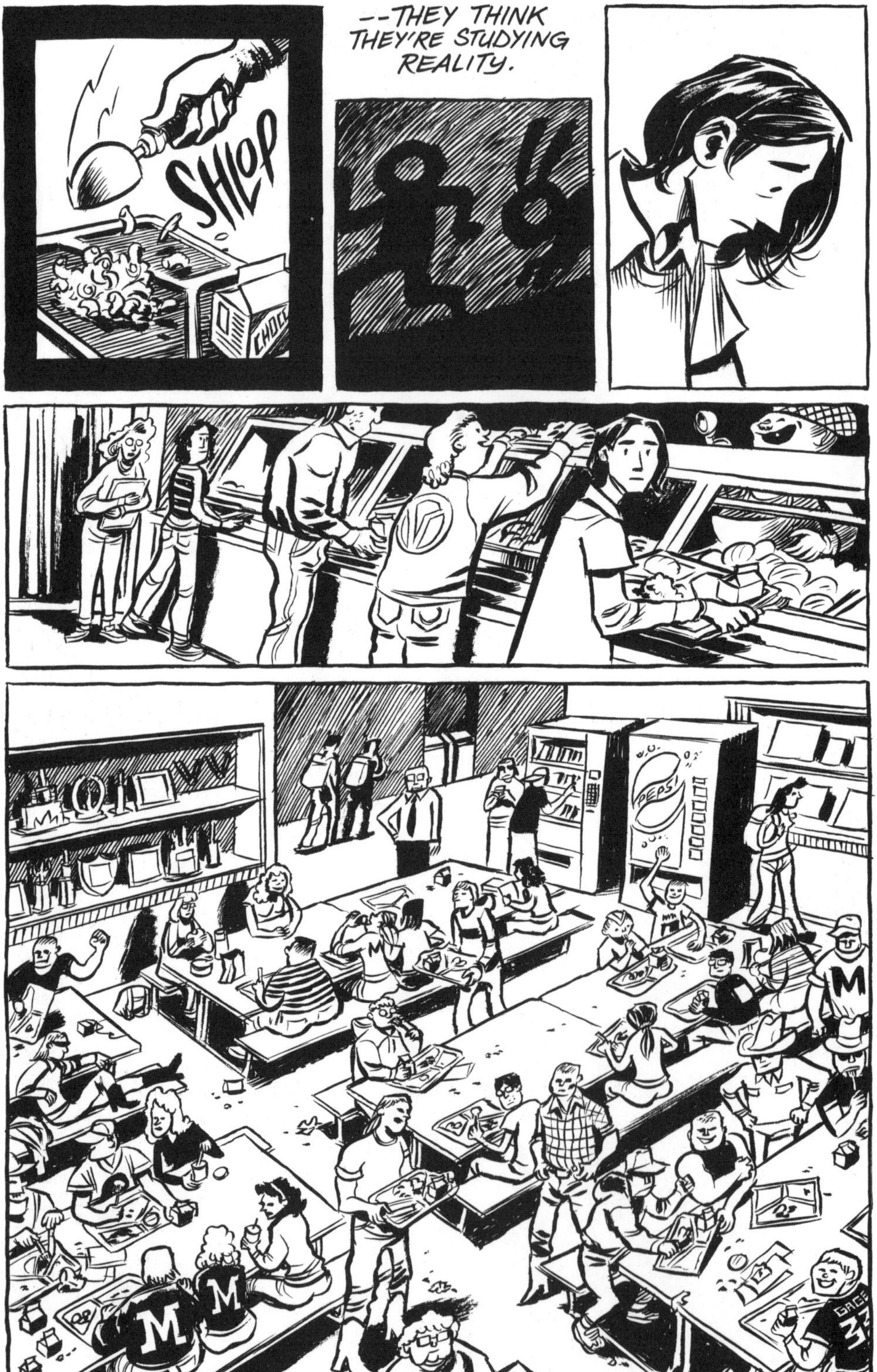
SHLOP
CHOC
--THEY THINK THEY'RE STUDYING REALITY.
PEPSI
M
M
M
M
GAGE

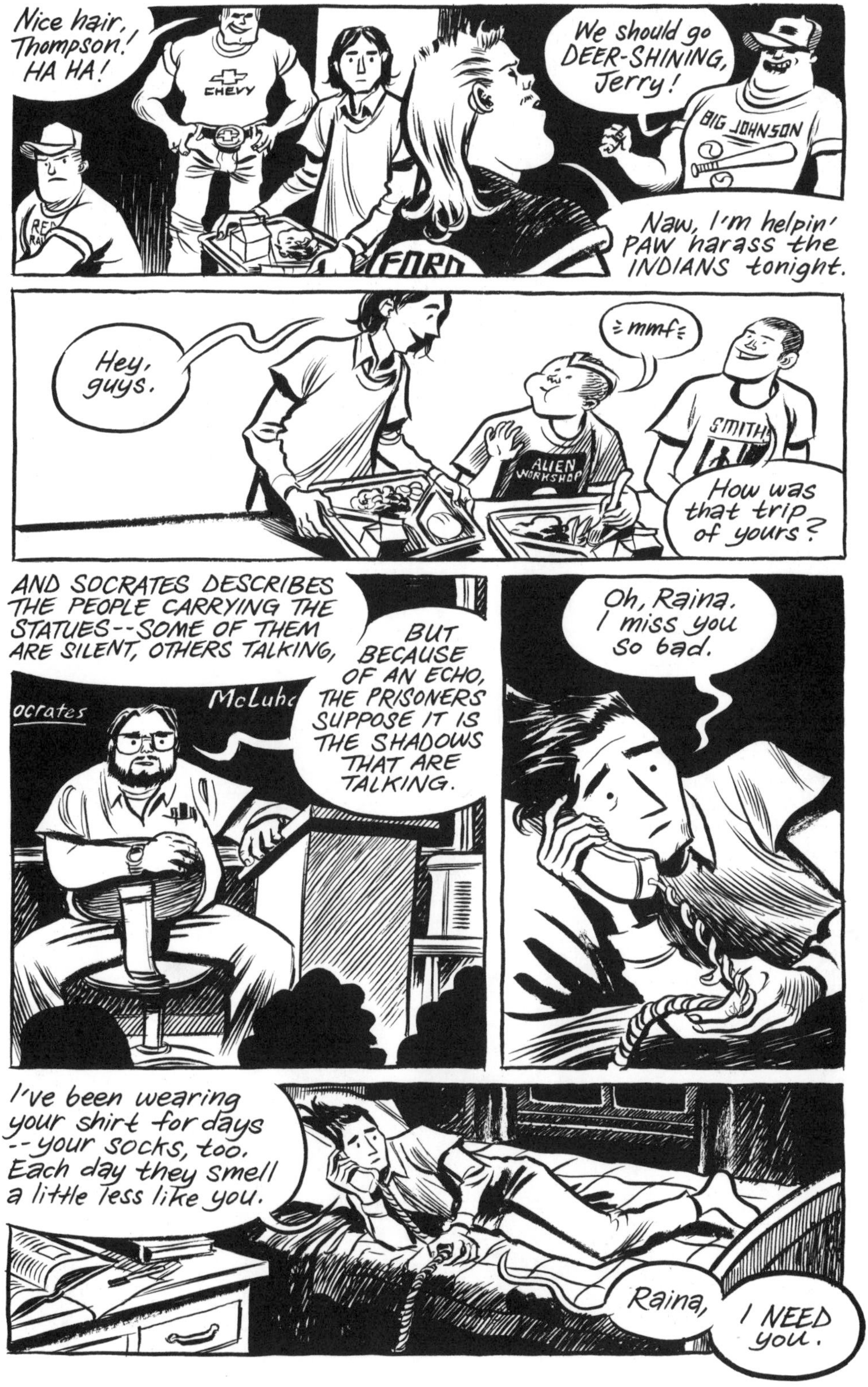

Nice hair, Thompson! HA HA!
CHEVY
We should go DEER-SHINING, Jerry!
BIG JOHNSON
FORD
Naw, I'm helpin' PAW harass the INDIANS tonight.
Hey, guys.
mmf
ALIEN WORKSHOP
SMITH
How was that trip of yours?
AND SOCRATES DESCRIBES THE PEOPLE CARRYING THE STATUES--SOME OF THEM ARE SILENT, OTHERS TALKING,
ocrates
McLuh
BUT BECAUSE OF AN ECHO, THE PRISONERS SUPPOSE IT IS THE SHADOWS THAT ARE TALKING.
Oh, Raina. I miss you so bad.
I've been wearing your shirt for days --your socks, too. Each day they smell a little less like you.
Raina,
I NEED you.

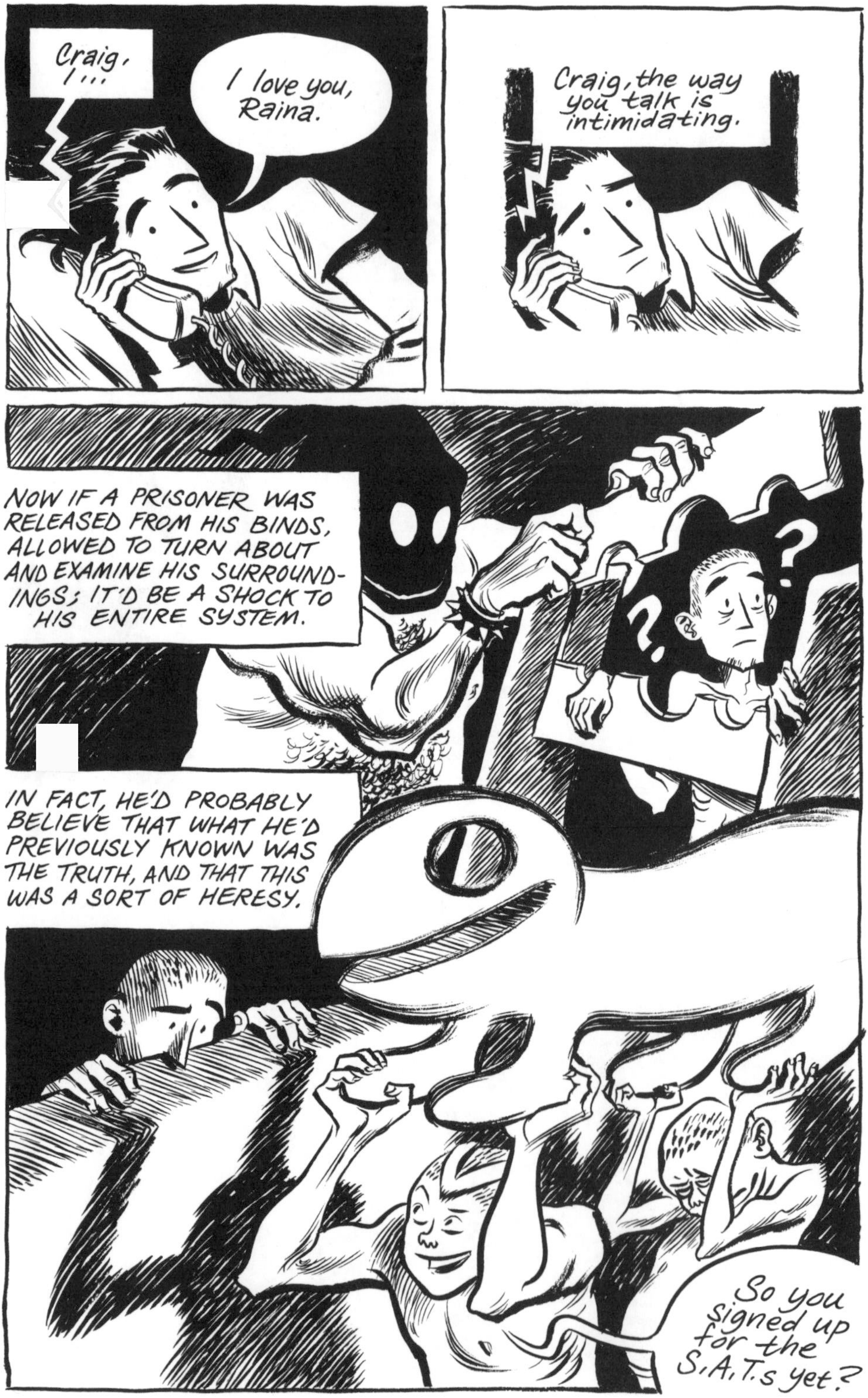
Craig, I...
I love you, Raina.
Craig, the way you talk is intimidating.
NOW IF A PRISONER WAS RELEASED FROM HIS BINDS, ALLOWED TO TURN ABOUT AND EXAMINE HIS SURROUNDINGS; IT'D BE A SHOCK TO HIS ENTIRE SYSTEM.
??
IN FACT, HE'D PROBABLY BELIEVE THAT WHAT HE'D PREVIOUSLY KNOWN WAS THE TRUTH, AND THAT THIS WAS A SORT OF HERESY.
So you signed up for the S.A.T.s yet?

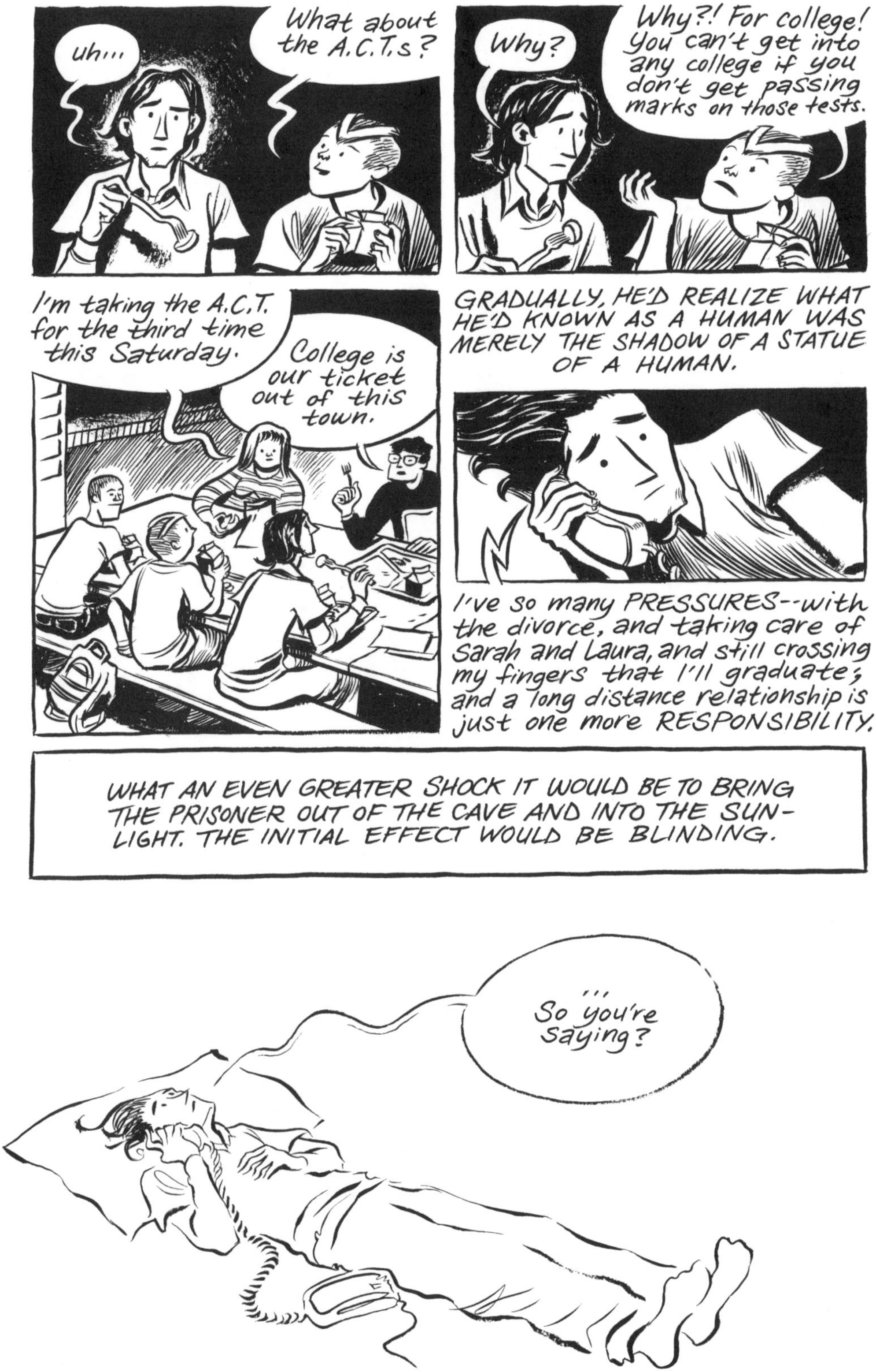
uh...
What about the A.C.T.s?
Why?
Why?! For college! You can't get into any college if you don't get passing marks on those tests.
I'm taking the A.C.T. for the third time this Saturday.
College is our ticket out of this town.
GRADUALLY, HE'D REALIZE WHAT HE'D KNOWN AS A HUMAN WAS MERELY THE SHADOW OF A STATUE OF A HUMAN.
I've so many PRESSURES--with the divorce, and taking care of Sarah and Laura, and still crossing my fingers that I'll graduate; and a long distance relationship is just one more RESPONSIBILITY.
WHAT AN EVEN GREATER SHOCK IT WOULD BE TO BRING THE PRISONER OUT OF THE CAVE AND INTO THE SUN-LIGHT. THE INITIAL EFFECT WOULD BE BLINDING.
... So you're saying?

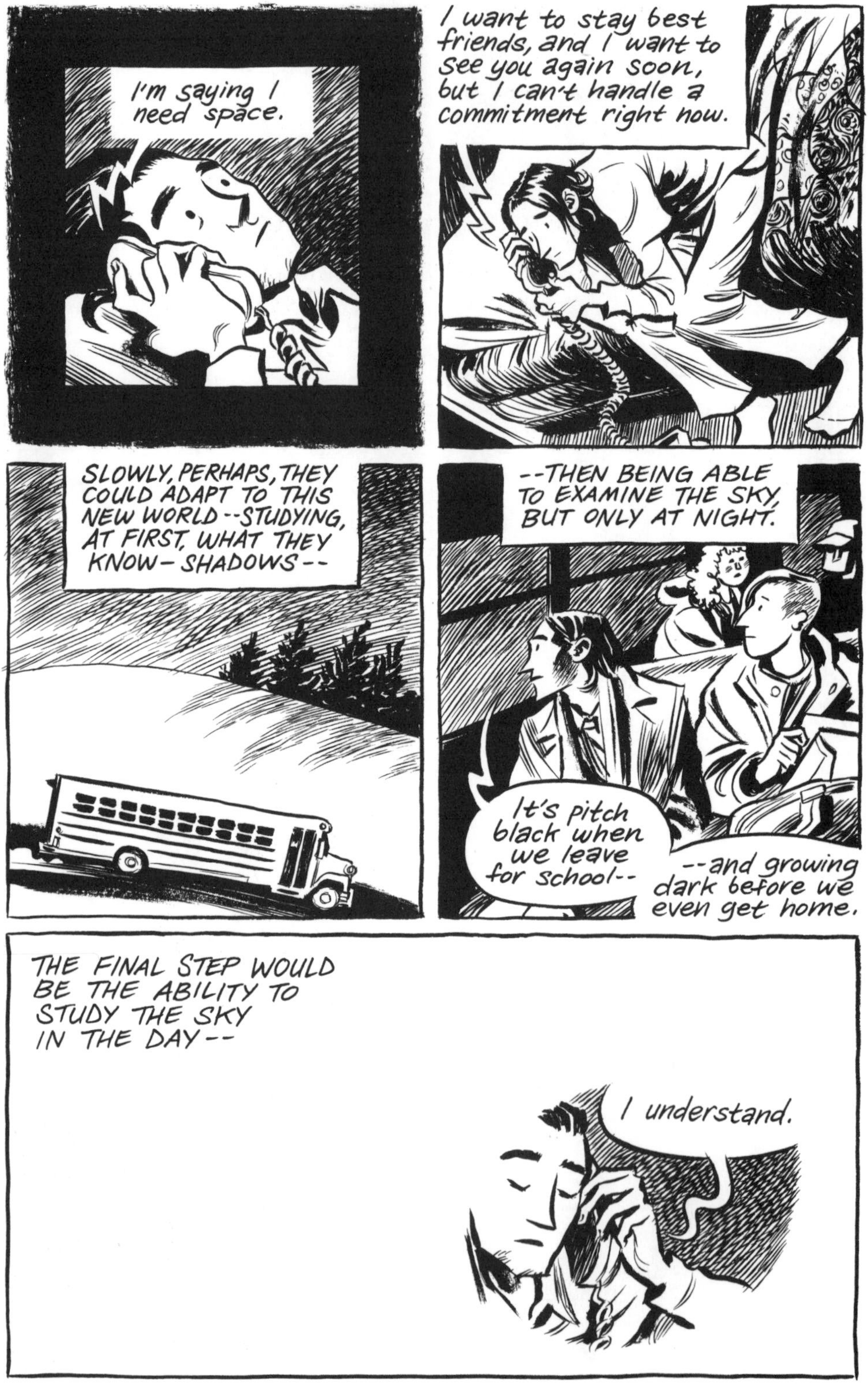
I'm saying I need space.
I want to stay best friends, and I want to see you again soon, but I can't handle a commitment right now.
SLOWLY, PERHAPS, THEY COULD ADAPT TO THIS NEW WORLD--STUDYING, AT FIRST, WHAT THEY KNOW- SHADOWS--
--THEN BEING ABLE TO EXAMINE THE SKY, BUT ONLY AT NIGHT.
It's pitch black when we leave for school--
--and growing dark before we even get home.
THE FINAL STEP WOULD BE THE ABILITY TO STUDY THE SKY IN THE DAY--
I understand.

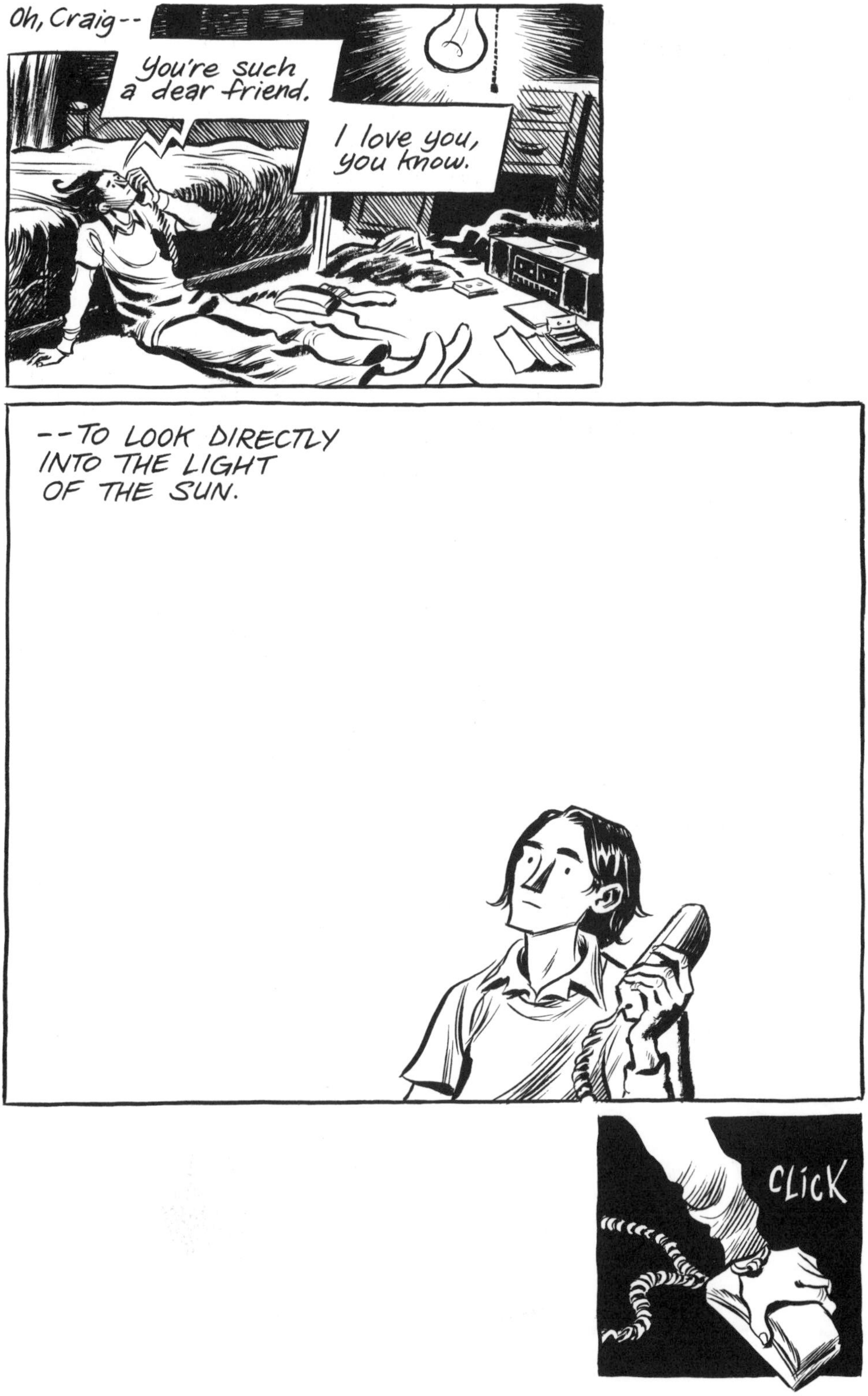
Oh, Craig--
You're such a dear friend.
I love you, you know.
--TO LOOK DIRECTLY INTO THE LIGHT OF THE SUN.
CLICK

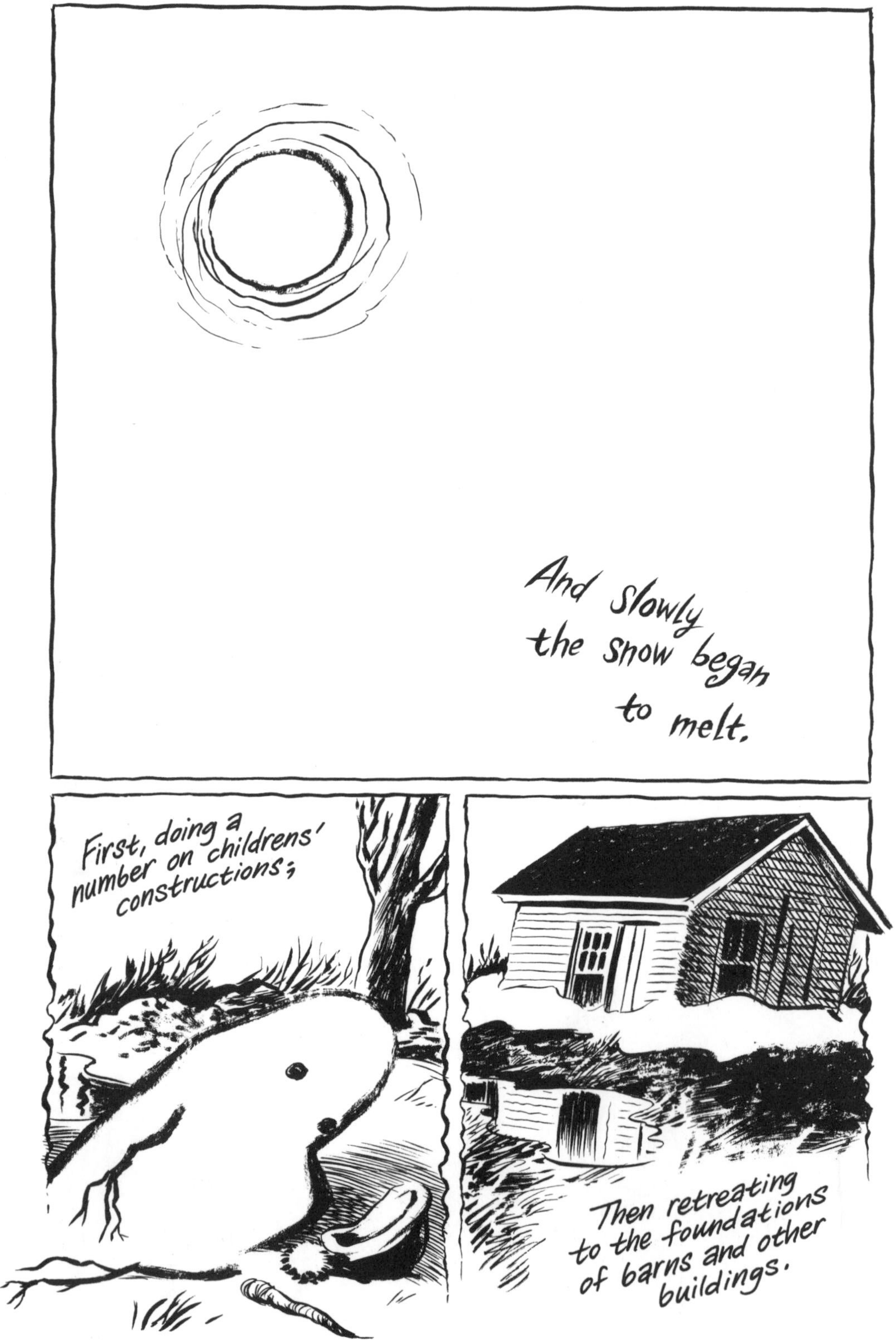
And slowly
the snow began
to melt.
First, doing a
number on childrens'
constructions;
Then retreating
to the foundations
of barns and other
buildings.

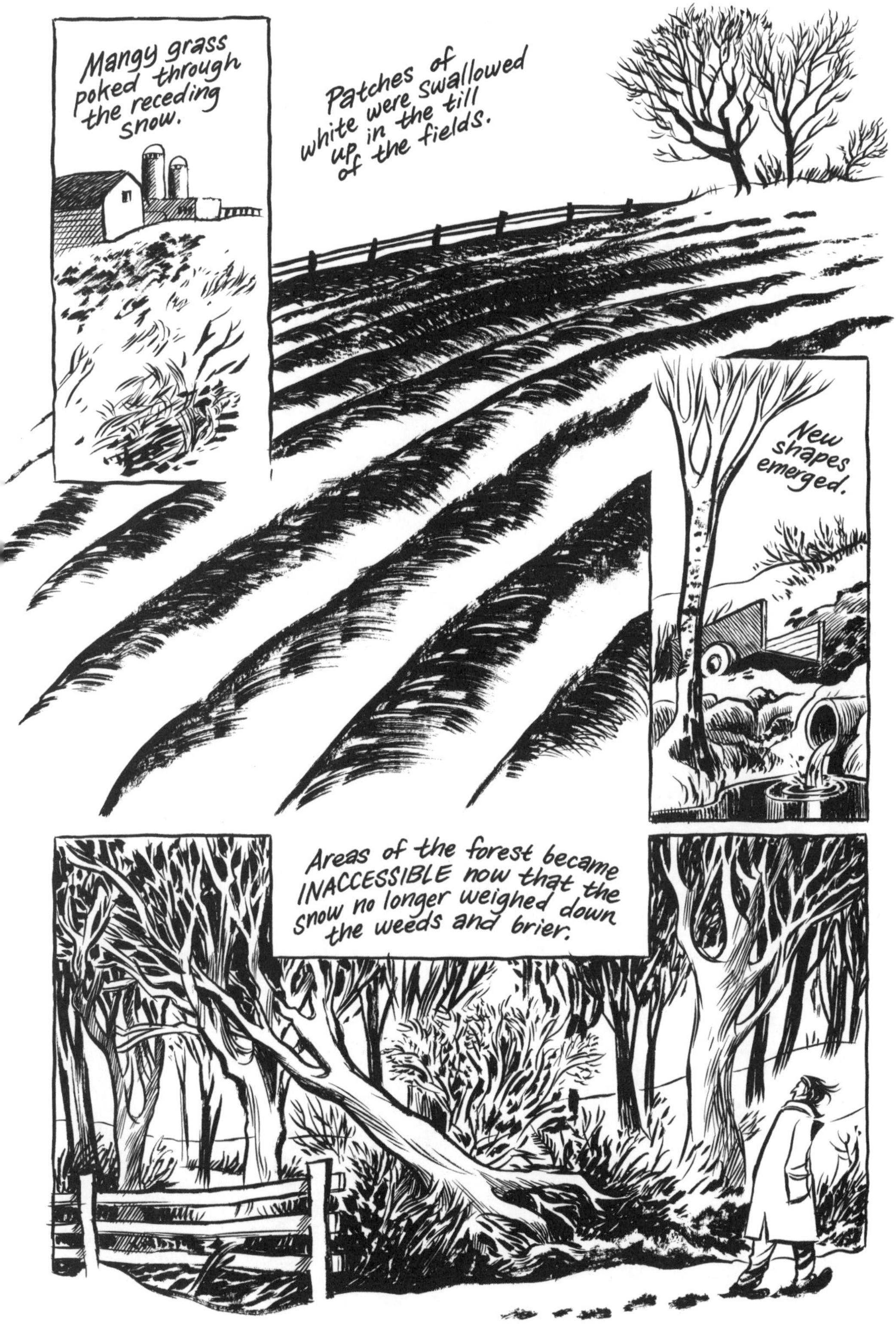
Mangy grass poked through the receding snow.
Patches of white were swallowed up in the till of the fields.
New shapes emerged.
Areas of the forest became INACCESSIBLE now that the snow no longer weighed down the weeds and brier.

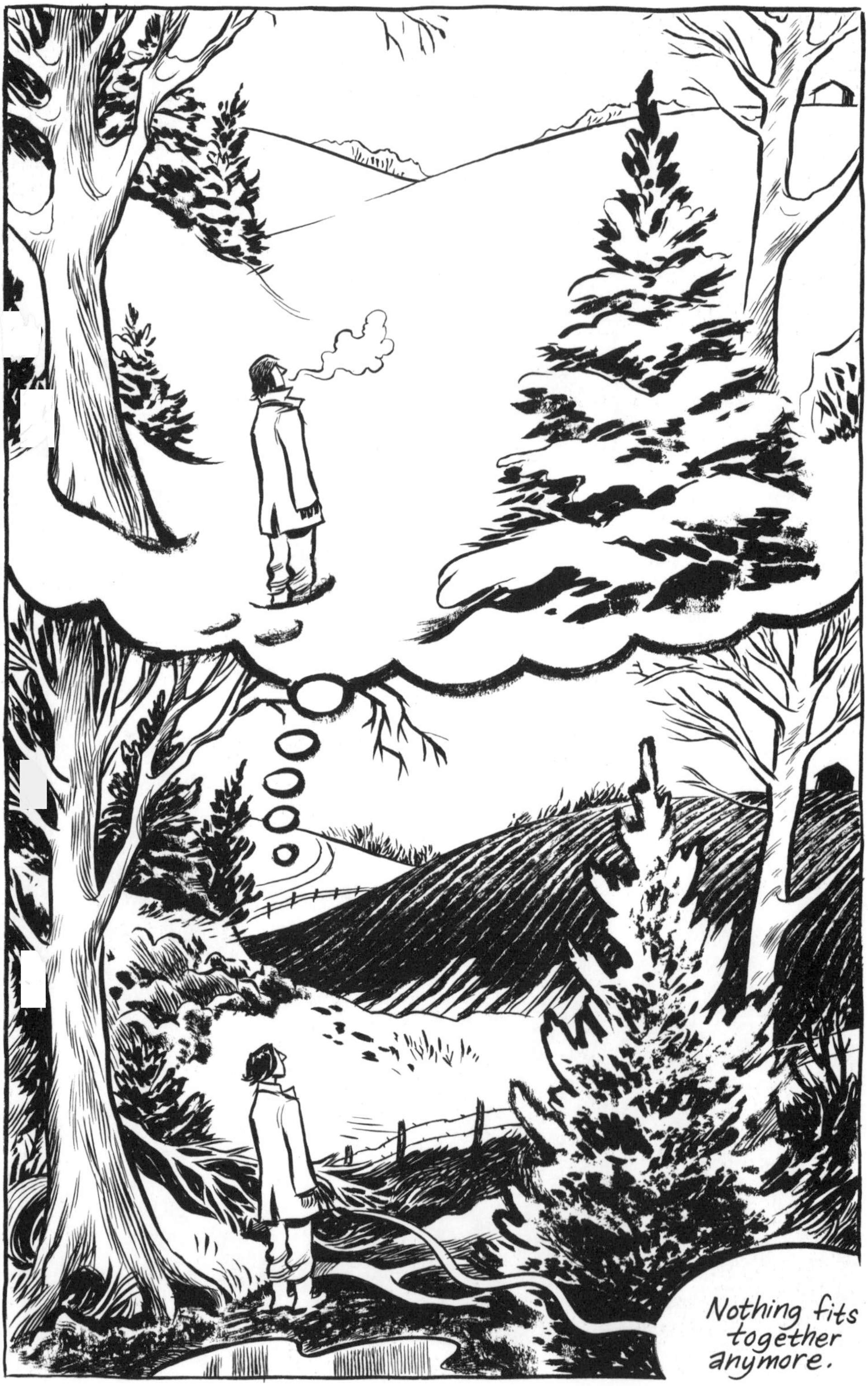
Nothing fits together anymore.

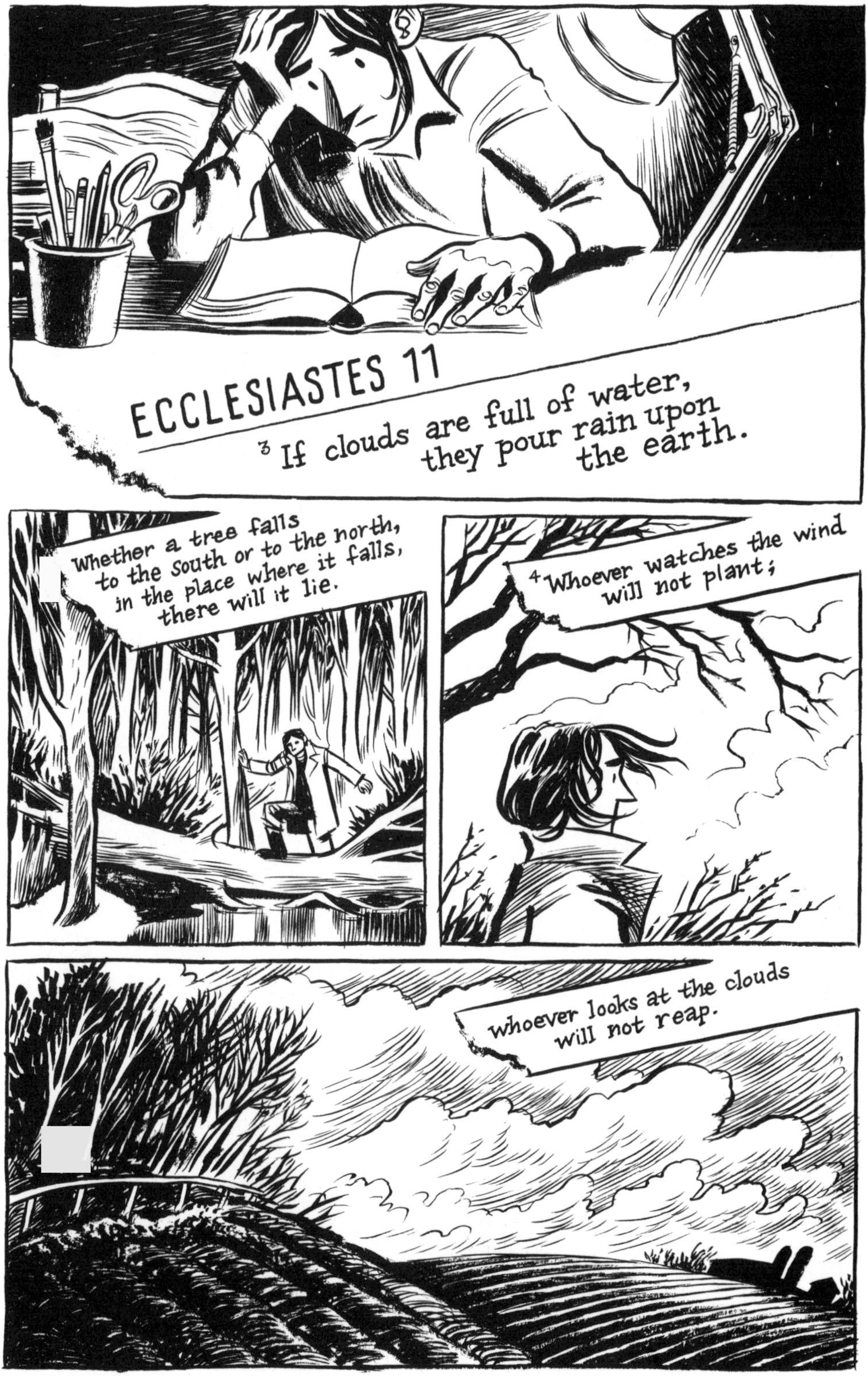
ECCLESIASTES 11
3 If clouds are full of water, they pour rain upon the earth.
Whether a tree falls to the South or to the north, in the place where it falls, there will it lie.
4 Whoever watches the wind will not plant;
whoever looks at the clouds will not reap.

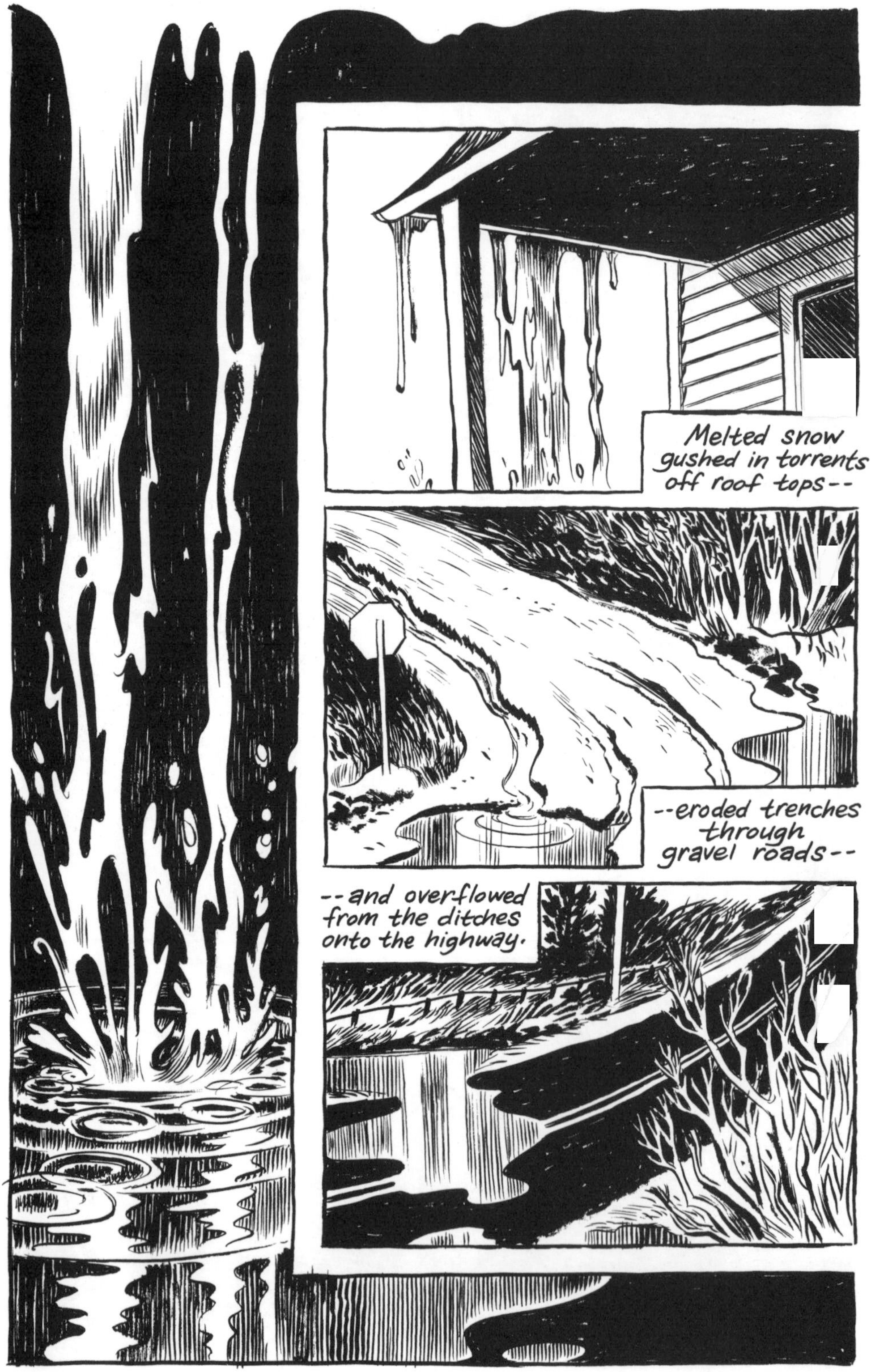
Melted snow gushed in torrents off roof tops--
--eroded trenches through gravel roads--
--and overflowed from the ditches onto the highway.

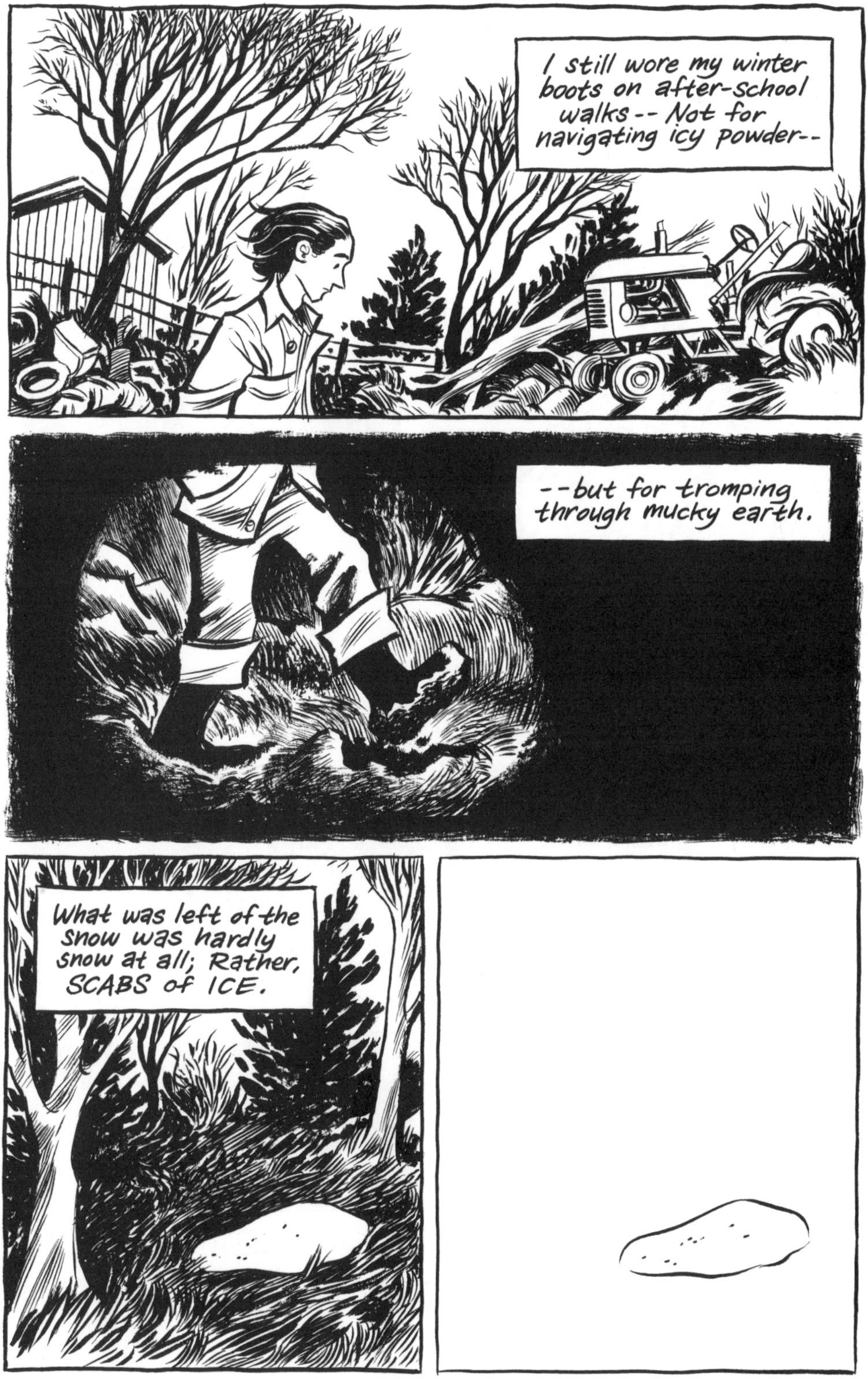
I still wore my winter boots on after-school walks -- Not for navigating icy powder--
--but for tromping through mucky earth.
What was left of the snow was hardly snow at all; Rather, SCABS of ICE.

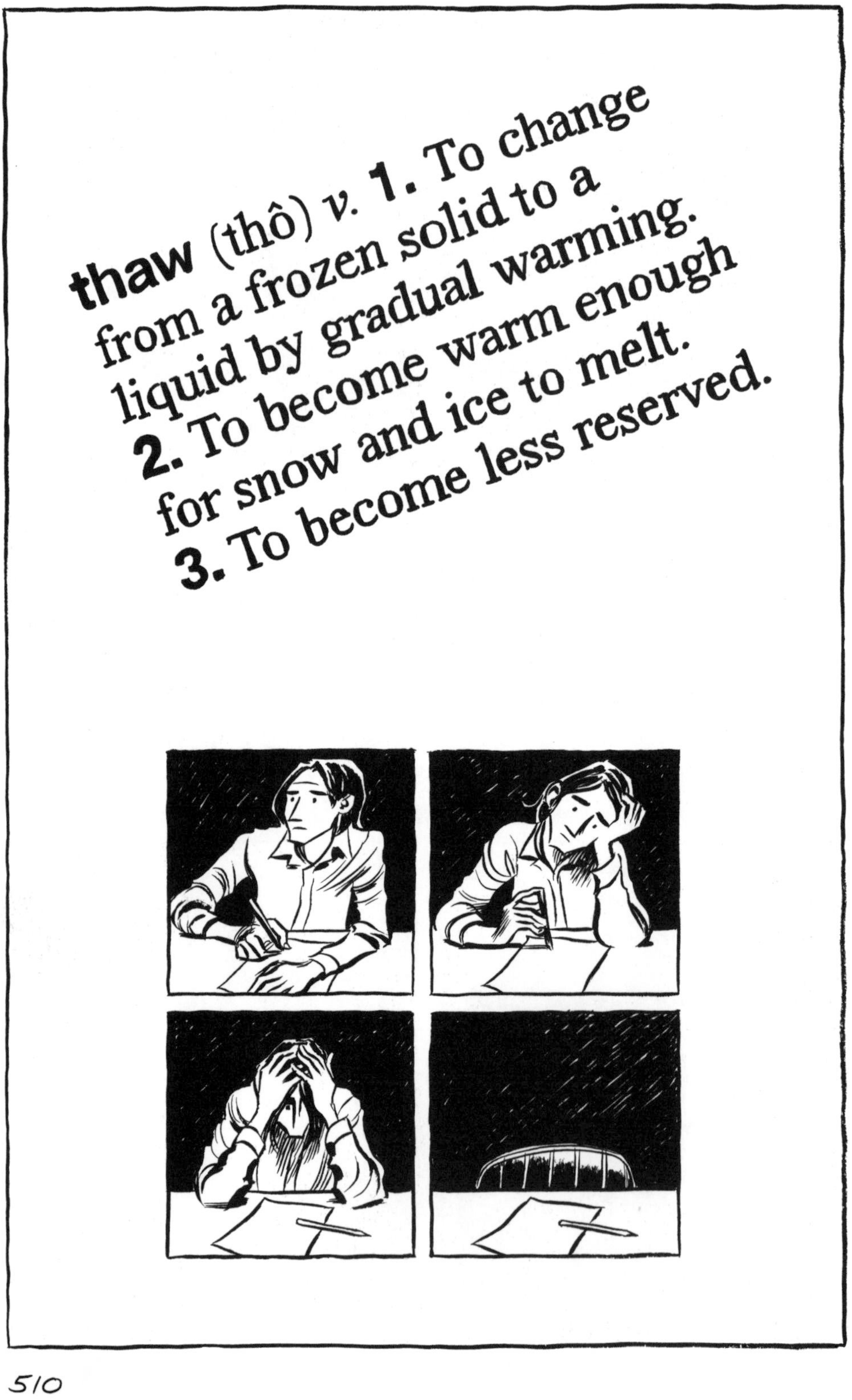
thaw (thô) v. 1. To change from a frozen solid to a liquid by gradual warming.
2. To become warm enough for snow and ice to melt.
3. To become less reserved.

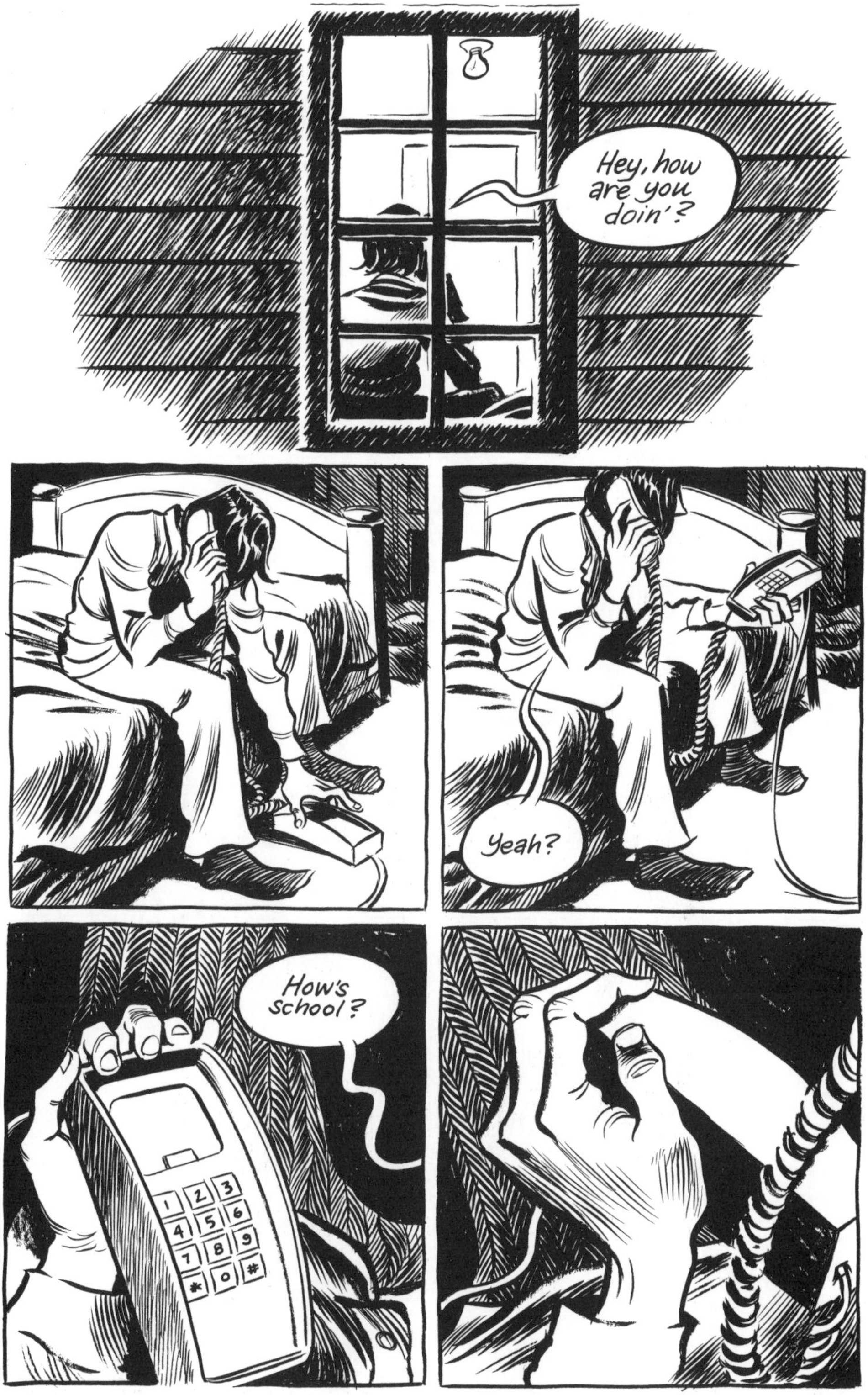
Hey, how are you doin'?
Yeah?
How's school?

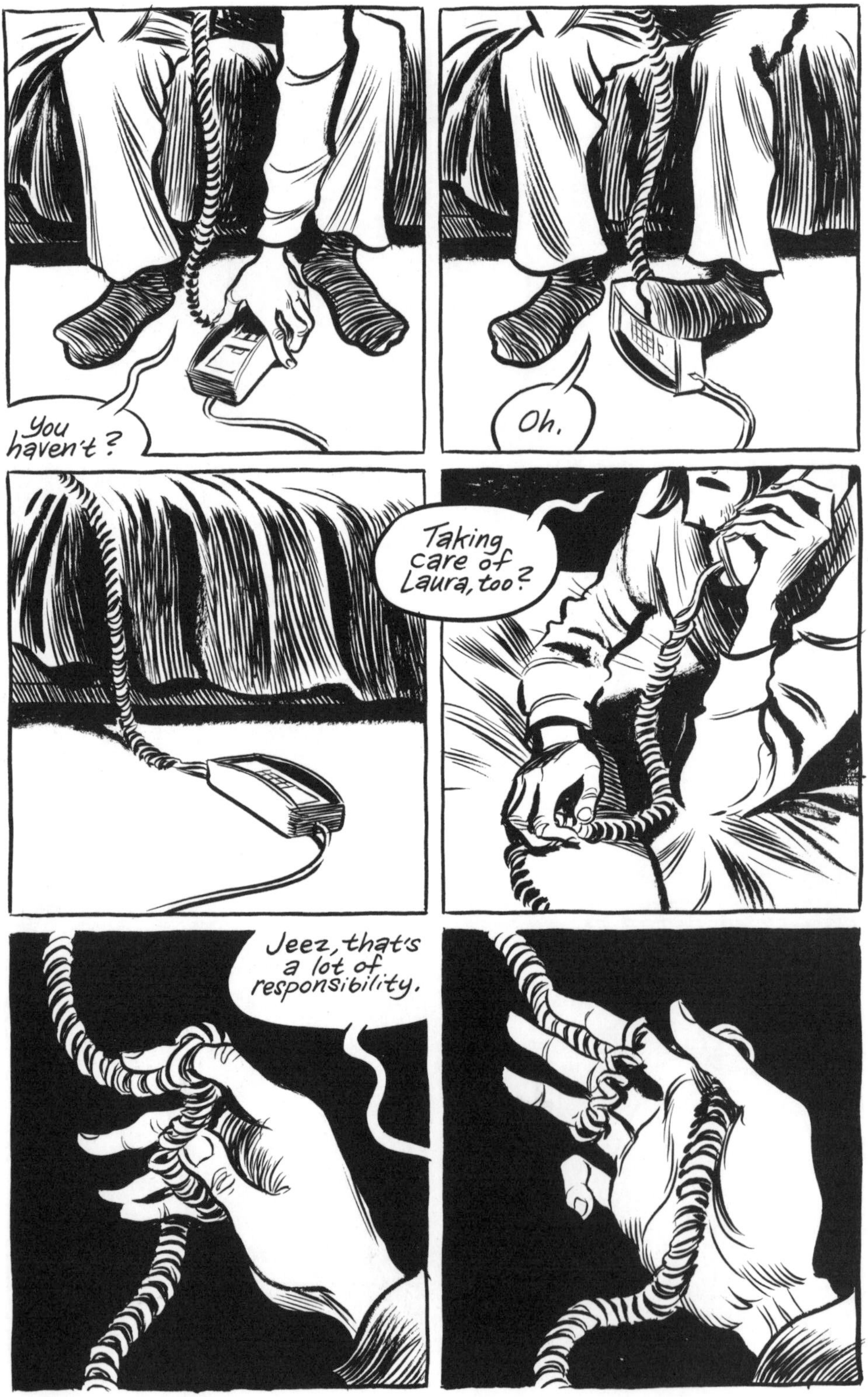
You haven't?
Oh.
Taking care of Laura, too?
Jeez, that's a lot of responsibility.

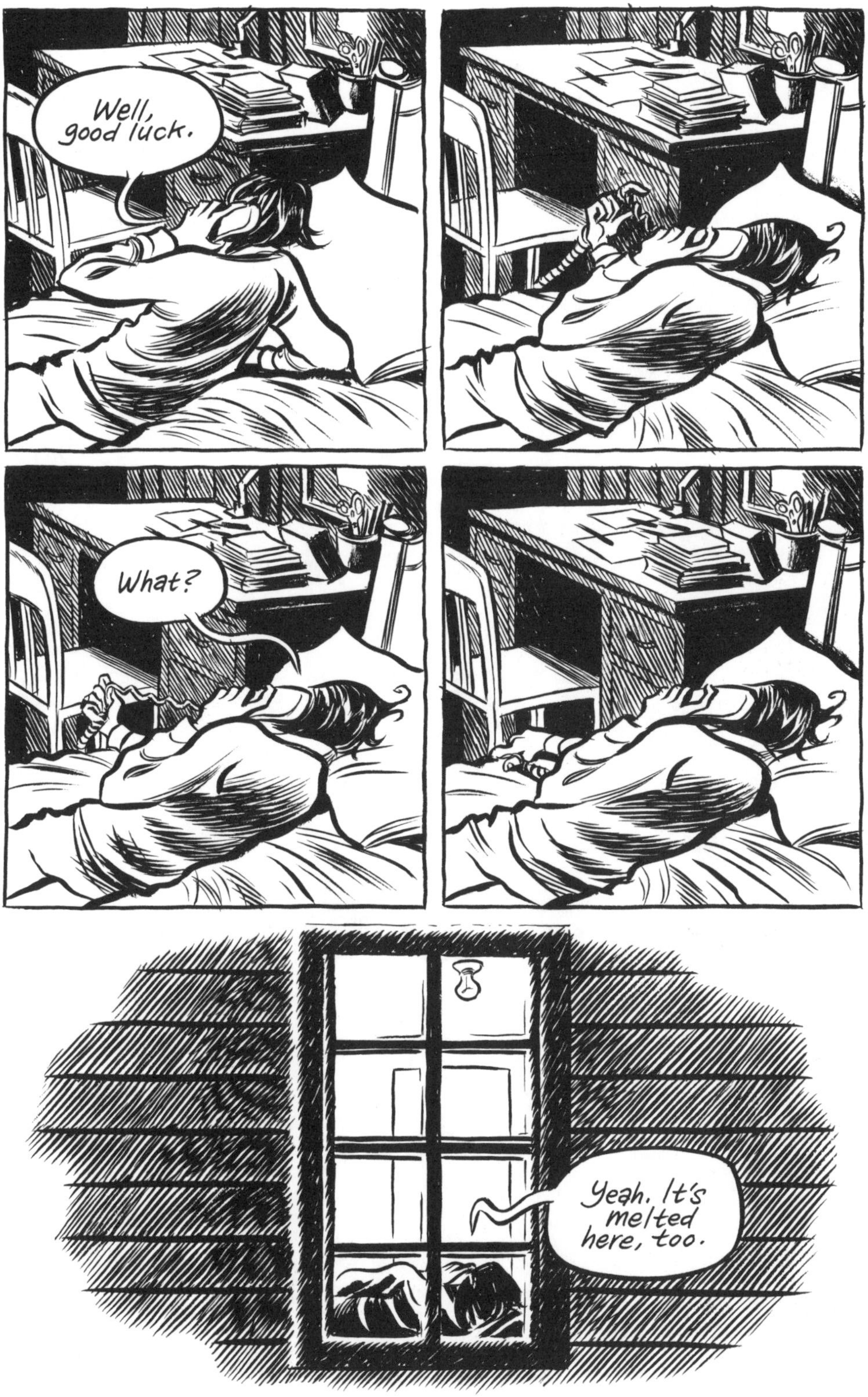
Well, good luck.
What?
Yeah. It's melted here, too.

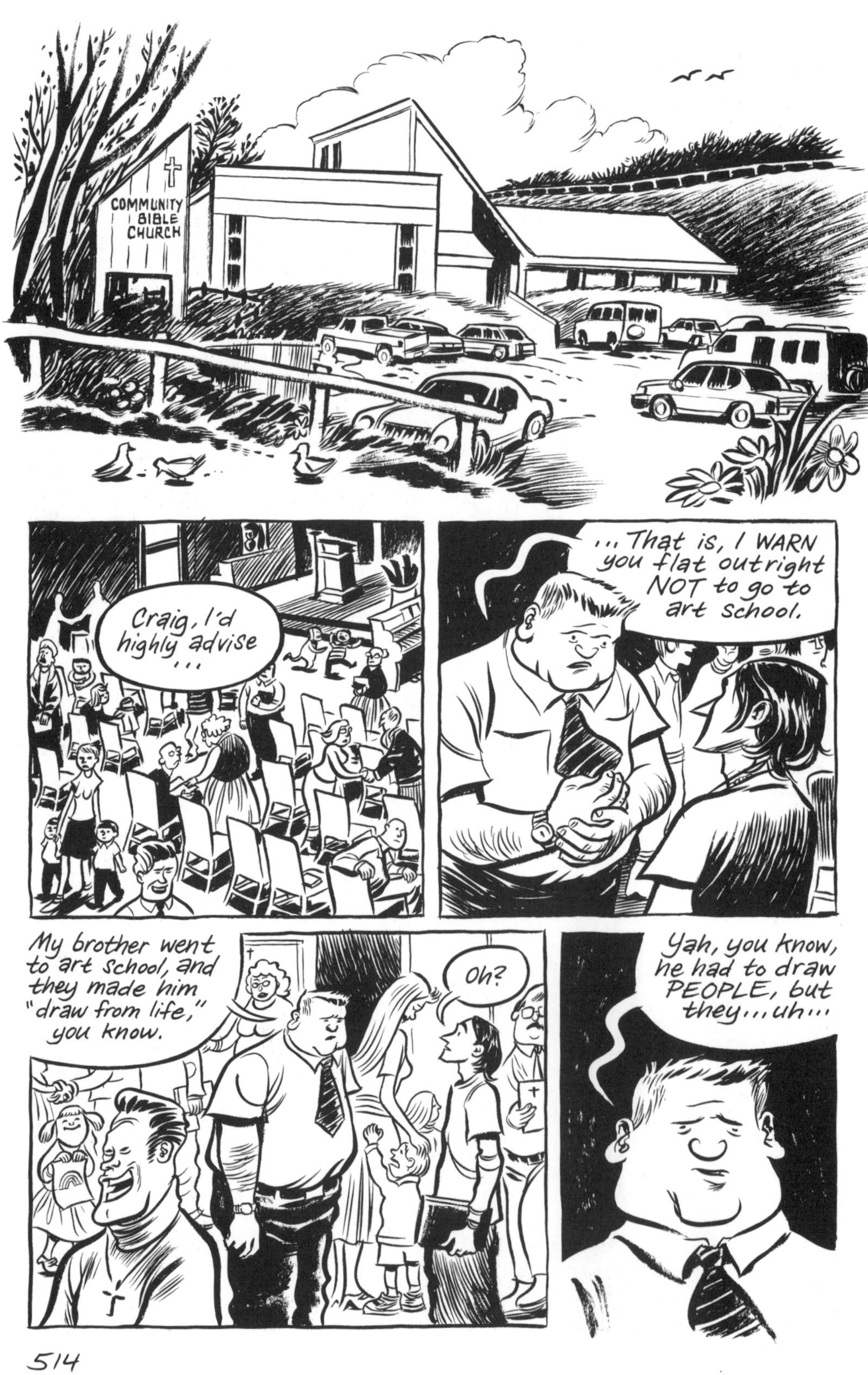
COMMUNITY BIBLE CHURCH
Craig, I'd highly advise ...
...That is, I WARN you flat outright NOT to go to art school.
My brother went to art school, and they made him "draw from life," you know.
Oh?
Yah, you know, he had to draw PEOPLE, but they...uh...

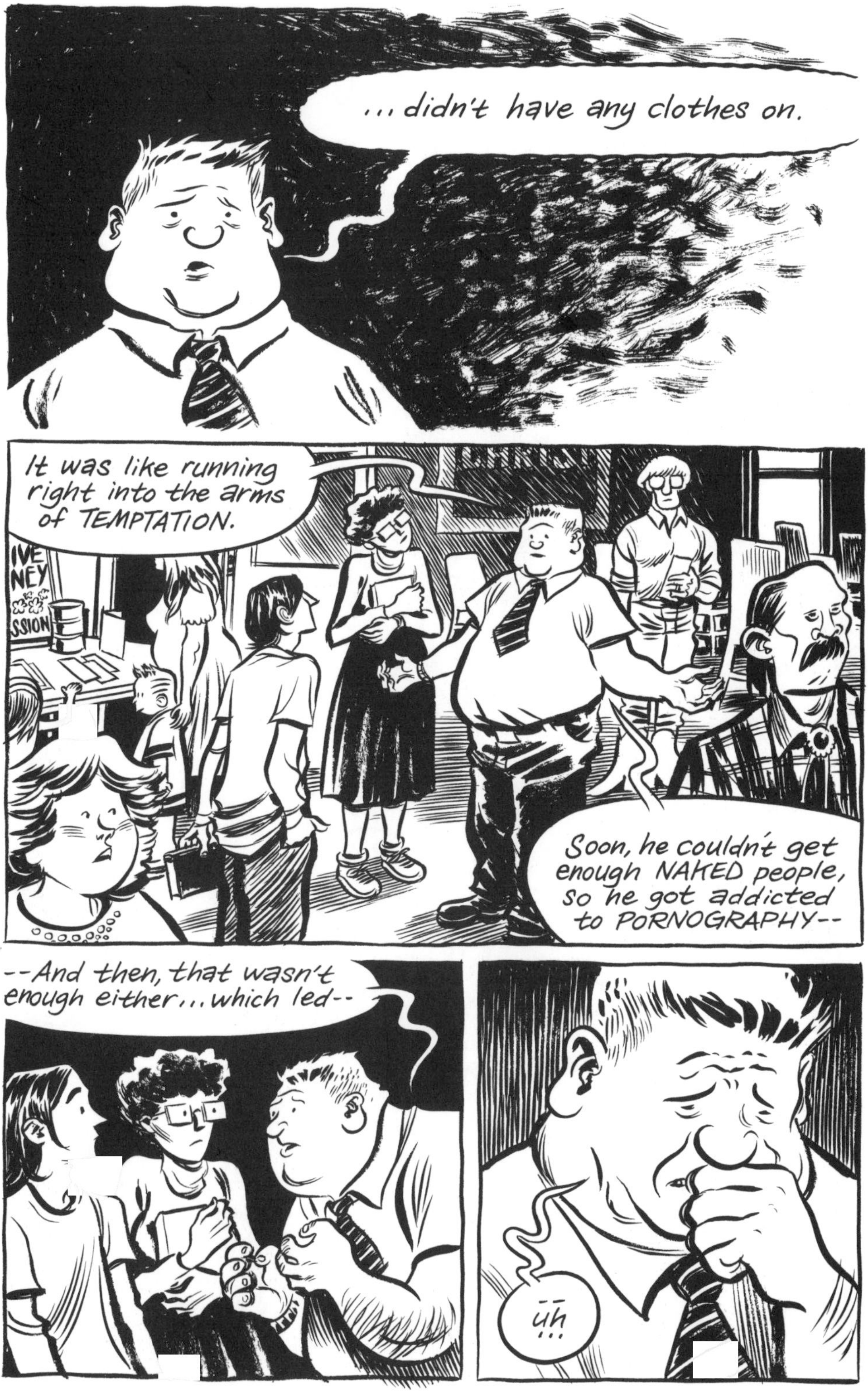
...didn't have any clothes on.
It was like running right into the arms of TEMPTATION.
Soon, he couldn't get enough NAKED people, so he got addicted to PORNOGRAPHY--
--And then, that wasn't enough either...which led--
uh

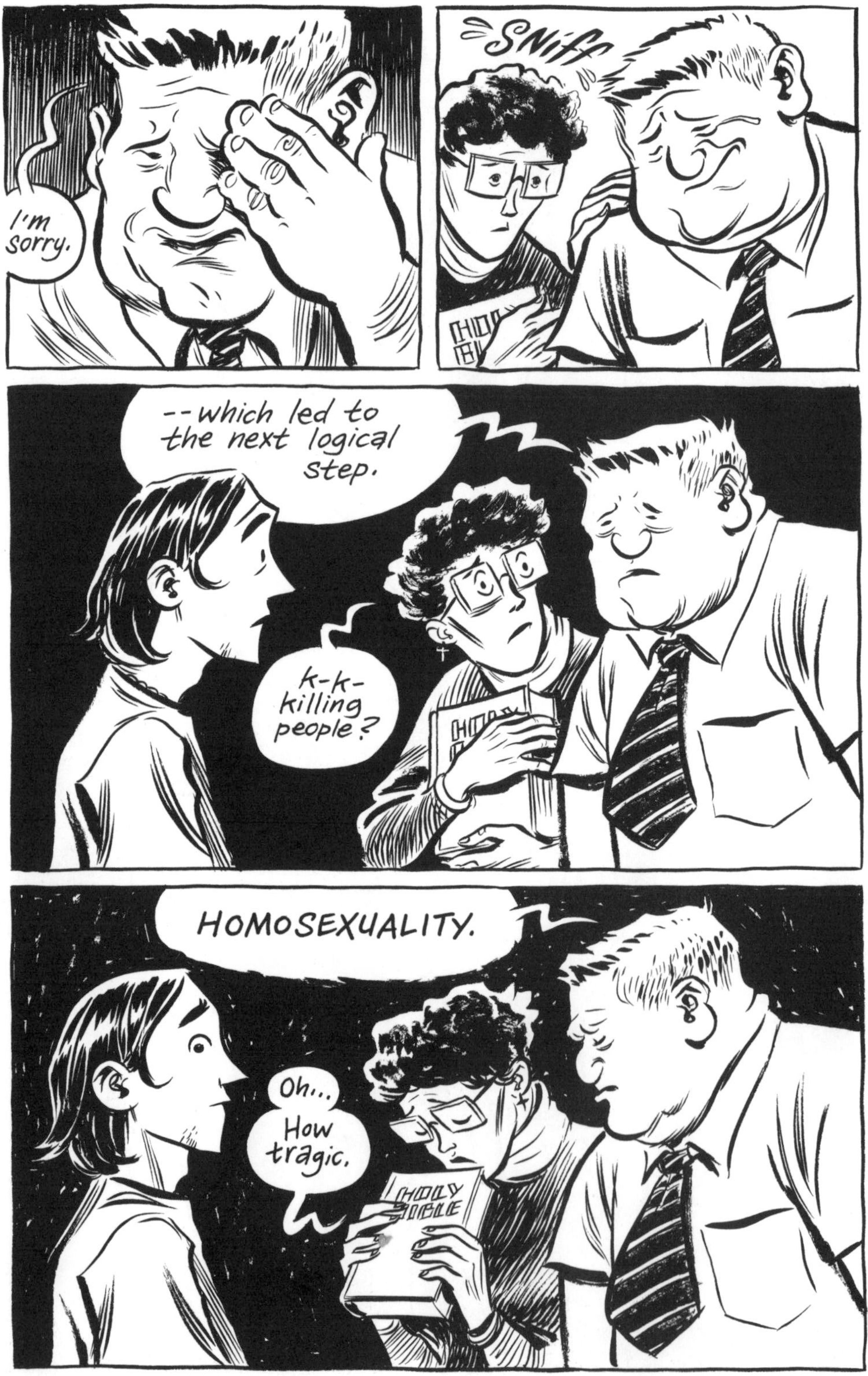
I'm sorry.
SNIFF
--which led to the next logical step.
k-k-killing people?
HOMOSEXUALITY.
Oh... How tragic.
HOLY BIBLE

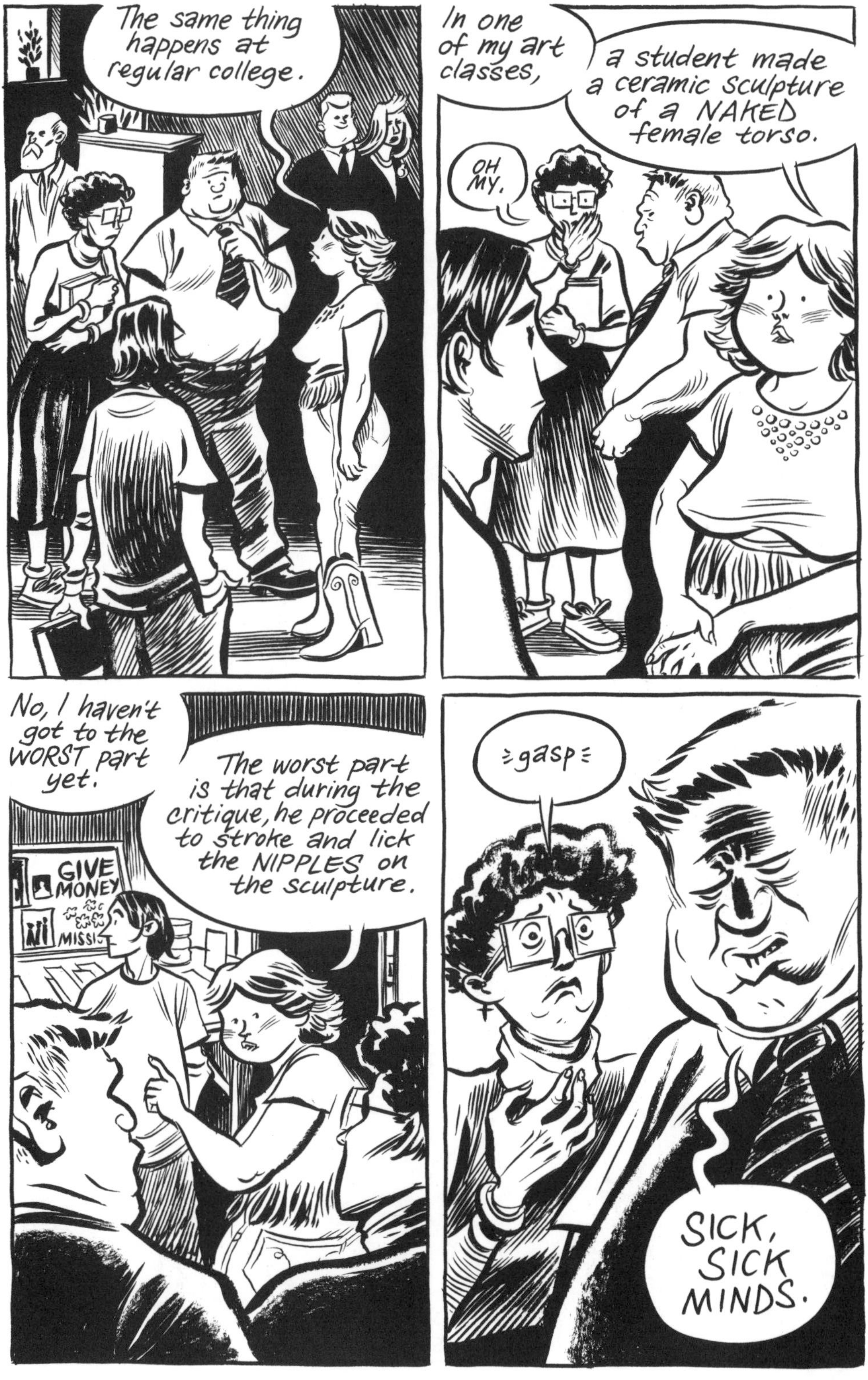
The same thing happens at regular college.
In one of my art classes,
a student made a ceramic sculpture of a NAKED female torso.
OH MY.
No, I haven't got to the WORST part yet.
The worst part is that during the critique, he proceeded to stroke and lick the NIPPLES on the sculpture.
GIVE MONEY
MISSI
gasp
SICK, SICK MINDS.

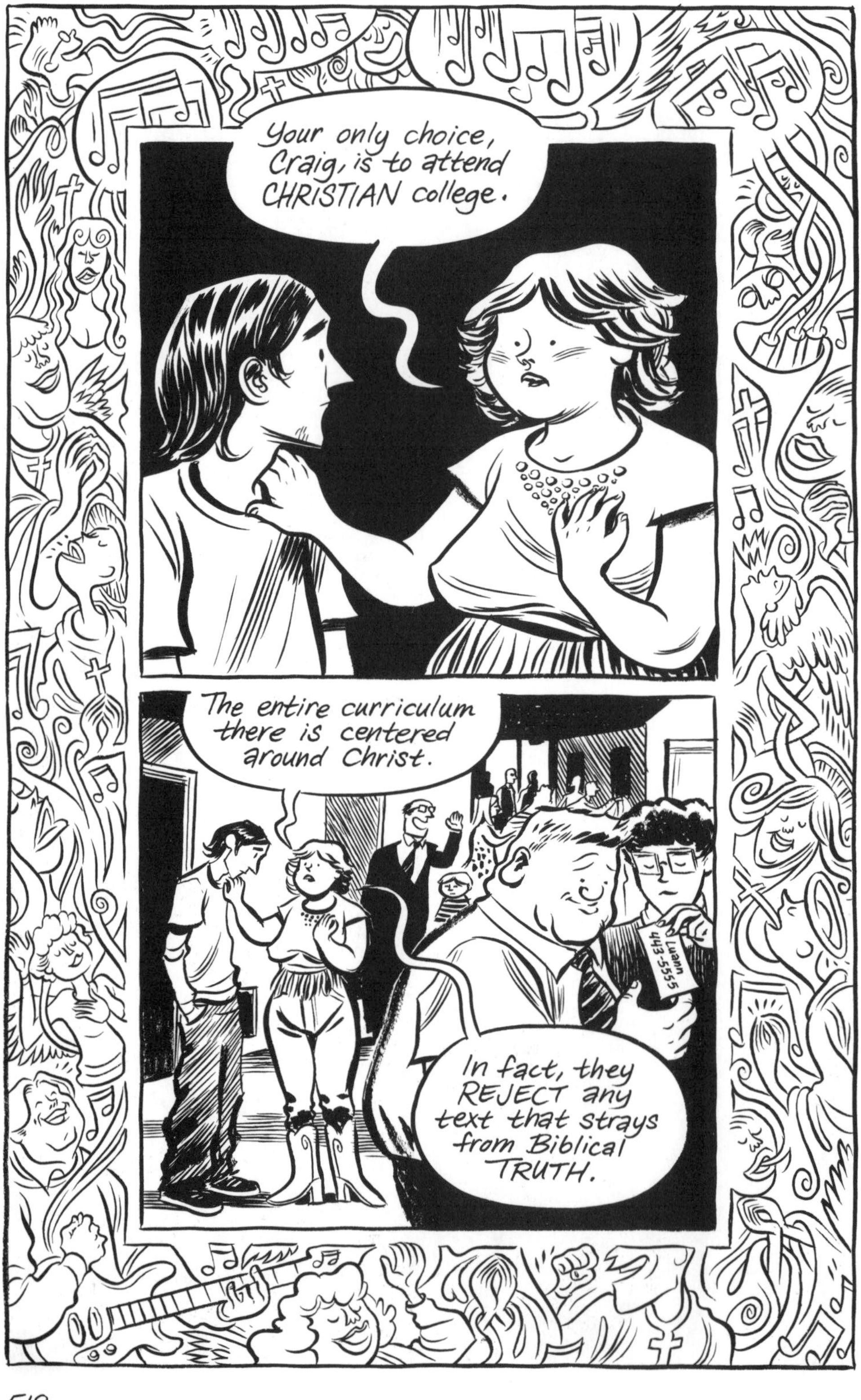
Your only choice, Craig, is to attend CHRISTIAN college.
The entire curriculum there is centered around Christ.
Luann 443-5555
In fact, they REJECT any text that strays from Biblical TRUTH.

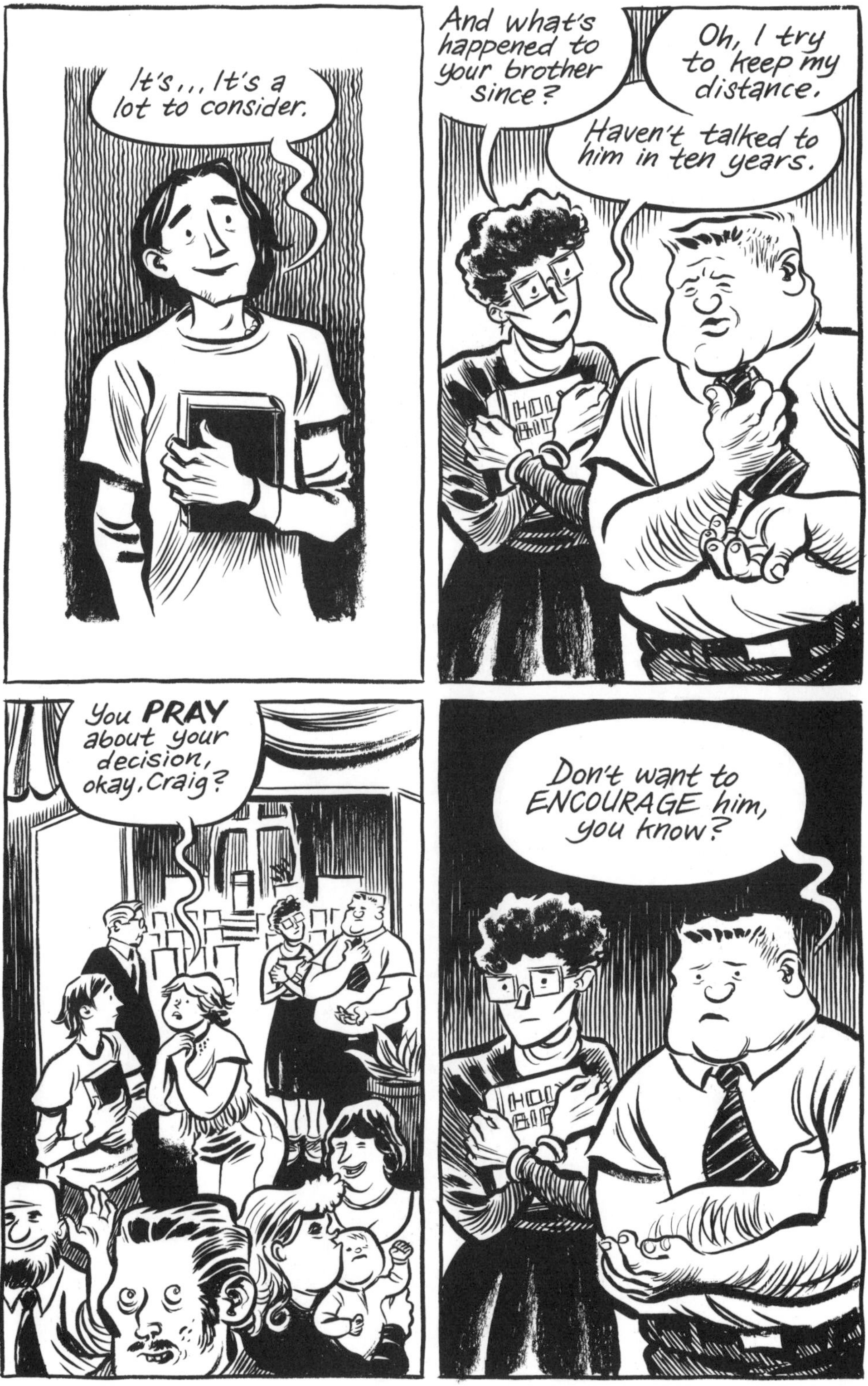
It's... It's a lot to consider.
And what's happened to your brother since?
Oh, I try to keep my distance.
Haven't talked to him in ten years.
You **PRAY** about your decision, okay, Craig?
Don't want to ENCOURAGE him, you know?

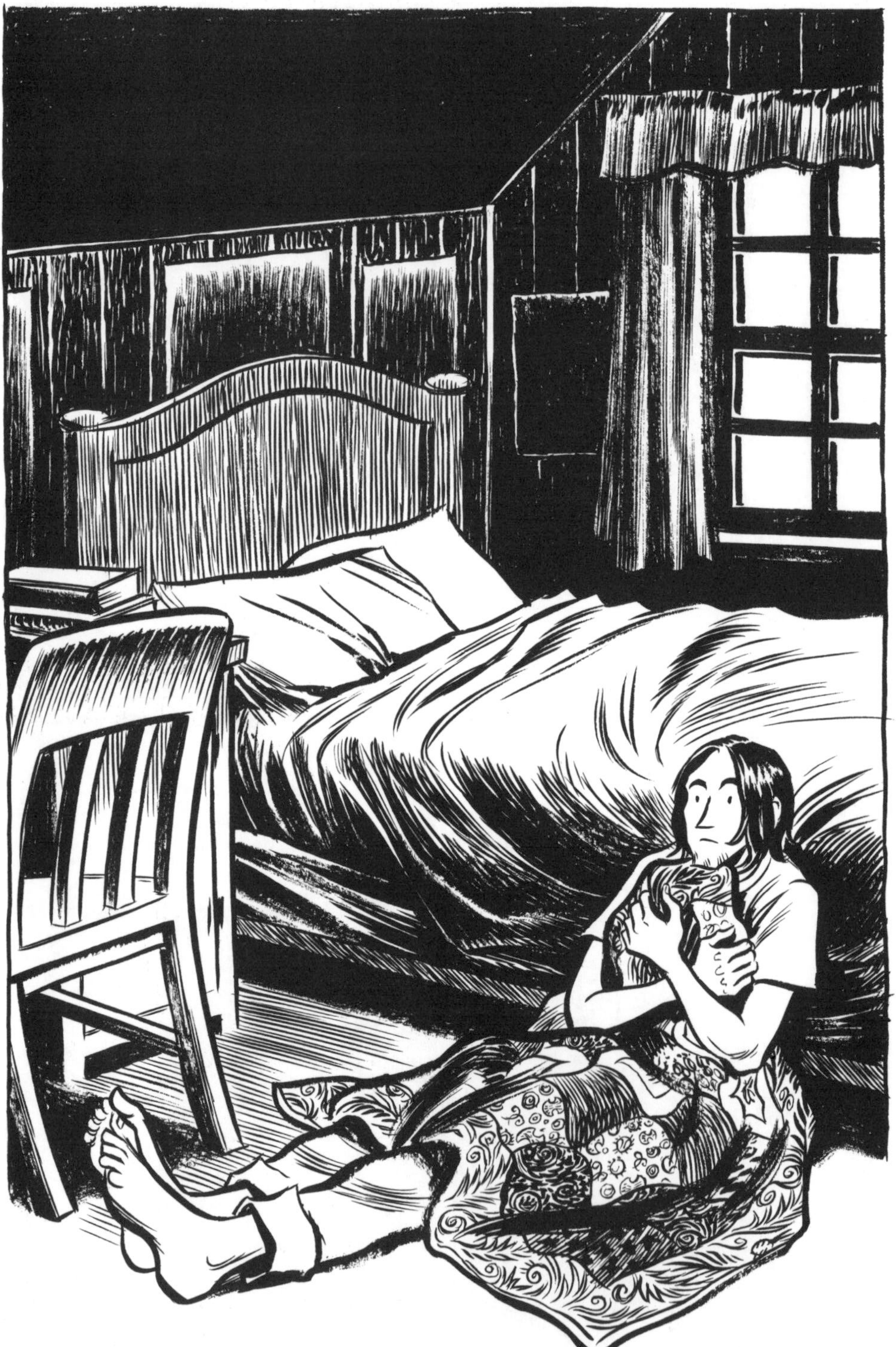

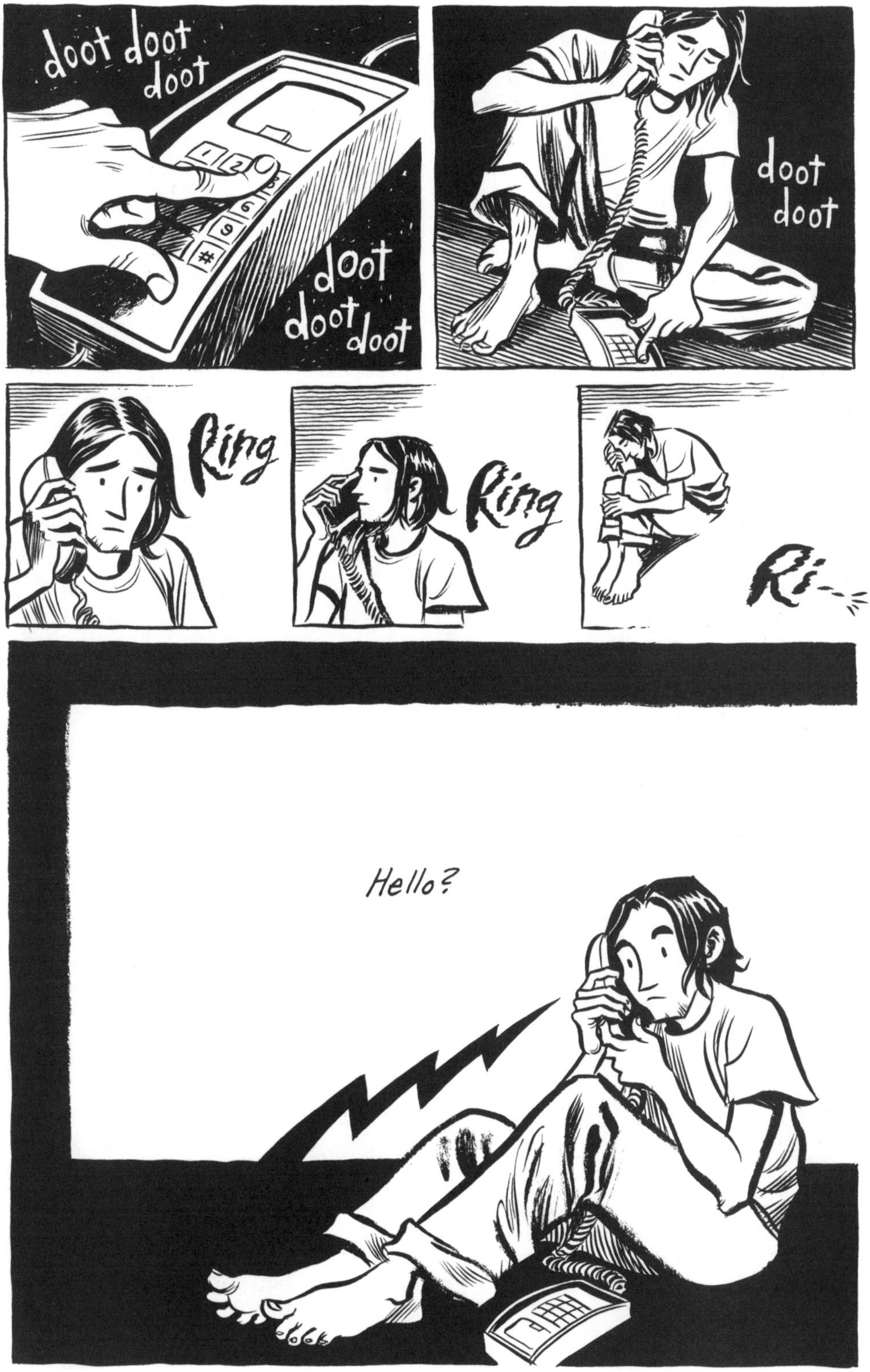
doot doot
doot
doot
doot doot
doot
doot
Ring
Ring
Ri---
Hello?

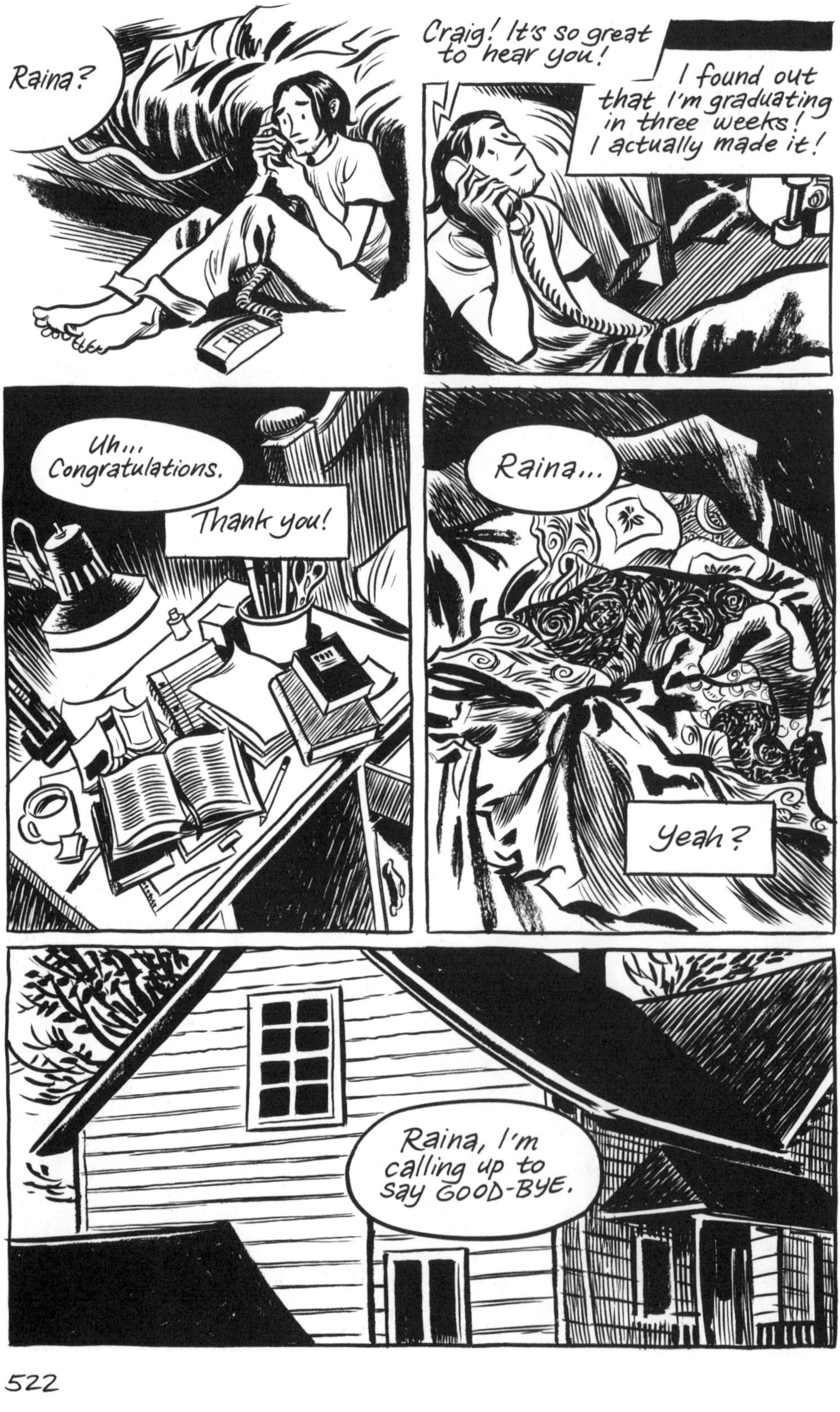
Raina?
Craig! It's so great to hear you!
I found out that I'm graduating in three weeks! I actually made it!
Uh... Congratulations.
Thank you!
Raina...
Yeah?
Raina, I'm calling up to say GOOD-BYE.

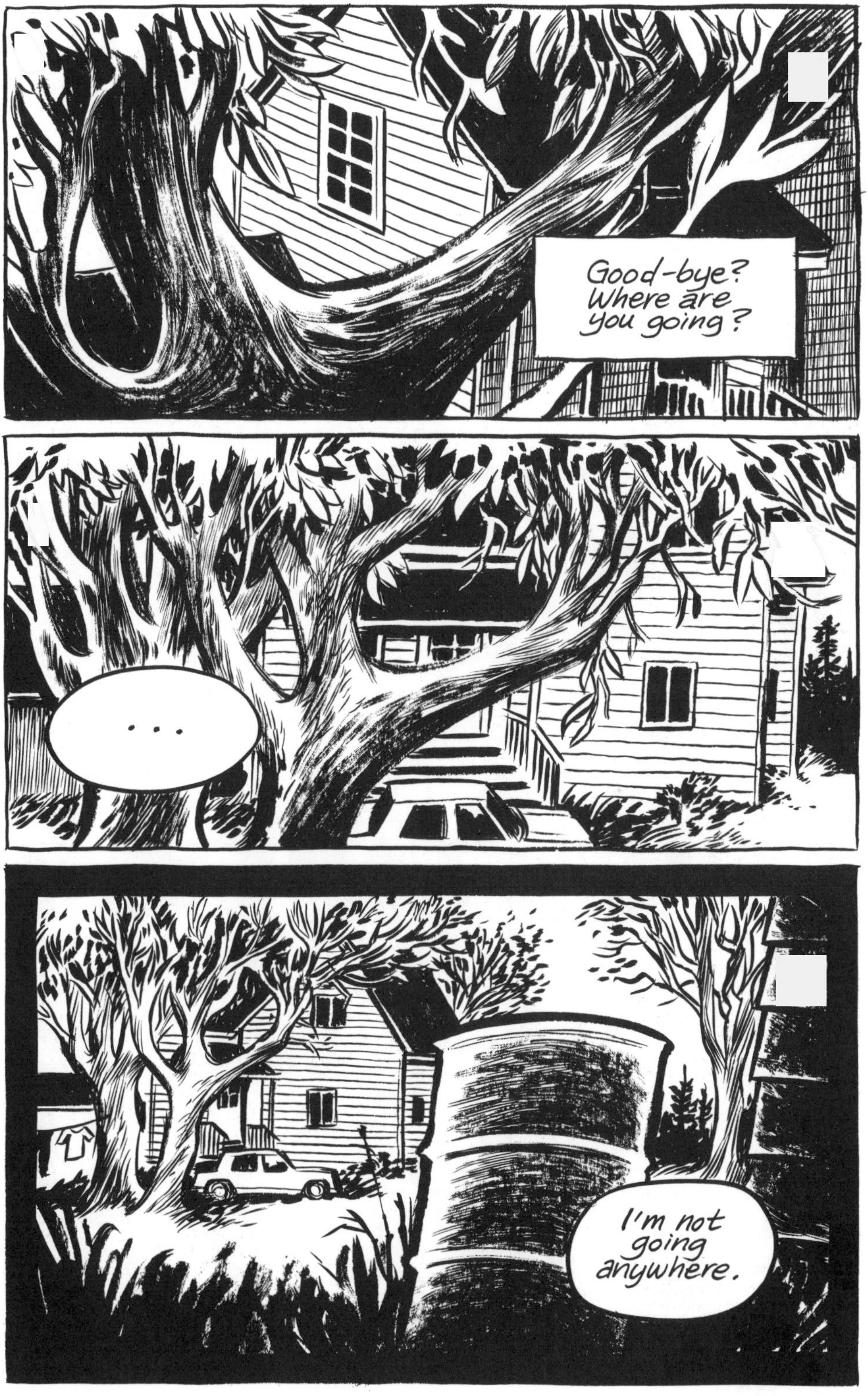
Good-bye? Where are you going?
...
I'm not going anywhere.

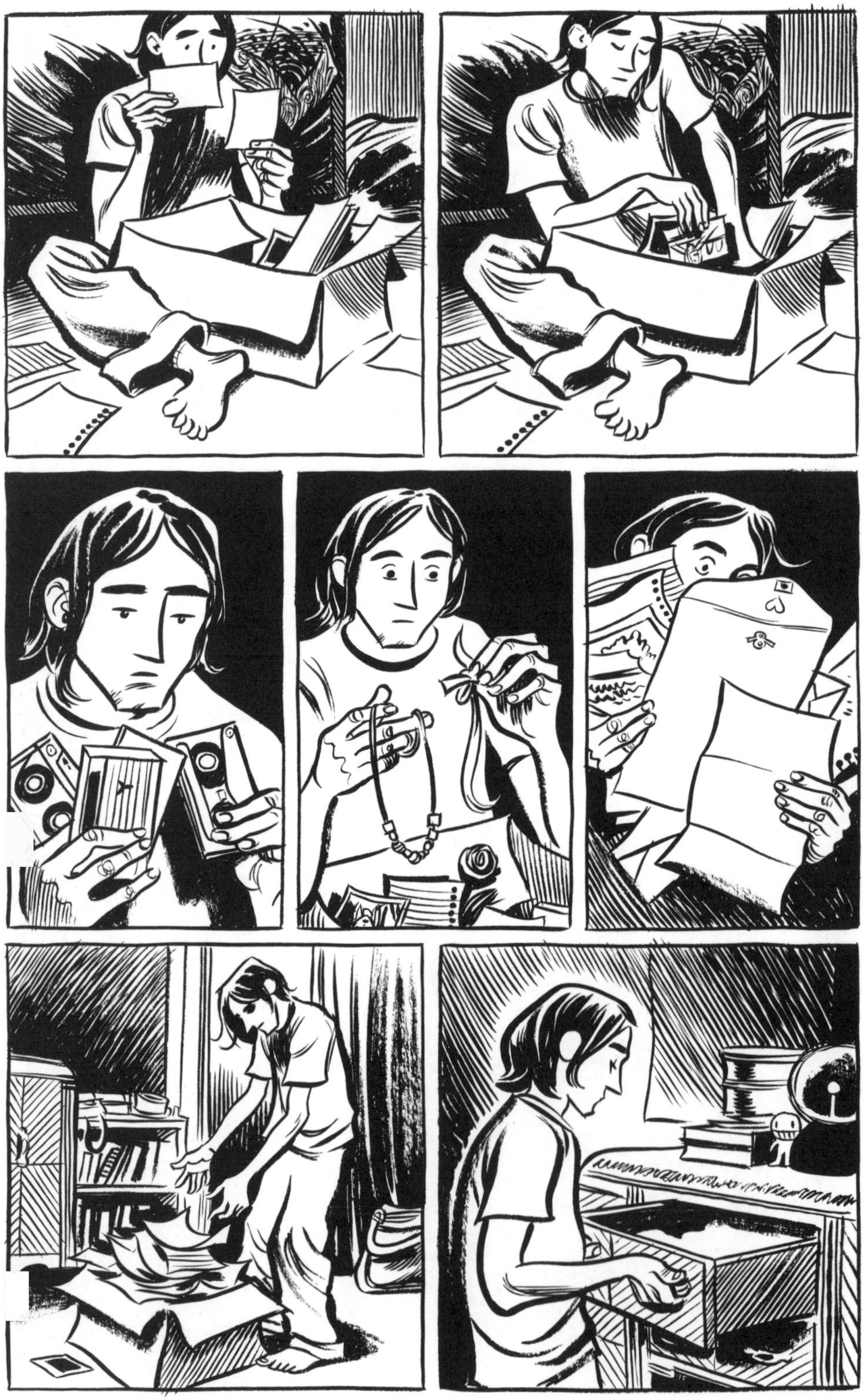

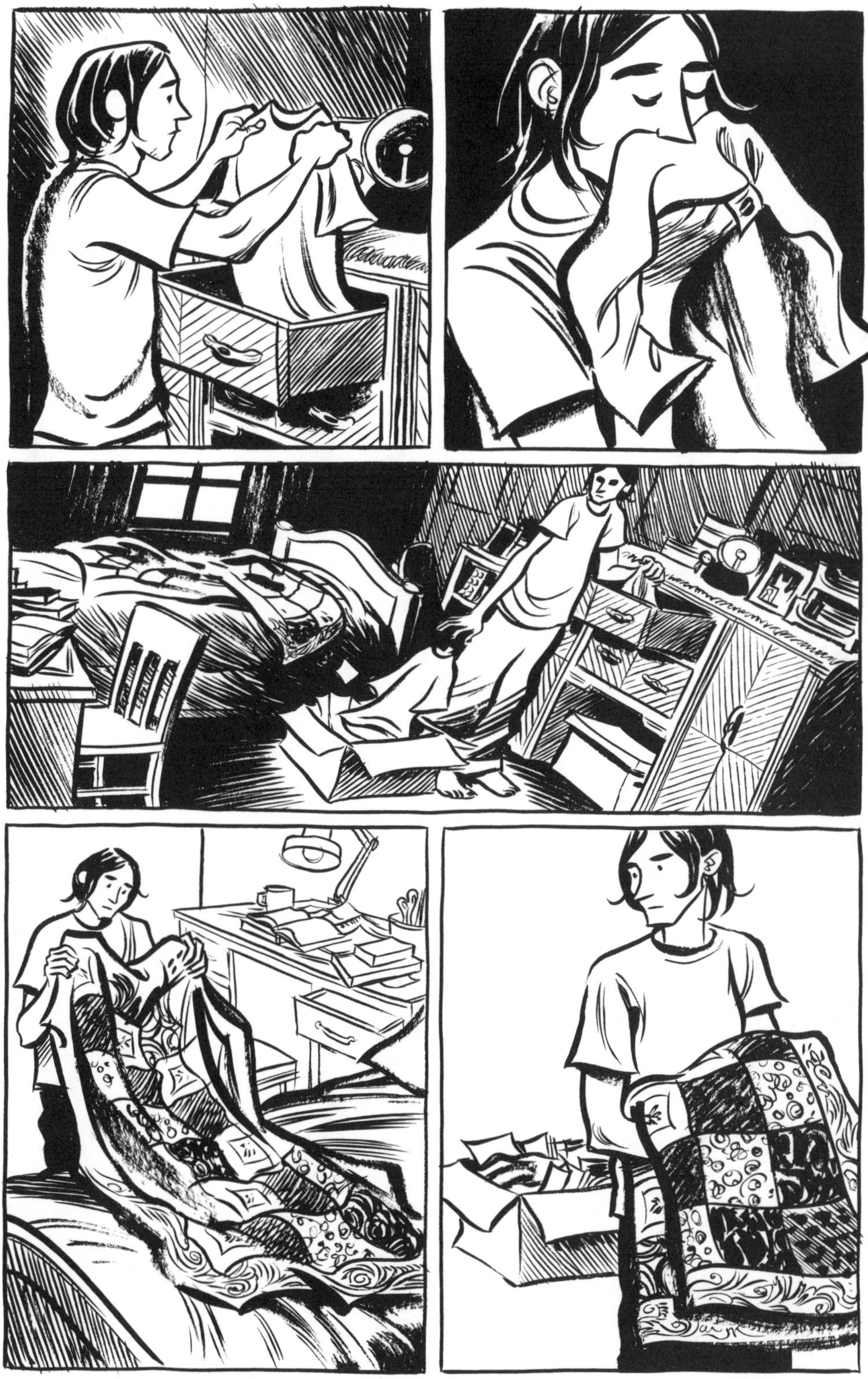

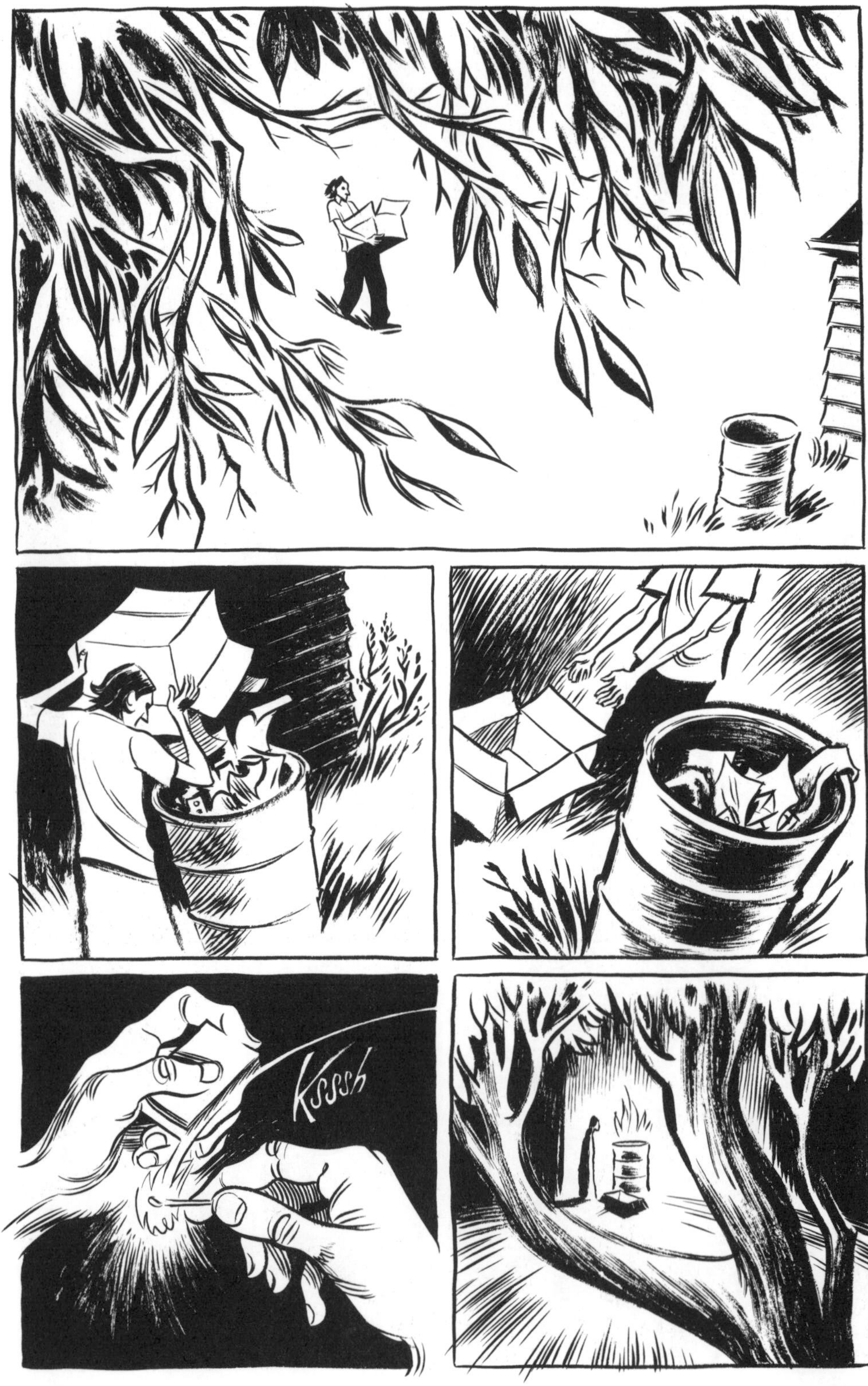
Ksssh

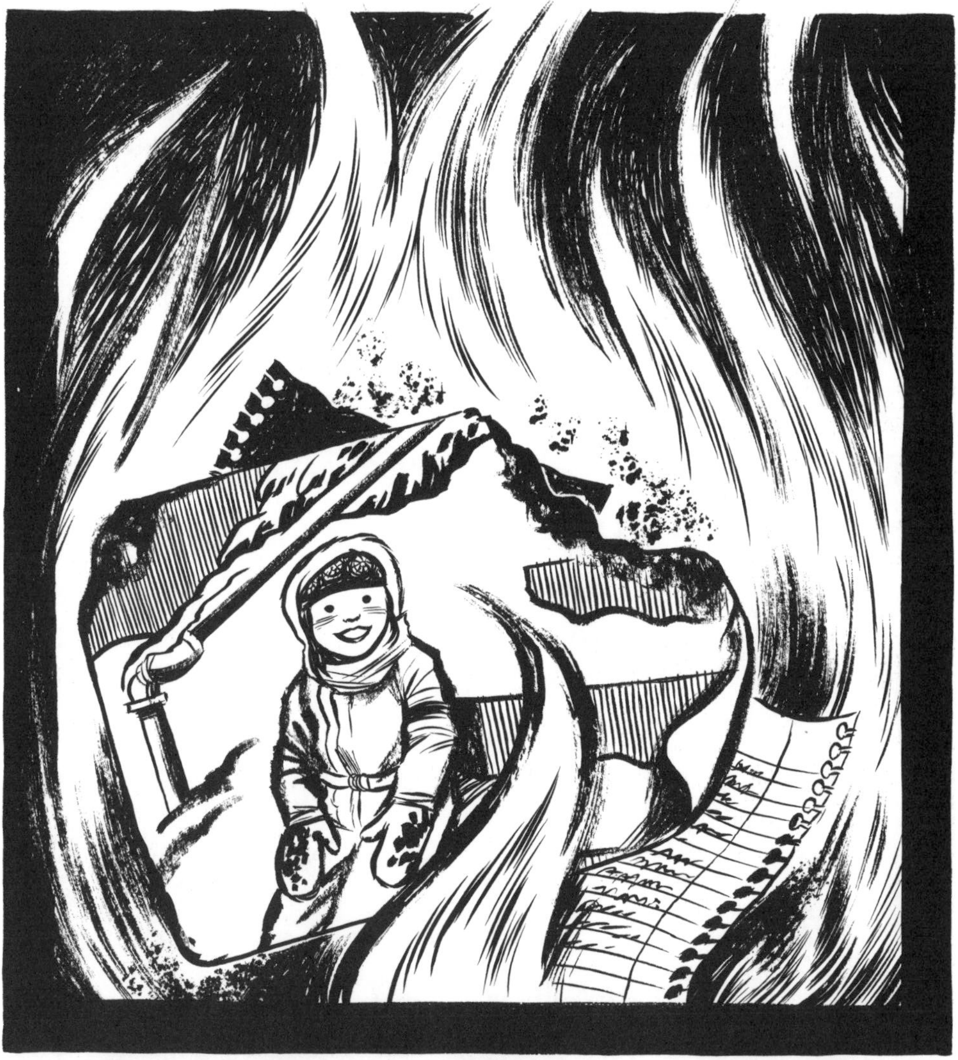

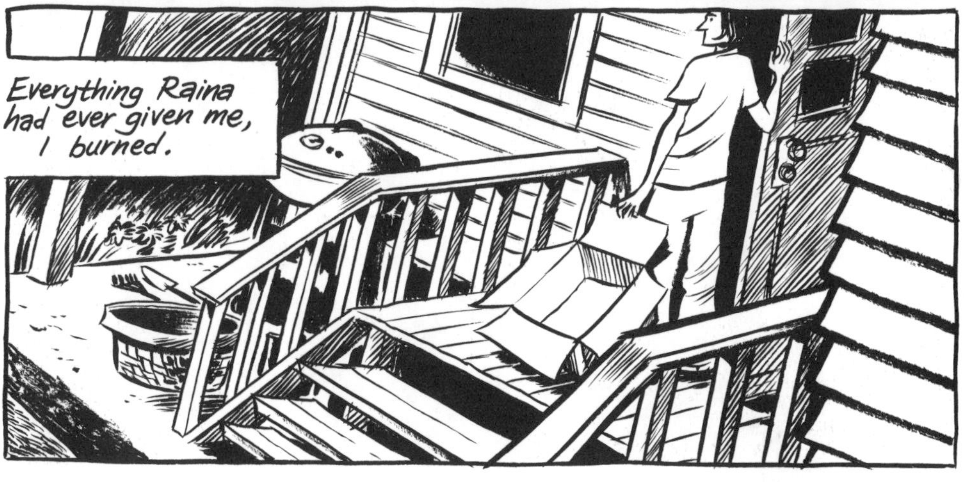
Everything Raina had ever given me, I burned.

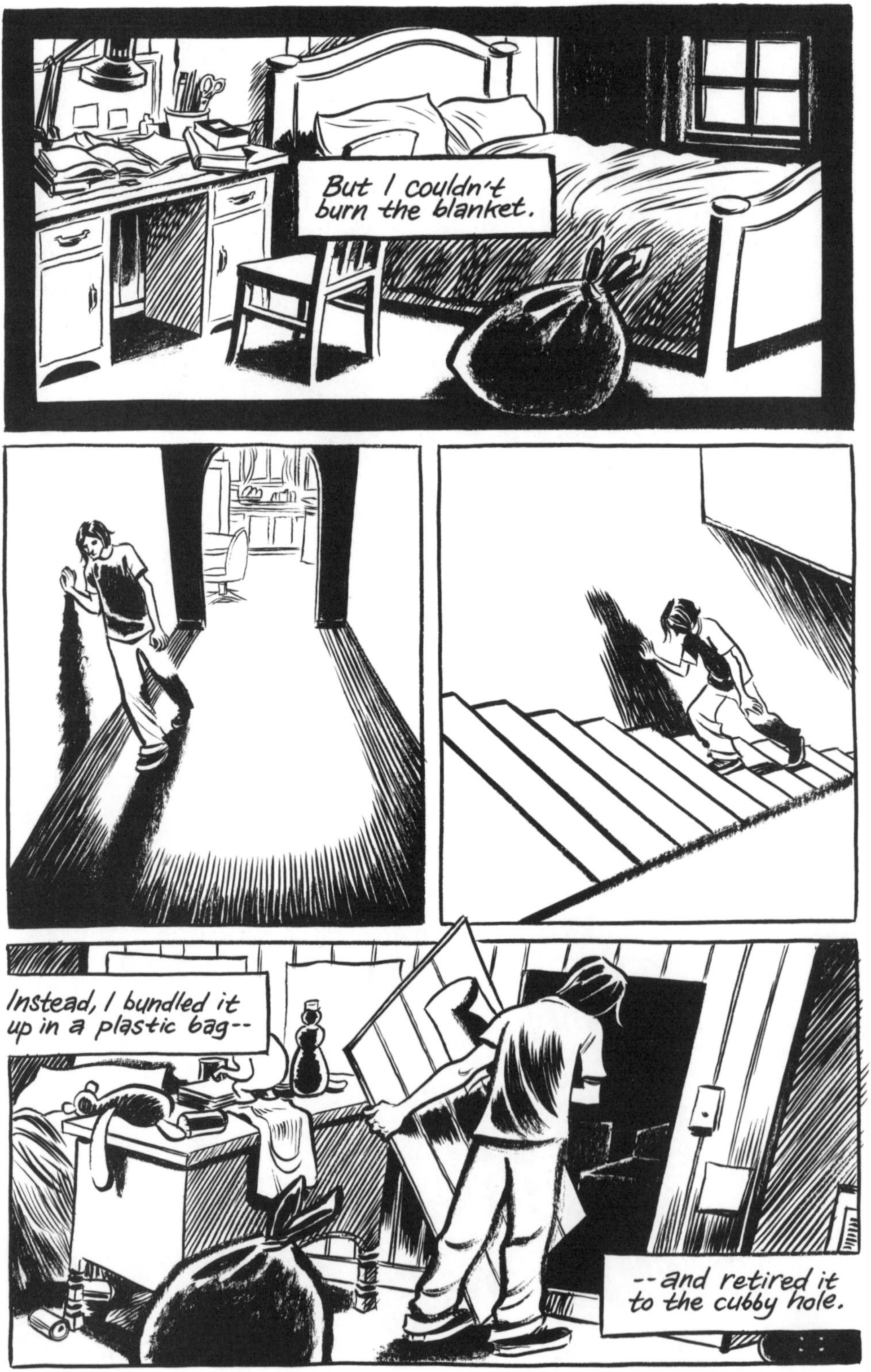
But I couldn't burn the blanket.
Instead, I bundled it up in a plastic bag--
--and retired it to the cubby hole.

I moved out of my
parents' home shortly
after my twentieth birthday.

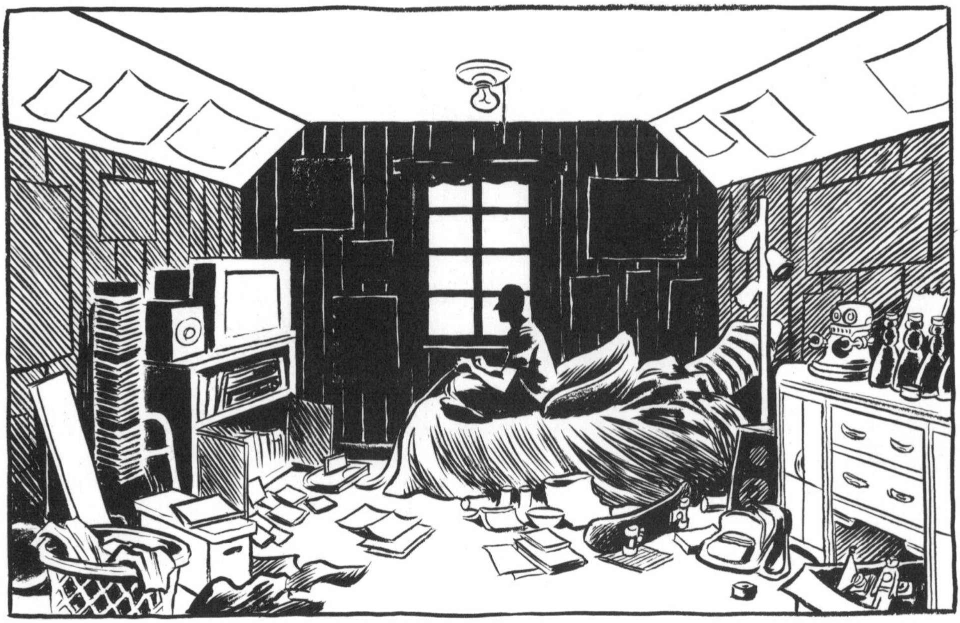

My brother moved into my room,
(because it was bigger).

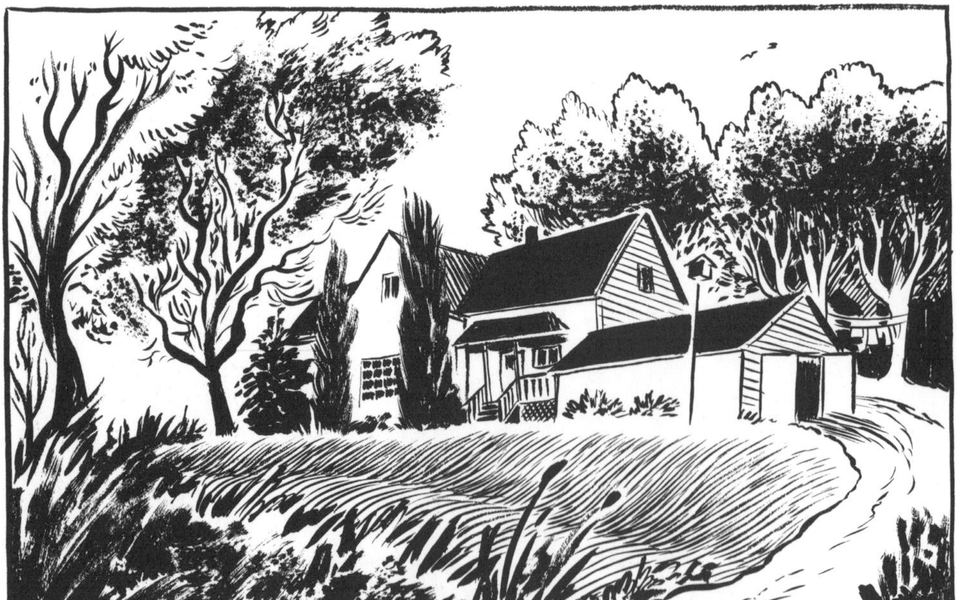

Upon his graduation,
I returned home to visit--

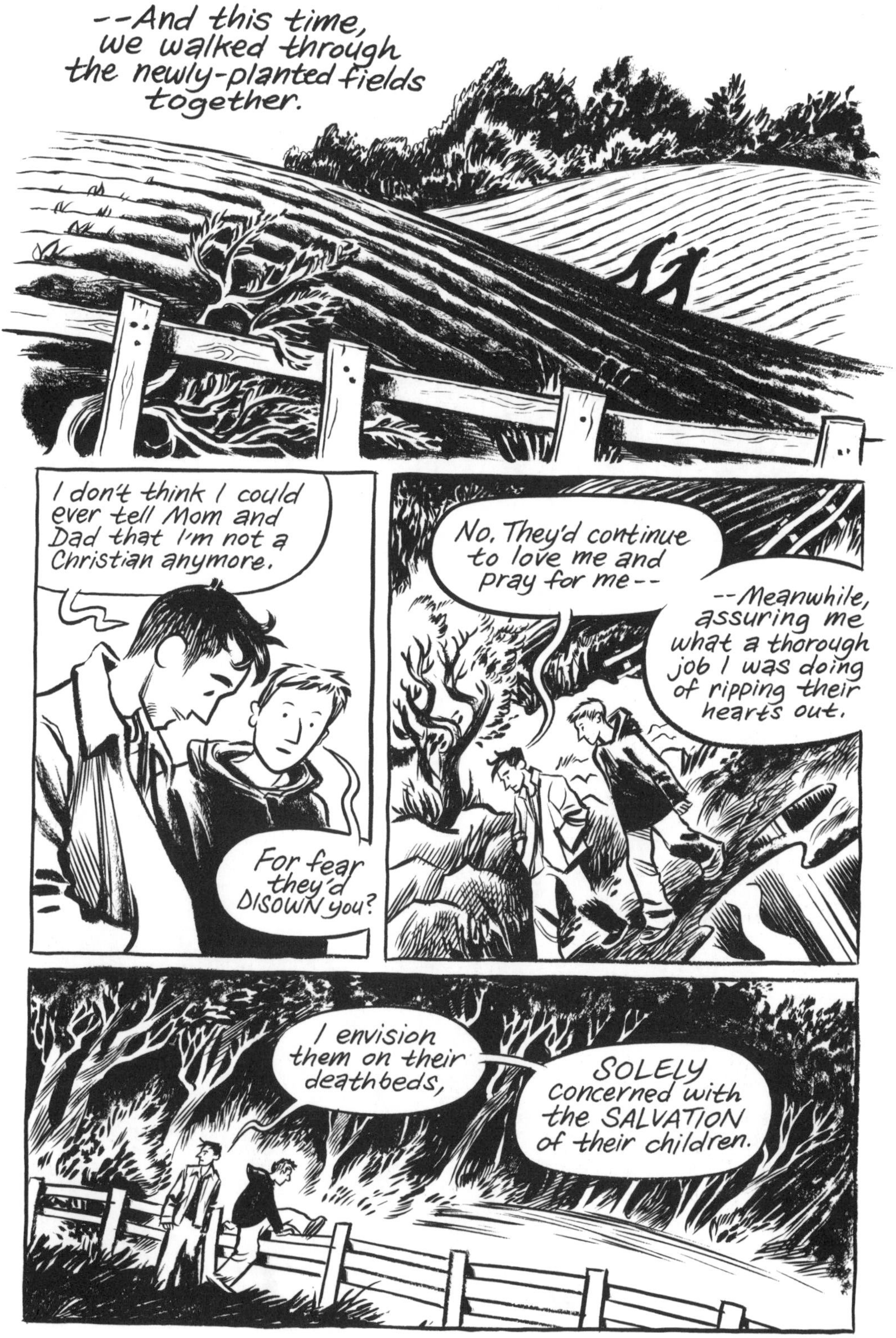
--And this time, we walked through the newly-planted fields together.
I don't think I could ever tell Mom and Dad that I'm not a Christian anymore.
For fear they'd DISOWN you?
No. They'd continue to love me and pray for me--
--Meanwhile, assuring me what a thorough job I was doing of ripping their hearts out.
I envision them on their deathbeds,
SOLELY concerned with the SALVATION of their children.

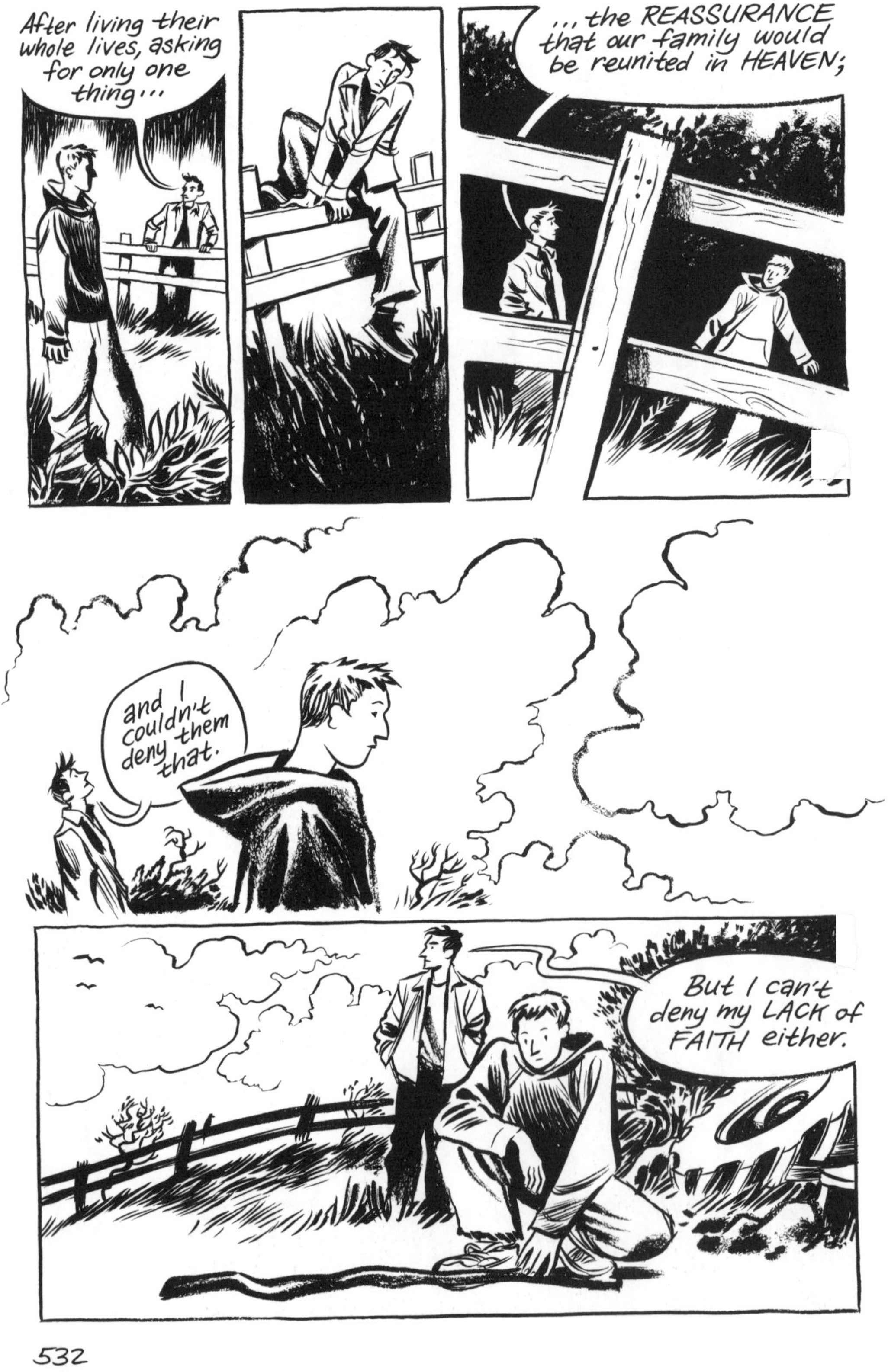
After living their whole lives, asking for only one thing...
... the REASSURANCE that our family would be reunited in HEAVEN;
and I couldn't deny them that.
But I can't deny my LACK of FAITH either.

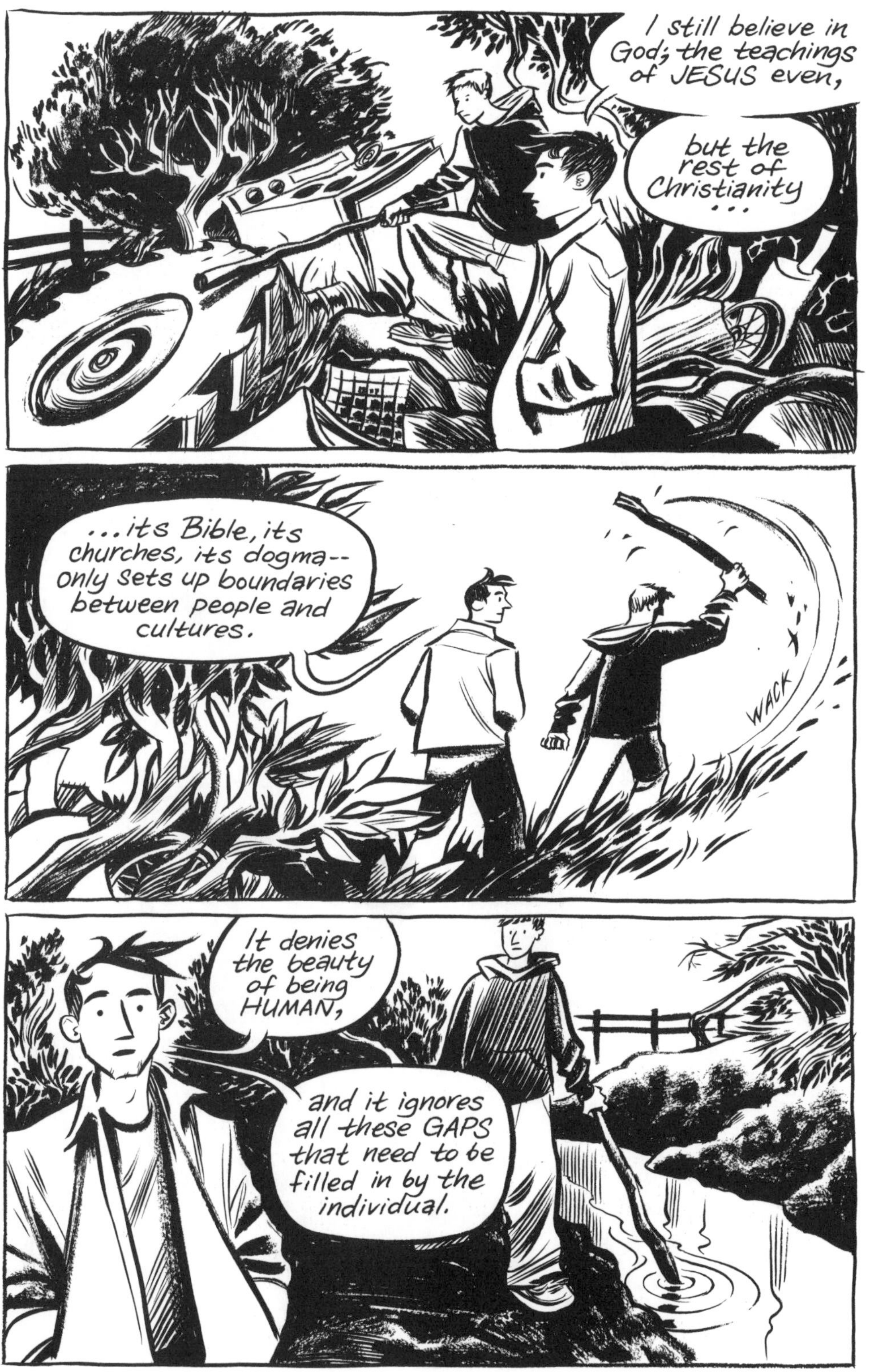
I still believe in God; the teachings of JESUS even,
but the rest of Christianity . . .
. . . its Bible, its churches, its dogma-- only sets up boundaries between people and cultures.
WACK
It denies the beauty of being HUMAN,
and it ignores all these GAPS that need to be filled in by the individual.

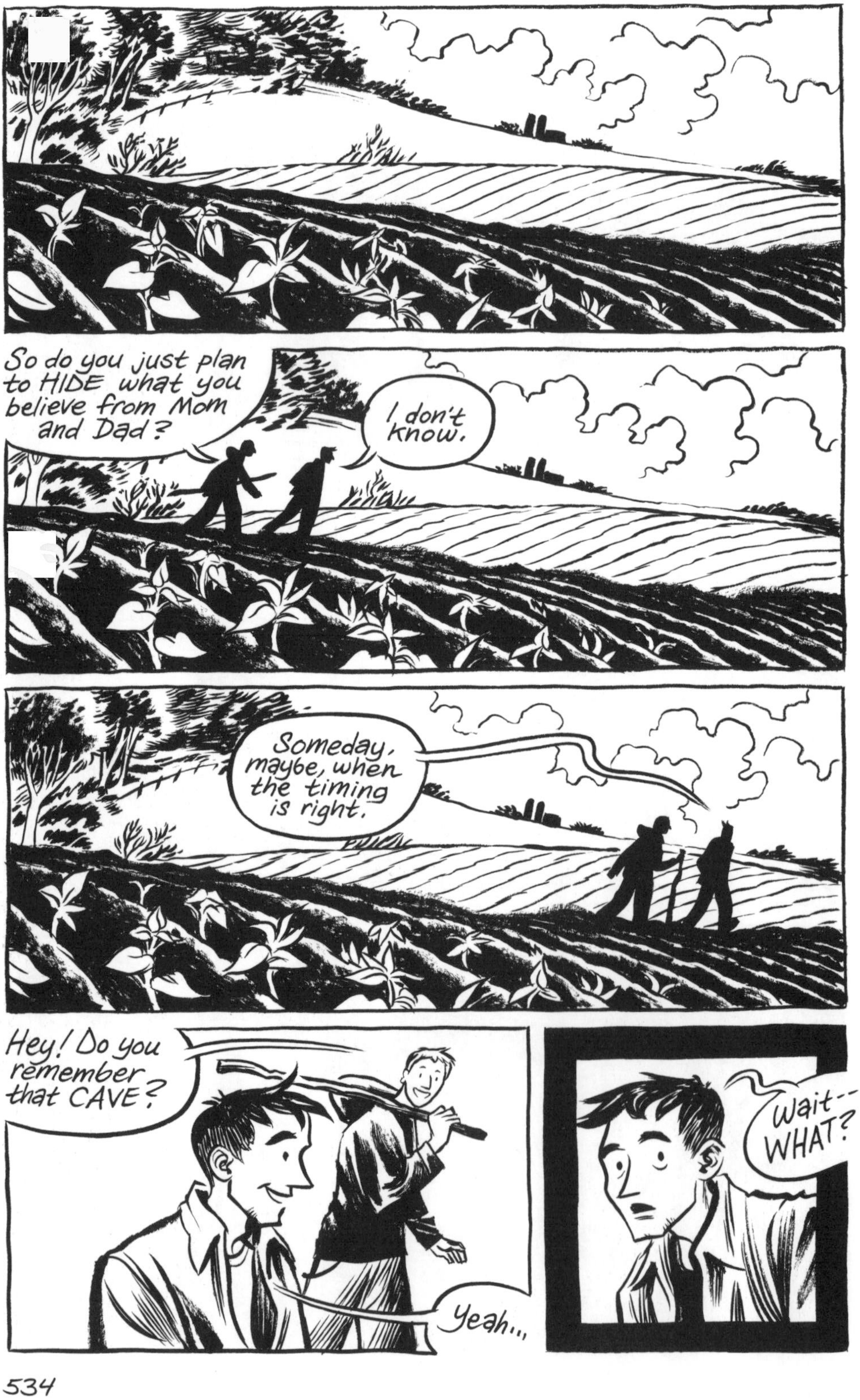

So do you just plan to HIDE what you believe from Mom and Dad?
I don't know.
Someday, maybe, when the timing is right.
Hey! Do you remember that CAVE?
Yeah...
Wait-- WHAT?

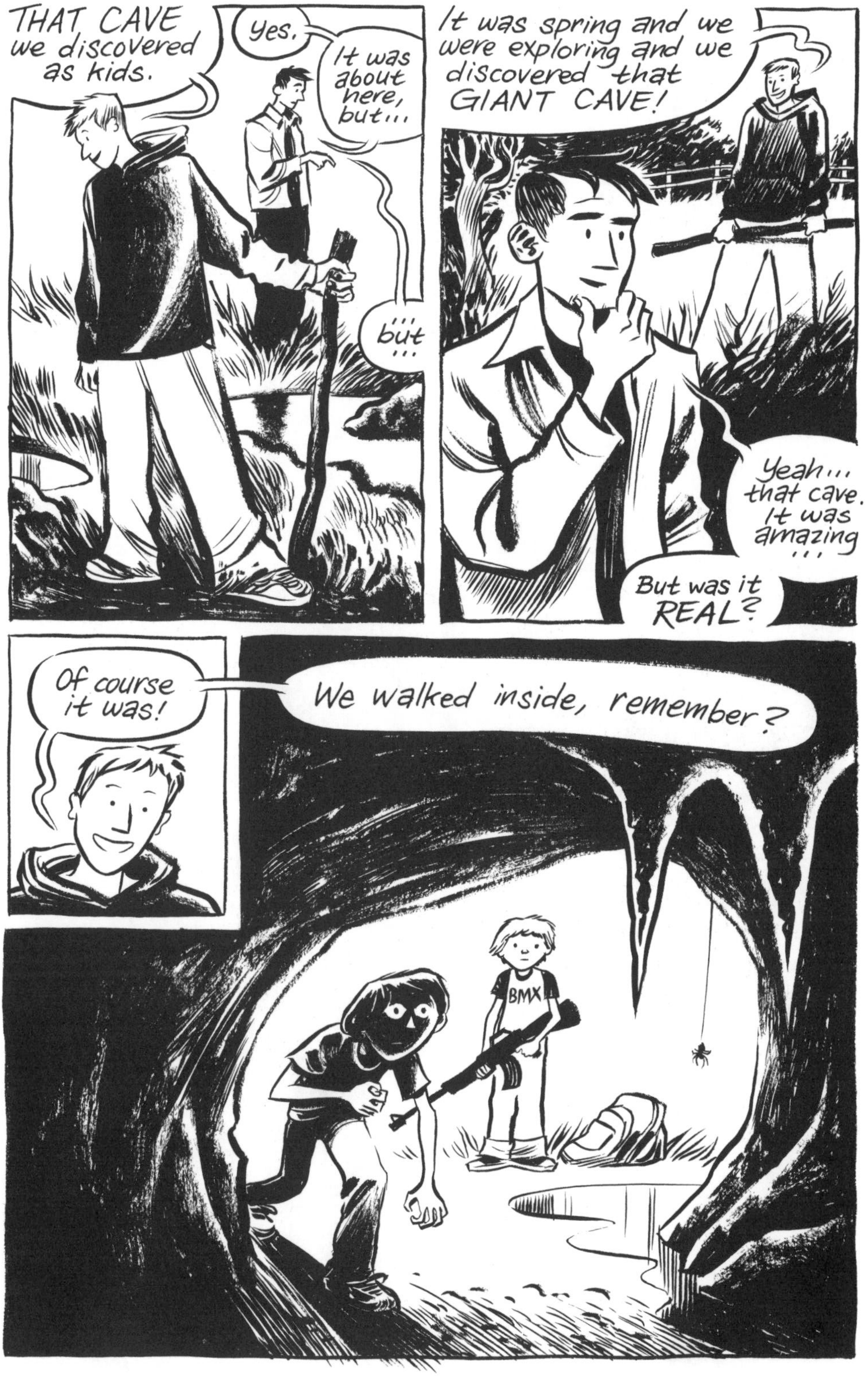
THAT CAVE we discovered as kids.
Yes.
It was about here, but...
... but ...
It was spring and we were exploring and we discovered that GIANT CAVE!
Yeah... that cave. It was amazing ...
But was it REAL?
Of course it was!
We walked inside, remember?
BMX

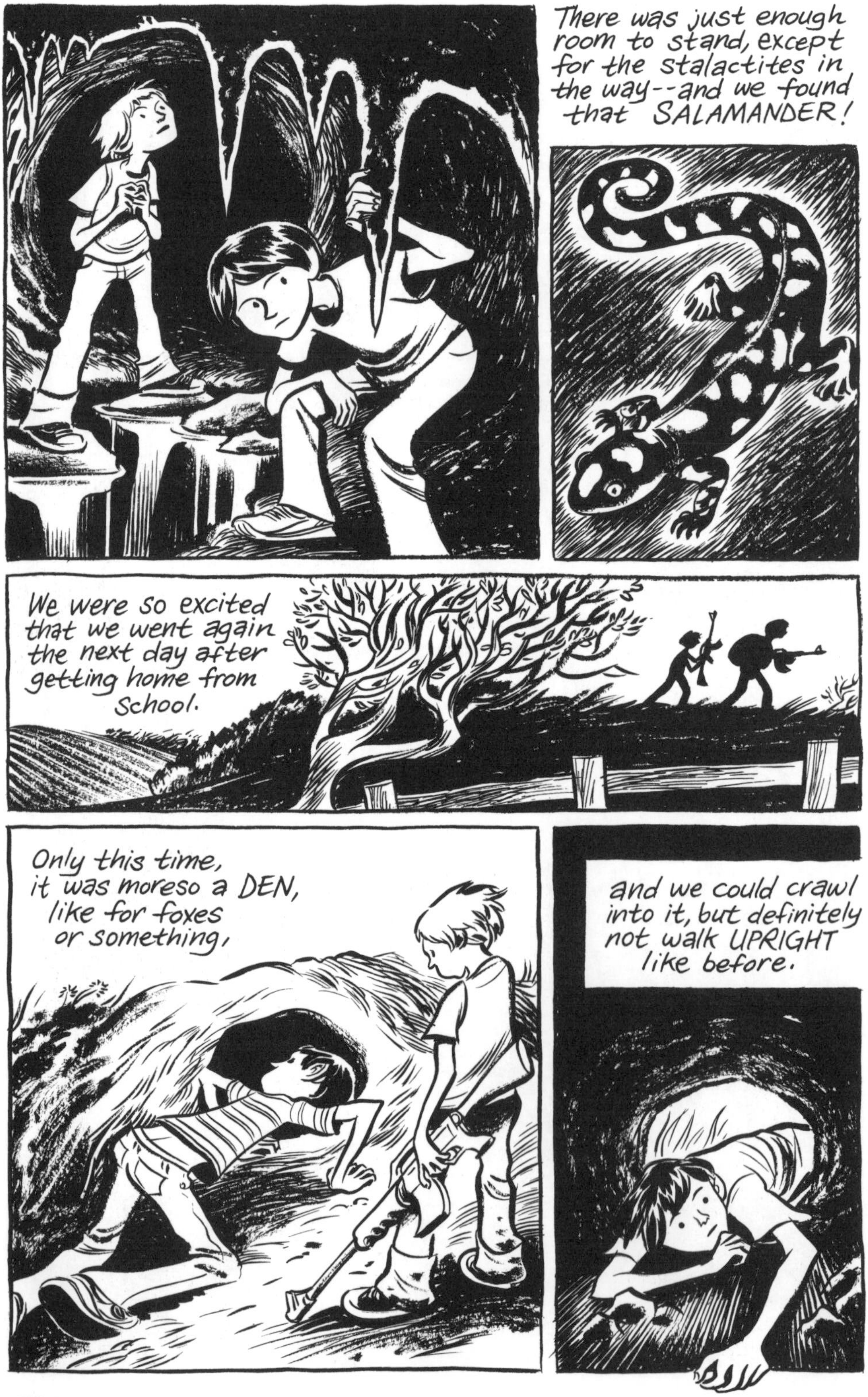
There was just enough room to stand, except for the stalactites in the way--and we found that SALAMANDER!
We were so excited that we went again the next day after getting home from school.
Only this time, it was moreso a DEN, like for foxes or something,
and we could crawl into it, but definitely not walk UPRIGHT like before.

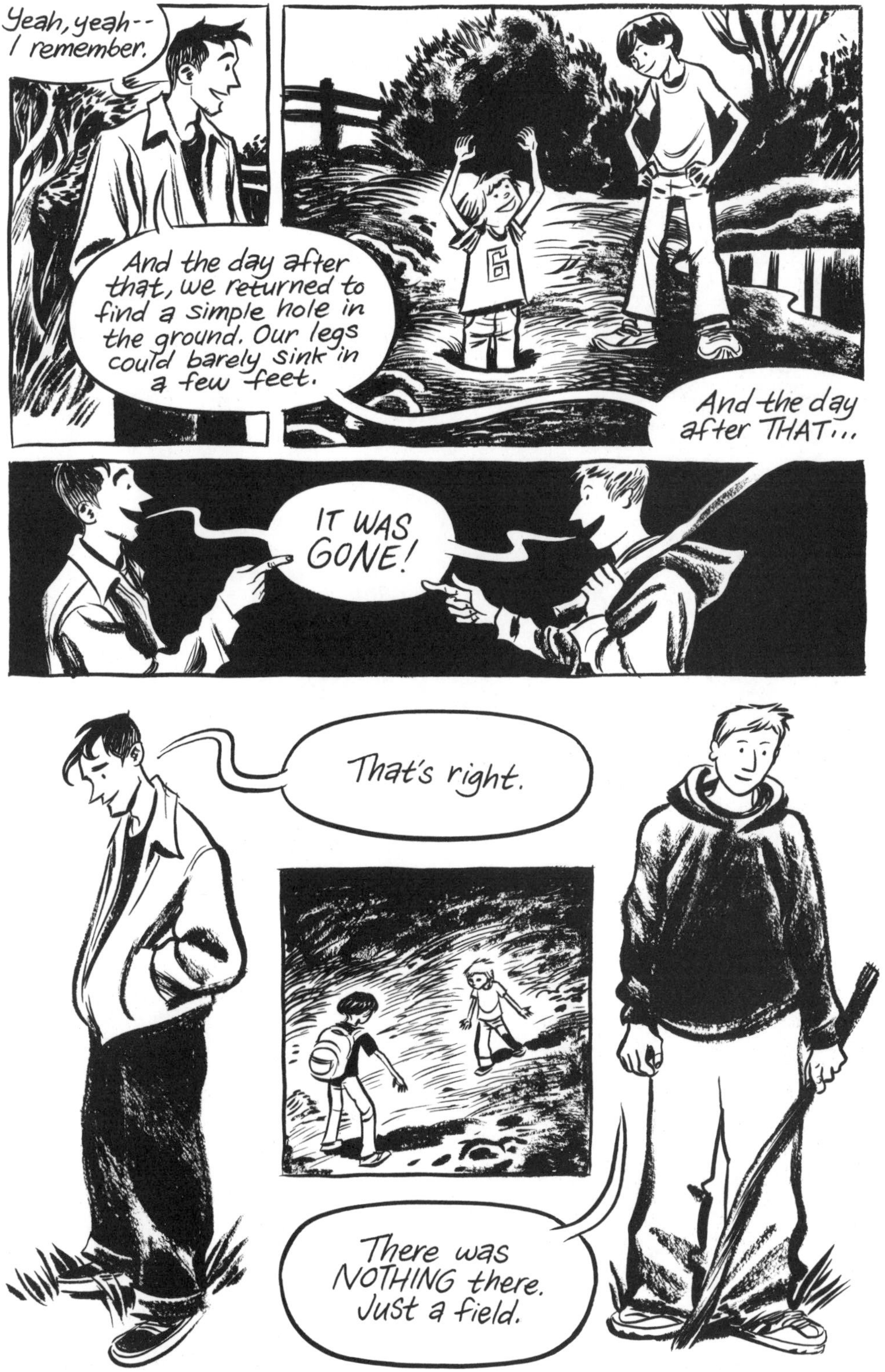
Yeah, yeah--
I remember.
And the day after that, we returned to find a simple hole in the ground. Our legs could barely sink in a few feet.
And the day after THAT...
IT WAS GONE!
That's right.
There was NOTHING there. Just a field.

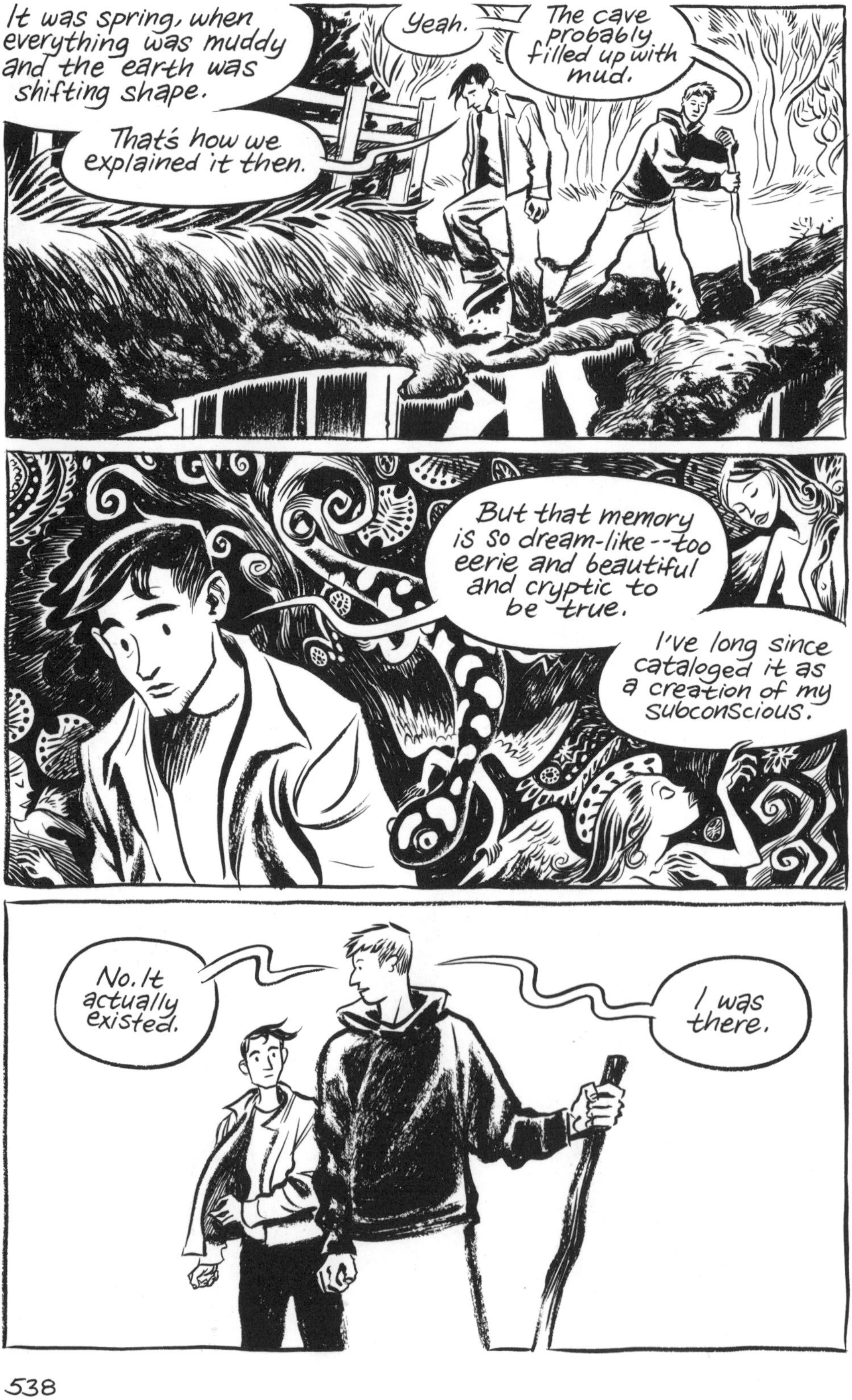
It was spring, when everything was muddy and the earth was shifting shape.
That's how we explained it then.
Yeah.
The cave probably filled up with mud.
But that memory is so dream-like--too eerie and beautiful and cryptic to be true.
I've long since cataloged it as a creation of my subconscious.
No. It actually existed.
I was there.

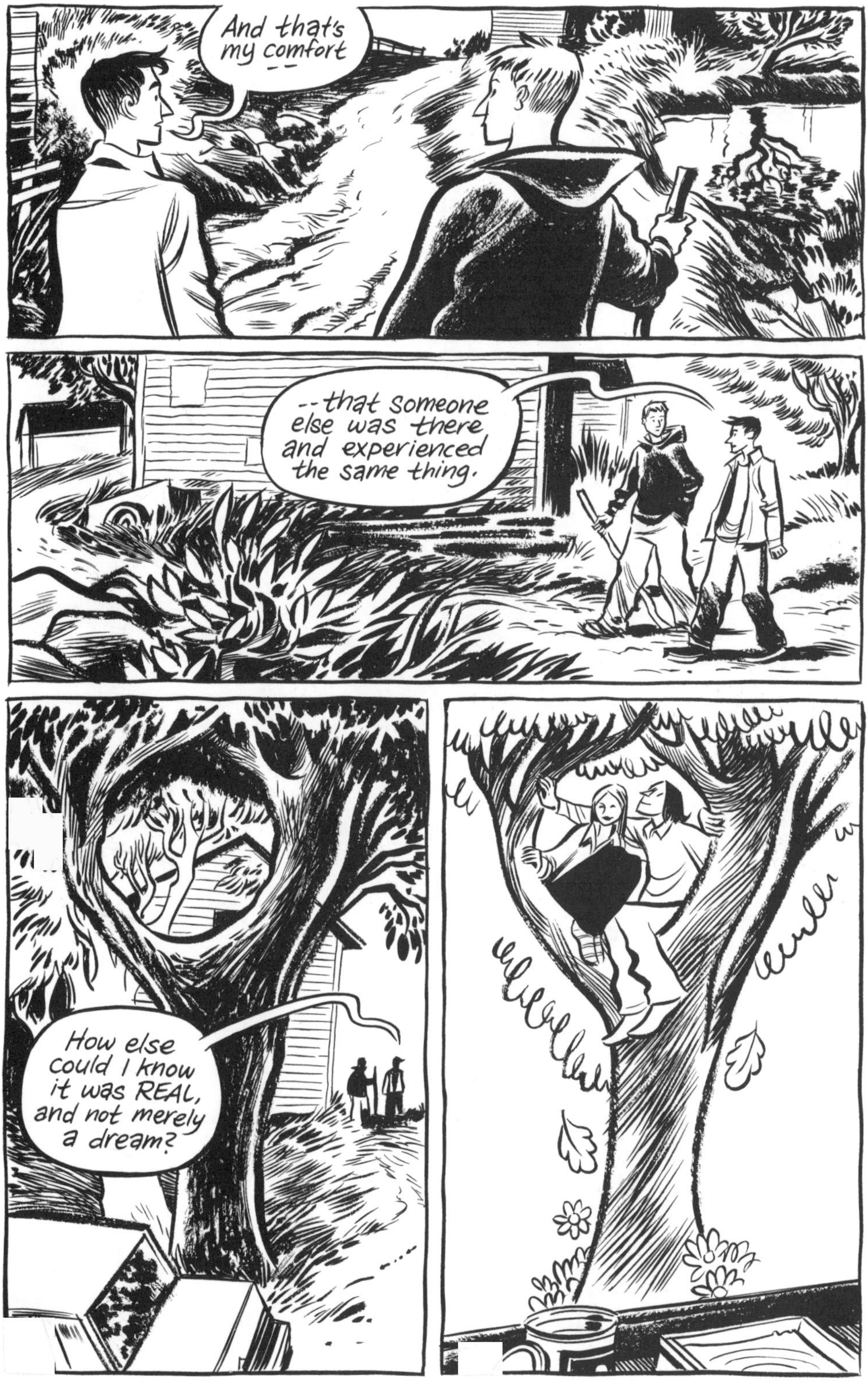
And that's my comfort --
--that someone else was there and experienced the same thing.
How else could I know it was REAL, and not merely a dream?

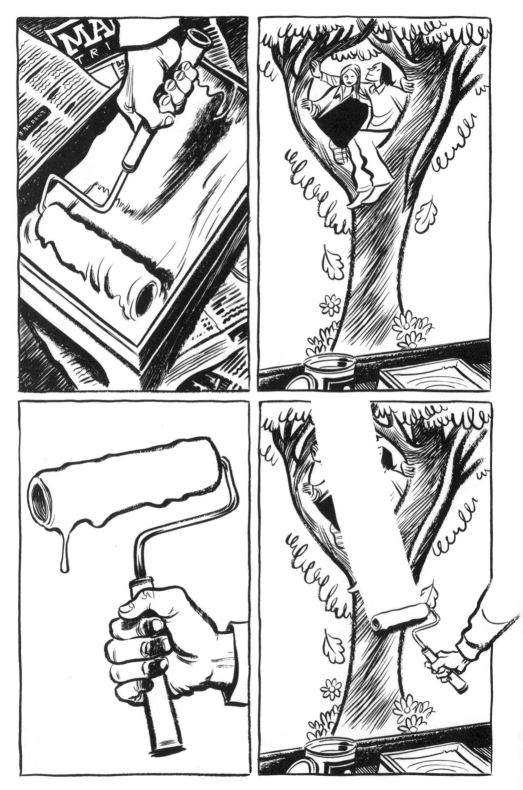

540

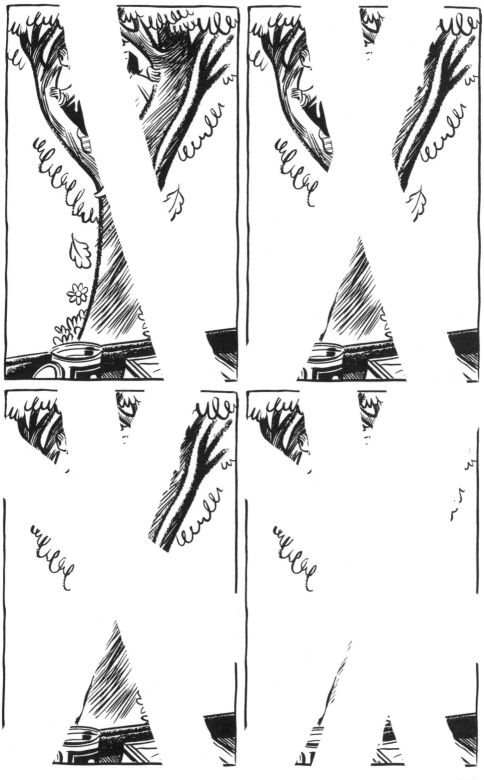

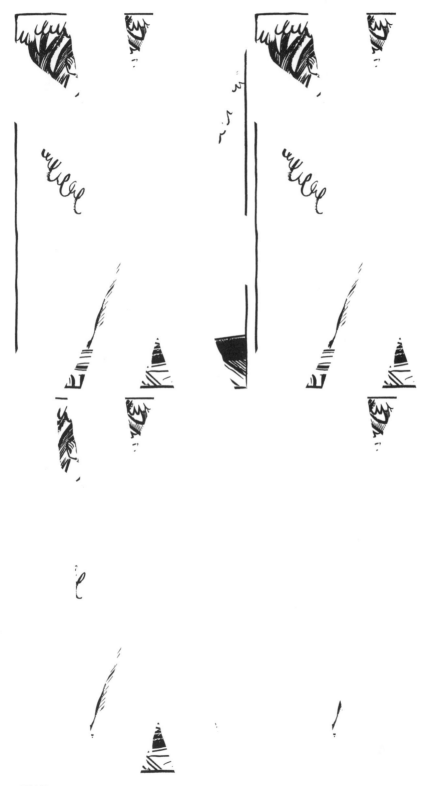

IX

Foot Notes

Upon moving out of my parents' home, I made a conscious effort to leave my Bible behind.

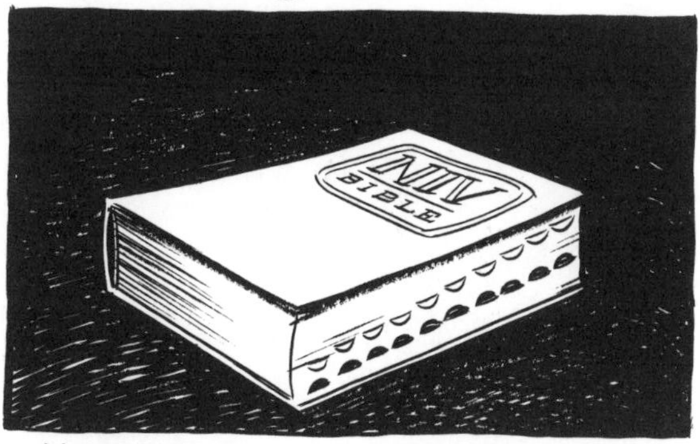
NIV
BIBLE

It was the book of ECCLESIASTES that prompted me to do so.

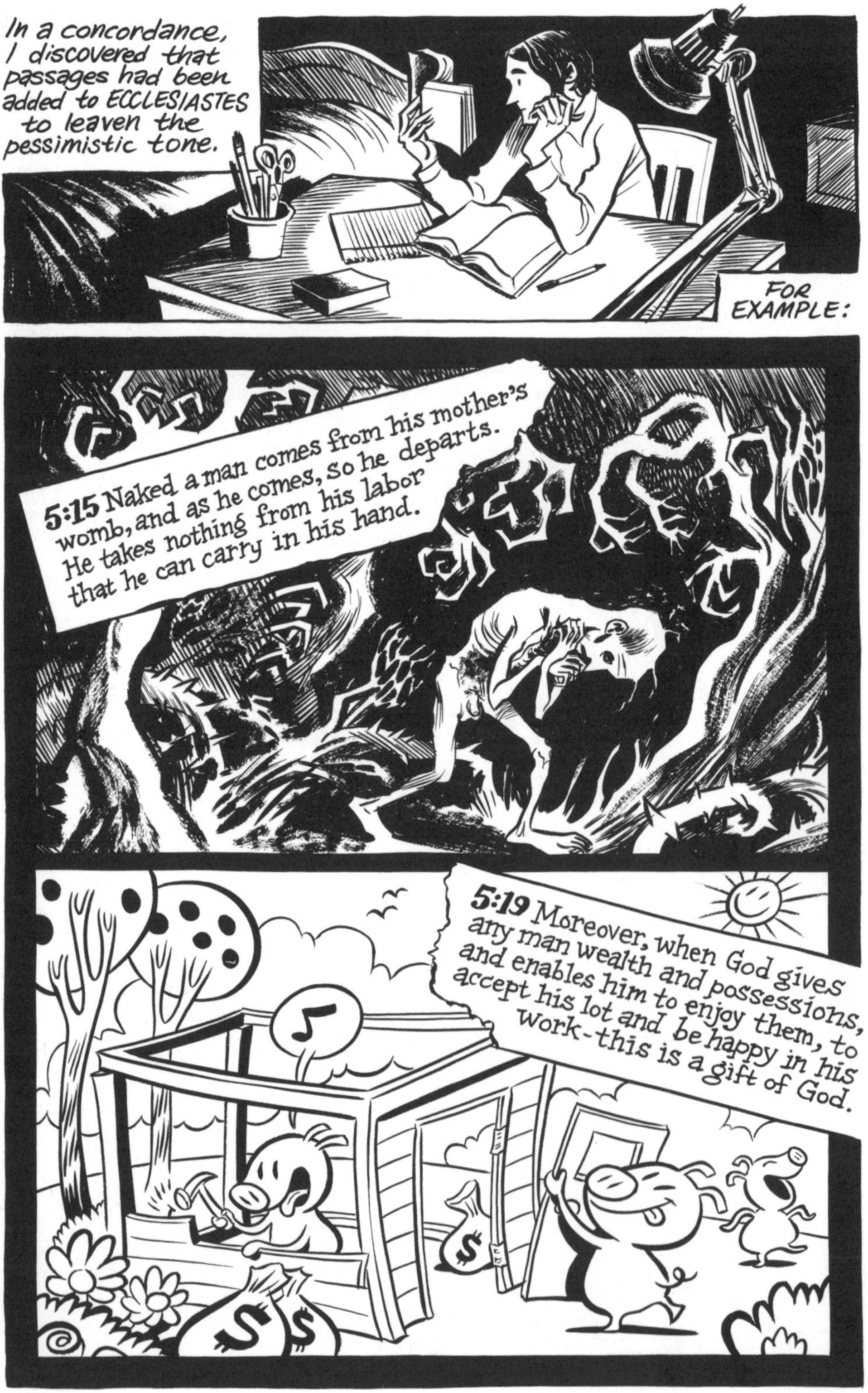
In a concordance, I discovered that passages had been added to ECCLESIASTES to leaven the pessimistic tone.
FOR EXAMPLE:
5:15 Naked a man comes from his mother's womb, and as he comes, so he departs. He takes nothing from his labor that he can carry in his hand.
5:19 Moreover, when God gives any man wealth and possessions, and enables him to enjoy them, to accept his lot and be happy in his work-this is a gift of God.

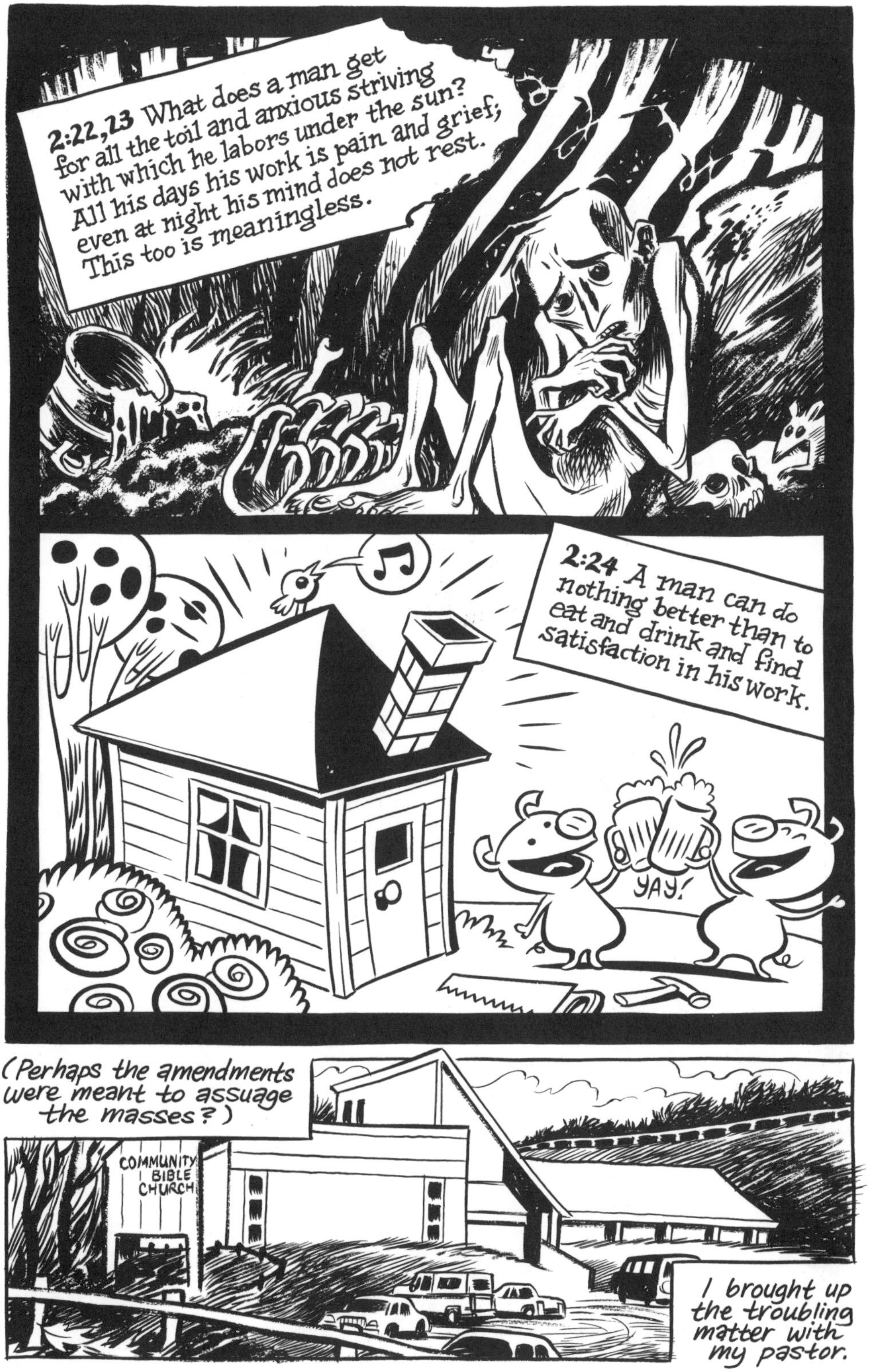
2:22,23 What does a man get for all the toil and anxious striving with which he labors under the sun? All his days his work is pain and grief; even at night his mind does not rest. This too is meaningless.
2:24 A man can do nothing better than to eat and drink and find satisfaction in his work.
YAY!
(Perhaps the amendments were meant to assuage the masses?)
COMMUNITY BIBLE CHURCH
I brought up the troubling matter with my pastor.

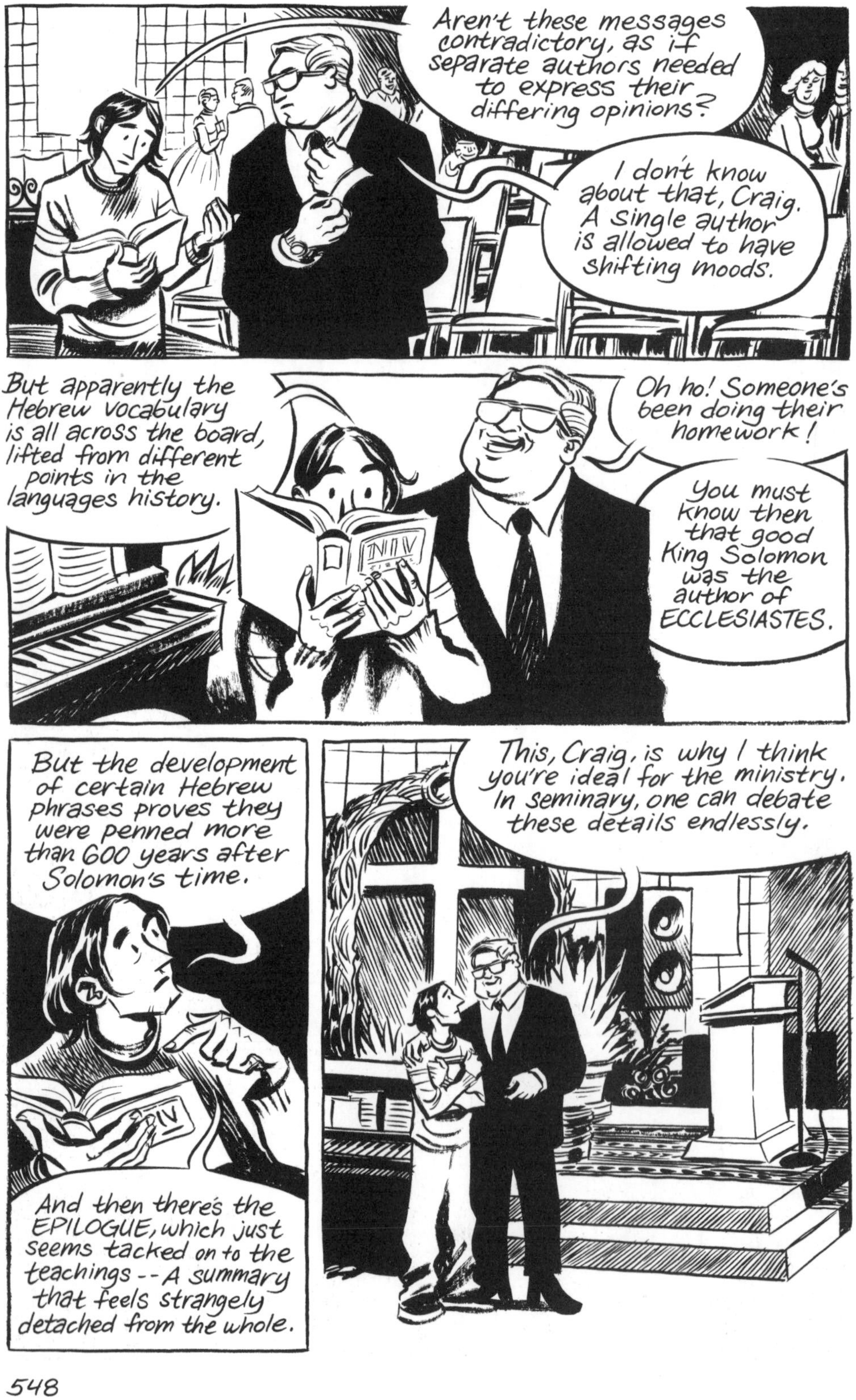
Aren't these messages contradictory, as if separate authors needed to express their differing opinions?
I don't know about that, Craig. A single author is allowed to have shifting moods.
But apparently the Hebrew vocabulary is all across the board, lifted from different points in the languages history.
Oh ho! Someone's been doing their homework!
You must know then that good King Solomon was the author of ECCLESIASTES.
But the development of certain Hebrew phrases proves they were penned more than 600 years after Solomon's time.
And then there's the EPILOGUE, which just seems tacked on to the teachings -- A summary that feels strangely detached from the whole.
This, Craig, is why I think you're ideal for the ministry. In seminary, one can debate these details endlessly.

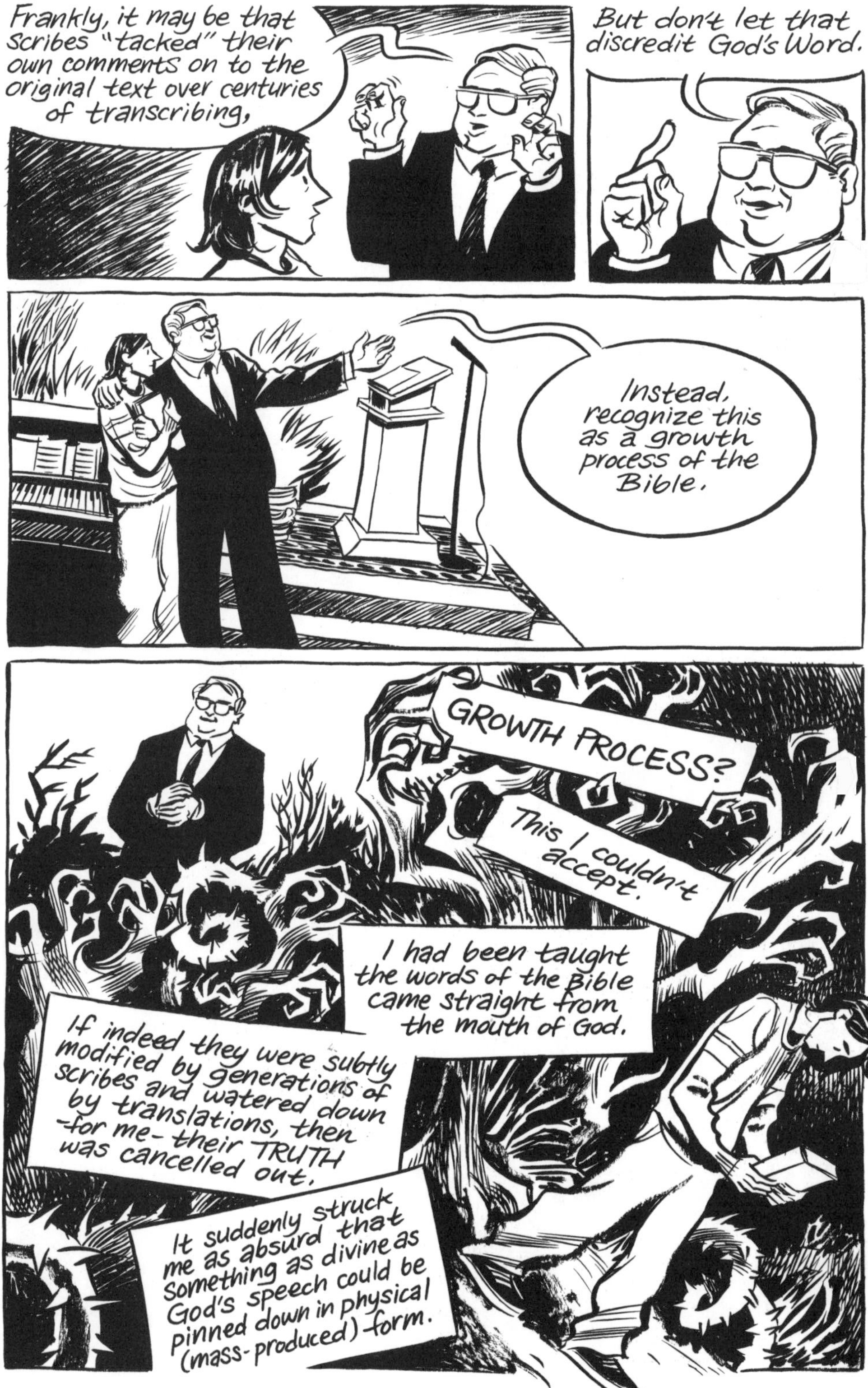
Frankly, it may be that scribes "tacked" their own comments on to the original text over centuries of transcribing,
But don't let that discredit God's Word.
Instead, recognize this as a growth process of the Bible.
GROWTH PROCESS?
This I couldn't accept.
I had been taught the words of the Bible came straight from the mouth of God.
If indeed they were subtly modified by generations of scribes and watered down by translations, then -for me- their TRUTH was cancelled out.
It suddenly struck me as absurd that something as divine as God's speech could be pinned down in physical (mass-produced) form.

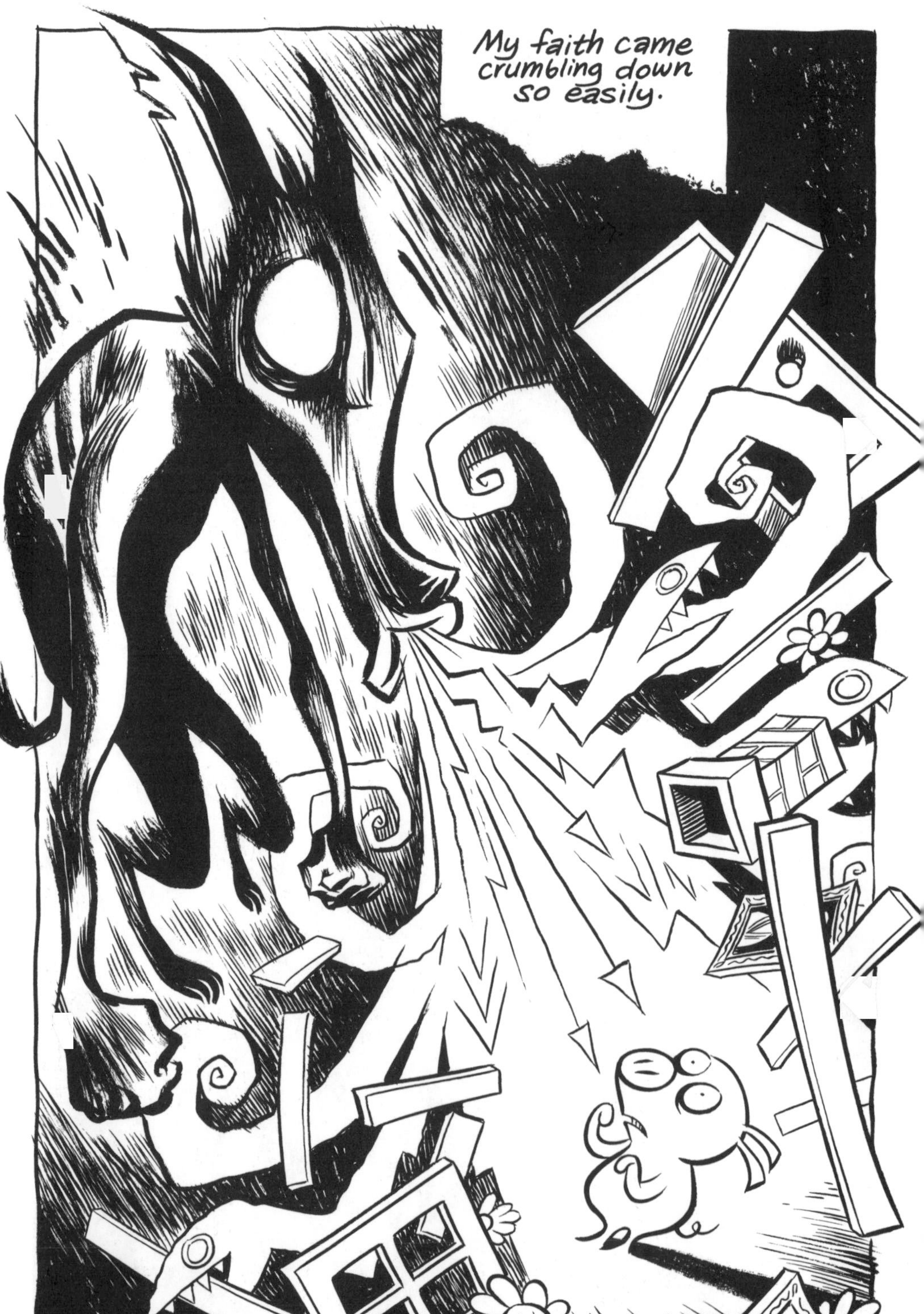
My faith came crumbling down so easily.

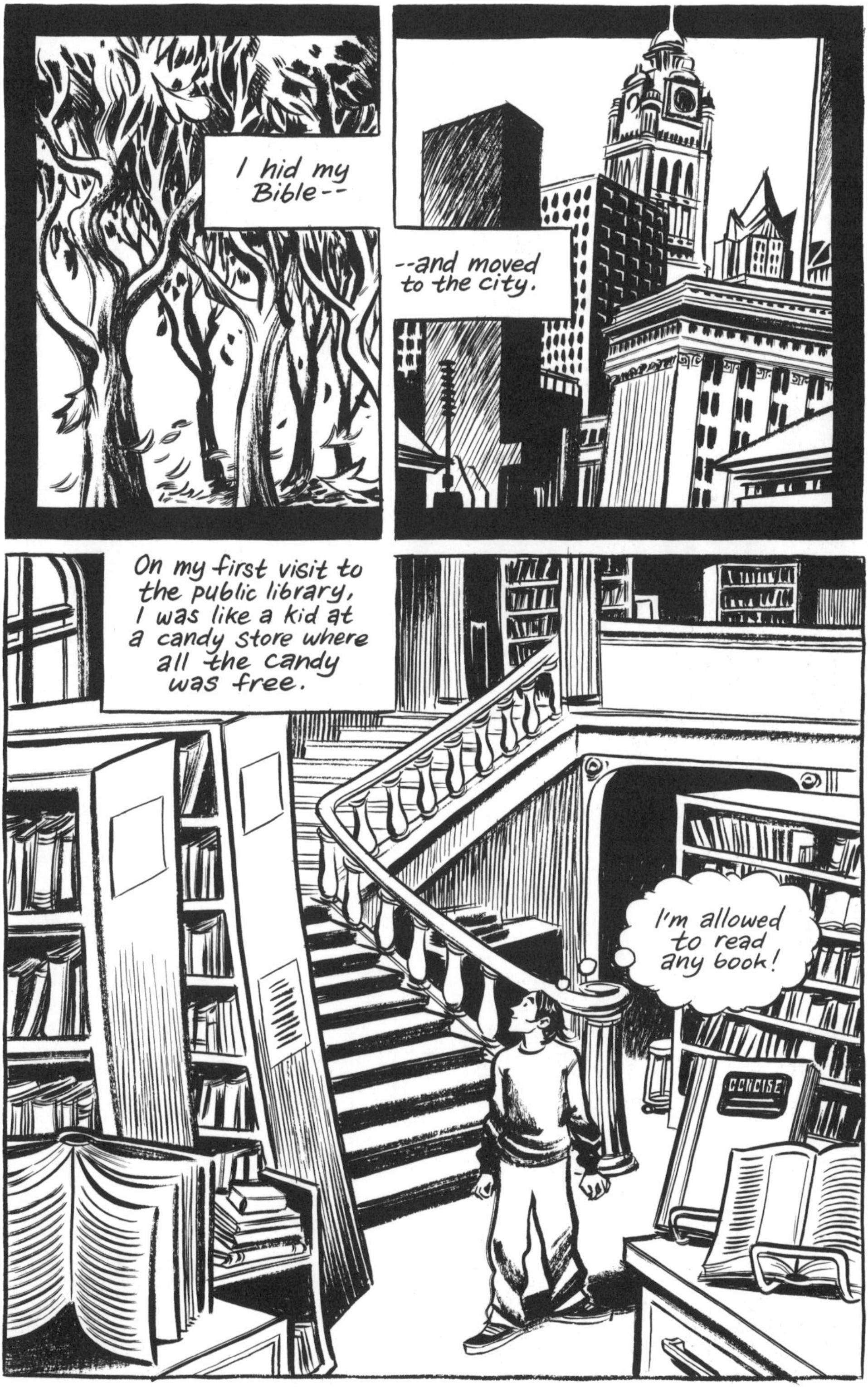
I hid my Bible--
--and moved to the city.
On my first visit to the public library, I was like a kid at a candy store where all the candy was free.
I'm allowed to read any book!
CONCISE

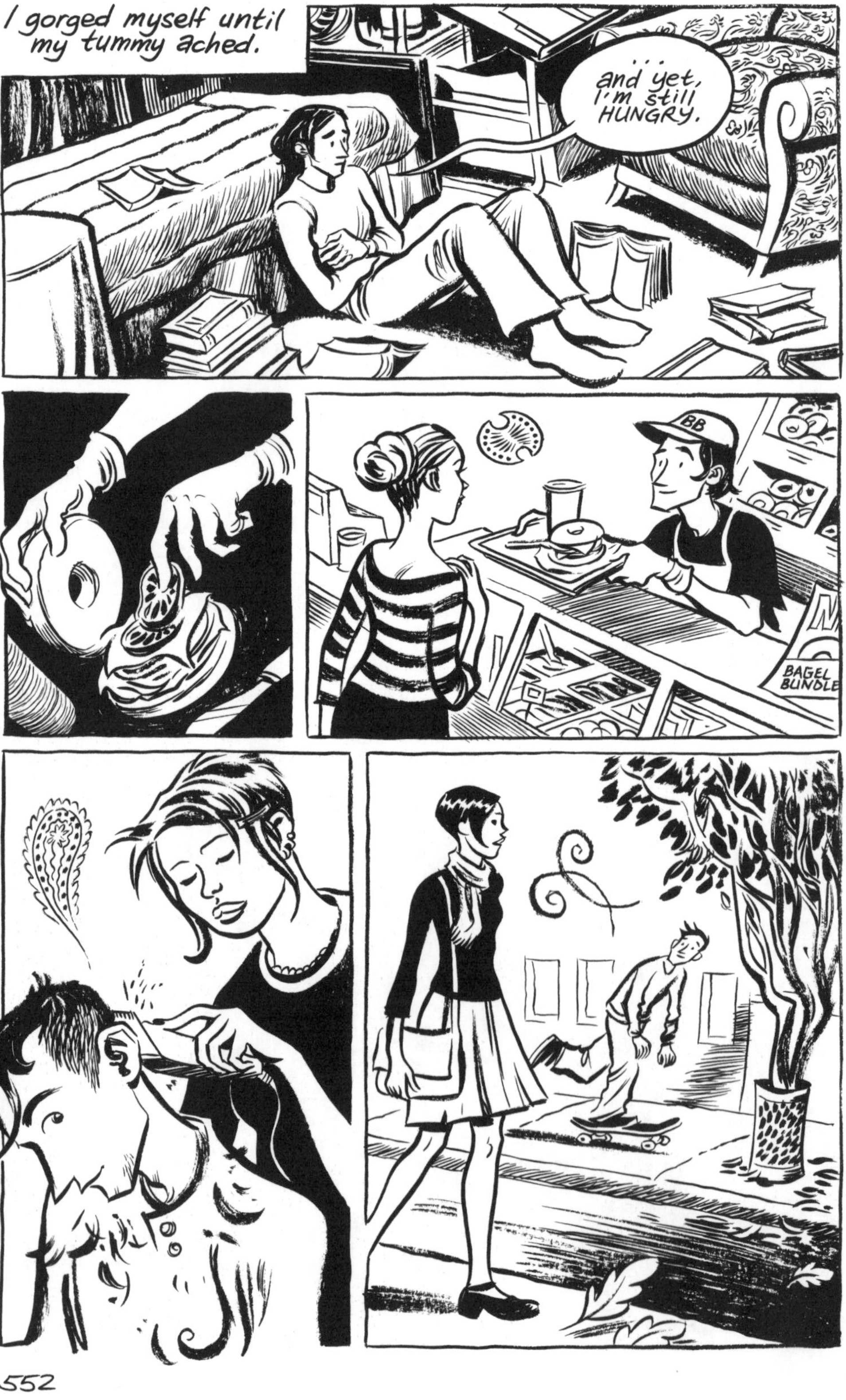

I gorged myself until my tummy ached.
... and yet, I'm still HUNGRY.
BB
BAGEL BUNDLE

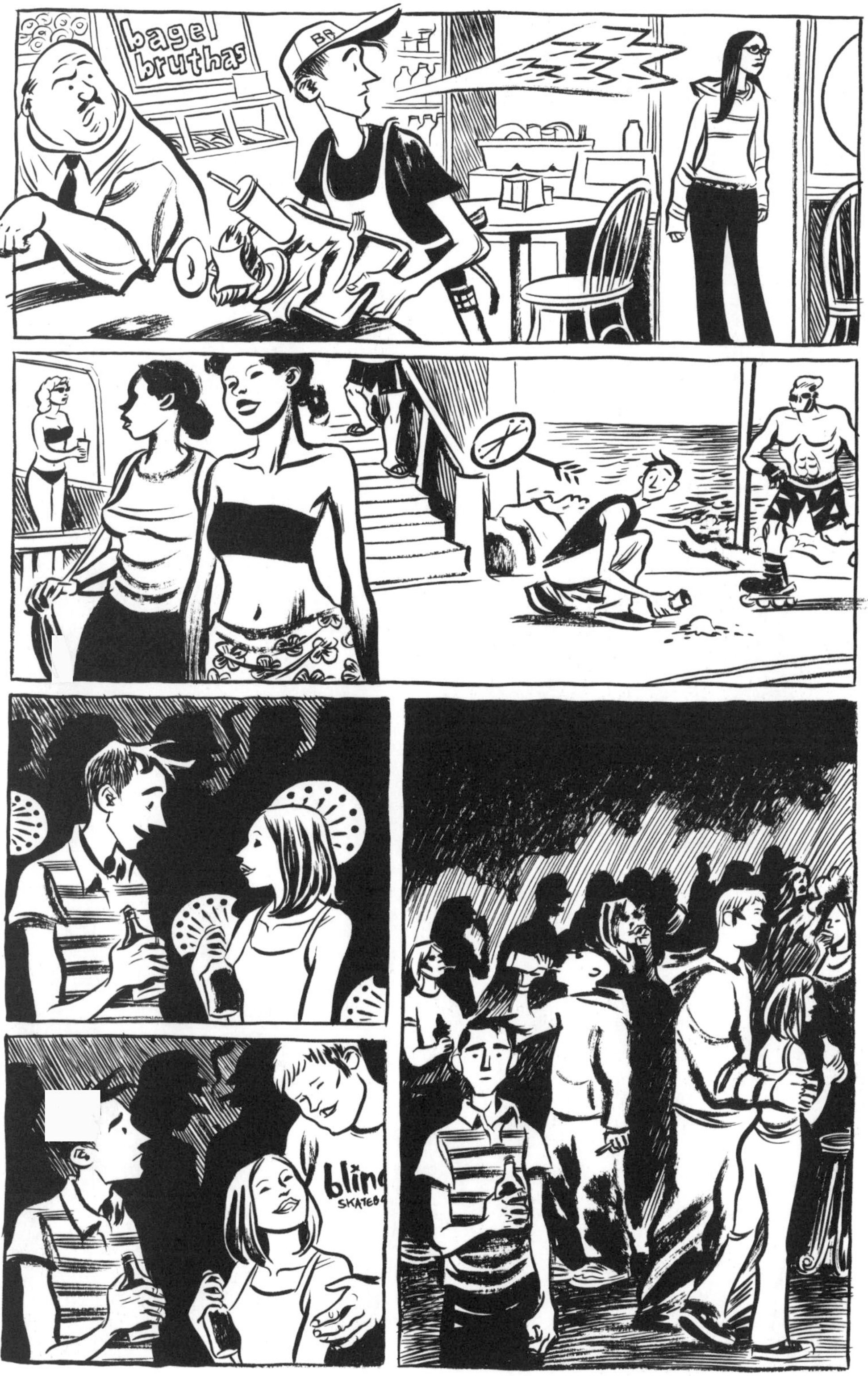
bagel bruthas
BR

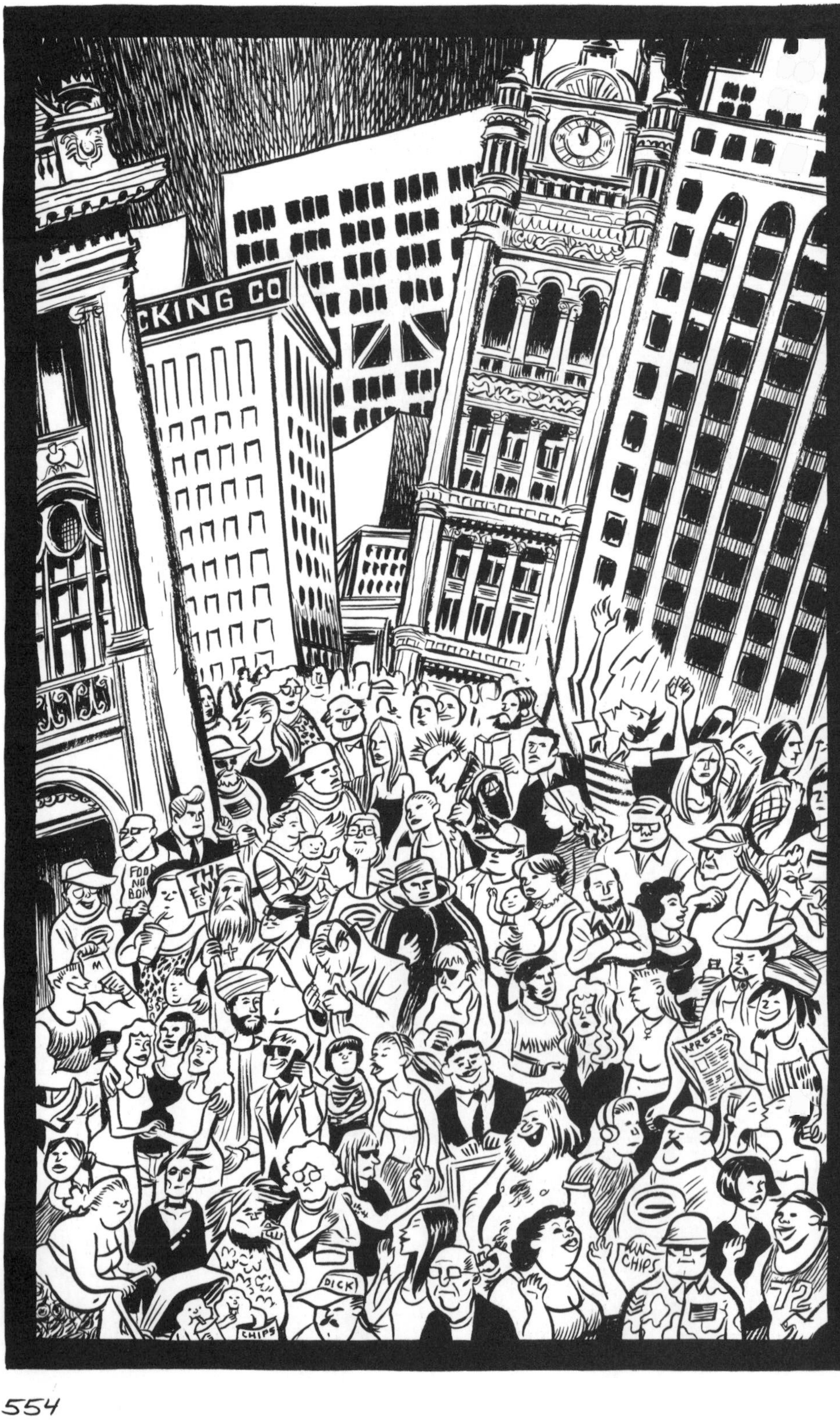
CKING CO
XPRESS
DICK
CHIPS
CHIPS
72

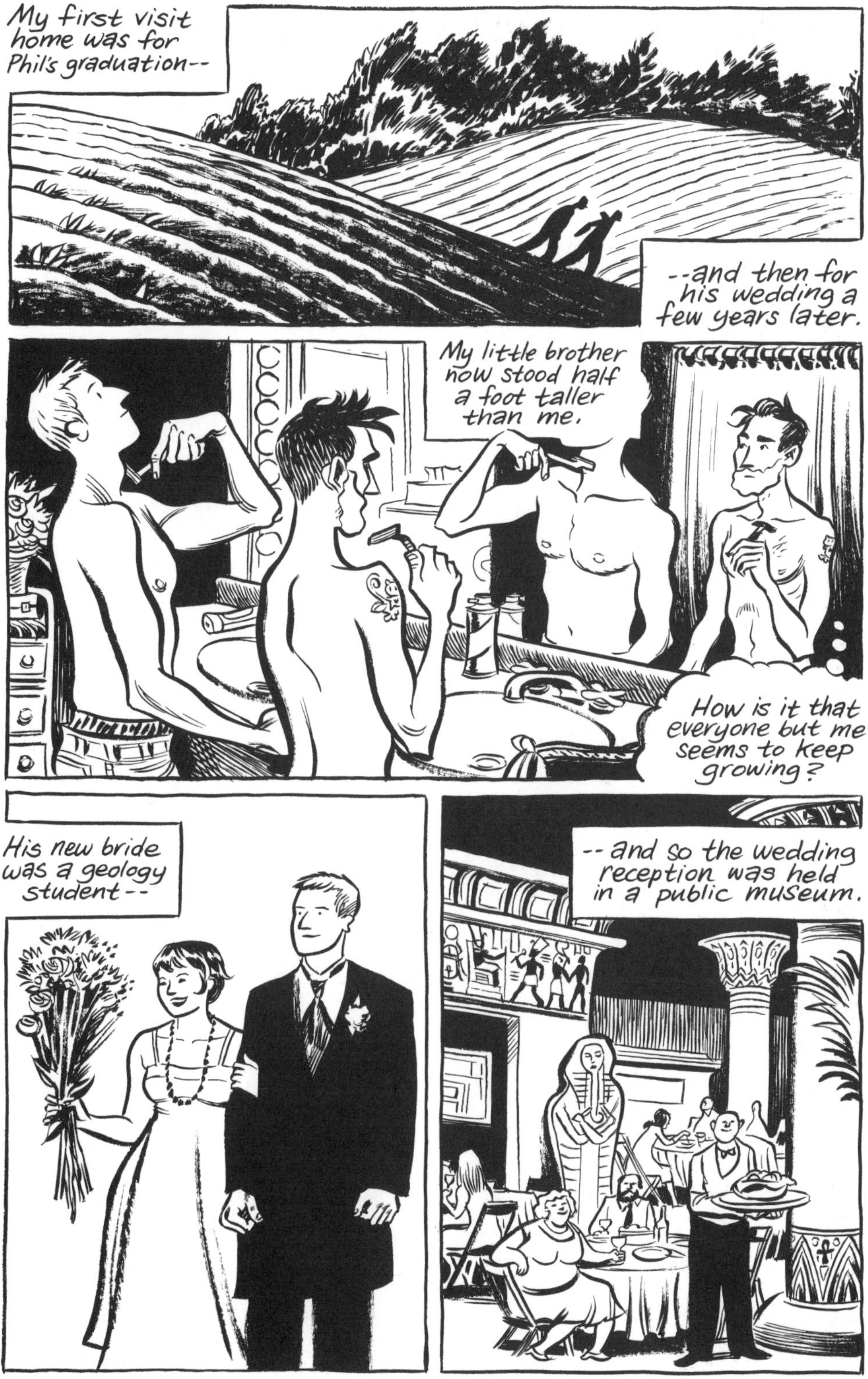
My first visit home was for Phil's graduation--
--and then for his wedding a few years later.
My little brother now stood half a foot taller than me.
How is it that everyone but me seems to keep growing?
His new bride was a geology student--
--and so the wedding reception was held in a public museum.

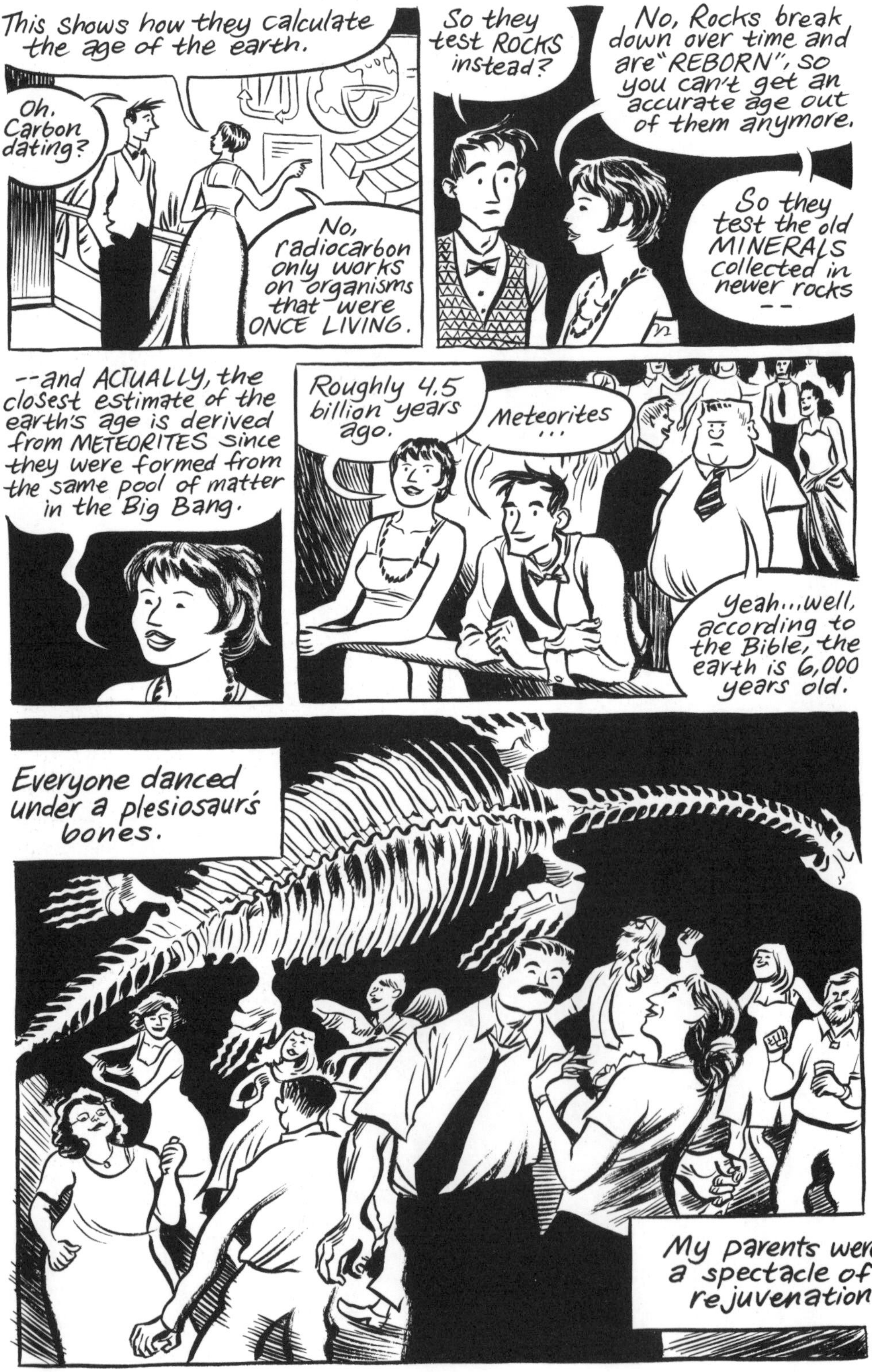
This shows how they calculate the age of the earth.
Oh. Carbon dating?
No, radiocarbon only works on organisms that were ONCE LIVING.
So they test ROCKS instead?
No, Rocks break down over time and are "REBORN", so you can't get an accurate age out of them anymore.
So they test the old MINERALS collected in newer rocks --
--and ACTUALLY, the closest estimate of the earth's age is derived from METEORITES since they were formed from the same pool of matter in the Big Bang.
Roughly 4.5 billion years ago.
Meteorites ...
Yeah...well, according to the Bible, the earth is 6,000 years old.
Everyone danced under a plesiosaur's bones.
My parents were a spectacle of rejuvenation.

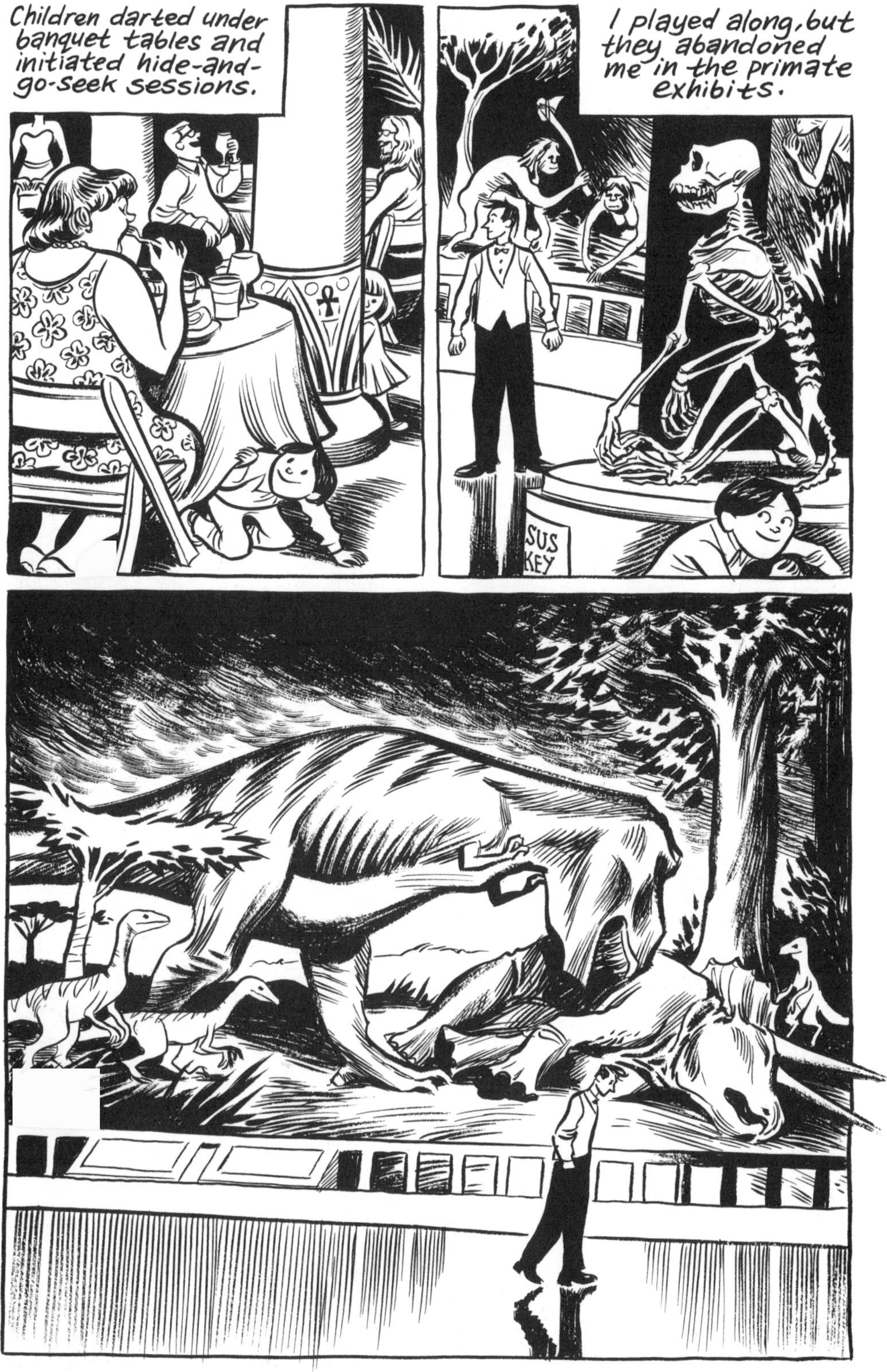

Children darted under banquet tables and initiated hide-and-go-seek sessions.
I played along, but they abandoned me in the primate exhibits.

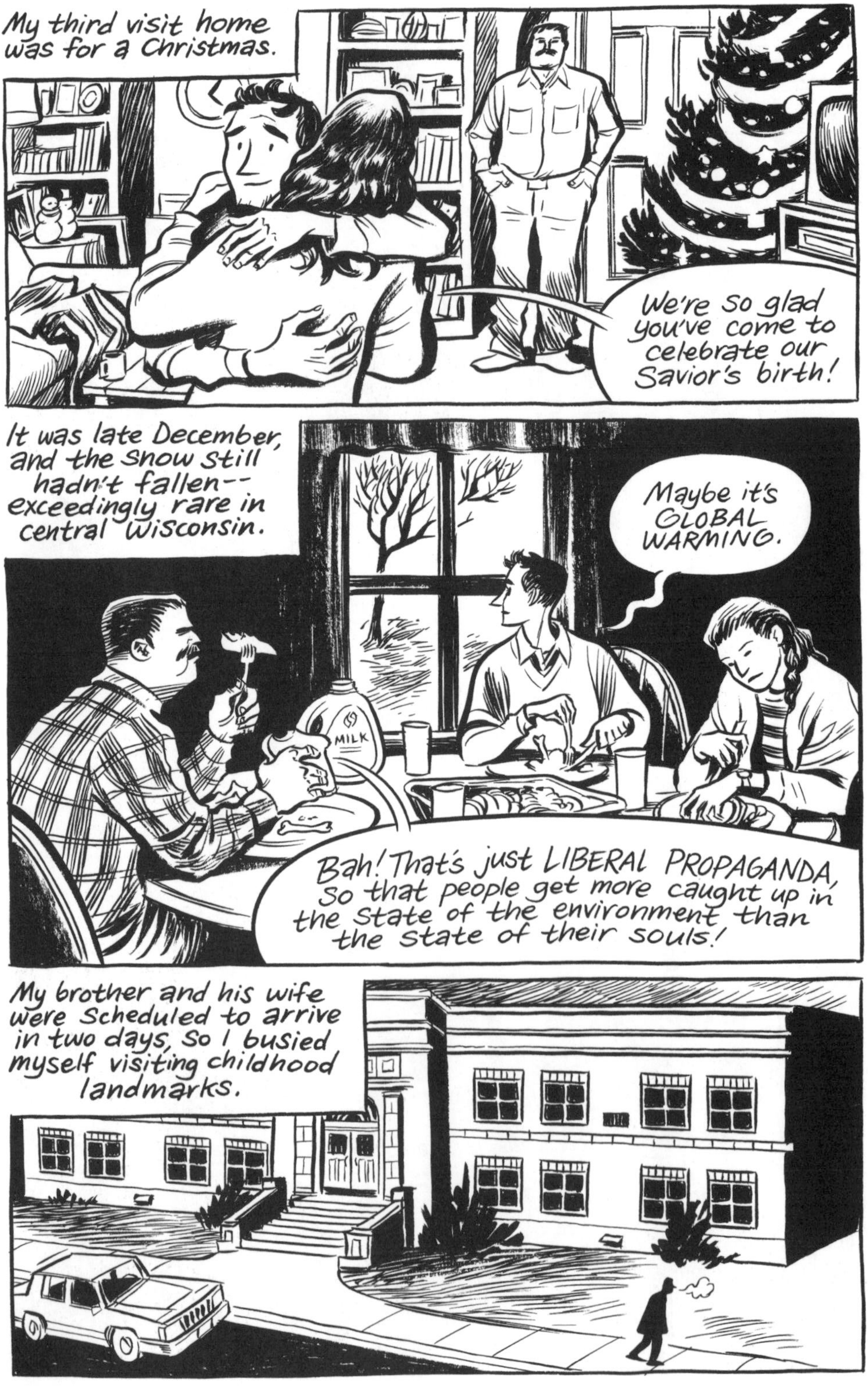
My third visit home was for a Christmas.
We're so glad you've come to celebrate our Savior's birth!
It was late December, and the snow still hadn't fallen-- exceedingly rare in central Wisconsin.
Maybe it's GLOBAL WARMING.
MILK
Bah! That's just LIBERAL PROPAGANDA, so that people get more caught up in the state of the environment than the state of their souls!
My brother and his wife were scheduled to arrive in two days, so I busied myself visiting childhood landmarks.

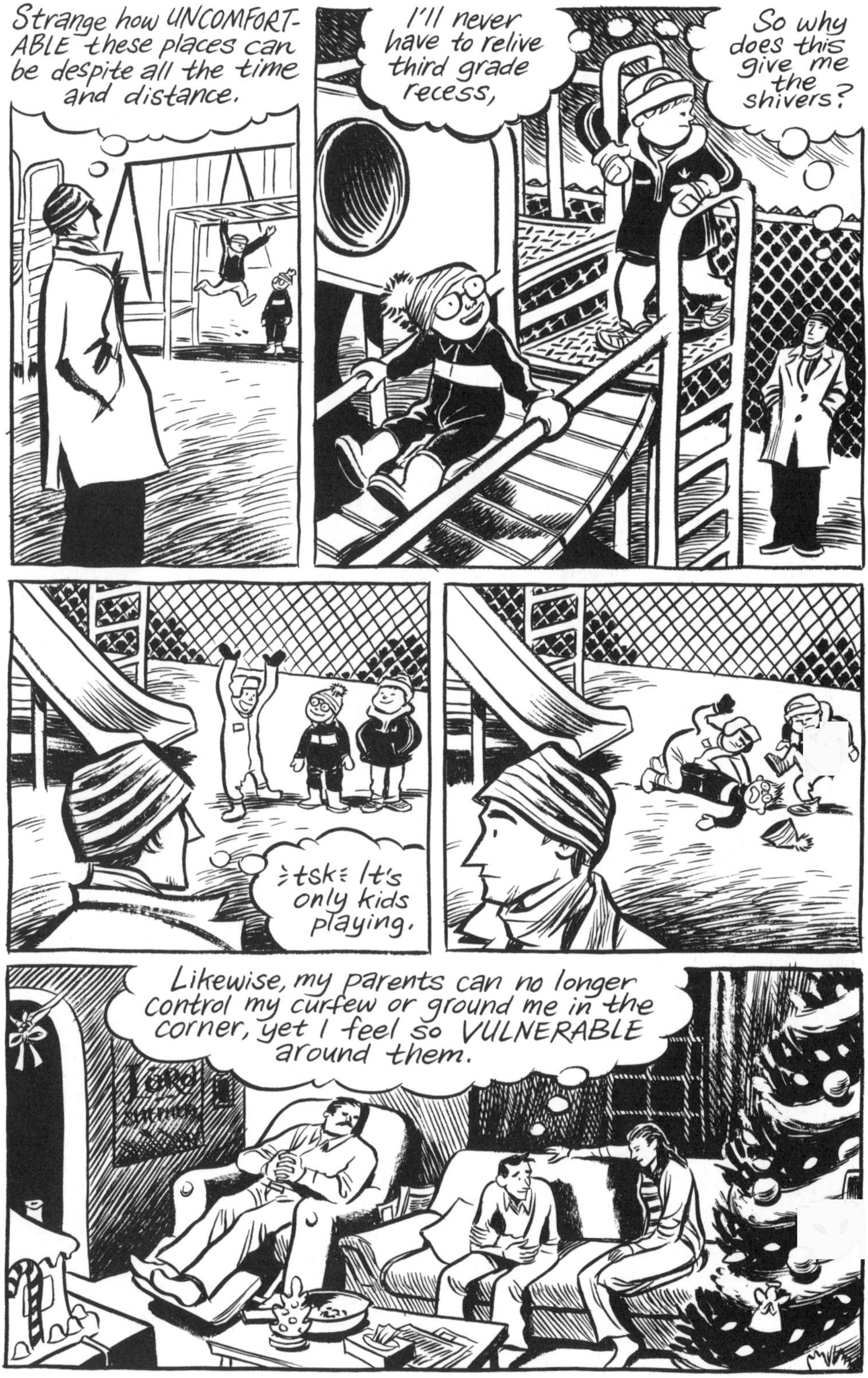
Strange how UNCOMFORTABLE these places can be despite all the time and distance.
I'll never have to relive third grade recess,
So why does this give me the shivers?
⩶tsk⩶ It's only kids playing.
Likewise, my parents can no longer control my curfew or ground me in the corner, yet I feel so VULNERABLE around them.

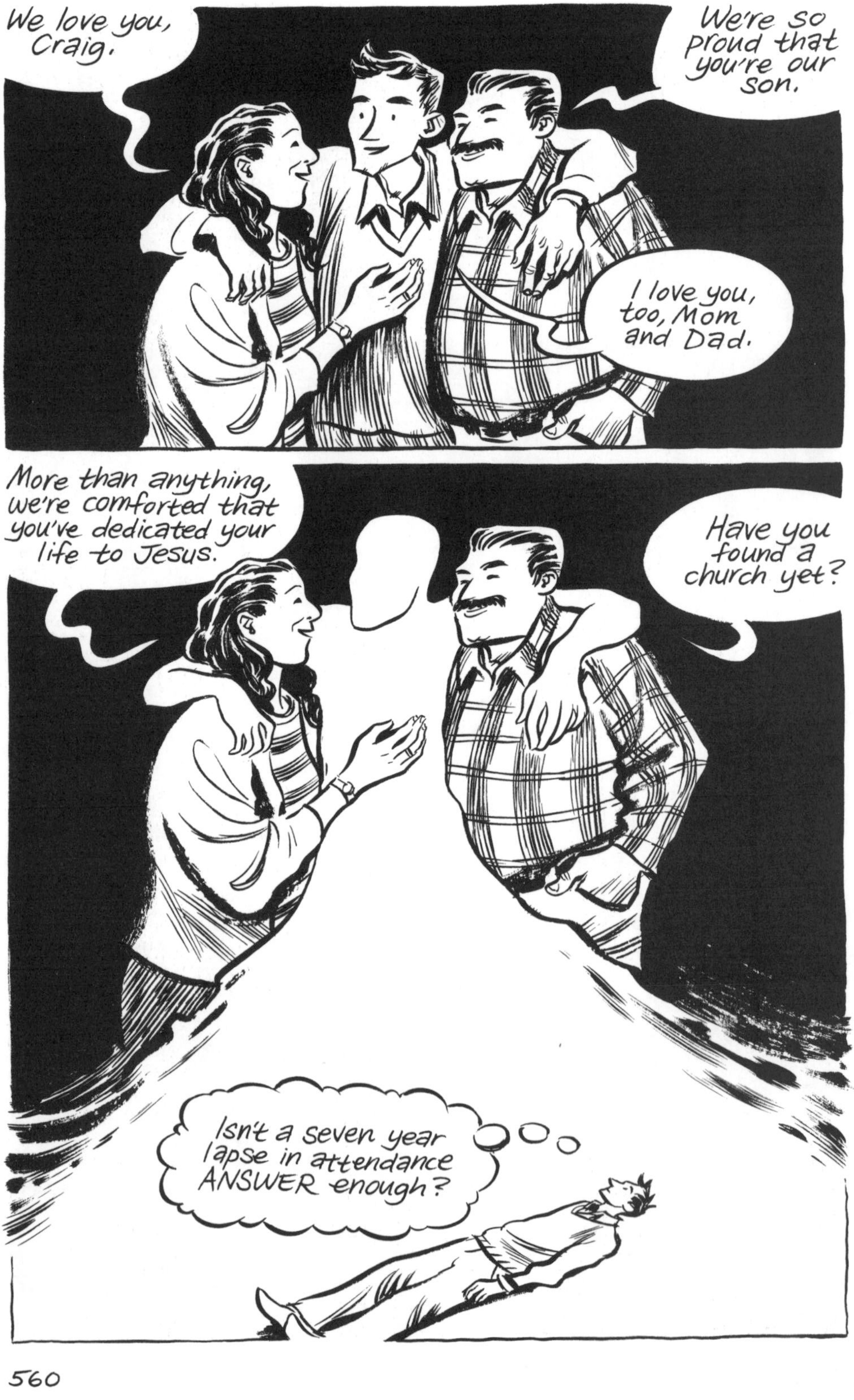
We love you, Craig.
We're so proud that you're our son.
I love you, too, Mom and Dad.
More than anything, we're comforted that you've dedicated your life to Jesus.
Have you found a church yet?
Isn't a seven year lapse in attendance ANSWER enough?

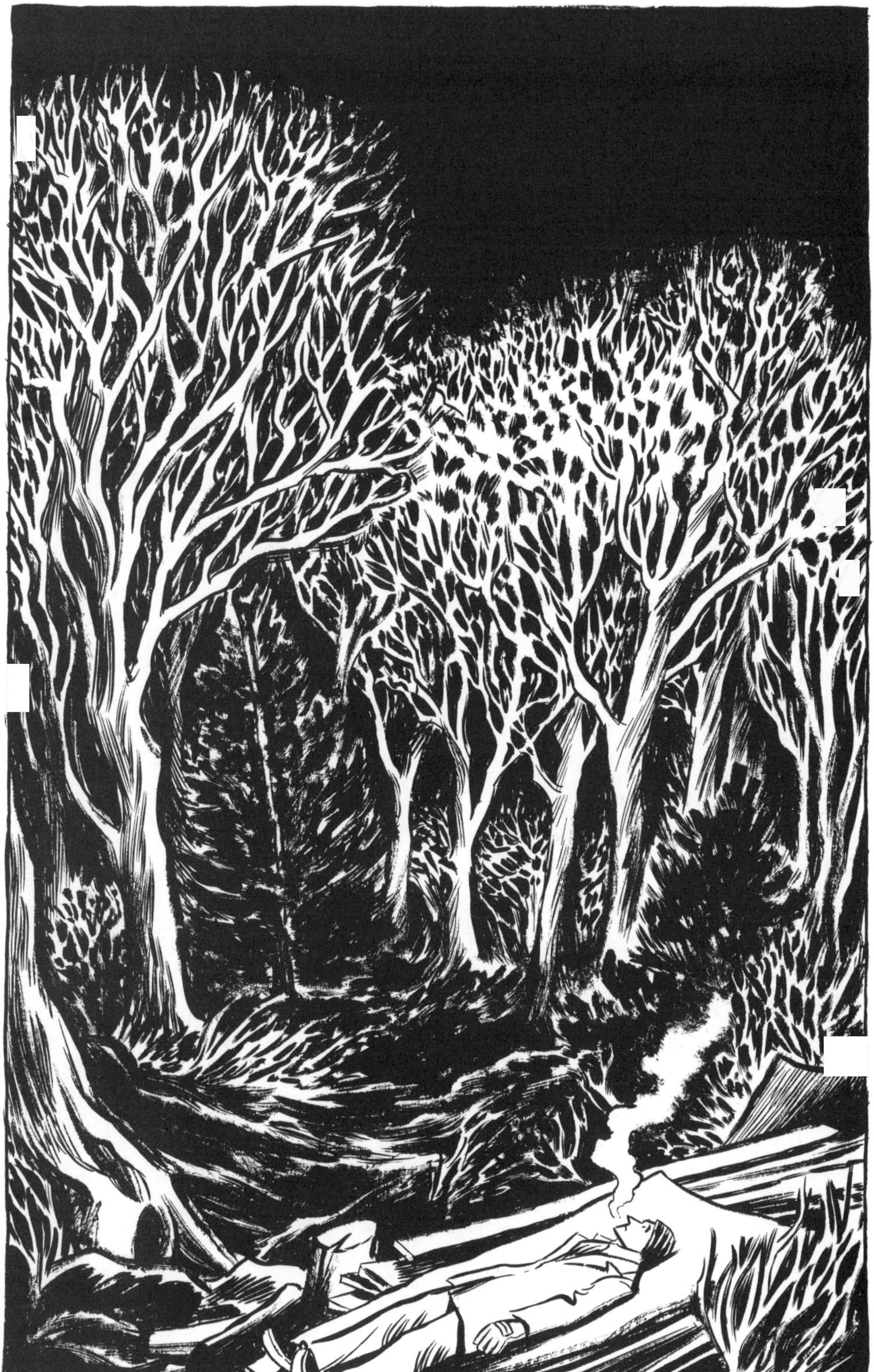

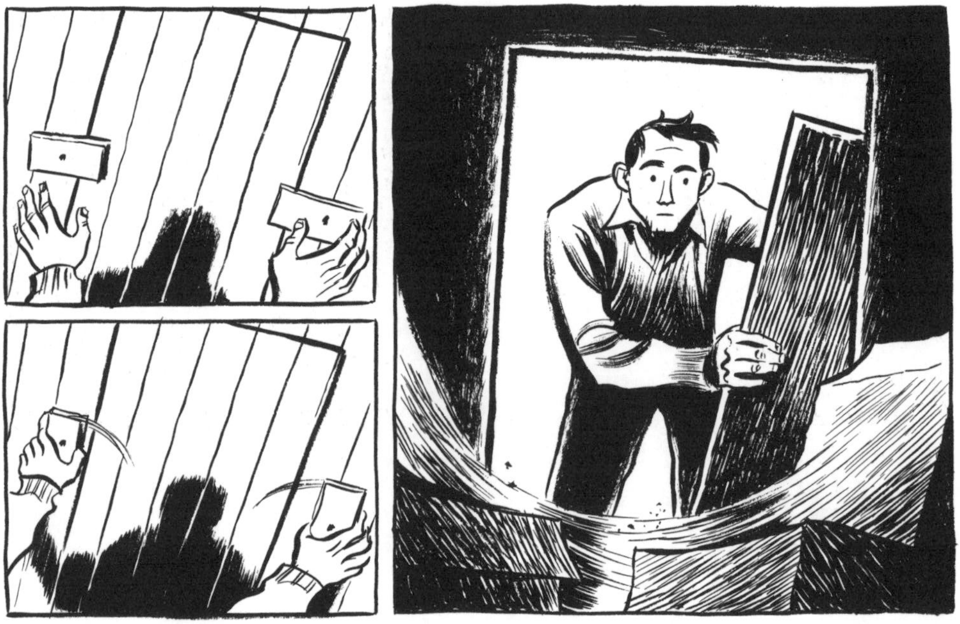

Once my parents retired
to bed, I explored.

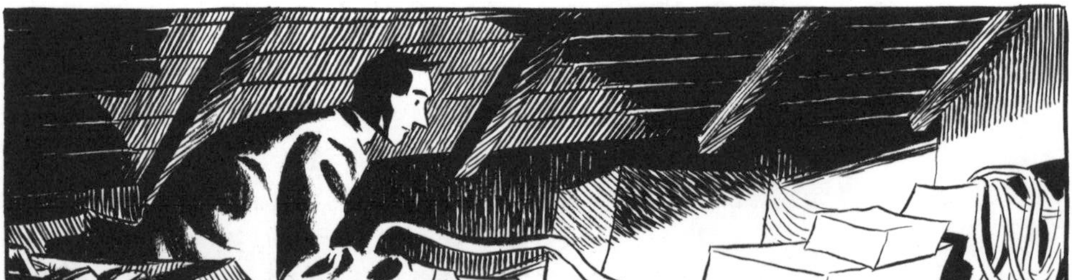

I couldn't
recall what
I was searching
for, but I knew
exactly when
I found it.

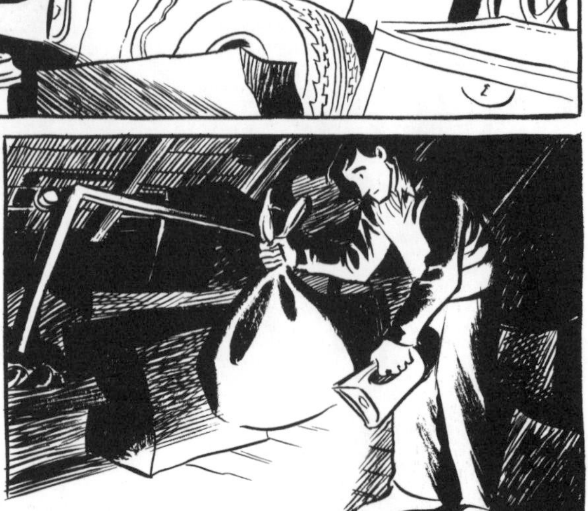

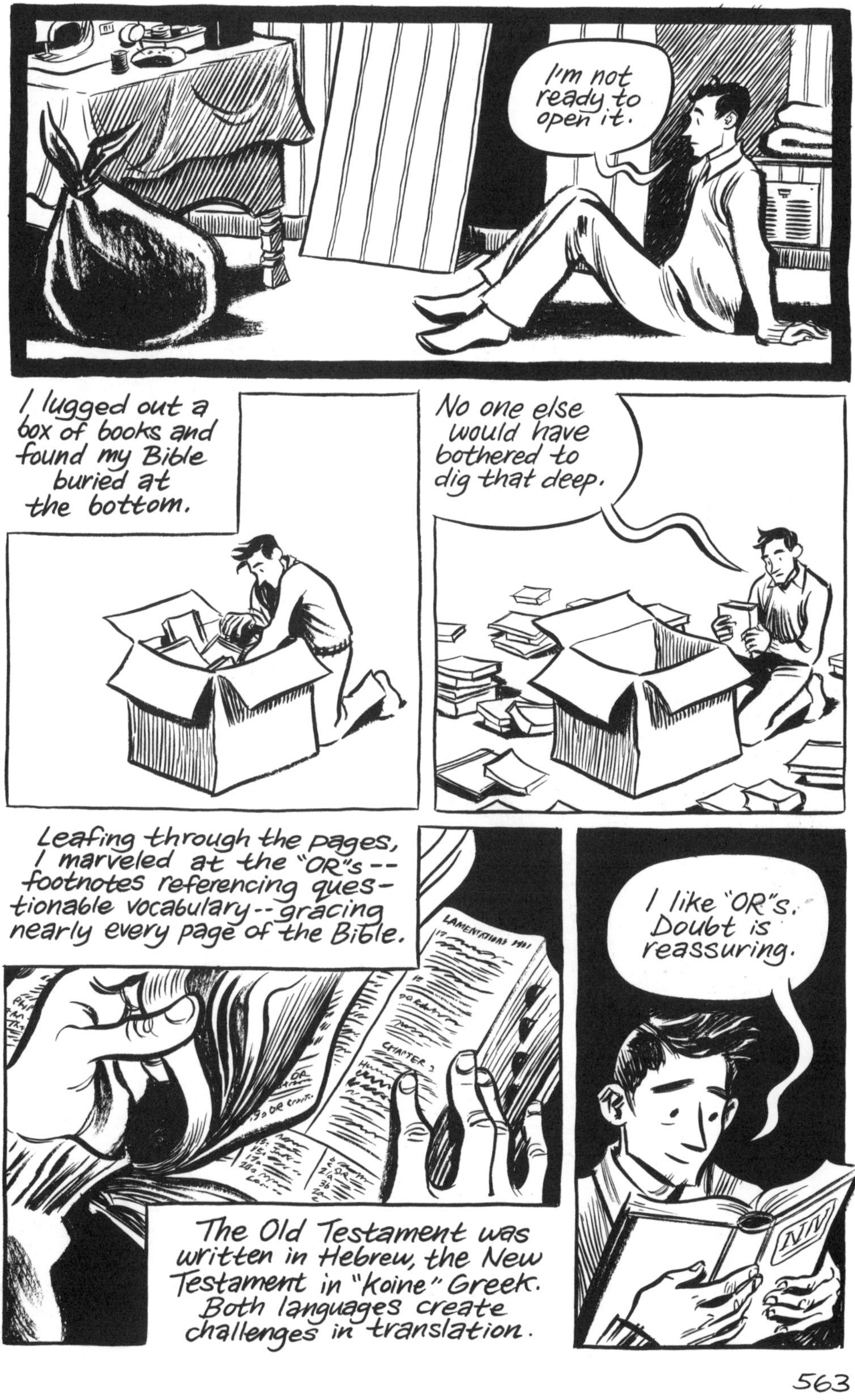
I'm not ready to open it.
I lugged out a box of books and found my Bible buried at the bottom.
No one else would have bothered to dig that deep.
Leafing through the pages, I marveled at the "OR"s -- footnotes referencing questionable vocabulary -- gracing nearly every page of the Bible.
I like "OR"s. Doubt is reassuring.
The Old Testament was written in Hebrew, the New Testament in "koine" Greek. Both languages create challenges in translation.
NIV

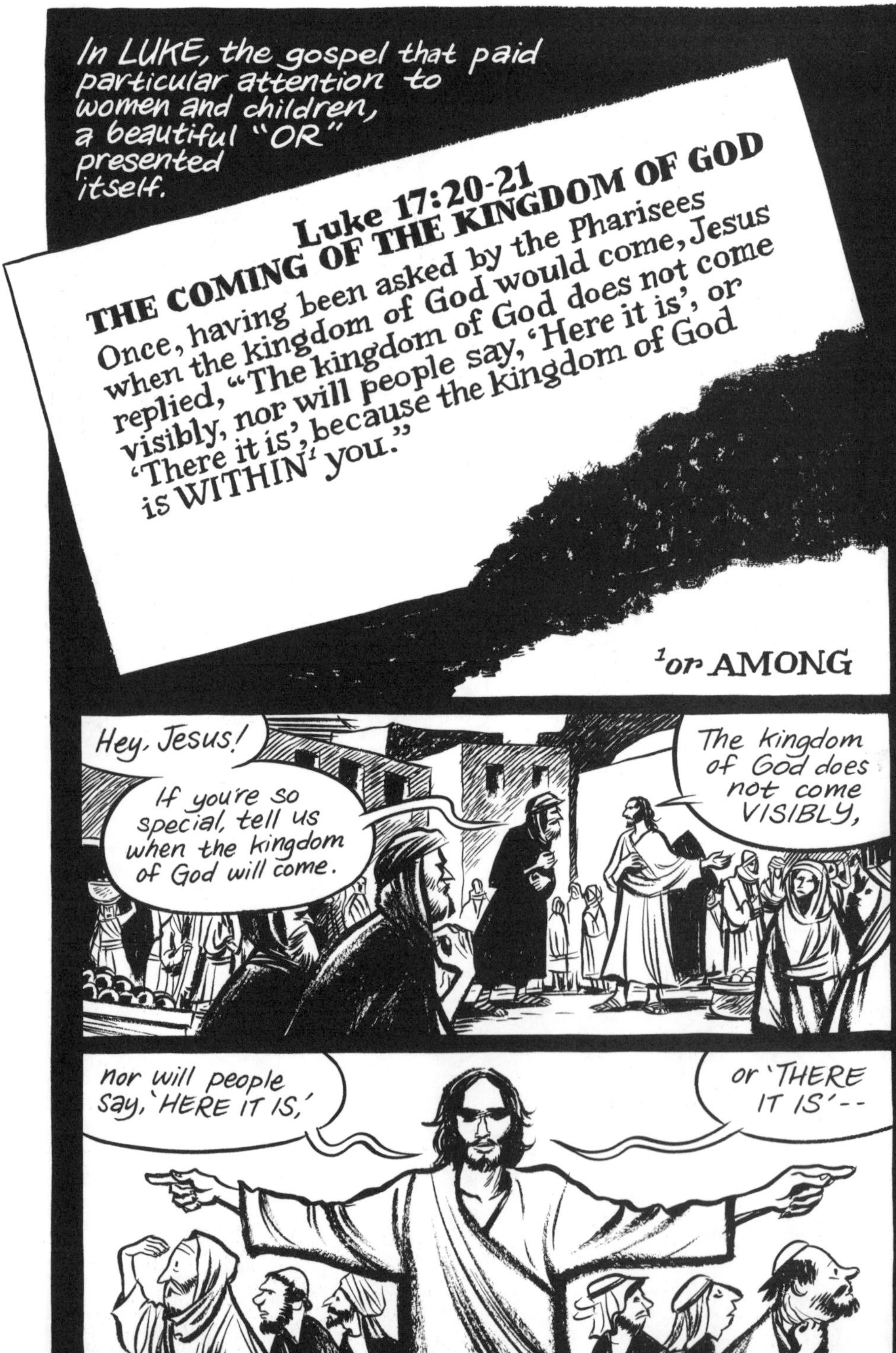
In LUKE, the gospel that paid particular attention to women and children, a beautiful "OR" presented itself.
Luke 17:20-21
THE COMING OF THE KINGDOM OF GOD
Once, having been asked by the Pharisees when the kingdom of God would come, Jesus replied, "The kingdom of God does not come visibly, nor will people say, 'Here it is', or 'There it is', because the Kingdom of God is WITHIN[1] you."
[1]or AMONG
Hey, Jesus!
If you're so special, tell us when the kingdom of God will come.
The kingdom of God does not come VISIBLY,
nor will people say, 'HERE IT IS,'
or 'THERE IT IS'--

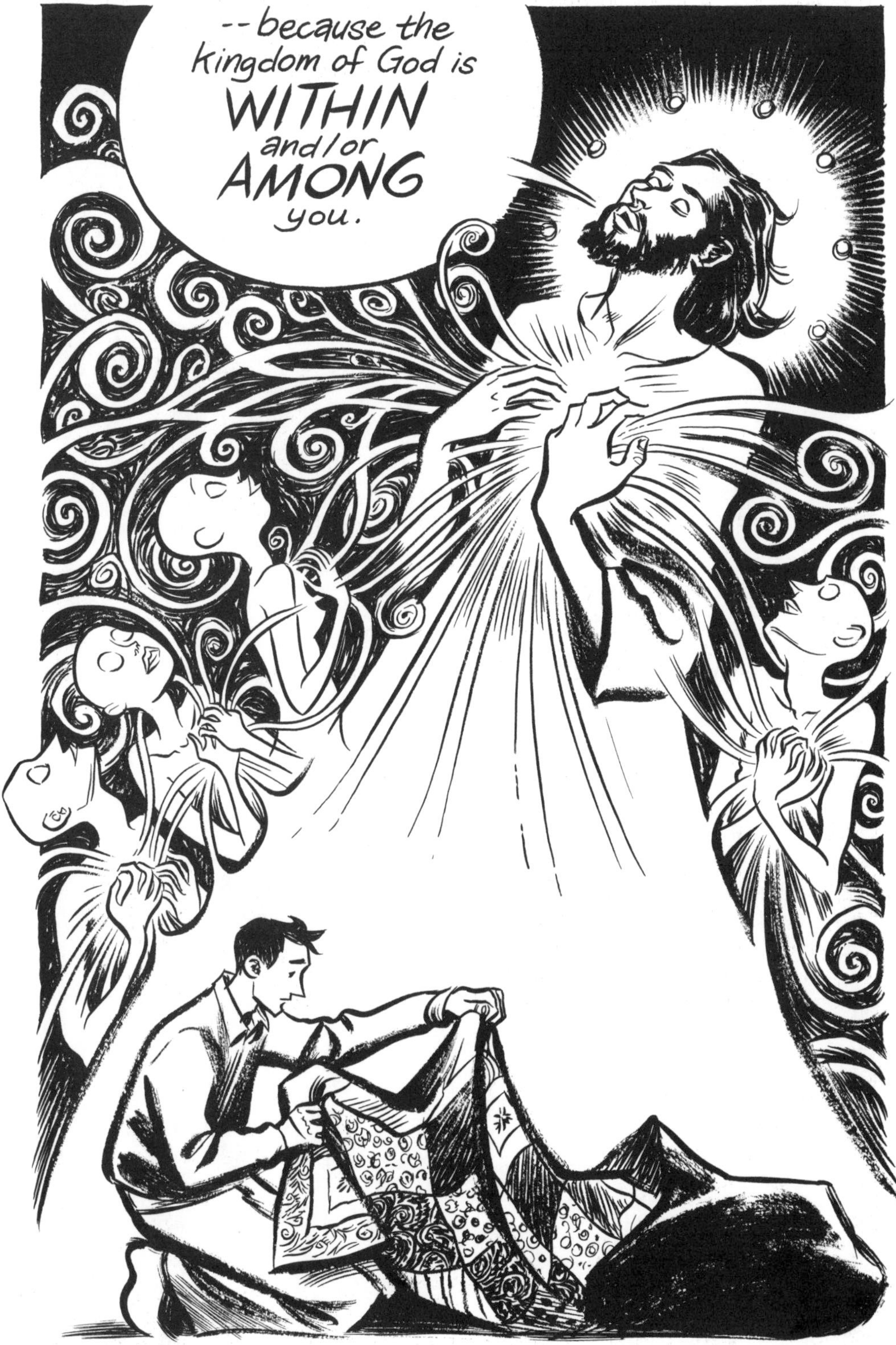
--because the kingdom of God is WITHIN and/or AMONG you.

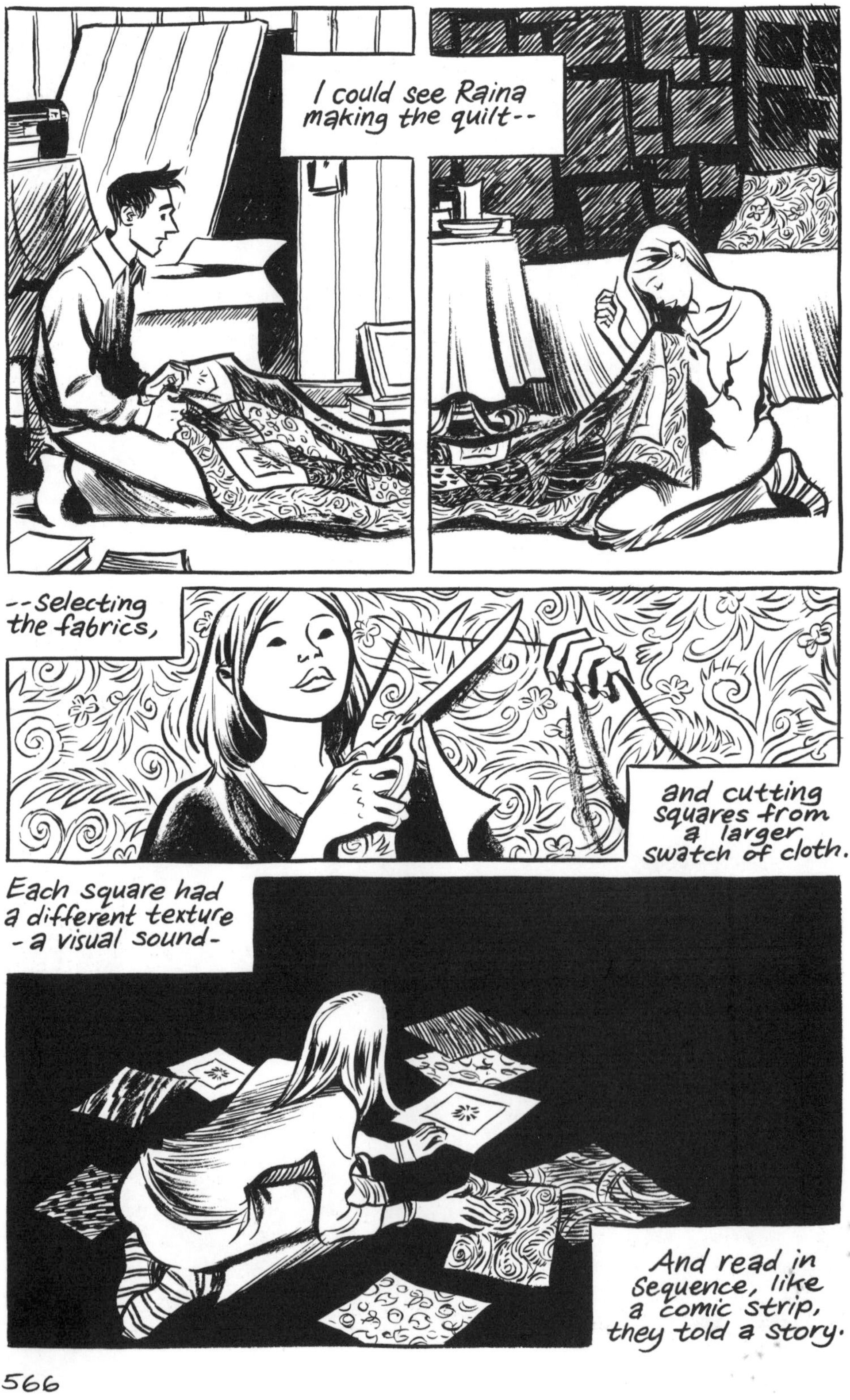
I could see Raina making the quilt--
--selecting the fabrics,
and cutting squares from a larger swatch of cloth.
Each square had a different texture -a visual sound-
And read in sequence, like a comic strip, they told a story.

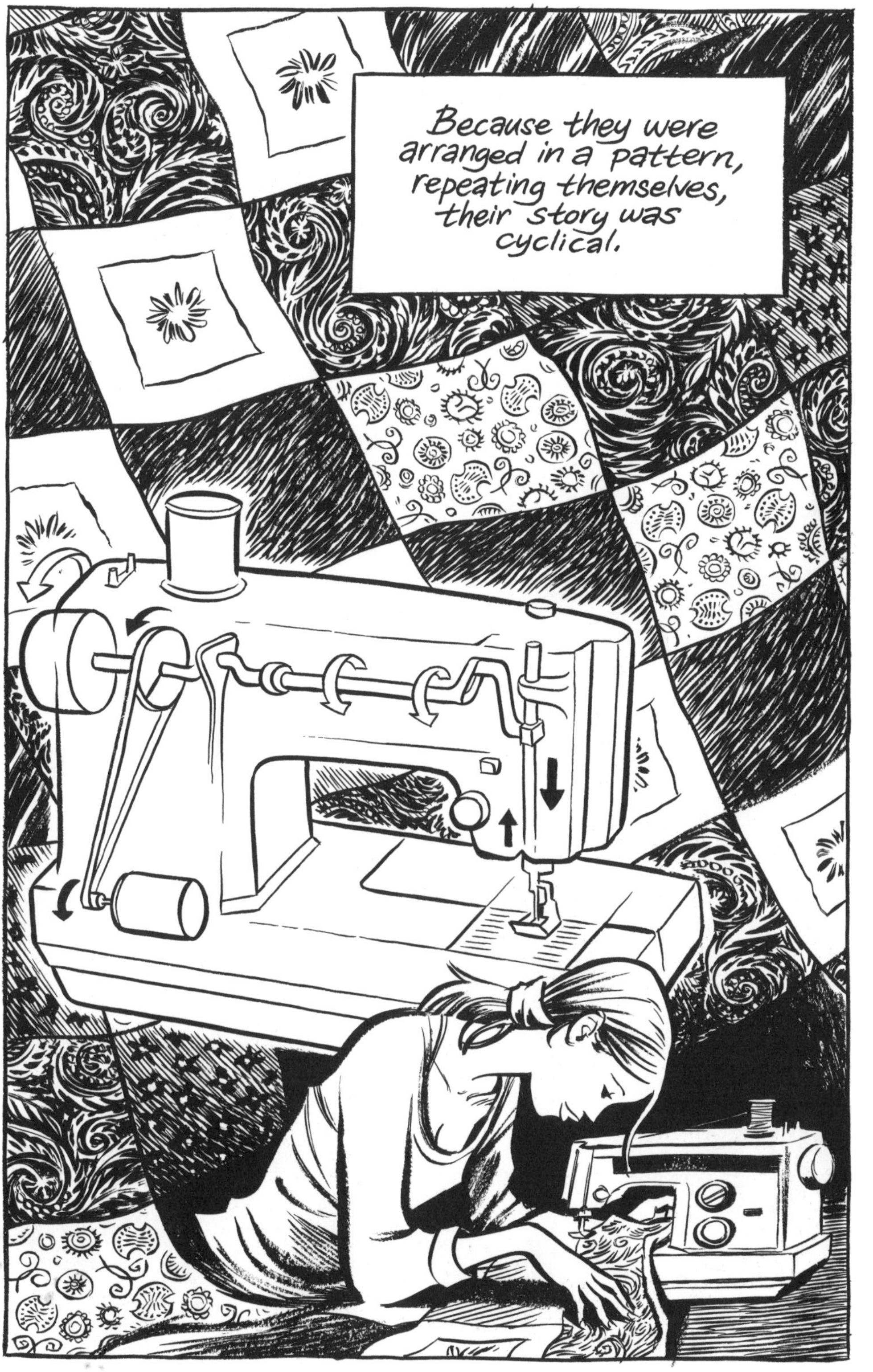
Because they were arranged in a pattern, repeating themselves, their story was cyclical.

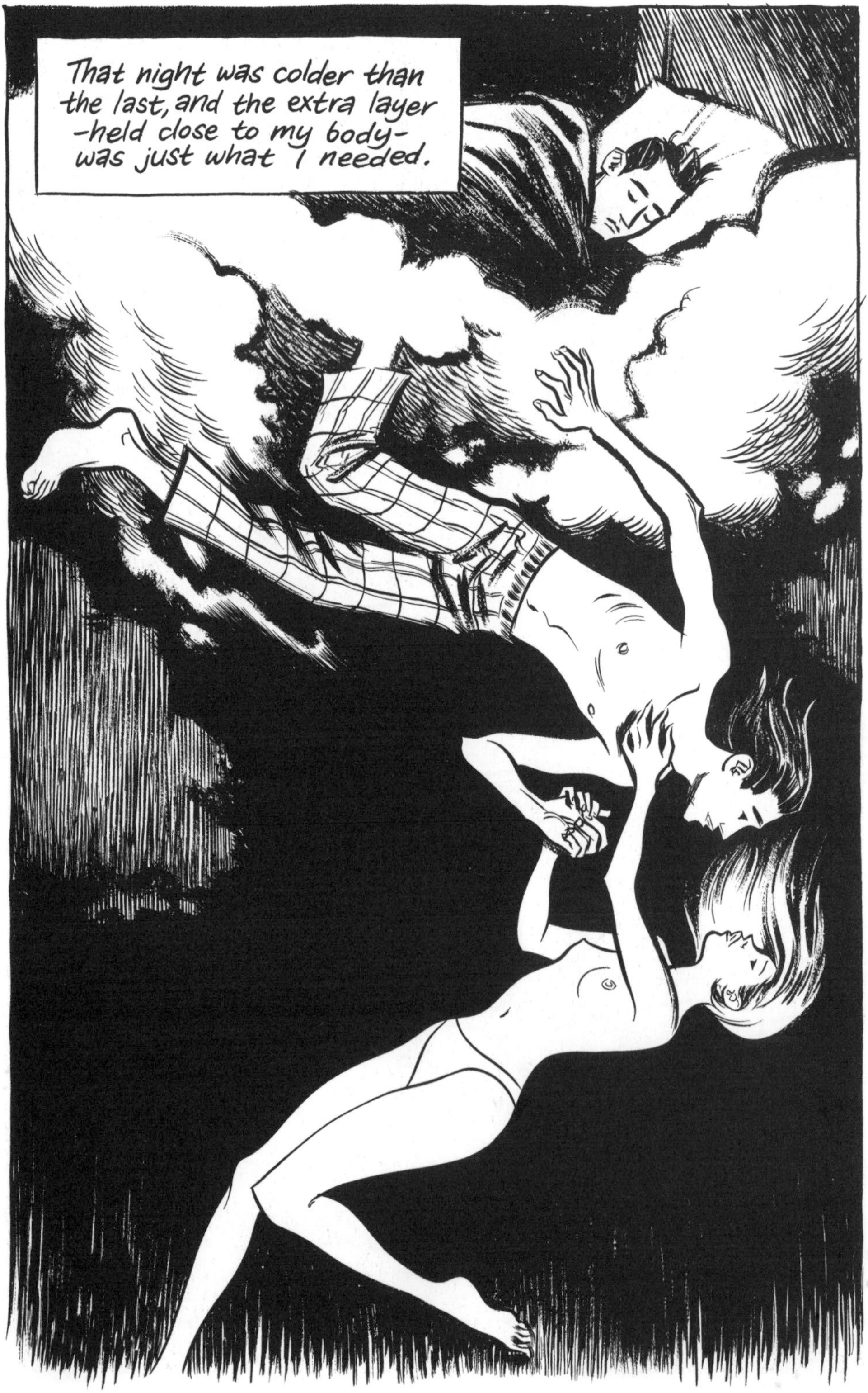
That night was colder than the last, and the extra layer -held close to my body- was just what I needed.

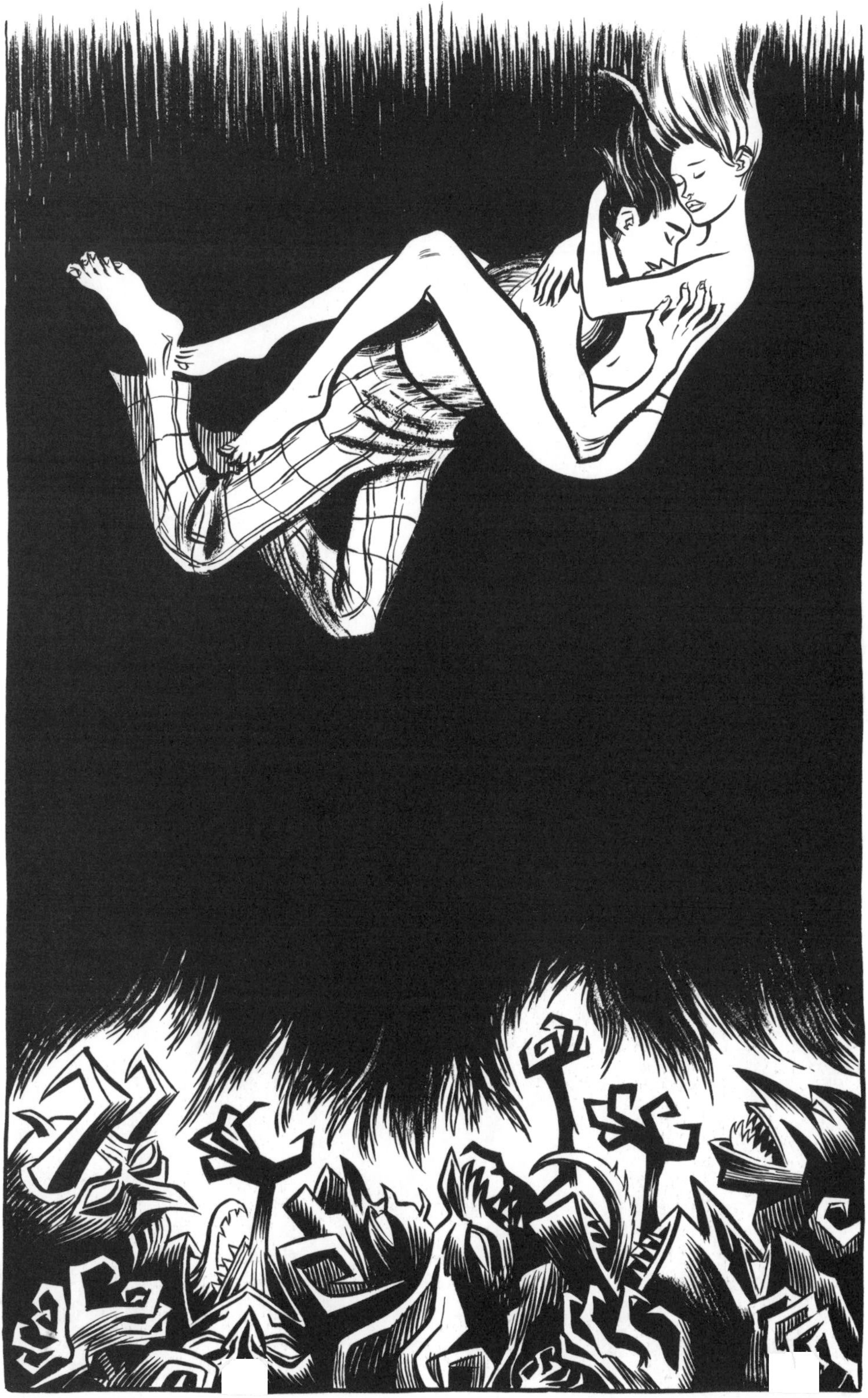

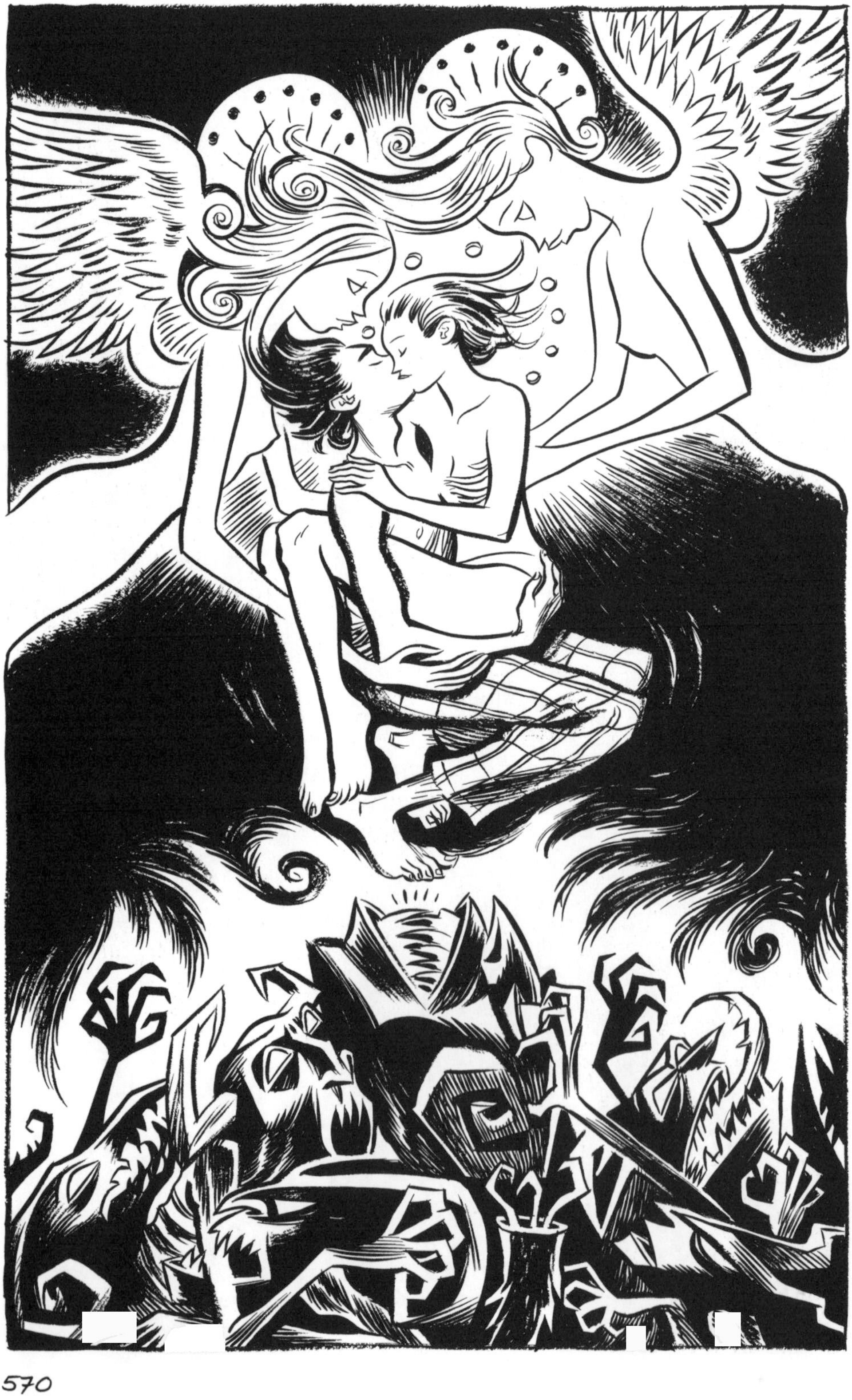

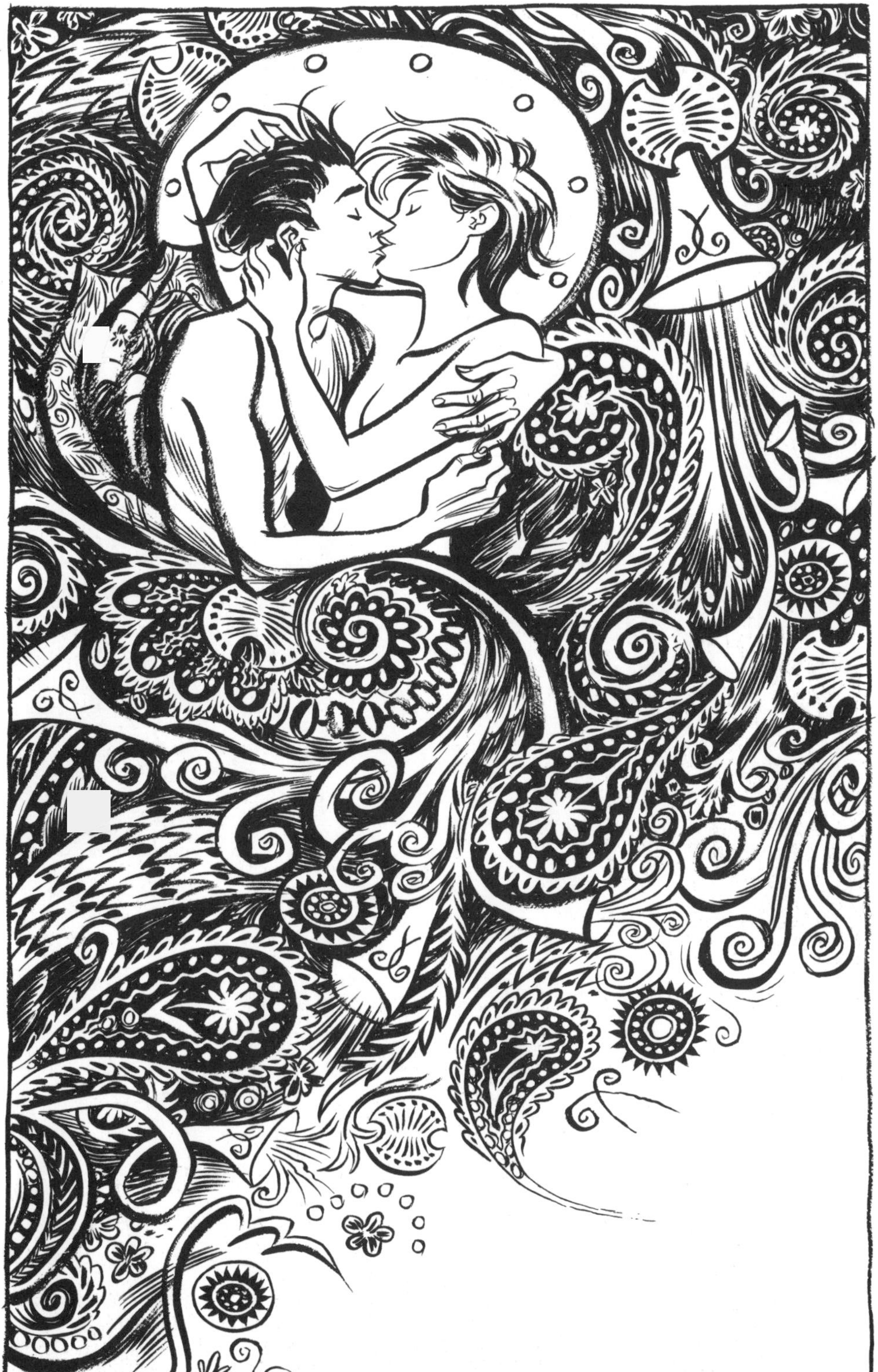

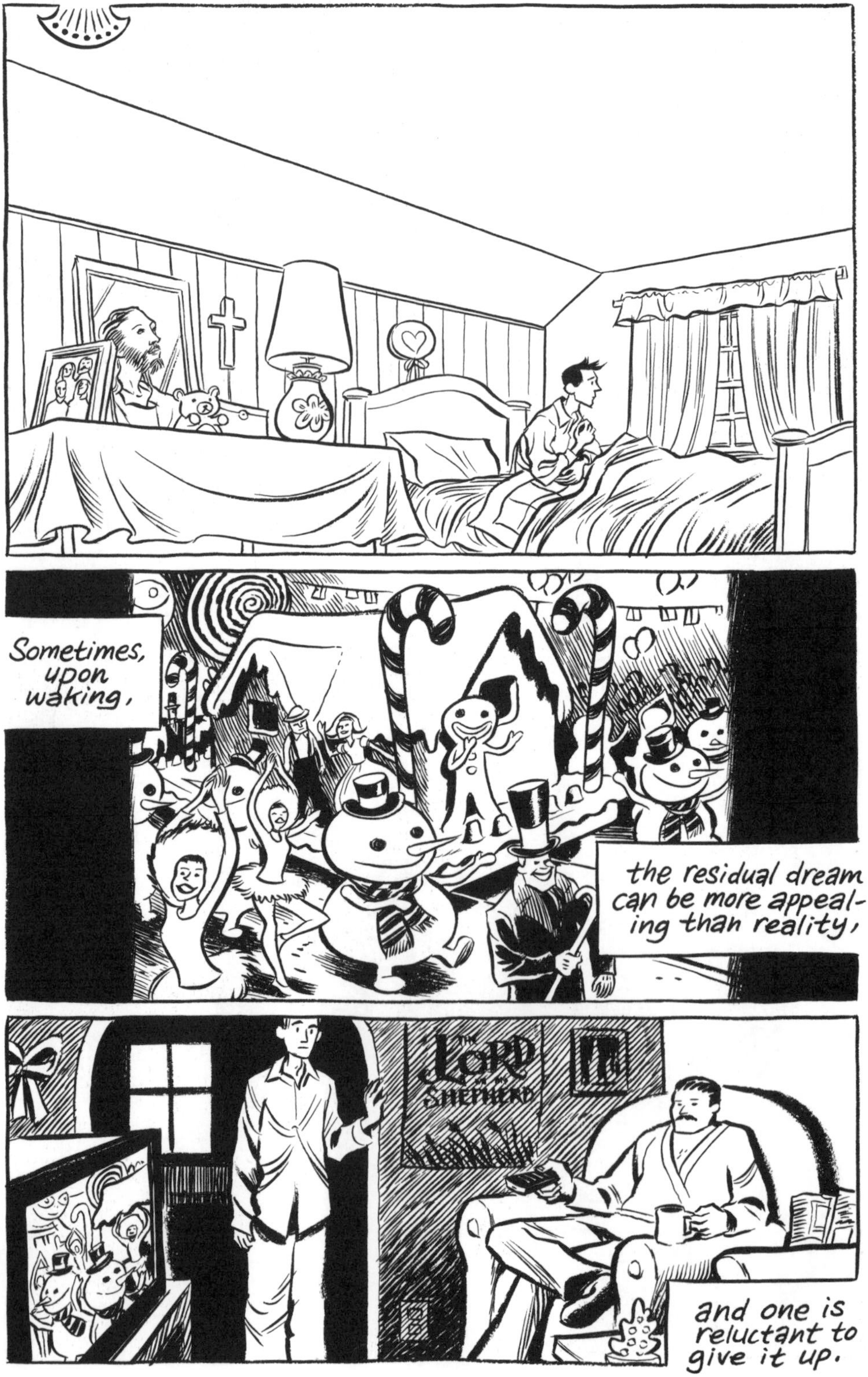
Sometimes, upon waking,
the residual dream can be more appealing than reality,
THE LORD
SHEPHERD
and one is reluctant to give it up.

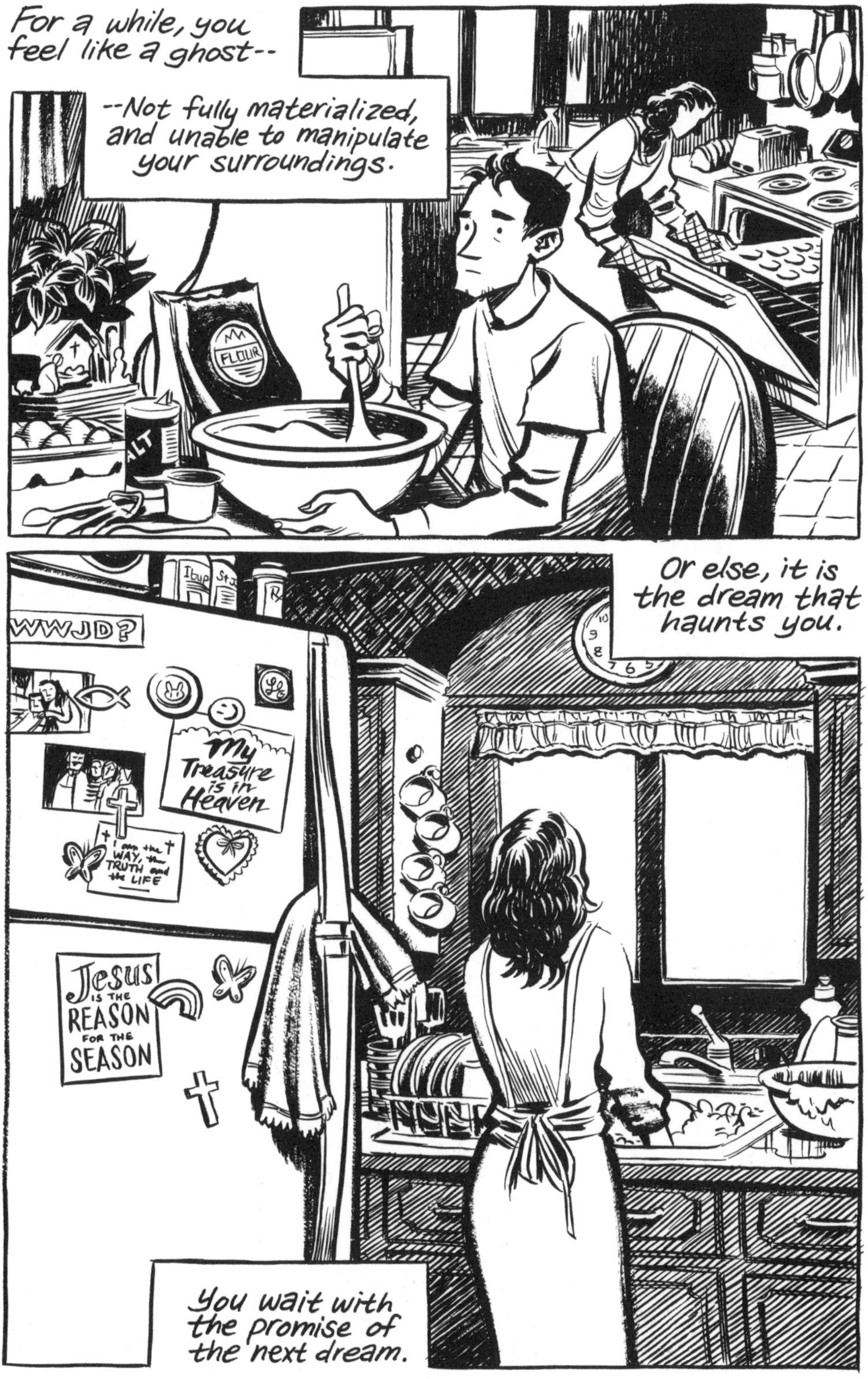
For a while, you feel like a ghost--
--Not fully materialized, and unable to manipulate your surroundings.
FLOUR
Or else, it is the dream that haunts you.
WWJD?
My Treasure is in Heaven
I am the WAY, the TRUTH and the LIFE
Jesus is the REASON for the SEASON
You wait with the promise of the next dream.

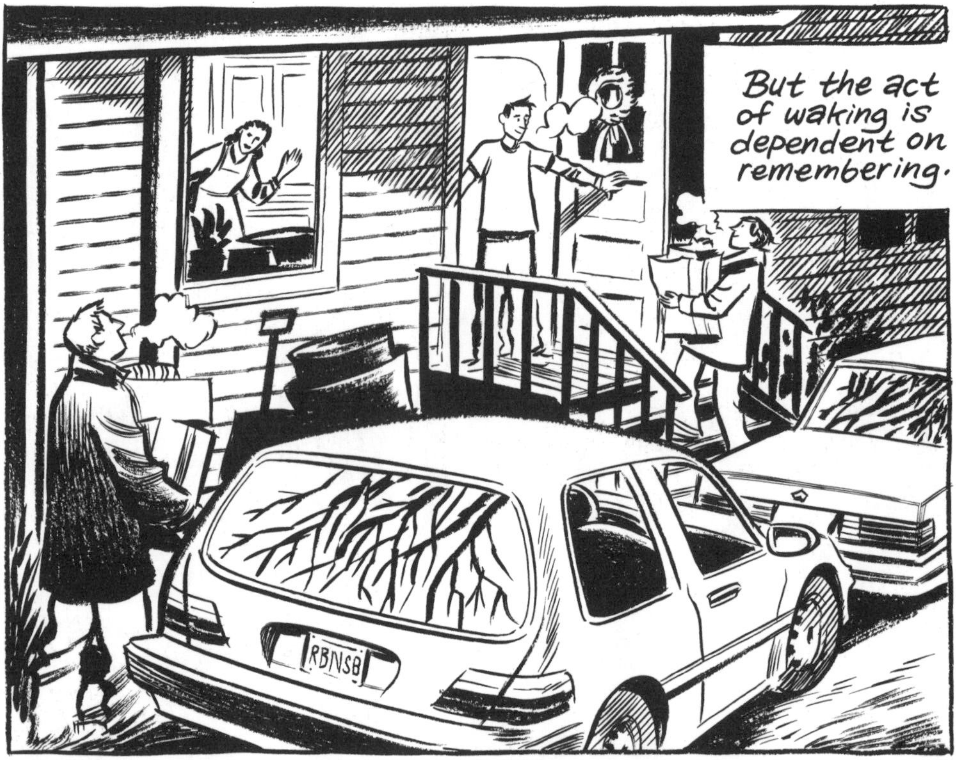
But the act of waking is dependent on remembering.
RBNSB

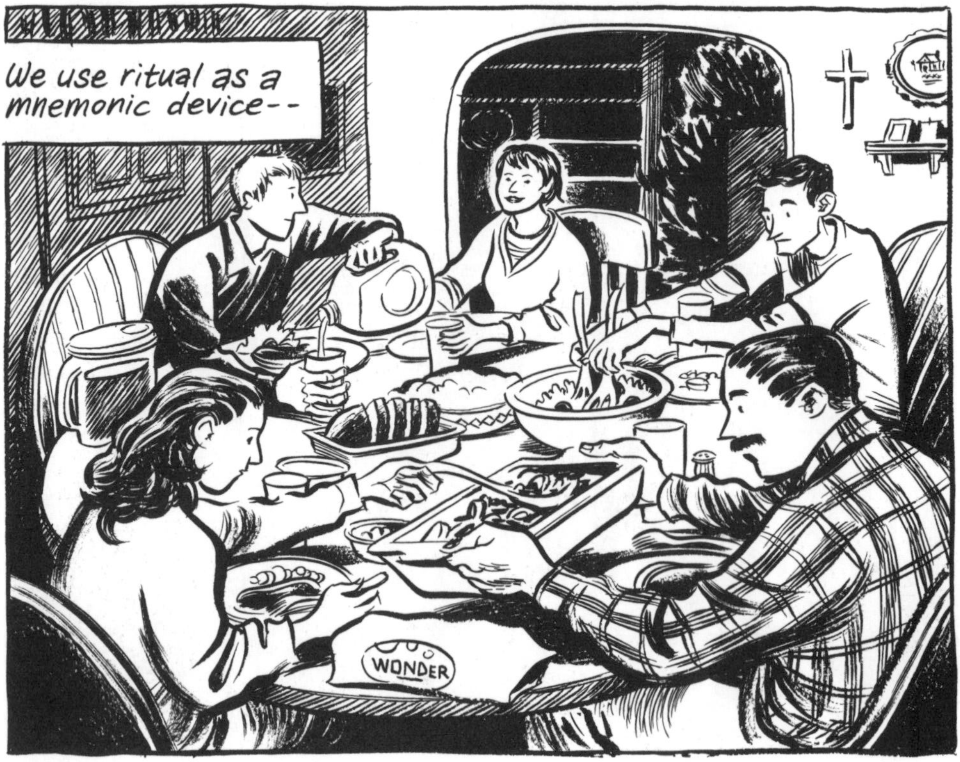
We use ritual as a mnemonic device--
WONDER

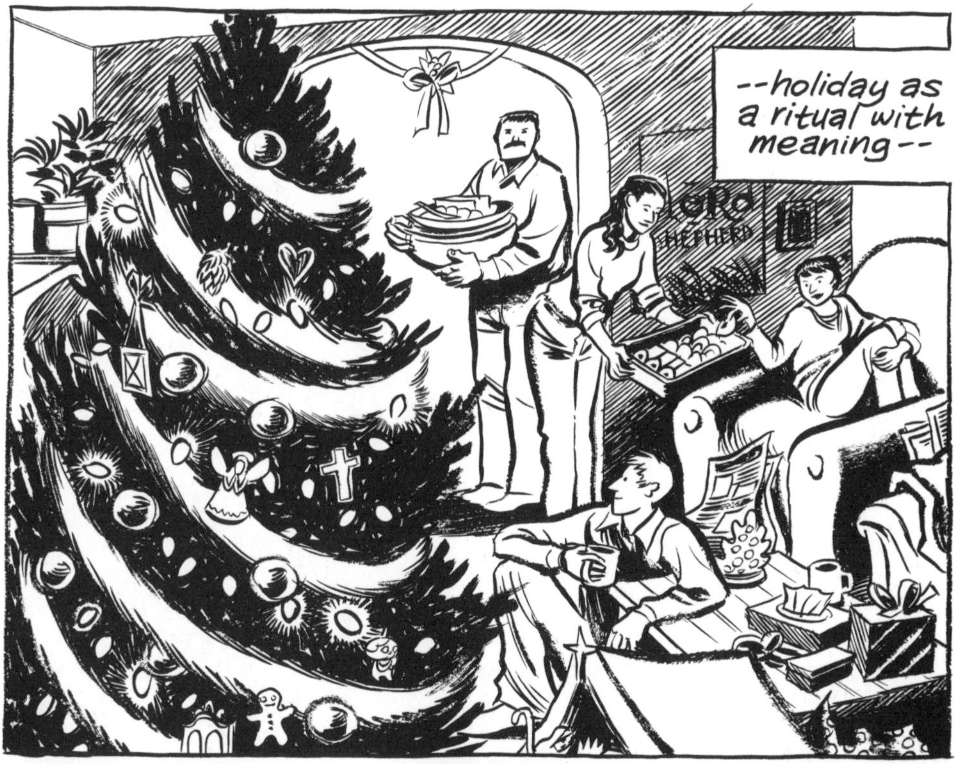
--holiday as a ritual with meaning--

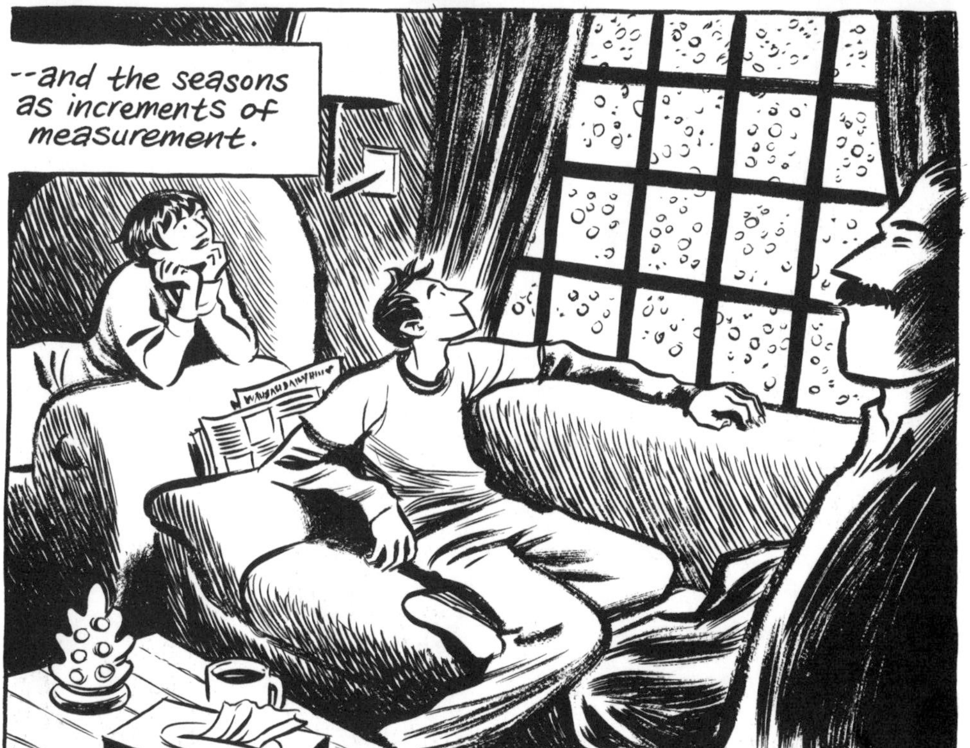
--and the seasons as increments of measurement.

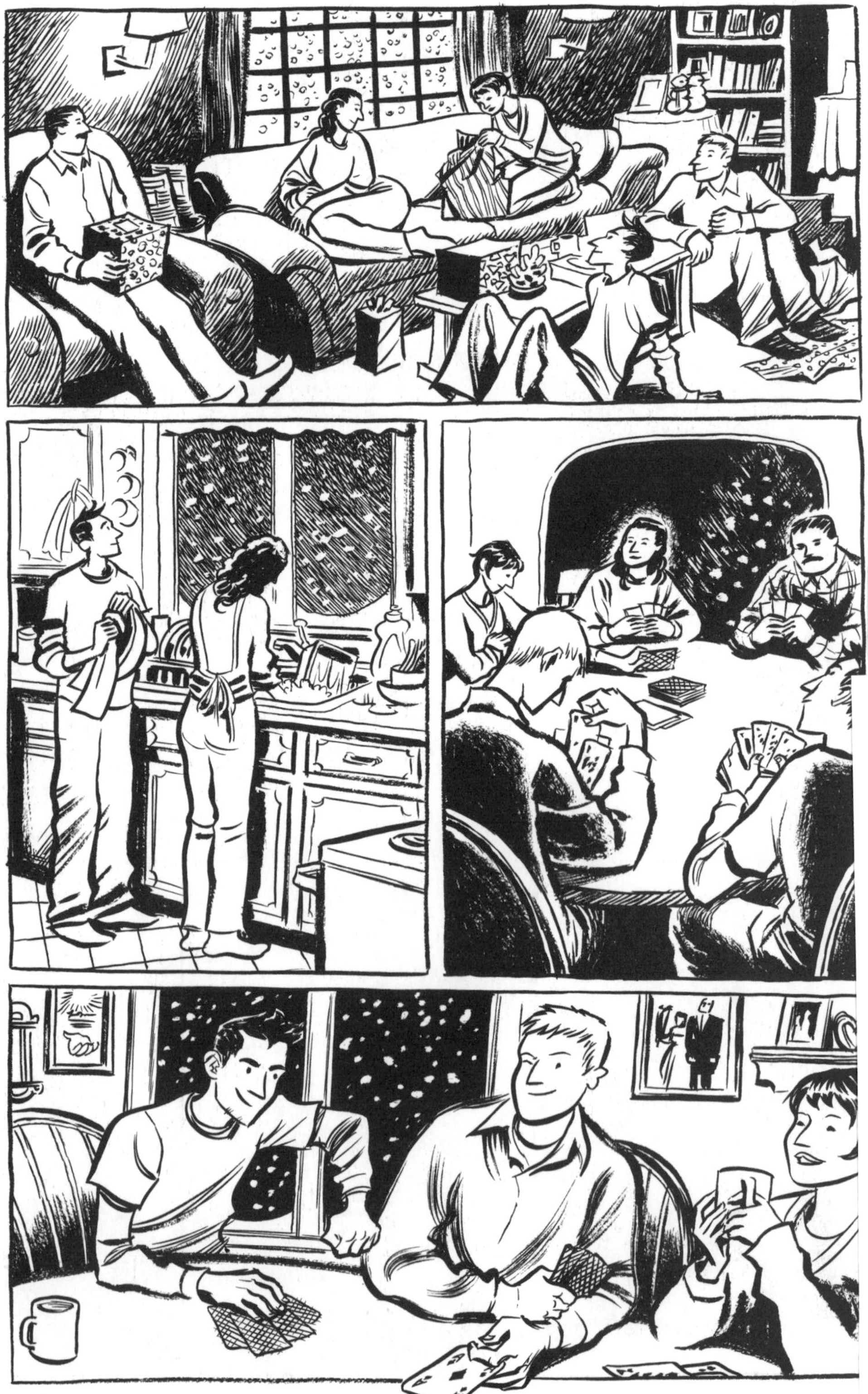

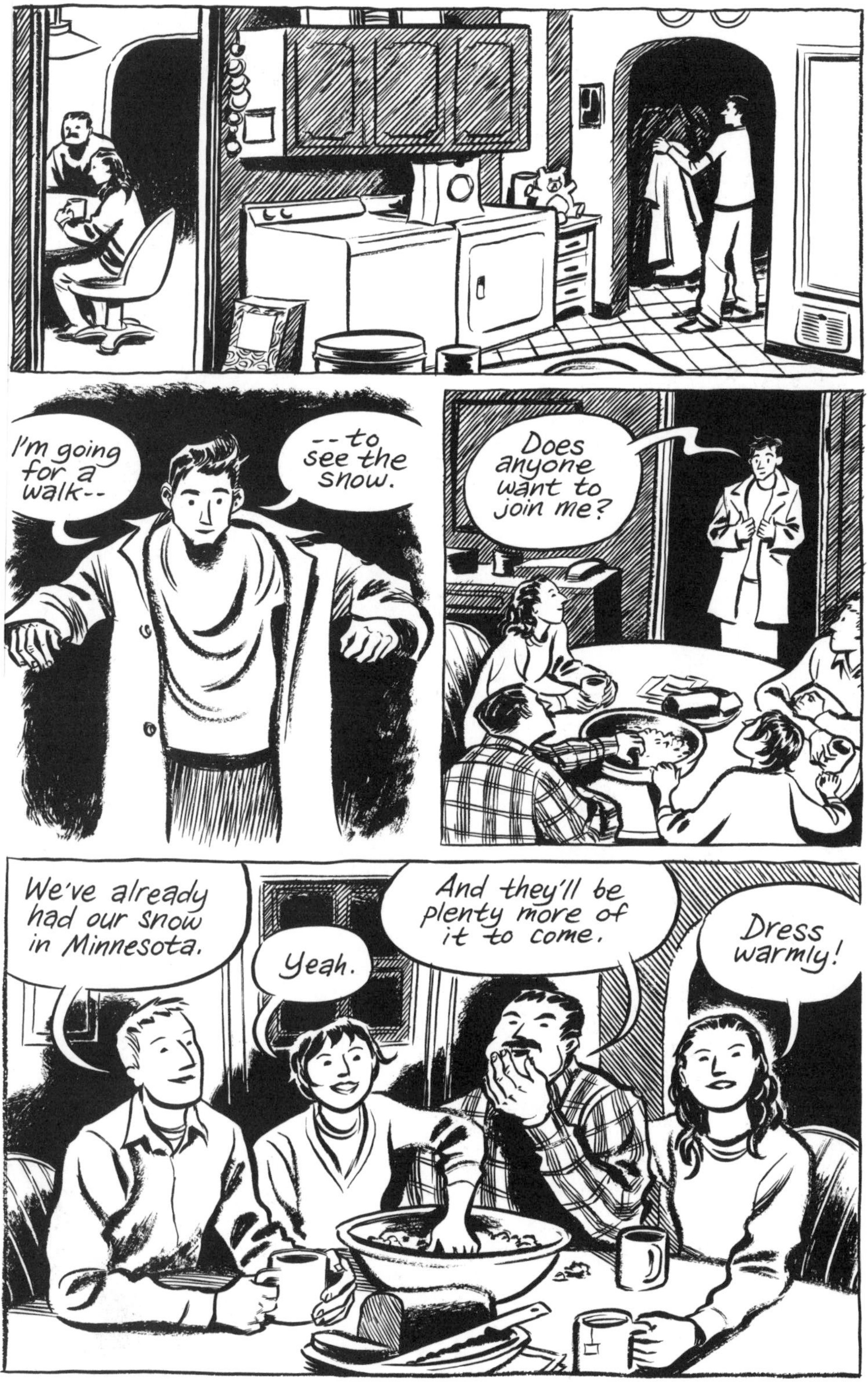

I'm going for a walk--
--to see the snow.
Does anyone want to join me?
We've already had our snow in Minnesota.
Yeah.
And they'll be plenty more of it to come.
Dress warmly!

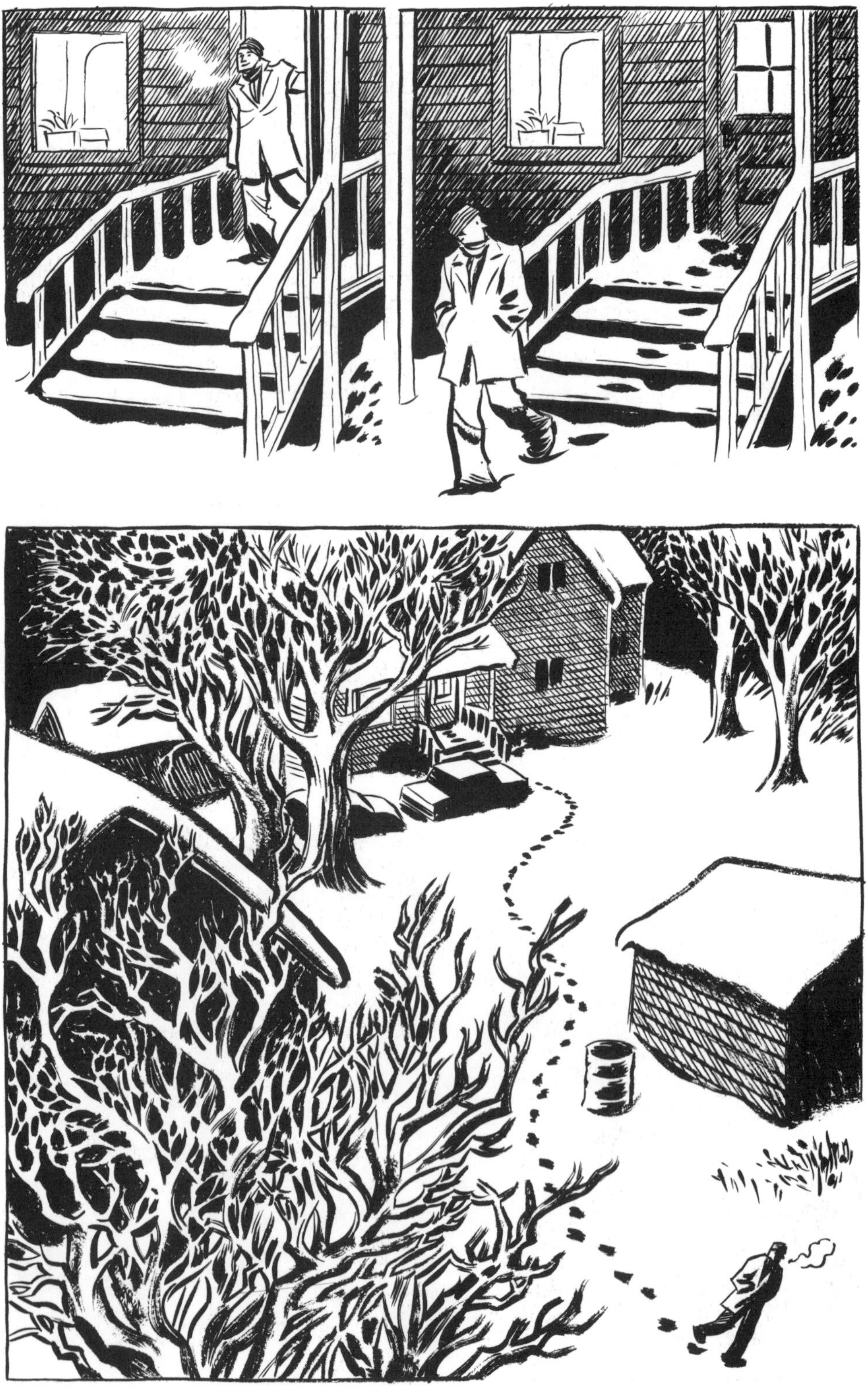

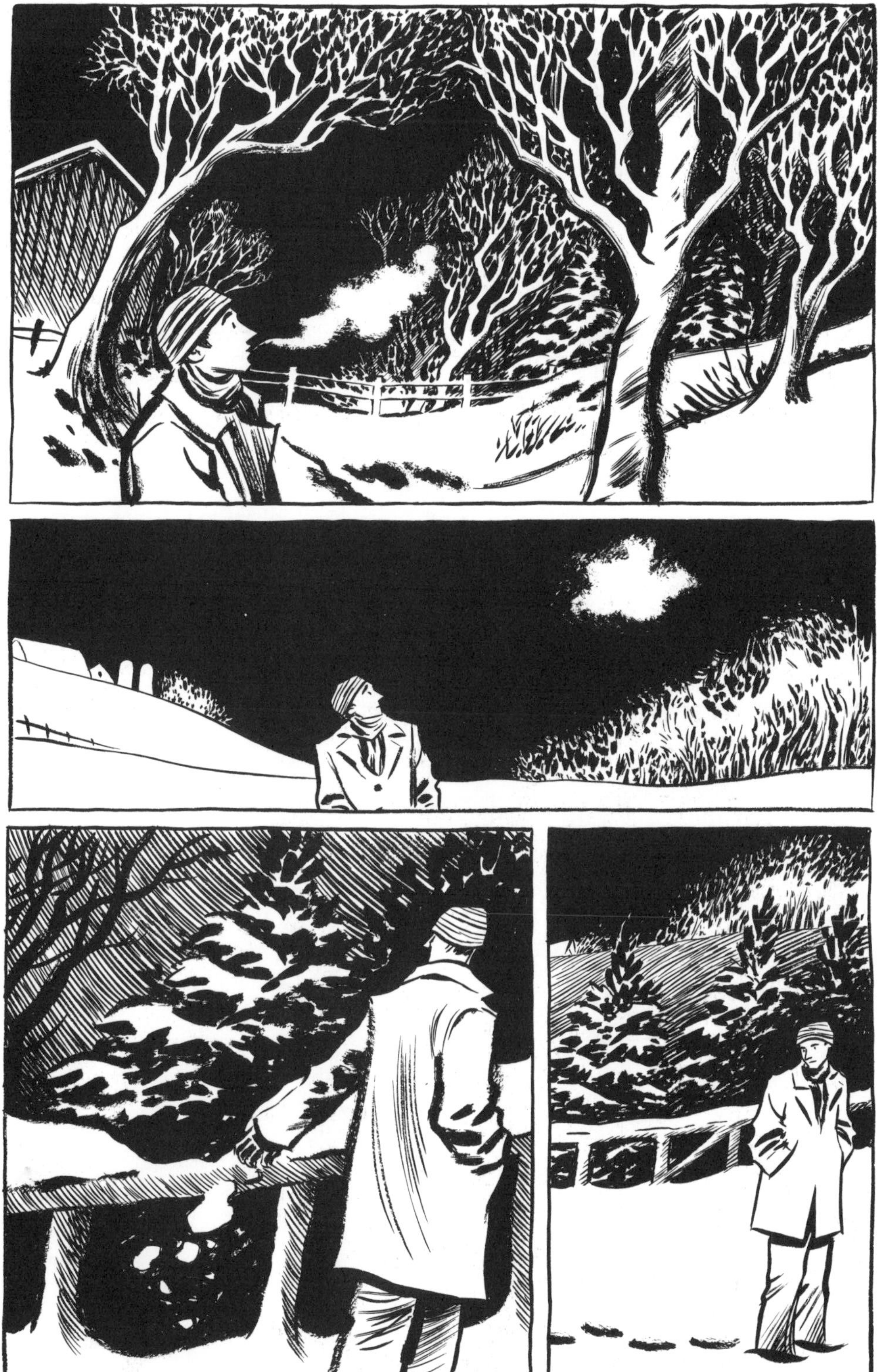

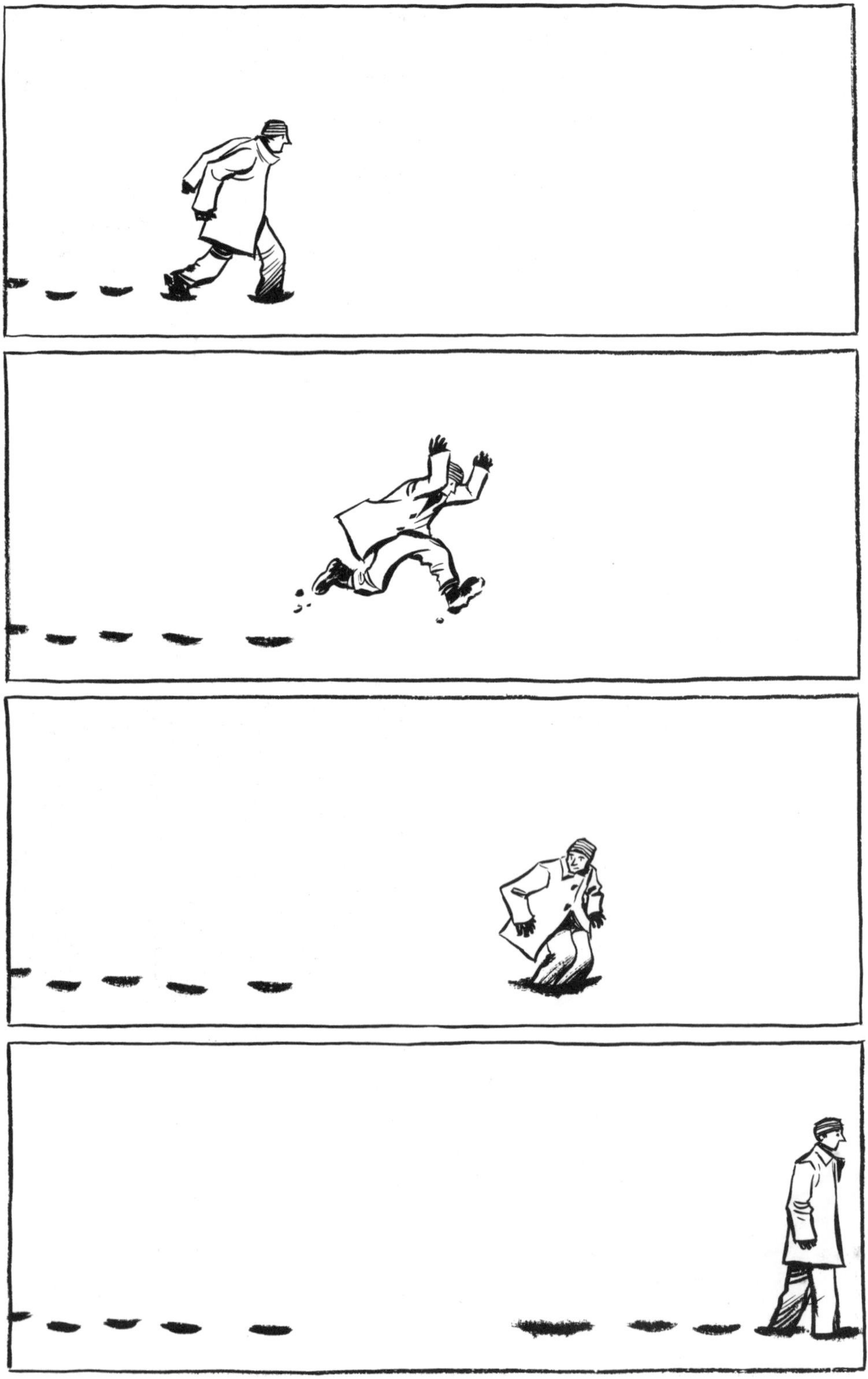

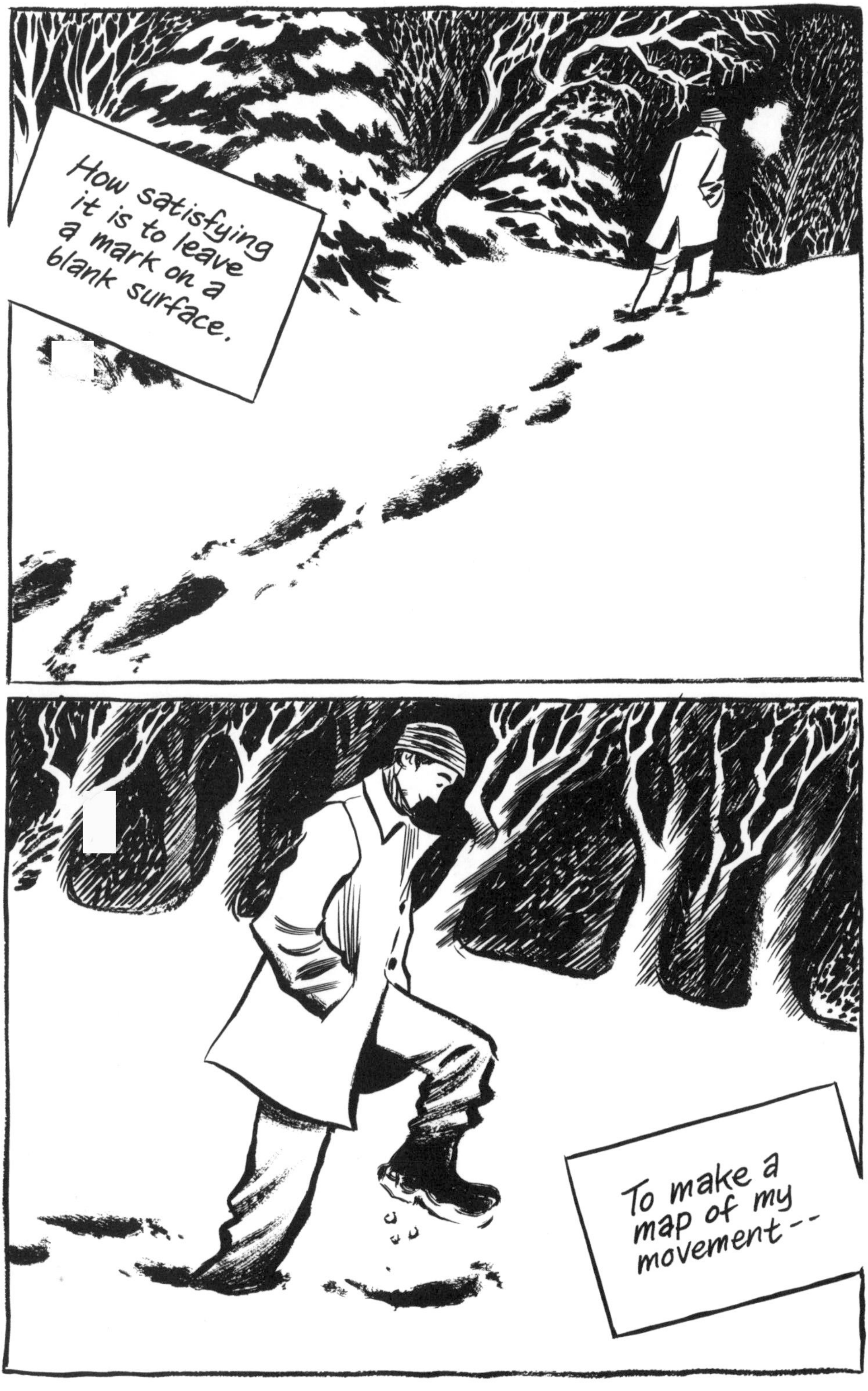
How satisfying it is to leave a mark on a blank surface.
To make a map of my movement--

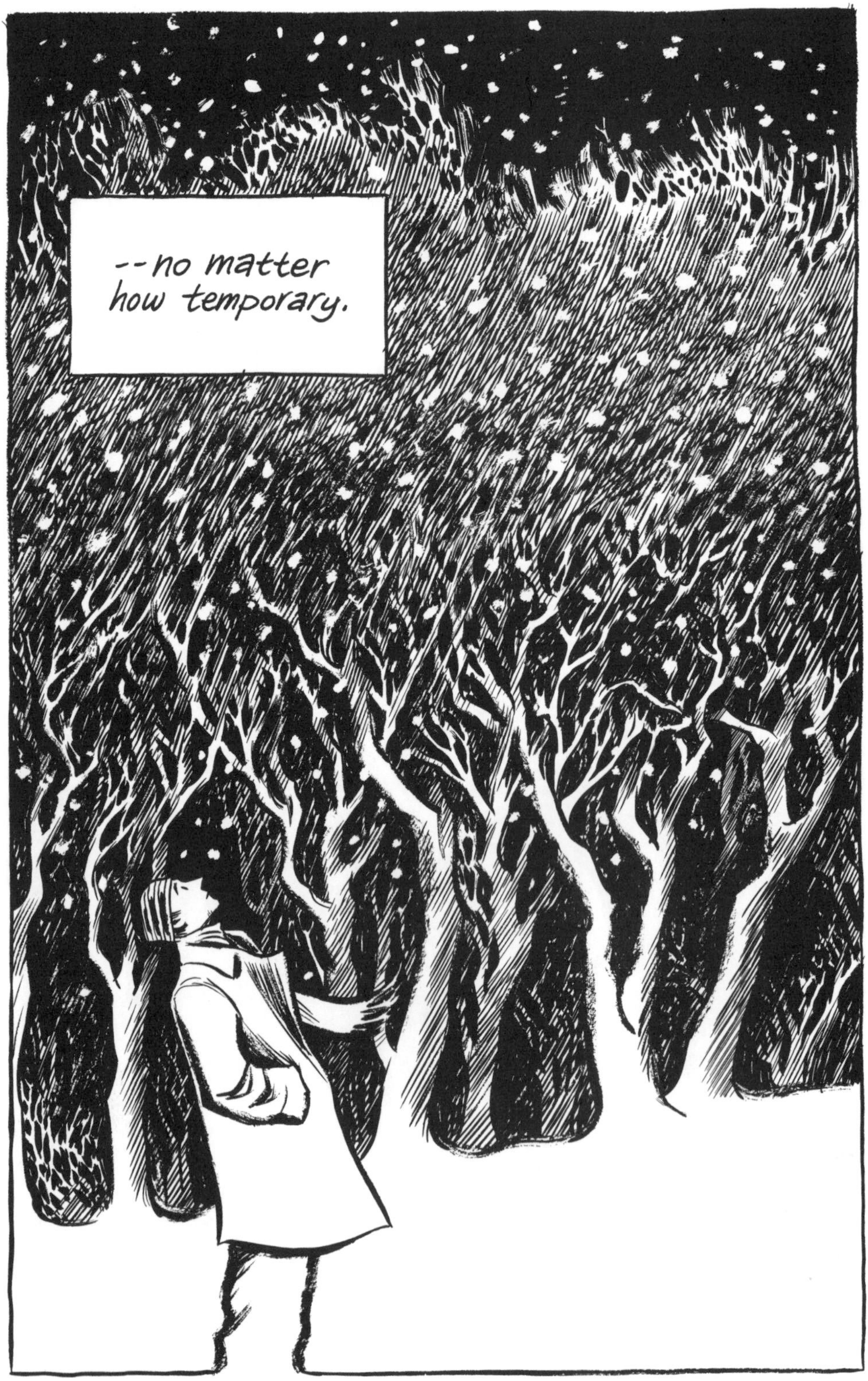
--no matter how temporary.

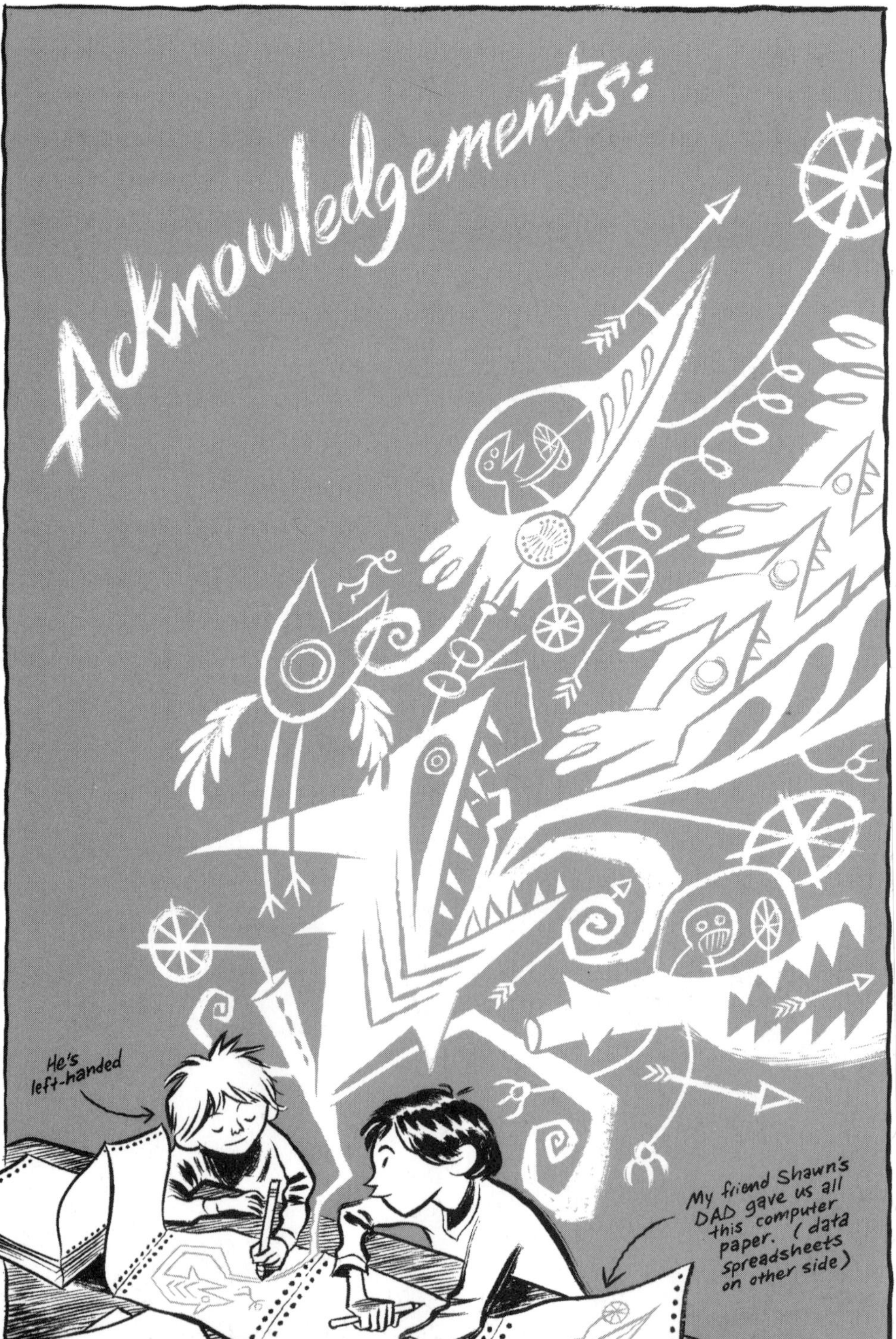
Acknowledgements:
He's left-handed
My friend Shawn's DAD gave us all this computer paper. (data spreadsheets on other side)

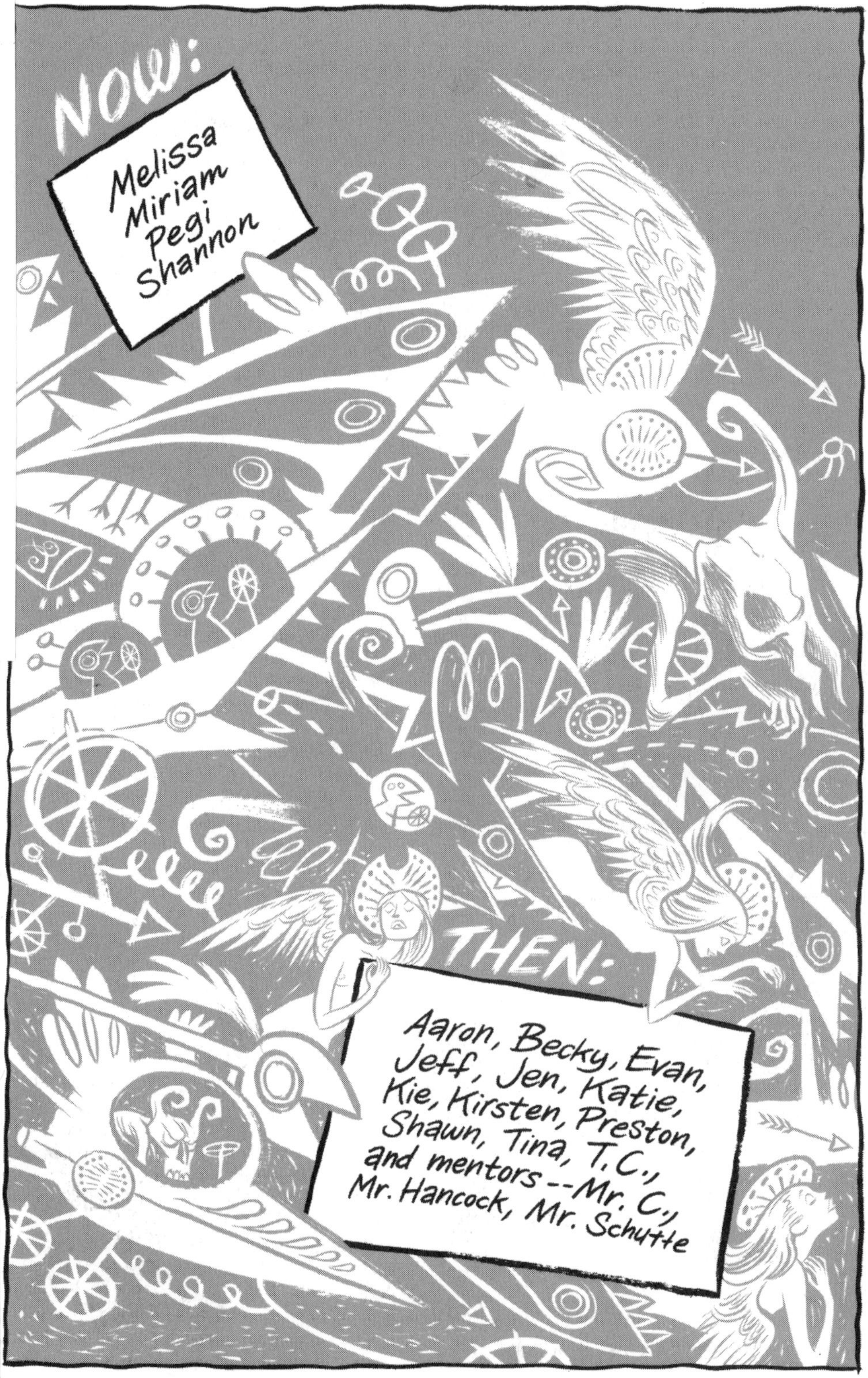
NOW:
Melissa
Miriam
Pegi
Shannon
THEN:
Aaron, Becky, Evan, Jeff, Jen, Katie, Kie, Kirsten, Preston, Shawn, Tina, T.C., and mentors--Mr. C., Mr. Hancock, Mr. Schutte

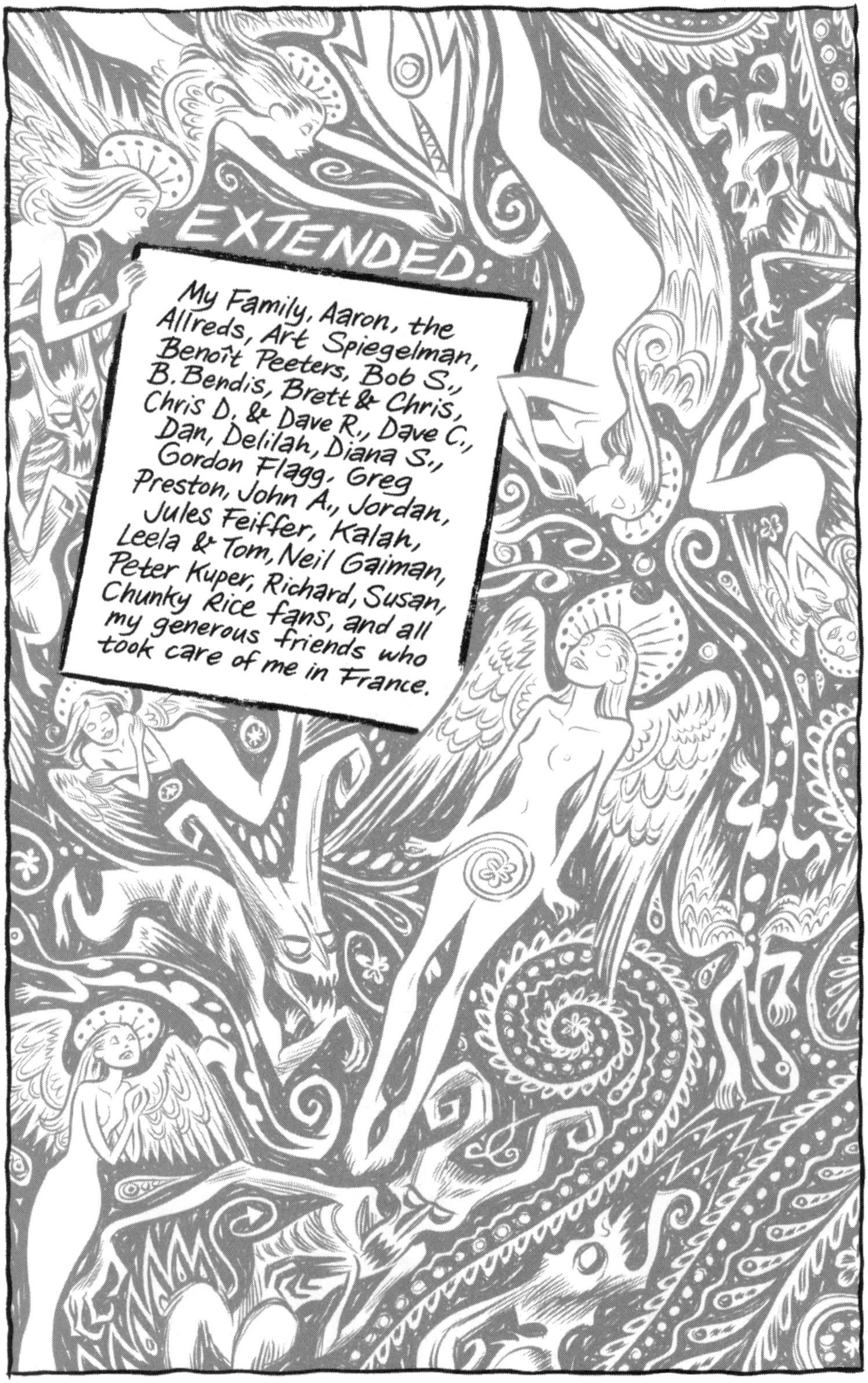
EXTENDED:
My Family, Aaron, the Allreds, Art Spiegelman, Benoît Peeters, Bob S., B. Bendis, Brett & Chris, Chris D. & Dave R., Dave C., Dan, Delilah, Diana S., Gordon Flagg, Greg Preston, John A., Jordan, Jules Feiffer, Kalah, Leela & Tom, Neil Gaiman, Peter Kuper, Richard, Susan, Chunky Rice fans, and all my generous friends who took care of me in France.

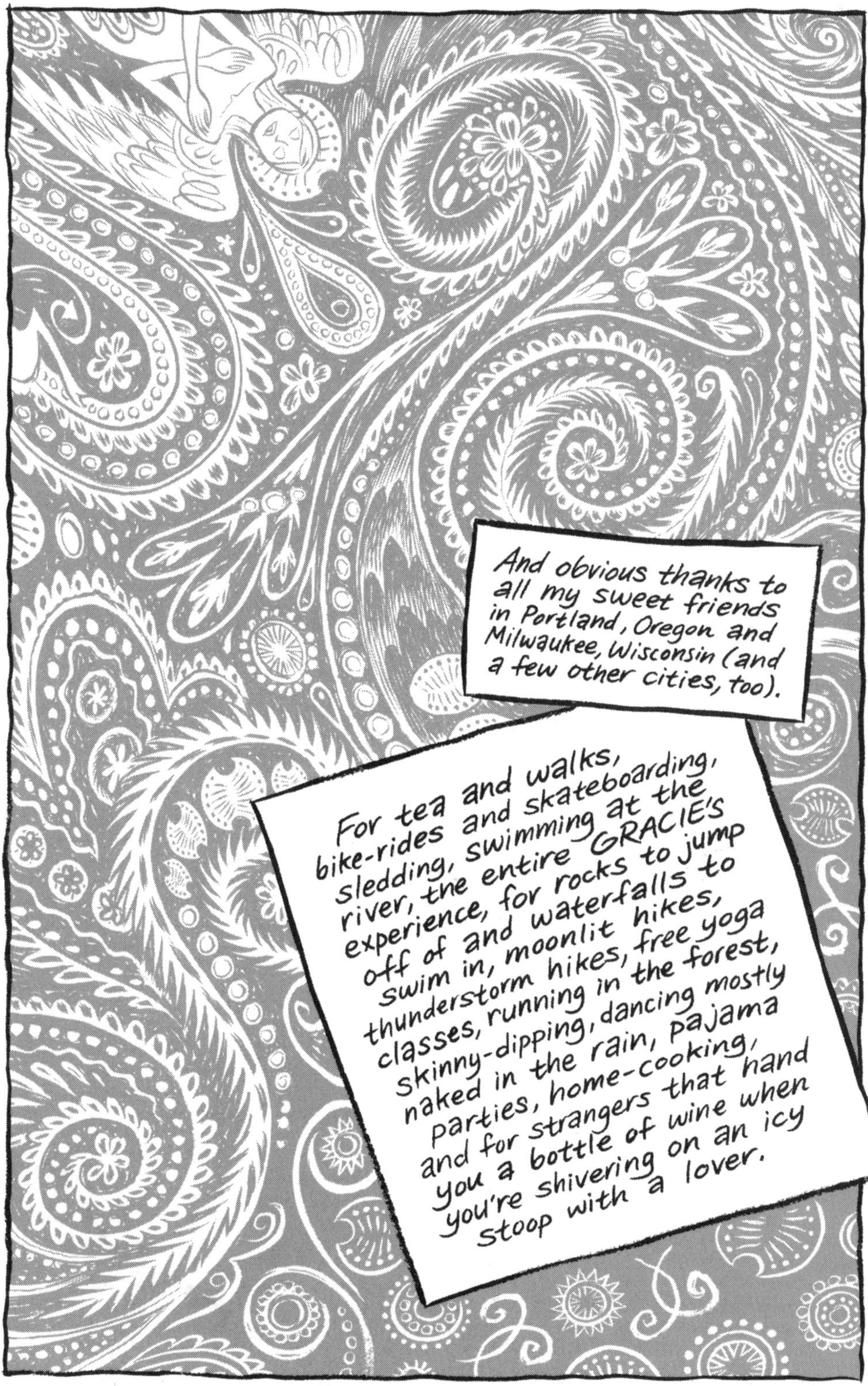
And obvious thanks to all my sweet friends in Portland, Oregon and Milwaukee, Wisconsin (and a few other cities, too).
For tea and walks, bike-rides and skateboarding, sledding, swimming at the river, the entire GRACIE'S experience, for rocks to jump off of and waterfalls to swim in, moonlit hikes, thunderstorm hikes, free yoga classes, running in the forest, skinny-dipping, dancing mostly naked in the rain, pajama parties, home-cooking, and for strangers that hand you a bottle of wine when you're shivering on an icy stoop with a lover.

EXTRA SPECIAL ACKNOWLEDGEMENTS:

Susan & Colin

Sarah & Joy

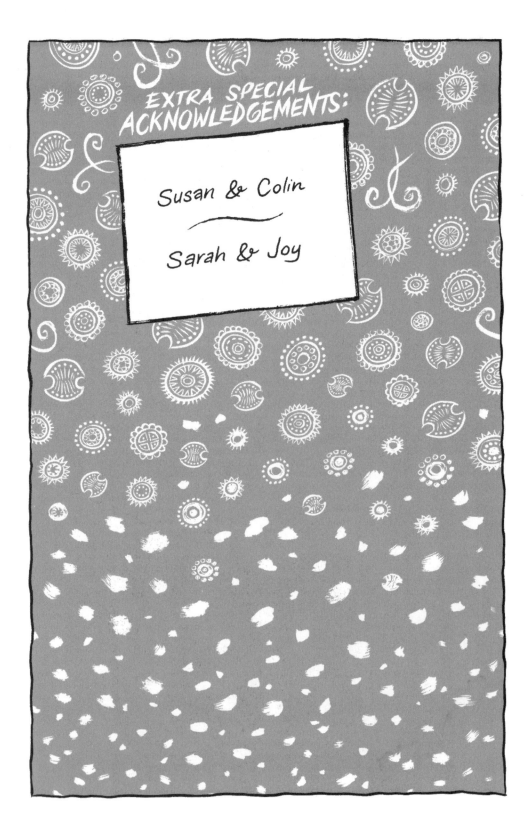

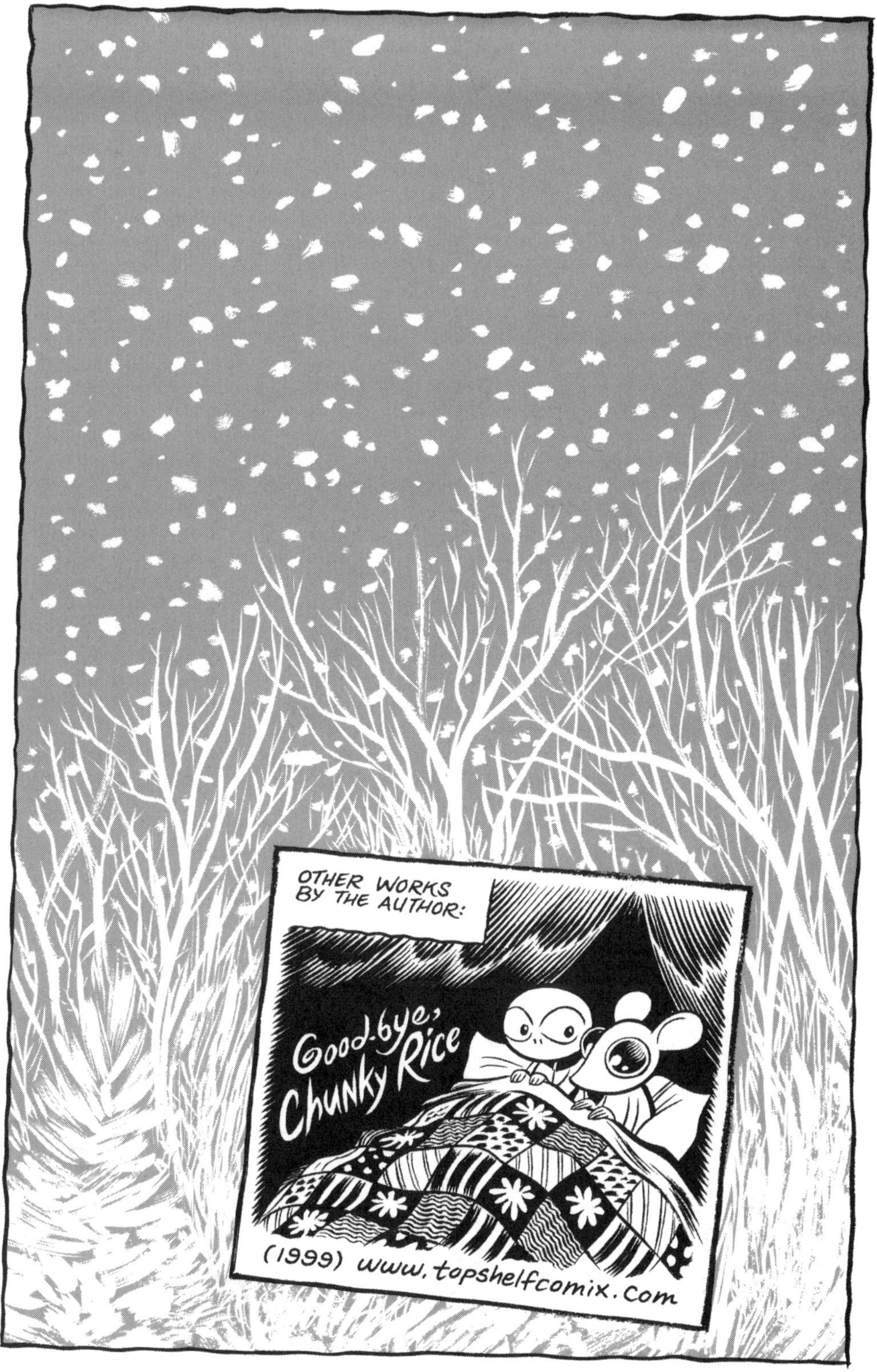
OTHER WORKS BY THE AUTHOR:
Good-bye, Chunky Rice
(1999) www.topshelfcomix.com